MW01011653

The Musical Theatre Codex
Index of Songs by Character Type

By Anita Anderson Endsley

Cover Art by Brittany Tovado

Printed in the United States of America

ISBN-13: 978-1974183760
ISBM-10: 1974183769

Dedication

To Chris for loyal support of "All-Things-Endsley"

To Nick for insightful navigation

To Ellis and Matti for unwavering expectation

Acknowledgements

Karen Noble
Dan LoBuono
Rusty Smith
Amanda Wansa Morgan

Table of Contents

The Musical Theatre Codex
Theory Of Theatrical Archetypes

The Musical Theatre Codex Theory of Theatrical Archetypes is an expansion of standard character types based on their contribution to the plot and interactions with other characters. This classification assists in connecting character type with the presentational qualities of actors. A commercial character type is not merely a "look". It is the assessment of physical "presence" along with demeanor to help define a commercial character type. Effective storytelling hinges on the use of believable actors.

Character archetypes can be traced back to the Aristotelian writing of Theophrastus' 30 character types in *The Characters* (c. 319 BC). Each type was characterized by his most *prominent trait*; i.e. The Insincere Man and The Stingy Man. Character *traits* were instrumental in clarifying plot of sketches written to define moral types. One millennium later, disposition and appearance are incorporated for more character development. In 16th Century Italy, The Commedia dell'arte "consisted of improvisations based around skeletal scenarios, employed stock characters...all of whom were distinguished by masks and emblematic costumes. Players, who usually specialized in one role, would often make slight alterations to masks and costumes in order to customize their character." (The Cassell Companion to Theatre, p.113).

During the 18th and 19th century stock companies of London's Drury Lane and Covent Garden Theatres Character labels evolved character *motives* that facilitate the development of the plot. The stock theatres utilized "a permanent troupe of actors who performed a limited repertory at one or more theatres." (The Cassell Companion to Theatre, p. 444)

For many centuries to follow, scripts have used believable characters to facilitate Suspension of Disbelief. Philosopher and poet Samuel Taylor Coleridge introduced this concept as the willingness of a reader or audience to put aside plausibility to believe a plot. Successful suspension also relies on characters being identifiable. Actors should have the appearance and demeanor the character requires. Believability suggests that antagonists be vocally and physically intimidating while Ingénues appear to be innocent and impressionable.

Using definitive character parameters, the plot for Cinderella can be set anytime, anywhere, with any set design and still be believable as long as Cinderella is visually and aurally an Ingénue and the stepfamily characterized as antagonistic. This categorization goes beyond "look" and "physical silhouette". The Codex theory focuses on demeanor, temperament, and quality of social relationships. This is exemplified in another Cinderella story entitled *Hairspray*. The lead female characters are non-traditionally written to identify ample-silhouetted Tracy Turnblad as Cinderella who is tormented by the antagonistic, yet beautiful, Amber Von Tussle along with her well-preserved-former-beauty-pageant-mother, Velma Von Tussle. In 1988, America was ready to challenge the norms of race and body image in this delightful cult classic film. Writer and Director, Sam Waters reassigned the protagonist from an Ingénue to a Character Ingénue. Set in 1962 Baltimore, MD, Waters made social heroes of the bountiful female Turnbads (one of whom is cast as a male in drag) as well as their socially discriminated counterparts Seaweed, Little Inez and Motormouth Mabel. Twenty years and one generation in advance of the start of the Civil Rights Movement, America was ready to reexamine its past social practices using the backdrop of Doo-wop and teen love. With Waters' non-traditional characters, his "Cinderella" was not a standard Ingénue, the secondary character romance was inter-racial, and racial integration was the conflict. As societal perspectives change, so do the limitations on a character descriptive. Traditionally homogenous stories are now cast multi-racially without apology or explanation. As entertainment continues to accommodate its nation's changing expectations, type should be detailed enough to keep up with current casting trends.

In this Musical Theatre Codex, the Theory of Theatrical Archetypes has a character breakdown with expanded titles and individual descriptions of temperament, demeanor, age range, life experience, and quality of social impact. The Codex consists of 9 character types for both male and female with examples from Grimm's fairytale archetypes of *Into The Woods*. Analysis for the Codex resources 178 musical scores from 1925 to current Broadway productions and extracts solos, duets and ensemble pieces to an assigned character type.

For an actor to know the character type that they are likely to portray is paramount to building a successful career. This knowledge increases marketability by knowing their fit within the industry and aiming straight for those opportunities. The job of casting stage, television or film requires finding the perfect actor for each character. Actors that know their character type can maximize their believability by choosing material that enhances their appeal. Audition material that fits character type and skill-set brings a cast-able clarity to performance and can increase the ability to book jobs.

Understanding the art of commercial storytelling can be an unpleasant perspective for an artist who is looking forward to devoting their life and livelihood to making art. It is suffocating for an actor to think that they must professionally view themselves as a "look"; a production perspective to attract target audiences. *This is **NOT** the message of knowing your character type.* The actor that assesses their physical presence, demeanor and skill set to discover their commercial character type increases the plausibility that they will be cast in a conventional medium. Knowledge is power. Awareness of traditional casting practices within the entertainment industry is also the first step to understanding the beauty of non-traditional-casting that expands the boundaries of convention.

The actor's arsenal begins with knowing how their vocal quality, vocal range, height and physique translate to stage and screen character types. The questions on the character type assessment consists of these questions:

- What characters are cast with actors that match my presence in profit-making theatre, television, and film?
- What characters have my vocal quality?
- What characters are written with my dependable vocal range?

Once these parameters are defined, research the material and productions in which similar actors have been cast. Fine-tuning character type and selecting material for that type and skill set is "perfect fit" material and power repertoire.

Character Type		Into The Woods Characters
Romantic Lead		**The Princes**
• Adult	• Idyllic	
• Attractive	• Charming	
• Glamorous	• Gallant	
• Chivalrous	• Courageous	
Ingénue		**Cinderella**
• Young	• Idealistic	
• Attractive	• Trusting	
• Dependant	• Impressionable	
• Innocent	• Unworldly	
Character Ingénue		**Rapunzel, Jack**
• Young	• Amusing	
• Attractive	• Quirky	
• Independent	• Strong-willed	
• Unique	• Worldly	
Character		**Baker and Baker's Wife**
• Adult	• Amusing and Cranky	
• Unique	• Curious	
• Independent	• Whimsical	
• Eccentric	• Offbeat	
Maternal and Paternal		**Jack's Mother**
• Nurturing	• Encouraging	
• Parental Role	• Affectionate	
• Protective	• Sympathetic	
• Trustworthy	• Comforting	
Mature		**The Old Man/Narrator**
• Middle-aged or older		
Juvenile		**Little Red Riding Hood**
• Under 18 years of age		
Antagonist		**The Witch**
• Adversarial	• Hostile	
• Domineering	• Nemesis	
• Opponent	• Aggressive	
• Arrogant	• Enemy	
Romantic Antagonist		**Transitioned Witch, Stepmother & Stepsisters**
• Attractive	• Opponent	
• Alluring	• Arrogant	
• Adversarial	• Nemesis	
• Domineering	• Aggressive	

How To Use This Book

Scores from 178 Musicals of Broadway, Off-Broadway, and Regional productions were analyzed to categorize into the following categories:

- Solo Songs by **Character Type**
- Solo Songs by **Vocal Type**
- Solo Songs by **Composer**
- Duet songs by **Character Type** and **Voicing**
- Ensemble Songs by **Voicing** and **Age Group**

Some songs listed as solo, that were originally written as duet or group number but have enough solo lines to be edited into a solo. These songs require editing and are identified with an asterisk (*) next to the title. Songs that require editing yield solo pieces seldom seen in auditions and performances.

Character Types

Character Types were determined first by Publishing House information. If no information was provided Character Types were determined by script and lyric references. Characters that make physical transitions, as the Witch in *Into The Woods*, are categorized according to the least-disguised character of the two.

Song Dates

Dates of each song signify the date the song was written regardless of the date the show was produced. Shows that are Pastiche (combination of songs from different sources) or a Juke Box Musical (combination of songs from a specific group) the year signifies when the song was written and not the date of the production.

Tempo

All songs are assigned one of three tempos; ballad, moderate tempo, and uptempo.

Categories

Categories denote the size of the role singing the song; leading role, supporting, and featured ensemble.

Ensemble Age Groups

Age assignments are identified by the age of characters singing the song. Any songs that are appropriate for any age is marked with a triangle Δ in the column marked "Any".

Vocal Types and Voicing

Vocal types and their range are identified with the categories names commonly used in musical theatre and choral arrangements. The term "Alto" is used instead of "Mezzo-Soprano" and is not a synonym for Contralto; a classical registration representing a female range that is lower than Mezzo-Soprano. The female categories are simply, Soprano and Alto. The category of Bari-tenor has been eliminated and songs are simply categorized into Tenor or Baritone. The following vocal ranges are identified using common practices in the profession and standard vocal pedagogy.

Vocal ranges are entered "at pitch"; male vocal ranges are input in the range in which they are sung.

Sort Order of Lists

Character Type Chapter
> First by Vocal Type
> Second by Year
> Third by Role

Vocal Type Chapters
> First by Character Type
> Second by Year
> Third by Show Name

Ensembles
> First by Voicing
> Second by Tempo

Duets
> First by Voicing
> Second by Character Type
> Third by Year

Composer
> First by Composer
> Second by Vocal Type
> Third by Tempo

Show
> First by Show Name
> Second by Year
> Third by Composer

Chart Legend
+   Ethnic Specific Roles
*   Songs that require editing from original setting to solo setting
Δ   Appropriate for any age group

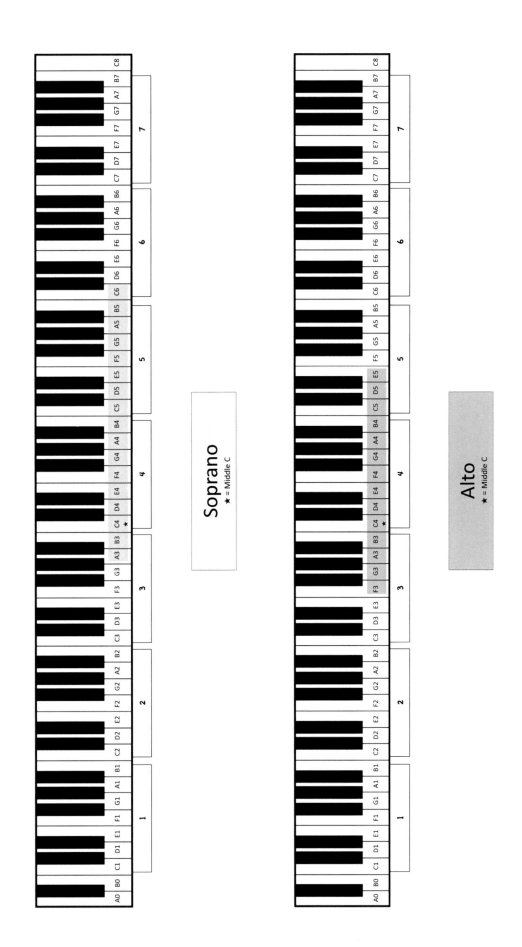

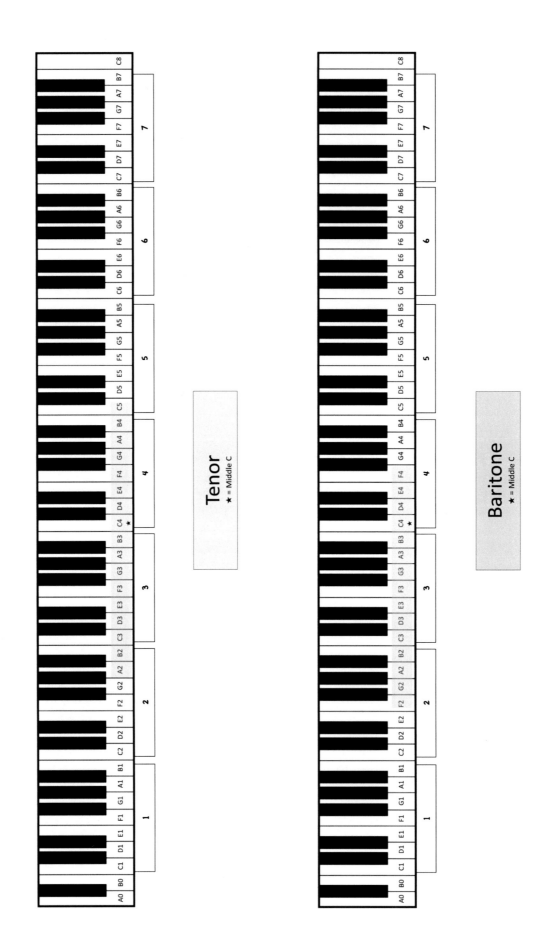

Tenor
★ = Middle C

Baritone
★ = Middle C

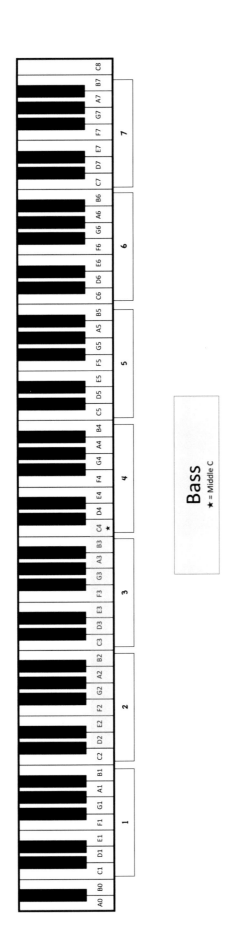

Bass
★ = Middle C

Romantic Lead Female

Show	Year	Role	Song	Tempo	Vocal Type	Range-Bottom	Range-Top	Category
Crazy For You (1992)	1924	Irene Roth	Naughty Baby	Moderate Tempo	Alto	Ab3	D#4	Supporting
No, No Nanette	1925	Lucille Early	Too Many Rings Around Rosie*	Uptempo	Alto	B3	D5	Lead
No, No Nanette	1925	Lucille Early	You Can Dance With Any Girl At	Uptempo	Alto	A3	D5	Lead
No, No Nanette	1925	Lucille Early	Where Has My Hubby Gone Blues	Ballad	Alto	G3	D5	Lead
No, No Nanette	1925	Sue Smith	Take A Little One Step*	Uptempo	Alto	G3	Cb5	Lead
Show Boat	1927	Julie	Can't Help Lovin' Dat Man	Moderate Tempo	Alto	Eb3	Ab4	Lead
Show Boat	1927	Julie	Bill	Ballad	Alto	F#3	G#4	Lead
Good News (1993 Revival)	1928	Professor Kenyan	Together*	Ballad	Alto	G3	B4	Lead
Good News (1993 Revival)	1928	Professor Kenyan	You're The Cream In My Coffee*	Uptempo	Alto	Db4	Eb5	Lead
Good News (1993 Revival)	1928	Professor Kenyan	Together Part 2*	Ballad	Alto	G3	C5	Lead
Good News (1993 Revival)	1931	Professor Kenyan	Life Is Just A Bowl Of Cherries	Uptempo	Alto	A3	Db5	Lead
Babes In Arms (1998)	1937	Baby Rose	Way Out West*	Moderate Tempo	Alto	B3	C5	Lead
Babes In Arms (1998)	1937	Baby Rose	Johnny One Note	Uptempo	Alto	Bb3	Bb4	Lead
Babes In Arms (1998)	1937	Baby Rose	Imagine*	Moderate Tempo	Alto	A3	C5	Lead
Kiss Me Kate	1948	Lilli Vanessi/Katherine	I Hate Men	Moderate Tempo	Alto	B3	C#5	Lead
South Pacific	1949	Nellie Forbush	A Cockeyed Optimist	Uptempo	Alto	A3	C5	Lead
South Pacific	1949	Nellie Forbush	I'm Gonna Wash That Man*	Uptempo	Alto	D3	E5	Lead
South Pacific	1949	Nellie Forbush	Honey Bun	Uptempo	Alto	Bb3	Bb4	Lead
South Pacific	1949	Nellie Forbush	Some Enchanted Evening Reprise	Ballad	Alto	Ab3	Bb4	Lead
South Pacific	1949	Nellie Forbush	Im In Love…Wonderful Guy*	Uptempo	Alto	B3	Db5	Lead
South Pacific	1949	Nellie Forbush	Im In Love….Wonderful Guy Repr	Uptempo	Alto	B3	C5	Lead
Pajama Game	1954	Babe Williams	I'm Not At All In Love*	Uptempo	Alto	A3	B4	Lead
Pajama Game	1954	Babe Williams	There Once Was A Man*	Uptempo	Alto	Bb3	Eb5	Lead
Pajama Game	1954	Babe Williams	Hey There Reprise	Ballad	Alto	A#3	Bb4	Lead
Pajama Game	1954	Babe Williams	Seven And A Half Cents*	Uptempo	Alto	A3	D5	Lead
West Side Story	1957	Anita+	A Boy Like That*	Moderate Tempo	Alto	Eb3	Cb5	Lead
Flower Drum Song 2002	1958	Helen Chao+	Love, Look Away (C Maj)	Ballad	Alto	B3	E5	Lead

Romantic Leading Female

* = Music Edit Required
+ = Ethnic Specific

Show	Year	Role	Song	Tempo	Vocal Type	Range-Bottom	Range-Top	Category
Flower Drum Song 2002	1958	Linda Low+	I Enjoy Being A Girl	Uptempo	Alto	A3	B4	Lead
Flower Drum Song 2002	1958	Linda Low+	I Enjoy Being A Girl Encore*	Moderate Tempo	Alto	A3	C♭5	Lead
Flower Drum Song 2002	1958	Linda Low+	I Enjoy Being A Girl Playoff*	Moderate Tempo	Alto	B♭3	E♭5	Lead
Flower Drum Song 2002	1958	Linda Low+	Fan Tan Fannie*	Uptempo	Alto	B3	B4	Lead
Bye Bye Birdie	1960	Rose Grant	An English Teacher	Uptempo	Alto	G♭3	B♭4	Lead
Bye Bye Birdie	1960	Rose Grant	Let's Settle Down (TV 1995)	Moderate Tempo	Alto	G3	D♭4	Lead
Bye Bye Birdie	1960	Rose Grant	What Did I Ever See In Him *	Uptempo	Alto	G3	B♭4	Lead
Bye Bye Birdie	1960	Rose Grant	Spanish Rose	Moderate Tempo	Alto	G3	C5	Lead
Bye Bye Birdie	1960	Rose Grant	What Did I Ever See In Him Repr	Uptempo	Alto	G3	B♭4	Lead
Bye Bye Birdie	1960	Rose Grant	An English Teacher Reprise	Uptempo	Alto	D♭4	B♭4	Lead
How To Succeed...	1961	Hedy La Rue	Love From A Heart Of Gold*	Ballad	Alto	B3	D5	Supporting
Mame	1966	Mame	It's Today*	Uptempo	Alto	A3	D5	Lead
Mame	1966	Mame	Open A New Window*	Uptempo	Alto	A3	D5	Lead
Mame	1966	Mame	That's How Young I Feel*	Uptempo	Alto	G3	B♭4	Lead
Mame	1966	Mame	If He Walked Into My Life	Ballad	Alto	F#3	B♭4	Lead
Mame	1966	Mame	It's Today Reprise*	Uptempo	Alto	F3	B♭4	Lead
Mame	1966	Mame	It's Today Reprise 2*	Moderate Tempo	Alto	A3	E♭5	Lead
Mame	1966	Mame	You're My Best Girl*	Ballad	Alto	G3	B♭4	Lead
Mame	1966	Mame	We Need A Little Christmas Rep*	Uptempo	Alto	C#4	D5	Lead
Mame	1966	Mame	We Need A Little Christmas*	Uptempo	Alto	F3	B♭4	Lead
Cabaret	1966	Sally Bowles	Don't Tell Mama	Uptempo	Alto	A3	A4	Lead
Cabaret	1966	Sally Bowles	Perfectly Marvelous *	Uptempo	Alto	F#3	A4	Lead
Cabaret	1966	Sally Bowles	Maybe This Time	Ballad	Alto	F#3	C5	Lead
Cabaret	1966	Sally Bowles	Cabaret	Uptempo	Alto	E3	B4	Lead
Follies	1971	Carolotta Champion	I'm Still Here	Moderate Tempo	Alto	E♭3	C5	Supporting
Follies	1971	Solange LaFitte	Ah, Paris *	Uptempo	Alto	C3	G4	Supporting
Pippin	1972	Catherine	There He Was	Uptempo	Alto	G#3	B4	Lead

Romantic Leading Female

Romantic Lead Female

* = Music Edit Required
+ = Ethnic Specific

Show	Year	Role	Song	Tempo	Vocal Type	Range-Bottom	Range-Top	Category
Pippin	1972	Catherine	Kind Of Woman*	Moderate Tempo	Alto	Ab3	C#5	Lead
Pippin	1972	Catherine	I Guess I'll Miss the Man	Ballad	Alto	F#3	B4	Lead
Cabaret	1972	Sally Bowles	Mein Herr	Moderate Tempo	Alto	F3	B4	Lead
Sugar	1972	Sugar Kane	Open Chicago	Uptempo	Alto	A3	C5	Lead
Sugar	1972	Sugar Kane	Hey Why Not!*	Uptempo	Alto	Bb3	Bb4	Lead
A Little Night Music	1973	Countess Charlotte Malcd	Everyday A Little Death	Uptempo	Alto	G3	B4	Supporting
A Little Night Music	1973	Desiree Armfeldt	Send In The Clowns	Ballad	Alto	G3	A4	Lead
Wiz, The	1974	Glinda	A Rested Body Is A Rested Mind	Moderate Tempo	Alto	C4	C5	Lead
They're Playing Our Song	1974	Sonia Walsk	Falling Reprise	Moderate Tempo	Alto	E3	A4	Lead
They're Playing Our Song	1974	Sonia Walsk	Workin' It Out*	Uptempo	Alto	F3	B4	Lead
They're Playing Our Song	1974	Sonia Walsk	If He Really Knew Me*	Ballad	Alto	G3	B4	Lead
They're Playing Our Song	1974	Sonia Walsk	They're Playing My Song*	Uptempo	Alto	G3	Cb5	Lead
They're Playing Our Song	1974	Sonia Walsk	If He Really Knew Me Reprise*	Ballad	Alto	G3	Ab4	Lead
They're Playing Our Song	1974	Sonia Walsk	Right*	Uptempo	Alto	A3	G4	Lead
They're Playing Our Song	1974	Sonia Walsk	Just For Tonight	Ballad	Alto	G3	A4	Lead
A Chorus Line	1975	Cassie	The Music And The Mirror	Moderate Tempo	Alto	A#3	D5	Lead
Cats	1981	Bombalurina	Macavity	Moderate Tempo	Alto	A3	C5	Supporting
Cats	1981	Demeter	Macavity	Moderate Tempo	Alto	A3	C5	Supporting
Nine	1982	Liliane La Fluer	Folies Bergeres*	Uptempo	Alto	G#3	B4	Supporting
Nine	1982	Luisa Contini	My Husband Makes Movies	Moderate Tempo	Alto	Eb3	C5	Lead
Nine	1982	Luisa Contini	Be On Your Own	Moderate Tempo	Alto	G#3	A4	Lead
Nine	1982	Stephanie Necrophorus	Folies Bergeres*	Uptempo	Alto	B3	B4	Supporting
Sunday...With Geroge	1984	Dot	Sunday In The Park With George	Moderate Tempo	Alto	E3	Db5	Lead
Sunday...With Geroge	1984	Dot	Color And Light (Part 2)	Moderate Tempo	Alto	B3	C5	Lead
Sunday...With Geroge	1984	Dot	Color And Light (Part 3)*	Uptempo	Alto	E4	E5	Lead
Sunday...With Geroge	1984	Dot	Everybody Loves Louis	Uptempo	Alto	A#3	C#5	Lead
Sunday...With Geroge	1984	Dot	We Do Not Belong Together*	Moderate Tempo	Alto	G3	D5	Lead
Sunday...With Geroge	1984	Dot	Move On*	Ballad	Alto	G#3	C#5	Lead

Romantic Leading Female

Romantic Lead Female

* = Music Edit Required
+ = Ethnic Specific

Show	Year	Role	Song	Tempo	Vocal Type	Range-Bottom	Range-Top	Category
Sunday...With Geroge	1984	Marie	Children And Art*	Ballad	Alto	Gb3	Db5	Lead
Les Miserables	1987	Fantine	I Have Dreamed (E Major)	Ballad	Alto	G3	C#5	Lead
Les Miserables	1987	Fantine	Come To Me	Ballad	Alto	C4	C5	Lead
Les Miserables	1987	Fantine	I Have Dreamed (Eb Major)	Ballad	Alto	Gb3	C5	Lead
City of Angels	1989	Bobbi	With Every Breath I Take	Ballad	Alto	E3	Db5	Lead
City of Angels	1989	Bobbi	With Every Breath I Take Reprise	Ballad	Alto	D#3	C5	Lead
City of Angels	1989	Gabby	What You Don't Know About Wor	Moderate Tempo	Alto	G3	F5	Lead
City of Angels	1989	Gabby	It Needs Work	Moderate Tempo	Alto	G#3	Cb5	Lead
Once On This Island	1990	Andrea+	Andrea Sequence*	Moderate Tempo	Alto	Bb3	C5	Lead
Once On This Island	1990	Erzulie+	Human Heart*	Ballad	Alto	B3	C#5	Lead
Will Rogers Follies	1991	Betty Blake	My Unknown Someone	Ballad	Alto	Ab3	C5	Lead
Will Rogers Follies	1991	Betty Blake	The Big Time*	Moderate Tempo	Alto	B3	D#5	Lead
Will Rogers Follies	1991	Betty Blake	My Big Mistake	Moderate Tempo	Alto	F3	D5	Lead
Will Rogers Follies	1991	Betty Blake	With You	Moderate Tempo	Alto	Eb4	C5	Lead
Will Rogers Follies	1991	Betty Blake	No Man Left For Me	Moderate Tempo	Alto	A3	C5	Lead
Miss Saigon	1991	Ellen Scott	I Still Believe*	Ballad	Alto	A3	Eb5	Lead
Miss Saigon	1991	Ellen Scott	Now I've Seen Her	Ballad	Alto	G#3	E5	Lead
Will Rogers Follies	1991	Ziegfield's Favorite	Will-A-Mania	Uptempo	Alto	G3	D5	Supporting
Goodbye Girl, The	1993	Actress	Too Good To Be Bad*	Moderate Tempo	Alto	A3	A4	Supporting
Goodbye Girl, The	1993	Paula McFadden	No More	Moderate Tempo	Alto	G3	C5	Lead
Goodbye Girl, The	1993	Paula McFadden	A Beat Behind*	Uptempo	Alto	F#3	B4	Lead
Goodbye Girl, The	1993	Paula McFadden	My Rules	Moderate Tempo	Alto	Ab3	C5	Lead
Goodbye Girl, The	1993	Paula McFadden	Don't Follow In My Footsteps*	Moderate Tempo	Alto	D#3	C#5	Lead
Goodbye Girl, The	1993	Paula McFadden	How Can I Win	Ballad	Alto	Ab3	D5	Lead
Goodbye Girl, The	1993	Paula McFadden	What A Guy	Ballad	Alto	F#3	C5	Lead
Victor/Victoria	1995	Parisienne	Paris By Night Reprise	Moderate Tempo	Alto	A3	C5	Supporting
Scarlet Pimpernel, The	1997	Marguerite St. Just	You Are My Home*	Ballad	Alto	C#4	F#5	Lead
Scarlet Pimpernel, The	1997	Marguerite St. Just	When I Look At You	Ballad	Alto	B3	E5	Lead

Romantic Leading Female

* = Music Edit Required
+ = Ethnic Specific

Show	Year	Role	Song	Tempo	Vocal Type	Range-Bottom	Range-Top	Category
Scarlet Pimpernel, The	1997	Marguerite St. Just	I'll Foget You	Ballad	Alto	G#3	D5	Lead
Scarlet Pimpernel, The	1997	Marguerite St. Just	Vivez*	Moderate Tempo	Alto	C#4	E5	Lead
Scarlet Pimpernel, The	1997	Marguerite St. Just	Only Love	Ballad	Alto	B♭3	E5	Lead
Scarlet Pimpernel, The	1997	Marguerite St. Just	Storybook*	Moderate Tempo	Alto	A3	E5	Lead
Steel Pier	1997	Rita Racine	Willing To Ride	Uptempo	Alto	G♭3	C5	Lead
Steel Pier	1997	Rita Racine	Love Bird*	Moderate Tempo	Alto	G3	C5	Lead
Steel Pier	1997	Rita Racine	Willing To Ride Reprise	Moderate Tempo	Alto	A♭3	B4	Lead
Steel Pier	1997	Rita Racine	Steel Pier Reprise*	Uptempo	Alto	A♭3	D♭5	Lead
Ragtime	1998	Evelyn Nesbit	Crime Of The Century*	Uptempo	Alto	B♭3	D5	Lead
Ragtime	1998	Evelyn Nesbit	Atlantic City (Part 1)*	Uptempo	Alto	B3	B4	Lead
Ragtime	1998	Evelyn Nesbit	Atlantic City (Part 3)*	Uptempo	Alto	B♭3	D5	Lead
Parade	1998	Lucille Frank	Waiting*	Moderate Tempo	Alto	A3	C5	Lead
Parade	1998	Lucille Frank	You Don't Know this Man	Ballad	Alto	G3	E♭5	Lead
Parade	1998	Lucille Frank	Do It Alone	Moderate Tempo	Alto	A3	E5	Lead
Parade	1998	Lucille Frank	All The Wasted Time*	Ballad	Alto	G3	E♭5	Lead
Parade	1998	Lucille Frank	Finale	Ballad	Alto	A3	C5	Lead
Aida	2000	Aida +	The Past Is Another Land	Ballad	Alto	A3	B4	Lead
Aida	2000	Aida +	Easy As Life	Moderate Tempo	Alto	G3	C5	Lead
Aida	2000	Aida +	Elaborate Lies Reprise	Ballad	Alto	G3	C5	Lead
Aida	2000	Aida +	The Gods Love Nubia	Alto	Alto	C4	E5	Lead
Aida	2000	Amneris	My Strongest Suit	Uptempo	Alto	G♭3	E♭5	Lead
Aida	2000	Amneris	My Strongest Suit Reprise	Ballad	Alto	B♭3	G4	Lead
Aida	2000	Amneris	I Know the Truth	Ballad	Alto	E3	D5	Lead
Aida	2000	Amneris	Every Story Reprise (Finale AII)	Ballad	Alto	G3	A♭4	Lead
Mamma Mia!	2001	Donna Sheridan	Money Money Money	Uptempo	Alto	G4	B♭4	Lead
Mamma Mia!	2001	Donna Sheridan	Mamma Mia*	Uptempo	Alto	F#3	A4	Lead
Mamma Mia!	2001	Donna Sheridan	Super Trouper*	Moderate Tempo	Alto	G3	G4	Lead

Romantic Leading Female

Romantic Lead Female

* = Music Edit Required
+ = Ethnic Specific

Show	Year	Role	Song	Tempo	Vocal Type	Range-Bottom	Range-Top	Category
Mamma Mia!	2001	Donna Sheridan	One Of Us*	Moderate Tempo	Alto	A3	C5	Lead
Mamma Mia!	2001	Donna Sheridan	SOS*	Uptempo	Alto	F4	A4	Lead
Mamma Mia!	2001	Donna Sheridan	One Last Summer*	Ballad	Alto	F#3	E4	Lead
Mamma Mia!	2001	Donna Sheridan	Slipping Through My Fingers*	Ballad	Alto	A3	C5	Lead
Mamma Mia!	2001	Donna Sheridan	The Winner Takes It All	Moderate Tempo	Alto	G3	C5	Lead
Mamma Mia!	2001	Donna Sheridan	I Do, I Do, I Do, I Do, I Do	Moderate Tempo	Alto	G3	C5	Lead
Thoroughly Modern Millie	2002	Muzzy Van Hossmere	Only In New York	Ballad	Alto	G#3	B4	Lead
Thoroughly Modern Millie	2002	Muzzy Van Hossmere	Long As I'm Here With You*	Uptempo	Alto	A3	C#5	Lead
Dirty Rotten Scoundrels	2005	Jolene Oakes	Oklahoma	Uptempo	Alto	G#3	C5	Supporting
All Shook Up	2005	Miss Sandra	Let Yourself Go	Moderate Tempo	Alto	E2	E4	Supporting
Dirty Rotten Scoundrels	2005	Muriel Eubanks	What's A Woman To Do	Moderate Tempo	Alto	G2	D4	Supporting
Dirty Rotten Scoundrels	2005	Muriel Eubanks	What's Was A Woman To Do Rep	Moderate Tempo	Alto	E3	Bb4	Supporting
Dirty Rotten Scoundrels	2005	Muriel Eubanks	Like Zis/Like Zat *	Moderate Tempo	Alto	E3	Bb4	Supporting
Legally Blonde	2007	Brooke Wyndam	Whipped Into Shape*	Uptempo	Alto	A3	G5	Supporting
Cutains	2007	Georgia Hendricks	Thinking of Him	Ballad	Alto	G3	Db5	Lead
Cutains	2007	Georgia Hendricks	Thataway *	Uptempo	Alto	B#3	B4	Lead
White Christmas	2008	Betty Haynes	Love And The Weather*	Uptempo	Alto	A3	C5	Lead
White Christmas	2008	Betty Haynes	Falling Out Of Love Can Be Fun*	Uptempo	Alto	G3	C5	Lead
White Christmas	2008	Betty Haynes	Love, You Didn't Do Right By Me	Moderate Tempo	Alto	A3	Bb4	Lead
In The Heights	2008	Vanessa+	It Won't Be Long Now	Uptempo	Alto	A3	E5	Lead
Next To Normal	2009	Diana	My Psychopharmacologist And I	Moderate Tempo	Alto	A3	C5	Lead
Next To Normal	2009	Diana	I Miss The Mountains	Moderate Tempo	Alto	G3	D5	Lead
Next To Normal	2009	Diana	You Don't Know*	Moderate Tempo	Alto	A3	B4	Lead
Next To Normal	2009	Diana	Didn't I See This Movie	Uptempo	Alto	A3	F#5	Lead
Next To Normal	2009	Diana	You Don't Know Reprise*	Uptempo	Alto	A3	A4	Lead
Next To Normal	2009	Diana	How Could I Forget*	Ballad	Alto	Bb3	Db5	Lead
Next To Normal	2009	Diana	The Break	Uptempo	Alto	B3	C5	Lead
Next To Normal	2009	Diana	Maybe*	Moderate Tempo	Alto	Eb3	Eb5	Lead

Romantic Leading Female

* = Music Edit Required
+ = Ethnic Specific

Show	Year	Role	Song	Tempo	Vocal Type	Range-Bottom	Range-Top	Category
Next To Normal	2009	Diana	So Anyway	Ballad	Alto	B3	C5	Lead
High Society 1998	1927	Tracy Lord	Let's Misbehave*	Uptempo	Soprano	B2	C#5	Lead
Of Thee I Sing	1931	Mary Turner	Of Thee I Sing*	Moderate Tempo	Soprano	C4	E5	Lead
Of Thee I Sing	1931	Mary Turner	A Kiss For Cinderella*	Moderate Tempo	Soprano	Ab4	G5	Lead
Of Thee I Sing	1931	Mary Turner	Who Cares Reprise*	Moderate Tempo	Soprano	C4	E5	Lead
Of Thee I Sing	1931	Mary Turner	I'm About To Be A Mother*	Moderate Tempo	Soprano	B3	A5	Lead
High Society 1998	1933	Tracy Lord	Once Upon A Time	Moderate Tempo	Soprano	F3	A4	Lead
Porgy and Bess	1935	Bess+	Bess, You Is My Woman*	Ballad	Soprano	D4	A#5	Lead
Porgy and Bess	1935	Bess+	What You Want Wid Bess*	Moderate Tempo	Soprano	Eb4	A5	Lead
Porgy and Bess	1935	Bess+	I Loves You Porgy*	Moderate Tempo	Soprano	Bb3	A5	Lead
Porgy and Bess	1935	Bess+	Summertime Reprise 2	Ballad	Soprano	E4	A5	Lead
Wizard Of Oz 1988	1939	Glenda	Come Out*	Moderate Tempo	Soprano	G3	C5	Lead
Kiss Me Kate	1948	Lilli Vanessi/Katherine	Wunderbar*	Ballad	Soprano	C4	G5	Lead
Kiss Me Kate	1948	Lilli Vanessi/Katherine	So In Love	Ballad	Soprano	A3	Db5	Lead
Kiss Me Kate	1948	Lilli Vanessi/Katherine	I Am Ashamed That Women Are	Moderate Tempo	Soprano	C4	Eb5	Lead
King and I, The	1951	Anna Leonowens	I Whistle A Happy Tune*	Uptempo	Soprano	D4	D5	Lead
King and I, The	1951	Anna Leonowens	Hello, Young Lovers	Ballad	Soprano	C#4	D5	Lead
King and I, The	1951	Anna Leonowens	Getting To Know You*	Moderate Tempo	Soprano	C#4	E5	Lead
King and I, The	1951	Anna Leonowens	Shall I Tell You What I Think....	Uptempo	Soprano	D3	C#5	Lead
King and I, The	1951	Anna Leonowens	Shall We Dance	Uptempo	Soprano	D4	C5	Lead
King and I, The	1951	Anna Leonowens	Hello, Young Lovers Reprise	Ballad	Soprano	C4	D5	Lead
King and I, The	1951	Lady Thiang+	Something Wonderful	Ballad	Soprano	C#4	G5	Lead
King and I, The	1951	Lady Thiang+	Western People Funny*	Moderate Tempo	Soprano	E4	G5	Lead
High Society 1998	1953	Tracy Lord	It's Alright With Me	Ballad	Soprano	C4	E5	Lead
High Society 1998	1955	Tracy Lord	High Society*	Uptempo	Soprano	Ab3	Eb5	Lead
Music Man, The	1957	Marian Paroo	My White Knight	Ballad	Soprano	C#4	Ab5	Lead
Music Man, The	1957	Marian Paroo	Will I Ever Leave You*	Moderate Tempo	Soprano	D4	F#5	Lead

Romantic Leading Female

* = Music Edit Required
+ = Ethnic Specific

Show	Year	Role	Song	Range-Bottom	Range-Top	Vocal Type	Tempo	Category
Music Man, The	1957	Marian Paroo	Till There Was You	Eb4	F5	Soprano	Ballad	Lead
Music Man, The	1957	Marian Paroo	Goodnight My Someone*	B3	E5	Soprano	Ballad	Lead
Sound Of Music, The	1959	Elsa Schraeder	How Can Love Survive	D4	F5	Soprano	Uptempo	Lead
Once Upon A Mattress	1959	Lady Larken	In A Little While*	Db4	Eb5	Soprano	Uptempo	Lead
Once Upon A Mattress	1959	Lady Larken	In A Little While Reprise*	D4	F5	Soprano	Ballad	Lead
Once Upon A Mattress	1959	Lady Larken	Yesterday I Loved You*	E4	F5	Soprano	Uptempo	Lead
Camelot	1960	Guenevere	The Simple Joys Of Maidenhood	B3	D#5	Soprano	Moderate Tempo	Lead
Camelot	1960	Guenevere	Camelot*	C4	D5	Soprano	Uptempo	Lead
Camelot	1960	Guenevere	The Lusty Month Of May*	D4	A5	Soprano	Uptempo	Lead
Camelot	1960	Guenevere	Before I Gaze At You Again	C4	Eb5	Soprano	Moderate Tempo	Lead
Camelot	1960	Guenevere	What Do The Simple Folk Do?*	Bb3	E5	Soprano	Moderate Tempo	Lead
Camelot	1960	Guenevere	I Loved You Once In Silence	Db4	Eb5	Soprano	Ballad	Lead
Camelot	1960	Nimue	Follow Me*	C#4	F#5	Soprano	Moderate Tempo	Supporting
She Loves Me	1963	Amalia Balash	No More Candy*	Db4	Fb5	Soprano	Moderate Tempo	Lead
She Loves Me	1963	Amalia Balash	I Don't Know His Name*	B#3	D#5	Soprano	Moderate Tempo	Lead
She Loves Me	1963	Amalia Balash	Will He Like Me	Bb3	F5	Soprano	Ballad	Lead
She Loves Me	1963	Amalia Balash	Dear Friend	C4	F5	Soprano	Uptempo	Lead
She Loves Me	1963	Amalia Balash	Where My Shoe (B Maj)*	E4	G5	Soprano	Uptempo	Lead
She Loves Me	1963	Amalia Balash	Vanilla Ice Cream	D4	B5	Soprano	Uptempo	Lead
She Loves Me	1963	Amalia Balash	Mr. Norwack, Will You Please	C4	E5	Soprano	Moderate Tempo	Lead
She Loves Me	1963	Amalia Balash	Where's My Shoe (G Maj)	C#4	F5	Soprano	Uptempo	Lead
Hello Dolly	1964	Irene Molloy	Ribbons Down My Back	A3	D5	Soprano	Ballad	Lead
Hello Dolly	1964	Irene Molloy	Motherhood	D4	E5	Soprano	Uptempo	Lead
Hello Dolly	1964	Irene Molloy	It Only Takes A Moment*	Ab3	Db4	Soprano	Ballad	Lead
Hello Dolly	1964	Irene Molloy	Ribbons Down My Back Reprise	B3	D5	Soprano	Ballad	Lead
Hello Dolly	1964	Irene Molloy	Dancing*	G3	E5	Soprano	Moderate Tempo	Lead
Annie	1977	Grace Farrell	N.Y.C. *	C4	F4	Soprano	Uptempo	Supporting
On The Twentieth Century	1978	Lily Garland	Veronique	E3	Ab6	Soprano	Uptempo	Lead

Romantic Leading Female

* = Music Edit Required
+ = Ethnic Specific

Show	Year	Role	Song	Tempo	Vocal Type	Range-Bottom	Range-Top	Category
On The Twentieth Century	1978	Lily Garland	Never*	Uptempo	Soprano	A3	A5	Lead
On The Twentieth Century	1978	Lily Garland	Our Private World*	Ballad	Soprano	A3	E5	Lead
On The Twentieth Century	1978	Lily Garland	I've Got It All*	Moderate Tempo	Soprano	B3	A5	Lead
On The Twentieth Century	1978	Lily Garland	Babette	Uptempo	Soprano	F#3	F#5	Lead
On The Twentieth Century	1978	Lily Garland	Sign Lily Sign*	Moderate Tempo	Soprano	B3	A5	Lead
Merrily We Roll Along 1994	1981	Beth	Not A Day Goes By	Ballad	Soprano	G3	B4	Lead
Nine	1982	Carla Albanese	A Call From The Vatican	Moderate Tempo	Soprano	A3	C6	Lead
Nine	1982	Carla Albanese	Simple	Ballad	Soprano	A3	E5	Lead
Nine	1982	Claudia Nardi	Unusual Way*	Ballad	Soprano	G#3	E5	Lead
Rags	1986	Rebecca Hershkowitz	Brand New World*	Moderate Tempo	Soprano	B3	G4	Lead
Rags	1986	Rebecca Hershkowitz	Children Of The Wind	Moderate Tempo	Soprano	A3	Bb5	Lead
Rags	1986	Rebecca Hershkowitz	If We Never Meet Again*	Ballad	Soprano	B2	C5	Lead
Rags	1986	Rebecca Hershkowitz	Penny A Tune	Uptempo	Soprano	E4	F#4	Lead
Rags	1986	Rebecca Hershkowitz	Blame It on The Summer Night	Moderate Tempo	Soprano	A3	D#5	Lead
Rags	1986	Rebecca Hershkowitz	Uptown*	Moderate Tempo	Soprano	C4	Eb5	Lead
Rags	1986	Rebecca Hershkowitz	Wanting*	Moderate Tempo	Soprano	A3	D#5	Lead
Rags	1986	Rebecca Hershkowitz	If We Never Meet Again Reprise	Ballad	Soprano	C4	D5	Lead
Rags	1986	Rebecca Hershkowitz	Dancing With Fools*	Uptempo	Soprano	Bb3	Gb5	Lead
Secret Garden, The	1991	Lily	Come To My Garden*	Moderate Tempo	Soprano	C4	G5	Lead
Secret Garden, The	1991	Lily	How Could I Ever Know*	Ballad	Soprano	Bb3	A5	Lead
Nick & Nora	1991	Tracy Gardner	Everybody Wants To Do A Musical	Moderate Tempo	Soprano	E2	G#5	Lead
Passion	1994	Clara	Happiness (Part 1)*	Moderate Tempo	Soprano	Bb3	Eb5	Lead
Passion	1994	Clara	Fourth Letter-How Could I Forget	Moderate Tempo	Soprano	F3	Db5	Lead
Passion	1994	Clara	Thinking Of You	Moderate Tempo	Soprano	Ab3	Db5	Lead
Passion	1994	Clara	Sunrise Letter*	Moderate Tempo	Soprano	Ab3	G5	Lead
Passion	1994	Clara	Forty Days	Uptempo	Soprano	Bb3	E5	Lead
Passion	1994	Clara	I Didn't Tell You	Ballad	Soprano	Ab3	F5	Lead
Passion	1994	Clara	I Am Writing To You	Moderate Tempo	Soprano	A3	C#5	Lead

Romantic Leading Female

Romantic Lead Female

Show	Year	Role	Song	Tempo	Vocal Type	Range-Bottom	Range-Top	Category
Victor/Victoria	1995	Victor	Le Jazz Hot	Moderate Tempo	Soprano	G#3	D5	Lead
Victor/Victoria	1995	Victor	Louis Says*	Uptempo	Soprano	E3	F4	Lead
Victor/Victoria	1995	Victoria	If I Were A Man	Moderate Tempo	Soprano	G3	A4	Lead
Victor/Victoria	1995	Victoria	Crazy World	Ballad	Soprano	Eb3	C5	Lead
Victor/Victoria	1995	Victoria	Almost A Love Song*	Ballad	Soprano	G#3	C5	Lead
Victor/Victoria	1995	Victoria	Living In The Shadows	Ballad	Soprano	E3	A4	Lead
Victor/Victoria	1995	Victoria	Living In The Shadows	Moderate Tempo	Soprano	E3	D5	Lead
Songs For A New World	1995	Woman 1	I'm Not Afraid Of Anything	Moderate Tempo	Soprano	A3	E5	Lead
Songs For A New World	1995	Woman 1	Christmas Lullaby	Ballad	Soprano	A3	E5	Lead
Songs For A New World	1995	Woman 1	I'd Give It All For You*	Moderate Tempo	Soprano	A3	F4	Lead
Songs For A New World	1995	Woman 1	Hear My Song*	Moderate Tempo	Soprano	A3	G4	Lead
Big	1996	Susan Lawrence	Stars, Stars, Stars	Ballad	Soprano	C4	D5	Lead
Big	1996	Susan Lawrence	One Special Man	Ballad	Soprano	G3	D5	Lead
Big	1996	Susan Lawrence	Dancing All The Time	Uptempo	Soprano	G3	D5	Lead
Big	1996	Susan Lawrence	My Secretary's In Love	Uptempo	Soprano	G3	D5	Lead
Big	1996	Susan Lawrence	Let's Not Move Too Fast	Ballad	Soprano	A3	C5	Lead
Big	1996	Susan Lawrence	Little Susan Lawrence	Uptempo	Soprano	Ab3	D5	Lead
Jekyll and Hyde	1997	Emma Crow	Emma's Reasons/The Engageme	Moderate Tempo	Soprano	Bb3	Db5	Lead
Jekyll and Hyde	1997	Emma Crow	Take Me As I Am	Ballad	Soprano	Bb3	F5	Lead
Jekyll and Hyde	1997	Emma Crow	Once Upon A Dream	Ballad	Soprano	B2	C#4	Lead
Jekyll and Hyde	1997	Emma Crow	In His Eyes*	Ballad	Soprano	Bb3	F5	Lead
Ragtime	1998	Mother	Goodbye My Love	Moderate Tempo	Soprano	G3	Db5	Lead
Ragtime	1998	Mother	What Kind Of Woman*	Moderate Tempo	Soprano	Bb3	Eb5	Lead
Ragtime	1998	Mother	New Music*	Ballad	Soprano	Bb3	D5	Lead
Ragtime	1998	Mother	Back To Before	Moderate Tempo	Soprano	G3	C5	Lead
Producers, The	2001	Ulla	When You've Got It Flaunt It!	Moderate Tempo	Soprano	Bb3	Eb5	Lead
Wicked	2003	Glinda	Openning*	Moderate Tempo	Soprano	A3	A5	Lead
Wicked	2003	Glinda	No One Mourns The Wicked*	Moderate Tempo	Soprano	C#4	B5	Lead

Romantic Leading Female

Show	Year	Role	Song	Tempo	Vocal Type	Range-Bottom	Range-Top	Category
Wicked	2003	Glinda	Popular*	Moderate Tempo	Soprano	G3	C5	Lead
Wicked	2003	Glinda	Thank Goodness (Part 3)	Uptempo	Soprano	Bb3	A5	Lead
Wicked	2003	Glinda	I'm Not That Girl Reprise	Ballad	Soprano	G3	D5	Lead
Wicked	2003	Glinda	For Good*	Ballad	Soprano	Ab3	Db5	Lead
Dirty Rotten Scoundrels	2005	Christine Colgate	Here I Am	Uptempo	Soprano	F3	E5	Lead
Dirty Rotten Scoundrels	2005	Christine Colgate	Nothing Is Too Wonderful To Be T	Ballad	Soprano	A3	F5	Lead
Light In The Piazza, The	2005	Margaret Johnson	Statues and Stories*	Uptempo	Soprano	A3	A5	Lead
Light In The Piazza, The	2005	Margaret Johnson	Dividing Day	Ballad	Soprano	G3	E5	Lead
Light In The Piazza, The	2005	Margaret Johnson	The Beauty Is Reprise	Moderate Tempo	Soprano	B#3	G5	Lead
Light In The Piazza, The	2005	Margaret Johnson	Fable	Uptempo	Soprano	C#4	F#5	Lead
Chitty Chitty Bang Bang	2005	Truly Scrumptious	Truly Scrumptious	Moderate Tempo	Soprano	C4	C5	Lead
Chitty Chitty Bang Bang	2005	Truly Scrumptious	Music Box	Ballad	Soprano	D4	Eb5	Lead
Chitty Chitty Bang Bang	2005	Truly Scrumptious	Toot Sweets *	Uptempo	Soprano	D4	Eb5	Lead
Grey Gardens	2006	Edie Beale (Act 2)	The Revolutionary Costume*	Uptempo	Soprano	Bb3	C5	Lead
Grey Gardens	2006	Edie Beale (Act 2)	Around The World	Moderate Tempo	Soprano	C4	C#5	Lead
Grey Gardens	2006	Edie Beale (Act 2)	Around The World Reprise	Ballad	Soprano	C4	C#5	Lead
Grey Gardens	2006	Edie Beale (Act 2)	Another Winter	Ballad	Soprano	F#3	C#5	Lead
Grey Gardens	2006	Edith Beale (Act 1)	The Five Fifteen*	Uptempo	Soprano	B3	B4	Lead
Grey Gardens	2006	Edith Beale (Act 1)	Hominy Grits*	Moderate Tempo	Soprano	B3	C#5	Lead
Grey Gardens	2006	Edith Beale (Act 1)	The Five Fifteen Reprise*	Ballad	Soprano	C4	A4	Lead
Grey Gardens	2006	Edith Beale (Act 1)	Will You?	Ballad	Soprano	C4	E5	Lead
Marry Poppins	2006	Mary Poppins	Practically Perfect*	Moderate Tempo	Soprano	A3	G#3	Lead
Marry Poppins	2006	Mary Poppins	A Spoonful Of Sugar*	Uptempo	Soprano	Cb4	Ab5	Lead
Marry Poppins	2006	Mary Poppins	Supercalifragilisticexpialidocious⟩	Uptempo	Soprano	C4	E5	Lead
Marry Poppins	2006	Mary Poppins	Anything Can Happen*	Moderate Tempo	Soprano	C4	D5	Lead

Romantic Leading Female

* = Music Edit Required
+ = Ethnic Specific

Show	Year	Role	Song	Tempo	Vocal Type	Range-Bottom	Range-Top	Category
No, No Nanette	1925	Bill Early	The Call Of TheSea*	Uptempo	Baritone	D3	F#4	Lead
No, No Nanette	1925	Bill Early	You Can Dance w/Any Girl At All*	Uptempo	Baritone	C3	F4	Lead
No, No Nanette	1925	Bill Early	Telephone Girlie*	Uptempo	Baritone	C3	F4	Lead
Good News (1993 Revival)	1928	Coach Johnson	You're The Cream In My Coffee*	Uptempo	Baritone	B2	Eb4	Lead
Good News (1993 Revival)	1928	Coach Johnson	Together*	Ballad	Baritone	G3	B4	Lead
Good News (1993 Revival)	1928	Coach Johnson	Together Part 2*	Ballad	Baritone	G2	C4	Lead
High Society 1998	1929	George Kittredge	I'll Worship You	Moderate Tempo	Baritone	G#2	F#4	Lead
Of Thee I Sing	1931	John P Wintergreen	Some Girls Can Bake A Pie*	Uptempo	Baritone	E3	F4	Lead
Of Thee I Sing	1931	John P Wintergreen	Of Thee I Sing*	Moderate Tempo	Baritone	C3	E4	Lead
Of Thee I Sing	1931	John P Wintergreen	Supreme Court Judges*	Uptempo	Baritone	B2	E4	Lead
Of Thee I Sing	1931	John P Wintergreen	Who Cares Reprise*	Moderate Tempo	Baritone	C3	E4	Lead
Anything Goes	1934	Billy Crocker	You're the Top *	Uptempo	Baritone	B2	F4	Lead
Anything Goes	1934	Billy Crocker	All Through The Night *	Ballad	Baritone	F3	G4	Lead
Oklahoma!	1943	Curly	Oh What A Beautiful Morning	Moderate Tempo	Baritone	D3	E4	Lead
Oklahoma!	1943	Curly	The Surrey w/The Fringe On Top	Uptempo	Baritone	D#3	E4	Lead
Oklahoma!	1943	Curly	People Will Say We're In Love*	Moderate Tempo	Baritone	C#3	F#4	Lead
Oklahoma!	1943	Curly	Poor Jud*	Ballad	Baritone	D#3	C#4	Lead
Annie Get Your Gun	1944	Frank Butler	There's No Business..Show Bus.	Uptempo	Baritone	Ab3	E4	Lead
Annie Get Your Gun	1944	Frank Butler	The Girl That I Marry*	Moderate Tempo	Baritone	D3	D4	Lead
Annie Get Your Gun	1944	Frank Butler	They Say That Falling In Love*	Ballad	Baritone	C3	D4	Lead
Annie Get Your Gun	1944	Frank Butler	My Defenses Are Down	Moderate Tempo	Baritone	Db3	Eb4	Lead
Annie Get Your Gun	1944	Frank Butler	An Old Fashioned Wedding	Uptempo	Baritone	B2	E4	Lead
Annie Get Your Gun	1944	Frank Butler	The Girl I Marry Reprise	Ballad	Baritone	A3	D4	Lead
Annie Get Your Gun	1944	Frank Butler	Show Business Reprise *	Moderate Tempo	Baritone	C3	F4	Lead
Brigadoon	1947	Tommy Albright	The Heather On The Hill *	Ballad	Baritone	Bb2	F4	Lead
Brigadoon	1947	Tommy Albright	Almost Like Being In Love *	Ballad	Baritone	C3	F#4	Lead
Brigadoon	1947	Tommy Albright	There But For You Go I	Ballad	Baritone	B2	F4	Lead
Brigadoon	1947	Tommy Albright	From This Day On *	Ballad	Baritone	D3	Eb4	Lead

Romantic Lead Male

* = Music Edit Required
+ = Ethnic Specitic

Show	Year	Role	Song	Tempo	Vocal Type	Range-Bottom	Range-Top	Category
Brigadoon	1947	Tommy Albright	From This Day On Reprise *	Ballad	Baritone	Eb3	Eb4	Lead
Kiss Me Kate	1948	Fred Graham/Petruchio	Wunderbar*	Ballad	Baritone	C3	G4	Lead
Kiss Me Kate	1948	Fred Graham/Petruchio	Were Thine That Speical Face	Moderate Tempo	Baritone	C3	F4	Lead
Kiss Me Kate	1948	Fred Graham/Petruchio	Where Is The Life...I Led	Moderate Tempo	Baritone	B2	F4	Lead
Kiss Me Kate	1948	Fred Graham/Petruchio	So In Love Reprise	Ballad	Baritone	B2	Eb4	Lead
South Pacific	1949	Emile De Becque	Some Enchanted Evening	Ballad	Baritone	C3	E4	Lead
South Pacific	1949	Emile De Becque	Some Enchanted Evening Reprise	Ballad	Baritone	C3	E4	Lead
South Pacific	1949	Emile De Becque	This Nearly Was Mine	Ballad	Baritone	B2	D4	Lead
South Pacific	1949	Emile De Becque	You've Got To Be...Taught Rep.	Moderate Tempo	Baritone	C#3	E4	Lead
Call Me Madam	1950	Cosmo Constantine	Lichtenburg*	Moderate Tempo	Baritone	Bb2	D4	Lead
Call Me Madam	1950	Cosmo Constantine	Marrying For Love*	Ballad	Baritone	G2	C4	Lead
Guys and Dolls	1950	Sky Masterson	I'll Know*	Ballad	Baritone	B2	D#4	Lead
Guys and Dolls	1950	Sky Masterson	My Time Of Day	Ballad	Baritone	Bb2	Db4	Lead
Guys and Dolls	1950	Sky Masterson	Luck Be A Lady*	Uptempo	Baritone	Db3	Eb4	Lead
King and I, The	1951	King of Siam+	A Puzzlement	Uptempo	Baritone	C3	E4	Lead
King and I, The	1951	King of Siam+	Song of the King	Moderate Tempo	Baritone	D3	D4	Lead
Wonderful Town	1953	Robert Baker	What A Waste*	Uptempo	Baritone	Ab2	F#4	Lead
Wonderful Town	1953	Robert Baker	A Quiet Girl	Ballad	Baritone	G2	C4	Lead
Wonderful Town	1953	Robert Baker	It's Love*	Moderate Tempo	Baritone	A2	F#4	Lead
My Fair Lady	1956	Henry Higgins	Why Can't The English	Uptempo	Baritone	B2	D4	Lead
My Fair Lady	1956	Henry Higgins	A Hymn to Him	Uptempo	Baritone	C#3	D4	Lead
My Fair Lady	1956	Henry Higgins	I've Grown Accustomed...	Ballad	Baritone	A2	B3	Lead
My Fair Lady	1956	Henry Higgins	I'm An Ordinary Man	Moderate Tempo	Baritone	Bb2	C4	Lead
Bells Are Ringing	1956	Jeff Moss	Independent	Uptempo	Baritone	D3	E4	Lead
Bells Are Ringing	1956	Jeff Moss	I Met A Girl	Uptempo	Baritone	C3	Gb4	Lead
Bells Are Ringing	1956	Jeff Moss	Long Before I Knew You *	Ballad	Baritone	B2	C4	Lead
Bells Are Ringing	1956	Jeff Moss	Just In Time *	Moderate Tempo	Baritone	C#3	D4	Lead

Romantic Lead Male

* = Music Edit Required
+ = Ethnic Specific

Show	Year	Role	Song	Tempo	Vocal Type	Range-Bottom	Range-Top	Category
Bells Are Ringing	1956	Jeff Moss	Long Before I Knew You Reprise	Moderate Tempo	Baritone	C3	C4	Lead
Bells Are Ringing	1956	Jeff Moss	Better Than A Dream *	Moderate Tempo	Baritone	E3	D4	Lead
Flower Drum Song 2002	1958	Chi-Yang Wang+	Gliding Through My Memory*	Moderate Tempo	Baritone	D3	G4	Lead
Sound Of Music, The	1959	Captain von Trapp	Edelweiss	Ballad	Baritone	E3	F4	Lead
Once Upon A Mattress	1959	Sir Harry	In A Little While*	Uptempo	Baritone	Db3	F4	Lead
Once Upon A Mattress	1959	Sir Harry	In A Little While Reprise*	Ballad	Baritone	D3	F4	Lead
Once Upon A Mattress	1959	Sir Harry	Yesterday I Loved You*	Uptempo	Baritone	F3	F4	Lead
Fantasticks, The	1960	El Gallo	Try To Remember *	Ballad	Baritone	A2	C4	Lead
Fantasticks, The	1960	El Gallo	Try To Remember Reprise	Moderate Tempo	Baritone	B2	C4	Lead
Fantasticks, The	1960	El Gallo	I Depends On What You Pay	Uptempo	Baritone	A2	G4	Lead
Fantasticks, The	1960	El Gallo	Round and Round *	Uptempo	Baritone	Ab2	F4	Lead
Camelot	1960	King Arthur	I Wonder What The King Is Doing	Uptempo	Baritone	Bb2	C4	Lead
Camelot	1960	King Arthur	Camelot*	Uptempo	Baritone	C3	D4	Lead
Camelot	1960	King Arthur	How To Handle A Woman*	Uptempo	Baritone	A2	D4	Lead
Camelot	1960	King Arthur	What Do The Simple Folk Do?*	Moderate Tempo	Baritone	Bb2	E4	Lead
Camelot	1960	King Arthur	Finalte Ultimo	Moderate Tempo	Baritone	Bb2	C4	Lead
Camelot	1960	Lancelot Du Lac	C'est Moi	Uptempo	Baritone	B2	D4	Lead
Camelot	1960	Lancelot Du Lac	If Ever I would Leave You	Ballad	Baritone	A2	D4	Lead
She Loves Me	1963	Georg Nowack	She Loves Me	Uptempo	Baritone	Eb3	F4	Lead
She Loves Me	1963	Georg Nowack	Three Letters*	Moderate Tempo	Baritone	D#3	E4	Lead
Funny Girl	1964	Nick Arnstein	I Want To Be Seen With You...*	Moderate Tempo	Baritone	Ab2	Eb4	Lead
Funny Girl	1964	Nick Arnstein	You Are Woman*	Moderate Tempo	Baritone	A#2	E4	Lead
Funny Girl	1964	Nick Arnstein	Don't Rain On My Parade (Nick)	Moderate Tempo	Baritone	G3	D4	Lead
Hair	1968	Claude	Manchester England	Moderate Tempo	Baritone	E3	F#4	Lead
Hair	1968	Claude	I Got Life	Uptempo	Baritone	C3	F4	Lead
Hair	1968	Claude	Where Do I Go	Moderate Tempo	Baritone	C4	F5	Lead
Hair	1968	Claude	Hair	Uptempo	Baritone	D3	G4	Lead
Hair	1968	Claude	Manchester England Reprise	Moderate Tempo	Baritone	E3	E4	Lead

Romantic Lead Male

* = Music Edit Required
+ = Ethnic Specific

Show	Year	Role	Song	Vocal Type	Range-Bottom	Range-Top	Category
1776	1969	Richard Henry Lee	The Lees of Old Virginia	Baritone	C3	F4	Lead
Applause	1970	Bill Sampson	Think How It's Gonna Be	Baritone	B2	F4	Lead
Applause	1970	Bill Sampson	One Of A Kind*	Baritone	Bb2	F4	Lead
Company (Revival)	1970	Peter	Have I Got A Girl For You	Baritone	B3	Gb5	Supporting
Follies	1971	Benjamin Stone	The Road You Didn't Take *	Baritone	A2	E4	Lead
Follies	1971	Benjamin Stone	Too Many Mornings *	Baritone	C3	E4	Lead
Follies	1971	Benjamin Stone	Live, Laugh, Love	Baritone	C#3	F4	Lead
Sugar	1972	Joe	Penniless Bums*	Baritone	C3	E4	Lead
Sugar	1972	Joe	The Beauty That Drives Men Mad	Baritone	D3	F4	Lead
Sugar	1972	Joe	Doin' It For Sugar*	Baritone	B3	E4	Lead
Sugar	1972	Joe	Shell Oil	Baritone	D3	B3	Lead
Sugar	1972	Joe	What Do You Give To A Man...*	Baritone	C3	E4	Lead
Sugar	1972	Joe	It Always Love	Baritone	C3	D4	Lead
A Little Night Music	1973	Count Carl-Magnus Malcolm	In Praise of Women	Baritone	C3	F4	Supporting
A Little Night Music	1973	Count Carl-Magnus Malcolm	It Would Have Been Wonderful *	Baritone	C3	E4	Supporting
A Little Night Music	1973	Frederik Egerman	Now	Baritone	Bb2	F4	Lead
A Little Night Music	1973	Frederik Egerman	You Must Meet My Wife	Baritone	C3	E4	Lead
A Little Night Music	1973	Frederik Egerman	It Would Have Been Wonderful *	Baritone	C3	E4	Lead
Annie	1977	Oliver Warbucks	N.Y.C.*	Baritone	C3	F4	Lead
Annie	1977	Oliver Warbucks	Something Was Missing	Baritone	Bb2	F4	Lead
Annie	1977	Oliver Warbucks	Why Should I Change A Thing	Baritone	Bb2	Gb4	Lead
Evita	1978	Juan Peron	The Art of the Possible	Baritone	Bb2	D4	Lead
Evita	1978	Juan Peron	She's A Diamond	Baritone	A2	F4	Lead
Best Little Whorehouse...	1978	Sheriff Ed Earl	Good Old Girl	Baritone	G3	F4	Lead
Dreamgirls	1981	Curtis Taylor, Jr +	Cadillac Car	Baritone	F3	G4	Lead
Dreamgirls	1981	Curtis Taylor, Jr +	When I First Saw You	Baritone	C3	E4	Lead
Cats	1981	Munkustrap	The Old Gumbie Cat	Baritone	E3	F4	Lead
Seven Brides/Seven Broth	1982	Adam	Bless Your Beautiful Hide*	Baritone	B2	G4	Lead

Romantic Lead Male

Romantic Lead Male

Show	Year	Role	Song	Tempo	Vocal Type	Range-Bottom	Range-Top	Category
Seven Brides/Seven Brothe	1982	Adam	Get A Wife*	Moderate Tempo	Baritone	F3	G4	Lead
Seven Brides/Seven Brothe	1982	Adam	Love Never Goes Away*	Ballad	Baritone	E3	E4	Lead
Seven Brides/Seven Brothe	1982	Adam	Sobbin' Women*	Uptempo	Baritone	C3	F4	Lead
Seven Brides/Seven Brothe	1982	Adam	A Woman Ought To Know Her Pla	Uptempo	Baritone	F#3	F#4	Lead
Seven Brides/Seven Brothe	1982	Adam	Love Never Goes Away Tag	Ballad	Baritone	B3	D4	Lead
Singin' In The Rain	1983	Don Lockwood	You Stepped Out Of A Dream*	Moderate Tempo	Baritone	C3	C4	Lead
Singin' In The Rain	1983	Don Lockwood	You Stepped Out Of A Dream Rep	Moderate Tempo	Baritone	C3	C4	Lead
Singin' In The Rain	1983	Don Lockwood	You Were Meant For Me	Moderate Tempo	Baritone	Bb2	Db4	Lead
Singin' In The Rain	1983	Don Lockwood	Meant For Me Playoff	Moderate Tempo	Baritone	C3	Db4	Lead
Singin' In The Rain	1983	Don Lockwood	Singin' In The Rain	Uptempo	Baritone	D3	D4	Lead
Singin' In The Rain	1983	Don Lockwood	Don's Would You	Moderate Tempo	Baritone	G2	C4	Lead
Singin' In The Rain	1983	Don Lockwood	Broadway Rhythm* (ms 115-182)	Uptempo	Baritone	C3	F4	Lead
LA Cage Aux Folles	1983	Georges	Song On The Sand	Ballad	Baritone	Ab2	E4	Lead
LA Cage Aux Folles	1983	Georges	Masculinity	Uptempo	Baritone	B2	E4	Lead
LA Cage Aux Folles	1983	Georges	Look Over There	Ballad	Baritone	B2	Eb4	Lead
LA Cage Aux Folles	1983	Georges	With You On My Arm	Moderate Tempo	Baritone	G#2	Eb4	Lead
LA Cage Aux Folles	1983	Georges	Song On The Sand Reprise	Ballad	Baritone	C3	D4	Lead
Into The Woods	1987	Cinderella's Prince	Agony*	Moderate Tempo	Baritone	C#3	E4	Lead
Into The Woods	1987	Cinderella's Prince	Agony II*	Moderate Tempo	Baritone	C#3	F4	Lead
Into The Woods	1987	Cinderella's Prince	Any Moment*	Uptempo	Baritone	B2	Eb5	Lead
Into The Woods	1987	Rapunzel's Prince	Agony*	Moderate Tempo	Baritone	C#3	E4	Lead
Into The Woods	1987	Rapunzel's Prince	Agony II*	Moderate Tempo	Baritone	C#3	F4	Lead
Into The Woods	1987	Wolf	Hello Little Girl	Uptempo	Baritone	Bb2	Gb4	Lead
City of Angels	1989	Stine	You're Nothing Without Me *	Uptempo	Baritone	D3	G4	Lead
City of Angels	1989	Stine	Funny	Moderate Tempo	Baritone	Bb2	F4	Lead
City of Angels	1989	Stine	Double Talk (Stine)	Moderate Tempo	Baritone	F3	G4	Lead
City of Angels	1989	Stine	I'm Nothing Without You *	Uptempo	Baritone	F3	G4	Lead

Romantic Lead Male

Romantic Lead Male

Show	Year	Role	Song	Tempo	Vocal Type	Range-Bottom	Range-Top	Category
Meet Me In St. Louis	1989	Warren Sheffield	Raving Beauty*	Ballad	Baritone	C3	Eb4	Lead
Phantom	1991	Count Philippe	Who Could Have Ever Dreamed...	Uptempo	Baritone	Bb2	E4	Lead
Phantom	1991	Count Philippe	Without Your Music	Moderate Tempo	Baritone	C3	F4	Lead
Children of Eden	1991	Father	Father's Day	Moderate Tempo	Baritone	B2	E4	Lead
Children of Eden	1991	Father	The Mark of Cain	Moderate Tempo	Baritone	B2	F4	Lead
Children of Eden	1991	Father	Precious Children	Ballad	Baritone	Bb2	Eb4	Lead
Children of Eden	1991	Father	The Hardest Part Of Love *	Uptempo	Baritone	D3	G4	Lead
Secret Garden, The	1991	Neville Craven	Disppear*	Moderate Tempo	Baritone	C3	F4	Lead
Nick & Nora	1991	Nick Charles	Look Who's Alone Now	Ballad	Baritone	Ab2	C4	Lead
Nick & Nora	1991	Nick Charles	As Long As You're Happy*	Uptempo	Baritone	A2	F4	Lead
Nick & Nora	1991	Nick Charles	Let' Go Home Nora	Ballad	Baritone	G3	B4	Lead
Assassins	1992	The Proprietor	Opening*	Moderate Tempo	Baritone	F#2	F4	Lead
Beauty and the Beast	1994	Lumiere	Be Our Guest	Uptempo	Baritone	F#2	E4	Support
Victor/Victoria	1995	Jazz Singer	Le Jazz Hot*	Moderate Tempo	Baritone	D3	F#4	Lead
Victor/Victoria	1995	King Marchan	King's Dilemma*	Uptempo	Baritone	A2	D4	Lead
Victor/Victoria	1995	King Marchan	Almost A Love Song*	Ballad	Baritone	G#2	Eb4	Lead
Songs For A New World	1995	Man 2	She Cries	Uptempo	Baritone	C3	G#4	Lead
Songs For A New World	1995	Man 2	I'd Give It All For You*	Moderate Tempo	Baritone	F#2	G4	Lead
Songs For A New World	1995	Man 2	Hear My Song*	Moderate Tempo	Baritone	F3	E4	Lead
Songs For A New World	1995	Man 2	The River Won't Flow*	Uptempo	Baritone	D3	A4	Lead
Lion King, The	1997	Mufasa	They Live In You*	Moderate Tempo	Baritone	C#3	F#4	Lead
Ragtime	1998	Coalhouse Walker, Jr.+	Now She Is Haunting Me (Part 1)	Ballad	Baritone	Bb2	D4	Lead
Ragtime	1998	Coalhouse Walker, Jr.+	On The Wheels Of A Dream*	Moderate Tempo	Baritone	Ab2	Fb4	Lead
Ragtime	1998	Coalhouse Walker, Jr.+	Coalhouse's Soliloguoy	Moderate Tempo	Baritone	G2	F4	Lead
Ragtime	1998	Coalhouse Walker, Jr.+	Sarah Brown Eyes*	Moderate Tempo	Baritone	A2	E4	Lead
Ragtime	1998	Coalhouse Walker, Jr.+	Make Them Hear You	Moderate Tempo	Baritone	Eb3	G#4	Lead
Ragtime	1998	Father	Journey On*	Uptempo	Baritone	B2	E4	Lead

Romantic Lead Male

Romantic Lead Male

* = Music Edit Required
+ = Ethnic Specific

Show	Year	Role	Song	Tempo	Vocal Type	Range-Bottom	Range-Top	Category
Ragtime	1998	Father	New Music*	Ballad	Baritone	Bb2	D4	Lead
Parade	1998	Gov. Jack Slaton	Pretty Music*	Uptempo	Baritone	C3	G4	Lead
Dirty Rotten Scoundrels	2005	Lawrence Jameson	Give Them What They Want *	Moderate Tempo	Baritone	C3	Eb4	Lead
Dirty Rotten Scoundrels	2005	Lawrence Jameson	All About Ruprecht	Uptempo	Baritone	D3	E4	Lead
Dirty Rotten Scoundrels	2005	Lawrence Jameson	Ruffjousin' Mit Shuffhousen	Uptempo	Baritone	C3	A4	Lead
Dirty Rotten Scoundrels	2005	Lawrence Jameson	Love Sneaks In	Ballad	Baritone	G2	D4	Lead
Dirty Rotten Scoundrels	2005	Lawrence Jameson	The More We Dance	Uptempo	Baritone	D3	G4	Lead
Dirty Rotten Scoundrels	2005	Lawrence Jameson	Dirty Rotten Number	Moderate Tempo	Baritone	C3	F4	Lead
Little Women	2005	Professor Bhaer	How I Am	Uptempo	Baritone	A2	F#4	Supporting
Grey Gardens	2006	Gould	Drift Away*	Ballad	Baritone	Eb3	F4	Lead
White Christmas	2008	Bob Wallace	Love And The Weather*	Uptempo	Baritone	Db3	E4	Lead
White Christmas	2008	Bob Wallace	Count Your Blessings*	Moderate Tempo	Baritone	C3	D4	Lead
White Christmas	2008	Bob Wallace	Blue Skies (Part 1-3)*	Moderate Tempo	Baritone	E3	F4	Lead
White Christmas	2008	Bob Wallace	How Deep Is The Ocean	Ballad	Baritone	C#3	D4	Lead
Addams Family, The	2010	Gomez Addams +	Trapped (US Tour)	Moderate Tempo	Baritone	C3	F4	Lead
Show Boat	1927	Gaylord Ravenal	Make Believe*	Ballad	Tenor	C3	G4	Lead
Show Boat	1927	Gaylord Ravenal	You Are Love*	Ballad	Tenor	D3	Bb4	Lead
Show Boat	1927	Gaylord Ravenal	You Are Love Reprise	Ballad	Tenor	C3	Ab4	Lead
Show Boat	1927	Gaylord Ravenal	I Have The Room Above Her	Moderate Tempo	Tenor	E3	Eb4	Lead
Show Boat	1927	Gaylord Ravenal	Where's The Mate For Me	Ballad	Tenor	D3	F#4	Lead
High Society 1998	1929	Dexter C.K. Haven	She's Got That Thing*	Uptempo	Tenor	A2	G4	Lead
High Society 1998	1933	Dexter C.K. Haven	Once Upon A Time	Moderate Tempo	Tenor	G2	E4	Lead
High Society 1998	1935	Dexter C.K. Haven	Just One Of Those Things	Uptempo	Tenor	B2	E4	Lead
Porgy and Bess	1935	Sporting Life+	It Ain't Necessarily So*	Moderate Tempo	Tenor	C4	A4	Lead
Porgy and Bess	1935	Sporting Life+	There's A Boat...Leaving Soon...	Moderate Tempo	Tenor	D3	Bb4	Lead
On The Town	1944	Gabey	Lonely Town	Ballad	Tenor	C4	F5	Lead

Romantic Lead Male

Romantic Lead Male

* = Music Edit Required
+ = Ethnic Specific

Show	Year	Role	Song	Tempo	Vocal Type	Range-Bottom	Range-Top	Category
On The Town	1944	Gabey	Lucky To Be Me	Uptempo	Tenor	B2	A4	Lead
Pajama Game	1954	Sid Sorokin	A New Town Is A Blue Town	Ballad	Tenor	Db3	G4	Lead
Pajama Game	1954	Sid Sorokin	Hey There*	Ballad	Tenor	F3	Ab4	Lead
Pajama Game	1954	Sid Sorokin	Once-A-Year Day*	Uptempo	Tenor	E3	F4	Lead
Pajama Game	1954	Sid Sorokin	Small Talk*	Uptempo	Tenor	Db3	Gb4	Lead
Pajama Game	1954	Sid Sorokin	There Once Was A Man*	Uptempo	Tenor	C#3	Gb4	Lead
Pajama Game	1954	Sid Sorokin	Hey There-Finale Act I	Ballad	Tenor	F3	Gb4	Lead
High Society 1998	1955	Dexter C.K. Haven	Little One*	Uptempo	Tenor	A2	D4	Lead
High Society 1998	1955	Dexter C.K. Haven	Little On Reprise	Uptempo	Tenor	Bb2	Ab3	Lead
High Society 1998	1955	Dexter C.K. Haven	True Love*	Ballad	Tenor	C3	F4	Lead
Candide	1956	Governor	My Love*	Moderate Tempo	Tenor	C3	A4	Lead
Candide	1956	Maximillion	Life Is Happiness Indeed*	Moderate Tempo	Tenor	D3	F4	Lead
Flower Drum Song 2002	1958	Chi-Yang Wang+	Chop Suey*	Moderate Tempo	Tenor	B2	D#4	Lead
Once Upon A Mattress	1959	Minstrel	Many Moons Ago	Moderate Tempo	Tenor	D3	G4	Lead
Unsinkable Molly Brown	1960	Johnny Brown	Colorado My Home	Moderate Tempo	Tenor	B2	F4	Lead
Unsinkable Molly Brown	1960	Johnny Brown	I've A'ready Started In	Moderate Tempo	Tenor	G3	E4	Lead
Unsinkable Molly Brown	1960	Johnny Brown	I'll Never Say No	Ballad	Tenor	Db3	F4	Lead
Unsinkable Molly Brown	1960	Johnny Brown	If I Knew	Ballad	Tenor	C3	F4	Lead
Unsinkable Molly Brown	1960	Johnny Brown	Chick-A-Pen	Ballad	Tenor	Db3	F4	Lead
Unsinkable Molly Brown	1960	Johnny Brown	Leadville Johnny Brown Soliloquy	Moderate Tempo	Tenor	C3	E4	Lead
Funny Girl	1964	Zeigfeld Tenor	His Love Makes Me Beautiful*	Moderate Tempo	Tenor	E3	A4	Supporting
Cabaret	1966	Clifford Bradshaw	Perfectly Marvelous *	Uptempo	Tenor	D3	E4	Lead
Cabaret	1966	Clifford Bradshaw	Why Should I Wake Up?	Moderate Tempo	Tenor	B2	E4	Lead
Sweet Charity	1966	Vittorio Vidal	Too Many Tomorrows	Ballad	Tenor	Bb2	G4	Lead
Company (Revival)	1970	Robert	Company	Uptempo	Tenor	A2	Ab4	Lead
Company (Revival)	1970	Robert	Someone Is Waiting	Ballad	Tenor	B2	E4	Lead
Company (Revival)	1970	Robert	Being Alive	Moderate Tempo	Tenor	D3	F4	Lead

Romantic Lead Male

* = Music Edit Required
+ = Ethnic Specitic

Show	Year	Role	Song	Tempo	Vocal Type	Range-Bottom	Range-Top	Category
Jesus Christ Superstar	1971	Jesus of Nazareth	Poor Jerusalem	Ballad	Tenor	A2	Ab4	Lead
Jesus Christ Superstar	1971	Jesus of Nazareth	Gethsemane	Ballad	Tenor	Bb2	Ab4	Lead
Jesus Christ Superstar	1971	Jesus of Nazareth	The Last Supper	Ballad	Tenor	F#2	C5	Lead
Grease	1971	Teen Angel	Beauty School Dropout	Moderate Tempo	Tenor	F#3	F#5	Supporting
Pacific Overtures	1976	Kayama+	Poems*	Moderate Tempo	Tenor	Eb3	F4	Lead
Pacific Overtures	1976	Kayama+	A Bowler Hat	Moderate Tempo	Tenor	G2	Eb4	Lead
Evita	1978	Magaldi	On This Nigh of a Thousand Stars	Ballad	Tenor	Bb2	G4	Supporting
Cats	1981	Munkustrap	Old Deuteronomy *	Ballad	Tenor	B2	G4	Lead
Singin' In The Rain	1983	Production Tenor	Beautiful Girl	Moderate Tempo	Tenor	F3	Bb4	Supporting
Phantom Of The Opera	1986	Raoul, Vicomte de Chagny	Prologue	Ballad	Tenor	C#3	E4	Lead
Phantom Of The Opera	1986	Raoul, Vicomte de Chagny	All I Ask Of You*	Ballad	Tenor	Ab3	G4	Lead
Chess	1988	Anatoly	Where I Want To Be	Moderate Tempo	Tenor	E3	G4	Lead
Chess	1988	Anatoly	Anthem	Moderate Tempo	Tenor	C3	G4	Lead
Chess	1988	Anatoly	You and I	Ballad	Tenor	G2	G4	Lead
Chess	1988	Anatoly	You and I Reprise	Ballad	Tenor	G3	F5	Lead
Chess	1988	Anatoly	Endgame*	Uptempo	Tenor	C3	A4	Lead
City of Angels	1989	Jimmy Powers	Ya Gotta Look Out For Yourself	Uptempo	Tenor	C3	D4	Supporting
City of Angels	1989	Jimmy Powers	Stay Wth Me	Ballad	Tenor	C3	G4	Supporting
Miss Saigon	1991	Chris Scott	Why God Why	Moderate Tempo	Tenor	G3	G4	Lead
Miss Saigon	1991	Chris Scott	The Confrontation (ms44-79)	Uptempo	Tenor	F3	B4	Lead
Miss Saigon	1991	Chris Scott	Sun And Moon*	Ballad	Tenor	A2	F#4	Lead
Passion	1994	Giorgio Bachetti	Happiness (Part 2)*	Moderate Tempo	Tenor	A2	C4	Lead
Passion	1994	Giorgio Bachetti	Is This What You Call Love?	Uptempo	Tenor	A#2	F4	Lead
Passion	1994	Giorgio Bachetti	No One Has Ever Loved Me	Ballad	Tenor	B2	D4	Lead
Rent	1996	Roger Davis	One Song Glory	Moderate Tempo	Tenor	D3	Ab4	Lead
Rent	1996	Tom Collins	Sante Fe*	Moderate Tempo	Tenor	F#2	F#4	Lead
Rent	1996	Tom Collins	I'll Cover You*	Moderate Tempo	Tenor	C3	G4	Lead

Romantic Lead Male

Romantic Lead Male

* = Music Edit Required
+ = Ethnic Specific

Show	Year	Role	Song	Tempo	Vocal Type	Range-Bottom	Range-Top	Category
Rent	1996	Tom Collins	I'll Cover You Reprise*	Ballad	Tenor	F#2	A4	Lead
Steel Pier	1997	Bill Kelly	Second Chance	Uptempo	Tenor	B2	E4	Lead
Steel Pier	1997	Bill Kelly	The Last Girl*	Moderate Tempo	Tenor	Bb2	G4	Lead
Steel Pier	1997	Bill Kelly	Leave The World Behind*	Moderate Tempo	Tenor	D3	Eb4	Lead
Steel Pier	1997	Bill Kelly	First You Dream*	Uptempo	Tenor	C3	F4	Lead
Jekyll and Hyde	1997	Dr. Henry Jekyll	Take Me As I Am	Ballad	Tenor	Bb2	Eb4	Lead
Scarlet Pimpernel, The	1997	Percy Blakeney	You Are My Home*	Ballad	Tenor	B2	G4	Lead
Scarlet Pimpernel, The	1997	Percy Blakeney	Prayer*	Ballad	Tenor	Bb2	Ab4	Lead
Scarlet Pimpernel, The	1997	Percy Blakeney	Into The Fire*	Uptempo	Tenor	D3	Ab4	Lead
Scarlet Pimpernel, The	1997	Percy Blakeney	When I Look At You Reprise	Ballad	Tenor	Db3	F4	Lead
Scarlet Pimpernel, The	1997	Percy Blakeney	She Was There	Ballad	Tenor	C#3	G#4	Lead
Scarlet Pimpernel, The	1997	Percy Blakeney	She Was There Tag	Moderate Tempo	Tenor	A3	G4	Lead
Parade	1998	Tom Watson	Watson's Lullaby	Ballad	Tenor	A#2	A3	Lead
Parade	1998	Tom Watson	...When The Flood Comes*	Uptempo	Tenor	B2	Eb4	Lead
Jane Eyre	2000	Edward Fairfax Rochester	Brave Enough For Love*	Uptempo	Tenor	Db3	Bb4	Lead
Full Monty, The	2000	Jerry Lukowski	Man *	Uptempo	Tenor	E3	B4	Lead
Full Monty, The	2000	Jerry Lukowski	Michael Jordan's Ball *	Uptempo	Tenor	G3	Bb4	Lead
Full Monty, The	2000	Jerry Lukowski	Breeze Off The River	Moderate Tempo	Tenor	C3	B4	Lead
Full Monty, The	2000	Jerry Lukowski	Man *	Uptempo	Tenor	E3	G4	Lead
Full Monty, The	2000	Jerry Lukowski	Man Reprise *	Uptempo	Tenor	A3	A4	Lead
Aida	2000	Radames	Fortune Favors the Brave	Uptempo	Tenor	Bb2	F4	Lead
Aida	2000	Radames	Elaborate Lies	Ballad	Tenor	Bb2	Ab4	Lead
Aida	2000	Radames	Like Father Like Son*	Uptempo	Tenor	G3	F4	Lead
Aida	2000	Radames	Radames' Letter	Ballad	Tenor	C3	G4	Lead
Aida	2000	Radames	Fortune Favors the Brave Reprise	Uptempo	Tenor	F3	G4	Lead
Producers, The	2001	Roger De Bris	Keep It Gay*	Uptempo	Tenor	G#2	G4	Lead
Producers, The	2001	Roger De Bris	Springtime For Hitler*	Moderate Tempo	Tenor	B2	G4	Lead

Romantic Lead Male

* = Music Edit Required
+ = Ethnic Specific

Show	Year	Role	Song	Tempo	Vocal Type	Range-Bottom	Range-Top	Category
Mamma Mia!	2001	Sam Carmichael	Knowing Me, Knowing You*	Moderate Tempo	Tenor	G2	F#4	Lead
Mamma Mia!	2001	Sam Carmichael	SOS*	Uptempo	Tenor	A3	Ab4	Lead
Producers, The	2001	Storm Trooper	Springtime For Hitler*	Moderate Tempo	Tenor	D3	Ab4	Lead
Hairspray	2002	Corny Collins	Hairspray	Uptempo	Tenor	E3	C5	Lead
Hairspray	2002	Corny Collins	Nicest Kids In Town*	Uptempo	Tenor	D3	F#4	Lead
Hairspray	2002	Corny Collins	Nicest Kids In Town Reprise	Uptempo	Tenor	B3	F#4	Lead
Sweet Smell Of Success	2002	Dallas	I Cannot Hear The City	Ballad	Tenor	A3	G4	Lead
Sweet Smell Of Success	2002	Dallas	Don't Know Where You Leave Off	Moderate Tempo	Tenor	A2	G4	Lead
Sweet Smell Of Success	2002	Dallas	One Track Mind	Uptempo	Tenor	E3	A4	Lead
Sweet Smell Of Success	2002	Dallas	I Cannot Hear... (Act 1 Finale)	Ballad	Tenor	A2	Bb4	Lead
A Man Of No Importance	2002	Robby Fay	Streets Of Dublin	Uptempo	Tenor	C4	E5	Lead
A Man Of No Importance	2002	Robby Fay	Love Who You Love Reprise	Ballad	Tenor	E3	F4	Lead
A Man Of No Importance	2002	Robby Fay	Confession *	Moderate Tempo	Tenor	Db3	F#4	Lead
Thoroughly Modern Millie	2002	Trevor Graydon	The Speed Test*	Uptempo	Tenor	A2	F4	Lead
Wicked	2003	Fiyero	Dancing Through Life*	Uptempo	Tenor	C3	A4	Lead
Wicked	2003	Fiyero	As Long As You're Mine*	Moderate Tempo	Tenor	G3	Bb4	Lead
Wicked	2003	Fiyero	Which Way Is The Party*	Uptempo	Tenor	C#3	A4	Lead
Drowsy Chaperon, The	2006	Adolpho	I Am Adolpho *	Moderate Tempo	Tenor	E2	A5	Lead
Cutains	2007	Aaron Fox	I Miss The Music	Ballad	Tenor	C3	Gb4	Lead
Cutains	2007	Aaron Fox	Thinking of Him Reprise*	Ballad	Tenor	A2	Gb4	Lead
In The Heights	2008	Benny+	Benny's Dispatch*	Uptempo	Tenor	B3	F#4	Lead
In The Heights	2008	Benny+	When You're Home*	Uptempo	Tenor	E3	G4	Lead
Addams Family, The	2010	Gomez Addams +	Live Before We Die	Moderate Tempo	Tenor	Bb3	D4	Lead

Romantic Lead Male

Ingenue Female

* = Music Edit Required
\+ = Ethnic Specific

Show	Year	Role	Song	Tempo	Vocal Type	Range-Bottom	Range-Top	Category
Good News (1993 Revival)	1927	Babe O'Day	The Varsity Drag	Uptempo	Alto	B♭3	C5	Lead
Good News (1993 Revival)	1927	Pat	Lucky In Love*	Uptempo	Alto	A3	C5	Supporting
Good News (1993 Revival)	1927	Pat	The Girl Of Pi Beta Phi	Moderate Tempo	Alto	G3	A4	Supporting
Good News (1993 Revival)	1928	Babe O'Day	Button Up Your Overcoat*	Uptempo	Alto	C4	C5	Lead
Good News (1993 Revival)	1930	Babe O'Day	Never Swat A Fly*	Uptempo	Alto	A3	C#5	Lead
Babes In Arms (1998)	1937	Billie Smith	All At Once*	Moderate Tempo	Alto	A3	B♭4	Lead
Babes In Arms (1998)	1937	Billie Smith	The Lady Is A Tramp	Uptempo	Alto	A♭3	B♭4	Lead
Babes In Arms (1998)	1937	Billie Smith	The Lady Is A Tramp Encore	Uptempo	Alto	A♭3	B♭4	Lead
Babes In Arms (1998)	1937	Billie Smith	The Lady Is A Tramp Reprise	Uptempo	Alto	A♭3	B♭4	Lead
Babes In Arms (1998)	1937	Billie Smith	My Funny Valentine	Ballad	Alto	A3	C5	Lead
Babes In Arms (1998)	1937	Billie Smith	Where Or When*	Moderate Tempo	Alto	B3	E5	Lead
Babes In Arms (1998)	1937	Billie Smith	Babes In Arms*	Uptempo	Alto	C4	E5	Lead
Babes In Arms (1998)	1937	Dolores Reynolds	I Wish I Were In Love Again*	Uptempo	Alto	A3	A4	Lead
Babes In Arms (1998)	1937	Dolores Reynolds	You Are So Fair*	Uptempo	Alto	B3	B4	Lead
Pal Joey	1940	Linda English	I Could Write A Book*	Moderate Tempo	Alto	D4	D5	Lead
Pal Joey	1940	Linda English	Take Him*	Moderate Tempo	Alto	C4	D5	Lead
State Fair 1996	1945	Margy Frake	It Might As Well Be Spring	Moderate Tempo	Alto	B♭3	B♭4	Lead
State Fair 1996	1945	Margy Frake	It Might As Well Be Spring Reprise	Moderate Tempo	Alto	B♭3	B♭4	Lead
Call Me Madam	1950	Princess Maria	The Ocarina*	Moderate Tempo	Alto	C4	D5	Lead
Call Me Madam	1950	Princess Maria	It's A Lovely Day Today*	Moderate Tempo	Alto	A3	B4	Lead
Call Me Madam	1950	Princess Maria	It's A Lovely Day Today Reprise 2*	Moderate Tempo	Alto	C4	D5	Lead
Flower Drum Song 2002	1958	Wu Mei-Li+	A Hundred Million Miracles*	Moderate Tempo	Alto	C4	E♭5	Lead
Flower Drum Song 2002	1958	Wu Mei-Li+	I Am Going To Like It Here	Moderate Tempo	Alto	B♭3	B♭4	Lead
Flower Drum Song 2002	1958	Wu Mei-Li+	You Are Beautiful Reprise*	Ballad	Alto	D4	D5	Lead
Flower Drum Song 2002	1958	Wu Mei-Li+	I Enjoy Being A Girl Reprise	Ballad	Alto	B♭3	D5	Lead
Flower Drum Song 2002	1958	Wu Mei-Li+	A Hundred Million Miracles Reprise*	Moderate Tempo	Alto	A♭3	B♭4	Lead
Flower Drum Song 2002	1958	Wu Mei-Li+	Love, Look Away (A♭ Maj)	Ballad	Alto	G3	C5	Lead

Ingenue Female

* = Music Edit Required
+ = Ethnic Specific

Show	Year	Role	Song	Tempo	Vocal Type	Range-Bottom	Range-Top	Category
Gypsy	1959	June	If Momma Was Married*	Moderate Tempo	Alto	G3	C5	Lead
Gypsy	1959	June	Broadway	Uptempo	Alto	E#4	D5	Lead
Sound Of Music, The	1959	Liesl von Trapp	You Are Sixteen*	Moderate Tempo	Alto	B3	C#5	Lead
Gypsy	1959	Louise	Little Lamb	Ballad	Alto	Db4	Eb5	Lead
Gypsy	1959	Louise	If Momma Was Married*	Moderate Tempo	Alto	G3	C5	Lead
Gypsy	1959	Louise	Let Me Entertain You*	Moderate Tempo	Alto	G3	C5	Lead
How To Succeed...	1961	Rosemary Pillkington	Happy To Keep His Dinner Warm	Moderate Tempo	Alto	A3	Db5	Lead
How To Succeed...	1961	Rosemary Pillkington	Paris Original*	Moderate Tempo	Alto	Bb3	D5	Lead
How To Succeed...	1961	Rosemary Pillkington	Happy To Keep...Dinner Warm Rep	Moderate Tempo	Alto	Bb3	Db5	Lead
How To Succeed...	1961	Rosemary Pillkington	I Believe In You Reprise*	Moderate Tempo	Alto	E4	B4	Lead
Anyone Can Whistle	1964	Fay Apple	There Won't Be Trumpets	Uptempo	Alto	G3	Bb4	Lead
Anyone Can Whistle	1964	Fay Apple	Come Play Wiz Me*	Uptempo	Alto	A3	D5	Lead
Anyone Can Whistle	1964	Fay Apple	Anyone Can Whistle	Ballad	Alto	G3	C5	Lead
Anyone Can Whistle	1964	Fay Apple	See What It Gets You	Uptempo	Alto	G3	Db5	Lead
Anyone Can Whistle	1964	Fay Apple	With So Little To Be Sure Of*	Moderate Tempo	Alto	A3	B4	Lead
Hair	1968	Crissy	Frank Mills	Ballad	Alto	A2	C5	Lead
Dear World	1969	Nina	I've Never Said I Love You	Ballad	Alto	Bb3	Eb5	Lead
Mack and Mabel	1974	Mabel Normand	Look What Happened to Mabel*	Uptempo	Alto	Gb3	C5	Lead
Mack and Mabel	1974	Mabel Normand	Mabel's Roses	Ballad	Alto	G3	D5	Lead
Mack and Mabel	1974	Mabel Normand	Wherever He Ain't	Uptempo	Alto	A3	C5	Lead
Mack and Mabel	1974	Mabel Normand	Time Heals Everything	Ballad	Alto	F#3	C#5	Lead
A Chorus Line	1975	Val	Dance: Ten; Looks: Three	Uptempo	Alto	Bb3	Db5	Supporting
Annie	1977	Star To Be	N.Y.C. *	Uptempo	Alto	Bb4	Eb5	Supporting
Cats	1981	Rumpleteezer	Mongojerrie and Rumpleteezer	Uptempo	Alto	E4	G5	Supporting
Big River	1985	Alice's Daughter +	How Blest We Are *	Ballad	Alto	C3	C5	Supporting
Nunsense	1985	Mary Leo	Benedicte*	Moderate Tempo	Alto	C4	G5	Lead
Once On This Island	1990	Ti Moune+	Waiting For Life	Uptempo	Alto	C#4	E5	Lead

* = Music Edit Required
+ = Ethnic Specific

Show	Year	Role	Song	Tempo	Vocal Type	Range-Bottom	Range-Top	Category
Once On This Island	1990	Ti Moune+	Forever Yours*	Ballad	Alto	A#3	C#5	Lead
Once On This Island	1990	Ti Moune+	Ti Moune*	Ballad	Alto	G3	C5	Lead
Once On This Island	1990	Ti Moune+	Waiting For Life Reprise	Uptempo	Alto	B3	C#5	Lead
State Fair 1996	1996	Margy Frake	The Next Time It Happens	Uptempo	Alto	Bb3	D5	Lead
Lion King, The	1997	Nala	Shadowland*	Ballad	Alto	E3	B4	Lead
Mamma Mia!	2001	Sophie Sheridan	Lay All Your Love On Me*	Moderate Tempo	Alto	C4	E5	Lead
Last Five Years, The	2002	Catherine Hiatt	Still Hurting	Ballad	Alto	A3	Db5	Lead
Last Five Years, The	2002	Catherine Hiatt	See I'm Smiling	Ballad	Alto	E3	C#5	Lead
Last Five Years, The	2002	Catherine Hiatt	I'm A Part Of That	Uptempo	Alto	Bb3	Eb5	Lead
Last Five Years, The	2002	Catherine Hiatt	A Summer In Ohio	Uptempo	Alto	F#3	E5	Lead
Last Five Years, The	2002	Catherine Hiatt	The Next Ten Minutes	Ballad	Alto	G#3	E#4	Lead
Last Five Years, The	2002	Catherine Hiatt	Climbing Uphill/Audition	Uptempo	Alto	G3	D5	Lead
Last Five Years, The	2002	Catherine Hiatt	I Can Do Better Than That	Uptempo	Alto	A3	D5	Lead
Last Five Years, The	2002	Catherine Hiatt	Goodbye Until Tomorrow	Moderate Tempo	Alto	F#3	Db5	Lead
Last Five Years, The	2002	Catherine Hiatt	When You Come To Me	Moderate Tempo	Alto	A3	D5	Lead
Hairspray	2002	Teen Girl	The New Kid In Town*	Uptempo	Alto	A3	D5	Featured Ensemble
All Shook Up	2005	Lorraine	It's Now Or Never *	Moderate Tempo	Alto	C4	F5	Supporting
Legally Blonde	2007	Elle Woods	So Much Better	Uptempo	Alto	G3	E5	Lead
Legally Blonde	2007	Elle Woods	Take It Like A Man	Moderate Tempo	Alto	Gb3	E5	Lead
Legally Blonde	2007	Elle Woods	Legally Blonde	Ballad	Alto	G3	Db5	Lead
Legally Blonde	2007	Elle Woods	Find My Way	Moderate Tempo	Alto	G3	B4	Lead
Legally Blonde	2007	Elle Woods	Legally Blonde Remix*	Uptempo	Alto	E4	D5	Lead
Legally Blonde	2007	Elle Woods	What You Want	Uptempo	Alto	Bb3	Db5	Lead
Legally Blonde	2007	Elle Woods	Chip On My Shoulder*	Uptempo	Alto	C4	Eb5	Lead
High School Musical	2007	Gabriella Montez	When There Was You And Me	Ballad	Alto	F#3	F5	Lead
High School Musical	2007	Gabriella Montez	Breaking Free*	Ballad	Alto	Bb3	D5	Lead
White Christmas	2008	Judy Haynes	Falling Out Of Love Can Be Fun*	Uptempo	Alto	G3	C5	Lead
In The Heights	2008	Nina Rosario+	Breathe	Moderate Tempo	Alto	F3	F5	Lead

Ingenue Female

* = Music Edit Required
+ = Ethnic Specific

Show	Year	Role	Song	Tempo	Vocal Type	Range-Bottom	Range-Top	Category
In The Heights	2008	Nina Rosario+	When You're Home*	Uptempo	Alto	C#4	E5	Lead
In The Heights	2008	Nina Rosario+	Everything's I Know	Ballad	Alto	Bb3	Db5	Lead
In The Heights	2008	Nina Rosario+	Alabanza*	Ballad	Alto	A3	A4	Lead
Heathers	2014	Heather McNamara	Lifeboat	Ballad	Alto	G3	Db5	Lead
No, No Nanette	1925	Nanette	I've Confessed To The Breeze*	Moderate Tempo	Soprano	B3	F5	Lead
No, No Nanette	1925	Nanette	I Want To Be Happy*	Uptempo	Soprano	C4	E5	Lead
No, No Nanette	1925	Nanette	No, No Nanette*	Uptempo	Soprano	Bb3	F5	Lead
No, No Nanette	1925	Nanette	Peach On The Beach*	Uptempo	Soprano	F#4	A4	Lead
No, No Nanette	1925	Nanette	Tea For Two*	Moderate Tempo	Soprano	Eb4	F5	Lead
No, No Nanette	1925	Nanette	Waiting For You*	Moderate Tempo	Soprano	Ab3	Eb5	Lead
Show Boat	1927	Magnolia	Make Believe	Ballad	Soprano	D4	Bb5	Lead
Show Boat	1927	Magnolia	You Are Love*	Ballad	Soprano	D4	Bb5	Lead
Show Boat	1927	Magnolia	Can't Help Reprise	Ballad	Soprano	Ab3	Eb5	Lead
Show Boat	1927	Magnolia	After The Ball	Moderate Tempo	Soprano	D4	Ab5	Lead
Show Boat	1927	Magnolia	Dance The Night Away*	Uptempo	Soprano	G3	C5	Lead
Anything Goes	1934	Hope Harcourt	All Through The Night *	Ballad	Soprano	C4	Eb5	Lead
Anything Goes	1934	Hope Harcourt	The Gypsy In Me	Moderate Tempo	Soprano	C3	G4	Lead
Anything Goes	1934	Hope Harcourt	Goodbye Little Dream, Goodbye	Ballad	Soprano	A3	Eb5	Lead
Porgy and Bess	1935	Clara+	Summertime	Moderate Tempo	Soprano	F#4	B5	Lead
Porgy and Bess	1935	Clara+	Summertime Reprise	Moderate Tempo	Soprano	E4	A5	Lead
Brigadoon	1947	Fiona MacLaren	Waitin For My Dearie *	Ballad	Soprano	C4	A5	Lead
Brigadoon	1947	Fiona MacLaren	The Heather On The Hill *	Ballad	Soprano	Bb2	G4	Lead
Brigadoon	1947	Fiona MacLaren	Almost Like Being In Love *	Ballad	Soprano	F4	A5	Lead
Brigadoon	1947	Fiona MacLaren	From This Day On *	Ballad	Soprano	F4	A5	Lead
Brigadoon	1947	Fiona MacLaren	Come To Me Bend To Me Reprise	Ballad	Soprano	D4	G5	Lead
Brigadoon	1947	Fiona MacLaren	The Heather On The Hill Reprise	Ballad	Soprano	C4	F5	Lead

* = Music Edit Required
+ = Ethnic Specific

Show	Year	Role	Song	Tempo	Vocal Type	Range-Bottom	Range-Top	Category
Brigadoon	1947	Fiona MacLaren	From This Day On Reprise *	Ballad	Soprano	Eb4	G5	Lead
Guys and Dolls	1950	Sarah Brown	I'll Know*	Ballad	Soprano	E4	G#5	Lead
Guys and Dolls	1950	Sarah Brown	If I Were A Bell	Uptempo	Soprano	Bb3	D5	Lead
Guys and Dolls	1950	Sarah Brown	Marry The Man Today*	Uptempo	Soprano	C4	Eb5	Lead
Guys and Dolls	1950	Sarah Brown	I'll Know (Finish)	Ballad	Soprano	Eb4	F5	Lead
King and I, The	1951	Tuptim+	My Lord And Master	Moderate Tempo	Soprano	D#4	A#5	Lead
King and I, The	1951	Tuptim+	We Kiss In The Shadow	Ballad	Soprano	D4	G5	Lead
King and I, The	1951	Tuptim+	I Have Dreamed	Ballad	Soprano	C4	G5	Lead
Wonderful Town	1953	Eileen Sherwood	A Little Bit In Love	Moderate Tempo	Soprano	C4	C#5	Lead
Wonderful Town	1953	Eileen Sherwood	Conversation Piece*	Uptempo	Soprano	D4	B4	Lead
Candide	1956	Cunegonde	Life Is Happiness Indeed*	Moderate Tempo	Soprano	F4	C6	Lead
Candide	1956	Cunegonde	Glitter And Be Gay	Moderate Tempo	Soprano	B2	E6	Lead
My Fair Lady	1956	Eliza Doolittle	Wouldn't It Be Loverly	Moderate Tempo	Soprano	C4	Eb5	Lead
My Fair Lady	1956	Eliza Doolittle	Just You Wait	Moderate Tempo	Soprano	A3	Eb4	Lead
My Fair Lady	1956	Eliza Doolittle	I Could Have Danced All Night*	Uptempo	Soprano	B3	G5	Lead
My Fair Lady	1956	Eliza Doolittle	Just You Wait Reprise	Ballad	Soprano	D4	C5	Lead
My Fair Lady	1956	Eliza Doolittle	Wouldn't It Be Loverly Reprise*	Ballad	Soprano	C4	D5	Lead
My Fair Lady	1956	Eliza Doolittle	Without You	Moderate Tempo	Soprano	B3	Eb5	Lead
My Fair Lady	1956	Eliza Doolittle	Show Me	Uptempo	Soprano	D4	G5	Lead
Cinderella (2013)	1957	Ella	In My Own Little Corner	Uptempo	Soprano	C4	C5	Lead
Cinderella (2013)	1957	Ella	In My Own Little Corner Reprise	Uptempo	Soprano	C4	C5	Lead
Cinderella (2013)	1957	Ella	Impossible*	Uptempo	Soprano	Bb2	D5	Lead
Cinderella (2013)	1957	Ella	Ten Minutes Ago*	Moderate Tempo	Soprano	C#4	D5	Lead
Cinderella (2013)	1957	Ella	Do I Love You...*	Ballad	Soprano	A4	E5	Lead
Cinderella (2013)	1957	Ella	When You're Driving....*	Uptempo	Soprano	B2	Bb4	Lead
Cinderella (2013)	1957	Ella	A Lovely Night*	Uptempo	Soprano	Bb3	Bb4	Lead
Cinderella (2013)	1957	Ella	A Lovely Night*	Uptempo	Soprano	C4	C5	Lead
Cinderella (2013)	1957	Ella	It's Possible	Uptempo	Soprano	C4	B4	Lead

Ingenue Female

* = Music Edit Required
+ = Ethnic Specific

Show	Year	Role	Song	Tempo	Vocal Type	Range-Bottom	Range-Top	Category
West Side Story	1957	Female Shark+	Somewhere	Ballad	Soprano	B3	F#5	Featured Ensemble
West Side Story	1957	Maria+	I Feel Pretty*	Uptempo	Soprano	C4	F5	Lead
West Side Story	1957	Maria+	I Have A Love*	Ballad	Soprano	Bb3	Bb5	Lead
Bye Bye Birdie	1960	Kim MacAfee	How Lovely To Be A Woman	Moderate Tempo	Soprano	D#4	F#4	Lead
Bye Bye Birdie	1960	Kim MacAfee	One Boy	Ballad	Soprano	Db4	F5	Lead
Bye Bye Birdie	1960	Kim MacAfee	What Did I Ever See In Him *	Uptempo	Soprano	G3	Bb4	Lead
Bye Bye Birdie	1960	Kim MacAfee	Lot of Livin' To Do *	Uptempo	Soprano	D4	E5	Lead
Fantasticks, The	1960	Luisa	Much More	Uptempo	Soprano	B3	F5	Lead
Fantasticks, The	1960	Luisa	Metaphor *	Uptempo	Soprano	Eb4	G5	Lead
Fantasticks, The	1960	Luisa	Soon It's Gonna Rain *	Moderate Tempo	Soprano	B2	F4	Lead
Fantasticks, The	1960	Luisa	They Were You *	Ballad	Soprano	B3	D5	Lead
Cinderella (2013)	1962	Ella	The Sweetest Sounds*	Moderate Tempo	Soprano	C#4	C5	Lead
A Funny Thing...Forum	1962	Philia	Lovely*	Moderate Tempo	Soprano	C#4	F5	Lead
A Funny Thing...Forum	1962	Philia	That'll Show Him	Moderate Tempo	Soprano	C4	G5	Lead
1776	1969	Martha Jefferson	He Plays The Violin	Moderate Tempo	Soprano	Bb3	D5	Supporting
Company (Revival)	1970	Kathy	You Could Drive a Person Crazy	Uptempo	Soprano	C#4	A5	Supporting
Grease	1971	Sandy Dumbrowski	It's Raining on Prom Night	Ballad	Soprano	A3	D5	Lead
Grease	1971	Sandy Dumbrowski	Hopelessly Devoted to You	Ballad	Soprano	A3	F5	Lead
Grease	1971	Sandy Dumbrowski	Look At Me I'm Sandra Dee Reprise	Ballad	Soprano	A3	C#5	Lead
Grease	1971	Sandy Dumbrowski	Since I Don't Have You	Ballad	Soprano	Ab3	Ab5	Lead
A Little Night Music	1973	Anne Egerman	Soon	Uptempo	Soprano	C4	G#5	Lead
Evita	1978	Mistress	Another Suitcase In Another Hall	Ballad	Soprano	A3	E5	Supporting
Sweeney Todd	1979	Johannah	Green Finch And Linnet Bird*	Uptempo	Soprano	C4	G5	Lead
Dreamgirls	1981	Deena Jones +	Heavy	Uptempo	Soprano	D3	D4	Lead
Dreamgirls	1981	Deena Jones +	One Night Only	Uptempo	Soprano	Ab3	D5	Lead
Singin' In The Rain	1983	Kathy Seldon	Lucky Star	Moderate Tempo	Soprano	Bb3	Eb5	Lead
Singin' In The Rain	1983	Kathy Seldon	Kathy's Would You	Moderate Tempo	Soprano	G3	C5	Lead
Baby	1983	Lizzie Fields	I Want It All *	Uptempo	Soprano	C4	Eb5	Lead

Ingenue Female

* = Music Edit Required
+ = Ethnic Specific

Show	Year	Role	Song	Tempo	Vocal Type	Range-Bottom	Range-Top	Category
Baby	1983	Lizzie Fields	The Story Goes On	Ballad	Soprano	G3	F5	Lead
Big River	1985	Mary Jane Wilkes	Leavin's Not The Only Way To Go	Ballad	Soprano	B3	B4	Supporting
Big River	1985	Mary Jane Wilkes	You Oughta Be Here With Me	Ballad	Soprano	B3	C#5	Supporting
Mystery Of Edwin Drood, The	1985	Rosa Bud	Moonfall	Ballad	Soprano	B3	G5	Lead
Mystery Of Edwin Drood, The	1985	Rosa Bud	Perfect Strangers*	Moderate Tempo	Soprano	C#4	F5	Lead
Mystery Of Edwin Drood	1985	Rosa Bud	Rosa's Confession	Uptempo	Soprano	A3	Ab5	Lead
Phantom Of The Opera	1986	Christine Daae	Think Of Me*	Moderate Tempo	Soprano	D4	C6	Lead
Phantom Of The Opera	1986	Christine Daae	Angel Of Music*	Moderate Tempo	Soprano	Bb3	F#5	Lead
Phantom Of The Opera	1986	Christine Daae	Phantom Of The Opera*	Moderate Tempo	Soprano	G3	E5	Lead
Phantom Of The Opera	1986	Christine Daae	All I Ask Of You*	Ballad	Soprano	Ab3	Ab5	Lead
Phantom Of The Opera	1986	Christine Daae	Twisted Every Way*	Ballad	Soprano	C4	Eb5	Lead
Phantom Of The Opera	1986	Christine Daae	Wishing You Were Somehow Here Aga	Ballad	Soprano	A3	G5	Lead
Phantom Of The Opera	1986	Christine Daae	The Point Of No Return*	Ballad	Soprano	C4	G5	Lead
Phantom Of The Opera	1986	Christine Daae	Raoul I've Been There	Moderate Tempo	Soprano	C#4	Ab5	Lead
Into The Woods	1987	Cinderella	On The Steps Of The Palace	Uptempo	Soprano	A3	E5	Lead
Into The Woods	1987	Cinderella	No One Is Alone	Ballad	Soprano	Bb3	Db5	Lead
Into The Woods	1987	Cinderella	No One Is Alone (Part 2)	Ballad	Soprano	Bb3	Db5	Lead
Meet Me In St. Louis	1989	Agnes Smith	Under The Bamboo Tree*	Moderate Tempo	Soprano	C4	Bb4	Lead
Meet Me In St. Louis	1989	Rose Smith	Raving Beauty*	Ballad	Soprano	Bb3	Db5	Lead
Phantom	1991	Christine Daae	Home*	Moderate Tempo	Soprano	D4	A5	Lead
Phantom	1991	Christine Daae	The Bistro*	Uptempo	Soprano	Bb3	B5	Lead
Phantom	1991	Christine Daae	Who Could Have Ever Dreamed Up Yo	Uptempo	Soprano	Bb3	Eb5	Lead
Phantom	1991	Christine Daae	My True Love	Moderate Tempo	Soprano	C4	F5	Lead
Phantom	1991	Christine Daae	Finale: You Are Music*	Ballad	Soprano	B4	G5	Lead
Phantom	1991	Christine Daee	Melody Of Paris	Uptempo	Soprano	B3	A5	Lead
Miss Saigon	1991	Kim+	The Movie In My Mind*	Ballad	Soprano	Ab3	Eb5	Lead
Miss Saigon	1991	Kim+	The Ceremony*	Ballad	Soprano	B3	D5	Lead

Ingenue Female

* = Music Edit Required
+ = Ethnic Specific

Show	Year	Role	Song	Tempo	Vocal Type	Range-Bottom	Range-Top	Category
Miss Saigon	1991	Kim+	I Still Believe*	Ballad	Soprano	A3	E5	Lead
Miss Saigon	1991	Kim+	There Is A Secret (ms 214-258)	Moderate Tempo	Soprano	A3	Db5	Lead
Miss Saigon	1991	Kim+	You Will Not Touch Him (ms 20-51)	Moderate Tempo	Soprano	C4	Eb5	Lead
Miss Saigon	1991	Kim+	I'd Give My Life For You*	Ballad	Soprano	G3	E5	Lead
Miss Saigon	1991	Kim+	Sun and Moon Reprise	Ballad	Soprano	E3	D5	Lead
Miss Saigon	1991	Kim+	Little God Of My Heart	Ballad	Soprano	A3	D5	Lead
Miss Saigon	1991	Kim+	Sun And Moon*	Ballad	Soprano	F#3	D5	Lead
A Christmas Carol	1997	Emily	A Place Called Home	Ballad	Soprano	Bb3	F5	Supporting
A Christmas Carol	1997	Grace Smythe	God Bless Us Everyone	Uptempo	Soprano	D4	C5	Lead
Marie Christine	1999	Lisette+	Tout Mi Mi	Ballad	Soprano	D4	C#5	Lead
Marie Christine	1999	Lisette+	Dansen Calinda	Ballad	Soprano	E4	C6	Lead
Marie Christine	1999	Lisette+	Tout Mimi Reprise	Ballad	Soprano	Bb3	Bb4	Lead
You're...Charlie Brown	1999	Sally	My New Philosophy	Uptempo	Soprano	B3	E5	Lead
Jane Eyre	2000	Blanche Ingram	The Finer Things	Uptempo	Soprano	Eb4	B5	Supporting
Jane Eyre	2000	Blanche Ingram	In the Virgin Morning*	Moderate Tempo	Soprano	B3	F5	Supporting
Jane Eyre	2000	School Girl	Rain	Moderate Tempo	Soprano	Bb3	E5	Supporting
Spitfire Grill	2001	Shelby Thorpe	Hannah Had A Son	Ballad	Soprano	D4	D5	Lead
Spitfire Grill	2001	Shelby Thorpe	When Hope Goes	Ballad	Soprano	A3	D5	Lead
Spitfire Grill	2001	Shelby Thorpe	Wild Bird	Ballad	Soprano	C4	D5	Lead
Mamma Mia!	2001	Sophie Sheridan	I Have A Dream	Ballad	Soprano	Ab4	Bb4	Lead
Mamma Mia!	2001	Sophie Sheridan	Honey Honey*	Uptempo	Soprano	C4	C5	Lead
Mamma Mia!	2001	Sophie Sheridan	The Name Of The Game*	Moderate Tempo	Soprano	F#3	B4	Lead
Mamma Mia!	2001	Sophie Sheridan	Under Attack*	Uptempo	Soprano	B3	C#5	Lead
Mamma Mia!	2001	Sophie Sheridan	I have A Dream Reprise	Ballad	Soprano	Ab3	Db5	Lead
Thoroughly Modern Millie	2002	Dorothy Brown	How The Other Half Lives*	Moderate Tempo	Soprano	B3	Eb5	Lead
Sweet Smell Of Success	2002	Susan	What If*	Uptempo	Soprano	A3	F5	Lead
Sweet Smell Of Success	2002	Susan	I Cannot Hear The City Reprise*	Ballad	Soprano	Ab3	G5	Lead
Caroline, Or Change	2004	Emmie Thibodeaux +	Duets: Nigh Mamma (ms 71-89)	Ballad	Soprano	F#4	C5	Supporting

Ingenue Female

Ingenue Female

* = Music Edit Required
+ = Ethnic Specific

Show	Year	Role	Song	Tempo	Vocal Type	Range-Bottom	Range-Top	Category
Caroline, Or Change	2004	Emmie Thibodeaux +	I Hate The Bus (ms 6-36)	Ballad	Soprano	G3	F#5	Supporting
Caroline, Or Change	2004	Emmie Thibodeaux +	Epilogue-Emmie's Dream (ms 9-73)	Uptempo	Soprano	Ab3	Db4	Supporting
Caroline, Or Change	2004	Emmie Thibodeaux +	The Bus (ms 71-89)	Ballad	Soprano	Bb2	Bb4	Supporting
Little Women	2005	Beth March	Off to Massachusettes*	Moderate Tempo	Soprano	C#4	F5	Lead
Little Women	2005	Beth March	Some Things Are Meant To Be	Uptempo	Soprano	B2	E5	Lead
Light In The Piazza, The	2005	Clara Johnson	The Beauty Is	Uptempo	Soprano	Cb4	G5	Lead
Light In The Piazza, The	2005	Clara Johnson	The Light in the Piazza	Moderate Tempo	Soprano	A3	F#5	Lead
Little Women	2005	Meg March	More Than I Am*	Moderate Tempo	Soprano	E4	E5	Lead
25th Annual...Spelling Bee	2005	Olive Ostrovsky	My Friend The Dictionary	Moderate Tempo	Soprano	B3	D5	Lead
25th Annual...Spelling Bee	2005	Olive Ostrovsky	The I Love You Song	Ballad	Soprano	D4	D5	Lead
25th Annual...Spelling Bee	2005	Olive Ostrovsky	Second Part 1*	Moderate Tempo	Soprano	C#4	D5	Lead
Grey Gardens	2006	Edie Beale (Act 1)	Daddy's Girl*	Uptempo	Soprano	C4	E5	Lead
Grey Gardens	2006	Edie Beale (Act 1)	The Telegram	Moderate Tempo	Soprano	C#4	F#5	Lead
Drowsy Chaperon, The	2006	Janet Van de Graff	Show Off *	Uptempo	Soprano	G3	C5	Lead
Drowsy Chaperon, The	2006	Janet Van de Graff	Accident Waiting To Happen *	Moderate Tempo	Soprano	C4	D5	Lead
Drowsy Chaperon, The	2006	Janet Van de Graff	Bride's Lament *	Ballad	Soprano	Ab3	F5	Lead
Spring Awakening	2006	Wendla	The Guilty One*	Moderate Tempo	Soprano	G3	A4	Lead
Spring Awakening	2006	Wendla	Whispering	Ballad	Soprano	B3	A4	Lead
Spring Awakening	2006	Wendla	Mama Who Bore Me	Moderate Tempo	Soprano	G3	A4	Lead
Spring Awakening	2006	Wendla	Those You've Known*	Moderate Tempo	Soprano	C4	D5	Lead
The Little Mermaid	2007	Ariel	The World Above	Uptempo	Soprano	A3	C5	Lead
The Little Mermaid	2007	Ariel	Part Of Your World	Uptempo	Soprano	C4	C5	Lead
The Little Mermaid	2007	Ariel	Ursula's Incantation (Ahs)*	Moderate Tempo	Soprano	F#4	E5	Lead
Cinderella (2013)	2013	Ella	He Was Tall	Moderate Tempo	Soprano	D4	C#5	Lead

Ingenue Female

47

* = Music Edit Required
+ = Ethnic Specific

Show	Year	Role	Song	Tempo	Vocal Type	Range-Bottom	Range-Top	Category
Good News (1993 Revival)	1927	Babe O'Day	The Varsity Drag	Uptempo	Alto	Bb3	C5	Lead
Good News (1993 Revival)	1927	Pat	Lucky In Love*	Uptempo	Alto	A3	C5	Supporting
Good News (1993 Revival)	1927	Pat	The Girl Of Pi Beta Phi	Moderate Tempo	Alto	G3	A4	Supporting
Good News (1993 Revival)	1928	Babe O'Day	Button Up Your Overcoat*	Uptempo	Alto	C4	C5	Lead
Good News (1993 Revival)	1930	Babe O'Day	Never Swat A Fly*	Uptempo	Alto	A3	C#5	Lead
Babes In Arms (1998)	1937	Billie Smith	All At Once*	Moderate Tempo	Alto	A3	Bb4	Lead
Babes In Arms (1998)	1937	Billie Smith	The Lady Is A Tramp	Uptempo	Alto	Ab3	Bb4	Lead
Babes In Arms (1998)	1937	Billie Smith	The Lady Is A Tramp Encore	Uptempo	Alto	Ab3	Bb4	Lead
Babes In Arms (1998)	1937	Billie Smith	The Lady Is A Tramp Reprise	Uptempo	Alto	Ab3	Bb4	Lead
Babes In Arms (1998)	1937	Billie Smith	My Funny Valentine	Ballad	Alto	A3	C5	Lead
Babes In Arms (1998)	1937	Billie Smith	Where Or When*	Moderate Tempo	Alto	B3	E5	Lead
Babes In Arms (1998)	1937	Billie Smith	Babes In Arms*	Uptempo	Alto	C4	E5	Lead
Babes In Arms (1998)	1937	Dolores Reynolds	I Wish I Were In Love Again*	Uptempo	Alto	A3	A4	Lead
Babes In Arms (1998)	1937	Dolores Reynolds	You Are So Fair*	Uptempo	Alto	B3	B4	Lead
Pal Joey	1940	Linda English	I Could Write A Book*	Moderate Tempo	Alto	D4	D5	Lead
Pal Joey	1940	Linda English	Take Him*	Moderate Tempo	Alto	C4	D5	Lead
State Fair 1996	1945	Margy Frake	It Might As Well Be Spring	Moderate Tempo	Alto	Bb3	Bb4	Lead
State Fair 1996	1945	Margy Frake	It Might As Well Be Spring Reprise	Moderate Tempo	Alto	Bb3	Bb4	Lead
Call Me Madam	1950	Princess Maria	The Ocarina*	Moderate Tempo	Alto	C4	D5	Lead
Call Me Madam	1950	Princess Maria	It's A Lovely Day Today*	Moderate Tempo	Alto	A3	B4	Lead
Call Me Madam	1950	Princess Maria	It's A Lovely Day Today Reprise 2*	Moderate Tempo	Alto	C4	D5	Lead
Flower Drum Song 2002	1958	Wu Mei-Li+	A Hundred Million Miracles*	Moderate Tempo	Alto	C4	Eb5	Lead
Flower Drum Song 2002	1958	Wu Mei-Li+	I Am Going To Like It Here	Moderate Tempo	Alto	Bb3	Bb4	Lead
Flower Drum Song 2002	1958	Wu Mei-Li+	You Are Beautiful Reprise*	Ballad	Alto	D4	D5	Lead
Flower Drum Song 2002	1958	Wu Mei-Li+	I Enjoy Being A Girl Reprise	Ballad	Alto	Bb3	D5	Lead
Flower Drum Song 2002	1958	Wu Mei-Li+	A Hundred Million Miracles Reprise*	Moderate Tempo	Alto	Ab3	Bb4	Lead
Flower Drum Song 2002	1958	Wu Mei-Li+	Love, Look Away (Ab Maj)	Ballad	Alto	G3	C5	Lead

Ingenue Female

* = Music Edit Required
+ = Ethnic Specific

Show	Year	Role	Song	Tempo	Vocal Type	Range-Bottom	Range-Top	Category
Gypsy	1959	June	If Momma Was Married*	Moderate Tempo	Alto	G3	C5	Lead
Gypsy	1959	June	Broadway	Uptempo	Alto	E#4	D5	Lead
Sound Of Music, The	1959	Liesl von Trapp	You Are Sixteen*	Moderate Tempo	Alto	B3	C#5	Lead
Gypsy	1959	Louise	Little Lamb	Ballad	Alto	Db4	Eb5	Lead
Gypsy	1959	Louise	If Momma Was Married*	Moderate Tempo	Alto	G3	C5	Lead
Gypsy	1959	Louise	Let Me Entertain You*	Moderate Tempo	Alto	G3	C5	Lead
How To Succeed...	1961	Rosemary Pillkington	Happy To Keep His Dinner Warm	Moderate Tempo	Alto	A3	Db5	Lead
How To Succeed...	1961	Rosemary Pillkington	Paris Original*	Moderate Tempo	Alto	Bb3	D5	Lead
How To Succeed...	1961	Rosemary Pillkington	Happy To Keep...Dinner Warm Rep	Moderate Tempo	Alto	Bb3	Db5	Lead
How To Succeed...	1961	Rosemary Pillkington	I Believe In You Reprise*	Moderate Tempo	Alto	E4	B4	Lead
Anyone Can Whistle	1964	Fay Apple	There Won't Be Trumpets	Uptempo	Alto	G3	Bb4	Lead
Anyone Can Whistle	1964	Fay Apple	Come Play Wiz Me*	Uptempo	Alto	A3	D5	Lead
Anyone Can Whistle	1964	Fay Apple	Anyone Can Whistle	Ballad	Alto	G3	C5	Lead
Anyone Can Whistle	1964	Fay Apple	See What It Gets You	Uptempo	Alto	G3	Db5	Lead
Anyone Can Whistle	1964	Fay Apple	With So Little To Be Sure Of*	Moderate Tempo	Alto	A3	B4	Lead
Hair	1968	Crissy	Frank Mills	Ballad	Alto	A2	C5	Lead
Dear World	1969	Nina	I've Never Said I Love You	Ballad	Alto	Bb3	Eb5	Lead
Mack and Mabel	1974	Mabel Normand	Look What Happened to Mabel*	Uptempo	Alto	Gb3	C5	Lead
Mack and Mabel	1974	Mabel Normand	Mabel's Roses	Ballad	Alto	G3	D5	Lead
Mack and Mabel	1974	Mabel Normand	Wherever He Ain't	Uptempo	Alto	A3	C5	Lead
Mack and Mabel	1974	Mabel Normand	Time Heals Everything	Ballad	Alto	F#3	C#5	Lead
A Chorus Line	1975	Val	Dance: Ten; Looks: Three	Uptempo	Alto	Bb3	Db5	Supporting
Annie	1977	Star To Be	N.Y.C. *	Uptempo	Alto	Bb4	Eb5	Supporting
Cats	1981	Rumpleteezer	Mongojerrie and Rumpleteezer	Uptempo	Alto	E4	G5	Supporting
Big River	1985	Alice's Daughter +	How Blest We Are *	Ballad	Alto	C3	C5	Supporting
Nunsense	1985	Mary Leo	Benedicte*	Moderate Tempo	Alto	C4	G5	Lead
Once On This Island	1990	Ti Moune+	Waiting For Life	Uptempo	Alto	C#4	E5	Lead

Ingenue Female

Ingenue Female

* = Music Edit Required
+ = Ethnic Specific

Show	Year	Role	Song	Tempo	Vocal Type	Range-Bottom	Range-Top	Category
Once On This Island	1990	Ti Moune+	Forever Yours*	Ballad	Alto	A#3	C#5	Lead
Once On This Island	1990	Ti Moune+	Ti Moune*	Ballad	Alto	G3	C5	Lead
Once On This Island	1990	Ti Moune+	Waiting For Life Reprise	Uptempo	Alto	B3	C#5	Lead
State Fair 1996	1996	Margy Frake	The Next Time It Happens	Uptempo	Alto	Bb3	D5	Lead
Lion King, The	1997	Nala	Shadowland*	Ballad	Alto	E3	B4	Lead
Mamma Mia!	2001	Sophie Sheridan	Lay All Your Love On Me*	Moderate Tempo	Alto	C4	E5	Lead
Last Five Years, The	2002	Catherine Hiatt	Still Hurting	Ballad	Alto	A3	Db5	Lead
Last Five Years, The	2002	Catherine Hiatt	See I'm Smiling	Ballad	Alto	E3	C#5	Lead
Last Five Years, The	2002	Catherine Hiatt	I'm A Part Of That	Uptempo	Alto	Bb3	Eb5	Lead
Last Five Years, The	2002	Catherine Hiatt	A Summer In Ohio	Uptempo	Alto	F#3	E5	Lead
Last Five Years, The	2002	Catherine Hiatt	The Next Ten Minutes	Ballad	Alto	G#3	E#4	Lead
Last Five Years, The	2002	Catherine Hiatt	Climbing Uphill/Audition	Uptempo	Alto	G3	D5	Lead
Last Five Years, The	2002	Catherine Hiatt	I Can Do Better Than That	Uptempo	Alto	A3	D5	Lead
Last Five Years, The	2002	Catherine Hiatt	Goodbye Until Tomorrow	Moderate Tempo	Alto	F#3	Db5	Lead
Last Five Years, The	2002	Catherine Hiatt	When You Come To Me	Moderate Tempo	Alto	A3	D5	Lead
Hairspray	2002	Teen Girl	The New Kid In Town*	Uptempo	Alto	A3	D5	Featured Ensemble
All Shook Up	2005	Lorraine	It's Now Or Never *	Moderate Tempo	Alto	C4	F5	Supporting
Legally Blonde	2007	Elle Woods	So Much Better	Uptempo	Alto	G3	E5	Lead
Legally Blonde	2007	Elle Woods	Take It Like A Man	Moderate Tempo	Alto	Gb3	E5	Lead
Legally Blonde	2007	Elle Woods	Legally Blonde	Ballad	Alto	G3	Db5	Lead
Legally Blonde	2007	Elle Woods	Find My Way	Moderate Tempo	Alto	G3	B4	Lead
Legally Blonde	2007	Elle Woods	Legally Blonde Remix*	Uptempo	Alto	E4	D5	Lead
Legally Blonde	2007	Elle Woods	What You Want	Uptempo	Alto	Bb3	Db5	Lead
Legally Blonde	2007	Elle Woods	Chip On My Shoulder*	Uptempo	Alto	C4	Eb5	Lead
High School Musical	2007	Gabriella Montez	When There Was You And Me	Ballad	Alto	F#3	F5	Lead
High School Musical	2007	Gabriella Montez	Breaking Free*	Ballad	Alto	Bb3	D5	Lead
White Christmas	2008	Judy Haynes	Falling Out Of Love Can Be Fun*	Uptempo	Alto	G3	C5	Lead
In The Heights	2008	Nina Rosario+	Breathe	Moderate Tempo	Alto	F3	F5	Lead

Ingenue Female

50

* = Music Edit Required
+ = Ethnic Specific

Show	Year	Role	Song	Tempo	Vocal Type	Range-Bottom	Range-Top	Category
In The Heights	2008	Nina Rosario+	When You're Home*	Uptempo	Alto	C#4	E5	Lead
In The Heights	2008	Nina Rosario+	Everything's I Know	Ballad	Alto	Bb3	Db5	Lead
In The Heights	2008	Nina Rosario+	Alabanza*	Ballad	Alto	A3	A4	Lead
Heathers	2014	Heather McNamara	Lifeboat	Ballad	Alto	G3	Db5	Lead
No, No Nanette	1925	Nanette	I've Confessed To The Breeze*	Moderate Tempo	Soprano	B3	F5	Lead
No, No Nanette	1925	Nanette	I Want To Be Happy*	Uptempo	Soprano	C4	E5	Lead
No, No Nanette	1925	Nanette	No, No Nanette*	Uptempo	Soprano	Bb3	F5	Lead
No, No Nanette	1925	Nanette	Peach On The Beach*	Uptempo	Soprano	F#4	A4	Lead
No, No Nanette	1925	Nanette	Tea For Two*	Moderate Tempo	Soprano	Eb4	F5	Lead
No, No Nanette	1925	Nanette	Waiting For You*	Moderate Tempo	Soprano	Ab3	Eb5	Lead
Show Boat	1927	Magnolia	Make Believe	Ballad	Soprano	D4	Bb5	Lead
Show Boat	1927	Magnolia	You Are Love*	Ballad	Soprano	D4	Bb5	Lead
Show Boat	1927	Magnolia	Can't Help Reprise	Ballad	Soprano	Ab3	Eb5	Lead
Show Boat	1927	Magnolia	After The Ball	Moderate Tempo	Soprano	D4	Ab5	Lead
Show Boat	1927	Magnolia	Dance The Night Away*	Uptempo	Soprano	G3	C5	Lead
Anything Goes	1934	Hope Harcourt	All Through The Night *	Ballad	Soprano	C4	Eb5	Lead
Anything Goes	1934	Hope Harcourt	The Gypsy In Me	Moderate Tempo	Soprano	C3	G4	Lead
Anything Goes	1934	Hope Harcourt	Goodbye Little Dream, Goodbye	Ballad	Soprano	A3	Eb5	Lead
Porgy and Bess	1935	Clara+	Summertime	Moderate Tempo	Soprano	F#4	B5	Lead
Porgy and Bess	1935	Clara+	Summertime Reprise	Moderate Tempo	Soprano	E4	A5	Lead
Brigadoon	1947	Fiona MacLaren	Waitin For My Dearie *	Ballad	Soprano	C4	A5	Lead
Brigadoon	1947	Fiona MacLaren	The Heather On The Hill *	Ballad	Soprano	Bb2	G4	Lead
Brigadoon	1947	Fiona MacLaren	Almost Like Being In Love *	Ballad	Soprano	F4	A5	Lead
Brigadoon	1947	Fiona MacLaren	From This Day On *	Ballad	Soprano	F4	A5	Lead
Brigadoon	1947	Fiona MacLaren	Come To Me Bend To Me Reprise	Ballad	Soprano	D4	G5	Lead
Brigadoon	1947	Fiona MacLaren	The Heather On The Hill Reprise	Ballad	Soprano	C4	F5	Lead

Ingenue Female

Ingenue Female

* = Music Edit Required
+ = Ethnic Specific

Show	Year	Role	Song	Tempo	Vocal Type	Range-Bottom	Range-Top	Category
Brigadoon	1947	Fiona MacLaren	From This Day On Reprise *	Ballad	Soprano	Eb4	G5	Lead
Guys and Dolls	1950	Sarah Brown	I'll Know*	Ballad	Soprano	E4	G#5	Lead
Guys and Dolls	1950	Sarah Brown	If I Were A Bell	Uptempo	Soprano	Bb3	D5	Lead
Guys and Dolls	1950	Sarah Brown	Marry The Man Today*	Uptempo	Soprano	C4	Eb5	Lead
Guys and Dolls	1950	Sarah Brown	I'll Know (Finish)	Ballad	Soprano	Eb4	F5	Lead
King and I, The	1951	Tuptim+	My Lord And Master	Moderate Tempo	Soprano	D#4	A#5	Lead
King and I, The	1951	Tuptim+	We Kiss In The Shadow	Ballad	Soprano	D4	G5	Lead
King and I, The	1951	Tuptim+	I Have Dreamed	Ballad	Soprano	C4	G5	Lead
Wonderful Town	1953	Eileen Sherwood	A Little Bit In Love	Moderate Tempo	Soprano	C4	C#5	Lead
Wonderful Town	1953	Eileen Sherwood	Conversation Piece*	Uptempo	Soprano	D4	B4	Lead
Candide	1956	Cunegonde	Life Is Happiness Indeed*	Moderate Tempo	Soprano	F4	C6	Lead
Candide	1956	Cunegonde	Glitter And Be Gay	Moderate Tempo	Soprano	B2	E6	Lead
My Fair Lady	1956	Eliza Doolittle	Wouldn't It Be Loverly	Moderate Tempo	Soprano	C4	Eb5	Lead
My Fair Lady	1956	Eliza Doolittle	Just You Wait	Moderate Tempo	Soprano	A3	Eb4	Lead
My Fair Lady	1956	Eliza Doolittle	I Could Have Danced All Night*	Uptempo	Soprano	B3	G5	Lead
My Fair Lady	1956	Eliza Doolittle	Just You Wait Reprise	Ballad	Soprano	D4	C5	Lead
My Fair Lady	1956	Eliza Doolittle	Wouldn't It Be Loverly Reprise*	Ballad	Soprano	C4	D5	Lead
My Fair Lady	1956	Eliza Doolittle	Without You	Moderate Tempo	Soprano	B3	Eb5	Lead
My Fair Lady	1956	Eliza Doolittle	Show Me	Uptempo	Soprano	D4	G5	Lead
Cinderella (2013)	1957	Ella	In My Own Little Corner	Uptempo	Soprano	C4	C5	Lead
Cinderella (2013)	1957	Ella	In My Own Little Corner Reprise	Uptempo	Soprano	C4	C5	Lead
Cinderella (2013)	1957	Ella	Impossible*	Uptempo	Soprano	Bb2	D5	Lead
Cinderella (2013)	1957	Ella	Ten Minutes Ago*	Moderate Tempo	Soprano	C#4	D5	Lead
Cinderella (2013)	1957	Ella	Do I Love You...*	Ballad	Soprano	A4	E5	Lead
Cinderella (2013)	1957	Ella	When You're Driving...*	Uptempo	Soprano	B2	Bb4	Lead
Cinderella (2013)	1957	Ella	A Lovely Night*	Uptempo	Soprano	Bb3	Bb4	Lead
Cinderella (2013)	1957	Ella	A Lovely Night*	Uptempo	Soprano	C4	C5	Lead
Cinderella (2013)	1957	Ella	It's Possible	Uptempo	Soprano	C4	B4	Lead

Ingenue Female

Ingenue Female

* = Music Edit Required
+ = Ethnic Specific

Show	Year	Role	Song	Tempo	Vocal Type	Range-Bottom	Range-Top	Category
West Side Story	1957	Female Shark+	Somewhere	Ballad	Soprano	B3	F#5	Featured Ensemble
West Side Story	1957	Maria+	I Feel Pretty*	Uptempo	Soprano	C4	F5	Lead
West Side Story	1957	Maria+	I Have A Love*	Ballad	Soprano	B♭3	B♭5	Lead
Bye Bye Birdie	1960	Kim MacAfee	How Lovely To Be A Woman	Moderate Tempo	Soprano	D#4	F#4	Lead
Bye Bye Birdie	1960	Kim MacAfee	One Boy	Ballad	Soprano	D♭4	F5	Lead
Bye Bye Birdie	1960	Kim MacAfee	What Did I Ever See In Him *	Uptempo	Soprano	G3	B♭4	Lead
Bye Bye Birdie	1960	Kim MacAfee	Lot of Livin' To Do *	Uptempo	Soprano	D4	E5	Lead
Fantasticks, The	1960	Luisa	Much More	Uptempo	Soprano	B3	F5	Lead
Fantasticks, The	1960	Luisa	Metaphor *	Uptempo	Soprano	E♭4	G5	Lead
Fantasticks, The	1960	Luisa	Soon It's Gonna Rain *	Moderate Tempo	Soprano	B2	F4	Lead
Fantasticks, The	1960	Luisa	They Were You *	Ballad	Soprano	B3	D5	Lead
Cinderella (2013)	1962	Ella	The Sweetest Sounds*	Moderate Tempo	Soprano	C#4	C5	Lead
A Funny Thing...Forum	1962	Philia	Lovely*	Moderate Tempo	Soprano	C#4	F5	Lead
A Funny Thing...Forum	1962	Philia	That'll Show Him	Moderate Tempo	Soprano	C4	G5	Lead
1776	1969	Martha Jefferson	He Plays The Violin	Moderate Tempo	Soprano	B♭3	D5	Supporting
Company (Revival)	1970	Kathy	You Could Drive a Person Crazy	Uptempo	Soprano	C#4	A5	Supporting
Grease	1971	Sandy Dumbrowski	It's Raining on Prom Night	Ballad	Soprano	A3	D5	Lead
Grease	1971	Sandy Dumbrowski	Hopelessly Devoted to You	Ballad	Soprano	A3	F5	Lead
Grease	1971	Sandy Dumbrowski	Look At Me I'm Sandra Dee Reprise	Ballad	Soprano	A3	C#5	Lead
Grease	1971	Sandy Dumbrowski	Since I Don't Have You	Ballad	Soprano	A♭3	A♭5	Lead
A Little Night Music	1973	Anne Egerman	Soon	Uptempo	Soprano	C4	G#5	Lead
Evita	1978	Mistress	Another Suitcase In Another Hall	Ballad	Soprano	A3	E5	Supporting
Sweeney Todd	1979	Johannah	Green Finch And Linnet Bird*	Uptempo	Soprano	C4	G5	Lead
Dreamgirls	1981	Deena Jones +	Heavy	Uptempo	Soprano	D3	D4	Lead
Dreamgirls	1981	Deena Jones +	One Night Only	Uptempo	Soprano	A♭3	D5	Lead
Singin' In The Rain	1983	Kathy Seldon	Lucky Star	Moderate Tempo	Soprano	B♭3	E♭5	Lead
Singin' In The Rain	1983	Kathy Seldon	Kathy's Would You	Moderate Tempo	Soprano	G3	C5	Lead
Baby	1983	Lizzie Fields	I Want It All *	Uptempo	Soprano	C4	E♭5	Lead

Ingenue Female

* = Music Edit Required
+ = Ethnic Specific

Show	Year	Role	Song	Tempo	Vocal Type	Range-Bottom	Range-Top	Category
Baby	1983	Lizzie Fields	The Story Goes On	Ballad	Soprano	G3	F5	Lead
Big River	1985	Mary Jane Wilkes	Leavin's Not The Only Way To Go	Ballad	Soprano	B3	B4	Supporting
Big River	1985	Mary Jane Wilkes	You Oughta Be Here With Me	Ballad	Soprano	B3	C#5	Supporting
Mystery Of Edwin Drood, The	1985	Rosa Bud	Moonfall	Ballad	Soprano	B3	G5	Lead
Mystery Of Edwin Drood, The	1985	Rosa Bud	Perfect Strangers*	Moderate Tempo	Soprano	C#4	F5	Lead
Mystery Of Edwin Drood	1985	Rosa Bud	Rosa's Confession	Uptempo	Soprano	A3	Ab5	Lead
Phantom Of The Opera	1986	Christine Daae	Think Of Me*	Moderate Tempo	Soprano	D4	C6	Lead
Phantom Of The Opera	1986	Christine Daae	Angel Of Music*	Moderate Tempo	Soprano	Bb3	F#5	Lead
Phantom Of The Opera	1986	Christine Daae	Phantom Of The Opera*	Moderate Tempo	Soprano	G3	E5	Lead
Phantom Of The Opera	1986	Christine Daae	All I Ask Of You*	Ballad	Soprano	Ab3	Ab5	Lead
Phantom Of The Opera	1986	Christine Daae	Twisted Every Way*	Ballad	Soprano	C4	Eb5	Lead
Phantom Of The Opera	1986	Christine Daae	Wishing You Were Somehow Here Aga	Ballad	Soprano	A3	G5	Lead
Phantom Of The Opera	1986	Christine Daae	The Point Of No Return*	Ballad	Soprano	C4	G5	Lead
Phantom Of The Opera	1986	Christine Daae	Raoul I've Been There	Moderate Tempo	Soprano	C#4	Ab5	Lead
Into The Woods	1987	Cinderella	On The Steps Of The Palace	Uptempo	Soprano	A3	E5	Lead
Into The Woods	1987	Cinderella	No One Is Alone	Ballad	Soprano	Bb3	Db5	Lead
Into The Woods	1987	Cinderella	No One Is Alone (Part 2)	Ballad	Soprano	Bb3	Db5	Lead
Meet Me In St. Louis	1989	Agnes Smith	Under The Bamboo Tree*	Moderate Tempo	Soprano	C4	Bb4	Lead
Meet Me In St. Louis	1989	Rose Smith	Raving Beauty*	Ballad	Soprano	Bb3	Db5	Lead
Phantom	1991	Christine Daae	Home*	Moderate Tempo	Soprano	D4	A5	Lead
Phantom	1991	Christine Daae	The Bistro*	Uptempo	Soprano	Bb3	B5	Lead
Phantom	1991	Christine Daae	Who Could Have Ever Dreamed Up Yo	Uptempo	Soprano	Bb3	Eb5	Lead
Phantom	1991	Christine Daae	My True Love	Moderate Tempo	Soprano	C4	F5	Lead
Phantom	1991	Christine Daae	Finale: You Are Music*	Ballad	Soprano	B4	G5	Lead
Phantom	1991	Christine Daee	Melody Of Paris	Uptempo	Soprano	B3	A5	Lead
Miss Saigon	1991	Kim+	The Movie In My Mind*	Ballad	Soprano	Ab3	Eb5	Lead
Miss Saigon	1991	Kim+	The Ceremony*	Ballad	Soprano	B3	D5	Lead

Ingenue Female

* = Music Edit Required
+ = Ethnic Specific

Show	Year	Role	Song	Tempo	Vocal Type	Range-Bottom	Range-Top	Category
Miss Saigon	1991	Kim+	I Still Believe*	Ballad	Soprano	A3	E5	Lead
Miss Saigon	1991	Kim+	There Is A Secret (ms 214-258)	Moderate Tempo	Soprano	A3	Db5	Lead
Miss Saigon	1991	Kim+	You Will Not Touch Him (ms 20-51)	Moderate Tempo	Soprano	C4	Eb5	Lead
Miss Saigon	1991	Kim+	I'd Give My Life For You*	Ballad	Soprano	G3	E5	Lead
Miss Saigon	1991	Kim+	Sun and Moon Reprise	Ballad	Soprano	E3	D5	Lead
Miss Saigon	1991	Kim+	Little God Of My Heart	Ballad	Soprano	A3	D5	Lead
Miss Saigon	1991	Kim+	Sun And Moon*	Ballad	Soprano	F#3	D5	Lead
A Christmas Carol	1997	Emily	A Place Called Home	Ballad	Soprano	Bb3	F5	Supporting
A Christmas Carol	1997	Grace Smythe	God Bless Us Everyone	Uptempo	Soprano	D4	C5	Lead
Marie Christine	1999	Lisette+	Tout Mi Mi	Ballad	Soprano	D4	C#5	Lead
Marie Christine	1999	Lisette+	Dansen Calinda	Ballad	Soprano	E4	C6	Lead
Marie Christine	1999	Lisette+	Tout Mimi Reprise	Ballad	Soprano	Bb3	Bb4	Lead
You're...Charlie Brown	1999	Sally	My New Philosophy	Uptempo	Soprano	B3	E5	Lead
Jane Eyre	2000	Blanche Ingram	The Finer Things	Uptempo	Soprano	Eb4	B5	Supporting
Jane Eyre	2000	Blanche Ingram	In the Virgin Morning*	Moderate Tempo	Soprano	B3	F5	Supporting
Jane Eyre	2000	School Girl	Rain	Moderate Tempo	Soprano	Bb3	E5	Supporting
Spitfire Grill	2001	Shelby Thorpe	Hannah Had A Son	Ballad	Soprano	D4	D5	Lead
Spitfire Grill	2001	Shelby Thorpe	When Hope Goes	Ballad	Soprano	A3	D5	Lead
Spitfire Grill	2001	Shelby Thorpe	Wild Bird	Ballad	Soprano	C4	D5	Lead
Mamma Mia!	2001	Sophie Sheridan	I Have A Dream	Ballad	Soprano	Ab4	Bb4	Lead
Mamma Mia!	2001	Sophie Sheridan	Honey Honey*	Uptempo	Soprano	C4	C5	Lead
Mamma Mia!	2001	Sophie Sheridan	The Name Of The Game*	Moderate Tempo	Soprano	F#3	B4	Lead
Mamma Mia!	2001	Sophie Sheridan	Under Attack*	Uptempo	Soprano	B3	C#5	Lead
Mamma Mia!	2001	Sophie Sheridan	I have A Dream Reprise	Ballad	Soprano	Ab3	Db5	Lead
Thoroughly Modern Millie	2002	Dorothy Brown	How The Other Half Lives*	Moderate Tempo	Soprano	B3	Eb5	Lead
Sweet Smell Of Success	2002	Susan	What If*	Uptempo	Soprano	A3	F5	Lead
Sweet Smell Of Success	2002	Susan	I Cannot Hear The City Reprise*	Ballad	Soprano	Ab3	G5	Lead
Caroline, Or Change	2004	Emmie Thibodeaux +	Duets: Nigh Mamma (ms 71-89)	Ballad	Soprano	F#4	C5	Supporting

Ingenue Female

55

Ingenue Female

* = Music Edit Required
+ = Ethnic Specific

Show	Year	Role	Song	Vocal Type	Range-Bottom	Range-Top	Category
Caroline, Or Change	2004	Emmie Thibodeaux +	I Hate The Bus (ms 6-36)	Soprano	G3	F#5	Supporting
Caroline, Or Change	2004	Emmie Thibodeaux +	Epilogue-Emmie's Dream (ms 9-73)	Soprano	Ab3	Db4	Supporting
Caroline, Or Change	2004	Emmie Thibodeaux +	The Bus (ms 71-89)	Soprano	Bb2	Bb4	Supporting
Little Women	2005	Beth March	Off to Massachusettes*	Soprano	C#4	F5	Lead
Little Women	2005	Beth March	Some Things Are Meant To Be	Soprano	B2	E5	Lead
Light In The Piazza, The	2005	Clara Johnson	The Beauty Is	Soprano	Cb4	G5	Lead
Light In The Piazza, The	2005	Clara Johnson	The Light in the Piazza	Soprano	A3	F#5	Lead
Little Women	2005	Meg March	More Than I Am*	Soprano	E4	E5	Lead
25th Annual...Spelling Bee	2005	Olive Ostrovsky	My Friend The Dictionary	Soprano	B3	D5	Lead
25th Annual...Spelling Bee	2005	Olive Ostrovsky	The I Love You Song	Soprano	D4	D5	Lead
25th Annual...Spelling Bee	2005	Olive Ostrovsky	Second Part 1*	Soprano	C#4	D5	Lead
Grey Gardens	2006	Edie Beale (Act 1)	Daddy's Girl*	Soprano	C4	E5	Lead
Grey Gardens	2006	Edie Beale (Act 1)	The Telegram	Soprano	C#4	F#5	Lead
Drowsy Chaperon, The	2006	Janet Van de Graff	Show Off *	Soprano	G3	C5	Lead
Drowsy Chaperon, The	2006	Janet Van de Graff	Accident Waiting To Happen *	Soprano	C4	D5	Lead
Drowsy Chaperon, The	2006	Janet Van de Graff	Bride's Lament *	Soprano	Ab3	F5	Lead
Spring Awakening	2006	Wendla	The Guilty One*	Soprano	G3	A4	Lead
Spring Awakening	2006	Wendla	Whispering	Soprano	B3	A4	Lead
Spring Awakening	2006	Wendla	Mama Who Bore Me	Soprano	G3	A4	Lead
Spring Awakening	2006	Wendla	Those You've Known*	Soprano	C4	D5	Lead
The Little Mermaid	2007	Ariel	The World Above	Soprano	A3	C5	Lead
The Little Mermaid	2007	Ariel	Part Of Your World	Soprano	C4	C5	Lead
The Little Mermaid	2007	Ariel	Ursula's Incantation (Ahs)*	Soprano	F#4	E5	Lead
Cinderella (2013)	2013	Ella	He Was Tall	Soprano	D4	C#5	Lead

Ingenue Female

56

Ingenue Male

* = Music Edit Required
+ = Ethnic Specific

Show	Year	Role	Song	Tempo	Vocal Type	Range-Bottom	Range-Top	Category
Good News (1993 Revival)	1927	Tom Marlowe	The Best Things In Life Are Free*	Ballad	Baritone	C3	E♭4	Lead
Good News (1993 Revival)	1927	Tom Marlowe	Lucky In Love*	Uptempo	Baritone	D3	F4	Lead
Good News (1993 Revival)	1928	Bobby Randall	Button Up Your Overcoat*	Uptempo	Baritone	E3	F#4	Supporting
Good News (1993 Revival)	1930	Bobby Randall	Never Swat A Fly*	Uptempo	Baritone	A2	E4	Supporting
Babes In Arms (1998)	1937	Marshall Blackstone	Babes In Arms*	Uptempo	Baritone	C3	E4	Lead
Babes In Arms (1998)	1937	Val LaMar	Where Or When*	Moderate Tempo	Baritone	B2	F4	Lead
Babes In Arms (1998)	1937	Val LaMar	All At Once*	Moderate Tempo	Baritone	A2	F4	Lead
Babes In Arms (1998)	1937	Val LaMar	Babes In Arms*	Uptempo	Baritone	C3	E4	Lead
Annie Get Your Gun	1944	Tommy Walker	I'll Share It All With You	Uptempo	Baritone	C#3	D4	Lead
State Fair 1996	1945	Wayne Frake	That's For Me	Moderate Tempo	Baritone	C3	F4	Lead
State Fair 1996	1947	Wayne Frake	So Far*	Moderate Tempo	Baritone	D3	E4	Lead
Damn Yankees	1955	Sohovic	Who's Got The Pain*	Uptempo	Baritone	G#3	D#4	Supporting
Sound Of Music, The	1959	Rolf Gruber	You Are Sixteen*	Moderate Tempo	Baritone	D3	E4	Lead
Fantasticks, The	1960	Matt	Soon It's Gonna Rain *	Moderate Tempo	Baritone	D4	A♭5	Lead
Mame	1966	Patrick Dennis	The Letter*	Uptempo	Baritone	D#3	D4	Lead
Mame	1966	Patrick Dennis	My Best Girl Reprise	Ballad	Baritone	C3	E4	Lead
Mame	1966	Patrick Dennis	My Best Girl Reprise 2	Ballad	Baritone	C3	E4	Lead
Dreamgirls	1981	CC White +	Family	Ballad	Baritone	D3	E4	Lead
Cats	1981	Mr. Mistoffolees	Mr. Mistoffolees	Uptempo	Baritone	C3	E♭4	Supporting
Cats	1981	Mungojerrie	Mongojerrie and Rumpleteezer	Uptempo	Baritone	E3	E4	Supporting
LA Cage Aux Folles	1983	Jean-Michel	Look Over There Reprise	Tenor	Baritone	D♭3	E♭4	Lead
Meet Me In St. Louis	1989	John Truitt	You Are For Loving*	Ballad	Baritone	D♭3	F4	Lead
Meet Me In St. Louis	1989	John Truitt	The Girl Next Door	Moderate Tempo	Baritone	D3	E4	Lead
Meet Me In St. Louis	1989	Lon Smith	Banjos*	Uptempo	Baritone	B♭2	F4	Lead
Once On This Island	1990	Daniel+	Forever Yours*	Ballad	Baritone	E#3	F#4	Lead
Once On This Island	1990	Daniel+	Some Girls	Moderate Tempo	Baritone	B2	F#4	Lead
Blood Brothers	1993	Edward	Long Sunday Afternoon *	Ballad	Baritone	E3	C4	Lead
State Fair 1996	1996	Wayne Frake	The Man I Used To Be*	Moderate Tempo	Baritone	C3	E♭4	Lead

Ingenue Male

57

Ingenue Male

* = Music Edit Required
+ = Ethnic Specific

Show	Year	Role	Song	Tempo	Vocal Type	Range-Bottom	Range-Top	Category
Parade	1998	Frankie Epps	Old Red Hills Of Home Finale*	Moderate Tempo	Baritone	E♭3	E♭4	Lead
Babes In Arms (1998)	1998	Irving de Quincy+	Light On Our Feet*	Uptempo	Baritone	F3	F4	Lead
Babes In Arms (1998)	1998	Ivor de Quincy+	Light On Our Feet*	Uptempo	Baritone	F3	F4	Lead
Marie Christine	1999	Jean L'Adrese+	All Eyes Look To You	Ballad	Baritone	A2	E4	Lead
All Shook Up	2005	Dean Hyde	It's Now Or Never *	Moderate Tempo	Baritone	C3	F4	Supporting
Little Women	2005	John Brooke	More Than I Am*	Moderate Tempo	Baritone	E3	E4	Supporting
Legally Blonde	2007	Padamadan+	Harvard Variation*	Uptempo	Baritone	B2	E4	Supporting
Addams Family, The	2010	Lucas Beineke	Crazier Than You *	Uptempo	Baritone	D3	E4	Supporting
Addams Family, The	2010	Lucas Beineke	One Normal Night	Uptempo	Baritone	D3	F4	Supporting
No, No Nanette	1925	Tom Trainor	I've Confessed To The Breeze*	Moderate Tempo	Tenor	D3	F4	Lead
No, No Nanette	1925	Tom Trainor	No, No Nanette*	Uptempo	Tenor	C3	E♭4	Lead
No, No Nanette	1925	Tom Trainor	Tea For Two*	Moderate Tempo	Tenor	E♭3	F4	Lead
No, No Nanette	1925	Tom Trainor	Waiting For You*	Moderate Tempo	Tenor	C3	E♭4	Lead
Crazy For You (1992)	1937	Bobby Child	I Can't Be Bothered Now	Uptempo	Tenor	D3	F4	Lead
Crazy For You (1992)	1937	Bobby Child	Things Are Looking Up	Uptempo	Tenor	C3	D4	Lead
Crazy For You (1992)	1937	Bobby Child	Shall We Dance	Uptempo	Tenor	D3	F♭4	Lead
Crazy For You (1992)	1937	Bobby Child	They Can't Take That Away	Moderate Tempo	Tenor	B♭2	E♭4	Lead
Crazy For You (1992)	1937	Bobby Child	Nice Work If You Can Get It	Uptempo	Tenor	D3	C4	Lead
Cinderella (2013)	1940	Topher	Loneliness Of Evening*	Ballad	Tenor	E♭3	A4	Lead
Brigadoon	1947	Charlie Dalrymple	I'll Go Home With Bonnie Jean	Uptempo	Tenor	B♭2	G4	Supporting
Brigadoon	1947	Charlie Dalrymple	Come To Me Bend To me	Ballad	Tenor	D3	G4	Supporting
Brigadoon	1947	Charlie Dalrymple	Go Home Reprise	Uptempo	Tenor	G3	G4	Supporting
South Pacific	1949	Lt. Jospeh Cable	Younger Than Springtime*	Ballad	Tenor	E3	G4	Lead
South Pacific	1949	Lt. Jospeh Cable	You've Got To Be Carefully Taught	Uptempo	Tenor	E3	G4	Lead
King and I, The	1951	Lun Tha+	We Kiss In The Shadow	Ballad	Tenor	D3	E4	Lead
King and I, The	1951	Lun Tha+	I Have Dreamed	Ballad	Tenor	C3	G4	Lead
Damn Yankees	1955	Joe Hardy	A Man Doesn't Know	Ballad	Tenor	C3	G♭4	Lead

Ingenue Male

58

Ingenue Male

* = Music Edit Required
+ = Ethnic Specific

Show	Year	Role	Song	Tempo	Vocal Type	Range-Bottom	Range-Top	Category
Damn Yankees	1955	Joe Hardy	Near To You	Ballad	Tenor	C3	C4	Lead
Damn Yankees	1955	Joe Hardy	Goodbye Old Girl	Ballad	Tenor	E♭3	F#4	Lead
Candide	1956	Candide	Life Is Happiness Indeed*	Moderate Tempo	Tenor	F3	G4	Lead
Candide	1956	Candide	It Must Be So	Ballad	Tenor	D3	E4	Lead
Candide	1956	Candide	Candide's Lament	Ballad	Tenor	C3	F4	Lead
Candide	1956	Candide	It Must Be Me	Ballad	Tenor	D3	E4	Lead
Candide	1956	Candide	Nothing More Than This	Moderate Tempo	Tenor	D3	F#4	Lead
Candide	1956	Candide	Universal Good Reprise*	Ballad	Tenor	D♭3	D♭4	Lead
My Fair Lady	1956	Freddy Eynsford Hill	On The Street Where You Live	Moderate Tempo	Tenor	C3	F4	Lead
My Fair Lady	1956	Freddy Eynsford Hill	On The Street Where You Live Reprise	Moderate Tempo	Tenor	C3	E4	Lead
West Side Story	1957	Tony	Something's Coming	Uptempo	Tenor	F#3	B♭4	Lead
West Side Story	1957	Tony	Maria	Ballad	Tenor	B2	B♭4	Lead
Cinderella (2013)	1957	Topher	Ten Minutes Ago*	Moderate Tempo	Tenor	C3	D4	Lead
Cinderella (2013)	1957	Topher	Do I Love You!...*	Ballad	Tenor	A3	E♭4	Lead
Cinderella (2013)	1957	Topher	Ten Minutes Ago Reprise	Moderate Tempo	Tenor	C3	D4	Lead
Flower Drum Song 2002	1958	Wang Ta+	You Are Beautiful	Ballad	Tenor	E♭3	G4	Lead
Flower Drum Song 2002	1958	Wang Ta+	You Are Beautiful Reprise*	Ballad	Tenor	F3	G4	Lead
Flower Drum Song 2002	1958	Wang Ta+	Sunday	Moderate Tempo	Tenor	C#4	E4	Lead
Flower Drum Song 2002	1958	Wang Ta+	Like A God	Uptempo	Tenor	C#3	G#4	Lead
Flower Drum Song 2002	1958	Wang Ta+	Like A God	Moderate Tempo	Tenor	B2	G4	Lead
Gypsy	1959	Tulsa	All I Need Is The Girl	Uptempo	Tenor	E3	G4	Lead
Fantasticks, The	1960	Matt	Metaphor *	Uptempo	Tenor	C♭3	E♭4	Lead
Fantasticks, The	1960	Matt	I Can See It *	Uptempo	Tenor	B2	E4	Lead
Fantasticks, The	1960	Matt	They Were You *	Ballad	Tenor	B2	D4	Lead
Fantasticks, The	1960	Matt	Metaphor Reprise *	Uptempo	Tenor	B2	D4	Lead
A Funny Thing...Forum	1962	Hero	Love I Hear	Uptempo	Tenor	B2	F#4	Lead
A Funny Thing...Forum	1962	Hero	Lovely*	Moderate Tempo	Tenor	D3	E4	Lead
Cinderella (2013)	1962	Topher	The Sweetest Sounds*	Moderate Tempo	Tenor	E3	E4	Lead

Ingenue Male

59

* = Music Edit Required
+ = Ethnic Specific

Show	Year	Role	Song	Tempo	Vocal Type	Range-Bottom	Range-Top	Category
Cinderella (2013)	1962	Topher	The Sweetest Sounds Reprise	Moderate Tempo	Tenor	A2	F♭4	Lead
110 In The Shade	1963	Jimmy Curry	Lizzie's Comin' Home *	Uptempo	Tenor	B2	E4	Supporting
Cabaret	1966	Nazi Youth	Tomorrow Belongs to Me	Ballad	Tenor	F3	F#4	Featured Ensemble
Pippin	1972	Pippin	Corner Of The Sky	Uptempo	Tenor	E3	C5	Lead
Pippin	1972	Pippin	War Is A Science*	Uptempo	Tenor	B♭2	G4	Lead
Pippin	1972	Pippin	Corner Of The Sky Reprise	Moderate Tempo	Tenor	D3	F4	Lead
Pippin	1972	Pippin	With You	Ballad	Tenor	C3	A♭4	Lead
Pippin	1972	Pippin	Morning Glow (C Major)	Moderate Tempo	Tenor	C3	F#4	Lead
Pippin	1972	Pippin	Morning Glow (D♭ Major)	Moderate Tempo	Tenor	D♭3	G4	Lead
Pippin	1972	Pippin	Extraordinary	Uptempo	Tenor	C3	G4	Lead
Pippin	1972	Pippin	Prayer For A Duck	Uptempo	Tenor	D3	F#4	Lead
Pippin	1972	Pippin	Corner of the Sky Last Reprise	Moderate Tempo	Tenor	D#3	F#4	Lead
Pippin	1972	Pippin	Love Song*	Ballad	Tenor	B2	G#4	Lead
Pippin	1972	Pippin	Think About The Sun*	Uptempo	Tenor	C3	G4	Lead
A Little Night Music	1973	Erik Egerman	Later	Uptempo	Tenor	C3	B4	Lead
A Chorus Line	1975	Mike	I Can Do That	Uptempo	Tenor	G4	A♭4	Lead
Sweeney Todd	1979	Anthony Hope	Ah, Miss (I & III)	Uptempo	Tenor	C3	F4	Lead
Sweeney Todd	1979	Anthony Hope	Johanna	Ballad	Tenor	C3	E♭4	Lead
Cats	1981	Skimbleshanks	Skimbleshanks	Uptempo	Tenor	A2	F4	Supporting
Seven Brides/Seven Brothers	1982	Gideon	Love Never Goes Away*	Ballad	Tenor	D3	G4	Lead
Joseph...Dream Coat	1982	Joseph	Any Dream Will Do	Ballad	Tenor	C4	F4	Lead
Joseph...Dream Coat	1982	Joseph	Close Every Door	Ballad	Tenor	C3	A4	Lead
Joseph...Dream Coat	1982	Joseph	Pharaoh's Dream Explained	Uptempo	Tenor	B2	E4	Lead
Joseph...Dream Coat	1982	Joseph	Any Dream Will Do Reprise	Ballad	Tenor	D3	F4	Lead
Joseph...Dream Coat	1982	Joseph	Any Dream Will Do (II)	Ballad	Tenor	C3	F4	Lead
LA Cage Aux Folles	1983	Jean-Michel	With Anne On My Arm	Moderate Tempo	Tenor	A#2	G4	Lead
Big River	1985	Tom Sawyer	Hand For The Hog	Uptempo	Tenor	C3	F4	Supporting
Cinderella (2013)	1985	Topher	Me, Who Am I*	Moderate Tempo	Tenor	B2	G4	Lead

* = Music Edit Required
+ = Ethnic Specific

Show	Year	Role	Song	Tempo	Vocal Type	Range-Bottom	Range-Top	Category
Les Miserables	1987	Male Student	Drink With Me*	Ballad	Tenor	D3	Eb4	Lead
Les Miserables	1987	Marius	Empty Chairs, Empty Tables (Bb Minor)	Ballad	Tenor	Bb2	Ab4	Lead
Les Miserables	1987	Marius	Empty Chairs, Empty Tables (A Minor)	Ballad	Tenor	A2	G4	Lead
Closer Than Ever	1989	Man One	She Loves Me Not *	Ballad	Tenor	Bb2	A4	Lead
Closer Than Ever	1989	Man One	What Am I Doin'	Uptempo	Tenor	C3	A4	Lead
Closer Than Ever	1989	Man One	One Of The Good Guys	Tenor	Tenor	C3	F4	Lead
Closer Than Ever	1989	Man One	Another Wedding Song *	Ballad	Tenor	B2	C4	Lead
Closer Than Ever	1989	Man One	Father of Fathers *	Ballad	Tenor	D3	G4	Lead
Children of Eden	1991	Abel	Lost in The Wilderness Reprise *	Moderate Tempo	Tenor	G3	G4	Supporting
Crazy For You (1992)	1992	Bobby Child	Krazy For You	Uptempo	Tenor	Eb3	Eb4	Lead
Blood Brothers	1993	Eddie	I'm Not Saying A Word	Moderate Tempo	Tenor	E2	A3	Lead
Lion King, The	1997	Simba	Endless Night*	Ballad	Tenor	E4	A4	Lead
Ragtime	1998	Younger Brother	New Music*	Ballad	Tenor	Bb2	D4	Lead
Ragtime	1998	Younger Brother	The Night That Goldman Spoke...(P 1 8	Uptempo	Tenor	B2	F#4	Lead
Aida	2000	Mereb +	How I Know You*	Ballad	Tenor	G2	A4	Supporting
Aida	2000	Mereb +	How I Know You Reprise	Ballad	Tenor	F3	G4	Supporting
Jane Eyre	2000	St. John Rivers	The Voice Across the Moors	Moderate Tempo	Tenor	C3	G4	Supporting
Mamma Mia!	2001	Sky	Lay All Your Love On Me*	Moderate Tempo	Tenor	G3	Ab4	Lead
Last Five Years, The	2002	Jamie Wellerstein	Shiksa Goddess	Uptempo	Tenor	A2	A4	Lead
Last Five Years, The	2002	Jamie Wellerstein	Moving Too Fast	Uptempo	Tenor	C3	Bb4	Lead
Last Five Years, The	2002	Jamie Wellerstein	The Schmuel Song	Uptempo	Tenor	C#3	Ab4	Lead
Last Five Years, The	2002	Jamie Wellerstein	The Next Ten Minutes	Ballad	Tenor	C#3	G#4	Lead
Last Five Years, The	2002	Jamie Wellerstein	If I Didn't Believe In You	Ballad	Tenor	Bb2	G4	Lead
Last Five Years, The	2002	Jamie Wellerstein	Nobody Needs To Know	Ballad	Tenor	C3	Ab4	Lead
Last Five Years, The	2002	Jamie Wellerstein	I Could Never Rescue You	Ballad	Tenor	C3	G4	Lead
Last Five Years, The	2002	Jamie Wellerstein	A Miracle Would Happen	Uptempo	Tenor	A2	A4	Lead
Thoroughly Modern Millie	2002	Jimmy Smith	What Do I Need With Love	Uptempo	Tenor	D3	G4	Lead

Ingenue Male

* = Music Edit Required
+ = Ethnic Specific

Show	Year	Role	Song	Tempo	Vocal Type	Range-Bottom	Range-Top	Category
Thoroughly Modern Millie	2002	Jimmy Smith	I Turned The Corner*	Moderate Tempo	Tenor	C#3	Ab4	Lead
Hairspray	2002	Link Larkin	It Takes Two	Ballad	Tenor	E3	F#4	Lead
Hairspray	2002	Link Larkin	Without Love*	Moderate Tempo	Tenor	C3	A4	Lead
Hairspray	2002	Seaweed Stubs+	Run And Tell That*	Uptempo	Tenor	F3	B4	Lead
Hairspray	2002	Seaweed Stubs+	Without Love*	Moderate Tempo	Tenor	G3	Ab4	Lead
Fame	2003	Nick	I Want To Make Magic	Moderate Tempo	Tenor	C3	G4	Lead
Fame	2003	Nick	Let's Play A Love Scene Reprise *	Ballad	Tenor	Db3	G4	Lead
25th Annual....Spelling Bee	2005	Chip Tolentino	Chip's Lament/...Unfortunate Erection	Uptempo	Tenor	C3	Ab4	Lead
Light In The Piazza, The	2005	Fabrizio Naccarelli	Il Mondo Era Vuoto	Moderate Tempo	Tenor	Bb2	Ab4	Lead
Light In The Piazza, The	2005	Fabrizio Naccarelli	Passegiata*	Moderate Tempo	Tenor	B3	G#4	Lead
Light In The Piazza, The	2005	Fabrizio Naccarelli	Love To Me	Moderate Tempo	Tenor	F4	F#5	Lead
Little Women	2005	Laurie Laurence	Take a Chance On Me	Uptempo	Tenor	B3	Bb4	Lead
Grey Gardens	2006	Joe Kennedy	Goin' Places*	Uptempo	Tenor	C3	F#4	Supporting
Drowsy Chaperon, The	2006	Robert Martin	Accident Waiting To Happen *	Moderate Tempo	Tenor	Eb3	A4	Lead
Drowsy Chaperon, The	2006	Robert Martin	Cold Feets *	Uptempo	Tenor	C3	Ab4	Lead
The Little Mermaid	2007	Flounder	She's In Love*	Uptempo	Tenor	G2	A#4	Lead
The Little Mermaid	2007	Prince Eric	Her Voice	Moderate Tempo	Tenor	C3	G4	Lead
The Little Mermaid	2007	Prince Eric	One Step Closer	Moderate Tempo	Tenor	B3	F#5	Lead
High School Musical	2007	Troy Bolton	What I've Been Looking For Reprise*	Ballad	Tenor	G3	F#4	Lead
High School Musical	2007	Troy Bolton	Breaking Free*	Ballad	Tenor	Bb2	Bb4	Lead
Legally Blonde	2007	Warner Huntington	Serious*	Uptempo	Tenor	F3	G4	Lead
Kinky Boots	2013	Charlie Price	Take What You Got*	Uptempo	Tenor	F#3	F#4	Lead
Kinky Boots	2013	Charlie Price	Step One	Uptempo	Tenor	Ab3	Ab4	Lead
Kinky Boots	2013	Charlie Price	Not My Father's Son*	Ballad	Tenor	F#3	F#4	Lead
Kinky Boots	2013	Charlie Price	The Soul of a Man	Uptempo	Tenor	C3	Bb4	Lead
Kinky Boots	2013	Charlie Price	Charlie's Soliloquy	Ballad	Tenor	Eb3	Cb4	Lead
Kinky Boots	2013	Charlie Price	Charlie's Soliloquy Reprise	Ballad	Tenor	F#3	C#4	Lead

Ingenue Male

62

* = Music Edit Required
+ = Ethnic Specific

Show	Year	Role	Song	Tempo	Vocal Type	Range-Bottom	Range-Top	Category
Crazy For You (1992)	1926	Polly Baker	Someone To Watch Over Me	Ballad	Alto	A♭2	C4	Lead
Good News (1993 Revival)	1927	Connie Lane	The Best Things In Life Are Free*	Ballad	Alto	A3	D5	Lead
Good News (1993 Revival)	1927	Connie Lane	Just Imagine	Ballad	Alto	B3	E5	Lead
Good News (1993 Revival)	1927	Connie Lane	Lucky In Love*	Uptempo	Alto	C4	E♭5	Lead
Show Boat	1927	Ellie	Life Upon The Wicked Stage*	Uptempo	Alto	G3	D5	Lead
Good News (1993 Revival)	1928	Connie Lane	My Lucky Star	Moderate Tempo	Alto	B♭3	D♭5	Lead
Crazy For You (1992)	1930	Polly Baker	Could You Use Me	Uptempo	Alto	A2	E♭4	Lead
Crazy For You (1992)	1930	Polly Baker	Embraceable You	Ballad	Alto	A3	B4	Lead
Crazy For You (1992)	1930	Polly Baker	I Got Rhythm	Uptempo	Alto	B♭3	E♭4	Lead
Crazy For You (1992)	1930	Polly Baker	But Not For Me	Ballad	Alto	B♭3	C5	Lead
Wizard Of Oz 1987	1939	Dorothy	Over The Rainbow	Ballad	Alto	G3	C5	Lead
Wizard Of Oz 1989	1939	Dorothy	Come Out*	Moderate Tempo	Alto	C4	D5	Lead
Wizard Of Oz 2002	1939	Dorothy	The Jitterbug*	Uptempo	Alto	A♭3	D5	Lead
Wizard Of Oz 2004	1939	Dorothy	Over The Rainbow Reprise*	Ballad	Alto	B3	C#5	Lead
Oklahoma!	1943	Ado Annie Carnes	I Cain't Say No Reprise	Moderate Tempo	Alto	C4	D5	Lead
Oklahoma!	1943	Ado Annie Carnes	I Cain't Say No	Moderate Tempo	Alto	C4	D5	Lead
Carousel	1945	Carrie Pipperidge	You're A Queer One Julie Jordan	Moderate Tempo	Alto	D4	E5	Lead
Carousel	1945	Carrie Pipperidge	When I Marry Mr. Snow	Ballad	Alto	D4	F5	Lead
Carousel	1945	Carrie Pipperidge	When I Marry Mr. Snow Reprise	Ballad	Alto	F#3	A4	Lead
Carousel	1945	Carrie Pipperidge	When The Children Are Asleep *	Moderate Tempo	Alto	E♭3	C5	Lead
Brigadoon	1947	Meg Brockie	The Love Of My Life	Uptempo	Alto	G3	C5	Supporting
Brigadoon	1947	Meg Brockie	My Mother's Wedding Day	Uptempo	Alto	C4	F5	Supporting
Kiss Me Kate	1948	Lois Lane/Bianca	Why Can't You Behave*	Moderate Tempo	Alto	G3	C♭5	Lead
Kiss Me Kate	1948	Lois Lane/Bianca	Always True To You*	Uptempo	Alto	A3	C#5	Lead
Kiss Me Kate	1948	Lois Lane/Bianca	Always True To You Encore	Uptempo	Alto	B♭3	A5	Lead
Cinderella (2013)	1957	Gabrielle	Stepsister's Lament*	Uptempo	Alto	C4	D5	Supporting
Cinderella (2013)	1957	Gabrielle	A Lovely Night*	Uptempo	Alto	B3	D5	Supporting
Once Upon A Mattress	1959	Princess Winifred	Happily Ever After	Moderate Tempo	Alto	A3	C♭5	Lead

Character Ingenue Female

Character Ingenue Female

* = Music Edit Required
+ = Ethnic Specific

Show	Year	Role	Song	Tempo	Vocal Type	Range-Bottom	Range-Top	Category
Fiddler on The Roof	1964	Hodel	Far From The Home I Love	Ballad	Alto	C4	E5	Supporting
Sweet Charity	1966	Charity	You Should See Yourself	Uptempo	Alto	B♭3	B♭4	Lead
Sweet Charity	1966	Charity	Charity's Soliloquy	Moderate Tempo	Alto	F3	A♭4	Lead
Sweet Charity	1966	Charity	If My Friends Could See Me Now	Uptempo	Alto	G#3	B♭4	Lead
Sweet Charity	1966	Charity	There's Gott Be Something Better...	Uptempo	Alto	B♭3	D♭5	Lead
Sweet Charity	1966	Charity	I'm The Bravest Individual	Uptempo	Alto	C4	E♭5	Lead
Sweet Charity	1966	Charity	Where Am I Going	Moderate Tempo	Alto	A3	A4	Lead
Sweet Charity	1966	Charity	I'm A Brass Band*	Uptempo	Alto	A#3	G#4	Lead
Hair	1968	Sheila	I Believe In Love	Uptempo	Alto	G3	C5	Lead
Hair	1968	Sheila	Easy To Be Hard	Ballad	Alto	C4	C5	Lead
Hair	1968	Sheila	Good Morning Starshine	Uptempo	Alto	C4	C5	Lead
Company (Revival)	1970	Marta	You Could Drive a Person Crazy	Uptempo	Alto	C#4	A5	Supporting
Company (Revival)	1970	Marta	Another Hundred People	Uptempo	Alto	A3	D5	Supporting
Grease	1971	Marty	Freddy My Love	Uptempo	Alto	C4	C5	Lead
Jesus Christ Superstar	1971	Mary Magdalene	Everything's Alright	Moderate Tempo	Alto	G#3	D5	Lead
Jesus Christ Superstar	1971	Mary Magdalene	Everything's Alright Reprise	Moderate Tempo	Alto	F#3	G4	Lead
Jesus Christ Superstar	1971	Mary Magdalene	I Don't Know How To Love Him	Ballad	Alto	A3	C5	Lead
Jesus Christ Superstar	1971	Mary Magdalene	Could We Start Again Please	Ballad	Alto	A3	F#5	Lead
Wiz, The	1974	Dorothy	Home Reprise	Moderate Tempo	Alto	G3	E5	Lead
A Chorus Line	1975	Maggie	At The Ballet	Moderate Tempo	Alto	A3	D5	Supporting
A Chorus Line	1975	Maggie	Mother *	Ballad	Alto	B3	D5	Supporting
Chicago	1975	Roxie Hart	Funny Honey	Ballad	Alto	F3	B♭4	Lead
Chicago	1975	Roxie Hart	Roxie	Moderate Tempo	Alto	G3	B♭4	Lead
Chicago	1975	Roxie Hart	My Own Best Friend	Moderate Tempo	Alto	E3	A4	Lead
Chicago	1975	Roxie Hart	Me and My Baby	Uptempo	Alto	B♭3	C4	Lead
Chicago	1975	Roxie Hart	Nowadays	Moderate Tempo	Alto	F#3	D5	Lead
Best Little Whorehouse....	1978	Mona's Girl	Hard Candy Christmas	Ballad	Alto	B♭3	C4	Featured Ensemble
Little Shop of Horrors	1982	Audrey	Somewhere That's Green	Ballad	Alto	B3	C5	Lead

Character Ingenue Female

* = Music Edit Required
+ = Ethnic Specific

Show	Year	Role	Song	Tempo	Vocal Type	Range-Bottom	Range-Top	Category
Little Shop of Horrors	1982	Audrey	Suddenly Seymour	Moderate Tempo	Alto	A2	C#4	Lead
Little Shop of Horrors	1982	Audrey	Somewhere That's Green Reprise	Ballad	Alto	B2	C5	Lead
7 Brides For 7 Brothers	1982	Milly	Wonderful Day*	Moderate Tempo	Alto	Ab3	Db5	Lead
7 Brides For 7 Brothers	1982	Milly	I'm Jumpin' In*	Moderate Tempo	Alto	Ab3	Bb4	Lead
7 Brides For 7 Brothers	1982	Milly	One Man*	Moderate Tempo	Alto	G3	Bb4	Lead
7 Brides For 7 Brothers	1982	Milly	I Married Seven Brothers*	Moderate Tempo	Alto	G3	Bb4	Lead
7 Brides For 7 Brothers	1982	Milly	Goin Co'tin*	Moderate Tempo	Alto	Bb3	Eb5	Lead
7 Brides For 7 Brothers	1982	Milly	Love Never Goes Away*	Ballad	Alto	G3	B5	Lead
7 Brides For 7 Brothers	1982	Milly	We Gotta Make It Through....Reprise	Ballad	Alto	A3	A4	Lead
7 Brides For 7 Brothers	1982	Milly	Glad That You Were Born*	Ballad	Alto	Db4	Bb4	Lead
Song & Dance	1985	Emma	Take That Look Off Your Face	Uptempo	Alto	B3	D5	Lead
Song & Dance	1985	Emma	Let Me Finish	Moderate Tempo	Alto	G#3	Eb5	Lead
Song & Dance	1985	Emma	So Much To Do In New York	Moderate Tempo	Alto	Ab3	Eb5	Lead
Song & Dance	1985	Emma	1st Letter Home	Moderate Tempo	Alto	A3	D5	Lead
Song & Dance	1985	Emma	English Girls	Uptempo	Alto	G3	C5	Lead
Song & Dance	1985	Emma	Capped Teeth And Ceasar Salad	Moderate Tempo	Alto	A3	B4	Lead
Song & Dance	1985	Emma	You Made Me Think You Were In Lo	Uptempo	Alto	A3	Bb4	Lead
Song & Dance	1985	Emma	Capped Teeth And Ceasar Salad Re	Ballad	Alto	Ab3	Bb4	Lead
Song & Dance	1985	Emma	So Much To Do In New York #2	Moderate Tempo	Alto	G3	Eb5	Lead
Song & Dance	1985	Emma	2nd Letter Home	Moderate Tempo	Alto	A3	A4	Lead
Song & Dance	1985	Emma	The Last Man In My Life	Ballad	Alto	G3	Eb5	Lead
Song & Dance	1985	Emma	Unexpectied Song	Ballad	Alto	F3	G5	Lead
Song & Dance	1985	Emma	Come Back With The Same Look...	Uptempo	Alto	A3	C5	Lead
Song & Dance	1985	Emma	Take That Look Off Your Face Repri	Uptempo	Alto	B3	E5	Lead
Song & Dance	1985	Emma	Tell Me On A Sunday	Ballad	Alto	G3	E5	Lead
Song & Dance	1985	Emma	I Love New York	Moderate Tempo	Alto	F3	Bb4	Lead

Character Ingenue Female

Character Ingenue Female

Show	Year	Role	Song	Tempo	Vocal Type	Range-Bottom	Range-Top	Category
Song & Dance	1985	Emma	So Much To Do In New York #3	Moderate Tempo	Alto	A3	Eb5	Lead
Song & Dance	1985	Emma	Married Man	Moderate Tempo	Alto	G#3	C5	Lead
Song & Dance	1985	Emma	I'm Very You	Uptempo	Alto	A#3	C5	Lead
Song & Dance	1985	Emma	3rd Letter Home	Moderate Tempo	Alto	G3	Eb5	Lead
Song & Dance	1985	Emma	Nothing Like You've Ever Known	Ballad	Alto	G3	C5	Lead
Song & Dance	1985	Emma	Let Me Finish Finale	Moderate Tempo	Alto	G#3	Eb5	Lead
Rags	1986	Bella Cohen	If We Never Meet Again*	Ballad	Alto	B2	C5	Lead
Rags	1986	Bella Cohen	Brand New World*	Moderate Tempo	Alto	C#4	D#5	Lead
Rags	1986	Bella Cohen	Penny A Tune	Uptempo	Alto	B3	D5	Lead
Rags	1986	Bella Cohen	Rags*	Uptempo	Alto	A3	D5	Lead
Rags	1986	Bella Cohen	Rags Reprise	Ballad	Alto	B#3	B4	Lead
Les Miserables	1987	Eponine	On My Own	Ballad	Alto	A3	C5	Lead
Les Miserables	1987	Eponine	A Little Fall Of Rain*	Ballad	Alto	F3	Db5	Lead
Chess	1988	Florence	Someone Else's Story	Ballad	Alto	F3	C5	Lead
Chess	1988	Florence	Nobody's Side	Uptempo	Alto	E3	E4	Lead
Chess	1988	Florence	Heaven Help My Heart	Ballad	Alto	A3	A4	Lead
Chess	1988	Florence	You and I*	Ballad	Alto	G3	Eb5	Lead
Chess	1988	Florence	I Know Him So Well	Ballad	Alto	F3	D5	Lead
Chess	1988	Florence	You and I Reprise	Ballad	Alto	G2	G4	Lead
Chess	1988	Florence	Anthem Reprise	Moderate Tempo	Alto	Ab3	D5	Lead
Meet Me In St. Louis	1989	Esther Smith	The Boy Next Door	Ballad	Alto	Ab3	Bb4	Lead
Meet Me In St. Louis	1989	Esther Smith	Under The Bamboo Tree*	Moderate Tempo	Alto	C4	Bb4	Lead
Meet Me In St. Louis	1989	Esther Smith	The Trolly Song*	Uptempo	Alto	A3	Bb4	Lead
Meet Me In St. Louis	1989	Esther Smith	You Are For Loving*	Ballad	Alto	Bb3	C5	Lead
Meet Me In St. Louis	1989	Esther Smith	Have Yourself A Merry Little Christm	Ballad	Alto	G3	C5	Lead
Meet Me In St. Louis	1989	Esther Smith	Over The Banister	Moderate Tempo	Alto	Bb3	Eb5	Lead
Children of Eden	1991	Yonah	Stranger To The Rain	Ballad	Alto	A3	D4	Supporting

Character Ingenue Female

* = Music Edit Required
+ = Ethnic Specific

Show	Year	Role	Song	Tempo	Vocal Type	Range-Bottom	Range-Top	Category
Children of Eden	1991	Yonah	Sailor Of The Skies	Ballad	Alto	G3	Bb4	Supporting
Kiss Of The Spider Woman	1993	Marta	Dear One*	Ballad	Alto	C4	Eb5	Lead
Kiss Of The Spider Woman	1993	Marta	I Do Miracles*	Moderate Tempo	Alto	E3	Bb4	Lead
Footloose	1998	Ariel Moore	Holding Out For A Hero	Uptempo	Alto	C4	C5	Lead
Footloose	1998	Ariel Moore	Almost Paradise*	Ballad	Alto	G3	C5	Lead
Footloose	1998	Featured Ensemble	Somebody's Eyes Are Watching	Ballad	Alto	Ab3	Bb4	Supporting
Spitfire Grill	2001	Percy Talbott	A Ring Around The Moon	Moderate Tempo	Alto	A3	E5	Lead
Spitfire Grill	2001	Percy Talbott	Coffee Cups And Gossip	Uptempo	Alto	C4	C5	Lead
Spitfire Grill	2001	Percy Talbott	Out Of The Frying Pan	Uptempo	Alto	A3	D5	Lead
Spitfire Grill	2001	Percy Talbott	The Colors of Paradise*	Uptempo	Alto	G3	F5	Lead
Spitfire Grill	2001	Percy Talbott	This Wide Woods Part 3	Moderate Tempo	Alto	E3	C#5	Lead
Spitfire Grill	2001	Percy Talbott	Shine	Ballad	Alto	G3	E5	Lead
Thoroughly Modern Millie	2002	Millie Dillmount	Not For The Life Of Me	Uptempo	Alto	Ab3	C5	Lead
Thoroughly Modern Millie	2002	Millie Dillmount	Jimmy	Uptempo	Alto	B3	D#4	Lead
Thoroughly Modern Millie	2002	Millie Dillmount	Forget About The Boy*	Uptempo	Alto	A3	Db5	Lead
Thoroughly Modern Millie	2002	Millie Dillmount	How The Other Half Lives*	Moderate Tempo	Alto	B3	Eb5	Lead
Thoroughly Modern Millie	2002	Millie Dillmount	The Speed Test*	Uptempo	Alto	A3	E5	Lead
Thoroughly Modern Millie	2002	Millie Dillmount	Gimmie Gimmie	Uptempo	Alto	Ab3	D5	Lead
Hairspray	2002	Penny Pingleton	Without Love*	Moderate Tempo	Alto	Eb3	Eb4	Lead
Hairspray	2002	Tracy Turnblad	Good Morning Baltimore	Uptempo	Alto	Bb3	C#5	Lead
Hairspray	2002	Tracy Turnblad	I Can Hear The Bells	Uptempo	Alto	A3	E5	Lead
Hairspray	2002	Tracy Turnblad	Welcome To The 60s*	Uptempo	Alto	G3	C#5	Lead
Hairspray	2002	Tracy Turnblad	Good Morning Baltimore Reprise	Ballad	Alto	Ab3	Bb4	Lead
Hairspray	2002	Tracy Turnblad	Without Love*	Moderate Tempo	Alto	A3	B4	Lead
Fame	2003	Carmen	There She Goes *	Uptempo	Alto	A3	C5	Lead
Fame	2003	Carmen	Fame! *	Uptempo	Alto	Eb4	Eb5	Lead
Fame	2003	Carmen	Bring In Tomorrow *	Ballad	Alto	D4	D	Lead

Character Ingenue Female

Character Ingenue Female

* = Music Edit Required
+ = Ethnic Specific

Show	Year	Role	Song	Tempo	Vocal Type	Range-Bottom	Range-Top	Category
Fame	2003	Carmen	In LA	Ballad	Alto	B♭3	E♭5	Lead
Avenue Q	2003	Kate Monster	Mix Tape *	Uptempo	Alto	F3	D5	Lead
Avenue Q	2003	Kate Monster	There's A Fine Fine Line	Moderate Tempo	Alto	G3	D5	Lead
Wicked	2003	Nessarose	Dancing Through Life*	Uptempo	Alto	A3	B4	Lead
All Shook Up	2005	Ed (Natalie In Drag)	Don't Be Cruel *	Uptempo	Alto	D4	D5	Lead
All Shook Up	2005	Ed (Natalie In Drag)	A Little Less Conversation	Uptempo	Alto	A♭3	E♭5	Supporting
Little Women	2005	Josephine March	Better	Uptempo	Alto	B3	B4	Lead
Little Women	2005	Josephine March	Our Finest Dreams	Uptempo	Alto	F#3	D♭5	Lead
Little Women	2005	Josephine March	Better Reprise	Uptempo	Alto	B2	B4	Lead
Little Women	2005	Josephine March	Astonishing	Uptempo	Alto	A♭3	E♭5	Lead
Little Women	2005	Josephine March	The Fire Within Me	Moderate Tempo	Alto	A♭3	B♭4	Lead
Little Women	2005	Josephine March	Volcanco Reprise	Ballad	Alto	A3	D5	Lead
All Shook Up	2005	Natalie Haller	Love Me Tender	Ballad	Alto	C4	C5	Lead
All Shook Up	2005	Natalie Haller	One Night With You	Moderate Tempo	Alto	C4	D5	Lead
All Shook Up	2005	Natalie Haller	Follow That Dream*	Uptempo	Alto	B3	D4	Supporting
All Shook Up	2005	Natalie Haller	Fools Fall In Love *	Ballad	Alto	A3	D5	Lead
All Shook Up	2005	Natalie Haller	If I Can Dream *	Moderate Tempo	Alto	C4	F5	Lead
Spring Awakening	2006	Ilse	The Dark I Know Well*	Moderate Tempo	Alto	A3	A4	Lead
Spring Awakening	2006	Ilse	Blue Wind	Ballad	Alto	G3	A4	Lead
Spring Awakening	2006	Ilse	Song of Purple Summer*	Moderate Tempo	Alto	G3	A4	Lead
Spring Awakening	2006	Martha	The Dark I Know Well*	Moderate Tempo	Alto	A3	A4	Lead
Next To Normal	2009	Natalie	Everything Else	Uptempo	Alto	G3	C5	Lead
Next To Normal	2009	Natalie	Superboy And The Invisible Girl	Uptempo	Alto	D4	D5	Lead
Next To Normal	2009	Natalie	Maybe*	Moderate Tempo	Alto	A♭3	D5	Lead
Addams Family, The	2010	Wednesday Addams	Pulled	Uptempo	Alto	B3	E♭5	Lead
Addams Family, The	2010	Wednesday Addams	One Normal Night	Uptempo	Alto	B♭3	B♭4	Lead
Addams Family, The	2010	Wednesday Addams	Crazier Than You *	Uptempo	Alto	A3	E5	Lead
Heathers	2014	Veronica Sawyer	Beautiful	Uptempo	Alto	G3	C5	Lead

Character Ingenue Female

68

* = Music Edit Required
+ = Ethnic Specific

Show	Year	Role	Song	Tempo	Vocal Type	Range-Bottom	Range-Top	Category
Heathers	2014	Veronica Sawyer	Fight For Me	Ballad	Alto	Bb3	D5	Lead
Heathers	2014	Veronica Sawyer	Dead Girl Walking*	Uptempo	Alto	A3	G5	Lead
Heathers	2014	Veronica Sawyer	The Me Inside Of Me	Moderate Tempo	Alto	Ab3	D5	Lead
Heathers	2014	Veronica Sawyer	Seventeen*	Ballad	Alto	A3	B4	Lead
Heathers	2014	Veronica Sawyer	Dead Girls Walking Reprise	Uptempo	Alto	A3	A5	Lead
Heathers	2014	Veronica Sawyer	Seventeen Reprise*	Moderate Tempo	Alto	A3	Gb5	Lead
Oklahoma!	1943	Laurey	Many A New Day	Uptempo	Soprano	C#4	E5	Lead
Oklahoma!	1943	Laurey	People Will Say We're In Love	Moderate Tempo	Soprano	C#4	F#5	Lead
Oklahoma!	1943	Laurey	Out Of My Dreams	Moderate Tempo	Soprano	E4	F5	Lead
On The Town	1944	Claire DeLune	Carried Away	Uptempo	Soprano	F3	G5	Lead
On The Town	1944	Claire DeLune	Ya Got Me *	Uptempo	Soprano	G3	Eb4	Lead
Carousel	1945	Julie Jordan	If I Loved You *	Ballad	Soprano	C4	Gb5	Lead
Carousel	1945	Julie Jordan	What's The Use In Wonderin'	Ballad	Soprano	C4	F5	Lead
Most Happy Fella, The	1956	Rosabella	I Don't Know*	Moderate Tempo	Soprano	Bb3	D5	Lead
Most Happy Fella, The	1956	Rosabella	Somebody Somewhere	Ballad	Soprano	E4	G5	Lead
Most Happy Fella, The	1956	Rosabella	Aren't You Glad?	Ballad	Soprano	C4	E5	Lead
Most Happy Fella, The	1956	Rosabella	No Home No Job	Uptempo	Soprano	D4	Eb5	Lead
Most Happy Fella, The	1956	Rosabella	Warm All Over	Ballad	Soprano	C#4	F#5	Lead
Most Happy Fella, The	1956	Rosabella	I Love Him*	Moderate Tempo	Soprano	D4	Eb5	Lead
Most Happy Fella, The	1956	Rosabella	Like A Woman Loves A Man	Moderate Tempo	Soprano	D4	G5	Lead
Most Happy Fella, The	1956	Rosabella	My Heart Is So Full Of You*	Ballad	Soprano	Db4	Gb5	Lead
Most Happy Fella, The	1956	Rosabella	Please Let Me Tell You	Uptempo	Soprano	D4	E5	Lead
Sound Of Music, The	1959	Maria Rainer	The Sound Of Music	Moderate Tempo	Soprano	B3	B4	Lead
Sound Of Music, The	1959	Maria Rainer	The Lonely Goatherd	Uptempo	Soprano	C4	Bb5	Lead
Sound Of Music, The	1959	Maria Rainer	Ordinary People*	Ballad	Soprano	B3	D5	Lead
Once Upon A Mattress	1959	Nightingale	Nightingale Lullaby	Moderate Tempo	Soprano	Gb4	G5	Supporting

Character Ingenue Female

Character Ingenue Female

* = Music Edit Required
+ = Ethnic Specific

Show	Year	Role	Song	Tempo	Vocal Type	Range-Bottom	Range-Top	Category
Anyone Can Whistle	1964	Baby Joan	I'm Like The Bluebird	Uptempo	Soprano	B3	C#5	Featured Ensemble
Company (Revival)	1970	Amy	Not Getting Married Today	Uptempo	Soprano	C#4	Ab5	Supporting
Wiz, The	1974	Dorothy	Soon As I Get Home	Uptempo	Soprano	C4	C#5	Lead
Wiz, The	1974	Dorothy	Home	Uptempo	Soprano	Bb3	D5	Lead
Wiz, The	1974	Dorothy	Be A Lion*	Ballad	Soprano	Bb3	Bb5	Lead
Dreamgirls	1981	Lorelle Robinson +	Ain't No Party *	Uptempo	Soprano	Bb3	E4	Lead
Ain't Misbehavin'	1988	Woman Two +	Yacht Club Swing	Uptempo	Soprano	Ab3	Ab5	Lead
Ain't Misbehavin'	1988	Woman Two +	Keepin' Out of Mischief Now	Ballad	Soprano	A3	C5	Lead
My Favorite Year	1992	K.C. Downing	Funny*	Moderate Tempo	Soprano	A3	E5	Lead
My Favorite Year	1992	K.C. Downing	Shut Up And Dance*	Moderate Tempo	Soprano	A3	C5	Lead
Beauty and the Beast	1994	Belle	Home	Ballad	Soprano	G3	E5	Lead
Beauty and the Beast	1994	Belle	Belle Reprise	Uptempo	Soprano	D4	D5	Lead
Beauty and the Beast	1994	Belle	Something There *	Uptempo	Soprano	A3	E5	Lead
Beauty and the Beast	1994	Belle	Home Reprise	Ballad	Soprano	C4	D5	Lead
Sunset Boulevard	1994	Betty Schaefer	Too Much In Love To Care*	Moderate Tempo	Soprano	A3	G5	Lead
Sunset Boulevard	1994	Betty Schaefer	Girl Meets Boy Reprise*	Uptempo	Soprano	A3	E5	Lead
Steel Pier	1997	Precious McGuire	Two Little Words	Uptempo	Soprano	C4	E6	Lead
Ragtime	1998	Sarah +	Your Daddy's Son (Bb Maj)	Ballad	Soprano	G3	F5	Lead
Ragtime	1998	Sarah +	Your Daddy's Son (Cb Maj)	Ballad	Soprano	Ab3	Gb5	Lead
Ragtime	1998	Sarah +	New Music*	Ballad	Soprano	Bb3	D5	Lead
Ragtime	1998	Sarah +	President (A Maj)*	Moderate Tempo	Soprano	A3	D5	Lead
Ragtime	1998	Sarah +	President (Bb Maj)*	Moderate Tempo	Soprano	Bb3	Eb5	Lead
Ragtime	1998	Sarah +	Justice*	Uptempo	Soprano	Ab3	C5	Lead
Seussical	2000	Gertrude McFuzz	The One Feather Tail	Moderate Tempo	Soprano	G3	C5	Lead
Seussical	2000	Gertrude McFuzz	Amayzing Gertrude*	Uptempo	Soprano	C#4	D6	Lead
Seussical	2000	Gertrude McFuzz	Notice Me, Horton*	Uptempo	Soprano	G3	C5	Lead
Seussical	2000	Gertrude McFuzz	For You*	Uptempo	Soprano	F3	C5	Lead
A Man Of No Importance	2002	Adele Rice	Princess	Moderate Tempo	Soprano	C4	E5	Supporting

Character Ingenue Female

* = Music Edit Required
+ = Ethnic Specific

Show	Year	Role	Song	Tempo	Vocal Type	Range-Bottom	Range-Top	Category
A Man Of No Importance	2002	Adele Rice	Love Who You Love (Adeke Reprise	Ballad	Soprano	A♭3	D♭5	Supporting

Character Ingenue Female

* = Music Edit Required
+ = Ethnic Specific

Show	Year	Role	Song	Tempo	Vocal Type	Range-Bottom	Range-Top	Category
Oklahoma!	1943	Will Parker	Kansas City	Uptempo	Baritone	E♭3	F4	Lead
On The Town	1944	Ozzie	Carried Away	Uptempo	Baritone	E2	F4	Lead
Kiss Me Kate	1948	Bill Calhoun/Lucentio	Bianca*	Uptempo	Baritone	G2	F4	Lead
Once Upon A Mattress	1959	Prince Dauntless	Song Of Love*	Uptempo	Baritone	C#3	E♭4	Lead
Hello Dolly	1964	Barnaby Tucker	Elegance*	Moderate Tempo	Baritone	C3	F4	Lead
Hello Dolly	1964	Cornelius Hackl	Put On Your Sunday Clothes	Uptempo	Baritone	C3	G#4	Lead
Hello Dolly	1964	Cornelius Hackl	It Only Takes A Moment*	Ballad	Baritone	B♭2	E♭4	Lead
Hello Dolly	1964	Cornelius Hackl	Elegance*	Moderate Tempo	Baritone	C3	F4	Lead
Company (Revival)	1970	Paul	Have I Got A Girl For You	Uptempo	Baritone	B4	G♭6	Supporting
Grease	1971	Johnny Casino	Born to Hand Jive	Uptempo	Baritone	A3	F#4	Supporting
You're A Good Man Charlie Brown	1971	Linus Van Pelt	My Blanket And Me	Moderate Tempo	Baritone	B2	D4	Lead
Annie	1977	Bert Healy	You're Never Fully Dressed	Uptempo	Baritone	E3	F#4	Supporting
Honk	1993	Ugly	Different	Ballad	Baritone	D♭3	F4	Lead
Honk	1993	Ugly	Hold Your Head Up High Reprise	Ballad	Baritone	C3	G4	Lead
Honk	1993	Ugly	Now I've Seen You	Moderate Tempo	Baritone	B♭2	G4	Lead
Avenue Q	2003	Princeton	What Do You...BA English	Moderate Tempo	Baritone	B2	D4	Lead
Avenue Q	2003	Princeton	Purpose	Uptempo	Baritone	B2	G3	Lead
25th Annual...Spelling Bee	2005	Leaf Coneybear	I'm Not That Smart	Uptempo	Baritone	A2	G4	Lead
25th Annual...Spelling Bee	2005	Leaf Coneybear	I'm Not Smart Reprise	Uptempo	Baritone	D3	F#4	Lead
Spring Awakening	2006	Georg	The Bitch Of Living*	Uptempo	Baritone	F3	D4	Lead
Kinky Boots	2013	Harry	Take What You Got*	Uptempo	Baritone	F#3	F#4	Supporting
Jersey Boys (2005)	1928	Frankie Castelluccio	I Can't Give You Anything But Love	Moderate Tempo	Tenor	E3	A♭4	Lead
Jersey Boys (2005)	1935	Frankie Valli	I'm In The Mood	Ballad	Tenor	E3	F5	Lead
On The Town	1944	Chip	Ya Got Me *	Uptempo	Tenor	E3	G♭4	Lead
Carousel	1945	Enoch Snow	When I Marry Mr. Snow Reprise	Ballad	Tenor	C4	D5	Lead
Carousel	1945	Enoch Snow	When The Children Are Asleep *	Moderate Tempo	Tenor	E♭3	C5	Lead

Character Ingenue Male

* = Music Edit Required
+ = Ethnic Specific

Show	Year	Role	Song	Tempo	Vocal Type	Range-Bottom	Range-Top	Category
Carousel	1945	Enoch Snow	Geranium In The Window *	Ballad	Tenor	D3	F#4	Lead
Jersey Boys (2005)	1946	Frankie Castelluccio	Sunday Kind Of Love	Uptempo	Tenor	D3	E5	Lead
Jersey Boys (2005)	1960	Frankie Valli	Stay*	Uptempo	Tenor	F3	D5	Lead
Jersey Boys (2005)	1962	Frankie Valli	Sherry*	Moderate Tempo	Tenor	G4	F5	Lead
Jersey Boys (2005)	1962	Frankie Valli	Big Girls Don't Cry	Uptempo	Tenor	Eb4	F5	Lead
She Loves Me	1963	Arpad Lazslo	Try Me	Uptempo	Tenor	B2	E4	Lead
Jersey Boys (2005)	1963	Frankie Valli	My Mother's Eyes	Ballad	Tenor	E3	F4	Lead
Jersey Boys (2005)	1963	Frankie Valli	Walk Like A Man	Moderate Tempo	Tenor	B3	F5	Lead
Jersey Boys (2005)	1964	Frankie Valli	Rag Doll	Moderate Tempo	Tenor	Bb3	F5	Lead
Jersey Boys (2005)	1965	Frankie Valli	Bye Bye Baby	Uptempo	Tenor	C#4	D5	Lead
Jersey Boys (2005)	1965	Frankie Valli	Work My Way Back To You	Uptempo	Tenor	G3	C5	Lead
Jersey Boys (2005)	1965	Frankie Valli	Let's Hang On!*	Uptempo	Tenor	Db3	D5	Lead
Jersey Boys (2005)	1966	Frankie Valli	Don't you Worry 'Bout Me*	Uptempo	Tenor	G3	C5	Lead
Jersey Boys (2005)	1967	Frankie Valli	Beggin'*	Uptempo	Tenor	B3	Bb4	Lead
Jersey Boys (2005)	1967	Frankie Valli	Can't Take My Eyes Off You	Uptempo	Tenor	D3	G4	Lead
1776	1969	Courier	Momma Look Sharp	Ballad	Tenor	Bb2	Db4	Supporting
Grease	1971	Doody	Those Magic Changes	Uptempo	Tenor	E3	Cb5	Lead
Grease	1971	Doody	Rock N Roll Party Queen	Uptempo	Tenor	A2	Ab3	Lead
Jersey Boys (2005)	1975	Frankie Valli	My Eyes Adored You	Ballad	Tenor	G3	Bb4	Lead
Jersey Boys (2005)	1976	Frankie Valli	Fallen Angel	Ballad	Tenor	Eb3	Ab4	Lead
Sweeney Todd	1979	Tobias Ragg	Perelli's Miracle Elixir*	Uptempo	Tenor	B2	A4	Lead
Sweeney Todd	1979	Tobias Ragg	Not While I'm Around*	Ballad	Tenor	Eb3	Ab4	Lead
Baby	1983	Danny Hooper	I Chose Right	Ballad	Tenor	D3	G4	Lead
Big River	1985	Huckleberry Finn	Waitin' For The Light To Shine	Ballad	Tenor	G#2	C#4	Lead
Big River	1985	Huckleberry Finn	I, Huckleberry, Me	Uptempo	Tenor	C3	F4	Lead
Big River	1985	Huckleberry Finn	River In The Rain *	Ballad	Tenor	A2	G4	Lead
Big River	1985	Huckleberry Finn	Worlds Apart *	Ballad	Tenor	B2	B4	Lead

Character Ingenue Male

* = Music Edit Required
+ = Ethnic Specific

Show	Year	Role	Song	Tempo	Vocal Type	Range-Bottom	Range-Top	Category
Big River	1985	Huckleberry Finn	Waitin' For...Light To Shine Reprise	Uptempo	Tenor	A2	F#4	Lead
Big River	1985	Huckleberry Finn	River in the Rain Reprise *	Ballad	Tenor	A2	D4	Lead
Big River	1985	Huckleberry Finn	Leavin's Not The Only Way To Go	Ballad	Tenor	B2	B3	Lead
Rags	1986	Ben	The Sound Of Love*	Uptempo	Tenor	Eb3	Ab4	Lead
Into The Woods	1987	Jack	I Guess This Is Goodbye	Ballad	Tenor	D#3	D#4	Lead
Into The Woods	1987	Jack	Giants In The Sky	Uptempo	Tenor	C3	F#4	Lead
Ain't Misbehavin'	1988	Man One +	How Ya Baby*	Uptempo	Tenor	C3	C5	Lead
Ain't Misbehavin'	1988	Man One +	The Viper's Drag*	Ballad	Tenor	C3	G4	Lead
Ain't Misbehavin'	1988	Man One +	That Ain't Right*	Ballad	Tenor	G2	Bb4	Lead
Secret Garden, The	1991	Dickon	Winter's On The Wing	Uptempo	Tenor	D3	F#4	Lead
Secret Garden, The	1991	Dickon	Winter's On The Wing Reprise	Ballad	Tenor	D3	E4	Lead
Secret Garden, The	1991	Dickon	Wick*	Uptempo	Tenor	F3	G4	Lead
My Favorite Year	1992	Benjy Stone	Larger Than Life	Moderate Tempo	Tenor	Eb3	F4	Lead
My Favorite Year	1992	Benjy Stone	Waldorf Reveal	Uptempo	Tenor	C3	F4	Lead
My Favorite Year	1992	Benjy Stone	My Favorite Year*	Moderate Tempo	Tenor	C3	G4	Lead
Kiss Of The Spider Woman	1993	Gabriel	Gabriel's Letter*	Moderate Tempo	Tenor	D#3	G4	Lead
Rent	1996	Angel Schunard	Today For You*	Uptempo	Tenor	Bb3	G4	Lead
Rent	1996	Angel Schunard	I'll Cover You*	Moderate Tempo	Tenor	G3	A4	Lead
Big	1996	Josh Baskin-Adult	We're Gonna Be Fine	Ballad	Tenor	Bb2	D4	Lead
Big	1996	Josh Baskin-Adult	I Want To Go Home	Ballad	Tenor	Ab2	B4	Lead
Big	1996	Josh Baskin-Adult	Fun	Uptempo	Tenor	C3	G4	Lead
Big	1996	Josh Baskin-Adult	Do You Want To Play Games	Uptempo	Tenor	E3	F4	Lead
Big	1996	Josh Baskin-Adult	Stars, Stars, Stars	Ballad	Tenor	C3	D4	Lead
Big	1996	Josh Baskin-Adult	Coffee Black	Uptempo	Tenor	C3	F4	Lead
Big	1996	Josh Baskin-Adult	When You're Big	Uptempo	Tenor	E3	F4	Lead
Big	1996	Josh Baskin-Adult	Cross The Line	Uptempo	Tenor	E3	D4	Lead
Big	1996	Josh Baskin-Adult	Big Boy Now	Ballad	Tenor	Db3	Eb4	Lead

Character Ingenue Male

* = Music Edit Required
+ = Ethnic Specific

Show	Year	Role	Song	Tempo	Vocal Type	Range-Bottom	Range-Top	Category
A Christmas Carol	1997	Scrooge-Young Adult	A Place Called Home	Ballad	Tenor	Bb2	D4	Supporting
Footloose	1998	Ren McCormick	I Can't Stand Still	Uptempo	Tenor	D3	C5	Lead
Footloose	1998	Ren McCormick	I'm Free	Uptempo	Tenor	D3	Ab4	Lead
Footloose	1998	Ren McCormick	Almost Paradise*	Ballad	Tenor	G2	A4	Lead
Footloose	1998	Ren McCormick	Dancing Is Not A Crime (Rap)	Uptempo	Tenor			Lead
Parade	1998	Young Soldier	Old Red Hills Of Home (Part 1)	Moderate Tempo	Tenor	D3	A4	Supporting
A Year With Frog and Toad	2002	Snail	The Letter #1	Moderate Tempo	Tenor	A2	Bb3	Lead
A Year With Frog and Toad	2002	Snail	Letter #2	Uptempo	Tenor	B2	E4	Supporting
A Year With Frog and Toad	2002	Snail	The Letter #3	Uptempo	Tenor	C#3	Eb4	Supporting
A Year With Frog and Toad	2002	Snail	I'm Coming Out Of My Shell	Uptempo	Tenor	E3	A4	Supporting
Wicked	2003	BOQ	Dancing Through Life*	Uptempo	Tenor	G3	G4	Lead
Wicked	2003	BOQ	March Of The Witch Hunters*	Uptempo	Tenor	G#3	G4	Lead
Color Purple, The	2005	Harpo	Brown Betty *	Moderate Tempo	Tenor	E3	G4	Lead
High School Musical	2007	Ryan Evans	What I've Been Looking For*	Uptempo	Tenor	A3	F#4	Lead
Next To Normal	2009	Gabe	I'm Alive	Uptempo	Tenor	G3	B4	Lead
Next To Normal	2009	Gabe	Aftershocks*	Uptempo	Tenor	D3	D4	Lead
Next To Normal	2009	Gabe	I'm Alive Reprise	Uptempo	Tenor	G3	G4	Lead
Next To Normal	2009	Gabe	There's A World	Ballad	Tenor	G3	G4	Lead
Next To Normal	2009	Henry	Perfect For You Reprise*	Moderate Tempo	Tenor	D3	G4	Lead

Character Ingenue Male

* = Music Edit Required
+ = Ethnic Specific

Show	Year	Role	Song	Tempo	Vocal Type	Range-Bottom	Range-Top	Category
No, No Nanette	1925	Betty Brown	The Three Happies*	Moderate Tempo	Alto	A3	C5	Supporting
No, No Nanette	1925	Flora Latham	The Three Happies*	Moderate Tempo	Alto	F4	Eb5	Supporting
Show Boat	1927	Queenie+	Can't Help Lovin' Dat Man*	Moderate Tempo	Alto	C3	D4	Lead
Show Boat	1927	Queenie+	Misery*	Ballad	Alto	A3	Eb5	Lead
Show Boat	1927	Queenie+	Bally-Hoo*	Uptempo	Alto	A3	Eb5	Lead
High Society 1998	1930	Liz Imbrie	I'm Getting Ready For You*	Uptempo	Alto	A#3	E5	Lead
Anything Goes	1934	Reno Sweeney	I Get A Kick Out of You	Uptempo	Alto	A3	D5	Lead
Anything Goes	1934	Reno Sweeney	You're the Top *	Uptempo	Alto	G3	D5	Lead
Anything Goes	1934	Reno Sweeney	Anything Goes	Uptempo	Alto	Ab3	C5	Lead
Anything Goes	1934	Reno Sweeney	Blow Gabriel Blow	Uptempo	Alto	G3	C5	Lead
Anything Goes	1934	Reno Sweeney	Buddy Beware	Moderate Tempo	Alto	A3	C#5	Lead
Anything Goes	1934	Reno Sweeney	Friendship *	Uptempo	Alto	Bb3	Eb5	Lead
Porgy and Bess	1935	Strawberry Woman+	Strawberry Woman	Ballad	Alto	G4	E5	Feat Ens
High Society 1998	1943	Liz Imbrie	He's A Right Guy	Ballad	Alto	F3	A4	Lead
Annie Get Your Gun	1944	Annie Oakley	Doin' What Comes Natur'lly	Uptempo	Alto	A3	C5	Lead
Annie Get Your Gun	1944	Annie Oakley	You Can't Get A Man With A Gun	Uptempo	Alto	Bb3	C5	Lead
Annie Get Your Gun	1944	Annie Oakley	Moonshine Lullaby	Ballad	Alto	Bb3	D5	Lead
Annie Get Your Gun	1944	Annie Oakley	No Business Reprise 2	Moderate Tempo	Alto	G3	C5	Lead
Annie Get Your Gun	1944	Annie Oakley	They Say That Falling In Love*	Ballad	Alto	A3	B4	Lead
Annie Get Your Gun	1944	Annie Oakley	You Can't Get A Man With A Gun Reprise	Moderate Tempo	Alto	Ab3	Ab4	Lead
Annie Get Your Gun	1944	Annie Oakley	Lost In His Arms	Ballad	Alto	Bb3	C5	Lead
Annie Get Your Gun	1944	Annie Oakley	I Got The Sun in the Morning	Moderate Tempo	Alto	Bb3	Bb4	Lead
Annie Get Your Gun	1944	Annie Oakley	The Girl That I Marry*	Moderate Tempo	Alto	B3	D4	Lead
On The Town	1944	Diana Dream	I Wish I Was Dead	Uptempo	Alto	C4	Db4	Feat Ens
On The Town	1944	Hildy	I Can Cook Too	Uptempo	Alto	A3	G#5	Lead
On The Town	1944	Hildy	Ya Got Me *	Uptempo	Alto	F3	Db5	Lead
Kiss Me Kate	1948	Hattie	Another Op'nin Another Show*	Uptempo	Alto	G3	E5	Supporting

Character Female

* = Music Edit Required
+ = Ethnic Specific

Show	Year	Role	Song	Tempo	Vocal Type	Range-Bottom	Range-Top	Category
South Pacific	1949	Bloody Mary	Bali Ha'i	Ballad	Alto	G3	G4	Lead
South Pacific	1949	Bloody Mary	Bali Ha'I Reprise	Ballad	Alto	D3	E4	Lead
South Pacific	1949	Bloody Mary	Happy Talk	Uptempo	Alto	A3	C5	Lead
Guys and Dolls	1950	Miss Adelaide	A Bushel And A Peck	Uptempo	Alto	B3	E♭3	Lead
Guys and Dolls	1950	Miss Adelaide	Adelaide's Lament	Moderate Tempo	Alto	A♭3	D5	Lead
Guys and Dolls	1950	Miss Adelaide	Adelaide's Lament Reprise	Ballad	Alto	D♭4	C♭5	Lead
Guys and Dolls	1950	Miss Adelaide	Take Back Your Mink	Uptempo	Alto	B♭3	D5	Lead
Guys and Dolls	1950	Miss Adelaide	Marry The Man Today*	Uptempo	Alto	C4	E♭5	Lead
Wonderful Town	1953	Ruth Sherwood	One Hundred Easy Ways To Lose A Man	Moderate Tempo	Alto	G3	A4	Lead
Wonderful Town	1953	Ruth Sherwood	Quiet Ruth	Ballad	Alto	F3	E4	Lead
Wonderful Town	1953	Ruth Sherwood	Conga*	Uptempo	Alto	F3	A4	Lead
Wonderful Town	1953	Ruth Sherwood	Swing*	Uptempo	Alto	E3	E4	Lead
Damn Yankees	1955	Gloria Thorpe	Shoeless Joe From Hanniibal, Mo	Uptempo	Alto	B♭3	D♭5	Supporting
Most Happy Fella, The	1956	Cleo	Ooh! My Feet!	Moderate Tempo	Alto	A#3	B♭4	Lead
Most Happy Fella, The	1956	Cleo	I Know How It Is*	Moderate Tempo	Alto	A♭3	B4	Lead
Most Happy Fella, The	1956	Cleo	I Like Everybody Reprise*	Uptempo	Alto	G#3	B4	Lead
Bells Are Ringing	1956	Ella Peterson	It's A Perfect Relationship	Uptempo	Alto	A♭3	C♭5	Lead
Bells Are Ringing	1956	Ella Peterson	Is It A Crime	Moderate Tempo	Alto	A3	C5	Lead
Bells Are Ringing	1956	Ella Peterson	Long Before I Knew You *	Ballad	Alto	B3	C#5	Lead
Bells Are Ringing	1956	Ella Peterson	The Party's Over	Ballad	Alto	F#3	B4	Lead
Bells Are Ringing	1956	Ella Peterson	I'm Going Back	Moderate Tempo	Alto	A#3	B4	Lead
Bells Are Ringing	1956	Ella Peterson	Better Than A Dream *	Moderate Tempo	Alto	A3	D5	Lead
Cinderella (2013)	1957	Charlotte	Stepsister's Lament*	Uptempo	Alto	C4	D5	Supporting
Cinderella (2013)	1957	Joy	A Lovely Night*	Uptempo	Alto	B3	D5	Supporting
Once Upon A Mattress	1959	Princess Winifred	Shy*	Uptempo	Alto	B3	C5	Lead
How To Succeed...	1961	Miss Jones	Brotherhood Of Man*	Uptempo	Alto	A#3	G5	Featured Ensemble
How To Succeed...	1961	Smitty	Been A Long Day*	Uptempo	Alto	B♭3	D5	Supporting

Character Female

Character Female

* = Music Edit Required
+ = Ethnic Specific

Show	Year	Role	Song	Tempo	Vocal Type	Range-Bottom	Range-Top	Category
Little Me	1962	Belle	Dimples*	Uptempo	Alto	A3	D5	Lead
Little Me	1962	Belle	I Needed Social Position*	Moderate Tempo	Alto	A♭3	C#5	Lead
Little Me	1962	Belle	Here's To Us*	Uptempo	Alto	F3	B♭4	Lead
Little Me	1962	Young Belle	Other Side Of The Tracks (Slow Version)	Ballad	Alto	B3	C5	Lead
Little Me	1962	Young Belle	On The Other Side Of The Tracks Reprise	Uptempo	Alto	A3	D5	Lead
Little Me	1962	Young Belle	Poor Little Hollywood Star	Moderate Tempo	Alto	G#3	E5	Lead
Little Me	1962	Young Belle	I Needed Social Position*	Moderate Tempo	Alto	A♭3	C#5	Lead
Funny Girl	1964	Fanny Brice	I'm The Greatest Start	Moderate Tempo	Alto	G#3	C5	Lead
Funny Girl	1964	Fanny Brice	Coronet Man	Moderate Tempo	Alto	A#3	D5	Lead
Funny Girl	1964	Fanny Brice	His Love Makes Me Beautiful*	Moderate Tempo	Alto	B♭3	E♭5	Lead
Funny Girl	1964	Fanny Brice	People	Ballad	Alto	A3	D♭5	Lead
Funny Girl	1964	Fanny Brice	You Are Woman*	Moderate Tempo	Alto	A#3	C#5	Lead
Funny Girl	1964	Fanny Brice	Don't Rain On My Parade	Uptempo	Alto	E3	B4	Lead
Funny Girl	1964	Fanny Brice	Sade, Sade Married Lady	Moderate Tempo	Alto	A3	F5	Lead
Funny Girl	1964	Fanny Brice	Who Are You Now	Ballad	Alto	B♭3	D♭4	Lead
Funny Girl	1964	Fanny Brice	The Music That Makes Me Dance	Ballad	Alto	G#3	E5	Lead
Funny Girl	1964	Fanny Brice	Don't Rain On My Parade Reprise	Moderate Tempo	Alto	E3	B4	Lead
Funny Girl	1964	Fanny Brice	Rat Tat Tat Tat Part 2*	Uptempo	Alto	B3	D#5	Lead
Annie Get Your Gun	1966	Annie Oakley	An Old Fashioned Wedding	Uptempo	Alto	B3	B4	Lead
Apple Tree, The	1966	Ella	Oh To Be A Movie Star	Uptempo	Alto	C4	D5	Lead
Apple Tree, The	1966	Eve	Here In Eden	Moderate Tempo	Alto	A3	B4	Lead
Apple Tree, The	1966	Eve	Feelings	Moderate Tempo	Alto	B3	E5	Lead
Apple Tree, The	1966	Eve	Go To Sleep Whoever You Are	Ballad	Alto	B3	B4	Lead
Apple Tree, The	1966	Eve	What Makes Me Love Him	Ballad	Alto	C3	C#5	Lead
Apple Tree, The	1966	Eve	Friends	Uptempo	Alto	B♭3	C5	Lead
Cabaret	1966	Faulein Kost	Married *	Ballad	Alto	F#3	B♭4	Supporting
Cabaret	1966	Faulein Kost	Tomorrow Belongs to Me Reprise *	Moderate Tempo	Alto	A3	B♭4	Supporting
Apple Tree, The	1966	Passionella	Gorgeous	Uptempo	Alto	C4	D5	Lead

Character Female

79

* = Music Edit Required
+ = Ethnic Specific

Show	Year	Role	Song	Tempo	Vocal Type	Range-Bottom	Range-Top	Category
Apple Tree, The	1966	Passionella	Wealth	Uptempo	Alto	B3	B4	Lead
Apple Tree, The	1966	Passionella	Oh To Be A Movie Star Reprise	Moderate Tempo	Alto	C4	D5	Lead
Apple Tree, The	1966	Princess Barbara	I've Got What You Want	Ballad	Alto	G3	C5	Lead
Apple Tree, The	1966	Princess Barbara	Tiger, Tiger	Uptempo	Alto	F3	A4	Lead
Hair	1968	Jeanie	Air	Uptempo	Alto	G3	G4	Lead
Hair	1968	Margaret Mead	My Conviction	Moderate Tempo	Alto	E3	A4	Lead
Follies	1971	Sally Durant	In Buddy's Eyes *	Ballad	Alto	F#3	D5	Lead
Godspell	1971	Soloist 1	Day By Day	Ballad	Alto	C4	A4	Supporting
Godspell	1971	Soloist 2	Learn Your Lesson Well	Uptempo	Alto	G3	Eb5	Supporting
Godspell	1971	Soloist 3	O Bless The Lord*	Moderate Tempo	Alto	B3	E5	Supporting
Godspell	1971	Soloist 5	Turn Back O Man*	Moderate Tempo	Alto	D3	D5	Supporting
Wiz, The	1974	Addaperle	He's The Wiz*	Moderate Tempo	Alto	F3	C5	Lead
Mack and Mabel	1974	Lottie Ames	Big Time*	Uptempo	Alto	F#3	Eb5	Supporting
Mack and Mabel	1974	Lottie Ames	Tap Your Troubles Away	Uptempo	Alto	F3	Bb4	Lead
A Chorus Line	1975	Bebe	At The Ballet	Moderate Tempo	Alto	A3	C#5	Supporting
A Chorus Line	1975	Diana +	Nothing	Uptempo	Alto	G3	B4	Lead
A Chorus Line	1975	Diana +	What I Did For Love	Ballad	Alto	Bb3	D#5	Lead
Chicago	1975	Mama Morton	When You're Good To Mama	Moderate Tempo	Alto	F#3	A4	Lead
Chicago	1975	Mama Morton	Class*	Ballad	Alto	F3	B4	Lead
Pacific Overtures	1976	Female	Prologue	Ballad	Alto	D3	Bb4	Lead
Best Little Whorehouse...	1978	Doatsey Mae	Doatsey Mae	Ballad	Alto	G3	C5	Supporting
Best Little Whorehouse...	1978	Mona Stangley	A Lil Ole Bitty Pissant Country Place	Uptempo	Alto	F3	D4	Lead
Best Little Whorehouse...	1978	Mona Stangley	Girl You're a Woman	Ballad	Alto	E2	G4	Lead
Best Little Whorehouse...	1978	Mona Stangley	No Lies	Uptempo	Alto	G3	B4	Lead
Best Little Whorehouse...	1978	Mona Stangley	Bus From Amarillo	Moderate Tempo	Alto	E3	Bb4	Lead
Sweeney Todd	1979	Mrs. Lovett	The Worst Pies In London	Uptempo	Alto	B3	Eb5	Lead
Sweeney Todd	1979	Mrs. Lovett	Poor Thing	Uptempo	Alto	F#3	B4	Lead
Sweeney Todd	1979	Mrs. Lovett	Wait	Moderate Tempo	Alto	Bb2	Eb5	Lead

Character Female

Character Female

* = Music Edit Required
+ = Ethnic Specific

Show	Year	Role	Song	Tempo	Vocal Type	Range-Bottom	Range-Top	Category
Sweeney Todd	1979	Mrs. Lovett	By The Sea	Uptempo	Alto	G3	E5	Lead
Dreamgirls	1981	Effie White +	I Am Changing	Ballad	Alto	Eb4	F5	Lead
Dreamgirls	1981	Effie White +	One Night Only	Ballad	Alto	Ab3	D5	Lead
Joseph...Dream Coat	1982	Narrator	Pharaoh Story	Moderate Tempo	Alto	A3	E5	Lead
Baby	1983	Pam Sakarian	I Want It All *	Uptempo	Alto	C4	Eb5	Lead
Baby	1983	Pam Sakarian	With You *	Ballad	Alto	G#3	D5	Lead
Sunday...Park With Geroge	1984	Nurse	The Day Off (Part 3)*	Moderate Tempo	Alto	B3	D5	Supporting
Mystery Of Edwin Drood, T	1985	Dick Datchery(Drood)	Out On A Limerick	Moderate Tempo	Alto	C3	E4	Lead
Big River	1985	Slave +	Crossing Over *	Ballad	Alto	G3	C5	Featured Ensemble
Into The Woods	1987	Baker's Wife	Maybe They're Magic	Uptempo	Alto	G#3	E5	Lead
Into The Woods	1987	Baker's Wife	It Takes Two	Moderate Tempo	Alto	A3	D5	Lead
Into The Woods	1987	Baker's Wife	Moments In The Woods	Uptempo	Alto	F3	D4	Lead
Ain't Misbehavin'	1988	Woman One +	I've Got A Feeling I'm Falling	Uptempo	Alto	F3	C5	Lead
Ain't Misbehavin'	1988	Woman One +	Cash For our Trash	Uptempo	Alto	B4	D5	Lead
Ain't Misbehavin'	1988	Woman One +	Mean To Me	Ballad	Alto	G3	G4	Lead
Ain't Misbehavin'	1988	Woman One +	Honeysuckle Rose*	Ballad	Alto	Bb4	F5	Lead
Ain't Misbehavin'	1988	Woman One +	Lounging At The Waldorf	Ballad	Alto	C4	D5	Lead
Ain't Misbehavin'	1988	Woman Two +	That Ain't Right*	Ballad	Alto	G2	Eb5	Lead
Meet Me In St. Louis	1989	Katie	A Touch Of Irish*	Uptempo	Alto	G3	Bb4	Lead
City of Angels	1989	Oolie	What You Don't Know About Women *	Moderate Tempo	Alto	G3	F5	Lead
City of Angels	1989	Oolie/Donna	You Can Always Count On Me	Moderate Tempo	Alto	Bb3	Db5	Supporting
Closer Than Ever	1989	Woman Two	You Want To Be My Friend	Uptempo	Alto	D4	E5	Lead
Closer Than Ever	1989	Woman Two	Miss Bird	Moderate Tempo	Alto	F3	Eb5	Lead
Closer Than Ever	1989	Woman Two	There *	Moderate Tempo	Alto	A3	D5	Lead
Closer Than Ever	1989	Woman Two	Another Wedding Song *	Ballad	Alto	B3	B4	Lead
Closer Than Ever	1989	Woman Two	Back On Base	Moderate Tempo	Alto	B3	G5	Lead
Closer Than Ever	1989	Woman Two	I've Been Here Before *	Ballad	Alto	Gb3	Cb5	Lead
Once On This Island	1990	Asaka+	Mama Will Provide*	Uptempo	Alto	B3	G5	Lead

Character Female

* = Music Edit Required
+ = Ethnic Specific

Show	Year	Role	Song	Tempo	Vocal Type	Range-Bottom	Range-Top	Category
Nick & Nora	1991	Maria Valdex	Boom Chicka Boom*	Uptempo	Alto	A3	Bb4	Lead
Secret Garden, The	1991	Martha	Hold On	Uptempo	Alto	F#3	B4	Lead
Secret Garden, The	1991	Martha	If I Had A Fine White Horse	Uptempo	Alto	G3	D5	Lead
Blood Brothers	1993	Mrs. Johnstone	Marilyn Monroe	Moderate Tempo	Alto	A3	A4	Lead
Blood Brothers	1993	Mrs. Johnstone	Easy Terms	Ballad	Alto	G3	A4	Lead
Blood Brothers	1993	Mrs. Johnstone	Easy Terms Reprise	Ballad	Alto	G3	F4	Lead
Blood Brothers	1993	Mrs. Johnstone	Bright New Day	Uptempo	Alto	D4	A4	Lead
Blood Brothers	1993	Mrs. Johnstone	Bright New Day Reprise *	Uptempo	Alto	D4	C5	Lead
Blood Brothers	1993	Mrs. Johnstone	Marilyn Monroe 2	Moderate Tempo	Alto	A3	A4	Lead
Blood Brothers	1993	Mrs. Johnstone	Light Romance	Ballad	Alto	G3	A4	Lead
Blood Brothers	1993	Mrs. Johnstone	Tell Me It's Not True	Ballad	Alto	F3	C5	Lead
Blood Brothers	1993	Mrs. Johnstone	Marilyn Monroe 3	Ballad	Alto	A3	B4	Lead
Songs For A New World	1995	Woman 2	Just One Step	Uptempo	Alto	F3	C#5	Lead
Songs For A New World	1995	Woman 2	Stars And The Moon	Moderate Tempo	Alto	A3	D5	Lead
Songs For A New World	1995	Woman 2	Surabaya Santa	Moderate Tempo	Alto	G3	Eb4	Lead
Songs For A New World	1995	Woman 2	The Flagmaker 1775	Moderate Tempo	Alto	A3	E5	Lead
Songs For A New World	1995	Woman 2	Hear My Song*	Moderate Tempo	Alto	A3	B4	Lead
Lion King, The	1997	Rafiki	Circle of Life*	Moderate Tempo	Alto	F#3	C5	Lead
Lion King, The	1997	Rafiki	Rafiki Mourns (Eulogy)	Ballad	Alto	G3	Eb5	Lead
Lion King, The	1997	Rafiki	He Lives In You*	Moderate Tempo	Alto	C4	E5	Lead
Ragtime	1998	Emma Goldman	He Wanted To Say*	Moderate Tempo	Alto	G3	Bb4	Lead
Footloose	1998	Irene	Let's Make Believe We're In Love	Moderate Tempo	Alto	G3	D4	Supporting
Footloose	1998	Rusty	Let's Hear It For the Boy	Uptempo	Alto	A3	D#5	Supporting
Marie Christine	1999	Magdelena	Cincincati*	Moderate Tempo	Alto	G3	F#3	Supporting
Marie Christine	1999	Magdelena	Paradise Is Burning Down*	Uptempo	Alto	Eb3	Eb5	Lead
Marie Christine	1999	Magdelena	A Lovely Wedding*	Uptempo	Alto	C4	C#5	Supporting
Marie Christine	1999	Magdelena	There's A Rumor	Moderate Tempo	Alto	F#3	C#5	Lead
Full Monty, The	2000	Georgie Bukatinsky	You Rule My World Reprise *	Ballad	Alto	G#3	D5	Supporting
Jane Eyre	2000	Jane Eyre	The Graveside	Ballad	Alto	A3	D5	Lead

Character Female

* = Music Edit Required
+ = Ethnic Specific

Show	Year	Role	Song	Tempo	Vocal Type	Range-Bottom	Range-Top	Category
Jane Eyre	2000	Jane Eyre	Sweet Liberty	Uptempo	Alto	A3	D5	Lead
Jane Eyre	2000	Jane Eyre	Secret Soul*	Uptempo	Alto	F#3	D4	Lead
Jane Eyre	2000	Jane Eyre	Painting Her Portrait	Uptempo	Alto	Bb3	D5	Lead
Jane Eyre	2000	Jane Eyre	In the Virgin Morning*	Moderate Tempo	Alto	G3	D5	Lead
Jane Eyre	2000	Jane Eyre	Sirens Reprise*	Moderate Tempo	Alto	G3	C5	Lead
Jane Eyre	2000	Jane Eyre	The Voice Across the Moors	Moderate Tempo	Alto	Ab3	E5	Supporting
Jane Eyre	2000	Jane Eyre	Brave Enough for Love	Uptempo	Alto			Lead
Seussical	2000	Mrs. Mayor	How To Raise A Child*	Uptempo	Alto	A3	Bb4	Lead
Seussical	2000	The Cat In The Hat	A Day For The Cat In The Hat*	Uptempo	Alto	E3	E4	Lead
Seussical	2000	The Cat In The Hat	How Lucky You Are	Moderate Tempo	Alto	D3	F4	Lead
Seussical	2000	The Cat In The Hat	Havin' A Hunch*	Uptempo	Alto	C#4	E5	Lead
Full Monty, The	2000	Vicki Nichols	Life With Harold	Uptempo	Alto	G3	D5	Supporting
Full Monty, The	2000	Vicki Nichols	You Rule My World Reprise *	Ballad	Alto	G#3	B4	Supporting
Mamma Mia!	2001	Rosie	Take A Chance On Me*	Moderate Tempo	Alto	F3	Bb4	Lead
Mamma Mia!	2001	Tanya	Does Your Mother Know*	Uptempo	Alto	A3	Ab4	Lead
Hairspray	2002	Motormouth Mabel+	Big Blonde And Beautiful*	Moderate Tempo	Alto	C4	E5	Lead
Hairspray	2002	Motormouth Mabel+	I Know Where I've Been	Ballad	Alto	E3	C5	Lead
Thoroughly Modern Millie	2002	Mrs. Meers	They Don't Know	Moderate Tempo	Alto	D#3	F4	Lead
Avenue Q	2003	Christmas Eve	The More You Love Someone	Ballad	Alto	B3	Eb5	Lead
Wicked	2003	Elphaba	The Wizard And I*	Moderate Tempo	Alto	G3	E5	Lead
Wicked	2003	Elphaba	I'm Not That Girl	Ballad	Alto	E3	B4	Lead
Wicked	2003	Elphaba	The Wizard and I Reprise	Moderate Tempo	Alto	A3	C5	Lead
Wicked	2003	Elphaba	Defying Gravity*	Uptempo	Alto	G3	F5	Lead
Wicked	2003	Elphaba	As Long As You're Mine*	Moderate Tempo	Alto	Bb3	Db5	Lead
Wicked	2003	Elphaba	No Good Deed	Uptempo	Alto	A3	D#5	Lead
Wicked	2003	Elphaba	For Good*	Ballad	Alto	Ab3	Db5	Lead
Avenue Q	2003	Gary Coleman	You Can Be As Loud As You Want	Uptempo	Alto	G3	Db5	Lead
Avenue Q	2003	Gary Coleman	Schadenfruede *	Uptempo	Alto	F3	C5	Lead

Character Female

* = Music Edit Required
+ = Ethnic Specific

Show	Year	Role	Song	Tempo	Vocal Type	Range-Bottom	Range-Top	Category
Fame	2003	Mabel	Mabel's Prayer	Moderate Tempo	Alto	D4	E5	Supporting
Fame	2003	Serena	Let's Play A Love Scene	Ballad	Alto	G#3	D#5	Lead
Fame	2003	Serena	Think of Meryl Streep	Uptempo	Alto	B3	D5	Lead
Fame	2003	Serena	Let's Play A Love Scene Reprise *	Ballad	Alto	A3	B4	Lead
Caroline, Or Change	2004	Dotty Moffett +	Lot's Wife (ms 6-42)	Moderate Tempo	Alto	G3	B4	Supporting
Caroline, Or Change	2004	Rose Gellman	Long Distance (ms 1-74)	Moderate Tempo	Alto	Bb3	D5	Supporting
Caroline, Or Change	2004	Rose Gellman	Noah Has A Problem (ms 6-59)	Uptempo	Alto	Ab3	Cb5	Supporting
Caroline, Or Change	2004	Rose Gellman	Rose Recovers (ms 3-27)	Ballad	Alto	G3	C5	Supporting
Caroline, Or Change	2004	Rose Gellman	Inside/Out (ms 11-54)	Uptempo	Alto	C4	D5	Supporting
Caroline, Or Change	2004	The Radio +	No One Waitin' (ms 1-18)	Alto	Alto	G3	D5	Supporting
Color Purple, The	2005	Celie+	Somebody Gonna Love You	Ballad	Alto	F3	A4	Lead
Color Purple, The	2005	Celie+	What About Love *	Ballad	Alto	B2	D5	Lead
Color Purple, The	2005	Celie+	I'm Here	Ballad	Alto	E3	G5	Lead
Color Purple, The	2005	Celie+	Bring My Nettie Back	Ballad	Alto	G3	G5	Lead
Color Purple, The	2005	Celie+	Dear God (Sofia)	Uptempo	Alto	G3	G4	Lead
Color Purple, The	2005	Celie+	Dear God (Shug)	Moderate Tempo	Alto	F3	B4	Lead
Color Purple, The	2005	Celie+	With These Hands	Moderate Tempo	Alto	Ab3	Eb5	Lead
Spamalot	2005	Marlene Cow	The Cow Song*	Moderate Tempo	Alto	F3	B4	Featured Ensemble
Drowsy Chaperon, The	2006	Drowsy Chaperone	As We Stumble Along	Moderate Tempo	Alto	F3	D5	Lead
Spring Awakening	2006	Female Solo	My Junk*	Uptempo	Alto	A3	E5	Featured Ensemble
Mary Poppins	2006	Mrs. Corry	Supercalifragilisticexpialidocious*	Uptempo	Alto	C4	D5	Lead
Curtains	2007	Carmen Bernstein	It's A Business	Moderate Tempo	Alto	Eb3	Bb4	Lead
Curtains	2007	Carmen Bernstein	Show People	Moderate Tempo	Alto	G3	Ab4	Lead
Curtains	2007	Carmen Bernstein	Show People Reprise *	Moderate Tempo	Alto	G3	Bb4	Lead
Legally Blonde	2007	Enid Hoops	Harvard Variation*	Uptempo	Alto	Bb3	C5	Supporting
Legally Blonde	2007	Paulette	Ireland	Moderate Tempo	Alto	A#3	B4	Lead
Legally Blonde	2007	Paulette	Ireland Reprise	Moderate Tempo	Alto	C4	Bb4	Lead
Legally Blonde	2007	Paulette	Find My Way	Ballad	Alto	Ab3	C5	Lead

Character Female

Character Female

* = Music Edit Required
+ = Ethnic Specific

Show	Year	Role	Song	Tempo	Vocal Type	Range-Bottom	Range-Top	Category
Billy Elliot	2008	Mrs. Wilkinson	Shine	Moderate Tempo	Alto	G♭3	B4	Lead
Billy Elliot	2008	Mrs. Wilkinson	Born To Boogie	Uptempo	Alto	G3	A4	Lead
Kinky Boots	2013	Lauren	The History of Wrong Guys	Uptempo	Alto	B♭3	D5	Lead
Heathers	2014	Martha Dunnstock	Kindergarten Boyfriend	Ballad	Alto	G3	E5	Supporting
No, No Nanette	1925	Winnie Winslow	The Three Happies*	Moderate Tempo	Soprano	C5	G5	Supporting
Porgy and Bess	1935	Serena+	My Man's Gone Now*	Moderate Tempo	Soprano	E4	B5	Lead
Crazy For You (1992)	1937	Patricia Fodor	Stiff Upper Lip	Uptempo	Soprano	D4	F5	Supporting
Peter Pan	1954	Peter Pan	I've Got To Crow	Uptempo	Soprano	B♭3	C5	Lead
Peter Pan	1954	Peter Pan	Neverland	Moderate Tempo	Soprano	E♭3	C5	Lead
Peter Pan	1954	Peter Pan	I'm Flying*	Uptempo	Soprano	A3	F5	Lead
Peter Pan	1954	Peter Pan	Wendy*	Moderate Tempo	Soprano	B♭3	C5	Lead
Peter Pan	1954	Peter Pan	Distant Melody	Ballad	Soprano	G♭3	A♭4	Lead
Peter Pan	1954	Peter Pan	Neverland Reprise	Moderate Tempo	Soprano	E3	B4	Lead
Cinderella (2013)	1957	F Godmother (Marie)	Impossible*	Uptempo	Soprano	F3	F4	Supporting
Cinderella (2013)	1957	F Godmother (Marie)	Fol-De-Rol	Uptempo	Soprano	A2	F#4	Supporting
110 In The Shade	1963	Lizzie Curry	Love Don't Turn Away	Uptempo	Soprano	D#4	F5	Lead
110 In The Shade	1963	Lizzie Curry	Raunchy	Uptempo	Soprano	G3	F5	Lead
110 In The Shade	1963	Lizzie Curry	Old Maid	Moderate Tempo	Soprano	B3	G#5	Lead
110 In The Shade	1963	Lizzie Curry	Simple Little Things	Ballad	Soprano	B3	E5	Lead
110 In The Shade	1963	Lizzie Curry	Is It Really Me	Ballad	Soprano	A3	E5	Lead
110 In The Shade	1963	Lizzie Curry	A Man And A Woman *	Ballad	Soprano	D4	G5	Lead
Anyone Can Whistle	1964	Soprano Cadenza	Cora's Chase*	Uptempo	Soprano	B4	D6	Feat Ens
Mame	1966	Anges Gooch	St. Bridget*	Ballad	Soprano	G3	F5	Lead
Mame	1966	Anges Gooch	Gooch's Song	Moderate Tempo	Soprano	G3	B♭5	Lead
Company (Revival)	1970	April	You Could Drive a Person Crazy	Uptempo	Soprano	C#4	A5	Supporting
Follies	1971	Sally Durant	Too Many Mornings *	Ballad	Soprano	C4	G#5	Lead
Follies	1971	Sally Durant	Losing My Mind	Ballad	Soprano	F3	B4	Lead

Character Female

85

* = Music Edit Required
+ = Ethnic Specific

Show	Year	Role	Song	Tempo	Vocal Type	Range-Bottom	Range-Top	Category
Follies	1971	Sally Durant	The Story of Lucy and Jesse	Uptempo	Soprano	G3	Bb4	Lead
Follies	1971	Sally Durant	Don't Look At Me*	Uptempo	Soprano	A3	B4	Lead
Chicago	1975	Mary Sunshine	A Little Good In Everyone	Moderate Tempo	Soprano	F3	B5	Supporting
Best Little Whorehouse...	1978	Jewel	Twenty-four Hours of Lovin'	Uptempo	Soprano	G3	G5	Supporting
Best Little Whorehouse...	1978	Jewel	No Lies	Uptempo	Soprano	C4	E5	Supporting
Mystery Of Edwin Drood	1985	Edwin Drood	The Writing On The Wall*	Uptempo	Soprano	G3	Gb5	Lead
Nunsense	1985	Mary Amnesia	So You Want To Be A Nun	Moderate Tempo	Soprano	C4	B5	Lead
Nunsense	1985	Mary Amnesia	I Could've Gone To Nashville	Ballad	Soprano	G3	E5	Lead
Chess	1988	Svetlana	You and I*	Ballad	Soprano	G3	Eb5	Supporting
Chess	1988	Svetlana	I Know Him So Well	Ballad	Soprano	F3	D5	Supporting
Ain't Misbehavin'	1988	Woman Three +	When The Nylons Are In Bloom Again	Uptempo	Soprano	C4	D5	Lead
Ain't Misbehavin'	1988	Woman Three +	Squeeze Me	Ballad	Soprano	Ab3	Db5	Lead
Assassins	1992	Squeaky Fromme	Unworthy Of Your Love*	Moderate Tempo	Soprano	A3	D5	Lead
Cinderella (2013)	1997	F Godmother (Marie)	There's Music In You*	Ballad	Soprano	C4	F5	Lead
Chitty Chitty Bang Bang	2005	Baroness Bomburst	The Bombie Samba	Uptempo	Soprano	B3	Eb5	Supporting
Chitty Chitty Bang Bang	2005	Baroness Bomburst	Chu-Chi Face	Moderate Tempo	Soprano	C4	F5	Supporting
25th Annual...Spelling Bee	2005	Rona Lisa Peretti	My Favorite Moment of the Bee	Moderate Tempo	Soprano	D4	D5	Lead
25th Annual...Spelling Bee	2005	Rona Lisa Peretti	Rona Moment #2	Moderate Tempo	Soprano	D4	D5	Lead
25th Annual...Spelling Bee	2005	Rona Lisa Peretti	Rona Moment #3	Moderate Tempo	Soprano	Db4	Db5	Lead
25th Annual...Spelling Bee	2005	Rona Lisa Peretti	The I Love You Song	Ballad	Soprano	D4	E5	Lead
Drowsy Chaperone, The	2006	Drowsy Chaperone	Show Off Encore	Uptempo	Soprano	A3	A5	Lead
Drowsy Chaperon, The	2006	Trix	I Do, I Do In The Sky	Uptempo	Soprano	A3	A5	Lead

Character Female

Character Male

* = Music Edit Required
+ = Ethnic Specific

Show	Year	Role	Song	Vocal Type	Range-Bottom	Range-Top	Category
Good News (1993 Revival)	1929	Pooch Kearney	Keep Your Sunny Side Up*	Baritone	Bb2	F4	Supporting
Of Thee I Sing	1931	Alexander Throttlebottom	The Senator From Minesota*	Baritone	Eb3	F4	Lead
Porgy and Bess	1935	Jim+	A Woman Is A Sometime Thing*	Baritone	D3	F4	Lead
Porgy and Bess	1935	Porgy+	Lonesome Road*	Baritone	A2	D4	Lead
Porgy and Bess	1935	Porgy+	It Takes A Long Pull To Get There*	Baritone	E3	G4	Lead
Porgy and Bess	1935	Porgy+	Oh, I Got Plenty O' Nuttin'*	Baritone	B2	D4	Lead
Porgy and Bess	1935	Porgy+	The Buzzard*	Baritone	Bb2	E4	Lead
Porgy and Bess	1935	Porgy+	Bess, You Is My Woman*	Baritone	Bb2	B5	Lead
Porgy and Bess	1935	Porgy+	I Got Plenty O' Nuttin' Reprise	Baritone	Bb2	Eb4	Lead
Porgy and Bess	1935	Porgy+	I Loves You Porgy*	Baritone	Db3	Db4	Lead
Porgy and Bess	1935	Porgy+	Oh, Bess, Oh, Where's My Bess*	Baritone	C#3	F4	Lead
Porgy and Bess	1935	Porgy+	Oh Lawd I'm On My Way*	Baritone	B2	E#4	Lead
Crazy For You (1992)	1937	Eugene Fodor	Stiff Upper Lip	Baritone	D3	F4	Supporting
Wizard Of Oz 1993	1939	Scarecrow	If I Only Had A Brain*	Baritone	D3	F#4	Lead
Oklahoma!	1943	Ali Hakim	It's A Scandal! It's A Outrage	Baritone	B2	F#4	Lead
Annie Get Your Gun	1944	Buffalo Bill	Show Business Reprise *	Baritone	C3	F4	Supporting
Annie Get Your Gun	1944	Charlie Davenport	Show Business Reprise *	Baritone	C3	F4	Supporting
On The Town	1944	Ozzie	Ya Got Me *	Baritone	Eb3	Fb4	Lead
Kiss Me Kate	1948	General Howell	From This Moment On	Baritone	B2	C#4	Supporting
South Pacific	1949	Luther Billis	Honey Bun Reprise	Baritone	Bb2	B3	Lead
Call Me Madam	1950	Kenneth Gibson	It's A Lovely Day Today*	Baritone	C3	D4	Lead
Call Me Madam	1950	Kenneth Gibson	It's A Lovely Day Today Reprise	Baritone	D3	D4	Lead
Call Me Madam	1950	Kenneth Gibson	Once Upon A Time Today	Baritone	E3	F4	Lead
Call Me Madam	1950	Kenneth Gibson	It's A Lovely Day Today Reprise 2*	Baritone	C3	D4	Lead
Call Me Madam	1950	Kenneth Gibson	You're Just In Love*	Baritone	D3	F4	Lead
Wonderful Town	1953	1st Editor	What A Waste*	Baritone	A2	D4	Lead
Wonderful Town	1953	2nd Editor	What A Waste*	Baritone	Bb2	Eb4	Lead
Pajama Game	1954	Hines	The Pajama Game	Baritone	Db3	F4	Lead

Character Male

87

* = Music Edit Required
+ = Ethnic Specific

Show	Year	Role	Song	Tempo	Vocal Type	Range-Bottom	Range-Top	Category
Pajama Game	1954	Hines	Think Of The Time I Save	Uptempo	Baritone	C3	D4	Lead
My Fair Lady	1956	Alfred Doolittle	With A Little Bit Of Luck*	Uptempo	Baritone	G2	E4	Lead
My Fair Lady	1956	Alfred Doolittle	Little Bit Of Luck Reprise	Uptempo	Baritone	G2	E4	Lead
My Fair Lady	1956	Alfred Doolittle	Get Me To The Church On Time	Uptempo	Baritone	B2	D4	Lead
Most Happy Fella, The	1956	Postman	I Seen Her At The Station	Moderate Tempo	Baritone	D3	E4	Feat Ens
Bells Are Ringing	1956	Sandor	Salzberg	Moderate Tempo	Baritone	E3	G4	Supporting
Bye Bye Birdie	1960	Albert Peterson	Put On A Happy Face	Uptempo	Baritone	B2	D#4	Lead
Bye Bye Birdie	1960	Albert Peterson	Baby Talk To me	Ballad	Baritone	C3	F#4	Lead
Bye Bye Birdie	1960	Albert Peterson	Rosie *	Moderate Tempo	Baritone	B2	D4	Lead
Bye Bye Birdie	1960	Albert Peterson	A Giant Step (TV 1995)	Uptempo	Baritone	D3	F#4	Lead
Little Me	1962	Benny Buchsbaum	To Be A Performer*	Uptempo	Baritone	D#3	F4	Lead
Little Me	1962	Benny Buchsbaum	Be A Performer Reprise*	Uptempo	Baritone	E3	E4	Lead
Little Me	1962	Bernie Buchsbaum	To Be A Performer*	Uptempo	Baritone	D#3	F4	Lead
Little Me	1962	Bernie Buchsbaum	Be A Performer Reprise*	Uptempo	Baritone	E3	E4	Lead
Little Me	1962	Fred Poitrane	Real Live Girl*	Ballad	Baritone	D3	C4	Lead
Little Me	1962	George Musgrove	I've Got Your Number*	Moderate Tempo	Baritone	E3	Ab4	Lead
Little Me	1962	Prince Chemey	Goodbye	Uptempo	Baritone	B2	F#4	Lead
A Funny Thing...Forum	1962	Prologus	Comedy Tonight*	Uptempo	Baritone	A2	F4	Lead
Little Me	1962	Val DuVal	Boom Boom*	Uptempo	Baritone	C#3	F#4	Lead
110 In The Shade	1963	File	Gonna Be Another Hot Day *	Moderate Tempo	Baritone	D3	F#4	Lead
110 In The Shade	1963	File	A Man And A Woman *	Ballad	Baritone	C3	D4	Lead
110 In The Shade	1963	File	Wonderful Music *	Uptempo	Baritone	Db3	F4	Lead
She Loves Me	1963	Headwaiter	A Romantic Atmosphere (D Maj)	Moderate Tempo	Baritone	G2	F4	Lead
She Loves Me	1963	Ladislav Sipos	Perpective	Uptempo	Baritone	D3	C#4	Lead
Oliver!	1963	Mr. Bumble	Boy For Sale	Ballad	Baritone	C3	G4	Lead
Funny Girl	1964	Eddie Ryan	Who Taught Her Everything...*	Moderate Tempo	Baritone	C3	F4	Supporting
Funny Girl	1964	Eddie Ryan	Rat Tat Tat Tat*	Uptempo	Baritone	D3	F#4	Lead
Funny Girl	1964	Eddie Ryan	If A Girl Isn't Pretty*	Moderate Tempo	Baritone	B2	F#4	Supporting
Apple Tree, The	1966	Adam	Eve	Moderate Tempo	Baritone	D3	Db4	Lead

* = Music Edit Required
+ = Ethnic Specific

Show	Year	Role	Song	Tempo	Vocal Type	Range-Bottom	Range-Top	Category
Apple Tree, The	1966	Adam	Beautiful World	Moderate Tempo	Baritone	C3	Eb4	Lead
Apple Tree, The	1966	Adam	It's A Fish	Uptempo	Baritone	Ab3	Eb4	Lead
Apple Tree, The	1966	Adam	Adam's Reprise	Moderate Tempo	Baritone	C3	Eb4	Lead
Apple Tree, The	1966	Flip	Real *	Moderate Tempo	Baritone	C3	Eb4	Lead
Cabaret	1966	Herr Ludwig	Tomorrow Belongs to Me Reprise *	Moderate Tempo	Baritone	C3	D4	Supporting
Sweet Charity	1966	Oscar Lindquist	Sweet Charity	Moderate Tempo	Baritone	Bb2	E4	Lead
Hair	1968	Ron	Aquarius	Moderate Tempo	Baritone	Eb3	Eb4	Lead
1776	1969	John Dickinson	Cool, Cool Considerate Men	Moderate Tempo	Baritone	A2	Gb4	Lead
Dear World	1969	President	The Spring Of Next Year*	Moderate Tempo	Baritone	G2	D4	Supporting
Dear World	1969	President	Just A Little Bit More*	Uptempo	Baritone	G2	Fb4	Supporting
Dear World	1969	President	Just A Little Bit More Reprise*	Uptempo	Baritone	Gb3	Eb4	Supporting
Dear World	1969	Sewerman	Pretty Garbage*	Moderate Tempo	Baritone	B2	E4	Supporting
Dear World	1969	Sewerman	Ugly Garbage*	Moderate Tempo	Baritone	A3	E4	Supporting
Applause	1970	Buzz Richards	Good Friends*	Moderate Tempo	Baritone	C3	F4	Lead
Company (Revival)	1970	David	Sorry Grateful	Ballad	Baritone	B2	E4	Supporting
Company (Revival)	1970	David	Have I Got A Girl For You	Uptempo	Baritone	B5	Gb7	Supporting
Company (Revival)	1970	Harry	Sorry Grateful	Ballad	Baritone	B2	E4	Supporting
Company (Revival)	1970	Harry	Have I Got A Girl For You	Uptempo	Baritone	B6	Gb8	Supporting
Follies	1971	Buddy Plummer	The Right Girl *	Uptempo	Baritone	C3	F4	Lead
Follies	1971	Buddy Plummer	Buddy's Blues	Uptempo	Baritone	Db3	F4	Lead
You're...Charlie Brown	1971	Charlie Brown	The Kite	Uptempo	Baritone	Bb2	Eb4	Lead
Jesus Christ Superstar	1971	King Herod	King Herod's Song	Uptempo	Baritone	B2	G4	Supporting
Sugar	1972	Jerry	Penniless Bums*	Uptempo	Baritone	C3	E4	Lead
Sugar	1972	Jerry	The Beauty That Drives Men Mad*	Uptempo	Baritone	D3	F4	Lead
Sugar	1972	Jerry	Doin' It For Sugar*	Moderate Tempo	Baritone	B3	E4	Lead
Sugar	1972	Jerry	Beautiful Through and Through*	Moderate Tempo	Baritone	C#3	E4	Lead
Sugar	1972	Jerry	Magic Nights	Moderate Tempo	Baritone	E3	F4	Lead

Character Male

* = Music Edit Required
+ = Ethnic Specific

Show	Year	Role	Song	Vocal Type	Range-Bottom	Range-Top	Category
Chicago	1975	Amos Hart	Mister Cellophane	Baritone	C3	F4	Lead
Pacific Overtures	1976	Male	Prologue	Baritone	D2	Bb3	Lead
Pacific Overtures	1976	Manjiro+	Poems*	Baritone	Eb3	F4	Lead
Pacific Overtures	1976	Reciter+	The Advantages Of Floating...*	Baritone	B2	E4	Lead
Pacific Overtures	1976	Soothsayer+	Chrysanthemum Tea*	Baritone	F2	D4	Lead
On The Twentieth Century	1978	Conductor Flanagan	I Have Written A Play	Baritone	C3	F4	Supporting
On The Twentieth Century	1978	Congressman	I Have Written A Play	Baritone	C3	F4	Supporting
On The Twentieth Century	1978	Doctor	I Have Written A Play	Baritone	Bb3	Eb5	Supporting
Cats	1981	Rum Tum Tugger	Rum Tum Tugger	Baritone	B2	F4	Supporting
Cats	1981	Rum Tum Tugger	Old Deuteronomy *	Baritone	B2	G4	Lead
Cats	1981	Rum Tum Tugger	Mr. Mistoffolees	Baritone	C3	Eb4	Lead
Joseph...Dream Coat	1982	Levi	One More Angel In Heaven	Baritone	D3	F4	Lead
Joseph...Dream Coat	1982	Napthali	Benjamin Calypso	Baritone	F3	F4	Supporting
Joseph...Dream Coat	1982	Reuben (Chevalier)	Those Canaan Days	Baritone	C3	F4	Supporting
LA Cage Aux Folles	1983	Albin	A Little More Mascara (Drag)	Baritone	Bb2	D4	Lead
LA Cage Aux Folles	1983	Albin	I Am What I Am (Drag)	Baritone	G#3	F4	Lead
LA Cage Aux Folles	1983	Albin	The Best Of Times (Drag)	Baritone	C3	Eb4	Lead
LA Cage Aux Folles	1983	Albin	With You On My Arm	Baritone	G#2	Eb4	Lead
LA Cage Aux Folles	1983	Albin	La Cage Aux Folles (Drag)	Baritone	Bb2	E4	Lead
Baby	1983	Nick Sakarian	At Night She Comes Home To Me *	Baritone	Db3	F#4	Lead
Baby	1983	Nick Sakarian	With You *	Baritone	A#2	D#4	Lead
Big River	1985	Duke	The Royal Nonesuch	Baritone	D3	F4	Supporting
Mystery Of Edwin Drood, The	1985	Durdle	Durdle's Confession	Baritone	C3	E4	Lead
Big River	1985	Jim +	Muddy Water	Baritone	B2	F4	Lead
Big River	1985	Jim +	River In The Rain *	Baritone	A2	E4	Lead
Big River	1985	Jim +	Worlds Apart *	Baritone	B2	C4	Lead
Big River	1985	Jim +	Free At Last	Baritone	C3	F4	Lead
Big River	1985	Pap	Guv'ment	Baritone	B2	F#4	Supporting

Character Male

* = Music Edit Required
+ = Ethnic Specific

Show	Year	Role	Song	Tempo	Vocal Type	Range-Bottom	Range-Top	Category
Big River	1985	Young Fool	Arkansas	Uptempo	Baritone	C3	E4	Supporting
Into The Woods	1987	Baker	It Takes Two	Moderate Tempo	Baritone	Bb2	F4	Lead
Into The Woods	1987	Baker	No More*	Ballad	Baritone	D3	Eb4	Lead
City of Angels	1989	Buddy Fiddler	The Buddy System	Moderate Tempo	Baritone	C3	D4	Lead
City of Angels	1989	Buddy Fiddler	Double Talk (Buddy)	Moderate Tempo	Baritone	C3	G4	Lead
City of Angels	1989	Munoz +	All You Have To Do Is Wait	Moderate Tempo	Baritone	F#3	D4	Supporting
Secret Garden, The	1991	Archibald Craven	A Bit of Earth*	Moderate Tempo	Baritone	D3	E4	Lead
Goodbye Girl, The	1993	Billy	A Beat Behind*	Uptempo	Baritone	E3	F#4	Supporting
Honk	1993	Bullfrog	Warts and All	Moderate Tempo	Baritone	A2	C#4	Supporting
Sunset Boulevard	1994	Manfred	The Lady's Paying*	Uptempo	Baritone	C3	F4	Lead
Sunset Boulevard	1994	Max Von Mayerling	The Grestest Star Of All	Moderate Tempo	Baritone	B2	Gb4	Lead
Sunset Boulevard	1994	Max Von Mayerling	New Ways To Dream Reprise	Ballad	Baritone	G2	E4	Lead
Victor/Victoria	1995	Toddy	Paris By Night*	Moderate Tempo	Baritone	Bb2	Eb4	Lead
Victor/Victoria	1995	Toddy	Trust Me*	Uptempo	Baritone	A2	D4	Lead
Lion King, The	1997	Zazu	The Morning Report*	Uptempo	Baritone	Eb3	F4	Supporting
Parade	1998	Leo Frank	How Can I Call This Home?	Uptempo	Baritone	A2	F4	Lead
Parade	1998	Leo Frank	Come Up To My Office*	Uptempo	Baritone	A2	F4	Lead
Parade	1998	Leo Frank	It's Hard To Speak My Heart	Ballad	Baritone	B2	E4	Lead
Parade	1998	Leo Frank	This Is Not Over Yet*	Uptempo	Baritone	D3	F#4	Lead
Parade	1998	Leo Frank	All The Wasted Time*	Ballad	Baritone	D3	Bb4	Lead
Parade	1998	Leo Frank	Sh'ma	Ballad	Baritone	G3	Eb4	Lead
Full Monty, The	2000	Dave Bukatinsky	You Rule My World *	Ballad	Baritone	C#3	B4	Lead
Full Monty, The	2000	Harold Nichols	You Rule My World *	Ballad	Baritone	C#3	G4	Lead
Seussical	2000	Horton	Horton Hears A Who (ms 17-119)	Moderate Tempo	Baritone	A2	E4	Lead
Seussical	2000	Horton	Alone In The Universe*	Moderate Tempo	Baritone	B2	E4	Lead
Seussical	2000	Horton	Alone In The Universe Reprise	Moderate Tempo	Baritone	C3	C5	Lead
Seussical	2000	Horton	Solla Sollew*	Moderate Tempo	Baritone	C3	D4	Lead
Seussical	2000	The Cat In The Hat	A Day For The Cat In The Hat*	Uptempo	Baritone	E3	E4	Lead

Character Male

* = Music Edit Required
+ = Ethnic Specific

Show	Year	Role	Song	Tempo	Vocal Type	Range-Bottom	Range-Top	Category
Seussical	2000	The Cat In The Hat	How Lucky You Are	Moderate Tempo	Baritone	D3	F4	Lead
Seussical	2000	The Cat In The Hat	Havin' A Hunch*	Uptempo	Baritone	C#3	E4	Lead
Seussical	2000	The Mayor	We're Whos Here Part 1*	Uptempo	Baritone	E3	E4	Supporting
Seussical	2000	The Mayor	How To Raise A Child*	Uptempo	Baritone	A2	E4	Lead
Mamma Mia!	2001	Harry Bright	Thank You For the Music*	Moderate Tempo	Baritone	A3	D5	Lead
Mamma Mia!	2001	Harry Bright	One Last Summer*	Ballad	Baritone	F#3	E4	Lead
Producers, The	2001	Leo Bloom	We Can Do It*	Uptempo	Baritone	Bb2	E4	Lead
Producers, The	2001	Leo Bloom	I Wanna Be A Producer*	Moderate Tempo	Baritone	A2	F4	Lead
Producers, The	2001	Leo Bloom	That Face*	Uptempo	Baritone	B2	F4	Lead
Producers, The	2001	Leo Bloom	Leo Goes To Rio*	Moderate Tempo	Baritone	C3	E4	Lead
Producers, The	2001	Leo Bloom	Til Him	Ballad	Baritone	C3	F4	Lead
Producers, The	2001	Max Bialystock	King Of Broadway*	Uptempo	Baritone	C#3	E4	Lead
Producers, The	2001	Max Bialystock	We Can Do It*	Uptempo	Baritone	Bb2	Eb4	Lead
Producers, The	2001	Max Bialystock	Along Came Bially*	Moderate Tempo	Baritone	Bb2	Eb4	Lead
Producers, The	2001	Max Bialystock	That Face Reprise*	Uptempo	Baritone	A2	Eb4	Lead
Producers, The	2001	Max Bialystock	Where Did We Go Right*	Uptempo	Baritone	A2	D4	Lead
Producers, The	2001	Max Bialystock	Betrayed	Uptempo	Baritone	B2	F4	Lead
Producers, The	2001	Max Bialystock	Til Him	Ballad	Baritone	C3	D#4	Lead
A Man Of No Importance	2002	Alfie Byrne	Man In The Mirror	Ballad	Baritone	Bb2	F4	Lead
A Man Of No Importance	2002	Alfie Byrne	Love Who You Love	Ballad	Baritone	B2	E4	Lead
A Man Of No Importance	2002	Alfie Byrne	Confession *	Moderate Tempo	Baritone	B2	D#4	Lead
A Man Of No Importance	2002	Alfie Byrne	Love's Never Lost	Ballad	Baritone	E3	C4	Lead
A Man Of No Importance	2002	Alfie Byrne	Welcome To The World	Ballad	Baritone	C3	C5	Lead
Hairspray	2002	Edna Turnblad	Welcome To The 60s*	Uptempo	Baritone	F2	G3	Lead
Hairspray	2002	Edna Turnblad	Timeless To Me*	Moderate Tempo	Baritone	F#2	D4	Lead
A Year With Frog and Toad	2002	Frog	He'll Never Know	Moderate Tempo	Baritone	B2	D4	Lead
A Year With Frog and Toad	2002	Toad	Seeds	Ballad	Baritone	A2	D4	Lead
A Year With Frog and Toad	2002	Toad	Alone	Ballad	Baritone	A2	G#4	Lead

* = Music Edit Required
+ = Ethnic Specific

Show	Year	Role	Song	Tempo	Vocal Type	Range-Bottom	Range-Top	Category
A Year With Frog and Toad	2002	Toad	He'll Never Know	Moderate Tempo	Baritone	C#3	E♭4	Lead
A Year With Frog and Toad	2002	Toad	Toad To The Rescue	Moderate Tempo	Baritone	E3	A4	Lead
A Year With Frog and Toad	2002	Toad	Merry Almost Christmas	Moderate Tempo	Baritone	E3	A4	Lead
Avenue Q	2003	Brian	I'm Not Wearing Underwear Today	Uptempo	Baritone	B2	E4	Lead
Avenue Q	2003	Brian	There Is Life Outside Your Apt	Uptempo	Baritone	B#2	E4	Lead
Wicked	2003	Doctor Dillamond	Something Bad*	Moderate Tempo	Baritone	C#3	D♭4	Lead
Wicked	2003	Salesman	No One Mourns The Wicked*	Moderate Tempo	Baritone	D3	E4	Supporting
Fame	2003	Schlomo	Bring In Tomorrow *	Ballad	Baritone	D3	F4	Lead
Wicked	2003	Wizard	A Sentimental Man	Moderate Tempo	Baritone	B2	F#4	Lead
Wicked	2003	Wizard	Wonderful*	Uptempo	Baritone	B2	E4	Lead
Dirty Rotten Scoundrels	2005	Andre Thibault	A Chimp In A Suit	Uptempo	Baritone	C3	E4	Supporting
Dirty Rotten Scoundrels	2005	Andre Thibault	Like Zis/Like Zat *	Moderate Tempo	Baritone	B♭3	E♭4	Supporting
Chitty Chitty Bang Bang	2005	Caratacus Potts	Hushabye Mountain	Ballad	Baritone	D#3	F4	Lead
Chitty Chitty Bang Bang	2005	Caratacus Potts	Truly Scrumptious Reprise	Ballad	Baritone	D♭3	D♭4	Lead
Chitty Chitty Bang Bang	2005	Caratacus Potts	You Two	Moderate Tempo	Baritone	D3	E4	Lead
Chitty Chitty Bang Bang	2005	Caratacus Potts	Toot Sweets *	Uptempo	Baritone	D3	E♭4	Lead
Chitty Chitty Bang Bang	2005	Caratacus Potts	Teamwork *	Uptempo	Baritone	E3	G4	Lead
Spamalot	2005	Herbert	Here You Are*	Moderate Tempo	Baritone	G2	B♭3	Supporting
Spamalot	2005	Sir Bedevere	Burn Her*	Uptempo	Baritone	F3	E4	Lead
Spamalot	2005	Sir Robin	You Won't Succeed On Broadway*	Uptempo	Baritone	D3	E4	Supporting
Mary Poppins	2006	Bank Chairman	Precision And Order*	Moderate Tempo	Baritone	C3	F4	Supporting
Mary Poppins	2006	Bert	Chim Chim Cher-ee	Moderate Tempo	Baritone	A2	D4	Lead
Mary Poppins	2006	Bert	Winds Can Change	Ballad	Baritone	C3	C4	Lead
Mary Poppins	2006	Bert	Chim Chim Cher-ee A1	Moderate Tempo	Baritone	C#3	E4	Lead
Mary Poppins	2006	Bert	Chim Chim Cher-ee Reprise	Moderate Tempo	Baritone	A2	D4	Lead
Mary Poppins	2006	Bert	Step In Time*	Uptempo	Baritone	B2	F#4	Lead
Mary Poppins	2006	Bert	A Spoonful Of Sugar Reprise*	Moderate Tempo	Baritone	B♭2	C#4	Lead
Mary Poppins	2006	Bert	All Me Own Work	Ballad	Baritone	C#3	D#4	Lead

Character Male

*= Music Edit Required
+ = Ethnic Specific

Show	Year	Role	Song	Tempo	Vocal Type	Range-Bottom	Range-Top	Category
Mary Poppins	2006	Bert	Twists And Turns	Ballad	Baritone	B2	E4	Lead
Mary Poppins	2006	Bert	Let's Go Fly A Kite*	Moderate Tempo	Baritone	Bb2	E4	Lead
Mary Poppins	2006	Bert	Jolly Holiday*	Uptempo	Baritone	B2	E4	Lead
Legally Blonde	2007	Aaron Schultz	Harvard Variation*	Uptempo	Baritone	C3	Eb4	Supporting
The Little Mermaid	2007	Chef Louis	Les Poisons	Uptempo	Baritone	Eb3	D4	Lead
Curtains	2007	Lieutenant Frank Cioffi	Show People	Moderate Tempo	Baritone	A2	F4	Lead
Curtains	2007	Lieutenant Frank Cioffi	Coffe Shop Nights	Ballad	Baritone	Ab2	D3	Lead
Curtains	2007	Lieutenant Frank Cioffi	A Tough Act To Follow *	Ballad	Baritone	A2	Eb4	Lead
Curtains	2007	Lieutenant Frank Cioffi	Show People Reprise *	Moderate Tempo	Baritone	B2	Bb3	Lead
White Christmas	2008	Phil Davis	The Best Things...Dancing	Moderate Tempo	Baritone	Db3	F4	Lead
In The Heights	2008	Usnavi De La Vega+	In The Heights (Rap)*	Uptempo	Baritone	D3	G4	Lead
In The Heights	2008	Usnavi De La Vega+	Finale (Rap)*	Moderate Tempo	Baritone	A3	C4	Lead
Show Boat	1927	Joe+	Ol' Man River	Ballad	Bass	F2	D4	Lead
Show Boat	1927	Joe+	Ol' Man River Reprise	Ballad	Bass	F2	D4	Lead
Show Boat	1927	Joe+	Ol' Man River - Act II	Ballad	Bass	Ab2	F4	Lead
Addams Family, The	2010	Lurch	Move Toward The Darkness	Ballad	Bass	G2	Eb4	Supporting
Anything Goes	1934	Moon Face Martin	Friendship *	Uptempo	Tenor	Bb2	Eb4	Supporting
Anything Goes	1934	Moon Face Martin	Be Like A Blue Bird	Moderate Tempo	Tenor	B#2	F#4	Supporting
Porgy and Bess	1935	Crab Man+	Crab Man	Ballad	Tenor	B3	G4	Feat Ens
Porgy and Bess	1935	Honey Man+	Honeyman	Ballad	Tenor	B3	G4	Feat Ens
Wizard Of Oz 1995	1939	Tin Man	If I Only Had A Heart*	Moderate Tempo	Tenor	D3	G4	Lead
Pal Joey	1940	Louis	The Flower Garden Of My Heart*	Moderate Tempo	Tenor	Eb3	G4	Feat Ens
Kiss Me Kate	1948	Paul	Too Darn Hot*	Uptempo	Tenor	C3	Gb4	Supporting
Cinderella (2013)	1949	Jean-Michel	Now Is the Time*	Uptempo	Tenor	Eb3	F4	Supporting
Cinderella (2013)	1949	Jean-Michel	Now Is The Time Reprise*	Uptempo	Tenor	C3	A4	Supporting
Guys and Dolls	1950	Nicely Nicely	Sit Down You're Rockin' The Boat*	Uptempo	Tenor	F3	C5	Supporting

Character Male

* = Music Edit Required
+ = Ethnic Specific

Show	Year	Role	Song	Tempo	Vocal Type	Range-Bottom	Range-Top	Category
Most Happy Fella, The	1956	Herman	I Like Everybody*	Uptempo	Tenor	G3	G4	Lead
Most Happy Fella, The	1956	Herman	I Like Everybody Reprise*	Uptempo	Tenor	F3	G4	Lead
Most Happy Fella, The	1956	Herman	I Made A Fist*	Moderate Tempo	Tenor	F3	A♭4	Lead
Most Happy Fella, The	1956	The Doctor	Love and Kindness	Moderate Tempo	Tenor	E3	A4	Supporting
Most Happy Fella, The	1956	The Doctor	A Song Of A Summer Night*	Moderate Tempo	Tenor	F3	F4	Supporting
Once Upon A Mattress	1959	Jester	Normandy*	Uptempo	Tenor	D#3	B4	Lead
Once Upon A Mattress	1959	Jester	Very Soft Shoes*	Moderate Tempo	Tenor	D3	F4	Lead
Jersey Boys (2005)	1961	Hal Miller	An Angel Cried	Uptempo	Tenor	A3	C5	Supporting
How To Succeed....	1961	J Pierpont Finch	How To Succeed	Uptempo	Tenor	E3	E4	Lead
How To Succeed....	1961	J Pierpont Finch	Rosemary*	Moderate Tempo	Tenor	B2	E4	Lead
How To Succeed....	1961	J Pierpont Finch	I Believe In You*	Uptempo	Tenor	F3	C4	Lead
How To Succeed....	1961	J Pierpont Finch	Brotherhood Of Man*	Uptempo	Tenor	F3	G4	Lead
She Loves Me	1963	Headwaiter	A Romantic Atmosphere (G Maj)	Moderate Tempo	Tenor	C#3	B4	Supporting
Fiddler on The Roof	1964	Motel	Miracle of Miracles	Uptempo	Tenor	E3	F#4	Supporting
Jersey Boys (2005)	1966	Bob Gaudio	Cry For Me	Ballad	Tenor	B♭2	G4	Lead
Sweet Charity	1966	Daddy Brubeck	The Rhythm Of Life*	Uptempo	Tenor	B2	G4	Lead
Cabaret	1966	Herr Schultz	Meeskite	Uptempo	Tenor	B2	A♭4	Supporting
Cabaret	1966	Master of Ceremonies	Wilkomen	Uptempo	Tenor	E3	G4	Lead
Cabaret	1966	Master of Ceremonies	Two Ladies	Uptempo	Tenor	G3	G4	Lead
Cabaret	1966	Master of Ceremonies	The Money Song	Moderate Tempo	Tenor	E♭2	A4	Lead
Cabaret	1966	Master of Ceremonies	If You Could See Her	Uptempo	Tenor	D3	F4	Lead
Hair	1968	Woof	Sodomy	Ballad	Tenor	D3	G4	Lead
Godspell	1971	Jesus	Save The People	Uptempo	Tenor	G3	G4	Lead
Godspell	1971	Jesus	Alas For You	Uptempo	Tenor	E3	G4	Lead
Godspell	1971	Jesus	Beautiful City (1972 Film)	Ballad	Tenor	E3	F#4	Lead
Godspell	1971	Jesus	All For The Best*	Uptempo	Tenor	D3	E4	Lead
Grease	1971	Roger	Mooning	Ballad	Tenor	F3	G4	Supporting
Grease	1971	Roger	Rock N Roll Party Queen	Uptempo	Tenor	A2	A♭3	Lead
You're A Good Man Charlie Br	1971	Snoopy	Snoopy	Ballad	Tenor	B2	G4	Lead

Character Male

* = Music Edit Required
+ = Ethnic Specific

Show	Year	Role	Song	Tempo	Vocal Type	Range-Bottom	Range-Top	Category
You're A Good Man Charlie Br	1971	Snoopy	Suppertime*	Uptempo	Tenor	C3	A4	Lead
Godspell	1971	Soloist 4	All Good Gifts	Ballad	Tenor	D3	A4	Supporting
Wiz, The	1974	Scarecrow	I Was Born...Day Before Yesterday*	Moderate Tempo	Tenor	E3	A4	Lead
Wiz, The	1974	Tin Man	Slide Some Oil To Me	Uptempo	Tenor	Eb3	Bb4	Lead
Wiz, The	1974	Tin Man	What Would I Do If I Could Feel	Ballad	Tenor	D3	A4	Lead
Jersey Boys (2005)	1975	Bob Gaudio	December 1963	Uptempo	Tenor	F3	G4	Lead
Pacific Overtures	1976	Fisherman+	Four Black Dragons*	Uptempo	Tenor	Eb3	Gb4	Supporting
Annie	1977	Rooster Hannigan	Easy Street *	Moderate Tempo	Tenor	A2	G4	Supporting
Best Little Whorehouse...	1978	Melvin P Thorpe	Texas Has A Whorehouse In It	Uptempo	Tenor	Bb2	E4	Supporting
On The Twentieth Century	1978	Owen O'Malley	Five Zeros*	Moderate Tempo	Tenor	Ab2	Ab4	Lead
Sweeney Todd	1979	Adolfo Pirelli	The Contest	Moderate Tempo	Tenor	B2	C4	Lead
Sweeney Todd	1979	Adolfo Pirelli	Pirelli's Death	Moderate Tempo	Tenor	Eb3	C5	Lead
Sweeney Todd	1979	The Beadle	Ladies In Their Sensitivities	Ballad	Tenor	D3	A4	Lead
Sweeney Todd	1979	The Beadle	Parlor Songs	Moderate Tempo	Tenor	D3	G4	Lead
Merrily We Roll Along 1994	1981	Charley Kringas	Franklin Shepard, Inc.	Uptempo	Tenor	C3	G4	Lead
Merrily We Roll Along 1994	1981	Charley Kringas	Old Friends II*	Moderate Tempo	Tenor	Bb2	D4	Lead
Merrily We Roll Along 1994	1981	Charley Kringas	Good Thing Going	Ballad	Tenor	C3	F4	Lead
Dreamgirls	1981	James Thunder Early +	Fake Your Way to the Top	Uptempo	Tenor	F3	Ab4	Supporting
Dreamgirls	1981	James Thunder Early +	I Want You Baby	Ballad	Tenor	Eb3	Db4	Lead
Dreamgirls	1981	James Thunder Early +	I Meant You No Harm	Ballad	Tenor	Bb2	G4	Lead
Joseph...Dream Coat	1982	Pharaoh (Elvis)	Song of the King	Uptempo	Tenor	B2	G#4	Supporting
Joseph...Dream Coat	1982	Pharaoh (Elvis)	Song of the King Reprise	Uptempo	Tenor	B2	G#4	Supporting
Little Shop of Horrors	1982	Seymour Krelborn	Grow For Me	Moderate Tempo	Tenor	Bb2	F4	Lead
Little Shop of Horrors	1982	Seymour Krelborn	Now*	Uptempo	Tenor	B2	G4	Lead
Singin' In The Rain	1983	Cosmo Brown	Make "Em Laugh	Uptempo	Tenor	C3	G4	Lead
Singin' In The Rain	1983	Cosmo Brown	Broadway Melody* (ms 1-30)	Uptempo	Tenor	Bb3	F4	Lead
Sunday...Park With Geroge	1984	Franz	The Day Off (Part 5)*	Moderate Tempo	Tenor	C3	Eb4	Supporting

Character Male

* = Music Edit Required
+ = Ethnic Specific

Show	Year	Role	Song	Tempo	Vocal Type	Range-Bottom	Range-Top	Category
Mystery Of Edwin Drood, The	1985	Bazzard	Never The Luck*	Moderate Tempo	Tenor	C3	G4	Lead
Mystery Of Edwin Drood, The	1985	Bazzard	Bazzard's Confession	Uptempo	Tenor	A2	G4	Lead
Rags	1986	Man	I Remember	Moderate Tempo	Tenor	E3	G4	Feat. Ens
Rags	1986	Nathan Hershkowitz	Uptown*	Moderate Tempo	Tenor	E3	G4	Lead
Rags	1986	Nathan Hershkowitz	What's Wrong With That*	Uptempo	Tenor	A2	G4	Lead
Rags	1986	Tim Sullivan	What's Wrong With That*	Uptempo	Tenor	A2	G4	Supporting
Ain't Misbehavin'	1988	Man Two +	Honeysuckle Rose*	Ballad	Tenor	D3	Ab4	Lead
Ain't Misbehavin'	1988	Man Two +	Lounging At The Waldorf	Ballad	Tenor	B3	E4	Lead
Ain't Misbehavin'	1988	Man Two +	Your Feets Too Big	Ballad	Tenor	G2	Eb4	Lead
Children of Eden	1991	Adam	A World Without You *	Moderate Tempo	Tenor	Db3	Ab4	Lead
Children of Eden	1991	Adam	Grateful Children *	Moderate Tempo	Tenor	B2	D#3	Lead
Secret Garden, The	1991	Archibald Craven	Race You...Top Of The Morning	Uptempo	Tenor	Eb3	Ab4	Lead
Secret Garden, The	1991	Archibald Craven	Where In The World	Uptempo	Tenor	F3	Fb4	Lead
Assassins	1992	The Balladeer	The Ballad Of Booth Part 1	Uptempo	Tenor	C#3	G#4	Lead
Assassins	1992	The Balladeer	The Ballad Of Booth Part 3	Uptempo	Tenor	C#3	Ab4	Lead
Assassins	1992	The Balladeer	The Ballad of Czolgosz (Part 1 & 2)	Uptempo	Tenor	D3	G4	Lead
Assassins	1992	The Balladeer	The Ballad of Guiteau*	Uptempo	Tenor	C3	G4	Lead
Assassins	1992	The Balladeer	Another National Anthem*	Moderate Tempo	Tenor	D3	F#4	Lead
Kiss Of The Spider Woman	1993	Molina	Her Name Is Aurora*	Moderate Tempo	Tenor	C3	C4	Lead
Kiss Of The Spider Woman	1993	Molina	Bluebloods*	Uptempo	Tenor	B2	C#4	Lead
Kiss Of The Spider Woman	1993	Molina	Dressing Them Up	Uptempo	Tenor	C3	F4	Lead
Kiss Of The Spider Woman	1993	Molina	Dear One*	Ballad	Tenor	C3	Eb4	Lead
Kiss Of The Spider Woman	1993	Molina	She's A Woman	Ballad	Tenor	C3	E4	Lead
Kiss Of The Spider Woman	1993	Molina	Mama, It's Me	Moderate Tempo	Tenor	C3	E4	Lead
Kiss Of The Spider Woman	1993	Molina	Only In the Movies	Uptempo	Tenor	B2	F4	Lead
Blood Brothers	1993	Narrator	Shoes Upon The Table	Uptempo	Tenor	G2	G3	Lead
Blood Brothers	1993	Narrator	Shoes Upon The Table Reprise	Uptempo	Tenor	G3	Bb4	Lead
Blood Brothers	1993	Narrator	Marilyn Monroe Reprise 1	Moderate Tempo	Tenor	A3	B4	Lead

Character Male

* = Music Edit Required
+ = Ethnic Specific

Show	Year	Role	Song	Tempo	Vocal Type	Range-Bottom	Range-Top	Category
Blood Brothers	1993	Narrator	Madman	Uptempo	Tenor	F2	C4	Lead
Beauty and the Beast	1994	Lefou	Gaston	Uptempo	Tenor	B2	E4	Supporting
Passion	1994	Lt. Torasso	Christmas Music	Moderate Tempo	Tenor	Eb3	F4	Lead
Rent	1996	Mark Cohen	Halloween	Moderate Tempo	Tenor	Eb3	Eb4	Lead
Rent	1996	Mark Cohen	You Are What You Own*	Uptempo	Tenor	D3	E4	Lead
A Christmas Carol	1997	Bob Cratchit	Christmas Together	Uptempo	Tenor	D3	D4	Supporting
A Christmas Carol	1997	Ghost...Past	The Lights of Long Ago	Uptempo	Tenor	E3	E4	Supporting
A Christmas Carol	1997	Ghost...Past	Abundance and Charity	Uptempo	Tenor	A#2	F#4	Supporting
A Christmas Carol	1997	Jacob Marley	Link By Link	Uptempo	Tenor	D3	Ab4	Lead
Cabaret	1997	Master of Cereomonies	I Don't Care Much	Ballad	Tenor	D3	F4	Lead
A Christmas Carol	1997	Scrooge-Adult	Yesterday, Tomorrow and Today	Ballad	Tenor	D3	E4	Lead
A Christmas Carol	1997	Scrooge-Adult	Nothing To Do With Me	Uptempo	Tenor	D3	Eb4	Lead
A Christmas Carol	1997	Scrooge-Adult	Will Tiny Tim Live	Ballad	Tenor	D3	E4	Lead
A Christmas Carol	1997	Scrooge-Adult	Christmas Day (Final Scene P2)	Uptempo	Tenor	C3	E4	Lead
Ragtime	1998	Harry Houdini	Harry Houdini Master...(Part 1&2)	Moderate Tempo	Tenor	Db3	Gb4	Lead
Ragtime	1998	Harry Houdini	Atlantic City (Part 3)*	Uptempo	Tenor	E3	G4	Lead
Ragtime	1998	Henry Ford	Henry Ford*	Uptempo	Tenor	D3	G4	Lead
Full Monty, The	2000	Malcolm MacGregor	You Walk With With Me *	Ballad	Tenor	F#3	A4	Lead
Spitfire Grill	2001	Joe Sutter	This Wide Woods Part 2	Uptempo	Tenor	E3	F4	Lead
Spitfire Grill	2001	Joe Sutter	Forest For The Trees	Uptempo	Tenor	D3	A4	Lead
Wicked	2003	Father	No One Mourns The Wicked*	Moderate Tempo	Tenor	D3	G4	Supporting
Fame	2003	Joe	I Can't Keep It Down *	Uptempo	Tenor	C3	Bb4	Supporting
Avenue Q	2003	Nicky	If You Were Gay	Uptempo	Tenor	C3	A4	Lead
Avenue Q	2003	Rod	My Girlfriend Who Lives In Canada	Uptempo	Tenor	B2	G4	Lead
Avenue Q	2003	Rod	Fantasies Come True	Ballad	Tenor	A2	D4	Lead
Caroline, Or Change	2004	The Dryer +	The Dryer (ms 1-24)	Moderate Tempo	Tenor	Bb2	C5	Supporting
Caroline, Or Change	2004	The Moon +	Moon Change (ms 1-12)	Ballad	Tenor	Bb2	G4	Supporting
Chitty Chitty Bang Bang	2005	Baron Bomburst	Chu-Chi Face	Moderate Tempo	Tenor	C3	G4	Supporting

Character Male

* = Music Edit Required
+ = Ethnic Specific

Show	Year	Role	Song	Tempo	Vocal Type	Range-Bottom	Range-Top	Category
All Shook Up	2005	Dennis	It Hurts Me	Ballad	Tenor	A2	Bb4	Supporting
Dirty Rotten Scoundrels	2005	Freddy Benson	Great Big Stuff	Uptempo	Tenor	D3	F#4	Lead
Spamalot	2005	Minstrel	Brave Sir Robin	Moderate Tempo	Tenor	A3	D4	Supporting
Spamalot	2005	Minstrel	Brave Sir Robin Reprise	Moderate Tempo	Tenor	A3	D4	Supporting
Spamalot	2005	Patsy	Always Look...Bright Side of Life*	Moderate Tempo	Tenor	B2	F4	Supporting
Drowsy Chaperon, The	2006	Gangster	Toledo Surprise *	Uptempo	Tenor	C3	Gb4	Supporting
Legally Blonde	2007	Emmett Forrest	Chip On My Shoulder*	Uptempo	Tenor	C3	A4	Lead
Legally Blonde	2007	Emmett Forrest	Legally Blonde (ms 101b-166)	Ballad	Tenor	E3	G4	Lead
The Little Mermaid	2007	Scuttle	Human Stuff*	Uptempo	Tenor	B2	G4	Lead
The Little Mermaid	2007	Scuttle	Positoovity	Uptempo	Tenor	G2	A4	Lead
The Little Mermaid	2007	Sebastian	The World Above Reprise	Moderate Tempo	Tenor	C3	E4	Lead
The Little Mermaid	2007	Sebastian	Kiss The Girl	Moderate Tempo	Tenor	D3	F4	Lead
The Little Mermaid	2007	Sebastian	Kiss The Girl*	Moderate Tempo	Tenor	A2	C4	Lead
In The Heights	2008	Piragua Guy+	Piragua	Uptempo	Tenor	E3	A4	Supporting
In The Heights	2008	Piragua Guy+	Piragua Reprise*	Uptempo	Tenor	D3	A4	Supporting
Next To Normal	2009	Dan	Who's Crazy*	Moderate Tempo	Tenor	G3	F4	Lead
Next To Normal	2009	Dan	He's Not Here	Ballad	Tenor	Eb3	G4	Lead
Next To Normal	2009	Dan	I Am The One*	Uptempo	Tenor	E3	F#4	Lead
Next To Normal	2009	Dan	I've Been	Uptempo	Tenor	E3	G4	Lead
Next To Normal	2009	Dan	A Light In The Dark*	Ballad	Tenor	D3	E4	Lead
Next To Normal	2009	Dan	It's Gonna Be Good Reprise*	Uptempo	Tenor	A2	F4	Lead
Next To Normal	2009	Dan	A Promies*	Uptempo	Tenor	C3	F4	Lead
Next To Normal	2009	Dr. Madden	Make Up Your Mind*	Moderate Tempo	Tenor	Ab3	Ab4	Lead
Next To Normal	2009	Dr. Madden	Make Up Your Mind Reprise	Moderate Tempo	Tenor	A3	G4	Lead
Next To Normal	2009	Dr. Madden	Open Your Eyes*	Moderate Tempo	Tenor	F3	A4	Lead
Kinky Boots	2013	Lola (Drag)	The Land of Lola	Uptempo	Tenor	F#3	F#4	Lead
Kinky Boots	2013	Lola (Drag)	The Sex Is In the Heel	Moderate Tempo	Tenor	A3	B4	Lead
Kinky Boots	2013	Lola (Drag)	Not My Father's Son*	Ballad	Tenor	E3	A4	Lead
Kinky Boots	2013	Lola (Drag)	What a Woman Wants	Moderate Tempo	Tenor	E3	A4	Lead

Character Male

* = Music Edit Required
+ = Ethnic Specific

Show	Year	Role	Song	Tempo	Vocal Type	Range-Bottom	Range-Top	Category
Kinky Boots	2013	Lola (Drag)	Hold Me In Your Heart	Ballad	Tenor	E3	B♭4	Lead

Maternal

* = Music Edit Required
+ = Ethnic Specific

Show	Year	Role	Song	Tempo	Vocal Type	Range-Bottom	Range-Top	Category
Fiddler on The Roof	1964	Golde	Sabbath Prayer	Ballad	Alto	D4	C5	Lead
Fiddler on The Roof	1964	Golde	Sunrise Sunset	Ballad	Alto	C4	D5	Lead
Pippin	1972	Berthe	No Time At All*	Uptempo	Alto	G3	A4	Lead
Wiz, The	1974	Aunt Em	The Feeling We Once Had	Moderate Tempo	Alto	G3	C5	Supporting
Meet Me In St. Louis	1989	Anna Smith	Wasn't It Fun*	Ballad	Alto	F3	C4	Lead
Meet Me In St. Louis	1989	Anna Smith	A Day In New York*	Uptempo	Alto	B3	E4	Lead
Meet Me In St. Louis	1989	Anna Smith	You'll Hear A Bill	Moderate Tempo	Alto	Bb3	D5	Lead
Meet Me In St. Louis	1989	Anna Smith	You'll Hear A Bell Reprise	Moderate Tempo	Alto	Bb3	Bb4	Lead
Once On This Island	1990	Mama Euralie+	Ti Moune*	Ballad	Alto	Gb3	Bb4	Lead
Children of Eden	1991	Eve	The Spark of Creation	Uptempo	Alto	G#3	Eb5	Lead
Children of Eden	1991	Eve	Grateful Children *	Moderate Tempo	Alto	B3	D#4	Lead
Children of Eden	1991	Eve	The Spark of Creation Reprise	Uptempo	Alto	Ab3	Db5	Supporting
Children of Eden	1991	Eve	Children Of Eden	Moderate Tempo	Alto	Ab3	Eb5	Lead
Children of Eden	1991	Mama Noah	The Spark Of Creation Reprise 2	Uptempo	Alto	A3	A4	Lead
Children of Eden	1991	Mama Noah	Ain't It Good	Moderate Tempo	Alto	A3	A5	Lead
My Favorite Year	1992	Belle Carroca	Rookie In The Ring*	Ballad	Alto	G3	Bb4	Lead
Honk	1993	Ida	The Joy of Motherhood*	Uptempo	Alto	G#3	C#5	Lead
Honk	1993	Ida	Different Pre-Reprise	Ballad	Alto	Ab3	A4	Lead
Honk	1993	Ida	Hold Your Head Up High	Moderate Tempo	Alto	G#3	C5	Lead
Honk	1993	Ida	Every Tear a Mother Cries	Ballad	Alto	F3	A4	Lead
Honk	1993	Maureen	The Joy of Motherhood*	Uptempo	Alto	G#3	C#5	Supporting
Footloose	1998	Ethel McCormick	Learning To Be Silent	Ballad	Alto	Ab3	D5	Lead
Parade	1998	Mrs. Phagan	My Child Will Forgive Me	Ballad	Alto	F#3	A4	Lead
Footloose	1998	Vi Moore	Learning To Be Silent	Ballad	Alto	Ab3	D5	Lead
Footloose	1998	Vi Moore	Can You Find It In Your Heart	Ballad	Alto	A3	Db5	Supporting
Little Women	2005	Marmee	Here Alone	Ballad	Alto	G3	Eb5	Lead
Little Women	2005	Marmee	Days of Plenty	Ballad	Alto	Eb3	Db5	Lead

Maternal

101

Maternal

* = Music Edit Required
+ = Ethnic Specific

Show	Year	Role	Song	Tempo	Vocal Type	Range-Bottom	Range-Top	Category
All Shook Up	2005	Sylvia	There's Always Me	Ballad	Alto	G3	F5	Supporting
Mary Poppins	2006	Winifred Banks	Being Mrs. Banks*	Moderate Tempo	Alto	G#3	B4	Lead
Mary Poppins	2006	Winifred Banks	Being Mrs. Banks*	Ballad	Alto	G#3	Db5	Lead
Mary Poppins	2006	Winifred Banks	A Man Has Dreams Reprise	Ballad	Alto	Bb2	C4	Lead
In The Heights	2008	Camila Rosario+	Enough*	Moderate Tempo	Alto	G3	Db5	Lead
Baby	1983	Arlene McNally	I Want It All *	Uptempo	Soprano	B3	Eb5	Lead
Baby	1983	Arlene McNally	And What If We'd Loved Like That *	Moderate Tempo	Soprano	D4	F5	Lead
Closer Than Ever	1989	Woman One	She Loves Me Not *	Ballad	Soprano	Bb3	Eb5	Lead
Closer Than Ever	1989	Woman One	The Bear, the Tiger, the Hampster...	Uptempo	Soprano	Ab3	Db4	Lead
Closer Than Ever	1989	Woman One	Life Story	Moderate Tempo	Soprano	Bb3	C5	Lead
Closer Than Ever	1989	Woman One	Patterns	Ballad	Soprano	Bb3	Eb5	Lead
Closer Than Ever	1989	Woman One	It's Never That Easy *	Ballad	Soprano	B3	G5	Lead
Beauty and the Beast	1994	Mrs. Potts	Home Reprise	Ballad	Soprano	G3	D5	Supporting
Beauty and the Beast	1994	Mrs. Potts	Beauty and the Beast	Ballad	Soprano	F3	B4	Supporting
Beauty and the Beast	1994	Mrs. Potts	Be Our Guest Reprise	Uptempo	Soprano	G3	G5	Supporting
Billy Elliot	2008	Dead Mum	The Letter *	Ballad	Soprano	G3	D5	Supporting
Addams Family, The	2010	Alice Beineke	Waiting	Moderate Tempo	Soprano	Ab3	E5	Supporting
Heathers	2014	Mrs. Fleming	Shine A Light*	Uptempo	Soprano	G3	F5	Supporting

Maternal

Paternal

* = Music Edit Required
+ = Ethnic Specific

Show	Year	Role	Song	Tempo	Vocal Type	Range-Bottom	Range-Top	Category
Fantasticks, The	1960	Bellomy	Never Say No *	Uptempo	Baritone	G3	E4	Supporting
Fantasticks, The	1960	Bellomy	Plant A Raddish *	Uptempo	Baritone	C3	F4	Supporting
Fantasticks, The	1960	Bellomy	It Depends On What You Pay Reprise *	Uptempo	Baritone	D3	G4	Supporting
Fantasticks, The	1960	Huckabee	Never Say No *	Uptempo	Baritone	C3	E4	Supporting
Fantasticks, The	1960	Huckabee	Plant A Raddish *	Uptempo	Baritone	C3	F4	Supporting
Fantasticks, The	1960	Huckabee	It Depends On What You Pay Reprise *	Uptempo	Baritone	D3	G4	Supporting
110 In The Shade	1963	H.C. Curry	Lizzie's Comin' Home *	Uptempo	Baritone	B2	E4	Supporting
Fiddler on The Roof	1964	Tevye	If I Were A Rich Man	Moderate Tempo	Baritone	Db3	F4	Lead
Fiddler on The Roof	1964	Tevye	Sabbath Prayer	Ballad	Baritone	D3	C4	Lead
Fiddler on The Roof	1964	Tevye	Sunrise Sunset	Ballad	Baritone	C3	D4	Lead
Fiddler on The Roof	1964	Tevye	Chavaleh	Ballad	Baritone	C3	C4	Lead
Fiddler on The Roof	1964	Tevye	Tevye's Monologue	Moderate Tempo	Baritone	Ab2	E4	Lead
Fiddler on The Roof	1964	Tevye	Tevye's Rebuttal	Moderate Tempo	Baritone	Ab2	E4	Lead
Baby	1983	Alan McNally	Easier To Love	Ballad	Baritone	C3	D4	Lead
Baby	1983	Alan McNally	And What If We'd Loved Like That *	Moderate Tempo	Baritone	D3	Gb4	Lead
Rags	1986	Avram Cohen	Three Sunny Rooms*	Moderate Tempo	Baritone	C3	D4	Lead
Meet Me In St. Louis	1989	Alonso Smith	Wasn't It Fun*	Ballad	Baritone	Ab2	Bb3	Lead
Closer Than Ever	1989	Man Two	She Loves Me Not *	Ballad	Baritone	C3	E4	Lead
Closer Than Ever	1989	Man Two	There *	Moderate Tempo	Baritone	A2	F4	Lead
Closer Than Ever	1989	Man Two	If I Sing	Ballad	Baritone	A2	Eb4	Lead
Closer Than Ever	1989	Man Two	Father of Fathers *	Ballad	Baritone	D3	F4	Lead
Once On This Island	1990	Tonton Julian+	Ti Moune*	Ballad	Baritone	G2	Eb4	Lead
Honk!	1993	Drake	A Poultry Tale	Uptempo	Baritone	C3	F4	Lead
Honk!	1993	Drake	The Collage	Uptempo	Baritone	G#2	E3	Lead
Blood Brothers	1993	Mr. Lyons	Miss Jones	Uptempo	Baritone	C3	D4	Supporting
Beauty and the Beast	1994	Maurice	No Matter What	Uptempo	Baritone	B2	Db4	Supporting
Beauty and the Beast	1994	Maurice	No Matter What Reprise	Uptempo	Baritone	Bb2	G3	Supporting
State Fair 1996	1996	Abel Frake	Boys And Girls Like You And Me*	Moderate Tempo	Baritone	Bb2	C4	Lead

Paternal

103

* = Music Edit Required
+ = Ethnic Specific

Show			Song			Range-Bottom	Range-Top	Category
Caroline, Or Change	2004	Stuart Gellman	Moon, Emmie, Stuart Trio (ms 6-76)	Ballad	Baritone	B♭2	E♭4	Supporting
Caroline, Or Change	2004	Stuart Gellman	There Is No God, Noah (ms 1-31)	Moderate Tempo	Baritone	E3	C#4	Supporting
Spamalot	2005	Dad	I Am Not Dead Yet	Uptempo	Baritone	C3	E4	Lead
Mary Poppins	2006	George Banks	Cherry Tree Lane*	Uptempo	Baritone	B♭2	E♭4	Lead
Mary Poppins	2006	George Banks	A Man Has Dreams	Ballad	Baritone	B♭2	E♭4	Lead
Billy Elliot	2008	Dad	Deep In The Ground *	Ballad	Baritone	B♭2	E♭4	Lead
In The Heights	2008	Kevin Rosario+	Inutil	Ballad	Baritone	C3	E4	Lead
In The Heights	2008	Kevin Rosario+	Atencion	Ballad	Baritone	F#3	D4	Lead
Addams Family, The	2010	Mal Geineke	In The Arms	Moderate Tempo	Baritone	C3	F4	Supporting
Children of Eden	1991	Noah	Blind Obedience	Ballad	Tenor	D3	A3	Lead
Children of Eden	1991	Noah	Noah's Lullaby	Ballad	Tenor	C3	D4	Lead
Children of Eden	1991	Noah	The Hardest Part Of Love *	Uptempo	Tenor	D3	G4	Lead
Footloose	1998	Rev. Shaw Moore	Heaven Help Me	Uptempo	Tenor	G2	E4	Lead
Footloose	1998	Rev. Shaw Moore	I Confess	Moderate Tempo	Tenor	B2	F4	Lead
Footloose	1998	Rev. Shaw Moore	Can You Find It In Your Heart	Ballad	Tenor	A2	C4	Lead
Ragtime	1998	Tateh	Journey On*	Uptempo	Tenor	D♭3	G♭4	Lead
Ragtime	1998	Tateh	Success (Part 1, 2 & 5)	Uptempo	Tenor	D3	F#4	Lead
Ragtime	1998	Tateh	Gliding (Part 1 & 2)	Moderate Tempo	Tenor	A2	F#4	Lead
Ragtime	1998	Tateh	Buffalo Nickel Photoplay Inc.	Uptempo	Tenor	B2	F#4	Lead
Hairspray	2002	Wilbur Turnblad	Timeless To Me	Moderate Tempo	Tenor	A#2	A4	Lead
Heathers	2014	Ram's Dad	My Dead Gay Son	Uptempo	Tenor	C3	A4	Supporting

* = Music Edit Required
+ = Ethnic Specific

Show	Year	Role	Song	Tempo	Vocal Type	Range-Bottom	Range-Top	Category
Porgy and Bess	1935	Maria+	I Hates Yo' Struttin' Style (Spoken)	Uptempo	Alto			Lead
Most Happy Fella, The	1956	Marie	A Long Time Ago*	Mod Tempo	Alto	D4	Eb5	Lead
Most Happy Fella, The	1956	Marie	Young People*	Mod Tempo	Alto	C4	E5	Lead
Bye Bye Birdie	1960	Mae Peterson	A Mother Doesn't... (TV '95)	Mod Tempo	Alto	F3	C5	Supporting
Oliver!	1963	Mrs. Bedwin	Where Is Love Reprise	Ballad	Alto	C#4	Bb4	Supporting
Hello Dolly	1964	Dolly Levi	I Put My Hand In	Uptempo	Alto	Eb3	G4	Lead
Hello Dolly	1964	Dolly Levi	Motherhood*	Uptempo	Alto	D3	F4	Lead
Hello Dolly	1964	Dolly Levi	Before The Parade Passes By	Mod Tempo	Alto	D3	F4	Lead
Hello Dolly	1964	Dolly Levi	Hello Dolly	Mod Tempo	Alto	Bb2	F4	Lead
Hello Dolly	1964	Dolly Levi	So Long Dearie	Uptempo	Alto	D3	G4	Lead
Hello Dolly	1964	Dolly Levi	I Put My Hand In	Uptempo	Alto	Ab3	C5	Lead
Hello Dolly	1964	Dolly Levi	Motherhood	Uptempo	Alto	F3	A4	Lead
Hello Dolly	1964	Dolly Levi	Before The Parade Passes By	Mod Tempo	Alto	F3	F4	Lead
Hello Dolly	1964	Dolly Levi	Dancing*	Mod Tempo	Alto	D3	D5	Lead
Hello Dolly	1964	Dolly Levi	Before The Parade Passes By Rep	Ballad	Alto	C3	F4	Lead
Funny Girl	1964	Mrs. Brice	Who Taught Her Everything...*	Mod Tempo	Alto	A3	Eb5	Supporting
Funny Girl	1964	Mrs. Brice	If A Girl Isn't Pretty*	Mod Tempo	Alto	G#3	C#5	Supporting
Cabaret	1966	Fraulein Scheider	So What?	Uptempo	Alto	F3	G4	Supporting
Cabaret	1966	Fraulein Scheider	What Would You Do	Ballad	Alto	F3	G4	Supporting
Dear World	1969	Countess Aurelia	I Don't Want To Know	Mod Tempo	Alto	G#3	A4	Lead
Dear World	1969	Countess Aurelia	Each Tomorrow Morning	Mod Tempo	Alto	E3	Bb4	Lead
Dear World	1969	Countess Aurelia	One Person*	Uptempo	Alto	F3	Bb4	Lead
Dear World	1969	Countess Aurelia	Thoughts	Uptempo	Alto	G3	D5	Lead
Dear World	1969	Countess Aurelia	And I Was Beautiful	Ballad	Alto	G3	D5	Lead
Dear World	1969	Countess Aurelia	Dear World*	Mod Tempo	Alto	E3	A4	Lead
Dear World	1969	Countess Aurelia	Kiss Her Now	Ballad	Alto	G#3	A4	Lead
Hello Dolly	1970	Dolly Levi	World Take Me Back	Mod Tempo	Alto	C4	E5	Lead
Hello Dolly	1970	Dolly Levi	Love, Look In MY Window	Ballad	Alto	C4	F5	Lead

Mature Female

* = Music Edit Required
+ = Ethnic Specific

Show	Year	Role	Song	Tempo	Vocal Type	Range-Bottom	Range-Top	Category
Grease	1971	Miss Lynch	Born to Hand Jive	Uptempo	Alto	D4	B4	Supporting
Follies	1971	Stella Deems	Who's That Woman *	Uptempo	Alto	E3	A4	Supporting
A Little Night Music	1973	Madame Armfeldt	Liaisons	Mod Tempo	Alto	G#3	F4	Lead
On The Twentieth Century	1978	Letitia Primrose	Repent	Uptempo	Alto	C4	F#5	Lead
On The Twentieth Century	1978	Letitia Primrose	Five Zeros*	Mod Tempo	Alto	Ab3	Eb5	Lead
Cats	1981	Grizabella	Grizabella the Glamour Cat	Ballad	Alto	G3	C5	Lead
Cats	1981	Grizabella	Memory	Ballad	Alto	G3	E5	Lead
Sunday...Park With Geroge	1984	Old Lady	Beautiful*	Ballad	Alto	F#3	B4	Supporting
Rags	1986	Rachel Halpern	Penny A Tune	Uptempo	Alto	G3	Bb4	Lead
Rags	1986	Rachel Halpern	Three Sunny Rooms*	Mod Tempo	Alto	G3	Bb4	Lead
Once On This Island	1990	Mama Euralie+	Come Down From The Tree	Mod Tempo	Alto	A3	E5	Lead
Nick & Nora	1991	Lorraine Bixby	Men*	Mod Tempo	Alto	F3	Cb5	Lead
Honk!	1993	Lowbutt	It Takes All Sorts*	Uptempo	Alto	C#4	D5	Supporting
Kiss Of The Spider Woman	1993	Mother	Dear One*	Ballad	Alto	Bb3	C5	Lead
Kiss Of The Spider Woman	1993	Mother	You Could Never Shame Me	Mod Tempo	Alto	F3	D5	Lead
Honk!	1993	Queenie	It Takes All Sorts*	Uptempo	Alto	C#4	D5	Supporting
Steel Pier	1997	Shelby Stevens	Everybody's Girl	Uptempo	Alto	G3	C5	Lead
Steel Pier	1997	Shelby Stevens	Everybody's Girl Encore	Uptempo	Alto	G3	Bb4	Lead
Steel Pier	1997	Shelby Stevens	Somebody Older	Mod Tempo	Alto	G3	Bb4	Lead
Full Monty, The	2000	Jeanette Burmeister	Jeanette's Showbiz Number	Mod Tempo	Alto	F3	Db5	Supporting
Jane Eyre	2000	Mrs. Fairfax	Perfectly Nice	Uptempo	Alto	A3	C#5	Lead
Jane Eyre	2000	Mrs. Fairfax	Slip of a Girl	Uptempo	Alto	F3	Bb4	Lead
Jane Eyre	2000	Mrs. Reed	Forgiveness Reprise	Mod Tempo	Alto	G#3	B4	Supporting
A Man Of No Importance	2002	Lily Byrne	The Burden of Life	Uptempo	Alto	F#3	C5	Lead
A Man Of No Importance	2002	Lily Byrne	Tell Me Why	Ballad	Alto	G3	Bb4	Lead
A Man Of No Importance	2002	Lily Byrne	The Girl That Was Me	Uptempo	Alto	A3	A4	Lead
A Man Of No Importance	2002	Lily Byrne	Burden of Life Part 1	Uptempo	Alto	Ab3	Ab4	Lead

* = Music Edit Required
+ = Ethnic Specific

Show	Year	Role	Song	Tempo	Vocal Type	Range-Bottom	Range-Top	Category
Wicked	2003	Madam Morrible	Thank Goodness (Part 3)	Uptempo	Alto	A3	B4	Lead
Wicked	2003	Madam Morrible	The Wizard and I*	Mod Tempo	Alto	Gb3	Bb4	Lead
Fame	2003	Miss Sherman	These Are My Children	Ballad	Alto	F3	C5	Supporting
Little Women	2005	Aunt March	Could You*	Uptempo	Alto	D3	F5	Supporting
All Shook Up	2005	Mayor Matilda Hyde	Devil In Disguise	Uptempo	Alto	C4	F#5	Supporting
Grey Gardens	2006	Edith Beale (Act 2)	The Girl Who Has Everything*	Mod Tempo	Alto	C4	Eb5	Lead
Grey Gardens	2006	Edith Beale (Act 2)	The Cake I Had*	Mod Tempo	Alto	E#3	A#4	Lead
Grey Gardens	2006	Edith Beale (Act 2)	Jerry Likes My Corn	Mod Tempo	Alto	G3	F5	Lead
Drowsy Chaperon, The	2006	Mrs. Tottendale	Love Is Always Lovely *	Mod Tempo	Alto	G3	Bb4	Supporting
In The Heights	2008	Abuela Claudia	Paciencia Y Fe	Uptempo	Alto	F3	C5	Lead
Billy Elliot	2008	Grandma	We'd Go Dancing	Mod Tempo	Alto	F3	G4	Supporting
Carousel	1945	Nettie Fowler	June Is Bustin' Out All Over *	Uptempo	Soprano	D4	E5	Lead
Carousel	1945	Nettie Fowler	You'll Never Walk Alone	Mod Tempo	Soprano	C4	G5	Lead
Carousel	1945	Nettie Fowler	June Is Bustin' Out All Over Reprise	Uptempo	Soprano	E4	E5	Lead
Carousel	1945	Nettie Fowler	June...Finale Act One	Uptempo	Soprano	E4	E5	Lead
Damn Yankees	1955	Meg Boyd	Six Months Out of Every Year	Uptempo	Soprano	A3	D5	Supporting
Damn Yankees	1955	Meg Boyd	A Man Doesn't Know	Ballad	Soprano	G3	Db5	Supporting
Damn Yankees	1955	Meg Boyd	There's Something...Empty Chair	Ballad	Soprano			Supporting
Damn Yankees	1955	Meg Boyd	Near To You*	Ballad	Soprano	B3	Eb5	Supporting
Damn Yankees	1955	Meg Boyd	A Man Doesn't Know Reprise	Ballad	Soprano	G3	D5	Supporting
Candide	1956	Old Lady	I Am Easily Assimilated*	Mod Tempo	Soprano	D4	A5	Lead
Sound Of Music, The	1959	Mother Abbess	Climb Every Mountain	Ballad	Soprano	C4	Ab5	Lead
1776	1969	Abigail Adams	Compliments	Uptempo	Soprano	D4	Eb5	Supporting
Dear World	1969	Countess Aurelia	Through The Bottom Of The Glass	Mod Tempo	Soprano	E3	A4	Lead
Dear World	1969	Madame Constance	Memory	Mod Tempo	Soprano	A3	F5	Lead
Dear World	1969	Madame Constance	Voices	Uptempo	Soprano	F4	E5	Lead
Dear World	1969	Madame Gabrielle	Dickie	Uptempo	Soprano	G3	E5	Lead

Mature Female

* = Music Edit Required
+ = Ethnic Specific

Show	Year	Role	Song	Tempo	Vocal Type	Range-Bottom	Range-Top	Category
Follies	1971	Emily Whitman	Rain On The Roof *	Uptempo	Soprano	B♭3	D5	Supporting
Follies	1971	Heidi Schiller	One More Kiss ×	Ballad	Soprano	D4	F5	Supporting
Cats	1981	Jellylorum	Gus: The Theatre Cat	Ballad	Soprano	A3	D5	Supporting
Cats	1981	Jennyanydots	Bustopher Jones *	Uptempo	Soprano	B3	F5	Supporting
Mary Poppins	2006	Bird Woman	Feed The Birds*	Uptempo	Soprano	G♭3	D♭5	Ensemble
White Christmas	2008	Martha Watson	Let Me sing And I'm Happy	Mod Tempo	Soprano	F3	G4	Lead
White Christmas	2008	Martha Watson	Falling Out Of Love Can Be Fun*	Uptempo	Soprano	G3	C5	Lead

Mature Female

* = Music Edit Rquired
+ = Ehtnic Specific

Show	Year	Role	Song	Tempo	Vocal Type	Range-Bottom	Range-Top	Category
No, No Nanette	1925	Jimmy Smith	I Want To Be Happy*	Uptempo	Baritone	C#3	F#4	Lead
Oklahoma!	1943	Old Man Carnes	The Farmer And The Cowman*	Moderate Tempo	Baritone	F3	F4	Supporting
On The Town	1944	Pitkin Bridgework	I Understand	Uptempo	Baritone	A2	D4	Supporting
Guys and Dolls	1950	Arvide	More I Cannot Wish You	Moderate Tempo	Baritone	D4	D5	Supporting
Damn Yankees	1955	Joe Boyd	Goodbye Old Girl	Ballad	Baritone	D3	E4	Lead
Damn Yankees	1955	Joe Boyd	Near To You	Ballad	Baritone	C3	C4	Supporting
Most Happy Fella, The	1956	Tony	Most Happy Fella (ms 74-109 & 131-157)	Uptempo	Baritone	E♭3	G4	Lead
Most Happy Fella, The	1956	Tony	Soon You Gonna Leave Me Joe	Moderate Tempo	Baritone	C#3	E4	Lead
Most Happy Fella, The	1956	Tony	Rosabella	Moderate Tempo	Baritone	E♭3	G4	Lead
Most Happy Fella, The	1956	Tony	Plenty Bambini	Ballad	Baritone	C#3	F#4	Lead
Most Happy Fella, The	1956	Tony	Old People Gotta Dance	Moderate Tempo	Baritone	C3	C4	Lead
Most Happy Fella, The	1956	Tony	My Heart Is So Full Of You*	Ballad	Baritone	D♭3	G♭4	Lead
Most Happy Fella, The	1956	Tony	Mamma, Mamma	Moderate Tempo	Baritone	C#3	G4	Lead
Most Happy Fella, The	1956	Tony	Tony's Thoughts	Ballad	Baritone	D3	F4	Lead
Most Happy Fella, The	1956	Tony	I Canno' Leave You Money	Moderate Tempo	Baritone	D#3	E♭4	Lead
Flower Drum Song 2002	1958	Chin+	My Best Love*	Ballad	Baritone	D#3	E4	Lead
A Funny Thing...Forum	1962	Pseudolus	Free*	Uptempo	Baritone	B2	F4	Lead
A Funny Thing...Forum	1962	Pseudolus	Pretty Little Picture*	Uptempo	Baritone	B2	F#4	Lead
A Funny Thing...Forum	1962	Pseudolus	Lovely Reprise*	Moderate Tempo	Baritone	D3	F4	Lead
A Funny Thing...Forum	1962	Sinex	Everybody Ought To Have A Maid*	Uptempo	Baritone	C#3	E4	Lead
Oliver!	1963	Fagin	Pick A Pocket Or Two	Uptempo	Baritone	D3	E♭4	Lead
Oliver!	1963	Fagin	Be Back Soon*	Uptempo	Baritone	C3	E4	Lead
Oliver!	1963	Fagin	Reviewing The Situation	Uptempo	Baritone	C3	F4	Lead
She Loves Me	1963	Mr. Maraczek	Days Gone By*	Uptempo	Baritone	B♭2	C4	Lead
She Loves Me	1963	Mr. Maraczek	Days Gone By Reprise	Uptempo	Baritone	B2	E4	Lead
Hello Dolly	1964	Horace Vandergelder	It Takes A Woman	Uptempo	Baritone	B2	G5	Lead
Hello Dolly	1964	Horace Vandergelder	Hello Dolly	Moderate Tempo	Baritone	B2	D4	Lead
Cabaret	1966	Herr Schultz	Married *	Ballad	Baritone	D3	F4	Supporting
Cabaret	1966	Herr Schultz	Married Reprise	Ballad	Baritone	C3	D4	Supporting

Mature Male

109

* = Music Edit Rquired
+ = Ehtnic Specific

Show	Year	Role	Song	Tempo	Vocal Type	Range-Bottom	Range-Top	Category
1776	1969	John Adams	Piddle, Twiddle, and Resolve	Uptempo	Baritone	D♭3	E♭4	Lead
1776	1969	John Adams	Is Anybody There? (ms 57-135)	Uptempo	Baritone	D3	E4	Lead
Company (Revival)	1970	Larry	Sorry Grateful	Ballad	Baritone	B2	E4	Supporting
Company (Revival)	1970	Larry	Have I Got A Girl For You	Uptempo	Baritone	B2	G♭4	Supporting
Follies	1971	Theodore Whitman	Rain On The Roof *	Uptempo	Baritone	B♭2	D4	Supporting
Sugar	1972	Sir Osgood	Beautiful Through and Through*	Moderate Tempo	Baritone	C#3	E♭4	Lead
Best Little Whorehouse...	1978	Governor	The Sidestep	Uptempo	Baritone	A2	E4	Supporting
Cats	1981	Asparagus	Gus: The Theatre Cat	Ballad	Baritone	A2	D4	Supporting
Cats	1981	Bustopher Jones	Bustopher Jones *	Uptempo	Baritone	C3	C4	Supporting
Little Shop of Horrors	1982	Mr. Mushnik	Mushnik and Son*	Uptempo	Baritone	A2	F4	Lead
Little Shop of Horrors	1982	Mr. Mushnik	Ya Never Know*	Uptempo	Baritone	C3	C4	Lead
Mystery Of Edwin Drood, The	1985	Chairman	There You Are*	Uptempo	Baritone	D3	D4	Lead
Mystery Of Edwin Drood, The	1985	Chairman	Both Sides Of The Coin*	Uptempo	Baritone	C3	F#4	Lead
Mystery Of Edwin Drood, The	1985	Chairman	Off To The Races*	Uptempo	Baritone	C3	F4	Lead
Mystery Of Edwin Drood, The	1985	Chrisparkle	Chrisparkle's Confession	Moderate Tempo	Baritone	D3	F4	Lead
Into The Woods	1987	Mysterious Man	No More*	Ballad	Baritone	B♭2	E4	Lead
Into The Woods	1987	Narrator	Act I Opening (Part 4)*	Uptempo	Baritone	G2	E4	Lead
Chess	1988	Molokov	The Soviet Machine	Uptempo	Baritone	A2	D4	Supporting
Phantom	1991	Gerard Carriere	You Are My Own*	Moderate Tempo	Baritone	G2	D4	Lead
Crazy For You (1992)	1992	Bella Zangler	What Causes That	Uptempo	Baritone	C3	F#4	Supporting
Sunset Boulevard	1994	Cecil B. DeMille	Surrender Reprise	Ballad	Baritone	A♭2	D♭4	Supporting
Parade	1998	Old Soldier	Old Red Hills Of Home (Part 2)*	Moderate Tempo	Baritone	C3	G4	Supporting
A Man Of No Importance	2002	Baldy O'Shea	The Cuddles That Mary Gave	Ballad	Baritone	E♭3	F4	Supporting
A Man Of No Importance	2002	Carney	Confussing Times	Ballad	Baritone	A2	A3	Supporting
Caroline, Or Change	2004	Mr. Stopnick	A Twenty Dollar Bil (ms 41-78)	Ballad	Baritone	C3	F4	Supporting
Chitty Chitty Bang Bang	2005	Grandpa Potts	Them Three	Uptempo	Baritone	C3	C4	Supporting
Chitty Chitty Bang Bang	2005	Grandpa Potts	Posh	Uptempo	Baritone	C3	C4	Supporting
Grey Gardens	2006	Major Bouvier	Marry Well*	Moderate Tempo	Baritone	A#2	E4	Supporting

Mature Male

* = Music Edit Rquired
+ = Ehtnic Specific

Show	Year	Role	Song	Tempo	Vocal Type	Range-Bottom	Range-Top	Category
Grey Gardens	2006	Norman Vincent Peale	Choose To Be Happy*	Moderate Tempo	Baritone	G2	E4	Supporting
Addams Family, The	2010	Uncle Fester	The Moon And Me	Ballad	Baritone	C3	E4	Supporting
High Society 1998	1929	Uncle Willie	She's Got That Thing*	Uptempo	Tenor	G2	G4	Lead
High Society 1998	1930	Uncle Willie	I'm Getting Ready For You*	Uptempo	Tenor	B♭2	E4	Lead
High Society 1998	1930	Uncle Willie	Say It With Gin	Uptempo	Tenor	C3	C4	Lead
Candide	1956	Martin	Words, Words, Words	Moderate Tempo	Tenor	A2	F4	Supporting
How To Succeed...	1961	JB Biggley	Grand Old Ivy*	Uptempo	Tenor	C3	G4	Lead
How To Succeed...	1961	JB Biggley	Love From A Heart Of Gold*	Ballad	Tenor	C#3	E4	Lead
How To Succeed...	1961	Twimble	Company Way*	Uptempo	Tenor	D3	G4	Supporting
A Funny Thing...Forum	1962	Hysterium	I'm Calm	Uptempo	Tenor	D3	F4	Lead
A Funny Thing...Forum	1962	Hysterium	Lovely Reprise*	Moderate Tempo	Tenor	E3	F4	Lead
Follies	1971	Roscoe	Beautiful Girls	Moderate Tempo	Tenor	D3	A4	Supporting
Cats	1981	Old Deuteronomy	Old Deuteronomy *	Ballad	Tenor	B2	G4	Lead
Cats	1981	Old Deuteronomy	The Moments of Happiness	Ballad	Tenor	B3	G5	Lead
Cats	1981	Old Deuteronomy	The Ad-Dressing of Cats	Moderate Tempo	Tenor	B♭2	G4	Lead

Mature Male

Juvenile Female

* = Music Edit Required
+ = Ethnic Specific

Show	Year	Role	Song	Tempo	Vocal Type	Range-Bottom	Range-Top	Category
110 In The Shade	1963	Girl	Cinderella	Uptempo	Alto	A3	D5	Featured Ensemble
Annie	1977	Annie	Maybe	Ballad	Alto	A3	C#5	Lead
Annie	1977	Annie	Tomorrow	Moderate Tempo	Alto	Bb3	Eb5	Lead
Into The Woods	1987	Little Red Riding Hood	I Know Things Now	Uptempo	Alto	C4	Eb5	Lead
Meet Me In St. Louis	1989	Tootie Smith	Under The Bamboo Tree*	Moderate Tempo	Alto	C4	Bb4	Lead
Secret Garden, The	1991	Mary Lennox	Show Me The Key (ms 52-92)	Moderate Tempo	Alto	B3	C#5	Lead
Secret Garden, The	1991	Mary Lennox	Storm III*	Moderate Tempo	Alto	B3	E5	Lead
Secret Garden, The	1991	Mary Lennox	The Girl I Mean To Be	Uptempo	Alto	Ab3	C5	Lead
Secret Garden, The	1991	Mary Lennox	Letter Song*	Moderate Tempo	Alto	Bb3	C5	Lead
Goodbye Girl, The	1993	Lucy McFadden	Good News, Bad News*	Moderate Tempo	Alto	Db4	Db5	Supporting
Hairspray	2002	Inez Stubs+	Run And Tell That*	Uptempo	Alto	F4	E5	Lead
Chitty Chitty Bang Bang	2005	Children	Teamwork*	Uptempo	Alto	C4	Eb5	Featured Ensemble
Mary Poppins	2006	Jane Banks	The Perfect Nanny*	Moderate Tempo	Alto	A3	B4	Lead
Mary Poppins	2006	Jane Banks	Anything Can Happen*	Moderate Tempo	Alto	C4	D5	Lead
13 The Musical	2008	Cassie (IF)	A Brand New You*	Uptempo	Alto	C4	F5	Supporting
13 The Musical	2008	Lucy (RAF)	It Can't Be True*	Uptempo	Alto	F#3	C5	Lead
13 The Musical	2008	Lucy (RAF)	Opportunity*	Uptempo	Alto	B3	E4	Lead
13 The Musical	2008	Patrice (CIF)	The Lamest Place In The World	Uptempo	Alto	B3	D#5	Lead
13 The Musical	2008	Patrice (CIF)	Good Enough	Ballad	Alto	G3	C5	Lead
13 The Musical	2008	Patrice (CIF)	Tell Her*	Ballad	Alto	Bb3	C5	Lead
13 The Musical	2008	Patrice (CIF)	If That's What It Is*	Moderate Tempo	Alto	Eb3	C5	Lead
13 The Musical	2008	Patrice (CIF)	What It Means To Be A Friend	Moderate Tempo	Alto	A3	E5	Lead
White Christmas	2008	Susan Waverly	Let Me sing And I'm Happy Rep	Uptempo	Alto	B3	B4	Lead
South Pacific	1949	Ngana	Dites-Moi Pourquoi*	Moderate Tempo	Soprano	D4	C5	Supporting
A Little Night Music	1973	Fredrika Armfeldt	The Glamorous Life	Uptempo	Soprano	C4	Eb5	Supporting
Les Miserables	1987	Young Cosette	Castle On The Cloud	Ballad	Soprano	A3	C5	Lead

Juvenile Female

Juvenile Female

Show	Year	Role	Song	Tempo	Vocal Type	Range-Bottom	Range-Top	Category
Jane Eyre	2000	Helen Burnes	Forgiveness	Ballad	Soprano	A3	C5	Supporting
Jane Eyre	2000	Young Jane Eyre	The Graveside	Ballad	Soprano	A3	D5	Supporting
Chitty Chitty Bang Bang	2005	Jemima Potts	Truy Scrumptious	Moderate Tempo	Soprano	C4	C5	Lead
Chitty Chitty Bang Bang	2005	Jemima Potts	Us Two	Ballad	Soprano	C4	C5	Lead

Juvenile Female

Juvenile Male

Show	Year	Role	Song	Tempo	Vocal Type	Range-Bottom	Range-Top	Category
Oliver!	1963	Artful Dodger	Consider Yourself (Part One)*	Uptempo	Alto	A3	F5	Lead
Mame	1966	Young Patrick Dennis	You're My Best Girl*	Ballad	Alto	A3	C5	Lead
Mame	1966	Young Patrick Dennis	The Letter*	Uptempo	Alto	C#4	Bb4	Lead
Les Miserables	1987	Gavroche	Look Down*	Moderate Tempo	Alto	C4	Db5	Supporting
Les Miserables	1987	Gavroche	Little People*	Uptempo	Alto	B3	D5	Supporting
Merrily We Roll Along 1994	1994	Frank, Jr.	Transition 7	Moderate Tempo	Alto	B2	C5	Supporting
Lion King, The	1997	Young Simba	I Just Can't Wait To Be King*	Uptempo	Alto	C4	C5	Supporting
Seussical	2000	JoJo	Alone In The Universe*	Moderate Tempo	Alto	Ab3	Ab4	Lead
Caroline, Or Change	2004	Noah Gellman	Noah Downstairs (ms 1-46)	Moderate Tempo	Alto	Bb3	Cb5	Lead
Chitty Chitty Bang Bang	2005	Children	Teamwork *	Uptempo	Alto	C4	Eb5	Featured Ensemble
Mary Poppins	2006	Michael Banks	The Perfect Nanny*	Moderate Tempo	Alto	A3	B4	Lead
Mary Poppins	2006	Michael Banks	Anything Can Happen*	Moderate Tempo	Alto	C4	D5	Lead
Billy Elliot	2008	Billy Elliot	Electricity	Ballad	Alto	F3	B4	Lead
Billy Elliot	2008	Billy Elliot	Billy's Reply *	Ballad	Alto	G3	D5	Lead
Billy Elliot	2008	Billy Elliot	The Letter *	Ballad	Alto	G3	D5	Lead
Billy Elliot	2008	Michael	Expressing Yourself	Uptempo	Alto	G3	B4	Supporting
Billy Elliot	2008	Michael	Expressing Yourself Playout	Uptempo	Alto	D4	Bb4	Supporting
King and I, The	1951	Louis Leonowens	A Puzzlement Reprise*	Uptempo	Baritone	G2	G3	Supporting
King and I, The	1951	Louis Leonowens	I Whistle A Happy Tune*	Uptempo	Baritone	B2	B3	Supporting
King and I, The	1951	Prince Chulalongkorn	A Puzzlement Reprise*	Uptempo	Baritone	G2	G3	Supporting
13 The Musical	2008	Brett (RAM)	Getting Ready*	Uptempo	Baritone	G3	F4	Supporting
South Pacific	1949	Jerome	Dites-Moi Pourquoi*	Moderate Tempo	Soprano	D4	C5	Supporting
Music Man, The	1957	Winthrop Paroo	Gary Indiana Reprise	Uptempo	Soprano	C4	Eb5	Lead
Oliver!	1963	Oliver Twist	Where Is Love	Ballad	Soprano	C4	C5	Lead
Oliver!	1963	Oliver Twist	Who Will Buy*	Moderate Tempo	Soprano	C4	C5	Lead
Cabaret	1966	Nazi Youth	Tomorrow Belongs to Me	Ballad	Soprano	F4	F#5	Featured Ensemble
Nine	1982	Young Guido Contini	Getting Tall	Moderate Tempo	Soprano	Ab3	F5	Supporting

Juvenile Male

* = Music Edit Required
+ = Ethnic Specific

Show	Year	Role	Song	Tempo	Vocal Type	Range-Bottom	Range-Top	Category
Secret Garden, The	1991	Colin Craven	Come To My Garden*	Moderate Tempo	Soprano	C4	E5	Lead
Secret Garden, The	1991	Colin Craven	Round-Shouldered Man	Uptempo	Soprano	A3	D5	Lead
A Christmas Carol	1997	Scrooge-Child	A Place Called Home	Ballad	Soprano	Bb2	A4	Lead
A Christmas Carol	1997	Tiny Tim	Christmas Together	Uptempo	Soprano	Bb4	C5	Supporting
A Christmas Carol	1997	Tiny Tim	God Bless Us Everyone	Uptempo	Soprano	D4	C5	Supporting
Chitty Chitty Bang Bang	2005	Jeremy Potts	Truy Scrumptious	Moderate Tempo	Soprano	C4	C5	Lead
Chitty Chitty Bang Bang	2005	Jeremy Potts	Us Two	Ballad	Soprano	C4	C5	Lead
The Little Mermaid	2007	Flounder	She's In Love*	Uptempo	Soprano	G3	A#5	Lead
Addams Family, The	2010	Pugsley Addams	What If	Ballad	Soprano	A3	C5	Supporting
Big	1996	Billy Kopecki	Talk To Her	Uptempo	Tenor	F2	Bb3	Supporting
Big	1996	Billy Kopecki	It's Time	Uptempo	Tenor	A2	C4	Supporting
Big	1996	Josh Baskin-Young	Talk To Her	Uptempo	Tenor	F2	Bb3	Supporting
Big	1996	Josh Baskin-Young	Opening	Uptempo	Tenor	A2	B3	Supporting
Big	1996	Josh Baskin-Young	I Want To Know	Ballad	Tenor	C3	F4	Supporting
13 The Musical	2008	Archie (CM)	Get Me What I Need	Uptempo	Tenor	C3	A4	Lead
13 The Musical	2008	Archie (CM)	Getting Ready*	Uptempo	Tenor	Eb3	Ab4	Lead
13 The Musical	2008	Evan Goldman (CM)	Becoming A Man	Uptempo	Tenor	D3	A4	Lead
13 The Musical	2008	Evan Goldman (CM)	Thirteen	Uptempo	Tenor	Bb2	Bb3	Lead
13 The Musical	2008	Evan Goldman (CM)	All Hail The Brain	Uptempo	Tenor	E3	G4	Lead
13 The Musical	2008	Evan Goldman (CM)	Terminal Illness	Uptempo	Tenor	Eb3	Ab4	Lead
13 The Musical	2008	Evan Goldman (CM)	Tell Her*	Ballad	Tenor	Bb2	G4	Lead
13 The Musical	2008	Evan Goldman (CM)	A Little More Homework*	Ballad	Tenor	C3	F4	Lead
13 The Musical	2008	Evan Goldman (CM)	Getting Ready*	Uptempo	Tenor	Db4	Bb4	Lead
13 The Musical	2008	Evan Goldman (CM)	Here I Come	Uptempo	Tenor	Eb3	Bb4	Lead
13 The Musical	2008	Evan Goldman (CM)	If That's What It Is*	Moderate Tempo	Tenor	C3	A4	Lead
13 The Musical	2008	Evan Goldman (CM)	Becoming A Man Reprise	Ballad	Tenor	E3	A4	Lead

Romantic Antagonist Female

* = Music Edit Required
+ = Ethnic Specific

Show	Year	Role	Song	Tempo	Vocal Type	Range-Bottom	Range-Top	Category
Pal Joey	1940	Gladys Bumps	You Mustn't Kick It...Encore	Uptempo	Alto	A3	C5	Lead
Pal Joey	1940	Gladys Bumps	That Terrific Rainbow	Moderate Tempo	Alto	B3	Bb4	Lead
Pal Joey	1940	Gladys Bumps	The Flower Garden Of My Heart*	Moderate Tempo	Alto	D4	F#5	Lead
Pal Joey	1940	Gladys Bumps	Plant You Now, Dig You Later	Uptempo	Alto	D4	D5	Lead
Pal Joey	1940	Melba	Zip	Moderate Tempo	Alto	F3	G4	Supporting
Pal Joey	1940	Vera Simpson	What Is A Man	Moderate Tempo	Alto	D4	Eb5	Lead
Pal Joey	1940	Vera Simpson	Bewitched Bothered...	Moderate Tempo	Alto	E4	D5	Lead
Pal Joey	1940	Vera Simpson	Bewitched...Encore	Moderate Tempo	Alto	F4	D5	Lead
Pal Joey	1940	Vera Simpson	Den Of Iniquity*	Uptempo	Alto	G4	Eb5	Lead
Pal Joey	1940	Vera Simpson	Take Him*	Moderate Tempo	Alto	C4	D5	Lead
Pal Joey	1940	Vera Simpson	Bewitched...Reprise	Moderate Tempo	Alto	D4	D5	Lead
Call Me Madam	1950	Sally Adams	The Hostess w/The Mostess	Uptempo	Alto	A3	B4	Lead
Call Me Madam	1950	Sally Adams	The Hostess...Encore	Uptempo	Alto	A3	B4	Lead
Call Me Madam	1950	Sally Adams	Washington Square Dance	Uptempo	Alto	Bb3	C5	Lead
Call Me Madam	1950	Sally Adams	Can You Use Any Money Today	Uptempo	Alto	Bb3	C5	Lead
Call Me Madam	1950	Sally Adams	Marrying For Love*	Ballad	Alto	F3	Bb4	Lead
Call Me Madam	1950	Sally Adams	The Best Thing For You	Moderate Tempo	Alto	A3	C5	Lead
Call Me Madam	1950	Sally Adams	Something To Dance About	Moderate Tempo	Alto	Bb3	C5	Lead
Call Me Madam	1950	Sally Adams	You're Just In Love*	Uptempo	Alto	D4	C5	Lead
Call Me Madam	1950	Sally Adams	The Best Thing For You Rep	Moderate Tempo	Alto	Bb3	Cb5	Lead
State Fair 1996	1953	Emily Arden	You Never Had It So Good	Uptempo	Alto	Bb3	Bb4	Lead
Pajama Game	1954	Gladys	Steam Heat*	Uptempo	Alto	C4	Eb5	Lead
Pajama Game	1954	Gladys	Hernando's Hideaway	Moderate Tempo	Alto	B3	C5	Lead
Damn Yankees	1955	Lola	Whatever Lola Wants	Moderate Tempo	Alto	G3	Db5	Lead
Damn Yankees	1955	Lola	A Little Brains A Little Talent	Uptempo	Alto	A3	B4	Lead
Damn Yankees	1955	Lola	Who's Got The Pain*	Uptempo	Alto	A3	B4	Lead
Cinderella (2013)	1957	Stepmother (Madam)	A Lovely Night*	Uptempo	Alto	B3	D5	Supporting

Romantic Antagonist Female

* = Music Edit Required
+ = Ethnic Specific

Show	Year	Role	Song	Tempo	Vocal Type	Range-Bottom	Range-Top	Category
Flower Drum Song 2002	1958	Madam Rita Liang	Grant Avenue*	Moderate Tempo	Alto	A3	C5	Lead
Once Upon A Mattress	1959	Queen Aggravain	Sensitivity*	Moderate Tempo	Alto	A3	B4	Lead
She Loves Me	1963	Ilona Ritter	I Resolve	Uptempo	Alto	Ab3	Bb4	Lead
She Loves Me	1963	Ilona Ritter	A Trip To The Library	Moderate Tempo	Alto	G3	C#5	Lead
Anyone Can Whistle	1964	Cora Hoover Hooper	Me And My Town*	Uptempo	Alto	A3	Eb5	Lead
Anyone Can Whistle	1964	Cora Hoover Hooper	There's A Parade In Town*	Uptempo	Alto	G3	Bb4	Lead
Anyone Can Whistle	1964	Cora Hoover Hooper	I've Got You To lean On*	Uptempo	Alto	Ab4	D5	Lead
Anyone Can Whistle	1964	Cora Hoover Hooper	Cora's Chase*	Uptempo	Alto	A3	E5	Lead
Sweet Charity	1966	Helene	There's Gotta Be Something...*	Uptempo	Alto	A3	Db5	Lead
Sweet Charity	1966	Nickie	There's Gotta Be Something...*	Uptempo	Alto	A3	Db4	Lead
Mame	1966	Vera Charles	The Man In The Moon	Ballad	Alto	Eb3	A4	Lead
Applause	1970	Eve Harrington	The Best Night Of My Life	Ballad	Alto	G#3	C#5	Lead
Applause	1970	Eve Harrington	Applause*	Moderate Tempo	Alto	G3	E5	Lead
Applause	1970	Eve Harrington	One Hallowe'en	Moderate Tempo	Alto	F3	Bb4	Lead
Applause	1970	Margo Channing	But Alive*	Uptempo	Alto	E3	F#4	Lead
Applause	1970	Margo Channing	Who's That Girl	Uptempo	Alto	E3	A4	Lead
Applause	1970	Margo Channing	Hurry Back	Ballad	Alto	Ab2	F4	Lead
Applause	1970	Margo Channing	Welcome To The Theatre	Moderate Tempo	Alto	D3	F#4	Lead
Applause	1970	Margo Channing	Something Greater*	Uptempo	Alto	D3	G4	Lead
Follies	1971	Phyllis Rogers Stone	Could I Leave You	Moderate Tempo	Alto	F#3	Bb4	Lead
Pippin	1972	Fastrada	Spread A Little Sunshine	Moderate Tempo	Alto	A2	F5	Lead
Sugar	1972	Sweet Sue	When You Meet A Man...*	Uptempo	Alto	Ab3	Eb5	Lead
A Chorus Line	1975	Sheila	At The Ballet	Moderate Tempo	Alto	E3	C#5	Lead
Chicago	1975	Velma Kelly	All That Jazz	Moderate Tempo	Alto	G2	Db5	Lead
Chicago	1975	Velma Kelly	I Can't Do It Alone	Uptempo	Alto	Bb3	D4	Lead
Chicago	1975	Velma Kelly	My Own Best Friend	Moderate Tempo	Alto	G3	A4	Lead
Chicago	1975	Velma Kelly	I Know A Girl	Uptempo	Alto	E3	A4	Lead

Romantic Antagonist Female

Romantic Antagonist Female

* = Music Edit Required
+ = Ethnic Specific

Show	Year	Role	Song	Tempo	Vocal Type	Range-Bottom	Range-Top	Category
Chicago	1975	Velma Kelly	Class*	Ballad	Alto	F3	B4	Lead
Chicago	1975	Velma Kelly	Nowadays	Moderate Tempo	Alto	F#3	D5	Lead
Evita	1978	Eva Peron	Buenos Aires	Uptempo	Alto	E3	F5	Lead
Evita	1978	Eva Peron	I'd Be...Good For You	Moderate Tempo	Alto	G#3	F5	Lead
Evita	1978	Eva Peron	Another Suitcase...	Ballad	Alto	A3	E5	Supporting
Evita	1978	Eva Peron	Don't Cry For Me Argentina	Alto	Alto	Ab3	Eb5	Lead
Evita	1978	Eva Peron	Rainbow High	Uptempo	Alto	G3	E5	Lead
Evita	1978	Eva Peron	The Actress Hasn't Learned...	Ballad	Alto	G#3	D#5	Lead
Evita	1978	Eva Peron	Waltz for Eva and Che	Uptempo	Alto	Ab3	F5	Lead
Evita	1978	Eva Peron	Eva's Final Broadcast	Ballad	Alto	Ab3	Db5	Lead
Evita	1978	Eva Peron	Lament	Ballad	Alto	Bb3	Db5	Lead
Nine	1982	Saraghina	Ti Voglio Bene*	Moderate Tempo	Alto	G3	Bb4	Lead
Singin' In The Rain	1983	Lina Lamont	What's Wrong With Me? (Eb Maj)	Moderate Tempo	Alto	C4	Eb5	Lead
Singin' In The Rain	1983	Lina Lamont	What's Wrong With Me? (C Maj)	Moderate Tempo	Alto	A3	C5	Lead
Mystery Of Edwin Drood	1985	Helena Landless	Helena's Confession	Moderate Tempo	Alto	G3	B4	Lead
Romance/Romance	1987	Jospehine Weninger	Goodbye Emil	Uptempo	Alto	A3	F5	Lead
Romance/Romance	1987	Jospehine Weninger	Goodbye Emil Reprise	Uptempo	Alto	Bb3	E5	Lead
Romance/Romance	1987	Jospehine Weninger	It's Not Too Late*	Moderate Tempo	Alto	G3	Cb5	Lead
Romance/Romance	1987	Jospehine Weninger	A Performance*	Moderate Tempo	Alto	G3	D#5	Lead
Romance/Romance	1987	Jospehine Weninger	I'll Remember The Song*	Uptempo	Alto	B3	D4	Lead
Romance/Romance	1987	Jospehine Weninger	Yes, It's Love	Uptempo	Alto	Ab3	C5	Lead
Romance/Romance	1987	Jospehine Weninger	A Rustic Country Inn*	Uptempo	Alto	G3	E5	Lead
Romance/Romance	1987	Jospehine Weninger	The Night It Had To End	Ballad	Alto	Ab3	Db5	Lead
Romance/Romance	1987	Monica	How Did I End Up Here	Uptempo	Alto	F3	C5	Lead
Romance/Romance	1987	Monica	Now	Uptempo	Alto	A3	D5	Lead
Romance/Romance	1987	Monica	Plan A and B	Uptempo	Alto	Ab3	A4	Lead
Into The Woods	1987	Witch	Stay With Me	Ballad	Alto	A#3	Db5	Lead

Romantic Antagonist Female

* = Music Edit Required
+ = Ethnic Specific

Show	Year	Role	Song	Tempo	Vocal Type	Range-Bottom	Range-Top	Category
Into The Woods	1987	Witch	Lament	Ballad	Alto	A3	D5	Lead
Into The Woods	1987	Witch	Last Midnight	Moderate Tempo	Alto	F3	Db5	Lead
City of Angels	1989	Mallory	Lost And Found	Ballad	Alto	G#3	F#5	Supporting
Miss Saigon	1991	Gigi Van Trahn+	The Movie In My Mind*	Ballad	Alto	Ab3	Eb5	Supporting
Nick & Nora	1991	Lily Connors	People Get Hurt	Uptempo	Alto	Ab3	Db5	Lead
Kiss Of The Spider Woman	1993	Aurora	Her Name Is Aurora*	Moderate Tempo	Alto	C3	A4	Lead
Kiss Of The Spider Woman	1993	Aurora	Spider Woman Fragment 1	Ballad	Alto	F3	F4	Lead
Kiss Of The Spider Woman	1993	Aurora	Where You Are*	Uptempo	Alto	Eb3	Gb4	Lead
Kiss Of The Spider Woman	1993	Aurora	I Do Miracles*	Moderate Tempo	Alto	B2	Ab4	Lead
Kiss Of The Spider Woman	1993	Aurora	Let's Make Love*	Uptempo	Alto	D3	A4	Lead
Kiss Of The Spider Woman	1993	Aurora	Good Times*	Uptempo	Alto	D#3	A4	Lead
Kiss Of The Spider Woman	1993	Spider Woman	Interrogation*	Moderate Tempo	Alto	F3	F4	Lead
Kiss Of The Spider Woman	1993	Spider Woman	Kiss Of The Spider Woman	Uptempo	Alto	C#3	A4	Lead
Merrily We Roll Along 1994	1994	Gussie Carnegie	Growing Up Part II	Moderate Tempo	Alto	G#3	Bb4	Lead
Merrily We Roll Along 1994	1994	Gussie Carnegie	Act 2 Opening	Moderate Tempo	Alto	B3	C5	Lead
Merrily We Roll Along 1994	1994	Gussie Carnegie	The Blob II	Uptempo	Alto	Ab3	Bb4	Lead
Merrily We Roll Along 1994	1994	Gussie Carnegie	Growing Up Act 2	Moderate Tempo	Alto	G3	A4	Lead
Sunset Boulevard	1994	Norma Desmond	Surrender	Ballad	Alto	F3	Bb4	Lead
Sunset Boulevard	1994	Norma Desmond	Once Upon A Time	Uptempo	Alto	A3	A4	Lead
Sunset Boulevard	1994	Norma Desmond	With One Look	Moderate Tempo	Alto	G3	D5	Lead
Sunset Boulevard	1994	Norma Desmond	New Ways To Dream	Ballad	Alto	B3	C5	Lead
Sunset Boulevard	1994	Norma Desmond	The Perfect Year*	Moderate Tempo	Alto	A3	Eb5	Lead
Sunset Boulevard	1994	Norma Desmond	As If We Never Said Goodbye	Moderate Tempo	Alto	G#3	C#5	Lead
Sunset Boulevard	1994	Norma Desmond	There's Been A Call*	Uptempo	Alto	C4	D5	Lead
Sunset Boulevard	1994	Norma Desmond	Phone Call	Moderate Tempo	Alto	F3	Ab4	Lead
State Fair 1996	1996	Emily Arden	That's The Way It Happens*	Moderate Tempo	Alto	B3	D5	Lead
Rent	1996	Maureen Johnson	Over The Moon	Moderate Tempo	Alto	C4	Eb5	Lead

Romantic Antagonist Female

* = Music Edit Required
+ = Ethnic Specific

Show	Year	Role	Song	Tempo	Vocal Type	Range-Bottom	Range-Top	Category
Rent	1996	Maureen Johnson	Take Me Or leave Me*	Uptempo	Alto	C4	F5	Lead
Rent	1996	Mimi Marquez	Out Tonight	Uptempo	Alto	A3	E5	Lead
Rent	1996	Mimi Marquez	Another Day*	Uptempo	Alto	B3	B4	Lead
Rent	1996	Mimi Marquez	Without You*	Moderate Tempo	Alto	A3	A4	Lead
Rent	1996	Mimi Marquez	Goodbye Love*	Moderate Tempo	Alto	A4	C5	Lead
Jekyll and Hyde	1997	Lucy Harris	No One Knows Who I Am	Ballad	Alto	C4	D5	Lead
Jekyll and Hyde	1997	Lucy Harris	Good and Evil	Moderate Tempo	Alto	G#3	E5	Lead
Jekyll and Hyde	1997	Lucy Harris	Someone Like You	Ballad	Alto	G2	Eb4	Lead
Jekyll and Hyde	1997	Lucy Harris	Sympathy, Tenderness	Ballad	Alto	D3	C#4	Lead
Jekyll and Hyde	1997	Lucy Harris	In His Eyes*	Ballad	Alto	Bb3	F5	Lead
Jekyll and Hyde	1997	Lucy Harris	A New Life	Ballad	Alto	B3	D5	Lead
Jekyll and Hyde	1997	Lucy Harris	Bring On The Men	Uptempo	Alto	G#3	E5	Lead
Jekyll and Hyde	1997	Lucy Harris	Sympathy.../Lucy's Death	Ballad	Alto	C#4	C#5	Lead
Marie Christine	1999	Mother+	Ton Grandpere Est Le Soleil*	Moderate Tempo	Alto	D3	E5	Lead
Marie Christine	1999	Mother+	Miracles and Mysteries	Moderate Tempo	Alto	E3	F5	Lead
Aida	2000	Amneris	Every Story is a Love Story	Ballad	Alto	G3	Ab4	Lead
Seussical	2000	Mayzie LaBird	Amayzing Mayzie*	Uptempo	Alto	G#3	D5	Lead
Seussical	2000	Mayzie LaBird	How Lucky You Are Reprise	Moderate Tempo	Alto	Bb3	D5	Lead
Seussical	2000	Mayzie LaBird	Mayzie In Palm Beach*	Uptempo	Alto	G3	C5	Lead
Hairspray	2002	Amber Von Tussle	Cooties	Uptempo	Alto	E4	E5	Lead
Sweet Smell Of Success	2002	Rita	Rita's Tune	Moderate Tempo	Alto	A3	Eb5	Lead
Hairspray	2002	Velma Von Tussle	Miss Baltimore Crabs	Uptempo	Alto	B3	Eb5	Lead
Hairspray	2002	Velma Von Tussle	Velma's Cha Cha	Moderate Tempo	Alto	Ab3	C#5	Lead
Sweet Smell Of Success	2002	Zanzibar Singer	Laughin' All The Way...	Uptempo	Alto	G#3	D4	Supporting
Avenue Q	2003	Lucy The Slut	Special	Moderate Tempo	Alto	G3	Db4	Supporting
Color Purple, The	2005	Shug Avery	Too Beautiful For Words *	Ballad	Alto	E3	F4	Lead
Color Purple, The	2005	Shug Avery	Push Da Button	Moderate Tempo	Alto	A3	Eb5	Lead
Color Purple, The	2005	Shug Avery	What About Love *	Ballad	Alto	E3	D5	Lead

Romantic Antagonist Female

* = Music Edit Required
+ = Ethnic Specific

Show	Year	Role	Song	Tempo	Vocal Type	Range-Bottom	Range-Top	Category
Color Purple, The	2005	Shug Avery	The Color Purple	Ballad	Alto	F#3	Db5	Lead
Spamalot	2005	The Lady Of The Lake	Come With Me*	Moderate Tempo	Alto	A3	C5	Lead
Spamalot	2005	The Lady Of The Lake	The Song That Goes….Rep*	Moderate Tempo	Alto	Ab3	Eb5	Lead
Spamalot	2005	The Lady Of The Lake	Find Your Grail*	Moderate Tempo	Alto	C#4	E5	Lead
Spamalot	2005	The Lady Of The Lake	Whatever Happened To My Part	Moderate Tempo	Alto	F#3	Eb5	Lead
Spamalot	2005	The Lady Of The Lake	Why Does He Never Notice Me	Ballad	Alto	F3	Db5	Lead
Pal Joey	2008	Gladys Bumps	Zip	Moderate Tempo	Alto	F3	G4	Lead
Addams Family, The	2010	Morticia Addams	Just Around The Corner *	Uptempo	Alto	G3	B4	Lead
Addams Family, The	2010	Morticia Addams	Live Before We Die	Moderate Tempo	Alto	Bb3	Ab4	Lead
Cinderella (2013)	2013	Stepmother (Madam)	A Lovely Night*	Uptempo	Alto	B3	D5	Lead
Heathers	2014	Heather Chandler	Candy*	Uptempo	Alto	Bb3	A5	Lead
Of Thee I Sing	1931	Diana Devereaux	The Most Beautiful Blossom	Ballad	Soprano	Eb4	F5	Lead
Of Thee I Sing	1931	Diana Devereaux	Because Reprise*	Uptempo	Soprano	E4	F5	Lead
Of Thee I Sing	1931	Diana Devereaux	Jilted*	Moderate Tempo	Soprano	D4	F5	Lead
Unsinkable Molly Brown	1960	Molly Tobin	I Ain't Down Yet*	Uptempo	Soprano	Ab3	F5	Lead
Unsinkable Molly Brown	1960	Molly Tobin	My Own Brass Bed	Ballad	Soprano	G3	Bb4	Lead
Unsinkable Molly Brown	1960	Molly Tobin	Beaiful People Of Denver	Uptempo	Soprano	F3	Bb4	Lead
Unsinkable Molly Brown	1960	Molly Tobin	Are You Sure*	Uptempo	Soprano	G3	Db5	Lead
Unsinkable Molly Brown	1960	Molly Tobin	Chick-A-Pen	Ballad	Soprano	G3	B4	Lead
Merrily We Roll Along 1994	1981	Mary Flynn	Old Friends	Moderate Tempo	Soprano	A3	A4	Lead
Merrily We Roll Along 1994	1981	Mary Flynn	Like It Was	Moderate Tempo	Soprano	G3	Bb4	Lead
Merrily We Roll Along 1994	1981	Mary Flynn	Now You Know*	Uptempo	Soprano	G3	D5	Lead
Phantom Of The Opera	1986	Carlotta Giudicelli	Hannibal Cadenza	Moderate Tempo	Soprano	C4	D6	Lead
Phantom Of The Opera	1986	Carlotta Giudicelli	Think Of Me*	Moderate Tempo	Soprano	E#4	G#5	Lead
Phantom Of The Opera	1986	Carlotta Giudicelli	Diva*	Moderate Tempo	Soprano	F4	E6	Lead
Phantom Of The Opera	1986	Carlotta Giudicelli	Prima Donna*	Moderate Tempo	Soprano	F4	F6	Lead

Romantic Antagonist Female

Romantic Antagonist Female

* = Music Edit Required
+ = Ethnic Specific

Show	Year	Role	Song	Tempo	Vocal Type	Range-Bottom	Range-Top	Category
Phantom Of The Opera	1986	Carlotta Giudicelli	Poor Fool He Makes Me Laugh*	Moderate Tempo	Soprano	F4	C6	Lead
Phantom	1991	Carlotta	This Place Is Mine	Uptempo	Soprano	B♭3	B♭5	Lead
Phantom	1991	Carlotta	This Is Mine Reprise	Moderate Tempo	Soprano	D4	G5	Lead
Victor/Victoria	1995	Norma Cassidy	Paris Makes Me Horny	Moderate Tempo	Soprano	B♭3	A5	Lead
Victor/Victoria	1995	Norma Cassidy	Chicago Illinois*	Uptempo	Soprano	A#3	E5	Lead
Marie Christine	1999	Marie Christine L'Adrese+	Prison In A Prison*	Uptempo	Soprano	G3	D5	Lead
Marie Christine	1999	Marie Christine L'Adrese+	Beautiful*	Moderate Tempo	Soprano	G3	D5	Lead
Marie Christine	1999	Marie Christine L'Adrese+	Way Back To Paradise*	Moderate Tempo	Soprano	D4	G5	Lead
Marie Christine	1999	Marie Christine L'Adrese+	To Find A Lover*	Moderate Tempo	Soprano	A3	G4	Lead
Marie Christine	1999	Marie Christine L'Adrese+	I Will Give	Ballad	Soprano	B♭3	F♭4	Lead
Marie Christine	1999	Marie Christine L'Adrese+	Tell Me	Moderate Tempo	Soprano	G3	F5	Lead
Marie Christine	1999	Marie Christine L'Adrese+	Marie's Soliloquy	Ballad	Soprano	A3	D5	Lead
Light In The Piazza, The	2005	Franca Naccarelli	The Joy You Feel	Moderate Tempo	Soprano	C4	G♭5	Lead

Romantic Antagonist Female

123

Show	Year	Role	Song	Tempo	Vocal Type	Range-Bottom	Range-Top	Category
Pal Joey	1940	Joey Evans	A Great Big Town	Uptempo	Baritone	E♭3	F4	Lead
Pal Joey	1940	Joey Evans	You Mustn't Kick It Around	Uptempo	Baritone	D3	F4	Lead
Pal Joey	1940	Joey Evans	I Could Write A Book*	Mod Tempo	Baritone	E♭3	E♭4	Lead
Pal Joey	1940	Joey Evans	Happy Hunting Horn	Mod Tempo	Baritone	A♭3	F4	Lead
Pal Joey	1940	Joey Evans	What Do I Care For A Dame	Uptempo	Baritone	D3	C#4	Lead
Pal Joey	1940	Joey Evans	Den Of Iniquity*	Uptempo	Baritone	G3	E♭4	Lead
Pal Joey	1940	Joey Evans	Do It The Hard Way	Mod Tempo	Baritone	C3	C4	Lead
Pal Joey	1940	Joey Evans	Finale-I Could Write A Book	Mod Tempo	Baritone	E♭3	E♭4	Lead
Carousel	1945	Billy Bigelow	If I Loved You *	Ballad	Baritone	B♭2	G♭4	Lead
Carousel	1945	Billy Bigelow	Soliloquy	Mod Tempo	Baritone	B2	G4	Lead
Carousel	1945	Billy Bigelow	If I Loved You Reprise	Ballad	Baritone	E♭3	G♭4	Lead
Carousel	1945	Billy Bigelow	The Highest Judge Of All	Mod Tempo	Baritone	D3	G4	Lead
Carousel	1945	Jigger Craigin	Stonecutter Cut It On Stone Reprise	Uptempo	Baritone	C3	F4	Lead
State Fair 1996	1945	Pat Gilbert	Isn't It Kinda Fun*	Uptempo	Baritone	C#3	D4	Lead
State Fair 1996	1945	Pat Gilbert	Isn't It Kinda Fun Reprise	Mod Tempo	Baritone	C3	G#4	Lead
Pajama Game	1954	Prez	Her Is*	Uptempo	Baritone	D♭3	F4	Lead
Pajama Game	1954	Prez	Her Is Reprise*	Uptempo	Baritone	A♭2	F4	Lead
Pajama Game	1954	Prez	Seven And A Half Cents*	Uptempo	Baritone	D3	E4	Lead
Most Happy Fella, The	1956	Joe	Don't Cry	Mod Tempo	Baritone	B♭2	E♭4	Lead
Most Happy Fella, The	1956	Joe	Getting' Out Of Town	Ballad	Baritone	D♭3	F4	Lead
Most Happy Fella, The	1956	Joe	Joey, Joey, Joey	Mod Tempo	Baritone	C3	F4	Lead
High Society 1998	1956	Mike Connor	You're Sensational	Ballad	Baritone	G2	F4	Lead
Music Man, The	1957	Harold Hill	Trouble	Uptempo	Baritone	A2	E4	Lead
Music Man, The	1957	Harold Hill	Seventy Six Trombones	Uptempo	Baritone	B2	F4	Lead
Music Man, The	1957	Harold Hill	The Sadder But Wiser Girl*	Uptempo	Baritone	C3	E4	Lead
Music Man, The	1957	Harold Hill	Marian The Librarian	Mod Tempo	Baritone	C3	F4	Lead
Music Man, The	1957	Harold Hill	76 Trombones	Mod Tempo	Baritone	G2	F4	Lead

* = Music Edit Required
+ = Ethnic Specific

Show	Year	Role	Song	Tempo	Vocal Type	Range-Bottom	Range-Top	Category
Music Man, The	1957	Harold Hill	Trouble Reprise	Uptempo	Baritone	A3	Eb4	Lead
Music Man, The	1957	Harold Hill	Till There Was You Reprise*	Ballad	Baritone	B2	C4	Lead
Bye Bye Birdie	1960	Conrad Birdie	Honestly Sincerely	Mod Tempo	Baritone	Ab2	F#4	Lead
Bye Bye Birdie	1960	Conrad Birdie	One Last Kiss	Mod Tempo	Baritone	Ab2	F4	Lead
Bye Bye Birdie	1960	Conrad Birdie	Lot of Livin' To Do *	Uptempo	Baritone	Db4	F4	Lead
A Funny Thing...Forum	1962	Miles	Bring Me My Bride*	Uptempo	Baritone	B2	F4	Lead
Anyone Can Whistle	1964	J. Bowden Hapgood	Everybody Says Don't	Uptempo	Baritone	G2	E4	Lead
Anyone Can Whistle	1964	J. Bowden Hapgood	With So Little To Be Sure Of*	Mod Tempo	Baritone	B2	E4	Lead
Mack and Mabel	1974	Mack Sennett	Movies Were Movies	Uptempo	Baritone	A2	Eb4	Lead
Mack and Mabel	1974	Mack Sennett	I Wont Send Roses	Ballad	Baritone	G2	Eb4	Lead
Mack and Mabel	1974	Mack Sennett	Make The World Laugh*	Uptempo	Baritone	A2	G4	Lead
Mack and Mabel	1974	Mack Sennett	Hundreds of Girls*	Uptempo	Baritone	B2	F4	Lead
Mack and Mabel	1974	Mack Sennett	I Promise You a Happy Ending	Ballad	Baritone	G2	D4	Lead
They're Playing Our Song	1974	Vernon Gersch	Falling	Mod Tempo	Baritone	A2	D4	Lead
They're Playing Our Song	1974	Vernon Gersch	If She Really Knew Me*	Ballad	Baritone	B2	Cb5	Lead
They're Playing Our Song	1974	Vernon Gersch	They're Playing My Song*	Uptempo	Baritone	C3	F4	Lead
They're Playing Our Song	1974	Vernon Gersch	If She Really Knew Me Reprise*	Ballad	Baritone	C3	D4	Lead
Chicago	1975	Billy Flynn	All I Care About Is Love	Mod Tempo	Baritone	A2	F#4	Lead
Chicago	1975	Billy Flynn	Razzle Dazzle	Uptempo	Baritone	D3	F4	Lead
On The Twentieth Century	1978	Oscar Jaffe	I Rise Again*	Mod Tempo	Baritone	B2	E4	Lead
On The Twentieth Century	1978	Oscar Jaffe	Together*	Uptempo	Baritone	C3	E4	Lead
On The Twentieth Century	1978	Oscar Jaffe	Our Private World*	Ballad	Baritone	A2	E4	Lead
On The Twentieth Century	1978	Oscar Jaffe	I've Got It All*	Mod Tempo	Baritone	B2	E5	Lead
On The Twentieth Century	1978	Oscar Jaffe	Five Zeros*	Mod Tempo	Baritone	Ab2	Ab4	Lead
On The Twentieth Century	1978	Oscar Jaffe	Last Will And Testament	Mod Tempo	Baritone	B2	F4	Lead
On The Twentieth Century	1978	Oscar Jaffe	Because Of Her	Mod Tempo	Baritone	B2	F4	Lead
Mystery Of Edwin Drood, The	1985	Neville Landless	Neville's Confesson	Mod Tempo	Baritone	Gb3	F4	Lead
City of Angels	1989	Stone	Double Talk	Uptempo	Baritone	A#2	D4	Lead

Romantic Antagonist Male

* = Music Edit Required
+ = Ethnic Specific

Show	Year	Role	Song	Tempo	Vocal Type	Range-Bottom	Range-Top	Category
City of Angels	1989	Stone	You're Nothing Without Me *	Uptempo	Baritone	E3	G4	Lead
City of Angels	1989	Stone	With Every Breath I Take Reprise *	Ballad	Baritone	G#2	F4	Lead
City of Angels	1989	Stone	I'm Nothing Without You *	Uptempo	Baritone	F3	G4	Lead
Once On This Island	1990	Agwe+	Rain*	Uptempo	Baritone	C#3	E4	Lead
Nick & Nora	1991	Victor Moisa	Class	Mod Tempo	Baritone	B2	F#4	Lead
Nick & Nora	1991	Victor Moisa	Class Reprise	Mod Tempo	Baritone	B2	F#3	Lead
Will Rogers Follies	1991	Will Rogers	Never Met A Man... (Act 1)	Mod Tempo	Baritone	B2	B♭3	Lead
Will Rogers Follies	1991	Will Rogers	Give A Man Enough Rope	Mod Tempo	Baritone	B♭2	F4	Lead
Will Rogers Follies	1991	Will Rogers	So Long Pa	Ballad	Baritone	B2	D4	Lead
Will Rogers Follies	1991	Will Rogers	The Big Time*	Mod Tempo	Baritone	G#2	D#4	Lead
Will Rogers Follies	1991	Will Rogers	Marry Me Now*	Mod Tempo	Baritone	E♭3	E♭4	Lead
Will Rogers Follies	1991	Will Rogers	Look Around	Ballad	Baritone	C#5	D4	Lead
Will Rogers Follies	1991	Will Rogers	The Campaign: Our Favorite Son	Mod Tempo	Baritone	C3	E♭4	Lead
Will Rogers Follies	1991	Will Rogers	Presents For Mrs. Rogers	Mod Tempo	Baritone	B2	D4	Lead
Will Rogers Follies	1991	Will Rogers	Never Met A Man...Reprise	Mod Tempo	Baritone	B♭2	D4	Lead
My Favorite Year	1992	Alan Swann	If The World Were Like The Movies	Ballad	Baritone	B♭2	E4	Lead
My Favorite Year	1992	Alan Swann	Exits	Mod Tempo	Baritone	G2	D4	Lead
My Favorite Year	1992	Alan Swann	The Lights Come Up*	Ballad	Baritone	B♭2	C4	Lead
My Favorite Year	1992	Alan Swann	Manhattan*	Uptempo	Baritone	G2	E♭4	Lead
Assassins	1992	John Wilkes Booth	Opening*	Mod Tempo	Baritone	D3	F4	Lead
Assassins	1992	John Wilkes Booth	The Ballad Of Booth Part 2	Mod Tempo	Baritone	F#2	F#4	Lead
Assassins	1992	John Wilkes Booth	Gun Song*	Mod Tempo	Baritone	C#3	E4	Lead
Assassins	1992	Leon Czolgosz	Gun Song*	Mod Tempo	Baritone	G2	B3	Lead
Beauty and the Beast	1994	Beast	How Long Must This Go On	Uptempo	Baritone	D3	C4	Lead
Beauty and the Beast	1994	Beast	If I Can't Love Her	Ballad	Baritone	B2	F4	Lead
Beauty and the Beast	1994	Beast	Something There *	Uptempo	Baritone	A2	E5	Lead
Beauty and the Beast	1994	Beast	If I Can't Love Her Reprise	Ballad	Baritone	D4	D5	Lead
Beauty and the Beast	1994	Gaston	Me	Uptempo	Baritone	B2	F4	Lead

Romantic Antagonist Male

* = Music Edit Required
+ = Ethnic Specific

Show	Year	Role	Song	Tempo	Vocal Type	Range-Bottom	Range-Top	Category
Beauty and the Beast	1994	Gaston	Gaston Reprise	Uptempo	Baritone	C3	E4	Lead
Beauty and the Beast	1994	Gaston	Maison Des Lune	Mod Tempo	Baritone	B2	E4	Lead
State Fair 1996	1996	Pat Gilbert	The Man I Used To Be Reprise	Mod Tempo	Baritone	C3	Eb4	Lead
Scarlet Pimpernel, The	1997	Chauvelin	Madame Guillotine*	Uptempo	Baritone	B2	F4	Lead
Scarlet Pimpernel, The	1997	Chauvelin	Falcon In The Dive*	Uptempo	Baritone	G2	G4	Lead
Scarlet Pimpernel, The	1997	Chauvelin	Where's The Girl	Mod Tempo	Baritone	B2	G4	Lead
Scarlet Pimpernel, The	1997	Chauvelin	The Riddle Part 1	Mod Tempo	Baritone	A2	D4	Lead
Scarlet Pimpernel, The	1997	Chauvelin	Where Is The Girl Reprise	Mod Tempo	Baritone	B2	G4	Lead
Steel Pier	1997	Mick Hamilton	Everybody Dance Part 1*	Uptempo	Baritone	D3	F4	Lead
Steel Pier	1997	Mick Hamilton	It's A Powerful Thing*	Uptempo	Baritone	C3	E4	Lead
Steel Pier	1997	Mick Hamilton	Dance With Me*	Uptempo	Baritone	Db3	Eb4	Lead
Steel Pier	1997	Mick Hamilton	Steel Pier Reprise*	Uptempo	Baritone	Bb2	E4	Lead
Parade	1998	Hugh Dorsey	Somethin' Ain't Right*	Mod Tempo	Baritone	C#3	F#4	Lead
Parade	1998	Hugh Dorsey	The Trial, Part 2: Twenty From Mariett	Uptempo	Baritone	Bb2	Eb4	Lead
Spring Awakening	2006	Hanschen	Word Of Your Body Reprise 2*	Ballad	Baritone	C3	E#4	Lead
Legally Blonde	2007	Professor Callahan	Blood In The Water	Mod Tempo	Baritone	C3	F#4	Supporting
Legally Blonde	2007	Professor Callahan	Whipped Into Shape*	Uptempo	Baritone	C3	F#4	Supporting
Addams Family, The	2010	Gomez Addams +	Happy/Sad	Ballad	Baritone	Eb3	Eb4	Lead
Once Upon A Mattress	1959	Minstrel	Normandy*	Uptempo	Tenor	D#3	B4	Lead
Unsinkable Molly Brown, The	1960	Prince Delong	Dolce Far Niente*	Ballad	Tenor	C3	Eb4	Lead
Unsinkable Molly Brown, The	1960	Prince Delong	Dolce Far Niente Reprise	Ballad	Tenor	D3	Eb4	Lead
110 In The Shade	1963	Bill Starbuck	The Rain Song *	Uptempo	Tenor	C3	Ab4	Lead
110 In The Shade	1963	Bill Starbuck	Melisande	Uptempo	Tenor	G2	G4	Lead
110 In The Shade	1963	Bill Starbuck	Evenin' Star	Ballad	Tenor	B3	Ab4	Lead
110 In The Shade	1963	Bill Starbuck	Wonderful Music *	Uptempo	Tenor	Db3	F4	Lead
She Loves Me	1963	Steven Kodaly	Ilona*	Mod Tempo	Tenor	C3	E4	Lead

Romantic Antagonist Male

* = Music Edit Required
+ = Ethnic Specific

Show	Year	Role	Song	Tempo	Vocal Type	Range-Bottom	Range-Top	Category
She Loves Me	1963	Steven Kodaly	Grand Knowing You	Uptempo	Tenor	D3	A4	Lead
1776	1969	Edward Rutledge	Molasses To Rum	Mod Tempo	Tenor	E3	A4	Lead
Grease	1971	Danny Zuko	Alone At the Drive-In Movie	Mod Tempo	Tenor	D3	D♭5	Lead
Pippin	1972	Leading Player	Magic To Do*	Uptempo	Tenor	E3	A4	Lead
Pippin	1972	Leading Player	Glory Part I & III*	Mod Tempo	Tenor	E3	G#4	Lead
Pippin	1972	Leading Player	Right On Track*	Mod Tempo	Tenor	E♭3	A♭4	Lead
Pippin	1972	Leading Player	Think About The Sun*	Uptempo	Tenor	G3	F4	Lead
Wiz, The	1974	The Wiz	So...Meet The Wizard	Uptempo	Tenor	E3	G4	Lead
Wiz, The	1974	The Wiz	Y'all Got It	Uptempo	Tenor	G3	A4	Lead
Wiz, The	1974	The Wiz	Believe In Yourself (F Major)	Mod Tempo	Tenor	C4	G5	Lead
Wiz, The	1974	The Wiz	Believe In Yourself (B♭ Major)	Mod Tempo	Tenor	F3	D5	Lead
Pacific Overtures	1976	Madam+	Welcome to Kanagawa*	Uptempo	Tenor	C3	E4	Lead
Evita	1978	Che Guevara	Peron's Latest Flame	Uptempo	Tenor	F2	F4	Lead
Merrily We Roll Along	1981	Franklin Shepard	Old Friends II*	Mod Tempo	Tenor	B♭2	D4	Lead
Merrily We Roll Along	1981	Franklin Shepard	Our Time Part 1 & 2*	Mod Tempo	Tenor	D♭3	B♭4	Lead
Nine	1982	Guido Contini	Guido's Song*	Uptempo	Tenor	G#2	F#4	Lead
Nine	1982	Guido Contini	Only With You	Mod Tempo	Tenor	G#2	E4	Lead
Nine	1982	Guido Contini	Script	Uptempo	Tenor	C3	F4	Lead
Nine	1982	Guido Contini	The Bells Of St. Sebastian*	Mod Tempo	Tenor	D4	G4	Lead
Nine	1982	Guido Contini	The Grand Canal*	Mod Tempo	Tenor	D#3	G4	Lead
Nine	1982	Guido Contini	I Can't Make This Movie	Mod Tempo	Tenor	G3	G4	Lead
Nine	1982	Guido Contini	Long Ago Reprise	Ballad	Tenor	B♭2	B♭3	Lead
Nine	1982	Guido Contini	Nine Reprise	Ballad	Tenor	B♭2	G4	Lead
Nine	1982	Guido Contini	Amour	Uptempo	Tenor	A2	B♭4	Lead
Sunday...Park With Geroge	1984	George	Color And Light (Part 1)	Uptempo	Tenor	B♭2	E♭4	Lead
Sunday...Park With Geroge	1984	George	Color And Light (Part 3)*	Uptempo	Tenor	D3	G4	Lead
Sunday...Park With Geroge	1984	George	The Day Off (Part 1)	Uptempo	Tenor	A#2	G4	Lead
Sunday...Park With Geroge	1984	George	The Day Off (Part 2)	Mod Tempo	Tenor	D#3	D#4	Lead

* = Music Edit Required
+ = Ethnic Specific

Show	Year	Role	Song	Tempo	Vocal Type	Range-Bottom	Range-Top	Category
Sunday...Park With Geroge	1984	George	Finishing The Hat	Mod Tempo	Tenor	Bb2	Ab5	Lead
Sunday...Park With Geroge	1984	George	We Do Not Belong Together*	Mod Tempo	Tenor	A2	E4	Lead
Sunday...Park With Geroge	1984	George	Beautiful*	Ballad	Tenor	C#3	F#4	Lead
Sunday...Park With Geroge	1984	George	Putting It Together (Part 7 & 9)	Uptempo	Tenor	D4	Gb4	Lead
Sunday...Park With Geroge	1984	George	Putting It Together (Part 16)*	Uptempo	Tenor	Db3	Gb4	Lead
Sunday...Park With Geroge	1984	George	Lesson #8	Ballad	Tenor	G#2	Eb4	Lead
Sunday...Park With Geroge	1984	George	Move On*	Ballad	Tenor	D#3	G4	Lead
Romance/Romance	1987	Alfred Von Wilmers	It's Not Too Late*	Mod Tempo	Tenor	Bb2	F4	Lead
Romance/Romance	1987	Alfred Von Wilmers	A Performance*	Mod Tempo	Tenor	A2	F#4	Lead
Romance/Romance	1987	Alfred Von Wilmers	I'll Remember The Song*	Uptempo	Tenor	B2	E4	Lead
Romance/Romance	1987	Alfred Von Wilmers	Happy, Happy, Happy	Ballad	Tenor	Bb2	F#4	Lead
Romance/Romance	1987	Alfred Von Wilmers	Women Of Vienna	Mod Tempo	Tenor	C3	F#4	Lead
Romance/Romance	1987	Alfred Von Wilmers	A Rustic Country Inn*	Uptempo	Tenor	C3	F4	Lead
Les Miserables	1987	Jean Valjean	Soliloquy	Mod Tempo	Tenor	C3	B4	Lead
Les Miserables	1987	Jean Valjean	Who Am I	Mod Tempo	Tenor	B3	B4	Lead
Les Miserables	1987	Jean Valjean	Bring Him Home	Ballad	Tenor	E3	A4	Lead
Romance/Romance	1987	Sam	There Are Things He Doesn't Say	Ballad	Tenor	Ab2	G4	Lead
Romance/Romance	1987	Sam	Moonlight Passing Through A Window	Ballad	Tenor	D3	F4	Lead
Romance/Romance	1987	Sam	Romantic Notions*	Mod Tempo	Tenor	B3	E4	Lead
Romance/Romance	1987	Sam	It's Not Too Late Reprise*	Mod Tempo	Tenor	Bb2	A4	Lead
	1988	Freddie	Endgame	Uptempo	Tenor	C#3	G4	Lead
	1988	Freddie	Florence Quits	Uptempo	Tenor	B2	B4	Lead
	1988	Freddie	One Night In Bangkok	Uptempo	Tenor	F3	A4	Lead
	1988	Freddie	Pity The Child	Uptempo	Tenor	Bb2	Db5	Lead
Miss Saigon	1991	John Thomas	Bui-Doi	Mod Tempo	Tenor	Ab2	Bb4	Lead
Miss Saigon	1991	Thuy+	Kim's Nightmare Part I	Uptempo	Tenor	C3	E4	Lead
Assassins	1992	Charles Guiteau	The Ballad of Guiteau*	Uptempo	Tenor	A2	Gb4	Lead

Romantic Antagonist Male

* = Music Edit Required
+ = Ethnic Specific

Show	Year	Role	Song	Tempo	Vocal Type	Range-Bottom	Range-Top	Category
Kiss Of The Spider Woman	1993	Valentin	Dear One*	Ballad	Tenor	Bb2	C4	Lead
Kiss Of The Spider Woman	1993	Valentin	Over The Wall 3 - Marta	Mod Tempo	Tenor	F3	A4	Lead
Kiss Of The Spider Woman	1993	Valentin	My First Woman*	Mod Tempo	Tenor	C3	G4	Lead
Kiss Of The Spider Woman	1993	Valentin	The Day After That*	Uptempo	Tenor	D3	Gb4	Lead
Merrily We Roll Along 1994	1994	Franklin Shepard	Growing Up Part I	Mod Tempo	Tenor	D3	E4	Lead
Sunset Boulevard	1994	Joe Gillis	It Took Her Three Days	Uptempo	Tenor	A2	E4	Lead
Sunset Boulevard	1994	Joe Gillis	Prologue	Mod Tempo	Tenor	D3	G4	Lead
Sunset Boulevard	1994	Joe Gillis	Let Me Take You Back Six Months	Mod Tempo	Tenor	C3	Eb4	Lead
Sunset Boulevard	1994	Joe Gillis	I Started Work	Uptempo	Tenor	C3	G4	Lead
Sunset Boulevard	1994	Joe Gillis	The Perfect Year*	Mod Tempo	Tenor	A2	D4	Lead
Sunset Boulevard	1994	Joe Gillis	I Had To Get Out	Uptempo	Tenor	C3	Eb4	Lead
Sunset Boulevard	1994	Joe Gillis	Sunset Boulevard	Uptempo	Tenor	C3	G4	Lead
Sunset Boulevard	1994	Joe Gillis	Girl Meets Boy Reprise*	Uptempo	Tenor	D3	E4	Lead
Sunset Boulevard	1994	Joe Gillis	I Should Have Stayed There	Uptempo	Tenor	A3	E4	Lead
Sunset Boulevard	1994	Joe Gillis	Too Much In Love To Care*	Mod Tempo	Tenor	F3	G4	Lead
Sunset Boulevard	1994	Joe Gillis	Sunset Blvd Reprise-What's Going On	Uptempo	Tenor	C#3	Gb4	Lead
Songs For A New World	1995	Man 1	On The Deck Of A Spanish Sailing Ship	Ballad	Tenor	F3	Bb4	Lead
Songs For A New World	1995	Man 1	The River Won't Flow*	Uptempo	Tenor	G3	C5	Lead
Songs For A New World	1995	Man 1	Steam Train*	Uptempo	Tenor	F3	C5	Lead
Songs For A New World	1995	Man 1	King Of the World	Uptempo	Tenor	E3	C5	Lead
Songs For A New World	1995	Man 1	Flying Home*	Ballad	Tenor	D#3	F4	Lead
Songs For A New World	1995	Man 1	Hear My Song*	Mod Tempo	Tenor	D3	C4	Lead
Rent	1996	Roger Davis	Another Day*	Uptempo	Tenor	F3	Gb4	Lead
Rent	1996	Roger Davis	Your Eyes*	Ballad	Tenor	B2	G4	Lead
Jekyll and Hyde	1997	Dr. Henry Jekyll	Lost In The Darkness	Ballad	Tenor	G2	E4	Lead
Jekyll and Hyde	1997	Dr. Henry Jekyll	This Is The Moment	Ballad	Tenor	B2	G#4	Lead
Jekyll and Hyde	1997	Dr. Henry Jekyll	What Streak of Madness/Obsession	Ballad	Tenor	C3	Eb4	Lead
Jekyll and Hyde	1997	Dr. Henry Jekyll	The Way Back/Angst 2	Uptempo	Tenor	B2	G4	Lead

Romantic Antagonist Male

* = Music Edit Required
+ = Ethnic Specific

Show	Year	Role	Song	Tempo	Vocal Type	Range-Bottom	Range-Top	Category
Jekyll and Hyde	1997	Dr. Henry Jekyll	Lost In The Darkness Reprise	Ball	Tenor	G2	E4	Lead
Jekyll and Hyde	1997	Dr. Henry Jekyll	Confrontation*	Uptempo	Tenor	B2	A4	Lead
Jekyll and Hyde	1997	Dr. Henry Jekyll	I Need To Know	Ballad	Tenor	B2	F#4	Lead
Footloose	1998	Chuck Cranston	The Girl Gets Around	Uptempo	Tenor	G#3	A4	Lead
Parade	1998	John Conley+	That's What He Said	Uptempo	Tenor	D3	G4	Lead
Parade	1998	John Conley+	Blues: Feel The Rain Fall*	Mod Tempo	Tenor	D3	Bb4	Lead
Marie Christine	1999	Dante Keyes	Nothing Beats Chicago	Uptempo	Tenor	B2	E4	Lead
Marie Christine	1999	Dante Keyes	Ocean Is Different	Mod Tempo	Tenor	C3	A4	Lead
Marie Christine	1999	Dante Keyes	I Don't Hear The Ocean*	Mod Tempo	Tenor	Eb3	F4	Lead
Marie Christine	1999	Dante Keyes	We Gonna Go To Chicago	Mod Tempo	Tenor	Db3	F4	Lead
Marie Christine	1999	Dante Keyes	The Scorpion*	Uptempo	Tenor	C3	Gb4	Lead
Marie Christine	1999	Dante Keyes	Your Name (Helena's Death)	Ballad	Tenor	G#2	A4	Lead
Marie Christine	1999	Dante Keyes	The Adventure Never Ends	Uptempo	Tenor	Bb2	Fb4	Lead
Marie Christine	1999	Dante Keyes	Danced With A Girl	Uptempo	Tenor	B2	E4	Lead
Marie Christine	1999	Paris L'Adrese+	No Turning Back	Ballad	Tenor	F3	Eb5	Supporting
Jane Eyre	2000	Edward Fairfax Rochester	As Good As You	Mod Tempo	Tenor	A2	E4	Lead
Jane Eyre	2000	Edward Fairfax Rochester	Secret Soul*	Uptempo	Tenor	B2	B4	Lead
Jane Eyre	2000	Edward Fairfax Rochester	Sirens	Uptempo	Tenor	Bb2	F4	Lead
Jane Eyre	2000	Edward Fairfax Rochester	The Gypsy (Drag)	Uptempo	Tenor	D4	A5	Lead
Jane Eyre	2000	Edward Fairfax Rochester	Farewell Good Angel	Uptempo	Tenor	G2	G4	Lead
Jane Eyre	2000	Edward Fairfax Rochester	Brave Enough for Love	Uptempo	Tenor			Lead
Spitfire Grill	2001	Caleb Thorpe	Digging Stone	Mod Tempo	Tenor	B2	G4	Lead
Sweet Smell Of Success	2002	Sidney	I Can Get You In JJ	Uptempo	Tenor	Db3	Ab4	Lead
Sweet Smell Of Success	2002	Sidney	At The Fountain	Mod Tempo	Tenor	F3	A4	Lead
Sweet Smell Of Success	2002	Sidney	Welcome To The Night Reprise*	Uptempo	Tenor	Db4	F4	Lead
Sweet Smell Of Success	2002	Sidney	Break It Up*	Uptempo	Tenor	E3	F4	Lead
Sweet Smell Of Success	2002	Sidney	I Could Get You In JJ Reprise	Mod Tempo	Tenor	D3	G#4	Lead
Sweet Smell Of Success	2002	Sidney	At The Fountain Reprise*	Mod Tempo	Tenor	A2	F4	Lead

Romantic Antagonist Male

* = Music Edit Required
+ = Ethnic Specific

Show	Year	Role	Song	Tempo	Vocal Type	Range-Bottom	Range-Top	Category
Sweet Smell Of Success	2002	Sidney	Finale (Part 3)	Uptempo	Tenor	E3	F4	Lead
All Shook Up	2005	Chad	Roustabout	Uptempo	Tenor	E3	G4	Lead
All Shook Up	2005	Chad	C'mon	Uptempo	Tenor	D♭3	G#4	Lead
All Shook Up	2005	Chad	Follow That Dream*	Uptempo	Tenor	A2	E4	Lead
All Shook Up	2005	Chad	Don't Be Cruel *	Uptempo	Tenor	B2	F#4	Lead
All Shook Up	2005	Chad	I Don't Want To	Ballad	Tenor	D3	G4	Lead
All Shook Up	2005	Chad	Jailhouse Rock *	Uptempo	Tenor	B2	C5	Lead
All Shook Up	2005	Chad	If I Can Dream *	Mod Tempo	Tenor	C3	G4	Lead
All Shook Up	2005	Chad	The Power of Love *	Mod Tempo	Tenor	E3	E♭4	Lead
Spring Awakening	2006	Melchoir	All That's Known	Mod Tempo	Tenor	D3	E4	Lead
Spring Awakening	2006	Melchoir	The Guilty One*	Mod Tempo	Tenor	G2	A3	Lead
Spring Awakening	2006	Melchoir	Left Behind	Ballad	Tenor	E3	B4	Lead
Spring Awakening	2006	Melchoir	Totally Fucked*	Uptempo	Tenor	B♭3	G4	Lead
Spring Awakening	2006	Melchoir	Those You've Known*	Mod Tempo	Tenor	D3	F4	Lead
Addams Family, The	2010	Gomez Addams +	Morticia	Mod Tempo	Tenor	A#2	A♭4	Lead
Addams Family, The	2010	Gomez Addams +	Not Today (US Tour)	Mod Tempo	Tenor	D3	G4	Lead
Addams Family, The	2010	Gomez Addams +	What If	Ballad	Tenor	C3	C4	Lead
Heathers	2014	Jason Dean (JD)	Freeze Your Brain	Mod Tempo	Tenor	B♭3	G#4	Lead
Heathers	2014	Jason Dean (JD)	Our Love Is God	Ballad	Tenor	F#3	F#4	Lead
Heathers	2014	Jason Dean (JD)	Meant To Be Yours	Uptempo	Tenor	G3	A♭4	Lead
Heathers	2014	Jason Dean (JD)	I Am Damaged	Ballad	Tenor	E3	F#4	Lead
Heathers	2014	Jason Dean (JD)	Seventeen*	Ballad	Tenor	A3	B4	Lead
Heathers	2014	Ram Sweeney	Blue*	Uptempo	Tenor	F#3	D5	Supporting

Romantic Antagonist Male

* = Music Edit Required
+ = Ethnic Specific

Show	Year	Role	Song	Tempo	Vocal Type	Range-Bottom	Range-Top	Category
Gypsy	1959	Rose	Some People	Uptempo	Alto	G#3	C5	Lead
Gypsy	1959	Rose	Small World	Moderate Tempo	Alto	F#3	B4	Lead
Gypsy	1959	Rose	You'll Never Get Away From Me*	Uptempo	Alto	F#3	B4	Lead
Gypsy	1959	Rose	Everything's Coming Up Roses	Uptempo	Alto	Bb3	C5	Lead
Gypsy	1959	Rose	Rose's Turn	Moderate Tempo	Alto	G3	C5	Lead
Gypsy	1959	Rose	Some People Reprise*	Ballad	Alto	G#3	A4	Lead
A Funny Thing...Forum	1962	Domina	That Dirty Old Man	Uptempo	Alto	B3	F5	Lead
Oliver!	1963	Nancy	It's A Fine Life*	Uptempo	Alto	Ab3	D5	Lead
Oliver!	1963	Nancy	Oom-Pah-Pah*	Uptempo	Alto	B3	C#5	Lead
Oliver!	1963	Nancy	As Long As He Needs Me	Ballad	Alto	F#3	C#5	Lead
Oliver!	1963	Nancy	As Long As He Needs Me Reprise	Moderate Tempo	Alto	G#3	C#5	Lead
Sweet Charity	1966	Dance Hall Girl	Big Spender*	Moderate Tempo	Alto	F3	B4	Feat Ensemble
Company (Revival)	1970	Joanne	The Little Things We Do Together	Uptempo	Alto	F3	A4	Supporting
Company (Revival)	1970	Joanne	The Ladies Who Lunch	Moderate Tempo	Alto	F3	Bb4	Supporting
Grease	1971	Betty Rizzo	Look At Me I'm Sandra Dee	Moderate Tempo	Alto	G3	Eb5	Lead
Grease	1971	Betty Rizzo	There Are Worse Things I Could Do	Ballad	Alto	A3	C4	Lead
Follies	1971	Hattie Walker	Broadway Baby	Moderate Tempo	Alto	A3	Bb4	Supporting
You're A Good Man Charlie B	1971	Lucy Van Pelt	Schroeder	Moderate Tempo	Alto	G3	E5	Lead
Wiz, The	1974	Evillene	Don't Nobody Bring Me No Bad News	Uptempo	Alto	Bb3	Db5	Lead
Annie	1977	Miss Hannigan	Little Girls	Uptempo	Alto	C4	D5	Lead
Annie	1977	Miss Hannigan	Easy Street*	Uptempo	Alto	Bb3	Ab4	Lead
Annie	1977	Miss Hannigan	Little Girl Reprise	Uptempo	Alto	E4	D5	Lead
Nunsense	1985	Mary Hubert	Tackle That Temptation*	Uptempo	Alto	A3	D5	Lead
Nunsense	1985	Mary Hubert	Holier Than Thou*	Uptempo	Alto	Bb3	F5	Lead
Nunsense	1985	Mary Robert Anne	Playing Second Fiddle	Uptempo	Alto	B3	B4	Lead
Nunsense	1985	Mary Robert Anne	Growing Up Catholic*	Ballad	Alto	Ab3	Db5	Lead
Nunsense	1985	Mary Robert Anne	Second Fiddle Reprise	Uptempo	Alto	E4	B4	Lead
Nunsense	1985	Mary Robert Anne	I Just Want To Be A Star*	Uptempo	Alto	G3	C5	Lead

* = Music Edit Required
+ = Ethnic Specific

Show	Year	Role	Song	Tempo	Vocal Type	Range-Bottom	Range-Top	Category
Mystery Of Edwin Drood	1985	Princess Puffer	The Wages Of Sin	Moderate Tempo	Alto	F3	C5	Lead
Mystery Of Edwin Drood	1985	Princess Puffer	Garden Path To Hell	Ballad	Alto	G3	A4	Lead
Mystery Of Edwin Drood	1985	Princess Puffer	Don't Quit While You're Ahead*	Moderate Tempo	Alto	F3	A4	Lead
Mystery Of Edwin Drood	1985	Princess Puffer	Puffer's Confession	Ballad	Alto	C4	C5	Lead
Les Miserables	1987	Madame Thenardier	Master of the House*	Uptempo	Alto	B3	D5	Supporting
Les Miserables	1987	Madame Thenardier	Beggars at the Wedding	Uptempo	Alto	C#4	D5	Supporting
Goodbye Girl, The	1993	Mrs. Crosby+	Too Good To Be Bad*	Uptempo	Alto	Bb3	F4	Supporting
Goodbye Girl, The	1993	Mrs. Crosby+	Too Good To Be Bad Play Off*	Uptempo	Alto	Bb3	F4	Supporting
Passion	1994	Fosca	I Read	Ballad	Alto	F3	D5	Lead
Passion	1994	Fosca	To Speak To Me Of Love	Moderate Tempo	Alto	E#3	C5	Lead
Passion	1994	Fosca	I Wish I Could Forget You*	Ballad	Alto	F3	C5	Lead
Passion	1994	Fosca	Loving You	Ballad	Alto	F#3	C5	Lead
Passion	1994	Fosca	All This Happiness	Moderate Tempo	Alto	B3	A4	Lead
Rent	1996	Joanne Jefferson	We're Okay	Uptempo	Alto	C4	C5	Lead
Rent	1996	Joanne Jefferson	Take Me Or leave Me*	Uptempo	Alto	C4	E5	Lead
Seussical	2000	Sour Kangaroo	Biggest Blame Fool (ms 9-29)*	Uptempo	Alto	Bb3	Db5	Lead
Spitfire Grill	2001	Hannah Ferguson	Hannah's Harangue	Moderate Tempo	Alto	G3	A4	Lead
Spitfire Grill	2001	Hannah Ferguson	Forgotten Lullaby	Ballad	Alto	G3	G4	Lead
Spitfire Grill	2001	Hannah Ferguson	Come Alive Again Part 2	Moderate Tempo	Alto	G3	A4	Lead
Spitfire Grill	2001	Hannah Ferguson	Way Back Home	Ballad	Alto	E3	B4	Lead
Caroline, Or Change	2004	Caroline Thibodeaux +	16 Feet Beneath the Sea (10-49)	Ballad	Alto	B3	D4	Lead
Caroline, Or Change	2004	Caroline Thibodeaux +	I Got Four Kids (ms 1-114)	Moderate Tempo	Alto	B3	Bb4	Lead
Caroline, Or Change	2004	Caroline Thibodeaux +	Lot's Wife (ms 67-151)	Moderate Tempo	Alto	F3	Eb5	Lead
Caroline, Or Change	2004	Caroline Thibodeaux +	Gonna Pass Me A Law (ms 1-37)	Ballad	Alto	G3	G4	Lead
Caroline, Or Change	2004	Caroline Thibodeaux +	Noah Go To Sleep (ms 60-98)	Moderate Tempo	Alto	Gb3	Db5	Lead
Caroline, Or Change	2004	Caroline Thibodeaux +	Underwater (ms 43-74)	Ballad	Alto	G3	F4	Lead
25th Annual...Spelling Bee	2005	Logainne	Woe Is Me	Uptempo	Alto	G3	D5	Lead
25th Annual...Spelling Bee	2005	Logainne	Woe Is Me Reprise	Uptempo	Alto	C4	C5	Lead

Antagonist Female

Antagonist Female

* = Music Edit Required
+ = Ethnic Specific

Show	Year	Role	Song	Tempo	Vocal Type	Range-Bottom	Range-Top	Category
25th Annual...Spelling Bee	2005	Marcy Park	I Speak Six Languages	Uptempo	Alto	B3	D5	Lead
Color Purple, The	2005	Sofia+	Hell No *	Moderate Tempo	Alto	E3	C5	Lead
Legally Blonde	2007	Vivianne Kensington	Legally Blonde Remix*	Uptempo	Alto	A3	E♭5	Lead
Mary Poppins	2006	Miss Andrew	Brimstone And Treacle (P1)	Moderate Tempo	Soprano	G#3	F5	Lead
The Little Mermaid	2007	Ursula	I Want The Good Times Back	Moderate Tempo	Soprano	F#3	A5	Lead
The Little Mermaid	2007	Ursula	Daddy's Little Angel	Moderate Tempo	Soprano	E♭3	C5	Lead
The Little Mermaid	2007	Ursula	Poor Unfortunate Soul	Moderate Tempo	Soprano	C4	A5	Lead
The Little Mermaid	2007	Ursula	Her Voice Reprise	Moderate Tempo	Soprano	D♭3	E♭4	Lead
The Little Mermaid	2007	Ursula	Ursula's Incantation*	Moderate Tempo	Soprano	G4	F#5	Lead
The Little Mermaid	2007	Ursula	I Want The Good Time Back Rep	Moderate Tempo	Soprano	F#3	A5	Lead

Antagonist Female

* = Music Edit Required
+ = Ethnic Specific

Show	Year	Role	Song	Tempo	Vocal Type	Range-Bottom	Range-Top	Category
Porgy and Bess	1935	Crown+	What You Want Wid Bess*	Mod Tempo	Baritone	Eb3	Ab4	Lead
Porgy and Bess	1935	Crown+	A Red-Headed Woman	Mod Tempo	Baritone	Db3	F4	Lead
Babes In Arms (1998)	1937	Peter	Imagine Reprise #2*	Mod Tempo	Baritone	E3	F4	Lead
Wizard Of Oz 1997	1939	Cowardly Lion	If I Only Had The Nerve*	Mod Tempo	Baritone	Bb2	D4	Lead
Wizard Of Oz 2001	1939	Cowardly Lion	King Of The Forest*	Mod Tempo	Baritone	C3	F4	Lead
Oklahoma!	1943	Jud Fry	Lonley Room	Ballad	Baritone	D3	C4	Lead
Oklahoma!	1943	Jud Fry	Poor Jud*	Ballad	Baritone	D#3	C#4	Lead
Kiss Me Kate	1948	First Man	Brush Up Your Shakespeare*	Mod Tempo	Baritone	B2	D4	Lead
Kiss Me Kate	1948	Second Man	Brush Up Your Shakespeare*	Mod Tempo	Baritone	B2	D4	Lead
Wonderful Town	1953	Wreck	Pass The Football	Mod Tempo	Baritone	Ab2	E4	Lead
Peter Pan	1954	Captain Hook	Hook's Tango*	Mod Tempo	Baritone	A2	D4	Lead
Peter Pan	1954	Captain Hook	Tarantella*	Uptempo	Baritone	D3	D4	Lead
Peter Pan	1954	Captain Hook	Captain Hook's Waltz*	Mod Tempo	Baritone	B2	G4	Lead
Damn Yankees	1955	Applegate	Those Were The Good Old Days	Uptempo	Baritone	A#2	D#4	Lead
Damn Yankees	1955	Applegate	Good Old Day Reprise	Uptempo	Baritone	A#2	E4	Lead
Camelot	1960	Mordred	The Seven Deadly Virtues	Uptempo	Baritone	C3	D4	Lead
How To Succeed...	1961	Bud Frump	Been A Long Day Reprise*	Uptempo	Baritone	Bb3	D4	Lead
A Funny Thing...Forum	1962	Marcus Lycus	The House Of Marcus Lycus	Mod Tempo	Baritone	B2	D#4	Lead
Oliver!	1963	Bill Sykes	My Name	Mod Tempo	Baritone	C#3	C4	Lead
Oliver!	1963	Fagin	Reviewing the Situation Reprise	Ballad	Baritone	C4	Eb5	Lead
110 In The Shade	1963	Noah Curry	Lizzie's Comin' Home *	Uptempo	Baritone	B2	E4	Supporting
Fiddler on The Roof	1964	Perchik	Now I Have Everything	Uptempo	Baritone	B2	E4	Supporting
Apple Tree, The	1966	Balladeer	I'll Tell You A Truth	Ballad	Baritone	E3	Eb4	Supporting
Apple Tree, The	1966	Balladeer	I'll Tell You A Truth Reprise	Ballad	Baritone	C3	F#4	Lead
Apple Tree, The	1966	Snake	Forbidden Fruit	Mod Tempo	Baritone	Eb3	G4	Supporting
Hair	1968	Berger	Going Down	Uptempo	Baritone	C3	F4	Lead
Hair	1968	Hud+	Colored Spade	Uptempo	Baritone	B2	D4	Lead
Jesus Christ Superstar	1971	Pontius Pilate	Pilate's Dream	Ballad	Baritone	A2	Bb3	Supporting

Antagonist Male

* = Music Edit Required
+ = Ethnic Specific

Show	Year	Role	Song	Tempo	Vocal Type	Range-Bottom	Range-Top	Category
Jesus Christ Superstar	1971	Pontius Pilate	Pilate and Christ	Mod Tempo	Baritone	Bb3	G#4	Supporting
Pippin	1972	Charles	War Is A Science*	Uptempo	Baritone	Bb2	E4	Lead
Pacific Overtures	1976	Thief+	Four Black Dragons*	Uptempo	Baritone	B2	C#4	Supporting
On The Twentieth Century	1978	Max Jacobs	Max Jacobs	Uptempo	Baritone	Bb2	F4	Lead
Sweeney Todd	1979	Sweeney Todd	The Barber And His Wife	Ballad	Baritone	G#2	Db4	Lead
Sweeney Todd	1979	Sweeney Todd	Epiphany*	Uptempo	Baritone	Bb2	F4	Lead
Sweeney Todd	1979	Sweeney Todd	My Friends*	Ballad	Baritone	Bb2	Eb4	Lead
Sweeney Todd	1979	Sweeney Todd	Johanna II*	Mod Tempo	Baritone	A2	Eb4	Lead
Sweeney Todd	1979	Sweeney Todd	Finale Scene II	Uptempo	Baritone	G2	C4	Lead
Little Shop of Horrors	1982	Orin Scrivello	Dentist!	Uptempo	Baritone	A2	F4	Lead
Little Shop of Horrors	1982	Voice of Audrey II	Git It (Feed Me)*	Mod Tempo	Baritone	B2	G4	Lead
Little Shop of Horrors	1982	Voice of Audrey II	Suppertime*	Mod Tempo	Baritone	G2	F4	Lead
Sunday...Park With Geroge	1984	Boatman	The Day Off (Part 6)	Mod Tempo	Baritone	E2	C4	Supporting
Rags	1986	Saul	Easy For You	Uptempo	Baritone	D3	D4	Lead
Les Miserables	1987	Thenardier	Master of the House*	Uptempo	Baritone	C3	D4	Supporting
Les Miserables	1987	Thenardier	Dog Eats Dog	Mod Tempo	Baritone	C3	E4	Supporting
Les Miserables	1987	Thenardier	Beggars at the Wedding	Uptempo	Baritone	G#2	C4	Supporting
Will Rogers Follies	1991	Clem Rogers	It's A Boy	Uptempo	Baritone	C#3	E4	Lead
Will Rogers Follies	1991	Clem Rogers	It's A Boy Reprise	Uptempo	Baritone	D#3	E4	Lead
Will Rogers Follies	1991	Clem Rogers	Clem's Retur	Mod Tempo	Baritone	C#3	D#4	Lead
Phantom	1991	Erik (Phantom)	You Are My Own*	Mod Tempo	Baritone	G2	E4	Lead
Phantom	1991	Phantom	Paris Is A Tomb	Ballad	Baritone	A2	C4	Lead
Phantom	1991	Phantom	Where In The World	Uptempo	Baritone	G2	F4	Lead
Phantom	1991	Phantom	Home*	Mod Tempo	Baritone	C3	G4	Lead
Phantom	1991	Phantom	Where In The World Reprise	Uptempo	Baritone	Bb2	F4	Lead
Phantom	1991	Phantom	My Mother Bore Me	Mod Tempo	Baritone	F2	F#4	Lead
My Favorite Year	1992	King Kaiser	The Gospel According To King*	Uptempo	Baritone	D3	C#4	Lead
Goodbye Girl, The	1993	Elliott Garfield	Elliott Garfield Grant	Uptempo	Baritone	C3	Gb4	Lead

Antagonist Male

* = Music Edit Required
+ = Ethnic Specific

Show	Year	Role	Song	Tempo	Vocal Type	Range-Bottom	Range-Top	Category
Goodbye Girl, The	1993	Elliott Garfield	Good News, Bad News*	Mod Tempo	Baritone	Bb3	F4	Lead
Goodbye Girl, The	1993	Elliott Garfield	Paula*	Mod Tempo	Baritone	G#2	E4	Lead
Goodbye Girl, The	1993	Elliott Garfield	I Can Play This Part	Ballad	Baritone	G#2	Eb4	Lead
Blood Brothers	1993	Mickey	Long Sunday Afternoon *	Ballad	Baritone	D3	E4	Lead
Lion King, The	1997	Scar	Be Prepared*	Uptempo	Baritone	A2	A3	Lead
Lion King, The	1997	Scar	Be Prepared Reprise*	Uptempo	Baritone	A2	D3	Lead
Parade	1998	Judge Roan	Judge Roan's Letter	Uptempo	Baritone	Eb2	D4	Lead
Parade	1998	Newt Lee+	The Trial, Part 5: Newt Lee's Testimony	Uptempo	Baritone	B2	F#3	Lead
Footloose	1998	Willard Hewitt	Mama Says	Uptempo	Baritone	Bb2	G4	Lead
Marie Christine	1999	Charles Gates	Good Looking Woman*	Mod Tempo	Baritone	G3	E5	Lead
Seussical	2000	Genghis Kahn Schmitz	The Military*	Uptempo	Baritone	G2	F4	Supporting
Full Monty, The	2000	Noah "Horse" Simmons	Big Black Man *	Uptempo	Baritone	G3	G4	Lead
Producers, The	2001	Franz Liebkind	In Old Bavaria	Mod Tempo	Baritone	F2	D4	Lead
Producers, The	2001	Franz Liebkind	Der Guten Tag Hop-Clop	Uptempo	Baritone	D#3	E4	Lead
Sweet Smell Of Success	2002	JJ Hunsecker	For Susan*	Mod Tempo	Baritone	C3	Eb4	Lead
Sweet Smell Of Success	2002	JJ Hunsecker	Don't Look Now*	Mod Tempo	Baritone	C3	G4	Lead
Chitty Chitty Bang Bang	2005	Childcatcher	Kiddy Widdy Winkies	Mod Tempo	Baritone	D3	E4	Supporting
Chitty Chitty Bang Bang	2005	Childcatcher	Childcatcher as Grandpa	Mod Tempo	Baritone	C3	C4	Supporting
Chitty Chitty Bang Bang	2005	Goan	Act English *	Mod Tempo	Baritone	C3	E4	Supporting
Spamalot	2005	King Arthur	Always Lok On The Bright Side of Life*	Mod Tempo	Baritone	C3	D4	Lead
Spamalot	2005	King Arthur	I'm All Alone*	Ballad	Baritone	A2	A3	Lead
25th Annual...Spelling Bee	2005	William Barfee	Magic Foot	Uptempo	Baritone	F3	A4	Lead
25th Annual...Spelling Bee	2005	William Barfee	Second Part 1*	Mod Tempo	Baritone	Db3	Eb4	Lead
Of Thee I Sing	1931	French Ambassador	The Illegitimate Daughter*	Uptempo	Tenor	C#3	G4	Lead
Of Thee I Sing	1931	French Ambassador	Illegitimate Daughter Reprise*	Uptempo	Tenor	D3	D4	Lead
Babes In Arms (1998)	1937	Gus Fielding	I Wish I Were In Love Again*	Uptempo	Tenor	C3	Ab4	Lead
Babes In Arms (1998)	1937	Gus Fielding	You Are So Fair*	Uptempo	Tenor	Eb3	F4	Lead

Antagonist Male

* = Music Edit Required
+ = Ethnic Specific

Show	Year	Role	Song	Tempo	Vocal Type	Range-Bottom	Range-Top	Category
Jersey Boys (2005)	1954	Tommy DeVito	Earth Angel	Ballad	Tenor	Bb3	Eb4	Lead
Candide	1956	Dr. Pangloss	Dear Boy	Uptempo	Tenor	Bb2	F#4	Lead
Candide	1956	Dr. Pangloss	The Venice Gavotte*	Uptempo	Tenor	Bb2	F4	Lead
Candide	1956	Vanderdenur	Bon Voyage*	Uptempo	Tenor	C3	Bb4	Supporting
West Side Story	1957	Riff	Cool	Mod Tempo	Tenor	C3	Eb4	Lead
West Side Story	1957	Riff	The Jet Song*	Uptempo	Tenor	Bb2	G4	Lead
How To Succeed...	1961	Bud Frump	Company Way Reprise*	Uptempo	Tenor	D3	G4	Lead
Sweet Charity	1966	Herman	I Love To Cry At Weddings*	Uptempo	Tenor	D3	B4	Lead
Hair	1968	Berger	Donna	Uptempo	Tenor	Eb3	Bb4	Lead
Godspell	1971	John The Baptist	Prepare Ye*	Ballad	Tenor	C#3	G#4	Lead
Godspell	1971	Judas	On The Willows	Ballad	Tenor	C3	F#4	Lead
Godspell	1971	Judas	All For The Best*	Uptempo	Tenor	C3	D4	Lead
Jesus Christ Superstar	1971	Judas Iscariot	Heaven On Their Minds	Uptempo	Tenor	D3	D5	Lead
Jesus Christ Superstar	1971	Judas Iscariot	Damned For All Time*	Uptempo	Tenor	D3	D5	Lead
Jesus Christ Superstar	1971	Judas Iscariot	Judas' Death	Uptempo	Tenor	D3	E5	Lead
Jesus Christ Superstar	1971	Judas Iscariot	Superstar	Uptempo	Tenor	E3	B4	Lead
Grease	1971	Kenicke	Greased Lightening	Uptempo	Tenor	E3	B4	Lead
Jesus Christ Superstar	1971	Simon Zealots	Simon Zealots*	Uptempo	Tenor	F3	Ab4	Supporting
Wiz, The	1974	Lion	Mean Ole Lion	Uptempo	Tenor	G2	Bb4	Lead
Wiz, The	1974	Lion	Be A Lion*	Ballad	Tenor	Ab3	Ab4	Lead
A Chorus Line	1975	Richie +	Gimmie The Ball (ms 231-269) *	Uptempo	Tenor	C#3	G4	Supporting
Pacific Overtures	1976	Mother+	Chrysanthemum Tea*	Mod Tempo	Tenor	D3	F4	Lead
Evita	1978	Che Guevara	Oh What A Circus	Uptempo	Tenor	B2	E4	Lead
Evita	1978	Che Guevara	Goodnight and Thank You	Uptempo	Tenor	B2	F4	Lead
Evita	1978	Che Guevara	High Flying Adored	Mod Tempo	Tenor	Bb2	G4	Lead
Evita	1978	Che Guevara	Rainbow Tour	Uptempo	Tenor	C3	E4	Lead
Evita	1978	Che Guevara	And the Money Kept Rolling In	Uptempo	Tenor	A2	G4	Lead

Antagonist Male

* = Music Edit Required
+ = Ethnic Specific

Show	Year	Role	Song	Tempo	Vocal Type	Range-Bottom	Range-Top	Category
Evita	1978	Che Guevara	Waltz for Eva and Che	Uptempo	Tenor	D3	G4	Lead
Mystery Of Edwin Drood, The	1985	John Jasper	A Man Could Go Quite Mad	Uptempo	Tenor	A2	G4	Lead
Mystery Of Edwin Drood, The	1985	John Jasper	Both Sides Of The Coin*	Uptempo	Tenor	C3	E4	Lead
Mystery Of Edwin Drood, The	1985	John Jasper	Jasper's Confession	Mod Tempo	Tenor	B2	A4	Lead
Phantom Of The Opera	1986	Phantom	Phantom Of The Opera*	Mod Tempo	Tenor	B2	G#4	Lead
Phantom Of The Opera	1986	Phantom	The Music Of The Night	Ballad	Tenor	G#2	G#4	Lead
Phantom Of The Opera	1986	Phantom	Stranger Than You Dreamt It*	Ballad	Tenor	D3	D4	Lead
Phantom Of The Opera	1986	Phantom	All I Ask Of You Reprise	Ballad	Tenor	G3	A4	Lead
Phantom Of The Opera	1986	Phantom	Why So Silent*	Ballad	Tenor	Eb3	Gb4	Lead
Phantom Of The Opera	1986	Phantom	Notes: No Doubt She'll Do Her Best	Ballad	Tenor	D#3	D#4	Lead
Phantom Of The Opera	1986	Phantom	The Point Of No Return*	Ballad	Tenor	C3	G4	Lead
Phantom Of The Opera	1986	Phantom	All I Ask Of You Reprise 2*	Ballad	Tenor	Db3	Ab4	Lead
Les Miserables	1987	Javert	Stars	Mod Tempo	Tenor	B2	E4	Lead
Les Miserables	1987	Javert	Javert's Suicide	Mod Tempo	Tenor	C3	F#4	Lead
Chess	1988	Arbiter	The Story of Chess	Mod Tempo	Tenor	B2	G4	Supporting
Chess	1988	Arbiter	The Arbiter	Uptempo	Tenor	E3	A4	Supporting
Chess	1988	Arbiter	The Arbiter Reprise	Uptempo	Tenor	E3	A4	Supporting
Once On This Island	1990	Papa Ge+	Forever Yours*	Uptempo	Tenor	C#3	G4	Lead
Once On This Island	1990	Papa Ge+	Promises/Forever Yours Reprise*	Mod Tempo	Tenor	C3	G4	Lead
Children of Eden	1991	Cain	Lost In The Wilderness *	Mod Tempo	Tenor	D3	G4	Lead
Miss Saigon	1991	Engineer+	If you Want To Die In Bed*	Mod Tempo	Tenor	A2	G4	Lead
Miss Saigon	1991	Engineer+	What A Waste*	Mod Tempo	Tenor	B2	F#4	Lead
Miss Saigon	1991	Engineer+	The American Dream*	Mod Tempo	Tenor	A2	A4	Lead
Assassins	1992	Giuseppe Zangara	How I Saved Roosevelt*	Uptempo	Tenor	D3	A4	Lead
Assassins	1992	John Hinkley	Unworthy Of Your Love*	Mod Tempo	Tenor	B2	E4	Lead
Honk	1993	Cat	You Can Play With Your Food	Uptempo	Tenor	C3	Ab4	Supporting
Jekyll and Hyde	1997	Mr. Edward Hyde	Alive	Uptempo	Tenor	B2	D4	Lead
Jekyll and Hyde	1997	Mr. Edward Hyde	Confrontation*	Uptempo	Tenor	B2	A4	Lead
Jekyll and Hyde	1997	Mr. Edward Hyde	Alive Reprise	Uptempo	Tenor	E3	A4	Lead

Antagonist Male

* = Music Edit Required
+ = Ethnic Specific

Show	Year	Role	Song	Tempo	Vocal Type	Range-Bottom	Range-Top	Category
Parade	1998	Britt Craig	Real Big News*	Uptempo	Tenor	F3	A4	Lead
Parade	1998	Britt Craig	Opening Act II	Mod Tempo	Tenor	F3	G4	Lead
Parade	1998	Britt Craig	Big News	Uptempo	Tenor	D3	Ab4	Lead
Parade	1998	Newt Lee+	Interrogation Sequence*	Mod Tempo	Tenor	Bb2	C4	Lead
Aida	2000	Zoser	Another Pyramid	Uptempo	Tenor	F3	E4	Supporting
Aida	2000	Zoser	Like Father Like Son*	Uptempo	Tenor	G3	Bb4	Supporting
Producers, The	2001	Franz Liebkind	Haben Sie Gehort Das Deutsche Band	Uptempo	Tenor	A2	G4	Lead
Fame	2003	Tyrone+	Tyrone's Rap	Uptempo	Tenor	Bb3	Bb4	Lead
Fame	2003	Tyrone+	Dancin' On The Sidewalk	Uptempo	Tenor	Bb2	Bb4	Lead
Chitty Chitty Bang Bang	2005	Boris	Act English *	Mod Tempo	Tenor	C3	G4	Supporting
Color Purple, The	2005	Mister+	Big Dog	Uptempo	Tenor	F3	Ab4	Lead
Color Purple, The	2005	Mister+	Mister's Song (2005)	Mod Tempo	Tenor	E3	G4	Lead
Color Purple, The	2005	Mister+	Mister's Song (2015)	Mod Tempo	Tenor	F3	Ab4	Lead
25th Annual...Spelling Bee	2005	Mitch Mahoney	Prayer of the Comfort Counselor	Uptempo	Tenor	E3	A4	Lead
25th Annual...Spelling Bee	2005	Mitch Mahoney	The I Love You Song	Ballad	Tenor	E3	G#4	Lead
Spring Awakening	2006	Moritz	The Bitch Of Living*	Uptempo	Tenor	C3	D4	Lead
Spring Awakening	2006	Moritz	And Then There Were None*	Uptempo	Tenor	E3	G#4	Lead
Spring Awakening	2006	Moritz	Don't Do Sadness	Uptempo	Tenor	B2	A4	Lead
Spring Awakening	2006	Moritz	Those You've Known*	Ballad	Tenor	D3	E4	Lead
The Little Mermaid	2007	Flotsam	Sweet Child	Ballad	Tenor	C3	C5	Supporting
The Little Mermaid	2007	Jetsom	Sweet Child	Ballad	Tenor	C3	C5	Supporting

Antagonist Male

* = Music Edit Required
+ = Ethnic Specific

Show	Year	Role	Song	Tempo	Range-Bottom	Range-Top	Category	Char Type
Marry Poppins	2006	Miss Andrew	Brimstone And Treacle (P1)	Moderate Tempo	G#3	F5	Lead	Antagonist Female
The Little Mermaid	2007	Ursula	I Want The Good Times Back	Moderate Tempo	F#3	A5	Lead	Antagonist Female
The Little Mermaid	2007	Ursula	Daddy's Little Angel	Moderate Tempo	Eb3	C5	Lead	Antagonist Female
The Little Mermaid	2007	Ursula	Poor Unfortunate Soul	Moderate Tempo	C4	A5	Lead	Antagonist Female
The Little Mermaid	2007	Ursula	Her Voice Reprise	Moderate Tempo	Db3	Eb4	Lead	Antagonist Female
The Little Mermaid	2007	Ursula	Ursula's Incantation*	Moderate Tempo	G4	F#5	Lead	Antagonist Female
The Little Mermaid	2007	Ursula	I Want The Good Time Back Reprise	Moderate Tempo	F#3	A5	Lead	Antagonist Female
No, No Nanette	1925	Winnie Winslow	The Three Happies*	Moderate Tempo	C5	G5	Supporting	Character Female
Porgy and Bess	1935	Serena+	My Man's Gone Now*	Moderate Tempo	E4	B5	Lead	Character Female
Crazy For You (1992)	1937	Patricia Fodor	Stiff Upper Lip	Uptempo	D4	F5	Supporting	Character Female
Peter Pan	1954	Peter Pan	I've Got To Crow	Uptempo	Bb3	C5	Lead	Character Female
Peter Pan	1954	Peter Pan	Neverland	Moderate Tempo	Eb3	C5	Lead	Character Female
Peter Pan	1954	Peter Pan	I'm Flying*	Uptempo	A3	F5	Lead	Character Female
Peter Pan	1954	Peter Pan	Wendy*	Moderate Tempo	Bb3	C5	Lead	Character Female
Peter Pan	1954	Peter Pan	Distant Melody	Ballad	Gb3	Ab4	Lead	Character Female
Peter Pan	1954	Peter Pan	Neverland Reprise	Moderate Tempo	E3	B4	Lead	Character Female
Cinderella (2013)	1957	F Godmother (Marie)	Impossible*	Uptempo	F3	F4	Supporting	Character Female
Cinderella (2013)	1957	F Godmother (Marie)	Fol-De-Rol	Uptempo	A2	F#4	Supporting	Character Female
110 In The Shade	1963	Lizzie Curry	Love Don't Turn Away	Uptempo	D#4	F5	Lead	Character Female
110 In The Shade	1963	Lizzie Curry	Raunchy	Uptempo	G3	F5	Lead	Character Female
110 In The Shade	1963	Lizzie Curry	Old Maid	Moderate Tempo	B3	G#5	Lead	Character Female
110 In The Shade	1963	Lizzie Curry	Simple Little Things	Ballad	B3	E5	Lead	Character Female
110 In The Shade	1963	Lizzie Curry	Is It Really Me	Ballad	A3	E5	Lead	Character Female
110 In The Shade	1963	Lizzie Curry	A Man And A Woman *	Ballad	D4	G5	Lead	Character Female
Anyone Can Whistle	1964	Soprano Cadenza	Cora's Chase*	Uptempo	B4	D6	Featured Ensemble	Character Female
Mame	1966	Anges Gooch	St. Bridget*	Ballad	G3	F5	Lead	Character Female
Mame	1966	Anges Gooch	Gooch's Song	Moderate Tempo	G3	Bb5	Lead	Character Female
Company (Revival)	1970	April	You Could Drive a Person Crazy	Uptempo	C#4	A5	Supporting	Character Female
Follies	1971	Sally Durant	Too Many Mornings *	Ballad	C4	G#5	Lead	Character Female
Follies	1971	Sally Durant	Losing My Mind	Ballad	F3	B4	Lead	Character Female

Soprano

* = Music Edit Required
+ = Ethnic Specific

Show	Year	Role	Song	Tempo	Range-Bottom	Range-Top	Category	Char Type
Follies	1971	Sally Durant	The Story of Lucy and Jesse	Uptempo	G3	Bb4	Lead	Character Female
Follies	1971	Sally Durant	Don't Look At Me*	Uptempo	A3	B4	Lead	Character Female
Chicago	1975	Mary Sunshine	A Little Good In Everyone	Moderate Tempo	F3	B5	Supporting	Character Female
Best Little Whorehouse...	1978	Jewel	Twenty-four Hours of Lovin'	Uptempo	G3	G5	Supporting	Character Female
Best Little Whorehouse...	1978	Jewel	No Lies	Uptempo	C4	E5	Supporting	Character Female
Mystery Of Edwin Drood, Th	1985	Edwin Drood	The Writing On The Wall*	Uptempo	G3	Gb5	Lead	Character Female
Nunsense	1985	Mary Amnesia	So You Want To Be A Nun	Moderate Tempo	C4	B5	Lead	Character Female
Nunsense	1985	Mary Amnesia	I Could've Gone To Nashville	Ballad	G3	E5	Lead	Character Female
Ain't Misbehavin'	1988	Woman Three +	When The Nylons Are In Bloom Again	Uptempo	C4	D5	Lead	Character Female
Ain't Misbehavin'	1988	Woman Three +	Squeeze Me	Ballad	Ab3	Db5	Lead	Character Female
Chess	1988	Svetlana	You and I*	Ballad	G3	Eb5	Supporting	Character Female
Chess	1988	Svetlana	I Know Him So Well	Ballad	F3	D5	Supporting	Character Female
Assassins	1992	Squeaky Fromme	Unworthy Of Your Love*	Moderate Tempo	A3	D5	Lead	Character Female
Cinderella (2013)	1997	F Godmother (Marie)	There's Music In You*	Ballad	C4	F5	Lead	Character Female
25th Annual...Spelling Bee	2005	Rona Lisa Peretti	My Favorite Moment of the Bee	Moderate Tempo	D4	D5	Lead	Character Female
25th Annual...Spelling Bee	2005	Rona Lisa Peretti	Rona Moment #2	Moderate Tempo	D4	D5	Lead	Character Female
25th Annual...Spelling Bee	2005	Rona Lisa Peretti	Rona Moment #3	Moderate Tempo	Db4	Db5	Lead	Character Female
25th Annual...Spelling Bee	2005	Rona Lisa Peretti	The I Love You Song	Ballad	D4	E5	Lead	Character Female
Chitty Chitty Bang Bang	2005	Baroness Bomburst	The Bombie Samba	Uptempo	B3	Eb5	Supporting	Character Female
Chitty Chitty Bang Bang	2005	Baroness Bomburst	Chu-Chi Face	Moderate Tempo	C4	F5	Supporting	Character Female
Drowsy Chaperon, The	2006	Drowsy Chaperone	Show Off Encore	Uptempo	A3	A5	Lead	Character Female
Drowsy Chaperon, The	2006	Trix	I Do, I Do In The Sky	Uptempo	A3	A5	Lead	Character Female
Oklahoma!	1943	Laurey	Many A New Day	Uptempo	C#4	E5	Lead	Character Ingenue Female
Oklahoma!	1943	Laurey	People Will Say We're In Love	Moderate Tempo	C#4	F#5	Lead	Character Ingenue Female
Oklahoma!	1943	Laurey	Out Of My Dreams	Moderate Tempo	E4	F5	Lead	Character Ingenue Female
On The Town	1944	Claire DeLune	Carried Away	Uptempo	F3	G5	Lead	Character Ingenue Female
On The Town	1944	Claire DeLune	Ya Got Me *	Uptempo	G3	Eb4	Lead	Character Ingenue Female
Carousel	1945	Julie Jordan	If I Loved You *	Ballad	C4	Gb5	Lead	Character Ingenue Female
Carousel	1945	Julie Jordan	What's The Use In Wonderin'	Ballad	C4	F5	Lead	Character Ingenue Female
Most Happy Fella, The	1956	Rosabella	I Don't Know*	Moderate Tempo	Bb3	D5	Lead	Character Ingenue Female

Soprano

* = Music Edit Required
+ = Ethnic Specific

Show	Year	Role	Song	Tempo	Range-Bottom	Range-Top	Category	Char Type
Most Happy Fella, The	1956	Rosabella	Somebody Somewhere	Ballad	E4	G5	Lead	Character Ingenue Female
Most Happy Fella, The	1956	Rosabella	Aren't You Glad?	Ballad	C4	E5	Lead	Character Ingenue Female
Most Happy Fella, The	1956	Rosabella	No Home No Job	Uptempo	D4	Eb5	Lead	Character Ingenue Female
Most Happy Fella, The	1956	Rosabella	Warm All Over	Ballad	C#4	F#5	Lead	Character Ingenue Female
Most Happy Fella, The	1956	Rosabella	I Love Him*	Moderate Tempo	D4	Eb5	Lead	Character Ingenue Female
Most Happy Fella, The	1956	Rosabella	Like A Woman Loves A Man	Moderate Tempo	D4	G5	Lead	Character Ingenue Female
Most Happy Fella, The	1956	Rosabella	My Heart Is So Full Of You*	Ballad	Db4	Gb5	Lead	Character Ingenue Female
Most Happy Fella, The	1956	Rosabella	Please Let Me Tell You	Uptempo	D4	F4	Lead	Character Ingenue Female
Most Happy Fella, The	1956	Rosabella	Please Let Me Tell You	Uptempo	D4	E5	Lead	Character Ingenue Female
Once Upon A Mattress	1959	Nightingale	Nightingale Lullaby	Moderate Tempo	Gb4	G5	Supporting	Character Ingenue Female
Sound Of Music, The	1959	Maria Rainer	The Sound Of Music	Moderate Tempo	B3	B4	Lead	Character Ingenue Female
Sound Of Music, The	1959	Maria Rainer	The Lonely Goatherd	Uptempo	C4	Bb5	Lead	Character Ingenue Female
Sound Of Music, The	1959	Maria Rainer	Ordinary People*	Ballad	B3	D5	Lead	Character Ingenue Female
Anyone Can Whistle	1964	Baby Joan	I'm Like The Bluebird	Uptempo	B3	C#5	Featured Ensemble	Character Ingenue Female
Company (Revival)	1970	Amy	Not Getting Married Today	Uptempo	C#4	Ab5	Supporting	Character Ingenue Female
Wiz, The	1974	Dorothy	Soon As I Get Home	Uptempo	C4	C#5	Lead	Character Ingenue Female
Wiz, The	1974	Dorothy	Home	Uptempo	Bb3	D5	Lead	Character Ingenue Female
Wiz, The	1974	Dorothy	Be A Lion*	Ballad	Bb3	Bb5	Lead	Character Ingenue Female
Dreamgirls	1981	Lorelle Robinson +	Ain't No Party *	Uptempo	Bb3	E4	Lead	Character Ingenue Female
Ain't Misbehavin'	1988	Woman Two +	Yacht Club Swing	Uptempo	Ab3	Ab5	Lead	Character Ingenue Female
Ain't Misbehavin'	1988	Woman Two +	Keepin' Out of Mischief Now	Ballad	A3	C5	Lead	Character Ingenue Female
My Favorite Year	1992	K.C. Downing	Funny*	Moderate Tempo	A3	E5	Lead	Character Ingenue Female
My Favorite Year	1992	K.C. Downing	Shut Up And Dance*	Moderate Tempo	A3	C5	Lead	Character Ingenue Female
Beauty and the Beast	1994	Belle	Home	Ballad	G3	E5	Lead	Character Ingenue Female
Beauty and the Beast	1994	Belle	Belle Reprise	Uptempo	D4	D5	Lead	Character Ingenue Female
Beauty and the Beast	1994	Belle	Something There *	Uptempo	A3	E5	Lead	Character Ingenue Female
Beauty and the Beast	1994	Belle	Home Reprise	Ballad	C4	D5	Lead	Character Ingenue Female
Sunset Boulevard	1994	Betty Schaefer	Too Much In Love To Care*	Moderate Tempo	A3	G5	Lead	Character Ingenue Female
Sunset Boulevard	1994	Betty Schaefer	Girl Meets Boy Reprise*	Uptempo	A3	E5	Lead	Character Ingenue Female
Steel Pier	1997	Precious McGuire	Two Little Words	Uptempo	C4	E6	Lead	Character Ingenue Female

Soprano

147

Soprano

* = Music Edit Required
+ = Ethnic Specific

Show	Year	Role	Song	Tempo	Range-Bottom	Range-Top	Category	Char Type
Ragtime	1998	Sarah	Your Daddy's Son (B♭Maj)	Ballad	G3	F5	Lead	Character Ingenue Female
Ragtime	1998	Sarah	Your Daddy's Son (C♭Maj)	Ballad	A♭3	G♭5	Lead	Character Ingenue Female
Ragtime	1998	Sarah	New Music*	Ballad	B♭3	D5	Lead	Character Ingenue Female
Ragtime	1998	Sarah	President (A Maj)*	Moderate Tempo	A3	D5	Lead	Character Ingenue Female
Ragtime	1998	Sarah	President (B♭Maj)*	Moderate Tempo	B♭3	E♭5	Lead	Character Ingenue Female
Ragtime	1998	Sarah	Justice*	Uptempo	A♭3	C5	Lead	Character Ingenue Female
Seussical	2000	Gertrude McFuzz	The One Feather Tail	Moderate Tempo	G3	C5	Lead	Character Ingenue Female
Seussical	2000	Gertrude McFuzz	Amayzing Gertrude*	Uptempo	C#4	D6	Lead	Character Ingenue Female
Seussical	2000	Gertrude McFuzz	Notice Me, Horton*	Uptempo	G3	C5	Lead	Character Ingenue Female
Seussical	2000	Gertrude McFuzz	For You*	Uptempo	F3	C5	Lead	Character Ingenue Female
A Man Of No Importance	2002	Adele Rice	Princess	Moderate Tempo	C4	E5	Supporting	Character Ingenue Female
A Man Of No Importance	2002	Adele Rice	Love Who You Love (Adele Reprise)	Ballad	A♭3	D♭5	Supporting	Character Ingenue Female
Into The Woods	2002	Rapunzel	Our Little World	Moderate Tempo			Lead	Character Ingenue Female
No, No Nanette	1925	Nanette	I've Confessed To The Breeze*	Moderate Tempo	B3	F5	Lead	Ingenue Female
No, No Nanette	1925	Nanette	I Want To Be Happy*	Uptempo	C4	E5	Lead	Ingenue Female
No, No Nanette	1925	Nanette	No, No Nanette*	Uptempo	B♭3	F5	Lead	Ingenue Female
No, No Nanette	1925	Nanette	Peach On The Beach*	Uptempo	F#4	A4	Lead	Ingenue Female
No, No Nanette	1925	Nanette	Tea For Two*	Moderate Tempo	E♭4	F5	Lead	Ingenue Female
No, No Nanette	1925	Nanette	Waiting For You*	Moderate Tempo	A♭3	E♭5	Lead	Ingenue Female
Show Boat	1927	Magnolia	Make Believe	Ballad	D4	B♭5	Lead	Ingenue Female
Show Boat	1927	Magnolia	You Are Love*	Ballad	D4	B♭5	Lead	Ingenue Female
Show Boat	1927	Magnolia	Can't Help Reprise	Ballad	A♭3	E♭5	Lead	Ingenue Female
Show Boat	1927	Magnolia	After The Ball	Moderate Tempo	D4	A♭5	Lead	Ingenue Female
Show Boat	1927	Magnolia	Dance The Night Away*	Uptempo	G3	C5	Lead	Ingenue Female
Anything Goes	1934	Hope Harcourt	All Through The Night *	Ballad	C4	E♭5	Lead	Ingenue Female
Anything Goes	1934	Hope Harcourt	The Gypsy In Me	Moderate Tempo	C3	G4	Lead	Ingenue Female
Anything Goes	1934	Hope Harcourt	Goodbye Little Dream, Goodbye	Ballad	A3	E♭5	Lead	Ingenue Female
Porgy and Bess	1935	Clara+	Summertime	Moderate Tempo	F#4	B5	Lead	Ingenue Female
Porgy and Bess	1935	Clara+	Summertime Reprise	Moderate Tempo	E4	A5	Lead	Ingenue Female

Soprano

* = Music Edit Required
+ = Ethnic Specific

Show	Year	Role	Song	Tempo	Range-Bottom	Range-Top	Category	Char Type
Brigadoon	1947	Fiona MacLaren	Waitin For My Dearie *	Ballad	C4	A5	Lead	Ingenue Female
Brigadoon	1947	Fiona MacLaren	The Heather On The Hill *	Ballad	B♭2	G4	Lead	Ingenue Female
Brigadoon	1947	Fiona MacLaren	Almost Like Being In Love *	Ballad	F4	A5	Lead	Ingenue Female
Brigadoon	1947	Fiona MacLaren	From This Day On *	Ballad	F4	A5	Lead	Ingenue Female
Brigadoon	1947	Fiona MacLaren	Come To Me Bend To Me Reprise	Ballad	D4	G5	Lead	Ingenue Female
Brigadoon	1947	Fiona MacLaren	The Heather On The Hill Reprise	Ballad	C4	F5	Lead	Ingenue Female
Brigadoon	1947	Fiona MacLaren	From This Day On Reprise *	Ballad	E♭4	G5	Lead	Ingenue Female
Guys and Dolls	1950	Sarah Brown	I'll Know*	Ballad	E4	G#5	Lead	Ingenue Female
Guys and Dolls	1950	Sarah Brown	If I Were A Bell	Uptempo	B♭3	D5	Lead	Ingenue Female
Guys and Dolls	1950	Sarah Brown	Marry The Man Today*	Uptempo	C4	E♭5	Lead	Ingenue Female
Guys and Dolls	1950	Sarah Brown	I'll Know (Finish)	Ballad	E♭4	F5	Lead	Ingenue Female
King and I, The	1951	Tuptim+	My Lord And Master	Moderate Tempo	D#4	A#5	Lead	Ingenue Female
King and I, The	1951	Tuptim+	We Kiss In The Shadow	Ballad	D4	G5	Lead	Ingenue Female
King and I, The	1951	Tuptim+	I Have Dreamed	Ballad	C4	G5	Lead	Ingenue Female
Wonderful Town	1953	Eileen Sherwood	A Little Bit In Love	Moderate Tempo	C4	C#5	Lead	Ingenue Female
Wonderful Town	1953	Eileen Sherwood	Conversation Piece*	Uptempo	D4	B4	Lead	Ingenue Female
Wonderful Town	1953	Eileen Sherwood	A Little Bit In Love	Moderate Tempo	C4	C#5	Lead	Ingenue Female
Candide	1956	Cunegonde	Life Is Happiness Indeed*	Moderate Tempo	F4	C6	Lead	Ingenue Female
Candide	1956	Cunegonde	Glitter And Be Gay	Moderate Tempo	B2	E6	Lead	Ingenue Female
My Fair Lady	1956	Eliza Doolittle	Wouldn't It Be Loverly	Moderate Tempo	C4	E♭5	Lead	Ingenue Female
My Fair Lady	1956	Eliza Doolittle	Just You Wait	Moderate Tempo	A3	E♭4	Lead	Ingenue Female
My Fair Lady	1956	Eliza Doolittle	I Could Have Danced All Night*	Uptempo	B3	G5	Lead	Ingenue Female
My Fair Lady	1956	Eliza Doolittle	Just You Wait Reprise	Ballad	D4	C5	Lead	Ingenue Female
My Fair Lady	1956	Eliza Doolittle	Wouldn't It Be Loverly Reprise*	Ballad	C4	D5	Lead	Ingenue Female
My Fair Lady	1956	Eliza Doolittle	Without You	Moderate Tempo	B3	E♭5	Lead	Ingenue Female
My Fair Lady	1956	Eliza Doolittle	Show Me	Uptempo	D4	G5	Lead	Ingenue Female
Cinderella (2013)	1957	Ella	In My Own Little Corner	Uptempo	C4	C5	Lead	Ingenue Female
Cinderella (2013)	1957	Ella	In My Own Little Corner Reprise	Uptempo	C4	C5	Lead	Ingenue Female
Cinderella (2013)	1957	Ella	Impossible*	Uptempo	B♭2	D5	Lead	Ingenue Female
Cinderella (2013)	1957	Ella	Ten Minutes Ago*	Moderate Tempo	C#4	D5	Lead	Ingenue Female
Cinderella (2013)	1957	Ella	Do I Love You...*	Ballad	A4	E5	Lead	Ingenue Female

Soprano

149

Soprano

* = Music Edit Required
+ = Ethnic Specific

Show	Year	Role	Song	Tempo	Range-Bottom	Range-Top	Category	Char Type
Cinderella (2013)	1957	Ella	When You're Driving....*	Uptempo	B2	Bb4	Lead	Ingenue Female
Cinderella (2013)	1957	Ella	A Lovely Night*	Uptempo	Bb3	Bb4	Lead	Ingenue Female
Cinderella (2013)	1957	Ella	A Lovely Night*	Uptempo	C4	C5	Lead	Ingenue Female
Cinderella (2013)	1957	Ella	It's Possible	Uptempo	C4	B4	Lead	Ingenue Female
West Side Story	1957	Maria+	I Feel Pretty*	Uptempo	C4	F5	Lead	Ingenue Female
West Side Story	1957	Female Shark+	Somewhere	Ballad	B3	F#5	Featured Ensemble	Ingenue Female
West Side Story	1957	Maria+	I Have A Love*	Ballad	Bb3	Bb5	Lead	Ingenue Female
Bye Bye Birdie	1960	Kim MacAfee	How Lovely To Be A Woman	Moderate Tempo	D#4	F#4	Lead	Ingenue Female
Bye Bye Birdie	1960	Kim MacAfee	One Boy	Ballad	Db4	F5	Lead	Ingenue Female
Bye Bye Birdie	1960	Kim MacAfee	What Did I Ever See In Him *	Uptempo	G3	Bb4	Lead	Ingenue Female
Bye Bye Birdie	1960	Kim MacAfee	Lot of Livin' To Do *	Uptempo	D4	E5	Lead	Ingenue Female
Fantasticks, The	1960	Luisa	Much More	Uptempo	B3	F5	Lead	Ingenue Female
Fantasticks, The	1960	Luisa	Metaphor *	Uptempo	Eb4	G5	Lead	Ingenue Female
Fantasticks, The	1960	Luisa	Soon It's Gonna Rain *	Moderate Tempo	B2	F4	Lead	Ingenue Female
Fantasticks, The	1960	Luisa	They Were You *	Ballad	B3	D5	Lead	Ingenue Female
A Funny Thing...Forum	1962	Philia	Lovely*	Moderate Tempo	C#4	F5	Lead	Ingenue Female
A Funny Thing...Forum	1962	Philia	That'll Show Him	Moderate Tempo	C4	G5	Lead	Ingenue Female
Cinderella (2013)	1962	Ella	The Sweetest Sounds*	Moderate Tempo	C#4	C5	Lead	Ingenue Female
1776	1969	Martha Jefferson	He Plays The Violin	Moderate Tempo	Bb3	D5	Supporting	Ingenue Female
Company (Revival)	1970	Kathy	You Could Drive a Person Crazy	Uptempo	C#4	A5	Supporting	Ingenue Female
Grease	1971	Sandy Dumbrowski	It's Raining on Prom Night	Ballad	A3	D5	Lead	Ingenue Female
Grease	1971	Sandy Dumbrowski	Hopelessly Devoted to You	Ballad	A3	F5	Lead	Ingenue Female
Grease	1971	Sandy Dumbrowski	Look At Me I'm Sandra Dee Reprise	Ballad	A3	C#5	Lead	Ingenue Female
Grease	1971	Sandy Dumbrowski	Since I Don't Have You	Ballad	Ab3	Ab5	Lead	Ingenue Female
A Little Night Music	1973	Anne Egerman	Soon	Uptempo	C4	G#5	Lead	Ingenue Female
Evita	1978	Mistress	Another Suitcase In Another Hall	Ballad	A3	E5	Supporting	Ingenue Female
Sweeney Todd	1979	Johannah	Green Finch And Linnet Bird*	Uptempo	C4	G5	Lead	Ingenue Female
Dreamgirls	1981	Deena Jones +	Heavy	Uptempo	D3	D4	Lead	Ingenue Female
Dreamgirls	1981	Deena Jones +	One Night Only	Uptempo	Ab3	D5	Lead	Ingenue Female
Baby	1983	Lizzie Fields	I Want It All *	Uptempo	C4	Eb5	Lead	Ingenue Female

Soprano

150

Soprano

* = Music Edit Required
+ = Ethnic Specific

Show	Year	Role	Song	Tempo	Range-Bottom	Range-Top	Category	Char Type
Baby	1983	Lizzie Fields	The Story Goes On	Ballad	G3	F5	Lead	Ingenue Female
Singin' In The Rain	1983	Kathy Seldon	Lucky Star	Moderate Tempo	Bb3	Eb5	Lead	Ingenue Female
Singin' In The Rain	1983	Kathy Seldon	Kathy's Would You	Moderate Tempo	G3	C5	Lead	Ingenue Female
Big River	1985	Mary Jane Wilkes	Leavin's Not The Only Way To Go	Ballad	B3	B4	Supporting	Ingenue Female
Big River	1985	Mary Jane Wilkes	You Oughta Be Here With Me	Ballad	B3	C#5	Supporting	Ingenue Female
Mystery Of Edwin Drood, Th	1985	Rosa Bud	Moonfall	Ballad	B3	G5	Lead	Ingenue Female
Mystery Of Edwin Drood, Th	1985	Rosa Bud	Perfect Strangers*	Moderate Tempo	C#4	F5	Lead	Ingenue Female
Mystery Of Edwin Drood, Th	1985	Rosa Bud	Rosa's Confession	Uptempo	A3	Ab5	Lead	Ingenue Female
Phantom Of The Opera	1986	Christine Daae	Think Of Me*	Moderate Tempo	D4	C6	Lead	Ingenue Female
Phantom Of The Opera	1986	Christine Daae	Angel Of Music*	Moderate Tempo	Bb3	F#5	Lead	Ingenue Female
Phantom Of The Opera	1986	Christine Daae	Phantom Of The Opera*	Moderate Tempo	G3	E5	Lead	Ingenue Female
Phantom Of The Opera	1986	Christine Daae	All I Ask Of You*	Ballad	Ab3	Ab5	Lead	Ingenue Female
Phantom Of The Opera	1986	Christine Daae	Twisted Every Way*	Ballad	C4	Eb5	Lead	Ingenue Female
Phantom Of The Opera	1986	Christine Daae	Wishing You Were Somehow Here Again	Ballad	A3	G5	Lead	Ingenue Female
Phantom Of The Opera	1986	Christine Daae	The Point Of No Return*	Ballad	C4	G5	Lead	Ingenue Female
Phantom Of The Opera	1986	Christine Daae	Raoul I've Been There	Moderate Tempo	C#4	Ab5	Lead	Ingenue Female
Into The Woods	1987	Cinderella	On The Steps Of The Palace	Uptempo	A3	E5	Lead	Ingenue Female
Into The Woods	1987	Cinderella	No One Is Alone	Ballad	Bb3	Db5	Lead	Ingenue Female
Into The Woods	1987	Cinderella	No One Is Alone (Part 2)	Ballad	Bb3	Db5	Lead	Ingenue Female
Meet Me In St. Louis	1989	Agnes Smith	Under The Bamboo Tree*	Moderate Tempo	C4	Bb4	Lead	Ingenue Female
Meet Me In St. Louis	1989	Rose Smith	Raving Beauty*	Ballad	Bb3	Db5	Lead	Ingenue Female
Miss Saigon	1991	Kim+	The Movie In My Mind*	Ballad	Ab3	Eb5	Lead	Ingenue Female
Miss Saigon	1991	Kim+	The Ceremony*	Ballad	B3	D5	Lead	Ingenue Female
Miss Saigon	1991	Kim+	I Still Believe*	Ballad	A3	E5	Lead	Ingenue Female
Miss Saigon	1991	Kim+	There Is A Secret (ms 214-258)	Moderate Tempo	A3	Db5	Lead	Ingenue Female
Miss Saigon	1991	Kim+	You Will Not Touch Him (ms 20-51)	Moderate Tempo	C4	Eb5	Lead	Ingenue Female
Miss Saigon	1991	Kim+	I'd Give My Life For You*	Ballad	G3	E5	Lead	Ingenue Female
Miss Saigon	1991	Kim+	Sun and Moon Reprise	Ballad	E3	D5	Lead	Ingenue Female
Miss Saigon	1991	Kim+	Little God Of My Heart	Ballad	A3	D5	Lead	Ingenue Female
Miss Saigon	1991	Kim+	Sun And Moon*	Ballad	F#3	D5	Lead	Ingenue Female

Soprano

* = Music Edit Required
+ = Ethnic Specific

Show	Year	Role	Song	Tempo	Range-Bottom	Range-Top	Category	Char Type
Phantom	1991	Christine Daee	Melody Of Paris	Uptempo	B3	A5	Lead	Ingenue Female
Phantom	1991	Christine Daae	Home*	Moderate Tempo	D4	A5	Lead	Ingenue Female
Phantom	1991	Christine Daae	The Bistro*	Uptempo	Bb3	B5	Lead	Ingenue Female
Phantom	1991	Christine Daae	Who Could Have Ever Dreamed Up You	Uptempo	Bb3	Eb5	Lead	Ingenue Female
Phantom	1991	Christine Daae	My True Love	Moderate Tempo	C4	F5	Lead	Ingenue Female
Phantom	1991	Christine Daae	Finale: You Are Music*	Ballad	B4	G5	Lead	Ingenue Female
A Christmas Carol	1997	Emily	A Place Called Home	Ballad	Bb3	F5	Supporting	Ingenue Female
A Christmas Carol	1997	Grace Smythe	God Bless Us Everyone	Uptempo	D4	C5	Lead	Ingenue Female
Marie Christine	1999	Lisette+	Tout Mi Mi	Ballad	D4	C#5	Lead	Ingenue Female
Marie Christine	1999	Lisette+	Dansen Calinda	Ballad	E4	C6	Lead	Ingenue Female
Marie Christine	1999	Lisette+	Tout Mimi Reprise	Ballad	Bb3	Bb4	Lead	Ingenue Female
Jane Eyre	2000	Blanche Ingram	The Finer Things	Uptempo	Eb4	B5	Supporting	Ingenue Female
Jane Eyre	2000	Blanche Ingram	In the Virgin Morning*	Moderate Tempo	B3	F5	Supporting	Ingenue Female
Jane Eyre	2000	School Girl	Rain	Moderate Tempo	Bb3	E5	Supporting	Ingenue Female
Mamma Mia!	2001	Sophie Sheridan	I Have A Dream	Ballad	Ab4	Bb4	Lead	Ingenue Female
Mamma Mia!	2001	Sophie Sheridan	Honey Honey*	Uptempo	C4	C5	Lead	Ingenue Female
Mamma Mia!	2001	Sophie Sheridan	The Name Of The Game*	Moderate Tempo	F#3	B4	Lead	Ingenue Female
Mamma Mia!	2001	Sophie Sheridan	Under Attack*	Uptempo	B3	C#5	Lead	Ingenue Female
Mamma Mia!	2001	Sophie Sheridan	I have A Dream Reprise	Ballad	Ab3	Db5	Lead	Ingenue Female
Spitfire Grill	2001	Shelby Thorpe	Hannah Had A Son	Ballad	D4	D5	Lead	Ingenue Female
Spitfire Grill	2001	Shelby Thorpe	When Hope Goes	Ballad	A3	D5	Lead	Ingenue Female
Spitfire Grill	2001	Shelby Thorpe	Wild Bird	Ballad	C4	D5	Lead	Ingenue Female
Sweet Smell Of Success	2002	Susan	What If*	Uptempo	A3	F5	Lead	Ingenue Female
Sweet Smell Of Success	2002	Susan	I Cannot Hear The City Reprise*	Ballad	Ab3	G5	Lead	Ingenue Female
Thoroughly Modern Millie	2002	Dorothy Brown	How The Other Half Lives*	Moderate Tempo	B3	Eb5	Lead	Ingenue Female
Caroline, Or Change	2004	Emmie Thibodeaux +	Duets: Nigh Mamma (ms 71-89)	Ballad	F#4	C5	Supporting	Ingenue Female
Caroline, Or Change	2004	Emmie Thibodeaux +	I Hate The Bus (ms 6-36)	Ballad	G3	F#5	Supporting	Ingenue Female
Caroline, Or Change	2004	Emmie Thibodeaux +	Epilogue-Emmie's Dream (ms 9-73)	Uptempo	Ab3	Db4	Supporting	Ingenue Female
Caroline, Or Change	2004	Emmie Thibodeaux +	The Bus (ms 71-89)	Ballad	Bb2	Bb4	Supporting	Ingenue Female
25th Annual...Spelling Bee	2005	Olive Ostrovsky	My Friend The Dictionary	Moderate Tempo	B3	D5	Lead	Ingenue Female

Soprano

* = Music Edit Required
+ = Ethnic Specific

Show	Year	Role	Song	Tempo	Range-Bottom	Range-Top	Category	Char Type
25th Annual...Spelling Bee	2005	Olive Ostrovsky	The I Love You Song	Ballad	D4	D5	Lead	Ingenue Female
25th Annual...Spelling Bee	2005	Olive Ostrovsky	Second Part 1*	Moderate Tempo	C#4	D5	Lead	Ingenue Female
Light In The Piazza, The	2005	Clara Johnson	The Beauty Is	Uptempo	Cb4	G5	Lead	Ingenue Female
Light In The Piazza, The	2005	Clara Johnson	The Light in the Piazza	Moderate Tempo	A3	F#5	Lead	Ingenue Female
Little Women	2005	Beth March	Off to Massachusettes*	Moderate Tempo	C#4	F5	Lead	Ingenue Female
Little Women	2005	Beth March	Some Things Are Meant To Be	Uptempo	B2	E5	Lead	Ingenue Female
Little Women	2005	Meg March	More Than I Am*	Moderate Tempo	E4	E5	Lead	Ingenue Female
Drowsy Chaperon, The	2006	Janet Van de Graff	Show Off *	Uptempo	G3	C5	Lead	Ingenue Female
Drowsy Chaperon, The	2006	Janet Van de Graff	Accident Waiting To Happen *	Moderate Tempo	C4	D5	Lead	Ingenue Female
Drowsy Chaperon, The	2006	Janet Van de Graff	Bride's Lament *	Ballad	Ab3	F5	Lead	Ingenue Female
Grey Gardens	2006	Edie Beale (Act 1)	Daddy's Girl*	Uptempo	C4	E5	Lead	Ingenue Female
Grey Gardens	2006	Edie Beale (Act 1)	The Telegram	Moderate Tempo	C#4	F#5	Lead	Ingenue Female
Spring Awakening	2006	Wendla	Mama Who Bore Me	Moderate Tempo	G3	A4	Lead	Ingenue Female
Spring Awakening	2006	Wendla	The Guilty One*	Moderate Tempo	G3	A4	Lead	Ingenue Female
Spring Awakening	2006	Wendla	Whispering	Ballad	B3	A4	Lead	Ingenue Female
Spring Awakening	2006	Wendla	Those You've Known*	Moderate Tempo	C4	D5	Lead	Ingenue Female
The Little Mermaid	2007	Ariel	The World Above	Uptempo	A3	C5	Lead	Ingenue Female
The Little Mermaid	2007	Ariel	Part Of Your World	Uptempo	C4	C5	Lead	Ingenue Female
The Little Mermaid	2007	Ariel	Ursula's Incantation (Ahs)*	Moderate Tempo	F#4	E5	Lead	Ingenue Female
Cinderella (2013)	2013	Ella	He Was Tall	Moderate Tempo	D4	C#5	Lead	Ingenue Female
South Pacific	1949	Ngana	Dites-Moi Pourquoi*	Moderate Tempo	D4	C5	Supporting	Juvenile Female
A Little Night Music	1973	Fredrika Armfeldt	The Glamorous Life	Uptempo	C4	Eb5	Supporting	Juvenile Female
Les Miserables	1987	Young Cosette	Castle On The Cloud	Ballad	A3	C5	Lead	Juvenile Female
Jane Eyre	2000	Helen Burnes	Forgiveness	Ballad	A3	C5	Supporting	Juvenile Female
Jane Eyre	2000	Young Jane Eyre	The Graveside	Ballad	A3	D5	Supporting	Juvenile Female
Chitty Chitty Bang Bang	2005	Jemima Potts	Truy Scrumptious	Moderate Tempo	C4	C5	Lead	Juvenile Female
Chitty Chitty Bang Bang	2005	Jemima Potts	Us Two	Ballad	C4	C5	Lead	Juvenile Female
South Pacific	1949	Jerome	Dites-Moi Pourquoi*	Moderate Tempo	D4	C5	Supporting	Juvenile Male
Music Man, The	1957	Winthrop Paroo	Gary Indiana Reprise	Uptempo	C4	Eb5	Lead	Juvenile Male
Oliver!	1963	Oliver Twist	Where Is Love	Ballad	C4	C5	Lead	Juvenile Male

Soprano

* = Music Edit Required
+ = Ethnic Specific

Show	Year	Role	Song	Tempo	Range-Bottom	Range-Top	Category	Char Type
Oliver!	1963	Oliver Twist	Who Will Buy*	Moderate Tempo	C4	C5	Lead	Juvenile Male
Cabaret	1966	Nazi Youth	Tomorrow Belongs to Me	Ballad	F4	F#5	Featured Ensembl	Juvenile Male
Nine	1982	Young Guido Contini	Getting Tall	Moderate Tempo	Ab3	F5	Supporting	Juvenile Male
Secret Garden, The	1991	Colin Craven	Round-Shouldered Man	Uptempo	A3	D5	Lead	Juvenile Male
Secret Garden, The	1991	Colin Craven	Come To My Garden*	Moderate Tempo	C4	E5	Lead	Juvenile Male
A Christmas Carol	1997	Scrooge-Child	A Place Called Home	Ballad	Bb2	A4	Lead	Juvenile Male
A Christmas Carol	1997	Tiny Tim	Christmas Together	Uptempo	Bb4	C5	Supporting	Juvenile Male
A Christmas Carol	1997	Tiny Tim	God Bless Us Everyone	Uptempo	D4	C5	Supporting	Juvenile Male
Chitty Chitty Bang Bang	2005	Jeremy Potts	Truy Scrumptious	Moderate Tempo	C4	C5	Lead	Juvenile Male
Chitty Chitty Bang Bang	2005	Jeremy Potts	Us Two	Ballad	C4	C5	Lead	Juvenile Male
The Little Mermaid	2007	Flounder	She's In Love*	Uptempo	G3	A#5	Lead	Juvenile Male
Addams Family, The	2010	Pugsley Addams	What If	Ballad	A3	C5	Supporting	Juvenile Male
Baby	1983	Arlene McNally	I Want It All *	Uptempo	B3	Eb5	Lead	Maternal
Baby	1983	Arlene McNally	And What If We'd Loved Like That *	Moderate Tempo	D4	F5	Lead	Maternal
Closer Than Ever	1989	Woman One	She Loves Me Not *	Ballad	Bb3	Eb5	Lead	Maternal
Closer Than Ever	1989	Woman One	The Bear, the Tiger, the Hampster...	Uptempo	Ab3	Db4	Lead	Maternal
Closer Than Ever	1989	Woman One	Life Story	Moderate Tempo	Bb3	C5	Lead	Maternal
Closer Than Ever	1989	Woman One	Patterns	Ballad	Bb3	Eb5	Lead	Maternal
Closer Than Ever	1989	Woman One	It's Never That Easy *	Ballad	B3	G5	Lead	Maternal
Beauty and the Beast	1994	Mrs. Potts	Home Reprise	Ballad	G3	D5	Supporting	Maternal
Beauty and the Beast	1994	Mrs. Potts	Beauty and the Beast	Ballad	F3	B4	Supporting	Maternal
Beauty and the Beast	1994	Mrs. Potts	Be Our Guest Reprise	Uptempo	G3	G5	Supporting	Maternal
Billy Elliot	2008	Dead Mum	The Letter *	Ballad	G3	D5	Supporting	Maternal
Addams Family, The	2010	Alice Beineke	Waiting	Moderate Tempo	Ab3	E5	Supporting	Maternal
Heathers	2014	Mrs. Fleming	Shine A Light*	Uptempo	G3	F5	Supporting	Maternal
Carousel	1945	Nettie Fowler	June Is Bustin' Out All Over *	Uptempo	D4	E5	Lead	Mature Female
Carousel	1945	Nettie Fowler	You'll Never Walk Alone	Moderate Tempo	C4	G5	Lead	Mature Female
Carousel	1945	Nettie Fowler	June Is Bustin' Out All Over Reprise	Uptempo	E4	E5	Lead	Mature Female
Carousel	1945	Nettie Fowler	June....Finale Act One	Uptempo	E4	E5	Lead	Mature Female

Soprano

Show	Year	Role	Song	Tempo	Range-Bottom	Range-Top	Category	Char Type
Damn Yankees	1955	Meg Boyd	Six Months Out of Every Year	Uptempo	A3	D5	Supporting	Mature Female
Damn Yankees	1955	Meg Boyd	A Man Doesn't Know	Ballad	G3	Db5	Supporting	Mature Female
Damn Yankees	1955	Meg Boyd	There's Something….Empty Chair	Ballad			Supporting	Mature Female
Damn Yankees	1955	Meg Boyd	Near To You*	Ballad	B3	Eb5	Supporting	Mature Female
Damn Yankees	1955	Meg Boyd	A Man Doesn't Know Reprise	Ballad	G3	D5	Supporting	Mature Female
Candide	1956	Old Lady	I Am Easily Assimilated*	Moderate Tempo	D4	A5	Lead	Mature Female
Sound Of Music, The	1959	Mother Abbess	Climb Every Mountain	Ballad	C4	Ab5	Lead	Mature Female
1776	1969	Abigail Adams	Compliments	Uptempo	D4	Eb5	Supporting	Mature Female
Dear World	1969	Madame Constance	Memory	Moderate Tempo	A3	F5	Lead	Mature Female
Dear World	1969	Countess Aurelia	Through The Bottom Of The Glass	Moderate Tempo	E3	A4	Lead	Mature Female
Dear World	1969	Madame Constance	Voices	Uptempo	F4	E5	Lead	Mature Female
Dear World	1969	Madame Gabrielle	Dickie	Uptempo	G3	E5	Lead	Mature Female
Follies	1971	Emily Whitman	Rain On The Roof *	Uptempo	Bb3	D5	Supporting	Mature Female
Follies	1971	Heidi Schiller	One More Kiss *	Ballad	D4	F5	Supporting	Mature Female
Cats	1981	Jellylorum	Gus: The Theatre Cat	Ballad	A3	D5	Supporting	Mature Female
Cats	1981	Jennyanydots	Bustopher Jones *	Uptempo	B3	F5	Supporting	Mature Female
Mary Poppins	2006	Bird Woman	Feed The Birds*	Ballad	Gb3	Db5	Lead	Mature Female
White Christmas	2008	Martha Watson	Let Me sing And I'm Happy	Moderate Tempo	F3	G4	Lead	Mature Female
White Christmas	2008	Martha Watson	Falling Out Of Love Can Be Fun*	Uptempo	G3	C5	Lead	Mature Female
Of Thee I Sing	1931	Diana Devereaux	The Most Beautiful Blossom	Ballad	Eb4	F5	Lead	Romantic Antagonist Female
Of Thee I Sing	1931	Diana Devereaux	Because Reprise*	Uptempo	E4	F5	Lead	Romantic Antagonist Female
Of Thee I Sing	1931	Diana Devereaux	Jilted*	Moderate Tempo	D4	F5	Lead	Romantic Antagonist Female
Unsinkable Molly Brown, Th	1960	Molly Tobin	I Ain't Down Yet*	Uptempo	Ab3	F5	Lead	Romantic Antagonist Female
Unsinkable Molly Brown, Th	1960	Molly Tobin	My Own Brass Bed	Ballad	G3	Bb4	Lead	Romantic Antagonist Female
Unsinkable Molly Brown, Th	1960	Molly Tobin	Beautiful People Of Denver	Uptempo	F3	Bb4	Lead	Romantic Antagonist Female
Unsinkable Molly Brown, Th	1960	Molly Tobin	Are You Sure*	Uptempo	G3	Db5	Lead	Romantic Antagonist Female
Unsinkable Molly Brown, Th	1960	Molly Tobin	Chick-A-Pen	Ballad	G3	B4	Lead	Romantic Antagonist Female
Merrily We Roll Along 1994	1981	Mary Flynn	Old Friends	Moderate Tempo	A3	A4	Lead	Romantic Antagonist Female
Merrily We Roll Along 1994	1981	Mary Flynn	Like It Was	Moderate Tempo	G3	Bb4	Lead	Romantic Antagonist Female

* = Music Edit Required
+ = Ethnic Specific

Show	Year	Role	Song	Tempo	Range-Bottom	Range-Top	Category	Char Type
Merrily We Roll Along 1994	1981	Mary Flynn	Now You Know*	Uptempo	G3	D5	Lead	Romantic Antagonist Female
Phantom Of The Opera	1986	Carlotta Giudicelli	Hannibal Cadenza	Moderate Tempo	C4	D6	Lead	Romantic Antagonist Female
Phantom Of The Opera	1986	Carlotta Giudicelli	Think Of Me*	Moderate Tempo	E#4	G#5	Lead	Romantic Antagonist Female
Phantom Of The Opera	1986	Carlotta Giudicelli	Diva*	Moderate Tempo	F4	E6	Lead	Romantic Antagonist Female
Phantom Of The Opera	1986	Carlotta Giudicelli	Prima Donna*	Moderate Tempo	F4	F6	Lead	Romantic Antagonist Female
Phantom Of The Opera	1986	Carlotta Giudicelli	Poor Fool He Makes Me Laugh*	Moderate Tempo	F4	C6	Lead	Romantic Antagonist Female
Phantom	1991	Carlotta	This Place Is Mine	Uptempo	Bb3	Bb5	Lead	Romantic Antagonist Female
Phantom	1991	Carlotta	This Is Mine Reprise	Moderate Tempo	D4	G5	Lead	Romantic Antagonist Female
Victor/Victoria	1995	Norma Cassidy	Paris Makes Me Horny	Moderate Tempo	Bb3	A5	Lead	Romantic Antagonist Female
Victor/Victoria	1995	Norma Cassidy	Chicago Illinois*	Uptempo	A#3	E5	Lead	Romantic Antagonist Female
Marie Christine	1999	Marie Christine+	Beautiful*	Moderate Tempo	G3	D5	Lead	Romantic Antagonist Female
Marie Christine	1999	Marie Christine+	Way Back To Paradise*	Moderate Tempo	D4	G5	Lead	Romantic Antagonist Female
Marie Christine	1999	Marie Christine+	To Find A Lover*	Moderate Tempo	A3	G4	Lead	Romantic Antagonist Female
Marie Christine	1999	Marie Christine+	I Will Give	Ballad	Bb3	Fb4	Lead	Romantic Antagonist Female
Marie Christine	1999	Marie Christine+	Tell Me	Moderate Tempo	G3	F5	Lead	Romantic Antagonist Female
Marie Christine	1999	Marie Christine+	Marie's Soliloquy	Ballad	A3	D5	Lead	Romantic Antagonist Female
Marie Christine	1999	Marie Christine+	Prison In A Prison*	Uptempo	G3	D5	Lead	Romantic Antagonist Female
Marie Christine	1999	Marie Christine+	Prison In A Prison*	Uptempo	G3	D5	Lead	Romantic Antagonist Female
Light In The Piazza, The	2005	Franca Naccarelli	The Joy You Feel	Moderate Tempo	C4	Gb5	Lead	Romantic Antagonist Female
High Society 1998	1927	Tracy Lord	Let's Misbehave*	Uptempo	B2	C#5	Lead	Romantic Lead Female
Of Thee I Sing	1931	Mary Turner	Of Thee I Sing*	Moderate Tempo	C4	E5	Lead	Romantic Lead Female
Of Thee I Sing	1931	Mary Turner	A Kiss For Cinderella*	Moderate Tempo	Ab4	G5	Lead	Romantic Lead Female
Of Thee I Sing	1931	Mary Turner	Who Cares Reprise*	Moderate Tempo	C4	E5	Lead	Romantic Lead Female
Of Thee I Sing	1931	Mary Turner	I'm About To Be A Mother*	Moderate Tempo	B3	A5	Lead	Romantic Lead Female
High Society 1998	1933	Tracy Lord	Once Upon A Time	Moderate Tempo	F3	A4	Lead	Romantic Lead Female
Porgy and Bess	1935	Bess+	Bess, You Is My Woman*	Ballad	D4	A#5	Lead	Romantic Lead Female
Porgy and Bess	1935	Bess+	What You Want Wid Bess*	Moderate Tempo	Eb4	A5	Lead	Romantic Lead Female
Porgy and Bess	1935	Bess+	I Loves You Porgy*	Moderate Tempo	Bb3	A5	Lead	Romantic Lead Female
Porgy and Bess	1935	Bess+	Summertime Reprise 2	Ballad	E4	A5	Lead	Romantic Lead Female
Wizard Of Oz 1988	1939	Glenda	Come Out*	Moderate Tempo	G3	C5	Lead	Romantic Lead Female
Kiss Me Kate	1948	Lilli Vanessi/Katherine	Wunderbar*	Ballad	C4	G5	Lead	Romantic Lead Female

Soprano

156

* = Music Edit Required
+ = Ethnic Specific

Show	Year	Role	Song	Tempo	Range-Bottom	Range-Top	Category	Char Type
Kiss Me Kate	1948	Lilli Vanessi/Katherine	So In Love	Ballad	A3	Db5	Lead	Romantic Lead Female
Kiss Me Kate	1948	Lilli Vanessi/Katherine	I Am Ashamed That Women Are So Sim	Moderate Tempo	C4	Eb5	Lead	Romantic Lead Female
King and I, The	1951	Anna Leonowens	I Whistle A Happy Tune*	Uptempo	D4	D5	Lead	Romantic Lead Female
King and I, The	1951	Anna Leonowens	Hello, Young Lovers	Ballad	C#4	D5	Lead	Romantic Lead Female
King and I, The	1951	Anna Leonowens	Getting To Know You*	Moderate Tempo	C#4	E5	Lead	Romantic Lead Female
King and I, The	1951	Anna Leonowens	Shall I Tell You What I Think...	Uptempo	D3	C#5	Lead	Romantic Lead Female
King and I, The	1951	Anna Leonowens	Shall We Dance	Uptempo	D4	C5	Lead	Romantic Lead Female
King and I, The	1951	Anna Leonowens	Hello, Young Lovers Reprise	Ballad	C4	D5	Lead	Romantic Lead Female
King and I, The	1951	Lady Thiang+	Something Wonderful	Ballad	C#4	G5	Lead	Romantic Lead Female
King and I, The	1951	Lady Thiang+	Western People Funny*	Moderate Tempo	E4	G5	Lead	Romantic Lead Female
High Society 1998	1953	Tracy Lord	It's Alright With Me	Ballad	C4	E5	Lead	Romantic Lead Female
High Society 1998	1955	Tracy Lord	High Society*	Uptempo	Ab3	Eb5	Lead	Romantic Lead Female
Music Man, The	1957	Marian Paroo	My White Knight	Ballad	C#4	Ab5	Lead	Romantic Lead Female
Music Man, The	1957	Marian Paroo	Will I Ever Leave You*	Moderate Tempo	D4	F#5	Lead	Romantic Lead Female
Music Man, The	1957	Marian Paroo	Till There Was You	Ballad	Eb4	F5	Lead	Romantic Lead Female
Music Man, The	1957	Marian Paroo	Goodnight My Someone*	Ballad	B3	E5	Lead	Romantic Lead Female
Once Upon A Mattress	1959	Lady Larken	In A Little While*	Uptempo	Db4	Eb5	Lead	Romantic Lead Female
Once Upon A Mattress	1959	Lady Larken	In A Little While Reprise*	Ballad	D4	F5	Lead	Romantic Lead Female
Once Upon A Mattress	1959	Lady Larken	Yesterday I Loved You*	Uptempo	E4	F5	Lead	Romantic Lead Female
Sound Of Music, The	1959	Elsa Schraeder	How Can Love Survive	Uptempo	D4	F5	Lead	Romantic Lead Female
Camelot	1960	Guenevere	The Simple Joys Of Maidenhood	Moderate Tempo	B3	D#5	Lead	Romantic Lead Female
Camelot	1960	Guenevere	Camelot*	Uptempo	C4	D5	Lead	Romantic Lead Female
Camelot	1960	Nimue	Follow Me*	Moderate Tempo	C#4	F#5	Supporting	Romantic Lead Female
Camelot	1960	Guenevere	The Lusty Month Of May*	Uptempo	D4	A5	Lead	Romantic Lead Female
Camelot	1960	Guenevere	Before I Gaze At You Again	Moderate Tempo	C4	Eb5	Lead	Romantic Lead Female
Camelot	1960	Guenevere	What Do The Simple Folk Do?*	Moderate Tempo	Bb3	E5	Lead	Romantic Lead Female
Camelot	1960	Guenevere	I Loved You Once In Silence	Ballad	Db4	Eb5	Lead	Romantic Lead Female
She Loves Me	1963	Amalia Balash	No More Candy*	Moderate Tempo	Db4	Fb5	Lead	Romantic Lead Female
She Loves Me	1963	Amalia Balash	I Don't Know His Name*	Moderate Tempo	B#3	D#5	Lead	Romantic Lead Female
She Loves Me	1963	Amalia Balash	Will He Like Me	Ballad	Bb3	F5	Lead	Romantic Lead Female
She Loves Me	1963	Amalia Balash	Dear Friend	Uptempo	C4	F5	Lead	Romantic Lead Female

Soprano

* = Music Edit Required
+ = Ethnic Specific

Show	Year	Role	Song	Tempo	Range-Bottom	Range-Top	Category	Char Type
She Loves Me	1963	Amalia Balash	Where My Shoe (B Maj)*	Uptempo	E4	G5	Lead	Romantic Lead Female
She Loves Me	1963	Amalia Balash	Vanilla Ice Cream	Uptempo	D4	B5	Lead	Romantic Lead Female
She Loves Me	1963	Amalia Balash	Mr. Norwack, Will You Please	Moderate Tempo	C4	E5	Lead	Romantic Lead Female
She Loves Me	1963	Amalia Balash	Where's My Shoe (G Maj)	Uptempo	C#4	F5	Lead	Romantic Lead Female
Hello Dolly	1964	Irene Molloy	Ribbons Down My Back	Ballad	A3	D5	Lead	Romantic Lead Female
Hello Dolly	1964	Irene Molloy	Motherhood	Uptempo	D4	E5	Lead	Romantic Lead Female
Hello Dolly	1964	Irene Molloy	It Only Takes A Moment*	Ballad	Ab3	Db4	Lead	Romantic Lead Female
Hello Dolly	1964	Irene Molloy	Ribbons Down My Back Reprise	Ballad	B3	D5	Lead	Romantic Lead Female
Hello Dolly	1964	Irene Molloy	Dancing*	Moderate Tempo	G3	E5	Lead	Romantic Lead Female
Annie	1977	Grace Farrell	N.Y.C. *	Uptempo	C4	F4	Supporting	Romantic Lead Female
On The Twentieth Century	1978	Lily Garland	Veronique	Uptempo	E3	Ab6	Lead	Romantic Lead Female
On The Twentieth Century	1978	Lily Garland	Never*	Uptempo	A3	A5	Lead	Romantic Lead Female
On The Twentieth Century	1978	Lily Garland	Our Private World*	Ballad	A3	E5	Lead	Romantic Lead Female
On The Twentieth Century	1978	Lily Garland	I've Got It All*	Moderate Tempo	B3	A5	Lead	Romantic Lead Female
On The Twentieth Century	1978	Lily Garland	Babette	Uptempo	F#3	F#5	Lead	Romantic Lead Female
Merrily We Roll Along	1994	Beth	Not A Day Goes By	Ballad	G3	B4	Lead	Romantic Lead Female
Nine	1982	Carla Albanese	A Call From The Vatican	Moderate Tempo	A3	C6	Lead	Romantic Lead Female
Nine	1982	Claudia Nardi	Unusual Way*	Ballad	G#3	E5	Lead	Romantic Lead Female
Nine	1982	Carla Albanese	Simple	Ballad	A3	E5	Lead	Romantic Lead Female
Rags	1986	Rebecca Hershkowitz	Brand New World*	Moderate Tempo	B3	G4	Lead	Romantic Lead Female
Rags	1986	Rebecca Hershkowitz	Children Of The Wind	Moderate Tempo	A3	Bb5	Lead	Romantic Lead Female
Rags	1986	Rebecca Hershkowitz	If We Never Meet Again*	Ballad	B2	C5	Lead	Romantic Lead Female
Rags	1986	Rebecca Hershkowitz	Penny A Tune	Uptempo	E4	F#4	Lead	Romantic Lead Female
Rags	1986	Rebecca Hershkowitz	Blame It on The Summer Night	Moderate Tempo	A3	D#5	Lead	Romantic Lead Female
Rags	1986	Rebecca Hershkowitz	Uptown*	Moderate Tempo	C4	Eb5	Lead	Romantic Lead Female
Rags	1986	Rebecca Hershkowitz	Wanting*	Moderate Tempo	A3	D#5	Lead	Romantic Lead Female
Rags	1986	Rebecca Hershkowitz	If We Never Meet Again Reprise 2	Ballad	C4	D5	Lead	Romantic Lead Female
Rags	1986	Rebecca Hershkowitz	Dancing With Fools*	Uptempo	Bb3	Gb5	Lead	Romantic Lead Female
Nick & Nora	1991	Tracy Gardner	Everybody Wants To Do A Musical	Moderate Tempo	E2	G#5	Lead	Romantic Lead Female
Secret Garden, The	1991	Lily	Come To My Garden*	Moderate Tempo	C4	G5	Lead	Romantic Lead Female
Secret Garden, The	1991	Lily	How Could I Ever Know*	Ballad	Bb3	A5	Lead	Romantic Lead Female

* = Music Edit Required
+ = Ethnic Specific

Show	Year	Role	Song	Tempo	Range-Bottom	Range-Top	Category	Char Type
Passion	1994	Clara	Happiness (Part 1)*	Moderate Tempo	Bb3	Eb5	Lead	Romantic Lead Female
Passion	1994	Clara	Fourth Letter-How Could I Forget You	Moderate Tempo	F3	Db5	Lead	Romantic Lead Female
Passion	1994	Clara	Thinking Of You	Moderate Tempo	Ab3	Db5	Lead	Romantic Lead Female
Passion	1994	Clara	Sunrise Letter*	Moderate Tempo	Ab3	G5	Lead	Romantic Lead Female
Passion	1994	Clara	Forty Days	Uptempo	Bb3	E5	Lead	Romantic Lead Female
Passion	1994	Clara	I Didn't Tell You	Ballad	Ab3	F5	Lead	Romantic Lead Female
Passion	1994	Clara	I Am Writing To You	Moderate Tempo	A3	C#5	Lead	Romantic Lead Female
Songs For A New World	1995	Woman 1	I'm Not Afraid Of Anything	Moderate Tempo	A3	E5	Lead	Romantic Lead Female
Songs For A New World	1995	Woman 1	Christmas Lullaby	Ballad	A3	E5	Lead	Romantic Lead Female
Songs For A New World	1995	Woman 1	I'd Give It All For You*	Moderate Tempo	A3	F4	Lead	Romantic Lead Female
Songs For A New World	1995	Woman 1	Hear My Song*	Moderate Tempo	A3	G4	Lead	Romantic Lead Female
Victor/Victoria	1995	Victor	If I Were A Man	Moderate Tempo	G3	A4	Lead	Romantic Lead Female
Victor/Victoria	1995	Victor	Le Jazz Hot	Moderate Tempo	G#3	D5	Lead	Romantic Lead Female
Victor/Victoria	1995	Victoria	Crazy World	Ballad	Eb3	C5	Lead	Romantic Lead Female
Victor/Victoria	1995	Victor	Louis Says*	Uptempo	E3	F4	Lead	Romantic Lead Female
Victor/Victoria	1995	Victoria	Almost A Love Song*	Ballad	G#3	C5	Lead	Romantic Lead Female
Victor/Victoria	1995	Victoria	Living In The Shadows	Ballad	E3	A4	Lead	Romantic Lead Female
Victor/Victoria	1995	Victoria	Living In The Shadows	Moderate Tempo	E3	D5	Lead	Romantic Lead Female
Big	1996	Susan Lawrence	Stars, Stars, Stars	Ballad	C4	D5	Lead	Romantic Lead Female
Big	1996	Susan Lawrence	One Special Man	Ballad	G3	D5	Lead	Romantic Lead Female
Big	1996	Susan Lawrence	Dancing All The Time	Uptempo	G3	D5	Lead	Romantic Lead Female
Big	1996	Susan Lawrence	My Secretary's In Love	Uptempo	G3	D5	Lead	Romantic Lead Female
Big	1996	Susan Lawrence	Let's Not Move Too Fast	Ballad	A3	C5	Lead	Romantic Lead Female
Big	1996	Susan Lawrence	Little Susan Lawrence	Uptempo	Ab3	D5	Lead	Romantic Lead Female
Jekyll and Hyde	1997	Emma Crow	Emma's Reasons/The Engagement Part	Moderate Tempo	Bb3	Db5	Lead	Romantic Lead Female
Jekyll and Hyde	1997	Emma Crow	Take Me As I Am	Ballad	Bb3	F5	Lead	Romantic Lead Female
Jekyll and Hyde	1997	Emma Crow	Once Upon A Dream	Ballad	B2	C#4	Lead	Romantic Lead Female
Jekyll and Hyde	1997	Emma Crow	In His Eyes*	Ballad	Bb3	F5	Lead	Romantic Lead Female
Ragtime	1998	Mother	Goodbye My Love	Moderate Tempo	G3	Db5	Lead	Romantic Lead Female
Ragtime	1998	Mother	What Kind Of Woman*	Moderate Tempo	Bb3	Eb5	Lead	Romantic Lead Female

Soprano

* = Music Edit Required
+ = Ethnic Specific

Show	Year	Role	Song	Tempo	Range-Bottom	Range-Top	Category	Char Type
Ragtime	1998	Mother	New Music*	Ballad	Bb3	D5	Lead	Romantic Lead Female
Ragtime	1998	Mother	Back To Before	Moderate Tempo	G3	C5	Lead	Romantic Lead Female
Producers, The	2001	Ulla	When You've Got It Flaunt It!	Moderate Tempo	Bb3	Eb5	Lead	Romantic Lead Female
Wicked	2003	Glinda	Openning*	Moderate Tempo	A3	A5	Lead	Romantic Lead Female
Wicked	2003	Glinda	No One Mourns The Wicked*	Moderate Tempo	C#4	B5	Lead	Romantic Lead Female
Wicked	2003	Glinda	Popular*	Moderate Tempo	G3	C5	Lead	Romantic Lead Female
Wicked	2003	Glinda	Thank Goodness (Part 3)	Uptempo	Bb3	A5	Lead	Romantic Lead Female
Wicked	2003	Glinda	I'm Not That Girl Reprise	Ballad	G3	D5	Lead	Romantic Lead Female
Wicked	2003	Glinda	For Good*	Ballad	Ab3	Db5	Lead	Romantic Lead Female
Chitty Chitty Bang Bang	2005	Truly Scrumptious	Truy Scrumptious	Moderate Tempo	C4	C5	Lead	Romantic Lead Female
Chitty Chitty Bang Bang	2005	Truly Scrumptious	Music Box	Ballad	D4	Eb5	Lead	Romantic Lead Female
Chitty Chitty Bang Bang	2005	Truly Scrumptious	Toot Sweets *	Uptempo	D4	Eb5	Lead	Romantic Lead Female
Dirty Rotten Scoundrels	2005	Christine Colgate	Here I Am	Uptempo	F3	E5	Lead	Romantic Lead Female
Dirty Rotten Scoundrels	2005	Christine Colgate	Nothing Is Too Wonderful To Be True	Ballad	A3	F5	Lead	Romantic Lead Female
Light In The Piazza, The	2005	Margaret Johnson	Statues and Stories*	Uptempo	A3	A5	Lead	Romantic Lead Female
Light In The Piazza, The	2005	Margaret Johnson	Dividing Day	Ballad	G3	E5	Lead	Romantic Lead Female
Light In The Piazza, The	2005	Margaret Johnson	The Beauty Is Reprise	Moderate Tempo	B#3	G5	Lead	Romantic Lead Female
Light In The Piazza, The	2005	Margaret Johnson	Fable	Uptempo	C#4	F#5	Lead	Romantic Lead Female
Grey Gardens	2006	Edie Beale (Act 2)	The Revolutionary Costume*	Uptempo	Bb3	C5	Lead	Romantic Lead Female
Grey Gardens	2006	Edie Beale (Act 2)	Around The World	Moderate Tempo	C4	C#5	Lead	Romantic Lead Female
Grey Gardens	2006	Edie Beale (Act 2)	Around The World Reprise	Ballad	C4	C#5	Lead	Romantic Lead Female
Grey Gardens	2006	Edie Beale (Act 2)	Another Winter	Ballad	F#3	C#5	Lead	Romantic Lead Female
Grey Gardens	2006	Edith Beale (Act 1)	The Five Fifteen*	Uptempo	B3	B4	Lead	Romantic Lead Female
Grey Gardens	2006	Edith Beale (Act 1)	Hominy Grits*	Moderate Tempo	B3	C#5	Lead	Romantic Lead Female
Grey Gardens	2006	Edith Beale (Act 1)	The Five Fifteen Reprise*	Ballad	C4	A4	Lead	Romantic Lead Female
Grey Gardens	2006	Edith Beale (Act 1)	Will You?	Ballad	C4	E5	Lead	Romantic Lead Female
Mary Poppins	2006	Mary Poppins	Practically Perfect*	Moderate Tempo	A3	G#3	Lead	Romantic Lead Female
Mary Poppins	2006	Mary Poppins	A Spoonful Of Sugar*	Uptempo	Cb4	Ab5	Lead	Romantic Lead Female
Mary Poppins	2006	Mary Poppins	Supercalifragilisticexpialidocious*	Uptempo	C4	E5	Lead	Romantic Lead Female
Mary Poppins	2006	Mary Poppins	Anything Can Happen*	Moderate Tempo	C4	D5	Lead	Romantic Lead Female

Soprano

* = Music Edit Required
+ = Ethnic Specific

Show	Year	Role	Song	Tempo	Range-Bottom	Range-Top	Category	Char Type
Gypsy	1959	Rose	Some People	Uptempo	G#3	C5	Lead	Antagonist Female
Gypsy	1959	Rose	Small World	Moderate Tempo	F#3	B4	Lead	Antagonist Female
Gypsy	1959	Rose	You'll Never Get Away From Me*	Uptempo	F#3	B4	Lead	Antagonist Female
Gypsy	1959	Rose	Everything's Coming Up Roses	Uptempo	Bb3	C5	Lead	Antagonist Female
Gypsy	1959	Rose	Rose's Turn	Moderate Tempo	G3	C5	Lead	Antagonist Female
Gypsy	1959	Rose	Some People Reprise*	Ballad	G#3	A4	Lead	Antagonist Female
A Funny Thing...Forum	1962	Domina	That Dirty Old Man	Uptempo	B3	F5	Lead	Antagonist Female
Oliver!	1963	Nancy	It's A Fine Life*	Uptempo	Ab3	D5	Lead	Antagonist Female
Oliver!	1963	Nancy	Oom-Pah-Pah*	Uptempo	B3	C#5	Lead	Antagonist Female
Oliver!	1963	Nancy	As Long As He Needs Me	Ballad	F#3	C#5	Lead	Antagonist Female
Oliver!	1963	Nancy	As Long As He Needs Me Reprise	Moderate Tempo	G#3	C#5	Lead	Antagonist Female
Sweet Charity	1966	Dance Hall Girl	Big Spender*	Moderate Tempo	F3	B4	Feat Ensemble	Antagonist Female
Company (Revival)	1970	Joanne	The Little Things We Do Together	Uptempo	F3	A4	Supporting	Antagonist Female
Company (Revival)	1970	Joanne	The Ladies Who Lunch	Moderate Tempo	F3	Bb4	Supporting	Antagonist Female
Follies	1971	Hattie Walker	Broadway Baby	Moderate Tempo	A3	Bb4	Supporting	Antagonist Female
Grease	1971	Betty Rizzo	Look At Me I'm Sandra Dee	Moderate Tempo	G3	Eb5	Lead	Antagonist Female
Grease	1971	Betty Rizzo	There Are Worse Things I Could Do	Ballad	A3	C4	Lead	Antagonist Female
You're A Good Man Charlie B	1971	Lucy Van Pelt	Schroeder	Moderate Tempo	G3	E5	Lead	Antagonist Female
Wiz, The	1974	Evillene	Don't Nobody Bring Me No Bad News	Uptempo	Bb3	Db5	Lead	Antagonist Female
Annie	1977	Miss Hannigan	Little Girls	Uptempo	C4	D5	Lead	Antagonist Female
Annie	1977	Miss Hannigan	Easy Street *	Uptempo	Bb3	Ab4	Lead	Antagonist Female
Annie	1977	Miss Hannigan	Little Girls Reprise	Uptempo	E4	D5	Lead	Antagonist Female
Mystery Of Edwin Drood, Th	1985	Princess Puffer	The Wages Of Sin	Moderate Tempo	F3	C5	Lead	Antagonist Female
Mystery Of Edwin Drood, Th	1985	Princess Puffer	Garden Path To Hell	Ballad	G3	A4	Lead	Antagonist Female
Mystery Of Edwin Drood, Th	1985	Princess Puffer	Don't Quit While You're Ahead*	Moderate Tempo	F3	A4	Lead	Antagonist Female
Mystery Of Edwin Drood, Th	1985	Princess Puffer	Puffer's Confession	Ballad	C4	C5	Lead	Antagonist Female
Nunsense	1985	Mary Robert Anne	I Just Want To Be A Star*	Uptempo	G3	C5	Lead	Antagonist Female
Nunsense	1985	Mary Robert Anne	Playing Second Fiddle	Uptempo	B3	B4	Lead	Antagonist Female
Nunsense	1985	Mary Hubert	Tackle That Temptation*	Uptempo	A3	D5	Lead	Antagonist Female
Nunsense	1985	Mary Robert Anne	Growing Up Catholic*	Ballad	Ab3	Db5	Lead	Antagonist Female
Nunsense	1985	Mary Robert Anne	Second Fiddle Reprise	Uptempo	E4	B4	Lead	Antagonist Female

Alto

Alto

* = Music Edit Required
+ = Ethnic Specific

Show	Year	Role	Song	Tempo	Range-Bottom	Range-Top	Category	Char Type
Nunsense	1985	Mary Hubert	Holier Than Thou*	Uptempo	Bb3	F5	Lead	Antagonist Female
Nunsense	1985	Mary Robert Anne	I Just Want To Be A Star*	Uptempo	G3	C5	Lead	Antagonist Female
Les Miserables	1987	Madame Thenardier	Master of the House*	Uptempo	B3	D5	Supporting	Antagonist Female
Les Miserables	1987	Madame Thenardier	Beggars at the Wedding	Uptempo	C#4	D5	Supporting	Antagonist Female
Goodbye Girl, The	1993	Mrs. Crosby+	Too Good To Be Bad*	Uptempo	Bb3	F4	Supporting	Antagonist Female
Goodbye Girl, The	1993	Mrs. Crosby+	Too Good To Be Bad Play Off*	Uptempo	Bb3	F4	Supporting	Antagonist Female
Passion	1994	Fosca	I Read	Ballad	F3	D5	Lead	Antagonist Female
Passion	1994	Fosca	To Speak To Me Of Love	Moderate Tempo	E#3	C5	Lead	Antagonist Female
Passion	1994	Fosca	I Wish I Could Forget You*	Ballad	F3	C5	Lead	Antagonist Female
Passion	1994	Fosca	Loving You	Ballad	F#3	C5	Lead	Antagonist Female
Passion	1994	Fosca	All This Happiness	Moderate Tempo	B3	A4	Lead	Antagonist Female
Rent	1996	Joanne Jefferson	We're Okay	Uptempo	C4	C5	Lead	Antagonist Female
Rent	1996	Joanne Jefferson	Take Me Or leave Me*	Uptempo	C4	E5	Lead	Antagonist Female
Seussical	2000	Sour Kangaroo	Biggest Blame Fool (ms 9-29)*	Uptempo	Bb3	Db5	Lead	Antagonist Female
Spitfire Grill	2001	Hannah Ferguson	Hannah's Harangue	Moderate Tempo	G3	A4	Lead	Antagonist Female
Spitfire Grill	2001	Hannah Ferguson	Forgotten Lullaby	Ballad	G3	G4	Lead	Antagonist Female
Spitfire Grill	2001	Hannah Ferguson	Come Alive Again Part 2	Moderate Tempo	G3	A4	Lead	Antagonist Female
Spitfire Grill	2001	Hannah Ferguson	Way Back Home	Ballad	E3	B4	Lead	Antagonist Female
Caroline, Or Change	2004	Caroline Thibodeaux +	16 Feet Beneath the Sea (10-49)	Ballad	B3	D4	Lead	Antagonist Female
Caroline, Or Change	2004	Caroline Thibodeaux +	I Got Four Kids (ms 1-114)	Moderate Tempo	B3	Bb4	Lead	Antagonist Female
Caroline, Or Change	2004	Caroline Thibodeaux +	Lot's Wife (ms 67-151)	Moderate Tempo	F3	Eb5	Lead	Antagonist Female
Caroline, Or Change	2004	Caroline Thibodeaux +	Gonna Pass Me A Law (ms 1-37)	Ballad	G3	G4	Lead	Antagonist Female
Caroline, Or Change	2004	Caroline Thibodeaux +	Noah Go To Sleep (ms 60-98)	Moderate Tempo	Gb3	Db5	Lead	Antagonist Female
Caroline, Or Change	2004	Caroline Thibodeaux +	Underwater (ms 43-74)	Ballad	G3	F4	Lead	Antagonist Female
25th Annual...Spelling Bee	2005	Logainne	Woe Is Me	Uptempo	G3	D5	Lead	Antagonist Female
25th Annual...Spelling Bee	2005	Logainne	Woe Is Me Reprise	Uptempo	C4	C5	Lead	Antagonist Female
25th Annual...Spelling Bee	2005	Marcy Park	I Speak Six Languages	Uptempo	B3	D5	Lead	Antagonist Female
Color Purple, The	2005	Sofia	Hell No *	Moderate Tempo	E3	C5	Lead	Antagonist Female
Legally Blonde	2007	Vivianne Kensington	Legally Blonde Remix*	Uptempo	A3	Eb5	Lead	Antagonist Female
No, No Nanette	1925	Flora Latham	The Three Happies*	Moderate Tempo	F4	Eb5	Supporting	Character Female

Alto

* = Music Edit Required
+ = Ethnic Specific

Show	Year	Role	Song	Tempo	Range-Bottom	Range-Top	Category	Char Type
No, No Nanette	1925	Betty Brown	The Three Happies*	Moderate Tempo	A3	C5	Supporting	Character Female
Show Boat	1927	Queenie+	Can't Help Lovin' Dat Man*	Moderate Tempo	C3	D4	Lead	Character Female
Show Boat	1927	Queenie+	Misery*	Ballad	A3	Eb5	Lead	Character Female
Show Boat	1927	Queenie+	Bally-Hoo*	Uptempo	A3	Eb5	Lead	Character Female
High Society 1998	1930	Liz Imbrie	I'm Getting Ready For You*	Uptempo	A#3	E5	Lead	Character Female
Anything Goes	1934	Reno Sweeney	I Get A Kick Out of You	Uptempo	A3	D5	Lead	Character Female
Anything Goes	1934	Reno Sweeney	You're the Top *	Uptempo	G3	D5	Lead	Character Female
Anything Goes	1934	Reno Sweeney	Anything Goes	Uptempo	Ab3	C5	Lead	Character Female
Anything Goes	1934	Reno Sweeney	Blow Gabriel Blow	Uptempo	G3	C5	Lead	Character Female
Anything Goes	1934	Reno Sweeney	Buddy Beware	Moderate Tempo	A3	C#5	Lead	Character Female
Anything Goes	1934	Reno Sweeney	Friendship *	Uptempo	Bb3	Eb5	Lead	Character Female
Porgy and Bess	1935	Strawberry Woman+	Strawberry Woman	Ballad	G4	E5	Featured Ensembl	Character Female
High Society 1998	1943	Liz Imbrie	He's A Right Guy	Ballad	F3	A4	Lead	Character Female
Annie Get Your Gun	1944	Annie Oakley	Doin' What Comes Natur'lly	Uptempo	A3	C5	Lead	Character Female
Annie Get Your Gun	1944	Annie Oakley	The Girl That I Marry*	Moderate Tempo	B3	B4	Lead	Character Female
Annie Get Your Gun	1944	Annie Oakley	You Can't Get A Man With A Gun	Uptempo	Bb3	C5	Lead	Character Female
Annie Get Your Gun	1944	Annie Oakley	Moonshine Lullaby	Ballad	Bb3	D5	Lead	Character Female
Annie Get Your Gun	1944	Annie Oakley	No Business Reprise 2	Moderate Tempo	G3	C5	Lead	Character Female
Annie Get Your Gun	1944	Annie Oakley	They Say That Falling In Love*	Ballad	A3	B4	Lead	Character Female
Annie Get Your Gun	1944	Annie Oakley	You Can't Get A Man With A Gun Repri	Moderate Tempo	Ab3	Ab4	Lead	Character Female
Annie Get Your Gun	1944	Annie Oakley	Lost In His Arms	Ballad	Bb3	C5	Lead	Character Female
Annie Get Your Gun	1944	Annie Oakley	I Got The Sun in the Morning	Moderate Tempo	Bb3	Bb4	Lead	Character Female
On The Town	1944	Diana Dream	I Wish I Was Dead	Uptempo	C4	Db4	Featured Ensembl	Character Female
On The Town	1944	Hildy	I Can Cook Too	Uptempo	A3	G#5	Lead	Character Female
On The Town	1944	Hildy	Ya Got Me *	Uptempo	F3	Db5	Lead	Character Female
Kiss Me Kate	1948	Hattie	Another Op'nin Another Show*	Uptempo	G3	E5	Supporting	Character Female
South Pacific	1949	Bloody Mary	Bali Ha'i	Ballad	G3	G4	Lead	Character Female
South Pacific	1949	Bloody Mary	Bali Ha'I Reprise	Ballad	D3	E4	Lead	Character Female
South Pacific	1949	Bloody Mary	Happy Talk	Uptempo	A3	C5	Lead	Character Female
Guys and Dolls	1950	Miss Adelaide	A Bushel And A Peck	Uptempo	B3	Eb3	Lead	Character Female

* = Music Edit Required
+ = Ethnic Specific

Show	Year	Role	Song	Tempo	Range-Bottom	Range-Top	Category	Char Type
Guys and Dolls	1950	Miss Adelaide	Adelaide's Lament	Moderate Tempo	Ab3	D5	Lead	Character Female
Guys and Dolls	1950	Miss Adelaide	Adelaide's Lament Reprise	Ballad	Db4	Cb5	Lead	Character Female
Guys and Dolls	1950	Miss Adelaide	Take Back Your Mink	Uptempo	Bb3	D5	Lead	Character Female
Guys and Dolls	1950	Miss Adelaide	Marry The Man Today*	Uptempo	C4	Eb5	Lead	Character Female
Wonderful Town	1953	Ruth Sherwood	One Hundred Easy Ways To Lose A Ma	Moderate Tempo	G3	A4	Lead	Character Female
Wonderful Town	1953	Ruth Sherwood	Quiet Ruth	Ballad	F3	E4	Lead	Character Female
Wonderful Town	1953	Ruth Sherwood	Conga*	Uptempo	F3	A4	Lead	Character Female
Wonderful Town	1953	Ruth Sherwood	Swing*	Uptempo	E3	E4	Lead	Character Female
Damn Yankees	1955	Gloria Thorpe	Shoeless Joe From Hanniibal, Mo	Uptempo	Bb3	Db5	Supporting	Character Female
Bells Are Ringing	1956	Ella Peterson	It's A Perfect Relationship	Uptempo	Ab3	Cb5	Lead	Character Female
Bells Are Ringing	1956	Ella Peterson	Is It A Crime	Moderate Tempo	A3	C5	Lead	Character Female
Bells Are Ringing	1956	Ella Peterson	Long Before I Knew You *	Ballad	B3	C#5	Lead	Character Female
Bells Are Ringing	1956	Ella Peterson	The Party's Over	Ballad	F#3	B4	Lead	Character Female
Bells Are Ringing	1956	Ella Peterson	I'm Going Back	Moderate Tempo	A#3	B4	Lead	Character Female
Bells Are Ringing	1956	Ella Peterson	Better Than A Dream *	Moderate Tempo	A3	D5	Lead	Character Female
Most Happy Fella, The	1956	Cleo	Ooh! My Feet!	Moderate Tempo	A#3	Bb4	Lead	Character Female
Most Happy Fella, The	1956	Cleo	I Know How It Is*	Moderate Tempo	Ab3	B4	Lead	Character Female
Most Happy Fella, The	1956	Cleo	I Like Everybody Reprise*	Uptempo	G#3	B4	Lead	Character Female
Cinderella (2013)	1957	Charlotte	Stepsister's Lament*	Uptempo	C4	D5	Supporting	Character Female
Cinderella (2013)	1957	Joy	A Lovely Night*	Uptempo	B3	D5	Supporting	Character Female
Once Upon A Mattress	1959	Princess Winifred	Shy*	Uptempo	B3	C5	Lead	Character Female
How To Succeed...	1961	Miss Jones	Brotherhood Of Man*	Uptempo	A#3	G5	Featured Ensembl	Character Female
How To Succeed...	1961	Smitty	Been A Long Day*	Uptempo	Bb3	D5	Supporting	Character Female
Little Me	1962	Young Belle	Other Side Of The Tracks (Slow Versio	Ballad	B3	C5	Lead	Character Female
Little Me	1962	Young Belle	On The Other Side Of The Tracks Repr	Uptempo	A3	D5	Lead	Character Female
Little Me	1962	Belle	Dimples*	Uptempo	A3	D5	Lead	Character Female
Little Me	1962	Young Belle	Poor Little Hollywood Star	Moderate Tempo	G#3	E5	Lead	Character Female
Little Me	1962	Young Belle	I Needed Social Position*	Moderate Tempo	Ab3	C#5	Lead	Character Female
Little Me	1962	Belle	I Needed Social Position*	Moderate Tempo	Ab3	C#5	Lead	Character Female
Little Me	1962	Belle	Here's To Us*	Uptempo	F3	Bb4	Lead	Character Female

* = Music Edit Required
+ = Ethnic Specific

Show	Year	Role	Song	Range-Bottom	Range-Top	Category	Char Type
Funny Girl	1964	Fanny Brice	I'm The Greatest Start	G#3	C5	Lead	Character Female
Funny Girl	1964	Fanny Brice	Coronet Man	A#3	D5	Lead	Character Female
Funny Girl	1964	Fanny Brice	His Love Makes Me Beautiful*	Bb3	Eb5	Lead	Character Female
Funny Girl	1964	Fanny Brice	People	A3	Db5	Lead	Character Female
Funny Girl	1964	Fanny Brice	You Are Woman*	A#3	C#5	Lead	Character Female
Funny Girl	1964	Fanny Brice	Don't Rain On My Parade	E3	B4	Lead	Character Female
Funny Girl	1964	Fanny Brice	Sade, Sade Married Lady	A3	F5	Lead	Character Female
Funny Girl	1964	Fanny Brice	Who Are You Now	Bb3	Db4	Lead	Character Female
Funny Girl	1964	Fanny Brice	The Music That Makes Me Dance	G#3	E5	Lead	Character Female
Funny Girl	1964	Fanny Brice	Don't Rain On My Parade Reprise	E3	B4	Lead	Character Female
Funny Girl	1964	Fanny Brice	Rat Tat Tat Part 2*	B3	D#5	Lead	Character Female
Annie Get Your Gun	1966	Annie Oakley	An Old Fashioned Wedding	B3	B4	Lead	Character Female
Apple Tree, The	1966	Ella	Oh To Be A Movie Star	C4	D5	Lead	Character Female
Apple Tree, The	1966	Eve	Here In Eden	A3	B4	Lead	Character Female
Apple Tree, The	1966	Eve	Feelings	B3	E5	Lead	Character Female
Apple Tree, The	1966	Eve	Go To Sleep Whoever You Are	B3	B4	Lead	Character Female
Apple Tree, The	1966	Eve	What Makes Me Love Him	C3	C#5	Lead	Character Female
Apple Tree, The	1966	Eve	Friends	Bb3	C5	Lead	Character Female
Apple Tree, The	1966	Passionella	Gorgeous	C4	D5	Lead	Character Female
Apple Tree, The	1966	Passionella	Wealth	B3	B4	Lead	Character Female
Apple Tree, The	1966	Passionella	Oh To Be A Movie Star Reprise	C4	D5	Lead	Character Female
Apple Tree, The	1966	Princess Barbara	I've Got What You Want	G3	C5	Lead	Character Female
Apple Tree, The	1966	Princess Barbara	Tiger, Tiger	F3	A4	Lead	Character Female
Cabaret	1966	Faulein Kost	Married *	F#3	Bb4	Supporting	Character Female
Cabaret	1966	Faulein Kost	Tomorrow Belongs to Me Reprise *	A3	Bb4	Supporting	Character Female
Hair	1968	Jeanie	Air	G3	G4	Lead	Character Female
Hair	1968	Margaret Mead	My Conviction	E3	A4	Lead	Character Female
Follies	1971	Sally Durant	In Buddy's Eyes *	F#3	D5	Lead	Character Female
Godspell	1971	Soloist 1	Day By Day	C4	A4	Supporting	Character Female
Godspell	1971	Soloist 2	Learn Your Lesson Well	G3	Eb5	Supporting	Character Female
Godspell	1971	Soloist 3	O Bless The Lord*	B3	E5	Supporting	Character Female

The tempo column (Moderate Tempo / Ballad / Uptempo) appears between Song and Range-Bottom:

Song	Tempo
I'm The Greatest Start	Moderate Tempo
Coronet Man	Moderate Tempo
His Love Makes Me Beautiful*	Moderate Tempo
People	Ballad
You Are Woman*	Moderate Tempo
Don't Rain On My Parade	Uptempo
Sade, Sade Married Lady	Moderate Tempo
Who Are You Now	Ballad
The Music That Makes Me Dance	Ballad
Don't Rain On My Parade Reprise	Moderate Tempo
Rat Tat Tat Part 2*	Uptempo
An Old Fashioned Wedding	Uptempo
Oh To Be A Movie Star	Uptempo
Here In Eden	Moderate Tempo
Feelings	Moderate Tempo
Go To Sleep Whoever You Are	Ballad
What Makes Me Love Him	Ballad
Friends	Uptempo
Gorgeous	Uptempo
Wealth	Uptempo
Oh To Be A Movie Star Reprise	Moderate Tempo
I've Got What You Want	Ballad
Tiger, Tiger	Uptempo
Married *	Ballad
Tomorrow Belongs to Me Reprise *	Moderate Tempo
Air	Uptempo
My Conviction	Moderate Tempo
In Buddy's Eyes *	Ballad
Day By Day	Ballad
Learn Your Lesson Well	Uptempo
O Bless The Lord*	Moderate Tempo

* = Music Edit Required
+ = Ethnic Specific

Show	Year	Role	Song	Tempo	Range-Bottom	Range-Top	Category	Char Type
Godspell	1971	Soloist 5	Turn Back O Man*	Moderate Tempo	D3	D5	Supporting	Character Female
Mack and Mabel	1974	Lottie Ames	Big Time*	Uptempo	F#3	Eb5	Supporting	Character Female
Mack and Mabel	1974	Lottie Ames	Tap Your Troubles Away	Uptempo	F3	Bb4	Lead	Character Female
Wiz, The	1974	Addaperle	He's The Wiz*	Moderate Tempo	F3	C5	Lead	Character Female
A Chorus Line	1975	Bebe	At The Ballet	Moderate Tempo	A3	C#5	Supporting	Character Female
A Chorus Line	1975	Diana +	Nothing	Uptempo	G3	B4	Lead	Character Female
A Chorus Line	1975	Diana +	What I Did For Love	Ballad	Bb3	D#5	Lead	Character Female
Chicago	1975	Mama Morton	When You're Good To Mama	Moderate Tempo	F#3	A4	Lead	Character Female
Chicago	1975	Mama Morton	Class*	Ballad	F3	B4	Lead	Character Female
Pacific Overtures	1976	Female	Prologue	Ballad	D3	Bb4	Lead	Character Female
Best Little Whorehouse...	1978	Doatsey Mae	Doatsey Mae	Ballad	G3	C5	Supporting	Character Female
Best Little Whorehouse...	1978	Mona Stangley	A Lil Ole Bitty Pissant Country Place	Uptempo	F3	D4	Lead	Character Female
Best Little Whorehouse...	1978	Mona Stangley	Girl You're a Woman	Ballad	E2	G4	Lead	Character Female
Best Little Whorehouse...	1978	Mona Stangley	No Lies	Uptempo	G3	B4	Lead	Character Female
Best Little Whorehouse...	1978	Mona Stangley	Bus From Amarillo	Moderate Tempo	E3	Bb4	Lead	Character Female
Sweeney Todd	1979	Mrs. Lovett	The Worst Pies In London	Uptempo	B3	Eb5	Lead	Character Female
Sweeney Todd	1979	Mrs. Lovett	Poor Thing	Uptempo	F#3	B4	Lead	Character Female
Sweeney Todd	1979	Mrs. Lovett	Wait	Moderate Tempo	Bb2	Eb5	Lead	Character Female
Sweeney Todd	1979	Mrs. Lovett	By The Sea	Uptempo	G3	E5	Lead	Character Female
Dreamgirls	1981	Effie White +	I Am Changing	Ballad	Eb4	F5	Lead	Character Female
Dreamgirls	1981	Effie White +	One Night Only	Ballad	Ab3	D5	Lead	Character Female
Joseph...Dream Coat	1982	Narrator	Pharaoh Story	Moderate Tempo	A3	E5	Lead	Character Female
Baby	1983	Pam Sakarian	I Want It All *	Uptempo	C4	Eb5	Lead	Character Female
Baby	1983	Pam Sakarian	With You *	Ballad	G#3	D5	Lead	Character Female
Sunday...Park With Geroge	1984	Nurse	The Day Off (Part 3)*	Moderate Tempo	B3	D5	Supporting	Character Female
Big River	1985	Slave +	Crossing Over *	Ballad	G3	C5	Featured Ensembl	Character Female
Mystery Of Edwin Drood, The	1985	Dick Datchery (Drood)	Out On A Limerick	Moderate Tempo	C3	E4	Lead	Character Female
Into The Woods	1987	Baker's Wife	Maybe They're Magic	Uptempo	G#3	E5	Lead	Character Female
Into The Woods	1987	Baker's Wife	It Takes Two	Moderate Tempo	A3	D5	Lead	Character Female
Into The Woods	1987	Baker's Wife	Moments In The Woods	Uptempo	F3	D4	Lead	Character Female
Ain't Misbehavin'	1988	Woman One +	I've Got A Feeling I'm Falling	Uptempo	F3	C5	Lead	Character Female

* = Music Edit Required
+ = Ethnic Specific

Show	Year	Role	Song	Tempo	Range-Bottom	Range-Top	Category	Char Type
Ain't Misbehavin'	1988	Woman One +	Cash For our Trash	Uptempo	B4	D5	Lead	Character Female
Ain't Misbehavin'	1988	Woman One +	Mean To Me	Ballad	G3	G4	Lead	Character Female
Ain't Misbehavin'	1988	Woman One +	Honeysuckle Rose*	Ballad	Bb4	F5	Lead	Character Female
Ain't Misbehavin'	1988	Woman One +	Lounging At The Waldorf	Ballad	C4	D5	Lead	Character Female
Ain't Misbehavin'	1988	Woman Two +	That Ain't Right*	Ballad	G2	Eb5	Lead	Character Female
City of Angels	1989	Oolie	What You Don't Know About Women *	Moderate Tempo	G3	F5	Lead	Character Female
City of Angels	1989	Oolie/Donna	You Can Always Count On Me	Moderate Tempo	Bb3	Db5	Supporting	Character Female
Closer Than Ever	1989	Woman Two	You Want To Be My Friend	Uptempo	D4	E5	Lead	Character Female
Closer Than Ever	1989	Woman Two	Miss Bird	Moderate Tempo	F3	Eb5	Lead	Character Female
Closer Than Ever	1989	Woman Two	There *	Moderate Tempo	A3	D5	Lead	Character Female
Closer Than Ever	1989	Woman Two	Another Wedding Song *	Ballad	B3	B4	Lead	Character Female
Closer Than Ever	1989	Woman Two	Back On Base	Moderate Tempo	G3	G5	Lead	Character Female
Closer Than Ever	1989	Woman Two	I've Been Here Before *	Ballad	Gb3	Cb5	Lead	Character Female
Meet Me In St. Louis	1989	Katie	A Touch Of Irish*	Uptempo	G3	Bb4	Lead	Character Female
Once On This Island	1990	Asaka+	Mama Will Provide*	Uptempo	B3	G5	Lead	Character Female
Nick & Nora	1991	Maria Valdex	Boom Chicka Boom*	Uptempo	A3	Bb4	Lead	Character Female
Secret Garden, The	1991	Martha	If I Had A Fine White Horse	Uptempo	G3	D5	Lead	Character Female
Secret Garden, The	1991	Martha	Hold On	Uptempo	F#3	B4	Lead	Character Female
Blood Brothers	1993	Mrs. Johnstone	Marilyn Monroe	Moderate Tempo	A3	A4	Lead	Character Female
Blood Brothers	1993	Mrs. Johnstone	Easy Terms	Ballad	G3	A4	Lead	Character Female
Blood Brothers	1993	Mrs. Johnstone	Easy Terms Reprise	Ballad	G3	F4	Lead	Character Female
Blood Brothers	1993	Mrs. Johnstone	Bright New Day	Uptempo	D4	A4	Lead	Character Female
Blood Brothers	1993	Mrs. Johnstone	Bright New Day Reprise *	Uptempo	D4	C5	Lead	Character Female
Blood Brothers	1993	Mrs. Johnstone	Marilyn Monroe 2	Moderate Tempo	A3	A4	Lead	Character Female
Blood Brothers	1993	Mrs. Johnstone	Light Romance	Ballad	G3	A4	Lead	Character Female
Blood Brothers	1993	Mrs. Johnstone	Tell Me It's Not True	Ballad	F3	C5	Lead	Character Female
Blood Brothers	1993	Mrs. Johnstone	Marilyn Monroe 3	Ballad	A3	B4	Lead	Character Female
Songs For A New World	1995	Woman 2	Just One Step	Uptempo	F3	C#5	Lead	Character Female
Songs For A New World	1995	Woman 2	Stars And The Moon	Moderate Tempo	A3	D5	Lead	Character Female
Songs For A New World	1995	Woman 2	Surabaya Santa	Moderate Tempo	G3	Eb4	Lead	Character Female
Songs For A New World	1995	Woman 2	The Flagmaker 1775	Moderate Tempo	A3	E5	Lead	Character Female

Alto

* = Music Edit Required
+ = Ethnic Specific

Show	Year	Role	Song	Tempo	Range-Bottom	Range-Top	Category	Char Type
Songs For A New World	1995	Woman 2	Hear My Song*	Moderate Tempo	A3	B4	Lead	Character Female
Lion King, The	1997	Rafiki	Circle of Life*	Moderate Tempo	F#3	C5	Lead	Character Female
Lion King, The	1997	Rafiki	Rafiki Mourns (Eulogy)	Ballad	G3	Eb5	Lead	Character Female
Lion King, The	1997	Rafiki	He Lives In You*	Moderate Tempo	C4	E5	Lead	Character Female
Footloose	1998	Irene	Let's Make Believe We're In Love	Moderate Tempo	G3	D4	Supporting	Character Female
Footloose	1998	Rusty	Let's Hear It For the Boy	Uptempo	A3	D#5	Supporting	Character Female
Ragtime	1998	Emma Goldman	He Wanted To Say*	Moderate Tempo	G3	Bb4	Lead	Character Female
Marie Christine	1999	Magdelena	Cincincati*	Moderate Tempo	G3	F#3	Supporting	Character Female
Marie Christine	1999	Magdelena	Paradise Is Burning Down*	Uptempo	Eb3	Eb5	Lead	Character Female
Marie Christine	1999	Magdelena	A Lovely Wedding*	Uptempo	C4	C#5	Supporting	Character Female
Marie Christine	1999	Magdelena	There's A Rumor	Moderate Tempo	F#3	C#5	Lead	Character Female
Full Monty, The	2000	Georgie Bukatinsky	You Rule My World Reprise *	Ballad	G#3	D5	Supporting	Character Female
Full Monty, The	2000	Vicki Nichols	Life With Harold	Uptempo	G3	D5	Supporting	Character Female
Full Monty, The	2000	Vicki Nichols	You Rule My World Reprise *	Ballad	G#3	B4	Supporting	Character Female
Jane Eyre	2000	Jane Eyre	The Graveside	Ballad	A3	D5	Lead	Character Female
Jane Eyre	2000	Jane Eyre	Sweet Liberty	Uptempo	A3	D5	Lead	Character Female
Jane Eyre	2000	Jane Eyre	Secret Soul*	Uptempo	F#3	D4	Lead	Character Female
Jane Eyre	2000	Jane Eyre	Painting Her Portrait	Uptempo	Bb3	D5	Lead	Character Female
Jane Eyre	2000	Jane Eyre	In the Virgin Morning*	Moderate Tempo	G3	D5	Lead	Character Female
Jane Eyre	2000	Jane Eyre	Sirens Reprise*	Moderate Tempo	G3	C5	Lead	Character Female
Jane Eyre	2000	Jane Eyre	The Voice Across the Moors	Moderate Tempo	Ab3	E5	Supporting	Character Female
Jane Eyre	2000	Jane Eyre	Brave Enough for Love	Uptempo	E3	E4	Lead	Character Female
Seussical	2000	The Cat In The Hat	A Day For The Cat In The Hat*	Uptempo	A3	Bb4	Lead	Character Female
Seussical	2000	Mrs. Mayor	How To Raise A Child*	Moderate Tempo	D3	F4	Lead	Character Female
Seussical	2000	The Cat In The Hat	How Lucky You Are	Uptempo	C#4	E5	Lead	Character Female
Seussical	2000	The Cat In The Hat	Havin' A Hunch*	Uptempo	A3	Ab4	Lead	Character Female
Mamma Mia!	2001	Tanya	Does Your Mother Know*	Moderate Tempo	F3	Bb4	Lead	Character Female
Mamma Mia!	2001	Rosie	Take A Chance On Me*	Moderate Tempo	C4	E5	Lead	Character Female
Hairspray	2002	Motormouth Mabel+	Big Blonde And Beautiful*	Ballad	E3	C5	Lead	Character Female
Hairspray	2002	Motormouth Mabel+	I Know Where I've Been	Moderate Tempo	D#3	F4	Lead	Character Female
Thoroughly Modern Millie	2002	Mrs. Meers	They Don't Know	Moderate Tempo	D#3	F4	Lead	Character Female

Alto

* = Music Edit Required
+ = Ethnic Specific

Show	Year	Role	Song	Tempo	Range-Bottom	Range-Top	Category	Char Type
Avenue Q	2003	Christmas Eve	The More You Love Someone	Ballad	B3	E♭5	Lead	Character Female
Avenue Q	2003	Gary Coleman	You Can Be As Loud As You Want	Uptempo	G3	D♭5	Lead	Character Female
Avenue Q	2003	Gary Coleman	Schadenfruede *	Uptempo	F3	C5	Lead	Character Female
Fame	2003	Mabel	Mabel's Prayer	Moderate Tempo	D4	E5	Supporting	Character Female
Fame	2003	Serena	Let's Play A Love Scene	Ballad	G#3	D#5	Lead	Character Female
Fame	2003	Serena	Think of Meryl Streep	Uptempo	B3	D5	Lead	Character Female
Fame	2003	Serena	Let's Play A Love Scene Reprise *	Ballad	A3	B4	Lead	Character Female
Wicked	2003	Elphaba	The Wizard And I*	Moderate Tempo	G3	E5	Lead	Character Female
Wicked	2003	Elphaba	I'm Not That Girl	Ballad	E3	B4	Lead	Character Female
Wicked	2003	Elphaba	The Wizard and I Reprise	Moderate Tempo	A3	C5	Lead	Character Female
Wicked	2003	Elphaba	Defying Gravity*	Uptempo	G3	F5	Lead	Character Female
Wicked	2003	Elphaba	As Long As You Are Mine*	Moderate Tempo	B♭3	D♭5	Lead	Character Female
Wicked	2003	Elphaba	No Good Deed	Uptempo	A3	D#5	Lead	Character Female
Wicked	2003	Elphaba	For Good*	Ballad	A♭3	D♭5	Lead	Character Female
Caroline, Or Change	2004	Dotty Moffett +	Lot's Wife (ms 6-42)	Moderate Tempo	G3	B4	Supporting	Character Female
Caroline, Or Change	2004	Rose Stopnick Gellman	Long Distance (ms 1-74)	Moderate Tempo	B♭3	D5	Supporting	Character Female
Caroline, Or Change	2004	Rose Stopnick Gellman	Noah Has A Problem (ms 6-59)	Uptempo	A♭3	C♭5	Supporting	Character Female
Caroline, Or Change	2004	Rose Stopnick Gellman	Rose Recovers (ms 3-27)	Ballad	G3	C5	Supporting	Character Female
Caroline, Or Change	2004	Rose Stopnick Gellman	Inside/Out (ms 11-54)	Uptempo	C4	D5	Supporting	Character Female
Caroline, Or Change	2004	The Radio +	No One Waitin' (ms 1-18)	Alto	G3	D5	Supporting	Character Female
Color Purple, The	2005	Celie+	Somebody Gonna Love You	Ballad	F3	A4	Lead	Character Female
Color Purple, The	2005	Celie+	What About Love *	Ballad	B2	D5	Lead	Character Female
Color Purple, The	2005	Celie+	I'm Here	Ballad	E3	G5	Lead	Character Female
Color Purple, The	2005	Celie+	Bring My Nettie Back	Ballad	G3	G5	Lead	Character Female
Color Purple, The	2005	Celie+	Dear God (Sofia)	Uptempo	G3	G4	Lead	Character Female
Color Purple, The	2005	Celie+	Dear God (Shug)	Moderate Tempo	F3	B4	Lead	Character Female
Color Purple, The	2005	Celie+	With These Hands	Moderate Tempo	A♭3	E♭5	Lead	Character Female
Spamalot	2005	Marlene Cow	The Cow Song*	Moderate Tempo	F3	B4	Featured Ensembl	Character Female
Drowsy Chaperon, The	2006	Drowsy Chaperone	As We Stumble Along	Moderate Tempo	F3	D5	Lead	Character Female
Mary Poppins	2006	Mrs. Corry	Supercalifragilisticexpialidocious*	Uptempo	C4	D5	Lead	Character Female
Spring Awakening	2006	Female Solo	My Junk*	Uptempo	A3	E5	Featured Ensembl	Character Female

* = Music Edit Required
+ = Ethnic Specific

Show	Year	Role	Song	Tempo	Range-Bottom	Range-Top	Category	Char Type
Cutains	2007	Carmen Bernstein	It's A Business	Moderate Tempo	Eb3	Bb4	Lead	Character Female
Cutains	2007	Carmen Bernstein	Show People	Moderate Tempo	G3	Ab4	Lead	Character Female
Cutains	2007	Carmen Bernstein	Show People Reprise *	Moderate Tempo	G3	Bb4	Lead	Character Female
Legally Blonde	2007	Enid Hoops	Harvard Variation*	Uptempo	Bb3	C5	Supporting	Character Female
Legally Blonde	2007	Paulette	Ireland	Moderate Tempo	A#3	B4	Lead	Character Female
Legally Blonde	2007	Paulette	Ireland Reprise	Moderate Tempo	C4	Bb4	Lead	Character Female
Legally Blonde	2007	Paulette	Find My Way	Ballad	Ab3	C5	Lead	Character Female
Billy Elliot	2008	Mrs. Wilkinson	Shine	Moderate Tempo	Gb3	B4	Lead	Character Female
Billy Elliot	2008	Mrs. Wilkinson	Born To Boogie	Uptempo	G3	A4	Lead	Character Female
Kinky Boots	2013	Lauren	The History of Wrong Guys	Uptempo	Bb3	D5	Lead	Character Female
Heathers	2014	Martha Dunnstock	Kindergarten Boyfriend	Ballad	G3	E5	Supporting	Character Female
Crazy For You (1992)	1926	Polly Baker	Someone To Watch Over Me	Ballad	Ab2	C4	Lead	Character Ingenue Female
Good News (1993 Revival)	1927	Connie Lane	The Best Things In Life Are Free*	Ballad	A3	D5	Lead	Character Ingenue Female
Good News (1993 Revival)	1927	Connie Lane	Just Imagine	Ballad	B3	E5	Lead	Character Ingenue Female
Good News (1993 Revival)	1927	Connie Lane	Lucky In Love*	Uptempo	C4	Eb5	Lead	Character Ingenue Female
Show Boat	1927	Ellie	Life Upon The Wicked Stage*	Uptempo	G3	D5	Lead	Character Ingenue Female
Good News (1993 Revival)	1928	Connie Lane	My Lucky Star	Moderate Tempo	Bb3	Db5	Lead	Character Ingenue Female
Crazy For You (1992)	1930	Polly Baker	Could You Use Me	Uptempo	A2	Eb4	Lead	Character Ingenue Female
Crazy For You (1992)	1930	Polly Baker	Embraceable You	Ballad	A3	B4	Lead	Character Ingenue Female
Crazy For You (1992)	1930	Polly Baker	I Got Rhythm	Uptempo	Bb3	Eb4	Lead	Character Ingenue Female
Crazy For You (1992)	1930	Polly Baker	But Not For Me	Ballad	Bb3	C5	Lead	Character Ingenue Female
Wizard Of Oz 1987	1939	Dorothy	Over The Rainbow	Ballad	G3	C5	Lead	Character Ingenue Female
Wizard Of Oz 1989	1939	Dorothy	Come Out*	Moderate Tempo	C4	D5	Lead	Character Ingenue Female
Wizard Of Oz 2002	1939	Dorothy	The Jitterbug*	Uptempo	Ab3	D5	Lead	Character Ingenue Female
Wizard Of Oz 2004	1939	Dorothy	Over The Rainbow Reprise*	Ballad	B3	C#5	Lead	Character Ingenue Female
Oklahoma!	1943	Ado Annie Carnes	I Cain't Say No Reprise	Moderate Tempo	C4	D5	Lead	Character Ingenue Female
Oklahoma!	1943	Ado Annie Carnes	I Cain't Say No	Moderate Tempo	C4	D5	Lead	Character Ingenue Female
Carousel	1945	Carrie Pipperidge	You're A Queer One Julie Jordan	Moderate Tempo	D4	E5	Lead	Character Ingenue Female
Carousel	1945	Carrie Pipperidge	When I Marry Mr. Snow	Ballad	D4	F5	Lead	Character Ingenue Female

* = Music Edit Required
+ = Ethnic Specific

Show	Year	Role	Song	Tempo	Range-Bottom	Range-Top	Category	Char Type
Carousel	1945	Carrie Pipperidge	When I Marry Mr. Snow Reprise	Ballad	F#3	A4	Lead	Character Ingenue Female
Carousel	1945	Carrie Pipperidge	When The Children Are Asleep *	Moderate Tempo	Eb3	C5	Lead	Character Ingenue Female
Brigadoon	1947	Meg Brockie	The Love Of My Life	Uptempo	G3	C5	Supporting	Character Ingenue Female
Brigadoon	1947	Meg Brockie	My Mother's Wedding Day	Uptempo	C4	F5	Supporting	Character Ingenue Female
Kiss Me Kate	1948	Lois Lane/Bianca	Why Can't You Behave*	Moderate Tempo	G3	Cb5	Lead	Character Ingenue Female
Kiss Me Kate	1948	Lois Lane/Bianca	Always True To You*	Uptempo	A3	C#5	Lead	Character Ingenue Female
Kiss Me Kate	1948	Lois Lane/Bianca	Always True To You Encore	Uptempo	Bb3	A5	Lead	Character Ingenue Female
Cinderella (2013)	1957	Gabrielle	Stepsister's Lament*	Uptempo	C4	D5	Supporting	Character Ingenue Female
Cinderella (2013)	1957	Gabrielle	A Lovely Night*	Uptempo	B3	D5	Supporting	Character Ingenue Female
Once Upon A Mattress	1959	Princess Winifred	Happily Ever After	Moderate Tempo	A3	Cb5	Lead	Character Ingenue Female
Fiddler on The Roof	1964	Hodel	Far From The Home I Love	Ballad	C4	E5	Supporting	Character Ingenue Female
Sweet Charity	1966	Charity Hope Valentine	You Should See Yourself	Uptempo	Bb3	Bb4	Lead	Character Ingenue Female
Sweet Charity	1966	Charity Hope Valentine	Charity's Soliloquy	Moderate Tempo	F3	Ab4	Lead	Character Ingenue Female
Sweet Charity	1966	Charity Hope Valentine	If My Friends Could See Me Now	Uptempo	G#3	Bb4	Lead	Character Ingenue Female
Sweet Charity	1966	Charity Hope Valentine	There's Gott Be Something Better...*	Uptempo	Bb3	Db5	Lead	Character Ingenue Female
Sweet Charity	1966	Charity Hope Valentine	I'm The Bravest Individual	Uptempo	C4	Eb5	Lead	Character Ingenue Female
Sweet Charity	1966	Charity Hope Valentine	Where Am I Going	Moderate Tempo	A3	A4	Lead	Character Ingenue Female
Sweet Charity	1966	Charity Hope Valentine	I'm A Brass Band*	Uptempo	A#3	G#4	Lead	Character Ingenue Female
Hair	1968	Sheila	I Believe In Love	Uptempo	G3	C5	Lead	Character Ingenue Female
Hair	1968	Sheila	Easy To Be Hard	Ballad	C4	C5	Lead	Character Ingenue Female
Hair	1968	Sheila	Good Morning Starshine	Uptempo	C4	C5	Lead	Character Ingenue Female
Company (Revival)	1970	Marta	You Could Drive a Person Crazy	Uptempo	C#4	A5	Supporting	Character Ingenue Female
Company (Revival)	1970	Marta	Another Hundred People	Uptempo	A3	D5	Supporting	Character Ingenue Female
Grease	1971	Marty	Freddy My Love	Uptempo	C4	C5	Lead	Character Ingenue Female
Jesus Christ Superstar	1971	Mary Magdalene	Everything's Alright	Moderate Tempo	G#3	D5	Lead	Character Ingenue Female
Jesus Christ Superstar	1971	Mary Magdalene	Everything's Alright Reprise	Moderate Tempo	F#3	G4	Lead	Character Ingenue Female
Jesus Christ Superstar	1971	Mary Magdalene	I Don't Know How To Love Him	Ballad	A3	C5	Lead	Character Ingenue Female
Jesus Christ Superstar	1971	Mary Magdalene	Could We Start Again Please	Ballad	A3	F#5	Lead	Character Ingenue Female
Wiz, The	1974	Dorothy	Home Reprise	Moderate Tempo	G3	E5	Lead	Character Ingenue Female
A Chorus Line	1975	Maggie	At The Ballet	Moderate Tempo	A3	D5	Supporting	Character Ingenue Female
A Chorus Line	1975	Maggie	Mother *	Ballad	B3	D5	Lead	Character Ingenue Female

Alto

* = Music Edit Required
+ = Ethnic Specific

Show	Year	Role	Song	Tempo	Range-Bottom	Range-Top	Category	Char Type
Chicago	1975	Roxie Hart	Funny Honey	Ballad	F3	Bb4	Lead	Character Ingenue Female
Chicago	1975	Roxie Hart	Roxie	Moderate Tempo	G3	Bb4	Lead	Character Ingenue Female
Chicago	1975	Roxie Hart	My Own Best Friend	Moderate Tempo	E3	A4	Lead	Character Ingenue Female
Chicago	1975	Roxie Hart	Me and My Baby	Uptempo	Bb3	C4	Lead	Character Ingenue Female
Chicago	1975	Roxie Hart	Nowadays	Moderate Tempo	F#3	D5	Lead	Character Ingenue Female
Best Little Whorehouse...	1978	Mona's Girl	Hard Candy Christmas	Ballad	Bb3	C4	Featured Ensembl	Character Ingenue Female
Little Shop of Horrors	1982	Audrey	Somewhere That's Green	Ballad	B3	C5	Lead	Character Ingenue Female
Little Shop of Horrors	1982	Audrey	Suddenly Seymour	Moderate Tempo	A2	C#4	Lead	Character Ingenue Female
Little Shop of Horrors	1982	Audrey	Somewhere That's Green Reprise	Ballad	B2	C5	Lead	Character Ingenue Female
Seven Brides/Seven Brother	1982	Milly	Wonderful Day*	Moderate Tempo	Ab3	Db5	Lead	Character Ingenue Female
Seven Brides/Seven Brother	1982	Milly	I'm Jumpin' In*	Moderate Tempo	Ab3	Bb4	Lead	Character Ingenue Female
Seven Brides/Seven Brother	1982	Milly	One Man*	Moderate Tempo	G3	Bb4	Lead	Character Ingenue Female
Seven Brides/Seven Brother	1982	Milly	I Married Seven Brothers*	Moderate Tempo	G3	Bb4	Lead	Character Ingenue Female
Seven Brides/Seven Brother	1982	Milly	Goin Co'tin*	Moderate Tempo	Bb3	Eb5	Lead	Character Ingenue Female
Seven Brides/Seven Brother	1982	Milly	Love Never Goes Away*	Ballad	G3	B5	Lead	Character Ingenue Female
Seven Brides/Seven Brother	1982	Milly	We Gotta Make It Through...Reprise*	Ballad	A3	A4	Lead	Character Ingenue Female
Seven Brides/Seven Brother	1982	Milly	Glad That You Were Born*	Ballad	Db4	Bb4	Lead	Character Ingenue Female
Song & Dance	1985	Emma	Take That Look Off Your Face	Uptempo	B3	D5	Lead	Character Ingenue Female
Song & Dance	1985	Emma	Let Me Finish	Moderate Tempo	G#3	Eb5	Lead	Character Ingenue Female
Song & Dance	1985	Emma	So Much To Do In New York	Moderate Tempo	Ab3	Eb5	Lead	Character Ingenue Female
Song & Dance	1985	Emma	1st Letter Home	Moderate Tempo	A3	D5	Lead	Character Ingenue Female
Song & Dance	1985	Emma	English Girls	Uptempo	G3	C5	Lead	Character Ingenue Female
Song & Dance	1985	Emma	Capped Teeth And Ceasar Salad	Moderate Tempo	A3	B4	Lead	Character Ingenue Female
Song & Dance	1985	Emma	You Made Me Think You Were In Love	Uptempo	A3	Bb4	Lead	Character Ingenue Female
Song & Dance	1985	Emma	Capped Teeth And Ceasar Salad Repris	Ballad	Ab3	Bb4	Lead	Character Ingenue Female
Song & Dance	1985	Emma	So Much To Do In New York #2	Moderate Tempo	G3	Eb5	Lead	Character Ingenue Female
Song & Dance	1985	Emma	2nd Letter Home	Moderate Tempo	A3	A4	Lead	Character Ingenue Female
Song & Dance	1985	Emma	The Last Man In My Life	Ballad	G3	Eb5	Lead	Character Ingenue Female
Song & Dance	1985	Emma	Unexpected Song	Ballad	F3	G5	Lead	Character Ingenue Female

Alto

Show	Year	Role	Song	Tempo	Range-Bottom	Range-Top	Category	Char Type
Song & Dance	1985	Emma	Come Back With The Same Look...	Uptempo	A3	C5	Lead	Character Ingenue Female
Song & Dance	1985	Emma	Take That Look Off Your Face Reprise	Uptempo	B3	E5	Lead	Character Ingenue Female
Song & Dance	1985	Emma	Tell Me On A Sunday	Ballad	G3	E5	Lead	Character Ingenue Female
Song & Dance	1985	Emma	I Love New York	Moderate Tempo	F3	Bb4	Lead	Character Ingenue Female
Song & Dance	1985	Emma	So Much To Do In New York #3	Moderate Tempo	A3	Eb5	Lead	Character Ingenue Female
Song & Dance	1985	Emma	Married Man	Moderate Tempo	G#3	C5	Lead	Character Ingenue Female
Song & Dance	1985	Emma	I'm Very You	Uptempo	A#3	C5	Lead	Character Ingenue Female
Song & Dance	1985	Emma	3rd Letter Home	Moderate Tempo	G3	Eb5	Lead	Character Ingenue Female
Song & Dance	1985	Emma	Nothing Like You've Ever Known	Ballad	G3	C5	Lead	Character Ingenue Female
Song & Dance	1985	Emma	Let Me Finish Finale	Moderate Tempo	G#3	Eb5	Lead	Character Ingenue Female
Rags	1986	Bella Cohen	If We Never Meet Again*	Ballad	B2	C5	Lead	Character Ingenue Female
Rags	1986	Bella Cohen	Brand New World*	Moderate Tempo	C#4	D#5	Lead	Character Ingenue Female
Rags	1986	Bella Cohen	Penny A Tune	Uptempo	B3	D5	Lead	Character Ingenue Female
Rags	1986	Bella Cohen	Rags*	Uptempo	A3	D5	Lead	Character Ingenue Female
Rags	1986	Bella Cohen	Rags Reprise	Ballad	B#3	B4	Lead	Character Ingenue Female
Les Miserables	1987	Eponine	On My Own	Ballad	A3	C5	Lead	Character Ingenue Female
Les Miserables	1987	Eponine	A Little Fall Of Rain*	Ballad	F3	Db5	Lead	Character Ingenue Female
Chess	1988	Florence	Someone Else's Story	Ballad	F3	C5	Lead	Character Ingenue Female
Chess	1988	Florence	Nobody's Side	Uptempo	E3	E4	Lead	Character Ingenue Female
Chess	1988	Florence	Heaven Help My Heart	Ballad	A3	A4	Lead	Character Ingenue Female
Chess	1988	Florence	You and I*	Ballad	G3	Eb5	Lead	Character Ingenue Female
Chess	1988	Florence	I Know Him So Well	Ballad	F3	D5	Lead	Character Ingenue Female
Chess	1988	Florence	You and I Reprise	Ballad	G2	G4	Lead	Character Ingenue Female
Chess	1988	Florence	Anthem Reprise	Moderate Tempo	Ab3	D5	Lead	Character Ingenue Female
Meet Me In St. Louis	1989	Esther Smith	The Boy Next Door	Ballad	Ab3	Bb4	Lead	Character Ingenue Female
Meet Me In St. Louis	1989	Esther Smith	Under The Bamboo Tree*	Moderate Tempo	C4	Bb4	Lead	Character Ingenue Female
Meet Me In St. Louis	1989	Esther Smith	The Trolly Song*	Uptempo	A3	Bb4	Lead	Character Ingenue Female
Meet Me In St. Louis	1989	Esther Smith	You Are For Loving*	Ballad	Bb3	C5	Lead	Character Ingenue Female
Meet Me In St. Louis	1989	Esther Smith	Have Yourself A Merry Little Christmas	Ballad	G3	C5	Lead	Character Ingenue Female
Meet Me In St. Louis	1989	Esther Smith	Over The Banister	Moderate Tempo	Bb3	Eb5	Lead	Character Ingenue Female

* = Music Edit Required
+ = Ethnic Specific

Show	Year	Role	Song	Tempo	Range-Bottom	Range-Top	Category	Char Type
Children of Eden	1991	Yonah	Stranger To The Rain	Ballad	A3	D4	Supporting	Character Ingenue Female
Children of Eden	1991	Yonah	Sailor Of The Skies	Ballad	G3	Bb4	Supporting	Character Ingenue Female
Kiss Of The Spider Woman	1993	Marta	Dear One*	Ballad	C4	Eb5	Lead	Character Ingenue Female
Kiss Of The Spider Woman	1993	Marta	I Do Miracles*	Moderate Tempo	E3	Bb4	Lead	Character Ingenue Female
Footloose	1998	Ariel Moore	Holding Out For A Hero	Uptempo	C4	C5	Lead	Character Ingenue Female
Footloose	1998	Ariel Moore	Almost Paradise*	Ballad	G3	C5	Lead	Character Ingenue Female
Footloose	1998	Featured Ensemble	Somebody's Eyes Are Watching	Ballad	Ab3	Bb4	Supporting	Character Ingenue Female
Spitfire Grill	2001	Percy Talbott	A Ring Around The Moon	Moderate Tempo	A3	E5	Lead	Character Ingenue Female
Spitfire Grill	2001	Percy Talbott	Coffee Cups And Gossip	Uptempo	C4	C5	Lead	Character Ingenue Female
Spitfire Grill	2001	Percy Talbott	Out Of The Frying Pan	Uptempo	A3	D5	Lead	Character Ingenue Female
Spitfire Grill	2001	Percy Talbott	The Colors of Paradise*	Uptempo	G3	F5	Lead	Character Ingenue Female
Spitfire Grill	2001	Percy Talbott	This Wide Woods Part 3	Moderate Tempo	E3	C#5	Lead	Character Ingenue Female
Spitfire Grill	2001	Percy Talbott	Shine	Ballad	G3	E5	Lead	Character Ingenue Female
Hairspray	2002	Penny Pingleton	Without Love*	Moderate Tempo	Eb3	Eb4	Lead	Character Ingenue Female
Hairspray	2002	Tracy Turnblad	Good Morning Baltimore	Uptempo	Bb3	C#5	Lead	Character Ingenue Female
Hairspray	2002	Tracy Turnblad	I Can Hear The Bells	Uptempo	A3	E5	Lead	Character Ingenue Female
Hairspray	2002	Tracy Turnblad	Welcome To The 60s*	Uptempo	G3	C#5	Lead	Character Ingenue Female
Hairspray	2002	Tracy Turnblad	Good Morning Baltimore Reprise	Ballad	Ab3	Bb4	Lead	Character Ingenue Female
Hairspray	2002	Tracy Turnblad	Without Love*	Moderate Tempo	A3	B4	Lead	Character Ingenue Female
Thoroughly Modern Millie	2002	Millie Dillmount	Gimmie Gimmie	Uptempo	Ab3	D5	Lead	Character Ingenue Female
Thoroughly Modern Millie	2002	Millie Dillmount	Not For The Life Of Me	Uptempo	Ab3	C5	Lead	Character Ingenue Female
Thoroughly Modern Millie	2002	Millie Dillmount	Jimmy	Uptempo	B3	D#4	Lead	Character Ingenue Female
Thoroughly Modern Millie	2002	Millie Dillmount	Forget About The Boy*	Uptempo	A3	Db5	Lead	Character Ingenue Female
Thoroughly Modern Millie	2002	Millie Dillmount	How The Other Half Lives*	Moderate Tempo	B3	Eb5	Lead	Character Ingenue Female
Thoroughly Modern Millie	2002	Millie Dillmount	The Speed Test*	Uptempo	A3	E5	Lead	Character Ingenue Female
Avenue Q	2003	Kate Monster	Mix Tape *	Uptempo	F3	D5	Lead	Character Ingenue Female
Avenue Q	2003	Kate Monster	There's A Fine Fine Line	Moderate Tempo	G3	D5	Lead	Character Ingenue Female
Fame	2003	Carmen	There She Goes *	Uptempo	A3	C5	Lead	Character Ingenue Female
Fame	2003	Carmen	Fame! *	Uptempo	Eb4	Eb5	Lead	Character Ingenue Female
Fame	2003	Carmen	Bring In Tomorrow *	Ballad	D4	D	Lead	Character Ingenue Female

Alto

Show	Year	Role	Song	Tempo	Range-Bottom	Range-Top	Category	Char Type
Fame	2003	Carmen	In LA	Ballad	Bb3	Eb5	Lead	Character Ingenue Female
Wicked	2003	Nessarose	Dancing Through Life*	Uptempo	A3	B4	Lead	Character Ingenue Female
All Shook Up	2005	Ed (Natalie In Drag)	Don't Be Cruel *	Uptempo	D4	D5	Lead	Character Ingenue Female
All Shook Up	2005	Ed (Natalie In Drag)	A Little Less Conversation	Uptempo	Ab3	Eb5	Supporting	Character Ingenue Female
All Shook Up	2005	Natalie Haller	Love Me Tender	Ballad	C4	C5	Lead	Character Ingenue Female
All Shook Up	2005	Natalie Haller	One Night With You	Moderate Tempo	C4	D5	Lead	Character Ingenue Female
All Shook Up	2005	Natalie Haller	Follow That Dream*	Uptempo	B3	D4	Supporting	Character Ingenue Female
All Shook Up	2005	Natalie Haller	Fools Fall In Love *	Ballad	A3	D5	Lead	Character Ingenue Female
All Shook Up	2005	Natalie Haller	If I Can Dream *	Moderate Tempo	C4	F5	Lead	Character Ingenue Female
Little Women	2005	Josephine March	Better	Uptempo	B3	B4	Lead	Character Ingenue Female
Little Women	2005	Josephine March	Our Finest Dreams	Uptempo	F#3	Db5	Lead	Character Ingenue Female
Little Women	2005	Josephine March	Better Reprise	Uptempo	B2	B4	Lead	Character Ingenue Female
Little Women	2005	Josephine March	Astonishing	Uptempo	Ab3	Eb5	Lead	Character Ingenue Female
Little Women	2005	Josephine March	The Fire Within Me	Moderate Tempo	Ab3	Bb4	Lead	Character Ingenue Female
Little Women	2005	Josephine March	Volcanco Reprise	Ballad	A3	D5	Lead	Character Ingenue Female
Spring Awakening	2006	Martha	The Dark I Know Well*	Moderate Tempo	A3	A4	Lead	Character Ingenue Female
Spring Awakening	2006	Ilse	The Dark I Know Well*	Moderate Tempo	A3	A4	Lead	Character Ingenue Female
Spring Awakening	2006	Ilse	Blue Wind	Ballad	G3	A4	Lead	Character Ingenue Female
Spring Awakening	2006	Ilse	Song of Purple Summer*	Moderate Tempo	G3	A4	Lead	Character Ingenue Female
Next To Normal	2009	Natalie	Everything Else	Uptempo	G3	C5	Lead	Character Ingenue Female
Next To Normal	2009	Natalie	Superboy And The Invisible Girl	Uptempo	D4	D5	Lead	Character Ingenue Female
Next To Normal	2009	Natalie	Maybe*	Moderate Tempo	Ab3	D5	Lead	Character Ingenue Female
Addams Family, The	2010	Wednesday Addams	Pulled	Uptempo	B3	Eb5	Lead	Character Ingenue Female
Addams Family, The	2010	Wednesday Addams	One Normal Night	Uptempo	Bb3	Bb4	Lead	Character Ingenue Female
Addams Family, The	2010	Wednesday Addams	Crazier Than You *	Uptempo	A3	E5	Lead	Character Ingenue Female
Heathers	2014	Veronica Sawyer	Beautiful	Uptempo	G3	C5	Lead	Character Ingenue Female
Heathers	2014	Veronica Sawyer	Fight For Me	Ballad	Bb3	D5	Lead	Character Ingenue Female
Heathers	2014	Veronica Sawyer	Dead Girl Walking*	Uptempo	A3	G5	Lead	Character Ingenue Female
Heathers	2014	Veronica Sawyer	The Me Inside Of Me	Moderate Tempo	Ab3	D5	Lead	Character Ingenue Female
Heathers	2014	Veronica Sawyer	Seventeen*	Ballad	A3	B4	Lead	Character Ingenue Female

Alto

* = Music Edit Required
+ = Ethnic Specific

Show	Year	Role	Song	Tempo	Range-Bottom	Range-Top	Category	Char Type
Heathers	2014	Veronica Sawyer	Dead Girls Walking Reprise	Uptempo	A3	A5	Lead	Character Ingenue Female
Heathers	2014	Veronica Sawyer	Seventeen Reprise*	Moderate Tempo	A3	Gb5	Lead	Character Ingenue Female
Good News (1993 Revival)	1927	Babe O'Day	The Varsity Drag	Uptempo	Bb3	C5	Lead	Ingenue Female
Good News (1993 Revival)	1927	Pat	Lucky In Love*	Uptempo	A3	C5	Supporting	Ingenue Female
Good News (1993 Revival)	1927	Pat	The Girl Of Pi Beta Phi	Moderate Tempo	G3	A4	Supporting	Ingenue Female
Good News (1993 Revival)	1928	Babe O'Day	Button Up Your Overcoat*	Uptempo	C4	C5	Lead	Ingenue Female
Good News (1993 Revival)	1930	Babe O'Day	Never Swat A Fly*	Uptempo	A3	C#5	Lead	Ingenue Female
Babes In Arms (1998)	1937	Dolores Reynolds	I Wish I Were In Love Again*	Uptempo	A3	A4	Lead	Ingenue Female
Babes In Arms (1998)	1937	Billie Smith	My Funny Valentine	Ballad	A3	C5	Lead	Ingenue Female
Babes In Arms (1998)	1937	Billie Smith	All At Once*	Moderate Tempo	A3	Bb4	Lead	Ingenue Female
Babes In Arms (1998)	1937	Billie Smith	The Lady Is A Tramp	Uptempo	Ab3	Bb4	Lead	Ingenue Female
Babes In Arms (1998)	1937	Billie Smith	The Lady Is A Tramp Encore	Uptempo	Ab3	Bb4	Lead	Ingenue Female
Babes In Arms (1998)	1937	Dolores Reynolds	You Are So Fair*	Uptempo	B3	B4	Lead	Ingenue Female
Babes In Arms (1998)	1937	Billie Smith	The Lady Is A Tramp Reprise	Uptempo	Ab3	Bb4	Lead	Ingenue Female
Babes In Arms (1998)	1937	Billie Smith	Babes In Arms*	Uptempo	C4	E5	Lead	Ingenue Female
Babes In Arms (1998)	1937	Billie Smith	Where Or When*	Moderate Tempo	B3	E5	Lead	Ingenue Female
Pal Joey	1940	Linda English	I Could Write A Book*	Moderate Tempo	D4	D5	Lead	Ingenue Female
Pal Joey	1940	Linda English	Take Him*	Moderate Tempo	C4	D5	Lead	Ingenue Female
State Fair 1996	1945	Margy Frake	It Might As Well Be Spring	Moderate Tempo	Bb3	Bb4	Lead	Ingenue Female
State Fair 1996	1945	Margy Frake	It Might As Well Be Spring Reprise	Moderate Tempo	Bb3	Bb4	Lead	Ingenue Female
Call Me Madam	1950	Princess Maria	The Ocarina*	Moderate Tempo	C4	D5	Lead	Ingenue Female
Call Me Madam	1950	Princess Maria	It's A Lovely Day Today*	Moderate Tempo	A3	B4	Lead	Ingenue Female
Call Me Madam	1950	Princess Maria	It's A Lovely Day Today Reprise 2*	Moderate Tempo	C4	D5	Lead	Ingenue Female
Flower Drum Song 2002	1958	Wu Mei-Li+	A Hundred Million Miracles*	Moderate Tempo	C4	Eb5	Lead	Ingenue Female
Flower Drum Song 2002	1958	Wu Mei-Li+	I Am Going To Like It Here	Moderate Tempo	Bb3	Bb4	Lead	Ingenue Female
Flower Drum Song 2002	1958	Wu Mei-Li+	You Are Beautiful Reprise*	Ballad	D4	D5	Lead	Ingenue Female
Flower Drum Song 2002	1958	Wu Mei-Li+	I Enjoy Being A Girl Reprise	Ballad	Bb3	D5	Lead	Ingenue Female
Flower Drum Song 2002	1958	Wu Mei-Li+	A Hundred Million Miracles Reprise*	Moderate Tempo	Ab3	Bb4	Lead	Ingenue Female
Flower Drum Song 2002	1958	Wu Mei-Li+	Love, Look Away (Ab Maj)	Ballad	G3	C5	Lead	Ingenue Female

* = Music Edit Required
+ = Ethnic Specific

Show	Year	Role	Song	Tempo	Range-Bottom	Range-Top	Category	Char Type
Gypsy	1959	June	If Momma Was Married*	Moderate Tempo	G3	C5	Lead	Ingenue Female
Gypsy	1959	June	Broadway	Uptempo	E#4	D5	Lead	Ingenue Female
Gypsy	1959	Louise	Little Lamb	Ballad	Db4	Eb5	Lead	Ingenue Female
Gypsy	1959	Louise	If Momma Was Married*	Moderate Tempo	G3	C5	Lead	Ingenue Female
Gypsy	1959	Louise	Let Me Entertain You*	Moderate Tempo	G3	C5	Lead	Ingenue Female
Sound Of Music, The	1959	Liesl von Trapp	You Are Sixteen*	Moderate Tempo	B3	C#5	Lead	Ingenue Female
How To Succeed....	1961	Rosemary Pillkington	Happy To Keep His Dinner Warm	Moderate Tempo	A3	Db5	Lead	Ingenue Female
How To Succeed....	1961	Rosemary Pillkington	Paris Original*	Moderate Tempo	Bb3	D5	Lead	Ingenue Female
How To Succeed....	1961	Rosemary Pillkington	Happy To Keep His Dinner Warm Repri	Moderate Tempo	Bb3	Db5	Lead	Ingenue Female
How To Succeed....	1961	Rosemary Pillkington	I Believe In You Reprise*	Moderate Tempo	E4	B4	Lead	Ingenue Female
Anyone Can Whistle	1964	Fay Apple	There Won't Be Trumpets	Uptempo	G3	Bb4	Lead	Ingenue Female
Anyone Can Whistle	1964	Fay Apple	Come Play Wiz Me*	Uptempo	A3	D5	Lead	Ingenue Female
Anyone Can Whistle	1964	Fay Apple	Anyone Can Whistle	Ballad	G3	C5	Lead	Ingenue Female
Anyone Can Whistle	1964	Fay Apple	See What It Gets You	Uptempo	G3	Db5	Lead	Ingenue Female
Anyone Can Whistle	1964	Fay Apple	With So Little To Be Sure Of*	Moderate Tempo	A3	B4	Lead	Ingenue Female
Hair	1968	Crissy	Frank Mills	Ballad	A2	C5	Lead	Ingenue Female
Dear World	1969	Nina	I've Never Said I Love You	Ballad	Bb3	Eb5	Lead	Ingenue Female
Mack and Mabel	1974	Mabel Normand	Look What Happened to Mabel*	Uptempo	Gb3	C5	Lead	Ingenue Female
Mack and Mabel	1974	Mabel Normand	Mabel's Roses	Ballad	G3	D5	Lead	Ingenue Female
Mack and Mabel	1974	Mabel Normand	Wherever He Ain't	Uptempo	A3	C5	Lead	Ingenue Female
Mack and Mabel	1974	Mabel Normand	Time Heals Everything	Ballad	F#3	C#5	Lead	Ingenue Female
A Chorus Line	1975	Val	Dance: Ten; Looks: Three	Uptempo	Bb3	Db5	Supporting	Ingenue Female
Annie	1977	Star To Be	N.Y.C. *	Uptempo	Bb4	Eb5	Supporting	Ingenue Female
Cats	1981	Rumpleteezer	Mongojerrie and Rumpleteezer	Uptempo	E4	G5	Supporting	Ingenue Female
Big River	1985	Alice's Daughter +	How Blest We Are *	Ballad	C3	C5	Supporting	Ingenue Female
Nunsense	1985	Mary Leo	Benedicte*	Moderate Tempo	C4	G5	Lead	Ingenue Female
Once On This Island	1990	Ti Moune+	Waiting For Life	Uptempo	C#4	E5	Lead	Ingenue Female
Once On This Island	1990	Ti Moune+	Forever Yours*	Ballad	A#3	C#5	Lead	Ingenue Female
Once On This Island	1990	Ti Moune+	Ti Moune*	Ballad	G3	C5	Lead	Ingenue Female
Once On This Island	1990	Ti Moune+	Waiting For Life Reprise	Uptempo	B3	C#5	Lead	Ingenue Female

Alto

* = Music Edit Required
+ = Ethnic Specific

Show	Year	Role	Song	Tempo	Range-Bottom	Range-Top	Category	Char Type
State Fair 1996	1996	Margy Frake	The Next Time It Happens	Uptempo	Bb3	D5	Lead	Ingenue Female
Lion King, The	1997	Nala	Shadowland*	Ballad	E3	B4	Lead	Ingenue Female
You're A Good Man Charlie B	1999	Sally	My New Philosophy	Uptempo	B3	E5	Lead	Ingenue Female
You're A Good Man Charlie B	1999	Sally	My New Philosophy	Uptempo	B3	E5	Lead	Ingenue Female
Mamma Mia!	2001	Sophie Sheridan	Lay All Your Love On Me*	Moderate Tempo	C4	E5	Lead	Ingenue Female
Hairspray	2002	Teen Girl	The New Kid In Town*	Uptempo	A3	D5	Featured Ensembl	Ingenue Female
Last Five Years, The	2002	Catherine Hiatt	Still Hurting	Ballad	A3	Db5	Lead	Ingenue Female
Last Five Years, The	2002	Catherine Hiatt	See I'm Smiling	Ballad	E3	C#5	Lead	Ingenue Female
Last Five Years, The	2002	Catherine Hiatt	I'm A Part Of That	Uptempo	Bb3	Eb5	Lead	Ingenue Female
Last Five Years, The	2002	Catherine Hiatt	A Summer In Ohio	Uptempo	F#3	E5	Lead	Ingenue Female
Last Five Years, The	2002	Catherine Hiatt	The Next Ten Minutes	Ballad	G#3	E#4	Lead	Ingenue Female
Last Five Years, The	2002	Catherine Hiatt	Climbing Uphill/Audition	Uptempo	G3	D5	Lead	Ingenue Female
Last Five Years, The	2002	Catherine Hiatt	I Can Do Better Than That	Uptempo	A3	D5	Lead	Ingenue Female
Last Five Years, The	2002	Catherine Hiatt	Goodbye Until Tomorrow	Moderate Tempo	F#3	Db5	Lead	Ingenue Female
Last Five Years, The	2002	Catherine Hiatt	When You Come To Me	Moderate Tempo	A3	D5	Lead	Ingenue Female
All Shook Up	2005	Lorraine	It's Now Or Never*	Moderate Tempo	C4	F5	Supporting	Ingenue Female
High School Musical	2007	Gabriella Montez	When There Was You And Me	Ballad	F#3	F5	Lead	Ingenue Female
High School Musical	2007	Gabriella Montez	Breaking Free*	Ballad	Bb3	D5	Lead	Ingenue Female
Legally Blonde	2007	Elle Woods	So Much Better	Uptempo	G3	E5	Lead	Ingenue Female
Legally Blonde	2007	Elle Woods	Take It Like A Man	Moderate Tempo	Gb3	E5	Lead	Ingenue Female
Legally Blonde	2007	Elle Woods	Legally Blonde	Ballad	G3	Db5	Lead	Ingenue Female
Legally Blonde	2007	Elle Woods	Find My Way	Moderate Tempo	G3	B4	Lead	Ingenue Female
Legally Blonde	2007	Elle Woods	Legally Blonde Remix*	Uptempo	E4	D5	Lead	Ingenue Female
Legally Blonde	2007	Elle Woods	What You Want	Uptempo	Bb3	Db5	Lead	Ingenue Female
Legally Blonde	2007	Elle Woods	Chip On My Shoulder*	Uptempo	C4	Eb5	Lead	Ingenue Female
In The Heights	2008	Nina Rosario+	Breathe	Moderate Tempo	F3	F5	Lead	Ingenue Female
In The Heights	2008	Nina Rosario+	When You're Home*	Uptempo	C#4	E5	Lead	Ingenue Female
In The Heights	2008	Nina Rosario+	Everything's I Know	Ballad	Bb3	Db5	Lead	Ingenue Female
In The Heights	2008	Nina Rosario+	Alabanza*	Ballad	A3	A4	Lead	Ingenue Female
White Christmas	2008	Judy Haynes	Falling Out Of Love Can Be Fun*	Uptempo	G3	C5	Lead	Ingenue Female

* = Music Edit Required
+ = Ethnic Specific

Show	Year	Role	Song	Tempo	Range-Bottom	Range-Top	Category	Char Type
Heathers	2014	Heather McNamara	Lifeboat	Ballad	G3	Db5	Lead	Ingenue Female
110 In The Shade	1963	Girl	Cinderella	Uptempo	A3	D5	Feat Ensemble	Juvenile Female
Annie	1977	Annie	Maybe	Ballad	A3	C#5	Lead	Juvenile Female
Annie	1977	Annie	Tomorrow	Moderate Tempo	Bb3	Eb5	Lead	Juvenile Female
Into The Woods	1987	Little Red Riding Hood	I Know Things Now	Uptempo	C4	Eb5	Lead	Juvenile Female
Meet Me In St. Louis	1989	Tootie Smith	Under The Bamboo Tree*	Moderate Tempo	C4	Bb4	Lead	Juvenile Female
Secret Garden, The	1991	Mary Lennox	Show Me The Key (ms 52-92)	Moderate Tempo	B3	C#5	Lead	Juvenile Female
Secret Garden, The	1991	Mary Lennox	Storm III*	Moderate Tempo	B3	E5	Lead	Juvenile Female
Secret Garden, The	1991	Mary Lennox	The Girl I Mean To Be	Uptempo	Ab3	C5	Lead	Juvenile Female
Secret Garden, The	1991	Mary Lennox	Letter Song*	Moderate Tempo	Bb3	C5	Lead	Juvenile Female
Goodbye Girl, The	1993	Lucy McFadden	Good News, Bad News*	Moderate Tempo	Db4	Db5	Supporting	Juvenile Female
Hairspray	2002	Inez Stubs+	Run And Tell That*	Uptempo	F4	E5	Lead	Juvenile Female
Chitty Chitty Bang Bang	2005	Children	Teamwork*	Uptempo	C4	Eb5	Featured Ensembl	Juvenile Female
Mary Poppins	2006	Jane Banks	The Perfect Nanny*	Moderate Tempo	A3	B4	Lead	Juvenile Female
Mary Poppins	2006	Jane Banks	Anything Can Happen*	Moderate Tempo	C4	D5	Lead	Juvenile Female
13 The Musical	2008	Cassie (IF)	A Brand New You*	Uptempo	C4	F5	Supporting	Juvenile Female
13 The Musical	2008	Lucy (RAF)	It Can't Be True*	Uptempo	F#3	C5	Lead	Juvenile Female
13 The Musical	2008	Lucy (RAF)	Opportunity*	Uptempo	B3	E4	Lead	Juvenile Female
13 The Musical	2008	Patrice (CIF)	The Lamest Place In The World	Uptempo	B3	D#5	Lead	Juvenile Female
13 The Musical	2008	Patrice (CIF)	Good Enough	Ballad	G3	C5	Lead	Juvenile Female
13 The Musical	2008	Patrice (CIF)	Tell Her*	Ballad	Bb3	C5	Lead	Juvenile Female
13 The Musical	2008	Patrice (CIF)	If That's What It Is*	Moderate Tempo	Eb3	C5	Lead	Juvenile Female
13 The Musical	2008	Patrice (CIF)	What It Means To Be A Friend	Moderate Tempo	A3	E5	Lead	Juvenile Female
White Christmas	2008	Susan Waverly	Let Me sing And I'm Happy Reprise	Uptempo	B3	B4	Lead	Juvenile Female
Oliver!	1963	Artful Dodger	Consider Yourself (Part One)*	Uptempo	A3	F5	Lead	Juvenile Male
Mame	1966	Young Patrick Dennis	You're My Best Girl*	Ballad	A3	C5	Lead	Juvenile Male
Mame	1966	Young Patrick Dennis	The Letter*	Uptempo	C#4	Bb4	Lead	Juvenile Male
Les Miserables	1987	Gavroche	Look Down*	Moderate Tempo	C4	Db5	Supporting	Juvenile Male

Alto

179

Alto

* = Music Edit Required
+ = Ethnic Specific

Show	Year	Role	Song	Tempo	Range-Bottom	Range-Top	Category	Char Type
Les Miserables	1987	Gavroche	Little People*	Uptempo	B3	D5	Supporting	Juvenile Male
Merrily We Roll Along 1994	1994	Frank, Jr.	Transition 7	Moderate Tempo	B2	C5	Supporting	Juvenile Male
Lion King, The	1997	Young Simba	I Just Can't Wait To Be King*	Uptempo	C4	C5	Supporting	Juvenile Male
Seussical	2000	JoJo	Alone In The Universe*	Moderate Tempo	Ab3	Ab4	Lead	Juvenile Male
Caroline, Or Change	2004	Noah Gellman	Noah Downstairs (ms 1-46)	Moderate Tempo	Bb3	Cb5	Lead	Juvenile Male
Chitty Chitty Bang Bang	2005	Children	Teamwork *	Uptempo	C4	Eb5	Featured Ensembl	Juvenile Male
Marry Poppins	2006	Michael Banks	The Perfect Nanny*	Moderate Tempo	A3	B4	Lead	Juvenile Male
Marry Poppins	2006	Michael Banks	Anything Can Happen*	Moderate Tempo	C4	D5	Lead	Juvenile Male
Billy Elliot	2008	Billy Elliot	Electricity	Ballad	F3	B4	Lead	Juvenile Male
Billy Elliot	2008	Billy Elliot	Billy's Reply *	Ballad	G3	D5	Lead	Juvenile Male
Billy Elliot	2008	Billy Elliot	The Letter *	Ballad	G3	D5	Lead	Juvenile Male
Billy Elliot	2008	Michael	Expressing Yourself	Uptempo	G3	B4	Supporting	Juvenile Male
Billy Elliot	2008	Michael	Expressing Yourself Playout	Uptempo	D4	Bb4	Supporting	Juvenile Male
Fiddler on The Roof	1964	Golde	Sabbath Prayer	Ballad	D4	C5	Lead	Maternal
Fiddler on The Roof	1964	Golde	Sunrise Sunset	Ballad	C4	D5	Lead	Maternal
Pippin	1972	Berthe	No Time At All*	Uptempo	G3	A4	Lead	Maternal
Wiz, The	1974	Aunt Em	The Feeling We Once Had	Moderate Tempo	G3	C5	Supporting	Maternal
Meet Me In St. Louis	1989	Anna Smith	Wasn't It Fun*	Ballad	F3	C4	Lead	Maternal
Meet Me In St. Louis	1989	Anna Smith	A Day In New York*	Uptempo	B3	E4	Lead	Maternal
Meet Me In St. Louis	1989	Anna Smith	You'll Hear A Bill	Moderate Tempo	Bb3	D5	Lead	Maternal
Meet Me In St. Louis	1989	Anna Smith	You'll Hear A Bell Reprise	Moderate Tempo	Bb3	Bb4	Lead	Maternal
Once On This Island	1990	Mama Euralie+	Ti Moune*	Ballad	Gb3	Bb4	Lead	Maternal
Children of Eden	1991	Eve	The Spark of Creation	Uptempo	G#3	Eb5	Lead	Maternal
Children of Eden	1991	Eve	Grateful Children *	Moderate Tempo	B3	D#4	Lead	Maternal
Children of Eden	1991	Eve	The Spark of Creation Reprise	Uptempo	Ab3	Db5	Supporting	Maternal
Children of Eden	1991	Eve	Children Of Eden	Moderate Tempo	Ab3	Eb5	Lead	Maternal
Children of Eden	1991	Mama Noah	The Spark Of Creation Reprise 2	Uptempo	A3	A4	Lead	Maternal
Children of Eden	1991	Mama Noah	Ain't It Good	Moderate Tempo	A3	A5	Lead	Maternal
My Favorite Year	1992	Belle Carroca	Rookie In The Ring*	Ballad	G3	Bb4	Lead	Maternal

Alto

180

* = Music Edit Required
+ = Ethnic Specific

Show	Year	Role	Song	Tempo	Range-Bottom	Range-Top	Category	Char Type
Honk	1993	Ida	The Joy of Motherhood*	Uptempo	G#3	C#5	Lead	Maternal
Honk	1993	Ida	Different Pre-Reprise	Ballad	Ab3	A4	Lead	Maternal
Honk	1993	Ida	Hold Your Head Up High	Moderate Tempo	G#3	C5	Lead	Maternal
Honk	1993	Ida	Every Tear a Mother Cries	Ballad	F3	A4	Lead	Maternal
Honk	1993	Maureen	The Joy of Motherhood*	Uptempo	G#3	C#5	Supporting	Maternal
Footloose	1998	Ethel McCormick	Learning To Be Silent	Ballad	Ab3	D5	Lead	Maternal
Footloose	1998	Vi Moore	Learning To Be Silent	Ballad	Ab3	D5	Lead	Maternal
Footloose	1998	Vi Moore	Can You Find It In Your Heart	Ballad	A3	Db5	Supporting	Maternal
Parade	1998	Mrs. Phagan	My Child Will Forgive Me	Ballad	F#3	A4	Lead	Maternal
All Shook Up	2005	Sylvia	There's Always Me	Ballad	G3	F5	Supporting	Maternal
Little Women	2005	Marmee	Here Alone	Ballad	G3	Eb5	Lead	Maternal
Little Women	2005	Marmee	Days of Plenty	Ballad	Eb3	Db5	Lead	Maternal
Mary Poppins	2006	Winifred Banks	Being Mrs. Banks*	Moderate Tempo	G#3	B4	Lead	Maternal
Mary Poppins	2006	Winifred Banks	Being Mrs. Banks*	Ballad	G#3	Db5	Lead	Maternal
Mary Poppins	2006	Winifred Banks	A Man Has Dreams Reprise	Ballad	Bb2	C4	Lead	Maternal
In The Heights	2008	Camila Rosario+	Enough*	Moderate Tempo	G3	Db5	Lead	Maternal
Porgy and Bess	1935	Maria+	I Hates Yo' Struttin' Style (Spoken)	Uptempo			Lead	Mature Female
Most Happy Fella, The	1956	Marie	A Long Time Ago*	Moderate Tempo	D4	Eb5	Lead	Mature Female
Most Happy Fella, The	1956	Marie	Young People*	Moderate Tempo	C4	E5	Lead	Mature Female
Bye Bye Birdie	1960	Mae Peterson	A Mother Doesn't Matter Anymore (TV	Moderate Tempo	F3	C5	Supporting	Mature Female
Oliver!	1963	Mrs. Bedwin	Where Is Love Reprise	Ballad	C#4	Bb4	Supporting	Mature Female
Funny Girl	1964	Mrs. Brice	Who Taught Her Everything...*	Moderate Tempo	A3	Eb5	Supporting	Mature Female
Funny Girl	1964	Mrs. Brice	If A Girl Isn't Pretty*	Moderate Tempo	G#3	C#5	Supporting	Mature Female
Hello Dolly	1964	Dolly Levi	I Put My Hand In	Uptempo	Eb3	G4	Lead	Mature Female
Hello Dolly	1964	Dolly Levi	Motherhood*	Uptempo	D3	F4	Lead	Mature Female
Hello Dolly	1964	Dolly Levi	Before The Parade Passes By	Moderate Tempo	D3	F4	Lead	Mature Female
Hello Dolly	1964	Dolly Levi	Hello Dolly	Moderate Tempo	Bb2	F4	Lead	Mature Female
Hello Dolly	1964	Dolly Levi	So Long Dearie	Uptempo	D3	G4	Lead	Mature Female

* = Music Edit Required
+ = Ethnic Specific

Show	Year	Role	Song	Tempo	Range-Bottom	Range-Top	Category	Char Type
Hello Dolly	1964	Dolly Levi	I Put My Hand In	Uptempo	Ab3	C5	Lead	Mature Female
Hello Dolly	1964	Dolly Levi	Motherhood	Uptempo	F3	A4	Lead	Mature Female
Hello Dolly	1964	Dolly Levi	Before The Parade Passes By	Moderate Tempo	F3	F4	Lead	Mature Female
Hello Dolly	1964	Dolly Levi	Dancing*	Moderate Tempo	D3	D5	Lead	Mature Female
Hello Dolly	1964	Dolly Levi	Before The Parade Passes By Reprise	Ballad	C3	F4	Lead	Mature Female
Cabaret	1966	Fraulein Scheider	So What?	Uptempo	F3	G4	Supporting	Mature Female
Cabaret	1966	Fraulein Scheider	What Would You Do	Ballad	F3	G4	Supporting	Mature Female
Dear World	1969	Countess Aurelia	Each Tomorrow Morning	Moderate Tempo	E3	Bb4	Lead	Mature Female
Dear World	1969	Countess Aurelia	One Person*	Uptempo	F3	Bb4	Lead	Mature Female
Dear World	1969	Countess Aurelia	Thoughts	Uptempo	G3	D5	Lead	Mature Female
Dear World	1969	Countess Aurelia	And I Was Beautiful	Ballad	G3	D5	Lead	Mature Female
Dear World	1969	Countess Aurelia	Dear World*	Moderate Tempo	E3	A4	Lead	Mature Female
Dear World	1969	Countess Aurelia	Kiss Her Now	Ballad	G#3	A4	Lead	Mature Female
Dear World	1969	Countess Aurelia	I Don't Want To Know	Moderate Tempo	G#3	A4	Lead	Mature Female
Hello Dolly	1970	Dolly Levi	World Take Me Back	Moderate Tempo	C4	E5	Lead	Mature Female
Hello Dolly	1970	Dolly Levi	Love, Look In MY Window	Ballad	C4	F5	Lead	Mature Female
Follies	1971	Stella Deems	Who's That Woman *	Uptempo	E3	A4	Supporting	Mature Female
Grease	1971	Miss Lynch	Born to Hand Jive	Uptempo	D4	B4	Supporting	Mature Female
A Little Night Music	1973	Madame Armfeldt	Liaisons	Uptempo	D3	F4	Lead	Mature Female
On The Twentieth Century	1978	Letitia Primrose	Repent	Uptempo	C4	F#5	Lead	Mature Female
On The Twentieth Century	1978	Letitia Primrose	Five Zeros*	Moderate Tempo	Ab3	Eb5	Lead	Mature Female
Cats	1981	Grizabella	Grizabella the Glamour Cat	Ballad	G3	C5	Lead	Mature Female
Cats	1981	Grizabella	Memory	Ballad	G3	E5	Lead	Mature Female
Sunday...Park With Geroge	1984	Old Lady	Beautiful*	Ballad	F#3	B4	Supporting	Mature Female
Rags	1986	Rachel Halpern	Penny A Tune	Uptempo	G3	Bb4	Lead	Mature Female
Rags	1986	Rachel Halpern	Three Sunny Rooms*	Moderate Tempo	G3	Bb4	Lead	Mature Female
Once On This Island	1990	Mama Euralie+	Come Down From The Tree	Moderate Tempo	A3	E5	Lead	Mature Female
Nick & Nora	1991	Lorraine Bixby	Men*	Moderate Tempo	F3	Cb5	Lead	Mature Female
Honk!	1993	Lowbutt	It Takes All Sorts*	Uptempo	C#4	D5	Supporting	Mature Female
Honk!	1993	Queenie	It Takes All Sorts*	Uptempo	C#4	D5	Supporting	Mature Female
Kiss Of The Spider Woman	1993	Mother	Dear One*	Ballad	Bb3	C5	Lead	Mature Female

* = Music Edit Required
+ = Ethnic Specific

Show	Year	Role	Song	Tempo	Range-Bottom	Range-Top	Category	Char Type
Kiss Of The Spider Woman	1993	Mother	You Could Never Shame Me	Moderate Tempo	F3	D5	Lead	Mature Female
Steel Pier	1997	Shelby Stevens	Everybody's Girl	Uptempo	G3	C5	Lead	Mature Female
Steel Pier	1997	Shelby Stevens	Everybody's Girl Encore	Uptempo	G3	Bb4	Lead	Mature Female
Steel Pier	1997	Shelby Stevens	Somebody Older	Moderate Tempo	G3	Bb4	Lead	Mature Female
Full Monty, The	2000	Jeanette Burmeister	Jeanette's Showbiz Number	Moderate Tempo	F3	Db5	Supporting	Mature Female
Jane Eyre	2000	Mrs. Fairfax	Perfectly Nice	Uptempo	A3	C#5	Lead	Mature Female
Jane Eyre	2000	Mrs. Fairfax	Slip of a Girl	Uptempo	F3	Bb4	Lead	Mature Female
Jane Eyre	2000	Mrs. Reed	Forgiveness Reprise	Moderate Tempo	G#3	B4	Supporting	Mature Female
A Man Of No Importance	2002	Lily Byrne	The Burden of Life	Uptempo	F#3	C5	Lead	Mature Female
A Man Of No Importance	2002	Lily Byrne	Tell Me Why	Ballad	G3	Bb4	Lead	Mature Female
A Man Of No Importance	2002	Lily Byrne	The Girl That Was Me	Uptempo	A3	A4	Lead	Mature Female
A Man Of No Importance	2002	Lily Byrne	Burden of Life Part 1	Uptempo	Ab3	Ab4	Lead	Mature Female
Fame	2003	Miss Sherman	These Are My Children	Ballad	F3	C5	Supporting	Mature Female
Wicked	2003	Madame Morrible	The Wizard And I*	Moderate Tempo	Gb3	Bb4	Lead	Mature Female
Wicked	2003	Madame Morrible	Thank Goodness (Part 3)	Uptempo	A3	B4	Lead	Mature Female
All Shook Up	2005	Mayor Matilda Hyde	Devil In Disguise	Uptempo	C4	F#5	Supporting	Mature Female
Little Women	2005	Aunt March	Could You*	Uptempo	D3	F5	Supporting	Mature Female
Drowsy Chaperon, The	2006	Mrs. Tottendale	Love Is Always Lovely *	Moderate Tempo	G3	Bb4	Supporting	Mature Female
Grey Gardens	2006	Edith Beale (Act 2)	The Girl Who Has Everything*	Moderate Tempo	C4	Eb5	Lead	Mature Female
Grey Gardens	2006	Edith Beale (Act 2)	The Cake I Had*	Moderate Tempo	E#3	A#4	Lead	Mature Female
Grey Gardens	2006	Edith Beale (Act 2)	Jerry Likes My Corn	Moderate Tempo	G3	F5	Lead	Mature Female
Billy Elliot	2008	Grandma	We'd Go Dancing	Moderate Tempo	F3	G4	Supporting	Mature Female
In The Heights	2008	Abuela Claudia	Paciencia Y Fe	Uptempo	F3	C5	Lead	Mature Female
Pal Joey	1940	Gladys Bumps	You Mustn't Kick It Around Encore	Uptempo	A3	C5	Lead	Romantic Antagonist Female
Pal Joey	1940	Gladys Bumps	That Terrific Rainbow	Moderate Tempo	B3	Bb4	Lead	Romantic Antagonist Female
Pal Joey	1940	Vera Simpson	What Is A Man	Moderate Tempo	D4	Eb5	Lead	Romantic Antagonist Female
Pal Joey	1940	Vera Simpson	Bewitched Bothered And Bewildered	Moderate Tempo	E4	D5	Lead	Romantic Antagonist Female
Pal Joey	1940	Vera Simpson	Bewitched...Encore	Moderate Tempo	F4	D5	Lead	Romantic Antagonist Female
Pal Joey	1940	Gladys Bumps	The Flower Garden Of My Heart*	Moderate Tempo	D4	F#5	Lead	Romantic Antagonist Female

* = Music Edit Required
+ = Ethnic Specific

Show	Year	Role	Song	Tempo	Range-Bottom	Range-Top	Category	Char Type
Pal Joey	1940	Melba	Zip	Moderate Tempo	F3	G4	Supporting	Romantic Antagonist Female
Pal Joey	1940	Gladys Bumps	Plant You Now, Dig You Later	Uptempo	D4	D5	Lead	Romantic Antagonist Female
Pal Joey	1940	Vera Simpson	Den Of Iniguity*	Uptempo	G4	Eb5	Lead	Romantic Antagonist Female
Pal Joey	1940	Vera Simpson	Take Him*	Moderate Tempo	C4	D5	Lead	Romantic Antagonist Female
Pal Joey	1940	Vera Simpson	Bewitched....Reprise	Moderate Tempo	D4	D5	Lead	Romantic Antagonist Female
Call Me Madam	1950	Sally Adams	The Hostess With The Mostess	Uptempo	A3	B4	Lead	Romantic Antagonist Female
Call Me Madam	1950	Sally Adams	The Hostess With The Mostess Encore	Uptempo	A3	B4	Lead	Romantic Antagonist Female
Call Me Madam	1950	Sally Adams	Washington Square Dance	Uptempo	Bb3	C5	Lead	Romantic Antagonist Female
Call Me Madam	1950	Sally Adams	Can You Use Any Money Today	Uptempo	Bb3	C5	Lead	Romantic Antagonist Female
Call Me Madam	1950	Sally Adams	Marrying For Love*	Ballad	F3	Bb4	Lead	Romantic Antagonist Female
Call Me Madam	1950	Sally Adams	The Best Thing For You	Moderate Tempo	A3	C5	Lead	Romantic Antagonist Female
Call Me Madam	1950	Sally Adams	Something To Dance About	Moderate Tempo	Bb3	C5	Lead	Romantic Antagonist Female
Call Me Madam	1950	Sally Adams	You're Just In Love*	Uptempo	D4	C5	Lead	Romantic Antagonist Female
Call Me Madam	1950	Sally Adams	The Best Thing For You Reprise	Moderate Tempo	Bb3	Cb5	Lead	Romantic Antagonist Female
State Fair 1996	1953	Emily Arden	You Never Had It So Good	Uptempo	Bb3	Bb4	Lead	Romantic Antagonist Female
Pajama Game	1954	Gladys	Steam Heat*	Uptempo	C4	Eb5	Lead	Romantic Antagonist Female
Pajama Game	1954	Gladys	Hernando's Hideaway	Moderate Tempo	B3	C5	Lead	Romantic Antagonist Female
Damn Yankees	1955	Lola	Whatever Lola Wants	Moderate Tempo	G3	Db5	Lead	Romantic Antagonist Female
Damn Yankees	1955	Lola	A Little Brains A Little Talent	Uptempo	A3	B4	Lead	Romantic Antagonist Female
Damn Yankees	1955	Lola	Who's Got The Pain	Uptempo	A3	B4	Lead	Romantic Antagonist Female
Cinderella (2013)	1957	Stepmother (Madam)	A Lovely Night*	Uptempo	B3	D5	Supporting	Romantic Antagonist Female
Flower Drum Song 2002	1958	Madam Rita Liang	Grant Avenue*	Moderate Tempo	A3	C5	Lead	Romantic Antagonist Female
Once Upon A Mattress	1959	Queen Aggravain	Sensitivity*	Moderate Tempo	A3	B4	Lead	Romantic Antagonist Female
She Loves Me	1963	Ilona Ritter	I Resolve	Uptempo	Ab3	Bb4	Lead	Romantic Antagonist Female
She Loves Me	1963	Ilona Ritter	A Trip To The Library	Moderate Tempo	G3	C#5	Lead	Romantic Antagonist Female
Anyone Can Whistle	1964	Cora Hoover Hooper	Me And My Town*	Uptempo	A3	Eb5	Lead	Romantic Antagonist Female
Anyone Can Whistle	1964	Cora Hoover Hooper	There's A Parade In Town*	Uptempo	G3	Bb4	Lead	Romantic Antagonist Female
Anyone Can Whistle	1964	Cora Hoover Hooper	I've Got You To lean On*	Uptempo	Ab4	D5	Lead	Romantic Antagonist Female
Anyone Can Whistle	1964	Cora Hoover Hooper	Cora's Chase*	Uptempo	A3	E5	Lead	Romantic Antagonist Female
Mame	1966	Vera Charles	The Man In The Moon	Ballad	Eb3	A4	Lead	Romantic Antagonist Female

Show	Year	Role	Song	Tempo	Range-Bottom	Range-Top	Category	Char Type
Sweet Charity	1966	Nickie	There's Gott Be Something Better...*	Uptempo	A3	Db4	Lead	Romantic Antagonist Female
Sweet Charity	1966	Helene	There's Gott Be Something Better...*	Uptempo	A3	Db5	Lead	Romantic Antagonist Female
Applause	1970	Margo Channing	But Alive*	Uptempo	E3	F#4	Lead	Romantic Antagonist Female
Applause	1970	Eve Harrington	The Best Night Of My Life	Ballad	G#3	C#5	Lead	Romantic Antagonist Female
Applause	1970	Margo Channing	Who's That Girl	Uptempo	E3	A4	Lead	Romantic Antagonist Female
Applause	1970	Eve Harrington	Applause*	Moderate Tempo	G3	E5	Lead	Romantic Antagonist Female
Applause	1970	Margo Channing	Hurry Back	Ballad	Ab2	F4	Lead	Romantic Antagonist Female
Applause	1970	Margo Channing	Welcome To The Theatre	Moderate Tempo	D3	F#4	Lead	Romantic Antagonist Female
Applause	1970	Eve Harrington	One Hallowe'en	Moderate Tempo	F3	Bb4	Lead	Romantic Antagonist Female
Applause	1970	Margo Channing	Something Greater*	Uptempo	D3	G4	Lead	Romantic Antagonist Female
Follies	1971	Phyllis Rogers Stone	Could I Leave You	Moderate Tempo	F#3	Bb4	Lead	Romantic Antagonist Female
Pippin	1972	Fastrada	Spread A Little Sunshine	Moderate Tempo	A2	F5	Lead	Romantic Antagonist Female
Sugar	1972	Sweet Sue	When You Meet A Man...*	Uptempo	Ab3	Eb5	Lead	Romantic Antagonist Female
A Chorus Line	1975	Sheila	At The Ballet	Moderate Tempo	E3	C#5	Lead	Romantic Antagonist Female
Chicago	1975	Velma Kelly	All That Jazz	Moderate Tempo	G2	Db5	Lead	Romantic Antagonist Female
Chicago	1975	Velma Kelly	I Can't Do It Alone	Uptempo	Bb3	D4	Lead	Romantic Antagonist Female
Chicago	1975	Velma Kelly	My Own Best Friend	Moderate Tempo	G3	A4	Lead	Romantic Antagonist Female
Chicago	1975	Velma Kelly	I Know A Girl	Uptempo	E3	A4	Lead	Romantic Antagonist Female
Chicago	1975	Velma Kelly	Class*	Ballad	F3	B4	Lead	Romantic Antagonist Female
Chicago	1975	Velma Kelly	Nowadays	Moderate Tempo	F#3	D5	Lead	Romantic Antagonist Female
Evita	1978	Eva Peron	Buenos Aires	Uptempo	E3	F5	Lead	Romantic Antagonist Female
Evita	1978	Eva Peron	I'd Be Surprisingly Good For You	Moderate Tempo	G#3	F5	Lead	Romantic Antagonist Female
Evita	1978	Eva Peron	Another Suitcase In Another Hall	Ballad	A3	E5	Supporting	Romantic Antagonist Female
Evita	1978	Eva Peron	Don't Cry For Me Argentina	Alto	Ab3	Eb5	Lead	Romantic Antagonist Female
Evita	1978	Eva Peron	Rainbow High	Uptempo	G3	E5	Lead	Romantic Antagonist Female
Evita	1978	Eva Peron	The Actress Hasn't Learned the Lines	Ballad	G#3	D#5	Lead	Romantic Antagonist Female
Evita	1978	Eva Peron	Waltz for Eva and Che	Uptempo	Ab3	F5	Lead	Romantic Antagonist Female
Evita	1978	Eva Peron	Eva's Final Broadcast	Ballad	Ab3	Db5	Lead	Romantic Antagonist Female
Evita	1978	Eva Peron	Lament	Ballad	Bb3	Db5	Lead	Romantic Antagonist Female
Nine	1982	Saraghina	Ti Voglio Bene*	Moderate Tempo	G3	Bb4	Lead	Romantic Antagonist Female

* = Music Edit Required
+ = Ethnic Specific

Show	Year	Role	Song	Tempo	Range-Bottom	Range-Top	Category	Char Type
Singin' In The Rain	1983	Lina Lamont	What's Wrong With Me? (E♭Maj)	Moderate Tempo	C4	E♭5	Lead	Romantic Antagonist Female
Singin' In The Rain	1983	Lina Lamont	What's Wrong With Me? (C Maj)	Moderate Tempo	A3	C5	Lead	Romantic Antagonist Female
Mystery Of Edwin Drood, The	1985	Helena Landless	Helena's Confession	Moderate Tempo	G3	B4	Lead	Romantic Antagonist Female
Into The Woods	1987	Witch	Stay With Me	Ballad	A#3	D♭5	Lead	Romantic Antagonist Female
Into The Woods	1987	Witch	Lament	Ballad	A3	D5	Lead	Romantic Antagonist Female
Into The Woods	1987	Witch	Last Midnight	Moderate Tempo	F3	D♭5	Lead	Romantic Antagonist Female
Romance/Romance	1987	Monica	How Did I End Up Here	Uptempo	F3	C5	Lead	Romantic Antagonist Female
Romance/Romance	1987	Monica	Now	Uptempo	A3	D5	Lead	Romantic Antagonist Female
Romance/Romance	1987	Josephine Weninger	Goodbye Emil	Uptempo	A3	F5	Lead	Romantic Antagonist Female
Romance/Romance	1987	Josephine Weninger	Goodbye Emil Reprise	Uptempo	B♭3	E5	Lead	Romantic Antagonist Female
Romance/Romance	1987	Josephine Weninger	It's Not Too Late*	Moderate Tempo	G3	C♭5	Lead	Romantic Antagonist Female
Romance/Romance	1987	Josephine Weninger	A Performance*	Moderate Tempo	G3	D#5	Lead	Romantic Antagonist Female
Romance/Romance	1987	Josephine Weninger	I'll Remember The Song*	Uptempo	B3	D4	Lead	Romantic Antagonist Female
Romance/Romance	1987	Josephine Weninger	Yes, It's Love	Uptempo	A♭3	C5	Lead	Romantic Antagonist Female
Romance/Romance	1987	Josephine Weninger	A Rustic Country Inn*	Uptempo	G3	E5	Lead	Romantic Antagonist Female
Romance/Romance	1987	Josephine Weninger	The Night It Had To End	Ballad	A♭3	D♭5	Lead	Romantic Antagonist Female
Romance/Romance	1987	Monica	Plan A and B	Uptempo	A♭3	A4	Lead	Romantic Antagonist Female
City of Angels	1989	Mallory	Lost And Found	Ballad	G#3	F#5	Supporting	Romantic Antagonist Female
Miss Saigon	1991	Gigi Van Trahn+	The Movie In My Mind*	Ballad	A♭3	E♭5	Supporting	Romantic Antagonist Female
Nick & Nora	1991	Lily Connors	People Get Hurt	Uptempo	A♭3	D♭5	Lead	Romantic Antagonist Female
Kiss Of The Spider Woman	1993	Aurora	Her Name Is Aurora*	Moderate Tempo	C3	A4	Lead	Romantic Antagonist Female
Kiss Of The Spider Woman	1993	Aurora	Spider Woman Fragment 1	Ballad	F3	F4	Lead	Romantic Antagonist Female
Kiss Of The Spider Woman	1993	Aurora	Where You Are*	Uptempo	E♭3	G♭4	Lead	Romantic Antagonist Female
Kiss Of The Spider Woman	1993	Spider Woman	Interrogation*	Moderate Tempo	F3	F4	Lead	Romantic Antagonist Female
Kiss Of The Spider Woman	1993	Aurora	I Do Miracles*	Moderate Tempo	B2	A♭4	Lead	Romantic Antagonist Female
Kiss Of The Spider Woman	1993	Aurora	Let's Make Love*	Uptempo	D3	A4	Lead	Romantic Antagonist Female
Kiss Of The Spider Woman	1993	Aurora	Good Times*	Uptempo	D#3	A4	Lead	Romantic Antagonist Female
Kiss Of The Spider Woman	1993	Spider Woman	Kiss Of The Spider Woman	Uptempo	C#3	A4	Lead	Romantic Antagonist Female
Merrily We Roll Along 1994	1994	Gussie Carnegie	Growing Up Part II	Moderate Tempo	G#3	B♭4	Lead	Romantic Antagonist Female
Merrily We Roll Along 1994	1994	Gussie Carnegie	Act 2 Opening	Moderate Tempo	B3	C5	Lead	Romantic Antagonist Female

* = Music Edit Required
+ = Ethnic Specific

Show	Year	Role	Song	Tempo	Range-Bottom	Range-Top	Category	Char Type
Merrily We Roll Along 1994	1994	Gussie Carnegie	The Blob II	Uptempo	Ab3	Bb4	Lead	Romantic Antagonist Female
Merrily We Roll Along 1994	1994	Gussie Carnegie	Growing Up Act 2	Moderate Tempo	G3	A4	Lead	Romantic Antagonist Female
Sunset Boulevard	1994	Norma Desmond	Surrender	Ballad	F3	Bb4	Lead	Romantic Antagonist Female
Sunset Boulevard	1994	Norma Desmond	Once Upon A Time	Uptempo	A3	A4	Lead	Romantic Antagonist Female
Sunset Boulevard	1994	Norma Desmond	With One Look	Moderate Tempo	G3	D5	Lead	Romantic Antagonist Female
Sunset Boulevard	1994	Norma Desmond	New Ways To Dream	Ballad	B3	C5	Lead	Romantic Antagonist Female
Sunset Boulevard	1994	Norma Desmond	The Perfect Year*	Moderate Tempo	A3	Eb5	Lead	Romantic Antagonist Female
Sunset Boulevard	1994	Norma Desmond	As If We Never Said Goodbye	Moderate Tempo	G#3	C#5	Lead	Romantic Antagonist Female
Sunset Boulevard	1994	Norma Desmond	There's Been A Call*	Uptempo	C4	D5	Lead	Romantic Antagonist Female
Sunset Boulevard	1994	Norma Desmond	Phone Call	Moderate Tempo	F3	Ab4	Lead	Romantic Antagonist Female
Rent	1996	Mimi Marquez	Out Tonight	Uptempo	A3	E5	Lead	Romantic Antagonist Female
Rent	1996	Mimi Marquez	Another Day*	Uptempo	B3	B4	Lead	Romantic Antagonist Female
Rent	1996	Maureen Johnson	Over The Moon	Moderate Tempo	C4	Eb5	Lead	Romantic Antagonist Female
Rent	1996	Maureen Johnson	Take Me Or leave Me*	Uptempo	C4	F5	Lead	Romantic Antagonist Female
Rent	1996	Mimi Marquez	Without You*	Moderate Tempo	A3	A4	Lead	Romantic Antagonist Female
Rent	1996	Mimi Marquez	Goodbye Love*	Moderate Tempo	A4	C5	Lead	Romantic Antagonist Female
State Fair 1996	1996	Emily Arden	That's The Way It Happens*	Moderate Tempo	B3	D5	Lead	Romantic Antagonist Female
Jekyll and Hyde	1997	Lucy Harris	No One Knows Who I Am	Ballad	C4	D5	Lead	Romantic Antagonist Female
Jekyll and Hyde	1997	Lucy Harris	Good and Evil	Moderate Tempo	G#3	E5	Lead	Romantic Antagonist Female
Jekyll and Hyde	1997	Lucy Harris	Someone Like You	Ballad	G2	Eb4	Lead	Romantic Antagonist Female
Jekyll and Hyde	1997	Lucy Harris	Sympathy, Tenderness	Ballad	D3	C#4	Lead	Romantic Antagonist Female
Jekyll and Hyde	1997	Lucy Harris	In His Eyes*	Ballad	Bb3	F5	Lead	Romantic Antagonist Female
Jekyll and Hyde	1997	Lucy Harris	A New Life	Ballad	B3	D5	Lead	Romantic Antagonist Female
Jekyll and Hyde	1997	Lucy Harris	Bring On The Men	Uptempo	G#3	E5	Lead	Romantic Antagonist Female
Jekyll and Hyde	1997	Lucy Harris	Sympathy, Tenderness/Lucy's Death	Ballad	C#4	C#5	Lead	Romantic Antagonist Female
Marie Christine	1999	Mother+	Ton Grandpere Est Le Soleil*	Moderate Tempo	D3	E5	Lead	Romantic Antagonist Female
Marie Christine	1999	Mother+	Miracles and Mysteries	Moderate Tempo	E3	F5	Lead	Romantic Antagonist Female
Aida	2000	Amneris	Every Story is a Love Story	Ballad	G3	Ab4	Lead	Romantic Antagonist Female
Seussical	2000	Mayzie LaBird	Amayzing Mayzie*	Uptempo	G#3	D5	Lead	Romantic Antagonist Female
Seussical	2000	Mayzie LaBird	How Lucky You Are Reprise	Moderate Tempo	Bb3	D5	Lead	Romantic Antagonist Female
Seussical	2000	Mayzie LaBird	Mayzie In Palm Beach*	Uptempo	G3	C5	Lead	Romantic Antagonist Female

* = Music Edit Required
+ = Ethnic Specific

Show	Year	Role	Song	Tempo	Range-Bottom	Range-Top	Category	Char Type
Hairspray	2002	Amber Von Tussle	Cooties	Uptempo	E4	E5	Lead	Romantic Antagonist Female
Hairspray	2002	Velma Von Tussle	Miss Baltimore Crabs	Uptempo	B3	Eb5	Lead	Romantic Antagonist Female
Hairspray	2002	Velma Von Tussle	Velma's Cha Cha	Moderate Tempo	Ab3	C#5	Lead	Romantic Antagonist Female
Into The Woods	2002	Witch	Our Little World	Moderate Tempo			Lead	Romantic Antagonist Female
Sweet Smell Of Success	2002	Zanzibar Singer	Laughin' All The Way To The Bank	Uptempo	G#3	D4	Supporting	Romantic Antagonist Female
Sweet Smell Of Success	2002	Rita	Rita's Tune	Moderate Tempo	A3	Eb5	Lead	Romantic Antagonist Female
Avenue Q	2003	Lucy The Slut	Special	Moderate Tempo	G3	Db4	Supporting	Romantic Antagonist Female
Color Purple, The	2005	Shug Avery+	Too Beautiful For Words *	Ballad	E3	F4	Lead	Romantic Antagonist Female
Color Purple, The	2005	Shug Avery+	Push Da Button	Moderate Tempo	A3	Eb5	Lead	Romantic Antagonist Female
Color Purple, The	2005	Shug Avery+	What About Love *	Ballad	E3	D5	Lead	Romantic Antagonist Female
Color Purple, The	2005	Shug Avery+	The Color Purple	Ballad	F#3	Db5	Lead	Romantic Antagonist Female
Spamalot	2005	The Lady Of The Lake	Come With Me*	Moderate Tempo	A3	C5	Lead	Romantic Antagonist Female
Spamalot	2005	The Lady Of The Lake	The Song That Goes Like This Reprise>	Moderate Tempo	Ab3	Eb5	Lead	Romantic Antagonist Female
Spamalot	2005	The Lady Of The Lake	Find Your Grail*	Moderate Tempo	C#4	E5	Lead	Romantic Antagonist Female
Spamalot	2005	The Lady Of The Lake	Whatever Happened To My Part	Moderate Tempo	F#3	Eb5	Lead	Romantic Antagonist Female
Spamalot	2005	The Lady Of The Lake	Why Does He Never Notice Me	Ballad	F3	Db5	Lead	Romantic Antagonist Female
Pal Joey	2008	Gladys Bumps	Zip	Moderate Tempo	F3	G4	Lead	Romantic Antagonist Female
Addams Family, The	2010	Morticia Addams	Just Around The Corner *	Uptempo	G3	B4	Lead	Romantic Antagonist Female
Addams Family, The	2010	Morticia Addams	Live Before We Die	Moderate Tempo	Bb3	Ab4	Lead	Romantic Antagonist Female
Heathers	2014	Heather Chandler	Candy*	Uptempo	Bb3	A5	Lead	Romantic Antagonist Female
Crazy For You (1992)	1924	Irene Roth	Naughty Baby	Moderate Tempo	Ab3	D#4	Supporting	Romantic Lead Female
No, No Nanette	1925	Lucille Early	Too Many Rings Around Rosie*	Uptempo	B3	D5	Lead	Romantic Lead Female
No, No Nanette	1925	Lucille Early	You Can Dance With Any Girl At All*	Uptempo	A3	D5	Lead	Romantic Lead Female
No, No Nanette	1925	Lucille Early	Where Has My Hubby Gone Blues*	Ballad	G3	D5	Lead	Romantic Lead Female
No, No Nanette	1925	Sue Smith	Take A Little One Step*	Uptempo	G3	Cb5	Lead	Romantic Lead Female
Show Boat	1927	Julie	Can't Help Lovin' Dat Man	Moderate Tempo	Eb3	Ab4	Lead	Romantic Lead Female
Show Boat	1927	Julie	Bill	Ballad	F#3	G#4	Lead	Romantic Lead Female
Good News (1993 Revival)	1928	Professor Kenyan	Together*	Ballad	G3	B4	Lead	Romantic Lead Female

Alto

Alto

* = Music Edit Required
+ = Ethnic Specific

Show	Year	Role	Song	Tempo	Range-Bottom	Range-Top	Category	Char Type
Good News (1993 Revival)	1928	Professor Kenyan	You're The Cream In My Coffee*	Uptempo	Db4	Eb5	Lead	Romantic Lead Female
Good News (1993 Revival)	1928	Professor Kenyan	Together Part 2*	Ballad	G3	C5	Lead	Romantic Lead Female
Good News (1993 Revival)	1931	Professor Kenyan	Life Is Just A Bowl Of Cherries	Uptempo	A3	Db5	Lead	Romantic Lead Female
Babes In Arms (1998)	1937	Baby Rose	Way Out West*	Moderate Tempo	B3	C5	Lead	Romantic Lead Female
Babes In Arms (1998)	1937	Baby Rose	Imagine*	Moderate Tempo	A3	C5	Lead	Romantic Lead Female
Babes In Arms (1998)	1937	Baby Rose	Johnny One Note	Uptempo	Bb3	Bb4	Lead	Romantic Lead Female
Kiss Me Kate	1948	Lilli Vanessi/Katherine	I Hate Men	Moderate Tempo	B3	C#5	Lead	Romantic Lead Female
South Pacific	1949	Nellie Forbush	A Cockeyed Optimist	Uptempo	A3	C5	Lead	Romantic Lead Female
South Pacific	1949	Nellie Forbush	I'm Gonna Wash That Man*	Uptempo	D3	E5	Lead	Romantic Lead Female
South Pacific	1949	Nellie Forbush	Honey Bun	Uptempo	Bb3	Bb4	Lead	Romantic Lead Female
South Pacific	1949	Nellie Forbush	Some Enchanted Evening Reprise 2	Ballad	Ab3	Bb4	Lead	Romantic Lead Female
South Pacific	1949	Nellie Forbush	Im In Love...Wonderful Guy*	Uptempo	B3	Db5	Lead	Romantic Lead Female
South Pacific	1949	Nellie Forbush	Im In Love...Wonderful Guy Reprise	Uptempo	B3	C5	Lead	Romantic Lead Female
Pajama Game	1954	Babe Williams	I'm Not At All In Love*	Uptempo	A3	B4	Lead	Romantic Lead Female
Pajama Game	1954	Babe Williams	There Once Was A Man*	Uptempo	Bb3	Eb5	Lead	Romantic Lead Female
Pajama Game	1954	Babe Williams	Hey There Reprise	Ballad	A#3	Bb4	Lead	Romantic Lead Female
Pajama Game	1954	Babe Williams	Seven And A Half Cents*	Uptempo	A3	D5	Lead	Romantic Lead Female
West Side Story	1957	Anita+	A Boy Like That*	Moderate Tempo	Eb3	Cb5	Lead	Romantic Lead Female
Flower Drum Song 2002	1958	Linda Low+	I Enjoy Being A Girl	Uptempo	A3	B4	Lead	Romantic Lead Female
Flower Drum Song 2002	1958	Linda Low+	I Enjoy Being A Girl Encore*	Moderate Tempo	A3	Cb5	Lead	Romantic Lead Female
Flower Drum Song 2002	1958	Linda Low+	I Enjoy Being A Girl Playoff*	Moderate Tempo	Bb3	Eb5	Lead	Romantic Lead Female
Flower Drum Song 2002	1958	Linda Low+	Fan Tan Fannie*	Uptempo	B3	B4	Lead	Romantic Lead Female
Flower Drum Song 2002	1958	Helen Chao+	Love, Look Away (C Maj)	Ballad	B3	E5	Lead	Romantic Lead Female
Bye Bye Birdie	1960	Rose Grant	An English Teacher	Uptempo	Gb3	Bb4	Lead	Romantic Lead Female
Bye Bye Birdie	1960	Rose Grant	Let's Settle Down (TV 1995)	Moderate Tempo	G3	Db4	Lead	Romantic Lead Female
Bye Bye Birdie	1960	Rose Grant	What Did I Ever See In Him *	Uptempo	G3	Bb4	Lead	Romantic Lead Female
Bye Bye Birdie	1960	Rose Grant	Spanish Rose	Moderate Tempo	G3	C5	Lead	Romantic Lead Female
Bye Bye Birdie	1960	Rose Grant	What Did I Ever See In Him Reprise	Uptempo	G3	Bb4	Lead	Romantic Lead Female
Bye Bye Birdie	1960	Rose Grant	An English Teacher Reprise	Uptempo	Db4	Bb4	Lead	Romantic Lead Female

Alto

189

* = Music Edit Required
+ = Ethnic Specific

Show	Year	Role	Song	Tempo	Range-Bottom	Range-Top	Category	Char Type
How To Succeed...	1961	Hedy La Rue	Love From A Heart Of Gold*	Ballad	B3	D5	Supporting	Romantic Lead Female
Cabaret	1966	Sally Bowles	Don't Tell Mama	Uptempo	A3	A4	Lead	Romantic Lead Female
Cabaret	1966	Sally Bowles	Perfectly Marvelous *	Uptempo	F#3	A4	Lead	Romantic Lead Female
Cabaret	1966	Sally Bowles	Maybe This Time	Ballad	F#3	C5	Lead	Romantic Lead Female
Cabaret	1966	Sally Bowles	Cabaret	Uptempo	E3	B4	Lead	Romantic Lead Female
Mame	1966	Mame	It's Today*	Uptempo	A3	D5	Lead	Romantic Lead Female
Mame	1966	Mame	Open A New Window*	Uptempo	A3	D5	Lead	Romantic Lead Female
Mame	1966	Mame	That's How Young I Feel*	Uptempo	G3	Bb4	Lead	Romantic Lead Female
Mame	1966	Mame	If He Walked Into My Life	Ballad	F#3	Bb4	Lead	Romantic Lead Female
Mame	1966	Mame	It's Today Reprise*	Uptempo	F3	Bb4	Lead	Romantic Lead Female
Mame	1966	Mame	It's Today Reprise 2*	Moderate Tempo	A3	Eb5	Lead	Romantic Lead Female
Mame	1966	Mame	You're My Best Girl*	Ballad	G3	Bb4	Lead	Romantic Lead Female
Mame	1966	Mame	We Need A Little Christmas*	Uptempo	C#4	D5	Lead	Romantic Lead Female
Mame	1966	Mame	We Need A Little Christmas*	Uptempo	F3	Bb4	Lead	Romantic Lead Female
Follies	1971	Carolotta Champion	I'm Still Here	Moderate Tempo	Eb3	C5	Supporting	Romantic Lead Female
Follies	1971	Solange LaFitte	Ah, Paris *	Uptempo	C3	G4	Supporting	Romantic Lead Female
Cabaret	1972	Sally Bowles	Mein Herr	Moderate Tempo	F3	B4	Lead	Romantic Lead Female
Pippin	1972	Catherine	There He Was	Uptempo	G#3	B4	Lead	Romantic Lead Female
Pippin	1972	Catherine	Kind Of Woman*	Moderate Tempo	Ab3	C#5	Lead	Romantic Lead Female
Pippin	1972	Catherine	I Guess I'll Miss the Man	Ballad	F#3	B4	Lead	Romantic Lead Female
Sugar	1972	Sugar Kane	Open Chicago	Uptempo	A3	C5	Lead	Romantic Lead Female
Sugar	1972	Sugar Kane	Hey Why Not! *	Uptempo	Bb3	Bb4	Lead	Romantic Lead Female
A Little Night Music	1973	Countess Charlotte Malc	Everyday A Little Death	Uptempo	G3	B4	Supporting	Romantic Lead Female
A Little Night Music	1973	Desiree Armfeldt	Send In The Clowns	Ballad	G3	A4	Lead	Romantic Lead Female
They're Playing Our Song	1974	Sonia Walsk	Falling Reprise	Moderate Tempo	E3	A4	Lead	Romantic Lead Female
They're Playing Our Song	1974	Sonia Walsk	Workin' It Out*	Uptempo	F3	B4	Lead	Romantic Lead Female
They're Playing Our Song	1974	Sonia Walsk	If He Really Knew Me*	Ballad	G3	B4	Lead	Romantic Lead Female
They're Playing Our Song	1974	Sonia Walsk	They're Playing My Song*	Uptempo	G3	Cb5	Lead	Romantic Lead Female
They're Playing Our Song	1974	Sonia Walsk	If He Really Knew Me Reprise*	Ballad	G3	Ab4	Lead	Romantic Lead Female
They're Playing Our Song	1974	Sonia Walsk	Right*	Uptempo	A3	G4	Lead	Romantic Lead Female

* = Music Edit Required
+ = Ethnic Specific

Show	Year	Role	Song	Tempo	Range-Bottom	Range-Top	Category	Char Type
They're Playing Our Song	1974	Sonia Walsk	Just For Tonight	Ballad	G3	A4	Lead	Romantic Lead Female
Wiz, The	1974	Glinda	A Rested Body Is A Rested Mind	Moderate Tempo	C4	C5	Lead	Romantic Lead Female
A Chorus Line	1975	Cassie	The Music And The Mirror	Moderate Tempo	A#3	D5	Lead	Romantic Lead Female
Cats	1981	Bombalurina	Macavity	Moderate Tempo	A3	C5	Supporting	Romantic Lead Female
Cats	1981	Demeter	Macavity	Moderate Tempo	A3	C5	Supporting	Romantic Lead Female
Nine	1982	Luisa Contini	My Husband Makes Movies	Moderate Tempo	Eb3	C5	Lead	Romantic Lead Female
Nine	1982	Stephanie Necrophorus	Folies Bergeres*	Uptempo	B3	B4	Supporting	Romantic Lead Female
Nine	1982	Liliane La Fluer	Folies Bergeres*	Uptempo	G#3	B4	Supporting	Romantic Lead Female
Nine	1982	Luisa Contini	Be On Your Own	Moderate Tempo	G#3	A4	Lead	Romantic Lead Female
Sunday...Park With Geroge	1984	Dot	Sunday In The Park With George	Moderate Tempo	E3	Db5	Lead	Romantic Lead Female
Sunday...Park With Geroge	1984	Dot	Color And Light (Part 2)	Moderate Tempo	B3	C5	Lead	Romantic Lead Female
Sunday...Park With Geroge	1984	Dot	Color And Light (Part 3)*	Uptempo	E4	E5	Lead	Romantic Lead Female
Sunday...Park With Geroge	1984	Dot	Everybody Loves Louis	Uptempo	A#3	C#5	Lead	Romantic Lead Female
Sunday...Park With Geroge	1984	Dot	We Do Not Belong Together*	Moderate Tempo	G3	D5	Lead	Romantic Lead Female
Sunday...Park With Geroge	1984	Marie	Children And Art*	Ballad	Gb3	Db5	Lead	Romantic Lead Female
Sunday...Park With Geroge	1984	Dot	Move On*	Ballad	G#3	C#5	Lead	Romantic Lead Female
Les Miserables	1987	Fantine	I Have Dreamed (E Major)	Ballad	G3	C#5	Lead	Romantic Lead Female
Les Miserables	1987	Fantine	Come To Me	Ballad	C4	C5	Lead	Romantic Lead Female
Les Miserables	1987	Fantine	I Have Dreamed (Eb Major)	Ballad	Gb3	C5	Lead	Romantic Lead Female
City of Angels	1989	Bobbi	With Every Breath I Take	Ballad	E3	Db5	Lead	Romantic Lead Female
City of Angels	1989	Bobbi	With Every Breath I Take Reprise *	Ballad	D#3	C5	Lead	Romantic Lead Female
City of Angels	1989	Gabby	What You Don't Know About Women *	Moderate Tempo	G3	F5	Lead	Romantic Lead Female
City of Angels	1989	Gabby	It Needs Work	Moderate Tempo	G#3	Cb5	Lead	Romantic Lead Female
Once On This Island	1990	Erzulie+	Human Heart*	Ballad	B3	C#5	Lead	Romantic Lead Female
Once On This Island	1990	Andrea+	Andrea Sequence*	Moderate Tempo	Bb3	C5	Lead	Romantic Lead Female
Miss Saigon	1991	Ellen Scott	I Still Believe*	Ballad	A3	Eb5	Lead	Romantic Lead Female
Miss Saigon	1991	Ellen Scott	Now I've Seen Her	Ballad	G#3	E5	Lead	Romantic Lead Female
Will Rogers Follies	1991	Ziegfield's Favorite	Will-A-Mania	Uptempo	G3	D5	Supporting	Romantic Lead Female
Will Rogers Follies	1991	Betty Blake	My Unknown Someone	Ballad	Ab3	C5	Lead	Romantic Lead Female
Will Rogers Follies	1991	Betty Blake	The Big Time*	Moderate Tempo	B3	D#5	Lead	Romantic Lead Female
Will Rogers Follies	1991	Betty Blake	My Big Mistake	Moderate Tempo	F3	D5	Lead	Romantic Lead Female

* = Music Edit Required
+ = Ethnic Specific

Show	Year	Role	Song	Tempo	Range-Bottom	Range-Top	Category	Char Type
Will Rogers Follies	1991	Betty Blake	With You	Moderate Tempo	Eb4	C5	Lead	Romantic Lead Female
Will Rogers Follies	1991	Betty Blake	No Man Left For Me	Moderate Tempo	A3	C5	Lead	Romantic Lead Female
Goodbye Girl, The	1993	Actress	Too Good To Be Bad*	Moderate Tempo	A3	A4	Supporting	Romantic Lead Female
Goodbye Girl, The	1993	Paula McFadden	No More	Moderate Tempo	G3	C5	Lead	Romantic Lead Female
Goodbye Girl, The	1993	Paula McFadden	A Beat Behind*	Uptempo	F#3	B4	Lead	Romantic Lead Female
Goodbye Girl, The	1993	Paula McFadden	My Rules	Moderate Tempo	Ab3	C5	Lead	Romantic Lead Female
Goodbye Girl, The	1993	Paula McFadden	Don't Follow In My Footsteps*	Moderate Tempo	D#3	C#5	Lead	Romantic Lead Female
Goodbye Girl, The	1993	Paula McFadden	How Can I Win	Ballad	Ab3	D5	Lead	Romantic Lead Female
Goodbye Girl, The	1993	Paula McFadden	What A Guy	Ballad	F#3	C5	Lead	Romantic Lead Female
Victor/Victoria	1995	Parisienne	Paris By Night Reprise	Moderate Tempo	A3	C5	Supporting	Romantic Lead Female
Scarlet Pimpernel, The	1997	Marguerite St. Just	You Are My Home*	Ballad	C#4	F#5	Lead	Romantic Lead Female
Scarlet Pimpernel, The	1997	Marguerite St. Just	When I Look At You	Ballad	B3	E5	Lead	Romantic Lead Female
Scarlet Pimpernel, The	1997	Marguerite St. Just	I'll Foget You	Ballad	G#3	D5	Lead	Romantic Lead Female
Scarlet Pimpernel, The	1997	Marguerite St. Just	Vivez*	Moderate Tempo	C#4	E5	Lead	Romantic Lead Female
Scarlet Pimpernel, The	1997	Marguerite St. Just	Only Love	Ballad	Bb3	E5	Lead	Romantic Lead Female
Scarlet Pimpernel, The	1997	Marguerite St. Just	Storybook*	Moderate Tempo	A3	E5	Lead	Romantic Lead Female
Steel Pier	1997	Rita Racine	Willing To Ride	Uptempo	Gb3	C5	Lead	Romantic Lead Female
Steel Pier	1997	Rita Racine	Love Bird*	Moderate Tempo	G3	C5	Lead	Romantic Lead Female
Steel Pier	1997	Rita Racine	Willing To Ride Reprise	Moderate Tempo	Ab3	B4	Lead	Romantic Lead Female
Steel Pier	1997	Rita Racine	Steel Pier Reprise*	Uptempo	Ab3	Db5	Lead	Romantic Lead Female
Parade	1998	Lucille Frank	Waiting*	Moderate Tempo	A3	C5	Lead	Romantic Lead Female
Parade	1998	Lucille Frank	You Don't Know this Man	Ballad	G3	Eb5	Lead	Romantic Lead Female
Parade	1998	Lucille Frank	Do It Alone	Moderate Tempo	A3	E5	Lead	Romantic Lead Female
Parade	1998	Lucille Frank	All The Wasted Time*	Ballad	G3	Eb5	Lead	Romantic Lead Female
Parade	1998	Lucille Frank	Finale	Ballad	A3	C5	Lead	Romantic Lead Female
Ragtime	1998	Evelyn Nesbit	Crime Of The Century*	Uptempo	Bb3	D5	Lead	Romantic Lead Female
Ragtime	1998	Evelyn Nesbit	Atlantic City (Part 1)*	Uptempo	B3	B4	Lead	Romantic Lead Female
Ragtime	1998	Evelyn Nesbit	Atlantic City (Part 3)*	Uptempo	Bb3	D5	Lead	Romantic Lead Female
Next To Normal	1999	Diana	So Anyway	Ballad	A3	C5	Lead	Romantic Lead Female
Aida	2000	Aida +	The Past Is Another Land	Ballad	A3	B4	Lead	Romantic Lead Female
Aida	2000	Aida +	Easy As Life	Moderate Tempo	G3	C5	Lead	Romantic Lead Female

* = Music Edit Required
+ = Ethnic Specific

Show	Year	Role	Song	Tempo	Range-Bottom	Range-Top	Category	Char Type
Aida	2000	Aida +	Elaborate Lies Reprise	Ballad	G3	C5	Lead	Romantic Lead Female
Aida	2000	Aida +	The Gods Love Nubia	Alto	C4	E5	Lead	Romantic Lead Female
Aida	2000	Amneris	My Strongest Suit	Uptempo	G♭3	E♭5	Lead	Romantic Lead Female
Aida	2000	Amneris	My Strongest Suit Reprise	Ballad	B♭3	G4	Lead	Romantic Lead Female
Aida	2000	Amneris	I Know the Truth	Ballad	E3	D5	Lead	Romantic Lead Female
Aida	2000	Amneris	Every Story Reprise (Finale AII)	Ballad	G3	A♭4	Lead	Romantic Lead Female
Mamma Mia!	2001	Donna Sheridan	Money Money Money	Uptempo	G4	B♭4	Lead	Romantic Lead Female
Mamma Mia!	2001	Donna Sheridan	Mamma Mia*	Uptempo	F#3	A4	Lead	Romantic Lead Female
Mamma Mia!	2001	Donna Sheridan	Super Trouper*	Moderate Tempo	G3	G4	Lead	Romantic Lead Female
Mamma Mia!	2001	Donna Sheridan	One Of Us*	Moderate Tempo	A3	C5	Lead	Romantic Lead Female
Mamma Mia!	2001	Donna Sheridan	SOS*	Uptempo	F4	A4	Lead	Romantic Lead Female
Mamma Mia!	2001	Donna Sheridan	One Last Summer*	Ballad	F#3	E4	Lead	Romantic Lead Female
Mamma Mia!	2001	Donna Sheridan	Slipping Through My Fingers*	Ballad	A3	C5	Lead	Romantic Lead Female
Mamma Mia!	2001	Donna Sheridan	The Winner Takes It All	Moderate Tempo	G3	C5	Lead	Romantic Lead Female
Mamma Mia!	2001	Donna Sheridan	I Do, I Do, I Do, I Do, I Do	Moderate Tempo	G3	C5	Lead	Romantic Lead Female
Thoroughly Modern Millie	2002	Muzzy Van Hossmere	Only In New York	Ballad	G#3	B4	Lead	Romantic Lead Female
Thoroughly Modern Millie	2002	Muzzy Van Hossmere	Long As I'm Here With You*	Uptempo	A3	C#5	Lead	Romantic Lead Female
All Shook Up	2005	Miss Sandra	Let Yourself Go	Moderate Tempo	E2	E4	Supporting	Romantic Lead Female
Dirty Rotten Scoundrels	2005	Jolene Oakes	Oklahoma	Uptempo	G#3	C5	Supporting	Romantic Lead Female
Dirty Rotten Scoundrels	2005	Muriel Eubanks	What's A Woman To Do	Moderate Tempo	G2	D4	Supporting	Romantic Lead Female
Dirty Rotten Scoundrels	2005	Muriel Eubanks	What's Was A Woman To Do Reprise	Moderate Tempo	E3	B♭4	Supporting	Romantic Lead Female
Dirty Rotten Scoundrels	2005	Muriel Eubanks	Like Zis/Like Zat *	Moderate Tempo	E3	B♭4	Supporting	Romantic Lead Female
Curtains	2007	Georgia Hendricks	Thinking of Him	Ballad	G3	D♭5	Lead	Romantic Lead Female
Curtains	2007	Georgia Hendricks	Thataway *	Uptempo	B#3	B4	Lead	Romantic Lead Female
Legally Blonde	2007	Brooke Wyndam	Whipped Into Shape*	Uptempo	A3	G5	Supporting	Romantic Lead Female
In The Heights	2008	Vanessa+	It Won't Be Long Now	Uptempo	A3	E5	Lead	Romantic Lead Female
White Christmas	2008	Betty Haynes	Love And The Weather*	Uptempo	A3	C5	Lead	Romantic Lead Female
White Christmas	2008	Betty Haynes	Falling Out Of Love Can Be Fun*	Uptempo	G3	C5	Lead	Romantic Lead Female
White Christmas	2008	Betty Haynes	Love, You Didn't Do Right By Me	Moderate Tempo	A3	B♭4	Lead	Romantic Lead Female
Next To Normal	2009	Diana	My Psychopharmacologist And I	Moderate Tempo	A3	C5	Lead	Romantic Lead Female
Next To Normal	2009	Diana	I Miss The Mountains	Moderate Tempo	G3	D5	Lead	Romantic Lead Female

Alto

* = Music Edit Required
+ = Ethnic Specific

Show	Year	Role	Song	Tempo	Range-Bottom	Range-Top	Category	Char Type
Next To Normal	2009	Diana	You Don't Know*	Moderate Tempo	A3	B4	Lead	Romantic Lead Female
Next To Normal	2009	Diana	Didn't I See This Movie	Uptempo	A3	F#5	Lead	Romantic Lead Female
Next To Normal	2009	Diana	You Don't Know Reprise*	Uptempo	A3	A4	Lead	Romantic Lead Female
Next To Normal	2009	Diana	How Could I Forget*	Ballad	B♭3	D♭5	Lead	Romantic Lead Female
Next To Normal	2009	Diana	The Break	Uptempo	B3	C5	Lead	Romantic Lead Female
Next To Normal	2009	Diana	Maybe*	Moderate Tempo	E♭3	E♭5	Lead	Romantic Lead Female
Next To Normal	2009	Diana	So Anyway	Ballad	B3	C5	Lead	Romantic Lead Female

* = Music Edit Required
+ = Ethnic Specific

Show	Year	Role	Song	Tempo	Range-Bottom	Range-Top	Category	Char Type
Of Thee I Sing	1931	French Ambassador	The Illegitimate Daughter*	Uptempo	C#3	G4	Lead	Antagonist Male
Of Thee I Sing	1931	French Ambassador	Illegitimate Daughter Reprise*	Uptempo	D3	D4	Lead	Antagonist Male
Babes In Arms (1998)	1937	Gus Fielding	I Wish I Were In Love Again*	Uptempo	C3	Ab4	Lead	Antagonist Male
Babes In Arms (1998)	1937	Gus Fielding	You Are So Fair*	Uptempo	Eb3	F4	Lead	Antagonist Male
Jersey Boys (2005)	1954	Tommy DeVito	Earth Angel	Ballad	Bb3	Eb4	Lead	Antagonist Male
Candide	1956	Dr. Pangloss	Dear Boy	Uptempo	Bb2	F#4	Lead	Antagonist Male
Candide	1956	Vanderdenur	Bon Voyage*	Uptempo	C3	Bb4	Supporting	Antagonist Male
Candide	1956	Dr. Pangloss	The Venice Gavotte*	Uptempo	Bb2	F4	Lead	Antagonist Male
West Side Story	1957	Riff	Cool	Moderate Tempo	C3	Eb4	Lead	Antagonist Male
West Side Story	1957	Riff	The Jet Song*	Uptempo	Bb2	G4	Lead	Antagonist Male
How To Succeed...	1961	Bud Frump	Company Way Reprise*	Uptempo	D3	G4	Lead	Antagonist Male
Sweet Charity	1966	Herman	I Love To Cry At Weddings*	Uptempo	D3	B4	Lead	Antagonist Male
Hair	1968	Berger	Donna	Uptempo	Eb3	Bb4	Lead	Antagonist Male
Godspell	1971	John The Baptist	Prepare Ye*	Ballad	C#3	G#4	Lead	Antagonist Male
Godspell	1971	Judas	On The Willows	Ballad	C3	F#4	Lead	Antagonist Male
Godspell	1971	Judas	All For The Best*	Uptempo	C3	D4	Lead	Antagonist Male
Grease	1971	Kenicke	Greased Lightening	Uptempo	E3	B4	Lead	Antagonist Male
Jesus Christ Superstar	1971	Judas Iscariot	Heaven On Their Minds	Uptempo	D3	D5	Lead	Antagonist Male
Jesus Christ Superstar	1971	Judas Iscariot	Damned For All Time*	Uptempo	D3	D5	Lead	Antagonist Male
Jesus Christ Superstar	1971	Judas Iscariot	Judas' Death	Uptempo	D3	E5	Lead	Antagonist Male
Jesus Christ Superstar	1971	Judas Iscariot	Superstar	Uptempo	E3	B4	Lead	Antagonist Male
Jesus Christ Superstar	1971	Simon Zealots	Simon Zealots*	Uptempo	F3	Ab4	Supporting	Antagonist Male
Wiz, The	1974	Lion	Mean Ole Lion	Uptempo	G2	Bb4	Lead	Antagonist Male
Wiz, The	1974	Lion	Be A Lion*	Ballad	Ab3	Ab4	Lead	Antagonist Male
A Chorus Line	1975	Richie +	Gimmie The Ball (ms 231-269) *	Uptempo	C#3	G4	Supporting	Antagonist Male
Pacific Overtures	1976	Mother+	Chrysanthemum Tea*	Moderate Tempo	D3	F4	Lead	Antagonist Male
Evita	1978	Che Guevara	Oh What A Circus	Uptempo	B2	E4	Lead	Antagonist Male
Evita	1978	Che Guevara	Goodnight and Thank You	Uptempo	B2	F4	Lead	Antagonist Male
Evita	1978	Che Guevara	High Flying Adored	Moderate Tempo	Bb2	G4	Lead	Antagonist Male
Evita	1978	Che Guevara	Rainbow Tour	Uptempo	C3	E4	Lead	Antagonist Male

Tenor

* = Music Edit Required
+ = Ethnic Specific

Show	Year	Role	Song	Tempo	Range-Bottom	Range-Top	Category	Char Type
Evita	1978	Che Guevara	And the Money Kept Rolling In	Uptempo	A2	G4	Lead	Antagonist Male
Evita	1978	Che Guevara	Waltz for Eva and Che	Uptempo	D3	G4	Lead	Antagonist Male
Mystery Of Edwin Drood, Th	1985	John Jasper	A Man Could Go Quite Mad	Uptempo	A2	G4	Lead	Antagonist Male
Mystery Of Edwin Drood, Th	1985	John Jasper	Both Sides Of The Coin*	Uptempo	C3	E4	Lead	Antagonist Male
Mystery Of Edwin Drood, Th	1985	John Jasper	Jasper's Confession	Moderate Tempo	B2	A4	Lead	Antagonist Male
Phantom Of The Opera	1986	Phantom	Phantom Of The Opera*	Moderate Tempo	B2	G#4	Lead	Antagonist Male
Phantom Of The Opera	1986	Phantom	The Music Of The Night	Ballad	G#2	G#4	Lead	Antagonist Male
Phantom Of The Opera	1986	Phantom	Stranger Than You Dreamt It*	Ballad	D3	D4	Lead	Antagonist Male
Phantom Of The Opera	1986	Phantom	All I Ask Of You Reprise	Ballad	G3	A4	Lead	Antagonist Male
Phantom Of The Opera	1986	Phantom	Why So Silent*	Ballad	Eb3	Gb4	Lead	Antagonist Male
Phantom Of The Opera	1986	Phantom	Notes: No Doubt She'll Do Her Best	Ballad	D#3	D#4	Lead	Antagonist Male
Phantom Of The Opera	1986	Phantom	The Point Of No Return*	Ballad	C3	G4	Lead	Antagonist Male
Phantom Of The Opera	1986	Phantom	All I Ask Of You Reprise 2*	Ballad	Db3	Ab4	Lead	Antagonist Male
Les Miserables	1987	Javert	Stars	Moderate Tempo	B2	E4	Lead	Antagonist Male
Les Miserables	1987	Javert	Javert's Suicide	Moderate Tempo	C3	F#4	Lead	Antagonist Male
Chess	1988	Arbiter	The Story of Chess	Moderate Tempo	B2	G4	Supporting	Antagonist Male
Chess	1988	Arbiter	The Arbiter	Uptempo	E3	A4	Supporting	Antagonist Male
Chess	1988	Arbiter	The Arbiter Reprise	Uptempo	E3	A4	Supporting	Antagonist Male
Once On This Island	1990	Papa Ge+	Forever Yours*	Uptempo	C#3	G4	Lead	Antagonist Male
Once On This Island	1990	Papa Ge+	Promises/Forever Yours Reprise*	Moderate Tempo	C3	G4	Lead	Antagonist Male
Children of Eden	1991	Cain	Lost In The Wilderness *	Moderate Tempo	D3	G4	Lead	Antagonist Male
Miss Saigon	1991	Engineer+	The American Dream*	Moderate Tempo	A2	A4	Lead	Antagonist Male
Miss Saigon	1991	Engineer+	If You Want To Die In Bed*	Moderate Tempo	A2	G4	Lead	Antagonist Male
Miss Saigon	1991	Engineer+	What A Waste*	Moderate Tempo	B2	F#4	Lead	Antagonist Male
Assassins	1992	Giuseppe Zangara	How I Saved Roosevelt*	Uptempo	D3	A4	Lead	Antagonist Male
Assassins	1992	John Hinkley	Unworthy Of Your Love*	Moderate Tempo	B2	E4	Lead	Antagonist Male
Honk	1993	Cat	You Can Play With Your Food	Uptempo	C3	Ab4	Supporting	Antagonist Male
Jekyll and Hyde	1997	Mr. Edward Hyde	Alive	Uptempo	B2	D4	Lead	Antagonist Male
Jekyll and Hyde	1997	Mr. Edward Hyde	Confrontation*	Uptempo	B2	A4	Lead	Antagonist Male
Jekyll and Hyde	1997	Mr. Edward Hyde	Alive Reprise	Uptempo	E3	A4	Lead	Antagonist Male
Parade	1998	Britt Craig	Big News	Uptempo	D3	Ab4	Lead	Antagonist Male

Tenor

Show	Year	Role	Song	Tempo	Range-Bottom	Range-Top	Category	Char Type
Parade	1998	Newt Lee+	Interrogation Sequence*	Moderate Tempo	Bb2	C4	Lead	Antagonist Male
Parade	1998	Britt Craig	Real Big News*	Uptempo	F3	A4	Lead	Antagonist Male
Parade	1998	Britt Craig	Opening Act II	Moderate Tempo	F3	G4	Lead	Antagonist Male
Aida	2000	Zoser	Another Pyramid	Uptempo	F3	E4	Supporting	Antagonist Male
Aida	2000	Zoser	Like Father Like Son*	Uptempo	G3	Bb4	Supporting	Antagonist Male
Producers, The	2001	Franz Liebkind	Haben Sie Gehort Das Deutsche Bar	Uptempo	A2	G4	Lead	Antagonist Male
Fame	2003	Tyrone+	Tyrone's Rap	Uptempo	Bb3	Bb4	Lead	Antagonist Male
Fame	2003	Tyrone+	Dancin' On The Sidewalk	Uptempo	Bb2	Bb4	Lead	Antagonist Male
25th Annual...Spelling Bee	2005	Mitch Mahoney	Prayer of the Comfort Counselor	Uptempo	E3	A4	Lead	Antagonist Male
25th Annual...Spelling Bee	2005	Mitch Mahoney	The I Love You Song	Ballad	E3	G#4	Lead	Antagonist Male
Chitty Chitty Bang Bang	2005	Boris	Act English *	Moderate Tempo	C3	G4	Supporting	Antagonist Male
Color Purple, The	2005	Mister+	Big Dog	Uptempo	F3	Ab4	Lead	Antagonist Male
Color Purple, The	2005	Mister+	Mister's Song (2005)	Moderate Tempo	E3	G4	Lead	Antagonist Male
Color Purple, The	2005	Mister+	Mister's Song (2015)	Moderate Tempo	F3	Ab4	Lead	Antagonist Male
Spring Awakening	2006	Moritz	The Bitch Of Living*	Uptempo	C3	D4	Lead	Antagonist Male
Spring Awakening	2006	Moritz	And Then There Were None*	Uptempo	E3	G#4	Lead	Antagonist Male
Spring Awakening	2006	Moritz	Don't Do Sadness	Uptempo	B2	A4	Lead	Antagonist Male
Spring Awakening	2006	Moritz	Those You've Known*	Ballad	D3	E4	Lead	Antagonist Male
The Little Mermaid	2007	Flotsam	Sweet Child	Ballad	C3	C5	Supporting	Antagonist Male
The Little Mermaid	2007	Jetsom	Sweet Child	Ballad	C3	C5	Supporting	Antagonist Male
Jersey Boys (2005)	1928	Frankie Castelluccio	I Can't Give You Anything But Love	Moderate Tempo	E3	Ab4	Lead	Character Ingenue Male
Jersey Boys (2005)	1935	Frankie Valli	I'm In The Mood	Ballad	E3	F5	Lead	Character Ingenue Male
On The Town	1944	Chip	Ya Got Me *	Uptempo	E3	Gb4	Lead	Character Ingenue Male
Carousel	1945	Enoch Snow	When I Marry Mr. Snow Reprise	Ballad	C4	D5	Lead	Character Ingenue Male
Carousel	1945	Enoch Snow	When The Children Are Asleep *	Moderate Tempo	Eb3	C5	Lead	Character Ingenue Male
Carousel	1945	Enoch Snow	Geranium In The Window *	Ballad	D3	F#4	Lead	Character Ingenue Male
Jersey Boys (2005)	1946	Frankie Castelluccio	Sunday Kind Of Love	Uptempo	D3	E5	Lead	Character Ingenue Male
Jersey Boys (2005)	1960	Frankie Valli	Stay*	Uptempo	F3	D5	Lead	Character Ingenue Male
Jersey Boys (2005)	1962	Frankie Valli	Sherry*	Moderate Tempo	G4	F5	Lead	Character Ingenue Male

Tenor

197

* = Music Edit Required
+ = Ethnic Specific

Show	Year	Role	Song	Tempo	Range-Bottom	Range-Top	Category	Char Type
Jersey Boys (2005)	1962	Frankie Valli	Big Girls Don't Cry	Uptempo	Eb4	F5	Lead	Character Ingenue Male
Jersey Boys (2005)	1963	Frankie Valli	My Mother's Eyes	Ballad	E3	F4	Lead	Character Ingenue Male
Jersey Boys (2005)	1963	Frankie Valli	Walk Like A Man	Moderate Tempo	B3	F5	Lead	Character Ingenue Male
She Loves Me	1963	Arpad Lazslo	Try Me	Uptempo	B2	E4	Lead	Character Ingenue Male
Jersey Boys (2005)	1964	Frankie Valli	Rag Doll	Moderate Tempo	Bb3	F5	Lead	Character Ingenue Male
Jersey Boys (2005)	1965	Frankie Valli	Bye Bye Baby	Uptempo	C#4	D5	Lead	Character Ingenue Male
Jersey Boys (2005)	1965	Frankie Valli	Work My Way Back To You	Uptempo	G3	C5	Lead	Character Ingenue Male
Jersey Boys (2005)	1965	Frankie Valli	Let's Hang On!*	Uptempo	Db3	D5	Lead	Character Ingenue Male
Jersey Boys (2005)	1966	Frankie Valli	Don't you Worry 'Bout Me*	Uptempo	G3	C5	Lead	Character Ingenue Male
Jersey Boys (2005)	1967	Frankie Valli	Beggin'*	Uptempo	B3	Bb4	Lead	Character Ingenue Male
Jersey Boys (2005)	1967	Frankie Valli	Can't Take My Eyes Off You	Uptempo	D3	G4	Lead	Character Ingenue Male
1776	1969	Courier	Momma Look Sharp	Ballad	Bb2	Db4	Supporting	Character Ingenue Male
Grease	1971	Doody	Those Magic Changes	Uptempo	E3	Cb5	Lead	Character Ingenue Male
Grease	1971	Doody	Rock N Roll Party Queen	Uptempo	A2	Ab3	Lead	Character Ingenue Male
Jersey Boys (2005)	1975	Frankie Valli	My Eyes Adored You	Ballad	G3	Bb4	Lead	Character Ingenue Male
Jersey Boys (2005)	1976	Frankie Valli	Fallen Angel	Ballad	Eb3	Ab4	Lead	Character Ingenue Male
Sweeney Todd	1979	Tobias Ragg	Perelli's Miracle Elixir*	Uptempo	B2	A4	Lead	Character Ingenue Male
Sweeney Todd	1979	Tobias Ragg	Not While I'm Around*	Ballad	Eb3	Ab4	Lead	Character Ingenue Male
Baby	1983	Danny Hooper	I Chose Right	Ballad	D3	G4	Lead	Character Ingenue Male
Big River	1985	Huckleberry Finn	Waitin' For The Light To Shine	Ballad	G#2	C#4	Lead	Character Ingenue Male
Big River	1985	Huckleberry Finn	I, Huckleberry, Me	Uptempo	C3	F4	Lead	Character Ingenue Male
Big River	1985	Huckleberry Finn	River In The Rain *	Ballad	A2	G4	Lead	Character Ingenue Male
Big River	1985	Huckleberry Finn	Worlds Apart *	Ballad	B2	B4	Lead	Character Ingenue Male
Big River	1985	Huckleberry Finn	Waitin' For The Light To Shine Repri	Uptempo	A2	F#4	Lead	Character Ingenue Male
Big River	1985	Huckleberry Finn	River in the Rain Reprise *	Ballad	A2	D4	Lead	Character Ingenue Male
Big River	1985	Huckleberry Finn	Leavin's Not The Only Way To Go	Ballad	B2	B3	Lead	Character Ingenue Male
Rags	1986	Ben	The Sound Of Love*	Uptempo	Eb3	Ab4	Lead	Character Ingenue Male
Into The Woods	1987	Jack	I Guess This Is Goodbye	Ballad	D#3	D#4	Lead	Character Ingenue Male
Into The Woods	1987	Jack	Giants In The Sky	Uptempo	C3	F#4	Lead	Character Ingenue Male
Ain't Misbehavin'	1988	Man One +	How Ya Baby*	Uptempo	C3	C5	Lead	Character Ingenue Male

Tenor

Show	Year	Role	Song	Tempo	Range-Bottom	Range-Top	Category	Char Type
Ain't Misbehavin'	1988	Man One +	The Viper's Drag*	Ballad	C3	G4	Lead	Character Ingenue Male
Ain't Misbehavin'	1988	Man One +	That Ain't Right*	Ballad	G2	Bb4	Lead	Character Ingenue Male
Secret Garden, The	1991	Dickon	Winter's On The Wing	Uptempo	D3	F#4	Lead	Character Ingenue Male
Secret Garden, The	1991	Dickon	Winter's On The Wing Reprise	Ballad	D3	E4	Lead	Character Ingenue Male
Secret Garden, The	1991	Dickon	Wick*	Uptempo	F3	G4	Lead	Character Ingenue Male
My Favorite Year	1992	Benjy Stone	Larger Than Life	Moderate Tempo	Eb3	F4	Lead	Character Ingenue Male
My Favorite Year	1992	Benjy Stone	Waldorf Reveal	Uptempo	C3	F4	Lead	Character Ingenue Male
My Favorite Year	1992	Benjy Stone	My Favorite Year*	Moderate Tempo	C3	G4	Lead	Character Ingenue Male
Kiss Of The Spider Woman	1993	Gabriel	Gabriel's Letter*	Moderate Tempo	D#3	G4	Lead	Character Ingenue Male
Big	1996	Josh Baskin-Adult	We're Gonna Be Fine	Ballad	Bb2	D4	Lead	Character Ingenue Male
Big	1996	Josh Baskin-Adult	I Want To Go Home	Ballad	Ab2	B4	Lead	Character Ingenue Male
Big	1996	Josh Baskin-Adult	Fun	Uptempo	C3	G4	Lead	Character Ingenue Male
Big	1996	Josh Baskin-Adult	Do You Want To Play Games	Uptempo	E3	F4	Lead	Character Ingenue Male
Big	1996	Josh Baskin-Adult	Stars, Stars, Stars	Ballad	C3	D4	Lead	Character Ingenue Male
Big	1996	Josh Baskin-Adult	Coffee Black	Uptempo	C3	F4	Lead	Character Ingenue Male
Big	1996	Josh Baskin-Adult	When You're Big	Uptempo	E3	F4	Lead	Character Ingenue Male
Big	1996	Josh Baskin-Adult	Cross The Line	Uptempo	E3	D4	Lead	Character Ingenue Male
Big	1996	Josh Baskin-Adult	Big Boy Now	Ballad	Db3	Eb4	Lead	Character Ingenue Male
Rent	1996	Angel Schunard	Today For You*	Uptempo	Bb3	G4	Lead	Character Ingenue Male
Rent	1996	Angel Schunard	I'll Cover You*	Moderate Tempo	G3	A4	Lead	Character Ingenue Male
A Christmas Carol	1997	Scrooge-Young Adult	A Place Called Home	Ballad	Bb2	D4	Supporting	Character Ingenue Male
Footloose	1998	Ren McCormick	I Can't Stand Still	Uptempo	D3	C5	Lead	Character Ingenue Male
Footloose	1998	Ren McCormick	I'm Free	Uptempo	D3	Ab4	Lead	Character Ingenue Male
Footloose	1998	Ren McCormick	Almost Paradise*	Ballad	G2	A4	Lead	Character Ingenue Male
Footloose	1998	Ren McCormick	Dancing Is Not A Crime (Rap)	Uptempo				Character Ingenue Male
Parade	1998	Young Soldier	Old Red Hills Of Home (Part 1)	Moderate Tempo	D3	A4	Supporting	Character Ingenue Male
A Year With Frog and Toad	2002	Snail	The Letter #1	Moderate Tempo	A2	Bb3	Lead	Character Ingenue Male
A Year With Frog and Toad	2002	Snail	Letter #2	Uptempo	B2	E4	Supporting	Character Ingenue Male
A Year With Frog and Toad	2002	Snail	The Letter #3	Uptempo	C#3	Eb4	Supporting	Character Ingenue Male
A Year With Frog and Toad	2002	Snail	I'm Coming Out Of My Shell	Uptempo	E3	A4	Supporting	Character Ingenue Male
Wicked	2003	BOQ	Dancing Through Life*	Uptempo	G3	G4	Lead	Character Ingenue Male

* = Music Edit Required
+ = Ethnic Specific

Show	Year	Role	Song	Tempo	Range-Bottom	Range-Top	Category	Char Type
Wicked	2003	BOQ	March Of The Witch Hunters*	Uptempo	G#3	G4	Lead	Character Ingenue Male
Color Purple, The	2005	Harpo	Brown Betty *	Moderate Tempo	E3	G4	Lead	Character Ingenue Male
High School Musical	2007	Ryan Evans	What I've Been Looking For*	Uptempo	A3	F#4	Lead	Character Ingenue Male
Next To Normal	2009	Gabe	I'm Alive	Uptempo	G3	B4	Lead	Character Ingenue Male
Next To Normal	2009	Gabe	Aftershocks*	Uptempo	D3	D4	Lead	Character Ingenue Male
Next To Normal	2009	Gabe	I'm Alive Reprise	Uptempo	G3	G4	Lead	Character Ingenue Male
Next To Normal	2009	Henry	Perfect For You Reprise*	Moderate Tempo	D3	G4	Lead	Character Ingenue Male
Next To Normal	2009	Gabe	There's A World	Ballad	G3	G4	Lead	Character Ingenue Male
Anything Goes	1934	Moon Face Martin	Friendship *	Uptempo	Bb2	Eb4	Supporting	Character Male
Anything Goes	1934	Moon Face Martin	Be Like A Blue Bird	Moderate Tempo	B#2	F#4	Supporting	Character Male
Porgy and Bess	1935	Honey Man+	Honeyman	Ballad	B3	G4	atured Enseml	Character Male
Porgy and Bess	1935	Crab Man+	Crab Man	Ballad	B3	G4	atured Enseml	Character Male
Wizard Of Oz 1995	1939	Tin Man	If I Only Had A Heart*	Moderate Tempo	D3	G4	Lead	Character Male
Pal Joey	1940	Louis	The Flower Garden Of My Heart*	Moderate Tempo	Eb3	G4	atured Enseml	Character Male
Kiss Me Kate	1948	Paul	Too Darn Hot*	Uptempo	C3	Gb4	Supporting	Character Male
Cinderella (2013)	1949	Jean-Michel	Now Is the Time*	Uptempo	Eb3	F4	Supporting	Character Male
Cinderella (2013)	1949	Jean-Michel	Now Is The Time Reprise*	Uptempo	C3	A4	Supporting	Character Male
Guys and Dolls	1950	Nicely Nicely	Sit Down You're Rockin' The Boat*	Uptempo	F3	C5	Supporting	Character Male
Most Happy Fella, The	1956	The Doctor	Love and Kindness	Moderate Tempo	E3	A4	Supporting	Character Male
Most Happy Fella, The	1956	Herman	I Like Everybody*	Uptempo	G3	G4	Lead	Character Male
Most Happy Fella, The	1956	Herman	I Like Everybody Reprise*	Uptempo	F3	G4	Lead	Character Male
Most Happy Fella, The	1956	The Doctor	A Song Of A Summer Night*	Uptempo	F3	F4	Supporting	Character Male
Most Happy Fella, The	1956	Herman	I Made A Fist*	Moderate Tempo	F3	Ab4	Lead	Character Male
Once Upon A Mattress	1959	Jester	Normandy*	Uptempo	D#3	B4	Lead	Character Male
Once Upon A Mattress	1959	Jester	Very Soft Shoes*	Moderate Tempo	D3	F4	Lead	Character Male
How To Succeed...	1961	J Pierpont Finch	How To Succeed	Uptempo	E3	E4	Lead	Character Male
How To Succeed...	1961	J Pierpont Finch	Rosemary*	Moderate Tempo	B2	E4	Lead	Character Male
How To Succeed...	1961	J Pierpont Finch	I Believe In You*	Uptempo	F3	C4	Lead	Character Male
How To Succeed...	1961	J Pierpont Finch	Brotherhood Of Man*	Uptempo	F3	G4	Lead	Character Male
Jersey Boys (2005)	1961	Hal Miller	An Angel Cried	Uptempo	A3	C5	Supporting	Character Male
She Loves Me	1963	Headwaiter	A Romantic Atmosphere (G Maj)	Moderate Tempo	C#3	B4	Supporting	Character Male

* = Music Edit Required
+ = Ethnic Specific

Show	Year	Role	Song	Tempo	Range-Bottom	Range-Top	Category	Char Type
Fiddler on The Roof	1964	Motel	Miracle of Miracles	Uptempo	E3	F#4	Supporting	Character Male
Cabaret	1966	Herr Schultz	Meeskite	Uptempo	B2	Ab4	Supporting	Character Male
Cabaret	1966	Master of Cereomonies	Wilkomen	Uptempo	E3	G4	Lead	Character Male
Cabaret	1966	Master of Cereomonies	Two Ladies	Uptempo	G3	G4	Lead	Character Male
Cabaret	1966	Master of Cereomonies	The Money Song	Moderate Tempo	Eb2	A4	Lead	Character Male
Cabaret	1966	Master of Cereomonies	If You Could See Her	Uptempo	D3	F4	Lead	Character Male
Jersey Boys (2005)	1966	Bob Gaudio	Cry For Me	Ballad	Bb2	G4	Lead	Character Male
Sweet Charity	1966	Daddy Brubeck	The Rhythm Of Life*	Uptempo	B2	G4	Lead	Character Male
Hair	1968	Woof	Sodomy	Ballad	D3	G4	Lead	Character Male
Godspell	1971	Jesus	Save The People	Uptempo	G3	G4	Lead	Character Male
Godspell	1971	Jesus	Alas For You	Uptempo	E3	G4	Lead	Character Male
Godspell	1971	Jesus	Beautiful City (1972 Film)	Ballad	E3	F#4	Lead	Character Male
Godspell	1971	Jesus	All For The Best*	Uptempo	D3	E4	Lead	Character Male
Godspell	1971	Soloist 4	All Good Gifts	Ballad	D3	A4	Supporting	Character Male
Grease	1971	Roger	Mooning	Ballad	F3	G4	Supporting	Character Male
Grease	1971	Roger	Rock N Roll Party Queen	Uptempo	A2	Ab3	Lead	Character Male
You're A Good Man Charlie	1971	Snoopy	Suppertime*	Uptempo	C3	A4	Lead	Character Male
You're A Good Man Charlie	1971	Snoopy	Snoopy	Ballad	B2	G4	Lead	Character Male
Wiz, The	1974	Scarecrow	I Was Born On The Day Before Yest	Moderate Tempo	E3	A4	Lead	Character Male
Wiz, The	1974	Tin Man	Slide Some Oil To Me	Uptempo	Eb3	Bb4	Lead	Character Male
Wiz, The	1974	Tin Man	What Would I Do If I Could Feel	Ballad	D3	A4	Lead	Character Male
Jersey Boys (2005)	1975	Bob Gaudio	December 1963	Uptempo	F3	G4	Lead	Character Male
Pacific Overtures	1976	Fisherman+	Four Black Dragons*	Uptempo	Eb3	Gb4	Supporting	Character Male
Annie	1977	Rooster Hannigan	Easy Street *	Moderate Tempo	A2	G4	Supporting	Character Male
Best Little Whorehouse...	1978	Melvin P Thorpe	Texas Has A Whorehouse In It	Uptempo	Bb2	E4	Supporting	Character Male
On The Twentieth Century	1978	Owen O'Malley	Five Zeros*	Moderate Tempo	Ab2	Ab4	Lead	Character Male
Sweeney Todd	1979	Adolfo Pirelli	The Contest	Moderate Tempo	B2	C4	Lead	Character Male
Sweeney Todd	1979	The Beadle	Ladies In Their Sensitivities	Ballad	D3	A4	Lead	Character Male
Sweeney Todd	1979	Adolfo Pirelli	Pirelli's Death	Moderate Tempo	Eb3	C5	Lead	Character Male
Sweeney Todd	1979	The Beadle	Parlor Songs	Moderate Tempo	D3	G4	Lead	Character Male
Dreamgirls	1981	James Thunder Early +	Fake Your Way to the Top	Uptempo	F3	Ab4	Supporting	Character Male

* = Music Edit Required
+ = Ethnic Specific

Show	Year	Role	Song	Tempo	Range-Bottom	Range-Top	Category	Char Type
Dreamgirls	1981	James Thunder Early +	I Want You Baby	Ballad	Eb3	Db4	Lead	Character Male
Dreamgirls	1981	James Thunder Early +	I Meant You No Harm	Ballad	Bb2	G4	Lead	Character Male
Merrily We Roll Along 1994	1981	Charley Kringas	Franklin Shepard, Inc.	Uptempo	C3	G4	Lead	Character Male
Merrily We Roll Along 1994	1981	Charley Kringas	Old Friends II*	Moderate Tempo	Bb2	D4	Lead	Character Male
Merrily We Roll Along 1994	1981	Charley Kringas	Good Thing Going	Ballad	C3	F4	Lead	Character Male
Joseph...Dream Coat	1982	Pharaoh (Elvis)	Song of the King	Uptempo	B2	G#4	Supporting	Character Male
Joseph...Dream Coat	1982	Pharaoh (Elvis)	Song of the King Reprise	Uptempo	B2	G#4	Supporting	Character Male
Little Shop of Horrors	1982	Seymour Krelborn	Grow For Me	Moderate Tempo	Bb2	F4	Lead	Character Male
Little Shop of Horrors	1982	Seymour Krelborn	Now*	Uptempo	B2	G4	Lead	Character Male
Singin' In The Rain	1983	Cosmo Brown	Make "Em Laugh	Uptempo	C3	G4	Lead	Character Male
Singin' In The Rain	1983	Cosmo Brown	Broadway Melody* (ms 1-30)	Uptempo	Bb3	F4	Lead	Character Male
Sunday...Park With Geroge	1984	Franz	The Day Off (Part 5)*	Moderate Tempo	C3	Eb4	Supporting	Character Male
Mystery Of Edwin Drood, Th	1985	Bazzard	Never The Luck*	Moderate Tempo	C3	G4	Lead	Character Male
Mystery Of Edwin Drood, Th	1985	Bazzard	Bazzard's Confession	Uptempo	A2	G4	Lead	Character Male
Rags	1986	Man	I Remember	Moderate Tempo	E3	G4	Featured Ensembl	Character Male
Rags	1986	Nathan Hershkowitz	Uptown*	Moderate Tempo	E3	G4	Lead	Character Male
Rags	1986	Tim Sullivan	What's Wrong With That*	Uptempo	A2	G4	Supporting	Character Male
Rags	1986	Nathan Hershkowitz	What's Wrong With That*	Uptempo	A2	G4	Lead	Character Male
Ain't Misbehavin'	1988	Man Two +	Honeysuckle Rose*	Ballad	D3	Ab4	Lead	Character Male
Ain't Misbehavin'	1988	Man Two +	Lounging At The Waldorf	Ballad	B3	E4	Lead	Character Male
Ain't Misbehavin'	1988	Man Two +	Your Feets Too Big	Ballad	G2	Eb4	Lead	Character Male
Children of Eden	1991	Adam	A World Without You *	Moderate Tempo	Db3	Ab4	Lead	Character Male
Children of Eden	1991	Adam	Grateful Children *	Moderate Tempo	B2	D#3	Lead	Character Male
Secret Garden, The	1991	Archibald Craven	Race You To The Top Of The Morning	Uptempo	Eb3	Ab4	Lead	Character Male
Secret Garden, The	1991	Archibald Craven	Where In The World	Uptempo	F3	Fb4	Lead	Character Male
Assassins	1992	The Balladeer	The Ballad Of Booth Part 1	Uptempo	C#3	G#4	Lead	Character Male
Assassins	1992	The Balladeer	The Ballad Of Booth Part 3	Uptempo	C#3	Ab4	Lead	Character Male
Assassins	1992	The Balladeer	The Ballad of Czolgosz (Part 1 & 2)	Uptempo	D3	G4	Lead	Character Male
Assassins	1992	The Balladeer	The Ballad of Guiteau*	Uptempo	C3	G4	Lead	Character Male
Assassins	1992	The Balladeer	Another National Anthem*	Moderate Tempo	D3	F#4	Lead	Character Male

Tenor

* = Music Edit Required
+ = Ethnic Specific

Show	Year	Role	Song	Tempo	Range-Bottom	Range-Top	Category	Char Type
Blood Brothers	1993	Narrator	Shoes Upon The Table	Uptempo	G2	G3	Lead	Character Male
Blood Brothers	1993	Narrator	Shoes Upon The Table Reprise	Uptempo	G3	Bb4	Lead	Character Male
Blood Brothers	1993	Narrator	Marilyn Monroe Reprise 1	Moderate Tempo	A3	B4	Lead	Character Male
Blood Brothers	1993	Narrator	Madman	Uptempo	F2	C4	Lead	Character Male
Kiss Of The Spider Woman	1993	Molina	Her Name Is Aurora*	Moderate Tempo	C3	C4	Lead	Character Male
Kiss Of The Spider Woman	1993	Molina	Bluebloods*	Uptempo	B2	C#4	Lead	Character Male
Kiss Of The Spider Woman	1993	Molina	Dressing Them Up	Uptempo	C3	F4	Lead	Character Male
Kiss Of The Spider Woman	1993	Molina	Dear One*	Ballad	C3	Eb4	Lead	Character Male
Kiss Of The Spider Woman	1993	Molina	She's A Woman	Ballad	C3	E4	Lead	Character Male
Kiss Of The Spider Woman	1993	Molina	Mama, It's Me	Moderate Tempo	C3	E4	Lead	Character Male
Kiss Of The Spider Woman	1993	Molina	Only In the Movies	Uptempo	B2	F4	Lead	Character Male
Beauty and the Beast	1994	Lefou	Gaston	Uptempo	B2	E4	Supporting	Character Male
Passion	1994	Lt. Torasso	Christmas Music	Moderate Tempo	Eb3	F4	Lead	Character Male
Rent	1996	Mark Cohen	Halloween	Moderate Tempo	Eb3	Eb4	Lead	Character Male
Rent	1996	Mark Cohen	You Are What You Own*	Uptempo	D3	E4	Lead	Character Male
A Christmas Carol	1997	Bob Cratchit	Christmas Together	Uptempo	D3	D4	Supporting	Character Male
A Christmas Carol	1997	Ghost...Past	The Lights of Long Ago	Uptempo	E3	E4	Supporting	Character Male
A Christmas Carol	1997	Ghost...Past	Abundance and Charity	Uptempo	A#2	F#4	Supporting	Character Male
A Christmas Carol	1997	Jacob Marley	Link By Link	Uptempo	D3	Ab4	Lead	Character Male
A Christmas Carol	1997	Scrooge-Adult	Yesterday, Tomorrow and Today	Ballad	D3	E4	Lead	Character Male
A Christmas Carol	1997	Scrooge-Adult	Nothing To Do With Me	Uptempo	D3	Eb4	Lead	Character Male
A Christmas Carol	1997	Scrooge-Adult	Will Tiny Tim Live	Ballad	D3	E4	Lead	Character Male
A Christmas Carol	1997	Scrooge-Adult	Christmas Day (Final Scene P2)	Uptempo	C3	E4	Lead	Character Male
Cabaret	1997	Master of Cereemonies	I Don't Care Much	Ballad	D3	F4	Lead	Character Male
Ragtime	1998	Henry Ford	Henry Ford*	Uptempo	D3	G4	Lead	Character Male
Ragtime	1998	Harry Houdini	Harry Houdini Master Escapist (Part	Moderate Tempo	Db3	Gb4	Lead	Character Male
Ragtime	1998	Harry Houdini	Atlantic City (Part 3)*	Uptempo	E3	G4	Lead	Character Male
Full Monty, The	2000	Malcolm MacGregor	You Walk With With Me *	Ballad	F#3	A4	Lead	Character Male
Spitfire Grill	2001	Joe Sutter	This Wide Woods Part 2	Uptempo	E3	F4	Lead	Character Male
Spitfire Grill	2001	Joe Sutter	Forest For The Trees	Uptempo	D3	A4	Lead	Character Male
Avenue Q	2003	Nicky	If You Were Gay	Uptempo	C3	A4	Lead	Character Male

Tenor

* = Music Edit Required
+ = Ethnic Specific

Show	Year	Role	Song	Tempo	Range-Bottom	Range-Top	Category	Char Type
Avenue Q	2003	Rod	My Girlfriend Who Lives In Canada	Uptempo	B2	G4	Lead	Character Male
Avenue Q	2003	Rod	Fantasies Come True	Ballad	A2	D4	Lead	Character Male
Fame	2003	Joe	I Can't Keep It Down *	Uptempo	C3	B♭4	Supporting	Character Male
Wicked	2003	Father	No One Mourns The Wicked*	Moderate Tempo	D3	G4	Supporting	Character Male
Caroline, Or Change	2004	The Dryer +	The Dryer (ms 1-24)	Moderate Tempo	B♭2	C5	Supporting	Character Male
Caroline, Or Change	2004	The Moon +	Moon Change (ms 1-12)	Ballad	B♭2	G4	Supporting	Character Male
All Shook Up	2005	Dennis	It Hurts Me	Ballad	A2	B♭4	Supporting	Character Male
Chitty Chitty Bang Bang	2005	Baron Bomburst	Chu-Chi Face	Moderate Tempo	C3	G4	Supporting	Character Male
Dirty Rotten Scoundrels	2005	Freddy Benson	Great Big Stuff	Uptempo	D3	F#4	Lead	Character Male
Spamalot	2005	Patsy	Always Lok On The Bright Side of Li	Moderate Tempo	B2	F4	Supporting	Character Male
Spamalot	2005	Minstrel	Brave Sir Robin	Moderate Tempo	A3	D4	Supporting	Character Male
Spamalot	2005	Minstrel	Brave Sir Robin Reprise	Moderate Tempo	A3	D4	Supporting	Character Male
Drowsy Chaperon, The	2006	Gangster	Toledo Surprise *	Uptempo	C3	G♭4	Supporting	Character Male
Legally Blonde	2007	Emmett Forrest	Chip On My Shoulder*	Uptempo	C3	A4	Lead	Character Male
Legally Blonde	2007	Emmett Forrest	Legally Blonde (ms 101b-166)	Ballad	E3	G4	Lead	Character Male
The Little Mermaid	2007	Scuttle	Human Stuff*	Uptempo	B2	G4	Lead	Character Male
The Little Mermaid	2007	Sebastian	The World Above Reprise	Moderate Tempo	C3	E4	Lead	Character Male
The Little Mermaid	2007	Scuttle	Positoovity	Uptempo	G2	A4	Lead	Character Male
The Little Mermaid	2007	Sebastian	Kiss The Girl	Moderate Tempo	D3	F4	Lead	Character Male
The Little Mermaid	2007	Sebastian	Kiss The Girl*	Moderate Tempo	A2	C4	Lead	Character Male
In The Heights	2008	Piragua Guy+	Piragua	Uptempo	E3	A4	Supporting	Character Male
In The Heights	2008	Piragua Guy+	Piragua Reprise*	Uptempo	D3	A4	Supporting	Character Male
Next To Normal	2009	Dan	Who's Crazy*	Moderate Tempo	G3	F4	Lead	Character Male
Next To Normal	2009	Dan	He's Not Here	Ballad	E♭3	G4	Lead	Character Male
Next To Normal	2009	Dan	I Am The One*	Uptempo	E3	F#4	Lead	Character Male
Next To Normal	2009	Dan	I've Been	Uptempo	E3	G4	Lead	Character Male
Next To Normal	2009	Dan	A Light In The Dark*	Ballad	D3	E4	Lead	Character Male
Next To Normal	2009	Dr. Madden	Make Up Your Mind*	Moderate Tempo	A♭3	A♭4	Lead	Character Male
Next To Normal	2009	Dan	It's Gonna Be Good Reprise*	Uptempo	A2	F4	Lead	Character Male
Next To Normal	2009	Dan	A Promies*	Uptempo	C3	F4	Lead	Character Male
Next To Normal	2009	Dr. Madden	Make Up Your Mind Reprise	Moderate Tempo	A3	G4	Lead	Character Male

Tenor

Tenor

Tenor

* = Music Edit Required
+ = Ethnic Specific

Show	Year	Role	Song	Tempo	Range-Bottom	Range-Top	Category	Char Type
Next To Normal	2009	Dr. Madden	Open Your Eyes*	Moderate Tempo	F3	A4	Lead	Character Male
Kinky Boots	2013	Lola (Drag)	The Land of Lola	Uptempo	F#3	F#4	Lead	Character Male
Kinky Boots	2013	Lola (Drag)	The Sex Is In the Heel	Moderate Tempo	A3	B4	Lead	Character Male
Kinky Boots	2013	Lola (Drag)	Not My Father's Son*	Ballad	E3	A4	Lead	Character Male
Kinky Boots	2013	Lola (Drag)	What a Woman Wants	Moderate Tempo	E3	A4	Lead	Character Male
Kinky Boots	2013	Lola (Drag)	Hold Me In Your Heart	Ballad	E3	Bb4	Lead	Character Male
No, No Nanette	1925	Tom Trainor	I've Confessed To The Breeze*	Moderate Tempo	D3	F4	Lead	Ingenue Male
No, No Nanette	1925	Tom Trainor	No, No Nanette*	Uptempo	C3	Eb4	Lead	Ingenue Male
No, No Nanette	1925	Tom Trainor	Tea For Two*	Moderate Tempo	Eb3	F4	Lead	Ingenue Male
No, No Nanette	1925	Tom Trainor	Waiting For You*	Moderate Tempo	C3	Eb4	Lead	Ingenue Male
Crazy For You (1992)	1937	Bobby Child	I Can't Be Bothered Now	Uptempo	D3	F4	Lead	Ingenue Male
Crazy For You (1992)	1937	Bobby Child	Things Are Looking Up	Uptempo	C3	D4	Lead	Ingenue Male
Crazy For You (1992)	1937	Bobby Child	Shall We Dance	Uptempo	D3	Fb4	Lead	Ingenue Male
Crazy For You (1992)	1937	Bobby Child	They Can't Take That Away	Moderate Tempo	Bb2	Eb4	Lead	Ingenue Male
Crazy For You (1992)	1937	Bobby Child	Nice Work If You Can Get It	Uptempo	D3	C4	Lead	Ingenue Male
Cinderella (2013)	1940	Topher	Loneliness Of Evening*	Ballad	Eb3	A4	Lead	Ingenue Male
Brigadoon	1947	Charlie Dalrymple	I'll Go Home With Bonnie Jean	Uptempo	Bb2	G4	Supporting	Ingenue Male
Brigadoon	1947	Charlie Dalrymple	Come To Me Bend To me	Ballad	D3	G4	Supporting	Ingenue Male
Brigadoon	1947	Charlie Dalrymple	Go Home Reprise	Uptempo	G3	G4	Supporting	Ingenue Male
South Pacific	1949	Lt. Jospeh Cable	Younger Than Springtime*	Ballad	E3	G4	Lead	Ingenue Male
South Pacific	1949	Lt. Jospeh Cable	You've Got To Be Carefully Taught	Uptempo	E3	G4	Lead	Ingenue Male
King and I, The	1951	Lun Tha+	We Kiss In The Shadow	Ballad	D3	E4	Lead	Ingenue Male
King and I, The	1951	Lun Tha+	I Have Dreamed	Ballad	C3	G4	Lead	Ingenue Male
Damn Yankees	1955	Joe Hardy	A Man Doesn't Know	Ballad	C3	Gb4	Lead	Ingenue Male
Damn Yankees	1955	Joe Hardy	Near To You	Ballad	C3	C4	Lead	Ingenue Male
Damn Yankees	1955	Joe Hardy	Goodbye Old Girl	Ballad	Eb3	F#4	Lead	Ingenue Male
Candide	1956	Candide	Life Is Happiness Indeed*	Moderate Tempo	F3	G4	Lead	Ingenue Male
Candide	1956	Candide	It Must Be So	Ballad	D3	E4	Lead	Ingenue Male
Candide	1956	Candide	Candide's Lament	Ballad	C3	F4	Lead	Ingenue Male
Candide	1956	Candide	It Must Be Me	Ballad	D3	E4	Lead	Ingenue Male

205

* = Music Edit Required
+ = Ethnic Specific

Show	Year	Role	Song	Tempo	Range-Bottom	Range-Top	Category	Char Type
Candide	1956	Candide	Nothing More Than This	Moderate Tempo	D3	F#4	Lead	Ingenue Male
Candide	1956	Candide	Universal Good Reprise*	Ballad	D♭3	D♭4	Lead	Ingenue Male
My Fair Lady	1956	Freddy Eynsford Hill	On The Street Where You Live	Moderate Tempo	C3	F4	Lead	Ingenue Male
My Fair Lady	1956	Freddy Eynsford Hill	On The Street Where You Live Repri	Moderate Tempo	C3	E4	Lead	Ingenue Male
Cinderella (2013)	1957	Topher	Ten Minutes Ago*	Moderate Tempo	C3	D4	Lead	Ingenue Male
Cinderella (2013)	1957	Topher	Do I Love You!...*	Ballad	A3	E♭4	Lead	Ingenue Male
Cinderella (2013)	1957	Topher	Ten Minutes Ago Reprise	Moderate Tempo	C3	D4	Lead	Ingenue Male
West Side Story	1957	Tony	Something's Coming	Uptempo	F#3	B♭4	Lead	Ingenue Male
West Side Story	1957	Tony	Maria	Ballad	B2	B♭4	Lead	Ingenue Male
Flower Drum Song 2002	1958	Wang Ta+	You Are Beautiful	Ballad	E♭3	G4	Lead	Ingenue Male
Flower Drum Song 2002	1958	Wang Ta+	You Are Beautiful Reprise*	Ballad	F3	G4	Lead	Ingenue Male
Flower Drum Song 2002	1958	Wang Ta+	Sunday	Moderate Tempo	C#4	E4	Lead	Ingenue Male
Flower Drum Song 2002	1958	Wang Ta+	Like A God	Uptempo	C#3	G#4	Lead	Ingenue Male
Flower Drum Song 2002	1958	Wang Ta+	Like A God	Moderate Tempo	B2	G4	Lead	Ingenue Male
Gypsy	1959	Tulsa	All I Need Is The Girl	Uptempo	E3	G4	Lead	Ingenue Male
Fantasticks, The	1960	Matt	Metaphor *	Uptempo	C♭3	E♭4	Lead	Ingenue Male
Fantasticks, The	1960	Matt	I Can See It *	Uptempo	B2	E4	Lead	Ingenue Male
Fantasticks, The	1960	Matt	They Were You *	Ballad	B2	D4	Lead	Ingenue Male
Fantasticks, The	1960	Matt	Metaphor Reprise *	Uptempo	B2	F#4	Lead	Ingenue Male
A Funny Thing...Forum	1962	Hero	Love I Hear	Uptempo	B2	E4	Lead	Ingenue Male
A Funny Thing...Forum	1962	Hero	Lovely*	Moderate Tempo	D3	E4	Lead	Ingenue Male
Cinderella (2013)	1962	Topher	The Sweetest Sounds*	Moderate Tempo	E3	E4	Lead	Ingenue Male
Cinderella (2013)	1962	Topher	The Sweetest Sounds Reprise	Moderate Tempo	A2	F♭4	Lead	Ingenue Male
110 In The Shade	1963	Jimmy Curry	Lizzie's Comin' Home *	Uptempo	B2	E4	Supporting	Ingenue Male
Cabaret	1966	Nazi Youth	Tomorrow Belongs to Me	Ballad	F3	F#4	Feat Ens	Ingenue Male
Pippin	1972	Pippin	Corner Of The Sky	Uptempo	E3	C5	Lead	Ingenue Male
Pippin	1972	Pippin	War Is A Science*	Uptempo	B♭2	G4	Lead	Ingenue Male
Pippin	1972	Pippin	Corner Of The Sky Reprise	Moderate Tempo	D3	F4	Lead	Ingenue Male
Pippin	1972	Pippin	With You	Ballad	C3	A♭4	Lead	Ingenue Male
Pippin	1972	Pippin	Morning Glow (C Major)	Moderate Tempo	C3	F#4	Lead	Ingenue Male

* = Music Edit Required
+ = Ethnic Specific

Show	Year	Role	Song	Tempo	Range-Bottom	Range-Top	Category	Char Type
Pippin	1972	Pippin	Morning Glow (Db Major)	Moderate Tempo	Db3	G4	Lead	Ingenue Male
Pippin	1972	Pippin	Extraordinary	Uptempo	C3	G4	Lead	Ingenue Male
Pippin	1972	Pippin	Prayer For A Duck	Uptempo	D3	F#4	Lead	Ingenue Male
Pippin	1972	Pippin	Corner Of the Sky Last Reprise	Moderate Tempo	D#3	F#4	Lead	Ingenue Male
Pippin	1972	Pippin	Love Song*	Ballad	B2	G#4	Lead	Ingenue Male
Pippin	1972	Pippin	Think About The Sun*	Uptempo	C3	G4	Lead	Ingenue Male
A Little Night Music	1973	Erik Egerman	Later	Uptempo	C3	B4	Lead	Ingenue Male
A Chorus Line	1975	Mike	I Can Do That	Uptempo	G4	Ab4	Lead	Ingenue Male
Sweeney Todd	1979	Anthony Hope	Ah, Miss (I & III)	Uptempo	C3	F4	Lead	Ingenue Male
Sweeney Todd	1979	Anthony Hope	Johanna	Ballad	C3	Eb4	Lead	Ingenue Male
Cats	1981	Skimbleshanks	Skimbleshanks	Uptempo	A2	F4	Supporting	Ingenue Male
Joseph...Dream Coat	1982	Joseph	Any Dream Will Do	Ballad	C4	F4	Lead	Ingenue Male
Joseph...Dream Coat	1982	Joseph	Close Every Door	Ballad	C3	A4	Lead	Ingenue Male
Joseph...Dream Coat	1982	Joseph	Pharaoh's Dream Explained	Uptempo	B2	E4	Lead	Ingenue Male
Joseph...Dream Coat	1982	Joseph	Any Dream Will Do Reprise	Ballad	D3	F4	Lead	Ingenue Male
Joseph...Dream Coat	1982	Joseph	Any Dream Will Do (II)	Ballad	C3	F4	Lead	Ingenue Male
Seven Brides/Seven Brothe	1982	Gideon	Love Never Goes Away*	Ballad	D3	G4	Lead	Ingenue Male
LA Cage Aux Folles	1983	Jean-Michel	With Anne On My Arm	Moderate Tempo	A#2	G4	Lead	Ingenue Male
Big River	1985	Tom Sawyer	Hand For The Hog	Uptempo	C3	F4	Supporting	Ingenue Male
Cinderella (2013)	1985	Topher	Me, Who Am I*	Moderate Tempo	B2	G4	Lead	Ingenue Male
Les Miserables	1987	Male Student	Drink With Me*	Ballad	D3	Eb4	Lead	Ingenue Male
Les Miserables	1987	Marius	Empty Chairs, Empty Tables (Bb Minor)	Ballad	Bb2	Ab4	Lead	Ingenue Male
Les Miserables	1987	Marius	Empty Chairs, Empty Tables (A Minc	Ballad	A2	G4	Lead	Ingenue Male
Closer Than Ever	1989	Man One	She Loves Me Not *	Ballad	Bb2	A4	Lead	Ingenue Male
Closer Than Ever	1989	Man One	What Am I Doin'	Uptempo	C3	A4	Lead	Ingenue Male
Closer Than Ever	1989	Man One	One Of The Good Guys	Tenor	C3	F4	Lead	Ingenue Male
Closer Than Ever	1989	Man One	Another Wedding Song *	Ballad	B2	C4	Lead	Ingenue Male
Closer Than Ever	1989	Man One	Father of Fathers *	Ballad	D3	G4	Lead	Ingenue Male
Children of Eden	1991	Abel	Lost in The Wilderness Reprise *	Moderate Tempo	G3	G4	Supporting	Ingenue Male
Crazy For You (1992)	1992	Bobby Child	Krazy For You	Uptempo	Eb3	Eb4	Lead	Ingenue Male
Blood Brothers	1993	Eddie	I'm Not Saying A Word	Moderate Tempo	E2	A3	Lead	Ingenue Male

Tenor

207

* = Music Edit Required
+ = Ethnic Specific

Show	Year	Role	Song	Tempo	Range-Bottom	Range-Top	Category	Char Type
Lion King, The	1997	Simba	Endless Night*	Ballad	E4	A4	Lead	Ingenue Male
Ragtime	1998	Younger Brother	New Music*	Ballad	Bb2	D4	Lead	Ingenue Male
Ragtime	1998	Younger Brother	The Night That Goldman Spoke...(P	Uptempo	B2	F#4	Lead	Ingenue Male
Aida	2000	Mereb +	How I Know You*	Ballad	G2	A4	Supporting	Ingenue Male
Aida	2000	Mereb +	How I Know You Reprise	Ballad	F3	G4	Supporting	Ingenue Male
Jane Eyre	2000	St. John Rivers	The Voice Across the Moors	Moderate Tempo	C3	G4	Supporting	Ingenue Male
Mamma Mia!	2001	Sky	Lay All Your Love On Me*	Moderate Tempo	G3	Ab4	Lead	Ingenue Male
Hairspray	2002	Link Larkin	It Takes Two	Ballad	E3	F#4	Lead	Ingenue Male
Hairspray	2002	Link Larkin	Without Love*	Moderate Tempo	C3	A4	Lead	Ingenue Male
Hairspray	2002	Seaweed Stubs+	Run And Tell That*	Uptempo	F3	B4	Lead	Ingenue Male
Hairspray	2002	Seaweed Stubs+	Without Love*	Moderate Tempo	G3	Ab4	Lead	Ingenue Male
Last Five Years, The	2002	Jamie Wellerstein	Shiksa Goddess	Uptempo	A2	A4	Lead	Ingenue Male
Last Five Years, The	2002	Jamie Wellerstein	Moving Too Fast	Uptempo	C3	Bb4	Lead	Ingenue Male
Last Five Years, The	2002	Jamie Wellerstein	The Schmuel Song	Uptempo	C#3	Ab4	Lead	Ingenue Male
Last Five Years, The	2002	Jamie Wellerstein	The Next Ten Minutes	Ballad	C#3	G#4	Lead	Ingenue Male
Last Five Years, The	2002	Jamie Wellerstein	If I Didn't Believe In You	Ballad	Bb2	G4	Lead	Ingenue Male
Last Five Years, The	2002	Jamie Wellerstein	Nobody Needs To Know	Ballad	C3	Ab4	Lead	Ingenue Male
Last Five Years, The	2002	Jamie Wellerstein	I Could Never Rescue You	Ballad	C3	G4	Lead	Ingenue Male
Last Five Years, The	2002	Jamie Wellerstein	A Miracle Would Happen	Uptempo	A2	A4	Lead	Ingenue Male
Thoroughly Modern Millie	2002	Jimmy Smith	What Do I Need With Love	Uptempo	D3	G4	Lead	Ingenue Male
Thoroughly Modern Millie	2002	Jimmy Smith	I Turned The Corner*	Moderate Tempo	C#3	Ab4	Lead	Ingenue Male
Fame	2003	Nick	I Want To Make Magic	Moderate Tempo	C3	G4	Lead	Ingenue Male
Fame	2003	Nick	Let's Play A Love Scene Reprise *	Ballad	Db3	G4	Lead	Ingenue Male
25th Annual...Spelling Bee	2005	Chip Tolentino	Chip's Lament/My Unfortunate Erec	Uptempo	C3	Ab4	Lead	Ingenue Male
Light In The Piazza, The	2005	Fabrizio Naccarelli	Il Mondo Era Vuoto	Moderate Tempo	Bb2	Ab4	Lead	Ingenue Male
Light In The Piazza, The	2005	Fabrizio Naccarelli	Passegiata*	Moderate Tempo	B3	G#4	Lead	Ingenue Male
Light In The Piazza, The	2005	Fabrizio Naccarelli	Love To Me	Moderate Tempo	F4	F#5	Lead	Ingenue Male
Little Women	2005	Laurie Laurence	Take a Chance On Me	Uptempo	B3	Bb4	Lead	Ingenue Male
Drowsy Chaperon, The	2006	Robert Martin	Accident Waiting To Happen *	Moderate Tempo	Eb3	A4	Lead	Ingenue Male

* = Music Edit Required
+ = Ethnic Specific

Show	Year	Role	Song	Tempo	Range-Bottom	Range-Top	Category	Char Type
Drowsy Chaperon, The	2006	Robert Martin	Cold Feets *	Uptempo	C3	Ab4	Lead	Ingenue Male
Grey Gardens	2006	Joe Kennedy	Goin' Places*	Uptempo	C3	F#4	Supporting	Ingenue Male
High School Musical	2007	Troy Bolton	What I've Been Looking For Reprise	Ballad	G3	F#4	Lead	Ingenue Male
High School Musical	2007	Troy Bolton	Breaking Free*	Ballad	Bb2	Bb4	Lead	Ingenue Male
Legally Blonde	2007	Warner Huntington	Serious*	Uptempo	F3	G4	Lead	Ingenue Male
The Little Mermaid	2007	Prince Eric	Her Voice	Moderate Tempo	C3	G4	Lead	Ingenue Male
The Little Mermaid	2007	Flounder	She's In Love*	Uptempo	G2	A#4	Lead	Ingenue Male
The Little Mermaid	2007	Prince Eric	One Step Closer	Moderate Tempo	B3	F#5	Lead	Ingenue Male
Kinky Boots	2013	Charlie Price	Take What You Got*	Uptempo	F#3	F#4	Lead	Ingenue Male
Kinky Boots	2013	Charlie Price	Step One	Uptempo	Ab3	Ab4	Lead	Ingenue Male
Kinky Boots	2013	Charlie Price	Not My Father's Son*	Ballad	F#3	F#4	Lead	Ingenue Male
Kinky Boots	2013	Charlie Price	The Soul of a Man	Uptempo	C3	Bb4	Lead	Ingenue Male
Kinky Boots	2013	Charlie Price	Charlie's Soliloquy	Ballad	Eb3	Cb4	Lead	Ingenue Male
Kinky Boots	2013	Charlie Price	Charlie's Soliloquy Reprise	Ballad	F#3	C#4	Lead	Ingenue Male
Big	1996	Billy Kopecki	Talk To Her	Uptempo	F2	Bb3	Supporting	Juvenile Male
Big	1996	Billy Kopecki	It's Time	Uptempo	A2	C4	Supporting	Juvenile Male
Big	1996	Josh Baskin-Young	Talk To Her	Uptempo	F2	Bb3	Supporting	Juvenile Male
Big	1996	Josh Baskin-Young	Opening	Uptempo	A2	B3	Supporting	Juvenile Male
Big	1996	Josh Baskin-Young	I Want To Know	Ballad	C3	F4	Supporting	Juvenile Male
13 The Musical	2008	Archie (CM)	Get Me What I Need	Uptempo	C3	A4	Lead	Juvenile Male
13 The Musical	2008	Archie (CM)	Getting Ready*	Uptempo	Eb3	Ab4	Lead	Juvenile Male
13 The Musical	2008	Evan Goldman (CM)	Becoming A Man	Uptempo	D3	A4	Lead	Juvenile Male
13 The Musical	2008	Evan Goldman (CM)	Thirteen	Uptempo	Bb2	Bb3	Lead	Juvenile Male
13 The Musical	2008	Evan Goldman (CM)	All Hail The Brain	Uptempo	E3	G4	Lead	Juvenile Male
13 The Musical	2008	Evan Goldman (CM)	Terminal Illness	Uptempo	Eb3	Ab4	Lead	Juvenile Male
13 The Musical	2008	Evan Goldman (CM)	Tell Her*	Ballad	Bb2	G4	Lead	Juvenile Male
13 The Musical	2008	Evan Goldman (CM)	A Little More Homework*	Ballad	C3	F4	Lead	Juvenile Male
13 The Musical	2008	Evan Goldman (CM)	Getting Ready*	Uptempo	Db4	Bb4	Lead	Juvenile Male
13 The Musical	2008	Evan Goldman (CM)	Here I Come	Uptempo	Eb3	Bb4	Lead	Juvenile Male

* = Music Edit Required
+ = Ethnic Specific

Show	Year	Role	Song	Tempo	Range-Bottom	Range-Top	Category	Char Type
13 The Musical	2008	Evan Goldman (CM)	If That's What It Is*	Moderate Tempo	C3	A4	Lead	Juvenile Male
13 The Musical	2008	Evan Goldman (CM)	Becoming A Man Reprise	Ballad	E3	A4	Lead	Juvenile Male
High Society 1998	1929	Uncle Willie	She's Got That Thing*	Uptempo	G2	G4	Lead	Mature Male
High Society 1998	1930	Uncle Willie	I'm Getting Ready For You*	Uptempo	Bb2	E4	Lead	Mature Male
High Society 1998	1930	Uncle Willie	Say It With Gin	Uptempo	C3	C4	Lead	Mature Male
Candide	1956	Martin	Words, Words, Words	Moderate Tempo	A2	F4	Supporting	Mature Male
How To Succeed....	1961	JB Biggley	Grand Old Ivy*	Uptempo	C3	G4	Lead	Mature Male
How To Succeed....	1961	JB Biggley	Love From A Heart Of Gold*	Ballad	C#3	E4	Lead	Mature Male
How To Succeed....	1961	Twimble	Company Way*	Uptempo	D3	G4	Supporting	Mature Male
A Funny Thing...Forum	1962	Hysterium	I'm Calm	Uptempo	D3	F4	Lead	Mature Male
A Funny Thing...Forum	1962	Hysterium	Lovely Reprise*	Moderate Tempo	E3	F4	Lead	Mature Male
Follies	1971	Roscoe	Beautiful Girls	Moderate Tempo	D3	A4	Supporting	Mature Male
Cats	1981	Old Deuteronomy	Old Deuteronomy *	Ballad	B2	G4	Lead	Mature Male
Cats	1981	Old Deuteronomy	The Moments of Happiness	Ballad	B3	G5	Lead	Mature Male
Cats	1981	Old Deuteronomy	The Ad-Dressing of Cats	Moderate Tempo	Bb2	G4	Lead	Mature Male
Children of Eden	1991	Noah	Blind Obedience	Ballad	D3	A3	Lead	Paternal
Children of Eden	1991	Noah	Noah's Lullaby	Ballad	C3	D4	Lead	Paternal
Children of Eden	1991	Noah	The Hardest Part Of Love *	Uptempo	D3	G4	Lead	Paternal
Footloose	1998	Rev. Shaw Moore	Heaven Help Me	Uptempo	G2	E4	Lead	Paternal
Footloose	1998	Rev. Shaw Moore	I Confess	Moderate Tempo	B2	F4	Lead	Paternal
Footloose	1998	Rev. Shaw Moore	Can You Find It In Your Heart	Ballad	A2	C4	Lead	Paternal
Ragtime	1998	Tateh	Journey On*	Uptempo	Db3	Gb4	Lead	Paternal
Ragtime	1998	Tateh	Success (Part 1, 2 & 5)	Uptempo	D3	F#4	Lead	Paternal
Ragtime	1998	Tateh	Gliding (Part 1 & 2)	Moderate Tempo	A2	F#4	Lead	Paternal
Ragtime	1998	Tateh	Buffalo Nickel Photoplay Inc.	Uptempo	B2	F#4	Lead	Paternal
Hairspray	2002	Wilbur Turnblad	Timeless To Me	Moderate Tempo	A#2	A4	Lead	Paternal
Heathers	2014	Ram's Dad	My Dead Gay Son	Uptempo	C3	A4	Supporting	Paternal
Once Upon A Mattress	1959	Minstrel	Normandy*	Uptempo	D#3	B4	Lead	Romantic Antagonist Male
Unsinkable Molly Brown	1960	Prince Delong	Dolce Far Niente*	Ballad	C3	Eb4	Lead	Romantic Antagonist Male

Tenor

* = Music Edit Required
+ = Ethnic Specific

Show	Year	Role	Song	Tempo	Range-Bottom	Range-Top	Category	Char Type
Unsinkable Molly Brown	1960	Prince Delong	Dolce Far Niente Reprise	Ballad	D3	E♭4	Lead	Romantic Antagonist Male
110 In The Shade	1963	Bill Starbuck	The Rain Song *	Uptempo	C3	A♭4	Lead	Romantic Antagonist Male
110 In The Shade	1963	Bill Starbuck	Melisande	Uptempo	G2	G4	Lead	Romantic Antagonist Male
110 In The Shade	1963	Bill Starbuck	Evenin' Star	Ballad	B3	A♭4	Lead	Romantic Antagonist Male
110 In The Shade	1963	Bill Starbuck	Wonderful Music *	Uptempo	D♭3	F4	Lead	Romantic Antagonist Male
She Loves Me	1963	Steven Kodaly	Ilona*	Moderate Tempo	C3	E4	Lead	Romantic Antagonist Male
She Loves Me	1963	Steven Kodaly	Grand Knowing You	Uptempo	D3	A4	Lead	Romantic Antagonist Male
1776	1969	Edward Rutledge	Molasses To Rum	Moderate Tempo	E3	A4	Lead	Romantic Antagonist Male
Grease	1971	Danny Zuko	Alone at a Drive-in Movie	Moderate Tempo	D3	D♭5	Lead	Romantic Antagonist Male
Pippin	1972	Leading Player	Magic To Do*	Uptempo	E3	A4	Lead	Romantic Antagonist Male
Pippin	1972	Leading Player	Glory Part I & III*	Moderate Tempo	E3	G#4	Lead	Romantic Antagonist Male
Pippin	1972	Leading Player	Right On Track*	Moderate Tempo	E♭3	A♭4	Lead	Romantic Antagonist Male
Pippin	1972	Leading Player	Think About The Sun*	Uptempo	G3	F4	Lead	Romantic Antagonist Male
Wiz, The	1974	The Wiz	So You Wanted To Meet The Wizard	Uptempo	E3	G4	Lead	Romantic Antagonist Male
Wiz, The	1974	The Wiz	Y'all Got It	Uptempo	G3	A4	Lead	Romantic Antagonist Male
Wiz, The	1974	The Wiz	Believe In Yourself (F Major)	Moderate Tempo	C4	G5	Lead	Romantic Antagonist Male
Wiz, The	1974	The Wiz	Believe In Yourself (B♭ Major)	Moderate Tempo	F3	D5	Lead	Romantic Antagonist Male
Pacific Overtures	1976	Madam+	Welcome to Kanagawa*	Uptempo	C3	E4	Lead	Romantic Antagonist Male
Evita	1978	Che Guevara	Peron's Latest Flame	Uptempo	F2	F4	Lead	Romantic Antagonist Male
Merrily We Roll Along 1994	1981	Franklin Shepard	Old Friends II*	Moderate Tempo	B♭2	D4	Lead	Romantic Antagonist Male
Merrily We Roll Along 1994	1981	Franklin Shepard	Our Time Part 1 & 2*	Moderate Tempo	D♭3	B♭4	Lead	Romantic Antagonist Male
Nine	1982	Guido Contini	Amour	Uptempo	A2	B♭4	Lead	Romantic Antagonist Male
Nine	1982	Guido Contini	Guido's Song*	Uptempo	G#2	F#4	Lead	Romantic Antagonist Male
Nine	1982	Guido Contini	Only With You	Moderate Tempo	G#2	E4	Lead	Romantic Antagonist Male
Nine	1982	Guido Contini	Script	Uptempo	C3	F4	Lead	Romantic Antagonist Male
Nine	1982	Guido Contini	The Bells Of St. Sebastian*	Moderate Tempo	D4	G4	Lead	Romantic Antagonist Male
Nine	1982	Guido Contini	The Grand Canal*	Moderate Tempo	D#3	G4	Lead	Romantic Antagonist Male
Nine	1982	Guido Contini	I Can't Make This Movie	Moderate Tempo	G3	G4	Lead	Romantic Antagonist Male
Nine	1982	Guido Contini	Long Ago Reprise	Ballad	B♭2	B♭3	Lead	Romantic Antagonist Male
Nine	1982	Guido Contini	Nine Reprise	Ballad	B♭2	G4	Lead	Romantic Antagonist Male

* = Music Edit Required
+ = Ethnic Specific

Show	Year	Role	Song	Tempo	Range-Bottom	Range-Top	Category	Char Type
Sunday...Park With Geroge	1984	George	Color And Light (Part 1)	Uptempo	Bb2	Eb4	Lead	Romantic Antagonist Male
Sunday...Park With Geroge	1984	George	Color And Light (Part 3)*	Uptempo	D3	G4	Lead	Romantic Antagonist Male
Sunday...Park With Geroge	1984	George	The Day Off (Part 1)	Uptempo	A#2	G4	Lead	Romantic Antagonist Male
Sunday...Park With Geroge	1984	George	The Day Off (Part 2)	Moderate Tempo	D#3	D#4	Lead	Romantic Antagonist Male
Sunday...Park With Geroge	1984	George	Finishing The Hat	Moderate Tempo	Bb2	Ab5	Lead	Romantic Antagonist Male
Sunday...Park With Geroge	1984	George	We Do Not Belong Together*	Moderate Tempo	A2	E4	Lead	Romantic Antagonist Male
Sunday...Park With Geroge	1984	George	Beautiful*	Ballad	C#3	F#4	Lead	Romantic Antagonist Male
Sunday...Park With Geroge	1984	George	Putting It Together (Part 7 & 9)	Uptempo	D4	Gb4	Lead	Romantic Antagonist Male
Sunday...Park With Geroge	1984	George	Putting It Together (Part 16)*	Uptempo	Db3	Gb4	Lead	Romantic Antagonist Male
Sunday...Park With Geroge	1984	George	Lesson #8	Ballad	G#2	Eb4	Lead	Romantic Antagonist Male
Sunday...Park With Geroge	1984	George	Move On*	Ballad	D#3	G4	Lead	Romantic Antagonist Male
Les Miserables	1987	Jean Valjean	Soliloquy	Moderate Tempo	C3	B4	Lead	Romantic Antagonist Male
Les Miserables	1987	Jean Valjean	Who Am I	Moderate Tempo	B3	B4	Lead	Romantic Antagonist Male
Les Miserables	1987	Jean Valjean	Bring Him Home	Ballad	E3	A4	Lead	Romantic Antagonist Male
Romance/Romance	1987	Sam	There Are Things He Doesn't Say	Ballad	Ab2	G4	Lead	Romantic Antagonist Male
Romance/Romance	1987	Sam	Moonlight Passing Through A Windo	Ballad	D3	F4	Lead	Romantic Antagonist Male
Romance/Romance	1987	Sam	Romantic Notions*	Ballad	B3	E4	Lead	Romantic Antagonist Male
Romance/Romance	1987	Alfred Von Wilmers	It's Not Too Late*	Moderate Tempo	Bb2	F4	Lead	Romantic Antagonist Male
Romance/Romance	1987	Alfred Von Wilmers	A Performance*	Moderate Tempo	A2	F#4	Lead	Romantic Antagonist Male
Romance/Romance	1987	Alfred Von Wilmers	I'll Remember The Song*	Uptempo	B2	E4	Lead	Romantic Antagonist Male
Romance/Romance	1987	Alfred Von Wilmers	Happy, Happy, Happy	Ballad	Bb2	F#4	Lead	Romantic Antagonist Male
Romance/Romance	1987	Alfred Von Wilmers	Women Of Vienna	Moderate Tempo	C3	F#4	Lead	Romantic Antagonist Male
Romance/Romance	1987	Alfred Von Wilmers	A Rustic Country Inn*	Uptempo	C3	F4	Lead	Romantic Antagonist Male
Romance/Romance	1987	Sam	It's Not Too Late Reprise*	Moderate Tempo	Bb2	A4	Lead	Romantic Antagonist Male
Chess	1988	Freddie	Endgame*	Uptempo	C#3	G4	Lead	Romantic Antagonist Male
Chess	1988	Freddie	Florence Quits	Uptempo	B2	B4	Lead	Romantic Antagonist Male
Chess	1988	Freddie	One Night In Bangkok	Uptempo	F3	A4	Lead	Romantic Antagonist Male
Chess	1988	Freddie	Pity The Child	Uptempo	Bb2	Db5	Lead	Romantic Antagonist Male
Miss Saigon	1991	John Thomas	Bui-Doi	Moderate Tempo	Ab2	Bb4	Lead	Romantic Antagonist Male
Miss Saigon	1991	Thuy+	Kim's Nightmare Part I	Uptempo	C3	E4	Lead	Romantic Antagonist Male

* = Music Edit Required
+ = Ethnic Specific

Show	Year	Role	Song	Tempo	Range-Bottom	Range-Top	Category	Char Type
Assassins	1992	Charles Guiteau	The Ballad of Guiteau*	Uptempo	A2	Gb4	Lead	Romantic Antagonist Male
Kiss Of The Spider Woman	1993	Valentin	Dear One*	Ballad	Bb2	C4	Lead	Romantic Antagonist Male
Kiss Of The Spider Woman	1993	Valentin	Over The Wall 3 - Marta	Moderate Tempo	F3	A4	Lead	Romantic Antagonist Male
Kiss Of The Spider Woman	1993	Valentin	My First Woman*	Moderate Tempo	C3	G4	Lead	Romantic Antagonist Male
Kiss Of The Spider Woman	1993	Valentin	The Day After That*	Uptempo	D3	Gb4	Lead	Romantic Antagonist Male
Merrily We Roll Along 1994	1994	Franklin Shepard	Growing Up Part I	Moderate Tempo	D3	E4	Lead	Romantic Antagonist Male
Sunset Boulevard	1994	Joe Gillis	Prologue	Moderate Tempo	D3	G4	Lead	Romantic Antagonist Male
Sunset Boulevard	1994	Joe Gillis	Let Me Take You Back Six Months	Moderate Tempo	C3	Eb4	Lead	Romantic Antagonist Male
Sunset Boulevard	1994	Joe Gillis	I Started Work	Uptempo	C3	G4	Lead	Romantic Antagonist Male
Sunset Boulevard	1994	Joe Gillis	The Perfect Year*	Moderate Tempo	A2	D4	Lead	Romantic Antagonist Male
Sunset Boulevard	1994	Joe Gillis	I Had To Get Out	Uptempo	C3	Eb4	Lead	Romantic Antagonist Male
Sunset Boulevard	1994	Joe Gillis	Sunset Boulevard	Uptempo	C3	G4	Lead	Romantic Antagonist Male
Sunset Boulevard	1994	Joe Gillis	Girl Meets Boy Reprise*	Uptempo	D3	E4	Lead	Romantic Antagonist Male
Sunset Boulevard	1994	Joe Gillis	I Should Have Stayed There	Uptempo	A3	E4	Lead	Romantic Antagonist Male
Sunset Boulevard	1994	Joe Gillis	Too Much In Love To Care*	Moderate Tempo	F3	G4	Lead	Romantic Antagonist Male
Sunset Boulevard	1994	Joe Gillis	Sunset Blvd Reprise-What's Going O	Uptempo	C#3	Gb4	Lead	Romantic Antagonist Male
Sunset Boulevard	1994	Joe Gillis	It Took Her Three Days	Uptempo	A2	E4	Lead	Romantic Antagonist Male
Songs For A New World	1995	Man 1	On The Deck Of A Spanish Sailing S	Ballad	F3	Bb4	Lead	Romantic Antagonist Male
Songs For A New World	1995	Man 1	The River Won't Flow*	Uptempo	G3	C5	Lead	Romantic Antagonist Male
Songs For A New World	1995	Man 1	Steam Train*	Uptempo	F3	C5	Lead	Romantic Antagonist Male
Songs For A New World	1995	Man 1	King Of the World	Uptempo	E3	C5	Lead	Romantic Antagonist Male
Songs For A New World	1995	Man 1	Flying Home*	Ballad	D#3	F4	Lead	Romantic Antagonist Male
Songs For A New World	1995	Man 1	Hear My Song*	Moderate Tempo	D3	C4	Lead	Romantic Antagonist Male
Rent	1996	Roger Davis	Another Day*	Uptempo	F3	Gb4	Lead	Romantic Antagonist Male
Rent	1996	Roger Davis	Your Eyes*	Ballad	B2	G4	Lead	Romantic Antagonist Male
Jekyll and Hyde	1997	Dr. Henry Jekyll	Lost In The Darkness	Ballad	G2	E4	Lead	Romantic Antagonist Male
Jekyll and Hyde	1997	Dr. Henry Jekyll	This Is The Moment	Ballad	B2	G#4	Lead	Romantic Antagonist Male
Jekyll and Hyde	1997	Dr. Henry Jekyll	What Streak of Madness/Obsession	Ballad	C3	Eb4	Lead	Romantic Antagonist Male
Jekyll and Hyde	1997	Dr. Henry Jekyll	The Way Back/Angst 2	Uptempo	B2	G4	Lead	Romantic Antagonist Male
Jekyll and Hyde	1997	Dr. Henry Jekyll	Lost In The Darkness Reprise	Ball	G2	E4	Lead	Romantic Antagonist Male
Jekyll and Hyde	1997	Dr. Henry Jekyll	Confrontation*	Uptempo	B2	A4	Lead	Romantic Antagonist Male

Tenor

* = Music Edit Required
+ = Ethnic Specific

Show	Year	Role	Song	Range-Bottom	Range-Top	Tempo	Category	Char Type
Jekyll and Hyde	1997	Dr. Henry Jekyll	I Need To Know	B2	F#4	Ballad	Lead	Romantic Antagonist Male
Footloose	1998	Chuck Cranston	The Girl Gets Around	G#3	A4	Uptempo	Supporting	Romantic Antagonist Male
Parade	1998	John Conley+	That's What He Said	D3	G4	Uptempo	Lead	Romantic Antagonist Male
Parade	1998	John Conley+	Blues: Feel The Rain Fall*	D3	Bb4	Moderate Tempo	Lead	Romantic Antagonist Male
Marie Christine	1999	Dante Keyes	Nothing Beats Chicago	B2	E4	Uptempo	Lead	Romantic Antagonist Male
Marie Christine	1999	Dante Keyes	Ocean Is Different	C3	A4	Moderate Tempo	Lead	Romantic Antagonist Male
Marie Christine	1999	Dante Keyes	I Don't Hear The Ocean*	Eb3	F4	Moderate Tempo	Lead	Romantic Antagonist Male
Marie Christine	1999	Dante Keyes	We Gonna Go To Chicago	Db3	F4	Moderate Tempo	Lead	Romantic Antagonist Male
Marie Christine	1999	Dante Keyes	The Scorpion*	C3	Gb4	Uptempo	Lead	Romantic Antagonist Male
Marie Christine	1999	Paris L'Adrese+	No Turning Back	F3	Eb5	Ballad	Supporting	Romantic Antagonist Male
Marie Christine	1999	Dante Keyes	Your Name (Helena's Death)	G#2	A4	Ballad	Lead	Romantic Antagonist Male
Marie Christine	1999	Dante Keyes	The Adventure Never Ends	Bb2	Fb4	Uptempo	Lead	Romantic Antagonist Male
Marie Christine	1999	Dante Keyes	Danced With A Girl	B2	E4	Uptempo	Lead	Romantic Antagonist Male
Jane Eyre	2000	Edward Fairfax Rochester	As Good As You	A2	E4	Moderate Tempo	Lead	Romantic Antagonist Male
Jane Eyre	2000	Edward Fairfax Rochester	Secret Soul*	B2	B4	Uptempo	Lead	Romantic Antagonist Male
Jane Eyre	2000	Edward Fairfax Rochester	Sirens	Bb2	F4	Uptempo	Lead	Romantic Antagonist Male
Jane Eyre	2000	Edward Fairfax Rochester	The Gypsy (Drag)	D4	A5	Uptempo	Lead	Romantic Antagonist Male
Jane Eyre	2000	Edward Fairfax Rochester	Farewell Good Angel	G2	G4	Uptempo	Lead	Romantic Antagonist Male
Jane Eyre	2000	Edward Fairfax Rochester	Brave Enough for Love			Uptempo	Lead	Romantic Antagonist Male
Spitfire Grill	2001	Caleb Thorpe	Digging Stone	B2	G4	Moderate Tempo	Lead	Romantic Antagonist Male
Sweet Smell Of Success	2002	Sidney	I Can Get You In JJ	Db3	Ab4	Uptempo	Lead	Romantic Antagonist Male
Sweet Smell Of Success	2002	Sidney	At The Fountain	F3	A4	Moderate Tempo	Lead	Romantic Antagonist Male
Sweet Smell Of Success	2002	Sidney	Welcome To The Night Reprise*	Db4	F4	Uptempo	Lead	Romantic Antagonist Male
Sweet Smell Of Success	2002	Sidney	Break It Up*	E3	F4	Uptempo	Lead	Romantic Antagonist Male
Sweet Smell Of Success	2002	Sidney	I Could Get You In JJ Reprise	D3	G#4	Moderate Tempo	Lead	Romantic Antagonist Male
Sweet Smell Of Success	2002	Sidney	At The Fountain Reprise*	A2	F4	Moderate Tempo	Lead	Romantic Antagonist Male
Sweet Smell Of Success	2002	Sidney	Finale (Part 3)	E3	F4	Uptempo	Lead	Romantic Antagonist Male
All Shook Up	2005	Chad	Roustabout	E3	G4	Uptempo	Lead	Romantic Antagonist Male
All Shook Up	2005	Chad	C'mon	Db3	G#4	Uptempo	Lead	Romantic Antagonist Male
All Shook Up	2005	Chad	Follow That Dream*	A2	E4	Uptempo	Lead	Romantic Antagonist Male
All Shook Up	2005	Chad	Don't Be Cruel *	B2	F#4	Uptempo	Lead	Romantic Antagonist Male

Tenor

Tenor

* = Music Edit Required
+ = Ethnic Specific

Show	Year	Role	Song	Tempo	Range-Bottom	Range-Top	Category	Char Type
All Shook Up	2005	Chad	I Don't Want To	Ballad	D3	G4	Lead	Romantic Antagonist Male
All Shook Up	2005	Chad	Jailhouse Rock *	Uptempo	B2	C5	Lead	Romantic Antagonist Male
All Shook Up	2005	Chad	If I Can Dream *	Moderate Tempo	C3	G4	Lead	Romantic Antagonist Male
All Shook Up	2005	Chad	The Power of Love *	Moderate Tempo	E3	Eb4	Lead	Romantic Antagonist Male
Spring Awakening	2006	Melchoir	All That's Known	Moderate Tempo	D3	E4	Lead	Romantic Antagonist Male
Spring Awakening	2006	Melchoir	The Guilty One*	Moderate Tempo	G2	A3	Lead	Romantic Antagonist Male
Spring Awakening	2006	Melchoir	Left Behind	Ballad	E3	B4	Lead	Romantic Antagonist Male
Spring Awakening	2006	Melchoir	Totally Fucked*	Uptempo	Bb3	G4	Lead	Romantic Antagonist Male
Spring Awakening	2006	Melchoir	Those You've Known*	Moderate Tempo	D3	F4	Lead	Romantic Antagonist Male
Addams Family, The	2010	Gomez Addams +	Morticia	Moderate Tempo	A#2	Ab4	Lead	Romantic Antagonist Male
Addams Family, The	2010	Gomez Addams +	Not Today (US Tour)	Moderate Tempo	D3	G4	Lead	Romantic Antagonist Male
Addams Family, The	2010	Gomez Addams +	What If	Ballad	C3	C4	Lead	Romantic Antagonist Male
Heathers	2014	Jason Dean (JD)	Freeze Your Brain	Moderate Tempo	Bb3	G#4	Lead	Romantic Antagonist Male
Heathers	2014	Jason Dean (JD)	Our Love Is God	Ballad	F#3	F#4	Lead	Romantic Antagonist Male
Heathers	2014	Jason Dean (JD)	Meant To Be Yours	Uptempo	G3	Ab4	Lead	Romantic Antagonist Male
Heathers	2014	Jason Dean (JD)	I Am Damaged	Ballad	E3	F#4	Lead	Romantic Antagonist Male
Heathers	2014	Jason Dean (JD)	Seventeen*	Ballad	A3	B4	Lead	Romantic Antagonist Male
Heathers	2014	Ram Sweeney	Blue*	Uptempo	F#3	D5	Supporting	Romantic Antagonist Male
Show Boat	1927	Gaylord Ravenal	Where's The Mate For Me	Ballad	D3	F#4	Lead	Romantic Lead Male
Show Boat	1927	Gaylord Ravenal	Make Believe*	Ballad	C3	G4	Lead	Romantic Lead Male
Show Boat	1927	Gaylord Ravenal	You Are Love*	Ballad	D3	Bb4	Lead	Romantic Lead Male
Show Boat	1927	Gaylord Ravenal	You Are Love Reprise	Ballad	C3	Ab4	Lead	Romantic Lead Male
Show Boat	1927	Gaylord Ravenal	I Have The Room Above Her	Moderate Tempo	E3	Eb4	Lead	Romantic Lead Male
High Society 1998	1929	Dexter C.K. Haven	She's Got That Thing*	Uptempo	A2	G4	Lead	Romantic Lead Male
High Society 1998	1933	Dexter C.K. Haven	Once Upon A Time	Moderate Tempo	G2	E4	Lead	Romantic Lead Male
High Society 1998	1935	Dexter C.K. Haven	Just One Of Those Things	Uptempo	B2	E4	Lead	Romantic Lead Male
Porgy and Bess	1935	Sporting Life+	It Ain't Necessarily So*	Moderate Tempo	C4	A4	Lead	Romantic Lead Male
Porgy and Bess	1935	Sporting Life+	There's A Boat That's Leaving Soon.	Moderate Tempo	D3	Bb4	Lead	Romantic Lead Male
On The Town	1944	Gabey	Lonely Town	Ballad	C4	F5	Lead	Romantic Lead Male
On The Town	1944	Gabey	Lucky To Be Me	Uptempo	B2	A4	Lead	Romantic Lead Male

Tenor

* = Music Edit Required
+ = Ethnic Specific

Show	Year	Role	Song	Tempo	Range-Bottom	Range-Top	Category	Char Type
Pajama Game	1954	Sid Sorokin	A New Town Is A Blue Town	Ballad	Db3	G4	Lead	Romantic Lead Male
Pajama Game	1954	Sid Sorokin	Hey There*	Ballad	F3	Ab4	Lead	Romantic Lead Male
Pajama Game	1954	Sid Sorokin	Once-A-Year Day*	Uptempo	E3	F4	Lead	Romantic Lead Male
Pajama Game	1954	Sid Sorokin	Small Talk*	Uptempo	Db3	Gb4	Lead	Romantic Lead Male
Pajama Game	1954	Sid Sorokin	There Once Was A Man*	Uptempo	C#3	Gb4	Lead	Romantic Lead Male
Pajama Game	1954	Sid Sorokin	Hey There-Finale Act I	Ballad	F3	Gb4	Lead	Romantic Lead Male
High Society 1998	1955	Dexter C.K. Haven	Little One*	Uptempo	A2	D4	Lead	Romantic Lead Male
High Society 1998	1955	Dexter C.K. Haven	Little On Reprise	Uptempo	Bb2	Ab3	Lead	Romantic Lead Male
High Society 1998	1955	Dexter C.K. Haven	True Love*	Ballad	C3	F4	Lead	Romantic Lead Male
Candide	1956	Maximillion	Life Is Happiness Indeed*	Moderate Tempo	D3	F4	Lead	Romantic Lead Male
Candide	1956	Governor	My Love*	Moderate Tempo	C3	A4	Lead	Romantic Lead Male
Flower Drum Song 2002	1958	Chi-Yang Wang+	Chop Suey*	Moderate Tempo	B2	D#4	Lead	Romantic Lead Male
Once Upon A Mattress	1959	Minstrel	Many Moons Ago	Moderate Tempo	D3	G4	Lead	Romantic Lead Male
Unsinkable Molly Brown, Th	1960	Johnny Brown	Colorado My Home	Moderate Tempo	B2	F4	Lead	Romantic Lead Male
Unsinkable Molly Brown, Th	1960	Johnny Brown	I've A'ready Started In	Moderate Tempo	G3	E4	Lead	Romantic Lead Male
Unsinkable Molly Brown, Th	1960	Johnny Brown	I'll Never Say No	Ballad	Db3	F4	Lead	Romantic Lead Male
Unsinkable Molly Brown, Th	1960	Johnny Brown	If I Knew	Ballad	C3	F4	Lead	Romantic Lead Male
Unsinkable Molly Brown, Th	1960	Johnny Brown	Chick-A-Pen	Ballad	Db3	F4	Lead	Romantic Lead Male
Unsinkable Molly Brown, Th	1960	Johnny Brown	Leadville Johnny Brown Soliloquy	Moderate Tempo	C3	E4	Lead	Romantic Lead Male
Funny Girl	1964	Zeigfeld Tenor	His Love Makes Me Beautiful*	Moderate Tempo	E3	A4	Supporting	Romantic Lead Male
Cabaret	1966	Clifford Bradshaw	Perfectly Marvelous *	Uptempo	D3	E4	Lead	Romantic Lead Male
Cabaret	1966	Clifford Bradshaw	Why Should I Wake Up?	Moderate Tempo	B2	E4	Lead	Romantic Lead Male
Sweet Charity	1966	Vittorio Vidal	Too Many Tomorrows	Ballad	Bb2	G4	Lead	Romantic Lead Male
Company (Revival)	1970	Robert	Company	Uptempo	A2	Ab4	Lead	Romantic Lead Male
Company (Revival)	1970	Robert	Someone Is Waiting	Ballad	B2	E4	Lead	Romantic Lead Male
Company (Revival)	1970	Robert	Being Alive	Moderate Tempo	D3	F4	Lead	Romantic Lead Male
Grease	1971	Teen Angel	Beauty School Dropout	Moderate Tempo	F#3	F#5	Supporting	Romantic Lead Male
Jesus Christ Superstar	1971	Jesus of Nazareth	Poor Jerusalem	Ballad	A2	Ab4	Lead	Romantic Lead Male
Jesus Christ Superstar	1971	Jesus of Nazareth	Gethsemane	Ballad	Bb2	Ab4	Lead	Romantic Lead Male
Jesus Christ Superstar	1971	Jesus of Nazareth	The Last Supper	Ballad	F#2	C5	Lead	Romantic Lead Male

Tenor

Tenor

Show	Year	Role	Song	Tempo	Range-Bottom	Range-Top	Category	Char Type
Pacific Overtures	1976	Kayama+	Poems*	Moderate Tempo	Eb3	F4	Lead	Romantic Lead Male
Pacific Overtures	1976	Kayama+	A Bowler Hat	Moderate Tempo	G2	Eb4	Lead	Romantic Lead Male
Evita	1978	Magaldi	On This Nigh of a Thousand Stars	Ballad	Bb2	G4	Supporting	Romantic Lead Male
Cats	1981	Munkustrap	Old Deuteronomy *	Ballad	B2	G4	Lead	Romantic Lead Male
Singin' In The Rain	1983	Production Tenor	Beautiful Girl	Moderate Tempo	F3	Bb4	Supporting	Romantic Lead Male
Phantom Of The Opera	1986	Raoul, Vicomte de Chagny	Prologue	Ballad	C#3	E4	Lead	Romantic Lead Male
Phantom Of The Opera	1986	Raoul, Vicomte de Chagny	All I Ask Of You*	Ballad	Ab3	G4	Lead	Romantic Lead Male
Chess	1988	Anatoly	Where I Want To Be	Moderate Tempo	E3	G4	Lead	Romantic Lead Male
Chess	1988	Anatoly	Anthem	Moderate Tempo	C3	G4	Lead	Romantic Lead Male
Chess	1988	Anatoly	You and I	Ballad	G2	G4	Lead	Romantic Lead Male
Chess	1988	Anatoly	You and I Reprise	Ballad	G3	F5	Lead	Romantic Lead Male
Chess	1988	Anatoly	Endgame*	Uptempo	C3	A4	Lead	Romantic Lead Male
City of Angels	1989	Jimmy Powers	Ya Gotta Look Out For Yourself	Uptempo	C3	D4	Supporting	Romantic Lead Male
City of Angels	1989	Jimmy Powers	Stay Wth Me	Ballad	C3	G4	Supporting	Romantic Lead Male
Miss Saigon	1991	Chris Scott	Why God Why	Moderate Tempo	G3	G4	Lead	Romantic Lead Male
Miss Saigon	1991	Chris Scott	The Confrontation (ms44-79)	Uptempo	F3	B4	Lead	Romantic Lead Male
Miss Saigon	1991	Chris Scott	Sun And Moon*	Ballad	A2	F#4	Lead	Romantic Lead Male
Passion	1994	Giorgio Bachetti	Happiness (Part 2)*	Moderate Tempo	A2	C4	Lead	Romantic Lead Male
Passion	1994	Giorgio Bachetti	Is This What You Call Love?	Uptempo	A#2	F4	Lead	Romantic Lead Male
Passion	1994	Giorgio Bachetti	No One Has Ever Loved Me	Ballad	B2	D4	Lead	Romantic Lead Male
Rent	1996	Roger Davis	One Song Glory	Moderate Tempo	D3	Ab4	Lead	Romantic Lead Male
Rent	1996	Tom Collins	Sante Fe*	Moderate Tempo	F#2	F#4	Lead	Romantic Lead Male
Rent	1996	Tom Collins	I'll Cover You*	Moderate Tempo	C3	G4	Lead	Romantic Lead Male
Rent	1996	Tom Collins	I'll Cover You Reprise*	Ballad	F#2	A4	Lead	Romantic Lead Male
Jekyll and Hyde	1997	Dr. Henry Jekyll	Take Me As I Am	Ballad	Bb2	Eb4	Lead	Romantic Lead Male
Scarlet Pimpernel, The	1997	Percy Blakeney	You Are My Home*	Ballad	B2	G4	Lead	Romantic Lead Male
Scarlet Pimpernel, The	1997	Percy Blakeney	Prayer*	Ballad	Bb2	Ab4	Lead	Romantic Lead Male
Scarlet Pimpernel, The	1997	Percy Blakeney	Into The Fire*	Uptempo	D3	Ab4	Lead	Romantic Lead Male
Scarlet Pimpernel, The	1997	Percy Blakeney	When I Look At You Reprise	Ballad	Db3	F4	Lead	Romantic Lead Male
Scarlet Pimpernel, The	1997	Percy Blakeney	She Was There	Ballad	C#3	G#4	Lead	Romantic Lead Male
Scarlet Pimpernel, The	1997	Percy Blakeney	She Was There Tag	Moderate Tempo	A3	G4	Lead	Romantic Lead Male

Tenor

* = Music Edit Required
+ = Ethnic Specific

Show	Year	Role	Song	Tempo	Range-Bottom	Range-Top	Category	Char Type
Steel Pier	1997	Bill Kelly	Second Chance	Uptempo	B2	E4	Lead	Romantic Lead Male
Steel Pier	1997	Bill Kelly	The Last Girl*	Moderate Tempo	Bb2	G4	Lead	Romantic Lead Male
Steel Pier	1997	Bill Kelly	Leave The World Behind*	Moderate Tempo	D3	Eb4	Lead	Romantic Lead Male
Steel Pier	1997	Bill Kelly	First You Dream*	Uptempo	C3	F4	Lead	Romantic Lead Male
Parade	1998	Tom Watson	Watson's Lullaby	Ballad	A#2	A3	Lead	Romantic Lead Male
Parade	1998	Tom Watson	Where Will You Stand...Flood Comes	Uptempo	B2	Eb4	Lead	Romantic Lead Male
Aida	2000	Radames	Fortune Favors the Brave	Uptempo	Bb2	F4	Lead	Romantic Lead Male
Aida	2000	Radames	Elaborate Lies	Ballad	Bb2	Ab4	Lead	Romantic Lead Male
Aida	2000	Radames	Like Father Like Son*	Uptempo	G3	F4	Lead	Romantic Lead Male
Aida	2000	Radames	Radames' Letter	Ballad	C3	G4	Lead	Romantic Lead Male
Aida	2000	Radames	Fortune Favors the Brave Reprise	Uptempo	F3	G4	Lead	Romantic Lead Male
Full Monty, The	2000	Jerry Lukowski	Man *	Uptempo	E3	B4	Lead	Romantic Lead Male
Full Monty, The	2000	Jerry Lukowski	Michael Jordan's Ball *	Uptempo	G3	Bb4	Lead	Romantic Lead Male
Full Monty, The	2000	Jerry Lukowski	Breeze Off The River	Moderate Tempo	C3	B4	Lead	Romantic Lead Male
Full Monty, The	2000	Jerry Lukowski	Man *	Uptempo	E3	G4	Lead	Romantic Lead Male
Full Monty, The	2000	Jerry Lukowski	Man Reprise *	Uptempo	A3	A4	Lead	Romantic Lead Male
Jane Eyre	2000	Edward Fairfax Rochester	Brave Enough For Love*	Uptempo	Db3	Bb4	Lead	Romantic Lead Male
Mamma Mia!	2001	Sam Carmichael	Knowing Me, Knowing You*	Moderate Tempo	G2	F#4	Lead	Romantic Lead Male
Mamma Mia!	2001	Sam Carmichael	SOS*	Uptempo	A3	Ab4	Lead	Romantic Lead Male
Producers, The	2001	Roger De Bris	Keep It Gay*	Uptempo	G#2	G4	Lead	Romantic Lead Male
Producers, The	2001	Storm Trooper	Springtime For Hitler*	Moderate Tempo	D3	Ab4	Lead	Romantic Lead Male
Producers, The	2001	Roger De Bris	Springtime For Hitler*	Moderate Tempo	B2	G4	Lead	Romantic Lead Male
A Man Of No Importance	2002	Robby Fay	Streets Of Dublin	Uptempo	C4	E5	Lead	Romantic Lead Male
A Man Of No Importance	2002	Robby Fay	Love Who You Love Reprise	Ballad	E3	F4	Lead	Romantic Lead Male
A Man Of No Importance	2002	Robby Fay	Confession *	Moderate Tempo	Db3	F#4	Lead	Romantic Lead Male
Hairspray	2002	Corny Collins	Hairspray	Uptempo	E3	C5	Lead	Romantic Lead Male
Hairspray	2002	Corny Collins	Nicest Kids In Town*	Uptempo	D3	F#4	Lead	Romantic Lead Male
Hairspray	2002	Corny Collins	Nicest Kids In Town Reprise	Uptempo	B3	F#4	Lead	Romantic Lead Male
Sweet Smell Of Success	2002	Dallas	I Cannot Hear The City	Ballad	A3	G4	Lead	Romantic Lead Male
Sweet Smell Of Success	2002	Dallas	Don't Know Where You Leave Off*	Moderate Tempo	A2	G4	Lead	Romantic Lead Male

Tenor

Tenor

* = Music Edit Required
+ = Ethnic Specific

Show	Year	Role	Song	Tempo	Range-Bottom	Range-Top	Category	Char Type
Sweet Smell Of Success	2002	Dallas	One Track Mind	Uptempo	E3	A4	Lead	Romantic Lead Male
Sweet Smell Of Success	2002	Dallas	I Cannot Hear The City (Act 1 Finale	Ballad	A2	Bb4	Lead	Romantic Lead Male
Thoroughly Modern Millie	2002	Trevor Graydon	The Speed Test*	Uptempo	A2	F4	Lead	Romantic Lead Male
Wicked	2003	Fiyero	Dancing Through Life*	Uptempo	C3	A4	Lead	Romantic Lead Male
Wicked	2003	Fiyero	As Long As You Are Mine*	Moderate Tempo	G3	Bb4	Lead	Romantic Lead Male
Wicked	2003	Fiyero	Which Way Is The Party*	Uptempo	C#3	A4	Lead	Romantic Lead Male
Drowsy Chaperon, The	2006	Adolpho	I Am Adolpho *	Moderate Tempo	E2	A5	Lead	Romantic Lead Male
Cutains	2007	Aaron Fox	I Miss The Music	Ballad	C3	Gb4	Lead	Romantic Lead Male
Cutains	2007	Aaron Fox	Thinking of Him Reprise*	Ballad	A2	Gb4	Lead	Romantic Lead Male
In The Heights	2008	Benny+	Benny's Dispatch*	Uptempo	B3	F#4	Lead	Romantic Lead Male
In The Heights	2008	Benny+	When You're Home*	Uptempo	E3	G4	Lead	Romantic Lead Male
Addams Family, The	2010	Gomez Addams +	Live Before We Die	Moderate Tempo	Bb3	D4	Lead	Romantic Lead Male

Tenor

219

Baritone

* = Music Edit Required
+ = Ethnic Specific

Show	Year	Role	Song	Tempo	Range-Bottom	Range-Top	Category	Char Type
Porgy and Bess	1935	Crown+	What You Want Wid Bess*	Moderate Tempo	Eb3	Ab4	Lead	Antagonist Male
Porgy and Bess	1935	Crown+	A Red-Headed Woman	Moderate Tempo	Db3	F4	Lead	Antagonist Male
Babes In Arms (1998)	1937	Peter	Imagine Reprise #2*	Moderate Tempo	E3	F4	Lead	Antagonist Male
Wizard Of Oz 1997	1939	Cowardly Lion	If I Only Had The Nerve*	Moderate Tempo	Bb2	D4	Lead	Antagonist Male
Wizard Of Oz 2001	1939	Cowardly Lion	King Of The Forest*	Moderate Tempo	C3	F4	Lead	Antagonist Male
Oklahoma!	1943	Jud Fry	Lonley Room	Ballad	D3	C4	Lead	Antagonist Male
Oklahoma!	1943	Jud Fry	Poor Jud*	Ballad	D#3	C#4	Lead	Antagonist Male
Kiss Me Kate	1948	First Man	Brush Up Your Shakespeare*	Moderate Tempo	B2	D4	Lead	Antagonist Male
Kiss Me Kate	1948	Second Man	Brush Up Your Shakespeare*	Moderate Tempo	B2	D4	Lead	Antagonist Male
Wonderful Town	1953	Wreck	Pass The Football	Moderate Tempo	Ab2	E4	Lead	Antagonist Male
Peter Pan	1954	Captain Hook	Hook's Tango*	Moderate Tempo	A2	D4	Lead	Antagonist Male
Peter Pan	1954	Captain Hook	Tarantella*	Uptempo	D3	D4	Lead	Antagonist Male
Peter Pan	1954	Captain Hook	Captain Hook's Waltz*	Moderate Tempo	B2	G4	Lead	Antagonist Male
Damn Yankees	1955	Applegate	Those Were The Good Old Days	Uptempo	A#2	D#4	Lead	Antagonist Male
Damn Yankees	1955	Applegate	Good Old Day Reprise	Uptempo	A#2	E4	Lead	Antagonist Male
Camelot	1960	Mordred	The Seven Deadly Virtues	Uptempo	C3	D4	Lead	Antagonist Male
How To Succeed...	1961	Bud Frump	Been A Long Day Reprise*	Uptempo	Bb3	D4	Lead	Antagonist Male
A Funny Thing....Forum	1962	Marcus Lycus	The House Of Marcus Lycus	Moderate Tempo	B2	D#4	Lead	Antagonist Male
110 In The Shade	1963	Noah Curry	Lizzie's Comin' Home *	Uptempo	B2	E4	Supporting	Antagonist Male
Oliver!	1963	Bill Sykes	My Name	Moderate Tempo	C#3	C4	Lead	Antagonist Male
Oliver!	1963	Fagin	Reviewing the Situation Reprise	Ballad	C4	Eb5	Lead	Antagonist Male
Fiddler on The Roof	1964	Perchik	Now I Have Everything	Uptempo	B2	E4	Supporting	Antagonist Male
Apple Tree, The	1966	Balladeer	I'll Tell You A Truth	Ballad	E3	Eb4	Supporting	Antagonist Male
Apple Tree, The	1966	Balladeer	I'll Tell You A Truth Reprise	Ballad	C3	F#4	Lead	Antagonist Male
Apple Tree, The	1966	Snake	Forbidden Fruit	Moderate Tempo	Eb3	G4	Supporting	Antagonist Male
Hair	1968	Berger	Going Down	Uptempo	C3	F4	Lead	Antagonist Male
Hair	1968	Hud+	Colored Spade	Uptempo	B2	D4	Lead	Antagonist Male
Jesus Christ Superstar	1971	Pontius Pilate	Pilate's Dream	Ballad	A2	Bb3	Supporting	Antagonist Male
Jesus Christ Superstar	1971	Pontius Pilate	Pilate and Christ	Moderate Tempo	Bb3	G#4	Supporting	Antagonist Male
Pippin	1972	Charles	War Is A Science*	Uptempo	Bb2	E4	Lead	Antagonist Male

Baritone

221

Show	Year	Role	Song	Tempo	Range-Bottom	Range-Top	Category	Char Type
Pacific Overtures	1976	Thief+	Four Black Dragons*	Uptempo	B2	C#4	Supporting	Antagonist Male
On The Twentieth Century	1978	Max Jacobs	Max Jacobs	Uptempo	Bb2	F4	Lead	Antagonist Male
Sweeney Todd	1979	Sweeney Todd	The Barber And His Wife	Ballad	G#2	Db4	Lead	Antagonist Male
Sweeney Todd	1979	Sweeney Todd	Epiphany*	Uptempo	Bb2	F4	Lead	Antagonist Male
Sweeney Todd	1979	Sweeney Todd	My Friends*	Ballad	Bb2	Eb4	Lead	Antagonist Male
Sweeney Todd	1979	Sweeney Todd	Johanna II*	Moderate Tempo	A2	Eb4	Lead	Antagonist Male
Sweeney Todd	1979	Sweeney Todd	Finale Scene II	Uptempo	G2	C4	Lead	Antagonist Male
Little Shop of Horrors	1982	Orin Scrivello	Dentist!	Uptempo	A2	F4	Lead	Antagonist Male
Little Shop of Horrors	1982	Voice of Audrey II	Git It (Feed Me)*	Moderate Tempo	B2	G4	Lead	Antagonist Male
Little Shop of Horrors	1982	Voice of Audrey II	Suppertime*	Moderate Tempo	G2	F4	Lead	Antagonist Male
Sunday...Park With Geroge	1984	Boatman	The Day Off (Part 6)	Moderate Tempo	E2	C4	Supporting	Antagonist Male
Rags	1986	Saul	Easy For You	Uptempo	D3	D4	Lead	Antagonist Male
Les Miserables	1987	Thenardier	Master of the House*	Uptempo	C3	D4	Supporting	Antagonist Male
Les Miserables	1987	Thenardier	Dog Eats Dog	Moderate Tempo	C3	E4	Supporting	Antagonist Male
Les Miserables	1987	Thenardier	Beggars at the Wedding	Uptempo	G#2	C4	Supporting	Antagonist Male
Phantom	1991	Phantom	Paris Is A Tomb	Ballad	A2	C4	Lead	Antagonist Male
Phantom	1991	Phantom	Where In The World	Uptempo	G2	F4	Lead	Antagonist Male
Phantom	1991	Phantom	Home*	Moderate Tempo	C3	G4	Lead	Antagonist Male
Phantom	1991	Phantom	Where In The World Reprise	Uptempo	Bb2	F4	Lead	Antagonist Male
Phantom	1991	Phantom	My Mother Bore Me	Moderate Tempo	F2	F#4	Lead	Antagonist Male
Phantom	1991	Erik (Phantom)	You Are My Own*	Moderate Tempo	G2	E4	Lead	Antagonist Male
Will Rogers Follies	1991	Clem Rogers	It's A Boy	Uptempo	C#3	E4	Lead	Antagonist Male
Will Rogers Follies	1991	Clem Rogers	It's A Boy Reprise	Uptempo	D#3	E4	Lead	Antagonist Male
Will Rogers Follies	1991	Clem Rogers	Clem's Retur	Moderate Tempo	C#3	D#4	Lead	Antagonist Male
My Favorite Year	1992	King Kaiser	The Gospel According To King*	Uptempo	D3	C#4	Lead	Antagonist Male
Blood Brothers	1993	Mickey	Long Sunday Afternoon *	Ballad	D3	E4	Lead	Antagonist Male
Goodbye Girl, The	1993	Elliott Garfield	Elliott Garfield Grant	Uptempo	C3	Gb4	Lead	Antagonist Male
Goodbye Girl, The	1993	Elliott Garfield	Good News, Bad News*	Moderate Tempo	Bb3	F4	Lead	Antagonist Male
Goodbye Girl, The	1993	Elliott Garfield	Paula*	Moderate Tempo	G#2	E4	Lead	Antagonist Male
Goodbye Girl, The	1993	Elliott Garfield	I Can Play This Part	Ballad	G#2	Eb4	Lead	Antagonist Male
Lion King, The	1997	Scar	Be Prepared*	Uptempo	A2	A3	Lead	Antagonist Male

Baritone

* = Music Edit Required
+ = Ethnic Specific

Show	Year	Role	Song	Tempo	Range-Bottom	Range-Top	Category	Char Type
Lion King, The	1997	Scar	Be Prepared Reprise*	Uptempo	A2	D3	Lead	Antagonist Male
Footloose	1998	Willard Hewitt	Mama Says	Uptempo	Bb2	G4	Lead	Antagonist Male
Parade	1998	Newt Lee+	The Trial, Part 5: Newt Lee's Testim	Uptempo	B2	F#3	Lead	Antagonist Male
Parade	1998	Judge Roan	Judge Roan's Letter	Uptempo	Eb2	D4	Lead	Antagonist Male
Marie Christine	1999	Charles Gates	Good Looking Woman*	Moderate Tempo	G3	E5	Lead	Antagonist Male
Marie Christine	1999	Charles Gates	Good Lookin' Woman*	Moderate Tempo	G3	E4	Lead	Antagonist Male
Full Monty, The	2000	Noah "Horse" Simmons	Big Black Man *	Uptempo	G3	G4	Lead	Antagonist Male
Seussical	2000	Genghis Kahn Schmitz	The Military*	Uptempo	G2	F4	Supporting	Antagonist Male
Producers, The	2001	Franz Liebkind	In Old Bavaria	Moderate Tempo	F2	D4	Lead	Antagonist Male
Producers, The	2001	Franz Liebkind	Der Guten Tag Hop-Clop	Uptempo	D#3	E4	Lead	Antagonist Male
Sweet Smell Of Success	2002	JJ Hunsecker	For Susan*	Moderate Tempo	C3	Eb4	Lead	Antagonist Male
Sweet Smell Of Success	2002	JJ Hunsecker	Don't Look Now*	Moderate Tempo	C3	G4	Lead	Antagonist Male
25th Annual...Spelling Bee	2005	William Barfee	Magic Foot	Uptempo	F3	A4	Lead	Antagonist Male
25th Annual...Spelling Bee	2005	William Barfee	Second Part 1*	Moderate Tempo	Db3	Eb4	Lead	Antagonist Male
Chitty Chitty Bang Bang	2005	Childcatcher	Kiddy Widdy Winkies	Moderate Tempo	D3	E4	Supporting	Antagonist Male
Chitty Chitty Bang Bang	2005	Childcatcher	Childcatcher as Grandpa	Moderate Tempo	C3	C4	Supporting	Antagonist Male
Chitty Chitty Bang Bang	2005	Goan	Act English *	Moderate Tempo	C3	E4	Supporting	Antagonist Male
Spamalot	2005	King Arthur	Always Lok On The Bright Side of Li	Moderate Tempo	C3	D4	Lead	Antagonist Male
Spamalot	2005	King Arthur	I'm All Alone*	Ballad	A2	A3	Lead	Antagonist Male
Camelot	1960	A Man	Guenevere*	Uptempo	D3	D4	Feat Ens	Any
Closer Than Ever	1989	Man Three (Pianist)	Father of Fathers *	Ballad	B2	E4	Lead	Any
Oklahoma!	1943	Will Parker	Kansas City	Uptempo	Eb3	F4	Lead	Character Ingenue Male
On The Town	1944	Ozzie	Carried Away	Uptempo	E2	F4	Lead	Character Ingenue Male
Kiss Me Kate	1948	Bill Calhoun/Lucentio	Bianca*	Uptempo	G2	F4	Lead	Character Ingenue Male
Once Upon A Mattress	1959	Prince Dauntless	Song Of Love*	Uptempo	C#3	Eb4	Lead	Character Ingenue Male
Hello Dolly	1964	Barnaby Tucker	Elegance*	Moderate Tempo	C3	F4	Lead	Character Ingenue Male
Hello Dolly	1964	Cornelius Hackl	Put On Your Sunday Clothes	Uptempo	C3	G#4	Lead	Character Ingenue Male
Hello Dolly	1964	Cornelius Hackl	It Only Takes A Moment*	Ballad	Bb2	Eb4	Lead	Character Ingenue Male
Hello Dolly	1964	Cornelius Hackl	Elegance*	Moderate Tempo	C3	F4	Lead	Character Ingenue Male

Baritone

* = Music Edit Required
+ = Ethnic Specific

Show	Year	Role	Song	Tempo	Range-Bottom	Range-Top	Category	Char Type
Company (Revival)	1970	Paul	Have I Got A Girl For You	Uptempo	B4	Gb6	Supporting	Character Ingenue Male
Grease	1971	Johnny Casino	Born to Hand Jive	Uptempo	A3	F#4	Supporting	Character Ingenue Male
You're A Good Man Charlie	1971	Linus Van Pelt	My Blanket And Me	Moderate Tempo	B2	D4	Lead	Character Ingenue Male
Annie	1977	Bert Healy	You're Never Fully Dressed	Uptempo	E3	F#4	Supporting	Character Ingenue Male
Honk	1993	Ugly	Different	Ballad	Db3	F4	Lead	Character Ingenue Male
Honk	1993	Ugly	Hold Your Head Up High Reprise	Ballad	C3	G4	Lead	Character Ingenue Male
Honk	1993	Ugly	Now I've Seen You	Moderate Tempo	Bb2	G4	Lead	Character Ingenue Male
Avenue Q	2003	Princeton	What Do You...BA English	Moderate Tempo	B2	D4	Lead	Character Ingenue Male
Avenue Q	2003	Princeton	Purpose	Uptempo	B2	G3	Lead	Character Ingenue Male
25th Annual...Spelling Bee	2005	Leaf Coneybear	I'm Not That Smart	Uptempo	A2	G4	Lead	Character Ingenue Male
25th Annual...Spelling Bee	2005	Leaf Coneybear	I'm Not Smart Reprise	Uptempo	D3	F#4	Lead	Character Ingenue Male
Spring Awakening	2006	Georg	The Bitch Of Living*	Uptempo	F3	D4	Lead	Character Ingenue Male
Kinky Boots	2013	Harry	Take What You Got*	Uptempo	F#3	F#4	Supporting	Character Ingenue Male
Good News (1993 Revival)	1929	Pooch Kearney	Keep Your Sunny Side Up*	Uptempo	Bb2	F4	Supporting	Character Male
Of Thee I Sing	1931	Alexander Throttlebottom	The Senator From Minesota*	Uptempo	Eb3	F4	Lead	Character Male
Porgy and Bess	1935	Jim+	A Woman Is A Sometime Thing*	Moderate Tempo	D3	F4	Lead	Character Male
Porgy and Bess	1935	Porgy+	Lonesome Road*	Ballad	A2	D4	Lead	Character Male
Porgy and Bess	1935	Porgy+	It Takes A Long Pull To Get There*	Moderate Tempo	E3	G4	Lead	Character Male
Porgy and Bess	1935	Porgy+	Oh, I Got Plenty O' Nuttin'*	Uptempo	B2	D4	Lead	Character Male
Porgy and Bess	1935	Porgy+	The Buzzard*	Moderate Tempo	Bb2	E4	Lead	Character Male
Porgy and Bess	1935	Porgy+	Bess, You Is My Woman*	Ballad	Bb2	B5	Lead	Character Male
Porgy and Bess	1935	Porgy+	I Got Plenty O' Nuttin' Reprise	Uptempo	Bb2	Eb4	Lead	Character Male
Porgy and Bess	1935	Porgy+	I Loves You Porgy*	Moderate Tempo	Db3	Db4	Lead	Character Male
Porgy and Bess	1935	Porgy+	Oh, Bess, Oh, Where's My Bess*	Moderate Tempo	C#3	F4	Lead	Character Male
Porgy and Bess	1935	Porgy+	Oh Lawd I'm On My Way*	Moderate Tempo	B2	E#4	Lead	Character Male
Crazy For You (1992)	1937	Eugene Fodor	Stiff Upper Lip	Uptempo	D3	F4	Supporting	Character Male
Wizard Of Oz 1993	1939	Scarecrow	If I Only Had A Brain*	Moderate Tempo	D3	F#4	Lead	Character Male
Oklahoma!	1943	Ali Hakim	It's A Scandal! It's A Outrage	Moderate Tempo	B2	F#4	Lead	Character Male
Annie Get Your Gun	1944	Buffalo Bill	Show Business Reprise *	Moderate Tempo	C3	F4	Supporting	Character Male
Annie Get Your Gun	1944	Charlie Davenport	Show Business Reprise *	Moderate Tempo	C3	F4	Supporting	Character Male

Baritone

* = Music Edit Required
+ = Ethnic Specific

Show	Year	Role	Song	Tempo	Range-Bottom	Range-Top	Category	Char Type
On The Town	1944	Ozzie	Ya Got Me *	Uptempo	Eb3	Fb4	Lead	Character Male
Kiss Me Kate	1948	General Howell	From This Moment On	Uptempo	B2	C#4	Supporting	Character Male
South Pacific	1949	Luther Billis	Honey Bun Reprise	Uptempo	Bb2	B3	Lead	Character Male
Call Me Madam	1950	Kenneth Gibson	It's A Lovely Day Today*	Moderate Tempo	C3	D4	Lead	Character Male
Call Me Madam	1950	Kenneth Gibson	It's A Lovely Day Today Reprise	Uptempo	D3	D4	Lead	Character Male
Call Me Madam	1950	Kenneth Gibson	Once Upon A Time Today	Moderate Tempo	E3	F4	Lead	Character Male
Call Me Madam	1950	Kenneth Gibson	It's A Lovely Day Today Reprise 2*	Moderate Tempo	C3	D4	Lead	Character Male
Wonderful Town	1953	1st Editor	You're Just In Love*	Uptempo	D3	F4	Lead	Character Male
Wonderful Town	1953	2nd Editor	What A Waste*	Uptempo	A2	D4	Lead	Character Male
Pajama Game	1954	Hines	What A Waste*	Uptempo	Bb2	Eb4	Lead	Character Male
Pajama Game	1954	Hines	The Pajama Game	Uptempo	Db3	F4	Lead	Character Male
Bells Are Ringing	1956	Sandor	Think Of The Time I Save	Moderate Tempo	C3	D4	Lead	Character Male
Most Happy Fella, The	1956	Postman	Salzberg	Moderate Tempo	E3	G4	Supporting	Character Male
My Fair Lady	1956	Alfred Doolittle	I Seen Her At The Station	Moderate Tempo	D3	E4	Featured Ensemble	Character Male
My Fair Lady	1956	Alfred Doolittle	With A Little Bit Of Luck*	Uptempo	G2	E4	Lead	Character Male
My Fair Lady	1956	Alfred Doolittle	Little Bit Of Luck Of Luck Reprise	Uptempo	G2	D4	Lead	Character Male
My Fair Lady	1956	Alfred Doolittle	Get Me To The Church On Time	Uptempo	B2	D#4	Lead	Character Male
Bye Bye Birdie	1960	Albert Peterson	Put On A Happy Face	Ballad	B2	F#4	Lead	Character Male
Bye Bye Birdie	1960	Albert Peterson	Baby Talk To me	Moderate Tempo	C3	D4	Lead	Character Male
Bye Bye Birdie	1960	Albert Peterson	Rosie *	Uptempo	B2	F#4	Lead	Character Male
Bye Bye Birdie	1960	Albert Peterson	A Giant Step (TV 1995)	Uptempo	D3	F4	Lead	Character Male
A Funny Thing...Forum	1962	Prologus	Comedy Tonight*	Uptempo	A2	F4	Lead	Character Male
Little Me	1962	Benny Buchsbaum	To Be A Performer*	Uptempo	D#3	F4	Lead	Character Male
Little Me	1962	Bernie Buchsbaum	To Be A Performer*	Uptempo	D#3	F4	Lead	Character Male
Little Me	1962	Val DuVal	Boom Boom*	Moderate Tempo	C#3	F#4	Lead	Character Male
Little Me	1962	George Musgrove	I've Got Your Number*	Moderate Tempo	E3	Ab4	Lead	Character Male
Little Me	1962	Fred Poitrane	Real Live Girl*	Ballad	D3	C4	Lead	Character Male
Little Me	1962	Benny Buchsbaum	Be A Performer Reprise*	Uptempo	E3	E4	Lead	Character Male
Little Me	1962	Bernie Buchsbaum	Be A Performer Reprise*	Uptempo	E3	E4	Lead	Character Male
Little Me	1962	Prince Chemey	Goodbye	Uptempo	B2	F#4	Lead	Character Male
110 In The Shade	1963	File	Gonna Be Another Hot Day *	Moderate Tempo	D3	F#4	Lead	Character Male
110 In The Shade	1963	File	A Man And A Woman *	Ballad	C3	D4	Lead	Character Male

Baritone

225

* = Music Edit Required
+ = Ethnic Specific

Show	Year	Role	Song	Tempo	Range-Bottom	Range-Top	Category	Char Type
110 In The Shade	1963	File	Wonderful Music *	Uptempo	Db3	F4	Lead	Character Male
Oliver!	1963	Mr. Bumble	Boy For Sale	Ballad	C3	G4	Lead	Character Male
She Loves Me	1963	Ladislav Sipos	Perpective	Uptempo	D3	C#4	Lead	Character Male
She Loves Me	1963	Headwaiter	A Romantic Atmosphere (D Maj)	Moderate Tempo	G2	F4	Lead	Character Male
Funny Girl	1964	Eddie Ryan	Who Taught Her Everything...*	Moderate Tempo	C3	F4	Supporting	Character Male
Funny Girl	1964	Eddie Ryan	Rat Tat Tat*	Uptempo	D3	F#4	Lead	Character Male
Funny Girl	1964	Eddie Ryan	If A Girl Isn't Pretty*	Moderate Tempo	B2	F#4	Supporting	Character Male
Apple Tree, The	1966	Adam	Adam's Reprise	Moderate Tempo	C3	Eb4	Lead	Character Male
Apple Tree, The	1966	Adam	Eve	Moderate Tempo	D3	Db4	Lead	Character Male
Apple Tree, The	1966	Adam	Beautiful World	Moderate Tempo	C3	Eb4	Lead	Character Male
Apple Tree, The	1966	Adam	It's A Fish	Uptempo	Ab3	Eb4	Lead	Character Male
Apple Tree, The	1966	Flip	Real *	Moderate Tempo	C3	Eb4	Lead	Character Male
Cabaret	1966	Herr Ludwig	Tomorrow Belongs to Me Reprise *	Moderate Tempo	C3	D4	Supporting	Character Male
Sweet Charity	1966	Oscar Lindquist	Sweet Charity	Moderate Tempo	Bb2	E4	Lead	Character Male
Hair	1968	Ron	Aquarius	Moderate Tempo	Eb3	Eb4	Lead	Character Male
1776	1969	John Dickinson	Cool, Cool Considerate Men	Moderate Tempo	A2	Gb4	Lead	Character Male
Dear World	1969	President	The Spring Of Next Year*	Moderate Tempo	G2	D4	Supporting	Character Male
Dear World	1969	President	Just A Little Bit More*	Uptempo	G2	Fb4	Supporting	Character Male
Dear World	1969	President	Just A Little Bit More Reprise*	Uptempo	Gb3	Eb4	Supporting	Character Male
Dear World	1969	Sewerman	Pretty Garbage*	Moderate Tempo	B2	E4	Supporting	Character Male
Dear World	1969	Sewerman	Ugly Garbage*	Moderate Tempo	A3	E4	Supporting	Character Male
Applause	1970	Buzz Richards	Good Friends*	Moderate Tempo	C3	F4	Lead	Character Male
Company (Revival)	1970	David	Sorry Grateful	Ballad	B2	E4	Supporting	Character Male
Company (Revival)	1970	David	Have I Got A Girl For You	Uptempo	B5	Gb7	Supporting	Character Male
Company (Revival)	1970	Harry	Sorry Grateful	Ballad	B2	E4	Supporting	Character Male
Company (Revival)	1970	Harry	Have I Got A Girl For You	Uptempo	B6	Gb8	Supporting	Character Male
Follies	1971	Buddy Plummer	The Right Girl *	Uptempo	C3	F4	Lead	Character Male
Follies	1971	Buddy Plummer	Buddy's Blues	Uptempo	Db3	F4	Lead	Character Male
Jesus Christ Superstar	1971	King Herod	King Herod's Song	Uptempo	B2	G4	Supporting	Character Male
You're A Good Man Charlie	1971	Charlie Brown	The Kite	Uptempo	Bb2	Eb4	Lead	Character Male

Baritone

Baritone

* = Music Edit Required
+ = Ethnic Specific

Show	Year	Role	Song	Tempo	Range-Bottom	Range-Top	Category	Char Type
Sugar	1972	Jerry	Penniless Bums*	Uptempo	C3	E4	Lead	Character Male
Sugar	1972	Jerry	The Beauty That Drives Men Mad*	Uptempo	D3	F4	Lead	Character Male
Sugar	1972	Jerry	Doin' It For Sugar*	Moderate Tempo	B3	E4	Lead	Character Male
Sugar	1972	Jerry	Beautiful Through and Through*	Moderate Tempo	C#3	E4	Lead	Character Male
Sugar	1972	Jerry	Magic Nights	Moderate Tempo	E3	F4	Lead	Character Male
Chicago	1975	Amos Hart	Mister Cellophane	Ballad	C3	F4	Lead	Character Male
Pacific Overtures	1976	Manjiro+	Poems*	Moderate Tempo	E♭3	F4	Lead	Character Male
Pacific Overtures	1976	Male	Prologue	Ballad	D2	B♭3	Lead	Character Male
Pacific Overtures	1976	Reciter+	The Advantages Of Floating...*	Uptempo	B2	E4	Lead	Character Male
Pacific Overtures	1976	Soothsayer+	Chrysanthemum Tea*	Moderate Tempo	F2	D4	Lead	Character Male
On The Twentieth Century	1978	Conductor Flanagan	I Have Written A Play	Moderate Tempo	C3	F4	Supporting	Character Male
On The Twentieth Century	1978	Congressman	I Have Written A Play	Moderate Tempo	C3	F4	Supporting	Character Male
On The Twentieth Century	1978	Doctor	I Have Written A Play	Moderate Tempo	B♭3	E♭5	Supporting	Character Male
Cats	1981	Rum Tum Tugger	Rum Tum Tugger	Uptempo	B2	F4	Supporting	Character Male
Cats	1981	Rum Tum Tugger	Old Deuteronomy *	Ballad	B2	G4	Lead	Character Male
Cats	1981	Rum Tum Tugger	Mr. Mistoffolees	Uptempo	C3	E♭4	Lead	Character Male
Joseph...Dream Coat	1982	Levi	One More Angel In Heaven	Moderate Tempo	D3	F4	Lead	Character Male
Joseph...Dream Coat	1982	Napthali	Benjamin Calypso	Uptempo	F3	F4	Supporting	Character Male
Joseph...Dream Coat	1982	Reuben (Chevalier)	Those Canaan Days	Ballad	C3	F4	Supporting	Character Male
Baby	1983	Nick Sakarian	At Night She Comes Home To Me *	Moderate Tempo	D♭3	F#4	Lead	Character Male
Baby	1983	Nick Sakarian	With You *	Ballad	A#2	D#4	Lead	Character Male
LA Cage Aux Folles	1983	Albin	A Little More Mascara (Drag)	Uptempo	B♭2	D4	Lead	Character Male
LA Cage Aux Folles	1983	Albin	I Am What I Am (Drag)	Moderate Tempo	G#3	F4	Lead	Character Male
LA Cage Aux Folles	1983	Albin	The Best Of Times (Drag)	Moderate Tempo	C3	E♭4	Lead	Character Male
LA Cage Aux Folles	1983	Albin	With You On My Arm	Moderate Tempo	G#2	E♭4	Lead	Character Male
LA Cage Aux Folles	1983	Albin	La Cage Aux Folles (Drag)	Moderate Tempo	B♭2	E4	Lead	Character Male
Big River	1985	Duke	The Royal Nonesuch	Uptempo	D3	F4	Supporting	Character Male
Big River	1985	Jim +	Muddy Water	Uptempo	B2	F4	Lead	Character Male
Big River	1985	Jim +	River In The Rain *	Ballad	A2	E4	Lead	Character Male
Big River	1985	Jim +	Worlds Apart *	Ballad	B2	C4	Lead	Character Male
Big River	1985	Jim +	Free At Last	Ballad	C3	F4	Lead	Character Male

Baritone

* = Music Edit Required
+ = Ethnic Specific

Show	Year	Role	Song	Tempo	Range-Bottom	Range-Top	Category	Char Type
Big River	1985	Pap	Guv'ment	Moderate Tempo	B2	F#4	Supporting	Character Male
Big River	1985	Young Fool	Arkansas	Uptempo	C3	E4	Supporting	Character Male
Mystery Of Edwin Drood, T	1985	Durdle	Durdle's Confession	Ballad	C3	E4	Lead	Character Male
Into The Woods	1987	Baker	It Takes Two	Moderate Tempo	Bb2	F4	Lead	Character Male
Into The Woods	1987	Baker	No More*	Ballad	D3	Eb4	Lead	Character Male
City of Angels	1989	Buddy Fiddler	The Buddy System	Moderate Tempo	C3	D4	Lead	Character Male
City of Angels	1989	Buddy Fiddler	Double Talk (Buddy)	Moderate Tempo	C3	G4	Lead	Character Male
City of Angels	1989	Munoz +	All You Have To Do Is Wait	Moderate Tempo	F#3	D4	Supporting	Character Male
Secret Garden, The	1991	Archibald Craven	A Bit of Earth*	Moderate Tempo	D3	E4	Supporting	Character Male
Goodbye Girl, The	1993	Billy	A Beat Behind*	Uptempo	E3	F#4	Supporting	Character Male
Honk	1993	Bullfrog	Warts and All	Moderate Tempo	A2	C#4	Supporting	Character Male
Sunset Boulevard	1994	Max Von Mayerling	The Grestest Star Of All	Moderate Tempo	B2	Gb4	Lead	Character Male
Sunset Boulevard	1994	Manfred	The Lady's Paying*	Uptempo	C3	F4	Lead	Character Male
Sunset Boulevard	1994	Max Von Mayerling	New Ways To Dream Reprise	Ballad	G2	E4	Lead	Character Male
Victor/Victoria	1995	Toddy	Paris By Night*	Moderate Tempo	Bb2	Eb4	Lead	Character Male
Victor/Victoria	1995	Toddy	Trust Me*	Uptempo	A2	D4	Lead	Character Male
Lion King, The	1997	Zazu	The Morning Report*	Uptempo	Eb3	F4	Supporting	Character Male
Parade	1998	Leo Frank	How Can I Call This Home?	Uptempo	A2	F4	Lead	Character Male
Parade	1998	Leo Frank	Come Up To My Office*	Uptempo	A2	F4	Lead	Character Male
Parade	1998	Leo Frank	It's Hard To Speak My Heart	Ballad	B2	E4	Lead	Character Male
Parade	1998	Leo Frank	This Is Not Over Yet*	Uptempo	D3	F#4	Lead	Character Male
Parade	1998	Leo Frank	All The Wasted Time*	Ballad	D3	Bb4	Lead	Character Male
Parade	1998	Leo Frank	Sh'ma	Ballad	G3	Eb4	Lead	Character Male
Full Monty, The	2000	Dave Bukatinsky	You Rule My World *	Ballad	C#3	B4	Lead	Character Male
Full Monty, The	2000	Harold Nichols	You Rule My World *	Ballad	C#3	G4	Lead	Character Male
Seussical	2000	Horton	Horton Hears A Who (ms 17-119)	Moderate Tempo	A2	E4	Lead	Character Male
Seussical	2000	The Mayor	We're Whos Here Part 1*	Uptempo	E3	E4	Supporting	Character Male
Seussical	2000	The Cat In The Hat	A Day For The Cat In The Hat*	Uptempo	E3	E4	Lead	Character Male
Seussical	2000	The Mayor	How To Raise A Child*	Uptempo	A2	E4	Lead	Character Male
Seussical	2000	Horton	Alone In The Universe*	Moderate Tempo	B2	E4	Lead	Character Male
Seussical	2000	The Cat In The Hat	How Lucky You Are	Moderate Tempo	D3	F4	Lead	Character Male

Baritone

* = Music Edit Required
+ = Ethnic Specific

Show	Year	Role	Song	Tempo	Range-Bottom	Range-Top	Category	Char Type
Seussical	2000	Horton	Alone In The Universe Reprise	Moderate Tempo	C3	C5	Lead	Character Male
Seussical	2000	Horton	Solla Sollew*	Moderate Tempo	C3	D4	Lead	Character Male
Seussical	2000	The Cat In The Hat	Havin' A Hunch*	Uptempo	C#3	E4	Lead	Character Male
Mamma Mia!	2001	Harry Bright	Thank You For the Music*	Moderate Tempo	A3	D5	Lead	Character Male
Mamma Mia!	2001	Harry Bright	One Last Summer*	Ballad	F#3	E4	Lead	Character Male
Producers, The	2001	Max Bialystock	King Of Broadway*	Uptempo	C#3	E4	Lead	Character Male
Producers, The	2001	Max Bialystock	We Can Do It*	Uptempo	Bb2	Eb4	Lead	Character Male
Producers, The	2001	Leo Bloom	We Can Do It*	Uptempo	Bb2	E4	Lead	Character Male
Producers, The	2001	Leo Bloom	I Wanna Be A Producer*	Moderate Tempo	A2	F4	Lead	Character Male
Producers, The	2001	Max Bialystock	Along Came Bially*	Moderate Tempo	Bb2	Eb4	Lead	Character Male
Producers, The	2001	Leo Bloom	That Face*	Uptempo	B2	F4	Lead	Character Male
Producers, The	2001	Max Bialystock	That Face Reprise*	Uptempo	A2	Eb4	Lead	Character Male
Producers, The	2001	Max Bialystock	Where Did We Go Right*	Uptempo	A2	D4	Lead	Character Male
Producers, The	2001	Leo Bloom	Leo Goes To Rio*	Moderate Tempo	C3	E4	Lead	Character Male
Producers, The	2001	Max Bialystock	Betrayed	Uptempo	B2	F4	Lead	Character Male
Producers, The	2001	Leo Bloom	Til Him	Ballad	C3	F4	Lead	Character Male
Producers, The	2001	Max Bialystock	Til Him	Ballad	C3	D#4	Lead	Character Male
A Man Of No Importance	2002	Alfie Byrne	Man In The Mirror	Ballad	Bb2	F4	Lead	Character Male
A Man Of No Importance	2002	Alfie Byrne	Love Who You Love	Ballad	B2	E4	Lead	Character Male
A Man Of No Importance	2002	Alfie Byrne	Confession *	Moderate Tempo	B2	D#4	Lead	Character Male
A Man Of No Importance	2002	Alfie Byrne	Love's Never Lost	Ballad	E3	C4	Lead	Character Male
A Man Of No Importance	2002	Alfie Byrne	Welcome To The World	Ballad	C3	C5	Lead	Character Male
A Year With Frog and Toad	2002	Frog	He'll Never Know	Moderate Tempo	B2	D4	Lead	Character Male
A Year With Frog and Toad	2002	Toad	Seeds	Ballad	A2	D4	Lead	Character Male
A Year With Frog and Toad	2002	Toad	Alone	Ballad	A2	G#4	Lead	Character Male
A Year With Frog and Toad	2002	Toad	He'll Never Know	Moderate Tempo	C#3	Eb4	Lead	Character Male
A Year With Frog and Toad	2002	Toad	Toad To The Rescue	Moderate Tempo	E3	A4	Lead	Character Male
A Year With Frog and Toad	2002	Toad	Merry Almost Christmas	Moderate Tempo	E3	A4	Lead	Character Male
Hairspray	2002	Edna Turnblad	Welcome To The 60s*	Uptempo	F2	G3	Lead	Character Male
Hairspray	2002	Edna Turnblad	Timeless To Me*	Moderate Tempo	F#2	D4	Lead	Character Male
Avenue Q	2003	Brian	I'm Not Wearing Underwear Today	Uptempo	B2	E4	Lead	Character Male

Baritone

229

* = Music Edit Required
+ = Ethnic Specific

Show	Year	Role	Song	Tempo	Range-Bottom	Range-Top	Category	Char Type
Avenue Q	2003	Brian	There Is Life Outside Your Apartmel	Uptempo	B#2	E4	Lead	Character Male
Fame	2003	Schlomo	Bring In Tomorrow *	Ballad	D3	F4	Lead	Character Male
Wicked	2003	Salesman	No One Mourns The Wicked*	Moderate Tempo	D3	E4	Supporting	Character Male
Wicked	2003	Doctor Dillamond	Something Bad*	Moderate Tempo	C#3	D♭4	Lead	Character Male
Wicked	2003	Wizard	A Sentimental Man	Moderate Tempo	B2	F#4	Lead	Character Male
Wicked	2003	Wizard	Wonderful*	Uptempo	B2	E4	Lead	Character Male
Chitty Chitty Bang Bang	2005	Caratacus Potts	Hushabye Mountain	Ballad	D#3	F4	Lead	Character Male
Chitty Chitty Bang Bang	2005	Caratacus Potts	Truly Scrumptious Reprise	Ballad	D♭3	D♭4	Lead	Character Male
Chitty Chitty Bang Bang	2005	Caratacus Potts	You Two	Moderate Tempo	D3	E4	Lead	Character Male
Chitty Chitty Bang Bang	2005	Caratacus Potts	Toot Sweets *	Uptempo	D3	E♭4	Lead	Character Male
Chitty Chitty Bang Bang	2005	Caratacus Potts	Teamwork *	Uptempo	E3	G4	Lead	Character Male
Dirty Rotten Scoundrels	2005	Andre Thibault	A Chimp In A Suit	Uptempo	C3	E4	Supporting	Character Male
Dirty Rotten Scoundrels	2005	Andre Thibault	Like Zis/Like Zat *	Moderate Tempo	B♭3	E♭4	Supporting	Character Male
Spamalot	2005	Sir Bedevere	Burn Her*	Uptempo	F3	E4	Lead	Character Male
Spamalot	2005	Sir Robin	You Won't Succeed On Broadway*	Uptempo	D3	E4	Lead	Character Male
Spamalot	2005	Herbert	Here You Are*	Moderate Tempo	G2	B♭3	Supporting	Character Male
Mary Poppins	2006	Bert	Jolly Holiday*	Uptempo	B2	E4	Lead	Character Male
Mary Poppins	2006	Bert	Chim Chim Cher-ee	Moderate Tempo	A2	D4	Lead	Character Male
Mary Poppins	2006	Bert	Winds Can Change	Ballad	C3	C4	Lead	Character Male
Mary Poppins	2006	Bank Chairman	Precision And Order*	Moderate Tempo	C3	F4	Supporting	Character Male
Mary Poppins	2006	Bert	Chim Chim Cher-ee A1	Moderate Tempo	C#3	E4	Lead	Character Male
Mary Poppins	2006	Bert	Chim Chim Cher-ee Reprise	Moderate Tempo	A2	D4	Lead	Character Male
Mary Poppins	2006	Bert	Step In Time*	Uptempo	B2	F#4	Lead	Character Male
Mary Poppins	2006	Bert	A Spoonful Of Sugar Reprise*	Moderate Tempo	B♭2	C#4	Lead	Character Male
Mary Poppins	2006	Bert	All Me Own Work	Ballad	C#3	D#4	Lead	Character Male
Mary Poppins	2006	Bert	Twists And Turns	Ballad	B2	E4	Lead	Character Male
Mary Poppins	2006	Bert	Let's Go Fly A Kite*	Moderate Tempo	B♭2	E4	Lead	Character Male
Cutains	2007	Lieutenant Frank Cioffi	Show People	Moderate Tempo	A2	F4	Lead	Character Male
Cutains	2007	Lieutenant Frank Cioffi	Coffe Shop Nights	Ballad	A♭2	D3	Lead	Character Male
Cutains	2007	Lieutenant Frank Cioffi	A Tough Act To Follow *	Ballad	A2	E♭4	Lead	Character Male
Cutains	2007	Lieutenant Frank Cioffi	Show People Reprise *	Moderate Tempo	B2	B♭3	Lead	Character Male

Baritone

230

Baritone

Show	Year	Role	Song	Tempo	Range-Bottom	Range-Top	Category	Char Type
Legally Blonde	2007	Aaron Schultz	Harvard Variation*	Uptempo	C3	Eb4	Supporting	Character Male
The Little Mermaid	2007	Chef Louis	Les Poisons	Uptempo	Eb3	D4	Lead	Character Male
In The Heights	2008	Usnavi De La Vega+	In The Heights (Rap)*	Uptempo	D3	G4	Lead	Character Male
In The Heights	2008	Usnavi De La Vega+	Finale (Rap)*	Moderate Tempo	A3	C4	Lead	Character Male
White Christmas	2008	Phil Davis	The Best Things...Dancing	Moderate Tempo	Db3	F4	Lead	Character Male
Good News (1993 Revival)	1927	Tom Marlowe	The Best Things In Life Are Free*	Ballad	C3	Eb4	Lead	Ingenue Male
Good News (1993 Revival)	1927	Tom Marlowe	Lucky In Love*	Uptempo	D3	F4	Lead	Ingenue Male
Good News (1993 Revival)	1928	Bobby Randall	Button Up Your Overcoat*	Uptempo	E3	F#4	Supporting	Ingenue Male
Good News (1993 Revival)	1930	Bobby Randall	Never Swat A Fly*	Uptempo	A2	E4	Supporting	Ingenue Male
Babes In Arms (1998)	1937	Val LaMar	Babes In Arms*	Uptempo	C3	E4	Lead	Ingenue Male
Babes In Arms (1998)	1937	Val LaMar	Where Or When*	Moderate Tempo	B2	F4	Lead	Ingenue Male
Babes In Arms (1998)	1937	Marshall Blackstone	Babes In Arms*	Uptempo	C3	E4	Lead	Ingenue Male
Babes In Arms (1998)	1937	Val LaMar	All At Once*	Moderate Tempo	A2	F4	Lead	Ingenue Male
Annie Get Your Gun	1944	Tommy Walker	I'll Share It All With You	Uptempo	C#3	D4	Lead	Ingenue Male
State Fair 1996	1945	Wayne Frake	That's For Me	Moderate Tempo	C3	F4	Lead	Ingenue Male
State Fair 1996	1947	Wayne Frake	So Far*	Moderate Tempo	D3	E4	Lead	Ingenue Male
Damn Yankees	1955	Sohovic	Who's Got The Pain	Uptempo	G#3	D#4	Supporting	Ingenue Male
Sound Of Music, The	1959	Rolf Gruber	You Are Sixteen*	Moderate Tempo	D3	E4	Lead	Ingenue Male
Fantasticks, The	1960	Matt	Soon It's Gonna Rain *	Moderate Tempo	D4	Ab5	Lead	Ingenue Male
Mame	1966	Patrick Dennis	The Letter*	Uptempo	D#3	D4	Lead	Ingenue Male
Mame	1966	Patrick Dennis	My Best Girl Reprise	Ballad	C3	E4	Lead	Ingenue Male
Mame	1966	Patrick Dennis	My Best Girl Reprise 2	Ballad	C3	E4	Lead	Ingenue Male
Cats	1981	Mr. Mistoffolees	Mr. Mistoffolees	Uptempo	C3	Eb4	Supporting	Ingenue Male
Cats	1981	Mungojerrie	Mongojerrie and Rumpleteezer	Uptempo	E3	E4	Supporting	Ingenue Male
Dreamgirls	1981	CC White +	Family	Ballad	D3	E4	Lead	Ingenue Male
LA Cage Aux Folles	1983	Jean-Michel	Look Over There Reprise	Tenor	Db3	Eb4	Lead	Ingenue Male
Meet Me In St. Louis	1989	Lon Smith	Banjos*	Uptempo	Bb2	F4	Lead	Ingenue Male
Meet Me In St. Louis	1989	John Truitt	You Are For Loving*	Ballad	Db3	F4	Lead	Ingenue Male
Meet Me In St. Louis	1989	John Truitt	The Girl Next Door	Moderate Tempo	D3	E4	Lead	Ingenue Male
Once On This Island	1990	Daniel+	Forever Yours*	Ballad	E#3	F#4	Lead	Ingenue Male

Baritone

231

Baritone

* = Music Edit Required
+ = Ethnic Specific

Show	Year	Role	Song	Tempo	Range-Bottom	Range-Top	Category	Char Type
Once On This Island	1990	Daniel+	Some Girls	Moderate Tempo	B2	F#4	Lead	Ingenue Male
Blood Brothers	1993	Edward	Long Sunday Afternoon *	Ballad	E3	C4	Lead	Ingenue Male
State Fair 1996	1996	Wayne Frake	The Man I Used To Be*	Moderate Tempo	C3	Eb4	Lead	Ingenue Male
Babes In Arms (1998)	1998	Irving de Quincy+	Light On Our Feet*	Uptempo	F3	F4	Lead	Ingenue Male
Babes In Arms (1998)	1998	Ivor de Quincy+	Light On Our Feet*	Uptempo	F3	F4	Lead	Ingenue Male
Parade	1998	Frankie Epps	Old Red Hills Of Home Finale*	Moderate Tempo	Eb3	Eb4	Lead	Ingenue Male
Marie Christine	1999	Jean L'Adrese+	All Eyes Look To You	Ballad	A2	E4	Lead	Ingenue Male
All Shook Up	2005	Dean Hyde	It's Now Or Never *	Moderate Tempo	C3	F4	Supporting	Ingenue Male
Little Women	2005	John Brooke	More Than I Am*	Moderate Tempo	E3	E4	Supporting	Ingenue Male
Legally Blonde	2007	Padamadan+	Harvard Variation*	Uptempo	B2	E4	Supporting	Ingenue Male
Addams Family, The	2010	Lucas Beineke	Crazier Than You *	Uptempo	D3	E4	Supporting	Ingenue Male
Addams Family, The	2010	Lucas Beineke	One Normal Night	Uptempo	D3	F4	Supporting	Ingenue Male
King and I, The	1951	Louis Leonowens	A Puzzlement Reprise*	Uptempo	G2	G3	Supporting	Juvenile Male
King and I, The	1951	Louis Leonowens	I Whistle A Happy Tune*	Uptempo	B2	B3	Supporting	Juvenile Male
King and I, The	1951	Prince Chulalongkorn	A Puzzlement Reprise*	Uptempo	G2	G3	Supporting	Juvenile Male
13 The Musical	2008	Brett (RAM)	Getting Ready*	Uptempo	G3	F4	Supporting	Juvenile Male
No, No Nanette	1925	Jimmy Smith	I Want To Be Happy*	Uptempo	C#3	F#4	Lead	Mature Male
Oklahoma!	1943	Old Man Carnes	The Farmer And The Cowman*	Moderate Tempo	F3	F4	Supporting	Mature Male
On The Town	1944	Pitkin Bridgework	I Understand	Uptempo	A2	D4	Supporting	Mature Male
Guys and Dolls	1950	Arvide	More I Cannot Wish You	Moderate Tempo	D4	D5	Supporting	Mature Male
Damn Yankees	1955	Joe Boyd	Goodbye Old Girl	Ballad	D3	E4	Lead	Mature Male
Damn Yankees	1955	Joe Boyd	Near To You*	Ballad	C3	C4	Supporting	Mature Male
Most Happy Fella, The	1956	Tony	Soon You Gonna Leave Me Joe	Moderate Tempo	C#3	E4	Lead	Mature Male
Most Happy Fella, The	1956	Tony	Rosabella	Moderate Tempo	Eb3	G4	Lead	Mature Male
Most Happy Fella, The	1956	Tony	Plenty Bambini	Ballad	C#3	F#4	Lead	Mature Male
Most Happy Fella, The	1956	Tony	Old People Gotta Dance	Moderate Tempo	C3	C4	Lead	Mature Male
Most Happy Fella, The	1956	Tony	My Heart Is So Full Of You*	Ballad	Db3	Gb4	Lead	Mature Male
Most Happy Fella, The	1956	Tony	Mamma, Mamma	Moderate Tempo	C#3	G4	Lead	Mature Male
Most Happy Fella, The	1956	Tony	Tony's Thoughts	Ballad	D3	F4	Lead	Mature Male
Most Happy Fella, The	1956	Tony	I Canno' Leave You Money	Moderate Tempo	D#3	Eb4	Lead	Mature Male

Baritone

Baritone

* = Music Edit Required
+ = Ethnic Specific

Show	Year	Role	Song	Tempo	Range-Bottom	Range-Top	Category	Char Type
Most Happy Fella, The	1956	Tony	Most Happy Fella (ms 74-109 & 131	Uptempo	Eb3	G4	Lead	Mature Male
Flower Drum Song 2002	1958	Chin+	My Best Love*	Ballad	D#3	E4	Lead	Mature Male
A Funny Thing...Forum	1962	Pseudolus	Free*	Uptempo	B2	F4	Lead	Mature Male
A Funny Thing...Forum	1962	Pseudolus	Pretty Little Picture*	Uptempo	B2	F#4	Lead	Mature Male
A Funny Thing...Forum	1962	Sinex	Everybody Ought To Have A Maid*	Uptempo	C#3	E4	Lead	Mature Male
A Funny Thing...Forum	1962	Pseudolus	Lovely Reprise*	Moderate Tempo	D3	F4	Lead	Mature Male
Oliver!	1963	Fagin	Pick A Pocket Or Two	Uptempo	D3	Eb4	Lead	Mature Male
Oliver!	1963	Fagin	Be Back Soon*	Uptempo	C3	E4	Lead	Mature Male
Oliver!	1963	Fagin	Reviewing The Situation	Uptempo	C3	F4	Lead	Mature Male
She Loves Me	1963	Mr. Maraczek	Days Gone By*	Uptempo	Bb2	C4	Lead	Mature Male
She Loves Me	1963	Mr. Maraczek	Days Gone By Reprise	Uptempo	B2	E4	Lead	Mature Male
Hello Dolly	1964	Horace Vandergelder	It Takes A Woman	Uptempo	B2	G5	Lead	Mature Male
Hello Dolly	1964	Horace Vandergelder	Hello Dolly	Moderate Tempo	B2	D4	Lead	Mature Male
Cabaret	1966	Herr Schultz	Married *	Ballad	D3	F4	Supporting	Mature Male
Cabaret	1966	Herr Schultz	Married Reprise	Ballad	C3	D4	Supporting	Mature Male
1776	1969	John Adams	Piddle, Twiddle, and Resolve	Uptempo	Db3	Eb4	Lead	Mature Male
1776	1969	John Adams	Is Anybody There? (ms 57-135)	Uptempo	D3	E4	Lead	Mature Male
Company (Revival)	1970	Larry	Sorry Grateful	Ballad	B2	E4	Supporting	Mature Male
Company (Revival)	1970	Larry	Have I Got A Girl For You	Uptempo	B2	Gb4	Supporting	Mature Male
Follies	1971	Theodore Whitman	Rain On The Roof *	Uptempo	Bb2	D4	Supporting	Mature Male
Sugar	1972	Sir Osgood	Beautiful Through and Through*	Moderate Tempo	C#3	Eb4	Lead	Mature Male
Best Little Whorehouse...	1978	Governor	The Sidestep	Uptempo	A2	E4	Supporting	Mature Male
Cats	1981	Asparagus	Gus: The Theatre Cat	Ballad	A2	D4	Supporting	Mature Male
Cats	1981	Bustopher Jones	Bustopher Jones *	Uptempo	C3	C4	Supporting	Mature Male
Little Shop of Horrors	1982	Mr. Mushnik	Mushnik and Son*	Uptempo	A2	F4	Lead	Mature Male
Little Shop of Horrors	1982	Mr. Mushnik	Ya Never Know*	Uptempo	C3	C4	Lead	Mature Male
Mystery Of Edwin Drood, T	1985	Chairman	There You Are*	Uptempo	D3	D4	Lead	Mature Male
Mystery Of Edwin Drood, T	1985	Chairman	Both Sides Of The Coin*	Uptempo	C3	F#4	Lead	Mature Male
Mystery Of Edwin Drood, T	1985	Chairman	Off To The Races*	Uptempo	C3	F4	Lead	Mature Male
Mystery Of Edwin Drood, T	1985	Chrisparkle	Chrisparkle's Confession	Moderate Tempo	D3	F4	Lead	Mature Male
Into The Woods	1987	Mysterious Man	No More*	Ballad	Bb2	E4	Lead	Mature Male

Baritone

233

Baritone

* = Music Edit Required
+ = Ethnic Specific

Show	Year	Role	Song	Tempo	Range-Bottom	Range-Top	Category	Char Type
Into The Woods	1987	Narrator	Act I Opening (Part 4)*	Uptempo	G2	E4	Lead	Mature Male
Chess	1988	Molokov	The Soviet Machine	Uptempo	A2	D4	Supporting	Mature Male
Phantom	1991	Gerard Carriere	You Are My Own*	Moderate Tempo	G2	D4	Lead	Mature Male
Crazy For You (1992)	1992	Bella Zangler	What Causes That	Uptempo	C3	F#4	Supporting	Mature Male
Sunset Boulevard	1994	Cecil B. DeMille	Surrender Reprise	Ballad	Ab2	Db4	Supporting	Mature Male
Parade	1998	Old Soldier	Old Red Hills Of Home (Part 2)*	Moderate Tempo	C3	G4	Supporting	Mature Male
A Man Of No Importance	2002	Baldy O'Shea	The Cuddles That Mary Gave	Ballad	Eb3	F4	Supporting	Mature Male
A Man Of No Importance	2002	Carney	Confussing Times	Ballad	A2	A3	Supporting	Mature Male
Caroline, Or Change	2004	Mr. Stopnick	A Twenty Dollar Bill and Why (ms 4	Ballad	C3	F4	Supporting	Mature Male
Chitty Chitty Bang Bang	2005	Grandpa Potts	Them Three	Uptempo	C3	C4	Supporting	Mature Male
Chitty Chitty Bang Bang	2005	Grandpa Potts	Posh	Uptempo	C3	C4	Supporting	Mature Male
Grey Gardens	2006	Major Bouvier	Marry Well*	Moderate Tempo	A#2	E4	Supporting	Mature Male
Grey Gardens	2006	Norman Vincent Peale	Choose To Be Happy*	Moderate Tempo	G2	E4	Supporting	Mature Male
Addams Family, The	2010	Uncle Fester	The Moon And Me	Ballad	C3	E4	Supporting	Mature Male
Fantasticks, The	1960	Bellomy	Never Say No *	Uptempo	G3	E4	Supporting	Paternal
Fantasticks, The	1960	Bellomy	Plant A Raddish *	Uptempo	C3	F4	Supporting	Paternal
Fantasticks, The	1960	Bellomy	It Depends On What You Pay Repris	Uptempo	D3	G4	Supporting	Paternal
Fantasticks, The	1960	Huckabee	Never Say No *	Uptempo	C3	E4	Supporting	Paternal
Fantasticks, The	1960	Huckabee	Plant A Raddish *	Uptempo	C3	F4	Supporting	Paternal
Fantasticks, The	1960	Huckabee	It Depends On What You Pay Repris	Uptempo	D3	G4	Supporting	Paternal
110 In The Shade	1963	H.C. Curry	Lizzie's Comin' Home *	Uptempo	B2	E4	Supporting	Paternal
Fiddler on The Roof	1964	Tevye	If I Were A Rich Man	Moderate Tempo	Db3	F4	Lead	Paternal
Fiddler on The Roof	1964	Tevye	Sabbath Prayer	Ballad	D3	C4	Lead	Paternal
Fiddler on The Roof	1964	Tevye	Sunrise Sunset	Ballad	C3	D4	Lead	Paternal
Fiddler on The Roof	1964	Tevye	Chavaleh	Ballad	C3	C4	Lead	Paternal
Fiddler on The Roof	1964	Tevye	Tevye's Monologue	Moderate Tempo	Ab2	E4	Lead	Paternal
Fiddler on The Roof	1964	Tevye	Tevye's Rebuttal	Moderate Tempo	Ab2	E4	Lead	Paternal
Baby	1983	Alan McNally	Easier To Love	Ballad	C3	D4	Lead	Paternal
Baby	1983	Alan McNally	And What If We'd Loved Like That *	Moderate Tempo	D3	Gb4	Lead	Paternal
Rags	1986	Avram Cohen	Three Sunny Rooms*	Moderate Tempo	C3	D4	Lead	Paternal

Baritone

* = Music Edit Required
+ = Ethnic Specific

Show	Year	Role	Song	Tempo	Range-Bottom	Range-Top	Category	Char Type
Closer Than Ever	1989	Man Two	She Loves Me Not *	Ballad	C3	E4	Lead	Paternal
Closer Than Ever	1989	Man Two	There *	Moderate Tempo	A2	F4	Lead	Paternal
Closer Than Ever	1989	Man Two	If I Sing	Ballad	A2	Eb4	Lead	Paternal
Closer Than Ever	1989	Man Two	Father of Fathers *	Ballad	D3	F4	Lead	Paternal
Meet Me In St. Louis	1989	Alonso Smith	Wasn't It Fun*	Ballad	Ab2	Bb3	Lead	Paternal
Once On This Island	1990	Tonton Julian+	Ti Moune*	Ballad	G2	Eb4	Lead	Paternal
Blood Brothers	1993	Mr. Lyons	Miss Jones	Uptempo	C3	D4	Supporting	Paternal
Honk!	1993	Drake	A Poultry Tale	Uptempo	C3	F4	Lead	Paternal
Honk!	1993	Drake	The Collage	Uptempo	G#2	E3	Lead	Paternal
Beauty and the Beast	1994	Maurice	No Matter What	Uptempo	B2	Db4	Supporting	Paternal
Beauty and the Beast	1994	Maurice	No Matter What Reprise	Uptempo	Bb2	G3	Supporting	Paternal
State Fair 1996	1996	Abel Frake	Boys And Girls Like You And Me*	Moderate Tempo	Bb2	C4	Lead	Paternal
Caroline, Or Change	2004	Stuart Gellman	Moon, Emmie, Stuart Trio (ms 6-76	Ballad	Bb2	Eb4	Supporting	Paternal
Caroline, Or Change	2004	Stuart Gellman	There Is No God, Noah (ms 1-31)	Moderate Tempo	E3	C#4	Supporting	Paternal
Spamalot	2005	Dad	I Am Not Dead Yet	Uptempo	C3	E4	Lead	Paternal
Marry Poppins	2006	George Banks	Cherry Tree Lane*	Uptempo	Bb2	Eb4	Lead	Paternal
Marry Poppins	2006	George Banks	A Man Has Dreams	Ballad	Bb2	Eb4	Lead	Paternal
Billy Elliot	2008	Dad	Deep In The Ground *	Ballad	Bb2	Eb4	Lead	Paternal
In The Heights	2008	Kevin Rosario+	Inutil	Ballad	C3	E4	Lead	Paternal
In The Heights	2008	Kevin Rosario+	Atencion	Ballad	F#3	D4	Lead	Paternal
Addams Family, The	2010	Mal Geineke	In The Arms	Moderate Tempo	C3	F4	Supporting	Paternal
Pal Joey	1940	Joey Evans	A Great Big Town	Uptempo	Eb3	F4	Lead	Romantic Antagonist Male
Pal Joey	1940	Joey Evans	You Mustn't Kick It Around	Uptempo	D3	F4	Lead	Romantic Antagonist Male
Pal Joey	1940	Joey Evans	I Could Write A Book*	Moderate Tempo	Eb3	Eb4	Lead	Romantic Antagonist Male
Pal Joey	1940	Joey Evans	Happy Hunting Horn	Moderate Tempo	Ab3	F4	Lead	Romantic Antagonist Male
Pal Joey	1940	Joey Evans	What Do I Care For A Dame	Uptempo	D3	C#4	Lead	Romantic Antagonist Male
Pal Joey	1940	Joey Evans	Den Of Iniguity*	Uptempo	G3	Eb4	Lead	Romantic Antagonist Male
Pal Joey	1940	Joey Evans	Do It The Hard Way	Moderate Tempo	C3	C4	Lead	Romantic Antagonist Male
Pal Joey	1940	Joey Evans	Finale-I Could Write A Book	Moderate Tempo	Eb3	Eb4	Lead	Romantic Antagonist Male

Baritone

* = Music Edit Required
+ = Ethnic Specific

Show	Year	Role	Song	Tempo	Range-Bottom	Range-Top	Category	Char Type
Carousel	1945	Billy Bigelow	If I Loved You *	Ballad	Bb2	Gb4	Lead	Romantic Antagonist Male
Carousel	1945	Billy Bigelow	Soliloquy	Moderate Tempo	B2	G4	Lead	Romantic Antagonist Male
Carousel	1945	Billy Bigelow	If I Loved You Reprise	Ballad	Eb3	Gb4	Lead	Romantic Antagonist Male
Carousel	1945	Billy Bigelow	The Highest Judge Of All	Moderate Tempo	D3	G4	Lead	Romantic Antagonist Male
Carousel	1945	Jigger Craigin	Stonecutter Cut It On Stone Reprise	Uptempo	C3	F4	Lead	Romantic Antagonist Male
State Fair 1996	1945	Pat Gilbert	Isn't It Kinda Fun*	Uptempo	C#3	D4	Lead	Romantic Antagonist Male
State Fair 1996	1945	Pat Gilbert	Isn't It Kinda Fun Reprise	Moderate Tempo	C3	G#4	Lead	Romantic Antagonist Male
Pajama Game	1954	Prez	Her Is*	Uptempo	Db3	F4	Lead	Romantic Antagonist Male
Pajama Game	1954	Prez	Her Is Reprise*	Uptempo	Ab2	F4	Lead	Romantic Antagonist Male
Pajama Game	1954	Prez	Seven And A Half Cents*	Uptempo	D3	E4	Lead	Romantic Antagonist Male
High Society 1998	1956	Mike Connor	You're Sensational	Ballad	G2	F4	Lead	Romantic Antagonist Male
Most Happy Fella, The	1956	Joe	Don't Cry	Moderate Tempo	Bb2	Eb4	Lead	Romantic Antagonist Male
Most Happy Fella, The	1956	Joe	Getting' Out Of Town	Ballad	Db3	F4	Lead	Romantic Antagonist Male
Music Man, The	1957	Harold Hill	Trouble	Uptempo	A2	E4	Lead	Romantic Antagonist Male
Music Man, The	1957	Harold Hill	Seventy Six Trombones	Uptempo	B2	F4	Lead	Romantic Antagonist Male
Music Man, The	1957	Harold Hill	The Sadder But Wiser Girl*	Uptempo	C3	E4	Lead	Romantic Antagonist Male
Music Man, The	1957	Harold Hill	Marian The Librarian	Moderate Tempo	C3	F4	Lead	Romantic Antagonist Male
Music Man, The	1957	Harold Hill	76 Trombones	Moderate Tempo	G2	F4	Lead	Romantic Antagonist Male
Music Man, The	1957	Harold Hill	Trouble Reprise	Uptempo	A3	Eb4	Lead	Romantic Antagonist Male
Music Man, The	1957	Harold Hill	Till There Was You Reprise	Ballad	B2	C4	Lead	Romantic Antagonist Male
Bye Bye Birdie	1960	Conrad Birdie	Honestly Sincerely	Moderate Tempo	Ab2	F#4	Lead	Romantic Antagonist Male
Bye Bye Birdie	1960	Conrad Birdie	One Last Kiss	Moderate Tempo	Ab2	F4	Lead	Romantic Antagonist Male
Bye Bye Birdie	1960	Conrad Birdie	Lot of Livin' To Do *	Uptempo	Db4	F4	Lead	Romantic Antagonist Male
A Funny Thing...Forum	1962	Miles	Bring Me My Bride*	Uptempo	B2	F4	Lead	Romantic Antagonist Male
Anyone Can Whistle	1964	J. Bowden Hapgood	Everybody Says Don't	Uptempo	G2	E4	Lead	Romantic Antagonist Male
Anyone Can Whistle	1964	J. Bowden Hapgood	With So Little To Be Sure Of*	Moderate Tempo	B2	E4	Lead	Romantic Antagonist Male
Mack and Mabel	1974	Mack Sennett	Movies Were Movies	Uptempo	A2	Eb4	Lead	Romantic Antagonist Male
Mack and Mabel	1974	Mack Sennett	I Wont Send Roses	Ballad	G2	Eb4	Lead	Romantic Antagonist Male
Mack and Mabel	1974	Mack Sennett	Make The World Laugh*	Uptempo	A2	G4	Lead	Romantic Antagonist Male
Mack and Mabel	1974	Mack Sennett	Hundreds of Girls*	Uptempo	B2	F4	Lead	Romantic Antagonist Male

Baritone

236

* = Music Edit Required
+ = Ethnic Specific

Show	Year	Role	Song	Tempo	Range-Bottom	Range-Top	Category	Char Type
Mack and Mabel	1974	Mack Sennett	I Promise You a Happy Ending	Ballad	G2	D4	Lead	Romantic Antagonist Male
They're Playing Our Song	1974	Vernon Gersch	Falling	Moderate Tempo	A2	D4	Lead	Romantic Antagonist Male
They're Playing Our Song	1974	Vernon Gersch	If She Really Knew Me*	Ballad	B2	C♭5	Lead	Romantic Antagonist Male
They're Playing Our Song	1974	Vernon Gersch	They're Playing My Song*	Uptempo	C3	F4	Lead	Romantic Antagonist Male
They're Playing Our Song	1974	Vernon Gersch	If She Really Knew Me Reprise*	Ballad	C3	D4	Lead	Romantic Antagonist Male
Chicago	1975	Billy Flynn	All I Care About Is Love	Moderate Tempo	A2	F#4	Lead	Romantic Antagonist Male
Chicago	1975	Billy Flynn	Razzle Dazzle	Uptempo	D3	F4	Lead	Romantic Antagonist Male
On The Twentieth Century	1978	Oscar Jaffe	I Rise Again*	Moderate Tempo	B2	E4	Lead	Romantic Antagonist Male
On The Twentieth Century	1978	Oscar Jaffe	Together*	Uptempo	C3	E4	Lead	Romantic Antagonist Male
On The Twentieth Century	1978	Oscar Jaffe	Our Private World*	Ballad	A2	E4	Lead	Romantic Antagonist Male
On The Twentieth Century	1978	Oscar Jaffe	I've Got It All*	Moderate Tempo	B2	E5	Lead	Romantic Antagonist Male
On The Twentieth Century	1978	Oscar Jaffe	Five Zeros*	Moderate Tempo	A♭2	A♭4	Lead	Romantic Antagonist Male
On The Twentieth Century	1978	Oscar Jaffe	Last Will And Testament	Moderate Tempo	B2	F4	Lead	Romantic Antagonist Male
On The Twentieth Century	1978	Oscar Jaffe	Because Of Her	Moderate Tempo	B2	F4	Lead	Romantic Antagonist Male
Mystery Of Edwin Drood, T	1985	Neville Landless	Neville's Confesson	Moderate Tempo	G♭3	F4	Lead	Romantic Antagonist Male
City of Angels	1989	Stone	Double Talk	Uptempo	A#2	D4	Lead	Romantic Antagonist Male
City of Angels	1989	Stone	You're Nothing Without Me *	Uptempo	E3	G4	Lead	Romantic Antagonist Male
City of Angels	1989	Stone	With Every Breath I Take Reprise *	Ballad	G#2	F4	Lead	Romantic Antagonist Male
City of Angels	1989	Stone	I'm Nothing Without You *	Uptempo	F3	G4	Lead	Romantic Antagonist Male
Once On This Island	1990	Agwe+	Rain*	Uptempo	C#3	E4	Lead	Romantic Antagonist Male
Nick & Nora	1991	Victor Moisa	Class	Moderate Tempo	B2	F#4	Lead	Romantic Antagonist Male
Nick & Nora	1991	Victor Moisa	Class Reprise	Moderate Tempo	B2	F#3	Lead	Romantic Antagonist Male
Will Rogers Follies	1991	Will Rogers	Never Met A Man I Didn't Like (Act	Moderate Tempo	B2	B♭3	Lead	Romantic Antagonist Male
Will Rogers Follies	1991	Will Rogers	Give A Man Enough Rope	Moderate Tempo	B♭2	F4	Lead	Romantic Antagonist Male
Will Rogers Follies	1991	Will Rogers	So Long Pa	Ballad	B2	D4	Lead	Romantic Antagonist Male
Will Rogers Follies	1991	Will Rogers	The Big Time*	Moderate Tempo	G#2	D#4	Lead	Romantic Antagonist Male
Will Rogers Follies	1991	Will Rogers	Marry Me Now*	Moderate Tempo	E♭3	E♭4	Lead	Romantic Antagonist Male
Will Rogers Follies	1991	Will Rogers	Look Around	Ballad	C#5	D4	Lead	Romantic Antagonist Male
Will Rogers Follies	1991	Will Rogers	The Campaign: Our Favorite Son	Moderate Tempo	C3	E♭4	Lead	Romantic Antagonist Male
Will Rogers Follies	1991	Will Rogers	Presents For Mrs. Rogers	Moderate Tempo	B2	D4	Lead	Romantic Antagonist Male
Will Rogers Follies	1991	Will Rogers	Never Met A Man I Didn't Like Repr	Moderate Tempo	B♭2	D4	Lead	Romantic Antagonist Male

Baritone

* = Music Edit Required
+ = Ethnic Specific

Show	Year	Role	Song	Tempo	Range-Bottom	Range-Top	Category	Char Type
Assassins	1992	John Wilkes Booth	Opening*	Moderate Tempo	D3	F4	Lead	Romantic Antagonist Male
Assassins	1992	John Wilkes Booth	The Ballad Of Booth Part 2	Moderate Tempo	F#2	F#4	Lead	Romantic Antagonist Male
Assassins	1992	Leon Czolgosz	Gun Song*	Moderate Tempo	G2	B3	Lead	Romantic Antagonist Male
Assassins	1992	John Wilkes Booth	Gun Song*	Moderate Tempo	C#3	E4	Lead	Romantic Antagonist Male
My Favorite Year	1992	Alan Swann	If The World Were Like The Movies	Ballad	Bb2	E4	Lead	Romantic Antagonist Male
My Favorite Year	1992	Alan Swann	Exits	Moderate Tempo	G2	D4	Lead	Romantic Antagonist Male
My Favorite Year	1992	Alan Swann	The Lights Come Up*	Ballad	Bb2	C4	Lead	Romantic Antagonist Male
My Favorite Year	1992	Alan Swann	Manhattan*	Uptempo	G2	Eb4	Lead	Romantic Antagonist Male
Beauty and the Beast	1994	Beast	How Long Must This Go On	Uptempo	D3	C4	Lead	Romantic Antagonist Male
Beauty and the Beast	1994	Beast	If I Can't Love Her	Ballad	B2	F4	Lead	Romantic Antagonist Male
Beauty and the Beast	1994	Beast	Something There *	Uptempo	A2	E5	Lead	Romantic Antagonist Male
Beauty and the Beast	1994	Beast	If I Can't Love Her Reprise	Ballad	D4	D5	Lead	Romantic Antagonist Male
Beauty and the Beast	1994	Gaston	Me	Uptempo	B2	F4	Lead	Romantic Antagonist Male
Beauty and the Beast	1994	Gaston	Gaston Reprise	Uptempo	C3	E4	Lead	Romantic Antagonist Male
Beauty and the Beast	1994	Gaston	Maison Des Lune	Moderate Tempo	B2	E4	Lead	Romantic Antagonist Male
State Fair 1996	1996	Pat Gilbert	The Man I Used To Be Reprise	Moderate Tempo	C3	Eb4	Lead	Romantic Antagonist Male
Scarlet Pimpernel, The	1997	Chauvelin	Falcon In The Dive*	Uptempo	G2	G4	Lead	Romantic Antagonist Male
Scarlet Pimpernel, The	1997	Chauvelin	Where's The Girl	Moderate Tempo	B2	G4	Lead	Romantic Antagonist Male
Scarlet Pimpernel, The	1997	Chauvelin	The Riddle Part 1	Moderate Tempo	A2	D4	Lead	Romantic Antagonist Male
Scarlet Pimpernel, The	1997	Chauvelin	Where Is The Girl Reprise	Moderate Tempo	B2	G4	Lead	Romantic Antagonist Male
Scarlet Pimpernel, The	1997	Chauvelin	Madame Guillotine*	Uptempo	B2	F4	Lead	Romantic Antagonist Male
Steel Pier	1997	Mick Hamilton	Everybody Dance Part 1*	Uptempo	D3	F4	Lead	Romantic Antagonist Male
Steel Pier	1997	Mick Hamilton	It's A Powerful Thing*	Uptempo	C3	E4	Lead	Romantic Antagonist Male
Steel Pier	1997	Mick Hamilton	Dance With Me*	Uptempo	Db3	Eb4	Lead	Romantic Antagonist Male
Steel Pier	1997	Mick Hamilton	Steel Pier Reprise*	Uptempo	Bb2	E4	Lead	Romantic Antagonist Male
Parade	1998	Hugh Dorsey	Somethin' Ain't Right*	Moderate Tempo	C#3	F#4	Lead	Romantic Antagonist Male
Parade	1998	Hugh Dorsey	The Trial, Part 2: Twenty From Mari	Uptempo	Bb2	Eb4	Lead	Romantic Antagonist Male
Spring Awakening	2006	Hanschen	Word Of Your Body Reprise 2*	Ballad	C3	E#4	Lead	Romantic Antagonist Male
Legally Blonde	2007	Professor Callahan	Blood In The Water	Moderate Tempo	C3	F#4	Supporting	Romantic Antagonist Male
Legally Blonde	2007	Professor Callahan	Whipped Into Shape*	Uptempo	C3	F#4	Supporting	Romantic Antagonist Male
Addams Family, The	2010	Gomez Addams +	Happy/Sad	Ballad	Eb3	Eb4	Lead	Romantic Antagonist Male

Baritone

* = Music Edit Required
+ = Ethnic Specific

Show	Year	Role	Song	Tempo	Range-Bottom	Range-Top	Category	Char Type
No, No Nanette	1925	Bill Early	The Call Of TheSea*	Uptempo	D3	F#4	Lead	Romantic Lead Male
No, No Nanette	1925	Bill Early	You Can Dance With Any Girl At All^	Uptempo	C3	F4	Lead	Romantic Lead Male
No, No Nanette	1925	Bill Early	Telephone Girlie*	Uptempo	C3	F4	Lead	Romantic Lead Male
Good News (1993 Revival)	1928	Coach Johnson	You're The Cream In My Coffee*	Uptempo	B2	E♭4	Lead	Romantic Lead Male
Good News (1993 Revival)	1928	Coach Johnson	Together*	Ballad	G3	B4	Lead	Romantic Lead Male
Good News (1993 Revival)	1928	Coach Johnson	Together Part 2*	Ballad	G2	C4	Lead	Romantic Lead Male
High Society 1998	1929	George Kittredge	I'll Worship You	Moderate Tempo	G#2	F#4	Lead	Romantic Lead Male
Of Thee I Sing	1931	John P Wintergreen	Some Girls Can Bake A Pie*	Uptempo	E3	F4	Lead	Romantic Lead Male
Of Thee I Sing	1931	John P Wintergreen	Of Thee I Sing*	Moderate Tempo	C3	E4	Lead	Romantic Lead Male
Of Thee I Sing	1931	John P Wintergreen	Supreme Court Judges*	Uptempo	B2	E4	Lead	Romantic Lead Male
Of Thee I Sing	1931	John P Wintergreen	Who Cares Reprise*	Moderate Tempo	C3	E4	Lead	Romantic Lead Male
Anything Goes	1934	Billy Crocker	You're the Top *	Uptempo	B2	F4	Lead	Romantic Lead Male
Anything Goes	1934	Billy Crocker	All Through The Night *	Ballad	F3	G4	Lead	Romantic Lead Male
Oklahoma!	1943	Curly	Oh What A Beautiful Morning	Moderate Tempo	D3	E4	Lead	Romantic Lead Male
Oklahoma!	1943	Curly	The Surrey With The Fringe On Top	Uptempo	D#3	E4	Lead	Romantic Lead Male
Oklahoma!	1943	Curly	People Will Say We're In Love	Moderate Tempo	C#3	F#4	Lead	Romantic Lead Male
Oklahoma!	1943	Curly	Poor Jud*	Ballad	D#3	C#4	Lead	Romantic Lead Male
Annie Get Your Gun	1944	Frank Butler	There's No Business Like Show Bus	Uptempo	A♭3	E4	Lead	Romantic Lead Male
Annie Get Your Gun	1944	Frank Butler	The Girl That I Marry*	Moderate Tempo	D3	D4	Lead	Romantic Lead Male
Annie Get Your Gun	1944	Frank Butler	They Say That Falling In Love*	Ballad	C3	D4	Lead	Romantic Lead Male
Annie Get Your Gun	1944	Frank Butler	My Defenses Are Down	Moderate Tempo	D♭3	E♭4	Lead	Romantic Lead Male
Annie Get Your Gun	1944	Frank Butler	An Old Fashioned Wedding	Uptempo	B2	E4	Lead	Romantic Lead Male
Annie Get Your Gun	1944	Frank Butler	The Girl I Marry Reprise	Ballad	A3	D4	Lead	Romantic Lead Male
Annie Get Your Gun	1944	Frank Butler	Show Business Reprise *	Moderate Tempo	C3	F4	Lead	Romantic Lead Male
Brigadoon	1947	Tommy Albright	The Heather On The Hill *	Ballad	B♭2	F4	Lead	Romantic Lead Male
Brigadoon	1947	Tommy Albright	Almost Like Being In Love *	Ballad	C3	F#4	Lead	Romantic Lead Male
Brigadoon	1947	Tommy Albright	There But For You Go I	Ballad	B2	F4	Lead	Romantic Lead Male
Brigadoon	1947	Tommy Albright	From This Day On *	Ballad	D3	E♭4	Lead	Romantic Lead Male
Brigadoon	1947	Tommy Albright	From This Day On Reprise *	Ballad	E♭3	E♭4	Lead	Romantic Lead Male
Kiss Me Kate	1948	Fred Graham/Petruchio	Wunderbar*	Ballad	C3	G4	Lead	Romantic Lead Male

* = Music Edit Required
+ = Ethnic Specific

Show	Year	Role	Song	Tempo	Range-Bottom	Range-Top	Category	Char Type
Kiss Me Kate	1948	Fred Graham/Petruchio	Were Thine That Speical Face	Moderate Tempo	C3	F4	Lead	Romantic Lead Male
Kiss Me Kate	1948	Fred Graham/Petruchio	Where Is The Life That Late I Led	Moderate Tempo	B2	F4	Lead	Romantic Lead Male
Kiss Me Kate	1948	Fred Graham/Petruchio	So In Love Reprise	Ballad	B2	Eb4	Lead	Romantic Lead Male
South Pacific	1949	Emile De Becque	Some Enchanted Evening	Ballad	C3	E4	Lead	Romantic Lead Male
South Pacific	1949	Emile De Becque	Some Enchanted Evening Reprise 2	Ballad	C3	D4	Lead	Romantic Lead Male
South Pacific	1949	Emile De Becque	This Nearly Was Mine	Ballad	B2	D4	Lead	Romantic Lead Male
South Pacific	1949	Emile De Becque	You've Got To Be Carefully Taught R	Moderate Tempo	C#3	E4	Lead	Romantic Lead Male
Call Me Madam	1950	Cosmo Constantine	Lichtenburg*	Moderate Tempo	Bb2	D4	Lead	Romantic Lead Male
Call Me Madam	1950	Cosmo Constantine	Marrying For Love*	Ballad	G2	C4	Lead	Romantic Lead Male
Guys and Dolls	1950	Sky Masterson	I'll Know*	Ballad	B2	D#4	Lead	Romantic Lead Male
Guys and Dolls	1950	Sky Masterson	My Time Of Day	Ballad	Bb2	Db4	Lead	Romantic Lead Male
Guys and Dolls	1950	Sky Masterson	Luck Be A Lady*	Uptempo	Db3	Eb4	Lead	Romantic Lead Male
King and I, The	1951	King of Siam+	A Puzzlement	Uptempo	C3	E4	Lead	Romantic Lead Male
King and I, The	1951	King of Siam+	Song of the King	Moderate Tempo	D3	D4	Lead	Romantic Lead Male
Wonderful Town	1953	Robert Baker	What A Waste*	Uptempo	Ab2	F#4	Lead	Romantic Lead Male
Wonderful Town	1953	Robert Baker	A Quiet Girl	Ballad	G2	C4	Lead	Romantic Lead Male
Wonderful Town	1953	Robert Baker	It's Love*	Moderate Tempo	A2	F#4	Lead	Romantic Lead Male
Bells Are Ringing	1956	Jeff Moss	Independent	Uptempo	D3	E4	Lead	Romantic Lead Male
Bells Are Ringing	1956	Jeff Moss	I Met A Girl	Uptempo	C3	Gb4	Lead	Romantic Lead Male
Bells Are Ringing	1956	Jeff Moss	Long Before I Knew You *	Ballad	B2	C4	Lead	Romantic Lead Male
Bells Are Ringing	1956	Jeff Moss	Just In Time *	Moderate Tempo	C#3	D4	Lead	Romantic Lead Male
Bells Are Ringing	1956	Jeff Moss	Long Before I Knew You Reprise	Moderate Tempo	C3	C4	Lead	Romantic Lead Male
Bells Are Ringing	1956	Jeff Moss	Better Than A Dream *	Moderate Tempo	E3	D4	Lead	Romantic Lead Male
Most Happy Fella, The	1956	Joe	Joey, Joey, Joey	Moderate Tempo	C3	F4	Lead	Romantic Lead Male
My Fair Lady	1956	Henry Higgins	Why Can't The English	Uptempo	B2	D4	Lead	Romantic Lead Male
My Fair Lady	1956	Henry Higgins	A Hymn to Him	Uptempo	C#3	D4	Lead	Romantic Lead Male
My Fair Lady	1956	Henry Higgins	I've Grown Accustomed To Her Face	Ballad	A2	B3	Lead	Romantic Lead Male
My Fair Lady	1956	Henry Higgins	I'm An Ordinary Man	Moderate Tempo	Bb2	C4	Lead	Romantic Lead Male
Flower Drum Song 2002	1958	Chi-Yang Wang+	Gliding Through My Memory*	Moderate Tempo	D3	G4	Lead	Romantic Lead Male
Once Upon A Mattress	1959	Sir Harry	In A Little While*	Uptempo	Db3	F4	Lead	Romantic Lead Male
Once Upon A Mattress	1959	Sir Harry	In A Little While Reprise*	Ballad	D3	F4	Lead	Romantic Lead Male

* = Music Edit Required
+ = Ethnic Specific

Show	Year	Role	Song	Tempo	Range-Bottom	Range-Top	Category	Char Type
Once Upon A Mattress	1959	Sir Harry	Yesterday I Loved You*	Uptempo	F3	F4	Lead	Romantic Lead Male
Sound Of Music, The	1959	Captain von Trapp	Edelweiss	Ballad	E3	F4	Lead	Romantic Lead Male
Camelot	1960	King Arthur	I Wonder What The King Is Doing To	Uptempo	Bb2	C4	Lead	Romantic Lead Male
Camelot	1960	King Arthur	Camelot*	Uptempo	C3	D4	Lead	Romantic Lead Male
Camelot	1960	Lancelot Du Lac	C'est Moi	Uptempo	B2	D4	Lead	Romantic Lead Male
Camelot	1960	King Arthur	How To Handle A Woman*	Uptempo	A2	D4	Lead	Romantic Lead Male
Camelot	1960	Lancelot Du Lac	If Ever I would Leave You	Ballad	A2	D4	Lead	Romantic Lead Male
Camelot	1960	King Arthur	What Do The Simple Folk Do?*	Moderate Tempo	Bb2	E4	Lead	Romantic Lead Male
Camelot	1960	King Arthur	Finalte Ultimo	Moderate Tempo	Bb2	C4	Lead	Romantic Lead Male
Fantasticks, The	1960	El Gallo	Try To Remember *	Ballad	A2	C4	Lead	Romantic Lead Male
Fantasticks, The	1960	El Gallo	Try To Remember Reprise	Moderate Tempo	B2	C4	Lead	Romantic Lead Male
Fantasticks, The	1960	El Gallo	I Depends On What You Pay	Uptempo	A2	G4	Lead	Romantic Lead Male
Fantasticks, The	1960	El Gallo	Round and Round *	Uptempo	Ab2	F4	Lead	Romantic Lead Male
She Loves Me	1963	Georg Nowack	Three Letters*	Moderate Tempo	D#3	E4	Lead	Romantic Lead Male
She Loves Me	1963	Georg Nowack	She Loves Me	Uptempo	Eb3	F4	Lead	Romantic Lead Male
Funny Girl	1964	Nick Arnstein	I Want To Be Seen With You...*	Moderate Tempo	Ab2	Eb4	Lead	Romantic Lead Male
Funny Girl	1964	Nick Arnstein	You Are Woman*	Moderate Tempo	A#2	E4	Lead	Romantic Lead Male
Funny Girl	1964	Nick Arnstein	Don't Rain On My Parade (Nick)	Moderate Tempo	G3	D4	Lead	Romantic Lead Male
Hair	1968	Claude	Manchester England	Moderate Tempo	E3	F#4	Lead	Romantic Lead Male
Hair	1968	Claude	I Got Life	Uptempo	C3	F4	Lead	Romantic Lead Male
Hair	1968	Claude	Where Do I Go	Moderate Tempo	C4	F5	Lead	Romantic Lead Male
Hair	1968	Claude	Hair	Uptempo	D3	G4	Lead	Romantic Lead Male
Hair	1968	Claude	Manchester England Reprise	Moderate Tempo	E3	E4	Lead	Romantic Lead Male
1776	1969	Richard Henry Lee	The Lees of Old Virginia	Uptempo	C3	F4	Lead	Romantic Lead Male
Applause	1970	Bill Sampson	Think How It's Gonna Be	Moderate Tempo	B2	F4	Lead	Romantic Lead Male
Applause	1970	Bill Sampson	One Of A Kind*	Uptempo	Bb2	F4	Lead	Romantic Lead Male
Company (Revival)	1970	Peter	Have I Got A Girl For You	Uptempo	B3	Gb5	Supporting	Romantic Lead Male
Follies	1971	Benjamin Stone	The Road You Didn't Take *	Uptempo	A2	E4	Lead	Romantic Lead Male
Follies	1971	Benjamin Stone	Too Many Mornings *	Ballad	C3	E4	Lead	Romantic Lead Male
Follies	1971	Benjamin Stone	Live, Laugh, Love	Uptempo	C#3	F4	Lead	Romantic Lead Male
Sugar	1972	Joe	Penniless Bums*	Uptempo	C3	E4	Lead	Romantic Lead Male

Baritone

Show	Year	Role	Song	Tempo	Range-Bottom	Range-Top	Category	Char Type
Sugar	1972	Joe	The Beauty That Drives Men Mad*	Uptempo	D3	F4	Lead	Romantic Lead Male
Sugar	1972	Joe	Doin' It For Sugar*	Moderate Tempo	B3	E4	Lead	Romantic Lead Male
Sugar	1972	Joe	Shell Oil	Moderate Tempo	D3	B3	Lead	Romantic Lead Male
Sugar	1972	Joe	What Do You Give To A Man...*	Uptempo	C3	E4	Lead	Romantic Lead Male
Sugar	1972	Joe	It Always Love	Uptempo	C3	D4	Lead	Romantic Lead Male
A Little Night Music	1973	Count Carl-Magnus Malcolm	In Praise of Women	Uptempo	C3	F4	Supporting	Romantic Lead Male
A Little Night Music	1973	Count Carl-Magnus Malcolm	It Would Have Been Wonderful *	Uptempo	C3	E4	Supporting	Romantic Lead Male
A Little Night Music	1973	Frederik Egerman	Now	Uptempo	B♭2	F4	Lead	Romantic Lead Male
A Little Night Music	1973	Frederik Egerman	You Must Meet My Wife	Uptempo	C3	E4	Lead	Romantic Lead Male
A Little Night Music	1973	Frederik Egerman	It Would Have Been Wonderful *	Uptempo	C3	E4	Lead	Romantic Lead Male
Annie	1977	Oliver Warbucks	N.Y.C. *	Uptempo	C3	F4	Lead	Romantic Lead Male
Annie	1977	Oliver Warbucks	Something Was Missing	Ballad	B♭2	F4	Lead	Romantic Lead Male
Annie	1977	Oliver Warbucks	Why Should I Change A Thing	Ballad	B♭2	G♭4	Lead	Romantic Lead Male
Best Little Whorehouse....	1978	Sherriff Ed Earl	Good Old Girl	Ballad	G3	F4	Lead	Romantic Lead Male
Evita	1978	Juan Peron	The Art of the Possible	Moderate Tempo	B♭2	D4	Lead	Romantic Lead Male
Evita	1978	Juan Peron	She's A Diamond	Moderate Tempo	A2	F4	Lead	Romantic Lead Male
Cats	1981	Munkustrap	The Old Gumbie Cat	Moderate Tempo	E3	F4	Lead	Romantic Lead Male
Dreamgirls	1981	Curtis Taylor, Jr +	Cadillac Car	Uptempo	F3	G4	Lead	Romantic Lead Male
Dreamgirls	1981	Curtis Taylor, Jr +	When I First Saw You	Ball	C3	E4	Lead	Romantic Lead Male
Seven Brides/Seven Brothe	1982	Adam	Bless Your Beautiful Hide*	Moderate Tempo	B2	G4	Lead	Romantic Lead Male
Seven Brides/Seven Brothe	1982	Adam	Get A Wife*	Moderate Tempo	F3	G4	Lead	Romantic Lead Male
Seven Brides/Seven Brothe	1982	Adam	Love Never Goes Away*	Ballad	E3	E4	Lead	Romantic Lead Male
Seven Brides/Seven Brothe	1982	Adam	Sobbin' Women*	Uptempo	C3	F4	Lead	Romantic Lead Male
Seven Brides/Seven Brothe	1982	Adam	A Woman Ought To Know Her Place	Uptempo	F#3	F#4	Lead	Romantic Lead Male
Seven Brides/Seven Brothe	1982	Adam	Love Never Goes Away Tag	Ballad	B3	D4	Lead	Romantic Lead Male
LA Cage Aux Folles	1983	Georges	Song On The Sand	Ballad	A♭2	E4	Lead	Romantic Lead Male
LA Cage Aux Folles	1983	Georges	Masculinity	Uptempo	B2	E4	Lead	Romantic Lead Male
LA Cage Aux Folles	1983	Georges	Look Over There	Ballad	B2	E♭4	Lead	Romantic Lead Male
LA Cage Aux Folles	1983	Georges	With You On My Arm	Moderate Tempo	G#2	E♭4	Lead	Romantic Lead Male
LA Cage Aux Folles	1983	Georges	Song On The Sand Reprise	Ballad	C3	D4	Lead	Romantic Lead Male
Singin' In The Rain	1983	Don Lockwood	You Stepped Out Of A Dream*	Moderate Tempo	C3	C4	Lead	Romantic Lead Male

Baritone

* = Music Edit Required
+ = Ethnic Specific

Show	Year	Role	Song	Tempo	Range-Bottom	Range-Top	Category	Char Type
Singin' In The Rain	1983	Don Lockwood	You Stepped Out Of A Dream Repris	Moderate Tempo	C3	C4	Lead	Romantic Lead Male
Singin' In The Rain	1983	Don Lockwood	You Were Meant For Me	Moderate Tempo	B♭2	D♭4	Lead	Romantic Lead Male
Singin' In The Rain	1983	Don Lockwood	Meant For Me Playoff	Moderate Tempo	C3	D♭4	Lead	Romantic Lead Male
Singin' In The Rain	1983	Don Lockwood	Singin' In The Rain	Uptempo	D3	D4	Lead	Romantic Lead Male
Singin' In The Rain	1983	Don Lockwood	Don's Would You	Moderate Tempo	G2	C4	Lead	Romantic Lead Male
Singin' In The Rain	1983	Don Lockwood	Broadway Rhythm* (ms 115-182)	Uptempo	C3	F4	Lead	Romantic Lead Male
Into The Woods	1987	Cinderella's Prince	Agony*	Moderate Tempo	C#3	E4	Lead	Romantic Lead Male
Into The Woods	1987	Cinderella's Prince	Agony II*	Moderate Tempo	C#3	F4	Lead	Romantic Lead Male
Into The Woods	1987	Cinderella's Prince	Any Moment*	Uptempo	B2	E♭5	Lead	Romantic Lead Male
Into The Woods	1987	Rapunzel's Prince	Agony*	Moderate Tempo	C#3	E4	Lead	Romantic Lead Male
Into The Woods	1987	Rapunzel's Prince	Agony II*	Moderate Tempo	C#3	F4	Lead	Romantic Lead Male
Into The Woods	1987	Wolf	Hello Little Girl	Uptempo	B♭2	G♭4	Lead	Romantic Lead Male
City of Angels	1989	Stine	You're Nothing Without Me *	Uptempo	D3	G4	Lead	Romantic Lead Male
City of Angels	1989	Stine	Funny	Moderate Tempo	B♭2	F4	Lead	Romantic Lead Male
City of Angels	1989	Stine	Double Talk (Stine)	Moderate Tempo	F3	G4	Lead	Romantic Lead Male
City of Angels	1989	Stine	I'm Nothing Without You *	Uptempo	F3	G4	Lead	Romantic Lead Male
Meet Me In St. Louis	1989	Warren Sheffield	Raving Beauty*	Ballad	C3	E♭4	Lead	Romantic Lead Male
Children of Eden	1991	Father	Father's Day	Moderate Tempo	B2	E4	Lead	Romantic Lead Male
Children of Eden	1991	Father	The Mark of Cain	Moderate Tempo	B2	F4	Lead	Romantic Lead Male
Children of Eden	1991	Father	Precious Children	Ballad	B♭2	E♭4	Lead	Romantic Lead Male
Children of Eden	1991	Father	The Hardest Part Of Love *	Uptempo	D3	G4	Lead	Romantic Lead Male
Nick & Nora	1991	Nick Charles	Look Who's Alone Now	Ballad	A♭2	C4	Lead	Romantic Lead Male
Nick & Nora	1991	Nick Charles	As Long As You're Happy*	Uptempo	A2	F4	Lead	Romantic Lead Male
Nick & Nora	1991	Nick Charles	Let' Go Home Nora	Ballad	G3	B4	Lead	Romantic Lead Male
Phantom	1991	Count Philippe	Who Could Have Ever Dreamed Up	Uptempo	B♭2	E4	Lead	Romantic Lead Male
Phantom	1991	Count Philippe	Without Your Music	Moderate Tempo	C3	F4	Lead	Romantic Lead Male
Secret Garden, The	1991	Neville Craven	Disppear*	Moderate Tempo	C3	F4	Lead	Romantic Lead Male
Assassins	1992	The Proprietor	Opening*	Moderate Tempo	F#2	F4	Lead	Romantic Lead Male
Beauty and the Beast	1994	Lumiere	Be Our Guest	Uptempo	F#2	E4	Support	Romantic Lead Male
Songs For A New World	1995	Man 2	The River Won't Flow*	Uptempo	D3	A4	Lead	Romantic Lead Male
Songs For A New World	1995	Man 2	She Cries	Uptempo	C3	G#4	Lead	Romantic Lead Male

Baritone

243

* = Music Edit Required
+ = Ethnic Specific

Show	Year	Role	Song	Tempo	Range-Bottom	Range-Top	Category	Char Type
Songs For A New World	1995	Man 2	I'd Give It All For You*	Moderate Tempo	F#2	G4	Lead	Romantic Lead Male
Songs For A New World	1995	Man 2	Hear My Song*	Moderate Tempo	F3	E4	Lead	Romantic Lead Male
Victor/Victoria	1995	Jazz Singer	Le Jazz Hot*	Moderate Tempo	D3	F#4	Lead	Romantic Lead Male
Victor/Victoria	1995	King Marchan	King's Dilemma*	Uptempo	A2	D4	Lead	Romantic Lead Male
Victor/Victoria	1995	King Marchan	Almost A Love Song*	Ballad	G#2	Eb4	Lead	Romantic Lead Male
Lion King, The	1997	Mufasa	They Live In You*	Moderate Tempo	C#3	F#4	Lead	Romantic Lead Male
Parade	1998	Gov. Jack Slaton	Pretty Music*	Uptempo	C3	G4	Lead	Romantic Lead Male
Ragtime	1998	Father	Journey On*	Uptempo	B2	E4	Lead	Romantic Lead Male
Ragtime	1998	Coalhouse Walker, Jr.	Now She Is Haunting Me (Part 1)	Ballad	Bb2	D4	Lead	Romantic Lead Male
Ragtime	1998	Father	New Music*	Ballad	Bb2	D4	Lead	Romantic Lead Male
Ragtime	1998	Coalhouse Walker, Jr.	On The Wheels Of A Dream*	Moderate Tempo	Ab2	Fb4	Lead	Romantic Lead Male
Ragtime	1998	Coalhouse Walker, Jr.	Coalhouse's Soliloguoy	Moderate Tempo	G2	F4	Lead	Romantic Lead Male
Ragtime	1998	Coalhouse Walker, Jr.	Sarah Brown Eyes*	Moderate Tempo	A2	E4	Lead	Romantic Lead Male
Ragtime	1998	Coalhouse Walker, Jr.	Make Them Hear You	Moderate Tempo	Eb3	G#4	Lead	Romantic Lead Male
Dirty Rotten Scoundrels	2005	Lawrence Jameson	Give Them What They Want *	Moderate Tempo	C3	Eb4	Lead	Romantic Lead Male
Dirty Rotten Scoundrels	2005	Lawrence Jameson	All About Ruprecht	Uptempo	D3	E4	Lead	Romantic Lead Male
Dirty Rotten Scoundrels	2005	Lawrence Jameson	Ruffjousin' Mit Shuffhousen	Uptempo	C3	A4	Lead	Romantic Lead Male
Dirty Rotten Scoundrels	2005	Lawrence Jameson	Love Sneaks In	Ballad	G2	D4	Lead	Romantic Lead Male
Dirty Rotten Scoundrels	2005	Lawrence Jameson	The More We Dance	Uptempo	D3	G4	Lead	Romantic Lead Male
Dirty Rotten Scoundrels	2005	Lawrence Jameson	Dirty Rotten Number	Moderate Tempo	C3	F4	Lead	Romantic Lead Male
Little Women	2005	Professor Bhaer	How I Am	Uptempo	A2	F#4	Supporting	Romantic Lead Male
Grey Gardens	2006	Gould	Drift Away*	Ballad	Eb3	F4	Lead	Romantic Lead Male
White Christmas	2008	Bob Wallace	Love And The Weather*	Uptempo	Db3	E4	Lead	Romantic Lead Male
White Christmas	2008	Bob Wallace	Count Your Blessings*	Moderate Tempo	C3	D4	Lead	Romantic Lead Male
White Christmas	2008	Bob Wallace	Blue Skies (Part 1-3)*	Moderate Tempo	E3	F4	Lead	Romantic Lead Male
White Christmas	2008	Bob Wallace	How Deep Is The Ocean	Ballad	C#3	D4	Lead	Romantic Lead Male
Addams Family, The	2010	Gomez Addams +	Trapped (US Tour)	Moderate Tempo	C3	F4	Lead	Romantic Lead Male

Bass

* = Music Edit Required
+ = Ethnic Specific

Show	Year	Role	Song	Tempo	Range-Bottom	Range-Top	Category	Char Type
Show Boat	1927	Joe+	Ol' Man River	Ballad	F2	D4	Lead	Character Male
Show Boat	1927	Joe+	Ol' Man River Reprise	Ballad	F2	D4	Lead	Character Male
Show Boat	1927	Joe+	Ol' Man River - Act II	Ballad	A♭2	F4	Lead	Character Male
Addams Family, The	2010	Lurch	Move Toward The Darkness	Ballad	G2	E♭4	Supporting	Character Male

Bass

* = Music Edit Required
+ = Ethnic Specific

Voicing	Char Types	Show	Year	Roles	Song	Tempo
Alto/Alto	AF/CF	Caroline or Change	2004	Caroline+ & Washing Machine	16 Feet Beneath The Sea	Ballad
Alto/Alto	AF/CF	Caroline or Change	2004	Caroline+ & Rose	Mr. Gellman's Shirt	Moderate Tempo
Alto/Alto	AF/CF	Caroline or Change	2004	Caroline+ & Dotty	Sunday Morning	Ballad
Alto/Alto	AF/JM	Caroline or Change	2004	Caroline+ & Noah	Gonna Pass Me a Law	Moderate Tempo
Alto/Alto	AF/MF	Nunsense	1985	Mary Hubert & Mother Superior	Just A Coupl'a Sisters	Uptempo
Alto/Alto	CF/AF	Mystery Of Edwin Drood, The	1985	Datchery & Puffer	Settling Up The Score	Uptempo
Alto/Alto	CF/CF	Little Me	1962	Young Belle & Belle	I Needed Social Position	Moderate Tempo
Alto/Alto	CF/CF	Full Monty, The	2000	Georgie & Vicki	You Rule My World Reprise	Ballad
Alto/Alto	CF/CF	Mamma Mia!	2001	Tanya & Rosie	Chiquitta*	Ballad
Alto/Alto	CF/M	Blood Brothers	1993	Mrs. Johnston/Mrs. Lyons	My Child	Ballad
Alto/Alto	CF/RAF	Chicago	1975	Matron & Velma	Class	Moderate Tempo
Alto/Alto	CF/RAF	Color Purple, The	2005	Celie+ & Shug+	What About Love	Ballad
Alto/Alto	CIF/CIF	Spring Awakening	2006	Martha & Ilse	The Dark I Know Well	Moderate Tempo
Alto/Alto	CIF/RAF	Chicago	1975	Roxie & Velma	My Own Best Friend	Moderate Tempo
Alto/Alto	CIF/RAF	Chicago	1975	Roxie & Velma	Nowadays Reprise	Ballad
Alto/Alto	IF/AF	Nunsense	1985	Mary Leo & Mary Hubert	The Biggest Ain't The Best	Uptempo
Alto/Alto	IF/IF	Gypsy	1959	June & Louise	If Momma Was Married	Uptempo
Alto/Alto	IF/IF	Producers, The	2001	Usherette 1 & Usherette 2	It's Opening Night Reprise*	Uptempo
Alto/Alto	JF/JF	Gypsy	1959	Baby June & Baby Louise	May We Entertain You	Uptempo
Alto/Alto	JF/JM	Mary Poppins	2006	Jane & Michael	The Perfect Nanny	Moderate Tempo
Alto/Alto	JF/RLF	Goodbye Girl, The	1993	Lucy & Paula	Footsteps	Moderate Tempo
Alto/Alto	M/M	Honk!	1993	Ida & Maureen	The Joy Of Motherhood	Moderate Tempo
Alto/Alto	M/M	Footloose	1998	Ethel & Vi	Learning To Be Silent	Ballad
Alto/Alto	M/MF	Honk!	1993	Lowbutt & Queenie	It Takes All Sorts	Uptempo
Alto/Alto	MF/CF	Most Happy Fella, The	1956	Marie & Cleo	I Don't Like This Dame	Uptempo
Alto/Alto	MF/CIF	Little Women	2005	Aunt March & Jo	Could You	Uptempo
Alto/Alto	MF/MF	Fame	2003	Bell & Sherman	Teacher's Argument	Uptempo
Alto/Alto	RAF/AF	Rent	1996	Maureen & Joanne	Take Me Or Leave Me	Uptempo
Alto/Alto	RAF/CIF	Kiss Of The Spider Woman	1993	Aurora & Marta	I Do Miracles	Moderate Tempo
Alto/Alto	RAF/RAF	Sweet Charity	1966	Nickie & Helene	Baby Dream Your Dream	Moderate Tempo
Alto/Alto	RLF/CF	City Of Angels	1989	Gabby & Oolie	What You Don't Know About Women	Uptempo
Alto/Alto	RLF/CF	Wicked	2003	Morrible & Elphaba	The Wizard and I	Moderate Tempo
Alto/Alto	RLF/CIF	Next To Normal	2009	Diana & Natalie	Why Stay	Uptempo
Alto/Alto	RLF/CIM	Next To Normal	2009	Diana & Natalie	Maybe*	Moderate Tempo
Alto/Alto	RLF/JF	High Society 1998	1953	Tracy & Dinah	I Love Paris	Moderate Tempo

RLF=Romantic Leading Female   RLM=Romantic Leading Male   MF=Mature Female   MM=Mature Male
IF=Ingenue Female   IM=Ingenue Male   JF=Juvenile Female JM=Juvenile Male
CIF=Character Ingenue Female   CIM=Character Ingenue Male   RAF=Rom. Antagonist Female   RAM=Rom. Antagonist Male
CF=Character Female   CM=Character Male   AF=Antagonist Female   AM=Antagonist Male
M=Maternal   P=Paternal

Duets

* = Music Edit Required
+ = Ethnic Specific

Voicing	Char Types	Show	Year	Roles	Song	Tempo
Alto/Alto	RLF/JM	Mame	1966	Mame & Young Patrick	You're My Best Girl	Ballad
Alto/Alto	RLF/RAF	Pal Joey	1940	Linda & Vera	Take Him	Moderate Tempo
Alto/Alto	RLF/RAF	Mame	1966	Mame & Vera	Bosom Buddies	Moderate Tempo
Alto/Alto	RLF/RLF	Nine	1982	Lileane & Stephanie	Folies Bergeres*	Uptempo
Alto/Alto	RLM/IF	White Christmas	2008	Betty Haynes & Judy Haynes	Sisters	Moderate Tempo
Alto/Bar	CF/CM	Little Me	1962	Young Belle & Noble Eggleston	I Love You	Moderate Tempo
Alto/Bar	CF/CM	Apple Tree, The	1966	Barbara & Sanjar	Forbidden Love (In Gaul)	Moderate Tempo
Alto/Bar	CF/CM	Guys And Dolls	2006	Adelaide & Nathan	Sue Me	Moderate Tempo
Alto/Bar	CF/RLM	Annie Get Your Gun	1949	Annie & Fank	They Say It's Wonderful Reprise	Ballad
Alto/Bar	CF/RLM	Annie Get Your Gun	1949	Annie & Fank	Anything You Can Do	Uptempo
Alto/Bar	CF/RLM	Bells Are Ringing	1956	Ella & Jeff	Long Before I Knew You	Ballad
Alto/Bar	CF/RLM	Bells Are Ringing	1956	Ella & Jeff	Just In Time*	Uptempo
Alto/Bar	CF/RLM	Funny Girl	1964	Fanny & Nick	I Want To Be Seen With You	Uptempo
Alto/Bar	CF/RLM	Into The Woods	1987	Baker's Wife & C's Prince	Any Moment	Moderate Tempo
Alto/Bar	CIF/CM	Fame	1988	Carmen & Schlomo	Bring On Tomorrow	Moderate Tempo
Alto/Bar	CIF/IM	Good News (1993 Revival)	1993	Connie & Tom	The Best Things In Life Are Free	Moderate Tempo
Alto/Bar	CIF/IM	Good News (1993 Revival)	1993	Connie & Tom	Lucky In Love	Uptempo
Alto/Bar	CIF/MM	Rags	1986	Bella & Avram Cohen	Rags	Uptempo
Alto/Bar	CIF/P	Beauty And The Beast	1999	Belle & Maurice	No Matter What	Moderate Tempo
Alto/Bar	CIF/RLM	Fiddler On The Roof	1964	Hodel & Perchik	Now I Have Everything	Uptempo
Alto/Bar	CM/CF	Les Miserables	1987	M. Thenardier & Thenardier	Beggar At The Feast	Uptempo
Alto/Bar	IF/IM	Sound Of Music, The	1959	Liesl & Rolf	You Are Sixteen	Moderate Tempo
Alto/Bar	IF/IM	Good News (1993 Revival)	1993	Babe & Bobby	Button Up Your Overcoat	Uptempo
Alto/Bar	IF/RAM	Anyone Can Whistle	1964	Fay & Hapgood	Come Play Wiz Me	Uptempo
Alto/Bar	IF/RAM	Anyone Can Whistle	1964	Fay & Hapgood	With So Little To Be Sure Of	Moderate Tempo
Alto/Bar	M/CIM	Honk!	1993	Ida & Ugly	Hold Your Head Up High Reprise	Ballad
Alto/Bar	M/P	Fiddler On The Roof	1964	Golde & Tevye	Do You Love Me	Moderate Tempo
Alto/Bar	MF/MM	Cabaret	1966	F. Schneider & H. Schultz	It Couldn't Please Me More	Moderate Tempo
Alto/Bar	MF/MM	Cabaret	1966	F. Schneider & H. Schultz	Married	Ballad
Alto/Bar	MF/MM	Follies	1971	Emily & Theodore	Rain On The Roof	Uptempo
Alto/Bar	MF/P	Rags	1986	Rachel & Avram	Three Sunny Rooms	Moderate Tempo
Alto/Bar	RAF/CM	Sunset Boulevard	1994	Norma & Max	The Final Scene	Ballad
Alto/Bar	RAF/IM	Damn Yankees	1955	Lola & Sohovik	Who's Got The Pain	Uptempo
Alto/Bar	RAF/RLF	Evita	1978	Eva & Peron	I'd Be Surprisingly Good For You	Moderate Tempo
Alto/Bar	RAF/RLM	Evita	1978	Eva & Peron	Dice Are Rolling	Moderate Tempo

RLF=Romantic Leading Female RLM=Romantic Leading Male
IF=Ingenue Female IM=Ingenue Male
CIF=Character Ingenue Female CIM=Character Ingenue Male
CF=Character Female CM=Character Male
M=Maternal P=Paternal

MF=Mature Female MM=Mature Male
JF=Juvenile Female JM=Juvenile Male
RAF=Rom. Antagonist Female RAM=Rom. Antagonist Male
AF=Antagonist Female AM=Antagonist Male

Duets

Duets

* = Music Edit Required
+ = Ethnic Specific

Voicing	Char Types	Show	Year	Roles	Song	Tempo
Alto/Bar	RLF/CM	Mamma Mia!	2001	Donna & Harry	One Last Summer	Ballad
Alto/Bar	RLF/RAM	City Of Angels	1989	Alaura & Stone	The Tennis Song	Uptempo
Alto/Bar	RLF/RAM	City Of Angels	1989	Bobbi & Stone	With Every Breath I Take Reprise	Ballad
Alto/Bar	RLF/RLM	No, No Nanette	1925	Lucille Early & Bill Early	You Can Dance With Any Girl At All	Uptempo
Alto/Bar	RLF/RLM	A Little Night Music	1973	Desiree & Frederik	You Must Meet My Wife	Moderate Tempo
Alto/Sop	CF/CF	Ain't Misbehavin	1988	Woman One & Woman Two	Find What They Like	Uptempo
Alto/Sop	CF/IF	Into The Woods	1987	Baker's Wife & Cinderella	A Very Nice Prince	Uptempo
Alto/Sop	CF/RLF	Wicked	2003	Elphaba & Glinda	Defying Gravity	Uptempo
Alto/Sop	CF/RLF	Wicked	2003	Elphaba & Glinda	For Good	Ballad
Alto/Sop	CIF/CIF	Carousel	1945	Carrie & Julie	You're A Queer One Julie Jordan	Uptempo
Alto/Sop	CIF/IF	Spitfire Grill	2001	Percy & Shelby	The Colors of Paradise	Uptempo
Alto/Sop	CM/IF	Guys And Dolls	2006	Adelaide & Sarah	Marry The Man Today	Uptempo
Alto/Sop	JM/M	Billy Elliot	2008	Billy & Mum	Dear Billy's Reply	Ballad
Alto/Sop	MF/IF	Cats	1981	Grizabella & Victoria	Memory Reprise	Ballad
Alto/Sop	RLF/IF	West Side Story	1957	Anita+ & Maria+	A Boy Like That	Moderate Tempo
Alto/Tenor	CF/CM	Avenue Q	2003	Gary & Nicky	Schadenfreude	Uptempo
Alto/Tenor	CF/CM	Cinderella (2013)	2013	Gabrielle & Jean-Michel	Now the Time Reprise	Moderate Tempo
Alto/Tenor	CF/IM	Les Miserables	1987	Eponine & Marius	A Little Fall Of Rain	Ballad
Alto/Tenor	CF/RLM	Wicked	2003	Elphaba & Fiyero	As Long As You Are Mine	Moderate Tempo
Alto/Tenor	CIF/AM	Jesus Christ Superstar	1971	Mary & Peter	Could We Start Again Please	Ballad
Alto/Tenor	CIF/CIM	Footloose	1998	Ariel & Ren	Almost Paradise	Ballad
Alto/Tenor	CIF/CIM	Wicked	2003	Nessarose & BOQ	Dancing Through Life*	Uptempo
Alto/Tenor	CIF/CIM	Next To Normal	2009	Natalie & Henry	Hey #3 Reprise	Moderate Tempo
Alto/Tenor	CIF/CM	Carousel	1945	Carrie & Enoch	When The Children Are Asleep	Moderate Tempo
Alto/Tenor	CIF/CM	Little Shop of Horrors	1982	Audrey & Seymour	Call Back In The Morning	Uptempo
Alto/Tenor	CIF/CM	Spitfire Grill	2001	Percy & Joe	This Wide Woods Part 4	Moderate Tempo
Alto/Tenor	CIF/IM	Thoroughly Modern Millie	2002	Millie & Jimmy	I Turned The Corner	Moderate Tempo
Alto/Tenor	CIF/RAM	Chess	1988	Florence & Freddie	Commie Newpapers	Uptempo
Alto/Tenor	CIF/RAM	Chess	1988	Florence & Freddie	You Want To Loose Your Only Friend	Uptempo
Alto/Tenor	CIF/RAM	Chess	1988	Florence & Freddie	So You Got What You Want	Uptempo
Alto/Tenor	CM/CM	Grease	1971	Jan & Roger	Mooning	Moderate Tempo
Alto/Tenor	CM/IF	How To Succeed...	1961	Finch & Rosemary	Rosemary	Moderate Tempo
Alto/Tenor	IF/CM	Legally Blonde	2007	Elle & Emmett	Legally Blonde	Ballad
Alto/Tenor	IF/IM	Mamma Mia!	2001	Sophie & Sky	Lay All Your Love On Me	Moderate Tempo
Alto/Tenor	IF/IM	Last Five Years, The	2002	Cathy & Jamie	The Next Ten Minutes	Ballad

RLF=Romantic Leading Female RLM=Romantic Leading Male MF=Mature Female MM=Mature Male
IF=Ingenue Female IM=Ingenue Male JF=Juvenile Female JM=Juvenile Male
CIF=Character Ingenue Female CIM=Character Ingenue Male RAF=Rom. Antagonist Female RAM=Rom. Antagonist Male
CF=Character Female CM=Character Male AF=Antagonist Female AM=Antagonist Male
M=Maternal P=Paternal

Duets

249

Duets

* = Music Edit Required
+ = Ethnic Specific

Voicing	Char Types	Show	Year	Roles	Song	Tempo
Alto/Tenor	IF/IM	High School Musical	2007	Gabriella & Troy	What I've Been Looking For Reprise	Ballad
Alto/Tenor	IF/IM	High School Musical	2007	Gabriella & Troy	If I Can't Take My Eyes Off You	Uptempo
Alto/Tenor	IF/IM	High School Musical	2007	Gabriella & Troy	Start Of Something New Reprise	Uptempo
Alto/Tenor	IF/IM	High School Musical	2007	Gabriella & Troy	Breaking Free	Uptempo
Alto/Tenor	IF/IM	Legally Blonde	2007	Elle & Warner	Serious	Moderate Tempo
Alto/Tenor	IF/IM	Legally Blonde	2007	Elle & Warner	Serious Reprise	Moderate Tempo
Alto/Tenor	RAF/RAM	Rent	1996	Mimi Marquez & Roger Davis	Light My Candle	Moderate Tempo
Alto/Tenor	RAF/RAM	Rent	1996	Mimi Marquez & Roger Davis	Goodbye Love	Moderate Tempo
Alto/Tenor	RLF/CIM	Next To Normal	2009	Diana & Gabe	Catch Me I'm Falling Reprise	Moderate Tempo
Alto/Tenor	RLF/CM	Next To Normal	2009	Diana & Dr. Madden	You Don't Know Reprise	Uptempo
Alto/Tenor	RLF/CM	Next To Normal	2009	Diana & Dan	How Could I Forget	Ballad
Alto/Tenor	RLF/IM	Scarlet Pimpernel, The	1997	Marguerite & Armad	You Are My Home (Garden Reprise)	Ballad
Alto/Tenor	RLF/IM	Aida	2000	Aida+ & Mereb+	How I Know You	Ballad
Alto/Tenor	RLF/RAM	Sunday...Park With Geroge	1984	Dot & George	We Do Not Belong Together	Moderate Tempo
Alto/Tenor	RLF/RLM	Aida	2000	Aida+ & Mereb+	Enchantment Passing Through	Ballad
Alto/Tenor	RLF/RLM	Aida	2000	Aida+ & Mereb+	Elaborate Lives	Ballad
Alto/Tenor	RLF/RLM	Aida	2000	Aida+ & Mereb+	Written In The Stars	Ballad
Alto/Tenor	RLF/RLM	Aida	2000	Aida+ & Mereb+	Elaborate Lives Reprise	Ballad
Alto/Tenor	RLF/RLM	Mamma Mia!	2001	Donna & Sam	SOS	Uptempo
Alto/Tenor	RLM/CM	Les Miserables	1987	Fantine & Jean Valjean	Come To Me	Ballad
Bar/Alto	AM/AF	Oliver!	1963	Mr. & Mrs. Sowerberry	That's Your Funeral*	Uptempo
Bar/Alto	AM/CF	Sweeney Todd	1979	Sweeney & Mrs. Lovett	My Friends	Ballad
Bar/Alto	AM/CF	Sweeney Todd	1979	Sweeney & Mrs. Lovett	A Little Priest	Uptempo
Bar/Alto	AM/CF	My Favorite Year	1992	King & Alice	Professional Show Biz Comedy	Uptempo
Bar/Alto	AM/RAM	Spamalot	2005	King Arthur & Lady of the Lake	Twice In Every Show	Moderate Tempo
Bar/Alto	AM/RLF	Goodbye Girl, The	1993	Elliot & Paula	My Rules	Uptempo
Bar/Alto	AM/RLF	Goodbye Girl, The	1993	Elliot & Paula	Paula	Moderate Tempo
Bar/Alto	Any/Any	Mystery Of Edwin Drood, The	1985	Male & Female	Perfect Strangers*	Moderate Tempo
Bar/Alto	CIM/CIF	Oklahoma!	1943	Will & Ado Annie	All 'Er Nothin'	Uptempo
Bar/Alto	CIM/CIF	Once Upon A Mattress	1959	Dauntless & Winifred	Song of Love	Uptempo
Bar/Alto	CIM/CIF	Follies	1971	Young Buddy & Young Sally	Love Will See Us Through	Uptempo
Bar/Alto	CM/AF	Gypsy	1959	Herbie & Rose	Small World	Moderate Tempo
Bar/Alto	CM/AF	Oliver!	1963	Mr. Bumble & Widow Corney	I Shall Scream	Uptempo
Bar/Alto	CM/AF	Oliver!	1963	Mr. Bumble & Widow Corney	Oliver Reprise	Uptempo

RLF=Romantic Leading Female   RLM=Romantic Leading Male   MF=Mature Female   MM=Mature Male
IF=Ingenue Female   IM=Ingenue Male   JF=Juvenile Female   JM=Juvenile Male
CIF=Character Ingenue Female   CIM=Character Ingenue Male   RAF=Rom. Antagonist Female   RAM=Rom. Antagonist Male
CF=Character Female   CM=Character Male   AF=Antagonist Female   AM=Antagonist Male
M=Maternal   P=Paternal

Duets

250

* = Music Edit Required
+ = Ethnic Specific

Voicing	Char Types	Show	Year	Roles	Song	Tempo
Bar/Alto	CM/AF	You're A Good Man Charlie Brown	1971	Charlie Brown & Lucy	The Doctor Is In	Moderate Tempo
Bar/Alto	CM/CF	Pajama Game	1954	Hines & Mabel	I'll Never Be Jealous Again	Uptempo
Bar/Alto	CM/CF	Little Me	1962	Mr. Pinchley & Belle	Deep Down Inside*	Uptempo
Bar/Alto	CM/CF	Baby	1983	Nick & Pam	Romance	Moderate Tempo
Bar/Alto	CM/CF	Baby	1983	Nick & Pam	Romance Reprise	Moderate Tempo
Bar/Alto	CM/CF	Into The Woods	1987	Baker & Baker's Wife	It Takes Two	Uptempo
Bar/Alto	CM/CF	Seussical	2000	The Mayor & Mrs. Mayor	How To Raise A Child	Uptempo
Bar/Alto	CM/IF	Call Me Madam	1950	Kenneth & Maria	It's A Lovely Day Today	Moderate Tempo
Bar/Alto	CM/IF	Call Me Madam	1950	Kenneth & Maria	It's A Lovely Day Today Reprise 2	Moderate Tempo
Bar/Alto	CM/IF	White Christmas	2008	Phil Davis & Judy Haynes	I Love A Piano*	Moderate Tempo
Bar/Alto	CM/JM	Seussical	2000	Horton & JoJo	Alone In The Universe	Moderate Tempo
Bar/Alto	CM/MF	Funny Girl	1964	Eddie & Mrs. Brice	Who Taught Her Everything	Moderate Tempo
Bar/Alto	CM/MF	Nick & Nora	1991	Max Bernheim & Lorraine Bixby	Max's Story	Moderate Tempo
Bar/Alto	CM/RAF	Call Me Madam	1950	Kenneth & Sally	You're Just In Love	Uptempo
Bar/Alto	CM/RLF	Bye Bye Birdie	1960	Albert & Rose	An English Teacher	Uptempo
Bar/Alto	CM/RLF	Bye Bye Birdie	1960	Albert & Rose	Rosie	Ballad
Bar/Alto	CM/RLF	Sugar	1972	Jerry & Sugar	We Could Be Close	Moderate Tempo
Bar/Alto	CM/RLF	Parade	1998	Leo Frank & Lucille Frank	This Is Not Over Yet	Uptempo
Bar/Alto	CM/RLF	Parade	1998	Leo Frank & Lucille Frank	All The Wasted Time	Ballad
Bar/Alto	CM/RLF	Dirty Rotten Scoundrels	2005	Andre & Muriel	Like Zis/Like Zat	Moderate Tempo
Bar/Alto	CM/RLF	In The Heights	2008	Usnavi & Vanessa	Champagne	Moderate Tempo
Bar/Alto	IF/IM	Babes In Arms (1998)	1937	Billie Smith & Val LaMar	Where Or When	Moderate Tempo
Bar/Alto	IF/IM	Babes In Arms (1998)	1937	Billie Smith & Val LaMar	All At Once	Moderate Tempo
Bar/Alto	IM/CIF	Show Boat	1927	Frank & Ellie	Goodbye My Lady Love	Uptempo
Bar/Alto	IM/CIF	Meet Me In St. Louis	1989	John & Esther	You Are For Loving	Ballad
Bar/Alto	IM/CIF	Addams Family, The	2010	Lucas & Wednesday	Crazier Than You	Uptempo
Bar/Alto	IM/IF	Cats	1981	Mungojerrie & Rumpleteazer	Mongojerrie and Rumpleteazer	Uptempo
Bar/Alto	IM/IF	Parade	1998	Frankie Epps & Mary Phagan	The Picture Show	Uptempo
Bar/Alto	IM/RAM	State Fair 1996	1947	Wayne Frake & Emily Arden	So Far	Moderate Tempo
Bar/Alto	MM/MF	Most Happy Fella, The	1956	Tony & Marie	A Long Time Ago	Moderate Tempo
Bar/Alto	MM/MF	A Man Of No Importance	2002	Carney & Lily	Books	Moderate Tempo
Bar/Alto	P/M	Meet Me In St. Louis	1989	Alonso & Anna Sith	Wasn't It Fun	Ballad
Bar/Alto	P/M	State Fair 1996	1996	Abel Frake & Melissa Frake	When I Go Out Walking With My Baby	Moderate Tempo
Bar/Alto	P/M	State Fair 1996	1996	Abel Frake & Melissa Frake	Boys And Girls Like You And Me	Moderate Tempo
Bar/Alto	RAM/CF	High Society 1998	1956	Mike & Liz	Who Wants To Be A Millionaire	Moderate Tempo

RLF=Romantic Leading Female   RLM=Romantic Leading Male   MF=Mature Female   MM=Mature Male
IF=Ingenue Female   IM=Ingenue Male   JF=Juvenile Female   JM=Juvenile Male
CIF=Character Ingenue Female   CIM=Character Ingenue Male   RAF=Rom. Antagonist Female   RAM=Rom. Antagonist Male
CF=Character Female   CM=Character Male   AF=Antagonist Female   AM=Antagonist Male
M=Maternal   P=Paternal

Duets

* = Music Edit Required
+ = Ethnic Specific

Voicing	Char Types	Show	Year	Roles	Song	Tempo
Bar/Alto	RAM/IF	Pal Joey	1940	Joey & Linda	I Could Write A Book	Moderate Tempo
Bar/Alto	RAM/IF	State Fair 1996	1945	Pat Gilbert & Margy Frake	Isn't It Kinda Fun	Uptempo
Bar/Alto	RAM/RAF	Sunday...Park With Geroge	1984	Jules & Yvonne	No Life	Moderate Tempo
Bar/Alto	RAM/RAF	Mystery Of Edwin Drood, The	1985	Neville & Helena	A British Subject*	Moderate Tempo
Bar/Alto	RAM/RAF	Merrily We Roll Along 1994	1994	Tyler & Dory	Transition 6	Uptempo
Bar/Alto	RAM/RAF	Addams Family, The	2010	Gomez & Morticia	Where Did We Go Wrong	Moderate Tempo
Bar/Alto	RAM/RAF	Addams Family, The	2010	Gomez & Morticia	Live Before We Die	Moderate Tempo
Bar/Alto	RAM/RLF	Pal Joey	1940	Joey & Vera	Den Of Iniquity	Uptempo
Bar/Alto	RAM/RLF	Pajama Game	1954	Ensemble	Seven And A Half Cents	Uptempo
Bar/Alto	RAM/RLF	They're Playing Our Song	1974	Vernon Gersch & Sonia Walsk	Workin' It Out*	Uptempo
Bar/Alto	RAM/RLF	They're Playing Our Song	1974	Vernon Gersch & Sonia Walsk	Right*	Uptempo
Bar/Alto	RAM/RLF	They're Playing Our Song	1974	Vernon Gersch & Sonia Walsk	When You're In My Arms*	Uptempo
Bar/Alto	RAM/RLF	Sunday...Park With Geroge	1984	George & Dot	Color And Light (Part 3)	Uptempo
Bar/Alto	RAM/RLF	Will Rogers Follies	1991	Will Rogers & Betty Blake	The Big Time*	Moderate Tempo
Bar/Alto	RAM/RLF	Will Rogers Follies	1991	Will Rogers & Betty Blake	Marry Me Now/Without You	Moderate Tempo
Bar/Alto	RAM/RLF	Scarlet Pimpernel, The	1997	Chauvelin & Marguerite	The Riddle Part 3*	Moderate Tempo
Bar/Alto	RAM/RLF	White Christmas	2008	Bob Wallace & Betty Haynes	Count Your Blessings	Moderate Tempo
Bar/Alto	RLM/CF	Anything Goes	1934	Billy & Reno	You're The Top	Uptempo
Bar/Alto	RLM/CIF	Seven Brides/Seven Brothers	1982	Adam & Gideon	A Woman Ought To Know...Reprise	Uptempo
Bar/Alto	RLM/CIF	Seven Brides/Seven Brothers	1982	Adam & Molly	Wonderful Day Reprise	Moderate Tempo
Bar/Alto	RLM/RAF	Call Me Madam	1950	Cosmo & Sally	Marrying For Love	Ballad
Bar/Alto	RLM/RAF	Flower Drum Song 2002	1958	Wang+ & Liang+	Don't Marry Me	Uptempo
Bar/Alto	RLM/RAF	Applause	1970	Bill & Margo	One Of A Kind	Uptempo
Bar/Alto	RLM/RAF	Applause	1970	Bill & Margo	Something Greater	Uptempo
Bar/Alto	RLM/RAF	Spamalot	2005	Sir Galahad & Lady of the Lake	The Song That Goes Like This	Moderate Tempo
Bar/Alto	RLM/RLF	South Pacific	1949	Emile & Nellie	Twin Soliloquies	Moderate Tempo
Bar/Alto	RLM/RLF	South Pacific	1949	Emile & Nellie	Some Enchanted Evening Reprise	Moderate Tempo
Bar/Alto	RLM/RLF	South Pacific	1949	Emile & Nellie	Cockeyed Optimist Reprise	Uptempo
Bar/Alto	RLM/RLF	South Pacific	1949	Emile & Nellie	Cockeyed Optimist Reprise	Uptempo
Bar/Alto	RLM/RLF	Sugar	1972	Joe & Sugar	What Do You Give To A Man...	Uptempo
Bar/Alto	RLM/RLF	Nick & Nora	1991	Nick Charles & Nora Charles	As Long As You're Happy	Uptempo
Bar/Alto	RLM/RLF	Nick & Nora	1991	Nick Charles & Nora Charles	Married Life	Moderate Tempo
Bar/Alto	RLM/RLF	Nick & Nora	1991	Nick Charles & Nora Charles	Is There Anything Better Than Dancing	Moderate Tempo
Bar/Alto	RLM/RLF	Good News (1993 Revival)	1993	Coach & Kenyon	You're The Cream In My Coffee	Uptempo
Bar/Alto	RLM/RLF	White Christmas	2008	Bob Wallace & Betty Haynes	Love And The Weather	Uptempo

RLF=Romantic Leading Female   RLM=Romantic Leading Male   MF=Mature Female   MM=Mature Male
IF=Ingenue Female   IM=Ingenue Male   JF=Juvenile Female   JM=Juvenile Male
CIF=Character Ingenue Female   CIM=Character Ingenue Male   RAF=Rom. Antagonist Female   RAM=Rom. Antagonist Male
CF=Character Female   CM=Character Male   AF=Antagonist Female   AM=Antagonist Male
M=Maternal   P=Paternal

Duets

* = Music Edit Required
+ = Ethnic Specific

Voicing	Char Types	Show	Year	Roles	Song	Tempo
Bar/Alto	RLM/RLF	White Christmas	2008	Bob Wallace & Betty Haynes	How Deep Is The Ocean Reprise	Moderate Tempo
Bar/Bar	AM/AM	Sweeney Todd	1979	Sweeney & Judge Turpin	Pretty Women (I & II)	Ballad
Bar/Bar	AM/RAM	My Favorite Year	1992	King & Alan	Musketeer Sketch Rehearsal PII*	Uptempo
Bar/Bar	CIM/CM	Spring Awakening	2006	Georg & Otto	The World Of You Body Reprise	Ballad
Bar/Bar	CM/CM	Kiss Me Kate	1948	First Man & Second Man	Brush Up Your Shakespeare	Uptempo
Bar/Bar	CM/CM	Little Me	1962	Benny & Bernie	To Be A Performer	Uptempo
Bar/Bar	CM/CM	Little Me	1962	Benny & Bernie	Be A Performer Reprise	Uptempo
Bar/Bar	CM/CM	Hair	1968	Ron & Tribe Member	What A Piece Of Work Is Man	Moderate Tempo
Bar/Bar	CM/CM	Full Monty, The	2000	Dave & Harold	You Rule My World	Ballad
Bar/Bar	CM/CM	Producers, The	2001	Max Bialystock & Leo Bloom	We Can Do It	Uptempo
Bar/Bar	CM/CM	Producers, The	2001	Max Bialystock & Leo Bloom	We Can Do It Reprise	Uptempo
Bar/Bar	CM/CM	Producers, The	2001	Max Bialystock & Leo Bloom	Where Did We Go Right	Uptempo
Bar/Bar	CM/CM	Producers, The	2001	Max Bialystock & Leo Bloom	Til Him	Ballad
Bar/Bar	CM/CM	Thoroughly Modern Millie	2002	Ching Ho & Bun Foo	Not For The Life Of Me Reprise II	Uptempo
Bar/Bar	CM/MM	Into The Woods	1987	Baker & Mysterious Man	No More	Ballad
Bar/Bar	CM/RLM	Sugar	1972	Jerry & Joe	Penniless Bums	Uptempo
Bar/Bar	CM/RLM	Sugar	1972	Jerry & Joe	The Beauty That Drives Men Mad	Uptempo
Bar/Bar	CM/RLM	Sugar	1972	Jerry & Joe	Doin' It For Sugar	Moderate Tempo
Bar/Bar	CM/RLM	LA Cage Aux Folles	1983	Albin & Georges	With You on My Arm Reprise	Moderate Tempo
Bar/Bar	CM/RLM	LA Cage Aux Folles	1983	Albin & Georges	Song On The Sand Reprise	Ballad
Bar/Bar	CM/RLM	City Of Angels	1989	Buddy & Stine	Double Talk	Uptempo
Bar/Bar	CM/RLM	Secret Garden, The	1991	Archibald & Neville	Lily's Eyes	Moderate Tempo
Bar/Bar	CM/RLM	Guys And Dolls	2006	Nathan & Sky	Travelling Light	Moderate Tempo
Bar/Bar	IM/CM	Cats	1981	Mistoffolees & Rum Tum Tigger	Mr. Mistoffolees	Uptempo
Bar/Bar	IM/IM	Babes In Arms (1998)	1937	Irving+ & Ivor+	Light On Our Feet	Uptempo
Bar/Bar	JM/JM	King and I, The	1951	Louis & Prince	A Puzzlement Reprise	Uptempo
Bar/Bar	MF/MM	Damn Yankees	1955	Boyd & Meg	A Man Doesn't Know Reprise 2	Moderate Tempo
Bar/Bar	MM/AM	Phantom	1991	Gerard & Erik	You Are My Own	Moderate Tempo
Bar/Bar	MM/CM	Sugar	1972	Sir Osgood & Jerry	Beautiful Through and Through	Moderate Tempo
Bar/Bar	MM/MM	Phantom Of The Opera	1986	Monsieurs Firmin & Andre	Notes	Uptempo
Bar/Bar	MM/MM	Phantom Of The Opera	1986	Monsieurs Firmin & Andre	Prima Donna*	Moderate Tempo
Bar/Bar	MM/MM	Chess	1988	Molokov & Walter	Endgame II	Uptempo
Bar/Bar	P/P	Fantasticks, The	1960	Bellomy & Hucklebee	Never Say No	Moderate Tempo
Bar/Bar	P/P	Fantasticks, The	1960	Bellomy & Hucklebee	Plant A Radish	Uptempo
Bar/Bar	RAM/AM	Will Rogers Follies	1991	Clem Rogers & Will Rogers	Will-A-Mania Reprise*	Ballad

RLF=Romantic Leading Female   RLM=Romantic Leading Male   MF=Mature Female   MM=Mature Male
IF=Ingenue Female   IM=Ingenue Male   JF=Juvenile Female   JM=Juvenile Male
CIF=Character Ingenue Female   CIM=Character Ingenue Male   RAF=Rom. Antagonist Female   RAM=Rom. Antagonist Male
CF=Character Female   CM=Character Male   AF=Antagonist Female   AM=Antagonist Male
M=Maternal   P=Paternal

Duets

* = Music Edit Required
+ = Ethnic Specific

Voicing	Char Types	Show	Year	Roles	Song	Tempo
Bar/Bar	RLF/RLM	Into The Woods	1987	C's Prince & R's Prince	Agony Reprise	Moderate Tempo
Bar/Bar	RLM/AM	Oklahoma!	1943	Curly & Jud Fry	Poor Jud	Ballad
Bar/Bar	RLM/CM	White Christmas	2008	Bob Wallace & Phil Davis	Happy Holiday	Uptempo
Bar/Bar	RLM/CM	White Christmas	2008	Bob Wallace & Phil Davis	Happy Holiday/Let Yourself Go	Uptempo
Bar/Bar	RLM/CM	White Christmas	2008	Bob Wallace & Phil Davis	Sisters Reprise	Moderate Tempo
Bar/Bar	RLM/MM	My Fair Lady	1956	Henry & Pickering	You Did It	Uptempo
Bar/Bar	RLM/RAM	City Of Angels	1989	Stine & Stone	You're Nothing Without Me	Uptempo
Bar/Bar	RLM/RAM	Assassins	1992	Proprietor & Booth	Opening	Moderate Tempo
Bar/Bar	RLM/RLM	A Little Night Music	1973	Carl-Magnus/Frederik	It Would Have Been Wonderful	Moderate Tempo
Bar/Bar	RLM/RLM	Into The Woods	1987	C's Prince & R's Prince	Agony	Moderate Tempo
Bar/Mute	CIF/MM	Once Upon A Mattress	1959	Sextimus & Dauntless	Man To Man Talk	Uptempo
Bar/Sop	AM/CF	Peter Pan	1954	Hook & Peter Pan	Oh, My Mysterious Lady	Uptempo
Bar/Sop	AM/IF	Phantom	1991	Phantom & Christine	Home	Moderate Tempo
Bar/Sop	AM/IF	Phantom	1991	Phantom & Christine	You Are Music	Moderate Tempo
Bar/Sop	AM/RLF	Rags	1986	Saul & Rebecca	Wanting	Moderate Tempo
Bar/Sop	AM/RLM	Porgy and Bess	1935	Crown & Bess	Crown!	Moderate Tempo
Bar/Sop	AM/RLM	Porgy and Bess	1935	Crown & Bess+	What You Want Wid Bess	Moderate Tempo
Bar/Sop	CF/CIF	Curtains	2007	Cioffi & Nikki	A Tough Act To Follow	Uptempo
Bar/Sop	CIM/CIF	My Favorite Year	1992	Benjy & K.C.	Shut Up And Dance	Moderate Tempo
Bar/Sop	CIM/RLF	Hello Dolly	1964	Cornelius & Irene	It Only Takes A Moment	Ballad
Bar/Sop	CM/CF	Most Happy Fella, The	1956	Tony & Rosabella	Finale-My Heart Is So Full....	Uptempo
Bar/Sop	CM/CF	110 In The Shade	1963	File & Lizzie	A Man And A Woman	Ballad
Bar/Sop	CM/IF	Mamma Mia!	2001	Harry & Sophie	Thank You For the Music*	Moderate Tempo
Bar/Sop	CM/RLF	Porgy and Bess	1935	Porgy+ & Bess+	Bess, You Is My Woman	Ballad
Bar/Sop	CM/RLF	Victor/Victoria	1995	Toddy & Victor	You And Me*	Moderate Tempo
Bar/Sop	CM/RLF	Producers, The	2001	Leo Bloom & Ulla	That Face	Uptempo
Bar/Sop	CM/RLF	Chitty Chitty Bang Bang	2005	Caratacus & Truly	Music Box/Truly	Moderate Tempo
Bar/Sop	MM/CIF	Most Happy Fella, The	1956	Tony & Rosabella	Cold And Dead	Ballad
Bar/Sop	MM/CIF	Most Happy Fella, The	1956	Tony & Rosabella	Happy To Make Your Acquaintance*	Moderate Tempo
Bar/Sop	MM/CIF	Most Happy Fella, The	1956	Tony & Rosabella	How Beautiful The Days*	Ballad
Bar/Sop	MM/CIF	Most Happy Fella, The	1956	Tony & Rosabella	My Heart Is So Full Of You*	Ballad
Bar/Sop	MM/IF	No, No Nanette	1925	Jimmy Smith & Nanette	I Want To Be Happy*	Uptempo
Bar/Sop	MM/MF	Cats	1981	Asparagus & Jellylorum	Gus: The Theatre Cat	Ballad
Bar/Sop	P/M	Bye Bye Birdie	1960	Mr. & Mrs. MacAfee	Kids	Uptempo
Bar/Sop	P/M	Baby	1983	Alan & Arlene	The Plaza Song	Moderate Tempo

RLF=Romantic Leading Female   RLM=Romantic Leading Male   MM=Mature Male
IF=Ingenue Female   IM=Ingenue Male   JM=Juvenile Male
CIF=Character Ingenue Female   CIM=Character Ingenue Male   RAM=Rom. Antagonist Male
CF=Character Female   CM=Character Male   AM=Antagonist Male
M=Maternal   P=Paternal

MF=Mature Female
JF=Juvenile Female
RAF=Rom. Antagonist Female
AF=Antagonist Female

* = Music Edit Required
+ = Ethnic Specific

Voicing	Char Types	Show	Year	Roles	Song	Tempo
Bar/Sop	P/M	Baby	1983	Alan & Arlene	And What If We Had Loved...	Moderate Tempo
Bar/Sop	P/M	Closer Than Ever	1989	Man Two & Woman One	Fandango	Uptempo
Bar/Sop	RAM/CIF	Carousel	1945	Billy & Julie	If I Loved You	Ballad
Bar/Sop	RAM/RLF	Music Man, The	1957	Harold & Marian	76 Trombones/Goodnight My Someone	Moderate Tempo
Bar/Sop	RAM/RLF	On The Twentieth Century	1978	Oscar Jaffe & Lily Garland	Our Private World	Ballad
Bar/Sop	RAM/RLF	On The Twentieth Century	1978	Oscar Jaffe & Lily Garland	I've Got It All	Moderate Tempo
Bar/Sop	RFM/CIF	Ragtime	1998	Coalhouse & Sarah	On The Wheels Of A Dram	Moderate Tempo
Bar/Sop	RLF/RLM	She Loves Me	1963	Amalia & Georg	Where's My Shoe	Uptempo
Bar/Sop	RLF/RLM	Romance/Romance	1987	Barb & Lenny	My Love For You	Uptempo
Bar/Sop	RLM/CF	Follies	1971	Ben & Sally	Don't Look At Me	Uptempo
Bar/Sop	RLM/CF	Follies	1971	Ben & Sally	Too Many Mornings	Moderate Tempo
Bar/Sop	RLM/CIF	Oklahoma!	1943	Curly & Laurey	People Will Say We're In Love	Moderate Tempo
Bar/Sop	RLM/CIF	Oklahoma!	1943	Curly & Laurey	People Will Say Reprise	Moderate Tempo
Bar/Sop	RLM/IF	Anything Goes	1934	Billy & Hope	All Through The Night	Ballad
Bar/Sop	RLM/IF	Anything Goes	1934	Billy & Hope	All Through The Night Reprise	Ballad
Bar/Sop	RLM/IF	My Fair Lady	1956	Henry & Eliza	The Rain In Spain	Uptempo
Bar/Sop	RLM/IF	Dreamgirls	1981	Curtis & Deena	When I First Saw You	Ballad
Bar/Sop	RLM/IF	Meet Me In St. Louis	1989	Warren & Rose	Raving Beauty	Ballad
Bar/Sop	RLM/RAF	Unsinkable Molly Brown, The	1960	Johnny Brown & Molly Tobin	I Ain't Down Yet Reprise	Uptempo
Bar/Sop	RLM/RLF	Of Thee I Sing	1931	Wintergreen & Mary Turner	Who Cares*	Uptempo
Bar/Sop	RLM/RLF	Of Thee I Sing	1931	Wintergreen & Mary Turner	Who Cares Reprise	Moderate Tempo
Bar/Sop	RLM/RLF	Once Upon A Mattress	1959	Sir Harry & Lady Larken	In A Little While	Uptempo
Bar/Sop	RLM/RLF	Once Upon A Mattress	1959	Sir Harry & Lady Larken	In A Little While Reprise	Ballad
Bar/Sop	RLM/RLF	Camelot	1960	Arthur & Guenevere	Camelot	Uptempo
Bar/Sop	RLM/RLF	Camelot	1960	Arthur & Guenevere	What Do The Simple Fold Do?	Moderate Tempo
Bar/Sop	RLM/RLF	She Loves Me	1963	Georg & Amalia	Finale Act II	Uptempo
Bar/Sop	RLM/RLF	Victor/Victoria	1995	King & Victoria	Almost A Love Song	Ballad
Bar/Sop	RLM/RLF	Ragtime	1998	Coalhouse & Sarah	Sarah Brown Eyes	Moderate Tempo
Bar/Tenor	AM/CM	Little Shop of Horrors	1982	Orin & Seymour	Now	Uptempo
Bar/Tenor	AM/CM	Spamalot	2005	King Arthur & Patsy	I'm All Alone	Ballad
Bar/Tenor	AM/IM	Pippin	1972	Charles & Pippin	War Is A Science*	Uptempo
Bar/Tenor	AM/IM	Sweeney Todd	1979	Sweeney & Anthony	Johanna II	Moderate Tempo
Bar/Tenor	CM/CM	Little Shop of Horrors	1982	Mushnik & Seymour	Mushnik And Son	Moderate Tempo
Bar/Tenor	CM/P	Hairspray	2003	Edna & Wilbur	Timeless To Me	Moderate Tempo
Bar/Tenor	CM/RLM	Full Monty, The	2000	Dave & Jerry	Man	Uptempo

RLF=Romantic Leading Female   RLM=Romantic Leading Male   MF=Mature Female   MM=Mature Male
IF=Ingenue Female   IM=Ingenue Male   JF=Juvenile Female   JM=Juvenile Male
CIF=Character Ingenue Female   CIM=Character Ingenue Male   RAF=Rom. Antagonist Female   RAM=Rom. Antagonist Male
CF=Character Female   CM=Character Male   AF=Antagonist Female   AM=Antagonist Male
M=Maternal   P=Paternal

Duets

* = Music Edit Required
+ = Ethnic Specific

Voicing	Char Types	Show	Year	Roles	Song	Tempo
Bar/Tenor	IM/MM	Crazy For You (1992)	1992	Bela & Bobby	What Causes That	Uptempo
Bar/Tenor	MM/IM	A Funny Thing...Forum	1962	Sinex & Hero	Impossible	Uptempo
Bar/Tenor	MM/MM	A Funny Thing...Forum	1962	Pseudolus & Hysterium	Lovely Reprise	Moderate Tempo
Bar/Tenor	RAM/CIM	My Favorite Year	1992	Swann & Benjy	Musketeer Sketch Rehearsal Pl	Uptempo
Bar/Tenor	RAM/CIM	My Favorite Year	1992	Alan & Benjy	The Lights Come Up	Ballad
Bar/Tenor	RAM/RLM	On The Twentieth Century	1978	Oscar Jaffe & Bruce Granit	Mine	Uptempo
Bar/Tenor	RLF/CM	Singin' In The Rain	1983	Don Lockwood & Cosmo Brown	Lucky Star Reprise (E♭ Maj)	Moderate Tempo
Bar/Tenor	RLM/CM	Singin' In The Rain	1983	Don Lockwood & Cosmo Brown	Fit As A Fiddle*	Uptempo
Bar/Tenor	RLM/CM	Singin' In The Rain	1983	Don Lockwood & Cosmo Brown	Moses Supposes	Uptempo
Bar/Tenor	RLM/IM	Fantasticks, The	1960	El Gallo & Matt	I Can See It	Uptempo
Sop/Alto	CF/CF	Best Little Whorehouse...	1978	Jewel & Mona	No Lies	Uptempo
Sop/Alto	CIF/CF	My Favorite Year	1992	K.C. & Alice	Funny	Moderate Tempo
Sop/Alto	CIF/CM	Most Happy Fella, The	1956	Rosabella & Cleo	I Know How It Is	Moderate Tempo
Sop/Alto	IF/CF	Wonderful Town	1953	Eileen & Ruth	Ohio	Ballad
Sop/Alto	IF/CF	Wonderful Town	1953	Eileen & Ruth	Ohio Reprise	Ballad
Sop/Alto	IF/CF	Wonderful Town	1953	Eileen & Ruth	The Wrong Note Rag*	Uptempo
Sop/Alto	IF/CF	Jane Eyre	2000	Blanche & Jane	In the Light Of The Morning	Moderate Tempo
Sop/Alto	IF/CIF	Cinderella (2013)	1957	Ella & Gabrielle	A Lovely Night Reprise	Moderate Tempo
Sop/Alto	IF/CIF	Little Women	2005	Beth & Jo	Some Things Are Meant To Be	Moderate Tempo
Sop/Alto	IF/IM	Cinderella (2013)	1957	Ella & Topher	Loneliness Of Evening	Ballad
Sop/Alto	IF/RLF	Bye Bye Birdie	1960	Kim & Rose	What Did I Ever See In Him	Uptempo
Sop/Alto	IF/RLF	A Little Night Music	1973	Anne & Charlotte	Every Day A Little Death	Uptempo
Sop/Alto	IF/RLF	Miss Saigon	1991	Kim+ & Ellen Scott	I Still Believe	Ballad
Sop/Alto	IF/RLF	Miss Saigon	1991	Kim+ & Ellen Scott	Room 317	Moderate Tempo
Sop/Alto	MF/MF	Dear World	1969	Gabrielle & Aurelia	Pearls	Ballad
Sop/Alto	RLF/CF	Wicked	2003	Glinda & Elphaba	What Is This Feeling*	Uptempo
Sop/Alto	RLF/CIF	Rags	1986	Rebecca & Bella	If We Never Meet Again	Ballad
Sop/Alto	RLF/CIF	Rags	1986	Rebecca & Bella	Brand New World Reprise	Moderate Tempo
Sop/Alto	RLF/CIF	Rags	1986	Rebecca & Bella	If We Never Meet Again Reprise	Ballad
Sop/Alto	RLF/MF	Music Man, The	1957	Marian Paroo & Mrs. Paroo	Piano Lesson	Uptempo
Sop/Alto	RLF/RAM	She Loves Me	1963	Amalia & Ilona	I Don't Know His Name	Moderate Tempo
Sop/Alto	RLF/RAM	Jekyll and Hyde	1997	Emma & Lucy	In His Eyes	Ballad
Sop/Bar	CIF/CM	Seussical	2000	Gertrude & Horton	Notice Me, Horton	Uptempo
Sop/Bar	CIF/RLM	Sound Of Music, The	1959	Maria & Captain	Ordinary People	Ballad

RLF=Romantic Leading Female	RLM=Romantic Leading Male	MF=Mature Female	MM=Mature Male
IF=Ingenue Female	IM=Ingenue Male	JF=Juvenile Female	JM=Juvenile Male
CIF=Character Ingenue Female	CIM=Character Ingenue Male	RAF=Rom. Antagonist Female	RAM=Rom. Antagonist Male
CF=Character Female	CM=Character Male	AF=Antagonist Female	AM=Antagonist Male
M=Maternal	P=Paternal		

* = Music Edit Required
+ = Ethnic Specific

Voicing	Char Types	Show	Year	Roles	Song	Tempo
Sop/Bar	CM/CF	Rags	1986	Man & Woman	Children Of The Wind Reprise	Moderate Tempo
Sop/Bar	IF/CM	Little Women	2005	Meg & John	More Than I Am	Moderate Tempo
Sop/Bar	IF/MM	Little Women	2005	Beth & Mr. Laurence	Off To Massachusettes	Moderate Tempo
Sop/Bar	IF/RLM	Brigadoon	1947	Fiona & Tommy	The Heather On The Hill	Moderate Tempo
Sop/Bar	IF/RLM	Brigadoon	1947	Fiona & Tommy	From This Day On	Ballad
Sop/Bar	IF/RLM	Songs For A New World	1995	Woman 1 & Man 2	I'd Give It All For You*	Moderate Tempo
Sop/Bar	IF/RLM	Guys And Dolls	2006	Sarah & Sky	I'll Know	Ballad
Sop/Bar	IF/RLM	Guys And Dolls	2006	Sarah & Sky	I've Never Been In Love Before	Ballad
Sop/Bar	MF/MM	1776	1969	Abigail & John	Til Then	Ballad
Sop/Bar	MF/MM	1776	1969	Abigail & John	Yours, Yours, Yours	Ballad
Sop/Bar	RLF/JM	King and I, The	1951	Anna & Louis	I Whistle A Happy Tune	Uptempo
Sop/Bar	RLF/P	Jekyll and Hyde	1997	Emma & Danvers	Letting Go	Ballad
Sop/Bar	RLF/RLM	Romance/Romance	1987	Barb & Lenny	Small Craft Warning	Moderate Tempo
Sop/Bar	RLF/RLM	Romance/Romance	1987	Barb & Lenny	Think Of The Odds	Moderate Tempo
Sop/Bar	RLF/RLM	Romance/Romance	1987	Barb & Lenny	Let's Not Talk About It	Ballad
Sop/Bar	RLF/RLM	Songs For A New World	1995	Woman 1 & Man 2	The World Was Dancing*	Moderate Tempo
Sop/Bar	RLF/RLM	Jekyll and Hyde	1997	Emma & Stride	Emma's Reasons	Moderate Tempo
Sop/Bar	RLF/RLM	Light In The Piazza, The	2005	Margaret & Signor	Let's Walk	Moderate Tempo
Sop/Bar	RLF/RLM	Grey Gardens	2006	Edith (AI) & Gould	Drift Away	Ballad
Sop/Bar	RLM/RLF	Kiss Me Kate	1948	Fred & Lilli	Wunderbar	Moderate Tempo
Sop/Sop	CF/IF	Mystery Of Edwin Drood, The	1985	Drood & Rosa Bud	Perfect Strangers	Moderate Tempo
Sop/Sop	CIF/CIF	Marie Christine	1999	Maid #1+ & Maid #2+	A Month Ago	Uptempo
Sop/Sop	CIF/MF	Sound Of Music, The	1959	Maria & Mother Superior	My Favorite Things*	Uptempo
Sop/Sop	IF/CF	Cinderella (2013)	1957	Ella & Marie	In My Own Little Corner Reprise	Uptempo
Sop/Sop	IF/CF	Cinderella (2013)	1957	Ella & Marie	Impossible	Uptempo
Sop/Sop	IF/CF	Cinderella (2013)	1957	Ella & Marie	It's Possible	Uptempo
Sop/Sop	IF/MF	Candide	1956	Cunegonde & Old Lady	We Are Women	Uptempo
Sop/Sop	IF/RLF	Light In The Piazza, The	2005	Clara & Margaret	Statues And Stories	Uptempo
Sop/Sop	IF/RLF	Grey Gardens	2006	Edie (AI) & Edith (AI)	Peas In A Pod	Moderate Tempo
Sop/Sop	JF/JM	Chitty Chitty Bang Bang	2005	Jeremia & Jeremy	Us Two/Chitty Prayer	Moderate Tempo
Sop/Sop	JM/JF	South Pacific	1949	Jerome & Ngana	Dites-Moi Pourquoi	Moderate Tempo
Sop/Sop	MF/IF	Follies	1971	Heidi & Young Heidi	One More Kiss	Ballad
Sop/Sop	MF/JF	Scarlet Pimpernel, The	1997	Helen & Chloe	Lullabye	Ballad
Sop/Sop	RAF/IF	Marie Christine	1999	Marie Christine+ & Lisette+	Way Back To Paradise*	Moderate Tempo
Sop/Sop	RLF/AF	Mary Poppins	2006	Mary Poppins & Miss Andrews	Brimstone And Treacle (P2)	Moderate Tempo

RLF=Romantic Leading Female   RLM=Romantic Leading Male   MM=Mature Male
IF=Ingenue Female   IM=Ingenue Male   JM=Juvenile Male
CIF=Character Ingenue Female   CIM=Character Ingenue Male   RAM=Rom. Antagonist Male
CF=Character Female   CM=Character Male   AM=Antagonist Male
M=Maternal   P=Paternal

MF=Mature Female
JF=Juvenile Female
RAF=Rom. Antagonist Female
AF=Antagonist Female

Duets

257

Duets

* = Music Edit Required
+ = Ethnic Specific

Voicing	Char Types	Show	Year	Roles	Song	Tempo
Sop/Sop	RLF/JM	Secret Garden, The	1991	Lily & Colin	Come To My Garden	Moderate Tempo
Sop/Sop	RLF/RLF	On The Twentieth Century	1978	Imelda & Mildred	Indian Maiden's Lament	Moderate Tempo
Sop/Tenor	CF/RLM	Company	1970	April & Robert	Barcelona	Ballad
Sop/Tenor	CIF/AM	Mystery Of Edwin Drood, The	1985	Drood & Jasper	Two Kinsmen	Uptempo
Sop/Tenor	IF/AM	Wiz, The	1974	Dorothy & Lion	Be A Lion	Ballad
Sop/Tenor	IF/IM	Fantasticks, The	1960	Luisa & Matt	Soon It's Gonna Rain	Moderate Tempo
Sop/Tenor	IF/IM	Fantasticks, The	1960	Luisa & Matt	They Were You	Ballad
Sop/Tenor	IF/IM	A Funny Thing...Forum	1962	Philia & Hero	Lovely	Moderate Tempo
Sop/Tenor	IF/IM	Les Miserables	1987	Cosette & Marius	A Heart Full Of Love*	Ballad
Sop/Tenor	IF/IM	Light In The Piazza, The	2005	Clara & Fabrizio	Passeggiata	Uptempo
Sop/Tenor	IF/IM	Light In The Piazza, The	2005	Clara & Fabrizio	Say It Somehow	Ballad
Sop/Tenor	IF/IM	Little Women	2005	Amy & Laurie	The Most Amazing Thing	Uptempo
Sop/Tenor	IF/IM	Drowsy Chaperone	2006	Janet & Robert	Accident Waiting To Happen	Moderate Tempo
Sop/Tenor	IF/RAM	Spring Awakening	2006	Wendla & Melchior	The Word Of Your Body	Ballad
Sop/Tenor	IF/RLM	Candide	1956	Cunegonde & Governor	My Love	Moderate Tempo
Sop/Tenor	IM/IF	Cinderella (2013)	1957	Ella & Topher	Ten Minutes Ago	Moderate Tempo
Sop/Tenor	RLF/CM	Secret Garden, The	1991	Lily & Archibald	How Could I Ever Know	Ballad
Sop/Tenor	RLF/CM	Dirty Rotten Scoundrels	2005	Christine & Freddy	Nothing Is Too Wonderful	Moderate Tempo
Sop/Tenor	RLF/P	Ragtime	1998	Mother & Tateh	Our Children	Moderate Tempo
Sop/Tenor	RLF/RAM	Jekyll and Hyde	1997	Emma & Jekyll	Take Me As I Am	Ballad
Tenor/Alto	AM/CIF	Spring Awakening	2006	Moritz & Ilse	Don't Do Sadness/Blue Wind	Uptempo
Tenor/Alto	AM/IF	Babes In Arms (1998)	1937	Gus & Dolores	I Wish I Were In Love Again	Uptempo
Tenor/Alto	AM/IF	Babes In Arms (1998)	1937	Gus & Dolores	You Are So Fair	Uptempo
Tenor/Alto	CIF/AM	Children of Eden	1991	Japeth & Yonah	In Whatever Time We Have	Moderate Tempo
Tenor/Alto	CIF/CIM	Next To Normal	2009	Natalie & Henry	Perfect For You	Moderate Tempo
Tenor/Alto	CIF/CIM	Next To Normal	2009	Natalie & Henry	Hey #2	Uptempo
Tenor/Alto	CIM/CF	On The Town	1944	Chip & Hildy	Come Up To My Place	Uptempo
Tenor/Alto	CIM/CIF	High School Musical	2007	Ryan & Sharpay	What I've Been Looking For	Uptempo
Tenor/Alto	CM/CF	Most Happy Fella, The	1956	Herman & Cleo	Big D*	Uptempo
Tenor/Alto	CM/CF	Most Happy Fella, The	1956	Herman & Cleo	I Like Everybody Reprise	Uptempo
Tenor/Alto	CM/CF	Most Happy Fella, The	1956	Herman & Cleo	I Made A Fist*	Moderate Tempo
Tenor/Alto	CM/CF	Ain't Misbehavin	1988	Man Two & Woman One	Honeysuckle Rose	Moderate Tempo
Tenor/Alto	CM/CF	Color Purple, The	2005	Harpo+ & Sofia+	Any Little Thing	Moderate Tempo
Tenor/Alto	CM/CIF	13 The Musical	2008	Evan & Patrice	Tell Her	Ballad

RLF=Romantic Leading Female   RLM=Romantic Leading Male   MM=Mature Male
IF=Ingenue Female   IM=Ingenue Male   JM=Juvenile Male
CIF=Character Ingenue Female   CIM=Character Ingenue Male   RAM=Rom. Antagonist Male
CF=Character Female   CM=Character Male   AM=Antagonist Male
M=Maternal   P=Paternal

MF=Mature Female
JF=Juvenile Female
RAF=Rom. Antagonist Female
AF=Antagonist Female

Duets

* = Music Edit Required
+ = Ethnic Specific

Voicing	Char Types	Show	Year	Roles	Song	Tempo
Tenor/Alto	CM/CIF	Next To Normal	2009	Dan & Natalie	Let There Be Lifht	Moderate Tempo
Tenor/Alto	CM/IF	A Chorus Line	1975	Ali & Kristine	Sing!	Uptempo
Tenor/Alto	CM/RAF	Pal Joey	1940	Louis & Gladys	The Flower Garden Of My Heart	Moderate Tempo
Tenor/Alto	CM/RAF	Kiss Of The Spider Woman	1993	Molina & Aurora	Her Name Is Aurora	Moderate Tempo
Tenor/Alto	CM/RAF	Kiss Of The Spider Woman	1993	Molina & Spider Woman	A Visit	Moderate Tempo
Tenor/Alto	IM/CF	Fame	2003	Nick & Serena	Let's Play A Love Scene Reprise	Moderate Tempo
Tenor/Alto	IM/CF	Hairspray	2003	Link & Tracy	It Takes Two	Ballad
Tenor/Alto	IM/CIF	Crazy For You (1992)	1930	Bobby & Polly	Could You Use Me	Uptempo
Tenor/Alto	IM/CIF	Crazy For You (1992)	1930	Bobby & Polly	Embraceable You	Ballad
Tenor/Alto	IM/IF	Flower Drum Song 2002	1958	Wang Ta+ & Wu Mei-Li	You Are Beautiful Reprise	Ballad
Tenor/Alto	IM/IF	Flower Drum Song 2002	1958	Wang Ta+ & Wu Mei-Li	Flower Boat	Ballad
Tenor/Alto	IM/IF	Follies	1971	Young Ben & Young Phyllis	You're Gonna Love Tomorrow	Uptempo
Tenor/Alto	IM/MF	Dear World	1969	Julian & Countess Aurelia	Each Tomorrow Morning Reprise 2	Moderate Tempo
Tenor/Alto	IM/RLF	Pippin	1972	Pippin & Catherine	Love Song	Ballad
Tenor/Alto	MM/RLF	How To Succeed...	1961	Biggley & Hedy	Love From A Heart Of Gold	Ballad
Tenor/Alto	RAM/CF	Jane Eyre	2000	Edward & Jane	Secret Soul	Ballad
Tenor/Alto	RAM/CF	Jane Eyre	2000	Edward & Jane	The Pledge	Moderate Tempo
Tenor/Alto	RAM/CF	Jane Eyre	2000	Edward & Jane	The Proposal	Moderate Tempo
Tenor/Alto	RAM/CF	Jane Eyre	2000	Edward & Jane	Siren Reprise	Moderate Tempo
Tenor/Alto	RAM/CF	Jane Eyre	2000	Edward & Jane	Brave Enough For Love	Moderate Tempo
Tenor/Alto	RAM/CIF	All Shook Up	2005	Chad & Natalie	Follow That Dream	Uptempo
Tenor/Alto	RAM/CIF	All Shook Up	2005	Chad & Ed	Blue Suede Shoes	Uptempo
Tenor/Alto	RAM/CIF	Heathers	2014	JD & Veronica	Seventeen	Ballad
Tenor/Alto	RAM/CIF	Heathers	2014	JD & Veronica	I Am Damaged	Ballad
Tenor/Alto	RAM/RAF	Evita	1978	Che & Eva	High Flying Adore	Uptempo
Tenor/Alto	RAM/RAF	Evita	1978	Che & Eva	Waltz of Eva And Che	Uptempo
Tenor/Alto	RLM/CIF	Chess	1988	Anatoly & Svetlana	Endgame III	Moderate Tempo
Tenor/Alto	RLM/CIF	Cabaret	1966	Clifford & Sally	Perfectly Marvelous	Uptempo
Tenor/Alto	RLM/CIF	Cabaret	1966	Clifford & Sally	Why Should I Wake Up?	Moderate Tempo
Tenor/Alto	RLM/CIF	Chess	1988	Anatoly & Florence	Terrace Duet	Moderate Tempo
Tenor/Alto	RLM/CIF	Chess	1988	Anatoly & Florence	You and I	Ballad
Tenor/Alto	RLM/CIF	Chess	1988	Anatoly & Florence	You and I Reprise	Ballad
Tenor/Alto	RLM/CIF	Thoroughly Modern Millie	2002	Trevor & Millie	The Speed Test	Uptempo
Tenor/Alto	RLM/IF	In The Heights	2008	Benny & Nina	Benny's Dispatch	Uptempo
Tenor/Alto	RLM/IF	In The Heights	2008	Benny & Nina	When The Sun Goes Down	Ballad

Duets

RLF=Romantic Leading Female RLM=Romantic Leading Male
IF=Ingenue Female IM=Ingenue Male
CIF=Character Ingenue Female CIM=Character Ingenue Male
CF=Character Female CM=Character Male
M=Maternal P=Paternal

MF=Mature Female MM=Mature Male
JF=Juvenile Female JM=Juvenile Male
RAF=Rom. Antagonist Female RAM=Rom. Antagonist Male
AF=Antagonist Female AM=Antagonist Male

* = Music Edit Required
+ = Ethnic Specific

Voicing	Char Types	Show	Year	Roles	Song	Tempo
Tenor/Alto	RLM/RLF	Pajama Game	1954	Sid & Babe	Small Talk	Uptempo
Tenor/Alto	RLM/RLF	Pajama Game	1954	Sid & Babe	There Once Was A Man	Uptempo
Tenor/Alto	RLM/RLF	Pajama Game	1954	Sid & Babe	There Once Was A Man Reprise	Uptempo
Tenor/Alto	RLM/RLF	Steel Pier	1997	Bill & Rita	Wet	Uptempo
Tenor/Alto	RLM/RLF	Curtains	2007	Aaron & Georgia	Thinking Of Him Reprise	Moderate Tempo
Tenor/Atlo	CIM/JF	Secret Garden, The	1991	Dickon & Mary	Show Me The Key	Moderate Tempo
Tenor/Atlo	CIM/JF	Secret Garden, The	1991	Dickon & Mary	Wick	Uptempo
Tenor/Atlo	CM/AF	Rent	1996	Mark Cohen & Joanne Jefferson	Tango Maureen	Moderate Tempo
Tenor/Atlo	CM/CF	Sunday...Park With Geroge	1984	Franz & Frieda	The Day Off (Part 5)	Moderate Tempo
Tenor/Atlo	RAM/MF	Sunday...Park With Geroge	1984	George & Old Lady	Beautiful	Ballad
Tenor/Atlo	RAM/RAF	Romance/Romance	1987	Alfred & Josephine	Little Comedy	Moderate Tempo
Tenor/Atlo	RAM/RAF	Romance/Romance	1987	Alfred & Josephine	It's Not Too Late	Moderate Tempo
Tenor/Atlo	RAM/RAF	Romance/Romance	1987	Alfred & Josephine	Great News	Uptempo
Tenor/Atlo	RAM/RAF	Romance/Romance	1987	Alfred & Josephine	A Performance	Moderate Tempo
Tenor/Atlo	RAM/RAF	Romance/Romance	1987	Alfred & Josephine	I'll Remember The Song	Moderate Tempo
Tenor/Atlo	RAM/RAF	Romance/Romance	1987	Alfred & Josephine	A Rustic Country Inn	Uptempo
Tenor/Atlo	RAM/RAF	Romance/Romance	1987	Alfred & Josephine	A Little Comedy Finale	Moderate Tempo
Tenor/Atlo	RAM/RAF	Romance/Romance	1987	Alfred & Josephine	It's Not Too Late Reprise	Moderate Tempo
Tenor/Atlo	RAM/RAF	Sunset Boulevard	1994	Joe Gillis & Norma Desmond	Salome	Moderate Tempo
Tenor/Atlo	RAM/RAF	Rent	1996	Roger Davis & Mimi Marquez	Another Day*	Uptempo
Tenor/Atlo	RAM/RAF	Rent	1996	Roger Davis & Mimi Marquez	I Should Tell You*	Ballad
Tenor/Atlo	RAM/RLF	Sunday...Park With Geroge	1984	George & Dot	Move On	Ballad
Tenor/Atlo	RLM/RLF	Scarlet Pimpernel, The	1997	Percy & Marguerite	You Are My Home*	Ballad
Tenor/Atlo	RLM/RLF	Scarlet Pimpernel, The	1997	Percy & Marguerite	Finale-When I Look At You	Moderate Tempo
Tenor/Atlo	RLM/RLF	Scarlet Pimpernel, The	1997	Percy & Marguerite	Believe	Moderate Tempo
Tenor/Atlo	RLM/RLF	Scarlet Pimpernel, The	1997	Percy & Marguerite	Believe Reprise	Moderate Tempo
Tenor/Bar	AM/CIM	Honk!	1993	Cat & Ugly	You Can Play With Your Good	Uptempo
Tenor/Bar	AM/MM	Mystery Of Edwin Drood, The	1985	Jasper & Chairman	Both Sides Of The Coin	Uptempo
Tenor/Bar	AM/RLM	Hair	1968	Berger & Claude	Hair	Uptempo
Tenor/Bar	CIM/CIM	Kinky Boots	2013	Charlie & Harry	Take What You Got	Uptempo
Tenor/Bar	CIM/CM	Baby	1983	Danny & Nick	At Night She Comes Home To Me	Moderate Tempo
Tenor/Bar	CIM/CM	Big River	1996	Huck & Jim	Muddy Water	Uptempo
Tenor/Bar	CIM/CM	Big River	1996	Huck & Jim	River In The Rain	Ballad
Tenor/Bar	CIM/CM	Big River	1996	Huck & Jim	Worlds Apart	Ballad
Tenor/Bar	CIM/CM	Big River	1996	Huck & Jim	River In The Rain Reprise	Ballad

RLF=Romantic Leading Female   RLM=Romantic Leading Male   MM=Mature Male
IF=Ingenue Female   IM=Ingenue Male   JM=Juvenile Female
CIF=Character Ingenue Female   CIM=Character Ingenue Male   RAM=Rom. Antagonist Male
CF=Character Female   CM=Character Male   AM=Antagonist Male
M=Maternal   P=Paternal

MF=Mature Female
JF=Juvenile Female
RAF=Rom. Antagonist Female
AF=Antagonist Female

Duets

* = Music Edit Required
+ = Ethnic Specific

Voicing	Char Types	Show	Year	Roles	Song	Tempo
Tenor/Bar	CM/CM	Pacific Overtures	1976	Observer 1 & Observer 2+	There Is No Other Way	Ballad
Tenor/Bar	CM/CM	On The Twentieth Century	1978	Owen O'Malley & Oliver Webb	Saddle Up*	Uptempo
Tenor/Bar	CM/CM	Rags	1986	American Male 1 & Male 2	Greenhorns*	Uptempo
Tenor/Bar	CM/RLM	The Little Mermaid	2007	Sebastian & King Triton	The World Above Reprise	Moderate Tempo
Tenor/Bar	IM/AM	Children of Eden	1991	Abel & Cain	Lost In The Wilderness	Moderate Tempo
Tenor/Bar	IM/AM	Blood Brothers	1993	Eddie & Mickey	Long Sunday Afternoon	Uptempo
Tenor/Bar	IM/AM	Blood Brothers	1993	Eddie & Mickey	My Friend	Uptempo
Tenor/Bar	IM/AM	Blood Brothers	1993	Eddie & Mickey	That Guy	Moderate Tempo
Tenor/Bar	IM/RAM	Spring Awakening	2006	Ernst & Hanschen	Word Of Your Body Reprise 2*	Ballad
Tenor/Bar	RAM/P	All Shook Up	2005	Chad & Jim	Don't Be Cruel	Moderate Tempo
Tenor/Bar	RLM/CM	Pacific Overtures	1976	Kayama+ & Majiro+	Poems	Moderate Tempo
Tenor/Sop	AM/CF	Assassins	1992	Hinkley & Fromme	Unworthy Of Your Love	Uptempo
Tenor/Sop	AM/IF	Mystery Of Edwin Drood, The	1985	Jasper & Rosa Bud	The Name Of Love	Moderate Tempo
Tenor/Sop	AM/IF	Mystery Of Edwin Drood, The	1985	Jasper & Rosa Bud	Moonfall Reprise	Moderate Tempo
Tenor/Sop	AM/IF	Phantom Of The Opera	1986	Phantom & Christine	Angel Of Music	Moderate Tempo
Tenor/Sop	AM/IF	Phantom Of The Opera	1986	Phantom & Christine	Phantom Of The Opera	Moderate Tempo
Tenor/Sop	CF/RAM	110 In The Shade	1963	Bill & Lizzie	You're Not Foolin' Me	Moderate Tempo
Tenor/Sop	CIM/IF	Baby	1983	Danny & Lizzie	What Could Be Better	Uptempo
Tenor/Sop	CIM/IF	Baby	1983	Danny & Lizzie	What Could Be Better Reprise	Uptempo
Tenor/Sop	CIM/IF	Big	1996	Josh & Susan	Stars, Stars, Stars	Ballad
Tenor/Sop	CIM/IF	Big	1996	Josh & Susan	I Want To Go Home Reprise	Ballad
Tenor/Sop	CIM/IF	Big	1996	Josh & Susan	Stars, Stars, Stars Reprise	Ballad
Tenor/Sop	CM/CF	Ain't Misbehavin	1988	Man One & Woman Two	That Ain't Right	Moderate Tempo
Tenor/Sop	CM/CF	Chitty Chitty Bang Bang	2005	Baron & Baroness	Chu-Chi Face	Moderate Tempo
Tenor/Sop	CM/JM	A Christmas Carol	1997	Cratchit & Tiny Tim	You Mean More to Me	Ballad
Tenor/Sop	CM/RLF	Rags	1986	Nathan & Rebecca	Uptown	Moderate Tempo
Tenor/Sop	CM/RLF	Secret Garden, The	1991	Archibald & Lily	A Girl In The Vallet	Moderate Tempo
Tenor/Sop	CM/RLF	Ragtime	1998	Harry Houdini & Evelyn	Atlantic City (Part 3)*	Uptempo
Tenor/Sop	IF/IM	Fantasticks, The	1960	Luis & Matt	Metaphor	Uptempo
Tenor/Sop	IM/IF	No, No Nanette	1925	Tom Trainor & Nanette	I've Confessed To The Breeze	Moderate Tempo
Tenor/Sop	IM/IF	No, No Nanette	1925	Tom Trainor & Nanette	Tea For Two	Moderate Tempo
Tenor/Sop	IM/IF	No, No Nanette	1925	Tom Trainor & Nanette	Waiting For You	Moderate Tempo
Tenor/Sop	IM/IF	King and I, The	1951	Lun Tha+ & Tuptim+	We Kiss In a Shadow	Ballad
Tenor/Sop	IM/IF	King and I, The	1951	Lun Tha+ & Tuptim+	I Have Dreamed	Ballad
Tenor/Sop	IM/IF	Candide	1956	Candide & Cunegonde	Oh Happy We	Uptempo

RLF=Romantic Leading Female   RLM=Romantic Leading Male   MM=Mature Male
IF=Ingenue Female   IM=Ingenue Male   JM=Juvenile Male
CIF=Character Ingenue Female   CIM=Character Ingenue Male   RAM=Rom. Antagonist Male
CF=Character Female   CM=Character Male   AM=Antagonist Male
M=Maternal   P=Paternal

MF=Mature Female
JF=Juvenile Female
RAF=Rom. Antagonist Female
AF=Antagonist Female

Duets

* = Music Edit Required
+ = Ethnic Specific

Voicing	Char Types	Show	Year	Roles	Song	Tempo
Tenor/Sop	IM/IF	Candide	1956	Candide & Cunegonde	You Were Dead, You Know	Moderate Tempo
Tenor/Sop	IM/IF	West Side Story	1957	Tony & Maria+	Tonight	Moderate Tempo
Tenor/Sop	IM/IF	West Side Story	1957	Tony & Maria+	One Hand, One Heart	Ballad
Tenor/Sop	IM/IF	110 In The Shade	1963	Jim & Snookie	Little Red Hat	Uptempo
Tenor/Sop	IM/IF	Sweeney Todd	1979	Anthony & Johanna	Kiss Me (I & II)	Uptempo
Tenor/Sop	IM/IF	Phantom Of The Opera	1986	Raoul & Christine	Why Have You Brought Us Here*	Uptempo
Tenor/Sop	IM/IF	Thoroughly Modern Millie	2002	Trevor & Dorothy	I'm Falling In Love With Someone	Ballad
Tenor/Sop	IM/IF	Thoroughly Modern Millie	2002	Trevor & Dorothy	Ah! Sweet Mystery Of Life	Moderate Tempo
Tenor/Sop	IM/MF	Damn Yankees	1955	Joe Hardy & Meg	A Man Doesn't Know Reprise	Ballad
Tenor/Sop	IM/MF	Damn Yankees	1955	Hardy & Meg	Near To You	Ballad
Tenor/Sop	MM/CF	High Society 1998	1930	Uncle Willie & Liz Imbrie	I'm Getting Ready For You	Uptempo
Tenor/Sop	RAM/CIF	Sunset Boulevard	1994	Joe Gillis & Betty Schaefer	Betty's Pitch	Moderate Tempo
Tenor/Sop	RAM/CIF	Sunset Boulevard	1994	Joe Gillis & Betty Schaefer	Girl Meets Boy	Moderate Tempo
Tenor/Sop	RAM/CIF	Sunset Boulevard	1994	Joe Gillis & Betty Schaefer	Too Much In Love To Care	Moderate Tempo
Tenor/Sop	RAM/CIF	Sunset Boulevard	1994	Joe Gillis & Betty Schaefer	Sunset Blvd Reprise-What's Going On	Uptempo
Tenor/Sop	RAM/IF	Miss Saigon	1991	John & Kim+	Please	Moderate Tempo
Tenor/Sop	RAM/RAF	Unsinkable Molly Brown, The	1960	Prince Delong & Molly Tobin	Dolce Far Niente	Ballad
Tenor/Sop	RAM/RAF	Marie Christine	1999	Dante & Marie+	I Don't Hear The Ocean	Moderate Tempo
Tenor/Sop	RAM/RAF	Marie Christine	1999	Dante & Marie+	I Will Love You	Ballad
Tenor/Sop	RAM/RAF	Marie Christine	1999	Dante & Marie+	I Will Love You Reprise	Ballad
Tenor/Sop	RAM/RLF	Nine	1982	Guido & Claudia	A Man Like You	Moderate Tempo
Tenor/Sop	RAM/RLF	Nine	1982	Guido & Claudia	Unusual Way	Ballad
Tenor/Sop	RLM/IF	Show Boat	1927	Gaylord & Magnolia	Make Believe	Ballad
Tenor/Sop	RLM/IF	Show Boat	1927	Gaylord & Magnolia	You Are Love	Ballad
Tenor/Sop	RLM/IF	Show Boat	1927	Gaylord & Magnolia	Why Do I Love You	Moderate Tempo
Tenor/Sop	RLM/IF	Phantom Of The Opera	1986	Raoul & Christine	All I Ask Of You	Ballad
Tenor/Sop	RLM/IF	Miss Saigon	1991	Chris & Kim+	This Money's Yours	Moderate Tempo
Tenor/Sop	RLM/IF	Miss Saigon	1991	Chris & Kim+	The Last Night Of the World*	Ballad
Tenor/Sop	RLM/IF	Miss Saigon	1991	Chris & Kim+	Sun And Moon	Ballad
Tenor/Sop	RLM/IF	Sweet Smell Of Success	2002	Dallas & Susan	Don't Know Where You Leave Off	Moderate Tempo
Tenor/Sop	RLM/IF	Sweet Smell Of Success	2002	Dallas & Susan	I Cannot Hear The City Reprise*	Ballad
Tenor/Sop	RLM/RLF	Passion	1994	Giorgio Bachetti & Clara	Happiness (Part 1)	Moderate Tempo
Tenor/Sop	RLM/RLF	Passion	1994	Giorgio Bachetti & Clara	Happiness (Part 2)	Moderate Tempo
Tenor/Sop	RLM/RLF	Passion	1994	Giorgio Bachetti & Clara	Every Waking Moment	Uptempo
Tenor/Sop	RLM/RLF	Passion	1994	Giorgio Bachetti & Clara	Sunrise Letter*	Moderate Tempo

RLF=Romantic Leading Female   RLM=Romantic Leading Male   MF=Mature Female   MM=Mature Male
IF=Ingenue Female   IM=Ingenue Male   JF=Juvenile Female   JM=Juvenile Male
CIF=Character Ingenue Female   CIM=Character Ingenue Male   RAF=Rom. Antagonist Female   RAM=Rom. Antagonist Male
CF=Character Female   CM=Character Male   AF=Antagonist Female   AM=Antagonist Male
M=Maternal   P=Paternal

Duets

* = Music Edit Required
+ = Ethnic Specific

Voicing	Char Types	Show	Year	Roles	Song	Tempo
Tenor/Sop	RLM/RLF	Wicked	2003	Fiyero & Glinda	Dancing Through Life*	Uptempo
Tenor/Srp	RLM/RLF	High Society 1998	1955	Dexter & Tracy	True Love	Ballad
Tenor/Tenor	AM/AM	The Little Mermaid	2007	Flotsam & Jetsom	Sweet Child	Ballad
Tenor/Tenor	AM/CM	Sweet Charity	1966	Herman & Wedding Guest	I Love To Cry At Weddings	Uptempo
Tenor/Tenor	CIM/CIM	Rags	1986	Ben & Tenor	For My Mary	Moderate Tempo
Tenor/Tenor	CIM/CM	Grease	1971	Doody & Roger	Rock N Roll Party Queen	Uptempo
Tenor/Tenor	CIM/RLM	Rent	1996	Angel Schunard & Tom Collins	You Okay, Honey	Moderate Tempo
Tenor/Tenor	CIM/RLM	Rent	1996	Angel & Tom	I'll Cover You	Moderate Tempo
Tenor/Tenor	CM/AM	Godspell	1971	Jesus & Judas	All For The Best	Uptempo
Tenor/Tenor	CM/CIM	Jersey Boys, The	2005	Bob & Frankie	Let's Hang On	Moderate Tempo
Tenor/Tenor	CM/CIM	Next To Normal	2009	Dan & Gabe	I Am The One Reprise	Moderate Tempo
Tenor/Tenor	CM/CM	Pacific Overtures	1976	Priest 1 & Priest 2+	Chrysanthemum Tea*	Moderate Tempo
Tenor/Tenor	CM/CM	Rags	1986	Tim & Nathan	What's Wrong With That	Uptempo
Tenor/Tenor	CM/CM	Ain't Misbehavin	1988	Man One & Man Two	The Ladies Who Sing With The Band	Uptempo
Tenor/Tenor	CM/CM	Ain't Misbehavin	1988	Man One & Man Two	Fat And Greasy	Moderate Tempo
Tenor/Tenor	CM/CM	Marie Christine	1999	McMahon & Leary	Better And Best	Moderate Tempo
Tenor/Tenor	CM/CM	Full Monty, The	2000	Ethan & Malcolm	You Walk With Me	Ballad
Tenor/Tenor	CM/IM	Drowsy Chaperone	2006	George & Robert	Cold Feets	Uptempo
Tenor/Tenor	CM/MM	How To Succeed...	1961	Finch & Twimble	Company Way	Uptempo
Tenor/Tenor	CM/MM	How To Succeed...	1961	Biggley & Finch	Grand Old Ivy	Uptempo
Tenor/Tenor	CM/RAM	Kiss Of The Spider Woman	1993	Monlina & Valentin	Bluebloods	Uptempo
Tenor/Tenor	CM/RAM	Kiss Of The Spider Woman	1993	Monlina & Valentin	I Draw A Line	Uptempo
Tenor/Tenor	CM/RAM	Rent	1996	Mark Cohen & Roger Davis	Rent*	Uptempo
Tenor/Tenor	CM/RAM	Rent	1996	Mark Cohen & Roger Davis	You Are What You Own	Uptempo
Tenor/Tenor	IM/CM	Kinky Boots	2013	Charlie & Lola (Drag)	I'm Not My Father's Son	Ballad
Tenor/Tenor	JM/JM	Big	1996	Billy & Young Josh	Talk To Her	Moderate Tempo
Tenor/Tenor	RAM/CM	Once Upon A Mattress	1959	Minstrel & Jester	Normancy	Uptempo
Tenor/Tenor	RAM/CM	Merrily We Roll Along 1994	1981	Franklin & Charley	Our Time Part 1 & 2	Moderate Tempo
Tenor/Tenor	RAM/CM	Assassins	1992	Guiteau & Balladeer	The Ballad of Guiteau	Uptempo
Tenor/Tenor	RAM/IM	Pippin	1972	Leading Player & Pippin	Right On Track	Moderate Tempo
Tenor/Tenor	RLM/RAM	Chess	1988	Anatoly & Freddie	Talking Chess	Uptempo
Tenor/Tenor	RLM/RAM	Miss Saigon	1991	Chris & John	The Telephone	Uptempo

RLF=Romantic Leading Female
IF=Ingenue Female
CIF=Character Ingenue Female
CF=Character Female
M=Maternal

RLM=Romantic Leading Male
IM=Ingenue Male
CIM=Character Ingenue Male
CM=Character Male
P=Paternal

MF=Mature Female
JF=Juvenile Female
RAF=Rom. Antagonist Female
AF=Antagonist Female

MM=Mature Male
JM=Juvenile Male
RAM=Rom. Antagonist Male
AM=Antagonist Male

Duets

Show	Year	Song	Tempo	Voicing	Scripted Age Group	Any Age Group
Parade	1998	The Trial, Part 4: The Factory Girls	Moderate Tempo	AAA	Adults	Δ
Sweet Charity	1966	There's Gott Be Something Better...	Uptempo	AAA	Adults	
White Christmas	2008	Falling Out Of Love Can Be Fun	Uptempo	AAA	Adults	
Once On This Island	1990	Ti Moune*	Ballad	AAB	Adults	Δ
Applause	1970	Good Friends	Moderate Tempo	AAB	Adults	
Oliver!	1963	It's A Fine Life Reprise	Uptempo	AABB	Adults	
Spitfire Grill	2001	The Colors of Paradise Reprise	Moderate Tempo	AAS	Adults	
Next To Normal	2009	Song Of Forgetting	Ballad	AAT	Adults	
Next To Normal	2009	Better Than Before	Moderate Tempo	AAT	Adults	
Next To Normal	2009	I Am The One*	Uptempo	AAT	Adults	
Next To Normal	2009	Catch Me I'm Falling	Moderate Tempo	AATT	Adults	
Next To Normal	2009	Just Another Day	Uptempo	AATT	Adults	
Next To Normal	2009	Wish I Were Here*	Uptempo	AATT	Adults	
Next To Normal	2009	Light	Moderate Tempo	AATTTT	Adults	
Next To Normal	2009	It's Gonna Be Good	Uptempo	AATTTT	Adults	
Merrily We Roll Along 1994	1981	Old Friends II	Moderate Tempo	ABB	Adults	
Nick & Nora	1991	Not Me	Moderate Tempo	ABB	Adults	
Singin' In The Rain	1983	Good Morning	Uptempo	ABT	Adults	Δ
Nick & Nora	1991	Swill	Moderate Tempo	ABTT	Adults	
Seven Brides/Seven Brothers	1982	Love Never Goes Away	Ballad	ATB	Adults	
Flower Drum Song 2002	1958	I Enjoy Being A Girl Playoff*	Moderate Tempo	ATB	Adults	
On The Twentieth Century	1978	Five Zeros	Moderate Tempo	ATB	Adults	
Parade	1998	A Rumblin' And A Rollin'	Moderate Tempo	ATB	Adults	
Ragtime	1998	He Wanted To Say	Moderate Tempo	ATB	Adults	
White Christmas	2008	What Can You With A General	Moderate Tempo	ATB	Adults	
Anyone Can Whistle	1964	Me And My Town	Uptempo	ATB	Adults	
Kiss Of The Spider Woman	1993	Where You Are	Uptempo	ATB	Adults	
No, No Nanette	1925	Take A Little One Step*	Uptempo	ATB	Adults	Δ
Pajama Game	1954	Steam Heat	Uptempo	ATB	Adults	
Producers, The	2001	Keep It Gay	Uptempo	ATB	Adults	
Spitfire Grill	2001	Ice And Snow	Uptempo	ATB	Adults	
Sunset Boulevard	1994	The Lady's Paying	Uptempo	ATB	Adults	
Thoroughly Modern Millie	2002	Long As I'm Here With You*	Uptempo	ATB	Adults	
Producers, The	2001	Keep It Gay	Uptempo	ATB	Adults	
Little Me	1962	The Truth	Uptempo	ATB	Adults	

Show	Year	Song	Tempo	Voicing	Scripted Age Group	Any Age Group
Kiss Of The Spider Woman	1993	Anything For Him	Moderate Tempo	ATT	Adults	
Miss Saigon	1991	The Heat Is On In Saigon	Uptempo	ATT	Adults	
Babes In Arms (1998)	1937	Imagine	Moderate Tempo	ATTBB	Adults	
Babes In Arms (1998)	1937	Way Out West	Moderate Tempo	ATTBB	Adults	
Most Happy Fella, The	1956	Nobody's Ever Gonna Love You	Moderate Tempo	BAA	Adults	
Seven Brides/Seven Brothers	1982	Wonderful Day Reprise	Moderate Tempo	Bar/Alto	Adults	Δ
A Funny Thing...Forum	1962	Everybody Ought To Have A Maid	Uptempo	BBB	Adults	
Wonderful Town	1953	What A Waste	Uptempo	BBB	Adults	
A Funny Thing...Forum	1962	Everybody Ought To Have A Maid Encore	Uptempo	BBBB	Adults	
South Pacific	1949	There Is Nothing Like A Dame	Uptempo	BT	Adults	
South Pacific	1949	Bloody Mary	Uptempo	BT	Adults	
Mamma Mia!	2001	Chiquitta*	Ballad	SA	Adults	
Mamma Mia!	2001	Slipping Through My Fingers*	Ballad	SA	Adults	
Nunsense	1985	Growing Up Catholic	Ballad	SA	Adults	
Best Little Whorehouse...	1978	Hard Candy Christmas	Moderate Tempo	SA	Adults	
Les Miserables	1987	Turning*	Moderate Tempo	SA	Adults	
Marie Christine	1999	Before The Morning	Moderate Tempo	SA	Adults	
Merrily We Roll Along 1994	1994	Transition 7	Moderate Tempo	SA	Adults	
Nine	1982	Overture Belle Donna	Moderate Tempo	SA	Adults	
Nunsense	1985	Lilac Bring Back Memories	Moderate Tempo	SA	Adults	
Nunsense	1985	Gloria In Excelsis Deo	Moderate Tempo	SA	Adults	
Oklahoma!	1943	Out Of My Dreams	Moderate Tempo	SA	Adults	Δ
Seven Brides/Seven Brothers	1982	Wonderful Day	Moderate Tempo	SA	Adults	Δ
Sweet Charity	1966	Big Spender	Moderate Tempo	SA	Adults	
Nine	1982	Nine	Moderate Tempo	SA	Adults	
Nine	1982	Ti Voglio Bene	Moderate Tempo	SA	Adults	
White Christmas	2008	I Love A Piano	Moderate Tempo	SA	Adults	
Annie	1977	It's A Hard-Knock Life	Uptempo	SA	Children	Δ
Annie	1977	It's A Hard-Knock Life Reprise	Uptempo	SA	Children	Δ
Brigadoon	1947	Jeannie's Packing Up	Uptempo	SA	Adults	
Good News (1993 Revival)	1927	He's A Ladies' Man	Uptempo	SA	Adults	
Hairspray	2002	Mama I'm A Big Girl Now	Uptempo	SA	Adults	Δ
Hairspray	2002	The Big Doll House	Uptempo	SA	Adults	
Little Shop of Horrors	1982	Little Shop of Horrors	Uptempo	SA	Adults	
Little Shop of Horrors	1982	Ya Never Know*	Uptempo	SA	Adults	

* = Music Edit Required
+ = Ethnic Specific

Show	Year	Song	Tempo	Voicing	Scripted Age Group	Any Age Group
Mamma Mia!	2001	Mamma Mia!	Uptempo	SA	Adults	
Music Man, The	1957	Pickalittle*	Uptempo	SA	Adults	Δ
Music Man, The	1957	Pickalittle Talkalittle Reprise	Uptempo	SA	Adults	Δ
My Fair Lady	1956	I Could Have Danced All Night*	Uptempo	SA	Adults	Δ
Nine	1982	Not Since Chaplin	Uptempo	SA	Adults	
Nunsense	1985	Nunsense Is Habit-Forming	Uptempo	SA	Adults	
Nunsense	1985	A Difficult Transition	Uptempo	SA	Adults	
Nunsense	1985	One Last Hope	Uptempo	SA	Adults	
Nunsense	1985	Mock Fifties	Uptempo	SA	Adults	
Nunsense	1985	Tackle That Temptation	Uptempo	SA	Adults	
Nunsense	1985	We've Got To Clean Out The Freezer	Uptempo	SA	Adults	
Nunsense	1985	Nunsense Reprise	Uptempo	SA	Adults	
Of Thee I Sing	1931	Who Is The Lucky Girl To Be	Uptempo	SA	Adults	
Oklahoma!	1943	Many A New Day	Uptempo	SA	Adults	Δ
Oliver!	1963	I'd Do Anything	Uptempo	SA	Children/Adults	Δ
Oliver!	1963	Be Back Soon	Uptempo	SA	Children/Adults	Δ
Pajama Game	1954	I'm Not At All In Love	Uptempo	SA	Adults	
Pal Joey	1940	A Great Bit Town Reprise	Uptempo	SA	Adults	
Seussical	2000	For You	Uptempo	SA	Adults	
Sound Of Music, The	1959	Maria	Uptempo	SA	Adults	Δ
South Pacific	1949	I'm Gonna Wash That Man*	Uptempo	SA	Adults	
South Pacific	1949	Bali Ha'i	Uptempo	SA	Adults	
Sunset Boulevard	1994	A Little Suffering	Uptempo	SA	Adults	
They're Playing Our Song	1974	Right	Uptempo	SA	Adults	
Thoroughly Modern Millie	2002	Not For The Life Of Me Reprise	Uptempo	SA	Adults	
Thoroughly Modern Millie	2002	Forget About The Boy	Uptempo	SA	Adults	
Victor/Victoria	1995	Chicago Illinois	Uptempo	SA	Adults	
West Side Story	1957	America	Uptempo	SA	Adults	
West Side Story	1957	I Feel Pretty*	Uptempo	SA	Adults	
Nunsense	1985	The Drive In	Uptempo	SA	Adults	Δ
Seussical	2000	Amayzing Mayzie	Uptempo	SA	Adults	
Seussical	2000	Amayzing Gertrude	Uptempo	SA	Adults	
Nunsense	1985	Holier Than Thou	Uptempo	SA	Adults	
Singin' In The Rain	1983	All I Do Is Deam Of You*	Uptempo	SA	Adults	
Pajama Game	1954	Racing With The Clock Reprise	Moderate Tempo	SA Unison	Adults	Δ

Ensemble

* = Music Edit Required
+ = Ethnic Specific

Show	Year	Song	Tempo	Voicing	Scripted Age Group	Any Age Group
Sound Of Music, The	1959	Morning Hymn	Moderate Tempo	SA Unison	Adults	
South Pacific	1949	Im In Love…Wonderful Guy	Uptempo	SA Unison	Adults	
Oliver!	1963	Food Glorious Food	Moderate Tempo	SAA	Children	Δ
Steel Pier	1997	Fralenger's Commercial	Moderate Tempo	SAA	Adults	
Will Rogers Follies	1991	The St. Louis Fair	Moderate Tempo	SAA	Adults	
Wizard Of Oz 1996	1939	If I Only Had A Heart	Moderate Tempo	SAA	Adults	Δ
Spring Awakening	2006	Mama Who Bore Me Reprise	Uptempo	SAA	Adults	
Steel Pier	1997	Steel Pier	Uptempo	SAA	Adults	
Wizard Of Oz 1999	1939	You're Out Of The Woods Reprise	Uptempo	SAA	Adults	Δ
Mame	1966	We Need A Little Christmas*	Uptempo	SAB	Children/Adults	Δ
Meet Me In St. Louis	1989	When I'm With You	Uptempo	SAB	Children/Adults	
Peter Pan	1954	Tender Shepherd	Ballad	SAT	Children	Δ
Caroline Or Change	2004	Laundry Quintet	Moderate Tempo	SAT	Adults	
Caroline Or Change	2004	Laundry Quintet Finish	Moderate Tempo	SAT	Adults	
Secret Garden, The	1991	A Bit Of Earth Reprise	Moderate Tempo	SAT	Adults	
Sound Of Music, The	1959	So Long Farewell	Moderate Tempo	SAT	Children/Adults	Δ
Nine	1982	Only You	Moderate Tempo	SAT	Adults	
Sound Of Music, The	1959	Do-Re-Mi	Uptempo	SAT	Children/Adults	Δ
Sound Of Music, The	1959	Lonely Goatherd*	Uptempo	SAT	Children/Adults	Δ
The Little Mermaid	2007	Positoovity	Uptempo	SAT	Adults	Δ
Sound Of Music, The	1959	My Favorite Things Reprise	Uptempo	SAT	Children/Adults	Δ
Addams Family, The	2010	Move Toward the Darkness	Ballad	SATB	Adults	
Annie Get Your Gun	1944	They Say It's Wonderful Reprise Act 2*	Ballad	SATB	Adults	
Brigadoon	1947	Once In The Highlands	Ballad	SATB	Adults	
Brigadoon	1947	Brigadoon	Ballad	SATB	Adults	
Candide	1956	Universal Good	Ballad	SATB	Adults	
Candide	1956	Universal Good Reprise	Ballad	SATB	Adults	
Carousel	1945	You'll Never Walk Along Reprise	Ballad	SATB	Adults	Δ
Chess	1988	Hymn of Chess	Ballad	SATB	Adults	
Chess	1988	Hungarian Folk Song	Ballad	SATB	Adults	
Curtains	2007	The Woman's Dead	Ballad	SATB	Adults	
Fiddler On The Roof	1964	Anatevka	Ballad	SATB	Adults	Δ
Hair	1968	Walking In Space	Ballad	SATB	Adults	
Jane Eyre	2000	Sympathies Exist	Ballad	SATB	Adults	Δ
Kiss Of The Spider Woman	1993	Dear One	Ballad	SATB	Adults	

Ensemble

268

* = Music Edit Required
+ = Ethnic Specific

Show	Year	Song	Tempo	Voicing	Scripted Age Group	Any Age Group
Les Miserables	1987	Drink With Me*	Ballad	SATB	Adults	
Lion King, The	1997	Can You Feel The Love Tonight*	Ballad	SATB	Adults	
Mamma Mia!	2001	Honey Honey*	Ballad	SATB	Adults	
Mamma Mia!	2001	One Last Summer	Ballad	SATB	Adults	
Most Happy Fella, The	1956	How Beautiful The Days	Ballad	SATB	Adults	Δ
Music Man, The	1957	It's You Reprise	Ballad	SATB	Adults	
My Fair Lady	1956	Get Me To The Church On Time Reprise	Ballad	SATB	Adults	
On The Twentieth Century	1978	Stranded*	Ballad	SATB	Adults	
Once On This Island	1990	A Part Of Us	Ballad	SATB	Adults	Δ
Parade	1998	It Don't Make Sense*	Ballad	SATB	Adults	
Porgy and Bess	1935	Gone, Gone, Gone	Ballad	SATB	Adults	
Porgy and Bess	1935	It Takes A Long Pull To Get There Reprise	Ballad	SATB	Adults	Δ
Rent	1996	I'll Cover You Reprise	Ballad	SATB	Adults	
Romance/Romance	1987	Romantic Notions	Ballad	SATB	Adults	
Scarlet Pimpernel, The	1997	You Are My Home	Ballad	SATB	Adults	
Sound Of Music, The	1959	The Sound Of Music Reprise	Ballad	SATB	Adults	
Spring Awakening	2006	Word Of Your Body Reprise 2	Ballad	SATB	Adults	
Sunday...Park With Geroge	1984	Sunday Finale	Ballad	SATB	Adults	
Sweeney Todd	1979	Quintet	Ballad	SATB	Adults	
Sweet Smell Of Success	2002	Psalm 151	Ballad	SATB	Adults	
Sweet Smell Of Success	2002	I Cannot Hear The City (Act 1 Finale)	Ballad	SATB	Adults	
Thoroughly Modern Millie	2002	Falling In Love With Love Reprise	Ballad	SATB	Adults	
Big River	1985	The Crossing	Ballad	SATB	Adults	
Aida	2000	The Gods Love Nubia	Ballad	SATB	Adults	
Big River	1985	How Blest We Are	Ballad	SATB	Adults	Δ
Color Purple, The	2005	The Color Purple Reprise	Ballad	SATB	Adults	Δ
Show Boat	1927	Misery*	Ballad	SATB	Adults	
Show Boat	1927	Ol' Man River	Ballad	SATB	Adults	
Songs For A New World	1995	On The Deck Of A Spanish Sailing Ship	Ballad	SATB	Adults	
Will Rogers Follies	1991	Will-A-Mania Reprise	Ballad	SATB	Adults	
You're A Good Man Charlie Brown	1971	Happiness	Ballad	SATB	Adults	Δ
A Chorus Line	1975	One (Bows)	Moderate Tempo	SATB	Adults	Δ
A Christmas Carol	1997	God Bless Us Everyone	Moderate Tempo	SATB	Children/Adults	Δ
A Funny Thing...Forum	1962	Funeral Sequence	Moderate Tempo	SATB	Adults	
A Little Night Music	1973	Remember	Moderate Tempo	SATB	Adults	

Ensemble

269

Ensemble

* = Music Edit Required
+ = Ethnic Specific

Show	Year	Song	Tempo	Voicing	Scripted Age Group	Any Age Group
A Little Night Music	1973	The Sun Won't Set	Moderate Tempo	SATB	Adults	
All Shook Up	2005	Can't Help Falling In Love*	Moderate Tempo	SATB	Adults	
All Shook Up	2005	If I Can Dream*	Moderate Tempo	SATB	Adults	Δ
Annie Get Your Gun	1946	Show Business Reprise *	Moderate Tempo	SATB	Adults	Δ
Applause	1970	Applause*	Moderate Tempo	SATB	Adults	Δ
Applause	1970	Applause Encore	Moderate Tempo	SATB	Adults	Δ
Applause	1970	Fasten Your Seatbelts	Moderate Tempo	SATB	Adults	
Assassins	1992	Another National Anthem	Moderate Tempo	SATB	Adults	
Assassins	1992	Something Just Broke	Moderate Tempo	SATB	Adults	
Assassins	1992	Take A Look Lee	Moderate Tempo	SATB	Adults	
Beauty and the Beast	1994	If I Could Love Her Finale	Moderate Tempo	SATB	Adults	
Beauty and the Beast	1994	Beauty and the Beast	Moderate Tempo	SATB	Adults	Δ
Best Little Whorehouse....	1978	Watch Dog Theme*	Moderate Tempo	SATB	Adults	
Billy Elliott	2008	The Stars Look Down	Moderate Tempo	SATB	Adults	
Billy Elliott	2008	Once We Were Kings	Moderate Tempo	SATB	Adults	
Call Me Madam	1950	Lichtenburg	Moderate Tempo	SATB	Adults	
Call Me Madam	1950	The Ocarina	Moderate Tempo	SATB	Adults	
Call Me Madam	1950	It's A Lovely Day Today Encore	Moderate Tempo	SATB	Adults	
Call Me Madam	1950	Lichtenburg Act II	Moderate Tempo	SATB	Adults	
Call Me Madam	1950	You're Just In Love Finale	Moderate Tempo	SATB	Adults	
Camelot	1960	Finalte Ultimo	Moderate Tempo	SATB	Adults	
Candide	1956	Voltaire Chorale	Moderate Tempo	SATB	Adults	
Candide	1956	Life Is Happiness Indeed	Moderate Tempo	SATB	Adults	
Candide	1956	Auto-da-fe	Moderate Tempo	SATB	Adults	
Candide	1956	I Am Easily Assimilated	Moderate Tempo	SATB	Adults	
Candide	1956	Quartet Finale	Moderate Tempo	SATB	Adults	
Candide	1956	Alleluia	Moderate Tempo	SATB	Adults	
Candide	1956	Ballad of Eldorado	Moderate Tempo	SATB	Adults	
Candide	1956	Make Our Garden Grow	Moderate Tempo	SATB	Adults	Δ
Cats	1981	Jellicle Songs for Jellicle Cats	Moderate Tempo	SATB	Adults	
Children of Eden	1991	In The Beginning*	Moderate Tempo	SATB	Adults	
Children of Eden	1991	Children of Eden*	Moderate Tempo	SATB	Adults	
Children of Eden	1991	Generations*	Moderate Tempo	SATB	Adults	
Dear World	1969	The Spring Of Next Year	Moderate Tempo	SATB	Adults	
Dear World	1969	Each Tomorrow Morning Reprise 1	Moderate Tempo	SATB	Adults	

Ensemble

270

* = Music Edit Required
+ = Ethnic Specific

Show	Year	Song	Tempo	Voicing	Scripted Age Group	Any Age Group
Dear World	1969	Dear World	Moderate Tempo	SATB	Adults	
Dear World	1969	Finale-Tomorrow Morning	Moderate Tempo	SATB	Adults	
Flower Drum Song 2002	1958	A Hundred Million Miracles	Moderate Tempo	SATB	Adults	∆
Flower Drum Song 2002	1958	Jazz Bit	Moderate Tempo	SATB	Adults	
Flower Drum Song 2002	1958	Grant Avenue	Moderate Tempo	SATB	Adults	
Flower Drum Song 2002	1958	A Hundred Million Miracles Reprise	Moderate Tempo	SATB	Adults	
Flower Drum Song 2002	1958	Chop Suey	Moderate Tempo	SATB	Adults	
Flower Drum Song 2002	1958	Finale: A Hundred Million Mirac	Moderate Tempo	SATB	Adults	
High Society 1998	1955	High Society Act II	Moderate Tempo	SATB	Adults	
High Society 1998	1956	True Love Finale	Moderate Tempo	SATB	Adults	
Kiss Me Kate	1948	Kiss Me Kate	Moderate Tempo	SATB	Adults	
Les Miserables	1987	Do You Hear the People Sing*	Moderate Tempo	SATB	Adults	∆
Les Miserables	1987	One Day More*	Moderate Tempo	SATB	Adults	
Lion King, The	1997	Weem-O-Wep	Moderate Tempo	SATB	Adults	
Lion King, The	1997	Shadowland*	Moderate Tempo	SATB	Adults	
Mamma Mia!	2001	Super Trouper*	Moderate Tempo	SATB	Adults	
Mamma Mia!	2001	The Name Of The Game*	Moderate Tempo	SATB	Adults	
Mamma Mia!	2001	One Of Us*	Moderate Tempo	SATB	Adults	
Mamma Mia!	2001	Knowing Me, Knowing You*	Moderate Tempo	SATB	Adults	
Marie Christine	1999	Mamzell' Marie	Moderate Tempo	SATB	Adults	
Marie Christine	1999	C'est L'Amour	Moderate Tempo	SATB	Adults	
Marie Christine	1999	Cincinati*	Moderate Tempo	SATB	Adults	
Mary Poppins	2006	Practically Perfect	Moderate Tempo	SATB	Children/Adults	∆
Mary Poppins	2006	Being Mrs. Banks*	Moderate Tempo	SATB	Adults	
Mary Poppins	2006	Precision And Order*	Moderate Tempo	SATB	Adults	∆
Mary Poppins	2006	Anything Can Happen	Moderate Tempo	SATB	Children/Adults	∆
Mary Poppins	2006	Let's Go Fly A Kite*	Moderate Tempo	SATB	Children/Adults	∆
Meet Me In St. Louis	1989	Meet Me In St. Louis Reprise 6B	Moderate Tempo	SATB	Adults	∆
Merrily We Roll Along 1994	1981	Merrily Rolling Along	Moderate Tempo	SATB	Adults	
Merrily We Roll Along 1994	1981	Our Time	Moderate Tempo	SATB	Adults	
Merrily We Roll Along 1994	1994	Transition 1	Moderate Tempo	SATB	Adults	
Merrily We Roll Along 1994	1994	Transition 3	Moderate Tempo	SATB	Adults	
Merrily We Roll Along 1994	1994	The Blob IV	Moderate Tempo	SATB	Adults	
Miss Saigon	1991	This Is The Hour	Moderate Tempo	SATB	Adults	
Miss Saigon	1991	You Wil Not Touch Him*	Moderate Tempo	SATB	Adults	

Ensemble

271

* = Music Edit Required
+ = Ethnic Specific

Show	Year	Song	Tempo	Voicing	Scripted Age Group	Any Age Group
Miss Saigon	1991	What A Waste*	Moderate Tempo	SATB	Adults	
Most Happy Fella, The	1956	Young People*	Moderate Tempo	SATB	Adults	
Music Man, The	1957	Pickalittle/Goodnight Ladies	Moderate Tempo	SATB	Adults	Δ
Music Man, The	1957	76 Trombones Reprise	Moderate Tempo	SATB	Children/Adults	Δ
My Fair Lady	1956	Ascot Gavotte	Moderate Tempo	SATB	Adults	
My Favorite Year	1992	Twenty Million People*	Moderate Tempo	SATB	Adults	
My Favorite Year	1992	Welcome To Brooklyn*	Moderate Tempo	SATB	Adults	
My Favorite Year	1992	My Favorite Year	Moderate Tempo	SATB	Adults	Δ
My Favorite Year	1992	Comedy Calvacade	Moderate Tempo	SATB	Adults	
Mystery Of Edwin Drood, The	1985	A British Subject	Moderate Tempo	SATB	Adults	
Mystery Of Edwin Drood, The	1985	Ceylon	Moderate Tempo	SATB	Adults	
Mystery Of Edwin Drood, The	1985	Don't Quit While You're Ahead	Moderate Tempo	SATB	Adults	Δ
Mystery Of Edwin Drood, The	1985	Perfect Strangers	Moderate Tempo	SATB	Adults	
No, No Nanette	1925	Bows and Exit	Moderate Tempo	SATB	Adults	
Of Thee I Sing	1931	Of The I Sing	Moderate Tempo	SATB	Adults	Δ
Of Thee I Sing	1931	Jilted	Moderate Tempo	SATB	Adults	
Of Thee I Sing	1931	Finale-Of Thee I Sing Reprise*	Moderate Tempo	SATB	Adults	
Once On This Island	1990	The Sad Tale Of The Beauxhommes	Moderate Tempo	SATB	Adults	
Pajama Game	1954	Sleep Tite	Moderate Tempo	SATB	Adults	
Parade	1998	Old Red Hills Of Home (Part 2)	Moderate Tempo	SATB	Adults	
Parade	1998	There Is A Fountain*	Moderate Tempo	SATB	Adults	
Parade	1998	The Trial, Part 3: Frankie's Testimony	Moderate Tempo	SATB	Adults	
Parade	1998	The Trial, Part 9: Closing Statemen/Verdict	Moderate Tempo	SATB	Adults	
Parade	1998	Old Red Hills Of Home Finale	Moderate Tempo	SATB	Adults	
Peter Pan	1954	Wendy	Moderate Tempo	SATB	Children/Adults	Δ
Phantom Of The Opera	1986	Hannibal Rehearsal	Moderate Tempo	SATB	Adults	
Phantom Of The Opera	1986	Poor Fool He Makes Me Laugh*	Moderate Tempo	SATB	Adults	
Phantom Of The Opera	1986	Masquerade*	Moderate Tempo	SATB	Adults	
Pippin	1972	Glory Part I & III	Moderate Tempo	SATB	Adults	
Pippin	1972	Morning Glow	Moderate Tempo	SATB	Adults	
Porgy and Bess	1935	A Woman Is A Sometime Thing	Moderate Tempo	SATB	Adults	
Porgy and Bess	1935	Overflow	Moderate Tempo	SATB	Adults	
Porgy and Bess	1935	My Man's Gone Now*	Moderate Tempo	SATB	Adults	
Porgy and Bess	1935	It Ain't Necessarily So	Moderate Tempo	SATB	Adults	
Porgy and Bess	1935	Dr. Jesus	Moderate Tempo	SATB	Adults	

* = Music Edit Required
+ = Ethnic Specific

Show	Year	Song	Tempo	Voicing	Scripted Age Group	Any Age Group
Porgy and Bess	1935	Oh, Dere's Somebody Knockin'	Moderate Tempo	SATB	Adults	
Porgy and Bess	1935	Clara, Clara	Moderate Tempo	SATB	Adults	
Porgy and Bess	1935	It Porgy Comoin' Home	Moderate Tempo	SATB	Adults	
Porgy and Bess	1935	Oh, Bess, Oh, Where's My Bess	Moderate Tempo	SATB	Adults	
Porgy and Bess	1935	Oh Lawd I'm On My Way	Moderate Tempo	SATB	Adults	
Producers, The	2001	I Wanna Be A Producer	Moderate Tempo	SATB	Adults	
Producers, The	2001	Springtime For Hitler	Moderate Tempo	SATB	Adults	
Rags	1986	Bread and Freedom*	Moderate Tempo	SATB	Adults	
Ragtime	1998	Prologue	Moderate Tempo	SATB	Adults	
Ragtime	1998	A Shtetl Iz Amereke	Moderate Tempo	SATB	Adults	
Ragtime	1998	Till We Reach That Day	Moderate Tempo	SATB	Adults	Δ
Ragtime	1998	Epilogue Two	Moderate Tempo	SATB	Adults	
Rent	1996	Life Support*	Moderate Tempo	SATB	Adults	
Rent	1996	Will I	Moderate Tempo	SATB	Adults	
Rent	1996	Sante Fe	Moderate Tempo	SATB	Adults	
Rent	1996	Seasons Of Love	Moderate Tempo	SATB	Adults	Δ
Rent	1996	Seasons Of Love B	Moderate Tempo	SATB	Adults	Δ
Rent	1996	Finale B-Medley	Moderate Tempo	SATB	Adults	
Romance/Romance	1987	So Glad I Married	Moderate Tempo	SATB	Adults	
Scarlet Pimpernel, The	1997	Storybook	Moderate Tempo	SATB	Adults	
Scarlet Pimpernel, The	1997	Scarlet Pimpernel	Moderate Tempo	SATB	Adults	
Scarlet Pimpernel, The	1997	The Creation Of Man	Moderate Tempo	SATB	Adults	
Scarlet Pimpernel, The	1997	The Riddle Part 3	Moderate Tempo	SATB	Adults	
Scarlet Pimpernel, The	1997	They Seek Him Here	Moderate Tempo	SATB	Adults	
Scarlet Pimpernel, The	1997	Vivez	Moderate Tempo	SATB	Adults	
Secret Garden, The	1991	The House Upon A Hill*	Moderate Tempo	SATB	Adults	
Secret Garden, The	1991	I Heard Someone Crying	Moderate Tempo	SATB	Children/Adults	
Secret Garden, The	1991	Finale-Come To My Garden	Moderate Tempo	SATB	Children/Adults	
Seussical	2000	Horton Hears A Who	Moderate Tempo	SATB	Adults	
Seussical	2000	Finale: Horton Sits On An Egg	Moderate Tempo	SATB	Adults	
Seussical	2000	Solla Sollew	Moderate Tempo	SATB	Children/Adults	Δ
Seven Brides/Seven Brothers	1982	Goin' Co'tin/Wonderful, Wonderful	Moderate Tempo	SATB	Adults	
She Loves Me	1963	Good Morning Good Day	Moderate Tempo	SATB	Adults	
She Loves Me	1963	Sound While Selling	Moderate Tempo	SATB	Adults	
She Loves Me	1963	Goodby Georg	Moderate Tempo	SATB	Adults	

* = Music Edit Required
+ = Ethnic Specific

Show	Year	Song	Tempo	Voicing	Scripted Age Group	Any Age Group
Show Boat	1927	Finale Act I - The Wedding	Moderate Tempo	SATB	Adults	
Show Boat	1927	Montage 1	Moderate Tempo	SATB	Adults	
Songs For A New World	1995	The World Was Dancing*	Moderate Tempo	SATB	Adults	
Songs For A New World	1995	Hear My Song*	Moderate Tempo	SATB	Adults	
Songs For A New World	1995	One Moment	Moderate Tempo	SATB	Adults	
Spamalot	2005	Fisch Schlapping Dance	Moderate Tempo	SATB	Adults	
Spamalot	2005	Find Your Grail	Moderate Tempo	SATB	Adults	
Spamalot	2005	The Cow Song	Moderate Tempo	SATB	Adults	
Spitfire Grill	2001	Shoot The Moon P1&P2	Moderate Tempo	SATB	Adults	
Spring Awakening	2006	Touch Me	Moderate Tempo	SATB	Adults	
Spring Awakening	2006	I Believe	Moderate Tempo	SATB	Adults	
Spring Awakening	2006	The Guilty One	Moderate Tempo	SATB	Adults	
Spring Awakening	2006	Song of Purple Summer	Moderate Tempo	SATB	Adults	
State Fair 1996	1947	All I Owe Ioway	Moderate Tempo	SATB	Adults	
Steel Pier	1997	The Last Girl	Moderate Tempo	SATB	Adults	
Steel Pier	1997	Leave The World Behind	Moderate Tempo	SATB	Adults	
Sunday...Park With Geroge	1984	Sunday	Moderate Tempo	SATB	Children/Adults	Δ
Sunday...Park With Geroge	1984	It's Hot Up Here	Moderate Tempo	SATB	Children/Adults	
Sunset Boulevard	1994	Let's Have Lunch	Moderate Tempo	SATB	Adults	
Sunset Boulevard	1994	Let's Have Lunch Reprise	Moderate Tempo	SATB	Adults	
Sunset Boulevard	1994	This Time Next Year	Moderate Tempo	SATB	Adults	
Sunset Boulevard	1994	Auld Lang Syne	Moderate Tempo	SATB	Adults	
Sunset Boulevard	1994	Paramount Conversations	Moderate Tempo	SATB	Adults	
Sweeney Todd	1979	The Ballad Of Sweeney Todd	Moderate Tempo	SATB	Adults	
Sweeney Todd	1979	God That's Good	Moderate Tempo	SATB	Adults	
Sweeney Todd	1979	Ballad Of Sweeney Todd #1	Moderate Tempo	SATB	Adults	
Sweeney Todd	1979	Ballad Of Sweeney Todd #5	Moderate Tempo	SATB	Adults	
Sweeney Todd	1979	Ballad Of Sweeney Todd #10B	Moderate Tempo	SATB	Adults	
Sweeney Todd	1979	Ballad Of Sweeney Todd #10B	Moderate Tempo	SATB	Adults	
Sweeney Todd	1979	Ballad Of Sweeney Todd #22	Moderate Tempo	SATB	Adults	
Sweeney Todd	1979	Ballad Of Sweeney Todd #25 Fogg's Asylum	Moderate Tempo	SATB	Adults	
Sweeney Todd	1979	Ballad Of Sweeney Todd #29B	Moderate Tempo	SATB	Adults	
Sweet Smell Of Success	2002	The Column	Moderate Tempo	SATB	Adults	
Sweet Smell Of Success	2002	Dirt	Moderate Tempo	SATB	Adults	
Sweet Smell Of Success	2002	At The Fountain Reprise	Moderate Tempo	SATB	Adults	

Ensemble

* = Music Edit Required
+ = Ethnic Specific

Show	Year	Song	Tempo	Voicing	Scripted Age Group	Any Age Group
The Little Mermaid	2007	Kiss The Girl	Moderate Tempo	SATB	Adults	
Unsinkable Molly Brown, The	1960	The Denver Police	Moderate Tempo	SATB	Adults	
Unsinkable Molly Brown, The	1960	Happy Birthday, Mrs. JJ Brown	Moderate Tempo	SATB	Adults	Δ
White Christmas	2008	Snow	Moderate Tempo	SATB	Adults	
White Christmas	2008	Blue Skies (Part 1-3)	Moderate Tempo	SATB	Adults	Δ
White Christmas	2008	White Christmas	Moderate Tempo	SATB	Adults	
Wicked	2003	No One Mourns The Wicked	Moderate Tempo	SATB	Adults	
Wicked	2003	Dear Old Shiz	Moderate Tempo	SATB	Adults	
Will Rogers Follies	1991	Let's Go Flying	Moderate Tempo	SATB	Adults	
Will Rogers Follies	1991	The Big Time	Moderate Tempo	SATB	Adults	Δ
Will Rogers Follies	1991	The Campaign: Our Favorite Son	Moderate Tempo	SATB	Adults	
Will Rogers Follies	1991	Presents For Mrs. Rogers	Moderate Tempo	SATB	Adults	
Will Rogers Follies	1991	Never Met A Man I Didn't Like Reprise	Moderate Tempo	SATB	Adults	Δ
Wiz, The	1974	He's The Wiz	Moderate Tempo	SATB	Adults	Δ
Wiz, The	1974	I Was Born On The Day Before Yesterday	Moderate Tempo	SATB	Adults	
Wizard Of Oz 1990	1939	Munchkinland Sequence	Moderate Tempo	SATB	Children/Adults	Δ
Wizard Of Oz 1998	1939	Poppies	Moderate Tempo	SATB	Adults	
Wonderful Town	1953	It's Love	Moderate Tempo	SATB	Adults	
Wonderful Town	1953	It's Love Reprise	Moderate Tempo	SATB	Adults	
You're A Good Man Charlie Brown	1971	Book Report	Moderate Tempo	SATB	Adults	Δ
You're A Good Man Charlie Brown	1971	Glee Club Rehearsal	Moderate Tempo	SATB	Adults	Δ
Wiz, The	1974	The Wiz	Moderate Tempo	SATB	Adults	Δ
Lion King, The	1997	Circle of Life*	Moderate Tempo	SATB	Adults	Δ
Lion King, The	1997	Circle of Life Finale Part 2*	Moderate Tempo	SATB	Adults	Δ
Little Shop of Horrors	1982	Downtown	Moderate Tempo	SATB	Adults	
Meet Me In St. Louis	1989	Meet Me In St. Louis	Moderate Tempo	SATB	Adults	Δ
Producers, The	2001	Along Came Bially	Moderate Tempo	SATB	Adults	
On The Twentieth Century	1978	Sign Lily Sign	Moderate Tempo	SATB	Adults	
Once On This Island	1990	One Small Girl	Moderate Tempo	SATB	Children/Adults	
Victor/Victoria	1995	Le Jazz Hot	Moderate Tempo	SATB	Adults	
Annie Get Your Gun	1944	I Got The Sun in the Morning*	Moderate Tempo	SATB	Adults	Δ
Candide	1956	Money, Money, Money	Moderate Tempo	SATB	Adults	
Cinderella (2013)	1997	There is Music In You	Moderate Tempo	SATB	Adults	Δ
Meet Me In St. Louis	1989	The First Noel	Moderate Tempo	SATB	Adults	
Show Boat	1927	Can't Help Lovin' Dat Man*	Moderate Tempo	SATB	Adults	Δ

Ensemble

* = Music Edit Required
+ = Ethnic Specific

Show	Year	Song	Tempo	Voicing	Scripted Age Group	Any Age Group
Company (Revival)	1970	Side By Side	Moderate Tempo	SATB	Adults	Δ
Singin' In The Rain	1983	You Stepped Out Of A Dream	Moderate Tempo	SATB	Adults	
110 In The Shade	1963	Another Hot Day*	Moderate Tempo	SATB	Adults	
25th Annual...Spelling Bee	2005	The Last Goodbye	Uptempo	SATB	Adults	Δ
110 In The Shade	1963	Hungry Men	Uptempo	SATB	Adults	
110 In The Shade	1963	The Rain Song Reprise	Uptempo	SATB	Adults	
13 The Musical	2008	Brand New You	Uptempo	SATB	Adults	Δ
25th Annual...Spelling Bee	2005	25th Annual...Spelling Bee	Uptempo	SATB	Adults	Δ
A Chorus Line	1975	I Hope I Get It	Uptempo	SATB	Adults	
A Christmas Carol	1997	Mr. Fezziwig's Annual Christmas Ball	Uptempo	SATB	Adults	
A Christmas Carol	1997	Christmas Together*	Uptempo	SATB	Adults	Δ
A Funny Thing...Forum	1962	Comedy Tonight	Uptempo	SATB	Adults	Δ
A Funny Thing...Forum	1962	Finale Ultimo	Uptempo	SATB	Adults	
All Shook Up	2005	All Shook Up	Uptempo	SATB	Adults	
All Shook Up	2005	C'mon Everybody Encore	Uptempo	SATB	Adults	
Annie Get Your Gun	1944	There's No Business Like Show Business*	Uptempo	SATB	Adults	Δ
Annie Get Your Gun	1944	I'll Share It All With You*	Uptempo	SATB	Adults	
Anyone Can Whistle	1964	Miracle Song	Uptempo	SATB	Adults	
Anyone Can Whistle	1964	Simple	Uptempo	SATB	Adults	
Anyone Can Whistle	1964	A-1 March	Uptempo	SATB	Adults	
Anyone Can Whistle	1964	Cora's Chase	Uptempo	SATB	Adults	
Anything Goes	1934	Bon Voyage	Uptempo	SATB	Adults	
Anything Goes	1934	Anything Goes*	Uptempo	SATB	Adults	
Anything Goes	1934	Blow Gabriel Blow*	Uptempo	SATB	Adults	
Applause	1970	Backstage Babble	Uptempo	SATB	Adults	
Applause	1970	But Alive	Uptempo	SATB	Adults	
Applause	1970	Backstage Babble Reprise	Uptempo	SATB	Adults	
Applause	1970	She's No Longer A Gypsy	Uptempo	SATB	Adults	
Applause	1970	Applause Finale	Uptempo	SATB	Adults	Δ
Assassins	1992	How I Saved Roosevelt	Uptempo	SATB	Adults	
Assassins	1992	Everybody's Got The Right	Uptempo	SATB	Adults	
Avenue Q	2003	The Avenue Q Theme	Uptempo	SATB	Adults	
Avenue Q	2003	For Now	Uptempo	SATB	Adults	
Babes In Arms (1998)	1937	Babes In Arms	Uptempo	SATB	Adults	Δ
Babes In Arms (1998)	1937	Babes In Arms Reprise	Uptempo	SATB	Adults	Δ

* = Music Edit Required
+ = Ethnic Specific

Show	Year	Song	Tempo	Voicing	Scripted Age Group	Any Age Group
Babes In Arms (1998)	1937	Finale Ultimo	Uptempo	SATB	Adults	
Brigadoon	1947	Down On MacConnachy Square	Uptempo	SATB	Adults	
Bye Bye Birdie	1960	The Telephone Hour	Uptempo	SATB	Teens/Adults	Δ
Call Me Madam	1950	Mrs. Sally Adams	Uptempo	SATB	Adults	
Call Me Madam	1950	Mrs. Sally Adams Reprise	Uptempo	SATB	Adults	
Camelot	1960	The Lusty Month Of May	Uptempo	SATB	Adults	
Camelot	1960	The Jousts	Uptempo	SATB	Adults	
Camelot	1960	Guenevere	Uptempo	SATB	Adults	
Candide	1956	The Best Of All Possible Worlds	Uptempo	SATB	Adults	
Candide	1956	Bon Voyage	Uptempo	SATB	Adults	
Candide	1956	What's The Use?	Uptempo	SATB	Adults	
Cats	1981	The Journey to the Heaviside Layer	Uptempo	SATB	Adults	
Chitty Chitty Bang Bang	2005	Chitty Chitty Bang Bang	Uptempo	SATB	Children/Adults	Δ
Chitty Chitty Bang Bang	2005	Vulgarian National Anthem	Uptempo	SATB	Adults	
Chitty Chitty Bang Bang	2005	Teamwork* (Children)	Uptempo	SATB	Children/Adults	Δ
Closer Than Ever	1989	Doors	Uptempo	SATB	Adults	
Closer Than Ever	1989	There's Nothing Like It	Uptempo	SATB	Adults	
Closer Than Ever	1989	Next Time/Wouldn't Go Back	Uptempo	SATB	Adults	
Closer Than Ever	1989	The March of Time	Uptempo	SATB	Adults	
Closer Than Ever	1989	Closer Than Ever	Uptempo	SATB	Adults	
Curtains	2007	In The Same Boat Parts 1-6	Uptempo	SATB	Adults	Δ
Dear World	1969	One Person	Uptempo	SATB	Adults	
Dear World	1969	Bows-Medley	Uptempo	SATB	Adults	
Fame	2003	Hard Work	Uptempo	SATB	Adults	
Fantasticks, The	1960	Happy Ending	Uptempo	SATB	Adults	Δ
Flower Drum Song 2002	1958	Fan Tan Fannie	Uptempo	SATB	Adults	
Flower Drum Song 2002	1958	I Am Going To Like It Here Reprise	Uptempo	SATB	Adults	
Footloose	1998	Footloose (Finale)	Uptempo	SATB	Adults	Δ
Godspell	1971	Prepare Ye Finale	Uptempo	SATB	Adults	Δ
Good News (1993 Revival)	1927	The Varsity Drag	Uptempo	SATB	Adults	
Good News (1993 Revival)	1927	Good News	Uptempo	SATB	Adults	
Grease	1972	Shakin' At The High School Hop	Uptempo	SATB	Adults	
Grease	1972	We Go Together Reprise (Finale Part 2)	Uptempo	SATB	Adults	
Grease	1972	Rock' N Roll Party Queen	Uptempo	SATB	Adults	
Hair	1968	Aquarius	Uptempo	SATB	Adults	

Ensemble

* = Music Edit Required
+ = Ethnic Specific

Show	Year	Song	Tempo	Voicing	Scripted Age Group	Any Age Group
Hair	1968	Initials	Uptempo	SATB	Adults	
Hair	1968	The Bed	Uptempo	SATB	Adults	
Heathers	2014	Big Fun	Uptempo	SATB	Adults	
Hello Dolly	1964	Hello Dolly Finale	Uptempo	SATB	Adults	
High School Musical	2007	Start of Something New*	Uptempo	SATB	Adults	Δ
High School Musical	2007	Stick to the Status Quo	Uptempo	SATB	Adults	Δ
High School Musical	2007	We're All In This Together	Uptempo	SATB	Adults	Δ
High Society 1998	1927	Let's Misbehave	Uptempo	SATB	Adults	
High Society 1998	1929	She's Got That Thing	Uptempo	SATB	Adults	
High Society 1998	1929	She's Got That Thing Reprise	Uptempo	SATB	Adults	
High Society 1998	1939	Well Did You Evah	Uptempo	SATB	Adults	
High Society 1998	1940	Throwing A Ball Tonight	Uptempo	SATB	Adults	
High Society 1998	1955	High Society	Uptempo	SATB	Adults	
Honk!	1993	Warts And All Reprise*	Uptempo	SATB	Adults	Δ
How To Succeed...	1961	Been A Long Day	Uptempo	SATB	Adults	Δ
How To Succeed...	1961	Company Way Finale Act II	Uptempo	SATB	Adults	
Jekyll and Hyde	1997	Façade	Uptempo	SATB	Adults	
Jekyll and Hyde	1997	Murder, Murder	Uptempo	SATB	Adults	
Kinky Boots	2013	Raise You Up	Uptempo	SATB	Adults	
Kiss Me Kate	1948	Another Op'nin Another Show*	Uptempo	SATB	Adults	Δ
Kiss Me Kate	1948	Too Darn Hot*	Uptempo	SATB	Adults	
Kiss Me Kate	1948	Cantiamo D'Amore	Uptempo	SATB	Adults	
Legally Blonde	2007	There, Right There	Uptempo	SATB	Adults	
Les Miserables	1987	The Wedding*	Uptempo	SATB	Adults	
Les Miserables	1987	Lovely Ladies *	Uptempo	SATB	Adults	
Little Me	1962	Deep Down Inside	Uptempo	SATB	Adults	
Little Me	1962	Here's To Us	Uptempo	SATB	Adults	
Mame	1966	Open A New Window*	Uptempo	SATB	Adults	Δ
Mame	1966	The Fox Hunt	Uptempo	SATB	Adults	
Mame	1966	That's How Young I Feel*	Uptempo	SATB	Adults	
Mame	1966	Curtain Call	Uptempo	SATB	Adults	
Mamma Mia!	2001	Dancing Queen	Uptempo	SATB	Adults	
Mamma Mia!	2001	Lay All Your Love On Me*	Uptempo	SATB	Adults	
Mamma Mia!	2001	Voulez Vous	Uptempo	SATB	Adults	
Mamma Mia!	2001	Under Attack*	Uptempo	SATB	Adults	

Show	Year	Song	Tempo	Voicing	Scripted Age Group	Any Age Group
Mamma Mia!	2001	Does Your Mother Know*	Uptempo	SATB	Adults	
Marie Christine	1999	Bird Inside The House	Uptempo	SATB	Adults	
Marie Christine	1999	Finale Act I (P 1-3)	Uptempo	SATB	Adults	
Marie Christine	1999	You're Looking At A Man*	Uptempo	SATB	Adults	
Mary Poppins	2006	Cherry Tree Lane*	Uptempo	SATB	Children/Adults	Δ
Mary Poppins	2006	Cherry Tree Lane (Part 2)	Uptempo	SATB	Children/Adults	Δ
Mary Poppins	2006	Jolly Holiday*	Uptempo	SATB	Children/Adults	Δ
Mary Poppins	2006	Cherry Tree Lane Reprise	Uptempo	SATB	Children/Adults	Δ
Mary Poppins	2006	A Spoonful Of Sugar*	Uptempo	SATB	Children/Adults	Δ
Mary Poppins	2006	Feed The Birds*	Uptempo	SATB	Adults	Δ
Mary Poppins	2006	Temper Temper	Uptempo	SATB	Adults	
Mary Poppins	2006	Chim Chim Cher-ee A2	Uptempo	SATB	Adults	Δ
Mary Poppins	2006	Step In Time*	Uptempo	SATB	Adults	Δ
Meet Me In St. Louis	1989	Skip To My Lou	Uptempo	SATB	Children/Adults	Δ
Meet Me In St. Louis	1989	Banjos*	Uptempo	SATB	Children/Adults	Δ
Meet Me In St. Louis	1989	Finale Act I	Uptempo	SATB	Adults	Δ
Merrily We Roll Along 1994	1981	Now You Know	Uptempo	SATB	Adults	
Merrily We Roll Along 1994	1981	It's A Hit	Uptempo	SATB	Adults	
Merrily We Roll Along 1994	1981	Opening Doors	Uptempo	SATB	Adults	
Merrily We Roll Along 1994	1994	That Frank	Uptempo	SATB	Adults	
Merrily We Roll Along 1994	1994	Transition 2	Uptempo	SATB	Adults	
Merrily We Roll Along 1994	1994	The Blob I	Uptempo	SATB	Adults	
Miss Saigon	1991	The Morning Of The Dragon	Uptempo	SATB	Adults	
Most Happy Fella, The	1956	The Most Happy Fella	Uptempo	SATB	Adults	Δ
Most Happy Fella, The	1956	Sposalizio	Uptempo	SATB	Adults	Δ
Most Happy Fella, The	1956	Big D	Uptempo	SATB	Adults	Δ
Most Happy Fella, The	1956	A Song Of A Summer Night*	Uptempo	SATB	Adults	Δ
Most Happy Fella, The	1956	Finale	Uptempo	SATB	Adults	
Music Man, The	1957	Iowa Stubborn	Uptempo	SATB	Adults	
Music Man, The	1957	The Wells Fargo Wagon	Uptempo	SATB	Adults	Δ
Music Man, The	1957	Shipoopi	Uptempo	SATB	Adults	
Music Man, The	1957	Shipoopi	Uptempo	SATB	Adults	
My Fair Lady	1956	With A Little Bit Of Luck*	Uptempo	SATB	Adults	
My Favorite Year	1992	Three Musketeer Sketch	Uptempo	SATB	Adults	
My Favorite Year	1992	The Gospel According To King	Uptempo	SATB	Adults	

* = Music Edit Required
+ = Ethnic Specific

Show	Year	Song	Tempo	Voicing	Scripted Age Group	Any Age Group
Mystery Of Edwin Drood, The	1985	There You Are	Uptempo	SATB	Adults	
Mystery Of Edwin Drood, The	1985	No Good Comes From Bad	Uptempo	SATB	Adults	
Mystery Of Edwin Drood, The	1985	Off To The Races	Uptempo	SATB	Adults	
Mystery Of Edwin Drood, The	1985	The Writing On The Wall*	Uptempo	SATB	Adults	
Nick & Nora	1991	May The Best Man Win	Uptempo	SATB	Adults	
No, No Nanette	1925	No, No Nanette*	Uptempo	SATB	Adults	
No, No Nanette	1925	Peach On The Beach	Uptempo	SATB	Adults	
No, No Nanette	1925	Finale	Uptempo	SATB	Adults	
Of Thee I Sing	1931	Wintergreen For President	Uptempo	SATB	Adults	
Of Thee I Sing	1931	The Dimple On My Knee	Uptempo	SATB	Adults	
Of Thee I Sing	1931	How Beautiful	Uptempo	SATB	Adults	
Of Thee I Sing	1931	Some Girls Can Bake A Pie	Uptempo	SATB	Adults	
Of Thee I Sing	1931	Love Is Sweeping The Country	Uptempo	SATB	Adults	
Of Thee I Sing	1931	Supreme Court Judges	Uptempo	SATB	Adults	
Of Thee I Sing	1931	Hello Good Morning	Uptempo	SATB	Adults	
Of Thee I Sing	1931	Who Cares	Uptempo	SATB	Adults	
Of Thee I Sing	1931	The Illegitimate Daughter	Uptempo	SATB	Adults	
Of Thee I Sing	1931	Posterity Is Just Around The Corner	Uptempo	SATB	Adults	
Of Thee I Sing	1931	Trumpeter Blow Your Horn	Uptempo	SATB	Adults	
Oklahoma!	1943	Oklahoma	Uptempo	SATB	Adults	Δ
Oklahoma!	1943	Oklahoma Encore	Uptempo	SATB	Adults	Δ
Oliver!	1963	Oliver	Uptempo	SATB	Children/Adults	Δ
Oliver!	1963	Consider Yourself (Part One)	Uptempo	SATB	Children/Adults	Δ
Oliver!	1963	Oom-Pah-Pah	Uptempo	SATB	Adults	
Oliver!	1963	Who Will Buy Part Two	Uptempo	SATB	Adults	Δ
Oliver!	1963	Bows-Consider Yourself	Uptempo	SATB	Children/Adults	Δ
On The Twentieth Century	1978	On The Twentieth Century*	Uptempo	SATB	Adults	
On The Twentieth Century	1978	Together	Uptempo	SATB	Adults	
On The Twentieth Century	1978	End Act I-On The Twentieth Century	Uptempo	SATB	Adults	
On The Twentieth Century	1978	She's A Nut	Uptempo	SATB	Adults	
Once On This Island	1990	Pray	Uptempo	SATB	Adults	
Once On This Island	1990	Some Say	Uptempo	SATB	Children/Adults	
Once On This Island	1990	Pray Reprise	Uptempo	SATB	Adults	
Once On This Island	1990	Why We Tell The Story	Uptempo	SATB	Children/Adults	Δ
Once Upon A Mattress	1959	Opening For A Princess	Uptempo	SATB	Adults	

* = Music Edit Required
+ = Ethnic Specific

Show	Year	Song	Tempo	Voicing	Scripted Age Group	Any Age Group
Once Upon A Mattress	1959	Finale	Uptempo	SATB	Adults	
Pacific Overtures	1976	The Advantages Of Floating...	Uptempo	SATB	Adults	
Pacific Overtures	1976	Next Part	Uptempo	SATB	Adults	
Pajama Game	1954	Once-A-Year Day	Uptempo	SATB	Adults	
Pajama Game	1954	The Pajama Game Closing	Uptempo	SATB	Adults	
Parade	1998	The Dream Of Atlatna	Uptempo	SATB	Adults	
Parade	1998	Real Big News	Uptempo	SATB	Adults	
Parade	1998	The Trial, Part 1: People Of Atlanta	Uptempo	SATB	Adults	
Parade	1998	The Trial, Part 2: Twenty From Marietta	Uptempo	SATB	Adults	
Parade	1998	Where Will You Stand...Flood Comes	Uptempo	SATB	Adults	
Passion	1994	Finale	Uptempo	SATB	Adults	
Peter Pan	1954	Ugg-A-Wugg	Uptempo	SATB	Children/Adults	
Phantom	1991	Dressing For The Night	Uptempo	SATB	Adults	
Phantom	1991	Phantom Fugue	Uptempo	SATB	Adults	
Phantom	1991	The Bistro	Uptempo	SATB	Adults	
Pippin	1972	Magic To Do	Uptempo	SATB	Adults	
Pippin	1972	War Is A Science	Uptempo	SATB	Adults	
Pippin	1972	No Time At All	Uptempo	SATB	Adults	
Pippin	1972	Think About The Sun	Uptempo	SATB	Adults	
Porgy and Bess	1935	Leavin' For The Promise Land	Uptempo	SATB	Adults	
Porgy and Bess	1935	Oh, I Got Plenty O' Nuttin'	Uptempo	SATB	Adults	
Porgy and Bess	1935	Oh I Can't Sit Down	Uptempo	SATB	Adults	
Porgy and Bess	1935	I Ain't Got No Shame	Uptempo	SATB	Adults	
Porgy and Bess	1935	Good Mornin' Sistuh!...*	Uptempo	SATB	Adults	
Producers, The	2001	Opening Night	Uptempo	SATB	Adults	
Producers, The	2001	King of Broadway	Uptempo	SATB	Adults	
Producers, The	2001	We Can Do It Reprise Act 1 Finale	Uptempo	SATB	Adults	
Producers, The	2001	Prisoners Of Love	Uptempo	SATB	Adults	
Rags	1986	Penny A Tune	Uptempo	SATB	Adults	
Rags	1986	Hard To Be A Prince	Uptempo	SATB	Adults	
Rags	1986	The Sound Of Love	Uptempo	SATB	Adults	
Ragtime	1998	Henry Ford	Uptempo	SATB	Adults	
Ragtime	1998	Atlantic City (Part 1)*	Uptempo	SATB	Adults	
Rent	1996	Rent	Uptempo	SATB	Adults	
Rent	1996	La Vie Boheme*	Uptempo	SATB	Adults	

* = Music Edit Required
+ = Ethnic Specific

Show	Year	Song	Tempo	Voicing	Scripted Age Group	Any Age Group
Rent	1996	Contact	Uptempo	SATB	Adults	
Romance/Romance	1987	Summer Share	Uptempo	SATB	Adults	
Scarlet Pimpernel, The	1997	Madame Guillotine	Uptempo	SATB	Adults	
Scarlet Pimpernel, The	1997	Into The Fire Reprise	Uptempo	SATB	Adults	
Secret Garden, The	1991	There's A Girl	Uptempo	SATB	Adults	
Secret Garden, The	1991	It's A Maze	Uptempo	SATB	Adults	
Secret Garden, The	1991	Storm I	Uptempo	SATB	Adults	
Secret Garden, The	1991	Storm Final	Uptempo	SATB	Adults	
Secret Garden, The	1991	Quartet	Uptempo	SATB	Adults	
Secret Garden, The	1991	Come Spirit Come Charm	Uptempo	SATB	Children/Adults	
Seussical	2000	Oh, The thinks You Can Think	Uptempo	SATB	Children/Adults	Δ
Seussical	2000	Chasing The Whos	Uptempo	SATB	Adults	
Seussical	2000	Egg, Nest, And Tree	Uptempo	SATB	Adults	
Seussical	2000	The People Versus Horton The Elephant	Uptempo	SATB	Adults	
She Loves Me	1963	Twelve Days Of Christmas	Uptempo	SATB	Adults	Δ
She Loves Me	1963	A Christmas Carol	Uptempo	SATB	Adults	
Show Boat	1927	Cotton Blossom	Uptempo	SATB	Adults	
Show Boat	1927	Can't Help Lovin' Dat Man*	Uptempo	SATB	Adults	
Show Boat	1927	Life Upon The Wicked Stage*	Uptempo	SATB	Adults	
Show Boat	1927	At The Fair	Uptempo	SATB	Adults	
Show Boat	1927	Dahomey	Uptempo	SATB	Adults	
Show Boat	1927	Life Upon The Wicked Stage	Uptempo	SATB	Adults	
Songs For A New World	1995	Steam Train*	Uptempo	SATB	Adults	
Sound Of Music, The	1959	The Concert	Uptempo	SATB	Children/Adults	Δ
Spamalot	2005	Burn Her	Uptempo	SATB	Adults	
Spamalot	2005	Knights Of The Round Table*	Uptempo	SATB	Adults	
Spamalot	2005	Lancelot	Uptempo	SATB	Adults	
Spamalot	2005	Finale Ensemble	Uptempo	SATB	Adults	
Spitfire Grill	2001	Something's Cooking	Uptempo	SATB	Adults	
Spring Awakening	2006	My Junk	Uptempo	SATB	Adults	
Spring Awakening	2006	Totally Fucked	Uptempo	SATB	Adults	
State Fair 1996	1947	A Grand Night For Singing	Uptempo	SATB	Adults	
State Fair 1996	1996	Our State Fair*	Uptempo	SATB	Adults	Δ
State Fair 2016	1996	State Fair Bows	Uptempo	SATB	Adults	Δ
Steel Pier	1997	Everybody Dance Part 1	Uptempo	SATB	Adults	

Ensemble

* = Music Edit Required
+ = Ethnic Specific

Show	Year	Song	Tempo	Voicing	Scripted Age Group	Any Age Group
Steel Pier	1997	Steel Pier Reprise	Uptempo	SATB	Adults	
Sugar	1972	Sun On My Face	Uptempo	SATB	Adults	
Sugar	1972	When You Meet A Man...	Uptempo	SATB	Adults	
Sunday...Park With Geroge	1984	Gossip Sequence	Uptempo	SATB	Adults	
Sunday...Park With Geroge	1984	The Day Off (Part 7)	Uptempo	SATB	Adults	
Sunday...Park With Geroge	1984	The One On The Left	Uptempo	SATB	Adults	
Sunday...Park With Geroge	1984	Putting It Together (Part 2 & 3)	Uptempo	SATB	Adults	
Sunday...Park With Geroge	1984	Putting It Together (Part 8)	Uptempo	SATB	Adults	
Sunday...Park With Geroge	1984	Putting It Together (Part 16)	Uptempo	SATB	Adults	
Sweeney Todd	1979	City On Fire	Uptempo	SATB	Adults	
Sweet Charity	1966	The Rhythm Of Life	Uptempo	SATB	Adults	
Sweet Smell Of Success	2002	Welcome To The Night	Uptempo	SATB	Adults	
Sweet Smell Of Success	2002	Break It Up	Uptempo	SATB	Adults	
Sweet Smell Of Success	2002	Finale*	Uptempo	SATB	Adults	
The Little Mermaid	2007	The Contest	Uptempo	SATB	Adults	
The Little Mermaid	2007	Under The Sea	Uptempo	SATB	Adults	Δ
They're Playing Our Song	1974	Workin' It Out	Uptempo	SATB	Adults	
Thoroughly Modern Millie	2002	Thoroughly Modern Millie	Uptempo	SATB	Adults	
Thoroughly Modern Millie	2002	Thoroughly Modern Millie Reprise	Uptempo	SATB	Adults	
Thoroughly Modern Millie	2002	Muquin (My Mammy)	Uptempo	SATB	Adults	
Unsinkable Molly Brown, The	1960	Are You Sure	Uptempo	SATB	Adults	
Unsinkable Molly Brown, The	1960	Bon Jour	Uptempo	SATB	Adults	
Unsinkable Molly Brown, The	1960	Keep-A-Hoppin'	Uptempo	SATB	Adults	
Unsinkable Molly Brown, The	1960	I Ain't Down Yet Fnale	Uptempo	SATB	Adults	
Victor/Victoria	1995	Louis Says	Uptempo	SATB	Adults	
Victor/Victoria	1995	Victor/Victoria	Uptempo	SATB	Adults	
West Side Story	1957	Tonight Quintet	Uptempo	SATB	Adults	
White Christmas	2008	Happy Holiday/Let Yourself Go	Uptempo	SATB	Adults	
White Christmas	2008	I've Got My Love To Keep Me Warm	Uptempo	SATB	Adults	
Les Miserables	1987	At the End of the Day	Uptempo	SATB	Adults	
Pajama Game	1954	Racing With The Clock	Uptempo	SATB	Adults	
They're Playing Our Song	1974	When You're In My Arms	Uptempo	SATB	Adults	
Damn Yankees	1955	Six Months Out Of Every Year	Uptempo	SATB	Adults	
Light In The Piazza, The	2005	Aiutami	Uptempo	SATB	Adults	
Lion King, The	1997	Hakuna Matata*	Uptempo	SATB	Adults	Δ

Ensemble

283

Ensemble

* = Music Edit Required
+ = Ethnic Specific

Show	Year	Song	Tempo	Voicing	Scripted Age Group	Any Age Group
Lion King, The	1997	One By One	Uptempo	SATB	Adults	
Little Shop of Horrors	1982	Don't Feed The Plant*	Uptempo	SATB	Adults	
Peter Pan	1954	I Won't Grow Up	Uptempo	SATB	Children/Adults	Δ
Peter Pan	1954	I Won't Grow Up Reprise*	Uptempo	SATB	Children/Adults	Δ
Seussical	2000	It's Possible*	Uptempo	SATB	Children/Teens	Δ
Mame	1966	Mame	Uptempo	SATB	Adults	
On The Twentieth Century	1978	Finale Part II-On The Twentieth Century	Uptempo	SATB	Adults	
Once On This Island	1990	Prologue-We Dance	Uptempo	SATB	Adults	
Once On This Island	1990	And The Gods Heard Her Prayer	Uptempo	SATB	Adults	
Seussical	2000	We're Whos Here Part 1-4	Uptempo	SATB	Children/Adults	
Seussical	2000	Finale-Oh, The Thinks You Can Think	Uptempo	SATB	Children/Adults	
Seussical	2000	Biggest Blame Fool	Uptempo	SATB	Children/Adults	
Rent	1996	Another Day	Uptempo	SATB	Adults	
Honk!	1993	Look At Him Reprise*	Uptempo	SATB	Adults	
Chitty Chitty Bang Bang	2005	Chitty Flies Home Finale	Uptempo	SATB	Children/Adults	
City of Angels	1989	Everybody's Gotta Be Somewhere	Uptempo	SATB	Adults	
Candide	1956	The Venice Gavotte	Uptempo	SATB	Adults	
Show Boat	1927	At The Fair	Uptempo	SATB	Adults	
Show Boat	1927	Bally-Hoo*	Uptempo	SATB	Adults	
Singin' In The Rain	1983	Singin' In The Rain Finale	Uptempo	SATB	Adults	Δ
Songs For A New World	1995	A New World	Uptempo	SATB	Adults	
Songs For A New World	1995	The River Won't Flow*	Uptempo	SATB	Adults	
Wicked	2003	One Short Day	Uptempo	SATB	Adults	
Wicked	2003	Opening Act II	Uptempo	SATB	Adults	
Wicked	2003	Thank Goodness (Part 1-3)	Uptempo	SATB	Adults	
Wicked	2003	Thank Goodness (Part 1-3)	Uptempo	SATB	Adults	
Wicked	2003	March Of The Witch Hunters	Uptempo	SATB	Adults	
Wicked	2003	Which Way Is The Party	Uptempo	SATB	Adults	
Will Rogers Follies	1991	Will-A-Mania	Uptempo	SATB	Adults	
Wiz, The	1974	Ease On Down The Road #1	Uptempo	SATB	Adults	Δ
Wiz, The	1974	Ease On Down The Road #2	Uptempo	SATB	Adults	Δ
Wiz, The	1974	Ease On Down The Road #3	Uptempo	SATB	Adults	Δ
Wiz, The	1974	Everbody Rejoice	Uptempo	SATB	Adults	Δ
Wiz, The	1974	Who Do You Think You Are	Uptempo	SATB	Adults	
Wizard Of Oz 1991	1939	Yellow Brick Road	Uptempo	SATB	Adults	Δ

Ensemble

284

Ensemble

* = Music Edit Required
+ = Ethnic Specific

Show	Year	Song	Tempo	Voicing	Scripted Age Group	Any Age Group
Wizard Of Oz 2000	1939	Mary Old Land Of Oz Reprise*	Uptempo	SATB	Adults	Δ
Wizard Of Oz 2003	1939	The Jitterbug	Uptempo	SATB	Adults	Δ
Wonderful Town	1953	Christopher Street	Uptempo	SATB	Adults	
Wonderful Town	1953	Conversation Piece	Uptempo	SATB	Adults	
Wonderful Town	1953	Swing	Uptempo	SATB	Adults	
Wonderful Town	1953	The Wrong Note Rag	Uptempo	SATB	Adults	
You're A Good Man Charlie Brown	1971	You're A Good Man Charlie Brown	Uptempo	SATB	Adults	Δ
You're A Good Man Charlie Brown	1971	Little Known Facts	Uptempo	SATB	Adults	Δ
You're A Good Man Charlie Brown	1999	Beethoven Day	Uptempo	SATB	Adults	Δ
Meet Me In St. Louis	1989	Under The Bamboo Tree	Moderate Tempo	SATB Unison	Children/Adults	Δ
Merrily We Roll Along 1994	1994	Transition 4	Moderate Tempo	SATB Unison	Adults	
Music Man, The	1957	Columbia Gem Of The Ocean	Moderate Tempo	SATB Unison	Adults	
Oklahoma!	1943	The Farmer And The Cowman	Moderate Tempo	SATB Unison	Adults	Δ
Sweeney Todd	1979	Ballad Of Sweeney Todd #27A	Moderate Tempo	SATB Unison	Adults	
Anyone Can Whistle	1964	There's A Parade In Town	Uptempo	SATB Unison	Adults	
Anyone Can Whistle	1964	Bluebird Incidental	Uptempo	SATB Unison	Adults	
Mame	1966	It's Today	Uptempo	SATB Unison	Adults	Δ
Merrily We Roll Along 1994	1994	Transition 5	Uptempo	SATB Unison	Adults	
Oklahoma!	1943	Finale Ultimo	Uptempo	SATB Unison	Adults	
Producers, The	2001	Goodbye	Uptempo	SATB Unison	Adults	
Sound Of Music, The	1959	So Long Reprise	Uptempo	SATB Unison	Children/Adults	Δ
You're A Good Man Charlie Brown	1971	The Baseball Game	Uptempo	SATB Unison	Adults	Δ
Ain't Misbehavin'	1988	Black and Blue	Ballad	SATT	Adults	
Miss Saigon	1991	The Transaction	Moderate Tempo	SATT	Adults	
Ain't Misbehavin'	1988	Ain't Misbehavin'	Uptempo	SATT	Adults	
Ain't Misbehavin'	1988	Lookin' Good But Feelin' Bad	Uptempo	SATT	Adults	
Ain't Misbehavin'	1988	Spreadin' Rhythm Around	Uptempo	SATT	Adults	
Sound Of Music, The	1959	No Way To Stop It	Uptempo	SBB	Adults	
Marie Christine	1999	Lover Bring Me Summer	Ballad	SSA	Adults	
Marie Christine	1999	In An Instant	Moderate Tempo	SSA	Adults	
My Favorite Year	1992	Maxford House	Moderate Tempo	SSA	Adults	
Nine	1982	Every Girl In Venice	Moderate Tempo	SSA	Adults	
Rags	1986	Brand New World	Moderate Tempo	SSA	Children/Adults	
Dear World	1969	Tea Party Trio	Uptempo	SSA	Adults	
The Little Mermaid	2007	Daughters Of Triton	Uptempo	SSA	Adults	Δ

Ensemble

285

Show	Year	Song	Tempo	Voicing	Scripted Age Group	Any Age Group
The Little Mermaid	2007	She's In Love	Uptempo	SSA	Adults	
Marie Christine	1999	Innocence Dies	Ballad	SSAA	Adults	
Miss Saigon	1991	The Ceremony*	Ballad	SSAA	Adults	
Mystery Of Edwin Drood, The	1985	Moonfall Quartet	Ballad	SSAA	Adults	
Camelot	1960	Follow Me	Moderate Tempo	SSAA	Adults	
Marie Christine	1999	And You Would Lie	Moderate Tempo	SSAA	Adults	
Nunsense	1985	Drive In	Moderate Tempo	SSAA	Adults	
Nine	1982	Be Italian #4	Moderate Tempo	SSAA	Children/Teens/Adults	
Nine	1982	Be Italian Finale	Moderate Tempo	SSAA	Children/Teens/Adults	
Mamma Mia!	2001	Gimmie Gimmie Gimmie	Uptempo	SSAA	Adults	
Nine	1982	Folies Bergeres*	Uptempo	SSAA	Adults	
Nine	1982	Wester Di Guido	Uptempo	SSAA	Adults	
Steel Pier	1997	Leave The World Behind	Uptempo	SSAA	Adults	
Nine	1982	Coda Di guido	Uptempo	SSAA	Children	
Oliver!	1963	Who Will Buy	Moderate Tempo	SSAB	Adults	Δ
Nine	1982	The Grand Canal	Moderate Tempo	SSAT	Children/Adults	
Passion	1994	Fifth Letter-Trio*	Moderate Tempo	SSB	Adults	
Sound Of Music, The	1959	Preludium	Ballad	SSMA	Adults	
Sound Of Music, The	1959	Finale Ultimo	Moderate Tempo	SSMA	Adults	
Sound Of Music, The	1959	Confitemini	Uptempo	SSMA	Adults	
Sound Of Music, The	1959	Alleluia	Uptempo	SSMA	Adults	
Sound Of Music, The	1959	Processional	Uptempo	SSMA	Adults	
Sound Of Music, The	1959	Gaudeamus	Uptempo	SSMA	Children/Adults	
Ragtime	1998	Nothing Like The City	Moderate Tempo	SSST	Adults	
Merrily We Roll Along 1994	1981	Not A Day Goes By Reprise	Ballad	SST	Adults	
Porgy and Bess	1935	Lo, Bess, Goin' To The Picnic	Moderate Tempo	STB	Adults	
Rags	1986	Kaddish	Moderate Tempo	STB	Adults	
A Funny Thing....Forum	1962	Pretty Little Picture	Uptempo	STB	Adults	
Ragtime	1998	Journey On	Uptempo	STB	Adults	
Unsinkable Molly Brown, The	1960	I Ain't Down Yet	Uptempo	STB	Adults	Δ
Unsinkable Molly Brown, The	1960	Belly Up To The Bar Boys	Uptempo	STB	Adults	
Phantom Of The Opera	1986	Whispering Child*	Moderate Tempo	STT	Adults	
Spring Awakening	2006	Those You've Known	Moderate Tempo	STT	Adults	
Merrily We Roll Along 1994	1981	Bobby and Jackie and Jack	Uptempo	STT	Adults	
The Little Mermaid	2007	If Only	Ballad	STTB	Adults	

* = Music Edit Required
+ = Ethnic Specific

Show	Year	Song	Tempo	Voicing	Scripted Age Group	Any Age Group
Music Man, The	1957	Lida Rose/Will I Ever Leave You	Moderate Tempo	STTBB	Adults	
No, No Nanette	1925	Where Has My Hubby Gone Blues	Ballad	TB	Adults	
Seven Brides/Seven Brothers	1982	Suitors Lament	Ballad	TB	Adults	
Seven Brides/Seven Brothers	1982	Lonesome Polecat	Ballad	TB	Adults	
Show Boat	1927	Ol' Man River	Ballad	TB	Adults	
Spamalot	2005	Monks Chat	Ballad	TB	Adults	
Little Me	1962	Real Live Girl	Ballad	TB	Children/Adults	
1776	1969	Cool, Cool Considerate Men	Moderate Tempo	TB	Adults	
Damn Yankees	1955	Heart	Moderate Tempo	TB	Adults	Δ
Dear World	1969	The Spring Of Next Year Reprise	Moderate Tempo	TB	Adults	
Dreamgirls	1981	Cadilac Car	Moderate Tempo	TB	Adults	
Flower Drum Song 2002	1958	Gliding Through My Memory	Moderate Tempo	TB	Adults	
On The Twentieth Century	1978	Life Is Like A Train	Moderate Tempo	TB	Adults	
Pacific Overtures	1976	Chrysanthemum Tea	Moderate Tempo	TB	Adults	
Spamalot	2005	All For One	Moderate Tempo	TB	Adults	
Spamalot	2005	Always Lok On The Bright Side of Life	Moderate Tempo	TB	Adults	
Spring Awakening	2006	The Mirror-Blue Nigh	Moderate Tempo	TB	Adults	
Sweet Smell Of Success	2002	Don't Look Now	Moderate Tempo	TB	Adults	
The Little Mermaid	2007	The Fathoms Below	Moderate Tempo	TB	Adults	
Victor/Victoria	1995	Paris By Night	Moderate Tempo	TB	Adults	
White Christmas	2008	The Old Man	Moderate Tempo	TB	Adults	
Wizard Of Oz 1992	1939	If I Only Had A Brain	Moderate Tempo	TB	Adults	Δ
Best Little Whorehouse...	1978	The Aggie Song	Moderate Tempo	TB	Adults	
Peter Pan	1954	Pirate Song*	Moderate Tempo	TB	Adults	
Big River	1985	The Boys	Uptempo	TB	Adults	
Damn Yankees	1955	The Game	Uptempo	TB	Adults	
Full Monty, The	2000	Let It Go	Uptempo	TB	Adults	
Jersey Boys	2005	You're the Apple of My Eye	Uptempo	TB	Adults	
Jersey Boys	2005	Walk Like A Man	Uptempo	TB	Adults	
Jersey Boys	2005	Dawn	Uptempo	TB	Adults	
Jersey Boys	2005	Who Loves You	Uptempo	TB	Adults	
Kiss Of The Spider Woman	1993	Over The Wall 1	Uptempo	TB	Adults	
Kiss Of The Spider Woman	1993	Over The Wall 2	Uptempo	TB	Adults	
Kiss Of The Spider Woman	1993	The Day After That	Uptempo	TB	Adults	
Kiss Of The Spider Woman	1993	Over The Wall 4	Uptempo	TB	Adults	

Ensemble

287

* = Music Edit Required
+ = Ethnic Specific

Show	Year	Song	Tempo	Voicing	Scripted Age Group	Any Age Group
Most Happy Fella, The	1956	Fresno Beauties*	Uptempo	TB	Adults	
Music Man, The	1957	Rock Island	Uptempo	TB	Adults	
My Favorite Year	1992	Musketeer Sketch Rehearsal PII	Uptempo	TB	Adults	
No, No Nanette	1925	Too Many Rings Around Rosie	Uptempo	TB	Adults	
No, No Nanette	1925	I Want To Be Happy*	Uptempo	TB	Adults	Δ
No, No Nanette	1925	No, No Nanette*	Uptempo	TB	Adults	
Of Thee I Sing	1931	Because, Because	Uptempo	TB	Adults	
Pacific Overtures	1976	Four Black Dragons	Uptempo	TB	Adults	
Producers, The	2001	It's Bad Luck To Say Good Luck	Uptempo	TB	Adults	
Ragtime	1998	What A Game!	Uptempo	TB	Children/Adults	
Scarlet Pimpernel, The	1997	Into The Fire	Uptempo	TB	Adults	
Seussical	2000	The Military	Uptempo	TB	Children/Adults	
Seven Brides/Seven Brothers	1982	Sobbin' Women	Uptempo	TB	Adults	
Seven Brides/Seven Brothers	1982	We Gotta Make It Through The Winter	Uptempo	TB	Adults	
Spamalot	2005	I Am Not Dead Yet	Uptempo	TB	Adults	
Spamalot	2005	We Are Not Dead Yet Reprise	Uptempo	TB	Adults	
Spamalot	2005	Run Away	Uptempo	TB	Adults	
Spring Awakening	2006	The Bitch Of Living	Uptempo	TB	Adults	
Spring Awakening	2006	And Then There Were None	Uptempo	TB	Adults	
Sugar	1972	Hey Why Not!	Uptempo	TB	Adults	
West Side Story	1957	Gee, Officer Krupke	Uptempo	TB	Adults	
West Side Story	1957	The Jet Song*	Uptempo	TB	Adults	
Will Rogers Follies	1991	Give A Man Enough Rope Reprise	Uptempo	TB	Adults	
Pacific Overtures	1976	Someone In A Tree	Uptempo	TB	Adults	
Pacific Overtures	1976	Please Hello	Uptempo	TB	Adults	
Mack and Mabel	1974	When Mabel Comes In The Room*	Uptempo	TB	Adults	
Seussical	2000	Monkey Around	Uptempo	TB	Adults	
My Fair Lady	1956	Wouldn't It Be Loverly Reprise*	Moderate Tempo	TB	Adults	
Passion	1994	Flashback (Parts 1-4)	Moderate Tempo	TBB	Adults	
Parade	1998	Blues: Feel The Rain Fall	Moderate Tempo	TBB	Antagonist Male	
Call Me Madam	1950	They Like Ike	Uptempo	TBB	Adults	
Pacific Overtures	1976	Someone In A Tree	Uptempo	Tenor	Adults	
Pacific Overtures	1976	Please Hello	Uptempo	Tenor	Adults	
Once Upon A Mattress	1959	The Minstrel, The Jester and I	Uptempo	Tenor/Tenor	Adults	
Nine	1982	The Bells Of St. Sebastian	Moderate Tempo	TSSAA	Adults	

* = Music Edit Required
+ = Ethnic Specific

Show	Year	Song	Tempo	Voicing	Scripted Age Group	Any Age Group
Marie Christine	1999	Map Your Heart	Moderate Tempo	TTA	Adults	
Annie Get Your Gun	1944	Moonshines Lullaby*	Ballad	TTB	Adults	
Kiss Of The Spider Woman	1993	Morphine Tango	Moderate Tempo	TTB	Adults	
Kiss Of The Spider Woman	1993	Morphine Tango @	Moderate Tempo	TTB	Adults	
Miss Saigon	1991	Bui-Doi	Moderate Tempo	TTB	Adults	
Most Happy Fella, The	1956	Benvenuta	Moderate Tempo	TTB	Adults	
Pacific Overtures	1976	Pretty Lady	Moderate Tempo	TTB	Adults	
Dear World	1969	Just A Little But More	Uptempo	TTB	Adults	
Dear World	1969	Just A Little Bit More Reprise	Uptempo	TTB	Adults	
Most Happy Fella, The	1956	Abbondanza	Uptempo	TTB	Adults	
Most Happy Fella, The	1956	Abbodanza	Uptempo	TTB	Adults	
The Little Mermaid	2007	Human Stuff	Uptempo	TTB	Adults	Δ
Music Man, The	1957	It's You	Ballad	TTB	Adults	
Music Man, The	1957	Lida Rose*	Ballad	TTB	Adults	Δ
Assassins	1992	Gun Song	Moderate Tempo	TTBB	Adults	
Babes In Arms (1998)	1937	Imagine Reprise*	Moderate Tempo	TTBB	Adults	
Babes In Arms (1998)	1937	Imagine Reprise #2*	Moderate Tempo	TTBB	Adults	
Most Happy Fella, The	1956	Standing On The Corner	Moderate Tempo	TTBB	Adults	Δ
Music Man, The	1957	Sincere	Moderate Tempo	TTBB	Adults	Δ
Music Man, The	1957	Lida Rose Reprise	Moderate Tempo	TTBB	Adults	Δ
Passion	1994	Transition-To Speak To Me Of Love	Moderate Tempo	TTBB	Adults	
Passion	1994	Soldier's Gossip (Scenet 7&8)	Moderate Tempo	TTBB	Adults	
Passion	1994	Transition-To Feel A Woman's Touch	Moderate Tempo	TTBB	Adults	
Passion	1994	Soldier's Gossip (Scene 11)	Moderate Tempo	TTBB	Adults	
Porgy and Bess	1935	Nobody Knows When The Lord Goin' Call	Moderate Tempo	TTBB	Adults	
Porgy and Bess	1935	It Takes A Long Pull To Get There	Moderate Tempo	TTBB	Adults	
State Fair 1996	1996	More Than Just A Friend	Moderate Tempo	TTBB	Adults	
Passion	1994	Soldier's Gossip (Scene 10)	Moderate Tempo	TTBB	Children/Adults	
Camelot	1960	Fie On Goodness!	Uptempo	TTBB	Adults	
Music Man, The	1957	Goodnight Ladies*	Uptempo	TTBB	Adults	
Passion	1994	Nightmare	Uptempo	TTBB	Adults	
Show Boat	1927	Till Good Luck Comes My Way	Uptempo	TTBB	Adults	
Wonderful Town	1953	My Darlin' Eileen	Ballad	TTBB		
Candide	1956	The Kings' Barcarolle	Moderate Tempo	TTBBB	Adults	
Sweeney Todd	1979	Ballad Of Sweeney Todd #12C	Moderate Tempo	TTT	Adults	

Ensemble

* = Music Edit Required
+ = Ethnic Specific

Show	Year	Song	Tempo	Voicing	Scripted Age Group	Any Age Group
Rent	1996	You'll See	Uptempo	TTTBB	Adults	
Hair	1968	Hashish	Ballad	Unison	Adults	
Nunsense	1985	Veni Creator Spititus	Ballad	Unison	Adults	
Chicago	1975	Cell Block Tango	Moderate Tempo	Unison	Teens	
Annie	1977	Hooverville	Uptempo	Unison	Adults	
Annie	1977	You're Nevery Fully Dressed (Children)	Uptempo	Unison	Children	Δ
Carousel	1945	June Is Bustin' Out All Over	Uptempo	Unison	Adults	
Curtains	2007	Show People*	Uptempo	Unison	Adults	
Follies	1971	Loveland	Uptempo	Unison	Adults	
King and I, The	1951	Getting To Know You*	Uptempo	Unison	Children/Adults	Δ
Kiss Me Kate	1948	We Open In Venice	Uptempo	Unison	Adults	
Company (Revival)	1970	What Would We Do Without You	Uptempo	Unison	Adults	
Wizard Of Oz 1994	1939	We're Off To See The Wizard	Uptempo	Unison	Adults	Δ
Wizard Of Oz 2005	1939	Ding Dong! The Witch Is Dead	Uptempo	Unison	Adults	Δ
Curtains	2007	What Kind of Man	Moderate Tempo	Unison/2 Part	Adults	
Billy Elliott	2008	Merry Christmas, Maggie Thatcher	Uptempo	Unison/2 Part	Adults	
Crazy For You (1992)	1992	Tonight's The Night	Uptempo	Unison/2 Part	Adults	
Funny Girl	1964	Henry Street	Uptempo	Unison/2 Part	Adults	
Crazy For You (1992)	1930	I Got Rhythm	Uptempo	Unison/2 Part	Adults	
Curtains	2007	Wide Open Spaces	Uptempo	Unison/2 Part	Adults	
Into The Woods	2008	Children Will Listen Act II Finale Part 3	Ballad	Unison/3 Part	Adults	Δ
Into The Woods	2008	Into The Woods Act II Finale Part 4	Moderate Tempo	Unison/3 Part	Adults	
Curtains	2007	He Did It	Uptempo	Unison/3 Part	Adults	

Ensemble

Composer	Vocal Range	Show	Year	Role	Song	Tempo	Range-Bottom	Range-Top	Char Type
Adler and Ross	Alto	Damn Yankees	1955	Lola	Whatever Lola Wants	Moderate Tempo	G3	Db5	Romantic Antagonist Female
Adler and Ross	Alto	Damn Yankees	1955	Gloria Thorpe	Shoeless Joe From Hannibal, Mo	Uptempo	Bb3	Db5	Character Female
Adler and Ross	Alto	Damn Yankees	1955	Lola	A Little Brains A Little Talent	Uptempo	A3	B4	Romantic Antagonist Female
Adler and Ross	Alto	Damn Yankees	1955	Lola	Who's Got The Pain*	Uptempo	A3	B4	Romantic Antagonist Female
Adler and Ross	Baritone	Damn Yankees	1955	Joe Boyd	Goodbye Old Girl	Ballad	D3	E4	Mature Male
Adler and Ross	Baritone	Damn Yankees	1955	Joe Boyd	Near To You	Ballad	C3	C4	Mature Male
Adler and Ross	Baritone	Damn Yankees	1955	Applegate	Those Were The Good Old Days	Uptempo	A#2	D#4	Antagonist Male
Adler and Ross	Baritone	Damn Yankees	1955	Applegate	Good Old Day Reprise	Uptempo	A#2	E4	Antagonist Male
Adler and Ross	Baritone	Damn Yankees	1955	Sohovic	Who's Got The Pain*	Uptempo	G#3	D#4	Ingenue Male
Adler and Ross	Soprano	Damn Yankees	1955	Meg Boyd	A Man Doesn't Know	Ballad	G3	Db5	Mature Female
Adler and Ross	Soprano	Damn Yankees	1955	Meg Boyd	There's Something About An Empty (	Ballad			Mature Female
Adler and Ross	Soprano	Damn Yankees	1955	Meg Boyd	Near To You*	Ballad	B3	Eb5	Mature Female
Adler and Ross	Soprano	Damn Yankees	1955	Meg Boyd	A Man Doesn't Know Reprise	Ballad	G3	D5	Mature Female
Adler and Ross	Soprano	Damn Yankees	1955	Meg Boyd	Six Months Out of Every Year	Uptempo	A3	D5	Mature Female
Adler and Ross	Tenor	Damn Yankees	1955	Joe Hardy	A Man Doesn't Know	Ballad	C3	Gb4	Ingenue Male
Adler and Ross	Tenor	Damn Yankees	1955	Joe Hardy	Near To You*	Ballad	C3	C4	Ingenue Male
Adler and Ross	Tenor	Damn Yankees	1955	Joe Hardy	Goodbye Old Girl	Ballad	Eb3	F#4	Ingenue Male
Adler, Richard	Alto	Pajama Game	1954	Babe Williams	Hey There Reprise	Ballad	A#3	Bb4	Romantic Lead Female
Adler, Richard	Alto	Pajama Game	1954	Gladys	Hernando's Hideaway	Moderate Tempo	B3	C5	Romantic Antagonist Female
Adler, Richard	Alto	Pajama Game	1954	Babe Williams	I'm Not At All In Love*	Uptempo	A3	B4	Romantic Lead Female
Adler, Richard	Alto	Pajama Game	1954	Babe Williams	There Once Was A Man*	Uptempo	Bb3	Eb5	Romantic Lead Female
Adler, Richard	Alto	Pajama Game	1954	Gladys	Steam Heat*	Uptempo	C4	Eb5	Romantic Antagonist Female
Adler, Richard	Alto	Pajama Game	1954	Babe Williams	Seven And A Half Cents*	Uptempo	A3	D5	Romantic Lead Female
Adler, Richard	Baritone	Pajama Game	1954	Hines	The Pajama Game	Uptempo	Db3	F4	Character Male
Adler, Richard	Baritone	Pajama Game	1954	Prez	Her Is*	Uptempo	Db3	F4	Romantic Antagonist Male
Adler, Richard	Baritone	Pajama Game	1954	Prez	Her Is Reprise*	Uptempo	Ab2	F4	Romantic Antagonist Male
Adler, Richard	Baritone	Pajama Game	1954	Hines	Think Of The Time I Save	Uptempo	C3	D4	Character Male
Adler, Richard	Baritone	Pajama Game	1954	Prez	Seven And A Half Cents*	Uptempo	D3	E4	Romantic Antagonist Male
Adler, Richard	Tenor	Pajama Game	1954	Sid Sorokin	A New Town Is A Blue Town	Ballad	Db3	G4	Romantic Lead Male
Adler, Richard	Tenor	Pajama Game	1954	Sid Sorokin	Hey There*	Ballad	F3	Ab4	Romantic Lead Male
Adler, Richard	Tenor	Pajama Game	1954	Sid Sorokin	Hey There-Finale Act I	Ballad	F3	Gb4	Romantic Lead Male
Adler, Richard	Tenor	Pajama Game	1954	Sid Sorokin	Once-A-Year Day*	Uptempo	E3	F4	Romantic Lead Male

Composer

Composer	Vocal Range	Show	Year	Role	Song	Tempo	Range-Bottom	Range-Top	Char Type
Adler, Richard	Tenor	Pajama Game	1954	Sid Sorokin	Small Talk*	Uptempo	Db3	Gb4	Romantic Lead Male
Adler, Richard	Tenor	Pajama Game	1954	Sid Sorokin	There Once Was A Man*	Uptempo	C#3	Gb4	Romantic Lead Male
Andersson and Ulvaeus	Alto	Chess	1988	Florence	Someone Else's Story	Ballad	F3	C5	Character Ingenue Female
Andersson and Ulvaeus	Alto	Chess	1988	Florence	Heaven Help My Heart	Ballad	A3	A4	Character Ingenue Female
Andersson and Ulvaeus	Alto	Chess	1988	Florence	You and I*	Ballad	G3	Eb5	Character Ingenue Female
Andersson and Ulvaeus	Alto	Chess	1988	Florence	I Know Him So Well	Ballad	F3	D5	Character Ingenue Female
Andersson and Ulvaeus	Alto	Chess	1988	Florence	You and I Reprise	Ballad	G2	G4	Character Ingenue Female
Andersson and Ulvaeus	Alto	Chess	1988	Florence	Anthem Reprise	Moderate Tempo	Ab3	D5	Character Ingenue Female
Andersson and Ulvaeus	Alto	Chess	1988	Florence	Nobody's Side	Uptempo	E3	E4	Character Ingenue Female
Andersson and Ulvaeus	Baritone	Chess	1988	Molokov	The Soviet Machine	Uptempo	A2	D4	Mature Male
Andersson and Ulvaeus	Soprano	Chess	1988	Svetlana	You and I*	Ballad	G3	Eb5	Character Female
Andersson and Ulvaeus	Soprano	Chess	1988	Svetlana	I Know Him So Well	Ballad	F3	D5	Character Female
Andersson and Ulvaeus	Tenor	Chess	1988	Anatoly	You and I	Ballad	G2	G4	Romantic Lead Male
Andersson and Ulvaeus	Tenor	Chess	1988	Anatoly	You and I Reprise	Ballad	G3	F5	Romantic Lead Male
Andersson and Ulvaeus	Tenor	Chess	1988	Anatoly	Where I Want To Be	Moderate Tempo	E3	G4	Romantic Lead Male
Andersson and Ulvaeus	Tenor	Chess	1988	Anatoly	Anthem	Moderate Tempo	C3	G4	Romantic Lead Male
Andersson and Ulvaeus	Tenor	Chess	1988	Arbiter	The Story of Chess	Moderate Tempo	B2	G4	Antagonist Male
Andersson and Ulvaeus	Tenor	Chess	1988	Arbiter	The Arbiter	Uptempo	E3	A4	Antagonist Male
Andersson and Ulvaeus	Tenor	Chess	1988	Arbiter	The Arbiter Reprise	Uptempo	E3	A4	Antagonist Male
Andersson and Ulvaeus	Tenor	Chess	1988	Freddie	Endgame*	Uptempo	C#3	G4	Romantic Antagonist Male
Andersson and Ulvaeus	Tenor	Chess	1988	Freddie	Florence Quits	Uptempo	B2	B4	Romantic Antagonist Male
Andersson and Ulvaeus	Tenor	Chess	1988	Freddie	One Night In Bangkok	Uptempo	F3	A4	Romantic Antagonist Male
Andersson and Ulvaeus	Tenor	Chess	1988	Freddie	Pity The Child	Uptempo	Bb2	Db5	Romantic Antagonist Male
Andersson and Ulvaeus	Tenor	Chess	1988	Anatoly	Endgame*	Uptempo	C3	A4	Romantic Lead Male
Andersson, Benny	Alto	Mamma Mia!	2001	Donna Sheridan	One Last Summer*	Ballad	F#3	E4	Romantic Lead Female
Andersson, Benny	Alto	Mamma Mia!	2001	Donna Sheridan	Slipping Through My Fingers*	Ballad	A3	C5	Romantic Lead Female
Andersson, Benny	Alto	Mamma Mia!	2001	Sophie Sheridan	Lay All Your Love On Me*	Moderate Tempo	C4	E5	Ingenue Female
Andersson, Benny	Alto	Mamma Mia!	2001	Donna Sheridan	Super Trouper*	Moderate Tempo	G3	G4	Romantic Lead Female
Andersson, Benny	Alto	Mamma Mia!	2001	Donna Sheridan	One Of Us*	Moderate Tempo	A3	C5	Romantic Lead Female
Andersson, Benny	Alto	Mamma Mia!	2001	Donna Sheridan	The Winner Takes It All	Moderate Tempo	G3	C5	Romantic Lead Female
Andersson, Benny	Alto	Mamma Mia!	2001	Rosie	Take A Chance On Me*	Moderate Tempo	F3	Bb4	Character Female
Andersson, Benny	Alto	Mamma Mia!	2001	Donna Sheridan	I Do, I Do, I Do, I Do, I Do	Moderate Tempo	G3	C5	Romantic Lead Female
Andersson, Benny	Alto	Mamma Mia!	2001	Donna Sheridan	Money Money Money	Uptempo	G4	Bb4	Romantic Lead Female
Andersson, Benny	Alto	Mamma Mia!	2001	Donna Sheridan	Mamma Mia!*	Uptempo	F#3	A4	Romantic Lead Female

Composer

Composer	Vocal Range	Show	Year	Role	Song	Tempo	Range-Bottom	Range-Top	Char Type
Andersson, Benny	Alto	Mamma Mia!	2001	Tanya	Does Your Mother Know*	Uptempo	A3	Ab4	Character Female
Andersson, Benny	Alto	Mamma Mia!	2001	Donna Sheridan	SOS*	Uptempo	F4	A4	Romantic Lead Female
Andersson, Benny	Baritone	Mamma Mia!	2001	Harry Bright	One Last Summer*	Ballad	F#3	E4	Character Male
Andersson, Benny	Baritone	Mamma Mia!	2001	Harry Bright	Thank You For the Music*	Moderate Tempo	A3	D5	Character Male
Andersson, Benny	Soprano	Mamma Mia!	2001	Sophie Sheridan	I Have A Dream	Ballad	Ab4	Bb4	Ingenue Female
Andersson, Benny	Soprano	Mamma Mia!	2001	Sophie Sheridan	I Have A Dream Reprise	Ballad	Ab3	Db5	Ingenue Female
Andersson, Benny	Soprano	Mamma Mia!	2001	Sophie Sheridan	The Name Of The Game*	Moderate Tempo	F#3	B4	Ingenue Female
Andersson, Benny	Soprano	Mamma Mia!	2001	Sophie Sheridan	Honey Honey*	Uptempo	C4	C5	Ingenue Female
Andersson, Benny	Soprano	Mamma Mia!	2001	Sophie Sheridan	Under Attack*	Uptempo	B3	C#5	Ingenue Female
Andersson, Benny	Tenor	Mamma Mia!	2001	Sky	Lay All Your Love On Me*	Moderate Tempo	G3	Ab4	Ingenue Male
Andersson, Benny	Tenor	Mamma Mia!	2001	Sam Carmichael	Knowing Me, Knowing You*	Moderate Tempo	G2	F#4	Romantic Lead Male
Andersson, Benny	Tenor	Mamma Mia!	2001	Sam Carmichael	SOS*	Uptempo	A3	Ab4	Romantic Lead Male
Bart, Lionel	Alto	Oliver!	1963	Nancy	As Long As He Needs Me	Ballad	F#3	C#5	Antagonist Female
Bart, Lionel	Alto	Oliver!	1963	Mrs. Bedwin	Where Is Love Reprise	Ballad	C#4	Bb4	Mature Female
Bart, Lionel	Alto	Oliver!	1963	Nancy	As Long As He Needs Me Reprise	Moderate Tempo	G#3	C#5	Antagonist Female
Bart, Lionel	Alto	Oliver!	1963	Artful Dodger	Consider Yourself (Part One)*	Uptempo	A3	F5	Juvenile Male
Bart, Lionel	Alto	Oliver!	1963	Nancy	It's A Fine Life*	Uptempo	Ab3	D5	Antagonist Female
Bart, Lionel	Alto	Oliver!	1963	Nancy	Oom-Pah-Pah*	Uptempo	B3	C#5	Antagonist Female
Bart, Lionel	Baritone	Oliver!	1963	Mr. Bumble	Boy For Sale	Ballad	C3	G4	Character Male
Bart, Lionel	Baritone	Oliver!	1963	Fagin	Reviewing the Situation Reprise	Ballad	C4	Eb5	Antagonist Male
Bart, Lionel	Baritone	Oliver!	1963	Bill Sykes	My Name	Moderate Tempo	C#3	C4	Antagonist Male
Bart, Lionel	Baritone	Oliver!	1963	Fagin	Pick A Pocket Or Two	Uptempo	D3	Eb4	Mature Male
Bart, Lionel	Baritone	Oliver!	1963	Fagin	Be Back Soon*	Uptempo	C3	E4	Mature Male
Bart, Lionel	Baritone	Oliver!	1963	Fagin	Reviewing The Situation	Uptempo	C3	F4	Mature Male
Bart, Lionel	Soprano	Oliver!	1963	Oliver Twist	Where Is Love	Ballad	C4	C5	Juvenile Male
Bart, Lionel	Soprano	Oliver!	1963	Oliver Twist	Who Will Buy*	Moderate Tempo	C4	C5	Juvenile Male
Benjamin and O'Keefe	Alto	Legally Blonde	2007	Elle Woods	Legally Blonde	Ballad	G3	Db5	Ingenue Female
Benjamin and O'Keefe	Alto	Legally Blonde	2007	Paulette	Find My Way	Ballad	Ab3	C5	Character Female
Benjamin and O'Keefe	Alto	Legally Blonde	2007	Elle Woods	Take It Like A Man	Moderate Tempo	Gb3	E5	Ingenue Female
Benjamin and O'Keefe	Alto	Legally Blonde	2007	Elle Woods	Find My Way	Moderate Tempo	G3	B4	Ingenue Female
Benjamin and O'Keefe	Alto	Legally Blonde	2007	Paulette	Ireland	Moderate Tempo	A#3	B4	Character Female
Benjamin and O'Keefe	Alto	Legally Blonde	2007	Paulette	Ireland Reprise	Moderate Tempo	C4	Bb4	Character Female
Benjamin and O'Keefe	Alto	Legally Blonde	2007	Brooke Wyndam	Whipped Into Shape*	Uptempo	A3	G5	Romantic Lead Female

Composer

Composer	Vocal Range	Show	Year	Role	Song	Tempo	Range-Bottom	Range-Top	Char Type
Benjamin and O'Keefe	Alto	Legally Blonde	2007	Elle Woods	So Much Better	Uptempo	G3	E5	Ingenue Female
Benjamin and O'Keefe	Alto	Legally Blonde	2007	Elle Woods	Legally Blonde Remix*	Uptempo	E4	D5	Ingenue Female
Benjamin and O'Keefe	Alto	Legally Blonde	2007	Elle Woods	What You Want	Uptempo	Bb3	Db5	Ingenue Female
Benjamin and O'Keefe	Alto	Legally Blonde	2007	Elle Woods	Chip On My Shoulder*	Uptempo	C4	Eb5	Ingenue Female
Benjamin and O'Keefe	Alto	Legally Blonde	2007	Enid Hoops	Harvard Variation*	Uptempo	Bb3	C5	Character Female
Benjamin and O'Keefe	Alto	Legally Blonde	2007	Vivianne Kensington	Legally Blonde Remix*	Uptempo	A3	Eb5	Antagonist Female
Benjamin and O'Keefe	Baritone	Legally Blonde	2007	Professor Callahan	Blood In The Water	Moderate Tempo	C3	F#4	Romantic Antagonist Male
Benjamin and O'Keefe	Baritone	Legally Blonde	2007	Aaron Schultz	Harvard Variation*	Uptempo	C3	Eb4	Character Male
Benjamin and O'Keefe	Baritone	Legally Blonde	2007	Padamadan	Harvard Variation*	Uptempo	B2	E4	Ingenue Male
Benjamin and O'Keefe	Baritone	Legally Blonde	2007	Professor Callahan	Whipped Into Shape*	Uptempo	C3	F#4	Romantic Antagonist Male
Benjamin and O'Keefe	Tenor	Legally Blonde	2007	Emmett Forrest	Legally Blonde (ms 101b-166)	Ballad	E3	G4	Character Male
Benjamin and O'Keefe	Tenor	Legally Blonde	2007	Emmett Forrest	Chip On My Shoulder*	Uptempo	C3	A4	Character Male
Benjamin and O'Keefe	Tenor	Legally Blonde	2007	Warner Huntington	Serious*	Uptempo	F3	G4	Ingenue Male
Berlin, Irving	Alto	Annie Get Your Gun	1944	Annie Oakley	Moonshine Lullaby	Ballad	Bb3	D5	Character Female
Berlin, Irving	Alto	Annie Get Your Gun	1944	Annie Oakley	They Say That Falling In Love*	Ballad	A3	B4	Character Female
Berlin, Irving	Alto	Annie Get Your Gun	1944	Annie Oakley	Lost In His Arms	Ballad	Bb3	C5	Character Female
Berlin, Irving	Alto	Call Me Madam	1950	Sally Adams	Marrying For Love*	Ballad	F3	Bb4	Romantic Antagonist Female
Berlin, Irving	Alto	Annie Get Your Gun	1944	Annie Oakley	The Girl That I Marry*	Moderate Tempo	B3	B4	Character Female
Berlin, Irving	Alto	Annie Get Your Gun	1944	Annie Oakley	No Business Reprise 2	Moderate Tempo	G3	C5	Character Female
Berlin, Irving	Alto	Annie Get Your Gun	1944	Annie Oakley	You Can't Get A Man With A Gun Rep	Moderate Tempo	Ab3	Ab4	Character Female
Berlin, Irving	Alto	Annie Get Your Gun	1944	Annie Oakley	I Got The Sun in the Morning	Moderate Tempo	Bb3	Bb4	Character Female
Berlin, Irving	Alto	Call Me Madam	1950	Princess Maria	The Ocarina*	Moderate Tempo	C4	D5	Ingenue Female
Berlin, Irving	Alto	Call Me Madam	1950	Princess Maria	It's A Lovely Day Today*	Moderate Tempo	A3	B4	Ingenue Female
Berlin, Irving	Alto	Call Me Madam	1950	Sally Adams	The Best Thing For You	Moderate Tempo	A3	C5	Romantic Antagonist Female
Berlin, Irving	Alto	Call Me Madam	1950	Sally Adams	Something To Dance About	Moderate Tempo	Bb3	C5	Romantic Antagonist Female
Berlin, Irving	Alto	Call Me Madam	1950	Princess Maria	It's A Lovely Day Today Reprise 2*	Moderate Tempo	C4	D5	Ingenue Female
Berlin, Irving	Alto	Call Me Madam	1950	Sally Adams	The Best Thing For You Reprise	Moderate Tempo	Bb3	Cb5	Romantic Antagonist Female
Berlin, Irving	Alto	White Christmas	2008	Betty Haynes	Love, You Didn't Do Right By Me	Moderate Tempo	A3	Bb4	Romantic Lead Female
Berlin, Irving	Alto	Annie Get Your Gun	1944	Annie Oakley	Doin' What Comes Natur'lly	Uptempo	A3	C5	Character Female
Berlin, Irving	Alto	Annie Get Your Gun	1944	Annie Oakley	You Can't Get A Man With A Gun	Uptempo	Bb3	C5	Character Female
Berlin, Irving	Alto	Annie Get Your Gun	1966	Annie Oakley	An Old Fashioned Wedding	Uptempo	B3	B4	Character Female
Berlin, Irving	Alto	Call Me Madam	1950	Sally Adams	The Hostess With The Mostess	Uptempo	A3	B4	Romantic Antagonist Female
Berlin, Irving	Alto	Call Me Madam	1950	Sally Adams	The Hostess With The Mostess Encor	Uptempo	A3	B4	Romantic Antagonist Female

Composer	Vocal Range	Show	Year	Role	Song	Tempo	Range-Bottom	Range-Top	Char Type
Berlin, Irving	Alto	Call Me Madam	1950	Sally Adams	Washington Square Dance	Uptempo	B♭3	C5	Romantic Antagonist Female
Berlin, Irving	Alto	Call Me Madam	1950	Sally Adams	Can You Use Any Money Today	Uptempo	B♭3	C5	Romantic Antagonist Female
Berlin, Irving	Alto	Call Me Madam	1950	Sally Adams	You're Just In Love*	Uptempo	D4	C5	Romantic Antagonist Female
Berlin, Irving	Alto	White Christmas	2008	Betty Haynes	Love And The Weather*	Uptempo	A3	C5	Romantic Lead Female
Berlin, Irving	Alto	White Christmas	2008	Betty Haynes	Falling Out Of Love Can Be Fun*	Uptempo	G3	C5	Romantic Lead Female
Berlin, Irving	Alto	White Christmas	2008	Judy Haynes	Falling Out Of Love Can Be Fun*	Uptempo	G3	C5	Ingenue Female
Berlin, Irving	Alto	White Christmas	2008	Susan Waverly	Let Me sing And I'm Happy Reprise	Uptempo	B3	B4	Juvenile Female
Berlin, Irving	Baritone	Annie Get Your Gun	1944	Frank Butler	They Say That Falling In Love*	Ballad	C3	D4	Romantic Lead Male
Berlin, Irving	Baritone	Annie Get Your Gun	1944	Frank Butler	The Girl I Marry Reprise	Ballad	A3	D4	Romantic Lead Male
Berlin, Irving	Baritone	Call Me Madam	1950	Cosmo Constantine	Marrying For Love*	Ballad	G2	C4	Romantic Lead Male
Berlin, Irving	Baritone	White Christmas	2008	Bob Wallace	How Deep Is The Ocean	Ballad	C#3	D4	Romantic Lead Male
Berlin, Irving	Baritone	Annie Get Your Gun	1944	Buffalo Bill	Show Business Reprise *	Moderate Tempo	C3	F4	Character Male
Berlin, Irving	Baritone	Annie Get Your Gun	1944	Charlie Davenport	Show Business Reprise *	Moderate Tempo	C3	F4	Character Male
Berlin, Irving	Baritone	Annie Get Your Gun	1944	Frank Butler	The Girl That I Marry*	Moderate Tempo	D3	D4	Romantic Lead Male
Berlin, Irving	Baritone	Annie Get Your Gun	1944	Frank Butler	My Defenses Are Down	Moderate Tempo	D♭3	E♭4	Romantic Lead Male
Berlin, Irving	Baritone	Annie Get Your Gun	1944	Frank Butler	Show Business Reprise *	Moderate Tempo	C3	F4	Romantic Lead Male
Berlin, Irving	Baritone	Call Me Madam	1950	Cosmo Constantine	Lichtenburg*	Moderate Tempo	B♭2	D4	Romantic Lead Male
Berlin, Irving	Baritone	Call Me Madam	1950	Kenneth Gibson	It's A Lovely Day Today*	Moderate Tempo	C3	D4	Character Male
Berlin, Irving	Baritone	Call Me Madam	1950	Kenneth Gibson	Once Upon A Time Today	Moderate Tempo	E3	F4	Character Male
Berlin, Irving	Baritone	Call Me Madam	1950	Kenneth Gibson	It's A Lovely Day Today Reprise 2*	Moderate Tempo	C3	D4	Character Male
Berlin, Irving	Baritone	White Christmas	2008	Phil Davis	The Best Things...Dancing	Moderate Tempo	D♭3	F4	Character Male
Berlin, Irving	Baritone	White Christmas	2008	Bob Wallace	Count Your Blessings*	Moderate Tempo	C3	D4	Romantic Lead Male
Berlin, Irving	Baritone	White Christmas	2008	Bob Wallace	Blue Skies (Part 1-3)*	Moderate Tempo	E3	F4	Romantic Lead Male
Berlin, Irving	Baritone	Annie Get Your Gun	1944	Frank Butler	There's No Business...Show Business	Uptempo	A♭3	E4	Romantic Lead Male
Berlin, Irving	Baritone	Annie Get Your Gun	1944	Frank Butler	An Old Fashioned Wedding	Uptempo	B2	E4	Romantic Lead Male
Berlin, Irving	Baritone	Annie Get Your Gun	1944	Tommy Walker	I'll Share It All With You	Uptempo	C#3	D4	Ingenue Male
Berlin, Irving	Baritone	Call Me Madam	1950	Kenneth Gibson	It's A Lovely Day Today Reprise	Uptempo	D3	D4	Character Male
Berlin, Irving	Baritone	Call Me Madam	1950	Kenneth Gibson	You're Just In Love*	Uptempo	D3	F4	Character Male
Berlin, Irving	Baritone	White Christmas	2008	Bob Wallace	Love And The Weather*	Uptempo	D♭3	E4	Romantic Lead Male
Berlin, Irving	Soprano	White Christmas	2008	Martha Watson	Let Me sing And I'm Happy	Moderate Tempo	F3	G4	Mature Female
Berlin, Irving	Soprano	White Christmas	2008	Martha Watson	Falling Out Of Love Can Be Fun*	Uptempo	G3	C5	Mature Female
Bernstein, Leonard	Alto	Wonderful Town	1953	Ruth Sherwood	Quiet Ruth	Ballad	F3	E4	Character Female
Bernstein, Leonard	Alto	West Side Story	1957	Anita+	A Boy Like That*	Moderate Tempo	E♭3	C♭5	Romantic Lead Female
Bernstein, Leonard	Alto	Wonderful Town	1953	Ruth Sherwood	100 Easy Ways To Lose A Man	Moderate Tempo	G3	A4	Character Female

Composer

Composer	Vocal Range	Show	Year	Role	Song	Tempo	Range-Bottom	Range-Top	Char Type
Bernstein, Leonard	Alto	On The Town	1944	Diana Dream	I Wish I Was Dead	Uptempo	C4	D♭4	Character Female
Bernstein, Leonard	Alto	On The Town	1944	Hildy	I Can Cook Too	Uptempo	A3	G#5	Character Female
Bernstein, Leonard	Alto	On The Town	1944	Hildy	Ya Got Me *	Uptempo	F3	D♭5	Character Female
Bernstein, Leonard	Alto	Wonderful Town	1953	Ruth Sherwood	Conga*	Uptempo	F3	A4	Character Female
Bernstein, Leonard	Alto	Wonderful Town	1953	Ruth Sherwood	Swing*	Uptempo	E3	E4	Character Female
Bernstein, Leonard	Baritone	Wonderful Town	1953	Robert Baker	A Quiet Girl	Ballad	G2	C4	Romantic Lead Male
Bernstein, Leonard	Baritone	Wonderful Town	1953	Wreck	Pass The Football	Moderate Tempo	A♭2	E4	Antagonist Male
Bernstein, Leonard	Baritone	Wonderful Town	1953	Robert Baker	It's Love*	Moderate Tempo	A2	F#4	Romantic Lead Male
Bernstein, Leonard	Baritone	On The Town	1944	Ozzie	Carried Away	Uptempo	E2	F4	Character Ingenue Male
Bernstein, Leonard	Baritone	On The Town	1944	Ozzie	Ya Got Me *	Uptempo	E♭3	F♭4	Character Male
Bernstein, Leonard	Baritone	On The Town	1944	Pitkin Bridgework	I Understand	Uptempo	A2	D4	Mature Male
Bernstein, Leonard	Baritone	Wonderful Town	1953	Robert Baker	What A Waste*	Uptempo	A♭2	F#4	Romantic Lead Male
Bernstein, Leonard	Baritone	Wonderful Town	1953	1st Editor	What A Waste*	Uptempo	A2	D4	Character Male
Bernstein, Leonard	Baritone	Wonderful Town	1953	2nd Editor	What A Waste*	Uptempo	B♭2	E♭4	Character Male
Bernstein, Leonard	Soprano	West Side Story	1957	Female Shark+	Somewhere	Ballad	B3	F#5	Ingenue Female
Bernstein, Leonard	Soprano	West Side Story	1957	Maria+	I Have A Love*	Ballad	B♭3	B♭5	Ingenue Female
Bernstein, Leonard	Soprano	Candide	1956	Cunegonde	Life Is Happiness Indeed*	Moderate Tempo	F4	C6	Ingenue Female
Bernstein, Leonard	Soprano	Candide	1956	Cunegonde	Glitter And Be Gay	Moderate Tempo	B2	E6	Ingenue Female
Bernstein, Leonard	Soprano	Candide	1956	Old Lady	I Am Easily Assimilated*	Moderate Tempo	D4	A5	Mature Female
Bernstein, Leonard	Soprano	Wonderful Town	1953	Eileen Sherwood	A Little Bit In Love	Moderate Tempo	C4	C#5	Ingenue Female
Bernstein, Leonard	Soprano	On The Town	1944	Claire DeLune	Carried Away	Uptempo	F3	G5	Character Ingenue Female
Bernstein, Leonard	Soprano	On The Town	1944	Claire DeLune	Ya Got Me *	Uptempo	G3	E♭4	Character Ingenue Female
Bernstein, Leonard	Soprano	West Side Story	1957	Maria+	I Feel Pretty*	Uptempo	C4	F5	Ingenue Female
Bernstein, Leonard	Soprano	Wonderful Town	1953	Eileen Sherwood	Conversation Piece*	Uptempo	D4	B4	Ingenue Female
Bernstein, Leonard	Tenor	Candide	1956	Candide	It Must Be So	Ballad	D3	E4	Ingenue Male
Bernstein, Leonard	Tenor	Candide	1956	Candide	Candide's Lament	Ballad	C3	F4	Ingenue Male
Bernstein, Leonard	Tenor	Candide	1956	Candide	It Must Be Me	Ballad	D3	E4	Ingenue Male
Bernstein, Leonard	Tenor	Candide	1956	Candide	Universal Good Reprise*	Ballad	D♭3	D♭4	Ingenue Male
Bernstein, Leonard	Tenor	On The Town	1944	Gabey	Lonely Town	Ballad	C4	F5	Romantic Lead Male
Bernstein, Leonard	Tenor	West Side Story	1957	Tony	Maria	Ballad	B2	B♭4	Ingenue Male
Bernstein, Leonard	Tenor	Candide	1956	Candide	Life Is Happiness Indeed*	Moderate Tempo	F3	G4	Ingenue Male
Bernstein, Leonard	Tenor	Candide	1956	Maximillion	Life Is Happiness Indeed*	Moderate Tempo	D3	F4	Romantic Lead Male
Bernstein, Leonard	Tenor	Candide	1956	Governor	My Love*	Moderate Tempo	C3	A4	Romantic Lead Male
Bernstein, Leonard	Tenor	Candide	1956	Martin	Words, Words, Words	Moderate Tempo	A2	F4	Mature Male

Composer	Vocal Range	Show	Year	Role	Song	Tempo	Range-Bottom	Range-Top	Char Type
Bernstein, Leonard	Tenor	Candide	1956	Candide	Nothing More Than This	Moderate Tempo	D3	F#4	Ingenue Male
Bernstein, Leonard	Tenor	West Side Story	1957	Riff	Cool	Moderate Tempo	C3	Eb4	Antagonist Male
Bernstein, Leonard	Tenor	Candide	1956	Dr. Pangloss	Dear Boy	Uptempo	Bb2	F#4	Antagonist Male
Bernstein, Leonard	Tenor	Candide	1956	Vanderdenur	Bon Voyage*	Uptempo	C3	Bb4	Antagonist Male
Bernstein, Leonard	Tenor	Candide	1956	Dr. Pangloss	The Venice Gavotte*	Uptempo	Bb2	F4	Antagonist Male
Bernstein, Leonard	Tenor	On The Town	1944	Chip	Ya Got Me *	Uptempo	E3	Gb4	Character Ingenue Male
Bernstein, Leonard	Tenor	On The Town	1944	Gabey	Lucky To Be Me	Uptempo	B2	A4	Romantic Lead Male
Bernstein, Leonard	Tenor	West Side Story	1957	Tony	Something's Coming	Uptempo	F#3	Bb4	Ingenue Male
Bernstein, Leonard	Tenor	West Side Story	1957	Riff	The Jet Song*	Uptempo	Bb2	G4	Antagonist Male
Bock, Jerry	Alto	Apple Tree, The	1966	Eve	Go To Sleep Whoever You Are	Ballad	B3	B4	Character Female
Bock, Jerry	Alto	Apple Tree, The	1966	Eve	What Makes Me Love Him	Ballad	C3	C#5	Character Female
Bock, Jerry	Alto	Apple Tree, The	1966	Princess Barbara	I've Got What You Want	Ballad	G3	C5	Character Female
Bock, Jerry	Alto	Fiddler on The Roof	1964	Golde	Sabbath Prayer	Ballad	D4	C5	Maternal
Bock, Jerry	Alto	Fiddler on The Roof	1964	Golde	Sunrise Sunset	Ballad	C4	D5	Maternal
Bock, Jerry	Alto	Fiddler on The Roof	1964	Hodel	Far From The Home I Love	Ballad	C4	E5	Character Ingenue Female
Bock, Jerry	Alto	Apple Tree, The	1966	Eve	Here In Eden	Moderate Tempo	A3	B4	Character Female
Bock, Jerry	Alto	Apple Tree, The	1966	Eve	Feelings	Moderate Tempo	B3	E5	Character Female
Bock, Jerry	Alto	Apple Tree, The	1966	Passionella	Oh To Be A Movie Star Reprise	Moderate Tempo	C4	D5	Character Female
Bock, Jerry	Alto	She Loves Me	1963	Ilona Ritter	A Trip To The Library	Moderate Tempo	G3	C#5	Romantic Antagonist Female
Bock, Jerry	Alto	Apple Tree, The	1966	Ella	Oh To Be A Movie Star	Uptempo	C4	D5	Character Female
Bock, Jerry	Alto	Apple Tree, The	1966	Eve	Friends	Uptempo	Bb3	C5	Character Female
Bock, Jerry	Alto	Apple Tree, The	1966	Passionella	Gorgeous	Uptempo	C4	D5	Character Female
Bock, Jerry	Alto	Apple Tree, The	1966	Passionella	Wealth	Uptempo	B3	B4	Character Female
Bock, Jerry	Alto	Apple Tree, The	1966	Princess Barbara	Tiger, Tiger	Uptempo	F3	A4	Character Female
Bock, Jerry	Alto	She Loves Me	1963	Ilona Ritter	I Resolve	Uptempo	Ab3	Bb4	Romantic Antagonist Female
Bock, Jerry	Baritone	Apple Tree, The	1966	Balladeer	I'll Tell You A Truth	Ballad	E3	Eb4	Antagonist Male
Bock, Jerry	Baritone	Apple Tree, The	1966	Balladeer	I'll Tell You A Truth Reprise	Ballad	C3	F#4	Antagonist Male
Bock, Jerry	Baritone	Fiddler on The Roof	1964	Tevye	Sabbath Prayer	Ballad	D3	C4	Paternal
Bock, Jerry	Baritone	Fiddler on The Roof	1964	Tevye	Sunrise Sunset	Ballad	C3	D4	Paternal
Bock, Jerry	Baritone	Fiddler on The Roof	1964	Tevye	Chavaleh	Ballad	C3	C4	Paternal
Bock, Jerry	Baritone	Apple Tree, The	1966	Adam	Eve	Moderate Tempo	D3	Db4	Character Male
Bock, Jerry	Baritone	Apple Tree, The	1966	Adam	Beautiful World	Moderate Tempo	C3	Eb4	Character Male
Bock, Jerry	Baritone	Apple Tree, The	1966	Adam	Adam's Reprise	Moderate Tempo	C3	Eb4	Character Male

Composer

Composer	Vocal Range	Show	Year	Role	Song	Tempo	Range-Bottom	Range-Top	Char Type
Bock, Jerry	Baritone	Apple Tree, The	1966	Flip	Real *	Moderate Tempo	C3	Eb4	Character Male
Bock, Jerry	Baritone	Apple Tree, The	1966	Snake	Forbidden Fruit	Moderate Tempo	Eb3	G4	Antagonist Male
Bock, Jerry	Baritone	Fiddler on The Roof	1964	Tevye	If I Were A Rich Man	Moderate Tempo	Db3	F4	Paternal
Bock, Jerry	Baritone	Fiddler on The Roof	1964	Tevye	Tevye's Monologue	Moderate Tempo	Ab2	E4	Paternal
Bock, Jerry	Baritone	Fiddler on The Roof	1964	Tevye	Tevye's Rebuttal	Moderate Tempo	Ab2	E4	Paternal
Bock, Jerry	Baritone	She Loves Me	1963	Georg Nowack	Three Letters*	Moderate Tempo	D#3	E4	Romantic Lead Male
Bock, Jerry	Baritone	She Loves Me	1963	Headwaiter	A Romantic Atmosphere (D Maj)	Moderate Tempo	G2	F4	Character Male
Bock, Jerry	Baritone	Apple Tree, The	1966	Adam	It's A Fish	Uptempo	Ab3	Eb4	Character Male
Bock, Jerry	Baritone	Fiddler on The Roof	1964	Perchik	Now I Have Everything	Uptempo	B2	E4	Antagonist Male
Bock, Jerry	Baritone	She Loves Me	1963	Mr. Maraczek	Days Gone By*	Uptempo	Bb2	C4	Mature Male
Bock, Jerry	Baritone	She Loves Me	1963	Ladislav Sipos	Perpective	Uptempo	D3	C#4	Character Male
Bock, Jerry	Baritone	She Loves Me	1963	Mr. Maraczek	Days Gone By Reprise	Uptempo	B2	E4	Mature Male
Bock, Jerry	Baritone	She Loves Me	1963	Georg Nowack	She Loves Me	Uptempo	Eb3	F4	Romantic Lead Male
Bock, Jerry	Soprano	She Loves Me	1963	Amalia Balash	Will He Like Me	Ballad	Bb3	F5	Romantic Lead Female
Bock, Jerry	Soprano	She Loves Me	1963	Amalia Balash	No More Candy*	Moderate Tempo	Db4	Fb5	Romantic Lead Female
Bock, Jerry	Soprano	She Loves Me	1963	Amalia Balash	I Don't Know His Name*	Moderate Tempo	B#3	D#5	Romantic Lead Female
Bock, Jerry	Soprano	She Loves Me	1963	Amalia Balash	Mr. Norwack, Will You Please	Moderate Tempo	C4	E5	Romantic Lead Female
Bock, Jerry	Soprano	She Loves Me	1963	Amalia Balash	Dear Friend	Uptempo	C4	F5	Romantic Lead Female
Bock, Jerry	Soprano	She Loves Me	1963	Amalia Balash	Where My Shoe (B Maj)*	Uptempo	E4	G5	Romantic Lead Female
Bock, Jerry	Soprano	She Loves Me	1963	Amalia Balash	Vanilla Ice Cream	Uptempo	D4	B5	Romantic Lead Female
Bock, Jerry	Soprano	She Loves Me	1963	Amalia Balash	Where's My Shoe (G Maj)	Uptempo	C#4	F5	Romantic Lead Female
Bock, Jerry	Tenor	She Loves Me	1963	Steven Kodaly	Ilona*	Moderate Tempo	C3	E4	Romantic Antagonist Male
Bock, Jerry	Tenor	She Loves Me	1963	Headwaiter	A Romantic Atmosphere (G Maj)	Moderate Tempo	C#3	B4	Character Male
Bock, Jerry	Tenor	Fiddler on The Roof	1964	Motel	Miracle of Miracles	Uptempo	E3	F#4	Character Male
Bock, Jerry	Tenor	She Loves Me	1963	Arpad Lazslo	Try Me	Uptempo	B2	E4	Character Ingenue Male
Bock, Jerry	Tenor	She Loves Me	1963	Steven Kodaly	Grand Knowing You	Uptempo	D3	A4	Romantic Antagonist Male
Bray, Russell and Willis	Alto	Color Purple, The	2005	Celie+	Somebody Gonna Love You	Ballad	F3	A4	Character Female
Bray, Russell and Willis	Alto	Color Purple, The	2005	Celie+	What About Love *	Ballad	B2	D5	Character Female
Bray, Russell and Willis	Alto	Color Purple, The	2005	Celie+	I'm Here	Ballad	E3	G5	Character Female
Bray, Russell and Willis	Alto	Color Purple, The	2005	Celie+	Bring My Nettie Back	Ballad	G3	G5	Character Female
Bray, Russell and Willis	Alto	Color Purple, The	2005	Shug Avery	Too Beautiful For Words *	Ballad	E3	F4	Romantic Antagonist Female
Bray, Russell and Willis	Alto	Color Purple, The	2005	Shug Avery	What About Love *	Ballad	E3	D5	Romantic Antagonist Female
Bray, Russell and Willis	Alto	Color Purple, The	2005	Shug Avery	The Color Purple	Ballad	F#3	Db5	Romantic Antagonist Female

Composer	Vocal Range	Show	Year	Role	Song	Tempo	Range-Bottom	Range-Top	Char Type
Bray, Russell and Willis	Alto	Color Purple, The	2005	Celie+	Dear God (Shug)	Moderate Tempo	F3	B4	Character Female
Bray, Russell and Willis	Alto	Color Purple, The	2005	Celie+	With These Hands	Moderate Tempo	Ab3	Eb5	Character Female
Bray, Russell and Willis	Alto	Color Purple, The	2005	Shug Avery	Push Da Button	Moderate Tempo	A3	Eb5	Romantic Antagonist Female
Bray, Russell and Willis	Alto	Color Purple, The	2005	Sofia	Hell No *	Moderate Tempo	E3	C5	Antagonist Female
Bray, Russell and Willis	Alto	Color Purple, The	2005	Celie+	Dear God (Sofia)	Uptempo	G3	G4	Character Female
Bray, Russell and Willis	Tenor	Color Purple, The	2005	Harpo	Brown Betty *	Moderate Tempo	E3	G4	Character Ingenue Male
Bray, Russell and Willis	Tenor	Color Purple, The	2005	Mister	Mister's Song (2005)	Moderate Tempo	E3	G4	Antagonist Male
Bray, Russell and Willis	Tenor	Color Purple, The	2005	Mister	Mister's Song (2015)	Moderate Tempo	F3	Ab4	Antagonist Male
Bray, Russell and Willis	Tenor	Color Purple, The	2005	Mister	Big Dog	Uptempo	F3	Ab4	Antagonist Male
Brooks, Mel	Baritone	Producers, The	2001	Leo Bloom	Til Him	Ballad	C3	F4	Character Male
Brooks, Mel	Baritone	Producers, The	2001	Max Bialystock	Til Him	Ballad	C3	D#4	Character Male
Brooks, Mel	Baritone	Producers, The	2001	Leo Bloom	I Wanna Be A Producer*	Moderate Tempo	A2	F4	Character Male
Brooks, Mel	Baritone	Producers, The	2001	Franz Liebkind	In Old Bavaria	Moderate Tempo	F2	D4	Antagonist Male
Brooks, Mel	Baritone	Producers, The	2001	Max Bialystock	Along Came Bially*	Moderate Tempo	Bb2	Eb4	Character Male
Brooks, Mel	Baritone	Producers, The	2001	Leo Bloom	Leo Goes To Rio*	Moderate Tempo	C3	E4	Character Male
Brooks, Mel	Baritone	Producers, The	2001	Max Bialystock	King Of Broadway*	Uptempo	C#3	E4	Character Male
Brooks, Mel	Baritone	Producers, The	2001	Max Bialystock	We Can Do It*	Uptempo	Bb2	Eb4	Character Male
Brooks, Mel	Baritone	Producers, The	2001	Leo Bloom	We Can Do It*	Uptempo	Bb2	E4	Character Male
Brooks, Mel	Baritone	Producers, The	2001	Franz Liebkind	Der Guten Tag Hop-Clop	Uptempo	D#3	E4	Antagonist Male
Brooks, Mel	Baritone	Producers, The	2001	Leo Bloom	That Face*	Uptempo	B2	F4	Character Male
Brooks, Mel	Baritone	Producers, The	2001	Max Bialystock	That Face Reprise*	Uptempo	A2	Eb4	Character Male
Brooks, Mel	Baritone	Producers, The	2001	Max Bialystock	Where Did We Go Right*	Uptempo	A2	D4	Character Male
Brooks, Mel	Baritone	Producers, The	2001	Max Bialystock	Betrayed	Uptempo	B2	F4	Character Male
Brooks, Mel	Soprano	Producers, The	2001	Ulla	When You've Got It Flaunt It!	Moderate Tempo	Bb3	Eb5	Romantic Lead Female
Brooks, Mel	Tenor	Producers, The	2001	Storm Trooper	Springtime For Hitler*	Moderate Tempo	D3	Ab4	Romantic Lead Male
Brooks, Mel	Tenor	Producers, The	2001	Roger De Bris	Springtime For Hitler*	Moderate Tempo	B2	G4	Romantic Lead Male
Brooks, Mel	Tenor	Producers, The	2001	Roger De Bris	Keep It Gay*	Uptempo	G#2	G4	Romantic Lead Male
Brooks, Mel	Tenor	Producers, The	2001	Franz Liebkind	Haben Sie Gehort Das Deutsche Ban	Uptempo	A2	G4	Antagonist Male
Brown, Jason Robert	Alto	13 The Musical	2008	Patrice (CIF)	Good Enough	Ballad	G3	C5	Juvenile Female
Brown, Jason Robert	Alto	13 The Musical	2008	Patrice (CIF)	Tell Her*	Ballad	Bb3	C5	Juvenile Female
Brown, Jason Robert	Alto	Last Five Years, The	2002	Catherine Hiatt	Still Hurting	Ballad	A3	Db5	Ingenue Female
Brown, Jason Robert	Alto	Last Five Years, The	2002	Catherine Hiatt	See I'm Smiling	Ballad	E3	C#5	Ingenue Female
Brown, Jason Robert	Alto	Last Five Years, The	2002	Catherine Hiatt	The Next Ten Minutes	Ballad	G#3	E#4	Ingenue Female

Composer

Composer	Vocal Range	Show	Year	Role	Song	Tempo	Range-Bottom	Range-Top	Char Type
Brown, Jason Robert	Alto	Parade	1998	Lucille Frank	You Don't Know this Man	Ballad	G3	Eb5	Romantic Lead Female
Brown, Jason Robert	Alto	Parade	1998	Mrs. Phagan	My Child Will Forgive Me	Ballad	F#3	A4	Maternal
Brown, Jason Robert	Alto	Parade	1998	Lucille Frank	All The Wasted Time*	Ballad	G3	Eb5	Romantic Lead Female
Brown, Jason Robert	Alto	Parade	1998	Lucille Frank	Finale	Ballad	A3	C5	Romantic Lead Female
Brown, Jason Robert	Alto	13 The Musical	2008	Patrice (CIF)	If That's What It Is*	Moderate Tempo	Eb3	C5	Juvenile Female
Brown, Jason Robert	Alto	13 The Musical	2008	Patrice (CIF)	What It Means To Be A Friend	Moderate Tempo	A3	E5	Juvenile Female
Brown, Jason Robert	Alto	Last Five Years, The	2002	Catherine Hiatt	Goodbye Until Tomorrow	Moderate Tempo	F#3	Db5	Ingenue Female
Brown, Jason Robert	Alto	Last Five Years, The	2002	Catherine Hiatt	When You Come To Me	Moderate Tempo	A3	D5	Ingenue Female
Brown, Jason Robert	Alto	Parade	1998	Lucille Frank	Waiting*	Moderate Tempo	A3	C5	Romantic Lead Female
Brown, Jason Robert	Alto	Parade	1998	Lucille Frank	Do It Alone	Moderate Tempo	A3	E5	Romantic Lead Female
Brown, Jason Robert	Alto	Songs For A New World	1995	Woman 2	Stars And The Moon	Moderate Tempo	A3	D5	Character Female
Brown, Jason Robert	Alto	Songs For A New World	1995	Woman 2	Surabaya Santa	Moderate Tempo	G3	Eb4	Character Female
Brown, Jason Robert	Alto	Songs For A New World	1995	Woman 2	The Flagmaker 1775	Moderate Tempo	A3	E5	Character Female
Brown, Jason Robert	Alto	Songs For A New World	1995	Woman 2	Hear My Song*	Moderate Tempo	A3	B4	Character Female
Brown, Jason Robert	Alto	13 The Musical	2008	Cassie (IF)	A Brand New You*	Uptempo	C4	F5	Juvenile Female
Brown, Jason Robert	Alto	13 The Musical	2008	Lucy (RAF)	It Can't Be True*	Uptempo	F#3	C5	Juvenile Female
Brown, Jason Robert	Alto	13 The Musical	2008	Lucy (RAF)	Opportunity*	Uptempo	B3	E4	Juvenile Female
Brown, Jason Robert	Alto	13 The Musical	2008	Patrice (CIF)	The Lamest Place In The World	Uptempo	B3	D#5	Juvenile Female
Brown, Jason Robert	Alto	Last Five Years, The	2002	Catherine Hiatt	I'm A Part Of That	Uptempo	Bb3	Eb5	Ingenue Female
Brown, Jason Robert	Alto	Last Five Years, The	2002	Catherine Hiatt	A Summer In Ohio	Uptempo	F#3	E5	Ingenue Female
Brown, Jason Robert	Alto	Last Five Years, The	2002	Catherine Hiatt	Climbing Uphill/Audition	Uptempo	G3	D5	Ingenue Female
Brown, Jason Robert	Alto	Last Five Years, The	2002	Catherine Hiatt	I Can Do Better Than That	Uptempo	A3	D5	Ingenue Female
Brown, Jason Robert	Alto	Songs For A New World	1995	Woman 2	Just One Step	Uptempo	F3	C#5	Character Female
Brown, Jason Robert	Baritone	Parade	1998	Leo Frank	It's Hard To Speak My Heart	Ballad	B2	E4	Character Male
Brown, Jason Robert	Baritone	Parade	1998	Leo Frank	All The Wasted Time*	Ballad	D3	Bb4	Character Male
Brown, Jason Robert	Baritone	Parade	1998	Leo Frank	Sh'ma	Ballad	G3	Eb4	Character Male
Brown, Jason Robert	Baritone	Parade	1998	Old Soldier	Old Red Hills Of Home (Part 2)*	Moderate Tempo	C3	G4	Mature Male
Brown, Jason Robert	Baritone	Parade	1998	Hugh Dorsey	Somethin' Ain't Right*	Moderate Tempo	C#3	F#4	Romantic Antagonist Male
Brown, Jason Robert	Baritone	Parade	1998	Frankie Epps	Old Red Hills Of Home Finale*	Moderate Tempo	Eb3	Eb4	Ingenue Male
Brown, Jason Robert	Baritone	Songs For A New World	1995	Man 2	I'd Give It All For You*	Moderate Tempo	F#2	G4	Romantic Lead Male
Brown, Jason Robert	Baritone	Songs For A New World	1995	Man 2	Hear My Song*	Moderate Tempo	F3	E4	Romantic Lead Male
Brown, Jason Robert	Baritone	13 The Musical	2008	Brett (RAM)	Getting Ready*	Uptempo	G3	F4	Juvenile Male
Brown, Jason Robert	Baritone	Parade	1998	Leo Frank	How Can I Call This Home?	Uptempo	A2	F4	Character Male
Brown, Jason Robert	Baritone	Parade	1998	Hugh Dorsey	The Trial, Part 2: Twenty From Marie	Uptempo	Bb2	Eb4	Romantic Antagonist Male

Composer

Composer	Vocal Range	Show	Year	Role	Song	Tempo	Range-Bottom	Range-Top	Char Type
Brown, Jason Robert	Baritone	Parade	1998	Leo Frank	Come Up To My Office*	Uptempo	A2	F4	Character Male
Brown, Jason Robert	Baritone	Parade	1998	Newt Lee+	The Trial, Part 5: Newt Lee's Testimo	Uptempo	B2	F#3	Antagonist Male
Brown, Jason Robert	Baritone	Parade	1998	Judge Roan	Judge Roan's Letter	Uptempo	Eb2	D4	Antagonist Male
Brown, Jason Robert	Baritone	Parade	1998	Gov. Jack Slaton	Pretty Music*	Uptempo	C3	G4	Romantic Lead Male
Brown, Jason Robert	Baritone	Parade	1998	Leo Frank	This Is Not Over Yet*	Uptempo	D3	F#4	Character Male
Brown, Jason Robert	Baritone	Songs For A New World	1995	Man 2	The River Won't Flow*	Uptempo	D3	A4	Romantic Lead Male
Brown, Jason Robert	Baritone	Songs For A New World	1995	Man 2	She Cries	Uptempo	C3	G#4	Romantic Lead Male
Brown, Jason Robert	Soprano	Songs For A New World	1995	Woman 1	Christmas Lullaby	Ballad	A3	E5	Romantic Lead Female
Brown, Jason Robert	Soprano	Songs For A New World	1995	Woman 1	I'm Not Afraid Of Anything	Moderate Tempo	A3	E5	Romantic Lead Female
Brown, Jason Robert	Soprano	Songs For A New World	1995	Woman 1	I'd Give It All For You*	Moderate Tempo	A3	F4	Romantic Lead Female
Brown, Jason Robert	Soprano	Songs For A New World	1995	Woman 1	Hear My Song*	Moderate Tempo	A3	G4	Romantic Lead Female
Brown, Jason Robert	Tenor	13 The Musical	2008	Evan Goldman (CM)	Tell Her*	Ballad	Bb2	G4	Juvenile Male
Brown, Jason Robert	Tenor	13 The Musical	2008	Evan Goldman (CM)	A Little More Homework*	Ballad	C3	F4	Juvenile Male
Brown, Jason Robert	Tenor	13 The Musical	2008	Evan Goldman (CM)	Becoming A Man Reprise	Ballad	E3	A4	Juvenile Male
Brown, Jason Robert	Tenor	Last Five Years, The	2002	Jamie Wellerstein	The Next Ten Minutes	Ballad	C#3	G#4	Ingenue Male
Brown, Jason Robert	Tenor	Last Five Years, The	2002	Jamie Wellerstein	If I Didn't Believe In You	Ballad	Bb2	G4	Ingenue Male
Brown, Jason Robert	Tenor	Last Five Years, The	2002	Jamie Wellerstein	Nobody Needs To Know	Ballad	C3	Ab4	Ingenue Male
Brown, Jason Robert	Tenor	Last Five Years, The	2002	Jamie Wellerstein	I Could Never Rescue You	Ballad	C3	G4	Ingenue Male
Brown, Jason Robert	Tenor	Parade	1998	Tom Watson	Watson's Lullaby	Ballad	A#2	A3	Romantic Lead Male
Brown, Jason Robert	Tenor	Songs For A New World	1995	Man 1	On The Deck Of A Spanish Sailing Sh	Ballad	F3	Bb4	Romantic Antagonist Male
Brown, Jason Robert	Tenor	Songs For A New World	1995	Man 1	Flying Home*	Ballad	D#3	F4	Romantic Antagonist Male
Brown, Jason Robert	Tenor	13 The Musical	2008	Evan Goldman (CM)	If That's What It Is*	Moderate Tempo	C3	A4	Juvenile Male
Brown, Jason Robert	Tenor	Parade	1998	Young Soldier	Old Red Hills Of Home (Part 1)	Moderate Tempo	D3	A4	Character Ingenue Male
Brown, Jason Robert	Tenor	Parade	1998	Newt Lee+	Interrogation Sequence*	Moderate Tempo	Bb2	C4	Antagonist Male
Brown, Jason Robert	Tenor	Parade	1998	Britt Craig	Opening Act II	Moderate Tempo	F3	G4	Antagonist Male
Brown, Jason Robert	Tenor	Parade	1998	John Conley+	Blues: Feel The Rain Fall*	Moderate Tempo	D3	Bb4	Romantic Antagonist Male
Brown, Jason Robert	Tenor	Songs For A New World	1995	Man 1	Hear My Song*	Moderate Tempo	D3	C4	Romantic Antagonist Male
Brown, Jason Robert	Tenor	13 The Musical	2008	Archie (CM)	Get Me What I Need	Uptempo	C3	A4	Juvenile Male
Brown, Jason Robert	Tenor	13 The Musical	2008	Archie (CM)	Getting Ready*	Uptempo	Eb3	Ab4	Juvenile Male
Brown, Jason Robert	Tenor	13 The Musical	2008	Evan Goldman (CM)	Becoming A Man	Uptempo	D3	A4	Juvenile Male
Brown, Jason Robert	Tenor	13 The Musical	2008	Evan Goldman (CM)	Thirteen	Uptempo	Bb2	Bb3	Juvenile Male
Brown, Jason Robert	Tenor	13 The Musical	2008	Evan Goldman (CM)	All Hail The Brain	Uptempo	E3	G4	Juvenile Male
Brown, Jason Robert	Tenor	13 The Musical	2008	Evan Goldman (CM)	Terminal Illness	Uptempo	Eb3	Ab4	Juvenile Male

Composer	Vocal Range	Show	Year	Role	Song	Tempo	Range-Bottom	Range-Top	Char Type
Brown, Jason Robert	Tenor	13 The Musical	2008	Evan Goldman (CM)	Getting Ready*	Uptempo	Db4	Bb4	Juvenile Male
Brown, Jason Robert	Tenor	13 The Musical	2008	Evan Goldman (CM)	Here I Come	Uptempo	Eb3	Bb4	Juvenile Male
Brown, Jason Robert	Tenor	Last Five Years, The	2002	Jamie Wellerstein	Shiksa Goddess	Uptempo	A2	A4	Ingenue Male
Brown, Jason Robert	Tenor	Last Five Years, The	2002	Jamie Wellerstein	Moving Too Fast	Uptempo	C3	Bb4	Ingenue Male
Brown, Jason Robert	Tenor	Last Five Years, The	2002	Jamie Wellerstein	The Schmuel Song	Uptempo	C#3	Ab4	Ingenue Male
Brown, Jason Robert	Tenor	Last Five Years, The	2002	Jamie Wellerstein	A Miracle Would Happen	Uptempo	A2	A4	Ingenue Male
Brown, Jason Robert	Tenor	Parade	1998	Britt Craig	Big News	Uptempo	D3	Ab4	Antagonist Male
Brown, Jason Robert	Tenor	Parade	1998	Britt Craig	Real Big News*	Uptempo	F3	A4	Antagonist Male
Brown, Jason Robert	Tenor	Parade	1998	John Conley+	That's What He Said	Uptempo	D3	G4	Romantic Antagonist Male
Brown, Jason Robert	Tenor	Parade	1998	Tom Watson	Where Will You Stand...Flood Comes*	Uptempo	B2	Eb4	Romantic Lead Male
Brown, Jason Robert	Tenor	Songs For A New World	1995	Man 1	The River Won't Flow*	Uptempo	G3	C5	Romantic Antagonist Male
Brown, Jason Robert	Tenor	Songs For A New World	1995	Man 1	Steam Train*	Uptempo	F3	C5	Romantic Antagonist Male
Brown, Jason Robert	Tenor	Songs For A New World	1995	Man 1	King Of the World	Uptempo	E3	C5	Romantic Antagonist Male
Brown, Nacio Herb	Alto	Singin' In The Rain	1983	Lina Lamont	What's Wrong With Me? (Eb Maj)	Moderate Tempo	C4	Eb5	Romantic Antagonist Female
Brown, Nacio Herb	Alto	Singin' In The Rain	1983	Lina Lamont	What's Wrong With Me? (C Maj)	Moderate Tempo	A3	C5	Romantic Antagonist Female
Brown, Nacio Herb	Baritone	Singin' In The Rain	1983	Don Lockwood	You Stepped Out Of A Dream*	Moderate Tempo	C3	C4	Romantic Lead Male
Brown, Nacio Herb	Baritone	Singin' In The Rain	1983	Don Lockwood	You Stepped Out Of A Dream Reprise	Moderate Tempo	C3	C4	Romantic Lead Male
Brown, Nacio Herb	Baritone	Singin' In The Rain	1983	Don Lockwood	You Were Meant For Me	Moderate Tempo	Bb2	Db4	Romantic Lead Male
Brown, Nacio Herb	Baritone	Singin' In The Rain	1983	Don Lockwood	Meant For Me Playoff	Moderate Tempo	C3	Db4	Romantic Lead Male
Brown, Nacio Herb	Baritone	Singin' In The Rain	1983	Don Lockwood	Don's Would You	Moderate Tempo	G2	C4	Romantic Lead Male
Brown, Nacio Herb	Baritone	Singin' In The Rain	1983	Don Lockwood	Singin' In The Rain	Uptempo	D3	D4	Romantic Lead Male
Brown, Nacio Herb	Baritone	Singin' In The Rain	1983	Don Lockwood	Broadway Rhythm* (ms 115-182)	Uptempo	C3	F4	Romantic Lead Male
Brown, Nacio Herb	Soprano	Singin' In The Rain	1983	Kathy Seldon	Lucky Star	Moderate Tempo	Bb3	Eb5	Ingenue Female
Brown, Nacio Herb	Soprano	Singin' In The Rain	1983	Kathy Seldon	Kathy's Would You	Moderate Tempo	G3	C5	Ingenue Female
Brown, Nacio Herb	Tenor	Singin' In The Rain	1983	Production Tenor	Beautiful Girl	Moderate Tempo	F3	Bb4	Romantic Lead Male
Brown, Nacio Herb	Tenor	Singin' In The Rain	1983	Cosmo Brown	Make "Em Laugh	Uptempo	C3	G4	Character Male
Brown, Nacio Herb	Tenor	Singin' In The Rain	1983	Cosmo Brown	Broadway Melody* (ms 1-30)	Uptempo	Bb3	F4	Character Male
Casey and Jacobs	Alto	Grease	1971	Betty Rizzo	There Are Worse Things I Could Do	Ballad	A3	C4	Antagonist Female
Casey and Jacobs	Alto	Grease	1971	Betty Rizzo	Look At Me I'm Sandra Dee	Moderate Tempo	G3	Eb5	Antagonist Female
Casey and Jacobs	Alto	Grease	1971	Marty	Freddy My Love	Uptempo	C4	C5	Character Ingenue Female
Casey and Jacobs	Alto	Grease	1971	Miss Lynch	Born to Hand Jive	Uptempo	D4	B4	Mature Female
Casey and Jacobs	Baritone	Grease	1971	Johnny Casino	Born to Hand Jive	Uptempo	A3	F#4	Character Ingenue Male
Casey and Jacobs	Soprano	Grease	1971	Sandy Dumbrowski	It's Raining on Prom Night	Ballad	A3	D5	Ingenue Female

Composer	Vocal Range	Show	Year	Role	Song	Tempo	Range-Bottom	Range-Top	Char Type
Casey and Jacobs	Soprano	Grease	1971	Sandy Dumbrowski	Hopelessly Devoted to You	Ballad	A3	F5	Ingenue Female
Casey and Jacobs	Soprano	Grease	1971	Sandy Dumbrowski	Look At Me I'm Sandra Dee Reprise	Ballad	A3	C#5	Ingenue Female
Casey and Jacobs	Soprano	Grease	1971	Sandy Dumbrowski	Since I Don't Have You	Ballad	A♭3	A♭5	Ingenue Female
Casey and Jacobs	Tenor	Grease	1971	Roger	Mooning	Ballad	F3	G4	Character Male
Casey and Jacobs	Tenor	Grease	1971	Danny Zuko	Alone at a Drive-in Movie	Moderate Tempo	D3	D♭5	Romantic Antagonist Male
Casey and Jacobs	Tenor	Grease	1971	Teen Angel	Beauty School Dropout	Moderate Tempo	F#3	F#5	Romantic Lead Male
Casey and Jacobs	Tenor	Grease	1971	Doody	Those Magic Changes	Uptempo	E3	C♭5	Character Ingenue Male
Casey and Jacobs	Tenor	Grease	1971	Doody	Rock N Roll Party Queen	Uptempo	A2	A♭3	Character Ingenue Male
Casey and Jacobs	Tenor	Grease	1971	Kenicke	Greased Lightening	Uptempo	E3	B4	Antagonist Male
Casey and Jacobs	Tenor	Grease	1971	Roger	Rock N Roll Party Queen	Uptempo	A2	A♭3	Character Male
Charlap, Mark	Baritone	Peter Pan	1954	Captain Hook	Hook's Tango*	Moderate Tempo	A2	D4	Antagonist Male
Charlap, Mark	Baritone	Peter Pan	1954	Captain Hook	Captain Hook's Waltz*	Moderate Tempo	B2	G4	Antagonist Male
Charlap, Mark	Baritone	Peter Pan	1954	Captain Hook	Tarantella*	Uptempo	D3	D4	Antagonist Male
Charlap, Mark	Soprano	Peter Pan	1954	Peter Pan	Distant Melody	Ballad	G♭3	A♭4	Character Female
Charlap, Mark	Soprano	Peter Pan	1954	Peter Pan	Neverland	Moderate Tempo	E♭3	C5	Character Female
Charlap, Mark	Soprano	Peter Pan	1954	Peter Pan	Wendy*	Moderate Tempo	B♭3	C5	Character Female
Charlap, Mark	Soprano	Peter Pan	1954	Peter Pan	Neverland Reprise	Moderate Tempo	E3	B4	Character Female
Charlap, Mark	Soprano	Peter Pan	1954	Peter Pan	I've Got To Crow	Uptempo	B♭3	C5	Character Female
Charlap, Mark	Soprano	Peter Pan	1954	Peter Pan	I'm Flying*	Uptempo	A3	F5	Character Female
Coleman, Cy	Alto	City of Angels	1989	Bobbi	With Every Breath I Take	Ballad	E3	D♭5	Romantic Lead Female
Coleman, Cy	Alto	City of Angels	1989	Bobbi	With Every Breath I Take Reprise *	Ballad	D#3	C5	Romantic Lead Female
Coleman, Cy	Alto	City of Angels	1989	Mallory	Lost And Found	Ballad	G#3	F#5	Romantic Antagonist Female
Coleman, Cy	Alto	Little Me	1962	Young Belle	Other Side Of The Tracks (Slow Vers)	Ballad	B3	C5	Character Female
Coleman, Cy	Alto	Will Rogers Follies	1991	Betty Blake	My Unknown Someone	Ballad	A♭3	C5	Romantic Lead Female
Coleman, Cy	Alto	City of Angels	1989	Gabby	What You Don't Know About Women	Moderate Tempo	G3	F5	Romantic Lead Female
Coleman, Cy	Alto	City of Angels	1989	Gabby	It Needs Work	Moderate Tempo	G#3	C♭5	Romantic Lead Female
Coleman, Cy	Alto	City of Angels	1989	Oolie	What You Don't Know About Women	Moderate Tempo	G3	F5	Character Female
Coleman, Cy	Alto	City of Angels	1989	Oolie/Donna	You Can Always Count On Me	Moderate Tempo	B♭3	D♭5	Character Female
Coleman, Cy	Alto	Little Me	1962	Young Belle	Poor Little Hollywood Star	Moderate Tempo	G#3	E5	Character Female
Coleman, Cy	Alto	Little Me	1962	Young Belle	I Needed Social Position*	Moderate Tempo	A♭3	C#5	Character Female
Coleman, Cy	Alto	Little Me	1962	Belle	I Needed Social Position*	Moderate Tempo	A♭3	C#5	Character Female
Coleman, Cy	Alto	On The Twentieth Century	1978	Letitia Primrose	Five Zeros*	Moderate Tempo	A♭3	E♭5	Mature Female
Coleman, Cy	Alto	Sweet Charity	1966	Dance Hall Girl	Big Spender*	Moderate Tempo	F3	B4	Antagonist Female

Composer	Vocal Range	Show	Year	Role	Song	Tempo	Range-Bottom	Range-Top	Char Type
Coleman, Cy	Alto	Sweet Charity	1966	Charity Hope Valentine	Charity's Soliloquy	Moderate Tempo	F3	Ab4	Character Ingenue Female
Coleman, Cy	Alto	Sweet Charity	1966	Charity Hope Valentine	Where Am I Going	Moderate Tempo	A3	A4	Character Ingenue Female
Coleman, Cy	Alto	Will Rogers Follies	1991	Betty Blake	The Big Time*	Moderate Tempo	B3	D#5	Romantic Lead Female
Coleman, Cy	Alto	Will Rogers Follies	1991	Betty Blake	My Big Mistake	Moderate Tempo	F3	D5	Romantic Lead Female
Coleman, Cy	Alto	Will Rogers Follies	1991	Betty Blake	With You	Moderate Tempo	Eb4	C5	Romantic Lead Female
Coleman, Cy	Alto	Will Rogers Follies	1991	Betty Blake	No Man Left For Me	Moderate Tempo	A3	C5	Romantic Lead Female
Coleman, Cy	Alto	Little Me	1962	Young Belle	On The Other Side Of The Tracks Rep	Uptempo	A3	D5	Character Female
Coleman, Cy	Alto	Little Me	1962	Belle	Dimples*	Uptempo	A3	D5	Character Female
Coleman, Cy	Alto	Little Me	1962	Belle	Here's To Us*	Uptempo	F3	Bb4	Character Female
Coleman, Cy	Alto	On The Twentieth Century	1978	Letitia Primrose	Repent	Uptempo	C4	F#5	Mature Female
Coleman, Cy	Alto	Sweet Charity	1966	Charity Hope Valentine	You Should See Yourself	Uptempo	Bb3	Bb4	Character Ingenue Female
Coleman, Cy	Alto	Sweet Charity	1966	Charity Hope Valentine	If My Friends Could See Me Now	Uptempo	G#3	Bb4	Character Ingenue Female
Coleman, Cy	Alto	Sweet Charity	1966	Nickie	There's Gotta Be Something Better...*	Uptempo	A3	Db4	Romantic Antagonist Female
Coleman, Cy	Alto	Sweet Charity	1966	Helene	There's Gotta Be Something Better...*	Uptempo	A3	Db5	Romantic Antagonist Female
Coleman, Cy	Alto	Sweet Charity	1966	Charity Hope Valentine	There's Gotta Be Something Better...*	Uptempo	Bb3	Db5	Character Ingenue Female
Coleman, Cy	Alto	Sweet Charity	1966	Charity Hope Valentine	I'm The Bravest Individual	Uptempo	C4	Eb5	Character Ingenue Female
Coleman, Cy	Alto	Sweet Charity	1966	Charity Hope Valentine	I'm A Brass Band*	Uptempo	A#3	G#4	Character Ingenue Female
Coleman, Cy	Alto	Will Rogers Follies	1991	Ziegfield's Favorite	Will-A-Mania	Uptempo	G3	D5	Romantic Lead Female
Coleman, Cy	Baritone	City of Angels	1989	Stone	With Every Breath I Take Reprise *	Ballad	G#2	F4	Romantic Antagonist Male
Coleman, Cy	Baritone	Little Me	1962	Fred Poitrane	Real Live Girl*	Ballad	D3	C4	Character Male
Coleman, Cy	Baritone	On The Twentieth Century	1978	Oscar Jaffe	Our Private World*	Ballad	A2	E4	Romantic Antagonist Male
Coleman, Cy	Baritone	Will Rogers Follies	1991	Will Rogers	So Long Pa	Ballad	B2	D4	Romantic Antagonist Male
Coleman, Cy	Baritone	Will Rogers Follies	1991	Will Rogers	Look Around	Ballad	C#5	D4	Romantic Antagonist Male
Coleman, Cy	Baritone	City of Angels	1989	Buddy Fiddler	The Buddy System	Moderate Tempo	C3	D4	Character Male
Coleman, Cy	Baritone	City of Angels	1989	Buddy Fiddler	Double Talk (Buddy)	Moderate Tempo	C3	G4	Character Male
Coleman, Cy	Baritone	City of Angels	1989	Munoz +	All You Have To Do Is Wait	Moderate Tempo	F#3	D4	Character Male
Coleman, Cy	Baritone	City of Angels	1989	Stine	Funny	Moderate Tempo	Bb2	F4	Romantic Lead Male
Coleman, Cy	Baritone	City of Angels	1989	Stine	Double Talk (Stine)	Moderate Tempo	F3	G4	Romantic Lead Male
Coleman, Cy	Baritone	Little Me	1962	George Musgrove	I've Got Your Number*	Moderate Tempo	E3	Ab4	Character Male
Coleman, Cy	Baritone	On The Twentieth Century	1978	Oscar Jaffe	I Rise Again*	Moderate Tempo	B2	E4	Romantic Antagonist Male
Coleman, Cy	Baritone	On The Twentieth Century	1978	Conductor Flanagan	I Have Written A Play	Moderate Tempo	C3	F4	Character Male
Coleman, Cy	Baritone	On The Twentieth Century	1978	Oscar Jaffe	I've Got It All*	Moderate Tempo	B2	E5	Romantic Antagonist Male
Coleman, Cy	Baritone	On The Twentieth Century	1978	Congressman	I Have Written A Play	Moderate Tempo	C3	F4	Character Male
Coleman, Cy	Baritone	On The Twentieth Century	1978	Oscar Jaffe	Five Zeros*	Moderate Tempo	Ab2	Ab4	Romantic Antagonist Male

Composer

Composer	Vocal Range	Show	Year	Role	Song	Tempo	Range-Bottom	Range-Top	Char Type
Coleman, Cy	Baritone	On The Twentieth Century	1978	Doctor	I Have Written A Play	Moderate Tempo	Bb3	Eb5	Character Male
Coleman, Cy	Baritone	On The Twentieth Century	1978	Oscar Jaffe	Last Will And Testament	Moderate Tempo	B2	F4	Romantic Antagonist Male
Coleman, Cy	Baritone	On The Twentieth Century	1978	Oscar Jaffe	Because Of Her	Moderate Tempo	B2	F4	Romantic Antagonist Male
Coleman, Cy	Baritone	Sweet Charity	1966	Oscar Lindquist	Sweet Charity	Moderate Tempo	Bb2	E4	Character Male
Coleman, Cy	Baritone	Will Rogers Follies	1991	Will Rogers	Never Met A Man I Didn't Like (Act 1	Moderate Tempo	B2	Bb3	Romantic Antagonist Male
Coleman, Cy	Baritone	Will Rogers Follies	1991	Will Rogers	Give A Man Enough Rope	Moderate Tempo	Bb2	F4	Romantic Antagonist Male
Coleman, Cy	Baritone	Will Rogers Follies	1991	Clem Rogers	Clem's Retur	Moderate Tempo	C#3	D#4	Antagonist Male
Coleman, Cy	Baritone	Will Rogers Follies	1991	Will Rogers	The Big Time*	Moderate Tempo	G#2	D#4	Romantic Antagonist Male
Coleman, Cy	Baritone	Will Rogers Follies	1991	Will Rogers	Marry Me Now*	Moderate Tempo	Eb3	Eb4	Romantic Antagonist Male
Coleman, Cy	Baritone	Will Rogers Follies	1991	Will Rogers	The Campaign: Our Favorite Son	Moderate Tempo	C3	Eb4	Romantic Antagonist Male
Coleman, Cy	Baritone	Will Rogers Follies	1991	Will Rogers	Presents For Mrs. Rogers	Moderate Tempo	B2	D4	Romantic Antagonist Male
Coleman, Cy	Baritone	Will Rogers Follies	1991	Will Rogers	Never Met A Man I Didn't Like Repris	Moderate Tempo	Bb2	D4	Romantic Antagonist Male
Coleman, Cy	Baritone	City of Angels	1989	Stine	You're Nothing Without Me *	Uptempo	D3	G4	Romantic Lead Male
Coleman, Cy	Baritone	City of Angels	1989	Stine	I'm Nothing Without You *	Uptempo	F3	G4	Romantic Lead Male
Coleman, Cy	Baritone	City of Angels	1989	Stone	Double Talk	Uptempo	A#2	D4	Romantic Antagonist Male
Coleman, Cy	Baritone	City of Angels	1989	Stone	You're Nothing Without Me *	Uptempo	E3	G4	Romantic Antagonist Male
Coleman, Cy	Baritone	City of Angels	1989	Stone	I'm Nothing Without You *	Uptempo	F3	G4	Romantic Antagonist Male
Coleman, Cy	Baritone	Little Me	1962	Benny Buchsbaum	To Be A Performer*	Uptempo	D#3	F4	Character Male
Coleman, Cy	Baritone	Little Me	1962	Bernie Buchsbaum	To Be A Performer*	Uptempo	D#3	F4	Character Male
Coleman, Cy	Baritone	Little Me	1962	Val DuVal	Boom Boom*	Uptempo	C#3	F#4	Character Male
Coleman, Cy	Baritone	Little Me	1962	Benny Buchsbaum	Be A Performer Reprise*	Uptempo	E3	E4	Character Male
Coleman, Cy	Baritone	Little Me	1962	Bernie Buchsbaum	Be A Performer Reprise*	Uptempo	E3	E4	Character Male
Coleman, Cy	Baritone	Little Me	1962	Prince Chemey	Goodbye	Uptempo	B2	F#4	Character Male
Coleman, Cy	Baritone	On The Twentieth Century	1978	Oscar Jaffe	Together*	Uptempo	C3	E4	Romantic Antagonist Male
Coleman, Cy	Baritone	On The Twentieth Century	1978	Max Jacobs	Max Jacobs	Uptempo	Bb2	F4	Antagonist Male
Coleman, Cy	Baritone	Will Rogers Follies	1991	Clem Rogers	It's A Boy	Uptempo	C#3	E4	Antagonist Male
Coleman, Cy	Baritone	Will Rogers Follies	1991	Clem Rogers	It's A Boy Reprise	Uptempo	D#3	E4	Antagonist Male
Coleman, Cy	Soprano	On The Twentieth Century	1978	Lily Garland	Our Private World*	Ballad	A3	E5	Romantic Lead Female
Coleman, Cy	Soprano	On The Twentieth Century	1978	Lily Garland	I've Got It All*	Moderate Tempo	B3	A5	Romantic Lead Female
Coleman, Cy	Soprano	On The Twentieth Century	1978	Lily Garland	Veronique	Uptempo	E3	Ab6	Romantic Lead Female
Coleman, Cy	Soprano	On The Twentieth Century	1978	Lily Garland	Never*	Uptempo	A3	A5	Romantic Lead Female
Coleman, Cy	Soprano	On The Twentieth Century	1978	Lily Garland	Babette	Uptempo	F#3	F#5	Romantic Lead Female
Coleman, Cy	Tenor	City of Angels	1989	Jimmy Powers	Stay Wth Me	Ballad	C3	G4	Romantic Lead Male
Coleman, Cy	Tenor	Sweet Charity	1966	Vittorio Vidal	Too Many Tomorrows	Ballad	Bb2	G4	Romantic Lead Male

Composer

Composer	Vocal Range	Show	Year	Role	Song	Tempo	Range-Bottom	Range-Top	Char Type
Coleman, Cy	Tenor	On The Twentieth Century	1978	Owen O'Malley	Five Zeros*	Moderate Tempo	Ab2	Ab4	Character Male
Coleman, Cy	Tenor	City of Angels	1989	Jimmy Powers	Ya Gotta Look Out For Yourself	Uptempo	C3	D4	Romantic Lead Male
Coleman, Cy	Tenor	Sweet Charity	1966	Daddy Brubeck	The Rhythm Of Life*	Uptempo	B2	G4	Character Male
Coleman, Cy	Tenor	Sweet Charity	1966	Herman	I Love To Cry At Weddings*	Uptempo	D3	B4	Antagonist Male
de Paul, Kaska, Hirshchbo	Alto	Seven Brides/Seven Brothe	1982	Milly	Love Never Goes Away*	Ballad	G3	B5	Character Ingenue Female
de Paul, Kaska, Hirshchbo	Alto	Seven Brides/Seven Brothe	1982	Milly	We Gotta Make It Through...Reprise*	Ballad	A3	A4	Character Ingenue Female
de Paul, Kaska, Hirshchbo	Alto	Seven Brides/Seven Brothe	1982	Milly	Glad That You Were Born*	Ballad	Db4	Bb4	Character Ingenue Female
de Paul, Kaska, Hirshchbo	Alto	Seven Brides/Seven Brothe	1982	Milly	Wonderful Day*	Moderate Tempo	Ab3	Db5	Character Ingenue Female
de Paul, Kaska, Hirshchbo	Alto	Seven Brides/Seven Brothe	1982	Milly	I'm Jumpin' In*	Moderate Tempo	Ab3	Bb4	Character Ingenue Female
de Paul, Kaska, Hirshchbo	Alto	Seven Brides/Seven Brothe	1982	Milly	One Man*	Moderate Tempo	G3	Bb4	Character Ingenue Female
de Paul, Kaska, Hirshchbo	Alto	Seven Brides/Seven Brothe	1982	Milly	I Married Seven Brothers*	Moderate Tempo	G3	Bb4	Character Ingenue Female
de Paul, Kaska, Hirshchbo	Alto	Seven Brides/Seven Brothe	1982	Milly	Goin Co'tin*	Moderate Tempo	Bb3	Eb5	Character Ingenue Female
de Paul, Kaska, Hirshchbo	Baritone	Seven Brides/Seven Brothe	1982	Adam	Love Never Goes Away*	Ballad	E3	E4	Romantic Lead Male
de Paul, Kaska, Hirshchbo	Baritone	Seven Brides/Seven Brothe	1982	Adam	Love Never Goes Away Tag	Ballad	B3	D4	Romantic Lead Male
de Paul, Kaska, Hirshchbo	Baritone	Seven Brides/Seven Brothe	1982	Adam	Bless Your Beautiful Hide*	Moderate Tempo	B2	G4	Romantic Lead Male
de Paul, Kaska, Hirshchbo	Baritone	Seven Brides/Seven Brothe	1982	Adam	Get A Wife*	Moderate Tempo	F3	G4	Romantic Lead Male
de Paul, Kaska, Hirshchbo	Baritone	Seven Brides/Seven Brothe	1982	Adam	Sobbin' Women*	Uptempo	C3	F4	Romantic Lead Male
de Paul, Kaska, Hirshchbo	Baritone	Seven Brides/Seven Brothe	1982	Adam	A Woman Ought To Know Her Place	Uptempo	F#3	F#4	Romantic Lead Male
de Paul, Kaska, Hirshchbo	Tenor	Seven Brides/Seven Brothe	1982	Gideon	Love Never Goes Away*	Ballad	D3	G4	Ingenue Male
Du Pres and Idle	Alto	Spamalot	2005	The Lady Of The Lake	Why Does He Never Notice Me	Ballad	F3	Db5	Romantic Antagonist Female
Du Pres and Idle	Alto	Spamalot	2005	The Lady Of The Lake	Come With Me*	Moderate Tempo	A3	C5	Romantic Antagonist Female
Du Pres and Idle	Alto	Spamalot	2005	The Lady Of The Lake	The Song That Goes Like This Repris	Moderate Tempo	Ab3	Eb5	Romantic Antagonist Female
Du Pres and Idle	Alto	Spamalot	2005	The Lady Of The Lake	Find Your Grail*	Moderate Tempo	C#4	E5	Romantic Antagonist Female
Du Pres and Idle	Alto	Spamalot	2005	Marlene Cow	The Cow Song*	Moderate Tempo	F3	B4	Character Female
Du Pres and Idle	Alto	Spamalot	2005	The Lady Of The Lake	Whatever Happened To My Part	Moderate Tempo	F#3	Eb5	Romantic Antagonist Female
Du Pres and Idle	Baritone	Spamalot	2005	King Arthur	I'm All Alone*	Ballad	A2	A3	Antagonist Male
Du Pres and Idle	Baritone	Spamalot	2005	King Arthur	Always Lok On The Bright Side of Lif	Moderate Tempo	C3	D4	Antagonist Male
Du Pres and Idle	Baritone	Spamalot	2005	Herbert	Here You Are*	Moderate Tempo	G2	Bb3	Character Male
Du Pres and Idle	Baritone	Spamalot	2005	Dad	I Am Not Dead Yet	Uptempo	C3	E4	Paternal
Du Pres and Idle	Baritone	Spamalot	2005	Sir Bedevere	Burn Her*	Moderate Tempo	F3	E4	Character Male
Du Pres and Idle	Baritone	Spamalot	2005	Sir Robin	You Won't Succeed On Broadway*	Uptempo	D3	E4	Character Male
Du Pres and Idle	Tenor	Spamalot	2005	Patsy	Always Lok On The Bright Side of Lif	Moderate Tempo	B2	F4	Character Male
Du Pres and Idle	Tenor	Spamalot	2005	Minstrel	Brave Sir Robin	Moderate Tempo	A3	D4	Character Male

Composer

Composer

Composer	Vocal Range	Show	Year	Role	Song	Tempo	Range-Bottom	Range-Top	Char Type
Du Pres and Idle	Tenor	Spamalot	2005	Minstrel	Brave Sir Robin Reprise	Moderate Tempo	A3	D4	Character Male
Edwards, Sherman	Baritone	1776	1969	John Dickinson	Cool, Cool Considerate Men	Moderate Tempo	A2	Gb4	Character Male
Edwards, Sherman	Baritone	1776	1969	John Adams	Piddle, Twiddle, and Resolve	Uptempo	Db3	Eb4	Mature Male
Edwards, Sherman	Baritone	1776	1969	John Adams	Is Anybody There? (ms 57-135)	Uptempo	D3	E4	Mature Male
Edwards, Sherman	Baritone	1776	1969	Richard Henry Lee	The Lees of Old Virginia	Uptempo	C3	F4	Romantic Lead Male
Edwards, Sherman	Soprano	1776	1969	Martha Jefferson	He Plays The Violin	Moderate Tempo	Bb3	D5	Ingenue Female
Edwards, Sherman	Soprano	1776	1969	Abigail Adams	Compliments	Uptempo	D4	Eb5	Mature Female
Edwards, Sherman	Tenor	1776	1969	Courier	Momma Look Sharp	Ballad	Bb2	Db4	Character Ingenue Male
Edwards, Sherman	Tenor	1776	1969	Edward Rutledge	Molasses To Rum	Moderate Tempo	E3	A4	Romantic Antagonist Male
Finn, William	Alto	25th Annual...Spelling Bee	2005	Logainne	Woe Is Me	Uptempo	G3	D5	Antagonist Female
Finn, William	Alto	25th Annual...Spelling Bee	2005	Logainne	Woe Is Me Reprise	Uptempo	C4	C5	Antagonist Female
Finn, William	Alto	25th Annual...Spelling Bee	2005	Marcy Park	I Speak Six Languages	Uptempo	B3	D5	Antagonist Female
Finn, William	Baritone	25th Annual...Spelling Bee	2005	William Barfee	Second Part 1*	Moderate Tempo	Db3	Eb4	Antagonist Male
Finn, William	Baritone	25th Annual...Spelling Bee	2005	Leaf Coneybear	I'm Not That Smart	Uptempo	A2	G4	Character Ingenue Male
Finn, William	Baritone	25th Annual...Spelling Bee	2005	Leaf Coneybear	I'm Not Smart Reprise	Uptempo	D3	F#4	Character Ingenue Male
Finn, William	Baritone	25th Annual...Spelling Bee	2005	William Barfee	Magic Foot	Uptempo	F3	A4	Antagonist Male
Finn, William	Soprano	25th Annual...Spelling Bee	2005	Olive Ostrovsky	The I Love You Song	Ballad	D4	D5	Ingenue Female
Finn, William	Soprano	25th Annual...Spelling Bee	2005	Rona Lisa Peretti	The I Love You Song	Ballad	D4	E5	Character Female
Finn, William	Soprano	25th Annual...Spelling Bee	2005	Olive Ostrovsky	My Friend The Dictionary	Moderate Tempo	B3	D5	Ingenue Female
Finn, William	Soprano	25th Annual...Spelling Bee	2005	Olive Ostrovsky	Second Part 1*	Moderate Tempo	C#4	D5	Ingenue Female
Finn, William	Soprano	25th Annual...Spelling Bee	2005	Rona Lisa Peretti	My Favorite Moment of the Bee	Moderate Tempo	D4	D5	Character Female
Finn, William	Soprano	25th Annual...Spelling Bee	2005	Rona Lisa Peretti	Rona Moment #2	Moderate Tempo	D4	D5	Character Female
Finn, William	Soprano	25th Annual...Spelling Bee	2005	Rona Lisa Peretti	Rona Moment #3	Moderate Tempo	Db4	Db5	Character Female
Finn, William	Tenor	25th Annual...Spelling Bee	2005	Mitch Mahoney	The I Love You Song	Ballad	E3	G#4	Antagonist Male
Finn, William	Tenor	25th Annual...Spelling Bee	2005	Chip Tolentino	Chip's Lament/My Unfortunate Erecti	Uptempo	C3	Ab4	Ingenue Male
Finn, William	Tenor	25th Annual...Spelling Bee	2005	Mitch Mahoney	Prayer of the Comfort Counselor	Uptempo	E3	A4	Antagonist Male
Flaherty, Stephen	Alto	A Man Of No Importance	2002	Lily Byrne	Tell Me Why	Ballad	G3	Bb4	Mature Female
Flaherty, Stephen	Alto	My Favorite Year	1992	Belle Carroca	Rookie In The Ring*	Ballad	G3	Bb4	Maternal
Flaherty, Stephen	Alto	Once On This Island	1990	Ti Moune+	Forever Yours*	Ballad	A#3	C#5	Ingenue Female
Flaherty, Stephen	Alto	Once On This Island	1990	Mama Euralie+	Ti Moune*	Ballad	Gb3	Bb4	Maternal
Flaherty, Stephen	Alto	Once On This Island	1990	Ti Moune+	Ti Moune*	Ballad	G3	C5	Ingenue Female
Flaherty, Stephen	Alto	Once On This Island	1990	Erzulie+	Human Heart*	Ballad	B3	C#5	Romantic Lead Female
Flaherty, Stephen	Alto	Once On This Island	1990	Mama Euralie+	Come Down From The Tree	Moderate Tempo	A3	E5	Mature Female

Composer	Vocal Range	Show	Year	Role	Song	Tempo	Range-Bottom	Range-Top	Char Type
Flaherty, Stephen	Alto	Once On This Island	1990	Andrea+	Andrea Sequence*	Moderate Tempo	Bb3	C5	Romantic Lead Female
Flaherty, Stephen	Alto	Ragtime	1998	Emma Goldman	He Wanted To Say*	Moderate Tempo	G3	Bb4	Character Female
Flaherty, Stephen	Alto	Seussical	2000	JoJo	Alone In The Universe*	Moderate Tempo	Ab3	Ab4	Juvenile Male
Flaherty, Stephen	Alto	Seussical	2000	The Cat In The Hat	How Lucky You Are	Moderate Tempo	D3	F4	Character Female
Flaherty, Stephen	Alto	Seussical	2000	Mayzie LaBird	How Lucky You Are Reprise	Moderate Tempo	Bb3	D5	Romantic Antagonist Female
Flaherty, Stephen	Alto	A Man Of No Importance	2002	Lily Byrne	The Burden of Life	Uptempo	F#3	C5	Mature Female
Flaherty, Stephen	Alto	A Man Of No Importance	2002	Lily Byrne	The Girl That Was Me	Uptempo	A3	A4	Mature Female
Flaherty, Stephen	Alto	A Man Of No Importance	2002	Lily Byrne	Burden of Life Part 1	Uptempo	Ab3	Ab4	Mature Female
Flaherty, Stephen	Alto	Once On This Island	1990	Ti Moune+	Waiting For Life	Uptempo	C#4	E5	Ingenue Female
Flaherty, Stephen	Alto	Once On This Island	1990	Asaka+	Mama Will Provide*	Uptempo	B3	G5	Character Female
Flaherty, Stephen	Alto	Once On This Island	1990	Ti Moune+	Waiting For Life Reprise	Uptempo	B3	C#5	Ingenue Female
Flaherty, Stephen	Alto	Ragtime	1998	Evelyn Nesbit	Crime Of The Century*	Uptempo	Bb3	D5	Romantic Lead Female
Flaherty, Stephen	Alto	Ragtime	1998	Evelyn Nesbit	Atlantic City (Part 1)*	Uptempo	B3	B4	Romantic Lead Female
Flaherty, Stephen	Alto	Ragtime	1998	Evelyn Nesbit	Atlantic City (Part 3)*	Uptempo	Bb3	D5	Romantic Lead Female
Flaherty, Stephen	Alto	Seussical	2000	Sour Kangaroo	Biggest Blame Fool (ms 9-29)*	Uptempo	Bb3	Db5	Antagonist Female
Flaherty, Stephen	Alto	Seussical	2000	The Cat In The Hat	A Day For The Cat In The Hat*	Uptempo	E3	E4	Character Female
Flaherty, Stephen	Alto	Seussical	2000	Mrs. Mayor	How To Raise A Child*	Uptempo	A3	Bb4	Character Female
Flaherty, Stephen	Alto	Seussical	2000	Mayzie LaBird	Amayzing Mayzie*	Uptempo	G#3	D5	Romantic Antagonist Female
Flaherty, Stephen	Alto	Seussical	2000	Mayzie LaBird	Mayzie In Palm Beach*	Uptempo	G3	C5	Romantic Antagonist Female
Flaherty, Stephen	Alto	Seussical	2000	The Cat In The Hat	Havin' A Hunch*	Uptempo	C#4	E5	Character Female
Flaherty, Stephen	Baritone	A Man Of No Importance	2002	Alfie Byrne	Man In The Mirror	Ballad	Bb2	F4	Character Male
Flaherty, Stephen	Baritone	A Man Of No Importance	2002	Alfie Byrne	Love Who You Love	Ballad	B2	E4	Character Male
Flaherty, Stephen	Baritone	A Man Of No Importance	2002	Alfie Byrne	Love's Never Lost	Ballad	E3	C4	Character Male
Flaherty, Stephen	Baritone	A Man Of No Importance	2002	Alfie Byrne	Welcome To The World	Ballad	C3	C5	Character Male
Flaherty, Stephen	Baritone	A Man Of No Importance	2002	Baldy O'Shea	The Cuddles That Mary Gave	Ballad	Eb3	F4	Mature Male
Flaherty, Stephen	Baritone	A Man Of No Importance	2002	Carney	Confussing Times	Ballad	A2	A3	Mature Male
Flaherty, Stephen	Baritone	My Favorite Year	1992	Alan Swann	If The World Were Like The Movies	Ballad	Bb2	E4	Romantic Antagonist Male
Flaherty, Stephen	Baritone	My Favorite Year	1992	Alan Swann	The Lights Come Up*	Ballad	Bb2	C4	Romantic Antagonist Male
Flaherty, Stephen	Baritone	Once On This Island	1990	Daniel+	Forever Yours*	Ballad	E#3	F#4	Ingenue Male
Flaherty, Stephen	Baritone	Once On This Island	1990	Tonton Julian+	Ti Moune*	Ballad	G2	Eb4	Paternal
Flaherty, Stephen	Baritone	Ragtime	1998	Coalhouse Walker, Jr.+	Now She Is Haunting Me (Part 1)	Ballad	Bb2	D4	Romantic Lead Male
Flaherty, Stephen	Baritone	Ragtime	1998	Father	New Music*	Ballad	Bb2	D4	Romantic Lead Male

Composer

Composer	Vocal Range	Show	Year	Role	Song	Tempo	Range-Bottom	Range-Top	Char Type
Flaherty, Stephen	Baritone	A Man Of No Importance	2002	Alfie Byrne	Confession *	Moderate Tempo	B2	D#4	Character Male
Flaherty, Stephen	Baritone	My Favorite Year	1992	Alan Swann	Exits	Moderate Tempo	G2	D4	Romantic Antagonist Male
Flaherty, Stephen	Baritone	Once On This Island	1990	Daniel+	Some Girls	Moderate Tempo	B2	F#4	Ingenue Male
Flaherty, Stephen	Baritone	Ragtime	1998	Coalhouse Walker, Jr.+	On The Wheels Of A Dream*	Moderate Tempo	A♭2	F♭4	Romantic Lead Male
Flaherty, Stephen	Baritone	Ragtime	1998	Coalhouse Walker, Jr.+	Coalhouse's Soliloguoy	Moderate Tempo	G2	F4	Romantic Lead Male
Flaherty, Stephen	Baritone	Ragtime	1998	Coalhouse Walker, Jr.+	Sarah Brown Eyes*	Moderate Tempo	A2	E4	Romantic Lead Male
Flaherty, Stephen	Baritone	Ragtime	1998	Coalhouse Walker, Jr.+	Make Them Hear You	Moderate Tempo	E♭3	G#4	Romantic Lead Male
Flaherty, Stephen	Baritone	Seussical	2000	Horton	Horton Hears A Who (ms 17-119)	Moderate Tempo	A2	E4	Character Male
Flaherty, Stephen	Baritone	Seussical	2000	Horton	Alone In The Universe*	Moderate Tempo	B2	E4	Character Male
Flaherty, Stephen	Baritone	Seussical	2000	The Cat In The Hat	How Lucky You Are	Moderate Tempo	D3	F4	Character Male
Flaherty, Stephen	Baritone	Seussical	2000	Horton	Alone In The Universe Reprise	Moderate Tempo	C3	C5	Character Male
Flaherty, Stephen	Baritone	Seussical	2000	Horton	Solla Sollew*	Moderate Tempo	C3	D4	Character Male
Flaherty, Stephen	Baritone	My Favorite Year	1992	King Kaiser	The Gospel According To King*	Uptempo	D3	C#4	Antagonist Male
Flaherty, Stephen	Baritone	My Favorite Year	1992	Alan Swann	Manhattan*	Uptempo	G2	E♭4	Romantic Antagonist Male
Flaherty, Stephen	Baritone	Once On This Island	1990	Agwe+	Rain*	Uptempo	C#3	E4	Romantic Antagonist Male
Flaherty, Stephen	Baritone	Ragtime	1998	Father	Journey On*	Uptempo	B2	E4	Romantic Lead Male
Flaherty, Stephen	Baritone	Seussical	2000	The Mayor	We're Whos Here Part 1*	Uptempo	E3	E4	Character Male
Flaherty, Stephen	Baritone	Seussical	2000	The Cat In The Hat	A Day For The Cat In The Hat*	Uptempo	E3	E4	Character Male
Flaherty, Stephen	Baritone	Seussical	2000	The Mayor	How To Raise A Child*	Uptempo	A2	E4	Character Male
Flaherty, Stephen	Baritone	Seussical	2000	Genghis Kahn Schmitz	The Military*	Uptempo	G2	F4	Antagonist Male
Flaherty, Stephen	Baritone	Seussical	2000	The Cat In The Hat	Havin' A Hunch*	Uptempo	C#3	E4	Character Male
Flaherty, Stephen	Soprano	A Man Of No Importance	2002	Adele Rice	Love Who You Love (Adeke Reprise)	Ballad	A♭3	D♭5	Character Ingenue Female
Flaherty, Stephen	Soprano	Ragtime	1998	Sarah+	Your Daddy's Son (B♭ Maj)	Ballad	G3	F5	Character Ingenue Female
Flaherty, Stephen	Soprano	Ragtime	1998	Sarah+	Your Daddy's Son (C♭ Maj)	Ballad	A♭3	G♭5	Character Ingenue Female
Flaherty, Stephen	Soprano	Ragtime	1998	Mother	New Music*	Ballad	B♭3	D5	Romantic Lead Female
Flaherty, Stephen	Soprano	Ragtime	1998	Sarah+	New Music*	Ballad	B♭3	D5	Character Ingenue Female
Flaherty, Stephen	Soprano	A Man Of No Importance	2002	Adele Rice	Princess	Moderate Tempo	C4	E5	Character Ingenue Female
Flaherty, Stephen	Soprano	My Favorite Year	1992	K.C. Downing	Funny*	Moderate Tempo	A3	E5	Character Ingenue Female
Flaherty, Stephen	Soprano	My Favorite Year	1992	K.C. Downing	Shut Up And Dance*	Moderate Tempo	A3	C5	Character Ingenue Female
Flaherty, Stephen	Soprano	Ragtime	1998	Mother	Goodbye My Love	Moderate Tempo	G3	D♭5	Romantic Lead Female
Flaherty, Stephen	Soprano	Ragtime	1998	Mother	What Kind Of Woman*	Moderate Tempo	B♭3	E♭5	Romantic Lead Female
Flaherty, Stephen	Soprano	Ragtime	1998	Sarah+	President (A Maj)*	Moderate Tempo	A3	D5	Character Ingenue Female
Flaherty, Stephen	Soprano	Ragtime	1998	Sarah+	President (B♭ Maj)*	Moderate Tempo	B♭3	E♭5	Character Ingenue Female
Flaherty, Stephen	Soprano	Ragtime	1998	Mother	Back To Before	Moderate Tempo	G3	C5	Romantic Lead Female

Composer

Composer	Vocal Range	Show	Year	Role	Song	Tempo	Range-Bottom	Range-Top	Char Type
Flaherty, Stephen	Soprano	Seussical	2000	Gertrude McFuzz	The One Feather Tail	Moderate Tempo	G3	C5	Character Ingenue Female
Flaherty, Stephen	Soprano	Ragtime	1998	Sarah+	Justice*	Uptempo	Ab3	C5	Character Ingenue Female
Flaherty, Stephen	Soprano	Seussical	2000	Gertrude McFuzz	Amayzing Gertrude*	Uptempo	C#4	D6	Character Ingenue Female
Flaherty, Stephen	Soprano	Seussical	2000	Gertrude McFuzz	Notice Me, Horton*	Uptempo	G3	C5	Character Ingenue Female
Flaherty, Stephen	Soprano	Seussical	2000	Gertrude McFuzz	For You*	Uptempo	F3	C5	Character Ingenue Female
Flaherty, Stephen	Tenor	A Man Of No Importance	2002	Robby Fay	Love Who You Love Reprise	Ballad	E3	F4	Romantic Lead Male
Flaherty, Stephen	Tenor	Ragtime	1998	Younger Brother	New Music*	Ballad	Bb2	D4	Ingenue Male
Flaherty, Stephen	Tenor	A Man Of No Importance	2002	Robby Fay	Confession *	Moderate Tempo	Db3	F#4	Romantic Lead Male
Flaherty, Stephen	Tenor	My Favorite Year	1992	Benjy Stone	Larger Than Life	Moderate Tempo	Eb3	F4	Character Ingenue Male
Flaherty, Stephen	Tenor	My Favorite Year	1992	Benjy Stone	My Favorite Year*	Moderate Tempo	C3	G4	Character Ingenue Male
Flaherty, Stephen	Tenor	Once On This Island	1990	Papa Ge+	Promises/Forever Yours Reprise*	Moderate Tempo	C3	G4	Antagonist Male
Flaherty, Stephen	Tenor	Ragtime	1998	Tateh	Gliding (Part 1 & 2)	Moderate Tempo	A2	F#4	Paternal
Flaherty, Stephen	Tenor	Ragtime	1998	Harry Houdini	Harry Houdini Master Escapist (Part	Moderate Tempo	Db3	Gb4	Character Male
Flaherty, Stephen	Tenor	A Man Of No Importance	2002	Robby Fay	Streets Of Dublin	Uptempo	C4	E5	Romantic Lead Male
Flaherty, Stephen	Tenor	My Favorite Year	1992	Benjy Stone	Waldorf Reveal	Uptempo	C3	F4	Character Ingenue Male
Flaherty, Stephen	Tenor	Once On This Island	1990	Papa Ge+	Forever Yours*	Uptempo	C#3	G4	Antagonist Male
Flaherty, Stephen	Tenor	Ragtime	1998	Tateh	Journey On*	Uptempo	Db3 Gb4	F#4	Paternal
Flaherty, Stephen	Tenor	Ragtime	1998	Tateh	Success (Part 1, 2 & 5)	Uptempo	D3	F#4	Paternal
Flaherty, Stephen	Tenor	Ragtime	1998	Henry Ford	Henry Ford*	Uptempo	D3	G4	Character Male
Flaherty, Stephen	Tenor	Ragtime	1998	Younger Brother	The Night That Goldman Spoke...(P 1	Uptempo	B2	F#4	Ingenue Male
Flaherty, Stephen	Tenor	Ragtime	1998	Harry Houdini	Atlantic City (Part 3)*	Uptempo	E3	G4	Character Male
Flaherty, Stephen	Tenor	Ragtime	1998	Tateh	Buffalo Nickel Photoplay Inc.	Uptempo	B2	F#4	Paternal
Frankel, Scott	Alto	Grey Gardens	2006	Edith Beale (Act 2)	The Girl Who Has Everything*	Moderate Tempo	C4	Eb5	Mature Female
Frankel, Scott	Alto	Grey Gardens	2006	Edith Beale (Act 2)	The Cake I Had*	Moderate Tempo	E#3	A#4	Mature Female
Frankel, Scott	Alto	Grey Gardens	2006	Edith Beale (Act 2)	Jerry Likes My Corn	Moderate Tempo	G3	F5	Mature Female
Frankel, Scott	Baritone	Grey Gardens	2006	Gould	Drift Away*	Ballad	Eb3	F4	Romantic Lead Male
Frankel, Scott	Baritone	Grey Gardens	2006	Major Bouvier	Marry Well*	Moderate Tempo	A#2	E4	Mature Male
Frankel, Scott	Baritone	Grey Gardens	2006	Norman Vincent Peale	Choose To Be Happy*	Moderate Tempo	G2	E4	Mature Male
Frankel, Scott	Baritone	Guys and Dolls	1950	Arvide	More I Cannot Wish You	Moderate Tempo	D4	D5	Mature Male
Frankel, Scott	Soprano	Grey Gardens	2006	Edie Beale (Act 2)	Around The World Reprise	Ballad	C4	C#5	Romantic Lead Female
Frankel, Scott	Soprano	Grey Gardens	2006	Edie Beale (Act 2)	Another Winter	Ballad	F#3	C#5	Romantic Lead Female
Frankel, Scott	Soprano	Grey Gardens	2006	Edith Beale (Act 1)	The Five Fifteen Reprise*	Ballad	C4	A4	Romantic Lead Female
Frankel, Scott	Soprano	Grey Gardens	2006	Edith Beale (Act 1)	Will You?	Ballad	C4	E5	Romantic Lead Female
Frankel, Scott	Soprano	Grey Gardens	2006	Edie Beale (Act 1)	The Telegram	Moderate Tempo	C#4	F#5	Ingenue Female

Composer

Composer	Vocal Range	Show	Year	Role	Song	Tempo	Range-Bottom	Range-Top	Char Type
Frankel, Scott	Soprano	Grey Gardens	2006	Edie Beale (Act 2)	Around The World	Moderate Tempo	C4	C#5	Romantic Lead Female
Frankel, Scott	Soprano	Grey Gardens	2006	Edith Beale (Act 1)	Hominy Grits*	Moderate Tempo	B3	C#5	Romantic Lead Female
Frankel, Scott	Soprano	Grey Gardens	2006	Edie Beale (Act 1)	Daddy's Girl*	Uptempo	C4	E5	Ingenue Female
Frankel, Scott	Soprano	Grey Gardens	2006	Edie Beale (Act 2)	The Revolutionary Costume*	Uptempo	Bb3	C5	Romantic Lead Female
Frankel, Scott	Soprano	Grey Gardens	2006	Edith Beale (Act 1)	The Five Fifteen*	Uptempo	B3	B4	Romantic Lead Female
Frankel, Scott	Tenor	Grey Gardens	2006	Joe Kennedy	Goin' Places*	Uptempo	C3	F#4	Ingenue Male
Gaudio, Bob	Tenor	Jersey Boys (2005)	1935	Frankie Valli	I'm In The Mood	Ballad	E3	F5	Character Ingenue Male
Gaudio, Bob	Tenor	Jersey Boys (2005)	1954	Tommy DeVito	Earth Angel	Ballad	Bb3	Eb4	Antagonist Male
Gaudio, Bob	Tenor	Jersey Boys (2005)	1963	Frankie Valli	My Mother's Eyes	Ballad	E3	F4	Character Ingenue Male
Gaudio, Bob	Tenor	Jersey Boys (2005)	1966	Bob Gaudio	Cry For Me	Ballad	Bb2	G4	Character Male
Gaudio, Bob	Tenor	Jersey Boys (2005)	1975	Frankie Valli	My Eyes Adored You	Ballad	G3	Bb4	Character Ingenue Male
Gaudio, Bob	Tenor	Jersey Boys (2005)	1976	Frankie Valli	Fallen Angel	Ballad	Eb3	Ab4	Character Ingenue Male
Gaudio, Bob	Tenor	Jersey Boys (2005)	1928	Frankie Castelluccio	I Can't Give You Anything But Love	Moderate Tempo	E3	Ab4	Character Ingenue Male
Gaudio, Bob	Tenor	Jersey Boys (2005)	1962	Frankie Valli	Sherry*	Moderate Tempo	G4	F5	Character Ingenue Male
Gaudio, Bob	Tenor	Jersey Boys (2005)	1963	Frankie Valli	Walk Like A Man	Moderate Tempo	B3	F5	Character Ingenue Male
Gaudio, Bob	Tenor	Jersey Boys (2005)	1964	Frankie Valli	Rag Doll	Moderate Tempo	Bb3	F5	Character Ingenue Male
Gaudio, Bob	Tenor	Jersey Boys (2005)	1946	Frankie Castelluccio	Sunday Kind Of Love	Uptempo	D3	E5	Character Ingenue Male
Gaudio, Bob	Tenor	Jersey Boys (2005)	1960	Frankie Valli	Stay*	Uptempo	F3	D5	Character Ingenue Male
Gaudio, Bob	Tenor	Jersey Boys (2005)	1961	Hal Miller	An Angel Cried	Uptempo	A3	C5	Character Male
Gaudio, Bob	Tenor	Jersey Boys (2005)	1962	Frankie Valli	Big Girls Don't Cry	Uptempo	Eb4	F5	Character Ingenue Male
Gaudio, Bob	Tenor	Jersey Boys (2005)	1965	Frankie Valli	Bye Bye Baby	Uptempo	C#4	D5	Character Ingenue Male
Gaudio, Bob	Tenor	Jersey Boys (2005)	1965	Frankie Valli	Work My Way Back To You	Uptempo	G3	C5	Character Ingenue Male
Gaudio, Bob	Tenor	Jersey Boys (2005)	1965	Frankie Valli	Let's Hang On!*	Uptempo	Db3	D5	Character Ingenue Male
Gaudio, Bob	Tenor	Jersey Boys (2005)	1966	Frankie Valli	Don't you Worry 'Bout Me*	Uptempo	G3	C5	Character Ingenue Male
Gaudio, Bob	Tenor	Jersey Boys (2005)	1967	Frankie Valli	Beggin'*	Uptempo	B3	Bb4	Character Ingenue Male
Gaudio, Bob	Tenor	Jersey Boys (2005)	1967	Frankie Valli	Can't Take My Eyes Off You	Uptempo	D3	G4	Character Ingenue Male
Gaudio, Bob	Tenor	Jersey Boys (2005)	1975	Bob Gaudio	December 1963	Uptempo	F3	G4	Character Male
Gershwin, George	Alto	Crazy For You (1992)	1926	Polly Baker	Someone To Watch Over Me	Ballad	Ab2	C4	Character Ingenue Female
Gershwin, George	Alto	Crazy For You (1992)	1930	Polly Baker	Embraceable You	Ballad	A3	B4	Character Ingenue Female
Gershwin, George	Alto	Crazy For You (1992)	1930	Polly Baker	But Not For Me	Ballad	Bb3	C5	Character Ingenue Female
Gershwin, George	Alto	Porgy and Bess	1935	Strawberry Woman+	Strawberry Woman	Ballad	G4	E5	Character Female
Gershwin, George	Alto	Crazy For You (1992)	1924	Irene Roth	Naughty Baby	Moderate Tempo	Ab3	D#4	Romantic Lead Female
Gershwin, George	Alto	Crazy For You (1992)	1930	Polly Baker	Could You Use Me	Uptempo	A2	Eb4	Character Ingenue Female

Composer

Composer	Vocal Range	Show	Year	Role	Song	Tempo	Range-Bottom	Range-Top	Char Type
Gershwin, George	Alto	Crazy For You (1992)	1930	Polly Baker	I Got Rhythm	Uptempo	Bb3	Eb4	Character Ingenue Female
Gershwin, George	Baritone	Porgy and Bess	1935	Porgy+	Lonesome Road*	Ballad	A2	D4	Character Male
Gershwin, George	Baritone	Porgy and Bess	1935	Porgy+	Bess, You Is My Woman*	Ballad	Bb2	B5	Character Male
Gershwin, George	Baritone	Of Thee I Sing	1931	John P Wintergreen	Of Thee I Sing*	Moderate Tempo	C3	E4	Romantic Lead Male
Gershwin, George	Baritone	Of Thee I Sing	1931	John P Wintergreen	Who Cares Reprise*	Moderate Tempo	C3	E4	Romantic Lead Male
Gershwin, George	Baritone	Porgy and Bess	1935	Jim+	A Woman Is A Sometime Thing*	Moderate Tempo	D3	F4	Character Male
Gershwin, George	Baritone	Porgy and Bess	1935	Porgy+	It Takes A Long Pull To Get There*	Moderate Tempo	E3	G4	Character Male
Gershwin, George	Baritone	Porgy and Bess	1935	Porgy+	The Buzzard*	Moderate Tempo	Bb2	E4	Character Male
Gershwin, George	Baritone	Porgy and Bess	1935	Crown+	What You Want Wid Bess*	Moderate Tempo	Eb3	Ab4	Antagonist Male
Gershwin, George	Baritone	Porgy and Bess	1935	Porgy+	I Loves You Porgy*	Moderate Tempo	Db3	Db4	Character Male
Gershwin, George	Baritone	Porgy and Bess	1935	Crown+	A Red-Headed Woman	Moderate Tempo	Db3	F4	Antagonist Male
Gershwin, George	Baritone	Porgy and Bess	1935	Porgy+	Oh, Bess, Oh, Where's My Bess*	Moderate Tempo	C#3	F4	Character Male
Gershwin, George	Baritone	Porgy and Bess	1935	Porgy+	Oh Lawd I'm On My Way*	Moderate Tempo	B2	E#4	Character Male
Gershwin, George	Baritone	Crazy For You (1992)	1992	Bella Zangler	What Causes That	Uptempo	C3	F#4	Mature Male
Gershwin, George	Baritone	Crazy For You (1992)	1937	Eugene Fodor	Stiff Upper Lip	Uptempo	D3	F4	Character Male
Gershwin, George	Baritone	Of Thee I Sing	1931	John P Wintergreen	Some Girls Can Bake A Pie*	Uptempo	E3	F4	Romantic Lead Male
Gershwin, George	Baritone	Of Thee I Sing	1931	John P Wintergreen	Supreme Court Judges*	Uptempo	B2	E4	Romantic Lead Male
Gershwin, George	Baritone	Of Thee I Sing	1931	Alexander Throttlebottom	The Senator From Minesota*	Uptempo	Eb3	F4	Character Male
Gershwin, George	Baritone	Porgy and Bess	1935	Porgy+	Oh, I Got Plenty O' Nuttin'*	Uptempo	B2	D4	Character Male
Gershwin, George	Baritone	Porgy and Bess	1935	Porgy+	I Got Plenty O' Nuttin' Reprise	Uptempo	Bb2	Eb4	Character Male
Gershwin, George	Soprano	Of Thee I Sing	1931	Diana Devereaux	The Most Beautiful Blossom	Ballad	Eb4	F5	Romantic Antagonist Female
Gershwin, George	Soprano	Porgy and Bess	1935	Bess+	Bess, You Is My Woman*	Ballad	D4	A#5	Romantic Lead Female
Gershwin, George	Soprano	Porgy and Bess	1935	Bess+	Summertime Reprise 2	Ballad	E4	A5	Romantic Lead Female
Gershwin, George	Soprano	Porgy and Bess	1935	Serena+	My Man's Gone Now*	Moderate Tempo	E4	B5	Character Female
Gershwin, George	Soprano	Of Thee I Sing	1931	Mary Turner	Of Thee I Sing*	Moderate Tempo	C4	E5	Romantic Lead Female
Gershwin, George	Soprano	Of Thee I Sing	1931	Mary Turner	A Kiss For Cinderella*	Moderate Tempo	Ab4	G5	Romantic Lead Female
Gershwin, George	Soprano	Of Thee I Sing	1931	Mary Turner	Who Cares Reprise*	Moderate Tempo	C4	E5	Romantic Lead Female
Gershwin, George	Soprano	Of Thee I Sing	1931	Diana Devereaux	Jilted*	Moderate Tempo	D4	F5	Romantic Antagonist Female
Gershwin, George	Soprano	Of Thee I Sing	1931	Mary Turner	I'm About To Be A Mother*	Moderate Tempo	B3	A5	Romantic Lead Female
Gershwin, George	Soprano	Porgy and Bess	1935	Clara+	Summertime	Moderate Tempo	F#4	B5	Ingenue Female
Gershwin, George	Soprano	Porgy and Bess	1935	Bess+	What You Want Wid Bess*	Moderate Tempo	Eb4	A5	Romantic Lead Female
Gershwin, George	Soprano	Porgy and Bess	1935	Bess+	I Loves You Porgy*	Moderate Tempo	Bb3	A5	Romantic Lead Female
Gershwin, George	Soprano	Porgy and Bess	1935	Clara+	Summertime Reprise	Moderate Tempo	E4	A5	Ingenue Female
Gershwin, George	Soprano	Crazy For You (1992)	1937	Patricia Fodor	Stiff Upper Lip	Uptempo	D4	F5	Character Female

Composer

Composer	Vocal Range	Show	Year	Role	Song	Tempo	Range-Bottom	Range-Top	Char Type
Gershwin, George	Soprano	Of Thee I Sing	1931	Diana Devereaux	Because Reprise*	Uptempo	E4	F5	Romantic Antagonist Female
Gershwin, George	Tenor	Porgy and Bess	1935	Honey Man+	Honeyman	Ballad	B3	G4	Character Male
Gershwin, George	Tenor	Porgy and Bess	1935	Crab Man+	Crab Man	Ballad	B3	G4	Character Male
Gershwin, George	Tenor	Crazy For You (1992)	1937	Bobby Child	They Can't Take That Away	Moderate Tempo	Bb2	Eb4	Ingenue Male
Gershwin, George	Tenor	Porgy and Bess	1935	Sporting Life+	It Ain't Necessarily So*	Moderate Tempo	C4	A4	Romantic Lead Male
Gershwin, George	Tenor	Porgy and Bess	1935	Sporting Life+	There's A Boat That's Leaving Soon...	Moderate Tempo	D3	Bb4	Romantic Lead Male
Gershwin, George	Tenor	Crazy For You (1992)	1992	Bobby Child	Krazy For You	Uptempo	Eb3	Eb4	Ingenue Male
Gershwin, George	Tenor	Crazy For You (1992)	1937	Bobby Child	I Can't Be Bothered Now	Uptempo	D3	F4	Ingenue Male
Gershwin, George	Tenor	Crazy For You (1992)	1937	Bobby Child	Things Are Looking Up	Uptempo	C3	D4	Ingenue Male
Gershwin, George	Tenor	Crazy For You (1992)	1937	Bobby Child	Shall We Dance	Uptempo	D3	Fb4	Ingenue Male
Gershwin, George	Tenor	Crazy For You (1992)	1937	Bobby Child	Nice Work If You Can Get It	Uptempo	D3	C4	Ingenue Male
Gershwin, George	Tenor	Of Thee I Sing	1931	French Ambassador	The Illegitimate Daughter*	Uptempo	C#3	G4	Antagonist Male
Gershwin, George	Tenor	Of Thee I Sing	1931	French Ambassador	Illegitimate Daughter Reprise*	Uptempo	D3	D4	Antagonist Male
Gesner, Clark	Alto	You're A Good Man Charlie	1971	Lucy Van Pelt	Schroeder	Moderate Tempo	G3	E5	Antagonist Female
Gesner, Clark	Baritone	You're A Good Man Charlie	1971	Linus Van Pelt	My Blanket And Me	Moderate Tempo	B2	D4	Character Ingenue Male
Gesner, Clark	Baritone	You're A Good Man Charlie	1971	Charlie Brown	The Kite	Uptempo	Bb2	Eb4	Character Male
Gesner, Clark	Tenor	You're A Good Man Charlie	1971	Snoopy	Snoopy	Ballad	B2	G4	Character Male
Gesner, Clark	Tenor	You're A Good Man Charlie	1971	Snoopy	Suppertime*	Uptempo	C3	A4	Character Male
Goggin, Dan	Alto	Nunsense	1985	Mary Robert Anne	Growing Up Catholic*	Ballad	Ab3	Db5	Antagonist Female
Goggin, Dan	Alto	Nunsense	1985	Mary Leo	Benedicte*	Moderate Tempo	C4	G5	Ingenue Female
Goggin, Dan	Alto	Nunsense	1985	Mary Robert Anne	Playing Second Fiddle	Uptempo	B3	B4	Antagonist Female
Goggin, Dan	Alto	Nunsense	1985	Mary Hubert	Tackle That Temptation*	Uptempo	A3	D5	Antagonist Female
Goggin, Dan	Alto	Nunsense	1985	Mary Robert Anne	Second Fiddle Reprise	Uptempo	E4	B4	Antagonist Female
Goggin, Dan	Alto	Nunsense	1985	Mary Robert Anne	I Just Want To Be A Star*	Uptempo	G3	C5	Antagonist Female
Goggin, Dan	Alto	Nunsense	1985	Mary Hubert	Holier Than Thou*	Uptempo	Bb3	F5	Antagonist Female
Goggin, Dan	Soprano	Nunsense	1985	Mary Amnesia	I Could've Gone To Nashville	Ballad	G3	E5	Character Female
Goggin, Dan	Soprano	Nunsense	1985	Mary Amnesia	So You Want To Be A Nun	Moderate Tempo	C4	B5	Character Female
Gordon, Paul	Alto	Jane Eyre	2000	Jane Eyre	The Graveside	Ballad	A3	D5	Character Female
Gordon, Paul	Alto	Jane Eyre	2000	Jane Eyre	In the Virgin Morning*	Moderate Tempo	G3	D5	Character Female
Gordon, Paul	Alto	Jane Eyre	2000	Jane Eyre	Sirens Reprise*	Moderate Tempo	G3	C5	Character Female
Gordon, Paul	Alto	Jane Eyre	2000	Jane Eyre	The Voice Across the Moors	Moderate Tempo	Ab3	E5	Character Female
Gordon, Paul	Alto	Jane Eyre	2000	Mrs. Reed	Forgiveness Reprise	Moderate Tempo	G#3	B4	Mature Female
Gordon, Paul	Alto	Jane Eyre	2000	Jane Eyre	Sweet Liberty	Uptempo	A3	D5	Character Female
Gordon, Paul	Alto	Jane Eyre	2000	Jane Eyre	Secret Soul*	Uptempo	F#3	D4	Character Female

Composer	Vocal Range	Show	Year	Role	Song	Tempo	Range-Bottom	Range-Top	Char Type
Gordon, Paul	Alto	Jane Eyre	2000	Jane Eyre	Painting Her Portrait	Uptempo	B♭3	D5	Character Female
Gordon, Paul	Alto	Jane Eyre	2000	Jane Eyre	Brave Enough for Love*	Uptempo	E3	E♭5	Character Female
Gordon, Paul	Alto	Jane Eyre	2000	Mrs. Fairfax	Perfectly Nice	Uptempo	A3	C#5	Mature Female
Gordon, Paul	Alto	Jane Eyre	2000	Mrs. Fairfax	Slip of a Girl	Uptempo	F3	B♭4	Mature Female
Gordon, Paul	Soprano	Jane Eyre	2000	Helen Burnes	Forgiveness	Ballad	A3	C5	Juvenile Female
Gordon, Paul	Soprano	Jane Eyre	2000	Young Jane Eyre	The Graveside	Ballad	A3	D5	Juvenile Female
Gordon, Paul	Soprano	Jane Eyre	2000	Blanche Ingram	In the Virgin Morning*	Moderate Tempo	B3	F5	Ingenue Female
Gordon, Paul	Soprano	Jane Eyre	2000	School Girl	Rain	Moderate Tempo	B♭3	E5	Ingenue Female
Gordon, Paul	Soprano	Jane Eyre	2000	Blanche Ingram	The Finer Things	Uptempo	E♭4	B5	Ingenue Female
Gordon, Paul	Tenor	Jane Eyre	2000	Edward Fairfax Rocheste	As Good As You	Moderate Tempo	A2	E4	Romantic Antagonist Male
Gordon, Paul	Tenor	Jane Eyre	2000	St. John Rivers	The Voice Across the Moors	Moderate Tempo	C3	G4	Ingenue Male
Gordon, Paul	Tenor	Jane Eyre	2000	Edward Fairfax Rocheste	Secret Soul*	Uptempo	B2	B4	Romantic Antagonist Male
Gordon, Paul	Tenor	Jane Eyre	2000	Edward Fairfax Rocheste	Sirens	Uptempo	B♭2	F4	Romantic Antagonist Male
Gordon, Paul	Tenor	Jane Eyre	2000	Edward Fairfax Rocheste	The Gypsy (Drag)	Uptempo	D4	A5	Romantic Antagonist Male
Gordon, Paul	Tenor	Jane Eyre	2000	Edward Fairfax Rocheste	Farewell Good Angel	Uptempo	G2	G4	Romantic Antagonist Male
Gordon, Paul	Tenor	Jane Eyre	2000	Edward Fairfax Rocheste	Brave Enough for Love	Uptempo	D♭3	B♭4	Romantic Antagonist Male
Gordon, Paul	Tenor	Jane Eyre	2000	Edward Fairfax Rocheste	Brave Enough for Love*	Uptempo	D♭3	B♭4	Romantic Lead Male
Guettel, Adam	Soprano	Light In The Piazza, The	2005	Margaret Johnson	Dividing Day	Ballad	G3	E5	Romantic Lead Female
Guettel, Adam	Soprano	Light In The Piazza, The	2005	Clara Johnson	The Light in the Piazza	Moderate Tempo	A3	F#5	Ingenue Female
Guettel, Adam	Soprano	Light In The Piazza, The	2005	Margaret Johnson	The Beauty Is Reprise	Moderate Tempo	B#3	G5	Romantic Lead Female
Guettel, Adam	Soprano	Light In The Piazza, The	2005	Franca Naccarelli	The Joy You Feel	Moderate Tempo	C4	G♭4	Romantic Antagonist Female
Guettel, Adam	Soprano	Light In The Piazza, The	2005	Clara Johnson	The Beauty Is	Uptempo	C♭4	G5	Ingenue Female
Guettel, Adam	Soprano	Light In The Piazza, The	2005	Margaret Johnson	Statues and Stories*	Uptempo	A3	A5	Romantic Lead Female
Guettel, Adam	Soprano	Light In The Piazza, The	2005	Margaret Johnson	Fable	Uptempo	C#4	F#5	Romantic Lead Female
Guettel, Adam	Tenor	Light In The Piazza, The	2005	Fabrizio Naccarelli	Il Mondo Era Vuoto	Moderate Tempo	B♭2	A♭4	Ingenue Male
Guettel, Adam	Tenor	Light In The Piazza, The	2005	Fabrizio Naccarelli	Passegiata*	Moderate Tempo	B3	G#4	Ingenue Male
Guettel, Adam	Tenor	Light In The Piazza, The	2005	Fabrizio Naccarelli	Love To Me	Moderate Tempo	F4	F#5	Ingenue Male
Hall, Carol	Alto	Best Little Whorehouse...	1978	Doatsey Mae	Doatsey Mae	Ballad	G3	C5	Character Female
Hall, Carol	Alto	Best Little Whorehouse...	1978	Mona Stangley	Girl You're a Woman	Ballad	E2	G4	Character Female
Hall, Carol	Alto	Best Little Whorehouse...	1978	Mona's Girl	Hard Candy Christmas	Ballad	B♭3	C4	Character Ingenue Female
Hall, Carol	Alto	Best Little Whorehouse...	1978	Mona Stangley	Bus From Amarillo	Moderate Tempo	E3	B♭4	Character Female
Hall, Carol	Alto	Best Little Whorehouse...	1978	Mona Stangley	A Lil Ole Bitty Pissant Country Place	Uptempo	F3	D4	Character Female
Hall, Carol	Alto	Best Little Whorehouse...	1978	Mona Stangley	No Lies	Uptempo	G3	B4	Character Female

Composer

Composer	Vocal Range	Show	Year	Role	Song	Tempo	Range-Bottom	Range-Top	Char Type
Hall, Carol	Baritone	Best Little Whorehouse...	1978	Sherriff Ed Earl	Good Old Girl	Ballad	G3	F4	Romantic Lead Male
Hall, Carol	Baritone	Best Little Whorehouse...	1978	Governor	The Sidestep	Uptempo	A2	E4	Mature Male
Hall, Carol	Soprano	Best Little Whorehouse...	1978	Jewel	Twenty-four Hours of Lovin'	Uptempo	G3	G5	Character Female
Hall, Carol	Soprano	Best Little Whorehouse...	1978	Jewel	No Lies	Uptempo	C4	E5	Character Female
Hall, Carol	Tenor	Best Little Whorehouse...	1978	Melvin P Thorpe	Texas Has A Whorehouse In It	Uptempo	Bb2	E4	Character Male
Hamlisch, Marvin	Alto	A Chorus Line	1975	Diana +	What I Did For Love	Ballad	Bb3	D#5	Character Female
Hamlisch, Marvin	Alto	A Chorus Line	1975	Maggie	Mother *	Ballad	B3	D5	Character Ingenue Female
Hamlisch, Marvin	Alto	Goodbye Girl, The	1993	Paula McFadden	How Can I Win	Ballad	Ab3	D5	Romantic Lead Female
Hamlisch, Marvin	Alto	Goodbye Girl, The	1993	Paula McFadden	What A Guy	Ballad	F#3	C5	Romantic Lead Female
Hamlisch, Marvin	Alto	They're Playing Our Song	1974	Sonia Walsk	If He Really Knew Me*	Ballad	G3	B4	Romantic Lead Female
Hamlisch, Marvin	Alto	They're Playing Our Song	1974	Sonia Walsk	If He Really Knew Me Reprise*	Ballad	G3	Ab4	Romantic Lead Female
Hamlisch, Marvin	Alto	They're Playing Our Song	1974	Sonia Walsk	Just For Tonight	Ballad	G3	A4	Romantic Lead Female
Hamlisch, Marvin	Alto	A Chorus Line	1975	Bebe	At The Ballet	Moderate Tempo	A3	C#5	Character Female
Hamlisch, Marvin	Alto	A Chorus Line	1975	Cassie	The Music And The Mirror	Moderate Tempo	A#3	D5	Romantic Lead Female
Hamlisch, Marvin	Alto	A Chorus Line	1975	Maggie	At The Ballet	Moderate Tempo	A3	D5	Character Ingenue Female
Hamlisch, Marvin	Alto	A Chorus Line	1975	Sheila	At The Ballet	Moderate Tempo	E3	C#5	Romantic Antagonist Female
Hamlisch, Marvin	Alto	Goodbye Girl, The	1993	Actress	Too Good To Be Bad*	Moderate Tempo	A3	A4	Romantic Lead Female
Hamlisch, Marvin	Alto	Goodbye Girl, The	1993	Lucy McFadden	Good News, Bad News*	Moderate Tempo	Db4	Db5	Juvenile Female
Hamlisch, Marvin	Alto	Goodbye Girl, The	1993	Paula McFadden	No More	Moderate Tempo	G3	C5	Romantic Lead Female
Hamlisch, Marvin	Alto	Goodbye Girl, The	1993	Paula McFadden	My Rules	Moderate Tempo	Ab3	C5	Romantic Lead Female
Hamlisch, Marvin	Alto	Goodbye Girl, The	1993	Paula McFadden	Don't Follow In My Footsteps*	Moderate Tempo	D#3	C#5	Romantic Lead Female
Hamlisch, Marvin	Alto	Sweet Smell Of Success	2002	Rita	Rita's Tune	Moderate Tempo	A3	Eb5	Romantic Antagonist Female
Hamlisch, Marvin	Alto	They're Playing Our Song	1974	Sonia Walsk	Falling Reprise	Moderate Tempo	E3	A4	Romantic Lead Female
Hamlisch, Marvin	Alto	A Chorus Line	1975	Diana +	Nothing	Uptempo	G3	B4	Character Female
Hamlisch, Marvin	Alto	A Chorus Line	1975	Val	Dance: Ten; Looks: Three	Uptempo	Bb3	Db5	Ingenue Female
Hamlisch, Marvin	Alto	Goodbye Girl, The	1993	Mrs. Crosby+	Too Good To Be Bad*	Uptempo	Bb3	F4	Antagonist Female
Hamlisch, Marvin	Alto	Goodbye Girl, The	1993	Mrs. Crosby+	Too Good To Be Bad Play Off*	Uptempo	Bb3	F4	Antagonist Female
Hamlisch, Marvin	Alto	Goodbye Girl, The	1993	Paula McFadden	A Beat Behind*	Uptempo	F#3	B4	Romantic Lead Female
Hamlisch, Marvin	Alto	Sweet Smell Of Success	2002	Zanzibar Singer	Laughin' All The Way To The Bank	Uptempo	G#3	D4	Romantic Antagonist Female
Hamlisch, Marvin	Alto	They're Playing Our Song	1974	Sonia Walsk	Workin' It Out*	Uptempo	F3	B4	Romantic Lead Female
Hamlisch, Marvin	Alto	They're Playing Our Song	1974	Sonia Walsk	They're Playing My Song*	Uptempo	G3	Cb5	Romantic Lead Female
Hamlisch, Marvin	Alto	They're Playing Our Song	1974	Sonia Walsk	Right*	Uptempo	A3	G4	Romantic Lead Female
Hamlisch, Marvin	Baritone	Goodbye Girl, The	1993	Elliott Garfield	I Can Play This Part	Ballad	G#2	Eb4	Antagonist Male

Composer

Composer	Vocal Range	Show	Year	Role	Song	Tempo	Range-Bottom	Range-Top	Char Type
Hamlisch, Marvin	Baritone	They're Playing Our Song	1974	Vernon Gersch	If She Really Knew Me*	Ballad	B2	Cb5	Romantic Antagonist Male
Hamlisch, Marvin	Baritone	They're Playing Our Song	1974	Vernon Gersch	If She Really Knew Me Reprise*	Ballad	C3	D4	Romantic Antagonist Male
Hamlisch, Marvin	Baritone	Goodbye Girl, The	1993	Elliott Garfield	Good News, Bad News*	Moderate Tempo	Bb3	F4	Antagonist Male
Hamlisch, Marvin	Baritone	Goodbye Girl, The	1993	Elliott Garfield	Paula*	Moderate Tempo	G#2	E4	Antagonist Male
Hamlisch, Marvin	Baritone	Sweet Smell Of Success	2002	JJ Hunsecker	For Susan*	Moderate Tempo	C3	Eb4	Antagonist Male
Hamlisch, Marvin	Baritone	Sweet Smell Of Success	2002	JJ Hunsecker	Don't Look Now*	Moderate Tempo	C3	G4	Antagonist Male
Hamlisch, Marvin	Baritone	They're Playing Our Song	1974	Vernon Gersch	Falling	Moderate Tempo	A2	D4	Romantic Antagonist Male
Hamlisch, Marvin	Baritone	Goodbye Girl, The	1993	Billy	A Beat Behind*	Uptempo	E3	F#4	Character Male
Hamlisch, Marvin	Baritone	Goodbye Girl, The	1993	Elliott Garfield	Elliott Garfield Grant	Uptempo	C3	Gb4	Antagonist Male
Hamlisch, Marvin	Baritone	They're Playing Our Song	1974	Vernon Gersch	They're Playing My Song*	Uptempo	C3	F4	Romantic Antagonist Male
Hamlisch, Marvin	Soprano	Sweet Smell Of Success	2002	Susan	I Cannot Hear The City Reprise*	Ballad	Ab3	G5	Ingenue Female
Hamlisch, Marvin	Soprano	Sweet Smell Of Success	2002	Susan	What If*	Uptempo	A3	F5	Ingenue Female
Hamlisch, Marvin	Tenor	Sweet Smell Of Success	2002	Dallas	I Cannot Hear The City	Ballad	A3	G4	Romantic Lead Male
Hamlisch, Marvin	Tenor	Sweet Smell Of Success	2002	Dallas	I Cannot Hear The City (Act 1 Finale	Ballad	A2	Bb4	Romantic Lead Male
Hamlisch, Marvin	Tenor	Sweet Smell Of Success	2002	Sidney	At The Fountain	Moderate Tempo	F3	A4	Romantic Antagonist Male
Hamlisch, Marvin	Tenor	Sweet Smell Of Success	2002	Dallas	Don't Know Where You Leave Off*	Moderate Tempo	A2	G4	Romantic Antagonist Male
Hamlisch, Marvin	Tenor	Sweet Smell Of Success	2002	Sidney	I Could Get You In JJ Reprise	Moderate Tempo	D3	G#4	Romantic Antagonist Male
Hamlisch, Marvin	Tenor	Sweet Smell Of Success	2002	Sidney	At The Fountain Reprise*	Moderate Tempo	A2	F4	Romantic Antagonist Male
Hamlisch, Marvin	Tenor	A Chorus Line	1975	Mike	I Can Do That	Uptempo	G4	Ab4	Ingenue Male
Hamlisch, Marvin	Tenor	A Chorus Line	1975	Richie +	Gimmie The Ball (ms 231-269) *	Uptempo	C#3	G4	Antagonist Male
Hamlisch, Marvin	Tenor	Sweet Smell Of Success	2002	Sidney	I Can Get You In JJ	Uptempo	Db3	Ab4	Romantic Antagonist Male
Hamlisch, Marvin	Tenor	Sweet Smell Of Success	2002	Sidney	Welcome To The Night Reprise*	Uptempo	Db4	F4	Romantic Antagonist Male
Hamlisch, Marvin	Tenor	Sweet Smell Of Success	2002	Dallas	One Track Mind	Uptempo	E3	A4	Romantic Lead Male
Hamlisch, Marvin	Tenor	Sweet Smell Of Success	2002	Sidney	Break It Up*	Uptempo	E3	F4	Romantic Antagonist Male
Hamlisch, Marvin	Tenor	Sweet Smell Of Success	2002	Sidney	Finale (Part 3)	Uptempo	E3	F4	Romantic Antagonist Male
Hart, Lorenz & Rodgers	Alto	Pal Joey	1940	Linda English	I Could Write A Book*	Moderate Tempo	D4	D5	Ingenue Female
Hart, Lorenz & Rodgers	Alto	Pal Joey	1940	Gladys Bumps	That Terrific Rainbow	Moderate Tempo	B3	Bb4	Romantic Antagonist Female
Hart, Lorenz & Rodgers	Alto	Pal Joey	1940	Vera Simpson	What Is A Man	Moderate Tempo	D4	Eb5	Romantic Antagonist Female
Hart, Lorenz & Rodgers	Alto	Pal Joey	1940	Vera Simpson	Bewitched Bothered And Bewildered	Moderate Tempo	E4	D5	Romantic Antagonist Female
Hart, Lorenz & Rodgers	Alto	Pal Joey	1940	Vera Simpson	Bewitched...Encore	Moderate Tempo	F4	D5	Romantic Antagonist Female
Hart, Lorenz & Rodgers	Alto	Pal Joey	1940	Gladys Bumps	The Flower Garden Of My Heart*	Moderate Tempo	D4	F#5	Romantic Antagonist Female
Hart, Lorenz & Rodgers	Alto	Pal Joey	1940	Melba	Zip	Moderate Tempo	F3	G4	Romantic Antagonist Female
Hart, Lorenz & Rodgers	Alto	Pal Joey	1940	Linda English	Take Him*	Moderate Tempo	C4	D5	Ingenue Female
Hart, Lorenz & Rodgers	Alto	Pal Joey	1940	Vera Simpson	Take Him*	Moderate Tempo	C4	D5	Romantic Antagonist Female

Composer

Composer	Vocal Range	Show	Year	Role	Song	Tempo	Range-Bottom	Range-Top	Char Type
Hart, Lorenz & Rodgers	Alto	Pal Joey	1940	Vera Simpson	Bewitched...Reprise	Moderate Tempo	D4	D5	Romantic Antagonist Female
Hart, Lorenz & Rodgers	Alto	Pal Joey	2008	Gladys Bumps	Zip	Moderate Tempo	F3	G4	Romantic Antagonist Female
Hart, Lorenz & Rodgers	Alto	Pal Joey	1940	Gladys Bumps	You Mustn't Kick It Around Encore	Uptempo	A3	C5	Romantic Antagonist Female
Hart, Lorenz & Rodgers	Alto	Pal Joey	1940	Gladys Bumps	Plant You Now, Dig You Later	Uptempo	D4	D5	Romantic Antagonist Female
Hart, Lorenz & Rodgers	Alto	Pal Joey	1940	Vera Simpson	Den Of Iniguity*	Uptempo	G4	Eb5	Romantic Antagonist Female
Hart, Lorenz & Rodgers	Baritone	Pal Joey	1940	Joey Evans	I Could Write A Book*	Moderate Tempo	Eb3	Eb4	Romantic Antagonist Male
Hart, Lorenz & Rodgers	Baritone	Pal Joey	1940	Joey Evans	Happy Hunting Horn	Moderate Tempo	Ab3	F4	Romantic Antagonist Male
Hart, Lorenz & Rodgers	Baritone	Pal Joey	1940	Joey Evans	Do It The Hard Way	Moderate Tempo	C3	C4	Romantic Antagonist Male
Hart, Lorenz & Rodgers	Baritone	Pal Joey	1940	Joey Evans	Finale-I Could Write A Book	Moderate Tempo	Eb3	Eb4	Romantic Antagonist Male
Hart, Lorenz & Rodgers	Baritone	Pal Joey	1940	Joey Evans	A Great Big Town	Uptempo	Eb3	F4	Romantic Antagonist Male
Hart, Lorenz & Rodgers	Baritone	Pal Joey	1940	Joey Evans	You Mustn't Kick It Around	Uptempo	D3	F4	Romantic Antagonist Male
Hart, Lorenz & Rodgers	Baritone	Pal Joey	1940	Joey Evans	What Do I Care For A Dame	Uptempo	D3	C#4	Romantic Antagonist Male
Hart, Lorenz & Rodgers	Baritone	Pal Joey	1940	Joey Evans	Den Of Iniguity*	Uptempo	G3	Eb4	Romantic Antagonist Male
Hart, Lorenz & Rodgers	Tenor	Pal Joey	1940	Louis	The Flower Garden Of My Heart*	Moderate Tempo	Eb3	G4	Character Male
Henderson, Ray	Alto	Good News (1993 Revival)	1927	Connie Lane	The Best Things In Life Are Free*	Ballad	A3	D5	Character Ingenue Female
Henderson, Ray	Alto	Good News (1993 Revival)	1927	Connie Lane	Just Imagine	Ballad	B3	E5	Character Ingenue Female
Henderson, Ray	Alto	Good News (1993 Revival)	1928	Professor Kenyan	Together*	Ballad	G3	B4	Romantic Lead Female
Henderson, Ray	Alto	Good News (1993 Revival)	1928	Professor Kenyan	Together Part 2*	Ballad	G3	C5	Romantic Lead Female
Henderson, Ray	Alto	Good News (1993 Revival)	1927	Pat	The Girl Of Pi Beta Phi	Moderate Tempo	G3	A4	Ingenue Female
Henderson, Ray	Alto	Good News (1993 Revival)	1928	Connie Lane	My Lucky Star	Moderate Tempo	Bb3	Db5	Character Ingenue Female
Henderson, Ray	Alto	Good News (1993 Revival)	1927	Babe O'Day	The Varsity Drag	Uptempo	Bb3	C5	Ingenue Female
Henderson, Ray	Alto	Good News (1993 Revival)	1927	Connie Lane	Lucky In Love*	Uptempo	C4	Eb5	Character Ingenue Female
Henderson, Ray	Alto	Good News (1993 Revival)	1927	Pat	Lucky In Love*	Uptempo	A3	C5	Ingenue Female
Henderson, Ray	Alto	Good News (1993 Revival)	1928	Babe O'Day	Button Up Your Overcoat*	Uptempo	C4	C5	Ingenue Female
Henderson, Ray	Alto	Good News (1993 Revival)	1928	Professor Kenyan	You're The Cream In My Coffee*	Uptempo	Db4	Eb5	Romantic Lead Female
Henderson, Ray	Alto	Good News (1993 Revival)	1930	Babe O'Day	Never Swat A Fly*	Uptempo	A3	C#5	Ingenue Female
Henderson, Ray	Alto	Good News (1993 Revival)	1931	Professor Kenyan	Life Is Just A Bowl Of Cherries	Uptempo	A3	Db5	Romantic Lead Female
Henderson, Ray	Baritone	Good News (1993 Revival)	1927	Tom Marlowe	The Best Things In Life Are Free*	Ballad	C3	Eb4	Ingenue Male
Henderson, Ray	Baritone	Good News (1993 Revival)	1928	Coach Johnson	Together*	Ballad	G3	B4	Romantic Lead Male
Henderson, Ray	Baritone	Good News (1993 Revival)	1928	Coach Johnson	Together Part 2*	Ballad	G2	C4	Romantic Lead Male
Henderson, Ray	Baritone	Good News (1993 Revival)	1927	Tom Marlowe	Lucky In Love*	Uptempo	D3	F4	Ingenue Male
Henderson, Ray	Baritone	Good News (1993 Revival)	1928	Bobby Randall	Button Up Your Overcoat*	Uptempo	E3	F#4	Ingenue Male
Henderson, Ray	Baritone	Good News (1993 Revival)	1928	Coach Johnson	You're The Cream In My Coffee*	Uptempo	B2	Eb4	Romantic Lead Male

Composer

Composer	Vocal Range	Show	Year	Role	Song	Tempo	Range-Bottom	Range-Top	Char Type
Henderson, Ray	Baritone	Good News (1993 Revival)	1929	Pooch Kearney	Keep Your Sunny Side Up*	Uptempo	Bb2	F4	Character Male
Henderson, Ray	Baritone	Good News (1993 Revival)	1930	Bobby Randall	Never Swat A Fly*	Uptempo	A2	E4	Ingenue Male
Herman, Jerry	Alto	Dear World	1969	Nina	I've Never Said I Love You	Ballad	Bb3	Eb5	Ingenue Female
Herman, Jerry	Alto	Dear World	1969	Countess Aurelia	And I Was Beautiful	Ballad	G3	D5	Mature Female
Herman, Jerry	Alto	Dear World	1969	Countess Aurelia	Kiss Her Now	Ballad	G#3	A4	Mature Female
Herman, Jerry	Alto	Hello Dolly	1964	Dolly Levi	Before The Parade Passes By Reprise	Ballad	C3	F4	Mature Female
Herman, Jerry	Alto	Hello Dolly	1970	Dolly Levi	Love, Look In MY Window	Ballad	C4	F5	Mature Female
Herman, Jerry	Alto	Mack and Mabel	1974	Mabel Normand	Mabel's Roses	Ballad	G3	D5	Ingenue Female
Herman, Jerry	Alto	Mack and Mabel	1974	Mabel Normand	Time Heals Everything	Ballad	F#3	C#5	Ingenue Female
Herman, Jerry	Alto	Mame	1966	Vera Charles	The Man In The Moon	Ballad	Eb3	A4	Romantic Antagonist Female
Herman, Jerry	Alto	Mame	1966	Young Patrick Dennis	You're My Best Girl*	Ballad	A3	C5	Juvenile Male
Herman, Jerry	Alto	Mame	1966	Mame	If He Walked Into My Life	Ballad	F#3	Bb4	Romantic Lead Female
Herman, Jerry	Alto	Mame	1966	Mame	You're My Best Girl*	Ballad	G3	Bb4	Romantic Lead Female
Herman, Jerry	Alto	Dear World	1969	Countess Aurelia	I Don't Want To Know	Moderate Tempo	G#3	A4	Mature Female
Herman, Jerry	Alto	Dear World	1969	Countess Aurelia	Each Tomorrow Morning	Moderate Tempo	E3	Bb4	Mature Female
Herman, Jerry	Alto	Dear World	1969	Countess Aurelia	Dear World*	Moderate Tempo	E3	A4	Mature Female
Herman, Jerry	Alto	Hello Dolly	1964	Dolly Levi	Before The Parade Passes By	Moderate Tempo	D3	F4	Mature Female
Herman, Jerry	Alto	Hello Dolly	1964	Dolly Levi	Hello Dolly	Moderate Tempo	Bb2	F4	Mature Female
Herman, Jerry	Alto	Hello Dolly	1964	Dolly Levi	Before The Parade Passes By	Moderate Tempo	F3	F4	Mature Female
Herman, Jerry	Alto	Hello Dolly	1964	Dolly Levi	Dancing*	Moderate Tempo	D3	D5	Mature Female
Herman, Jerry	Alto	Hello Dolly	1970	Dolly Levi	World Take Me Back	Moderate Tempo	C4	E5	Mature Female
Herman, Jerry	Alto	Mame	1966	Mame	It's Today Reprise 2*	Moderate Tempo	A3	Eb5	Romantic Lead Female
Herman, Jerry	Alto	Dear World	1969	Countess Aurelia	One Person*	Uptempo	F3	Bb4	Mature Female
Herman, Jerry	Alto	Dear World	1969	Countess Aurelia	Thoughts	Uptempo	G3	D5	Mature Female
Herman, Jerry	Alto	Hello Dolly	1964	Dolly Levi	I Put My Hand In	Uptempo	Eb3	G4	Mature Female
Herman, Jerry	Alto	Hello Dolly	1964	Dolly Levi	Motherhood*	Uptempo	D3	F4	Mature Female
Herman, Jerry	Alto	Hello Dolly	1964	Dolly Levi	So Long Dearie	Uptempo	D3	G4	Mature Female
Herman, Jerry	Alto	Hello Dolly	1964	Dolly Levi	I Put My Hand In	Uptempo	Ab3	C5	Mature Female
Herman, Jerry	Alto	Hello Dolly	1964	Dolly Levi	Motherhood	Uptempo	F3	A4	Mature Female
Herman, Jerry	Alto	Mack and Mabel	1974	Lottie Ames	Big Time*	Uptempo	F#3	Eb5	Character Female
Herman, Jerry	Alto	Mack and Mabel	1974	Lottie Ames	Tap Your Troubles Away	Uptempo	F3	Bb4	Character Female
Herman, Jerry	Alto	Mack and Mabel	1974	Mabel Normand	Look What Happened to Mabel*	Uptempo	Gb3	C5	Ingenue Female
Herman, Jerry	Alto	Mack and Mabel	1974	Mabel Normand	Wherever He Ain't	Uptempo	A3	C5	Ingenue Female

Composer

Composer	Vocal Range	Show	Year	Role	Song	Tempo	Range-Bottom	Range-Top	Char Type
Herman, Jerry	Alto	Mame	1966	Mame	It's Today*	Uptempo	A3	D5	Romantic Lead Female
Herman, Jerry	Alto	Mame	1966	Mame	Open A New Window*	Uptempo	A3	D5	Romantic Lead Female
Herman, Jerry	Alto	Mame	1966	Mame	We Need A Little Christmas*	Uptempo	F3	Bb4	Romantic Lead Female
Herman, Jerry	Alto	Mame	1966	Young Patrick Dennis	The Letter*	Uptempo	C#4	Bb4	Juvenile Male
Herman, Jerry	Alto	Mame	1966	Mame	That's How Young I Feel*	Uptempo	G3	Bb4	Romantic Lead Female
Herman, Jerry	Alto	Mame	1966	Mame	It's Today Reprise*	Uptempo	F3	Bb4	Romantic Lead Female
Herman, Jerry	Alto	Mame	1966	Mame	We Need A Little Christmas*	Uptempo	C#4	D5	Romantic Lead Female
Herman, Jerry	Baritone	Hello Dolly	1964	Cornelius Hackl	It Only Takes A Moment*	Ballad	Bb2	Eb4	Character Ingenue Male
Herman, Jerry	Baritone	LA Cage Aux Folles	1983	Georges	Song On The Sand	Ballad	Ab2	E4	Romantic Lead Male
Herman, Jerry	Baritone	LA Cage Aux Folles	1983	Georges	Look Over There	Ballad	B2	Eb4	Romantic Lead Male
Herman, Jerry	Baritone	LA Cage Aux Folles	1983	Georges	Song On The Sand Reprise	Ballad	C3	D4	Romantic Antagonist Male
Herman, Jerry	Baritone	Mack and Mabel	1974	Mack Sennett	I Wont Send Roses	Ballad	G2	Eb4	Romantic Antagonist Male
Herman, Jerry	Baritone	Mack and Mabel	1974	Mack Sennett	I Promise You a Happy Ending	Ballad	G2	D4	Ingenue Male
Herman, Jerry	Baritone	Mame	1966	Patrick Dennis	My Best Girl Reprise	Ballad	C3	E4	Ingenue Male
Herman, Jerry	Baritone	Mame	1966	Patrick Dennis	My Best Girl Reprise 2	Ballad	C3	E4	Character Male
Herman, Jerry	Baritone	Dear World	1969	President	The Spring Of Next Year*	Moderate Tempo	G2	D4	Character Male
Herman, Jerry	Baritone	Dear World	1969	Sewerman	Pretty Garbage*	Moderate Tempo	B2	E4	Character Male
Herman, Jerry	Baritone	Dear World	1969	Sewerman	Ugly Garbage*	Moderate Tempo	A3	E4	Character Ingenue Male
Herman, Jerry	Baritone	Hello Dolly	1964	Barnaby Tucker	Elegance*	Moderate Tempo	C3	F4	Character Ingenue Male
Herman, Jerry	Baritone	Hello Dolly	1964	Cornelius Hackl	Elegance*	Moderate Tempo	C3	F4	Mature Male
Herman, Jerry	Baritone	Hello Dolly	1964	Horace Vandergelder	Hello Dolly	Moderate Tempo	B2	D4	Character Male
Herman, Jerry	Baritone	LA Cage Aux Folles	1983	Albin	I Am What I Am (Drag)	Moderate Tempo	G#3	F4	Character Male
Herman, Jerry	Baritone	LA Cage Aux Folles	1983	Albin	The Best Of Times (Drag)	Moderate Tempo	C3	Eb4	Character Male
Herman, Jerry	Baritone	LA Cage Aux Folles	1983	Albin	With You On My Arm	Moderate Tempo	G#2	Eb4	Character Male
Herman, Jerry	Baritone	LA Cage Aux Folles	1983	Albin	La Cage Aux Folles (Drag)	Moderate Tempo	Bb2	E4	Romantic Lead Male
Herman, Jerry	Baritone	LA Cage Aux Folles	1983	Georges	With You On My Arm	Moderate Tempo	G#2	Eb4	Ingenue Male
Herman, Jerry	Baritone	LA Cage Aux Folles	1983	Jean-Michel	Look Over There Reprise	Tenor	Db3	Eb4	Character Male
Herman, Jerry	Baritone	Dear World	1969	President	Just A Little Bit More*	Uptempo	G2	Fb4	Character Male
Herman, Jerry	Baritone	Dear World	1969	President	Just A Little Bit More Reprise*	Uptempo	Gb3	Eb4	Character Ingenue Male
Herman, Jerry	Baritone	Hello Dolly	1964	Cornelius Hackl	Put On Your Sunday Clothes	Uptempo	C3	G#4	Mature Male
Herman, Jerry	Baritone	Hello Dolly	1964	Horace Vandergelder	It Takes A Woman	Uptempo	G#2	G5	Mature Male
Herman, Jerry	Baritone	LA Cage Aux Folles	1983	Albin	A Little More Mascara (Drag)	Uptempo	Bb2	D4	Character Male
Herman, Jerry	Baritone	LA Cage Aux Folles	1983	Georges	Masculinity	Uptempo	B2	E4	Romantic Lead Male

Composer

Composer	Vocal Range	Show	Year	Role	Song	Tempo	Range-Bottom	Range-Top	Char Type
Herman, Jerry	Baritone	Mack and Mabel	1974	Mack Sennett	Movies Were Movies	Uptempo	A2	Eb4	Romantic Antagonist Male
Herman, Jerry	Baritone	Mack and Mabel	1974	Mack Sennett	Make The World Laugh*	Uptempo	A2	G4	Romantic Antagonist Male
Herman, Jerry	Baritone	Mack and Mabel	1974	Mack Sennett	Hundreds of Girls*	Uptempo	B2	F4	Romantic Antagonist Male
Herman, Jerry	Baritone	Mame	1966	Patrick Dennis	The Letter*	Uptempo	D#3	D4	Ingenue Male
Herman, Jerry	Soprano	Hello Dolly	1964	Irene Molloy	Ribbons Down My Back	Ballad	A3	D5	Romantic Lead Female
Herman, Jerry	Soprano	Hello Dolly	1964	Irene Molloy	It Only Takes A Moment*	Ballad	Ab3	Db4	Romantic Lead Female
Herman, Jerry	Soprano	Hello Dolly	1964	Irene Molloy	Ribbons Down My Back Reprise	Ballad	B3	D5	Romantic Lead Female
Herman, Jerry	Soprano	Mame	1966	Anges Gooch	St. Bridget*	Ballad	G3	F5	Character Female
Herman, Jerry	Soprano	Dear World	1969	Madame Constance	Memory	Moderate Tempo	A3	F5	Mature Female
Herman, Jerry	Soprano	Dear World	1969	Countess Aurelia	Through The Bottom Of The Glass	Moderate Tempo	E3	A4	Mature Female
Herman, Jerry	Soprano	Hello Dolly	1964	Irene Molloy	Dancing*	Moderate Tempo	G3	E5	Romantic Lead Female
Herman, Jerry	Soprano	Mame	1966	Anges Gooch	Gooch's Song	Moderate Tempo	G3	Bb5	Character Female
Herman, Jerry	Soprano	Dear World	1969	Madame Constance	Voices	Uptempo	F4	E5	Mature Female
Herman, Jerry	Soprano	Dear World	1969	Madame Gabrielle	Dickie	Uptempo	G3	E5	Mature Female
Herman, Jerry	Soprano	Hello Dolly	1964	Irene Molloy	Motherhood	Uptempo	D4	E5	Romantic Lead Female
Herman, Jerry	Tenor	LA Cage Aux Folles	1983	Jean-Michel	With Anne On My Arm	Moderate Tempo	A#2	G4	Ingenue Male
Herrmann, Keith	Alto	Romance/Romance	1987	Jospehine Weninger	The Night It Had To End	Ballad	Ab3	Db5	Romantic Antagonist Female
Herrmann, Keith	Alto	Romance/Romance	1987	Jospehine Weninger	It's Not Too Late*	Moderate Tempo	G3	Cb5	Romantic Antagonist Female
Herrmann, Keith	Alto	Romance/Romance	1987	Jospehine Weninger	A Performance*	Moderate Tempo	G3	D#5	Romantic Antagonist Female
Herrmann, Keith	Alto	Romance/Romance	1987	Monica	How Did I End Up Here	Uptempo	F3	C5	Romantic Antagonist Female
Herrmann, Keith	Alto	Romance/Romance	1987	Monica	Now	Uptempo	A3	D5	Romantic Antagonist Female
Herrmann, Keith	Alto	Romance/Romance	1987	Jospehine Weninger	Goodbye Emil	Uptempo	A3	F5	Romantic Antagonist Female
Herrmann, Keith	Alto	Romance/Romance	1987	Jospehine Weninger	Goodbye Emil Reprise	Uptempo	Bb3	E5	Romantic Antagonist Female
Herrmann, Keith	Alto	Romance/Romance	1987	Jospehine Weninger	I'll Remember The Song*	Uptempo	B3	D4	Romantic Antagonist Female
Herrmann, Keith	Alto	Romance/Romance	1987	Jospehine Weninger	Yes, It's Love	Uptempo	Ab3	C5	Romantic Antagonist Female
Herrmann, Keith	Alto	Romance/Romance	1987	Jospehine Weninger	A Rustic Country Inn*	Uptempo	G3	E5	Romantic Antagonist Female
Herrmann, Keith	Alto	Romance/Romance	1987	Monica	Plan A and B	Uptempo	Ab3	A4	Romantic Antagonist Female
Herrmann, Keith	Tenor	Romance/Romance	1987	Sam	There Are Things He Doesn't Say	Ballad	Ab2	G4	Romantic Antagonist Male
Herrmann, Keith	Tenor	Romance/Romance	1987	Sam	Moonlight Passing Through A Window	Ballad	D3	F4	Romantic Antagonist Male
Herrmann, Keith	Tenor	Romance/Romance	1987	Sam	Romantic Notions*	Ballad	B3	E4	Romantic Antagonist Male
Herrmann, Keith	Tenor	Romance/Romance	1987	Alfred Von Wilmers	Happy, Happy, Happy	Ballad	Bb2	F#4	Romantic Antagonist Male
Herrmann, Keith	Tenor	Romance/Romance	1987	Alfred Von Wilmers	It's Not Too Late*	Moderate Tempo	Bb2	F4	Romantic Antagonist Male
Herrmann, Keith	Tenor	Romance/Romance	1987	Alfred Von Wilmers	A Performance*	Moderate Tempo	A2	F#4	Romantic Antagonist Male
Herrmann, Keith	Tenor	Romance/Romance	1987	Alfred Von Wilmers	Women Of Vienna	Moderate Tempo	C3	F#4	Romantic Antagonist Male

Composer

Composer	Vocal Range	Show	Year	Role	Song	Tempo	Range-Bottom	Range-Top	Char Type
Herrmann, Keith	Tenor	Romance/Romance	1987	Sam	It's Not Too Late Reprise*	Moderate Tempo	B♭2	A4	Romantic Antagonist Male
Herrmann, Keith	Tenor	Romance/Romance	1987	Alfred Von Wilmers	I'll Remember The Song*	Uptempo	B2	E4	Romantic Antagonist Male
Herrmann, Keith	Tenor	Romance/Romance	1987	Alfred Von Wilmers	A Rustic Country Inn*	Uptempo	C3	F4	Romantic Antagonist Male
Holmes, Rupert	Alto	Mystery Of Edwin Drood, Th	1985	Princess Puffer	Garden Path To Hell	Ballad	G3	A4	Antagonist Female
Holmes, Rupert	Alto	Mystery Of Edwin Drood, Th	1985	Princess Puffer	Puffer's Confession	Ballad	C4	C5	Antagonist Female
Holmes, Rupert	Alto	Mystery Of Edwin Drood, Th	1985	Princess Puffer	The Wages Of Sin	Moderate Tempo	F3	C5	Antagonist Female
Holmes, Rupert	Alto	Mystery Of Edwin Drood, Th	1985	Princess Puffer	Don't Quit While You're Ahead*	Moderate Tempo	F3	A4	Antagonist Female
Holmes, Rupert	Alto	Mystery Of Edwin Drood, Th	1985	Dick Datchery	Out On A Limerick	Moderate Tempo	C3	E4	Character Male
Holmes, Rupert	Alto	Mystery Of Edwin Drood, Th	1985	Helena Landless	Helena's Confession	Moderate Tempo	G3	B4	Romantic Antagonist Female
Holmes, Rupert	Baritone	Mystery Of Edwin Drood, Th	1985	Durdle	Durdle's Confession	Ballad	C3	E4	Character Male
Holmes, Rupert	Baritone	Mystery Of Edwin Drood, Th	1985	Chrisparkle	Chrisparkle's Confession	Moderate Tempo	D3	F4	Mature Male
Holmes, Rupert	Baritone	Mystery Of Edwin Drood, Th	1985	Neville Landless	Neville's Confession	Moderate Tempo	G♭3	F4	Romantic Antagonist Male
Holmes, Rupert	Baritone	Mystery Of Edwin Drood, Th	1985	Chairman	There You Are*	Uptempo	D3	D4	Mature Male
Holmes, Rupert	Baritone	Mystery Of Edwin Drood, Th	1985	Chairman	Both Sides Of The Coin*	Uptempo	C3	F#4	Mature Male
Holmes, Rupert	Baritone	Mystery Of Edwin Drood, Th	1985	Chairman	Off To The Races*	Uptempo	C3	F4	Mature Male
Holmes, Rupert	Soprano	Mystery Of Edwin Drood, Th	1985	Rosa Bud	Moonfall	Ballad	B3	G5	Ingenue Female
Holmes, Rupert	Soprano	Mystery Of Edwin Drood, Th	1985	Rosa Bud	Perfect Strangers*	Moderate Tempo	C#4	F5	Ingenue Female
Holmes, Rupert	Soprano	Mystery Of Edwin Drood, Th	1985	Rosa Bud	Rosa's Confession	Uptempo	A3	A♭5	Ingenue Female
Holmes, Rupert	Soprano	Mystery Of Edwin Drood, Th	1985	Edwin Drood	The Writing On The Wall*	Uptempo	G3	G♭5	Character Female
Holmes, Rupert	Tenor	Mystery Of Edwin Drood, Th	1985	Bazzard	Never The Luck*	Moderate Tempo	C3	G4	Character Male
Holmes, Rupert	Tenor	Mystery Of Edwin Drood, Th	1985	John Jasper	Jasper's Confession	Moderate Tempo	B2	A4	Antagonist Male
Holmes, Rupert	Tenor	Mystery Of Edwin Drood, Th	1985	John Jasper	A Man Could Go Quite Mad	Uptempo	A2	G4	Antagonist Male
Holmes, Rupert	Tenor	Mystery Of Edwin Drood, Th	1985	John Jasper	Both Sides Of The Coin*	Uptempo	C3	E4	Antagonist Male
Holmes, Rupert	Tenor	Mystery Of Edwin Drood, Th	1985	Bazzard	Bazzard's Confession	Uptempo	A2	G4	Character Male
Howland, Jason	Alto	Little Women	2005	Josephine March	Volcano Reprise	Ballad	A3	D5	Character Ingenue Female
Howland, Jason	Alto	Little Women	2005	Marmee	Here Alone	Ballad	G3	E♭5	Maternal
Howland, Jason	Alto	Little Women	2005	Marmee	Days of Plenty	Ballad	E♭3	D♭5	Maternal
Howland, Jason	Alto	Little Women	2005	Josephine March	The Fire Within Me	Moderate Tempo	A♭3	B♭4	Character Ingenue Female
Howland, Jason	Alto	Little Women	2005	Aunt March	Could You*	Uptempo	D3	F5	Mature Female
Howland, Jason	Alto	Little Women	2005	Josephine March	Better	Uptempo	B3	B4	Character Ingenue Female
Howland, Jason	Alto	Little Women	2005	Josephine March	Our Finest Dreams	Uptempo	F#3	D♭5	Character Ingenue Female
Howland, Jason	Alto	Little Women	2005	Josephine March	Better Reprise	Uptempo	B2	B4	Character Ingenue Female
Howland, Jason	Alto	Little Women	2005	Josephine March	Astonishing	Uptempo	A♭3	E♭5	Character Ingenue Female
Howland, Jason	Baritone	Little Women	2005	John Brooke	More Than I Am*	Moderate Tempo	E3	E4	Ingenue Male

Composer

321

Composer	Vocal Range	Show	Year	Role	Song	Tempo	Range-Bottom	Range-Top	Char Type
Howland, Jason	Baritone	Little Women	2005	Professor Bhaer	How I Am	Uptempo	A2	F#4	Romantic Lead Male
Howland, Jason	Soprano	Little Women	2005	Beth March	Off to Massachusettes*	Moderate Tempo	C#4	F5	Ingenue Female
Howland, Jason	Soprano	Little Women	2005	Meg March	More Than I Am*	Moderate Tempo	E4	E5	Ingenue Female
Howland, Jason	Soprano	Little Women	2005	Beth March	Some Things Are Meant To Be	Uptempo	B2	E5	Ingenue Female
Howland, Jason	Tenor	Little Women	2005	Laurie Laurence	Take a Chance On Me	Uptempo	B3	Bb4	Ingenue Male
John, Elton	Alto	Aida	2000	Aida +	The Gods Love Nubia	Alto	C4	E5	Romantic Lead Female
John, Elton	Alto	Aida	2000	Aida +	The Past Is Another Land	Ballad	A3	B4	Romantic Lead Female
John, Elton	Alto	Aida	2000	Aida +	Elaborate Lies Reprise	Ballad	G3	C5	Romantic Lead Female
John, Elton	Alto	Aida	2000	Amneris	Every Story is a Love Story	Ballad	G3	Ab4	Romantic Antagonist Female
John, Elton	Alto	Aida	2000	Amneris	My Strongest Suit Reprise	Ballad	Bb3	G4	Romantic Lead Female
John, Elton	Alto	Aida	2000	Amneris	I Know the Truth	Ballad	E3	D5	Romantic Lead Female
John, Elton	Alto	Aida	2000	Amneris	Every Story Reprise (Finale AII)	Ballad	G3	Ab4	Romantic Lead Female
John, Elton	Alto	Billy Elliot	2008	Billy Elliot	Electricity	Ballad	F3	B4	Juvenile Male
John, Elton	Alto	Billy Elliot	2008	Billy Elliot	Billy's Reply *	Ballad	G3	D5	Juvenile Male
John, Elton	Alto	Billy Elliot	2008	Billy Elliot	The Letter *	Ballad	G3	D5	Juvenile Male
John, Elton	Alto	Lion King, The	1997	Nala	Shadowland*	Ballad	E3	B4	Ingenue Female
John, Elton	Alto	Lion King, The	1997	Rafiki	Rafiki Mourns (Eulogy)	Ballad	G3	Eb5	Character Female
John, Elton	Alto	Aida	2000	Aida +	Easy As Life	Moderate Tempo	G3	C5	Romantic Lead Female
John, Elton	Alto	Billy Elliot	2008	Grandma	We'd Go Dancing	Moderate Tempo	F3	G4	Mature Female
John, Elton	Alto	Billy Elliot	2008	Mrs. Wilkinson	Shine	Moderate Tempo	Gb3	B4	Character Female
John, Elton	Alto	Lion King, The	1997	Rafiki	Circle of Life*	Moderate Tempo	F#3	C5	Character Female
John, Elton	Alto	Lion King, The	1997	Rafiki	He Lives In You*	Moderate Tempo	C4	E5	Character Female
John, Elton	Alto	Aida	2000	Amneris	My Strongest Suit	Uptempo	Gb3	Eb5	Romantic Lead Female
John, Elton	Alto	Billy Elliot	2008	Michael	Expressing Yourself	Uptempo	G3	B4	Juvenile Male
John, Elton	Alto	Billy Elliot	2008	Michael	Expressing Yourself Playout	Uptempo	D4	Bb4	Juvenile Male
John, Elton	Alto	Billy Elliot	2008	Mrs. Wilkinson	Born To Boogie	Uptempo	G3	A4	Character Female
John, Elton	Alto	Lion King, The	1997	Young Simba	I Just Can't Wait To Be King*	Uptempo	C4	C5	Juvenile Male
John, Elton	Baritone	Billy Elliot	2008	Dad	Deep In The Ground *	Ballad	Bb2	Eb4	Paternal
John, Elton	Baritone	Lion King, The	1997	Mufasa	They Live In You*	Moderate Tempo	C#3	F#4	Romantic Lead Male
John, Elton	Baritone	Lion King, The	1997	Scar	Be Prepared*	Uptempo	A2	A3	Antagonist Male
John, Elton	Baritone	Lion King, The	1997	Scar	Be Prepared Reprise*	Uptempo	A2	D3	Antagonist Male
John, Elton	Baritone	Lion King, The	1997	Zazu	The Morning Report*	Uptempo	Eb3	F4	Character Male
John, Elton	Soprano	Billy Elliot	2008	Dead Mum	The Letter *	Ballad	G3	D5	Maternal
John, Elton	Tenor	Aida	2000	Mereb +	How I Know You*	Ballad	G2	A4	Ingenue Male

Composer	Vocal Range	Show	Year	Role	Song	Tempo	Range-Bottom	Range-Top	Char Type
John, Elton	Tenor	Aida	2000	Mereb +	How I Know You Reprise	Ballad	F3	G4	Ingenue Male
John, Elton	Tenor	Aida	2000	Radames	Elaborate Lies	Ballad	B♭2	A♭4	Romantic Lead Male
John, Elton	Tenor	Aida	2000	Radames	Radames' Letter	Ballad	C3	G4	Romantic Lead Male
John, Elton	Tenor	Lion King, The	1997	Simba	Endless Night*	Ballad	E4	A4	Ingenue Male
John, Elton	Tenor	Aida	2000	Radames	Fortune Favors the Brave	Uptempo	B♭2	F4	Romantic Lead Male
John, Elton	Tenor	Aida	2000	Radames	Like Father Like Son*	Uptempo	G3	F4	Romantic Lead Male
John, Elton	Tenor	Aida	2000	Radames	Fortune Favors the Brave Reprise	Uptempo	F3	G4	Romantic Lead Male
John, Elton	Tenor	Aida	2000	Zoser	Another Pyramid	Uptempo	F3	E4	Antagonist Male
John, Elton	Tenor	Aida	2000	Zoser	Like Father Like Son*	Uptempo	G3	B♭4	Antagonist Male
Kander, John	Alto	Cabaret	1966	Faulein Kost	Married *	Ballad	F#3	B♭4	Character Female
Kander, John	Alto	Cabaret	1966	Fraulein Scheider	What Would You Do	Ballad	F3	G4	Mature Female
Kander, John	Alto	Cabaret	1966	Sally Bowles	Maybe This Time	Ballad	F#3	C5	Romantic Lead Female
Kander, John	Alto	Chicago	1975	Mama Morton	Class*	Ballad	F3	B4	Character Female
Kander, John	Alto	Chicago	1975	Roxie Hart	Funny Honey	Ballad	F3	B♭4	Character Ingenue Female
Kander, John	Alto	Chicago	1975	Velma Kelly	Class*	Ballad	F3	B4	Romantic Antagonist Female
Kander, John	Alto	Cutains	2007	Georgia Hendricks	Thinking of Him	Ballad	G3	D♭5	Romantic Lead Female
Kander, John	Alto	Kiss Of The Spider Woman	1993	Aurora	Spider Woman Fragment 1	Ballad	F3	F4	Romantic Antagonist Female
Kander, John	Alto	Kiss Of The Spider Woman	1993	Mother	Dear One*	Ballad	B♭3	C5	Mature Female
Kander, John	Alto	Kiss Of The Spider Woman	1993	Marta	Dear One*	Ballad	C4	E♭5	Character Ingenue Female
Kander, John	Alto	Cabaret	1966	Faulein Kost	Tomorrow Belongs to Me Reprise *	Moderate Tempo	A3	B♭4	Character Female
Kander, John	Alto	Cabaret	1972	Sally Bowles	Mein Herr	Moderate Tempo	F3	B4	Romantic Lead Female
Kander, John	Alto	Chicago	1975	Mama Morton	When You're Good To Mama	Moderate Tempo	F#3	A4	Character Female
Kander, John	Alto	Chicago	1975	Roxie Hart	Roxie	Moderate Tempo	G3	B♭4	Character Ingenue Female
Kander, John	Alto	Chicago	1975	Roxie Hart	My Own Best Friend	Moderate Tempo	E3	A4	Character Ingenue Female
Kander, John	Alto	Chicago	1975	Roxie Hart	Nowadays	Moderate Tempo	F#3	D5	Character Ingenue Female
Kander, John	Alto	Chicago	1975	Velma Kelly	All That Jazz	Moderate Tempo	G2	D♭5	Romantic Antagonist Female
Kander, John	Alto	Chicago	1975	Velma Kelly	My Own Best Friend	Moderate Tempo	G3	A4	Romantic Antagonist Female
Kander, John	Alto	Chicago	1975	Velma Kelly	Nowadays	Moderate Tempo	F#3	D5	Romantic Antagonist Female
Kander, John	Alto	Cutains	2007	Carmen Bernstein	It's A Business	Moderate Tempo	E♭3	B♭4	Character Female
Kander, John	Alto	Cutains	2007	Carmen Bernstein	Show People	Moderate Tempo	G3	A♭4	Character Female
Kander, John	Alto	Cutains	2007	Carmen Bernstein	Show People Reprise *	Moderate Tempo	G3	B♭4	Character Female
Kander, John	Alto	Kiss Of The Spider Woman	1993	Aurora	Her Name Is Aurora*	Moderate Tempo	C3	A4	Romantic Antagonist Female
Kander, John	Alto	Kiss Of The Spider Woman	1993	Spider Woman	Interrogation*	Moderate Tempo	F3	F4	Romantic Antagonist Female

Composer

Composer	Vocal Range	Show	Year	Role	Song	Tempo	Range-Bottom	Range-Top	Char Type
Kander, John	Alto	Kiss Of The Spider Woman	1993	Marta	I Do Miracles*	Moderate Tempo	E3	Bb4	Character Ingenue Female
Kander, John	Alto	Kiss Of The Spider Woman	1993	Aurora	I Do Miracles*	Moderate Tempo	B2	Ab4	Romantic Antagonist Female
Kander, John	Alto	Kiss Of The Spider Woman	1993	Mother	You Could Never Shame Me	Moderate Tempo	F3	D5	Mature Female
Kander, John	Alto	Steel Pier	1997	Rita Racine	Love Bird*	Moderate Tempo	G3	C5	Romantic Lead Female
Kander, John	Alto	Steel Pier	1997	Shelby Stevens	Somebody Older	Moderate Tempo	G3	Bb4	Mature Female
Kander, John	Alto	Steel Pier	1997	Rita Racine	Willing To Ride Reprise	Moderate Tempo	Ab3	B4	Romantic Lead Female
Kander, John	Alto	Cabaret	1966	Fraulein Scheider	So What?	Uptempo	F3	G4	Mature Female
Kander, John	Alto	Cabaret	1966	Sally Bowles	Don't Tell Mama	Uptempo	A3	A4	Romantic Lead Female
Kander, John	Alto	Cabaret	1966	Sally Bowles	Perfectly Marvelous *	Uptempo	F#3	A4	Romantic Lead Female
Kander, John	Alto	Cabaret	1966	Sally Bowles	Cabaret	Uptempo	E3	B4	Romantic Lead Female
Kander, John	Alto	Chicago	1975	Roxie Hart	Me and My Baby	Uptempo	Bb3	C4	Character Ingenue Female
Kander, John	Alto	Chicago	1975	Velma Kelly	I Can't Do It Alone	Uptempo	Bb3	D4	Romantic Antagonist Female
Kander, John	Alto	Chicago	1975	Velma Kelly	I Know A Girl	Uptempo	E3	A4	Romantic Antagonist Female
Kander, John	Alto	Cutains	2007	Georgia Hendricks	Thataway *	Uptempo	B#3	B4	Romantic Lead Female
Kander, John	Alto	Kiss Of The Spider Woman	1993	Aurora	Where You Are*	Uptempo	Eb3	Gb4	Romantic Antagonist Female
Kander, John	Alto	Kiss Of The Spider Woman	1993	Aurora	Let's Make Love*	Uptempo	D3	A4	Romantic Antagonist Female
Kander, John	Alto	Kiss Of The Spider Woman	1993	Aurora	Good Times*	Uptempo	D#3	A4	Romantic Antagonist Female
Kander, John	Alto	Kiss Of The Spider Woman	1993	Spider Woman	Kiss Of The Spider Woman	Uptempo	C#3	A4	Romantic Antagonist Female
Kander, John	Alto	Steel Pier	1997	Rita Racine	Willing To Ride	Uptempo	Gb3	C5	Romantic Lead Female
Kander, John	Alto	Steel Pier	1997	Shelby Stevens	Everybody's Girl	Uptempo	G3	C5	Mature Female
Kander, John	Alto	Steel Pier	1997	Shelby Stevens	Everybody's Girl Encore	Uptempo	G3	Bb4	Mature Female
Kander, John	Alto	Steel Pier	1997	Rita Racine	Steel Pier Reprise*	Uptempo	Ab3	Db5	Romantic Lead Female
Kander, John	Baritone	Cabaret	1966	Herr Schultz	Married *	Ballad	D3	F4	Mature Male
Kander, John	Baritone	Cabaret	1966	Herr Schultz	Married Reprise	Ballad	C3	D4	Mature Male
Kander, John	Baritone	Chicago	1975	Amos Hart	Mister Cellophane	Ballad	C3	F4	Character Male
Kander, John	Baritone	Cutains	2007	Lieutenant Frank Cioffi	Coffe Shop Nights	Ballad	Ab2	D3	Character Male
Kander, John	Baritone	Cutains	2007	Lieutenant Frank Cioffi	A Tough Act To Follow *	Ballad	A2	Eb4	Character Male
Kander, John	Baritone	Cabaret	1966	Herr Ludwig	Tomorrow Belongs to Me Reprise *	Moderate Tempo	C3	D4	Character Male
Kander, John	Baritone	Chicago	1975	Billy Flynn	All I Care About Is Love	Moderate Tempo	A2	F#4	Romantic Antagonist Male
Kander, John	Baritone	Cutains	2007	Lieutenant Frank Cioffi	Show People	Moderate Tempo	A2	F4	Character Male
Kander, John	Baritone	Cutains	2007	Lieutenant Frank Cioffi	Show People Reprise *	Moderate Tempo	B2	Bb3	Character Male
Kander, John	Baritone	Chicago	1975	Billy Flynn	Razzle Dazzle	Uptempo	D3	F4	Romantic Antagonist Male
Kander, John	Baritone	Steel Pier	1997	Mick Hamilton	Everybody Dance Part 1*	Uptempo	D3	F4	Romantic Antagonist Male

Composer	Vocal Range	Show	Year	Role	Song	Tempo	Range-Bottom	Range-Top	Char Type
Kander, John	Baritone	Steel Pier	1997	Mick Hamilton	It's A Powerful Thing*	Uptempo	C3	E4	Romantic Antagonist Male
Kander, John	Baritone	Steel Pier	1997	Mick Hamilton	Dance With Me*	Uptempo	Db3	Eb4	Romantic Antagonist Male
Kander, John	Baritone	Steel Pier	1997	Mick Hamilton	Steel Pier Reprise*	Uptempo	Bb2	E4	Romantic Antagonist Male
Kander, John	Soprano	Cabaret	1966	Nazi Youth	Tomorrow Belongs to Me	Ballad	F4	F#5	Juvenile Male
Kander, John	Soprano	Chicago	1975	Mary Sunshine	A Little Good In Everyone	Moderate Tempo	F3	B5	Character Female
Kander, John	Soprano	Steel Pier	1997	Precious McGuire	Two Little Words	Uptempo	C4	E6	Character Ingenue Female
Kander, John	Tenor	Cabaret	1966	Nazi Youth	Tomorrow Belongs to Me	Ballad	F3	F#4	Ingenue Male
Kander, John	Tenor	Cabaret	1997	Master of Cereomonies	I Don't Care Much	Ballad	D3	F4	Character Male
Kander, John	Tenor	Cutains	2007	Aaron Fox	I Miss The Music	Ballad	C3	Gb4	Romantic Lead Male
Kander, John	Tenor	Cutains	2007	Aaron Fox	Thinking of Him Reprise*	Ballad	A2	Gb4	Romantic Lead Male
Kander, John	Tenor	Kiss Of The Spider Woman	1993	Valentin	Dear One*	Ballad	Bb2	C4	Romantic Antagonist Male
Kander, John	Tenor	Kiss Of The Spider Woman	1993	Molina	Dear One*	Ballad	C3	Eb4	Character Male
Kander, John	Tenor	Kiss Of The Spider Woman	1993	Molina	She's A Woman	Ballad	C3	E4	Character Male
Kander, John	Tenor	Cabaret	1966	Clifford Bradshaw	Why Should I Wake Up?	Moderate Tempo	B2	E4	Romantic Lead Male
Kander, John	Tenor	Cabaret	1966	Clifford Bradshaw	The Money Song	Moderate Tempo	Eb2	A4	Character Male
Kander, John	Tenor	Kiss Of The Spider Woman	1993	Molina	Her Name Is Aurora*	Moderate Tempo	C3	C4	Character Male
Kander, John	Tenor	Kiss Of The Spider Woman	1993	Valentin	Over The Wall 3 - Marta	Moderate Tempo	F3	A4	Romantic Antagonist Male
Kander, John	Tenor	Kiss Of The Spider Woman	1993	Gabriel	Gabriel's Letter*	Moderate Tempo	D#3	G4	Character Ingenue Male
Kander, John	Tenor	Kiss Of The Spider Woman	1993	Valentin	My First Woman*	Moderate Tempo	C3	G4	Romantic Antagonist Male
Kander, John	Tenor	Kiss Of The Spider Woman	1993	Molina	Mama, It's Me	Moderate Tempo	C3	E4	Character Male
Kander, John	Tenor	Steel Pier	1997	Bill Kelly	The Last Girl*	Moderate Tempo	Bb2	G4	Romantic Lead Male
Kander, John	Tenor	Steel Pier	1997	Bill Kelly	Leave The World Behind*	Moderate Tempo	D3	Eb4	Romantic Lead Male
Kander, John	Tenor	Cabaret	1966	Clifford Bradshaw	Perfectly Marvelous *	Uptempo	D3	E4	Romantic Lead Male
Kander, John	Tenor	Cabaret	1966	Herr Schultz	Meeskite	Uptempo	B2	Ab4	Character Male
Kander, John	Tenor	Cabaret	1966	Master of Cereomonies	Wilkomen	Uptempo	E3	G4	Character Male
Kander, John	Tenor	Cabaret	1966	Master of Cereomonies	Two Ladies	Uptempo	G3	G4	Character Male
Kander, John	Tenor	Cabaret	1966	Master of Cereomonies	If You Could See Her	Uptempo	D3	F4	Character Male
Kander, John	Tenor	Kiss Of The Spider Woman	1993	Molina	Bluebloods*	Uptempo	B2	C#4	Character Male
Kander, John	Tenor	Kiss Of The Spider Woman	1993	Molina	Dressing Them Up	Uptempo	C3	F4	Character Male
Kander, John	Tenor	Kiss Of The Spider Woman	1993	Valentin	The Day After That*	Uptempo	D3	Gb4	Romantic Antagonist Male
Kander, John	Tenor	Kiss Of The Spider Woman	1993	Molina	Only In the Movies	Uptempo	B2	F4	Character Male
Kander, John	Tenor	Steel Pier	1997	Bill Kelly	Second Chance	Uptempo	B2	E4	Romantic Lead Male
Kander, John	Tenor	Steel Pier	1997	Bill Kelly	First You Dream*	Uptempo	C3	F4	Romantic Lead Male
Kern, Jerome	Alto	Show Boat	1927	Julie	Bill	Ballad	F#3	G#4	Romantic Lead Female

Composer

Composer	Vocal Range	Show	Year	Role	Song	Tempo	Range-Bottom	Range-Top	Char Type
Kern, Jerome	Alto	Show Boat	1927	Queenie+	Misery*	Ballad	A3	Eb5	Character Female
Kern, Jerome	Alto	Show Boat	1927	Julie	Can't Help Lovin' Dat Man	Moderate Tempo	Eb3	Ab4	Romantic Lead Female
Kern, Jerome	Alto	Show Boat	1927	Queenie+	Can't Help Lovin' Dat Man*	Moderate Tempo	C3	D4	Character Female
Kern, Jerome	Alto	Show Boat	1927	Ellie	Life Upon The Wicked Stage*	Uptempo	G3	D5	Character Ingenue Female
Kern, Jerome	Alto	Show Boat	1927	Queenie+	Bally-Hoo*	Uptempo	A3	Eb5	Character Female
Kern, Jerome	Bass	Show Boat	1927	Joe+	Ol' Man River	Ballad	F2	D4	Character Male
Kern, Jerome	Bass	Show Boat	1927	Joe+	Ol' Man River Reprise	Ballad	F2	D4	Character Male
Kern, Jerome	Bass	Show Boat	1927	Joe+	Ol' Man River - Act II	Ballad	Ab2	F4	Character Male
Kern, Jerome	Soprano	Show Boat	1927	Magnolia	Make Believe	Ballad	D4	Bb5	Ingenue Female
Kern, Jerome	Soprano	Show Boat	1927	Magnolia	You Are Love*	Ballad	D4	Bb5	Ingenue Female
Kern, Jerome	Soprano	Show Boat	1927	Magnolia	Can't Help Reprise	Ballad	Ab3	Eb5	Ingenue Female
Kern, Jerome	Soprano	Show Boat	1927	Magnolia	After The Ball	Moderate Tempo	D4	A5	Ingenue Female
Kern, Jerome	Soprano	Show Boat	1927	Magnolia	Dance The Night Away*	Uptempo	G3	C5	Ingenue Female
Kern, Jerome	Tenor	Show Boat	1927	Gaylord Ravenal	Where's The Mate For Me	Ballad	D3	F#4	Romantic Lead Male
Kern, Jerome	Tenor	Show Boat	1927	Gaylord Ravenal	Make Believe*	Ballad	C3	G4	Romantic Lead Male
Kern, Jerome	Tenor	Show Boat	1927	Gaylord Ravenal	You Are Love*	Ballad	D3	Bb4	Romantic Lead Male
Kern, Jerome	Tenor	Show Boat	1927	Gaylord Ravenal	You Are Love Reprise	Ballad	C3	Ab4	Romantic Lead Male
Kitt, Tom	Tenor	Show Boat	1927	Gaylord Ravenal	I Have The Room Above Her	Moderate Tempo	E3	E4	Romantic Lead Male
Kitt, Tom	Alto	Next To Normal	2009	Diana	How Could I Forget*	Ballad	Bb3	Db5	Romantic Lead Female
Kitt, Tom	Alto	Next To Normal	2009	Diana	So Anyway	Ballad	B3	C5	Romantic Lead Female
Kitt, Tom	Alto	Next To Normal	2009	Diana	My Psychopharmacologist And I	Moderate Tempo	A3	C5	Romantic Lead Female
Kitt, Tom	Alto	Next To Normal	2009	Diana	I Miss The Mountains	Moderate Tempo	G3	D5	Romantic Lead Female
Kitt, Tom	Alto	Next To Normal	2009	Diana	You Don't Know*	Moderate Tempo	A3	B4	Romantic Lead Female
Kitt, Tom	Alto	Next To Normal	2009	Diana	Maybe*	Moderate Tempo	Eb3	Eb5	Romantic Lead Female
Kitt, Tom	Alto	Next To Normal	2009	Natalie	Maybe*	Moderate Tempo	Ab3	D5	Character Ingenue Female
Kitt, Tom	Alto	Next To Normal	2009	Natalie	Everything Else	Uptempo	G3	C5	Character Ingenue Female
Kitt, Tom	Alto	Next To Normal	2009	Natalie	Superboy And The Invisible Girl	Uptempo	D4	D5	Character Ingenue Female
Kitt, Tom	Alto	Next To Normal	2009	Diana	Didn't I See This Movie	Uptempo	A3	F#5	Romantic Lead Female
Kitt, Tom	Alto	Next To Normal	2009	Diana	You Don't Know Reprise*	Uptempo	A3	A4	Romantic Lead Female
Kitt, Tom	Alto	Next To Normal	2009	Diana	The Break	Uptempo	B3	C5	Romantic Lead Female
Kitt, Tom	Tenor	Next To Normal	2009	Dan	He's Not Here	Ballad	Eb3	G4	Character Male
Kitt, Tom	Tenor	Next To Normal	2009	Dan	A Light In The Dark*	Ballad	D3	E4	Character Male
Kitt, Tom	Tenor	Next To Normal	2009	Gabe	There's A World	Ballad	G3	G4	Character Ingenue Male

Composer

Composer	Vocal Range	Show	Year	Role	Song	Tempo	Range-Bottom	Range-Top	Char Type
Kitt, Tom	Tenor	Next To Normal	2009	Dan	Who's Crazy*	Moderate Tempo	G3	F4	Character Male
Kitt, Tom	Tenor	Next To Normal	2009	Dr. Madden	Make Up Your Mind*	Moderate Tempo	Ab3	Ab4	Character Male
Kitt, Tom	Tenor	Next To Normal	2009	Dr. Madden	Make Up Your Mind Reprise	Moderate Tempo	A3	G4	Character Male
Kitt, Tom	Tenor	Next To Normal	2009	Henry	Perfect For You Reprise*	Moderate Tempo	D3	G4	Character Ingenue Male
Kitt, Tom	Tenor	Next To Normal	2009	Dr. Madden	Open Your Eyes*	Moderate Tempo	F3	A4	Character Male
Kitt, Tom	Tenor	Next To Normal	2009	Dan	I Am The One*	Uptempo	E3	F#4	Character Male
Kitt, Tom	Tenor	Next To Normal	2009	Gabe	I'm Alive	Uptempo	G3	B4	Character Ingenue Male
Kitt, Tom	Tenor	Next To Normal	2009	Gabe	I've Been	Uptempo	E3	G4	Character Male
Kitt, Tom	Tenor	Next To Normal	2009	Gabe	Aftershocks*	Uptempo	D3	D4	Character Ingenue Male
Kitt, Tom	Tenor	Next To Normal	2009	Dan	It's Gonna Be Good Reprise*	Uptempo	A2	F4	Character Male
Kitt, Tom	Tenor	Next To Normal	2009	Dan	A Promies*	Uptempo	C3	F4	Character Male
Kitt, Tom	Tenor	Next To Normal	2009	Gabe	I'm Alive Reprise	Uptempo	G3	G4	Character Ingenue Male
Krieger, Henry	Alto	Dreamgirls	1981	Effie White +	I Am Changing	Ballad	Eb4	F5	Character Female
Krieger, Henry	Alto	Dreamgirls	1981	Effie White +	One Night Only	Ballad	Ab3	D5	Character Female
Krieger, Henry	Baritone	Dreamgirls	1981	Curtis Taylor, Jr +	When I First Saw You	Ball	C3	E4	Romantic Lead Male
Krieger, Henry	Baritone	Dreamgirls	1981	CC White +	Family	Ballad	D3	E4	Ingenue Male
Krieger, Henry	Baritone	Dreamgirls	1981	Curtis Taylor, Jr +	Cadillac Car	Uptempo	F3	G4	Romantic Lead Male
Krieger, Henry	Soprano	Dreamgirls	1981	Deena Jones +	Heavy	Uptempo	D3	D4	Ingenue Female
Krieger, Henry	Soprano	Dreamgirls	1981	Deena Jones +	One Night Only	Uptempo	Ab3	D5	Ingenue Female
Krieger, Henry	Soprano	Dreamgirls	1981	Lorelle Robinson +	Ain't No Party *	Uptempo	Bb3	E4	Character Ingenue Female
Krieger, Henry	Tenor	Dreamgirls	1981	James Thunder Early +	I Want You Baby	Ballad	Eb3	Db4	Character Male
Krieger, Henry	Tenor	Dreamgirls	1981	James Thunder Early +	I Meant You No Harm	Ballad	Bb2	G4	Character Male
Krieger, Henry	Tenor	Dreamgirls	1981	James Thunder Early +	Fake Your Way to the Top	Uptempo	F3	Ab4	Character Male
La Chuissa, Michael John	Alto	Marie Christine	1999	Mother+	Ton Grandpere Est Le Soleil*	Moderate Tempo	D3	E5	Romantic Antagonist Female
La Chuissa, Michael John	Alto	Marie Christine	1999	Mother+	Miracles and Mysteries	Moderate Tempo	E3	F5	Romantic Antagonist Female
La Chuissa, Michael John	Alto	Marie Christine	1999	Magdelena	Cincincati*	Moderate Tempo	G3	F#3	Character Female
La Chuissa, Michael John	Alto	Marie Christine	1999	Magdelena	There's A Rumor	Moderate Tempo	F#3	C#5	Character Female
La Chuissa, Michael John	Alto	Marie Christine	1999	Magdelena	Paradise Is Burning Down*	Uptempo	Eb3	Eb5	Character Female
La Chuissa, Michael John	Alto	Marie Christine	1999	Magdelena	A Lovely Wedding*	Uptempo	C4	C#5	Character Female
La Chuissa, Michael John	Baritone	Marie Christine	1999	Jean L'Adrese+	All Eyes Look To You	Ballad	A2	E4	Ingenue Male
La Chuissa, Michael John	Baritone	Marie Christine	1999	Charles Gates	Good Looking Woman*	Moderate Tempo	G3	E5	Antagonist Male
La Chuissa, Michael John	Soprano	Marie Christine	1999	Lisette+	Tout Mi Mi	Ballad	D4	C#5	Ingenue Female
La Chuissa, Michael John	Soprano	Marie Christine	1999	Lisette+	Dansen Calinda	Ballad	E4	C6	Ingenue Female
La Chuissa, Michael John	Soprano	Marie Christine	1999	Marie Christine L'Adrese	I Will Give	Ballad	Bb3	Fb4	Romantic Antagonist Female

Composer

Composer	Vocal Range	Show	Year	Role	Song	Tempo	Range-Bottom	Range-Top	Char Type
La Chuissa, Michael John	Soprano	Marie Christine	1999	Marie Christine L'Adrese	Marie's Soliloquy	Ballad	A3	D5	Romantic Antagonist Female
La Chuissa, Michael John	Soprano	Marie Christine	1999	Lisette+	Tout Mimi Reprise	Ballad	Bb3	Bb4	Ingenue Female
La Chuissa, Michael John	Soprano	Marie Christine	1999	Marie Christine L'Adrese	Beautiful*	Moderate Tempo	G3	D5	Romantic Antagonist Female
La Chuissa, Michael John	Soprano	Marie Christine	1999	Marie Christine L'Adrese	Way Back To Paradise*	Moderate Tempo	D4	G5	Romantic Antagonist Female
La Chuissa, Michael John	Soprano	Marie Christine	1999	Marie Christine L'Adrese	To Find A Lover*	Moderate Tempo	A3	G4	Romantic Antagonist Female
La Chuissa, Michael John	Soprano	Marie Christine	1999	Marie Christine L'Adrese	Tell Me	Moderate Tempo	G3	F5	Romantic Antagonist Female
La Chuissa, Michael John	Soprano	Marie Christine	1999	Marie Christine L'Adrese	Prison In A Prison*	Uptempo	G3	D5	Romantic Antagonist Female
La Chuissa, Michael John	Tenor	Marie Christine	1999	Paris L'Adrese+	No Turning Back	Ballad	F3	Eb5	Romantic Antagonist Male
La Chuissa, Michael John	Tenor	Marie Christine	1999	Dante Keyes	Your Name (Helena's Death)	Ballad	G#2	A4	Romantic Antagonist Male
La Chuissa, Michael John	Tenor	Marie Christine	1999	Dante Keyes	Ocean Is Different	Moderate Tempo	C3	A4	Romantic Antagonist Male
La Chuissa, Michael John	Tenor	Marie Christine	1999	Dante Keyes	I Don't Hear The Ocean*	Moderate Tempo	Eb3	F4	Romantic Antagonist Male
La Chuissa, Michael John	Tenor	Marie Christine	1999	Dante Keyes	We Gonna Go To Chicago	Moderate Tempo	Db3	F4	Romantic Antagonist Male
La Chuissa, Michael John	Tenor	Marie Christine	1999	Dante Keyes	Nothing Beats Chicago	Uptempo	B2	E4	Romantic Antagonist Male
La Chuissa, Michael John	Tenor	Marie Christine	1999	Dante Keyes	The Scorpion*	Uptempo	C3	Gb4	Romantic Antagonist Male
La Chuissa, Michael John	Tenor	Marie Christine	1999	Dante Keyes	The Adventure Never Ends	Uptempo	Bb2	Fb4	Romantic Antagonist Male
La Chuissa, Michael John	Tenor	Marie Christine	1999	Dante Keyes	Danced With A Girl	Uptempo	B2	E4	Romantic Antagonist Male
Lambert and Morrison	Alto	Drowsy Chaperon, The	2006	Drowsy Chaperone	As We Stumble Along	Moderate Tempo	F3	D5	Character Female
Lambert and Morrison	Alto	Drowsy Chaperon, The	2006	Mrs. Tottendale	Love Is Always Lovely *	Moderate Tempo	G3	Bb4	Mature Female
Lambert and Morrison	Soprano	Drowsy Chaperon, The	2006	Janet Van de Graff	Bride's Lament *	Ballad	Ab3	F5	Ingenue Female
Lambert and Morrison	Soprano	Drowsy Chaperon, The	2006	Janet Van de Graff	Accident Waiting To Happen *	Moderate Tempo	C4	D5	Ingenue Female
Lambert and Morrison	Soprano	Drowsy Chaperon, The	2006	Drowsy Chaperone	Show Off Encore	Uptempo	A3	A5	Character Female
Lambert and Morrison	Soprano	Drowsy Chaperon, The	2006	Janet Van de Graff	Show Off *	Uptempo	G3	C5	Ingenue Female
Lambert and Morrison	Soprano	Drowsy Chaperon, The	2006	Trix	I Do, I Do In The Sky	Uptempo	A3	A5	Character Female
Lambert and Morrison	Tenor	Drowsy Chaperon, The	2006	Adolpho	I Am Adolpho *	Moderate Tempo	E2	A5	Romantic Lead Male
Lambert and Morrison	Tenor	Drowsy Chaperon, The	2006	Robert Martin	Accident Waiting To Happen *	Moderate Tempo	Eb3	A4	Ingenue Male
Lambert and Morrison	Tenor	Drowsy Chaperon, The	2006	Gangster	Toledo Surprise *	Uptempo	C3	Gb4	Character Male
Lambert and Morrison	Tenor	Drowsy Chaperon, The	2006	Robert Martin	Cold Feets *	Uptempo	C3	Ab4	Ingenue Male
Larson, Jonathan	Alto	Rent	1996	Maureen Johnson	Over The Moon	Moderate Tempo	C4	Eb5	Romantic Antagonist Female
Larson, Jonathan	Alto	Rent	1996	Mimi Marquez	Without You*	Moderate Tempo	A3	A4	Romantic Antagonist Female
Larson, Jonathan	Alto	Rent	1996	Mimi Marquez	Goodbye Love*	Moderate Tempo	A4	C5	Romantic Antagonist Female
Larson, Jonathan	Alto	Rent	1996	Mimi Marquez	Out Tonight	Uptempo	A3	E5	Romantic Antagonist Female
Larson, Jonathan	Alto	Rent	1996	Mimi Marquez	Another Day*	Uptempo	B3	B4	Romantic Antagonist Female
Larson, Jonathan	Alto	Rent	1996	Joanne Jefferson	We're Okay	Uptempo	C4	C5	Antagonist Female

Composer

Composer	Vocal Range	Show	Year	Role	Song	Tempo	Range-Bottom	Range-Top	Char Type
Larson, Jonathan	Alto	Rent	1996	Joanne Jefferson	Take Me Or leave Me*	Uptempo	C4	E5	Antagonist Female
Larson, Jonathan	Alto	Rent	1996	Maureen Johnson	Take Me Or leave Me*	Uptempo	C4	F5	Romantic Antagonist Female
Larson, Jonathan	Tenor	Rent	1996	Tom Collins	I'll Cover You Reprise*	Ballad	F#2	A4	Romantic Lead Male
Larson, Jonathan	Tenor	Rent	1996	Roger Davis	Your Eyes*	Ballad	B2	G4	Romantic Antagonist Male
Larson, Jonathan	Tenor	Rent	1996	Roger Davis	One Song Glory	Moderate Tempo	D3	A♭4	Romantic Lead Male
Larson, Jonathan	Tenor	Rent	1996	Tom Collins	Sante Fe*	Moderate Tempo	F#2	F#4	Romantic Lead Male
Larson, Jonathan	Tenor	Rent	1996	Angel Schunard	I'll Cover You*	Moderate Tempo	G3	A4	Character Ingenue Male
Larson, Jonathan	Tenor	Rent	1996	Tom Collins	I'll Cover You*	Moderate Tempo	C3	G4	Romantic Lead Male
Larson, Jonathan	Tenor	Rent	1996	Mark Cohen	Halloween	Moderate Tempo	E♭3	E♭4	Character Male
Larson, Jonathan	Tenor	Rent	1996	Angel Schunard	Today For You*	Uptempo	B♭3	G4	Character Ingenue Male
Larson, Jonathan	Tenor	Rent	1996	Roger Davis	Another Day*	Uptempo	F3	G♭4	Romantic Antagonist Male
Larson, Jonathan	Tenor	Rent	1996	Mark Cohen	You Are What You Own*	Uptempo	D3	E4	Character Male
Lauper, Cyndi	Alto	Kinky Boots	2013	Lauren	The History of Wrong Guys	Uptempo	B♭3	D5	Character Female
Lauper, Cyndi	Baritone	Kinky Boots	2013	Harry	Take What You Got*	Uptempo	F#3	F#4	Character Ingenue Male
Lauper, Cyndi	Tenor	Kinky Boots	2013	Charlie Price	Not My Father's Son*	Ballad	F#3	F#4	Ingenue Male
Lauper, Cyndi	Tenor	Kinky Boots	2013	Charlie Price	Charlie's Soliloquy	Ballad	E♭3	C♭4	Ingenue Male
Lauper, Cyndi	Tenor	Kinky Boots	2013	Charlie Price	Charlie's Soliloquy Reprise	Ballad	F#3	C#4	Ingenue Male
Lauper, Cyndi	Tenor	Kinky Boots	2013	Lola (Drag)	Not My Father's Son*	Ballad	E3	A4	Character Male
Lauper, Cyndi	Tenor	Kinky Boots	2013	Lola (Drag)	Hold Me In Your Heart	Ballad	E3	B♭4	Character Male
Lauper, Cyndi	Tenor	Kinky Boots	2013	Lola (Drag)	The Sex Is In the Heel	Moderate Tempo	A3	B4	Character Male
Lauper, Cyndi	Tenor	Kinky Boots	2013	Lola (Drag)	What a Woman Wants	Moderate Tempo	E3	A4	Character Male
Lauper, Cyndi	Tenor	Kinky Boots	2013	Charlie Price	Take What You Got*	Uptempo	F#3	F#4	Ingenue Male
Lauper, Cyndi	Tenor	Kinky Boots	2013	Charlie Price	Step One	Uptempo	A♭3	A♭4	Ingenue Male
Lauper, Cyndi	Tenor	Kinky Boots	2013	Charlie Price	The Soul of a Man	Uptempo	C3	B♭4	Ingenue Male
Lauper, Cyndi	Tenor	Kinky Boots	2013	Lola (Drag)	The Land of Lola	Uptempo	F#3	F#4	Character Male
Lippa, Andrew	Alto	Addams Family, The	2010	Morticia Addams	Live Before We Die	Moderate Tempo	B♭3	A♭4	Romantic Antagonist Female
Lippa, Andrew	Alto	Addams Family, The	2010	Morticia Addams	Just Around The Corner *	Uptempo	G3	B4	Romantic Antagonist Female
Lippa, Andrew	Alto	Addams Family, The	2010	Wednesday Addams	Pulled	Uptempo	B3	E♭5	Character Ingenue Female
Lippa, Andrew	Alto	Addams Family, The	2010	Wednesday Addams	One Normal Night	Uptempo	B♭3	B♭4	Character Ingenue Female
Lippa, Andrew	Alto	Addams Family, The	2010	Wednesday Addams	Crazier Than You *	Uptempo	A3	E5	Character Ingenue Female
Lippa, Andrew	Alto	You're....Charlie Brown	1999	Sally	My New Philosophy	Uptempo	B3	E5	Ingenue Female
Lippa, Andrew	Baritone	Addams Family, The	2010	Gomez Addams +	Happy/Sad	Ballad	E♭3	E♭4	Romantic Antagonist Male
Lippa, Andrew	Baritone	Addams Family, The	2010	Uncle Fester	The Moon And Me	Ballad	C3	E4	Mature Male

Composer	Vocal Range	Show	Year	Role	Song	Tempo	Range-Bottom	Range-Top	Char Type
Lippa, Andrew	Baritone	Addams Family, The	2010	Gomez Addams +	Trapped (US Tour)	Moderate Tempo	C3	F4	Romantic Lead Male
Lippa, Andrew	Baritone	Addams Family, The	2010	Mal Geineke	In The Arms	Moderate Tempo	C3	F4	Paternal
Lippa, Andrew	Baritone	Addams Family, The	2010	Lucas Beineke	Crazier Than You *	Uptempo	D3	E4	Ingenue Male
Lippa, Andrew	Baritone	Addams Family, The	2010	Lucas Beineke	One Normal Night	Uptempo	D3	F4	Ingenue Male
Lippa, Andrew	Bass	Addams Family, The	2010	Lurch	Move Toward The Darkness	Ballad	G2	Eb4	Character Male
Lippa, Andrew	Soprano	Addams Family, The	2010	Pugsley Addams	What If	Ballad	A3	C5	Juvenile Male
Lippa, Andrew	Soprano	Addams Family, The	2010	Alice Beineke	Waiting	Moderate Tempo	Ab3	E5	Maternal
Lippa, Andrew	Tenor	Addams Family, The	2010	Gomez Addams +	What If	Ballad	C3	C4	Romantic Antagonist Male
Lippa, Andrew	Tenor	Addams Family, The	2010	Gomez Addams +	Morticia	Moderate Tempo	A#2	Ab4	Romantic Antagonist Male
Lippa, Andrew	Tenor	Addams Family, The	2010	Gomez Addams +	Live Before We Die	Moderate Tempo	Bb3	D4	Romantic Lead Male
Lippa, Andrew	Tenor	Addams Family, The	2010	Gomez Addams +	Not Today (US Tour)	Moderate Tempo	D3	G4	Romantic Antagonist Male
Loesser, Frank	Alto	Guys and Dolls	1950	Miss Adelaide	Adelaide's Lament Reprise	Ballad	Db4	Cb5	Character Female
Loesser, Frank	Alto	How To Succeed...	1961	Hedy La Rue	Love From A Heart Of Gold*	Ballad	B3	D5	Romantic Lead Female
Loesser, Frank	Alto	Guys and Dolls	1950	Miss Adelaide	Adelaide's Lament	Moderate Tempo	Ab3	D5	Character Female
Loesser, Frank	Alto	How To Succeed...	1961	Rosemary Pillkington	Happy To Keep His Dinner Warm	Moderate Tempo	A3	Db5	Ingenue Female
Loesser, Frank	Alto	How To Succeed...	1961	Rosemary Pillkington	Paris Original*	Moderate Tempo	Bb3	D5	Ingenue Female
Loesser, Frank	Alto	How To Succeed...	1961	Rosemary Pillkington	Happy To Keep His Dinner Warm Rep	Moderate Tempo	Bb3	Db5	Ingenue Female
Loesser, Frank	Alto	How To Succeed...	1961	Rosemary Pillkington	I Believe In You Reprise*	Moderate Tempo	E4	B4	Ingenue Female
Loesser, Frank	Alto	Most Happy Fella, The	1956	Cleo	Ooh! My Feet!	Moderate Tempo	A#3	Bb4	Character Female
Loesser, Frank	Alto	Most Happy Fella, The	1956	Marie	A Long Time Ago*	Moderate Tempo	D4	Eb5	Mature Female
Loesser, Frank	Alto	Most Happy Fella, The	1956	Marie	Young People*	Moderate Tempo	C4	E5	Mature Female
Loesser, Frank	Alto	Most Happy Fella, The	1956	Cleo	I Know How It Is*	Moderate Tempo	Ab3	B4	Character Female
Loesser, Frank	Alto	Guys and Dolls	1950	Miss Adelaide	A Bushel And A Peck	Uptempo	B3	Eb3	Character Female
Loesser, Frank	Alto	Guys and Dolls	1950	Miss Adelaide	Take Back Your Mink	Uptempo	Bb3	D5	Character Female
Loesser, Frank	Alto	Guys and Dolls	1950	Miss Adelaide	Marry The Man Today*	Uptempo	C4	Eb5	Character Female
Loesser, Frank	Alto	How To Succeed...	1961	Miss Jones	Brotherhood Of Man*	Uptempo	A#3	G5	Character Female
Loesser, Frank	Alto	How To Succeed...	1961	Smitty	Been A Long Day*	Uptempo	Bb3	D5	Character Female
Loesser, Frank	Alto	Most Happy Fella, The	1956	Cleo	I Like Everybody Reprise*	Uptempo	G#3	B4	Character Female
Loesser, Frank	Baritone	Guys and Dolls	1950	Sky Masterson	I'll Know*	Ballad	B2	D#4	Romantic Lead Male
Loesser, Frank	Baritone	Guys and Dolls	1950	Sky Masterson	My Time Of Day	Ballad	Bb2	Db4	Romantic Lead Male
Loesser, Frank	Baritone	Most Happy Fella, The	1956	Tony	Plenty Bambini	Ballad	C#3	F#4	Romantic Lead Male
Loesser, Frank	Baritone	Most Happy Fella, The	1956	Tony	My Heart Is So Full Of You*	Ballad	Db3	Gb4	Mature Male

Composer

Composer	Vocal Range	Show	Year	Role	Song	Tempo	Range-Bottom	Range-Top	Char Type
Loesser, Frank	Baritone	Most Happy Fella, The	1956	Tony	Tony's Thoughts	Ballad	D3	F4	Mature Male
Loesser, Frank	Baritone	Most Happy Fella, The	1956	Joe	Getting' Out Of Town	Ballad	Db3	F4	Romantic Antagonist Male
Loesser, Frank	Baritone	Most Happy Fella, The	1956	Joe	Joey, Joey, Joey	Moderate Tempo	C3	F4	Romantic Antagonist Male
Loesser, Frank	Baritone	Most Happy Fella, The	1956	Tony	Soon You Gonna Leave Me Joe	Moderate Tempo	C#3	E4	Mature Male
Loesser, Frank	Baritone	Most Happy Fella, The	1956	Tony	Rosabella	Moderate Tempo	Eb3	G4	Mature Male
Loesser, Frank	Baritone	Most Happy Fella, The	1956	Postman	I Seen Her At The Station	Moderate Tempo	D3	E4	Character Male
Loesser, Frank	Baritone	Most Happy Fella, The	1956	Joe	Don't Cry	Moderate Tempo	Bb2	Eb4	Romantic Antagonist Male
Loesser, Frank	Baritone	Most Happy Fella, The	1956	Tony	Old People Gotta Dance	Moderate Tempo	C3	C4	Mature Male
Loesser, Frank	Baritone	Most Happy Fella, The	1956	Tony	Mamma, Mamma	Moderate Tempo	C#3	G4	Mature Male
Loesser, Frank	Baritone	Most Happy Fella, The	1956	Tony	I Canno' Leave You Money	Moderate Tempo	D#3	Eb4	Mature Male
Loesser, Frank	Baritone	Most Happy Fella, The	1956	Tony	Most Happy Fella* (ms 74-109 & 131-	Uptempo	Eb3	G4	Mature Male
Loesser, Frank	Baritone	Guys and Dolls	1950	Sky Masterson	Luck Be A Lady*	Uptempo	Db3	Eb4	Romantic Lead Male
Loesser, Frank	Baritone	How To Succeed...	1961	Bud Frump	Been A Long Day Reprise*	Uptempo	Bb3	D4	Antagonist Male
Loesser, Frank	Soprano	Guys and Dolls	1950	Sarah Brown	I'll Know*	Ballad	E4	G#5	Ingenue Female
Loesser, Frank	Soprano	Guys and Dolls	1950	Sarah Brown	I'll Know (Finish)	Ballad	Eb4	F5	Ingenue Female
Loesser, Frank	Soprano	Most Happy Fella, The	1956	Rosabella	Somebody Somewhere	Ballad	E4	G5	Character Ingenue Female
Loesser, Frank	Soprano	Most Happy Fella, The	1956	Rosabella	Aren't You Glad?	Ballad	C4	E5	Character Ingenue Female
Loesser, Frank	Soprano	Most Happy Fella, The	1956	Rosabella	Warm All Over	Ballad	C#4	F#5	Character Ingenue Female
Loesser, Frank	Soprano	Most Happy Fella, The	1956	Rosabella	My Heart Is So Full Of You*	Ballad	Db4	Gb5	Character Ingenue Female
Loesser, Frank	Soprano	Most Happy Fella, The	1956	Rosabella	I Don't Know*	Moderate Tempo	Bb3	D5	Character Ingenue Female
Loesser, Frank	Soprano	Most Happy Fella, The	1956	Rosabella	I Love Him*	Moderate Tempo	D4	Eb5	Character Ingenue Female
Loesser, Frank	Soprano	Most Happy Fella, The	1956	Rosabella	Like A Woman Loves A Man	Moderate Tempo	D4	G5	Character Ingenue Female
Loesser, Frank	Soprano	Guys and Dolls	1950	Sarah Brown	If I Were A Bell	Uptempo	Bb3	D5	Ingenue Female
Loesser, Frank	Soprano	Guys and Dolls	1950	Sarah Brown	Marry The Man Today*	Uptempo	C4	Eb5	Ingenue Female
Loesser, Frank	Soprano	Most Happy Fella, The	1956	Rosabella	No Home No Job	Uptempo	D4	Eb5	Character Ingenue Female
Loesser, Frank	Soprano	Most Happy Fella, The	1956	Rosabella	Please Let Me Tell You	Uptempo	D4	E5	Character Ingenue Female
Loesser, Frank	Tenor	How To Succeed...	1961	JB Biggley	Love From A Heart Of Gold*	Ballad	C#3	E4	Mature Male
Loesser, Frank	Tenor	How To Succeed...	1961	J Pierpont Finch	Rosemary*	Moderate Tempo	B2	E4	Character Male
Loesser, Frank	Tenor	Most Happy Fella, The	1956	The Doctor	Love and Kindness	Moderate Tempo	E3	A4	Character Male
Loesser, Frank	Tenor	Most Happy Fella, The	1956	Herman	I Made A Fist*	Moderate Tempo	F3	Ab4	Character Male
Loesser, Frank	Tenor	Guys and Dolls	1950	Nicely Nicely	Sit Down You're Rockin' The Boat*	Uptempo	F3	C5	Character Male
Loesser, Frank	Tenor	How To Succeed...	1961	Bud Frump	Company Way Reprise*	Uptempo	D3	G4	Antagonist Male
Loesser, Frank	Tenor	How To Succeed...	1961	J Pierpont Finch	How To Succeed	Uptempo	E3	E4	Character Male

Composer

Composer	Vocal Range	Show	Year	Role	Song	Tempo	Range-Bottom	Range-Top	Char Type
Loesser, Frank	Tenor	How To Succeed...	1961	J Pierpont Finch	I Believe In You*	Uptempo	F3	C4	Character Male
Loesser, Frank	Tenor	How To Succeed...	1961	J Pierpont Finch	Brotherhood Of Man*	Uptempo	F3	G4	Character Male
Loesser, Frank	Tenor	How To Succeed...	1961	JB Biggley	Grand Old Ivy*	Uptempo	C3	G4	Mature Male
Loesser, Frank	Tenor	How To Succeed...	1961	Twimble	Company Way*	Uptempo	D3	G4	Mature Male
Loesser, Frank	Tenor	Most Happy Fella, The	1956	Herman	I Like Everybody*	Uptempo	G3	G4	Character Male
Loesser, Frank	Tenor	Most Happy Fella, The	1956	Herman	I Like Everybody Reprise*	Uptempo	F3	G4	Character Male
Loesser, Frank	Tenor	Most Happy Fella, The	1956	The Doctor	A Song Of A Summer Night*	Uptempo	F3	F4	Character Male
Loewe, Frederick	Alto	Brigadoon	1947	Meg Brockie	The Love Of My Life	Uptempo	G3	C5	Character Ingenue Female
Loewe, Frederick	Alto	Brigadoon	1947	Meg Brockie	My Mother's Wedding Day	Uptempo	C4	F5	Character Ingenue Female
Loewe, Frederick	Baritone	Brigadoon	1947	Tommy Albright	The Heather On The Hill *	Ballad	Bb2	F4	Romantic Lead Male
Loewe, Frederick	Baritone	Brigadoon	1947	Tommy Albright	Almost Like Being In Love *	Ballad	C3	F#4	Romantic Lead Male
Loewe, Frederick	Baritone	Brigadoon	1947	Tommy Albright	There But For You Go I	Ballad	B2	F4	Romantic Lead Male
Loewe, Frederick	Baritone	Brigadoon	1947	Tommy Albright	From This Day On *	Ballad	D3	Eb4	Romantic Lead Male
Loewe, Frederick	Baritone	Brigadoon	1947	Tommy Albright	From This Day On Reprise *	Ballad	Eb3	Eb4	Romantic Lead Male
Loewe, Frederick	Baritone	Camelot	1960	Lancelot Du Lac	If Ever I would Leave You	Ballad	A2	D4	Romantic Lead Male
Loewe, Frederick	Baritone	My Fair Lady	1956	Henry Higgins	I've Grown Accustomed To Her Face	Ballad	A2	B3	Romantic Lead Male
Loewe, Frederick	Baritone	Camelot	1960	King Arthur	What Do The Simple Folk Do?*	Moderate Tempo	Bb2	E4	Romantic Lead Male
Loewe, Frederick	Baritone	Camelot	1960	King Arthur	Finalte Ultimo	Moderate Tempo	Bb2	C4	Romantic Lead Male
Loewe, Frederick	Baritone	My Fair Lady	1956	Henry Higgins	I'm An Ordinary Man	Moderate Tempo	Bb2	C4	Romantic Lead Male
Loewe, Frederick	Baritone	Camelot	1960	King Arthur	I Wonder What The King Is Doing To	Uptempo	Bb2	C4	Romantic Lead Male
Loewe, Frederick	Baritone	Camelot	1960	King Arthur	Camelot*	Uptempo	C3	D4	Romantic Lead Male
Loewe, Frederick	Baritone	Camelot	1960	Lancelot Du Lac	C'est Moi	Uptempo	B2	D4	Romantic Lead Male
Loewe, Frederick	Baritone	Camelot	1960	King Arthur	How To Handle A Woman*	Uptempo	A2	D4	Romantic Lead Male
Loewe, Frederick	Baritone	Camelot	1960	Mordred	The Seven Deadly Virtues	Uptempo	C3	D4	Antagonist Male
Loewe, Frederick	Baritone	Camelot	1960	A Man	Guenevere*	Uptempo	D3	D4	Adults
Loewe, Frederick	Baritone	My Fair Lady	1956	Henry Higgins	Why Can't The English	Uptempo	B2	D4	Romantic Lead Male
Loewe, Frederick	Baritone	My Fair Lady	1956	Alfred Doolittle	With A Little Bit Of Luck*	Uptempo	G2	E4	Character Male
Loewe, Frederick	Baritone	My Fair Lady	1956	Alfred Doolittle	Little Bit Of Luck Of Luck Reprise	Uptempo	G2	E4	Character Male
Loewe, Frederick	Baritone	My Fair Lady	1956	Alfred Doolittle	Get Me To The Church On Time	Uptempo	B2	D4	Character Male
Loewe, Frederick	Baritone	My Fair Lady	1956	Henry Higgins	A Hymn to Him	Uptempo	C#3	D4	Romantic Lead Male
Loewe, Frederick	Soprano	Brigadoon	1947	Fiona MacLaren	Waitin For My Dearie *	Ballad	C4	A5	Ingenue Female
Loewe, Frederick	Soprano	Brigadoon	1947	Fiona MacLaren	The Heather On The Hill *	Ballad	Bb2	G4	Ingenue Female
Loewe, Frederick	Soprano	Brigadoon	1947	Fiona MacLaren	Almost Like Being In Love *	Ballad	F4	A5	Ingenue Female
Loewe, Frederick	Soprano	Brigadoon	1947	Fiona MacLaren	From This Day On *	Ballad	F4	A5	Ingenue Female

Composer	Vocal Range	Show	Year	Role	Song	Tempo	Range-Bottom	Range-Top	Char Type
Loewe, Frederick	Soprano	Brigadoon	1947	Fiona MacLaren	Come To Me Bend To Me Reprise	Ballad	D4	G5	Ingenue Female
Loewe, Frederick	Soprano	Brigadoon	1947	Fiona MacLaren	The Heather On The Hill Reprise	Ballad	C4	F5	Ingenue Female
Loewe, Frederick	Soprano	Brigadoon	1947	Fiona MacLaren	From This Day On Reprise *	Ballad	Eb4	G5	Ingenue Female
Loewe, Frederick	Soprano	Camelot	1960	Guenevere	I Loved You Once In Silence	Ballad	Db4	Eb5	Romantic Lead Female
Loewe, Frederick	Soprano	My Fair Lady	1956	Eliza Doolittle	Just You Wait Reprise	Ballad	D4	C5	Ingenue Female
Loewe, Frederick	Soprano	My Fair Lady	1956	Eliza Doolittle	Wouldn't It Be Lovely Reprise*	Ballad	C4	D5	Ingenue Female
Loewe, Frederick	Soprano	Camelot	1960	Guenevere	The Simple Joys Of Maidenhood	Moderate Tempo	B3	D#5	Romantic Lead Female
Loewe, Frederick	Soprano	Camelot	1960	Nimue	Follow Me*	Moderate Tempo	C#4	F#5	Romantic Lead Female
Loewe, Frederick	Soprano	Camelot	1960	Guenevere	Before I Gaze At You Again	Moderate Tempo	C4	Eb5	Romantic Lead Female
Loewe, Frederick	Soprano	Camelot	1960	Guenevere	What Do The Simple Folk Do?*	Moderate Tempo	Bb3	E5	Romantic Lead Female
Loewe, Frederick	Soprano	My Fair Lady	1956	Eliza Doolittle	Wouldn't It Be Loverly	Moderate Tempo	C4	Eb5	Ingenue Female
Loewe, Frederick	Soprano	My Fair Lady	1956	Eliza Doolittle	Just You Wait	Moderate Tempo	A3	Eb4	Ingenue Female
Loewe, Frederick	Soprano	My Fair Lady	1956	Eliza Doolittle	Without You	Moderate Tempo	B3	Eb5	Ingenue Female
Loewe, Frederick	Soprano	Camelot	1960	Guenevere	Camelot*	Uptempo	C4	D5	Romantic Lead Female
Loewe, Frederick	Soprano	Camelot	1960	Guenevere	The Lusty Month Of May*	Uptempo	D4	A5	Romantic Lead Female
Loewe, Frederick	Soprano	My Fair Lady	1956	Eliza Doolittle	I Could Have Danced All Night*	Uptempo	B3	G5	Ingenue Female
Loewe, Frederick	Soprano	My Fair Lady	1956	Eliza Doolittle	Show Me	Uptempo	D4	G5	Ingenue Female
Loewe, Frederick	Tenor	Brigadoon	1947	Charlie Dalrymple	Come To Me Bend To me	Ballad	D3	G4	Ingenue Male
Loewe, Frederick	Tenor	My Fair Lady	1956	Freddy Eynsford Hill	On The Street Where You Live	Moderate Tempo	C3	F4	Ingenue Male
Loewe, Frederick	Tenor	My Fair Lady	1956	Freddy Eynsford Hill	On The Street Where You Live Repris	Moderate Tempo	C3	E4	Ingenue Male
Loewe, Frederick	Tenor	Brigadoon	1947	Charlie Dalrymple	I'll Go Home With Bonnie Jean	Uptempo	Bb2	G4	Ingenue Male
Loewe, Frederick	Tenor	Brigadoon	1947	Charlie Dalrymple	Go Home Reprise	Uptempo	G3	G4	Ingenue Male
Lopez and Marx	Alto	Avenue Q	2003	Christmas Eve	The More You Love Someone	Ballad	B3	Eb5	Character Female
Lopez and Marx	Alto	Avenue Q	2003	Kate Monster	There's A Fine Fine Line	Moderate Tempo	G3	D5	Character Ingenue Female
Lopez and Marx	Alto	Avenue Q	2003	Lucy The Slut	Special	Moderate Tempo	G3	Db4	Romantic Antagonist Female
Lopez and Marx	Alto	Avenue Q	2003	Gary Coleman	You Can Be As Loud As You Want	Uptempo	G3	Db5	Character Female
Lopez and Marx	Alto	Avenue Q	2003	Gary Coleman	Schadenfruede *	Uptempo	F3	C5	Character Female
Lopez and Marx	Alto	Avenue Q	2003	Kate Monster	Mix Tape *	Uptempo	F3	D5	Character Ingenue Female
Lopez and Marx	Baritone	Avenue Q	2003	Princeton	What Do You...BA English	Moderate Tempo	B2	D4	Character Ingenue Male
Lopez and Marx	Baritone	Avenue Q	2003	Brian	I'm Not Wearing Underwear Today	Uptempo	B2	E4	Character Male
Lopez and Marx	Baritone	Avenue Q	2003	Brian	There Is Life Outside Your Apartmen	Uptempo	B#2	E4	Character Male
Lopez and Marx	Baritone	Avenue Q	2003	Princeton	Purpose	Uptempo	B2	G3	Character Ingenue Male
Lopez and Marx	Tenor	Avenue Q	2003	Rod	Fantasies Come True	Ballad	A2	D4	Character Male
Lopez and Marx	Tenor	Avenue Q	2003	Nicky	If You Were Gay	Uptempo	C3	A4	Character Male

Composer

Composer	Vocal Range	Show	Year	Role	Song	Tempo	Range-Bottom	Range-Top	Char Type
Lopez and Marx	Tenor	Avenue Q	2003	Rod	My Girlfriend Who Lives In Canada	Uptempo	B2	G4	Character Male
MacDermot, Galt	Alto	Hair	1968	Crissy	Frank Mills	Ballad	A2	C5	Ingenue Female
MacDermot, Galt	Alto	Hair	1968	Sheila	Easy To Be Hard	Ballad	C4	C5	Character Ingenue Female
MacDermot, Galt	Alto	Hair	1968	Margaret Mead	My Conviction	Moderate Tempo	E3	A4	Character Female
MacDermot, Galt	Alto	Hair	1968	Jeanie	Air	Uptempo	G3	G4	Character Female
MacDermot, Galt	Alto	Hair	1968	Sheila	I Believe In Love	Uptempo	G3	C5	Character Ingenue Female
MacDermot, Galt	Alto	Hair	1968	Sheila	Good Morning Starshine	Uptempo	C4	C5	Character Ingenue Female
MacDermot, Galt	Baritone	Hair	1968	Claude	Manchester England	Moderate Tempo	E3	F#4	Romantic Lead Male
MacDermot, Galt	Baritone	Hair	1968	Claude	Where Do I Go	Moderate Tempo	C4	F5	Romantic Lead Male
MacDermot, Galt	Baritone	Hair	1968	Claude	Manchester England Reprise	Moderate Tempo	E3	E4	Romantic Lead Male
MacDermot, Galt	Baritone	Hair	1968	Ron	Aquarius	Moderate Tempo	Eb3	Eb4	Character Male
MacDermot, Galt	Baritone	Hair	1968	Berger	Going Down	Uptempo	C3	F4	Antagonist Male
MacDermot, Galt	Baritone	Hair	1968	Claude	I Got Life	Uptempo	C3	F4	Romantic Lead Male
MacDermot, Galt	Baritone	Hair	1968	Claude	Hair	Uptempo	D3	G4	Romantic Lead Male
MacDermot, Galt	Baritone	Hair	1968	Hud+	Colored Spade	Uptempo	B2	D4	Antagonist Male
MacDermot, Galt	Tenor	Hair	1968	Woof	Sodomy	Ballad	D3	G4	Character Male
MacDermot, Galt	Tenor	Hair	1968	Berger	Donna	Uptempo	Eb3	Bb4	Antagonist Male
Maltby Jr., Richard	Alto	Closer Than Ever	1989	Woman Two	Another Wedding Song *	Ballad	B3	B4	Character Female
Maltby Jr., Richard	Alto	Closer Than Ever	1989	Woman Two	I've Been Here Before *	Ballad	Gb3	Cb5	Character Female
Maltby Jr., Richard	Alto	Closer Than Ever	1989	Woman Two	Miss Bird	Moderate Tempo	F3	Eb5	Character Female
Maltby Jr., Richard	Alto	Closer Than Ever	1989	Woman Two	There *	Moderate Tempo	A3	D5	Character Female
Maltby Jr., Richard	Alto	Closer Than Ever	1989	Woman Two	Back On Base	Moderate Tempo	G3	G5	Character Female
Maltby Jr., Richard	Alto	Closer Than Ever	1989	Woman Two	You Want To Be My Friend	Uptempo	D4	E5	Character Female
Maltby Jr., Richard	Baritone	Closer Than Ever	1989	Man Three (Pianist)	Father of Fathers *	Ballad	B2	E4	Adults
Maltby Jr., Richard	Baritone	Closer Than Ever	1989	Man Two	She Loves Me Not *	Ballad	C3	E4	Paternal
Maltby Jr., Richard	Baritone	Closer Than Ever	1989	Man Two	If I Sing	Ballad	A2	Eb4	Paternal
Maltby Jr., Richard	Baritone	Closer Than Ever	1989	Man Two	Father of Fathers *	Ballad	D3	F4	Paternal
Maltby Jr., Richard	Baritone	Closer Than Ever	1989	Man Two	There *	Moderate Tempo	A2	F4	Paternal
Maltby Jr., Richard	Soprano	Closer Than Ever	1989	Woman One	She Loves Me Not *	Ballad	Bb3	Eb5	Maternal
Maltby Jr., Richard	Soprano	Closer Than Ever	1989	Woman One	Patterns	Ballad	Bb3	Eb5	Maternal
Maltby Jr., Richard	Soprano	Closer Than Ever	1989	Woman One	It's Never That Easy *	Ballad	B3	G5	Maternal
Maltby Jr., Richard	Soprano	Closer Than Ever	1989	Woman One	Life Story	Moderate Tempo	Bb3	C5	Maternal
Maltby Jr., Richard	Soprano	Closer Than Ever	1989	Woman One	The Bear, the Tiger, the Hampster...	Uptempo	Ab3	Db4	Maternal
Maltby Jr., Richard	Tenor	Closer Than Ever	1989	Man One	She Loves Me Not *	Ballad	Bb2	A4	Ingenue Male

Composer

Composer	Vocal Range	Show	Year	Role	Song	Tempo	Range-Bottom	Range-Top	Char Type
Maltby Jr., Richard	Tenor	Closer Than Ever	1989	Man One	Another Wedding Song *	Ballad	B2	C4	Ingenue Male
Maltby Jr., Richard	Tenor	Closer Than Ever	1989	Man One	Father of Fathers *	Ballad	D3	G4	Ingenue Male
Maltby Jr., Richard	Tenor	Closer Than Ever	1989	Man One	One Of The Good Guys	Tenor	C3	F4	Ingenue Male
Maltby Jr., Richard	Tenor	Closer Than Ever	1989	Man One	What Am I Doin'	Uptempo	C3	A4	Ingenue Male
Mancini, Henry	Alto	Victor/Victoria	1995	Parisienne	Paris By Night Reprise	Moderate Tempo	A3	C5	Romantic Lead Female
Mancini, Henry	Baritone	Victor/Victoria	1995	King Marchan	Almost A Love Song*	Ballad	G#2	Eb4	Romantic Lead Male
Mancini, Henry	Baritone	Victor/Victoria	1995	Toddy	Paris By Night*	Moderate Tempo	Bb2	Eb4	Character Male
Mancini, Henry	Baritone	Victor/Victoria	1995	Jazz Singer	Le Jazz Hot*	Moderate Tempo	D3	F#4	Romantic Lead Male
Mancini, Henry	Baritone	Victor/Victoria	1995	Toddy	Trust Me*	Uptempo	A2	D4	Character Male
Mancini, Henry	Baritone	Victor/Victoria	1995	King Marchan	King's Dilemma*	Uptempo	A2	D4	Romantic Lead Male
Mancini, Henry	Soprano	Victor/Victoria	1995	Victoria	Crazy World	Ballad	Eb3	C5	Romantic Lead Female
Mancini, Henry	Soprano	Victor/Victoria	1995	Victoria	Almost A Love Song*	Ballad	G#3	C5	Romantic Lead Female
Mancini, Henry	Soprano	Victor/Victoria	1995	Victoria	Living In The Shadows	Ballad	E3	A4	Romantic Lead Female
Mancini, Henry	Soprano	Victor/Victoria	1995	Victoria	If I Were A Man	Moderate Tempo	G3	A4	Romantic Lead Female
Mancini, Henry	Soprano	Victor/Victoria	1995	Victor	Le Jazz Hot	Moderate Tempo	G#3	D5	Romantic Lead Female
Mancini, Henry	Soprano	Victor/Victoria	1995	Norma Cassidy	Paris Makes Me Horny	Moderate Tempo	Bb3	A5	Romantic Antagonist Female
Mancini, Henry	Soprano	Victor/Victoria	1995	Victoria	Living In The Shadows	Moderate Tempo	E3	D5	Romantic Lead Female
Mancini, Henry	Soprano	Victor/Victoria	1995	Victor	Louis Says*	Uptempo	E3	F4	Romantic Lead Female
Mancini, Henry	Soprano	Victor/Victoria	1995	Norma Cassidy	Chicago Illinois*	Uptempo	A#3	E5	Romantic Antagonist Female
Margoshes, Steve	Alto	Fame	2003	Carmen	Bring In Tomorrow *	Ballad	D4	D	Character Ingenue Female
Margoshes, Steve	Alto	Fame	2003	Carmen	In LA	Ballad	Bb3	Eb5	Character Ingenue Female
Margoshes, Steve	Alto	Fame	2003	Miss Sherman	These Are My Children	Ballad	F3	C5	Mature Female
Margoshes, Steve	Alto	Fame	2003	Serena	Let's Play A Love Scene	Ballad	G#3	D#5	Character Female
Margoshes, Steve	Alto	Fame	2003	Serena	Let's Play A Love Scene Reprise *	Ballad	A3	B4	Character Female
Margoshes, Steve	Alto	Fame	2003	Mabel	Mabel's Prayer	Moderate Tempo	D4	E5	Character Female
Margoshes, Steve	Alto	Fame	2003	Carmen	There She Goes *	Uptempo	A3	C5	Character Ingenue Female
Margoshes, Steve	Alto	Fame	2003	Carmen	Fame! *	Uptempo	Eb4	Eb5	Character Ingenue Female
Margoshes, Steve	Alto	Fame	2003	Serena	Think of Meryl Streep	Uptempo	B3	D5	Character Female
Margoshes, Steve	Baritone	Fame	2003	Schlomo	Bring In Tomorrow *	Ballad	D3	F4	Character Male
Margoshes, Steve	Tenor	Fame	2003	Nick	Let's Play A Love Scene Reprise *	Ballad	Db3	G4	Ingenue Male
Margoshes, Steve	Tenor	Fame	2003	Nick	I Want To Make Magic	Moderate Tempo	C3	G4	Ingenue Male
Margoshes, Steve	Tenor	Fame	2003	Joe	I Can't Keep It Down *	Uptempo	C3	Bb4	Character Male
Margoshes, Steve	Tenor	Fame	2003	Tyrone+	Tyrone's Rap	Uptempo	Bb3	Bb4	Antagonist Male
Margoshes, Steve	Tenor	Fame	2003	Tyrone+	Dancin' On The Sidewalk	Uptempo	Bb2	Bb4	Antagonist Male

Composer

Composer	Vocal Range	Show	Year	Role	Song	Tempo	Range-Bottom	Range-Top	Char Type
Menken, Alan	Alto	Little Shop of Horrors	1982	Audrey	Somewhere That's Green	Ballad	B3	C5	Character Ingenue Female
Menken, Alan	Alto	Little Shop of Horrors	1982	Audrey	Somewhere That's Green Reprise	Ballad	B2	C5	Character Ingenue Female
Menken, Alan	Alto	Little Shop of Horrors	1982	Audrey	Suddenly Seymour	Moderate Tempo	A2	C#4	Character Ingenue Female
Menken, Alan	Baritone	Beauty and the Beast	1994	Beast	If I Can't Love Her	Ballad	B2	F4	Romantic Antagonist Male
Menken, Alan	Baritone	Beauty and the Beast	1994	Beast	If I Can't Love Her Reprise	Ballad	D4	D5	Romantic Antagonist Male
Menken, Alan	Baritone	Beauty and the Beast	1994	Gaston	Maison Des Lune	Moderate Tempo	B2	E4	Romantic Antagonist Male
Menken, Alan	Baritone	Little Shop of Horrors	1982	Voice of Audrey II	Git It (Feed Me)*	Moderate Tempo	B2	G4	Antagonist Male
Menken, Alan	Baritone	Little Shop of Horrors	1982	Voice of Audrey II	Suppertime*	Moderate Tempo	G2	F4	Antagonist Male
Menken, Alan	Baritone	Beauty and the Beast	1994	Beast	How Long Must This Go On	Uptempo	D3	C4	Romantic Antagonist Male
Menken, Alan	Baritone	Beauty and the Beast	1994	Beast	Something There *	Uptempo	A2	E5	Romantic Antagonist Male
Menken, Alan	Baritone	Beauty and the Beast	1994	Gaston	Me	Uptempo	B2	F4	Romantic Antagonist Male
Menken, Alan	Baritone	Beauty and the Beast	1994	Gaston	Gaston Reprise	Uptempo	C3	E4	Romantic Antagonist Male
Menken, Alan	Baritone	Beauty and the Beast	1994	Lumiere	Be Our Guest	Uptempo	F#2	E4	Romantic Lead Male
Menken, Alan	Baritone	Beauty and the Beast	1994	Maurice	No Matter What	Uptempo	B2	Db4	Paternal
Menken, Alan	Baritone	Beauty and the Beast	1994	Maurice	No Matter What Reprise	Uptempo	Bb2	G3	Paternal
Menken, Alan	Baritone	Little Shop of Horrors	1982	Mr. Mushnik	Mushnik and Son*	Uptempo	A2	F4	Mature Male
Menken, Alan	Baritone	Little Shop of Horrors	1982	Mr. Mushnik	Ya Never Know*	Uptempo	C3	C4	Mature Male
Menken, Alan	Baritone	Little Shop of Horrors	1982	Orin Scrivello	Dentist!	Uptempo	A2	F4	Antagonist Male
Menken, Alan	Baritone	The Little Mermaid	2007	Chef Louis	Les Poisons	Uptempo	Eb3	D4	Character Male
Menken, Alan	Soprano	A Christmas Carol	1997	Emily	A Place Called Home	Ballad	Bb3	F5	Ingenue Female
Menken, Alan	Soprano	A Christmas Carol	1997	Scrooge-Child	A Place Called Home	Ballad	Bb2	A4	Juvenile Male
Menken, Alan	Soprano	Beauty and the Beast	1994	Belle	Home	Ballad	G3	E5	Character Ingenue Female
Menken, Alan	Soprano	Beauty and the Beast	1994	Belle	Home Reprise	Ballad	C4	D5	Character Ingenue Female
Menken, Alan	Soprano	Beauty and the Beast	1994	Mrs. Potts	Home Reprise	Ballad	G3	D5	Maternal
Menken, Alan	Soprano	Beauty and the Beast	1994	Mrs. Potts	Beauty and the Beast	Ballad	F3	B4	Maternal
Menken, Alan	Soprano	The Little Mermaid	2007	Ursula	I Want The Good Times Back	Moderate Tempo	F#3	A5	Antagonist Female
Menken, Alan	Soprano	The Little Mermaid	2007	Ursula	Daddy's Little Angel	Moderate Tempo	Eb3	C5	Antagonist Female
Menken, Alan	Soprano	The Little Mermaid	2007	Ursula	Poor Unfortunate Soul	Moderate Tempo	C4	A5	Antagonist Female
Menken, Alan	Soprano	The Little Mermaid	2007	Ursula	I Want The Good Time Back Reprise	Moderate Tempo	F#3	A5	Antagonist Female
Menken, Alan	Soprano	The Little Mermaid	2007	Ursula	Her Voice Reprise	Moderate Tempo	Db3	Eb4	Antagonist Female
Menken, Alan	Soprano	The Little Mermaid	2007	Ursula	Ursula's Incantation*	Moderate Tempo	G4	F#5	Antagonist Female
Menken, Alan	Soprano	The Little Mermaid	2007	Ariel	Ursula's Incantation (Ahs)*	Moderate Tempo	F#4	E5	Ingenue Female
Menken, Alan	Soprano	A Christmas Carol	1997	Grace Smythe	God Bless Us Everyone	Uptempo	D4	C5	Ingenue Female
Menken, Alan	Soprano	A Christmas Carol	1997	Tiny Tim	Christmas Together	Uptempo	Bb4	C5	Juvenile Male

Composer

Composer	Vocal Range	Show	Year	Role	Song	Tempo	Range-Bottom	Range-Top	Char Type
Menken, Alan	Soprano	A Christmas Carol	1997	Tiny Tim	God Bless Us Everyone	Uptempo	D4	C5	Juvenile Male
Menken, Alan	Soprano	Beauty and the Beast	1994	Belle	Belle Reprise	Uptempo	D4	D5	Character Ingenue Female
Menken, Alan	Soprano	Beauty and the Beast	1994	Belle	Something There *	Uptempo	A3	E5	Character Ingenue Female
Menken, Alan	Soprano	Beauty and the Beast	1994	Mrs. Potts	Be Our Guest Reprise	Uptempo	G3	G5	Maternal
Menken, Alan	Soprano	The Little Mermaid	2007	Ariel	The World Above	Uptempo	A3	C5	Ingenue Female
Menken, Alan	Soprano	The Little Mermaid	2007	Ariel	Part Of Your World	Uptempo	C4	C5	Ingenue Female
Menken, Alan	Soprano	The Little Mermaid	2007	Flounder	She's In Love*	Uptempo	G3	A#5	Juvenile Male
Menken, Alan	Tenor	A Christmas Carol	1997	Scrooge-Adult	Yesterday, Tomorrow and Today	Ballad	D3	E4	Character Male
Menken, Alan	Tenor	A Christmas Carol	1997	Scrooge-Adult	Will Tiny Tim Live	Ballad	D3	E4	Character Male
Menken, Alan	Tenor	A Christmas Carol	1997	Scrooge-Young Adult	A Place Called Home	Ballad	Bb2	D4	Character Ingenue Male
Menken, Alan	Tenor	The Little Mermaid	2007	Flotsam	Sweet Child	Ballad	C3	C5	Antagonist Male
Menken, Alan	Tenor	The Little Mermaid	2007	Jetsom	Sweet Child	Ballad	C3	C5	Antagonist Male
Menken, Alan	Tenor	Little Shop of Horrors	1982	Seymour Krelborn	Grow For Me	Moderate Tempo	Bb2	F4	Character Male
Menken, Alan	Tenor	The Little Mermaid	2007	Prince Eric	Her Voice	Moderate Tempo	C3	G4	Ingenue Male
Menken, Alan	Tenor	The Little Mermaid	2007	Sebastian	The World Above Reprise	Moderate Tempo	C3	E4	Character Male
Menken, Alan	Tenor	The Little Mermaid	2007	Prince Eric	One Step Closer	Moderate Tempo	B3	F#5	Ingenue Male
Menken, Alan	Tenor	The Little Mermaid	2007	Sebastian	Kiss The Girl	Moderate Tempo	D3	F4	Character Male
Menken, Alan	Tenor	The Little Mermaid	2007	Sebastian	Kiss The Girl*	Moderate Tempo	A2	C4	Character Male
Menken, Alan	Tenor	A Christmas Carol	1997	Bob Cratchit	Christmas Together	Uptempo	D3	D4	Character Male
Menken, Alan	Tenor	A Christmas Carol	1997	Ghost...Past	The Lights of Long Ago	Uptempo	E3	E4	Character Male
Menken, Alan	Tenor	A Christmas Carol	1997	Ghost...Past	Abundance and Charity	Uptempo	A#2	F#4	Character Male
Menken, Alan	Tenor	A Christmas Carol	1997	Jacob Marley	Link By Link	Uptempo	D3	Ab4	Character Male
Menken, Alan	Tenor	A Christmas Carol	1997	Scrooge-Adult	Nothing To Do With Me	Uptempo	D3	Eb4	Character Male
Menken, Alan	Tenor	A Christmas Carol	1997	Scrooge-Adult	Christmas Day (Final Scene P2)	Uptempo	C3	E4	Character Male
Menken, Alan	Tenor	Beauty and the Beast	1994	Lefou	Gaston	Uptempo	B2	E4	Character Male
Menken, Alan	Tenor	Little Shop of Horrors	1982	Seymour Krelborn	Now*	Uptempo	B2	G4	Character Male
Menken, Alan	Tenor	The Little Mermaid	2007	Scuttle	Human Stuff*	Uptempo	B2	G4	Character Male
Menken, Alan	Tenor	The Little Mermaid	2007	Scuttle	Positoovity	Uptempo	G2	A4	Character Male
Menken, Alan	Tenor	The Little Mermaid	2007	Flounder	She's In Love*	Uptempo	G2	A#4	Ingenue Male
Miller, Roger	Alto	Big River	1985	Alice's Daughter +	How Blest We Are *	Ballad	C3	C5	Ingenue Female
Miller, Roger	Alto	Big River	1985	Slave +	Crossing Over *	Ballad	G3	C5	Character Female
Miller, Roger	Baritone	Big River	1985	Jim +	River In The Rain *	Ballad	A2	E4	Character Male
Miller, Roger	Baritone	Big River	1985	Jim +	Worlds Apart *	Ballad	B2	C4	Character Male
Miller, Roger	Baritone	Big River	1985	Jim +	Free At Last	Ballad	C3	F4	Character Male
Miller, Roger	Baritone	Big River	1985	Pap	Guv'ment	Moderate Tempo	B2	F#4	Character Male

Composer

Composer	Vocal Range	Show	Year	Role	Song	Tempo	Range-Bottom	Range-Top	Char Type
Miller, Roger	Baritone	Big River	1985	Duke	The Royal Nonesuch	Uptempo	D3	F4	Character Male
Miller, Roger	Baritone	Big River	1985	Jim +	Muddy Water	Uptempo	B2	F4	Character Male
Miller, Roger	Baritone	Big River	1985	Young Fool	Arkansas	Uptempo	C3	E4	Character Male
Miller, Roger	Soprano	Big River	1985	Mary Jane Wilkes	Leavin's Not The Only Way To Go	Ballad	B3	B4	Ingenue Female
Miller, Roger	Soprano	Big River	1985	Mary Jane Wilkes	You Oughta Be Here With Me	Ballad	B3	C#5	Ingenue Female
Miller, Roger	Tenor	Big River	1985	Huckleberry Finn	Waitin' For The Light To Shine	Ballad	G#2	C#4	Character Ingenue Male
Miller, Roger	Tenor	Big River	1985	Huckleberry Finn	River In The Rain *	Ballad	A2	G4	Character Ingenue Male
Miller, Roger	Tenor	Big River	1985	Huckleberry Finn	Worlds Apart *	Ballad	B2	B4	Character Ingenue Male
Miller, Roger	Tenor	Big River	1985	Huckleberry Finn	River in the Rain Reprise *	Ballad	A2	D4	Character Ingenue Male
Miller, Roger	Tenor	Big River	1985	Huckleberry Finn	Leavin's Not The Only Way To Go	Ballad	B2	B3	Character Ingenue Male
Miller, Roger	Tenor	Big River	1985	Huckleberry Finn	I, Huckleberry, Me	Uptempo	C3	F4	Character Ingenue Male
Miller, Roger	Tenor	Big River	1985	Huckleberry Finn	Waitin' For The Light To Shine Repris	Uptempo	A2	F#4	Character Ingenue Male
Miller, Roger	Tenor	Big River	1985	Tom Sawyer	Hand For The Hog	Uptempo	C3	F4	Ingenue Male
Miranda, Lin-Manuel	Alto	In The Heights	2008	Nina Rosario+	Everything's I Know	Ballad	Bb3	Db5	Ingenue Female
Miranda, Lin-Manuel	Alto	In The Heights	2008	Nina Rosario+	Alabanza*	Ballad	A3	A4	Ingenue Female
Miranda, Lin-Manuel	Alto	In The Heights	2008	Camila Rosario+	Enough*	Moderate Tempo	G3	Db5	Maternal
Miranda, Lin-Manuel	Alto	In The Heights	2008	Nina Rosario+	Breathe	Moderate Tempo	F3	F5	Ingenue Female
Miranda, Lin-Manuel	Alto	In The Heights	2008	Abuela Claudia	Paciencia Y Fe	Uptempo	F3	C5	Mature Female
Miranda, Lin-Manuel	Alto	In The Heights	2008	Nina Rosario+	When You're Home*	Uptempo	C#4	E5	Ingenue Female
Miranda, Lin-Manuel	Alto	In The Heights	2008	Vanessa+	It Won't Be Long Now	Uptempo	A3	E5	Romantic Lead Female
Miranda, Lin-Manuel	Baritone	In The Heights	2008	Kevin Rosario+	Inutil	Ballad	C3	E4	Paternal
Miranda, Lin-Manuel	Baritone	In The Heights	2008	Kevin Rosario+	Atencion	Ballad	F#3	D4	Paternal
Miranda, Lin-Manuel	Baritone	In The Heights	2008	Usnavi De La Vega+	Finale (Rap)*	Moderate Tempo	A3	C4	Character Male
Miranda, Lin-Manuel	Baritone	In The Heights	2008	Usnavi De La Vega+	In The Heights (Rap)*	Uptempo	D3	G4	Character Male
Miranda, Lin-Manuel	Tenor	In The Heights	2008	Benny+	Benny's Dispatch*	Uptempo	B3	F#4	Romantic Lead Male
Miranda, Lin-Manuel	Tenor	In The Heights	2008	Benny+	When You're Home*	Uptempo	E3	G4	Romantic Lead Male
Miranda, Lin-Manuel	Tenor	In The Heights	2008	Piragua Guy+	Piragua	Uptempo	E3	A4	Character Male
Miranda, Lin-Manuel	Tenor	In The Heights	2008	Piragua Guy+	Piragua Reprise*	Uptempo	D3	A4	Character Male
Porter, Cole	Alto	High Society 1998	1943	Liz Imbrie	He's A Right Guy	Ballad	F3	A4	Character Female
Porter, Cole	Alto	Anything Goes	1934	Reno Sweeney	Buddy Beware	Moderate Tempo	A3	C#5	Character Female
Porter, Cole	Alto	Kiss Me Kate	1948	Lilli Vanessi/Katherine	I Hate Men	Moderate Tempo	B3	C#5	Romantic Lead Female
Porter, Cole	Alto	Kiss Me Kate	1948	Lois Lane/Bianca	Why Can't You Behave*	Moderate Tempo	G3	Cb5	Character Ingenue Female
Porter, Cole	Alto	Anything Goes	1934	Reno Sweeney	I Get A Kick Out of You	Uptempo	A3	D5	Character Male
Porter, Cole	Alto	Anything Goes	1934	Reno Sweeney	You're the Top *	Uptempo	G3	D5	Character Female
Porter, Cole	Alto	Anything Goes	1934	Reno Sweeney	Anything Goes	Uptempo	Ab3	C5	Character Female

Composer

338

Composer	Vocal Range	Show	Year	Role	Song	Tempo	Range-Bottom	Range-Top	Char Type
Porter, Cole	Alto	Anything Goes	1934	Reno Sweeney	Blow Gabriel Blow	Uptempo	G3	C5	Character Female
Porter, Cole	Alto	Anything Goes	1934	Reno Sweeney	Friendship *	Uptempo	Bb3	Eb5	Character Female
Porter, Cole	Alto	High Society 1998	1930	Liz Imbrie	I'm Getting Ready For You*	Uptempo	A#3	E5	Character Female
Porter, Cole	Alto	Kiss Me Kate	1948	Hattie	Another Op'nin Another Show*	Uptempo	G3	E5	Character Female
Porter, Cole	Alto	Kiss Me Kate	1948	Lois Lane/Bianca	Always True To You*	Uptempo	A3	C#5	Character Ingenue Female
Porter, Cole	Alto	Kiss Me Kate	1948	Lois Lane/Bianca	Always True To You Encore	Uptempo	Bb3	A5	Character Ingenue Female
Porter, Cole	Baritone	Anything Goes	1934	Billy Crocker	All Through The Night *	Ballad	F3	G4	Romantic Lead Male
Porter, Cole	Baritone	High Society 1998	1956	Mike Connor	You're Sensational	Ballad	G2	F4	Romantic Antagonist Male
Porter, Cole	Baritone	Kiss Me Kate	1948	Fred Graham/Petruchio	Wunderbar*	Ballad	C3	G4	Romantic Lead Male
Porter, Cole	Baritone	Kiss Me Kate	1948	Fred Graham/Petruchio	So In Love Reprise	Ballad	B2	Eb4	Romantic Lead Male
Porter, Cole	Baritone	High Society 1998	1929	George Kittredge	I'll Worship You	Moderate Tempo	G#2	F#4	Romantic Lead Male
Porter, Cole	Baritone	Kiss Me Kate	1948	First Man	Brush Up Your Shakespeare*	Moderate Tempo	B2	D4	Antagonist Male
Porter, Cole	Baritone	Kiss Me Kate	1948	Fred Graham/Petruchio	Were Thine That Speical Face	Moderate Tempo	C3	F4	Romantic Lead Male
Porter, Cole	Baritone	Kiss Me Kate	1948	Fred Graham/Petruchio	Where Is The Life That Late I Led	Moderate Tempo	B2	F4	Romantic Lead Male
Porter, Cole	Baritone	Kiss Me Kate	1948	Second Man	Brush Up Your Shakespeare*	Moderate Tempo	B2	D4	Antagonist Male
Porter, Cole	Baritone	Anything Goes	1934	Billy Crocker	You're the Top *	Uptempo	B2	F4	Romantic Lead Male
Porter, Cole	Baritone	Kiss Me Kate	1948	Bill Calhoun/Lucentio	Bianca*	Uptempo	G2	F4	Character Ingenue Male
Porter, Cole	Baritone	Kiss Me Kate	1948	General Howell	From This Moment On	Uptempo	B2	C#4	Character Male
Porter, Cole	Soprano	Anything Goes	1934	Hope Harcourt	All Through The Night *	Ballad	C4	Eb5	Ingenue Female
Porter, Cole	Soprano	Anything Goes	1934	Hope Harcourt	Goodbye Little Dream, Goodbye	Ballad	A3	Eb5	Ingenue Female
Porter, Cole	Soprano	High Society 1998	1953	Tracy Lord	It's Alright With Me	Ballad	C4	E5	Romantic Lead Female
Porter, Cole	Soprano	Kiss Me Kate	1948	Lilli Vanessi/Katherine	Wunderbar*	Ballad	C4	G5	Romantic Lead Female
Porter, Cole	Soprano	Kiss Me Kate	1948	Lilli Vanessi/Katherine	So In Love	Ballad	A3	Db5	Romantic Lead Female
Porter, Cole	Soprano	Anything Goes	1934	Hope Harcourt	The Gypsy In Me	Moderate Tempo	C3	G4	Ingenue Female
Porter, Cole	Soprano	High Society 1998	1933	Tracy Lord	Once Upon A Time	Moderate Tempo	F3	A4	Romantic Lead Female
Porter, Cole	Soprano	Kiss Me Kate	1948	Lilli Vanessi/Katherine	I Am Ashamed That Women Are So S	Moderate Tempo	C4	Eb5	Romantic Lead Female
Porter, Cole	Soprano	Anything Goes	1934	Hope Harcourt	Let's Misbehave*	Uptempo	B2	C#5	Ingenue Female
Porter, Cole	Soprano	High Society 1998	1955	Tracy Lord	High Society*	Uptempo	Ab3	Eb5	Romantic Lead Female
Porter, Cole	Tenor	High Society 1998	1955	Dexter C.K. Haven	True Love*	Ballad	C3	F4	Romantic Lead Female
Porter, Cole	Tenor	Anything Goes	1934	Moon Face Martin	Be Like A Blue Bird	Moderate Tempo	B#2	F#4	Character Male
Porter, Cole	Tenor	High Society 1998	1933	Dexter C.K. Haven	Once Upon A Time	Moderate Tempo	G2	E4	Romantic Lead Male
Porter, Cole	Tenor	Anything Goes	1934	Moon Face Martin	Friendship *	Uptempo	Bb2	Eb4	Character Male
Porter, Cole	Tenor	High Society 1998	1929	Uncle Willie	She's Got That Thing*	Uptempo	G2	G4	Mature Male
Porter, Cole	Tenor	High Society 1998	1929	Dexter C.K. Haven	She's Got That Thing*	Uptempo	A2	G4	Romantic Lead Male

Composer	Vocal Range	Show	Year	Role	Song	Tempo	Range-Bottom	Range-Top	Char Type
Porter, Cole	Tenor	High Society 1998	1930	Uncle Willie	I'm Getting Ready For You*	Uptempo	Bb2	E4	Mature Male
Porter, Cole	Tenor	High Society 1998	1930	Uncle Willie	Say It With Gin	Uptempo	C3	C4	Mature Male
Porter, Cole	Tenor	High Society 1998	1935	Dexter C.K. Haven	Just One Of Those Things	Uptempo	B2	E4	Romantic Lead Male
Porter, Cole	Tenor	High Society 1998	1955	Dexter C.K. Haven	Little One*	Uptempo	A2	D4	Romantic Lead Male
Porter, Cole	Tenor	High Society 1998	1955	Dexter C.K. Haven	Little On Reprise	Uptempo	Bb2	Ab3	Romantic Lead Male
Porter, Cole	Tenor	Kiss Me Kate	1948	Paul	Too Darn Hot*	Uptempo	C3	Gb4	Character Male
Presley, Elvis	Alto	All Shook Up	2005	Natalie Haller	Love Me Tender	Ballad	C4	C5	Character Ingenue Female
Presley, Elvis	Alto	All Shook Up	2005	Natalie Haller	Fools Fall In Love *	Ballad	A3	D5	Character Ingenue Female
Presley, Elvis	Alto	All Shook Up	2005	Sylvia	There's Always Me	Ballad	G3	F5	Maternal
Presley, Elvis	Alto	All Shook Up	2005	Lorraine	It's Now Or Never *	Moderate Tempo	C4	F5	Ingenue Female
Presley, Elvis	Alto	All Shook Up	2005	Miss Sandra	Let Yourself Go	Moderate Tempo	E2	E4	Romantic Lead Female
Presley, Elvis	Alto	All Shook Up	2005	Natalie Haller	One Night With You	Moderate Tempo	C4	D5	Character Ingenue Female
Presley, Elvis	Alto	All Shook Up	2005	Natalie Haller	If I Can Dream *	Moderate Tempo	C4	F5	Character Ingenue Female
Presley, Elvis	Alto	All Shook Up	2005	Ed (Natalie In Drag)	Don't Be Cruel *	Uptempo	D4	D5	Character Ingenue Female
Presley, Elvis	Alto	All Shook Up	2005	Ed (Natalie In Drag)	A Little Less Conversation	Uptempo	Ab3	Eb5	Character Ingenue Female
Presley, Elvis	Alto	All Shook Up	2005	Mayor Matilda Hyde	Devil In Disguise	Uptempo	C4	F#5	Mature Female
Presley, Elvis	Alto	All Shook Up	2005	Natalie Haller	Follow That Dream*	Uptempo	B3	D4	Character Ingenue Female
Presley, Elvis	Baritone	All Shook Up	2005	Dean Hyde	It's Now Or Never *	Moderate Tempo	C3	F4	Ingenue Male
Presley, Elvis	Tenor	All Shook Up	2005	Chad	I Don't Want To	Ballad	D3	G4	Romantic Antagonist Male
Presley, Elvis	Tenor	All Shook Up	2005	Dennis	It Hurts Me	Ballad	A2	Bb4	Character Male
Presley, Elvis	Tenor	All Shook Up	2005	Chad	If I Can Dream *	Moderate Tempo	C3	G4	Romantic Antagonist Male
Presley, Elvis	Tenor	All Shook Up	2005	Chad	The Power of Love *	Moderate Tempo	E3	Eb4	Romantic Antagonist Male
Presley, Elvis	Tenor	All Shook Up	2005	Chad	Roustabout	Uptempo	E3	G4	Romantic Antagonist Male
Presley, Elvis	Tenor	All Shook Up	2005	Chad	C'mon	Uptempo	Db3	G#4	Romantic Antagonist Male
Presley, Elvis	Tenor	All Shook Up	2005	Chad	Follow That Dream*	Uptempo	A2	E4	Romantic Antagonist Male
Presley, Elvis	Tenor	All Shook Up	2005	Chad	Don't Be Cruel *	Uptempo	B2	F#4	Romantic Antagonist Male
Presley, Elvis	Tenor	All Shook Up	2005	Chad	Jailhouse Rock *	Uptempo	B2	C5	Romantic Antagonist Male
Ralph & Hugh	Alto	Meet Me In St. Louis	1989	Esther Smith	The Boy Next Door	Ballad	Ab3 Bb4		Character Ingenue Female
Ralph & Hugh	Alto	Meet Me In St. Louis	1989	Anna Smith	Wasn't It Fun*	Ballad	F3	C4	Maternal
Ralph & Hugh	Alto	Meet Me In St. Louis	1989	Esther Smith	You Are For Loving*	Ballad	Bb3	C5	Character Ingenue Female
Ralph & Hugh	Alto	Meet Me In St. Louis	1989	Esther Smith	Have Yourself A Merry Little Christma	Ballad	G3	C5	Character Ingenue Female
Ralph & Hugh	Alto	Meet Me In St. Louis	1989	Esther Smith	Under The Bamboo Tree*	Moderate Tempo	C4	Bb4	Character Ingenue Female
Ralph & Hugh	Alto	Meet Me In St. Louis	1989	Tootie Smith	Under The Bamboo Tree*	Moderate Tempo	C4	Bb4	Juvenile Female

Composer

Composer	Vocal Range	Show	Year	Role	Song	Tempo	Range-Bottom	Range-Top	Char Type
Ralph & Hugh	Alto	Meet Me In St. Louis	1989	Anna Smith	You'll Hear A Bill	Moderate Tempo	Bb3	D5	Maternal
Ralph & Hugh	Alto	Meet Me In St. Louis	1989	Esther Smith	Over The Banister	Moderate Tempo	Bb3	Eb5	Character Ingenue Female
Ralph & Hugh	Alto	Meet Me In St. Louis	1989	Anna Smith	You'll Hear A Bell Reprise	Moderate Tempo	Bb3	Bb4	Maternal
Ralph & Hugh	Alto	Meet Me In St. Louis	1989	Esther Smith	The Trolly Song*	Uptempo	A3	Bb4	Character Ingenue Female
Ralph & Hugh	Alto	Meet Me In St. Louis	1989	Katie	A Touch Of Irish*	Uptempo	G3	Bb4	Character Female
Ralph & Hugh	Alto	Meet Me In St. Louis	1989	Anna Smith	A Day In New York*	Uptempo	B3	E4	Maternal
Ralph & Hugh	Baritone	Meet Me In St. Louis	1989	Alonso Smith	Wasn't It Fun*	Ballad	Ab2	Bb3	Paternal
Ralph & Hugh	Baritone	Meet Me In St. Louis	1989	John Truitt	You Are For Loving*	Ballad	Db3	F4	Ingenue Male
Ralph & Hugh	Baritone	Meet Me In St. Louis	1989	Warren Sheffield	Raving Beauty*	Ballad	C3	Eb4	Romantic Lead Male
Ralph & Hugh	Baritone	Meet Me In St. Louis	1989	John Truitt	The Girl Next Door	Moderate Tempo	D3	E4	Ingenue Male
Ralph & Hugh	Baritone	Meet Me In St. Louis	1989	Lon Smith	Banjos*	Uptempo	Bb2	F4	Ingenue Male
Ralph & Hugh	Soprano	Meet Me In St. Louis	1989	Rose Smith	Raving Beauty*	Ballad	Bb3	Db5	Ingenue Female
Ralph & Hugh	Soprano	Meet Me In St. Louis	1989	Agnes Smith	Under The Bamboo Tree*	Moderate Tempo	C4	Bb4	Ingenue Female
Reale, Robert	Baritone	A Year With Frog and Toad	2002	Toad	Seeds	Ballad	A2	D4	Character Male
Reale, Robert	Baritone	A Year With Frog and Toad	2002	Toad	Alone	Ballad	A2	G#4	Character Male
Reale, Robert	Baritone	A Year With Frog and Toad	2002	Frog	He'll Never Know	Moderate Tempo	B2	D4	Character Male
Reale, Robert	Baritone	A Year With Frog and Toad	2002	Toad	He'll Never Know	Moderate Tempo	C#3	Eb4	Character Male
Reale, Robert	Baritone	A Year With Frog and Toad	2002	Toad	Toad To The Rescue	Moderate Tempo	E3	A4	Character Male
Reale, Robert	Baritone	A Year With Frog and Toad	2002	Toad	Merry Almost Christmas	Moderate Tempo	E3	A4	Character Male
Reale, Robert	Tenor	A Year With Frog and Toad	2002	Snail	The Letter #1	Moderate Tempo	A2	Bb3	Character Ingenue Male
Reale, Robert	Tenor	A Year With Frog and Toad	2002	Snail	Letter #2	Uptempo	B2	E4	Character Ingenue Male
Reale, Robert	Tenor	A Year With Frog and Toad	2002	Snail	The Letter #3	Uptempo	C#3	Eb4	Character Ingenue Male
Reale, Robert	Tenor	A Year With Frog and Toad	2002	Snail	I'm Coming Out Of My Shell	Uptempo	E3	A4	Character Ingenue Male
Rodgers, Mary	Alto	Once Upon A Mattress	1959	Queen Aggravain	Sensitivity*	Moderate Tempo	A3	B4	Romantic Antagonist Female
Rodgers, Mary	Alto	Once Upon A Mattress	1959	Princess Winifred	Happily Ever After	Moderate Tempo	A3	Cb5	Character Ingenue Female
Rodgers, Mary	Alto	Once Upon A Mattress	1959	Princess Winifred	Shy*	Uptempo	B3	C5	Character Female
Rodgers, Mary	Baritone	Once Upon A Mattress	1959	Sir Harry	In A Little While Reprise*	Ballad	D3	F4	Romantic Lead Male
Rodgers, Mary	Baritone	Once Upon A Mattress	1959	Sir Harry	In A Little While*	Uptempo	Db3	F4	Romantic Lead Male
Rodgers, Mary	Baritone	Once Upon A Mattress	1959	Prince Dauntless	Song Of Love*	Uptempo	C#3	Eb4	Character Ingenue Male
Rodgers, Mary	Baritone	Once Upon A Mattress	1959	Sir Harry	Yesterday I Loved You*	Uptempo	F3	F4	Romantic Lead Male
Rodgers, Mary	Soprano	Once Upon A Mattress	1959	Lady Larken	In A Little While Reprise*	Ballad	D4	F5	Romantic Lead Female
Rodgers, Mary	Soprano	Once Upon A Mattress	1959	Nightingale	Nightingale Lullaby	Moderate Tempo	Gb4	G5	Character Ingenue Female

Composer

Composer	Vocal Range	Show	Year	Role	Song	Tempo	Range-Bottom	Range-Top	Char Type
Rodgers, Mary	Soprano	Once Upon A Mattress	1959	Lady Larken	In A Little While*	Uptempo	Db4	Eb5	Romantic Lead Female
Rodgers, Mary	Soprano	Once Upon A Mattress	1959	Lady Larken	Yesterday I Loved You*	Uptempo	E4	F5	Romantic Lead Female
Rodgers, Mary	Tenor	Once Upon A Mattress	1959	Minstrel	Many Moons Ago	Moderate Tempo	D3	G4	Romantic Lead Male
Rodgers, Mary	Tenor	Once Upon A Mattress	1959	Jester	Very Soft Shoes*	Moderate Tempo	D3	F4	Character Male
Rodgers, Mary	Tenor	Once Upon A Mattress	1959	Minstrel	Normandy*	Uptempo	D#3	B4	Romantic Antagonist Male
Rodgers, Mary	Tenor	Once Upon A Mattress	1959	Jester	Normandy*	Uptempo	D#3	B4	Character Male
Rodgers, Richard	Alto	Babes In Arms (1998)	1937	Billie Smith	My Funny Valentine	Ballad	A3	C5	Ingenue Female
Rodgers, Richard	Alto	Carousel	1945	Carrie Pipperidge	When I Marry Mr. Snow	Ballad	D4	F5	Character Ingenue Female
Rodgers, Richard	Alto	Carousel	1945	Carrie Pipperidge	When I Marry Mr. Snow Reprise	Ballad	F#3	A4	Character Ingenue Female
Rodgers, Richard	Alto	Flower Drum Song 2002	1958	Wu Mei-Li+	You Are Beautiful Reprise*	Ballad	D4	D5	Ingenue Female
Rodgers, Richard	Alto	Flower Drum Song 2002	1958	Wu Mei-Li+	I Enjoy Being A Girl Reprise	Ballad	Bb3	D5	Ingenue Female
Rodgers, Richard	Alto	Flower Drum Song 2002	1958	Wu Mei-Li+	Love, Look Away (Ab Maj)	Ballad	G3	C5	Ingenue Female
Rodgers, Richard	Alto	Flower Drum Song 2002	1958	Helen Chao+	Love, Look Away (C Maj)	Ballad	B3	E5	Romantic Lead Female
Rodgers, Richard	Alto	South Pacific	1949	Bloody Mary	Bali Ha'i	Ballad	G3	G4	Character Female
Rodgers, Richard	Alto	South Pacific	1949	Bloody Mary	Bali Ha'I Reprise	Ballad	D3	E4	Character Female
Rodgers, Richard	Alto	South Pacific	1949	Nellie Forbush	Some Enchanted Evening Reprise 2	Ballad	Ab3	Bb4	Romantic Lead Female
Rodgers, Richard	Alto	Babes In Arms (1998)	1937	Baby Rose	Way Out West*	Moderate Tempo	B3	C5	Romantic Lead Female
Rodgers, Richard	Alto	Babes In Arms (1998)	1937	Baby Rose	Imagine*	Moderate Tempo	A3	C5	Romantic Lead Female
Rodgers, Richard	Alto	Babes In Arms (1998)	1937	Billie Smith	All At Once*	Moderate Tempo	A3	Bb4	Ingenue Female
Rodgers, Richard	Alto	Carousel	1945	Carrie Pipperidge	You're A Queer One Julie Jordan	Moderate Tempo	D4	E5	Character Ingenue Female
Rodgers, Richard	Alto	Carousel	1945	Carrie Pipperidge	When The Children Are Asleep *	Moderate Tempo	Eb3	C5	Character Ingenue Female
Rodgers, Richard	Alto	Flower Drum Song 2002	1958	Wu Mei-Li+	A Hundred Million Miracles*	Moderate Tempo	C4	Eb5	Ingenue Female
Rodgers, Richard	Alto	Flower Drum Song 2002	1958	Wu Mei-Li+	I Am Going To Like It Here	Moderate Tempo	Bb3	Bb4	Ingenue Female
Rodgers, Richard	Alto	Flower Drum Song 2002	1958	Linda Low+	I Enjoy Being A Girl Encore*	Moderate Tempo	A3	Cb5	Romantic Lead Female
Rodgers, Richard	Alto	Flower Drum Song 2002	1958	Linda Low+	I Enjoy Being A Girl Playoff*	Moderate Tempo	Bb3	Eb5	Romantic Lead Female
Rodgers, Richard	Alto	Flower Drum Song 2002	1958	Madam Rita Liang	Grant Avenue*	Moderate Tempo	A3	C5	Romantic Antagonist Female
Rodgers, Richard	Alto	Flower Drum Song 2002	1958	Wu Mei-Li+	A Hundred Million Miracles Reprise*	Moderate Tempo	Ab3	Bb4	Ingenue Female
Rodgers, Richard	Alto	Oklahoma!	1943	Ado Annie Carnes	I Cain't Say No Reprise	Moderate Tempo	C4	D5	Character Ingenue Female
Rodgers, Richard	Alto	Sound Of Music, The	1959	Liesl von Trapp	You Are Sixteen*	Moderate Tempo	B3	C#5	Ingenue Female
Rodgers, Richard	Alto	State Fair 1996	1945	Margy Frake	It Might As Well Be Spring	Moderate Tempo	Bb3	Bb4	Ingenue Female
Rodgers, Richard	Alto	State Fair 1996	1945	Margy Frake	It Might As Well Be Spring Reprise	Moderate Tempo	Bb3	Bb4	Ingenue Female
Rodgers, Richard	Alto	State Fair 1996	1996	Emily Arden	That's The Way It Happens*	Moderate Tempo	B3	D5	Romantic Antagonist Female
Rodgers, Richard	Alto	Oklahoma!	1943	Ado Annie Carnes	I Cain't Say No	Moderate Tempo	C4	D5	Character Ingenue Female

Composer

Composer	Vocal Range	Show	Year	Role	Song	Tempo	Range-Bottom	Range-Top	Char Type
Rodgers, Richard	Alto	Babes In Arms (1998)	1937	Billie Smith	Where Or When*	Moderate Tempo	B3	E5	Ingenue Female
Rodgers, Richard	Alto	Babes In Arms (1998)	1937	Dolores Reynolds	I Wish I Were In Love Again*	Uptempo	A3	A4	Ingenue Female
Rodgers, Richard	Alto	Babes In Arms (1998)	1937	Billie Smith	The Lady Is A Tramp	Uptempo	Ab3	Bb4	Ingenue Female
Rodgers, Richard	Alto	Babes In Arms (1998)	1937	Billie Smith	The Lady Is A Tramp Encore	Uptempo	Ab3	Bb4	Ingenue Female
Rodgers, Richard	Alto	Babes In Arms (1998)	1937	Dolores Reynolds	You Are So Fair*	Uptempo	B3	B4	Ingenue Female
Rodgers, Richard	Alto	Babes In Arms (1998)	1937	Baby Rose	Johnny One Note	Uptempo	Bb3	Bb4	Romantic Lead Female
Rodgers, Richard	Alto	Babes In Arms (1998)	1937	Billie Smith	The Lady Is A Tramp Reprise	Uptempo	Ab3	Bb4	Ingenue Female
Rodgers, Richard	Alto	Cinderella (2013)	1957	Charlotte	Stepsister's Lament*	Uptempo	C4	D5	Character Female
Rodgers, Richard	Alto	Cinderella (2013)	1957	Gabrielle	Stepsister's Lament*	Uptempo	C4	D5	Character Ingenue Female
Rodgers, Richard	Alto	Cinderella (2013)	1957	Gabrielle	A Lovely Night*	Uptempo	B3	D5	Character Ingenue Female
Rodgers, Richard	Alto	Cinderella (2013)	1957	Joy	A Lovely Night*	Uptempo	B3	D5	Character Female
Rodgers, Richard	Alto	Cinderella (2013)	1957	Stepmother (Madam)	A Lovely Night*	Uptempo	B3	D5	Romantic Antagonist Female
Rodgers, Richard	Alto	Flower Drum Song 2002	1958	Linda Low+	I Enjoy Being A Girl	Uptempo	A3	B4	Romantic Lead Female
Rodgers, Richard	Alto	Flower Drum Song 2002	1958	Linda Low+	Fan Tan Fannie*	Uptempo	B3	B4	Romantic Lead Female
Rodgers, Richard	Alto	South Pacific	1949	Nellie Forbush	A Cockeyed Optimist	Uptempo	A3	C5	Romantic Lead Female
Rodgers, Richard	Alto	South Pacific	1949	Nellie Forbush	I'm Gonna Wash That Man*	Uptempo	D3	E5	Romantic Lead Female
Rodgers, Richard	Alto	South Pacific	1949	Bloody Mary	Happy Talk	Uptempo	A3	C5	Character Female
Rodgers, Richard	Alto	South Pacific	1949	Nellie Forbush	Honey Bun	Uptempo	Bb3	Bb4	Romantic Lead Female
Rodgers, Richard	Alto	South Pacific	1949	Nellie Forbush	Im In Love…Wonderful Guy*	Uptempo	Bb3	Db5	Romantic Lead Female
Rodgers, Richard	Alto	South Pacific	1949	Nellie Forbush	Im In Love…Wonderful Guy Reprise	Uptempo	B3	C5	Romantic Lead Female
Rodgers, Richard	Alto	State Fair 1996	1953	Emily Arden	You Never Had It So Good	Uptempo	Bb3	Bb4	Romantic Antagonist Female
Rodgers, Richard	Alto	State Fair 1996	1996	Margy Frake	The Next Time It Happens	Uptempo	Bb3	D5	Ingenue Female
Rodgers, Richard	Alto	Babes In Arms (1998)	1937	Billie Smith	Babes In Arms*	Uptempo	C4	E5	Ingenue Female
Rodgers, Richard	Baritone	Carousel	1945	Billy Bigelow	If I Loved You *	Ballad	Bb2	Gb4	Romantic Antagonist Male
Rodgers, Richard	Baritone	Carousel	1945	Billy Bigelow	If I Loved You Reprise	Ballad	Eb3	Gb4	Romantic Antagonist Male
Rodgers, Richard	Baritone	Flower Drum Song 2002	1958	Chin+	My Best Love*	Ballad	D#3	E4	Mature Male
Rodgers, Richard	Baritone	Oklahoma!	1943	Jud Fry	Lonley Room	Ballad	D3	C4	Antagonist Male
Rodgers, Richard	Baritone	Oklahoma!	1943	Curly	Poor Jud*	Ballad	D#3	C#4	Romantic Lead Male
Rodgers, Richard	Baritone	Oklahoma!	1943	Jud Fry	Poor Jud*	Ballad	D#3	C#4	Antagonist Male
Rodgers, Richard	Baritone	Sound Of Music, The	1959	Captain von Trapp	Edelweiss	Ballad	E3	F4	Romantic Lead Male
Rodgers, Richard	Baritone	South Pacific	1949	Emile De Becque	Some Enchanted Evening	Ballad	C3	E4	Romantic Lead Male
Rodgers, Richard	Baritone	South Pacific	1949	Emile De Becque	Some Enchanted Evening Reprise 2	Ballad	C3	E4	Romantic Lead Male
Rodgers, Richard	Baritone	South Pacific	1949	Emile De Becque	This Nearly Was Mine	Ballad	B2	D4	Romantic Lead Male
Rodgers, Richard	Baritone	Babes In Arms (1998)	1937	Val LaMar	Where Or When*	Moderate Tempo	B2	F4	Ingenue Male

Composer

Composer	Vocal Range	Show	Year	Role	Song	Tempo	Range-Bottom	Range-Top	Char Type
Rodgers, Richard	Baritone	Babes In Arms (1998)	1937	Val LaMar	All At Once*	Moderate Tempo	A2	F4	Ingenue Male
Rodgers, Richard	Baritone	Babes In Arms (1998)	1937	Peter	Imagine Reprise #2*	Moderate Tempo	E3	F4	Antagonist Male
Rodgers, Richard	Baritone	Carousel	1945	Billy Bigelow	Soliloquy	Moderate Tempo	B2	G4	Romantic Antagonist Male
Rodgers, Richard	Baritone	Carousel	1945	Billy Bigelow	The Highest Judge Of All	Moderate Tempo	D3	G4	Romantic Antagonist Male
Rodgers, Richard	Baritone	Flower Drum Song 2002	1958	Chi-Yang Wang+	Gliding Through My Memory*	Moderate Tempo	D3	G4	Romantic Lead Male
Rodgers, Richard	Baritone	King and I, The	1951	King of Siam+	Song of the King	Moderate Tempo	D3	D4	Romantic Lead Male
Rodgers, Richard	Baritone	Oklahoma!	1943	Curly	Oh What A Beautiful Morning	Moderate Tempo	D3	E4	Romantic Lead Male
Rodgers, Richard	Baritone	Oklahoma!	1943	Curly	People Will Say We're In Love	Moderate Tempo	C#3	F#4	Romantic Lead Male
Rodgers, Richard	Baritone	Oklahoma!	1943	Ali Hakim	It's A Scandal! It's A Outrage	Moderate Tempo	B2	F#4	Character Male
Rodgers, Richard	Baritone	Oklahoma!	1943	Old Man Carnes	The Farmer And The Cowman*	Moderate Tempo	F3	F4	Mature Male
Rodgers, Richard	Baritone	Sound Of Music, The	1959	Rolf Gruber	You Are Sixteen*	Moderate Tempo	D3	E4	Ingenue Male
Rodgers, Richard	Baritone	South Pacific	1949	Emile De Becque	You've Got To Be Carefully Taught Re	Moderate Tempo	C#3	E4	Romantic Lead Male
Rodgers, Richard	Baritone	State Fair 1996	1945	Wayne Frake	That's For Me	Moderate Tempo	C3	F4	Ingenue Male
Rodgers, Richard	Baritone	State Fair 1996	1945	Pat Gilbert	Isn't It Kinda Fun Reprise	Moderate Tempo	C3	G#4	Romantic Antagonist Male
Rodgers, Richard	Baritone	State Fair 1996	1947	Wayne Frake	So Far*	Moderate Tempo	D3	E4	Ingenue Male
Rodgers, Richard	Baritone	State Fair 1996	1996	Wayne Frake	The Man I Used To Be*	Moderate Tempo	C3	Eb4	Ingenue Male
Rodgers, Richard	Baritone	State Fair 1996	1996	Pat Gilbert	The Man I Used To Be Reprise	Moderate Tempo	C3	Eb4	Romantic Antagonist Male
Rodgers, Richard	Baritone	State Fair 1996	1996	Abel Frake	Boys And Girls Like You And Me*	Moderate Tempo	Bb2	C4	Paternal
Rodgers, Richard	Baritone	Babes In Arms (1998)	1937	Val LaMar	Babes In Arms*	Uptempo	C3	E4	Ingenue Male
Rodgers, Richard	Baritone	Babes In Arms (1998)	1937	Marshall Blackstone	Babes In Arms*	Uptempo	C3	E4	Ingenue Male
Rodgers, Richard	Baritone	Babes In Arms (1998)	1998	Irving de Quincy+	Light On Our Feet*	Uptempo	F3	F4	Ingenue Male
Rodgers, Richard	Baritone	Babes In Arms (1998)	1998	Ivor de Quincy+	Light On Our Feet*	Uptempo	F3	F4	Ingenue Male
Rodgers, Richard	Baritone	Carousel	1945	Jigger Craigin	Stonecutter Cut It On Stone Reprise	Uptempo	C3	F4	Romantic Antagonist Male
Rodgers, Richard	Baritone	King and I, The	1951	King of Siam+	A Puzzlement	Uptempo	C3	E4	Romantic Lead Male
Rodgers, Richard	Baritone	King and I, The	1951	Louis Leonowens	A Puzzlement Reprise*	Uptempo	G2	G3	Juvenile Male
Rodgers, Richard	Baritone	King and I, The	1951	Louis Leonowens	I Whistle A Happy Tune*	Uptempo	B2	B3	Juvenile Male
Rodgers, Richard	Baritone	King and I, The	1951	Prince Chulalongkorn	A Puzzlement Reprise*	Uptempo	G2	G3	Juvenile Male
Rodgers, Richard	Baritone	Oklahoma!	1943	Curly	The Surrey With The Fringe On Top	Uptempo	D#3	E4	Romantic Lead Male
Rodgers, Richard	Baritone	Oklahoma!	1943	Will Parker	Kansas City	Uptempo	Eb3	F4	Character Ingenue Male
Rodgers, Richard	Baritone	South Pacific	1949	Luther Billis	Honey Bun Reprise	Uptempo	Bb2	B3	Character Male
Rodgers, Richard	Baritone	State Fair 1996	1945	Pat Gilbert	Isn't It Kinda Fun*	Uptempo	C#3	D4	Romantic Antagonist Male
Rodgers, Richard	Soprano	Carousel	1945	Julie Jordan	If I Loved You *	Ballad	C4	Gb5	Character Ingenue Female
Rodgers, Richard	Soprano	Carousel	1945	Julie Jordan	What's The Use In Wonderin'	Ballad	C4	F5	Character Ingenue Female
Rodgers, Richard	Soprano	Cinderella (2013)	1957	Ella	Do I Love You...*	Ballad	A4	E5	Ingenue Female
Rodgers, Richard	Soprano	Cinderella (2013)	1997	Fairy Godmother (Marie)	There's Music In You*	Ballad	C4	F5	Character Female

Composer	Vocal Range	Show	Year	Role	Song	Tempo	Range-Bottom	Range-Top	Char Type
Rodgers, Richard	Soprano	King and I, The	1951	Anna Leonowens	Hello, Young Lovers	Ballad	C#4	D5	Romantic Lead Female
Rodgers, Richard	Soprano	King and I, The	1951	Anna Leonowens	Hello, Young Lovers Reprise	Ballad	C4	D5	Romantic Lead Female
Rodgers, Richard	Soprano	King and I, The	1951	Lady Thiang+	Something Wonderful	Ballad	C#4	G5	Romantic Lead Female
Rodgers, Richard	Soprano	King and I, The	1951	Tuptim+	We Kiss In The Shadow	Ballad	D4	G5	Ingenue Female
Rodgers, Richard	Soprano	King and I, The	1951	Tuptim+	I Have Dreamed	Ballad	C4	G5	Ingenue Female
Rodgers, Richard	Soprano	Sound Of Music, The	1959	Mother Abbess	Climb Every Mountain	Ballad	C4	A♭5	Mature Female
Rodgers, Richard	Soprano	Sound Of Music, The	1959	Maria Rainer	Ordinary People*	Ballad	B3	D5	Character Ingenue Female
Rodgers, Richard	Soprano	Carousel	1945	Nettie Fowler	You'll Never Walk Alone	Moderate Tempo	C4	G5	Mature Female
Rodgers, Richard	Soprano	Cinderella (2013)	1957	Ella	Ten Minutes Ago*	Moderate Tempo	C#4	D5	Ingenue Female
Rodgers, Richard	Soprano	Cinderella (2013)	1962	Ella	The Sweetest Sounds*	Moderate Tempo	C#4	C5	Ingenue Female
Rodgers, Richard	Soprano	Cinderella (2013)	2013	Ella	He Was Tall	Moderate Tempo	D4	C#5	Ingenue Female
Rodgers, Richard	Soprano	King and I, The	1951	Anna Leonowens	Getting To Know You*	Moderate Tempo	C#4	E5	Romantic Lead Female
Rodgers, Richard	Soprano	King and I, The	1951	Lady Thiang+	Western People Funny*	Moderate Tempo	E4	G5	Romantic Lead Female
Rodgers, Richard	Soprano	King and I, The	1951	Tuptim+	My Lord And Master	Moderate Tempo	D#4	A#5	Ingenue Female
Rodgers, Richard	Soprano	Oklahoma!	1943	Laurey	People Will Say We're In Love	Moderate Tempo	C#4	F#5	Character Ingenue Female
Rodgers, Richard	Soprano	Oklahoma!	1943	Laurey	Out Of My Dreams	Moderate Tempo	E4	F5	Character Ingenue Female
Rodgers, Richard	Soprano	Sound Of Music, The	1959	Maria Rainer	The Sound Of Music	Moderate Tempo	B3	B4	Character Ingenue Female
Rodgers, Richard	Soprano	South Pacific	1949	Jerome	Dites-Moi Pourquoi*	Moderate Tempo	D4	C5	Juvenile Male
Rodgers, Richard	Soprano	South Pacific	1949	Ngana	Dites-Moi Pourquoi*	Moderate Tempo	D4	C5	Juvenile Female
Rodgers, Richard	Soprano	Carousel	1945	Nettie Fowler	June Is Bustin' Out All Over *	Uptempo	D4	E5	Mature Female
Rodgers, Richard	Soprano	Carousel	1945	Nettie Fowler	June Is Bustin' Out All Over Reprise	Uptempo	E4	E5	Mature Female
Rodgers, Richard	Soprano	Carousel	1945	Nettie Fowler	June...Finale Act One	Uptempo	E4	E5	Mature Female
Rodgers, Richard	Soprano	Cinderella (2013)	1957	Ella	In My Own Little Corner	Uptempo	C4	C5	Ingenue Female
Rodgers, Richard	Soprano	Cinderella (2013)	1957	Ella	In My Own Little Corner Reprise	Uptempo	C4	C5	Ingenue Female
Rodgers, Richard	Soprano	Cinderella (2013)	1957	Ella	Impossible*	Uptempo	B♭2	D5	Ingenue Female
Rodgers, Richard	Soprano	Cinderella (2013)	1957	Ella	When You're Driving...*	Uptempo	B2	B♭4	Ingenue Female
Rodgers, Richard	Soprano	Cinderella (2013)	1957	Ella	A Lovely Night*	Uptempo	B♭3	B♭4	Ingenue Female
Rodgers, Richard	Soprano	Cinderella (2013)	1957	Ella	A Lovely Night*	Uptempo	C4	C5	Ingenue Female
Rodgers, Richard	Soprano	Cinderella (2013)	1957	Ella	It's Possible	Uptempo	C4	B4	Ingenue Female
Rodgers, Richard	Soprano	Cinderella (2013)	1957	Fairy Godmother (Marie)	Impossible*	Uptempo	F3	F4	Character Female
Rodgers, Richard	Soprano	Cinderella (2013)	1957	Fairy Godmother (Marie)	Fol-De-Rol	Uptempo	A2	F#4	Character Female
Rodgers, Richard	Soprano	King and I, The	1951	Anna Leonowens	I Whistle A Happy Tune*	Uptempo	D4	D5	Romantic Lead Female
Rodgers, Richard	Soprano	King and I, The	1951	Anna Leonowens	Shall I Tell You What I Think...	Uptempo	D3	C#5	Romantic Lead Female
Rodgers, Richard	Soprano	King and I, The	1951	Anna Leonowens	Shall We Dance	Uptempo	D4	C5	Romantic Lead Female
Rodgers, Richard	Soprano	Oklahoma!	1943	Laurey	Many A New Day	Uptempo	C#4	E5	Character Ingenue Female

Composer

345

Composer	Vocal Range	Show	Year	Role	Song	Tempo	Range-Bottom	Range-Top	Char Type
Rodgers, Richard	Soprano	Sound Of Music, The	1959	Maria Rainer	The Lonely Goatherd	Uptempo	C4	B♭5	Character Ingenue Female
Rodgers, Richard	Soprano	Sound Of Music, The	1959	Elsa Schraeder	How Can Love Survive	Uptempo	D4	F5	Romantic Lead Female
Rodgers, Richard	Tenor	Carousel	1945	Enoch Snow	When I Marry Mr. Snow Reprise	Ballad	C4	D5	Character Ingenue Male
Rodgers, Richard	Tenor	Carousel	1945	Enoch Snow	Geranium In The Window *	Ballad	D3	F#4	Character Ingenue Male
Rodgers, Richard	Tenor	Cinderella (2013)	1940	Topher	Loneliness Of Evening*	Ballad	E♭3	A4	Ingenue Male
Rodgers, Richard	Tenor	Cinderella (2013)	1957	Topher	Do I Love You!...*	Ballad	A3	E♭4	Ingenue Male
Rodgers, Richard	Tenor	Flower Drum Song 2002	1958	Wang Ta+	You Are Beautiful	Ballad	E♭3	G4	Ingenue Male
Rodgers, Richard	Tenor	Flower Drum Song 2002	1958	Wang Ta+	You Are Beautiful Reprise*	Ballad	F3	G4	Ingenue Male
Rodgers, Richard	Tenor	King and I, The	1951	Lun Tha+	We Kiss In The Shadow	Ballad	D3	E4	Ingenue Male
Rodgers, Richard	Tenor	King and I, The	1951	Lun Tha+	I Have Dreamed	Ballad	C3	G4	Ingenue Male
Rodgers, Richard	Tenor	South Pacific	1949	Lt. Jospeh Cable	Younger Than Springtime*	Ballad	E3	G4	Ingenue Male
Rodgers, Richard	Tenor	Carousel	1945	Enoch Snow	When The Children Are Asleep *	Moderate Tempo	E♭3	C5	Character Ingenue Male
Rodgers, Richard	Tenor	Cinderella (2013)	1957	Topher	Ten Minutes Ago*	Moderate Tempo	C3	D4	Ingenue Male
Rodgers, Richard	Tenor	Cinderella (2013)	1957	Topher	Ten Minutes Ago Reprise	Moderate Tempo	C3	D4	Ingenue Male
Rodgers, Richard	Tenor	Cinderella (2013)	1962	Topher	The Sweetest Sounds*	Moderate Tempo	E3	E4	Ingenue Male
Rodgers, Richard	Tenor	Cinderella (2013)	1962	Topher	The Sweetest Sounds Reprise	Moderate Tempo	A2	F♭4	Ingenue Male
Rodgers, Richard	Tenor	Cinderella (2013)	1985	Topher	Me, Who Am I*	Moderate Tempo	B2	G4	Ingenue Male
Rodgers, Richard	Tenor	Flower Drum Song 2002	1958	Wang Ta+	Sunday	Moderate Tempo	C#4	E4	Ingenue Male
Rodgers, Richard	Tenor	Flower Drum Song 2002	1958	Chi-Yang Wang+	Chop Suey*	Moderate Tempo	B2	D#4	Romantic Lead Male
Rodgers, Richard	Tenor	Flower Drum Song 2002	1958	Wang Ta+	Like A God	Moderate Tempo	B2	G4	Ingenue Male
Rodgers, Richard	Tenor	Babes In Arms (1998)	1937	Gus Fielding	I Wish I Were In Love Again*	Uptempo	C3	A♭4	Antagonist Male
Rodgers, Richard	Tenor	Babes In Arms (1998)	1937	Gus Fielding	You Are So Fair*	Uptempo	E♭3	F4	Antagonist Male
Rodgers, Richard	Tenor	Cinderella (2013)	1949	Jean-Michel	Now Is the Time*	Uptempo	E♭3	F4	Character Male
Rodgers, Richard	Tenor	Cinderella (2013)	1949	Jean-Michel	Now Is The Time Reprise*	Uptempo	C3	A4	Character Male
Rodgers, Richard	Tenor	Flower Drum Song 2002	1958	Wang Ta+	Like A God	Uptempo	C#3	G#4	Ingenue Male
Rodgers, Richard	Tenor	South Pacific	1949	Lt. Jospeh Cable	You've Got To Be Carefully Taught	Uptempo	E3	G4	Ingenue Male
Rusell, Willy	Alto	Blood Brothers	1993	Mrs. Johnstone	Easy Terms	Ballad	G3	A4	Character Female
Rusell, Willy	Alto	Blood Brothers	1993	Mrs. Johnstone	Easy Terms Reprise	Ballad	G3	F4	Character Female
Rusell, Willy	Alto	Blood Brothers	1993	Mrs. Johnstone	Light Romance	Ballad	G3	A4	Character Female
Rusell, Willy	Alto	Blood Brothers	1993	Mrs. Johnstone	Tell Me It's Not True	Ballad	F3	C5	Character Female
Rusell, Willy	Alto	Blood Brothers	1993	Mrs. Johnstone	Marilyn Monroe 3	Ballad	A3	B4	Character Female
Rusell, Willy	Alto	Blood Brothers	1993	Mrs. Johnstone	Marilyn Monroe	Moderate Tempo	A3	A4	Character Female
Rusell, Willy	Alto	Blood Brothers	1993	Mrs. Johnstone	Marilyn Monroe 2	Moderate Tempo	A3	A4	Character Female
Rusell, Willy	Alto	Blood Brothers	1993	Mrs. Johnstone	Bright New Day	Uptempo	D4	A4	Character Female

Composer

Composer	Vocal Range	Show	Year	Role	Song	Tempo	Range-Bottom	Range-Top	Char Type
Rusell, Willy	Alto	Blood Brothers	1993	Mrs. Johnstone	Bright New Day Reprise *	Uptempo	D4	C5	Character Female
Rusell, Willy	Baritone	Blood Brothers	1993	Edward	Long Sunday Afternoon *	Ballad	E3	C4	Ingenue Male
Rusell, Willy	Baritone	Blood Brothers	1993	Mickey	Long Sunday Afternoon *	Ballad	D3	E4	Antagonist Male
Rusell, Willy	Baritone	Blood Brothers	1993	Mr. Lyons	Miss Jones	Uptempo	C3	D4	Paternal
Rusell, Willy	Tenor	Blood Brothers	1993	Eddie	I'm Not Saying A Word	Moderate Tempo	E2	A3	Ingenue Male
Rusell, Willy	Tenor	Blood Brothers	1993	Narrator	Marilyn Monroe Reprise 1	Moderate Tempo	A3	B4	Character Male
Rusell, Willy	Tenor	Blood Brothers	1993	Narrator	Shoes Upon The Table	Uptempo	G2	G3	Character Male
Rusell, Willy	Tenor	Blood Brothers	1993	Narrator	Shoes Upon The Table Reprise	Uptempo	G3	Bb4	Character Male
Rusell, Willy	Tenor	Blood Brothers	1993	Narrator	Madman	Uptempo	F2	C4	Character Male
Schmidt, Harvey	Alto	110 In The Shade	1963	Girl	Cinderella	Uptempo	A3	D5	Juvenile Female
Schmidt, Harvey	Baritone	110 In The Shade	1963	File	A Man And A Woman *	Ballad	C3	D4	Character Male
Schmidt, Harvey	Baritone	110 In The Shade	1960	El Gallo	Try To Remember *	Ballad	A2	C4	Romantic Lead Male
Schmidt, Harvey	Baritone	110 In The Shade	1963	File	Gonna Be Another Hot Day *	Moderate Tempo	D3	F#4	Character Male
Schmidt, Harvey	Baritone	Fantasticks, The	1960	El Gallo	Try To Remember Reprise	Moderate Tempo	B2	C4	Romantic Lead Male
Schmidt, Harvey	Baritone	Fantasticks, The	1960	Matt	Soon It's Gonna Rain *	Moderate Tempo	D4	Ab5	Ingenue Male
Schmidt, Harvey	Baritone	Fantasticks, The	1963	File	Wonderful Music *	Uptempo	Db3	F4	Character Male
Schmidt, Harvey	Baritone	110 In The Shade	1963	H.C. Curry	Lizzie's Comin' Home *	Uptempo	B2	E4	Paternal
Schmidt, Harvey	Baritone	110 In The Shade	1963	Noah Curry	Lizzie's Comin' Home *	Uptempo	B2	E4	Antagonist Male
Schmidt, Harvey	Baritone	Fantasticks, The	1960	Bellomy	Never Say No *	Uptempo	G3	E4	Paternal
Schmidt, Harvey	Baritone	Fantasticks, The	1960	Bellomy	Plant A Raddish *	Uptempo	C3	F4	Paternal
Schmidt, Harvey	Baritone	Fantasticks, The	1960	Bellomy	It Depends On What You Pay Reprise	Uptempo	D3	G4	Paternal
Schmidt, Harvey	Baritone	Fantasticks, The	1960	El Gallo	It Depends On What You Pay	Uptempo	A2	G4	Romantic Lead Male
Schmidt, Harvey	Baritone	Fantasticks, The	1960	El Gallo	Round and Round *	Uptempo	Ab2	F4	Romantic Lead Male
Schmidt, Harvey	Baritone	Fantasticks, The	1960	Huckabee	Never Say No *	Uptempo	C3	E4	Paternal
Schmidt, Harvey	Baritone	Fantasticks, The	1960	Huckabee	Plant A Raddish *	Uptempo	C3	F4	Paternal
Schmidt, Harvey	Baritone	Fantasticks, The	1960	Huckabee	It Depends On What You Pay Reprise	Uptempo	D3	G4	Paternal
Schmidt, Harvey	Soprano	110 In The Shade	1963	Lizzie Curry	Simple Little Things	Ballad	B3	E5	Character Female
Schmidt, Harvey	Soprano	110 In The Shade	1963	Lizzie Curry	Is It Really Me	Ballad	A3	E5	Character Female
Schmidt, Harvey	Soprano	110 In The Shade	1963	Lizzie Curry	A Man And A Woman *	Ballad	D4	G5	Character Female
Schmidt, Harvey	Soprano	Fantasticks, The	1960	Luisa	They Were You *	Ballad	B3	D5	Ingenue Female
Schmidt, Harvey	Soprano	110 In The Shade	1963	Lizzie Curry	Old Maid	Moderate Tempo	B3	G#5	Character Female
Schmidt, Harvey	Soprano	Fantasticks, The	1960	Luisa	Soon It's Gonna Rain *	Moderate Tempo	B2	F4	Ingenue Female
Schmidt, Harvey	Soprano	110 In The Shade	1963	Lizzie Curry	Love Don't Turn Away	Uptempo	D#4	F5	Character Female
Schmidt, Harvey	Soprano	110 In The Shace	1963	Lizzie Curry	Raunchy	Uptempo	G3	F5	Character Female
Schmidt, Harvey	Soprano	Fantasticks, The	1960	Luisa	Much More	Uptempo	B3	F5	Ingenue Female

Composer

Composer	Vocal Range	Show	Year	Role	Song	Range-Bottom	Range-Top	Char Type
Schmidt, Harvey	Soprano	Fantasticks, The	1960	Luisa	Metaphor *	Eb4	G5	Ingenue Female
Schmidt, Harvey	Tenor	110 In The Shade	1963	Bill Starbuck	Evenin' Star	B3	Ab4	Romantic Antagonist Male
Schmidt, Harvey	Tenor	Fantasticks, The	1960	Matt	They Were You *	B2	D4	Ingenue Male
Schmidt, Harvey	Tenor	110 In The Shade	1963	Bill Starbuck	The Rain Song *	C3	Ab4	Romantic Antagonist Male
Schmidt, Harvey	Tenor	110 In The Shade	1963	Bill Starbuck	Melisande	G2	G4	Romantic Antagonist Male
Schmidt, Harvey	Tenor	110 In The Shade	1963	Bill Starbuck	Wonderful Music *	Db3	F4	Romantic Antagonist Male
Schmidt, Harvey	Tenor	110 In The Shade	1963	Jimmy Curry	Lizzie's Comin' Home *	B2	E4	Ingenue Male
Schmidt, Harvey	Tenor	Fantasticks, The	1960	Matt	Metaphor *	Cb3	Eb4	Ingenue Male
Schmidt, Harvey	Tenor	Fantasticks, The	1960	Matt	I Can See It *	B2	E4	Ingenue Male
Schmidt, Harvey	Tenor	Fantasticks, The	1960	Matt	Metaphor Reprise *	B2	D4	Ingenue Male
Schonberg, Claude-Michel	Alto	Les Miserables	1987	Eponine	On My Own	A3	C5	Character Ingenue Female
Schonberg, Claude-Michel	Alto	Les Miserables	1987	Eponine	A Little Fall Of Rain*	F3	Db5	Character Ingenue Female
Schonberg, Claude-Michel	Alto	Les Miserables	1987	Fantine	I Have Dreamed (E Major)	G3	C#5	Romantic Lead Female
Schonberg, Claude-Michel	Alto	Les Miserables	1987	Fantine	Come To Me	C4	C5	Romantic Lead Female
Schonberg, Claude-Michel	Alto	Les Miserables	1987	Fantine	I Have Dreamed (Eb Major)	Gb3	C5	Romantic Lead Female
Schonberg, Claude-Michel	Alto	Miss Saigon	1991	Gigi Van Trahn+	The Movie In My Mind*	Ab3	Eb5	Romantic Antagonist Female
Schonberg, Claude-Michel	Alto	Miss Saigon	1991	Ellen Scott	I Still Believe*	A3	Eb5	Romantic Lead Female
Schonberg, Claude-Michel	Alto	Miss Saigon	1991	Ellen Scott	Now I've Seen Her	G#3	E5	Romantic Lead Female
Schonberg, Claude-Michel	Alto	Les Miserables	1987	Gavroche	Look Down*	C4	Db5	Juvenile Male
Schonberg, Claude-Michel	Alto	Les Miserables	1987	Gavroche	Little People*	B3	D5	Juvenile Male
Schonberg, Claude-Michel	Alto	Les Miserables	1987	Madame Thenardier	Master of the House*	B3	D5	Antagonist Female
Schonberg, Claude-Michel	Alto	Les Miserables	1987	Madame Thenardier	Beggars at the Wedding	C#4	D5	Antagonist Female
Schonberg, Claude-Michel	Baritone	Les Miserables	1987	Thenardier	Dog Eats Dog	C3	E4	Antagonist Male
Schonberg, Claude-Michel	Baritone	Les Miserables	1987	Thenardier	Master of the House*	C3	D4	Antagonist Male
Schonberg, Claude-Michel	Baritone	Les Miserables	1987	Thenardier	Beggars at the Wedding	G#2	C4	Antagonist Male
Schonberg, Claude-Michel	Soprano	Les Miserables	1987	Young Cosette	Castle On The Cloud	A3	C5	Juvenile Female
Schonberg, Claude-Michel	Soprano	Miss Saigon	1991	Kim+	The Movie In My Mind*	Ab3	Eb5	Ingenue Female
Schonberg, Claude-Michel	Soprano	Miss Saigon	1991	Kim+	The Ceremony*	B3	D5	Ingenue Female
Schonberg, Claude-Michel	Soprano	Miss Saigon	1991	Kim+	I Still Believe*	A3	E5	Ingenue Female
Schonberg, Claude-Michel	Soprano	Miss Saigon	1991	Kim+	I'd Give My Life For You*	G3	E5	Ingenue Female
Schonberg, Claude-Michel	Soprano	Miss Saigon	1991	Kim+	Sun and Moon Reprise	E3	D5	Ingenue Female
Schonberg, Claude-Michel	Soprano	Miss Saigon	1991	Kim+	Little God Of My Heart	A3	D5	Ingenue Female
Schonberg, Claude-Michel	Soprano	Miss Saigon	1991	Kim+	Sun And Moon*	F#3	D5	Ingenue Female

Note: The Tempo column (between Song and Range-Bottom) reads top to bottom: Uptempo, Ballad, Ballad, Uptempo, Uptempo, Uptempo, Uptempo, Uptempo, Uptempo, Uptempo, Ballad, Ballad, Ballad, Ballad, Ballad, Ballad, Ballad, Ballad, Moderate Tempo, Uptempo, Uptempo, Uptempo, Moderate Tempo, Uptempo, Uptempo, Ballad, Ballad, Ballad, Ballad, Ballad, Ballad, Ballad, Ballad.

Composer

Composer	Vocal Range	Show	Year	Role	Song	Tempo	Range-Bottom	Range-Top	Char Type
Schonberg, Claude-Michel	Soprano	Miss Saigon	1991	Kim+	There Is A Secret (ms 214-258)	Moderate Tempo	A3	Db5	Ingenue Female
Schonberg, Claude-Michel	Soprano	Miss Saigon	1991	Kim+	You Will Not Touch Him (ms 20-51)	Moderate Tempo	C4	Eb5	Ingenue Female
Schonberg, Claude-Michel	Tenor	Les Miserables	1987	Jean Valjean	Bring Him Home	Ballad	E3	A4	Romantic Antagonist Male
Schonberg, Claude-Michel	Tenor	Les Miserables	1987	Male Student	Drink With Me*	Ballad	D3	Eb4	Ingenue Male
Schonberg, Claude-Michel	Tenor	Les Miserables	1987	Marius	Empty Chairs, Empty Tables (Bb Minor)	Ballad	Bb2	Ab4	Ingenue Male
Schonberg, Claude-Michel	Tenor	Les Miserables	1987	Marius	Empty Chairs, Empty Tables (A Minor)	Ballad	A2	G4	Ingenue Male
Schonberg, Claude-Michel	Tenor	Miss Saigon	1991	Chris Scott	Sun And Moon*	Ballad	A2	F#4	Romantic Lead Male
Schonberg, Claude-Michel	Tenor	Les Miserables	1987	Javert	Stars	Moderate Tempo	B2	E4	Antagonist Male
Schonberg, Claude-Michel	Tenor	Les Miserables	1987	Javert	Javert's Suicide	Moderate Tempo	C3	F#4	Antagonist Male
Schonberg, Claude-Michel	Tenor	Les Miserables	1987	Jean Valjean	Soliloquy	Moderate Tempo	C3	B4	Romantic Antagonist Male
Schonberg, Claude-Michel	Tenor	Les Miserables	1987	Jean Valjean	Who Am I	Moderate Tempo	B3	B4	Romantic Antagonist Male
Schonberg, Claude-Michel	Tenor	Miss Saigon	1991	Chris Scott	Why God Why	Moderate Tempo	G3	G4	Romantic Lead Male
Schonberg, Claude-Michel	Tenor	Miss Saigon	1991	Engineer+	If you Want To Die In Bed*	Moderate Tempo	A2	G4	Antagonist Male
Schonberg, Claude-Michel	Tenor	Miss Saigon	1991	John Thomas	Bui-Doi	Moderate Tempo	Ab2	Bb4	Romantic Antagonist Male
Schonberg, Claude-Michel	Tenor	Miss Saigon	1991	Engineer+	What A Waste*	Moderate Tempo	B2	F#4	Antagonist Male
Schonberg, Claude-Michel	Tenor	Miss Saigon	1991	Engineer+	The American Dream*	Moderate Tempo	A2	A4	Antagonist Male
Schonberg, Claude-Michel	Tenor	Miss Saigon	1991	Chris Scott	The Confrontation (ms44-79)	Uptempo	F3	B4	Romantic Lead Male
Schonberg, Claude-Michel	Tenor	Miss Saigon	1991	Thuy+	Kim's Nightmare Part I	Uptempo	C3	E4	Romantic Antagonist Male
Schwartz, Stephen	Alto	Children of Eden	1991	Yonah	Stranger To The Rain	Ballad	A3	D4	Character Ingenue Female
Schwartz, Stephen	Alto	Children of Eden	1991	Yonah	Sailor Of The Skies	Ballad	G3	Bb4	Character Ingenue Female
Schwartz, Stephen	Alto	Godspell	1971	Soloist 1	Day By Day	Ballad	C4	A4	Character Female
Schwartz, Stephen	Alto	Pippin	1972	Catherine	I Guess I'll Miss the Man	Ballad	F#3	B4	Romantic Lead Female
Schwartz, Stephen	Alto	Rags	1986	Bella Cohen	If We Never Meet Again*	Ballad	B2	C5	Character Ingenue Female
Schwartz, Stephen	Alto	Rags	1986	Bella Cohen	Rags Reprise	Ballad	B#3	B4	Character Ingenue Female
Schwartz, Stephen	Alto	Wicked	2003	Elphaba	I'm Not That Girl	Ballad	E3	B4	Character Female
Schwartz, Stephen	Alto	Wicked	2003	Elphaba	For Good*	Ballad	Ab3	Db5	Character Female
Schwartz, Stephen	Alto	Children of Eden	1991	Eve	Grateful Children *	Moderate Tempo	B3	D#4	Maternal
Schwartz, Stephen	Alto	Children of Eden	1991	Eve	Children Of Eden	Moderate Tempo	Ab3	Eb5	Maternal
Schwartz, Stephen	Alto	Children of Eden	1991	Mama Noah	Ain't It Good	Moderate Tempo	A3	A5	Maternal
Schwartz, Stephen	Alto	Godspell	1971	Soloist 3	O Bless The Lord*	Moderate Tempo	B3	E5	Character Female
Schwartz, Stephen	Alto	Godspell	1971	Soloist 5	Turn Back O Man*	Moderate Tempo	D3	D5	Character Female
Schwartz, Stephen	Alto	Pippin	1972	Fastrada	Spread A Little Sunshine	Moderate Tempo	A2	F5	Romantic Antagonist Female
Schwartz, Stephen	Alto	Pippin	1972	Catherine	Kind Of Woman*	Moderate Tempo	Ab3	C#5	Romantic Lead Female
Schwartz, Stephen	Alto	Rags	1986	Bella Cohen	Brand New World*	Moderate Tempo	C#4	D#5	Character Ingenue Female

Composer

Composer	Vocal Range	Show	Year	Role	Song	Tempo	Range-Bottom	Range-Top	Char Type
Schwartz, Stephen	Alto	Rags	1986	Rachel Halpern	Three Sunny Rooms*	Moderate Tempo	G3	Bb4	Mature Female
Schwartz, Stephen	Alto	Wicked	2003	Madame Morrible	The Wizard And I*	Moderate Tempo	Gb3	Bb4	Mature Female
Schwartz, Stephen	Alto	Wicked	2003	Elphaba	The Wizard And I*	Moderate Tempo	G3	E5	Character Female
Schwartz, Stephen	Alto	Wicked	2003	Elphaba	The Wizard and I Reprise	Moderate Tempo	A3	C5	Character Female
Schwartz, Stephen	Alto	Wicked	2003	Elphaba	As Long As You Are Mine*	Moderate Tempo	Bb3	Db5	Character Female
Schwartz, Stephen	Alto	Children of Eden	1991	Eve	The Spark of Creation	Uptempo	G#3	Eb5	Maternal
Schwartz, Stephen	Alto	Children of Eden	1991	Eve	The Spark of Creation Reprise	Uptempo	Ab3	Db5	Maternal
Schwartz, Stephen	Alto	Children of Eden	1991	Mama Noah	The Spark Of Creation Reprise 2	Uptempo	A3	A4	Maternal
Schwartz, Stephen	Alto	Godspell	1971	Soloist 2	Learn Your Lesson Well	Uptempo	G3	Eb5	Character Female
Schwartz, Stephen	Alto	Pippin	1972	Berthe	No Time At All*	Uptempo	G3	A4	Maternal
Schwartz, Stephen	Alto	Pippin	1972	Catherine	There He Was	Uptempo	G#3	B4	Romantic Lead Female
Schwartz, Stephen	Alto	Rags	1986	Rachel Halpern	Penny A Tune	Uptempo	G3	Bb4	Mature Female
Schwartz, Stephen	Alto	Rags	1986	Bella Cohen	Penny A Tune	Uptempo	B3	D5	Character Ingenue Female
Schwartz, Stephen	Alto	Rags	1986	Bella Cohen	Rags*	Uptempo	A3	D5	Character Ingenue Female
Schwartz, Stephen	Alto	Wicked	2003	Nessarose	Dancing Through Life*	Uptempo	A3	B4	Character Ingenue Female
Schwartz, Stephen	Alto	Wicked	2003	Elphaba	Defying Gravity*	Uptempo	G3	F5	Character Female
Schwartz, Stephen	Alto	Wicked	2003	Madame Morrible	Thank Goodness (Part 3)	Uptempo	A3	B4	Mature Female
Schwartz, Stephen	Alto	Wicked	2003	Elphaba	No Good Deed	Uptempo	A3	D#5	Character Female
Schwartz, Stephen	Baritone	Children of Eden	1991	Father	Precious Children	Ballad	Bb2	Eb4	Romantic Lead Male
Schwartz, Stephen	Baritone	Children of Eden	1991	Father	Father's Day	Moderate Tempo	B2	E4	Romantic Lead Male
Schwartz, Stephen	Baritone	Children of Eden	1991	Father	The Mark of Cain	Moderate Tempo	B2	F4	Romantic Lead Male
Schwartz, Stephen	Baritone	Rags	1986	Avram Cohen	Three Sunny Rooms*	Moderate Tempo	C3	D4	Paternal
Schwartz, Stephen	Baritone	Wicked	2003	Salesman	No One Mourns The Wicked*	Moderate Tempo	D3	E4	Character Male
Schwartz, Stephen	Baritone	Wicked	2003	Doctor Dillamond	Something Bad*	Moderate Tempo	C#3	Db4	Character Male
Schwartz, Stephen	Baritone	Wicked	2003	Wizard	A Sentimental Man	Moderate Tempo	B2	F#4	Character Male
Schwartz, Stephen	Baritone	Children of Eden	1991	Father	The Hardest Part Of Love *	Uptempo	D3	G4	Romantic Lead Male
Schwartz, Stephen	Baritone	Pippin	1972	Charles	War Is A Science*	Uptempo	Bb2	E4	Antagonist Male
Schwartz, Stephen	Baritone	Rags	1986	Saul	Easy For You	Uptempo	D3	D4	Antagonist Male
Schwartz, Stephen	Baritone	Wicked	2003	Wizard	Wonderful*	Uptempo	B2	E4	Character Male
Schwartz, Stephen	Soprano	Rags	1986	Rebecca Hershkowitz	If We Never Meet Again*	Ballad	B2	C5	Romantic Lead Female
Schwartz, Stephen	Soprano	Rags	1986	Rebecca Hershkowitz	If We Never Meet Again Reprise 2	Ballad	C4	D5	Romantic Lead Female
Schwartz, Stephen	Soprano	Wicked	2003	Glinda	I'm Not That Girl Reprise	Ballad	G3	D5	Romantic Lead Female
Schwartz, Stephen	Soprano	Wicked	2003	Glinda	For Good*	Ballad	Ab3	Db5	Romantic Lead Female

Composer	Vocal Range	Show	Year	Role	Song	Tempo	Range-Bottom	Range-Top	Char Type
Schwartz, Stephen	Soprano	Rags	1986	Rebecca Hershkowitz	Brand New World*	Moderate Tempo	B3	G4	Romantic Lead Female
Schwartz, Stephen	Soprano	Rags	1986	Rebecca Hershkowitz	Children Of The Wind	Moderate Tempo	A3	Bb5	Romantic Lead Female
Schwartz, Stephen	Soprano	Rags	1986	Rebecca Hershkowitz	Blame It on The Summer Night	Moderate Tempo	A3	D#5	Romantic Lead Female
Schwartz, Stephen	Soprano	Rags	1986	Rebecca Hershkowitz	Uptown*	Moderate Tempo	C4	Eb5	Romantic Lead Female
Schwartz, Stephen	Soprano	Rags	1986	Rebecca Hershkowitz	Wanting*	Moderate Tempo	A3	D#5	Romantic Lead Female
Schwartz, Stephen	Soprano	Wicked	2003	Glinda	Opening*	Moderate Tempo	A3	A5	Romantic Lead Female
Schwartz, Stephen	Soprano	Wicked	2003	Glinda	No One Mourns The Wicked*	Moderate Tempo	C#4	B5	Romantic Lead Female
Schwartz, Stephen	Soprano	Wicked	2003	Glinda	Popular*	Moderate Tempo	G3	C5	Romantic Lead Female
Schwartz, Stephen	Soprano	Rags	1986	Rebecca Hershkowitz	Penny A Tune	Uptempo	E4	F#4	Romantic Lead Female
Schwartz, Stephen	Soprano	Rags	1986	Rebecca Hershkowitz	Dancing With Fools*	Uptempo	Bb3	Gb5	Romantic Lead Female
Schwartz, Stephen	Soprano	Wicked	2003	Glinda	Thank Goodness (Part 3)	Uptempo	Bb3	A5	Romantic Lead Female
Schwartz, Stephen	Tenor	Children of Eden	1991	Noah	Blind Obedience	Ballad	D3	A3	Paternal
Schwartz, Stephen	Tenor	Children of Eden	1991	Noah	Noah's Lullaby	Ballad	C3	D4	Paternal
Schwartz, Stephen	Tenor	Godspell	1971	Jesus	Beautiful City (1972 Film)	Ballad	E3	F#4	Character Male
Schwartz, Stephen	Tenor	Godspell	1971	John The Baptist	Prepare Ye*	Ballad	C#3	G#4	Antagonist Male
Schwartz, Stephen	Tenor	Godspell	1971	Judas	On The Willows	Ballad	C3	F#4	Antagonist Male
Schwartz, Stephen	Tenor	Godspell	1971	Soloist 4	All Good Gifts	Ballad	D3	A4	Character Male
Schwartz, Stephen	Tenor	Pippin	1972	Pippin	With You	Ballad	C3	Ab4	Ingenue Male
Schwartz, Stephen	Tenor	Pippin	1972	Pippin	Love Song*	Ballad	B2	G#4	Ingenue Male
Schwartz, Stephen	Tenor	Children of Eden	1991	Abel	Lost in The Wilderness Reprise *	Moderate Tempo	G3	G4	Ingenue Male
Schwartz, Stephen	Tenor	Children of Eden	1991	Adam	A World Without You *	Moderate Tempo	Db3	Ab4	Character Male
Schwartz, Stephen	Tenor	Children of Eden	1991	Adam	Grateful Children *	Moderate Tempo	B2	D#3	Character Male
Schwartz, Stephen	Tenor	Children of Eden	1991	Cain	Lost In The Wilderness *	Moderate Tempo	D3	G4	Antagonist Male
Schwartz, Stephen	Tenor	Pippin	1972	Leading Player	Glory Part I & III*	Moderate Tempo	E3	G#4	Romantic Antagonist Male
Schwartz, Stephen	Tenor	Pippin	1972	Pippin	Corner Of The Sky Reprise	Moderate Tempo	D3	F4	Ingenue Male
Schwartz, Stephen	Tenor	Pippin	1972	Pippin	Morning Glow (C Major)	Moderate Tempo	C3	F#4	Ingenue Male
Schwartz, Stephen	Tenor	Pippin	1972	Pippin	Morning Glow (Db Major)	Moderate Tempo	Db3	G4	Ingenue Male
Schwartz, Stephen	Tenor	Pippin	1972	Leading Player	Right On Track*	Moderate Tempo	Eb3	Ab4	Romantic Antagonist Male
Schwartz, Stephen	Tenor	Pippin	1972	Pippin	Corner Of the Sky Last Reprise	Moderate Tempo	D#3	F#4	Ingenue Male
Schwartz, Stephen	Tenor	Rags	1986	Man	I Remember	Moderate Tempo	E3	G4	Character Male
Schwartz, Stephen	Tenor	Rags	1986	Nathan Hershkowitz	Uptown*	Moderate Tempo	E3	G4	Character Male
Schwartz, Stephen	Tenor	Wicked	2003	Father	No One Mourns The Wicked*	Moderate Tempo	D3	G4	Character Male
Schwartz, Stephen	Tenor	Wicked	2003	Fiyero	As Long As You Are Mine*	Moderate Tempo	G3	Bb4	Romantic Lead Male
Schwartz, Stephen	Tenor	Children of Eden	1991	Noah	The Hardest Part Of Love *	Uptempo	D3	G4	Paternal

Composer

Composer	Vocal Range	Show	Year	Role	Song	Tempo	Range-Bottom	Range-Top	Char Type
Schwartz, Stephen	Tenor	Godspell	1971	Jesus	Save The People	Uptempo	G3	G4	Character Male
Schwartz, Stephen	Tenor	Godspell	1971	Jesus	Alas For You	Uptempo	E3	G4	Character Male
Schwartz, Stephen	Tenor	Godspell	1971	Jesus	All For The Best*	Uptempo	D3	E4	Character Male
Schwartz, Stephen	Tenor	Godspell	1971	Judas	All For The Best*	Uptempo	C3	D4	Antagonist Male
Schwartz, Stephen	Tenor	Pippin	1972	Leading Player	Magic To Do*	Uptempo	E3	A4	Romantic Antagonist Male
Schwartz, Stephen	Tenor	Pippin	1972	Pippin	Corner Of The Sky	Uptempo	E3	C5	Ingenue Male
Schwartz, Stephen	Tenor	Pippin	1972	Pippin	War Is A Science*	Uptempo	Bb2	G4	Ingenue Male
Schwartz, Stephen	Tenor	Pippin	1972	Pippin	Extraordinary	Uptempo	C3	G4	Ingenue Male
Schwartz, Stephen	Tenor	Pippin	1972	Pippin	Prayer For A Duck	Uptempo	D3	F#4	Ingenue Male
Schwartz, Stephen	Tenor	Pippin	1972	Leading Player	Think About The Sun*	Uptempo	G3	F4	Romantic Antagonist Male
Schwartz, Stephen	Tenor	Pippin	1972	Pippin	Think About The Sun*	Uptempo	C3	G4	Ingenue Male
Schwartz, Stephen	Tenor	Rags	1986	Ben	The Sound Of Love*	Uptempo	Eb3	Ab4	Character Ingenue Male
Schwartz, Stephen	Tenor	Rags	1986	Tim Sullivan	What's Wrong With That*	Uptempo	A2	G4	Character Male
Schwartz, Stephen	Tenor	Rags	1986	Nathan Hershkowitz	What's Wrong With That*	Uptempo	A2	G4	Character Male
Schwartz, Stephen	Tenor	Wicked	2003	Fiyero	Dancing Through Life*	Uptempo	C3	A4	Romantic Lead Male
Schwartz, Stephen	Tenor	Wicked	2003	BOQ	Dancing Through Life*	Uptempo	G3	G4	Character Ingenue Male
Schwartz, Stephen	Tenor	Wicked	2003	BOQ	March Of The Witch Hunters*	Uptempo	G#3	G4	Character Ingenue Male
Schwartz, Stephen	Tenor	Wicked	2003	Fiyero	Which Way Is The Party*	Uptempo	C#3	A4	Romantic Lead Male
Shaiman, Marc	Alto	Hairspray	2002	Motormouth Mabel+	I Know Where I've Been	Ballad	E3	C5	Character Female
Shaiman, Marc	Alto	Hairspray	2002	Tracy Turnblad	Good Morning Baltimore Reprise	Ballad	Ab3	Bb4	Character Ingenue Female
Shaiman, Marc	Alto	Hairspray	2002	Motormouth Mabel+	Big Blonde And Beautiful*	Moderate Tempo	C4	E5	Character Female
Shaiman, Marc	Alto	Hairspray	2002	Penny Pingleton	Without Love*	Moderate Tempo	Eb3	Eb4	Character Ingenue Female
Shaiman, Marc	Alto	Hairspray	2002	Tracy Turnblad	Without Love*	Moderate Tempo	A3	B4	Character Ingenue Female
Shaiman, Marc	Alto	Hairspray	2002	Velma Von Tussle	Velma's Cha Cha	Moderate Tempo	Ab3	C#5	Romantic Antagonist Female
Shaiman, Marc	Alto	Hairspray	2002	Amber Von Tussle	Cooties	Uptempo	E4	E5	Romantic Antagonist Female
Shaiman, Marc	Alto	Hairspray	2002	Inez Stubs+	Run And Tell That*	Uptempo	F4	E5	Juvenile Female
Shaiman, Marc	Alto	Hairspray	2002	Teen Girl	The New Kid In Town*	Uptempo	A3	D5	Ingenue Female
Shaiman, Marc	Alto	Hairspray	2002	Tracy Turnblad	Good Morning Baltimore	Uptempo	Bb3	C#5	Character Ingenue Female
Shaiman, Marc	Alto	Hairspray	2002	Tracy Turnblad	I Can Hear The Bells	Uptempo	A3	E5	Character Ingenue Female
Shaiman, Marc	Alto	Hairspray	2002	Tracy Turnblad	Welcome To The 60s*	Uptempo	G3	C#5	Character Ingenue Female
Shaiman, Marc	Alto	Hairspray	2002	Velma Von Tussle	Miss Baltimore Crabs	Uptempo	B3	Eb5	Romantic Antagonist Female
Shaiman, Marc	Baritone	Hairspray	2002	Edna Turnblad	Timeless To Me*	Moderate Tempo	F#2	D4	Character Male
Shaiman, Marc	Baritone	Hairspray	2002	Edna Turnblad	Welcome To The 60s*	Uptempo	F2	G3	Character Male
Shaiman, Marc	Tenor	Hairspray	2002	Link Larkin	It Takes Two	Ballad	E3	F#4	Ingenue Male

Composer

Composer	Vocal Range	Show	Year	Role	Song	Tempo	Range-Bottom	Range-Top	Char Type
Shaiman, Marc	Tenor	Hairspray	2002	Link Larkin	Without Love*	Moderate Tempo	C3	A4	Ingenue Male
Shaiman, Marc	Tenor	Hairspray	2002	Seaweed Stubs+	Without Love*	Moderate Tempo	G3	Ab4	Ingenue Male
Shaiman, Marc	Tenor	Hairspray	2002	Wilbur Turnblad	Timeless To Me	Moderate Tempo	A#2	A4	Paternal
Shaiman, Marc	Tenor	Hairspray	2002	Corny Collins	Hairspray	Uptempo	E3	C5	Romantic Lead Male
Shaiman, Marc	Tenor	Hairspray	2002	Corny Collins	Nicest Kids In Town*	Uptempo	D3	F#4	Romantic Lead Male
Shaiman, Marc	Tenor	Hairspray	2002	Corny Collins	Nicest Kids In Town Reprise	Uptempo	B3	F#4	Romantic Lead Male
Shaiman, Marc	Tenor	Hairspray	2002	Seaweed Stubs+	Run And Tell That*	Uptempo	F3	B4	Ingenue Male
Sheik, Duncan	Alto	Spring Awakening	2006	Ilse	Blue Wind	Ballad	G3	A4	Character Ingenue Female
Sheik, Duncan	Alto	Spring Awakening	2006	Martha	The Dark I Know Well*	Moderate Tempo	A3	A4	Character Ingenue Female
Sheik, Duncan	Alto	Spring Awakening	2006	Ilse	The Dark I Know Well*	Moderate Tempo	A3	A4	Character Ingenue Female
Sheik, Duncan	Alto	Spring Awakening	2006	Ilse	Song of Purple Summer*	Moderate Tempo	G3	A4	Character Ingenue Female
Sheik, Duncan	Alto	Spring Awakening	2006	Female Solo	My Junk*	Uptempo	A3	E5	Character Female
Sheik, Duncan	Baritone	Spring Awakening	2006	Hanschen	Word Of Your Body Reprise 2*	Ballad	C3	E#4	Romantic Antagonist Male
Sheik, Duncan	Baritone	Spring Awakening	2006	Georg	The Bitch Of Living*	Uptempo	F3	D4	Character Ingenue Male
Sheik, Duncan	Soprano	Spring Awakening	2006	Wendla	Whispering	Ballad	B3	A4	Ingenue Female
Sheik, Duncan	Soprano	Spring Awakening	2006	Wendla	Mama Who Bore Me	Moderate Tempo	G3	A4	Ingenue Female
Sheik, Duncan	Soprano	Spring Awakening	2006	Wendla	The Guilty One*	Moderate Tempo	G3	A4	Ingenue Female
Sheik, Duncan	Soprano	Spring Awakening	2006	Wendla	Those You've Known*	Moderate Tempo	C4	D5	Ingenue Female
Sheik, Duncan	Tenor	Spring Awakening	2006	Melchoir	Left Behind	Ballad	E3	B4	Romantic Antagonist Male
Sheik, Duncan	Tenor	Spring Awakening	2006	Moritz	Those You've Known*	Ballad	D3	E4	Antagonist Male
Sheik, Duncan	Tenor	Spring Awakening	2006	Melchoir	All That's Known	Moderate Tempo	D3	E4	Romantic Antagonist Male
Sheik, Duncan	Tenor	Spring Awakening	2006	Melchoir	The Guilty One*	Moderate Tempo	G2	A3	Romantic Antagonist Male
Sheik, Duncan	Tenor	Spring Awakening	2006	Melchoir	Those You've Known*	Moderate Tempo	D3	F4	Romantic Antagonist Male
Sheik, Duncan	Tenor	Spring Awakening	2006	Moritz	The Bitch Of Living*	Uptempo	C3	D4	Antagonist Male
Sheik, Duncan	Tenor	Spring Awakening	2006	Moritz	And Then There Were None*	Uptempo	E3	G#4	Antagonist Male
Sheik, Duncan	Tenor	Spring Awakening	2006	Moritz	Don't Do Sadness	Uptempo	B2	A4	Antagonist Male
Sheik, Duncan	Tenor	Spring Awakening	2006	Melchoir	Totally Fucked*	Uptempo	Bb3	G4	Romantic Antagonist Male
Sherman and Sherman	Alto	Chitty Chitty Bang Bang	2005	Children	Teamwork *	Uptempo	C4	Eb5	Juvenile Female
Sherman and Sherman	Alto	Chitty Chitty Bang Bang	2005	Children	Teamwork *	Uptempo	C4	Eb5	Juvenile Male
Sherman and Sherman	Baritone	Chitty Chitty Bang Bang	2005	Caratacus Potts	Hushabye Mountain	Ballad	D#3	F4	Character Male
Sherman and Sherman	Baritone	Chitty Chitty Bang Bang	2005	Caratacus Potts	Truly Scrumptious Reprise	Ballad	Db3	Db4	Character Male
Sherman and Sherman	Baritone	Chitty Chitty Bang Bang	2005	Caratacus Potts	You Two	Moderate Tempo	D3	E4	Character Male
Sherman and Sherman	Baritone	Chitty Chitty Bang Bang	2005	Childcatcher	Kiddy Widdy Winkies	Moderate Tempo	D3	E4	Antagonist Male
Sherman and Sherman	Baritone	Chitty Chitty Bang Bang	2005	Childcatcher	Childcatcher as Grandpa	Moderate Tempo	C3	C4	Antagonist Male
Sherman and Sherman	Baritone	Chitty Chitty Bang Bang	2005	Goan	Act English *	Moderate Tempo	C3	E4	Antagonist Male

Composer

Composer	Vocal Range	Show	Year	Role	Song	Tempo	Range-Bottom	Range-Top	Char Type
Sherman and Sherman	Baritone	Chitty Chitty Bang Bang	2005	Caratacus Potts	Toot Sweets *	Uptempo	D3	Eb4	Character Male
Sherman and Sherman	Baritone	Chitty Chitty Bang Bang	2005	Caratacus Potts	Teamwork *	Uptempo	E3	G4	Character Male
Sherman and Sherman	Baritone	Chitty Chitty Bang Bang	2005	Grandpa Potts	Them Three	Uptempo	C3	C4	Mature Male
Sherman and Sherman	Baritone	Chitty Chitty Bang Bang	2005	Grandpa Potts	Posh	Uptempo	C3	C4	Mature Male
Sherman and Sherman	Soprano	Chitty Chitty Bang Bang	2005	Jemima Potts	Us Two	Ballad	C4	C5	Juvenile Female
Sherman and Sherman	Soprano	Chitty Chitty Bang Bang	2005	Jeremy Potts	Us Two	Ballad	C4	C5	Juvenile Male
Sherman and Sherman	Soprano	Chitty Chitty Bang Bang	2005	Truly Scrumptious	Music Box	Ballad	D4	Eb5	Romantic Lead Female
Sherman and Sherman	Soprano	Chitty Chitty Bang Bang	2005	Baroness Bomburst	Chu-Chi Face	Moderate Tempo	C4	F5	Character Female
Sherman and Sherman	Soprano	Chitty Chitty Bang Bang	2005	Jemima Potts	Truly Scrumptious	Moderate Tempo	C4	C5	Juvenile Female
Sherman and Sherman	Soprano	Chitty Chitty Bang Bang	2005	Jeremy Potts	Truly Scrumptious	Moderate Tempo	C4	C5	Juvenile Male
Sherman and Sherman	Soprano	Chitty Chitty Bang Bang	2005	Truly Scrumptious	Truly Scrumptious	Moderate Tempo	C4	C5	Romantic Lead Female
Sherman and Sherman	Soprano	Chitty Chitty Bang Bang	2005	Baroness Bomburst	The Bombie Samba	Uptempo	B3	Eb5	Character Female
Sherman and Sherman	Soprano	Chitty Chitty Bang Bang	2005	Truly Scrumptious	Toot Sweets *	Uptempo	D4	Eb5	Romantic Lead Female
Sherman and Sherman	Tenor	Chitty Chitty Bang Bang	2005	Baron Bomburst	Chu-Chi Face	Moderate Tempo	C3	G4	Character Male
Sherman and Sherman	Tenor	Chitty Chitty Bang Bang	2005	Boris	Act English *	Moderate Tempo	C3	G4	Antagonist Male
Sherman, Richard	Alto	Mary Poppins	2006	Winifred Banks	Being Mrs. Banks*	Ballad	G#3	Db5	Maternal
Sherman, Richard	Alto	Mary Poppins	2006	Winifred Banks	A Man Has Dreams Reprise	Ballad	Bb2	C4	Maternal
Sherman, Richard	Alto	Mary Poppins	2006	Jane Banks	The Perfect Nanny*	Moderate Tempo	A3	B4	Juvenile Female
Sherman, Richard	Alto	Mary Poppins	2006	Michael Banks	The Perfect Nanny*	Moderate Tempo	A3	B4	Juvenile Male
Sherman, Richard	Alto	Mary Poppins	2006	Winifred Banks	Being Mrs. Banks*	Moderate Tempo	G#3	B4	Maternal
Sherman, Richard	Alto	Mary Poppins	2006	Jane Banks	Anything Can Happen*	Moderate Tempo	C4	D5	Juvenile Female
Sherman, Richard	Alto	Mary Poppins	2006	Michael Banks	Anything Can Happen*	Moderate Tempo	C4	D5	Juvenile Male
Sherman, Richard	Alto	Mary Poppins	2006	Mrs. Corry	Supercalifragilisticexpialidocious*	Uptempo	C4	D5	Character Female
Sherman, Richard	Baritone	Mary Poppins	2006	Bert	Winds Can Change	Ballad	C3	C4	Character Male
Sherman, Richard	Baritone	Mary Poppins	2006	George Banks	A Man Has Dreams	Ballad	Bb2	Eb4	Paternal
Sherman, Richard	Baritone	Mary Poppins	2006	Bert	All Me Own Work	Ballad	C#3	D#4	Character Male
Sherman, Richard	Baritone	Mary Poppins	2006	Bert	Twists And Turns	Ballad	B2	E4	Character Male
Sherman, Richard	Baritone	Mary Poppins	2006	Bert	Chim Chim Cher-ee	Moderate Tempo	A2	D4	Character Male
Sherman, Richard	Baritone	Mary Poppins	2006	Bank Chairman	Precision And Order*	Moderate Tempo	C3	F4	Character Male
Sherman, Richard	Baritone	Mary Poppins	2006	Bert	Chim Chim Cher-ee A1	Moderate Tempo	C#3	E4	Character Male
Sherman, Richard	Baritone	Mary Poppins	2006	Bert	Chim Chim Cher-ee Reprise	Moderate Tempo	A2	D4	Character Male
Sherman, Richard	Baritone	Mary Poppins	2006	Bert	A Spoonful Of Sugar Reprise*	Moderate Tempo	Bb2	C#4	Character Male
Sherman, Richard	Baritone	Mary Poppins	2006	Bert	Let's Go Fly A Kite*	Moderate Tempo	Bb2	E4	Character Male
Sherman, Richard	Baritone	Mary Poppins	2006	George Banks	Cherry Tree Lane*	Uptempo	Bb2	Eb4	Paternal

Composer

Composer	Vocal Range	Show	Year	Role	Song	Tempo	Range-Bottom	Range-Top	Char Type
Sherman, Richard	Baritone	Mary Poppins	2006	Bert	Jolly Holiday*	Uptempo	B2	E4	Character Male
Sherman, Richard	Baritone	Mary Poppins	2006	Bert	Step In Time*	Uptempo	B2	F#4	Character Male
Sherman, Richard	Soprano	Mary Poppins	2006	Mary Poppins	Practically Perfect*	Moderate Tempo	A3	G#3	Romantic Lead Female
Sherman, Richard	Soprano	Mary Poppins	2006	Miss Andrew	Brimstone And Treacle (P1)	Moderate Tempo	G#3	F5	Antagonist Female
Sherman, Richard	Soprano	Mary Poppins	2006	Mary Poppins	Anything Can Happen*	Moderate Tempo	C4	D5	Romantic Lead Female
Sherman, Richard	Soprano	Mary Poppins	2006	Bird Woman	Feed The Birds*	Uptempo	Gb3	Db5	Mature Female
Sherman, Richard	Soprano	Mary Poppins	2006	Mary Poppins	A Spoonful Of Sugar*	Uptempo	Cb4	Ab5	Romantic Lead Female
Sherman, Richard	Soprano	Mary Poppins	2006	Mary Poppins	Supercalifragilisticexpialidocious*	Uptempo	C4	E5	Romantic Lead Female
Shire, David	Alto	Baby	1983	Pam Sakarian	With You *	Ballad	G#3	D5	Character Female
Shire, David	Alto	Baby	1983	Pam Sakarian	I Want It All *	Uptempo	C4	Eb5	Character Female
Shire, David	Baritone	Baby	1983	Alan McNally	Easier To Love	Ballad	C3	D4	Paternal
Shire, David	Baritone	Baby	1983	Nick Sakarian	With You *	Ballad	A#2	D#4	Character Male
Shire, David	Baritone	Baby	1983	Alan McNally	And What If We'd Loved Like That *	Moderate Tempo	D3	Gb4	Paternal
Shire, David	Baritone	Baby	1983	Nick Sakarian	At Night She Comes Home To Me *	Moderate Tempo	Db3	F#4	Character Male
Shire, David	Soprano	Baby	1983	Lizzie Fields	The Story Goes On	Ballad	G3	F5	Ingenue Female
Shire, David	Soprano	Big	1996	Susan Lawrence	Stars, Stars, Stars	Ballad	C4	D5	Romantic Lead Female
Shire, David	Soprano	Big	1996	Susan Lawrence	One Special Man	Ballad	G3	D5	Romantic Lead Female
Shire, David	Soprano	Big	1996	Susan Lawrence	Let's Not Move Too Fast	Ballad	A3	C5	Romantic Lead Female
Shire, David	Soprano	Baby	1983	Arlene McNally	And What If We'd Loved Like That *	Moderate Tempo	D4	F5	Maternal
Shire, David	Soprano	Baby	1983	Arlene McNally	I Want It All *	Uptempo	B3	Eb5	Maternal
Shire, David	Soprano	Baby	1983	Lizzie Fields	I Want It All *	Uptempo	C4	Eb5	Ingenue Female
Shire, David	Soprano	Big	1996	Susan Lawrence	Dancing All The Time	Uptempo	G3	D5	Romantic Lead Female
Shire, David	Soprano	Big	1996	Susan Lawrence	My Secretary's In Love	Uptempo	G3	D5	Romantic Lead Female
Shire, David	Soprano	Big	1996	Susan Lawrence	Little Susan Lawrence	Uptempo	Ab3	D5	Romantic Lead Female
Shire, David	Tenor	Baby	1983	Danny Hooper	I Chose Right	Ballad	D3	G4	Character Ingenue Male
Shire, David	Tenor	Big	1996	Josh Baskin-Adult	We're Gonna Be Fine	Ballad	Bb2	D4	Character Ingenue Male
Shire, David	Tenor	Big	1996	Josh Baskin-Adult	I Want To Go Home	Ballad	Ab2	B4	Character Ingenue Male
Shire, David	Tenor	Big	1996	Josh Baskin-Adult	Stars, Stars, Stars	Ballad	C3	D4	Character Ingenue Male
Shire, David	Tenor	Big	1996	Josh Baskin-Adult	Big Boy Now	Ballad	Db3	Eb4	Character Ingenue Male
Shire, David	Tenor	Big	1996	Josh Baskin-Young	I Want To Know	Ballad	C3	F4	Juvenile Male
Shire, David	Tenor	Big	1996	Billy Kopecki	Talk To Her	Uptempo	F2	Bb3	Juvenile Male
Shire, David	Tenor	Big	1996	Billy Kopecki	It's Time	Uptempo	A2	C4	Juvenile Male
Shire, David	Tenor	Big	1996	Josh Baskin-Adult	Fun	Uptempo	C3	G4	Character Ingenue Male

Composer	Vocal Range	Show	Year	Role	Song	Tempo	Range-Bottom	Range-Top	Char Type
Shire, David	Tenor	Big	1996	Josh Baskin-Adult	Do You Want To Play Games	Uptempo	E3	F4	Character Ingenue Male
Shire, David	Tenor	Big	1996	Josh Baskin-Adult	Coffee Black	Uptempo	C3	F4	Character Ingenue Male
Shire, David	Tenor	Big	1996	Josh Baskin-Adult	When You're Big	Uptempo	E3	F4	Character Ingenue Male
Shire, David	Tenor	Big	1996	Josh Baskin-Adult	Cross The Line	Uptempo	E3	D4	Character Ingenue Male
Shire, David	Tenor	Big	1996	Josh Baskin-Young	Talk To Her	Uptempo	F2	Bb3	Juvenile Male
Shire, David	Tenor	Big	1996	Josh Baskin-Young	Opening	Uptempo	A2	B3	Juvenile Male
Simon, Lucy	Alto	Secret Garden, The	1991	Mary Lennox	Show Me The Key (ms 52-92)	Moderate Tempo	B3	C#5	Juvenile Female
Simon, Lucy	Alto	Secret Garden, The	1991	Mary Lennox	Storm III*	Moderate Tempo	B3	E5	Juvenile Female
Simon, Lucy	Alto	Secret Garden, The	1991	Mary Lennox	Letter Song*	Moderate Tempo	Bb3	C5	Juvenile Female
Simon, Lucy	Alto	Secret Garden, The	1991	Martha	If I Had A Fine White Horse	Uptempo	G3	D5	Character Female
Simon, Lucy	Alto	Secret Garden, The	1991	Mary Lennox	The Girl I Mean To Be	Uptempo	Ab3	C5	Juvenile Female
Simon, Lucy	Alto	Secret Garden, The	1991	Marha	Hold On	Uptempo	F#3	B4	Character Female
Simon, Lucy	Bar/Bar	Secret Garden, The	1991	Archibald & Neville	Lily's Eyes	Moderate Tempo			CM/RLM
Simon, Lucy	Baritone	Secret Garden, The	1991	Archibald Craven	A Bit of Earth*	Moderate Tempo	D3	E4	Character Male
Simon, Lucy	Baritone	Secret Garden, The	1991	Neville Craven	Disppear*	Moderate Tempo	C3	F4	Romantic Lead Male
Simon, Lucy	Soprano	Secret Garden, The	1991	Lily	How Could I Ever Know*	Ballad	Bb3	A5	Romantic Lead Female
Simon, Lucy	Soprano	Secret Garden, The	1991	Colin Craven	Come To My Garden*	Moderate Tempo	C4	E5	Juvenile Male
Simon, Lucy	Soprano	Secret Garden, The	1991	Lily	Come To My Garden*	Moderate Tempo	C4	G5	Romantic Lead Female
Simon, Lucy	Soprano	Secret Garden, The	1991	Colin Craven	Round-Shouldered Man	Uptempo	A3	D5	Juvenile Male
Simon, Lucy	Tenor	Secret Garden, The	1991	Dickon	Winter's On The Wing Reprise	Ballad	D3	E4	Character Ingenue Male
Simon, Lucy	Tenor	Secret Garden, The	1991	Dickon	Winter's On The Wing	Uptempo	D3	F#4	Character Ingenue Male
Simon, Lucy	Tenor	Secret Garden, The	1991	Archibald Craven	Race You To The Top Of The Morning	Uptempo	Eb3	Ab4	Character Male
Simon, Lucy	Tenor	Secret Garden, The	1991	Dickon	Wick*	Uptempo	F3	G4	Character Ingenue Male
Simon, Lucy	Tenor	Secret Garden, The	1991	Archibald Craven	Where In The World	Uptempo	F3	Fb4	Character Male
Small, Charlie	Alto	Wiz, The	1974	Aunt Em	The Feeling We Once Had	Moderate Tempo	G3	C5	Maternal
Small, Charlie	Alto	Wiz, The	1974	Addaperle	He's The Wiz*	Moderate Tempo	F3	C5	Character Female
Small, Charlie	Alto	Wiz, The	1974	Glinda	A Rested Body Is A Rested Mind	Moderate Tempo	C4	C5	Romantic Lead Female
Small, Charlie	Alto	Wiz, The	1974	Dorothy	Home Reprise	Moderate Tempo	G3	E5	Character Ingenue Female
Small, Charlie	Alto	Wiz, The	1974	Evillene	Don't Nobody Bring Me No Bad News	Uptempo	Bb3	Db5	Antagonist Female
Small, Charlie	Soprano	Wiz, The	1974	Dorothy	Be A Lion*	Ballad	Bb3	Bb5	Character Ingenue Female
Small, Charlie	Soprano	Wiz, The	1974	Dorothy	Soon As I Get Home	Uptempo	C4	C#5	Character Ingenue Female
Small, Charlie	Soprano	Wiz, The	1974	Dorothy	Home	Uptempo	Bb3	D5	Character Ingenue Female
Small, Charlie	Tenor	Wiz, The	1974	Lion	Be A Lion*	Ballad	Ab3	Ab4	Antagonist Male
Small, Charlie	Tenor	Wiz, The	1974	Tin Man	What Would I Do If I Could Feel	Ballad	D3	A4	Character Male

Composer	Vocal Range	Show	Year	Role	Song	Tempo	Range-Bottom	Range-Top	Char Type
Small, Charlie	Tenor	Wiz, The	1974	Scarecrow	I Was Born On The Day Before Yeste	Moderate Tempo	E3	A4	Character Male
Small, Charlie	Tenor	Wiz, The	1974	The Wiz	Believe In Yourself (F Major)	Moderate Tempo	C4	G5	Romantic Antagonist Male
Small, Charlie	Tenor	Wiz, The	1974	The Wiz	Believe In Yourself (B♭ Major)	Moderate Tempo	F3	D5	Romantic Antagonist Male
Small, Charlie	Tenor	Wiz, The	1974	Tin Man	Slide Some Oil To Me	Uptempo	E♭3	B♭4	Character Male
Small, Charlie	Tenor	Wiz, The	1974	Lion	Mean Ole Lion	Uptempo	G2	B♭4	Antagonist Male
Small, Charlie	Tenor	Wiz, The	1974	The Wiz	So You Wanted To Meet The Wizard	Uptempo	E3	G4	Romantic Antagonist Male
Small, Charlie	Tenor	Wiz, The	1974	The Wiz	Y'all Got It	Uptempo	G3	A4	Romantic Antagonist Male
Snow, Tom	Alto	Footloose	1998	Ariel Moore	Almost Paradise*	Ballad	G3	C5	Character Ingenue Female
Snow, Tom	Alto	Footloose	1998	Ethel McCormick	Learning To Be Silent	Ballad	A♭3	D5	Maternal
Snow, Tom	Alto	Footloose	1998	Featured Ensemble	Somebody's Eyes Are Watching	Ballad	A♭3	B♭4	Character Ingenue Female
Snow, Tom	Alto	Footloose	1998	Vi Moore	Learning To Be Silent	Ballad	A♭3	D5	Maternal
Snow, Tom	Alto	Footloose	1998	Vi Moore	Can You Find It In Your Heart	Ballad	A3	D♭5	Maternal
Snow, Tom	Alto	Footloose	1998	Irene	Let's Make Believe We're In Love	Moderate Tempo	G3	D4	Character Female
Snow, Tom	Alto	Footloose	1998	Ariel Moore	Holding Out For A Hero	Uptempo	C4	C5	Character Ingenue Female
Snow, Tom	Alto	Footloose	1998	Rusty	Let's Hear It For the Boy	Uptempo	A3	D#5	Character Female
Snow, Tom	Baritone	Footloose	1998	Willard Hewitt	Mama Says	Uptempo	B♭2	G4	Antagonist Male
Snow, Tom	Tenor	Footloose	1998	Ren McCormick	Almost Paradise*	Ballad	G2	A4	Character Ingenue Male
Snow, Tom	Tenor	Footloose	1998	Rev. Shaw Moore	Can You Find It In Your Heart	Ballad	A2	C4	Paternal
Snow, Tom	Tenor	Footloose	1998	Rev. Shaw Moore	I Confess	Moderate Tempo	B2	F4	Paternal
Snow, Tom	Tenor	Footloose	1998	Chuck Cranston	The Girl Gets Around	Uptempo	G#3	A4	Romantic Antagonist Male
Snow, Tom	Tenor	Footloose	1998	Ren McCormick	I Can't Stand Still	Uptempo	D3	C5	Character Ingenue Male
Snow, Tom	Tenor	Footloose	1998	Ren McCormick	I'm Free	Uptempo	D3	A♭4	Character Ingenue Male
Snow, Tom	Tenor	Footloose	1998	Rev. Shaw Moore	Heaven Help Me	Uptempo	G2	E4	Paternal
Sondheim, Stephen	Alto	A Little Night Music	1973	Desiree Armfeldt	Send In The Clowns	Ballad	G3	A4	Romantic Lead Female
Sondheim, Stephen	Alto	Anyone Can Whistle	1964	Fay Apple	Anyone Can Whistle	Ballad	G3	C5	Ingenue Female
Sondheim, Stephen	Alto	Follies	1971	Sally Durant	In Buddy's Eyes *	Ballad	F#3	D5	Character Female
Sondheim, Stephen	Alto	Into The Woods	1987	Witch	Stay With Me	Ballad	A#3	D♭5	Romantic Antagonist Female
Sondheim, Stephen	Alto	Into The Woods	1987	Witch	Lament	Ballad	A3	D5	Romantic Antagonist Female
Sondheim, Stephen	Alto	Pacific Overtures	1976	Female	Prologue	Ballad	D3	B♭4	Character Female
Sondheim, Stephen	Alto	Passion	1994	Fosca	I Read	Ballad	F3	D5	Antagonist Female
Sondheim, Stephen	Alto	Passion	1994	Fosca	I Wish I Could Forget You*	Ballad	F3	C5	Antagonist Female
Sondheim, Stephen	Alto	Passion	1994	Fosca	Loving You	Ballad	F#3	C5	Antagonist Female
Sondheim, Stephen	Alto	Sunday...Park With Geroge	1984	Old Lady	Beautiful*	Ballad	F#3	B4	Mature Female

Composer

Composer	Vocal Range	Show	Year	Role	Song	Tempo	Range-Bottom	Range-Top	Char Type
Sondheim, Stephen	Alto	Sunday...Park With Geroge	1984	Marie	Children And Art*	Ballad	Gb3	Db5	Romantic Lead Female
Sondheim, Stephen	Alto	Sunday...Park With Geroge	1984	Dot	Move On*	Ballad	G#3	C#5	Romantic Lead Female
Sondheim, Stephen	Alto	Anyone Can Whistle	1964	Fay Apple	With So Little To Be Sure Of*	Moderate Tempo	A3	B4	Ingenue Female
Sondheim, Stephen	Alto	Company (Revival)	1970	Joanne	The Ladies Who Lunch	Moderate Tempo	F3	Bb4	Antagonist Female
Sondheim, Stephen	Alto	Follies	1971	Carolotta Champion	I'm Still Here	Moderate Tempo	Eb3	C5	Romantic Lead Female
Sondheim, Stephen	Alto	Follies	1971	Hattie Walker	Broadway Baby	Moderate Tempo	A3	Bb4	Antagonist Female
Sondheim, Stephen	Alto	Follies	1971	Phyllis Rogers Stone	Could I Leave You	Moderate Tempo	F#3	Bb4	Romantic Antagonist Female
Sondheim, Stephen	Alto	Into The Woods	1987	Baker's Wife	It Takes Two	Moderate Tempo	A3	D5	Character Female
Sondheim, Stephen	Alto	Into The Woods	1987	Witch	Last Midnight	Moderate Tempo	F3	Db5	Romantic Antagonist Female
Sondheim, Stephen	Alto	Merrily We Roll Along 1994	1994	Gussie Carnegie	Growing Up Part II	Moderate Tempo	G#3	Bb4	Romantic Antagonist Female
Sondheim, Stephen	Alto	Merrily We Roll Along 1994	1994	Gussie Carnegie	Act 2 Opening	Moderate Tempo	B3	C5	Romantic Antagonist Female
Sondheim, Stephen	Alto	Merrily We Roll Along 1994	1994	Gussie Carnegie	Growing Up Act 2	Moderate Tempo	G3	A4	Romantic Antagonist Female
Sondheim, Stephen	Alto	Merrily We Roll Along 1994	1994	Frank, Jr.	Transition 7	Moderate Tempo	B2	C5	Juvenile Male
Sondheim, Stephen	Alto	Passion	1994	Fosca	To Speak To Me Of Love	Moderate Tempo	E#3	C5	Antagonist Female
Sondheim, Stephen	Alto	Passion	1994	Fosca	All This Happiness	Moderate Tempo	B3	A4	Antagonist Female
Sondheim, Stephen	Alto	Sunday...Park With Geroge	1984	Dot	Sunday In The Park With George	Moderate Tempo	E3	Db5	Romantic Lead Female
Sondheim, Stephen	Alto	Sunday...Park With Geroge	1984	Dot	Color And Light (Part 2)	Moderate Tempo	B3	C5	Romantic Lead Female
Sondheim, Stephen	Alto	Sunday...Park With Geroge	1984	Dot	We Do Not Belong Together*	Moderate Tempo	G3	D5	Romantic Lead Female
Sondheim, Stephen	Alto	Sweeney Todd	1979	Mrs. Lovett	Wait	Moderate Tempo	Bb2	Eb5	Character Female
Sondheim, Stephen	Alto	Sunday...Park With Geroge	1984	Nurse	The Day Off (Part 3)*	Moderate Tempo	B3	D5	Character Female
Sondheim, Stephen	Alto	A Funny Thing...Forum	1962	Domina	That Dirty Old Man	Uptempo	B3	F5	Antagonist Female
Sondheim, Stephen	Alto	A Little Night Music	1973	Countess Charlotte Malc	Everyday A Little Death	Uptempo	G3	B4	Romantic Lead Female
Sondheim, Stephen	Alto	A Little Night Music	1973	Madame Armfeldt	Liaisons	Uptempo	D3	F4	Mature Female
Sondheim, Stephen	Alto	Anyone Can Whistle	1964	Cora Hoover Hooper	Me And My Town*	Uptempo	A3	Eb5	Romantic Antagonist Female
Sondheim, Stephen	Alto	Anyone Can Whistle	1964	Fay Apple	There Won't Be Trumpets	Uptempo	G3	Bb4	Ingenue Female
Sondheim, Stephen	Alto	Anyone Can Whistle	1964	Fay Apple	Come Play Wiz Me*	Uptempo	A3	D5	Ingenue Female
Sondheim, Stephen	Alto	Anyone Can Whistle	1964	Cora Hoover Hooper	There's A Parade In Town*	Uptempo	G3	Bb4	Romantic Antagonist Female
Sondheim, Stephen	Alto	Anyone Can Whistle	1964	Cora Hoover Hooper	I've Got You To lean On*	Uptempo	Ab4	D5	Romantic Antagonist Female
Sondheim, Stephen	Alto	Anyone Can Whistle	1964	Fay Apple	See What It Gets You	Uptempo	G3	Db5	Ingenue Female
Sondheim, Stephen	Alto	Anyone Can Whistle	1964	Cora Hoover Hooper	Cora's Chase*	Uptempo	A3	E5	Romantic Antagonist Female
Sondheim, Stephen	Alto	Company (Revival)	1970	Joanne	The Little Things We Do Together	Uptempo	F3	A4	Antagonist Female
Sondheim, Stephen	Alto	Company (Revival)	1970	Marta	You Could Drive a Person Crazy	Uptempo	C#4	A5	Character Ingenue Female
Sondheim, Stephen	Alto	Company (Revival)	1970	Marta	Another Hundred People	Uptempo	A3	D5	Character Ingenue Female

Composer	Vocal Range	Show	Year	Role	Song	Tempo	Range-Bottom	Range-Top	Char Type
Sondheim, Stephen	Alto	Follies	1971	Solange LaFitte	Ah, Paris *	Uptempo	C3	G4	Romantic Lead Female
Sondheim, Stephen	Alto	Follies	1971	Stella Deems	Who's That Woman *	Uptempo	E3	A4	Mature Female
Sondheim, Stephen	Alto	Into The Woods	1987	Baker's Wife	Maybe They're Magic	Uptempo	G#3	E5	Character Female
Sondheim, Stephen	Alto	Into The Woods	1987	Baker's Wife	Moments In The Woods	Uptempo	F3	D4	Character Female
Sondheim, Stephen	Alto	Into The Woods	1987	Little Red Riding Hood	I Know Things Now	Uptempo	C4	Eb5	Juvenile Female
Sondheim, Stephen	Alto	Merrily We Roll Along	1994	Gussie Carnegie	The Blob II	Uptempo	Ab3	Bb4	Romantic Antagonist Female
Sondheim, Stephen	Alto	Sunday...Park With Geroge	1984	Dot	Color And Light (Part 3)*	Uptempo	E4	E5	Romantic Lead Female
Sondheim, Stephen	Alto	Sunday...Park With Geroge	1984	Dot	Everybody Loves Louis	Uptempo	A#3	C#5	Romantic Lead Female
Sondheim, Stephen	Alto	Sweeney Todd	1979	Mrs. Lovett	The Worst Pies In London	Uptempo	B3	Eb5	Character Female
Sondheim, Stephen	Alto	Sweeney Todd	1979	Mrs. Lovett	Poor Thing	Uptempo	F#3	B4	Character Female
Sondheim, Stephen	Alto	Sweeney Todd	1979	Mrs. Lovett	By The Sea	Uptempo	G3	E5	Character Female
Sondheim, Stephen	Baritone	Company (Revival)	1970	David	Sorry Grateful	Ballad	B2	E4	Character Male
Sondheim, Stephen	Baritone	Company (Revival)	1970	Harry	Sorry Grateful	Ballad	B2	E4	Character Male
Sondheim, Stephen	Baritone	Company (Revival)	1970	Larry	Sorry Grateful	Ballad	B2	E4	Mature Male
Sondheim, Stephen	Baritone	Follies	1971	Benjamin Stone	Too Many Mornings *	Ballad	C3	E4	Romantic Lead Male
Sondheim, Stephen	Baritone	Into The Woods	1987	Baker	No More*	Ballad	D3	Eb4	Character Male
Sondheim, Stephen	Baritone	Into The Woods	1987	Mysterious Man	No More*	Ballad	Bb2	E4	Mature Male
Sondheim, Stephen	Baritone	Pacific Overtures	1976	Male	Prologue	Ballad	D2	Bb3	Character Male
Sondheim, Stephen	Baritone	Sweeney Todd	1979	Sweeney Todd	The Barber And His Wife	Ballad	G#2	Db4	Antagonist Male
Sondheim, Stephen	Baritone	Sweeney Todd	1979	Sweeney Todd	My Friends*	Ballad	Bb2	Eb4	Antagonist Male
Sondheim, Stephen	Baritone	A Funny Thing...Forum	1962	Marcus Lycus	The House Of Marcus Lycus	Moderate Tempo	B2	D#4	Antagonist Male
Sondheim, Stephen	Baritone	A Funny Thing...Forum	1962	Pseudolus	Lovely Reprise*	Moderate Tempo	D3	F4	Mature Male
Sondheim, Stephen	Baritone	Anyone Can Whistle	1964	J. Bowden Hapgood	With So Little To Be Sure Of*	Moderate Tempo	B2	E4	Romantic Antagonist Male
Sondheim, Stephen	Baritone	Assassins	1992	The Proprietor	Opening*	Moderate Tempo	F#2	F4	Romantic Lead Male
Sondheim, Stephen	Baritone	Assassins	1992	John Wilkes Booth	Opening*	Moderate Tempo	D3	F4	Romantic Antagonist Male
Sondheim, Stephen	Baritone	Assassins	1992	John Wilkes Booth	The Ballad Of Booth Part 2	Moderate Tempo	F#2	F#4	Romantic Antagonist Male
Sondheim, Stephen	Baritone	Assassins	1992	Leon Czolgosz	Gun Song*	Moderate Tempo	G2	B3	Romantic Antagonist Male
Sondheim, Stephen	Baritone	Assassins	1992	John Wilkes Booth	Gun Song*	Moderate Tempo	C#3	E4	Romantic Antagonist Male
Sondheim, Stephen	Baritone	Into The Woods	1987	Baker	It Takes Two	Moderate Tempo	Bb2	F4	Character Male
Sondheim, Stephen	Baritone	Into The Woods	1987	Cinderella's Prince	Agony*	Moderate Tempo	C#3	E4	Romantic Lead Male
Sondheim, Stephen	Baritone	Into The Woods	1987	Cinderella's Prince	Agony II*	Moderate Tempo	C#3	F4	Romantic Lead Male
Sondheim, Stephen	Baritone	Into The Woods	1987	Rapunzel's Prince	Agony*	Moderate Tempo	C#3	E4	Romantic Lead Male
Sondheim, Stephen	Baritone	Into The Woods	1987	Rapunzel's Prince	Agony II*	Moderate Tempo	C#3	F4	Romantic Lead Male
Sondheim, Stephen	Baritone	Pacific Overtures	1976	Soothsayer+	Chrysanthemum Tea*	Moderate Tempo	F2	D4	Character Male

Composer

Composer	Vocal Range	Show	Year	Role	Song	Tempo	Range-Bottom	Range-Top	Char Type
Sondheim, Stephen	Baritone	Pacific Overtures	1976	Manjiro+	Poems*	Moderate Tempo	Eb3	F4	Character Female
Sondheim, Stephen	Baritone	Sunday...Park With Geroge	1984	Boatman	The Day Off (Part 6)	Moderate Tempo	E2	C4	Antagonist Male
Sondheim, Stephen	Baritone	Sweeney Todd	1979	Sweeney Todd	Johanna II*	Moderate Tempo	A2	Eb4	Antagonist Male
Sondheim, Stephen	Baritone	A Funny Thing...Forum	1962	Prologus	Comedy Tonight*	Uptempo	A2	F4	Character Male
Sondheim, Stephen	Baritone	A Funny Thing...Forum	1962	Pseudolus	Free*	Uptempo	B2	F4	Mature Male
Sondheim, Stephen	Baritone	A Funny Thing...Forum	1962	Pseudolus	Pretty Little Picture*	Uptempo	B2	F#4	Mature Male
Sondheim, Stephen	Baritone	A Funny Thing...Forum	1962	Sinex	Everybody Ought To Have A Maid*	Uptempo	C#3	E4	Mature Male
Sondheim, Stephen	Baritone	A Funny Thing...Forum	1962	Miles	Bring Me My Bride*	Uptempo	B2	F4	Romantic Antagonist Male
Sondheim, Stephen	Baritone	A Little Night Music	1973	Count Carl-Magnus Malc	In Praise of Women	Uptempo	C3	F4	Romantic Lead Male
Sondheim, Stephen	Baritone	A Little Night Music	1973	Count Carl-Magnus Malc	It Would Have Been Wonderful *	Uptempo	C3	E4	Romantic Lead Male
Sondheim, Stephen	Baritone	A Little Night Music	1973	Frederik Egerman	Now	Uptempo	Bb2	F4	Romantic Lead Male
Sondheim, Stephen	Baritone	A Little Night Music	1973	Frederik Egerman	You Must Meet My Wife	Uptempo	C3	E4	Romantic Lead Male
Sondheim, Stephen	Baritone	A Little Night Music	1973	Frederik Egerman	It Would Have Been Wonderful *	Uptempo	C3	E4	Romantic Lead Male
Sondheim, Stephen	Baritone	Anyone Can Whistle	1964	J. Bowden Hapgood	Everybody Says Don't	Uptempo	G2	E4	Romantic Antagonist Male
Sondheim, Stephen	Baritone	Company (Revival)	1970	David	Have I Got A Girl For You	Uptempo	B5	Gb7	Character Male
Sondheim, Stephen	Baritone	Company (Revival)	1970	Harry	Have I Got A Girl For You	Uptempo	B6	Gb8	Character Male
Sondheim, Stephen	Baritone	Company (Revival)	1970	Larry	Have I Got A Girl For You	Uptempo	B2	Gb4	Mature Male
Sondheim, Stephen	Baritone	Company (Revival)	1970	Paul	Have I Got A Girl For You	Uptempo	B4	Gb6	Character Ingenue Male
Sondheim, Stephen	Baritone	Company (Revival)	1970	Peter	Have I Got A Girl For You	Uptempo	B3	Gb5	Romantic Lead Male
Sondheim, Stephen	Baritone	Follies	1971	Benjamin Stone	The Road You Didn't Take *	Uptempo	A2	F4	Romantic Lead Male
Sondheim, Stephen	Baritone	Follies	1971	Benjamin Stone	Live, Laugh, Love	Uptempo	C#3	F4	Romantic Lead Male
Sondheim, Stephen	Baritone	Follies	1971	Buddy Plummer	The Right Girl *	Uptempo	C3	F4	Character Male
Sondheim, Stephen	Baritone	Follies	1971	Buddy Plummer	Buddy's Blues	Uptempo	Db3	F4	Character Male
Sondheim, Stephen	Baritone	Follies	1971	Theodore Whitman	Rain On The Roof *	Uptempo	Bb2	D4	Mature Male
Sondheim, Stephen	Baritone	Into The Woods	1987	Cinderella's Prince	Any Moment*	Uptempo	B2	Eb5	Romantic Lead Male
Sondheim, Stephen	Baritone	Into The Woods	1987	Narrator	Act I Opening (Part 4)*	Uptempo	G2	E4	Mature Male
Sondheim, Stephen	Baritone	Into The Woods	1987	Wolf	Hello Little Girl	Uptempo	Bb2	Gb4	Romantic Lead Male
Sondheim, Stephen	Baritone	Pacific Overtures	1976	Reciter+	The Advantages Of Floating....*	Uptempo	B2	E4	Character Male
Sondheim, Stephen	Baritone	Pacific Overtures	1976	Thief+	Four Black Dragons*	Uptempo	B2	C#4	Antagonist Male
Sondheim, Stephen	Baritone	Sweeney Todd	1979	Sweeney Todd	Epiphany*	Uptempo	Bb2	F4	Antagonist Male
Sondheim, Stephen	Baritone	Sweeney Todd	1979	Sweeney Todd	Finale Scene II	Uptempo	G2	C4	Antagonist Male
Sondheim, Stephen	Soprano	Follies	1971	Heidi Schiller	One More Kiss *	Ballad	D4	F5	Mature Female
Sondheim, Stephen	Soprano	Follies	1971	Sally Durant	Too Many Mornings *	Ballad	C4	G#5	Character Female

Composer	Vocal Range	Show	Year	Role	Song	Tempo	Range-Bottom	Range-Top	Char Type
Sondheim, Stephen	Soprano	Follies	1971	Sally Durant	Losing My Mind	Ballad	F3	B4	Character Female
Sondheim, Stephen	Soprano	Into The Woods	1987	Cinderella	No One Is Alone	Ballad	Bb3	Db5	Ingenue Female
Sondheim, Stephen	Soprano	Into The Woods	1987	Cinderella	No One Is Alone (Part 2)	Ballad	Bb3	Db5	Ingenue Female
Sondheim, Stephen	Soprano	Merrily We Roll Along 1994	1981	Beth	Not A Day Goes By	Ballad	G3	B4	Romantic Lead Female
Sondheim, Stephen	Soprano	Passion	1994	Clara	I Didn't Tell You	Ballad	Ab3	F5	Romantic Lead Female
Sondheim, Stephen	Soprano	A Funny Thing...Forum	1962	Philia	Lovely*	Moderate Tempo	C#4	F5	Ingenue Female
Sondheim, Stephen	Soprano	A Funny Thing...Forum	1962	Philia	That'll Show Him	Moderate Tempo	C4	G5	Ingenue Female
Sondheim, Stephen	Soprano	Assassins	1992	Lynette Squeaky Fromm	Unworthy Of Your Love*	Moderate Tempo	A3	D5	Character Female
Sondheim, Stephen	Soprano	Merrily We Roll Along 1994	1981	Mary Flynn	Old Friends	Moderate Tempo	A3	A4	Romantic Antagonist Female
Sondheim, Stephen	Soprano	Merrily We Roll Along 1994	1981	Mary Flynn	Like It Was	Moderate Tempo	G3	Bb4	Romantic Antagonist Female
Sondheim, Stephen	Soprano	Passion	1994	Clara	Happiness (Part 1)*	Moderate Tempo	Bb3	Eb5	Romantic Lead Female
Sondheim, Stephen	Soprano	Passion	1994	Clara	Fourth Letter-How Could I Forget You	Moderate Tempo	F3	Db5	Romantic Lead Female
Sondheim, Stephen	Soprano	Passion	1994	Clara	Thinking Of You	Moderate Tempo	Ab3	Db5	Romantic Lead Female
Sondheim, Stephen	Soprano	Passion	1994	Clara	Sunrise Letter*	Moderate Tempo	Ab3	G5	Romantic Lead Female
Sondheim, Stephen	Soprano	Passion	1994	Clara	I Am Writing To You	Moderate Tempo	A3	C#5	Romantic Lead Female
Sondheim, Stephen	Soprano	A Little Night Music	1973	Anne Egerman	Soon	Uptempo	C4	G#5	Ingenue Female
Sondheim, Stephen	Soprano	A Little Night Music	1973	Fredrika Armfeldt	The Glamorous Life	Uptempo	C4	Eb5	Juvenile Female
Sondheim, Stephen	Soprano	Anyone Can Whistle	1964	Soprano Cadenza	Cora's Chase*	Uptempo	B4	D6	Character Female
Sondheim, Stephen	Soprano	Anyone Can Whistle	1964	Baby Joan	I'm Like The Bluebird	Uptempo	B3	C#5	Character Ingenue Female
Sondheim, Stephen	Soprano	Company (Revival)	1970	Amy	Not Getting Married Today	Uptempo	C#4	Ab5	Character Ingenue Female
Sondheim, Stephen	Soprano	Company (Revival)	1970	April	You Could Drive a Person Crazy	Uptempo	C#4	A5	Character Female
Sondheim, Stephen	Soprano	Company (Revival)	1970	Kathy	You Could Drive a Person Crazy	Uptempo	C#4	A5	Ingenue Female
Sondheim, Stephen	Soprano	Follies	1971	Emily Whitman	Rain On The Roof *	Uptempo	Bb3	D5	Mature Female
Sondheim, Stephen	Soprano	Follies	1971	Sally Durant	The Story of Lucy and Jesse	Uptempo	G3	Bb4	Character Female
Sondheim, Stephen	Soprano	Follies	1971	Sally Durant	Don't Look At Me*	Uptempo	A3	B4	Character Female
Sondheim, Stephen	Soprano	Into The Woods	1987	Cinderella	On The Steps Of The Palace	Uptempo	A3	E5	Ingenue Female
Sondheim, Stephen	Soprano	Merrily We Roll Along 1994	1981	Mary Flynn	Now You Know*	Uptempo	G3	D5	Romantic Antagonist Female
Sondheim, Stephen	Soprano	Passion	1994	Clara	Forty Days	Uptempo	Bb3	E5	Romantic Lead Female
Sondheim, Stephen	Soprano	Sweeney Todd	1979	Johannah	Green Finch And Linnet Bird*	Uptempo	C4	G5	Ingenue Female
Sondheim, Stephen	Tenor	Company (Revival)	1970	Robert	Someone Is Waiting	Ballad	B2	E4	Romantic Lead Male
Sondheim, Stephen	Tenor	Into The Woods	1987	Jack	I Guess This Is Goodbye	Ballad	D#3	D#4	Character Ingenue Male
Sondheim, Stephen	Tenor	Merrily We Roll Along 1994	1981	Charley Kringas	Good Thing Going	Ballad	C3	F4	Character Male
Sondheim, Stephen	Tenor	Passion	1994	Giorgio Bachetti	No One Has Ever Loved Me	Ballad	B2	D4	Romantic Lead Male

Composer

Composer	Vocal Range	Show	Year	Role	Song	Tempo	Range-Bottom	Range-Top	Char Type
Sondheim, Stephen	Tenor	Sunday...Park With Geroge	1984	George	Beautiful*	Ballad	C#3	F#4	Romantic Antagonist Male
Sondheim, Stephen	Tenor	Sunday...Park With Geroge	1984	George	Lesson #8	Ballad	G#2	Eb4	Romantic Antagonist Male
Sondheim, Stephen	Tenor	Sunday...Park With Geroge	1984	George	Move On*	Ballad	D#3	G4	Romantic Antagonist Male
Sondheim, Stephen	Tenor	Sweeney Todd	1979	Anthony Hope	Johanna	Ballad	C3	Eb4	Ingenue Male
Sondheim, Stephen	Tenor	Sweeney Todd	1979	The Beadle	Ladies In Their Sensitivities	Ballad	D3	A4	Character Male
Sondheim, Stephen	Tenor	Sweeney Todd	1979	Tobias Ragg	Not While I'm Around*	Ballad	Eb3	Ab4	Character Ingenue Male
Sondheim, Stephen	Tenor	A Funny Thing...Forum	1962	Hero	Lovely*	Moderate Tempo	D3	E4	Ingenue Male
Sondheim, Stephen	Tenor	A Funny Thing...Forum	1962	Hysterium	Lovely Reprise*	Moderate Tempo	E3	F4	Mature Male
Sondheim, Stephen	Tenor	Assassins	1992	John Hinkley	Unworthy Of Your Love*	Moderate Tempo	B2	E4	Antagonist Male
Sondheim, Stephen	Tenor	Assassins	1992	The Balladeer	Another National Anthem*	Moderate Tempo	D3	F#4	Character Male
Sondheim, Stephen	Tenor	Company (Revival)	1970	Robert	Being Alive	Moderate Tempo	D3	F4	Romantic Lead Male
Sondheim, Stephen	Tenor	Follies	1971	Roscoe	Beautiful Girls	Moderate Tempo	D3	A4	Mature Male
Sondheim, Stephen	Tenor	Merrily We Roll Along 1994	1981	Franklin Shepard	Old Friends II*	Moderate Tempo	Bb2	D4	Romantic Antagonist Male
Sondheim, Stephen	Tenor	Merrily We Roll Along 1994	1981	Charley Kringas	Old Friends II*	Moderate Tempo	Bb2	D4	Character Male
Sondheim, Stephen	Tenor	Merrily We Roll Along 1994	1981	Franklin Shepard	Our Time Part 1 & 2*	Moderate Tempo	Db3	Bb4	Romantic Antagonist Male
Sondheim, Stephen	Tenor	Merrily We Roll Along 1994	1994	Franklin Shepard	Growing Up Part I	Moderate Tempo	D3	E4	Romantic Antagonist Male
Sondheim, Stephen	Tenor	Pacific Overtures	1976	Mother+	Chrysanthemum Tea*	Moderate Tempo	D3	F4	Antagonist Male
Sondheim, Stephen	Tenor	Pacific Overtures	1976	Kayama+	Poems*	Moderate Tempo	Eb3	F4	Romantic Lead Male
Sondheim, Stephen	Tenor	Pacific Overtures	1976	Kayama+	A Bowler Hat	Moderate Tempo	G2	Eb4	Romantic Lead Male
Sondheim, Stephen	Tenor	Passion	1994	Giorgio Bachetti	Happiness (Part 2)*	Moderate Tempo	A2	C4	Romantic Lead Male
Sondheim, Stephen	Tenor	Passion	1994	Lt. Torasso	Christmas Music	Moderate Tempo	Eb3	F4	Character Male
Sondheim, Stephen	Tenor	Sunday...Park With Geroge	1984	George	The Day Off (Part 2)	Moderate Tempo	D#3	D#4	Romantic Antagonist Male
Sondheim, Stephen	Tenor	Sunday...Park With Geroge	1984	Franz	The Day Off (Part 5)*	Moderate Tempo	C3	Eb4	Character Male
Sondheim, Stephen	Tenor	Sunday...Park With Geroge	1984	George	Finishing The Hat	Moderate Tempo	Bb2	A5	Romantic Antagonist Male
Sondheim, Stephen	Tenor	Sunday...Park With Geroge	1984	George	We Do Not Belong Together*	Moderate Tempo	A2	E4	Romantic Antagonist Male
Sondheim, Stephen	Tenor	Sweeney Todd	1979	Adolfo Pirelli	The Contest	Moderate Tempo	B2	C4	Character Male
Sondheim, Stephen	Tenor	Sweeney Todd	1979	Adolfo Pirelli	Pirelli's Death	Moderate Tempo	Eb3	C5	Character Male
Sondheim, Stephen	Tenor	Sweeney Todd	1979	The Beadle	Parlor Songs	Moderate Tempo	D3	G4	Character Male
Sondheim, Stephen	Tenor	A Funny Thing...Forum	1962	Hero	Love I Hear	Uptempo	B2	F#4	Ingenue Male
Sondheim, Stephen	Tenor	A Funny Thing...Forum	1962	Hysterium	I'm Calm	Uptempo	D3	F4	Mature Male
Sondheim, Stephen	Tenor	A Little Night Music	1973	Erik Egerman	Later	Uptempo	C3	B4	Ingenue Male
Sondheim, Stephen	Tenor	Assassins	1992	The Balladeer	The Ballad Of Booth Part 1	Uptempo	C#3	G#4	Character Male
Sondheim, Stephen	Tenor	Assassins	1992	The Balladeer	The Ballad Of Booth Part 3	Uptempo	C#3	Ab4	Character Male

Composer

Composer	Vocal Range	Show	Year	Role	Song	Tempo	Range-Bottom	Range-Top	Char Type
Sondheim, Stephen	Tenor	Assassins	1992	Giuseppe Zangara	How I Saved Roosevelt*	Uptempo	D3	A4	Antagonist Male
Sondheim, Stephen	Tenor	Assassins	1992	The Balladeer	The Ballad of Czolgosz (Part 1 & 2)	Uptempo	D3	G4	Character Male
Sondheim, Stephen	Tenor	Assassins	1992	Charles Guiteau	The Ballad of Guiteau*	Uptempo	A2	Gb4	Romantic Antagonist Male
Sondheim, Stephen	Tenor	Assassins	1992	The Balladeer	The Ballad of Guiteau*	Uptempo	C3	G4	Character Male
Sondheim, Stephen	Tenor	Company (Revival)	1970	Robert	Company	Uptempo	A2	Ab4	Romantic Lead Male
Sondheim, Stephen	Tenor	Into The Woods	1987	Jack	Giants In The Sky	Uptempo	C3	F#4	Character Ingenue Male
Sondheim, Stephen	Tenor	Merrily We Roll Along 1994	1981	Charley Kringas	Franklin Shepard, Inc.	Uptempo	C3	G4	Character Male
Sondheim, Stephen	Tenor	Pacific Overtures	1976	Fisherman+	Four Black Dragons*	Uptempo	Eb3	Gb4	Character Male
Sondheim, Stephen	Tenor	Pacific Overtures	1976	Madam+	Welcome to Kanagawa*	Uptempo	C3	E4	Romantic Antagonist Male
Sondheim, Stephen	Tenor	Passion	1994	Giorgio Bachetti	Is This What You Call Love?	Uptempo	A#2	F4	Romantic Lead Male
Sondheim, Stephen	Tenor	Sunday...Park With Geroge	1984	George	Color And Light (Part 1)	Uptempo	Bb2	Eb4	Romantic Antagonist Male
Sondheim, Stephen	Tenor	Sunday...Park With Geroge	1984	George	Color And Light (Part 3)*	Uptempo	D3	G4	Romantic Antagonist Male
Sondheim, Stephen	Tenor	Sunday...Park With Geroge	1984	George	The Day Off (Part 1)	Uptempo	A#2	G4	Romantic Antagonist Male
Sondheim, Stephen	Tenor	Sunday...Park With Geroge	1984	George	Putting It Together (Part 7 & 9)	Uptempo	D4	Gb4	Romantic Antagonist Male
Sondheim, Stephen	Tenor	Sunday...Park With Geroge	1984	George	Putting It Together (Part 16)*	Uptempo	Db3	Gb4	Romantic Antagonist Male
Sondheim, Stephen	Tenor	Sweeney Todd	1979	Anthony Hope	Ah, Miss (I & III)	Uptempo	C3	F4	Ingenue Male
Sondheim, Stephen	Tenor	Sweeney Todd	1979	Tobias Ragg	Perelli's Miracle Elixir*	Uptempo	B2	A4	Character Ingenue Male
Stiles, George	Alto	Honk	1993	Ida	Different Pre-Reprise	Ballad	Ab3	A4	Maternal
Stiles, George	Alto	Honk	1993	Ida	Every Tear a Mother Cries	Ballad	F3	A4	Maternal
Stiles, George	Alto	Honk	1993	Ida	Hold Your Head Up High	Moderate Tempo	G#3	C5	Maternal
Stiles, George	Alto	Honk	1993	Ida	The Joy of Motherhood*	Uptempo	G#3	C#5	Maternal
Stiles, George	Alto	Honk!	1993	Lowbutt	It Takes All Sorts*	Uptempo	C#4	D5	Mature Female
Stiles, George	Alto	Honk	1993	Maureen	The Joy of Motherhood*	Uptempo	G#3	C#5	Maternal
Stiles, George	Alto	Honk!	1993	Queenie	It Takes All Sorts*	Uptempo	C#4	D5	Mature Female
Stiles, George	Baritone	Honk	1993	Ugly	Different	Ballad	Db3	F4	Character Ingenue Male
Stiles, George	Baritone	Honk	1993	Ugly	Hold Your Head Up High Reprise	Ballad	C3	G4	Character Ingenue Male
Stiles, George	Baritone	Honk	1993	Bullfrog	Warts and All	Moderate Tempo	A2	C#4	Character Male
Stiles, George	Baritone	Honk	1993	Ugly	Now I've Seen You	Moderate Tempo	Bb2	G4	Character Ingenue Male
Stiles, George	Baritone	Honk!	1993	Drake	A Poultry Tale	Uptempo	C3	F4	Paternal
Stiles, George	Baritone	Honk!	1993	Drake	The Collage	Uptempo	G#2	E3	Paternal
Stothart, Herbert	Alto	Wizard Of Oz 1987	1939	Dorothy	Over The Rainbow	Ballad	G3	C5	Character Ingenue Female
Stothart, Herbert	Alto	Wizard Of Oz 2004	1939	Dorothy	Over The Rainbow Reprise*	Ballad	B3	C#5	Character Ingenue Female
Stothart, Herbert	Alto	Wizard Of Oz 1989	1939	Dorothy	Come Out*	Moderate Tempo	C4	D5	Character Ingenue Female
Stothart, Herbert	Alto	Wizard Of Oz 2002	1939	Dorothy	The Jitterbug*	Uptempo	Ab3	D5	Character Ingenue Female

Composer

Composer	Vocal Range	Show	Year	Role	Song	Tempo	Range-Bottom	Range-Top	Char Type
Stothart, Herbert	Baritone	Wizard Of Oz 1993	1939	Scarecrow	If I Only Had A Brain*	Moderate Tempo	D3	F#4	Character Male
Stothart, Herbert	Baritone	Wizard Of Oz 1997	1939	Cowardly Lion	If I Only Had The Nerve*	Moderate Tempo	Bb2	D4	Antagonist Male
Stothart, Herbert	Baritone	Wizard Of Oz 2001	1939	Cowardly Lion	King Of The Forest*	Moderate Tempo	C3	F4	Antagonist Male
Stothart, Herbert	Soprano	Wizard Of Oz 1988	1939	Glenda	Come Out*	Moderate Tempo	G3	C5	Romantic Lead Female
Stothart, Herbert	Tenor	Wizard Of Oz 1995	1939	Tin Man	If I Only Had A Heart*	Moderate Tempo	D3	G4	Character Male
Strouse, Charles	Alto	Annie	1977	Annie	Maybe	Ballad	A3	C#5	Juvenile Female
Strouse, Charles	Alto	Annie	1977	Annie	Tomorrow	Moderate Tempo	Bb3	Eb5	Juvenile Female
Strouse, Charles	Alto	Bye Bye Birdie	1960	Mae Peterson	A Mother Doesn't Matter Anymore (T	Moderate Tempo	F3	C5	Mature Female
Strouse, Charles	Alto	Bye Bye Birdie	1960	Rose Grant	Let's Settle Down (TV 1995)	Moderate Tempo	G3	Db4	Romantic Lead Female
Strouse, Charles	Alto	Bye Bye Birdie	1960	Rose Grant	Spanish Rose	Moderate Tempo	G3	C5	Romantic Lead Female
Strouse, Charles	Alto	Nick & Nora	1991	Lorraine Bixby	Men*	Moderate Tempo	F3	Cb5	Mature Female
Strouse, Charles	Alto	Annie	1977	Miss Hannigan	Little Girls	Uptempo	C4	D5	Antagonist Female
Strouse, Charles	Alto	Annie	1977	Miss Hannigan	Easy Street *	Uptempo	Bb3	Ab4	Antagonist Female
Strouse, Charles	Alto	Annie	1977	Miss Hannigan	Little Girls Reprise	Uptempo	E4	D5	Antagonist Female
Strouse, Charles	Alto	Annie	1977	Star To Be	N.Y.C. *	Uptempo	Bb4	Eb5	Ingenue Female
Strouse, Charles	Alto	Bye Bye Birdie	1960	Rose Grant	An English Teacher	Uptempo	Gb3	Bb4	Romantic Lead Female
Strouse, Charles	Alto	Bye Bye Birdie	1960	Rose Grant	What Did I Ever See In Him *	Uptempo	G3	Bb4	Romantic Lead Female
Strouse, Charles	Alto	Bye Bye Birdie	1960	Rose Grant	What Did I Ever See In Him Reprise	Uptempo	G3	Bb4	Romantic Lead Female
Strouse, Charles	Alto	Bye Bye Birdie	1960	Rose Grant	An English Teacher Reprise	Uptempo	Db4	Bb4	Romantic Lead Female
Strouse, Charles	Alto	Nick & Nora	1991	Lily Connors	People Get Hurt	Uptempo	Ab3	Db5	Romantic Antagonist Female
Strouse, Charles	Alto	Nick & Nora	1991	Maria Valdex	Boom Chicka Boom*	Uptempo	A3	Bb4	Character Female
Strouse, Charles	Baritone	Annie	1977	Oliver Warbucks	Something Was Missing	Ballad	Bb2	F4	Romantic Lead Male
Strouse, Charles	Baritone	Annie	1977	Oliver Warbucks	Why Should I Change A Thing	Ballad	Bb2	Gb4	Romantic Lead Male
Strouse, Charles	Baritone	Bye Bye Birdie	1960	Albert Peterson	Baby Talk To me	Ballad	C3	F#4	Character Male
Strouse, Charles	Baritone	Nick & Nora	1991	Nick Charles	Look Who's Alone Now	Ballad	Ab2	C4	Romantic Lead Male
Strouse, Charles	Baritone	Nick & Nora	1991	Nick Charles	Let' Go Home Nora	Ballad	G3	B4	Romantic Lead Male
Strouse, Charles	Baritone	Bye Bye Birdie	1960	Albert Peterson	Rosie *	Moderate Tempo	B2	D4	Character Male
Strouse, Charles	Baritone	Bye Bye Birdie	1960	Conrad Birdie	Honestly Sincerely	Moderate Tempo	Ab2	F#4	Romantic Antagonist Male
Strouse, Charles	Baritone	Bye Bye Birdie	1960	Conrad Birdie	One Last Kiss	Moderate Tempo	Ab2	F4	Romantic Antagonist Male
Strouse, Charles	Baritone	Nick & Nora	1991	Victor Moisa	Class	Moderate Tempo	B2	F#4	Romantic Antagonist Male
Strouse, Charles	Baritone	Nick & Nora	1991	Victor Moisa	Class Reprise	Moderate Tempo	B2	F#3	Romantic Antagonist Male
Strouse, Charles	Baritone	Annie	1977	Bert Healy	You're Never Fully Dressed	Uptempo	E3	F#4	Character Ingenue Male

Composer

Composer	Vocal Range	Show	Year	Role	Song	Tempo	Range-Bottom	Range-Top	Char Type
Strouse, Charles	Baritone	Annie	1977	Oliver Warbucks	N.Y.C. *	Uptempo	C3	F4	Romantic Lead Male
Strouse, Charles	Baritone	Bye Bye Birdie	1960	Albert Peterson	Put On A Happy Face	Uptempo	B2	D#4	Character Male
Strouse, Charles	Baritone	Bye Bye Birdie	1960	Albert Peterson	A Giant Step (TV 1995)	Uptempo	D3	F#4	Character Male
Strouse, Charles	Baritone	Bye Bye Birdie	1960	Conrad Birdie	Lot of Livin' To Do *	Uptempo	Db4	F4	Romantic Antagonist Male
Strouse, Charles	Baritone	Nick & Nora	1991	Nick Charles	As Long As You're Happy*	Uptempo	A2	F4	Romantic Lead Male
Strouse, Charles	Soprano	Bye Bye Birdie	1960	Kim MacAfee	One Boy	Ballad	Db4	F5	Ingenue Female
Strouse, Charles	Soprano	Bye Bye Birdie	1960	Kim MacAfee	How Lovely To Be A Woman	Moderate Tempo	D#4	F#4	Ingenue Female
Strouse, Charles	Soprano	Nick & Nora	1991	Tracy Gardner	Everybody Wants To Do A Musical	Moderate Tempo	E2	G#5	Romantic Lead Female
Strouse, Charles	Soprano	Annie	1977	Grace Farrell	N.Y.C. *	Uptempo	C4	F4	Romantic Lead Female
Strouse, Charles	Soprano	Bye Bye Birdie	1960	Kim MacAfee	What Did I Ever See In Him *	Uptempo	G3	Bb4	Ingenue Female
Strouse, Charles	Soprano	Bye Bye Birdie	1960	Kim MacAfee	Lot of Livin' To Do *	Uptempo	D4	E5	Ingenue Female
Strouse, Charles	Tenor	Annie	1977	Rooster Hannigan	Easy Street *	Moderate Tempo	A2	G4	Character Male
Strouse, Charles	Alto	Applause	1970	Eve Harrington	The Best Night Of My Life	Ballad	G#3	C#5	Romantic Antagonist Female
Strouse, Charles	Alto	Applause	1970	Margo Channing	Hurry Back	Ballad	Ab2	F4	Romantic Antagonist Female
Strouse, Charles	Alto	Applause	1970	Eve Harrington	Applause*	Moderate Tempo	G3	E5	Romantic Antagonist Female
Strouse, Charles	Alto	Applause	1970	Margo Channing	Welcome To The Theatre	Moderate Tempo	D3	F#4	Romantic Antagonist Female
Strouse, Charles	Alto	Applause	1970	Eve Harrington	One Hallowe'en	Moderate Tempo	F3	Bb4	Romantic Antagonist Female
Strouse, Charles	Alto	Applause	1970	Margo Channing	But Alive*	Uptempo	E3	F#4	Romantic Antagonist Female
Strouse, Charles	Alto	Applause	1970	Margo Channing	Who's That Girl	Uptempo	E3	A4	Romantic Antagonist Female
Strousse, Charles	Alto	Applause	1970	Margo Channing	Something Greater*	Uptempo	D3	G4	Romantic Antagonist Female
Strousse, Charles	Baritone	Applause	1970	Bill Sampson	Think How It's Gonna Be	Moderate Tempo	B2	F4	Romantic Lead Male
Strousse, Charles	Baritone	Applause	1970	Buzz Richards	Good Friends*	Moderate Tempo	C3	F4	Character Male
Strousse, Charles	Baritone	Applause	1970	Bill Sampson	One Of A Kind*	Uptempo	Bb2	F4	Romantic Lead Male
Styne, Jule	Alto	Gypsy	1959	Louise	Little Lamb	Ballad	Db4	Eb5	Ingenue Female
Styne, Jule	Alto	Gypsy	1959	Rose	Some People Reprise*	Ballad	G#3	A4	Antagonist Female
Styne, Jule	Alto	Gypsy	1959	June	If Momma Was Married*	Moderate Tempo	G3	C5	Ingenue Female
Styne, Jule	Alto	Gypsy	1959	Louise	If Momma Was Married*	Moderate Tempo	G3	C5	Ingenue Female
Styne, Jule	Alto	Gypsy	1959	Louise	Let Me Entertain You*	Moderate Tempo	G3	C5	Ingenue Female
Styne, Jule	Alto	Gypsy	1959	Rose	Small World	Moderate Tempo	F#3	B4	Antagonist Female
Styne, Jule	Alto	Gypsy	1959	Rose	Rose's Turn	Moderate Tempo	G3	C5	Antagonist Female
Styne, Jule	Alto	Gypsy	1959	June	Broadway	Uptempo	E#4	D5	Ingenue Female
Styne, Jule	Alto	Gypsy	1959	Rose	Some People	Uptempo	G#3	C5	Antagonist Female
Styne, Jule	Alto	Gypsy	1959	Rose	You'll Never Get Away From Me*	Uptempo	F#3	B4	Antagonist Female
Styne, Jule	Alto	Gypsy	1959	Rose	Everything's Coming Up Roses	Uptempo	Bb3	C5	Antagonist Female

Composer

Composer	Vocal Range	Show	Year	Role	Song	Tempo	Range-Bottom	Range-Top	Char Type
Styne, Julie	Tenor	Gypsy	1959	Tulsa	All I Need Is The Girl	Uptempo	E3	G4	Ingenue Male
Styne, Julie	Alto	Bells Are Ringing	1956	Ella Peterson	Long Before I Knew You *	Ballad	B3	C#5	Character Female
Styne, Julie	Alto	Bells Are Ringing	1956	Ella Peterson	The Party's Over	Ballad	F#3	B4	Character Female
Styne, Julie	Alto	Funny Girl	1964	Fanny Brice	People	Ballad	A3	Db5	Character Female
Styne, Julie	Alto	Funny Girl	1964	Fanny Brice	Who Are You Now	Ballad	Bb3	Db4	Character Female
Styne, Julie	Alto	Funny Girl	1964	Fanny Brice	The Music That Makes Me Dance	Ballad	G#3	E5	Character Female
Styne, Julie	Alto	Bells Are Ringing	1956	Ella Peterson	Is It A Crime	Moderate Tempo	A3	C5	Character Female
Styne, Julie	Alto	Bells Are Ringing	1956	Ella Peterson	I'm Going Back	Moderate Tempo	A#3	B4	Character Female
Styne, Julie	Alto	Bells Are Ringing	1956	Ella Peterson	Better Than A Dream *	Moderate Tempo	A3	D5	Character Female
Styne, Julie	Alto	Funny Girl	1964	Fanny Brice	I'm The Greatest Start	Moderate Tempo	G#3	C5	Character Female
Styne, Julie	Alto	Funny Girl	1964	Fanny Brice	Coronet Man	Moderate Tempo	A#3	D5	Character Female
Styne, Julie	Alto	Funny Girl	1964	Fanny Brice	His Love Makes Me Beautiful*	Moderate Tempo	Bb3	Eb5	Character Female
Styne, Julie	Alto	Funny Girl	1964	Fanny Brice	You Are Woman*	Moderate Tempo	A#3	C#5	Character Female
Styne, Julie	Alto	Funny Girl	1964	Fanny Brice	Sade, Sade Married Lady	Moderate Tempo	A3	F5	Character Female
Styne, Julie	Alto	Funny Girl	1964	Fanny Brice	Don't Rain On My Parade Reprise	Moderate Tempo	E3	B4	Character Female
Styne, Julie	Alto	Funny Girl	1964	Mrs. Brice	Who Taught Her Everything....*	Moderate Tempo	A3	Eb5	Mature Female
Styne, Julie	Alto	Funny Girl	1964	Mrs. Brice	If A Girl Isn't Pretty*	Moderate Tempo	G#3	C#5	Mature Female
Styne, Julie	Alto	Bells Are Ringing	1956	Ella Peterson	It's A Perfect Relationship	Uptempo	Ab3	Cb5	Character Female
Styne, Julie	Alto	Funny Girl	1964	Fanny Brice	Don't Rain On My Parade	Uptempo	E3	B4	Character Female
Styne, Julie	Alto	Funny Girl	1964	Fanny Brice	Rat Tat Tat Tat Part 2*	Uptempo	B3	D#5	Character Female
Styne, Julie	Alto	Sugar	1972	Sugar Kane	Open Chicago	Uptempo	A3	C5	Romantic Lead Female
Styne, Julie	Alto	Sugar	1972	Sugar Kane	Hey Why Not!*	Uptempo	Bb3	Bb4	Romantic Lead Female
Styne, Julie	Alto	Sugar	1972	Sweet Sue	When You Meet A Man...*	Uptempo	Ab3	Eb5	Romantic Antagonist Female
Styne, Julie	Baritone	Bells Are Ringing	1956	Jeff Moss	Long Before I Knew You *	Ballad	B2	C4	Romantic Lead Male
Styne, Julie	Baritone	Bells Are Ringing	1956	Jeff Moss	Just In Time *	Moderate Tempo	C#3	D4	Romantic Lead Male
Styne, Julie	Baritone	Bells Are Ringing	1956	Jeff Moss	Long Before I Knew You Reprise	Moderate Tempo	C3	C4	Romantic Lead Male
Styne, Julie	Baritone	Bells Are Ringing	1956	Jeff Moss	Better Than A Dream *	Moderate Tempo	E3	D4	Romantic Lead Male
Styne, Julie	Baritone	Bells Are Ringing	1956	Sandor	Salzberg	Moderate Tempo	E3	G4	Character Male
Styne, Julie	Baritone	Funny Girl	1964	Eddie Ryan	Who Taught Her Everything...*	Moderate Tempo	C3	F4	Character Male
Styne, Julie	Baritone	Funny Girl	1964	Eddie Ryan	If A Girl Isn't Pretty*	Moderate Tempo	B2	F#4	Character Male
Styne, Julie	Baritone	Funny Girl	1964	Nick Arnstein	I Want To Be Seen With You...*	Moderate Tempo	Ab2	Eb4	Romantic Lead Male
Styne, Julie	Baritone	Funny Girl	1964	Nick Arnstein	You Are Woman*	Moderate Tempo	A#2	E4	Romantic Lead Male
Styne, Julie	Baritone	Funny Girl	1964	Nick Arnstein	Don't Rain On My Parade (Nick)	Moderate Tempo	G3	D4	Romantic Lead Male
Styne, Julie	Baritone	Sugar	1972	Jerry	Doin' It For Sugar*	Moderate Tempo	B3	E4	Character Male

Composer

Composer	Vocal Range	Show	Year	Role	Song	Tempo	Range-Bottom	Range-Top	Char Type
Styne, Julie	Baritone	Sugar	1972	Joe	Doin' It For Sugar*	Moderate Tempo	B3	E4	Romantic Lead Male
Styne, Julie	Baritone	Sugar	1972	Joe	Shell Oil	Moderate Tempo	D3	B3	Romantic Lead Male
Styne, Julie	Baritone	Sugar	1972	Sir Osgood	Beautiful Through and Through*	Moderate Tempo	C#3	Eb4	Mature Male
Styne, Julie	Baritone	Sugar	1972	Jerry	Beautiful Through and Through*	Moderate Tempo	C#3	E4	Character Male
Styne, Julie	Baritone	Sugar	1972	Jerry	Magic Nights	Moderate Tempo	E3	F4	Character Male
Styne, Julie	Baritone	Bells Are Ringing	1956	Jeff Moss	Independent	Uptempo	D3	E4	Romantic Lead Male
Styne, Julie	Baritone	Bells Are Ringing	1956	Jeff Moss	I Met A Girl	Uptempo	C3	Gb4	Romantic Lead Male
Styne, Julie	Baritone	Funny Girl	1964	Eddie Ryan	Rat Tat Tat*	Uptempo	D3	F#4	Character Male
Styne, Julie	Baritone	Sugar	1972	Jerry	Penniless Bums*	Uptempo	C3	E4	Character Male
Styne, Julie	Baritone	Sugar	1972	Joe	Penniless Bums*	Uptempo	C3	E4	Romantic Lead Male
Styne, Julie	Baritone	Sugar	1972	Jerry	The Beauty That Drives Men Mad*	Uptempo	D3	F4	Character Male
Styne, Julie	Baritone	Sugar	1972	Joe	The Beauty That Drives Men Mad*	Uptempo	D3	F4	Romantic Lead Male
Styne, Julie	Baritone	Sugar	1972	Joe	What Do You Give To A Man...*	Uptempo	C3	E4	Romantic Lead Male
Styne, Julie	Baritone	Sugar	1972	Joe	It Always Love	Uptempo	C3	D4	Romantic Lead Male
Styne, Julie	Tenor	Funny Girl	1964	Zeigfeld Tenor	His Love Makes Me Beautiful*	Moderate Tempo	E3	A4	Romantic Lead Male
Tesori, Jeanine	Alto	Caroline, Or Change	2004	The Radio +	No One Waitin' (ms 1-18)	Alto	G3	D5	Character Female
Tesori, Jeanine	Alto	Caroline, Or Change	2004	Caroline Thibodeaux +	16 Feet Beneath the Sea (10-49)	Ballad	B3	D4	Antagonist Female
Tesori, Jeanine	Alto	Caroline, Or Change	2004	Caroline Thibodeaux +	Gonna Pass Me A Law (ms 1-37)	Ballad	G3	G4	Antagonist Female
Tesori, Jeanine	Alto	Caroline, Or Change	2004	Caroline Thibodeaux +	Underwater (ms 43-74)	Ballad	G3	F4	Antagonist Female
Tesori, Jeanine	Alto	Caroline, Or Change	2004	Rose Stopnick Gellman	Rose Recovers (ms 3-27)	Ballad	G3	C5	Character Female
Tesori, Jeanine	Alto	Thoroughly Modern Millie	2002	Muzzy Van Hossmere	Only In New York	Ballad	G#3	B4	Romantic Lead Female
Tesori, Jeanine	Alto	Caroline, Or Change	2004	Caroline Thibodeaux +	I Got Four Kids (ms 1-114)	Moderate Tempo	Bb3	Bb4	Antagonist Female
Tesori, Jeanine	Alto	Caroline, Or Change	2004	Caroline Thibodeaux +	Lot's Wife (ms 67-151)	Moderate Tempo	F3	Eb5	Antagonist Female
Tesori, Jeanine	Alto	Caroline, Or Change	2004	Caroline Thibodeaux +	Noah Go To Sleep (ms 60-98)	Moderate Tempo	Gb3	Db5	Antagonist Female
Tesori, Jeanine	Alto	Caroline, Or Change	2004	Dotty Moffett +	Lot's Wife (ms 6-42)	Moderate Tempo	G3	B4	Character Female
Tesori, Jeanine	Alto	Caroline, Or Change	2004	Noah Gellman	Noah Downstairs (ms 1-46)	Moderate Tempo	Bb3	Cb5	Juvenile Male
Tesori, Jeanine	Alto	Caroline, Or Change	2004	Rose Stopnick Gellman	Long Distance (ms 1-74)	Moderate Tempo	Bb3	D5	Character Female
Tesori, Jeanine	Alto	Thoroughly Modern Millie	2002	Mrs. Meers	They Don't Know	Moderate Tempo	D#3	F4	Character Female
Tesori, Jeanine	Alto	Thoroughly Modern Millie	2002	Millie Dillmount	How The Other Half Lives*	Moderate Tempo	B3	Eb5	Character Ingenue Female
Tesori, Jeanine	Alto	Caroline, Or Change	2004	Rose Stopnick Gellman	Noah Has A Problem (ms 6-59)	Uptempo	Ab3	Cb5	Character Female
Tesori, Jeanine	Alto	Caroline, Or Change	2004	Rose Stopnick Gellman	Inside/Out (ms 11-54)	Uptempo	C4	D5	Character Female
Tesori, Jeanine	Alto	Thoroughly Modern Millie	2002	Millie Dillmount	Not For The Life Of Me	Uptempo	Ab3	C5	Character Ingenue Female
Tesori, Jeanine	Alto	Thoroughly Modern Millie	2002	Millie Dillmount	Jimmy	Uptempo	B3	D#4	Character Ingenue Female
Tesori, Jeanine	Alto	Thoroughly Modern Millie	2002	Millie Dillmount	Forget About The Boy*	Uptempo	A3	Db5	Character Ingenue Female

Composer

Composer	Vocal Range	Show	Year	Role	Song	Tempo	Range-Bottom	Range-Top	Char Type
Tesori, Jeanine	Alto	Thoroughly Modern Millie	2002	Muzzy Van Hossmere	Long As I'm Here With You*	Uptempo	A3	C#5	Romantic Lead Female
Tesori, Jeanine	Alto	Thoroughly Modern Millie	2002	Millie Dillmount	Gimmie Gimmie	Uptempo	Ab3	D5	Character Ingenue Female
Tesori, Jeanine	Alto	Thoroughly Modern Millie	2002	Millie Dillmount	The Speed Test*	Uptempo	A3	E5	Character Ingenue Female
Tesori, Jeanine	Baritone	Caroline, Or Change	2004	Mr. Stopnick	A Twenty Dollar Bill and Why (ms 41	Ballad	C3	F4	Mature Male
Tesori, Jeanine	Baritone	Caroline, Or Change	2004	Stuart Gellman	Moon, Emmie, Stuart Trio (ms 6-76)	Ballad	Bb2	Eb4	Paternal
Tesori, Jeanine	Baritone	Caroline, Or Change	2004	Stuart Gellman	There Is No God, Noah (ms 1-31)	Moderate Tempo	E3	C#4	Paternal
Tesori, Jeanine	Soprano	Caroline, Or Change	2004	Emmie Thibodeaux +	Duets: Nigh Mamma (ms 71-89)	Ballad	F#4	C5	Ingenue Female
Tesori, Jeanine	Soprano	Caroline, Or Change	2004	Emmie Thibodeaux +	I Hate The Bus (ms 6-36)	Ballad	G3	F#5	Ingenue Female
Tesori, Jeanine	Soprano	Caroline, Or Change	2004	Emmie Thibodeaux +	The Bus (ms 71-89)	Ballad	Bb2	Bb4	Ingenue Female
Tesori, Jeanine	Soprano	Thoroughly Modern Millie	2002	Dorothy Brown	How The Other Half Lives*	Moderate Tempo	B3	Eb5	Ingenue Female
Tesori, Jeanine	Soprano	Caroline, Or Change	2004	Emmie Thibodeaux +	Epilogue-Emmie's Dream (ms 9-73)	Uptempo	Ab3	Db4	Ingenue Female
Tesori, Jeanine	Tenor	Caroline, Or Change	2004	The Moon +	Moon Change (ms 1-12)	Ballad	Bb2	G4	Character Male
Tesori, Jeanine	Tenor	Caroline, Or Change	2004	The Dryer +	The Dryer (ms 1-24)	Moderate Tempo	Bb2	C5	Character Male
Tesori, Jeanine	Tenor	Thoroughly Modern Millie	2002	Jimmy Smith	I Turned The Corner*	Moderate Tempo	C#3	Ab4	Ingenue Male
Tesori, Jeanine	Tenor	Thoroughly Modern Millie	2002	Jimmy Smith	What Do I Need With Love	Uptempo	D3	G4	Ingenue Male
Tesori, Jeanine	Tenor	Thoroughly Modern Millie	2002	Trevor Graydon	The Speed Test*	Uptempo	A2	F4	Romantic Lead Male
Valcq, James	Alto	Spitfire Grill	2001	Hannah Ferguson	Forgotten Lullaby	Ballad	G3	G4	Antagonist Female
Valcq, James	Alto	Spitfire Grill	2001	Percy Talbott	Shine	Ballad	G3	E5	Character Ingenue Female
Valcq, James	Alto	Spitfire Grill	2001	Hannah Ferguson	Way Back Home	Ballad	E3	B4	Antagonist Female
Valcq, James	Alto	Spitfire Grill	2001	Percy Talbott	A Ring Around The Moon	Moderate Tempo	A3	E5	Character Ingenue Female
Valcq, James	Alto	Spitfire Grill	2001	Hannah Ferguson	Hannah's Harangue	Moderate Tempo	G3	A4	Antagonist Female
Valcq, James	Alto	Spitfire Grill	2001	Percy Talbott	This Wide Woods Part 3	Moderate Tempo	E3	C#5	Character Ingenue Female
Valcq, James	Alto	Spitfire Grill	2001	Hannah Ferguson	Come Alive Again Part 2	Moderate Tempo	G3	A4	Antagonist Female
Valcq, James	Alto	Spitfire Grill	2001	Percy Talbott	Coffee Cups And Gossip	Uptempo	C4	C5	Character Ingenue Female
Valcq, James	Alto	Spitfire Grill	2001	Percy Talbott	Out Of The Frying Pan	Uptempo	A3	D5	Character Ingenue Female
Valcq, James	Alto	Spitfire Grill	2001	Percy Talbott	The Colors of Paradise*	Uptempo	G3	F5	Character Ingenue Female
Valcq, James	Soprano	Spitfire Grill	2001	Shelby Thorpe	Hannah Had A Son	Ballad	D4	D5	Ingenue Female
Valcq, James	Soprano	Spitfire Grill	2001	Shelby Thorpe	When Hope Goes	Ballad	A3	D5	Ingenue Female
Valcq, James	Soprano	Spitfire Grill	2001	Shelby Thorpe	Wild Bird	Ballad	C4	D5	Ingenue Female
Valcq, James	Tenor	Spitfire Grill	2001	Caleb Thorpe	Digging Stone	Moderate Tempo	B2	G4	Romantic Antagonist Male
Valcq, James	Tenor	Spitfire Grill	2001	Joe Sutter	This Wide Woods Part 2	Uptempo	E3	F4	Character Male
Valcq, James	Tenor	Spitfire Grill	2001	Joe Sutter	Forest For The Trees	Uptempo	D3	A4	Character Male
Various	Alto	High School Musical	2007	Gabriella Montez	When There Was You And Me	Ballad	F#3	F5	Ingenue Female
Various	Alto	High School Musical	2007	Gabriella Montez	Breaking Free*	Ballad	Bb3	D5	Ingenue Female

Composer

Composer	Vocal Range	Show	Year	Role	Song	Tempo	Range-Bottom	Range-Top	Char Type
Various	Tenor	High School Musical	2007	Troy Bolton	What I've Been Looking For Reprise*	Ballad	G3	F#4	Ingenue Male
Various	Tenor	High School Musical	2007	Troy Bolton	Breaking Free*	Ballad	Bb2	Bb4	Ingenue Male
Various	Tenor	High School Musical	2007	Ryan Evans	What I've Been Looking For*	Uptempo	A3	F#4	Character Ingenue Male
Waller, Fats	Alto	Ain't Misbehavin'	1988	Woman One +	Mean To Me	Ballad	G3	G4	Character Female
Waller, Fats	Alto	Ain't Misbehavin'	1988	Woman One +	Honeysuckle Rose*	Ballad	Bb4	F5	Character Female
Waller, Fats	Alto	Ain't Misbehavin'	1988	Woman One +	Lounging At The Waldorf	Ballad	C4	D5	Character Female
Waller, Fats	Alto	Ain't Misbehavin'	1988	Woman Two +	That Ain't Right*	Ballad	G2	Eb5	Character Female
Waller, Fats	Alto	Ain't Misbehavin'	1988	Woman One +	I've Got A Feeling I'm Falling	Uptempo	F3	C5	Character Female
Waller, Fats	Alto	Ain't Misbehavin'	1988	Woman One +	Cash For our Trash	Uptempo	B4	D5	Character Female
Waller, Fats	Soprano	Ain't Misbehavin'	1988	Woman Three +	Squeeze Me	Ballad	Ab3	Db5	Character Female
Waller, Fats	Soprano	Ain't Misbehavin'	1988	Woman Two +	Keepin' Out of Mischief Now	Ballad	A3	C5	Character Ingenue Female
Waller, Fats	Soprano	Ain't Misbehavin'	1988	Woman Three +	When The Nylons Are In Bloom Again	Uptempo	C4	D5	Character Ingenue Female
Waller, Fats	Soprano	Ain't Misbehavin'	1988	Woman Two +	Yacht Club Swing	Uptempo	Ab3	Ab5	Character Ingenue Female
Waller, Fats	Tenor	Ain't Misbehavin'	1988	Man One +	The Viper's Drag*	Ballad	C3	G4	Character Ingenue Male
Waller, Fats	Tenor	Ain't Misbehavin'	1988	Man One +	That Ain't Right*	Ballad	G2	Bb4	Character Ingenue Male
Waller, Fats	Tenor	Ain't Misbehavin'	1988	Man Two +	Honeysuckle Rose*	Ballad	D3	Ab4	Character Male
Waller, Fats	Tenor	Ain't Misbehavin'	1988	Man Two +	Lounging At The Waldorf	Ballad	B3	E4	Character Male
Waller, Fats	Tenor	Ain't Misbehavin'	1988	Man Two +	Your Feets Too Big	Ballad	G2	Eb4	Character Male
Waller, Fats	Tenor	Ain't Misbehavin'	1988	Man One +	How Ya Baby*	Uptempo	C3	C5	Character Ingenue Male
Waters, Daniel	Alto	Heathers	2014	Heather McNamara	Lifeboat	Ballad	G3	Db5	Ingenue Female
Waters, Daniel	Alto	Heathers	2014	Martha Dunnstock	Kindergarten Boyfriend	Ballad	G3	E5	Character Female
Waters, Daniel	Alto	Heathers	2014	Veronica Sawyer	Fight For Me	Ballad	Bb3	D5	Character Ingenue Female
Waters, Daniel	Alto	Heathers	2014	Veronica Sawyer	Seventeen*	Ballad	A3	B4	Character Ingenue Female
Waters, Daniel	Alto	Heathers	2014	Veronica Sawyer	The Me Inside Of Me	Moderate Tempo	Ab3	D5	Character Ingenue Female
Waters, Daniel	Alto	Heathers	2014	Veronica Sawyer	Seventeen Reprise*	Moderate Tempo	A3	Gb5	Character Ingenue Female
Waters, Daniel	Alto	Heathers	2014	Heather Chandler	Candy*	Uptempo	Bb3	A5	Romantic Antagonist Female
Waters, Daniel	Alto	Heathers	2014	Veronica Sawyer	Beautiful	Uptempo	G3	C5	Character Ingenue Female
Waters, Daniel	Alto	Heathers	2014	Veronica Sawyer	Dead Girl Walking*	Uptempo	A3	G5	Character Ingenue Female
Waters, Daniel	Alto	Heathers	2014	Veronica Sawyer	Dead Girls Walking Reprise	Uptempo	A3	A5	Character Ingenue Female
Waters, Daniel	Soprano	Heathers	2014	Mrs. Fleming	Shine A Light*	Uptempo	G3	F5	Maternal
Waters, Daniel	Tenor	Heathers	2014	Jason Dean (JD)	Our Love Is God	Ballad	F#3	F#4	Romantic Antagonist Male
Waters, Daniel	Tenor	Heathers	2014	Jason Dean (JD)	I Am Damaged	Ballad	E3	F#4	Romantic Antagonist Male
Waters, Daniel	Tenor	Heathers	2014	Jason Dean (JD)	Seventeen*	Ballad	A3	B4	Romantic Antagonist Male

Composer

Composer	Vocal Range	Show	Year	Role	Song	Tempo	Range-Bottom	Range-Top	Char Type
Waters, Daniel	Tenor	Heathers	2014	Jason Dean (JD)	Freeze Your Brain	Moderate Tempo	Bb3	G#4	Romantic Antagonist Male
Waters, Daniel	Tenor	Heathers	2014	Jason Dean (JD)	Meant To Be Yours	Uptempo	G3	Ab4	Romantic Antagonist Male
Waters, Daniel	Tenor	Heathers	2014	Ram Sweeney	Blue*	Uptempo	F#3	D5	Romantic Antagonist Male
Waters, Daniel	Tenor	Heathers	2014	Ram's Dad	My Dead Gay Son	Uptempo	C3	A4	Paternal
Webber, Andrew Lloyd	Alto	Evita	1978	Eva Peron	Don't Cry For Me Argentina	Alto	Ab3	Eb5	Romantic Antagonist Female
Webber, Andrew Lloyd	Alto	Cats	1981	Grizabella	Grizabella the Glamour Cat	Ballad	G3	C5	Mature Female
Webber, Andrew Lloyd	Alto	Cats	1981	Grizabella	Memory	Ballad	G3	E5	Mature Female
Webber, Andrew Lloyd	Alto	Evita	1978	Eva Peron	Another Suitcase In Another Hall	Ballad	A3	E5	Romantic Antagonist Female
Webber, Andrew Lloyd	Alto	Evita	1978	Eva Peron	The Actress Hasn't Learned the Lines	Ballad	G#3	D#5	Romantic Antagonist Female
Webber, Andrew Lloyd	Alto	Evita	1978	Eva Peron	Eva's Final Broadcast	Ballad	Ab3	Db5	Romantic Antagonist Female
Webber, Andrew Lloyd	Alto	Evita	1978	Eva Peron	Lament	Ballad	Bb3	Db5	Romantic Antagonist Female
Webber, Andrew Lloyd	Alto	Jesus Christ Superstar	1971	Mary Magdalene	I Don't Know How To Love Him	Ballad	A3	C5	Character Ingenue Female
Webber, Andrew Lloyd	Alto	Jesus Christ Superstar	1971	Mary Magdalene	Could We Start Again Please	Ballad	A3	F#5	Character Ingenue Female
Webber, Andrew Lloyd	Alto	Song & Dance	1985	Emma	Capped Teeth And Ceasar Salad Rep	Ballad	Ab3	Bb4	Character Ingenue Female
Webber, Andrew Lloyd	Alto	Song & Dance	1985	Emma	The Last Man In My Life	Ballad	G3	Eb5	Character Ingenue Female
Webber, Andrew Lloyd	Alto	Song & Dance	1985	Emma	Unexpected Song	Ballad	F3	G5	Character Ingenue Female
Webber, Andrew Lloyd	Alto	Song & Dance	1985	Emma	Tell Me On A Sunday	Ballad	G3	E5	Character Ingenue Female
Webber, Andrew Lloyd	Alto	Song & Dance	1985	Emma	Nothing Like You've Ever Known	Ballad	G3	C5	Character Ingenue Female
Webber, Andrew Lloyd	Alto	Sunset Boulevard	1994	Norma Desmond	Surrender	Ballad	F3	Bb4	Romantic Antagonist Female
Webber, Andrew Lloyd	Alto	Sunset Boulevard	1994	Norma Desmond	New Ways To Dream	Ballad	B3	C5	Romantic Antagonist Female
Webber, Andrew Lloyd	Alto	Cats	1981	Bombalurina	Macavity	Moderate Tempo	A3	C5	Romantic Lead Female
Webber, Andrew Lloyd	Alto	Cats	1981	Demeter	Macavity	Moderate Tempo	A3	C5	Romantic Lead Female
Webber, Andrew Lloyd	Alto	Evita	1978	Eva Peron	I'd Be Surprisingly Good For You	Moderate Tempo	G#3	F5	Romantic Antagonist Female
Webber, Andrew Lloyd	Alto	Jesus Christ Superstar	1971	Mary Magdalene	Everything's Alright	Moderate Tempo	G#3	D5	Character Ingenue Female
Webber, Andrew Lloyd	Alto	Jesus Christ Superstar	1971	Mary Magdalene	Everything's Alright Reprise	Moderate Tempo	F#3	G4	Character Ingenue Female
Webber, Andrew Lloyd	Alto	Joseph...Dream Coat	1982	Narrator	Pharaoh Story	Moderate Tempo	A3	E5	Character Female
Webber, Andrew Lloyd	Alto	Song & Dance	1985	Emma	Let Me Finish	Moderate Tempo	G#3	Eb5	Character Ingenue Female
Webber, Andrew Lloyd	Alto	Song & Dance	1985	Emma	So Much To Do In New York	Moderate Tempo	Ab3	Eb5	Character Ingenue Female
Webber, Andrew Lloyd	Alto	Song & Dance	1985	Emma	1st Letter Home	Moderate Tempo	A3	D5	Character Ingenue Female
Webber, Andrew Lloyd	Alto	Song & Dance	1985	Emma	Capped Teeth And Ceasar Salad	Moderate Tempo	A3	B4	Character Ingenue Female
Webber, Andrew Lloyd	Alto	Song & Dance	1985	Emma	So Much To Do In New York #2	Moderate Tempo	G3	Eb5	Character Ingenue Female
Webber, Andrew Lloyd	Alto	Song & Dance	1985	Emma	2nd Letter Home	Moderate Tempo	A3	A4	Character Ingenue Female
Webber, Andrew Lloyd	Alto	Song & Dance	1985	Emma	I Love New York	Moderate Tempo	F3	Bb4	Character Ingenue Female

Composer

Composer	Vocal Range	Show	Year	Role	Song	Tempo	Range-Bottom	Range-Top	Char Type
Webber, Andrew Lloyd	Alto	Song & Dance	1985	Emma	So Much To Do In New York #3	Moderate Tempo	A3	Eb5	Character Ingenue Female
Webber, Andrew Lloyd	Alto	Song & Dance	1985	Emma	Married Man	Moderate Tempo	G#3	C5	Character Ingenue Female
Webber, Andrew Lloyd	Alto	Song & Dance	1985	Emma	3rd Letter Home	Moderate Tempo	G3	Eb5	Character Ingenue Female
Webber, Andrew Lloyd	Alto	Song & Dance	1985	Emma	Let Me Finish Finale	Moderate Tempo	G#3	Eb5	Character Ingenue Female
Webber, Andrew Lloyd	Alto	Sunset Boulevard	1994	Norma Desmond	With One Look	Moderate Tempo	G3	D5	Romantic Antagonist Female
Webber, Andrew Lloyd	Alto	Sunset Boulevard	1994	Norma Desmond	The Perfect Year*	Moderate Tempo	A3	Eb5	Romantic Antagonist Female
Webber, Andrew Lloyd	Alto	Sunset Boulevard	1994	Norma Desmond	As If We Never Said Goodbye	Moderate Tempo	G#3	C#5	Romantic Antagonist Female
Webber, Andrew Lloyd	Alto	Sunset Boulevard	1994	Norma Desmond	Phone Call	Moderate Tempo	F3	Ab4	Romantic Antagonist Female
Webber, Andrew Lloyd	Alto	Cats	1981	Rumpleteezer	Mongojerrie and Rumpleteezer	Uptempo	E4	G5	Ingenue Female
Webber, Andrew Lloyd	Alto	Evita	1978	Eva Peron	Buenos Aires	Uptempo	E3	F5	Romantic Antagonist Female
Webber, Andrew Lloyd	Alto	Evita	1978	Eva Peron	Rainbow High	Uptempo	G3	E5	Romantic Antagonist Female
Webber, Andrew Lloyd	Alto	Evita	1978	Eva Peron	Waltz for Eva and Che	Uptempo	Ab3	F5	Romantic Antagonist Female
Webber, Andrew Lloyd	Alto	Song & Dance	1985	Emma	Take That Look Off Your Face	Uptempo	B3	D5	Character Ingenue Female
Webber, Andrew Lloyd	Alto	Song & Dance	1985	Emma	English Girls	Uptempo	G3	C5	Character Ingenue Female
Webber, Andrew Lloyd	Alto	Song & Dance	1985	Emma	You Made Me Think You Were In Love	Uptempo	A3	Bb4	Character Ingenue Female
Webber, Andrew Lloyd	Alto	Song & Dance	1985	Emma	Come Back With The Same Look...	Uptempo	A3	C5	Character Ingenue Female
Webber, Andrew Lloyd	Alto	Song & Dance	1985	Emma	Take That Look Off Your Face Reprise	Uptempo	B3	E5	Character Ingenue Female
Webber, Andrew Lloyd	Alto	Song & Dance	1985	Emma	I'm Very You	Uptempo	A#3	C5	Character Ingenue Female
Webber, Andrew Lloyd	Alto	Sunset Boulevard	1994	Norma Desmond	Once Upon A Time	Uptempo	A3	A4	Romantic Antagonist Female
Webber, Andrew Lloyd	Alto	Sunset Boulevard	1994	Norma Desmond	There's Been A Call*	Uptempo	C4	D5	Romantic Antagonist Female
Webber, Andrew Lloyd	Baritone	Cats	1981	Asparagus	Gus: The Theatre Cat	Ballad	A2	D4	Mature Male
Webber, Andrew Lloyd	Baritone	Cats	1981	Rum Tum Tugger	Old Deuteronomy *	Ballad	B2	G4	Character Male
Webber, Andrew Lloyd	Baritone	Jesus Christ Superstar	1971	Pontius Pilate	Pilate's Dream	Ballad	A2	Bb3	Antagonist Male
Webber, Andrew Lloyd	Baritone	Joseph...Dream Coat	1982	Reuben (Chevalier)	Those Canaan Days	Ballad	C3	F4	Character Male
Webber, Andrew Lloyd	Baritone	Sunset Boulevard	1994	Cecil B. DeMille	Surrender Reprise	Ballad	Ab2	Db4	Mature Male
Webber, Andrew Lloyd	Baritone	Sunset Boulevard	1994	Max Von Mayerling	New Ways To Dream Reprise	Ballad	G2	E4	Character Male
Webber, Andrew Lloyd	Baritone	Cats	1981	Munkustrap	The Old Gumbie Cat	Moderate Tempo	E3	F4	Romantic Lead Male
Webber, Andrew Lloyd	Baritone	Evita	1978	Juan Peron	The Art of the Possible	Moderate Tempo	Bb2	D4	Romantic Lead Male
Webber, Andrew Lloyd	Baritone	Evita	1978	Juan Peron	She's A Diamond	Moderate Tempo	A2	F4	Romantic Lead Male
Webber, Andrew Lloyd	Baritone	Jesus Christ Superstar	1971	Pontius Pilate	Pilate and Christ	Moderate Tempo	Bb3	G#4	Antagonist Male
Webber, Andrew Lloyd	Baritone	Joseph...Dream Coat	1982	Levi	One More Angel In Heaven	Moderate Tempo	D3	F4	Character Male
Webber, Andrew Lloyd	Baritone	Sunset Boulevard	1994	Max Von Mayerling	The Grestest Star Of All	Moderate Tempo	B2	Gb4	Character Male
Webber, Andrew Lloyd	Baritone	Cats	1981	Bustopher Jones	Bustopher Jones *	Uptempo	C3	C4	Mature Male

Composer

Composer	Vocal Range	Show	Year	Role	Song	Tempo	Range-Bottom	Range-Top	Char Type
Webber, Andrew Lloyd	Baritone	Cats	1981	Mr. Mistoffolees	Mr. Mistoffolees	Uptempo	C3	Eb4	Ingenue Male
Webber, Andrew Lloyd	Baritone	Cats	1981	Mungojerrie	Mongojerrie and Rumpleteezer	Uptempo	E3	E4	Ingenue Male
Webber, Andrew Lloyd	Baritone	Cats	1981	Rum Tum Tugger	Rum Tum Tugger	Uptempo	B2	F4	Character Male
Webber, Andrew Lloyd	Baritone	Cats	1981	Rum Tum Tugger	Mr. Mistoffolees	Uptempo	C3	Eb4	Character Male
Webber, Andrew Lloyd	Baritone	Jesus Christ Superstar	1971	King Herod	King Herod's Song	Uptempo	B2	G4	Character Male
Webber, Andrew Lloyd	Baritone	Joseph...Dream Coat	1982	Napthali	Benjamin Calypso	Uptempo	F3	F4	Character Male
Webber, Andrew Lloyd	Baritone	Sunset Boulevard	1994	Manfred	The Lady's Paying*	Uptempo	C3	F4	Character Male
Webber, Andrew Lloyd	Soprano	Cats	1981	Jellylorum	Gus: The Theatre Cat	Ballad	A3	D5	Mature Female
Webber, Andrew Lloyd	Soprano	Evita	1978	Mistress	Another Suitcase In Another Hall	Ballad	A3	E5	Ingenue Female
Webber, Andrew Lloyd	Soprano	Phantom Of The Opera	1986	Christine Daae	All I Ask Of You*	Ballad	Ab3	Ab5	Ingenue Female
Webber, Andrew Lloyd	Soprano	Phantom Of The Opera	1986	Christine Daae	Twisted Every Way*	Ballad	C4	Eb5	Ingenue Female
Webber, Andrew Lloyd	Soprano	Phantom Of The Opera	1986	Christine Daae	Wishing You Were Somehow Here Ag	Ballad	A3	G5	Ingenue Female
Webber, Andrew Lloyd	Soprano	Phantom Of The Opera	1986	Christine Daae	The Point Of No Return*	Ballad	C4	G5	Ingenue Female
Webber, Andrew Lloyd	Soprano	Phantom Of The Opera	1986	Carlotta Giudicelli	Hannibal Cadenza	Moderate Tempo	C4	D6	Romantic Antagonist Female
Webber, Andrew Lloyd	Soprano	Phantom Of The Opera	1986	Carlotta Giudicelli	Think Of Me*	Moderate Tempo	E#4	G#5	Romantic Antagonist Female
Webber, Andrew Lloyd	Soprano	Phantom Of The Opera	1986	Christine Daae	Think Of Me*	Moderate Tempo	D4	C6	Ingenue Female
Webber, Andrew Lloyd	Soprano	Phantom Of The Opera	1986	Christine Daae	Angel Of Music*	Moderate Tempo	Bb3	F#5	Ingenue Female
Webber, Andrew Lloyd	Soprano	Phantom Of The Opera	1986	Christine Daae	Phantom Of The Opera*	Moderate Tempo	G3	E5	Ingenue Female
Webber, Andrew Lloyd	Soprano	Phantom Of The Opera	1986	Carlotta Giudicelli	Diva*	Moderate Tempo	F4	E6	Romantic Antagonist Female
Webber, Andrew Lloyd	Soprano	Phantom Of The Opera	1986	Carlotta Giudicelli	Prima Donna*	Moderate Tempo	F4	F6	Romantic Antagonist Female
Webber, Andrew Lloyd	Soprano	Phantom Of The Opera	1986	Carlotta Giudicelli	Poor Fool He Makes Me Laugh*	Moderate Tempo	F4	C6	Romantic Antagonist Female
Webber, Andrew Lloyd	Soprano	Phantom Of The Opera	1986	Christine Daae	Raoul I've Been There	Moderate Tempo	C#4	Ab5	Ingenue Female
Webber, Andrew Lloyd	Soprano	Sunset Boulevard	1994	Betty Schaefer	Too Much In Love To Care*	Moderate Tempo	A3	G5	Character Ingenue Female
Webber, Andrew Lloyd	Soprano	Cats	1981	Jennyanydots	Bustopher Jones *	Uptempo	B3	F5	Mature Female
Webber, Andrew Lloyd	Soprano	Sunset Boulevard	1994	Betty Schaefer	Girl Meets Boy Reprise*	Uptempo	A3	E5	Character Ingenue Female
Webber, Andrew Lloyd	Tenor	Cats	1981	Munkustrap	Old Deuteronomy *	Ballad	B2	G4	Romantic Lead Male
Webber, Andrew Lloyd	Tenor	Cats	1981	Old Deuteronomy	Old Deuteronomy *	Ballad	B2	G4	Mature Male
Webber, Andrew Lloyd	Tenor	Cats	1981	Old Deuteronomy	The Moments of Happiness	Ballad	B3	G5	Mature Male
Webber, Andrew Lloyd	Tenor	Evita	1978	Magaldi	On This Nigh of a Thousand Stars	Ballad	Bb2	G4	Romantic Lead Male
Webber, Andrew Lloyd	Tenor	Jesus Christ Superstar	1971	Jesus of Nazareth	Poor Jerusalem	Ballad	A2	Ab4	Romantic Lead Male
Webber, Andrew Lloyd	Tenor	Jesus Christ Superstar	1971	Jesus of Nazareth	Gethsemane	Ballad	Bb2	Ab4	Romantic Lead Male
Webber, Andrew Lloyd	Tenor	Jesus Christ Superstar	1971	Jesus of Nazareth	The Last Supper	Ballad	F#2	C5	Romantic Lead Male
Webber, Andrew Lloyd	Tenor	Joseph...Dream Coat	1982	Joseph	Any Dream Will Do	Ballad	C4	F4	Ingenue Male
Webber, Andrew Lloyd	Tenor	Joseph...Dream Coat	1982	Joseph	Close Every Door	Ballad	C3	A4	Ingenue Male

Composer

Composer	Vocal Range	Show	Year	Role	Song	Tempo	Range-Bottom	Range-Top	Char Type
Webber, Andrew Lloyd	Tenor	Joseph...Dream Coat	1982	Joseph	Any Dream Will Do Reprise	Ballad	D3	F4	Ingenue Male
Webber, Andrew Lloyd	Tenor	Joseph...Dream Coat	1982	Joseph	Any Dream Will Do (II)	Ballad	C3	F4	Ingenue Male
Webber, Andrew Lloyd	Tenor	Phantom Of The Opera	1986	Raoul, Vicomte de Chag	Prologue	Ballad	C#3	E4	Romantic Lead Male
Webber, Andrew Lloyd	Tenor	Phantom Of The Opera	1986	Phantom	The Music Of The Night	Ballad	G#2	G#4	Antagonist Male
Webber, Andrew Lloyd	Tenor	Phantom Of The Opera	1986	Phantom	Stranger Than You Dreamt It*	Ballad	D3	D4	Antagonist Male
Webber, Andrew Lloyd	Tenor	Phantom Of The Opera	1986	Raoul, Vicomte de Chag	All I Ask Of You*	Ballad	Ab3	G4	Romantic Lead Male
Webber, Andrew Lloyd	Tenor	Phantom Of The Opera	1986	Phantom	All I Ask Of You Reprise	Ballad	G3	A4	Antagonist Male
Webber, Andrew Lloyd	Tenor	Phantom Of The Opera	1986	Phantom	Why So Silent*	Ballad	Eb3	Gb4	Antagonist Male
Webber, Andrew Lloyd	Tenor	Phantom Of The Opera	1986	Phantom	Notes: No Doubt She'll Do Her Best	Ballad	D#3	D#4	Antagonist Male
Webber, Andrew Lloyd	Tenor	Phantom Of The Opera	1986	Phantom	The Point Of No Return*	Ballad	C3	G4	Antagonist Male
Webber, Andrew Lloyd	Tenor	Phantom Of The Opera	1986	Phantom	All I Ask Of You Reprise 2*	Ballad	Db3	Ab4	Antagonist Male
Webber, Andrew Lloyd	Tenor	Cats	1981	Old Deuteronomy	The Ad-Dressing of Cats	Moderate Tempo	Bb2	G4	Mature Male
Webber, Andrew Lloyd	Tenor	Evita	1978	Che Guevara	High Flying Adored	Moderate Tempo	Bb2	G4	Antagonist Male
Webber, Andrew Lloyd	Tenor	Phantom Of The Opera	1986	Phantom	Phantom Of The Opera*	Moderate Tempo	B2	G#4	Antagonist Male
Webber, Andrew Lloyd	Tenor	Sunset Boulevard	1994	Joe Gillis	Prologue	Moderate Tempo	D3	G4	Romantic Antagonist Male
Webber, Andrew Lloyd	Tenor	Sunset Boulevard	1994	Joe Gillis	Let Me Take You Back Six Months	Moderate Tempo	C3	Eb4	Romantic Antagonist Male
Webber, Andrew Lloyd	Tenor	Sunset Boulevard	1994	Joe Gillis	The Perfect Year*	Moderate Tempo	A2	D4	Romantic Antagonist Male
Webber, Andrew Lloyd	Tenor	Sunset Boulevard	1994	Joe Gillis	Too Much In Love To Care*	Moderate Tempo	F3	G4	Romantic Antagonist Male
Webber, Andrew Lloyd	Tenor	Cats	1981	Skimbleshanks	It Took Her Three Days	Uptempo	A2	E4	Romantic Antagonist Male
Webber, Andrew Lloyd	Tenor	Evita	1978	Che Guevara	Skimbleshanks	Uptempo	A2	F4	Ingenue Male
Webber, Andrew Lloyd	Tenor	Evita	1978	Che Guevara	Oh What A Circus	Uptempo	B2	E4	Antagonist Male
Webber, Andrew Lloyd	Tenor	Evita	1978	Che Guevara	Goodnight and Thank You	Uptempo	B2	F4	Antagonist Male
Webber, Andrew Lloyd	Tenor	Evita	1978	Che Guevara	Peron's Latest Flame	Uptempo	F2	F4	Romantic Antagonist Male
Webber, Andrew Lloyd	Tenor	Evita	1978	Che Guevara	Rainbow Tour	Uptempo	C3	E4	Antagonist Male
Webber, Andrew Lloyd	Tenor	Evita	1978	Che Guevara	And the Money Kept Rolling In	Uptempo	A2	G4	Antagonist Male
Webber, Andrew Lloyd	Tenor	Evita	1978	Che Guevara	Waltz for Eva and Che	Uptempo	D3	G4	Antagonist Male
Webber, Andrew Lloyd	Tenor	Jesus Christ Superstar	1971	Judas Iscariot	Heaven On Their Minds	Uptempo	D3	D5	Antagonist Male
Webber, Andrew Lloyd	Tenor	Jesus Christ Superstar	1971	Judas Iscariot	Damned For All Time*	Uptempo	D3	D5	Antagonist Male
Webber, Andrew Lloyd	Tenor	Jesus Christ Superstar	1971	Judas Iscariot	Judas' Death	Uptempo	D3	E5	Antagonist Male
Webber, Andrew Lloyd	Tenor	Jesus Christ Superstar	1971	Judas Iscariot	Superstar	Uptempo	E3	B4	Antagonist Male
Webber, Andrew Lloyd	Tenor	Jesus Christ Superstar	1971	Simon Zealots	Simon Zealots*	Uptempo	F3	Ab4	Antagonist Male
Webber, Andrew Lloyd	Tenor	Joseph...Dream Coat	1982	Joseph	Pharaoh's Dream Explained	Uptempo	B2	E4	Ingenue Male
Webber, Andrew Lloyd	Tenor	Joseph...Dream Coat	1982	Pharaoh (Elvis)	Song of the King	Uptempo	B2	G#4	Character Male
Webber, Andrew Lloyd	Tenor	Joseph...Dream Coat	1982	Pharaoh (Elvis)	Song of the King Reprise	Uptempo	B2	G#4	Character Male

Composer

Composer	Vocal Range	Show	Year	Role	Song	Tempo	Range-Bottom	Range-Top	Char Type
Webber, Andrew Lloyd	Tenor	Sunset Boulevard	1994	Joe Gillis	I Started Work	Uptempo	C3	G4	Romantic Antagonist Male
Webber, Andrew Lloyd	Tenor	Sunset Boulevard	1994	Joe Gillis	I Had To Get Out	Uptempo	C3	Eb4	Romantic Antagonist Male
Webber, Andrew Lloyd	Tenor	Sunset Boulevard	1994	Joe Gillis	Sunset Boulevard	Uptempo	C3	G4	Romantic Antagonist Male
Webber, Andrew Lloyd	Tenor	Sunset Boulevard	1994	Joe Gillis	Girl Meets Boy Reprise	Uptempo	D3	E4	Romantic Antagonist Male
Webber, Andrew Lloyd	Tenor	Sunset Boulevard	1994	Joe Gillis	I Should Have Stayed There	Uptempo	A3	E4	Romantic Antagonist Male
Webber, Andrew Lloyd	Tenor	Sunset Boulevard	1994	Joe Gillis	Sunset Blvd Reprise-What's Going On	Uptempo	C#3	Gb4	Romantic Antagonist Male
Wildhorn, Frank	Alto	Jekyll and Hyde	1997	Lucy Harris	No One Knows Who I Am	Ballad	C4	D5	Romantic Antagonist Female
Wildhorn, Frank	Alto	Jekyll and Hyde	1997	Lucy Harris	Someone Like You	Ballad	G2	Eb4	Romantic Antagonist Female
Wildhorn, Frank	Alto	Jekyll and Hyde	1997	Lucy Harris	Sympathy, Tenderness	Ballad	D3	C#4	Romantic Antagonist Female
Wildhorn, Frank	Alto	Jekyll and Hyde	1997	Lucy Harris	In His Eyes*	Ballad	Bb3	F5	Romantic Antagonist Female
Wildhorn, Frank	Alto	Jekyll and Hyde	1997	Lucy Harris	A New Life	Ballad	B3	D5	Romantic Antagonist Female
Wildhorn, Frank	Alto	Jekyll and Hyde	1997	Lucy Harris	Sympathy, Tenderness/Lucy's Death	Ballad	C#4	C#5	Romantic Antagonist Female
Wildhorn, Frank	Alto	Scarlet Pimpernel, The	1997	Marguerite St. Just	You Are My Home*	Ballad	C#4	F#5	Romantic Lead Female
Wildhorn, Frank	Alto	Scarlet Pimpernel, The	1997	Marguerite St. Just	When I Look At You	Ballad	B3	E5	Romantic Lead Female
Wildhorn, Frank	Alto	Scarlet Pimpernel, The	1997	Marguerite St. Just	I'll Foget You	Ballad	G#3	D5	Romantic Lead Female
Wildhorn, Frank	Alto	Scarlet Pimpernel, The	1997	Marguerite St. Just	Only Love	Ballad	Bb3	E5	Romantic Lead Female
Wildhorn, Frank	Alto	Jekyll and Hyde	1997	Lucy Harris	Good and Evil	Moderate Tempo	G#3	E5	Romantic Antagonist Female
Wildhorn, Frank	Alto	Scarlet Pimpernel, The	1997	Marguerite St. Just	Storybook*	Moderate Tempo	A3	E5	Romantic Antagonist Female
Wildhorn, Frank	Alto	Scarlet Pimpernel, The	1997	Marguerite St. Just	Vivez*	Moderate Tempo	C#4	E5	Romantic Lead Female
Wildhorn, Frank	Alto	Jekyll and Hyde	1997	Lucy Harris	Bring On The Men	Uptempo	G#3	E5	Romantic Antagonist Female
Wildhorn, Frank	Bar/Sop	Scarlet Pimpernel, The	1997	Chauvelin	Madame Guillotine*	Uptempo	B2	F4	Romantic Antagonist Male
Wildhorn, Frank	Baritone	Scarlet Pimpernel, The	1997	Chauvelin	Where's The Girl	Moderate Tempo	B2	G4	Romantic Antagonist Male
Wildhorn, Frank	Baritone	Scarlet Pimpernel, The	1997	Chauvelin	The Riddle Part 1	Moderate Tempo	A2	D4	Romantic Antagonist Male
Wildhorn, Frank	Baritone	Scarlet Pimpernel, The	1997	Chauvelin	Where Is The Girl Reprise	Moderate Tempo	B2	G4	Romantic Antagonist Male
Wildhorn, Frank	Baritone	Scarlet Pimpernel, The	1997	Chauvelin	Falcon In The Dive*	Uptempo	G2	G4	Romantic Antagonist Male
Wildhorn, Frank	Soprano	Jekyll and Hyde	1997	Emma Crow	Take Me As I Am	Ballad	Bb3	F5	Romantic Lead Female
Wildhorn, Frank	Soprano	Jekyll and Hyde	1997	Emma Crow	Once Upon A Dream	Ballad	B2	C#4	Romantic Lead Female
Wildhorn, Frank	Soprano	Jekyll and Hyde	1997	Emma Crow	In His Eyes*	Ballad	Bb3	F5	Romantic Lead Female
Wildhorn, Frank	Soprano	Jekyll and Hyde	1997	Emma Crow	Emma's Reasons/The Engagement P	Moderate Tempo	Bb3	Db5	Romantic Lead Female
Wildhorn, Frank	Tenor	Jekyll and Hyde	1997	Dr. Henry Jekyll	Lost In The Darkness Reprise	Ball	G2	E4	Romantic Lead Male
Wildhorn, Frank	Tenor	Jekyll and Hyde	1997	Dr. Henry Jekyll	Lost In The Darkness	Ballad	G2	E4	Romantic Lead Male
Wildhorn, Frank	Tenor	Jekyll and Hyde	1997	Dr. Henry Jekyll	Take Me As I Am	Ballad	Bb2	Eb4	Romantic Lead Male
Wildhorn, Frank	Tenor	Jekyll and Hyde	1997	Dr. Henry Jekyll	This Is The Moment	Ballad	B2	G#4	Romantic Antagonist Male
Wildhorn, Frank	Tenor	Jekyll and Hyde	1997	Dr. Henry Jekyll	What Streak of Madness/Obsession	Ballad	C3	Eb4	Romantic Antagonist Male

Composer

Composer	Vocal Range	Show	Year	Role	Song	Tempo	Range-Bottom	Range-Top	Char Type
Wildhorn, Frank	Tenor	Jekyll and Hyde	1997	Dr. Henry Jekyll	I Need To Know	Ballad	B2	F#4	Romantic Antagonist Male
Wildhorn, Frank	Tenor	Scarlet Pimpernel, The	1997	Percy Blakeney	You Are My Home*	Ballad	B2	G4	Romantic Lead Male
Wildhorn, Frank	Tenor	Scarlet Pimpernel, The	1997	Percy Blakeney	Prayer*	Ballad	Bb2	Ab4	Romantic Lead Male
Wildhorn, Frank	Tenor	Scarlet Pimpernel, The	1997	Percy Blakeney	When I Look At You Reprise	Ballad	Db3	F4	Romantic Lead Male
Wildhorn, Frank	Tenor	Scarlet Pimpernel, The	1997	Percy Blakeney	She Was There	Ballad	C#3	G#4	Romantic Lead Male
Wildhorn, Frank	Tenor	Scarlet Pimpernel, The	1997	Percy Blakeney	She Was There Tag	Moderate Tempo	A3	G4	Romantic Lead Male
Wildhorn, Frank	Tenor	Jekyll and Hyde	1997	Dr. Henry Jekyll	The Way Back/Angst 2	Uptempo	B2	G4	Romantic Antagonist Male
Wildhorn, Frank	Tenor	Jekyll and Hyde	1997	Dr. Henry Jekyll	Confrontation*	Uptempo	B2	A4	Romantic Antagonist Male
Wildhorn, Frank	Tenor	Jekyll and Hyde	1997	Mr. Edward Hyde	Alive	Uptempo	B2	D4	Antagonist Male
Wildhorn, Frank	Tenor	Jekyll and Hyde	1997	Mr. Edward Hyde	Confrontation*	Uptempo	B2	A4	Antagonist Male
Wildhorn, Frank	Tenor	Jekyll and Hyde	1997	Mr. Edward Hyde	Alive Reprise	Uptempo	E3	A4	Antagonist Male
Wildhorn, Frank	Tenor	Scarlet Pimpernel, The	1997	Percy Blakeney	Into The Fire*	Uptempo	D3	Ab4	Romantic Lead Male
Willson, Meredith	Soprano	Unsinkable Molly Brown, Th	1960	Molly Tobin	My Own Brass Bed	Ballad	G3	Bb4	Romantic Antagonist Female
Willson, Meredith	Soprano	Unsinkable Molly Brown, Th	1960	Molly Tobin	Chick-A-Pen	Ballad	G3	B4	Romantic Antagonist Female
Willson, Meredith	Soprano	Unsinkable Molly Brown, Th	1960	Molly Tobin	I Ain't Down Yet*	Uptempo	Ab3	F5	Romantic Antagonist Female
Willson, Meredith	Soprano	Unsinkable Molly Brown, Th	1960	Molly Tobin	Beautiful People Of Denver	Uptempo	F3	Bb4	Romantic Antagonist Female
Willson, Meredith	Soprano	Unsinkable Molly Brown, Th	1960	Molly Tobin	Are You Sure*	Uptempo	G3	Db5	Romantic Antagonist Female
Willson, Meredith	Tenor	Unsinkable Molly Brown, Th	1960	Johnny Brown	I'll Never Say No	Ballad	Db3	F4	Romantic Lead Male
Willson, Meredith	Tenor	Unsinkable Molly Brown, Th	1960	Johnny Brown	If I Knew	Ballad	C3	F4	Romantic Lead Male
Willson, Meredith	Tenor	Unsinkable Molly Brown, Th	1960	Johnny Brown	Chick-A-Pen	Ballad	Db3	F4	Romantic Lead Male
Willson, Meredith	Tenor	Unsinkable Molly Brown, Th	1960	Prince Delong	Dolce Far Niente*	Ballad	C3	Eb4	Romantic Antagonist Male
Willson, Meredith	Tenor	Unsinkable Molly Brown, Th	1960	Prince Delong	Dolce Far Niente Reprise	Ballad	D3	Eb4	Romantic Antagonist Male
Willson, Meredith	Tenor	Unsinkable Molly Brown, Th	1960	Johnny Brown	Colorado My Home	Moderate Tempo	B2	F4	Romantic Lead Male
Willson, Meredith	Tenor	Unsinkable Molly Brown, Th	1960	Johnny Brown	I've A'ready Started In	Moderate Tempo	G3	E4	Romantic Lead Male
Willson, Meredith	Tenor	Unsinkable Molly Brown, Th	1960	Johnny Brown	Leadville Johnny Brown Soliloquy	Moderate Tempo	C3	E4	Romantic Lead Male
Wilson, Meredith	Baritone	Music Man, The	1957	Harold Hill	Till There Was You Reprise	Ballad	B2	C4	Romantic Antagonist Male
Wilson, Meredith	Baritone	Music Man, The	1957	Harold Hill	Marian The Librarian	Moderate Tempo	C3	F4	Romantic Antagonist Male
Wilson, Meredith	Baritone	Music Man, The	1957	Harold Hill	76 Trombones	Moderate Tempo	G2	F4	Romantic Antagonist Male
Wilson, Meredith	Baritone	Music Man, The	1957	Harold Hill	Trouble	Uptempo	A2	E4	Romantic Antagonist Male
Wilson, Meredith	Baritone	Music Man, The	1957	Harold Hill	Seventy Six Trombones	Uptempo	B2	F4	Romantic Antagonist Male
Wilson, Meredith	Baritone	Music Man, The	1957	Harold Hill	The Sadder But Wiser Girl*	Uptempo	C3	E4	Romantic Antagonist Male
Wilson, Meredith	Baritone	Music Man, The	1957	Harold Hill	Trouble Reprise	Uptempo	A3	Eb4	Romantic Antagonist Male
Wilson, Meredith	Soprano	Music Man, The	1957	Marian Paroo	My White Knight	Ballad	C#4	Ab5	Romantic Lead Female

Composer

Composer	Vocal Range	Show	Year	Role	Song	Tempo	Range-Bottom	Range-Top	Char Type
Wilson, Meredith	Soprano	Music Man, The	1957	Marian Paroo	Till There Was You	Ballad	Eb4	F5	Romantic Lead Female
Wilson, Meredith	Soprano	Music Man, The	1957	Marian Paroo	Goodnight My Someone*	Ballad	B3	E5	Romantic Lead Female
Wilson, Meredith	Soprano	Music Man, The	1957	Marian Paroo	Will I Ever Leave You*	Moderate Tempo	D4	F#5	Romantic Lead Female
Wilson, Meredith	Soprano	Music Man, The	1957	Winthrop Paroo	Gary Indiana Reprise	Uptempo	C4	Eb5	Juvenile Male
Yazbek, David	Alto	Full Monty, The	2000	Georgie Bukatinsky	You Rule My World Reprise *	Ballad	G#3	D5	Character Female
Yazbek, David	Alto	Full Monty, The	2000	Vicki Nichols	You Rule My World Reprise *	Ballad	G#3	B4	Character Female
Yazbek, David	Alto	Dirty Rotten Scoundrels	2005	Muriel Eubanks	What's A Woman To Do	Moderate Tempo	G2	D4	Romantic Lead Female
Yazbek, David	Alto	Dirty Rotten Scoundrels	2005	Muriel Eubanks	What's Was A Woman To Do Reprise	Moderate Tempo	E3	Bb4	Romantic Lead Female
Yazbek, David	Alto	Dirty Rotten Scoundrels	2005	Muriel Eubanks	Like Zis/Like Zat *	Moderate Tempo	E3	Bb4	Romantic Lead Female
Yazbek, David	Alto	Full Monty, The	2000	Jeanette Burmeister	Jeanette's Showbiz Number	Moderate Tempo	F3	Db5	Mature Female
Yazbek, David	Alto	Dirty Rotten Scoundrels	2005	Jolene Oakes	Oklahoma	Uptempo	G#3	C5	Romantic Lead Female
Yazbek, David	Alto	Full Monty, The	2000	Vicki Nichols	Life With Harold	Uptempo	G3	D5	Character Female
Yazbek, David	Baritone	Dirty Rotten Scoundrels	2005	Lawrence Jameson	Love Sneaks In	Ballad	G2	D4	Romantic Lead Male
Yazbek, David	Baritone	Full Monty, The	2000	Dave Bukatinsky	You Rule My World *	Ballad	C#3	B4	Character Male
Yazbek, David	Baritone	Full Monty, The	2000	Harold Nichols	You Rule My World *	Ballad	C#3	G4	Character Male
Yazbek, David	Baritone	Dirty Rotten Scoundrels	2005	Andre Thibault	Like Zis/Like Zat *	Moderate Tempo	Bb3	Eb4	Character Male
Yazbek, David	Baritone	Dirty Rotten Scoundrels	2005	Lawrence Jameson	Give Them What They Want *	Moderate Tempo	C3	Eb4	Romantic Lead Male
Yazbek, David	Baritone	Dirty Rotten Scoundrels	2005	Lawrence Jameson	Dirty Rotten Number	Moderate Tempo	C3	F4	Romantic Lead Male
Yazbek, David	Baritone	Dirty Rotten Scoundrels	2005	Andre Thibault	A Chimp In A Suit	Uptempo	C3	E4	Character Male
Yazbek, David	Baritone	Dirty Rotten Scoundrels	2005	Lawrence Jameson	All About Ruprecht	Uptempo	D3	E4	Romantic Lead Male
Yazbek, David	Baritone	Dirty Rotten Scoundrels	2005	Lawrence Jameson	Ruffjousin' Mit Shuffhousen	Uptempo	C3	A4	Romantic Lead Male
Yazbek, David	Baritone	Dirty Rotten Scoundrels	2005	Lawrence Jameson	The More We Dance	Uptempo	D3	G4	Romantic Lead Male
Yazbek, David	Baritone	Full Monty, The	2000	Noah "Horse" Simmons	Big Black Man *	Uptempo	G3	G4	Antagonist Male
Yazbek, David	Soprano	Dirty Rotten Scoundrels	2005	Christine Colgate	Nothing Is Too Wonderful To Be True	Ballad	A3	F5	Romantic Lead Female
Yazbek, David	Soprano	Dirty Rotten Scoundrels	2005	Christine Colgate	Here I Am	Uptempo	F3	E5	Romantic Lead Female
Yazbek, David	Tenor	Full Monty, The	2000	Malcolm MacGregor	You Walk With With Me *	Ballad	F#3	A4	Character Male
Yazbek, David	Tenor	Full Monty, The	2000	Jerry Lukowski	Breeze Off The River	Moderate Tempo	C3	B4	Romantic Lead Male
Yazbek, David	Tenor	Dirty Rotten Scoundrels	2005	Freddy Benson	Great Big Stuff	Uptempo	D3	F#4	Character Male
Yazbek, David	Tenor	Full Monty, The	2000	Jerry Lukowski	Man *	Uptempo	E3	B4	Romantic Lead Male
Yazbek, David	Tenor	Full Monty, The	2000	Jerry Lukowski	Michael Jordan's Ball *	Uptempo	G3	Bb4	Romantic Lead Male
Yazbek, David	Tenor	Full Monty, The	2000	Jerry Lukowski	Man *	Uptempo	E3	G4	Romantic Lead Male
Yazbek, David	Tenor	Full Monty, The	2000	Jerry Lukowski	Man Reprise *	Uptempo	A3	A4	Romantic Lead Male
Yeston, Maury	Alto	Nine	1982	Luisa Contini	My Husband Makes Movies	Moderate Tempo	Eb3	C5	Romantic Lead Female
Yeston, Maury	Alto	Nine	1982	Saraghina	Ti Voglio Bene*	Moderate Tempo	G3	Bb4	Romantic Antagonist Female

Composer	Vocal Range	Show	Year	Role	Song	Tempo	Range-Bottom	Range-Top	Char Type
Yeston, Maury	Alto	Nine	1982	Luisa Contini	Be On Your Own	Moderate Tempo	G#3	A4	Romantic Lead Female
Yeston, Maury	Alto	Nine	1982	Stephanie Necrophorus	Folies Bergeres*	Uptempo	B3	B4	Romantic Lead Female
Yeston, Maury	Alto	Nine	1982	Liliane La Fluer	Folies Bergeres*	Uptempo	G#3	B4	Romantic Lead Female
Yeston, Maury	Baritone	Phantom	1991	Phantom	Paris Is A Tomb	Ballad	A2	C4	Antagonist Male
Yeston, Maury	Baritone	Phantom	1991	Phantom	Home*	Moderate Tempo	C3	G4	Antagonist Male
Yeston, Maury	Baritone	Phantom	1991	Count Philippe	Without Your Music	Moderate Tempo	C3	F4	Romantic Lead Male
Yeston, Maury	Baritone	Phantom	1991	Phantom	My Mother Bore Me	Moderate Tempo	F2	F#4	Antagonist Male
Yeston, Maury	Baritone	Phantom	1991	Gerard Carriere	You Are My Own*	Moderate Tempo	G2	D4	Mature Male
Yeston, Maury	Baritone	Phantom	1991	Erik (Phantom)	You Are My Own*	Uptempo	G2	E4	Antagonist Male
Yeston, Maury	Baritone	Phantom	1991	Phantom	Where In The World	Uptempo	G2	F4	Antagonist Male
Yeston, Maury	Baritone	Phantom	1991	Count Philippe	Who Could Have Ever Dreamed Up Y	Uptempo	Bb2	E4	Romantic Lead Male
Yeston, Maury	Baritone	Phantom	1991	Phantom	Where In The World Reprise	Uptempo	Bb2	F4	Antagonist Male
Yeston, Maury	Soprano	Nine	1982	Claudio Nardi	Unusual Way*	Ballad	G#3	E5	Romantic Lead Female
Yeston, Maury	Soprano	Nine	1982	Carla Albanese	Simple	Ballad	A3	E5	Romantic Lead Female
Yeston, Maury	Soprano	Phantom	1991	Christine Daae	Finale: You Are Music*	Ballad	B4	G5	Ingenue Female
Yeston, Maury	Soprano	Nine	1982	Carla Albanese	A Call From The Vatican	Moderate Tempo	A3	C6	Romantic Lead Female
Yeston, Maury	Soprano	Nine	1982	Young Guido Contini	Getting Tall	Moderate Tempo	Ab3	F5	Juvenile Male
Yeston, Maury	Soprano	Phantom	1991	Christine Daae	Home*	Moderate Tempo	D4	A5	Ingenue Female
Yeston, Maury	Soprano	Phantom	1991	Carlotta	This Is Mine Reprise	Moderate Tempo	D4	G5	Romantic Antagonist Female
Yeston, Maury	Soprano	Phantom	1991	Christine Daae	My True Love	Moderate Tempo	C4	F5	Ingenue Female
Yeston, Maury	Soprano	Phantom	1991	Christine Daee	Melody Of Paris	Uptempo	B3	A5	Ingenue Female
Yeston, Maury	Soprano	Phantom	1991	Carlotta	This Place Is Mine	Uptempo	Bb3	Bb5	Romantic Antagonist Female
Yeston, Maury	Soprano	Phantom	1991	Christine Daae	The Bistro*	Uptempo	Bb3	B5	Ingenue Female
Yeston, Maury	Soprano	Phantom	1991	Christine Daae	Who Could Have Ever Dreamed Up Y	Uptempo	Bb3	Eb5	Ingenue Female
Yeston, Maury	Tenor	Nine	1982	Guido Contini	Long Ago Reprise	Ballad	Bb2	Bb3	Romantic Antagonist Male
Yeston, Maury	Tenor	Nine	1982	Guido Contini	Nine Reprise	Ballad	Bb2	G4	Romantic Antagonist Male
Yeston, Maury	Tenor	Nine	1982	Guido Contini	Only With You	Moderate Tempo	G#2	E4	Romantic Antagonist Male
Yeston, Maury	Tenor	Nine	1982	Guido Contini	The Bells Of St. Sebastian*	Moderate Tempo	D4	G4	Romantic Antagonist Male
Yeston, Maury	Tenor	Nine	1982	Guido Contini	The Grand Canal*	Moderate Tempo	D#3	G4	Romantic Antagonist Male
Yeston, Maury	Tenor	Nine	1982	Guido Contini	I Can't Make This Movie	Moderate Tempo	G3	G4	Romantic Antagonist Male
Yeston, Maury	Tenor	Nine	1982	Guido Contini	Guido's Song*	Uptempo	G#2	F#4	Romantic Antagonist Male
Yeston, Maury	Tenor	Nine	1982	Guido Contini	Script	Uptempo	C3	F4	Romantic Antagonist Male
Yeston, Maury	Tenor	Nine	1982	Guido Contini	Amour	Uptempo	A2	Bb4	Romantic Antagonist Male
Youmans, Vincent	Alto	No, No Nanette	1925	Lucille Early	Where Has My Hubby Gone Blues*	Ballad	G3	D5	Romantic Lead Female

Composer

Composer	Vocal Range	Show	Year	Role	Song	Tempo	Range-Bottom	Range-Top	Char Type
Youmans, Vincent	Alto	No, No Nanette	1925	Flora Latham	The Three Happies*	Moderate Tempo	F4	E♭5	Character Female
Youmans, Vincent	Alto	No, No Nanette	1925	Betty Brown	The Three Happies*	Moderate Tempo	A3	C5	Character Female
Youmans, Vincent	Alto	No, No Nanette	1925	Lucille Early	Too Many Rings Around Rosie*	Uptempo	B3	D5	Romantic Lead Female
Youmans, Vincent	Alto	No, No Nanette	1925	Lucille Early	You Can Dance With Any Girl At All*	Uptempo	A3	D5	Romantic Lead Female
Youmans, Vincent	Alto	No, No Nanette	1925	Sue Smith	Take A Little One Step*	Uptempo	G3	C♭5	Romantic Lead Female
Youmans, Vincent	Baritone	No, No Nanette	1925	Bill Early	The Call Of TheSea*	Uptempo	D3	F#4	Romantic Lead Male
Youmans, Vincent	Baritone	No, No Nanette	1925	Jimmy Smith	I Want To Be Happy*	Uptempo	C#3	F#4	Mature Male
Youmans, Vincent	Baritone	No, No Nanette	1925	Bill Early	You Can Dance With Any Girl At All*	Uptempo	C3	F4	Romantic Lead Male
Youmans, Vincent	Baritone	No, No Nanette	1925	Bill Early	Telephone Girlie*	Uptempo	C3	F4	Romantic Lead Male
Youmans, Vincent	Soprano	No, No Nanette	1925	Nanette	I've Confessed To The Breeze*	Moderate Tempo	B3	F5	Ingenue Female
Youmans, Vincent	Soprano	No, No Nanette	1925	Winnie Winslow	The Three Happies*	Moderate Tempo	C5	G5	Character Female
Youmans, Vincent	Soprano	No, No Nanette	1925	Nanette	Tea For Two*	Moderate Tempo	E♭4	F5	Ingenue Female
Youmans, Vincent	Soprano	No, No Nanette	1925	Nanette	Waiting For You*	Moderate Tempo	A♭3	E♭5	Ingenue Female
Youmans, Vincent	Soprano	No, No Nanette	1925	Nanette	I Want To Be Happy*	Uptempo	C4	E5	Ingenue Female
Youmans, Vincent	Soprano	No, No Nanette	1925	Nanette	No, No Nanette*	Uptempo	B♭3	F5	Ingenue Female
Youmans, Vincent	Soprano	No, No Nanette	1925	Nanette	Peach On The Beach*	Uptempo	F#4	A4	Ingenue Female
Youmans, Vincent	Tenor	No, No Nanette	1925	Tom Trainor	I've Confessed To The Breeze*	Moderate Tempo	D3	F4	Ingenue Male
Youmans, Vincent	Tenor	No, No Nanette	1925	Tom Trainor	Tea For Two*	Moderate Tempo	E♭3	F4	Ingenue Male
Youmans, Vincent	Tenor	No, No Nanette	1925	Tom Trainor	Waiting For You*	Moderate Tempo	C3	E♭4	Ingenue Male
Youmans, Vincent	Tenor	No, No Nanette	1925	Tom Trainor	No, No Nanette*	Uptempo	C3	E♭4	Ingenue Male

Composer

* = Music Edit Required
+ = Ethnic Specific

Show	Composer	Year	Role	Song	Tempo	Vocal Type	Range-Bottom	Range-Top	Category	Character Type
1776	Edwards, Sherman	1969	Abigail Adams	Compliments	Uptempo	Soprano	D4	Eb5	Supporting	Mature Female
1776	Edwards, Sherman	1969	Courier	Momma Look Sharp	Ballad	Tenor	Bb2	Db4	Supporting	Character Ingenue Male
1776	Edwards, Sherman	1969	Edward Rutledge	Molasses To Rum	Moderate Tempo	Tenor	E3	A4	Lead	Romantic Antagonist Male
1776	Edwards, Sherman	1969	Ensemble	Cool, Cool Considerate Men	Moderate Tempo	TB			Ensemble	Adults
1776	Edwards, Sherman	1969	John Adams	Piddle, Twiddle, and Resolve	Uptempo	Baritone	Db3	Eb4	Lead	Mature Male
1776	Edwards, Sherman	1969	John Adams	Is Anybody There? (ms 57-135)	Uptempo	Baritone	D3	E4	Lead	Mature Male
1776	Edwards, Sherman	1969	John Dickinson	Cool, Cool Considerate Men	Moderate Tempo	Baritone	A2	Gb4	Lead	Character Male
1776	Edwards, Sherman	1969	Martha Jefferson	He Plays The Violin	Moderate Tempo	Soprano	Bb3	D5	Supporting	Ingenue Female
1776	Edwards, Sherman	1969	Richard Henry Lee	The Lees of Old Virginia	Uptempo	Baritone	C3	F4	Lead	Romantic Lead Male
1776	Edwards, Sherman	1969	Abigail & John	Til Then	Ballad	Sop/Bar			Duet	MF/MM
1776	Edwards, Sherman	1969	Abigail & John	Yours, Yours, Yours	Ballad	Sop/Bar			Duet	MF/MM
110 In The Shade	Schmidt, Harvey	1963	Bill Starbuck	The Rain Song *	Uptempo	Tenor	C3	Ab4	Lead	Romantic Antagonist Male
110 In The Shade	Schmidt, Harvey	1963	Bill Starbuck	Melisande	Uptempo	Tenor	G2	G4	Lead	Romantic Antagonist Male
110 In The Shade	Schmidt, Harvey	1963	Bill Starbuck	Evenin' Star	Ballad	Tenor	B3	Ab4	Lead	Romantic Antagonist Male
110 In The Shade	Schmidt, Harvey	1963	Bill Starbuck	Wonderful Music *	Uptempo	Tenor	Db3	F4	Lead	Romantic Antagonist Male
110 In The Shade	Schmidt, Harvey	1963	Ensemble	Another Hot Day*	Moderate Tempo	ST/AB			Ensemble	Adults
110 In The Shade	Schmidt, Harvey	1963	Ensemble	Hungry Men	Uptempo	SATB			Ensemble	Adults
110 In The Shade	Schmidt, Harvey	1963	Ensemble	The Rain Song Reprise	Uptempo	SATB			Ensemble	Teens
110 In The Shade	Schmidt, Harvey	1963	File	Gonna Be Another Hot Day *	Moderate Tempo	Baritone	D3	F#4	Lead	Character Male
110 In The Shade	Schmidt, Harvey	1963	File	A Man And A Woman *	Ballad	Baritone	C3	D4	Lead	Character Male
110 In The Shade	Schmidt, Harvey	1963	File	Wonderful Music *	Uptempo	Baritone	Db3	F4	Lead	Character Male
110 In The Shade	Schmidt, Harvey	1963	Girl	Cinderella	Uptempo	Alto	A3	D5	Featured Ensemble	Juvenile Female
110 In The Shade	Schmidt, Harvey	1963	H.C. Curry	Lizzie's Comin' Home *	Uptempo	Baritone	B2	E4	Supporting	Paternal
110 In The Shade	Schmidt, Harvey	1963	Jimmy Curry	Lizzie's Comin' Home *	Uptempo	Tenor	B2	E4	Supporting	Ingenue Male
110 In The Shade	Schmidt, Harvey	1963	Lizzie Curry	Love Don't Turn Away	Uptempo	Soprano	D#4	F5	Lead	Character Female
110 In The Shade	Schmidt, Harvey	1963	Lizzie Curry	Raunchy	Uptempo	Soprano	G3	F5	Lead	Character Female
110 In The Shade	Schmidt, Harvey	1963	Lizzie Curry	Old Maid	Moderate Tempo	Soprano	B3	G#5	Lead	Character Female
110 In The Shade	Schmidt, Harvey	1963	Lizzie Curry	Simple Little Things	Ballad	Soprano	B3	E5	Lead	Character Female
110 In The Shade	Schmidt, Harvey	1963	Lizzie Curry	Is It Really Me	Ballad	Soprano	A3	E5	Lead	Character Female
110 In The Shade	Schmidt, Harvey	1963	Lizzie Curry	A Man And A Woman *	Ballad	Soprano	D4	G5	Lead	Character Female
110 In The Shade	Schmidt, Harvey	1963	Noah Curry	Lizzie's Comin' Home *	Uptempo	Baritone	B2	E4	Supporting	Antagonist Male
110 In The Shade	Schmidt, Harvey	1963	File & Lizzie	You're Not Foolin' Me	Moderate Tempo	Tenor/Sop			Duet	CF/RAM
110 In The Shade	Schmidt, Harvey	1963	File & Lizzie	A Man And A Woman	Ballad	Bar/Sop			Duet	CM/CF
110 In The Shade	Schmidt, Harvey	1963	Jim & Snookie	Little Red Hat	Uptempo	Tenor/Sop			Duet	IM/IF
13 The Musical	Brown, Jason Robert	2008	Archie (CM)	Get Me What I Need	Uptempo	Tenor	C3	A4	Lead	Juvenile Male
13 The Musical	Brown, Jason Robert	2008	Archie (CM)	Getting Ready*	Uptempo	Tenor	Eb3	Ab4	Lead	Juvenile Male
13 The Musical	Brown, Jason Robert	2008	Brett (RAM)	Getting Ready*	Uptempo	Baritone	G3	F4	Supporting	Juvenile Male
13 The Musical	Brown, Jason Robert	2008	Cassie (IF)	A Brand New You*	Uptempo	Alto	C4	F5	Supporting	Juvenile Female
13 The Musical	Brown, Jason Robert	2008	Ensemble	Brand New You	Uptempo	SATB			Ensemble	Children
13 The Musical	Brown, Jason Robert	2008	Evan Goldman (CM)	Becoming A Man	Uptempo	Tenor	D3	A4	Lead	Juvenile Male
13 The Musical	Brown, Jason Robert	2008	Evan Goldman (CM)	Thirteen	Uptempo	Tenor	Bb2	Bb3	Lead	Juvenile Male
13 The Musical	Brown, Jason Robert	2008	Evan Goldman (CM)	All Hail The Brain	Uptempo	Tenor	E3	G4	Lead	Juvenile Male

Shows

Songs by Character Type

* = Music Edit Required
+ = Ethnic Specific

Show	Composer	Year	Role	Song	Tempo	Vocal Type	Range-Bottom	Range-Top	Category	Character Type
13 The Musical	Brown, Jason Robert	2008	Evan Goldman (CM)	Terminal Illness	Uptempo	Tenor	E♭3	A♭4	Lead	Juvenile Male
13 The Musical	Brown, Jason Robert	2008	Evan Goldman (CM)	Tell Her*	Ballad	Tenor	B♭2	G4	Lead	Juvenile Male
13 The Musical	Brown, Jason Robert	2008	Evan Goldman (CM)	A Little More Homework*	Ballad	Tenor	C3	F4	Lead	Juvenile Male
13 The Musical	Brown, Jason Robert	2008	Evan Goldman (CM)	Getting Ready*	Uptempo	Tenor	D♭4	B♭4	Lead	Juvenile Male
13 The Musical	Brown, Jason Robert	2008	Evan Goldman (CM)	Here I Come	Uptempo	Tenor	E♭3	B♭4	Lead	Juvenile Male
13 The Musical	Brown, Jason Robert	2008	Evan Goldman (CM)	If That's What It Is*	Moderate Tempo	Tenor	C3	A4	Lead	Juvenile Male
13 The Musical	Brown, Jason Robert	2008	Evan Goldman (CM)	Becoming A Man Reprise	Ballad	Tenor	E3	A4	Lead	Juvenile Male
13 The Musical	Brown, Jason Robert	2008	Lucy (RAF)	It Can't Be True*	Uptempo	Alto	F#3	C5	Lead	Juvenile Female
13 The Musical	Brown, Jason Robert	2008	Lucy (RAF)	Opportunity*	Uptempo	Alto	B3	E4	Lead	Juvenile Female
13 The Musical	Brown, Jason Robert	2008	Patrice (CIF)	The Lamest Place In The World	Uptempo	Alto	B3	D#5	Lead	Juvenile Female
13 The Musical	Brown, Jason Robert	2008	Patrice (CIF)	Good Enough	Ballad	Alto	G3	C5	Lead	Juvenile Female
13 The Musical	Brown, Jason Robert	2008	Patrice (CIF)	Tell Her*	Ballad	Alto	B♭3	C5	Lead	Juvenile Female
13 The Musical	Brown, Jason Robert	2008	Patrice (CIF)	If That's What It Is*	Moderate Tempo	Alto	E♭3	C5	Lead	Juvenile Female
13 The Musical	Brown, Jason Robert	2008	Patrice (CIF)	What It Means To Be A Friend	Moderate Tempo	Alto	A3	E5	Lead	Juvenile Female
13 The Musical	Brown, Jason Robert	2008	Evan & Patrice	Tell Her	Ballad	Tenor/Alto			Duet	CM/CIF
25th Annual...Spelling Bee	Finn, William	2005	Chip Tolentino	Chip's Lament/My Unfortunate Erection	Uptempo	Tenor	C3	A♭4	Lead	Ingenue Male
25th Annual...Spelling Bee	Finn, William	2005	Ensemble	25th Annual...Spelling Bee	Uptempo	SATB			Ensemble	Teens/Adults
25th Annual...Spelling Bee	Finn, William	2005	Ensemble	The Last Goodbye	up	SATB			Ensemble	Teens/Adults
25th Annual...Spelling Bee	Finn, William	2005	Leaf Coneybear	I'm Not That Smart	Uptempo	Baritone	A2	G4	Lead	Character Ingenue Male
25th Annual...Spelling Bee	Finn, William	2005	Leaf Coneybear	I'm Not Smart Reprise	Uptempo	Baritone	D3	F#4	Lead	Character Ingenue Male
25th Annual...Spelling Bee	Finn, William	2005	Logainne	Woe Is Me	Uptempo	Alto	G3	D5	Lead	Antagonist Female
25th Annual...Spelling Bee	Finn, William	2005	Logainne	Woe Is Me Reprise	Uptempo	Alto	C4	C5	Lead	Antagonist Female
25th Annual...Spelling Bee	Finn, William	2005	Marcy Park	I Speak Six Languages	Uptempo	Alto	B3	D5	Lead	Antagonist Female
25th Annual...Spelling Bee	Finn, William	2005	Mitch Mahoney	Prayer of the Comfort Counselor	Uptempo	Tenor	E3	A4	Lead	Antagonist Male
25th Annual...Spelling Bee	Finn, William	2005	Mitch Mahoney	The I Love You Song	Ballad	Tenor	E3	G#4	Lead	Antagonist Male
25th Annual...Spelling Bee	Finn, William	2005	Olive Ostrovsky	My Friend The Dictionary	Moderate Tempo	Soprano	B3	D5	Lead	Ingenue Female
25th Annual...Spelling Bee	Finn, William	2005	Olive Ostrovsky	The I Love You Song	Ballad	Soprano	D4	D5	Lead	Ingenue Female
25th Annual...Spelling Bee	Finn, William	2005	Olive Ostrovsky	Second Part 1*	Moderate Tempo	Soprano	C#4	D5	Lead	Ingenue Female
25th Annual...Spelling Bee	Finn, William	2005	Rona Lisa Peretti	My Favorite Moment of the Bee	Moderate Tempo	Soprano	D4	D5	Lead	Character Female
25th Annual...Spelling Bee	Finn, William	2005	Rona Lisa Peretti	Rona Moment #2	Moderate Tempo	Soprano	D4	D5	Lead	Character Female
25th Annual...Spelling Bee	Finn, William	2005	Rona Lisa Peretti	Rona Moment #3	Moderate Tempo	Soprano	D♭4	D♭5	Lead	Character Female
25th Annual...Spelling Bee	Finn, William	2005	Rona Lisa Peretti	The I Love You Song	Ballad	Soprano	D4	E5	Lead	Character Female
25th Annual...Spelling Bee	Finn, William	2005	William Barfee	Magic Foot	Uptempo	Baritone	F3	A4	Lead	Antagonist Male
25th Annual...Spelling Bee	Finn, William	2005	William Barfee	Second Part 1*	Moderate Tempo	Baritone	D♭3	E♭4	Lead	Antagonist Male
A Chorus Line	Hamlisch, Marvin	1975	Bebe	At The Ballet	Moderate Tempo	Alto	A3	C#5	Supporting	Character Female
A Chorus Line	Hamlisch, Marvin	1975	Cassie	The Music And The Mirror	Moderate Tempo	Alto	A#3	D5	Lead	Romantic Lead Female
A Chorus Line	Hamlisch, Marvin	1975	Diana +	Nothing	Uptempo	Alto	G3	B4	Lead	Character Female
A Chorus Line	Hamlisch, Marvin	1975	Diana +	What I Did For Love	Ballad	Alto	B♭3	D#5	Lead	Character Female
A Chorus Line	Hamlisch, Marvin	1975	Ensemble	I Hope I Get It	Uptempo	SATB			Ensemble	Adults
A Chorus Line	Hamlisch, Marvin	1975	Ensemble	One (Bows)	Moderate Tempo	SATB			Ensemble	Adults
A Chorus Line	Hamlisch, Marvin	1975	Maggie	At The Ballet	Moderate Tempo	Alto	A3	D5	Supporting	Character Ingenue Female
A Chorus Line	Hamlisch, Marvin	1975	Maggie	Mother *	Ballad	Alto	B3	D5	Lead	Character Ingenue Female

Shows

* = Music Edit Required
+ = Ethnic Specific

Show	Composer	Year	Role	Song	Tempo	Vocal Type	Range-Bottom	Range-Top	Category	Character Type
A Chorus Line	Hamlisch, Marvin	1975	Mike	I Can Do That	Uptempo	Tenor	G4	Ab4	Lead	Ingenue Male
A Chorus Line	Hamlisch, Marvin	1975	Richie +	Gimmie The Ball (ms 231-269) *	Uptempo	Tenor	C#3	G4	Supporting	Antagonist Male
A Chorus Line	Hamlisch, Marvin	1975	Sheila	At The Ballet	Moderate Tempo	Alto	E3	C#5	Lead	Romantic Antagonist Female
A Chorus Line	Hamlisch, Marvin	1975	Val	Dance: Ten; Looks: Three	Uptempo	Alto	Bb3	Db5	Supporting	Ingenue Female
A Chorus Line	Hamlisch, Marvin	1975	All & Kristine	Sing!	Uptempo	Tenor/Alto			Duet	CM/IF
A Christmas Carol	Menken, Alan	1997	Bob Cratchit	Christmas Together	Uptempo	Tenor	D3	D4	Supporting	Character Male
A Christmas Carol	Menken, Alan	1997	Emily	A Place Called Home	Ballad	Soprano	Bb3	F5	Supporting	Ingenue Female
A Christmas Carol	Menken, Alan	1997	Ensemble	Mr. Fezziwig's Annual Christmas Ball	Uptempo	SATB			Ensemble	Adults
A Christmas Carol	Menken, Alan	1997	Ensemble	Christmas Together*	Uptempo	SATB			Ensemble	Adults
A Christmas Carol	Menken, Alan	1997	Ensemble	God Bless Us Everyone	Moderate Tempo	SATB			Ensemble	Adults
A Christmas Carol	Menken, Alan	1997	Ghost...Past	The Lights of Long Ago	Uptempo	Tenor	E3	E4	Supporting	Character Male
A Christmas Carol	Menken, Alan	1997	Ghost...Past	Abundance and Charity	Uptempo	Tenor	A#2	F#4	Supporting	Character Male
A Christmas Carol	Menken, Alan	1997	Grace Smythe	God Bless Us Everyone	Uptempo	Soprano	D4	C5	Lead	Ingenue Female
A Christmas Carol	Menken, Alan	1997	Jacob Marley	Link By Link	Uptempo	Tenor	D3	Ab4	Lead	Character Male
A Christmas Carol	Menken, Alan	1997	Scrooge-Adult	Yesterday, Tomorrow and Today	Ballad	Tenor	D3	E4	Lead	Character Male
A Christmas Carol	Menken, Alan	1997	Scrooge-Adult	Nothing To Do With Me	Uptempo	Tenor	D3	Eb4	Lead	Character Male
A Christmas Carol	Menken, Alan	1997	Scrooge-Adult	Will Tiny Tim Live	Ballad	Tenor	D3	E4	Lead	Character Male
A Christmas Carol	Menken, Alan	1997	Scrooge-Adult	Christmas Day (Final Scene P2)	Uptempo	Tenor	C3	E4	Lead	Character Male
A Christmas Carol	Menken, Alan	1997	Scrooge-Child	A Place Called Home	Ballad	Soprano	Bb2	A4	Lead	Juvenile Male
A Christmas Carol	Menken, Alan	1997	Scrooge-Young Adult	A Place Called Home	Ballad	Tenor	Bb2	D4	Supporting	Character Ingenue Male
A Christmas Carol	Menken, Alan	1997	Tiny Tim	Christmas Together	Uptempo	Soprano	Bb4	C5	Supporting	Juvenile Male
A Christmas Carol	Menken, Alan	1997	Tiny Tim	God Bless Us Everyone	Uptempo	Soprano	D4	C5	Supporting	Juvenile Male
A Christmas Carol	Menken, Alan	1997	Cratchit & Tiny Tim	You Mean More to Me	Ballad	Tenor/Sop			Duet	CM/JM
A Funny Thing...Forum	Sondheim, Stephen	1962	Prologus	Comedy Tonight*	Uptempo	Baritone	A2	F4	Lead	Character Male
A Funny Thing...Forum	Sondheim, Stephen	1962	Ensemble	Comedy Tonight	Uptempo	SATB			Ensemble	Adults
A Funny Thing...Forum	Sondheim, Stephen	1962	Hero	Love I Hear	Uptempo	Tenor	B2	F#4	Lead	Ingenue Male
A Funny Thing...Forum	Sondheim, Stephen	1962	Pseudolus	Free*	Uptempo	Baritone	B2	F4	Lead	Mature Male
A Funny Thing...Forum	Sondheim, Stephen	1962	Marcus Lycus	The House Of Marcus Lycus	Moderate Tempo	Baritone	B2	D#4	Lead	Antagonist Male
A Funny Thing...Forum	Sondheim, Stephen	1962	Philia	Lovely*	Moderate Tempo	Soprano	C#4	F5	Lead	Ingenue Female
A Funny Thing...Forum	Sondheim, Stephen	1962	Hero	Lovely*	Moderate Tempo	Tenor	D3	E4	Lead	Ingenue Male
A Funny Thing...Forum	Sondheim, Stephen	1962	Philia & Hero	Lovely	Moderate Tempo	Sop/Tenor			Duet	IF/IM
A Funny Thing...Forum	Sondheim, Stephen	1962	Pseudolus	Pretty Little Picture*	Uptempo	Baritone	B2	F#4	Lead	Mature Male
A Funny Thing...Forum	Sondheim, Stephen	1962	Ensemble	Pretty Little Picture	Uptempo	STB			Ensemble	Adults
A Funny Thing...Forum	Sondheim, Stephen	1962	Sinex	Everybody Ought To Have A Maid*	Uptempo	Baritone	C#3	E4	Lead	Mature Male
A Funny Thing...Forum	Sondheim, Stephen	1962	Ensemble	Everybody Ought To Have A Maid	Uptempo	BBB			Ensemble	Adults
A Funny Thing...Forum	Sondheim, Stephen	1962	Ensemble	Everybody Ought To Have A Maid Encor	Uptempo	BBBB			Ensemble	Adults
A Funny Thing...Forum	Sondheim, Stephen	1962	Hysterium	I'm Calm	Uptempo	Tenor	D3	F4	Lead	Mature Male
A Funny Thing...Forum	Sondheim, Stephen	1962	Sinex & Hero	Impossible	Uptempo	Bar/Tenor			Duet	MM/IM
A Funny Thing...Forum	Sondheim, Stephen	1962	Miles	Bring Me My Bride*	Uptempo	Baritone	B2	F4	Lead	Romantic Antagonist Male
A Funny Thing...Forum	Sondheim, Stephen	1962	Domina	That Dirty Old Man	Uptempo	Alto	B3	F5	Lead	Antagonist Female
A Funny Thing...Forum	Sondheim, Stephen	1962	Philia	That'll Show Him	Uptempo	Soprano	C4	G5	Lead	Ingenue Female
A Funny Thing...Forum	Sondheim, Stephen	1962	Pseudolus	Lovely Reprise*	Moderate Tempo	Baritone	D3	F4	Lead	Mature Male
A Funny Thing...Forum	Sondheim, Stephen	1962	Hysterium	Lovely Reprise*	Moderate Tempo	Tenor	E3	F4	Lead	Mature Male

Shows

Songs by Character Type

Show	Composer	Year	Role	Song	Tempo	Vocal Type	Range-Bottom	Range-Top	Category	Character Type
A Funny Thing...Forum	Sondheim, Stephen	1962	Pseudolus & Hysterium	Lovely Reprise	Moderate Tempo	Bar/Tenor			Duet	MM/MM
A Funny Thing...Forum	Sondheim, Stephen	1962	Ensemble	Funeral Sequence	Moderate Tempo	SATB			Ensemble	Adults
A Funny Thing...Forum	Sondheim, Stephen	1962	Ensemble	Finale Ultimo	Uptempo	SATB			Ensemble	Adults
A Little Night Music	Sondheim, Stephen	1973	Anne Egerman	Soon	Uptempo	Soprano	C4	G#5	Lead	Ingenue Female
A Little Night Music	Sondheim, Stephen	1973	Count Carl-Magnus Malcolm	In Praise of Women	Uptempo	Baritone	C3	F4	Supporting	Romantic Lead Male
A Little Night Music	Sondheim, Stephen	1973	Count Carl-Magnus Malcolm	It Would Have Been Wonderful *	Uptempo	Baritone	C3	E4	Supporting	Romantic Lead Male
A Little Night Music	Sondheim, Stephen	1973	Countess Charlotte Malcolm	Everyday A Little Death	Uptempo	Alto	G3	B4	Supporting	Romantic Lead Female
A Little Night Music	Sondheim, Stephen	1973	Desiree Armfeldt	Send In The Clowns	Ballad	Alto	G3	A4	Lead	Romantic Lead Female
A Little Night Music	Sondheim, Stephen	1973	Ensemble	Remember	Moderate Tempo	SATB			Ensemble	Adults
A Little Night Music	Sondheim, Stephen	1973	Ensemble	The Sun Won't Set	Moderate Tempo	SATB			Ensemble	Adults
A Little Night Music	Sondheim, Stephen	1973	Erik Egerman	Later	Uptempo	Tenor	C3	B4	Lead	Ingenue Male
A Little Night Music	Sondheim, Stephen	1973	Frederik Egerman	Now	Uptempo	Baritone	Bb2	F4	Lead	Romantic Lead Male
A Little Night Music	Sondheim, Stephen	1973	Frederik Egerman	You Must Meet My Wife	Uptempo	Baritone	C3	E4	Lead	Romantic Lead Male
A Little Night Music	Sondheim, Stephen	1973	Frederik Egerman	It Would Have Been Wonderful *	Uptempo	Baritone	C3	E4	Lead	Romantic Lead Male
A Little Night Music	Sondheim, Stephen	1973	Fredrika Armfeldt	The Glamorous Life	Uptempo	Soprano	C4	Eb5	Supporting	Juvenile Female
A Little Night Music	Sondheim, Stephen	1973	Madame Armfeldt	Liaisons	Uptempo	Alto	D3	F4	Lead	Mature Female
A Little Night Music	Sondheim, Stephen	1973	Desiree & Frederik	You Must Meet My Wife	Moderate Tempo	Alto/Bar			Duet	RLF/RLM
A Little Night Music	Sondheim, Stephen	1973	Anne & Charlotte	Every Day A Little Death	Uptempo	Sop/Alto			Duet	IF/RLF
A Little Night Music	Sondheim, Stephen	1973	Carl-Magnus/Frederik	It Would Have Been Wonderful	Moderate Tempo	Bar/Bar			Duet	RLM/RLM
A Man Of No Importance	Flaherty, Stephen	2002	Adele Rice	Princess	Moderate Tempo	Soprano	C4	E5	Supporting	Character Ingenue Female
A Man Of No Importance	Flaherty, Stephen	2002	Adele Rice	Love Who You Love (Adeke Reprise)	Ballad	Soprano	Ab3	Db5	Supporting	Character Ingenue Female
A Man Of No Importance	Flaherty, Stephen	2002	Alfie Byrne	Man In The Mirror	Ballad	Baritone	Bb2	F4	Lead	Character Male
A Man Of No Importance	Flaherty, Stephen	2002	Alfie Byrne	Love Who You Love	Ballad	Baritone	B2	E4	Lead	Character Male
A Man Of No Importance	Flaherty, Stephen	2002	Alfie Byrne	Confession *	Moderate Tempo	Baritone	B2	D#4	Lead	Character Male
A Man Of No Importance	Flaherty, Stephen	2002	Alfie Byrne	Love's Never Lost	Ballad	Baritone	E3	C4	Lead	Character Male
A Man Of No Importance	Flaherty, Stephen	2002	Baldy O'Shea	Welcome To The World	Ballad	Baritone	C3	C5	Lead	Character Male
A Man Of No Importance	Flaherty, Stephen	2002	Carney	The Cuddles That Mary Gave	Ballad	Baritone	Eb3	F4	Supporting	Mature Male
A Man Of No Importance	Flaherty, Stephen	2002	Carney	Confussing Times	Ballad	Baritone	A2	A3	Supporting	Mature Male
A Man Of No Importance	Flaherty, Stephen	2002	Lily Byrne	The Burden of Life	Uptempo	Alto	F#3	C5	Lead	Mature Female
A Man Of No Importance	Flaherty, Stephen	2002	Lily Byrne	Tell Me Why	Ballad	Alto	G3	Bb4	Lead	Mature Female
A Man Of No Importance	Flaherty, Stephen	2002	Lily Byrne	The Girl That Was Me	Uptempo	Alto	A3	A4	Lead	Mature Female
A Man Of No Importance	Flaherty, Stephen	2002	Lily Byrne	Burden of Life Part 1	Uptempo	Alto	Ab3	Ab4	Lead	Mature Female
A Man Of No Importance	Flaherty, Stephen	2002	Robby Fay	Streets Of Dublin	Uptempo	Tenor	C4	E5	Lead	Romantic Lead Male
A Man Of No Importance	Flaherty, Stephen	2002	Robby Fay	Love Who You Love Reprise	Ballad	Tenor	E3	F4	Lead	Romantic Lead Male
A Man Of No Importance	Flaherty, Stephen	2002	Robby Fay	Confession *	Moderate Tempo	Tenor	Db3	F#4	Lead	Romantic Lead Male
A Man Of No Importance	Flaherty, Stephen	2002	Carney & Lily	Books	Moderate Tempo	Bar/Alto			Duet	MM/MF
A Year With Frog and Toad	Reale, Robert	2002	Frog	He'll Never Know	Moderate Tempo	Baritone	B2	D4	Lead	Character Male
A Year With Frog and Toad	Reale, Robert	2002	Snail	The Letter #1	Moderate Tempo	Tenor	A2	Bb3	Lead	Character Ingenue Male
A Year With Frog and Toad	Reale, Robert	2002	Snail	Letter #2	Uptempo	Tenor	B2	E4	Supporting	Character Ingenue Male
A Year With Frog and Toad	Reale, Robert	2002	Snail	The Letter #3	Uptempo	Tenor	C#3	Eb4	Supporting	Character Ingenue Male
A Year With Frog and Toad	Reale, Robert	2002	Snail	I'm Coming Out Of My Shell	Uptempo	Tenor	E3	A4	Supporting	Character Ingenue Male
A Year With Frog and Toad	Reale, Robert	2002	Toad	Seeds	Ballad	Baritone	A2	D4	Lead	Character Male

Shows

Songs by Character Type

* = Music Edit Required
+ = Ethnic Specific

Show	Composer	Year	Role	Song	Tempo	Vocal Type	Range-Bottom	Range-Top	Category	Character Type
A Year With Frog and Toad	Reale, Robert	2002	Toad	Alone	Ballad	Baritone	A2	G#4	Lead	Character Male
A Year With Frog and Toad	Reale, Robert	2002	Toad	He'll Never Know	Moderate Tempo	Baritone	C#3	Eb4	Lead	Character Male
A Year With Frog and Toad	Reale, Robert	2002	Toad	Toad To The Rescue	Moderate Tempo	Baritone	E3	A4	Lead	Character Male
A Year With Frog and Toad	Reale, Robert	2002	Toad	Merry Almost Christmas	Moderate Tempo	Baritone	E3	A4	Lead	Character Male
Addams Family, The	Lippa, Andrew	2010	Alice Beineke	Waiting	Moderate Tempo	Soprano	Ab3	E5	Supporting	Maternal
Addams Family, The	Lippa, Andrew	2010	Ensemble	Move Toward the Darkness	Ballad	SATB			Ensemble	Adults
Addams Family, The	Lippa, Andrew	2010	Gomez Addams +	Trapped (US Tour)	Moderate Tempo	Baritone	C3	F4	Lead	Romantic Lead Male
Addams Family, The	Lippa, Andrew	2010	Gomez Addams +	Morticia	Moderate Tempo	Tenor	A#2	Ab4	Lead	Romantic Antagonist Male
Addams Family, The	Lippa, Andrew	2010	Gomez Addams +	Happy/Sad	Ballad	Baritone	Eb3	Eb4	Lead	Romantic Antagonist Male
Addams Family, The	Lippa, Andrew	2010	Gomez Addams +	Live Before We Die	Moderate Tempo	Tenor	Bb3	D4	Lead	Romantic Lead Male
Addams Family, The	Lippa, Andrew	2010	Gomez Addams +	Not Today (US Tour)	Moderate Tempo	Tenor	D3	G4	Lead	Romantic Antagonist Male
Addams Family, The	Lippa, Andrew	2010	Gomez Addams +	What If	Ballad	Tenor	C3	C4	Lead	Romantic Antagonist Male
Addams Family, The	Lippa, Andrew	2010	Lucas Beineke	Crazier Than You *	Uptempo	Baritone	D3	E4	Supporting	Ingenue Male
Addams Family, The	Lippa, Andrew	2010	Lucas Beineke	One Normal Night	Uptempo	Baritone	D3	F4	Supporting	Ingenue Male
Addams Family, The	Lippa, Andrew	2010	Lurch	Move Toward The Darkness	Ballad	Bass	G2	Eb4	Supporting	Character Male
Addams Family, The	Lippa, Andrew	2010	Mal Geineke	In The Arms	Moderate Tempo	Baritone	C3	F4	Supporting	Paternal
Addams Family, The	Lippa, Andrew	2010	Morticia Addams	Just Around The Corner *	Uptempo	Alto	G3	B4	Lead	Romantic Antagonist Female
Addams Family, The	Lippa, Andrew	2010	Morticia Addams	Live Before We Die	Moderate Tempo	Alto	Bb3	Ab4	Lead	Romantic Antagonist Female
Addams Family, The	Lippa, Andrew	2010	Pugsley Addams	What If	Ballad	Soprano	A3	C5	Supporting	Juvenile Male
Addams Family, The	Lippa, Andrew	2010	Uncle Fester	The Moon And Me	Ballad	Baritone	C3	E4	Supporting	Mature Male
Addams Family, The	Lippa, Andrew	2010	Wednesday Addams	Pulled	Uptempo	Alto	B3	Eb5	Lead	Character Ingenue Female
Addams Family, The	Lippa, Andrew	2010	Wednesday Addams	One Normal Night	Uptempo	Alto	Bb3	Bb4	Lead	Character Ingenue Female
Addams Family, The	Lippa, Andrew	2010	Wednesday Addams	Crazier Than You *	Uptempo	Alto	A3	E5	Lead	Character Ingenue Female
Addams Family, The	Lippa, Andrew	2010	Gomez & Mortica	Where Did We Go Wrong	Moderate Tempo	Bar/Alto			Duet	RAM/RAF
Addams Family, The	Lippa, Andrew	2010	Lucas & Wednesday	Crazier Than You	Uptempo	Bar/Alto			Duet	IM/CIF
Addams Family, The	Lippa, Andrew	2010	Gomez & Mortica	Live Before We Die	Moderate Tempo	Bar/Alto			Duet	RAM/RAF
Aida	John, Elton	2000	Aida +	The Past Is Another Land	Ballad	Alto	A3	B4	Lead	Romantic Lead Female
Aida	John, Elton	2000	Aida +	Easy As Life	Moderate Tempo	Alto	G3	C5	Lead	Romantic Lead Female
Aida	John, Elton	2000	Aida +	Elaborate Lies Reprise	Ballad	Alto	G3	C5	Lead	Romantic Lead Female
Aida	John, Elton	2000	Aida +	The Gods Love Nubia	Alto	Alto	C4	E5	Lead	Romantic Lead Female
Aida	John, Elton	2000	Amneris	Every Story is a Love Story	Ballad	Alto	G3	Ab4	Lead	Romantic Antagonist Female
Aida	John, Elton	2000	Amneris	My Strongest Suit	Uptempo	Alto	Gb3	Eb5	Lead	Romantic Lead Female
Aida	John, Elton	2000	Amneris	My Strongest Suit Reprise	Ballad	Alto	Bb3	G4	Lead	Romantic Lead Female
Aida	John, Elton	2000	Amneris	I Know the Truth	Ballad	Alto	E3	D5	Lead	Romantic Lead Female
Aida	John, Elton	2000	Amneris	Every Story Reprise (Finale AII)	Ballad	Alto	G3	Ab4	Lead	Romantic Lead Female
Aida	John, Elton	2000	Ensemble	The Gods Love Nubia	Ballad	SATB			Ensemble	Adults
Aida	John, Elton	2000	Mereb +	How I Know You*	Ballad	Tenor	G2	A4	Supporting	Ingenue Male
Aida	John, Elton	2000	Mereb +	How I Know You Reprise	Ballad	Tenor	F3	G4	Supporting	Ingenue Male
Aida	John, Elton	2000	Radames	Fortune Favors the Brave	Uptempo	Tenor	Bb2	F4	Lead	Romantic Lead Male
Aida	John, Elton	2000	Radames	Elaborate Lies	Ballad	Tenor	Bb2	Ab4	Lead	Romantic Lead Male
Aida	John, Elton	2000	Radames	Like Father Like Son*	Uptempo	Tenor	G3	F4	Lead	Romantic Lead Male

Shows

383

* = Music Edit Required
+ = Ethnic Specific

Show	Composer	Year	Role	Song	Tempo	Vocal Type	Range-Bottom	Range-Top	Category	Character Type
Aida	John, Elton	2000	Radames	Radames' Letter	Ballad	Tenor	C3	G4	Lead	Romantic Lead Male
Aida	John, Elton	2000	Radames	Fortune Favors the Brave Reprise	Uptempo	Tenor	F3	G4	Lead	Romantic Lead Male
Aida	John, Elton	2000	Zoser	Another Pyramid	Uptempo	Tenor	F3	E4	Supporting	Antagonist Male
Aida	John, Elton	2000	Zoser	Like Father Like Son*	Uptempo	Tenor	G3	Bb4	Supporting	Antagonist Male
Aida	John, Elton	2000	Aida+ & Mereb	How I Know You	Ballad	Alto/Tenor			Duet	RLF/1M
Aida	John, Elton	2000	Aida+ & Mereb	Enchantment Passing Through	Ballad	Alto/Tenor			Duet	RLF/RLM
Aida	John, Elton	2000	Aida+ & Mereb	Elaborate Lives	Ballad	Alto/Tenor			Duet	RLF/RLM
Aida	John, Elton	2000	Aida+ & Mereb	Written In The Stars	Ballad	Alto/Tenor			Duet	RLF/RLM
Aida	John, Elton	2000	Aida+ & Mereb	Elaborate Lives Reprise	Ballad	Alto/Tenor			Duet	RLF/RLM
Ain't Misbehavin	Waller, Fats	1988	Man Two & Woman One	Honeysuckle Rose	Moderate Tempo	Tenor/Alto			Duet	CM/CF
Ain't Misbehavin	Waller, Fats	1988	Man One & Man Two	The Ladies Who Sing With The Band	Uptempo	Tenor/Tenor			Duet	CM/CM
Ain't Misbehavin	Waller, Fats	1988	Ensemble	Off Time	Uptempo	SATT				Ensemble
Ain't Misbehavin	Waller, Fats	1988	Ensemble	This Joint Is Jumpin'	Uptempo	SATT				Ensemble
Ain't Misbehavin	Waller, Fats	1988	Ensemble	Lounging At The Waldorf	Moderate Tempo	SATT				Ensemble
Ain't Misbehavin	Waller, Fats	1988	Man One & Woman Two	That Ain't Right	Moderate Tempo	Tenor/Sop			Duet	CM/CF
Ain't Misbehavin	Waller, Fats	1988	Woman One & Woman Two	Find What They Like	Uptempo	Alto/Sop			Duet	CF/CF
Ain't Misbehavin	Waller, Fats	1988	Man One & Man Two	Fat And Greasy	Moderate Tempo	Tenor/Tenor			Duet	CM/CM
Ain't Misbehavin'	Waller, Fats	1988	Ensemble	Finale	Uptempo	SATT				Ensemble
Ain't Misbehavin'	Waller, Fats	1988	Ensemble	Black and Blue	Ballad	SATT				Adults
Ain't Misbehavin'	Waller, Fats	1988	Ensemble	Ain't Misbehavin'	Uptempo	SATT				Adults
Ain't Misbehavin'	Waller, Fats	1988	Ensemble	Lookin' Good But Feelin' Bad	Uptempo	SATT				Adults
Ain't Misbehavin'	Waller, Fats	1988	Ensemble	Spreadin' Rhythm Around	Uptempo	SATT				Adults
Ain't Misbehavin'	Waller, Fats	1988	Man One +	How Ya Baby*	Uptempo	Tenor	C3	C5	Lead	Character Ingenue Male
Ain't Misbehavin'	Waller, Fats	1988	Man One +	The Viper's Drag*	Ballad	Tenor	C3	G4	Lead	Character Ingenue Male
Ain't Misbehavin'	Waller, Fats	1988	Man One +	That Ain't Right*	Ballad	Tenor	G2	Bb4	Lead	Character Ingenue Male
Ain't Misbehavin'	Waller, Fats	1988	Man Two +	Honeysuckle Rose*	Ballad	Tenor	D3	A4	Lead	Character Male
Ain't Misbehavin'	Waller, Fats	1988	Man Two +	Lounging At The Waldorf	Ballad	Tenor	B3	E4	Lead	Character Male
Ain't Misbehavin'	Waller, Fats	1988	Man Two +	Your Feets Too Big	Ballad	Tenor	G2	Eb4	Lead	Character Male
Ain't Misbehavin'	Waller, Fats	1988	Woman One +	I've Got A Feeling I'm Falling	Uptempo	Alto	F3	C5	Lead	Character Female
Ain't Misbehavin'	Waller, Fats	1988	Woman One +	Cash For our Trash	Uptempo	Alto	B4	D5	Lead	Character Female
Ain't Misbehavin'	Waller, Fats	1988	Woman One +	Mean To Me	Ballad	Alto	G3	G4	Lead	Character Female
Ain't Misbehavin'	Waller, Fats	1988	Woman One +	Honeysuckle Rose*	Ballad	Alto	Bb4	F5	Lead	Character Female
Ain't Misbehavin'	Waller, Fats	1988	Woman One +	Lounging At The Waldorf	Ballad	Alto	C4	D5	Lead	Character Female
Ain't Misbehavin'	Waller, Fats	1988	Woman Three +	When The Nylons Are In Bloom Again	Uptempo	Soprano	C4	D5	Lead	Character Female
Ain't Misbehavin'	Waller, Fats	1988	Woman Three +	Squeeze Me	Ballad	Soprano	Ab3	Db5	Lead	Character Female
Ain't Misbehavin'	Waller, Fats	1988	Woman Two +	That Ain't Right*	Ballad	Alto	G2	Eb5	Lead	Character Female
Ain't Misbehavin'	Waller, Fats	1988	Woman Two +	Yacht Club Swing	Uptempo	Soprano	Ab3	Ab5	Lead	Character Ingenue Female
Ain't Misbehavin'	Waller, Fats	1988	Woman Two +	Keepin' Out of Mischief Now	Ballad	Soprano	A3	C5	Lead	Character Ingenue Female
All Shook Up	Presley, Elvis	2005	Chad	Roustabout	Uptempo	Tenor	E3	G4	Lead	Romantic Antagonist Male
All Shook Up	Presley, Elvis	2005	Chad	C'mon	Uptempo	Tenor	Db3	G#4	Lead	Romantic Antagonist Male
All Shook Up	Presley, Elvis	2005	Chad	Follow That Dream*	Uptempo	Tenor	A2	E4	Lead	Romantic Antagonist Male
All Shook Up	Presley, Elvis	2005	Chad	Don't Be Cruel *	Uptempo	Tenor	B2	F#4	Lead	Romantic Antagonist Male
All Shook Up	Presley, Elvis	2005	Chad	I Don't Want To	Ballad	Tenor	D3	G4	Lead	Romantic Antagonist Male

Shows

Songs by Character Type

* = Music Edit Required
+ = Ethnic Specific

Show	Composer	Year	Role	Song	Tempo	Vocal Type	Range-Bottom	Range-Top	Category	Character Type
All Shook Up	Presley, Elvis	2005	Chad	Jailhouse Rock *	Uptempo	Tenor	B2	C5	Lead	Romantic Antagonist Male
All Shook Up	Presley, Elvis	2005	Chad	If I Can Dream *	Moderate Tempo	Tenor	C3	G4	Lead	Romantic Antagonist Male
All Shook Up	Presley, Elvis	2005	Chad	The Power of Love *	Moderate Tempo	Tenor	E3	Eb4	Lead	Romantic Antagonist Male
All Shook Up	Presley, Elvis	2005	Dean Hyde	It's Now Or Never *	Moderate Tempo	Baritone	C3	F4	Supporting	Ingenue Male
All Shook Up	Presley, Elvis	2005	Dennis	It Hurts Me	Ballad	Tenor	A2	Bb4	Supporting	Character Male
All Shook Up	Presley, Elvis	2005	Ed (Natalie In Drag)	Don't Be Cruel *	Uptempo	Alto	D4	D5	Lead	Character Ingenue Female
All Shook Up	Presley, Elvis	2005	Ed (Natalie In Drag)	A Little Less Conversation	Uptempo	Alto	Ab3	Eb5	Supporting	Character Ingenue Female
All Shook Up	Presley, Elvis	2005	Ensemble	Can't Help Falling In Love*	Moderate Tempo	SATB			Ensemble	Adults
All Shook Up	Presley, Elvis	2005	Ensemble	All Shook Up	Uptempo	SATB			Ensemble	Adults
All Shook Up	Presley, Elvis	2005	Ensemble	If I Can Dream*	Moderate Tempo	SATB			Ensemble	Adults
All Shook Up	Presley, Elvis	2005	Ensemble	C'mon Everybody Encore	Uptempo	SATB			Ensemble	Adults
All Shook Up	Presley, Elvis	2005	Lorraine	It's Now Or Never *	Moderate Tempo	Alto	C4	F5	Supporting	Ingenue Female
All Shook Up	Presley, Elvis	2005	Mayor Matilda Hyde	Devil In Disguise	Uptempo	Alto	C4	F#5	Supporting	Mature Female
All Shook Up	Presley, Elvis	2005	Miss Sandra	Let Yourself Go	Moderate Tempo	Alto	E2	E4	Supporting	Romantic Lead Female
All Shook Up	Presley, Elvis	2005	Natalie Haller	Love Me Tender	Ballad	Alto	C4	C5	Lead	Character Ingenue Female
All Shook Up	Presley, Elvis	2005	Natalie Haller	One Night With You	Moderate Tempo	Alto	C4	D5	Lead	Character Ingenue Female
All Shook Up	Presley, Elvis	2005	Natalie Haller	Follow That Dream*	Uptempo	Alto	B3	D4	Supporting	Character Ingenue Female
All Shook Up	Presley, Elvis	2005	Natalie Haller	Fools Fall In Love *	Ballad	Alto	A3	D5	Lead	Character Ingenue Female
All Shook Up	Presley, Elvis	2005	Natalie Haller	If I Can Dream *	Moderate Tempo	Alto	C4	F5	Lead	Character Ingenue Female
All Shook Up	Presley, Elvis	2005	Sylvia	There's Always Me	Ballad	Alto	G3	F5	Supporting	Maternal
All Shook Up	Presley, Elvis	2005	Chad & Natalie	Follow That Dream	Uptempo	Tenor/Alto			Duet	RAM/CIF
All Shook Up	Presley, Elvis	2005	Ensemble	Heartbreak Hotel	Moderate Tempo	SATB			Ensemble	Ensemble
All Shook Up	Presley, Elvis	2005	Chad & Ed	Blue Suede Shoes	Uptempo	Tenor/Alto			Duet	RAM/CIF
All Shook Up	Presley, Elvis	2005	Chad & Jim	Don't Be Cruel	Moderate Tempo	Tenor/Bar			Duet	RAM/P
Annie	Strouse, Charles	1977	Annie	Maybe	Ballad	Alto	A3	C#5	Lead	Juvenile Female
Annie	Strouse, Charles	1977	Annie	Tomorrow	Moderate Tempo	Alto	Bb3	Eb5	Lead	Juvenile Female
Annie	Strouse, Charles	1977	Bert Healy	You're Never Fully Dressed	Uptempo	Baritone	E3	F#4	Supporting	Character Ingenue Male
Annie	Strouse, Charles	1977	Ensemble	Hooverville	Uptempo	Unison			Ensemble	Adults
Annie	Strouse, Charles	1977	Ensemble	It's A Hard-Knock Life	Uptempo	SA			Ensemble	Children
Annie	Strouse, Charles	1977	Ensemble	It's A Hard-Knock Life Reprise	Uptempo	SA			Ensemble	Children
Annie	Strouse, Charles	1977	Ensemble	You're Nevery Fully Dressed (Children)	Uptempo	Unison			Ensemble	Children
Annie	Strouse, Charles	1977	Grace Farrell	N.Y.C. *	Uptempo	Soprano	C4	F4	Supporting	Romantic Lead Female
Annie	Strouse, Charles	1977	Miss Hannigan	Little Girls	Uptempo	Alto	C4	D5	Lead	Romantic Antagonist Female
Annie	Strouse, Charles	1977	Miss Hannigan	Easy Street *	Uptempo	Alto	Bb3	Ab4	Lead	Romantic Antagonist Female
Annie	Strouse, Charles	1977	Miss Hannigan	Little Girls Reprise	Uptempo	Alto	E4	D5	Lead	Romantic Antagonist Female
Annie	Strouse, Charles	1977	Oliver Warbucks	N.Y.C. *	Uptempo	Baritone	C3	F4	Lead	Romantic Lead Male
Annie	Strouse, Charles	1977	Oliver Warbucks	Something Was Missing	Ballad	Baritone	Bb2	F4	Lead	Romantic Lead Male
Annie	Strouse, Charles	1977	Oliver Warbucks	Why Should I Change A Thing	Ballad	Baritone	Bb2	G4	Lead	Romantic Lead Male
Annie	Strouse, Charles	1977	Rooster Hannigan	Easy Street *	Moderate Tempo	Tenor	A2	G4	Supporting	Character Male
Annie	Strouse, Charles	1977	Star To Be	N.Y.C. *	Uptempo	Alto	Bb4	Eb5	Supporting	Ingenue Female
Annie Get Your Gun	Berlin, Irving	1944	Annie Oakley	Doin' What Comes Natur'lly	Uptempo	Alto	A3	C5	Lead	Character Female
Annie Get Your Gun	Berlin, Irving	1944	Annie Oakley	The Girl That I Marry*	Moderate Tempo	Alto	B3	B4	Lead	Character Female

Songs by Character Type

* = Music Edit Required
+ = Ethnic Specific

Show	Composer	Year	Role	Song	Tempo	Vocal Type	Range-Bottom	Range-Top	Category	Character Type
Annie Get Your Gun	Berlin, Irving	1944	Annie Oakley	You Can't Get A Man With A Gun	Uptempo	Alto	Bb3	C5	Lead	Character Female
Annie Get Your Gun	Berlin, Irving	1944	Annie Oakley	Moonshine Lullaby	Ballad	Alto	Bb3	D5	Lead	Character Female
Annie Get Your Gun	Berlin, Irving	1944	Annie Oakley	No Business Reprise 2	Moderate Tempo	Alto	G3	C5	Lead	Character Female
Annie Get Your Gun	Berlin, Irving	1944	Annie Oakley	They Say That Falling In Love*	Ballad	Alto	A3	B4	Lead	Character Female
Annie Get Your Gun	Berlin, Irving	1944	Annie Oakley	You Can't Get A Man With A Gun Repris	Moderate Tempo	Alto	Ab3	Ab4	Lead	Character Female
Annie Get Your Gun	Berlin, Irving	1944	Annie Oakley	Lost In His Arms	Ballad	Alto	Bb3	C5	Lead	Character Female
Annie Get Your Gun	Berlin, Irving	1944	Annie Oakley	I Got The Sun in the Morning	Moderate Tempo	Alto	Bb3	Bb4	Lead	Character Female
Annie Get Your Gun	Berlin, Irving	1944	Buffalo Bill	Show Business Reprise *	Moderate Tempo	Baritone	C3	F4	Supporting	Character Male
Annie Get Your Gun	Berlin, Irving	1944	Charlie Davenport	Show Business Reprise *	Moderate Tempo	Baritone	C3	F4	Supporting	Character Male
Annie Get Your Gun	Berlin, Irving	1944	Ensemble	There's No Business Like Show Busines	Uptempo	SATB			Ensemble	Adults
Annie Get Your Gun	Berlin, Irving	1944	Ensemble	I Got The Sun in the Morning*	Moderate Tempo	SATB			Ensemble	Adults
Annie Get Your Gun	Berlin, Irving	1944	Ensemble	They Say It's Wonderful Reprise Act 2*	Ballad	SATB			Ensemble	Adults
Annie Get Your Gun	Berlin, Irving	1944	Ensemble	I'll Share It All With You*	Uptempo	SATB			Ensemble	Adults
Annie Get Your Gun	Berlin, Irving	1944	Ensemble	Moonshines Lullaby*	Ballad	TTB			Ensemble	Adults
Annie Get Your Gun	Berlin, Irving	1944	Frank Butler	There's No Business Like Show Busines	Uptempo	Baritone	Ab3	E4	Lead	Romantic Lead Male
Annie Get Your Gun	Berlin, Irving	1944	Frank Butler	The Girl That I Marry*	Moderate Tempo	Baritone	D3	D4	Lead	Romantic Lead Male
Annie Get Your Gun	Berlin, Irving	1944	Frank Butler	They Say That Falling In Love*	Ballad	Baritone	C3	D4	Lead	Romantic Lead Male
Annie Get Your Gun	Berlin, Irving	1944	Frank Butler	My Defenses Are Down	Moderate Tempo	Baritone	Db3	Eb4	Lead	Romantic Lead Male
Annie Get Your Gun	Berlin, Irving	1944	Frank Butler	An Old Fashioned Wedding	Uptempo	Baritone	B2	E4	Lead	Romantic Lead Male
Annie Get Your Gun	Berlin, Irving	1944	Frank Butler	The Girl I Marry Reprise	Ballad	Baritone	A3	D4	Lead	Romantic Lead Male
Annie Get Your Gun	Berlin, Irving	1944	Frank Butler	Show Business Reprise *	Moderate Tempo	Baritone	C3	F4	Lead	Romantic Lead Male
Annie Get Your Gun	Berlin, Irving	1944	Tommy Walker	I'll Share It All With You	Uptempo	Baritone	C#3	D4	Lead	Ingenue Male
Annie Get Your Gun	Berlin, Irving	1946	Ensemble	Show Business Reprise *	Moderate Tempo	SATB			Ensemble	Adults
Annie Get Your Gun	Berlin, Irving	1949	Annie & Fank	They Say It's Wonderful Reprise	Ballad	Alto/Bar			Duet	CF/RLM
Annie Get Your Gun	Berlin, Irving	1949	Annie & Fank	Anything You Can Do	Uptempo	Alto/Bar			Duet	CF/RLM
Annie Get Your Gun	Berlin, Irving	1966	Annie Oakley	An Old Fashioned Wedding	Uptempo	Alto	B3	B4	Lead	Character Female
Anyone Can Whistle	Sondheim, Stephen	1964	Ensemble	Me And My Town	Uptempo	ATB			Ensemble	Adults
Anyone Can Whistle	Sondheim, Stephen	1964	Cora Hoover Hooper	Me And My Town*	Uptempo	Alto	A3	Eb5	Lead	Romantic Antagonist Female
Anyone Can Whistle	Sondheim, Stephen	1964	Ensemble	Miracle Song	Uptempo	SATB			Ensemble	Adults
Anyone Can Whistle	Sondheim, Stephen	1964	Fay Apple	There Won't Be Trumpets	Uptempo	Alto	G3	Bb4	Lead	Ingenue Female
Anyone Can Whistle	Sondheim, Stephen	1964	Ensemble	Simple	Uptempo	SATB			Ensemble	Adults
Anyone Can Whistle	Sondheim, Stephen	1964	Ensemble	A-1 March	Uptempo	SATB			Ensemble	Adults
Anyone Can Whistle	Sondheim, Stephen	1964	Fay Apple	Come Play Wiz Me*	Uptempo	Alto	A3	D5	Lead	Ingenue Female
Anyone Can Whistle	Sondheim, Stephen	1964	Fay & Hapgood	Come Play Wiz Me	Uptempo	Alto/Bar			Duet	IF/RAM
Anyone Can Whistle	Sondheim, Stephen	1964	Fay Apple	Anyone Can Whistle	Ballad	Alto	G3	C5	Lead	Ingenue Female
Anyone Can Whistle	Sondheim, Stephen	1964	Cora Hoover Hooper	There's A Parade In Town*	Uptempo	Alto	G3	Bb4	Lead	Romantic Antagonist Female
Anyone Can Whistle	Sondheim, Stephen	1964	Ensemble	There's A Parade In Town	Uptempo	SATB Unison			Ensemble	Adults
Anyone Can Whistle	Sondheim, Stephen	1964	J. Bowden Hapgood	Everybody Says Don't	Uptempo	Baritone	G2	E4	Lead	Romantic Antagonist Male
Anyone Can Whistle	Sondheim, Stephen	1964	Cora Hoover Hooper	I've Got You To Jean On*	Uptempo	Alto	Ab4	D5	Lead	Romantic Antagonist Female
Anyone Can Whistle	Sondheim, Stephen	1964	Fay Apple	See What It Gets You	Uptempo	Alto	G3	Db5	Lead	Ingenue Female
Anyone Can Whistle	Sondheim, Stephen	1964	Cora Hoover Hooper	Cora's Chase*	Uptempo	Alto	A3	E5	Lead	Romantic Antagonist Female
Anyone Can Whistle	Sondheim, Stephen	1964	Soprano Cadenza	Cora's Chase*	Uptempo	Soprano	B4	D6	Featured Ensemble	Character Female

Shows

Songs by Character Type

Show	Composer	Year	Role	Song	Tempo	Vocal Type	Range-Bottom	Range-Top	Category	Character Type
Anyone Can Whistle	Sondheim, Stephen	1964	Ensemble	Cora's Chase	Uptempo	SATB			Ensemble	Adults
Anyone Can Whistle	Sondheim, Stephen	1964	J. Bowden Hapgood	With So Little To Be Sure Of*	Moderate Tempo	Baritone	B2	E4	Lead	Romantic Antagonist Male
Anyone Can Whistle	Sondheim, Stephen	1964	Fay Apple	With So Little To Be Sure Of*	Moderate Tempo	Alto	A3	B4	Lead	Ingenue Female
Anyone Can Whistle	Sondheim, Stephen	1964	Fay & Hapgood	With So Little To Be Sure Of	Moderate Tempo	Alto/Bar			Duet	IF/RAM
Anyone Can Whistle	Sondheim, Stephen	1964	Baby Joan	I'm Like The Bluebird	Uptempo	Soprano	B3	C#5	Featured Ensemble	Character Ingenue Female
Anyone Can Whistle	Sondheim, Stephen	1964	Ensemble	Bluebird Incidental	Uptempo	SATB Unison			Ensemble	Adults
Anything Goes	Porter, Cole	1934	Billy Crocker	You're the Top *	Uptempo	Baritone	B2	F4	Lead	Romantic Lead Male
Anything Goes	Porter, Cole	1934	Billy Crocker	All Through The Night *	Ballad	Baritone	F3	G4	Lead	Romantic Lead Male
Anything Goes	Porter, Cole	1934	Ensemble	Bon Voyage	Uptempo	SATB			Ensemble	Adults
Anything Goes	Porter, Cole	1934	Ensemble	Anything Goes*	Uptempo	SATB			Ensemble	Adults
Anything Goes	Porter, Cole	1934	Ensemble	Blow Gabriel Blow*	Uptempo	SATB			Ensemble	Adults
Anything Goes	Porter, Cole	1934	Hope Harcourt	All Through The Night *	Ballad	Soprano	C4	Eb5	Lead	Ingenue Female
Anything Goes	Porter, Cole	1934	Hope Harcourt	The Gypsy In Me	Moderate Tempo	Soprano	C3	G4	Lead	Ingenue Female
Anything Goes	Porter, Cole	1934	Hope Harcourt	Goodbye Little Dream, Goodbye	Ballad	Soprano	A3	Eb5	Lead	Ingenue Female
Anything Goes	Porter, Cole	1934	Moon Face Martin	Friendship *	Uptempo	Tenor	Bb2	Eb4	Supporting	Character Male
Anything Goes	Porter, Cole	1934	Moon Face Martin	Be Like A Blue Bird	Moderate Tempo	Tenor	B#2	F#4	Supporting	Character Male
Anything Goes	Porter, Cole	1934	Reno Sweeney	I Get A Kick Out of You	Uptempo	Alto	A3	D5	Lead	Character Female
Anything Goes	Porter, Cole	1934	Reno Sweeney	You're the Top *	Uptempo	Alto	G3	D5	Lead	Character Female
Anything Goes	Porter, Cole	1934	Reno Sweeney	Anything Goes	Uptempo	Alto	Ab3	C5	Lead	Character Female
Anything Goes	Porter, Cole	1934	Reno Sweeney	Blow Gabriel Blow	Uptempo	Alto	G3	C5	Lead	Character Female
Anything Goes	Porter, Cole	1934	Reno Sweeney	Buddy Beware	Moderate Tempo	Alto	A3	C#5	Lead	Character Female
Anything Goes	Porter, Cole	1934	Reno Sweeney	Friendship *	Uptempo	Alto	Bb3	Eb5	Lead	Character Female
Anything Goes	Porter, Cole	1934	Billy & Reno	You're The Top	Uptempo	Bar/Alto			Duet	RLM/CF
Anything Goes	Porter, Cole	1934	Billy & Hope	All Through The Night	Ballad	Bar/Sop			Duet	RLM/IF
Anything Goes	Porter, Cole	1934	Billy & Hope	All Through The Night Reprise	Ballad	Bar/Sop			Duet	RLM/IF
Applause	Strousse, Charles	1970	Ensemble	Backstage Babble	Uptempo	SATB			Ensemble	Adults
Applause	Strousse, Charles	1970	Bill Sampson	Think How It's Gonna Be	Moderate Tempo	Baritone	B2	F4	Lead	Romantic Lead Male
Applause	Strousse, Charles	1970	Margo Channing	But Alive*	Uptempo	Alto	E3	F#4	Lead	Romantic Antagonist Female
Applause	Strousse, Charles	1970	Ensemble	But Alive	Uptempo	SATB			Ensemble	Adults
Applause	Strousse, Charles	1970	Eve Harrington	The Best Night Of My Life	Ballad	Alto	G#3	C#5	Lead	Romantic Antagonist Female
Applause	Strousse, Charles	1970	Margo Channing	Who's That Girl	Uptempo	Alto	E3	A4	Lead	Romantic Antagonist Female
Applause	Strousse, Charles	1970	Ensemble	Backstage Babble Reprise	Uptempo	SATB			Ensemble	Adults
Applause	Strousse, Charles	1970	Eve Harrington	Applause*	Moderate Tempo	Alto	G3	E5	Lead	Romantic Antagonist Female
Applause	Strousse, Charles	1970	Ensemble	Applause*	Moderate Tempo	SATB			Ensemble	Adults
Applause	Strousse, Charles	1970	Ensemble	Applause Encore	Moderate Tempo	SATB			Ensemble	Adults
Applause	Strousse, Charles	1970	Margo Channing	Hurry Back	Ballad	Alto	Ab2	F4	Lead	Romantic Antagonist Female
Applause	Strousse, Charles	1970	Ensemble	Fasten Your Seatbelts	Moderate Tempo	SATB			Ensemble	Adults
Applause	Strousse, Charles	1970	Margo Channing	Welcome To The Theatre	Moderate Tempo	Alto	D3	F#4	Lead	Romantic Antagonist Female
Applause	Strousse, Charles	1970	Buzz Richards	Good Friends*	Moderate Tempo	Baritone	C3	F4	Lead	Character Male
Applause	Strousse, Charles	1970	Ensemble	Good Friends	Moderate Tempo	AAB			Ensemble	Adults
Applause	Strousse, Charles	1970	Ensemble	She's No Longer A Gypsy	Uptempo	SATB			Ensemble	Adults
Applause	Strousse, Charles	1970	Bill Sampson	One Of A Kind*	Uptempo	Baritone	Bb2	F4	Lead	Romantic Lead Male
Applause	Strousse, Charles	1970	Bill & Margo	One Of A Kind	Uptempo	Bar/Alto			Duet	RLM/RAF

Shows

Songs by Character Type

* = Music Edit Required
+ = Ethnic Specific

Show	Composer	Year	Role	Song	Tempo	Vocal Type	Range-Bottom	Range-Top	Category	Character Type
Applause	Strousse, Charles	1970	Eve Harrington	One Hallowe'en	Moderate Tempo	Alto	F3	B♭4	Lead	Romantic Antagonist Female
Applause	Strousse, Charles	1970	Margo Channing	Something Greater*	Uptempo	Alto	D3	G4	Lead	Romantic Antagonist Female
Applause	Strousse, Charles	1970	Bill & Margo	Something Greater	Uptempo	Bar/Alto			Duet	RLM/RAF
Applause	Strousse, Charles	1970	Ensemble	Applause Finale	Uptempo	SATB			Ensemble	Adults
Apple Tree, The	Bock, Jerry	1966	Adam	Eve	Moderate Tempo	Baritone	D3	D♭4	Lead	Character Male
Apple Tree, The	Bock, Jerry	1966	Adam	Beautiful World	Moderate Tempo	Baritone	C3	E♭4	Lead	Character Male
Apple Tree, The	Bock, Jerry	1966	Adam	It's A Fish	Uptempo	Baritone	A♭3	E♭4	Lead	Character Male
Apple Tree, The	Bock, Jerry	1966	Adam	Adam's Reprise	Moderate Tempo	Baritone	C3	E♭4	Lead	Character Male
Apple Tree, The	Bock, Jerry	1966	Balladeer	I'll Tell You A Truth	Ballad	Baritone	E3	E♭4	Supporting	Antagonist Male
Apple Tree, The	Bock, Jerry	1966	Balladeer	I'll Tell You A Truth Reprise	Ballad	Baritone	C3	F#4	Lead	Antagonist Male
Apple Tree, The	Bock, Jerry	1966	Ella	Oh To Be A Movie Star	Uptempo	Alto	C4	D5	Lead	Character Female
Apple Tree, The	Bock, Jerry	1966	Eve	Here In Eden	Moderate Tempo	Alto	A3	B4	Lead	Character Female
Apple Tree, The	Bock, Jerry	1966	Eve	Feelings	Moderate Tempo	Alto	B3	E5	Lead	Character Female
Apple Tree, The	Bock, Jerry	1966	Eve	Go To Sleep Whoever You Are	Ballad	Alto	B3	B4	Lead	Character Female
Apple Tree, The	Bock, Jerry	1966	Eve	What Makes Me Love Him	Ballad	Alto	C3	C#5	Lead	Character Female
Apple Tree, The	Bock, Jerry	1966	Eve	Friends	Uptempo	Alto	B♭3	C5	Lead	Character Female
Apple Tree, The	Bock, Jerry	1966	Flip	Real *	Moderate Tempo	Baritone	C3	E♭4	Lead	Character Male
Apple Tree, The	Bock, Jerry	1966	Passionella	Gorgeous	Uptempo	Alto	C4	D5	Lead	Character Female
Apple Tree, The	Bock, Jerry	1966	Passionella	Wealth	Uptempo	Alto	B3	B4	Lead	Character Female
Apple Tree, The	Bock, Jerry	1966	Passionella	Oh To Be A Movie Star Reprise	Moderate Tempo	Alto	C4	D5	Lead	Character Female
Apple Tree, The	Bock, Jerry	1966	Princess Barbara	I've Got What You Want	Ballad	Alto	G3	C5	Lead	Character Female
Apple Tree, The	Bock, Jerry	1966	Princess Barbara	Tiger, Tiger	Uptempo	Alto	F3	A4	Lead	Character Female
Apple Tree, The	Bock, Jerry	1966	Snake	Forbidden Fruit	Moderate Tempo	Baritone	E♭3	G4	Supporting	Antagonist Male
Apple Tree, The	Bock, Jerry	1966	Barbara & Sanjar	Forbidden Love (In Gaul)	Moderate Tempo	Alto/Bar			Duet	CF/CM
Assassins	Sondheim, Stephen	1992	The Proprietor	Opening*	Moderate Tempo	Baritone	F#2	F4	Lead	Romantic Lead Male
Assassins	Sondheim, Stephen	1992	Proprietor & Booth	Opening	Moderate Tempo	Bar/Bar	D3	F4	Duet	RLM/RAM
Assassins	Sondheim, Stephen	1992	The Balladeer	The Ballad Of Booth Part 1	Uptempo	Tenor	C#3	G#4	Lead	Character Male
Assassins	Sondheim, Stephen	1992	John Wilkes Booth	The Ballad Of Booth Part 2	Moderate Tempo	Baritone	F#2	F#4	Lead	Romantic Antagonist Male
Assassins	Sondheim, Stephen	1992	The Balladeer	The Ballad Of Booth Part 3	Uptempo	Tenor	C#3	A4	Lead	Character Male
Assassins	Sondheim, Stephen	1992	Giuseppe Zangara	How I Saved Roosevelt*	Uptempo	Tenor	D3	A4	Lead	Antagonist Male
Assassins	Sondheim, Stephen	1992	Ensemble	How I Saved Roosevelt	Uptempo	SATB			Ensemble	Adults
Assassins	Sondheim, Stephen	1992	Leon Czolgosz	Gun Song*	Moderate Tempo	Baritone	G2	B3	Lead	Romantic Antagonist Male
Assassins	Sondheim, Stephen	1992	John Wilkes Booth	Gun Song*	Moderate Tempo	Baritone	C#3	E4	Lead	Romantic Antagonist Male
Assassins	Sondheim, Stephen	1992	Ensemble	Gun Song	Moderate Tempo	TTBB			Ensemble	Adults
Assassins	Sondheim, Stephen	1992	The Balladeer	The Ballad of Czolgosz (Part 1 & 2)	Uptempo	Tenor	D3	G4	Lead	Character Male
Assassins	Sondheim, Stephen	1992	John Hinkley	Unworthy Of Your Love*	Moderate Tempo	Tenor	B2	E4	Lead	Antagonist Male
Assassins	Sondheim, Stephen	1992	Lynette Squeaky Fromme	Unworthy Of Your Love*	Moderate Tempo	Soprano	A3	D5	Lead	Character Female
Assassins	Sondheim, Stephen	1992	Hinkley & Fromme	Unworthy Of Your Love	Moderate Tempo	Tenor/Sop			Duet	AM/CF
Assassins	Sondheim, Stephen	1992	Charles Guiteau	The Ballad Of Guiteau*	Uptempo	Tenor	A2	G♭4	Lead	Romantic Antagonist Male
Assassins	Sondheim, Stephen	1992	The Balladeer	The Ballad Of Guiteau*	Uptempo	Tenor	C3	G4	Lead	Character Male
Assassins	Sondheim, Stephen	1992	Guiteau & Balladeer	The Ballad of Guiteau	Uptempo	Tenor/Tenor			Duet	RAM/CM

Shows

* = Music Edit Required
+ = Ethnic Specific

Show	Composer	Year	Role	Song	Tempo	Vocal Type	Range-Bottom	Range-Top	Category	Character Type
Assassins	Sondheim, Stephen	1992	The Balladeer	Another National Anthem*	Moderate Tempo	Tenor	D3	F#4	Lead	Character Male
Assassins	Sondheim, Stephen	1992	Ensemble	Another National Anthem	Moderate Tempo	SATB			Ensemble	Adults
Assassins	Sondheim, Stephen	1992	Ensemble	Something Just Broke	Moderate Tempo	SATB			Ensemble	Adults
Assassins	Sondheim, Stephen	1992	Ensemble	Everybody's Got The Right	Uptempo	SATB			Ensemble	Adults
Assassins	Sondheim, Stephen	1992	Ensemble	Take A Look Lee	Moderate Tempo	SATB			Ensemble	Adults
Avenue Q	Lopez and Marx	2003	Brian	I'm Not Wearing Underwear Today	Uptempo	Baritone	B2	E4	Lead	Character Male
Avenue Q	Lopez and Marx	2003	Brian	There Is Life Outside Your Apartment	Uptempo	Baritone	B#2	E4	Lead	Character Male
Avenue Q	Lopez and Marx	2003	Christmas Eve	The More You Love Someone	Ballad	Alto	B3	Eb5	Lead	Character Female
Avenue Q	Lopez and Marx	2003	Ensemble	The Avenue Q Theme	Uptempo	SATB			Ensemble	Adults
Avenue Q	Lopez and Marx	2003	Ensemble	For Now	Uptempo	SATB			Ensemble	Adults
Avenue Q	Lopez and Marx	2003	Gary Coleman	You Can Be As Loud As You Want	Uptempo	Alto	G3	Db5	Lead	Character Female
Avenue Q	Lopez and Marx	2003	Gary Coleman	Schadenfruede *	Uptempo	Alto	F3	C5	Lead	Character Female
Avenue Q	Lopez and Marx	2003	Kate Monster	Mix Tape *	Uptempo	Alto	F3	D5	Lead	Character Ingenue Female
Avenue Q	Lopez and Marx	2003	Kate Monster	There's A Fine Fine Line	Moderate Tempo	Alto	G3	D5	Lead	Character Ingenue Female
Avenue Q	Lopez and Marx	2003	Lucy The Slut	Special	Moderate Tempo	Alto	G3	Db4	Supporting	Romantic Antagonist Female
Avenue Q	Lopez and Marx	2003	Nicky	If You Were Gay	Uptempo	Tenor	C3	A4	Lead	Character Male
Avenue Q	Lopez and Marx	2003	Princeton	What Do You...BA English	Moderate Tempo	Baritone	B2	D4	Lead	Character Ingenue Male
Avenue Q	Lopez and Marx	2003	Princeton	Purpose	Uptempo	Baritone	B2	G3	Lead	Character Ingenue Male
Avenue Q	Lopez and Marx	2003	Rod	My Girlfriend Who Lives In Canada	Uptempo	Tenor	B2	G4	Lead	Character Male
Avenue Q	Lopez and Marx	2003	Rod	Fantasies Come True	Ballad	Tenor	A2	D4	Lead	Character Male
Avenue Q	Lopez and Marx	2003	Gary & Nicky	Schadenfreude	Uptempo	Alto/Tenor			Duet	CF/CM
Babes In Arms (1998)	Rodgers, Richard	1937	Val LaMar	Where Or When*	Moderate Tempo	Baritone	B2	F4	Lead	Ingenue Male
Babes In Arms (1998)	Rodgers, Richard	1937	Billie Smith	Where Or When*	Moderate Tempo	Alto	B3	E5	Lead	Ingenue Female
Babes In Arms (1998)	Rodgers, Richard	1937	Billie Smith & Val LaMar	Where Or When	Moderate Tempo	Bar/Alto			Duet	IF/IM
Babes In Arms (1998)	Rodgers, Richard	1937	Val LaMar	Babes In Arms*	Uptempo	Baritone	C3	E4	Lead	Ingenue Male
Babes In Arms (1998)	Rodgers, Richard	1937	Marshall Blackstone	Babes In Arms*	Uptempo	Baritone	C3	E4	Lead	Ingenue Male
Babes In Arms (1998)	Rodgers, Richard	1937	Billie Smith	Babes In Arms*	Uptempo	Alto	C3	E4	Lead	Ingenue Female
Babes In Arms (1998)	Rodgers, Richard	1937	Ensemble	Babes In Arms	Uptempo	SATB			Ensemble	Adults
Babes In Arms (1998)	Rodgers, Richard	1937	Gus Fielding	I Wish I Were In Love Again*	Uptempo	Tenor	C3	Ab4	Lead	Antagonist Male
Babes In Arms (1998)	Rodgers, Richard	1937	Dolores Reynolds	I Wish I Were In Love Again*	Uptempo	Alto	A3	A4	Lead	Ingenue Female
Babes In Arms (1998)	Rodgers, Richard	1937	Gus & Dolores	I Wish I Were In Love Again	Uptempo	Tenor/Alto			Duet	AM/IF
Babes In Arms (1998)	Rodgers, Richard	1937	Ensemble	Babes In Arms Reprise	Uptempo	SATB			Ensemble	Adults
Babes In Arms (1998)	Rodgers, Richard	1937	Irving+ & Ivor+	Light On Our Feet	Uptempo	Bar/Bar			Duet	IM/IM
Babes In Arms (1998)	Rodgers, Richard	1937	Baby Rose	Way Out West*	Moderate Tempo	Alto	B3	C5	Lead	Romantic Lead Female
Babes In Arms (1998)	Rodgers, Richard	1937	Ensemble	Way Out West	Moderate Tempo	ATTBB			Ensemble	Adults
Babes In Arms (1998)	Rodgers, Richard	1937	Billie Smith	My Funny Valentine	Ballad	Alto	A3	C5	Lead	Ingenue Female
Babes In Arms (1998)	Rodgers, Richard	1937	Baby Rose	Johnny One Note	Uptempo	Alto	Bb3	Bb4	Lead	Romantic Lead Female
Babes In Arms (1998)	Rodgers, Richard	1937	Baby Rose	Imagine*	Moderate Tempo	Alto	A3	C5	Lead	Romantic Lead Female
Babes In Arms (1998)	Rodgers, Richard	1937	Ensemble	Imagine	Moderate Tempo	ATTBB			Ensemble	Adults
Babes In Arms (1998)	Rodgers, Richard	1937	Val LaMar	All At Once*	Moderate Tempo	Baritone	A2	F4	Lead	Ingenue Male
Babes In Arms (1998)	Rodgers, Richard	1937	Billie Smith	All At Once*	Moderate Tempo	Alto	A3	Bb4	Lead	Ingenue Female
Babes In Arms (1998)	Rodgers, Richard	1937	Billie Smith & Val LaMar	All At Once	Moderate Tempo	Bar/Alto			Duet	IF/IM
Babes In Arms (1998)	Rodgers, Richard	1937	Ensemble	Imagine Reprise*	Moderate Tempo	TTBB			Ensemble	Adults

Shows

* = Music Edit Required
+ = Ethnic Specific

Show	Composer	Year	Role	Song	Tempo	Vocal Type	Range-Bottom	Range-Top	Category	Character Type
Babes In Arms (1998)	Rodgers, Richard	1937	Ensemble	Imagine Reprise #2*	Moderate Tempo	TTBB			Ensemble	Adults
Babes In Arms (1998)	Rodgers, Richard	1937	Peter	Imagine Reprise #2*	Moderate Tempo	Baritone	E3	F4	Lead	Antagonist Male
Babes In Arms (1998)	Rodgers, Richard	1937	Billie Smith	The Lady Is A Tramp	Uptempo	Alto	Ab3	Bb4	Lead	Ingenue Female
Babes In Arms (1998)	Rodgers, Richard	1937	Billie Smith	The Lady Is A Tramp Encore	Uptempo	Alto	Ab3	Bb4	Lead	Ingenue Female
Babes In Arms (1998)	Rodgers, Richard	1937	Gus Fielding	You Are So Fair*	Uptempo	Tenor	Eb3	F4	Lead	Antagonist Male
Babes In Arms (1998)	Rodgers, Richard	1937	Dolores Reynolds	You Are So Fair*	Uptempo	Alto	B3	B4	Lead	Ingenue Female
Babes In Arms (1998)	Rodgers, Richard	1937	Gus & Dolores	You Are So Fair	Uptempo	Tenor/Alto			Duet	AM/IF
Babes In Arms (1998)	Rodgers, Richard	1937	Billie Smith	The Lady Is A Tramp Reprise	Uptempo	Alto	Ab3	Bb4	Lead	Ingenue Female
Babes In Arms (1998)	Rodgers, Richard	1937	Ensemble	Finale Ultimo	Uptempo	SATB			Ensemble	Adults
Babes In Arms (1998)	Rodgers, Richard	1998	Irving de Quincy+	Light On Our Feet*	Uptempo	Baritone	F3	F4	Lead	Ingenue Male
Babes In Arms (1998)	Rodgers, Richard	1998	Ivor de Quincy+	Light On Our Feet*	Uptempo	Baritone	F3	F4	Lead	Ingenue Male
Baby	Shire, David	1983	Alan McNally	Easier To Love	Ballad	Baritone	C3	D4	Lead	Paternal
Baby	Shire, David	1983	Alan McNally	And What If We'd Loved Like That *	Moderate Tempo	Baritone	D3	Gb4	Lead	Paternal
Baby	Shire, David	1983	Arlene McNally	I Want It All *	Uptempo	Soprano	B3	Eb5	Lead	Maternal
Baby	Shire, David	1983	Arlene McNally	And What If We'd Loved Like That *	Moderate Tempo	Soprano	D4	F5	Lead	Maternal
Baby	Shire, David	1983	Danny Hooper	I Chose Right	Ballad	Tenor	D3	G4	Lead	Character Ingenue Male
Baby	Shire, David	1983	Lizzie Fields	I Want It All *	Uptempo	Soprano	C4	Eb5	Lead	Ingenue Female
Baby	Shire, David	1983	Lizzie Fields	The Story Goes On	Ballad	Soprano	G3	F5	Lead	Ingenue Female
Baby	Shire, David	1983	Nick Sakarian	At Night She Comes Home To Me *	Moderate Tempo	Baritone	Db3	F#4	Lead	Character Male
Baby	Shire, David	1983	Nick Sakarian	With You *	Ballad	Baritone	A#2	D#4	Lead	Character Male
Baby	Shire, David	1983	Pam Sakarian	I Want It All *	Uptempo	Alto	C4	Eb5	Lead	Character Female
Baby	Shire, David	1983	Pam Sakarian	With You *	Ballad	Alto	G#3	D5	Lead	Character Female
Baby	Shire, David	1983	Danny & Lizzie	What Could Be Better	Uptempo	Tenor/Sop			Duet	CIM/IF
Baby	Shire, David	1983	Alan & Arlene	The Plaza Song	Moderate Tempo	Bar/Sop			Duet	P/M
Baby	Shire, David	1983	Danny & Nick	At Night She Comes Home To Me	Moderate Tempo	Tenor/Bar			Duet	CIM/CM
Baby	Shire, David	1983	Danny & Lizzie	What Could Be Better Reprise	Uptempo	Tenor/Sop			Duet	CIM/IF
Baby	Shire, David	1983	Nick & Pam	Romance	Moderate Tempo	Bar/Alto			Duet	CM/CF
Baby	Shire, David	1983	Nick & Pam	Romance Reprise	Moderate Tempo	Bar/Alto			Duet	CM/CF
Baby	Shire, David	1983	Alan & Arlene	And What If We Had Loved...	Moderate Tempo	Bar/Sop			Duet	P/M
Beauty and the Beast	Menken, Alan	1994	Beast	How Long Must This Go On	Uptempo	Baritone	D3	C4	Lead	Romantic Antagonist Male
Beauty and the Beast	Menken, Alan	1994	Beast	If I Can't Love Her	Ballad	Baritone	B2	F4	Lead	Romantic Antagonist Male
Beauty and the Beast	Menken, Alan	1994	Beast	Something There *	Uptempo	Baritone	A2	E5	Lead	Romantic Antagonist Male
Beauty and the Beast	Menken, Alan	1994	Beast	If I Can't Love Her Reprise	Ballad	Baritone	D4	D5	Lead	Romantic Antagonist Male
Beauty and the Beast	Menken, Alan	1994	Belle	Home	Ballad	Soprano	G3	E5	Lead	Character Ingenue Female
Beauty and the Beast	Menken, Alan	1994	Belle	Belle Reprise	Uptempo	Soprano	D4	D5	Lead	Character Ingenue Female
Beauty and the Beast	Menken, Alan	1994	Belle	Something There *	Uptempo	Soprano	A3	E5	Lead	Character Ingenue Female
Beauty and the Beast	Menken, Alan	1994	Belle	Home Reprise	Ballad	Soprano	C4	D5	Lead	Character Ingenue Female
Beauty and the Beast	Menken, Alan	1994	Ensemble	If I Could Love Her Finale	Moderate Tempo	SATB			Ensemble	Adults
Beauty and the Beast	Menken, Alan	1994	Ensemble	Beauty and the Beast	Moderate Tempo	SATB			Ensemble	Children/Adults
Beauty and the Beast	Menken, Alan	1994	Gaston	Me	Uptempo	Baritone	B2	F4	Lead	Romantic Antagonist Male
Beauty and the Beast	Menken, Alan	1994	Gaston	Gaston Reprise	Uptempo	Baritone	C3	E4	Lead	Romantic Antagonist Male
Beauty and the Beast	Menken, Alan	1994	Gaston	Maison Des Lune	Moderate Tempo	Baritone	B2	E4	Lead	Romantic Antagonist Male

Songs by Character Type

Show	Composer	Year	Role	Song	Tempo	Vocal Type	Range-Bottom	Range-Top	Category	Character Type
Beauty and the Beast	Menken, Alan	1994	Lefou	Gaston	Uptempo	Tenor	B2	E4	Supporting	Character Male
Beauty and the Beast	Menken, Alan	1994	Lumiere	Be Our Guest	Uptempo	Baritone	F#2	E4	Support	Romantic Lead Male
Beauty and the Beast	Menken, Alan	1994	Maurice	No Matter What	Uptempo	Baritone	B2	D♭4	Supporting	Paternal
Beauty and the Beast	Menken, Alan	1994	Maurice	No Matter What Reprise	Uptempo	Baritone	B♭2	G3	Supporting	Paternal
Beauty and the Beast	Menken, Alan	1994	Mrs. Potts	Home Reprise	Ballad	Soprano	G3	D5	Supporting	Maternal
Beauty and the Beast	Menken, Alan	1994	Mrs. Potts	Beauty and the Beast	Ballad	Soprano	F3	B4	Supporting	Maternal
Beauty and the Beast	Menken, Alan	1994	Mrs. Potts	Beauty and the Beast Reprise	Uptempo	Soprano	G3	G5	Supporting	Maternal
Beauty And The Beast	Menken, Alan	1999	Belle & Maurice	No Matter What	Moderate Tempo	Alto/Bar			Duet	CIF/P
Bells Are Ringing	Styne, Julie	1956	Ella Peterson	It's A Perfect Relationship	Uptempo	Alto	A♭3	C♭5	Lead	Character Female
Bells Are Ringing	Styne, Julie	1956	Ella Peterson	Is It A Crime	Moderate Tempo	Alto	A3	C5	Lead	Character Female
Bells Are Ringing	Styne, Julie	1956	Ella Peterson	Long Before I Knew You *	Ballad	Alto	B3	C#5	Lead	Character Female
Bells Are Ringing	Styne, Julie	1956	Ella Peterson	The Party's Over	Ballad	Alto	F#3	B4	Lead	Character Female
Bells Are Ringing	Styne, Julie	1956	Ella Peterson	I'm Going Back	Moderate Tempo	Alto	A#3	B4	Lead	Character Female
Bells Are Ringing	Styne, Julie	1956	Ella Peterson	Better Than A Dream *	Moderate Tempo	Alto	A3	D5	Lead	Character Female
Bells Are Ringing	Styne, Julie	1956	Jeff Moss	Independent	Uptempo	Baritone	D3	E4	Lead	Romantic Lead Male
Bells Are Ringing	Styne, Julie	1956	Jeff Moss	I Met A Girl	Uptempo	Baritone	C3	G♭4	Lead	Romantic Lead Male
Bells Are Ringing	Styne, Julie	1956	Jeff Moss	Long Before I Knew You *	Ballad	Baritone	B2	C4	Lead	Romantic Lead Male
Bells Are Ringing	Styne, Julie	1956	Jeff Moss	Just In Time *	Moderate Tempo	Baritone	C#3	D4	Lead	Romantic Lead Male
Bells Are Ringing	Styne, Julie	1956	Jeff Moss	Long Before I Knew You Reprise	Moderate Tempo	Baritone	C3	C4	Lead	Romantic Lead Male
Bells Are Ringing	Styne, Julie	1956	Jeff Moss	Better Than A Dream *	Moderate Tempo	Baritone	E3	D4	Lead	Romantic Lead Male
Bells Are Ringing	Styne, Julie	1956	Sandor	Salzberg	Moderate Tempo	Baritone	E3	G4	Supporting	Character Male
Bells Are Ringing	Styne, Julie	1956	Ella & Jeff	Long Before I Knew You	Ballad	Alto/Bar			Duet	CF/RLM
Bells Are Ringing	Styne, Julie	1956	Ella & Jeff	Just In Time*	Uptempo	Alto/Bar			Duet	CF/RLM
Best Little Whorehouse...	Hall, Carol	1978	Doatsey Mae	Doatsey Mae	Ballad	Alto	G3	C5	Supporting	Character Female
Best Little Whorehouse...	Hall, Carol	1978	Ensemble	Watch Dog Theme*	Moderate Tempo	SATB			Ensemble	Adults
Best Little Whorehouse...	Hall, Carol	1978	Ensemble	Hard Candy Christmas	Moderate Tempo	SA			Ensemble	Adults
Best Little Whorehouse...	Hall, Carol	1978	Ensemble	The Aggie Song	Moderate Tempo	TB			Ensemble	Adults
Best Little Whorehouse...	Hall, Carol	1978	Governor	The Sidestep	Uptempo	Baritone	A2	E4	Supporting	Mature Male
Best Little Whorehouse...	Hall, Carol	1978	Jewel	Twenty-four Hours of Lovin'	Uptempo	Soprano	G3	G5	Supporting	Character Female
Best Little Whorehouse...	Hall, Carol	1978	Jewel	No Lies	Uptempo	Soprano	C4	E5	Supporting	Character Female
Best Little Whorehouse...	Hall, Carol	1978	Melvin P Thorpe	Texas Has A Whorehouse In It	Uptempo	Tenor	B♭2	E4	Supporting	Character Male
Best Little Whorehouse...	Hall, Carol	1978	Mona Stangley	A Lil Ole Bitty Pissant Country Place	Uptempo	Alto	F3	D4	Supporting	Character Female
Best Little Whorehouse...	Hall, Carol	1978	Mona Stangley	Girl You're a Woman	Ballad	Alto	E2	G4	Lead	Character Female
Best Little Whorehouse...	Hall, Carol	1978	Mona Stangley	No Lies	Uptempo	Alto	G3	B4	Lead	Character Female
Best Little Whorehouse...	Hall, Carol	1978	Mona Stangley	Bus From Amarillo	Moderate Tempo	Alto	E3	B♭4	Lead	Character Female
Best Little Whorehouse...	Hall, Carol	1978	Mona's Girl	Hard Candy Christmas	Ballad	Alto	B♭3	C4	Featured Ensemble	Character Ingenue Female
Best Little Whorehouse...	Hall, Carol	1978	Sherriff Ed Earl	Good Old Girl	Ballad	Baritone	G3	F4	Lead	Romantic Lead Male
Best Little Whorehouse...	Hall, Carol	1978	Jewel & Mona	No Lies	Uptempo	Sop/Alto			Duet	CF/CF
Big	Shire, David	1996	Billy Kopecki	Talk To Her	Uptempo	Tenor	F2	B♭3	Supporting	Juvenile Male
Big	Shire, David	1996	Billy Kopecki	It's Time	Uptempo	Tenor	A2	C4	Supporting	Juvenile Male
Big	Shire, David	1996	Josh Baskin-Adult	We're Gonna Be Fine	Ballad	Tenor	B♭2	D4	Lead	Character Ingenue Male
Big	Shire, David	1996	Josh Baskin-Adult	I Want To Go Home	Ballad	Tenor	A♭2	B4	Lead	Character Ingenue Male
Big	Shire, David	1996	Josh Baskin-Adult	Fun	Uptempo	Tenor	C3	G4	Lead	Character Ingenue Male

Shows

Songs by Character Type

* = Music Edit Required
+ = Ethnic Specific

Show	Composer	Year	Role	Song	Tempo	Vocal Type	Range-Bottom	Range-Top	Category	Character Type
Big	Shire, David	1996	Josh Baskin-Adult	Do You Want To Play Games	Uptempo	Tenor	E3	F4	Lead	Character Ingenue Male
Big	Shire, David	1996	Josh Baskin-Adult	Stars, Stars, Stars	Ballad	Tenor	C3	D4	Lead	Character Ingenue Male
Big	Shire, David	1996	Josh Baskin-Adult	Coffee Black	Uptempo	Tenor	C3	F4	Lead	Character Ingenue Male
Big	Shire, David	1996	Josh Baskin-Adult	When You're Big	Uptempo	Tenor	E3	D4	Lead	Character Ingenue Male
Big	Shire, David	1996	Josh Baskin-Adult	Cross The Line	Uptempo	Tenor	E3	D4	Lead	Character Ingenue Male
Big	Shire, David	1996	Josh Baskin-Adult	Big Boy Now	Ballad	Tenor	D♭3	E♭4	Lead	Character Ingenue Male
Big	Shire, David	1996	Josh Baskin-Young	Talk To Her	Uptempo	Tenor	F2	B♭3	Supporting	Juvenile Male
Big	Shire, David	1996	Josh Baskin-Young	Opening	Uptempo	Tenor	A2	B3	Supporting	Juvenile Male
Big	Shire, David	1996	Josh Baskin-Young	I Want To Know	Ballad	Tenor	C3	D4	Supporting	Juvenile Male
Big	Shire, David	1996	Susan Lawrence	Stars, Stars, Stars	Ballad	Soprano	C4	D5	Lead	Romantic Lead Female
Big	Shire, David	1996	Susan Lawrence	One Special Man	Ballad	Soprano	G3	D5	Lead	Romantic Lead Female
Big	Shire, David	1996	Susan Lawrence	Dancing All The Time	Uptempo	Soprano	G3	D5	Lead	Romantic Lead Female
Big	Shire, David	1996	Susan Lawrence	My Secretary's In Love	Uptempo	Soprano	G3	D5	Lead	Romantic Lead Female
Big	Shire, David	1996	Susan Lawrence	Let's Not Move Too Fast	Ballad	Soprano	A3	C5	Lead	Romantic Lead Female
Big	Shire, David	1996	Susan Lawrence	Little Susan Lawrence	Uptempo	Soprano	A♭3	D5	Lead	Romantic Lead Female
Big	Shire, David	1996	Billy & Young Josh	Talk To Her	Moderate Tempo	Tenor/Tenor			Duet	JM/JM
Big	Shire, David	1996	Josh & Susan	Stars, Stars, Stars	Ballad	Tenor/Sop			Duet	CIM/1F
Big	Shire, David	1996	Josh & Susan	I Want To Go Home Reprise	Ballad	Tenor/Sop			Duet	CIM/1F
Big	Shire, David	1996	Josh & Susan	Stars, Stars, Stars Reprise	Ballad	Tenor/Sop			Duet	CIM/1F
Big River	Miller, Roger	1985	Alice's Daughter +	How Blest We Are *	Ballad	Alto	C3	C5	Supporting	Ingenue Female
Big River	Miller, Roger	1985	Duke	The Royal Nonesuch	Uptempo	Baritone	D3	F4	Supporting	Character Male
Big River	Miller, Roger	1985	Ensemble	The Boys	Ballad	TB			Ensemble	Adults
Big River	Miller, Roger	1985	Ensemble	The Crossing	Ballad	SATB			Ensemble	Adults
Big River	Miller, Roger	1985	Ensemble	How Blest We Are	Ballad	SATB			Ensemble	Adults
Big River	Miller, Roger	1985	Huckleberry Finn	Waitin' For The Light To Shine	Ballad	Tenor	G#2	C#4	Lead	Character Ingenue Male
Big River	Miller, Roger	1985	Huckleberry Finn	I, Huckleberry, Me	Uptempo	Tenor	C3	F4	Lead	Character Ingenue Male
Big River	Miller, Roger	1985	Huckleberry Finn	River In The Rain *	Ballad	Tenor	A2	G4	Lead	Character Ingenue Male
Big River	Miller, Roger	1985	Huckleberry Finn	Worlds Apart *	Ballad	Tenor	B2	B4	Lead	Character Ingenue Male
Big River	Miller, Roger	1985	Huckleberry Finn	Waitin' For The Light To Shine Reprise	Uptempo	Tenor	A2	F#4	Lead	Character Ingenue Male
Big River	Miller, Roger	1985	Huckleberry Finn	River in the Rain Reprise *	Ballad	Tenor	A2	D4	Lead	Character Ingenue Male
Big River	Miller, Roger	1985	Huckleberry Finn	Leavin's Not The Only Way To Go	Ballad	Tenor	B2	B3	Lead	Character Ingenue Male
Big River	Miller, Roger	1985	Jim +	Muddy Water	Uptempo	Baritone	B2	F4	Lead	Character Male
Big River	Miller, Roger	1985	Jim +	River In The Rain *	Ballad	Baritone	A2	E4	Lead	Character Male
Big River	Miller, Roger	1985	Jim +	Worlds Apart *	Ballad	Baritone	B2	C4	Lead	Character Male
Big River	Miller, Roger	1985	Jim +	Free At Last	Ballad	Baritone	C3	B4	Lead	Character Male
Big River	Miller, Roger	1985	Mary Jane Wilkes	Leavin's Not The Only Way To Go	Ballad	Soprano	B3	B4	Supporting	Ingenue Female
Big River	Miller, Roger	1985	Mary Jane Wilkes	You Oughta Be Here With Me	Ballad	Soprano	B3	C#5	Supporting	Ingenue Female
Big River	Miller, Roger	1985	Pap	Guv'ment	Moderate Tempo	Baritone	G3	C5	Supporting	Character Male
Big River	Miller, Roger	1985	Slave +	Crossing Over *	Ballad	Alto	C3	E4	Featured Ensemble	Character Female
Big River	Miller, Roger	1985	Tom Sawyer	Hand For The Hog	Uptempo	Tenor			Supporting	Ingenue Male
Big River	Miller, Roger	1985	Young Fool	Arkansas	Uptempo	Baritone	C3	E4	Supporting	Character Male
Big River	Miller, Roger	1996	Huck & Jim	Muddy Water	Ballad	Tenor/Bar			Duet	CIM/CM
Big River	Miller, Roger	1996	Huck & Jim	River In The Rain	Ballad	Tenor/Bar			Duet	CIM/CM
Big River	Miller, Roger	1996	Huck & Jim	Worlds Apart	Ballad	Tenor/Bar			Duet	CIM/CM

Shows

Songs by Character Type

Show	Composer	Year	Role	Song	Tempo	Vocal Type	Range-Bottom	Range-Top	Category	Character Type
Big River	Miller, Roger	1996	Huck & Jim	River In The Rain Reprise	Ballad	Tenor/Bar			Duet	CIM/CM
Billy Elliot	John, Elton	2008	Billy Elliot	Electricity	Ballad	Alto	F3	B4	Lead	Juvenile Male
Billy Elliot	John, Elton	2008	Billy Elliot	Billy's Reply *	Ballad	Alto	G3	D5	Lead	Juvenile Male
Billy Elliot	John, Elton	2008	Billy Elliot	The Letter *	Ballad	Alto	G3	D5	Lead	Juvenile Male
Billy Elliot	John, Elton	2008	Dad	Deep In The Ground *	Ballad	Baritone	Bb2	Eb4	Lead	Paternal
Billy Elliot	John, Elton	2008	Dead Mum	The Letter *	Ballad	Soprano	G3	D5	Supporting	Maternal
Billy Elliot	John, Elton	2008	Grandma	We'd Go Dancing	Moderate Tempo	Alto	F3	G4	Supporting	Mature Female
Billy Elliot	John, Elton	2008	Michael	Expressing Yourself	Uptempo	Alto	G3	B4	Supporting	Juvenile Male
Billy Elliot	John, Elton	2008	Michael	Expressing Yourself Playout	Uptempo	Alto	D4	Bb4	Supporting	Juvenile Male
Billy Elliot	John, Elton	2008	Mrs. Wilkinson	Shine	Moderate Tempo	Alto	Gb3	B4	Lead	Character Female
Billy Elliot	John, Elton	2008	Mrs. Wilkinson	Born To Boogie	Uptempo	Alto	G3	A4	Lead	Character Female
Billy Elliot	John, Elton	2008	Billy & Mum	Dear Billy's Reply	Ballad	Alto/Sop			Duet	JM/M
Billy Elliott	John, Elton	2008	Ensemble	The Stars Look Down	Moderate Tempo	SATB			Ensemble	Adults
Billy Elliott	John, Elton	2008	Ensemble	Merry Christmas, Maggie Thatcher	Uptempo	Unison/2 Part			Ensemble	Adults
Billy Elliott	John, Elton	2008	Ensemble	Once We Were Kings	Moderate Tempo	SATB			Ensemble	Adults
Blood Brothers	Rusell, Willy	1993	Eddie	I'm Not Saying A Word	Moderate Tempo	Tenor	E2	A3	Lead	Ingenue Male
Blood Brothers	Rusell, Willy	1993	Edward	Long Sunday Afternoon *	Ballad	Baritone	E3	C4	Lead	Ingenue Male
Blood Brothers	Rusell, Willy	1993	Mickey	Long Sunday Afternoon *	Ballad	Baritone	D3	E4	Lead	Antagonist Male
Blood Brothers	Rusell, Willy	1993	Mr. Lyons	Miss Jones	Uptempo	Baritone	C3	D4	Supporting	Paternal
Blood Brothers	Rusell, Willy	1993	Mrs. Johnstone	Marilyn Monroe	Moderate Tempo	Alto	A3	A4	Lead	Character Female
Blood Brothers	Rusell, Willy	1993	Mrs. Johnstone	Easy Terms	Ballad	Alto	G3	A4	Lead	Character Female
Blood Brothers	Rusell, Willy	1993	Mrs. Johnstone	Easy Terms Reprise	Ballad	Alto	G3	F4	Lead	Character Female
Blood Brothers	Rusell, Willy	1993	Mrs. Johnstone	Bright New Day	Uptempo	Alto	D4	A4	Lead	Character Female
Blood Brothers	Rusell, Willy	1993	Mrs. Johnstone	Bright New Day Reprise *	Uptempo	Alto	D4	C5	Lead	Character Female
Blood Brothers	Rusell, Willy	1993	Mrs. Johnstone	Marilyn Monroe 2	Moderate Tempo	Alto	A3	A4	Lead	Character Female
Blood Brothers	Rusell, Willy	1993	Mrs. Johnstone	Light Romance	Ballad	Alto	G3	A4	Lead	Character Female
Blood Brothers	Rusell, Willy	1993	Mrs. Johnstone	Tell Me It's Not True	Ballad	Alto	F3	C5	Lead	Character Female
Blood Brothers	Rusell, Willy	1993	Mrs. Johnstone	Marilyn Monroe 3	Ballad	Alto	A3	B4	Lead	Character Female
Blood Brothers	Rusell, Willy	1993	Narrator	Shoes Upon The Table	Uptempo	Tenor	G2	G3	Lead	Character Male
Blood Brothers	Rusell, Willy	1993	Narrator	Shoes Upon The Table Reprise	Uptempo	Tenor	G3	Bb4	Lead	Character Male
Blood Brothers	Rusell, Willy	1993	Narrator	Marilyn Monroe Reprise 1	Moderate Tempo	Tenor	A3	B4	Lead	Character Male
Blood Brothers	Rusell, Willy	1993	Narrator	Madman	Uptempo	Tenor	F2	C4	Lead	Character Male
Blood Brothers	Rusell, Willy	1993	Mrs. Johnston/Mrs. Lyons	My Child	Ballad	Alto/Alto			Duet	CF/M
Blood Brothers	Rusell, Willy	1993	Eddie & Mickey	Long Sunday Afternoon	Uptempo	Tenor/Bar			Duet	IM/AM
Blood Brothers	Rusell, Willy	1993	Eddie & Mickey	My Friend	Uptempo	Tenor/Bar			Duet	IM/AM
Blood Brothers	Rusell, Willy	1993	Eddie & Mickey	That Guy	Moderate Tempo	Tenor/Bar			Duet	IM/AM
Brigadoon	Loewe, Frederick	1947	Charlie Dalrymple	I'll Go Home With Bonnie Jean	Uptempo	Tenor	Bb2	G4	Supporting	Ingenue Male
Brigadoon	Loewe, Frederick	1947	Charlie Dalrymple	Come To Me Bend To me	Ballad	Tenor	D3	G4	Supporting	Ingenue Male
Brigadoon	Loewe, Frederick	1947	Charlie Dalrymple	Go Home Reprise	Uptempo	Tenor	G3	G4	Supporting	Ingenue Male
Brigadoon	Loewe, Frederick	1947	Ensemble	Once In The Highlands	Ballad	SATB			Ensemble	Adults
Brigadoon	Loewe, Frederick	1947	Ensemble	Brigadoon	Ballad	SATB			Ensemble	Adults
Brigadoon	Loewe, Frederick	1947	Ensemble	Jeannie's Packing Up	Uptempo	SA			Ensemble	Adults
Brigadoon	Loewe, Frederick	1947	Ensemble	Down On MacConnachy Square	Uptempo	SATB			Ensemble	Adults
Brigadoon	Loewe, Frederick	1947	Fiona MacLaren	Waitin For My Dearie *	Ballad	Soprano	C4	A5	Lead	Ingenue Female

Songs by Character Type

* = Music Edit Required
+ = Ethnic Specific

Show	Composer	Year	Role	Song	Tempo	Vocal Type	Range-Bottom	Range-Top	Category	Character Type
Brigadoon	Loewe, Frederick	1947	Fiona MacLaren	The Heather On The Hill *	Ballad	Soprano	Bb2	G4	Lead	Ingenue Female
Brigadoon	Loewe, Frederick	1947	Fiona MacLaren	Almost Like Being In Love *	Ballad	Soprano	F4	A5	Lead	Ingenue Female
Brigadoon	Loewe, Frederick	1947	Fiona MacLaren	From This Day On *	Ballad	Soprano	F4	A5	Lead	Ingenue Female
Brigadoon	Loewe, Frederick	1947	Fiona MacLaren	Come To Me Bend To Me Reprise	Ballad	Soprano	D4	G5	Lead	Ingenue Female
Brigadoon	Loewe, Frederick	1947	Fiona MacLaren	The Heather On The Hill Reprise	Ballad	Soprano	C4	F5	Lead	Ingenue Female
Brigadoon	Loewe, Frederick	1947	Fiona MacLaren	From This Day On Reprise *	Ballad	Soprano	Eb4	G5	Lead	Ingenue Female
Brigadoon	Loewe, Frederick	1947	Meg Brockie	The Love Of My Life	Uptempo	Alto	G3	C5	Supporting	Character Ingenue Female
Brigadoon	Loewe, Frederick	1947	Meg Brockie	My Mother's Wedding Day	Uptempo	Alto	C4	F5	Supporting	Character Ingenue Female
Brigadoon	Loewe, Frederick	1947	Tommy Albright	The Heather On The Hill *	Ballad	Baritone	Bb2	F4	Lead	Romantic Lead Male
Brigadoon	Loewe, Frederick	1947	Tommy Albright	Almost Like Being In Love *	Ballad	Baritone	C3	F#4	Lead	Romantic Lead Male
Brigadoon	Loewe, Frederick	1947	Tommy Albright	There But For You Go I	Ballad	Baritone	B2	F4	Lead	Romantic Lead Male
Brigadoon	Loewe, Frederick	1947	Tommy Albright	From This Day On *	Ballad	Baritone	D3	Eb4	Lead	Romantic Lead Male
Brigadoon	Loewe, Frederick	1947	Tommy Albright	From This Day On Reprise *	Ballad	Baritone	Eb3	Eb4	Lead	Romantic Lead Male
Brigadoon	Loewe, Frederick	1947	Fiona & Tommy	The Heather On The Hill	Moderate Tempo	Sop/Bar			Duet	IF/RLM
Brigadoon	Loewe, Frederick	1947	Fiona & Tommy	From This Day On	Ballad	Sop/Bar			Duet	IF/RLM
Bye Bye Birdie	Strouse, Charles	1960	Albert Peterson	Put On A Happy Face	Uptempo	Baritone	B2	D#4	Lead	Character Male
Bye Bye Birdie	Strouse, Charles	1960	Albert Peterson	Baby Talk To me	Ballad	Baritone	C3	F#4	Lead	Character Male
Bye Bye Birdie	Strouse, Charles	1960	Albert Peterson	Rosie *	Moderate Tempo	Baritone	B2	D4	Lead	Character Male
Bye Bye Birdie	Strouse, Charles	1960	Albert Peterson	A Giant Step (TV 1995)	Uptempo	Baritone	D3	F#4	Lead	Character Male
Bye Bye Birdie	Strouse, Charles	1960	Conrad Birdie	Honestly Sincerely	Moderate Tempo	Baritone	Ab2	F#4	Lead	Romantic Antagonist Male
Bye Bye Birdie	Strouse, Charles	1960	Conrad Birdie	One Last Kiss	Moderate Tempo	Baritone	Ab2	F4	Lead	Romantic Antagonist Male
Bye Bye Birdie	Strouse, Charles	1960	Conrad Birdie	Lot of Livin' To Do *	Uptempo	Baritone	Db4	F4	Lead	Romantic Antagonist Male
Bye Bye Birdie	Strouse, Charles	1960	Ensemble	The Telephone Hour	Uptempo	SATB			Ensemble	Teens/Adults
Bye Bye Birdie	Strouse, Charles	1960	Kim MacAfee	How Lovely To Be A Woman	Moderate Tempo	Soprano	D#4	F#4	Lead	Ingenue Female
Bye Bye Birdie	Strouse, Charles	1960	Kim MacAfee	One Boy	Ballad	Soprano	Db4	F5	Lead	Ingenue Female
Bye Bye Birdie	Strouse, Charles	1960	Kim MacAfee	What Did I Ever See In Him *	Uptempo	Soprano	G3	Bb4	Lead	Ingenue Female
Bye Bye Birdie	Strouse, Charles	1960	Kim MacAfee	Lot of Livin' To Do *	Uptempo	Soprano	D4	E5	Lead	Ingenue Female
Bye Bye Birdie	Strouse, Charles	1960	Mae Peterson	A Mother Doesn't Matter Anymore (TV)	Moderate Tempo	Alto	F3	C5	Supporting	Mature Female
Bye Bye Birdie	Strouse, Charles	1960	Rose Grant	An English Teacher	Uptempo	Alto	Gb3	Bb4	Lead	Romantic Lead Female
Bye Bye Birdie	Strouse, Charles	1960	Rose Grant	Let's Settle Down (TV 1995)	Moderate Tempo	Alto	G3	Db4	Lead	Romantic Lead Female
Bye Bye Birdie	Strouse, Charles	1960	Rose Grant	What Did I Ever See In Him *	Uptempo	Alto	G3	Bb4	Lead	Romantic Lead Female
Bye Bye Birdie	Strouse, Charles	1960	Rose Grant	Spanish Rose	Moderate Tempo	Alto	G3	C5	Lead	Romantic Lead Female
Bye Bye Birdie	Strouse, Charles	1960	Rose Grant	What Did I Ever See In Him Reprise	Uptempo	Alto	G3	Bb4	Lead	Romantic Lead Female
Bye Bye Birdie	Strouse, Charles	1960	Rose Grant	An English Teacher Reprise	Uptempo	Alto	Db4	Bb4	Lead	Romantic Lead Female
Bye Bye Birdie	Strouse, Charles	1960	Albert & Rose	An English Teacher	Uptempo	Bar/Alto			Duet	CM/RLF
Bye Bye Birdie	Strouse, Charles	1960	Kim & Rose	What Did I Ever See In Him	Uptempo	Sop/Alto			Duet	IF/RLF
Bye Bye Birdie	Strouse, Charles	1960	Mr. & Mrs. MacAfee	Kids	Uptempo	Bar/Sop			Duet	P/M
Bye Bye Birdie	Strouse, Charles	1960	Albert & Rose	Rosie	Ballad	Bar/Alto			Duet	CM/RLF
Cabaret	Kander, John	1966	Clifford Bradshaw	Perfectly Marvelous *	Uptempo	Tenor	D3	E4	Lead	Romantic Lead Male
Cabaret	Kander, John	1966	Clifford Bradshaw	Why Should I Wake Up?	Moderate Tempo	Tenor	B2	E4	Lead	Romantic Lead Male
Cabaret	Kander, John	1966	Faulein Kost	Married *	Ballad	Alto	F#3	Bb4	Supporting	Character Female

Shows

Songs by Character Type

* = Music Edit Required
+ = Ethnic Specific

Show	Composer	Year	Role	Song	Tempo	Vocal Type	Range-Bottom	Range-Top	Category	Character Type
Cabaret	Kander, John	1966	Faulein Kost	Tomorrow Belongs to Me Reprise *	Moderate Tempo	Alto	A3	Bb4	Supporting	Character Female
Cabaret	Kander, John	1966	Fraulein Scheider	So What?	Uptempo	Alto	F3	G4	Supporting	Mature Female
Cabaret	Kander, John	1966	Fraulein Scheider	What Would You Do	Ballad	Alto	F3	G4	Supporting	Mature Female
Cabaret	Kander, John	1966	Herr Ludwig	Tomorrow Belongs to Me Reprise *	Moderate Tempo	Baritone	C3	D4	Supporting	Character Male
Cabaret	Kander, John	1966	Herr Schultz	Meeskite	Uptempo	Tenor	B2	Ab4	Supporting	Character Male
Cabaret	Kander, John	1966	Herr Schultz	Married *	Ballad	Baritone	D3	F4	Supporting	Mature Male
Cabaret	Kander, John	1966	Herr Schultz	Married Reprise	Ballad	Baritone	C3	D4	Supporting	Mature Male
Cabaret	Kander, John	1966	Master of Ceremonies	Wilkomen	Uptempo	Tenor	E3	G4	Lead	Character Male
Cabaret	Kander, John	1966	Master of Ceremonies	Two Ladies	Uptempo	Tenor	G3	G4	Lead	Character Male
Cabaret	Kander, John	1966	Master of Ceremonies	The Money Song	Moderate Tempo	Tenor	Eb2	A4	Lead	Character Male
Cabaret	Kander, John	1966	Master of Ceremonies	If You Could See Her	Uptempo	Tenor	D3	F4	Lead	Character Male
Cabaret	Kander, John	1966	Nazi Youth	Tomorrow Belongs to Me	Ballad	Tenor	F3	F#4	Featured Ensemble	Ingenue Male
Cabaret	Kander, John	1966	Nazi Youth	Tomorrow Belongs to Me	Ballad	Soprano	F4	F#5	Featured Ensemble	Juvenile Male
Cabaret	Kander, John	1966	Sally Bowles	Don't Tell Mama	Uptempo	Alto	A3	A4	Lead	Romantic Lead Female
Cabaret	Kander, John	1966	Sally Bowles	Perfectly Marvelous *	Uptempo	Alto	F#3	A4	Lead	Romantic Lead Female
Cabaret	Kander, John	1966	Sally Bowles	Maybe This Time	Ballad	Alto	F#3	C5	Lead	Romantic Lead Female
Cabaret	Kander, John	1966	Sally Bowles	Cabaret	Uptempo	Alto	E3	B4	Lead	Romantic Lead Female
Cabaret	Kander, John	1966	Clifford & Sally	Perfeclty Marvelous	Uptempo	Tenor/Alto			Duet	RLM/CIF
Cabaret	Kander, John	1966	F. Schneider & H. Schultz	It Couldn't Please Me More	Moderate Tempo	Alto/Bar			Duet	MF/MM
Cabaret	Kander, John	1966	Clifford & Sally	Why Should I Wake Up?	Moderate Tempo	Tenor/Alto			Duet	RLM/CIF
Cabaret	Kander, John	1966	F. Schneider & H. Schultz	Married	Ballad	Alto/Bar			Duet	MF/MM
Cabaret	Kander, John	1972	Sally Bowles	Mein Herr	Moderate Tempo	Alto	F3	B4	Lead	Romantic Lead Female
Cabaret	Kander, John	1997	Master of Ceremonies	I Don't Care Much	Ballad	Tenor	D3	F4	Lead	Character Male
Call Me Madam	Berlin, Irving	1950	Ensemble	Mrs. Sally Adams	Uptempo	SATB			Ensemble	Adults
Call Me Madam	Berlin, Irving	1950	Sally Adams	The Hostess With The Mostess	Uptempo	Alto	A3	B4	Lead	Romantic Antagonist Female
Call Me Madam	Berlin, Irving	1950	Sally Adams	The Hostess With The Mostess Encore	Uptempo	Alto	A3	B4	Lead	Romantic Antagonist Female
Call Me Madam	Berlin, Irving	1950	Sally Adams	Washington Square Dance	Uptempo	Alto	Bb3	C5	Lead	Romantic Antagonist Female
Call Me Madam	Berlin, Irving	1950	Cosmo Constantine	Lichtenburg*	Moderate Tempo	Baritone	Bb2	D4	Lead	Romantic Lead Male
Call Me Madam	Berlin, Irving	1950	Ensemble	Lichtenburg	Moderate Tempo	SATB			Ensemble	Adults
Call Me Madam	Berlin, Irving	1950	Sally Adams	Can You Use Any Money Today	Uptempo	Alto	Bb3	C5	Lead	Romantic Antagonist Female
Call Me Madam	Berlin, Irving	1950	Cosmo Constantine	Marrying For Love*	Ballad	Baritone	G2	C4	Lead	Romantic Lead Male
Call Me Madam	Berlin, Irving	1950	Sally Adams	Marrying For Love*	Ballad	Alto	F3	Bb4	Lead	Romantic Antagonist Female
Call Me Madam	Berlin, Irving	1950	Cosmo & Sally	Marrying For Love	Ballad	Bar/Alto			Duet	RLM/RAF
Call Me Madam	Berlin, Irving	1950	Princess Maria	The Ocarina*	Moderate Tempo	Alto	C4	D5	Lead	Ingenue Female
Call Me Madam	Berlin, Irving	1950	Ensemble	The Ocarina	Moderate Tempo	SATB			Ensemble	Adults
Call Me Madam	Berlin, Irving	1950	Kenneth Gibson	It's A Lovely Day Today*	Moderate Tempo	Baritone	C3	D4	Lead	Character Male
Call Me Madam	Berlin, Irving	1950	Princess Maria	It's A Lovely Day Today*	Moderate Tempo	Alto	A3	B4	Lead	Ingenue Female
Call Me Madam	Berlin, Irving	1950	Kenneth & Maria	It's A Lovely Day Today	Moderate Tempo	Bar/Alto			Duet	CM/IF
Call Me Madam	Berlin, Irving	1950	Ensemble	It's A Lovely Day Today Encore	Moderate Tempo	SATB			Ensemble	Adults
Call Me Madam	Berlin, Irving	1950	Kenneth Gibson	The Best Thing For You	Uptempo	Baritone	D3	D4	Lead	Character Male
Call Me Madam	Berlin, Irving	1950	Sally Adams	It's A Lovely Day Today Reprise	Moderate Tempo	Alto	A3	C5	Lead	Romantic Antagonist Female
Call Me Madam	Berlin, Irving	1950	Ensemble	Lichtenburg Act II	Moderate Tempo	SATB			Ensemble	Adults
Call Me Madam	Berlin, Irving	1950	Sally Adams	Something To Dance About	Moderate Tempo	Alto	Bb3	C5	Lead	Romantic Antagonist Female

Shows

Songs by Character Type

* = Music Edit Required
\+ = Ethnic Specific

Show	Composer	Year	Role	Song	Tempo	Vocal Type	Range-Bottom	Range-Top	Category	Character Type
Call Me Madam	Berlin, Irving	1950	Kenneth Gibson	Once Upon A Time Today	Moderate Tempo	Baritone	E3	F4	Lead	Character Male
Call Me Madam	Berlin, Irving	1950	Ensemble	They Like Ike	Uptempo	TBB			Ensemble	Adults
Call Me Madam	Berlin, Irving	1950	Kenneth Gibson	It's A Lovely Day Today Reprise 2*	Moderate Tempo	Baritone	C3	D4	Lead	Character Male
Call Me Madam	Berlin, Irving	1950	Princess Maria	It's A Lovely Day Today Reprise 2*	Moderate Tempo	Alto	C4	D5	Lead	Ingenue Female
Call Me Madam	Berlin, Irving	1950	Kenneth & Maria	It's A Lovely Day Today Reprise 2	Moderate Tempo	Bar/Alto			Duet	CM/IF
Call Me Madam	Berlin, Irving	1950	Kenneth Gibson	You're Just In Love*	Uptempo	Baritone	D3	F4	Lead	Character Male
Call Me Madam	Berlin, Irving	1950	Sally Adams	You're Just In Love*	Uptempo	Alto	D4	C5	Lead	Romantic Antagonist Female
Call Me Madam	Berlin, Irving	1950	Kenneth & Sally	You're Just In Love	Uptempo	Bar/Alto			Duet	CM/RAF
Call Me Madam	Berlin, Irving	1950	Sally Adams	The Best Thing For You Reprise	Moderate Tempo	Alto	Bb3	Cb5	Lead	Romantic Antagonist Female
Call Me Madam	Berlin, Irving	1950	Ensemble	Mrs. Sally Adams Reprise	Uptempo	SATB			Ensemble	Adults
Call Me Madam	Berlin, Irving	1950	Ensemble	You're Just In Love Finale	Moderate Tempo	SATB			Ensemble	Adults
Camelot	Loewe, Frederick	1960	King Arthur	I Wonder What The King Is Doing Tonig	Uptempo	Baritone	Bb2	C4	Lead	Romantic Lead Male
Camelot	Loewe, Frederick	1960	Guenevere	The Simple Joys Of Maidenhood	Moderate Tempo	Soprano	B3	D#5	Lead	Romantic Lead Female
Camelot	Loewe, Frederick	1960	King Arthur	Camelot*	Uptempo	Baritone	C3	D4	Lead	Romantic Lead Male
Camelot	Loewe, Frederick	1960	Guenevere	Camelot*	Uptempo	Soprano	C4	D5	Lead	Romantic Lead Female
Camelot	Loewe, Frederick	1960	Arthur & Guenevere	Camelot	Uptempo	Bar/Sop			Duet	RLM/RLF
Camelot	Loewe, Frederick	1960	Nimue	Follow Me*	Moderate Tempo	Soprano	C#4	F#5	Lead	Romantic Lead Female
Camelot	Loewe, Frederick	1960	Ensemble	Follow Me	Moderate Tempo	SSAA			Supporting	Adults
Camelot	Loewe, Frederick	1960	Lancelot Du Lac	C'est Moi	Uptempo	Baritone	B2	D4	Lead	Romantic Lead Male
Camelot	Loewe, Frederick	1960	Guenevere	The Lusty Month Of May*	Uptempo	Soprano	D4	A5	Lead	Romantic Lead Female
Camelot	Loewe, Frederick	1960	Ensemble	The Lusty Month Of May	Uptempo	SATB			Ensemble	Adults
Camelot	Loewe, Frederick	1960	King Arthur	How To Handle A Woman*	Uptempo	Baritone	A2	D4	Lead	Romantic Lead Male
Camelot	Loewe, Frederick	1960	Ensemble	The Jousts	Uptempo	SATB			Ensemble	Adults
Camelot	Loewe, Frederick	1960	Guenevere	Before I Gaze At You Again	Moderate Tempo	Soprano	C4	Eb5	Lead	Romantic Lead Female
Camelot	Loewe, Frederick	1960	Lancelot Du Lac	If Ever I would Leave You	Ballad	Baritone	A2	D4	Lead	Romantic Lead Male
Camelot	Loewe, Frederick	1960	Mordred	The Seven Deadly Virtues	Uptempo	Baritone	C3	D4	Lead	Antagonist Male
Camelot	Loewe, Frederick	1960	Guenevere	What Do The Simple Folk Do?*	Moderate Tempo	Soprano	Bb3	E5	Lead	Romantic Lead Female
Camelot	Loewe, Frederick	1960	King Arthur	What Do The Simple Folk Do?*	Moderate Tempo	Baritone	Bb2	E4	Lead	Romantic Lead Male
Camelot	Loewe, Frederick	1960	Arthur & Guenevere	What Do The Simple Fold Do?	Moderate Tempo	Bar/Sop			Duet	RLM/RLF
Camelot	Loewe, Frederick	1960	Guenevere	I Loved You Once In Silence	Ballad	Soprano	Db4	Eb5	Lead	Romantic Lead Female
Camelot	Loewe, Frederick	1960	Ensemble	Fie On Goodness!	Uptempo	TTBB			Ensemble	Adults
Camelot	Loewe, Frederick	1960	A Man	Guenevere*	Uptempo	Baritone	D3	D4	Featured Ensemble	Adults
Camelot	Loewe, Frederick	1960	Ensemble	Guenevere	Uptempo	SATB			Ensemble	Adults
Camelot	Loewe, Frederick	1960	Ensemble	Finalte Ultimo	Moderate Tempo	SATB			Ensemble	Adults
Camelot	Loewe, Frederick	1960	King Arthur	Finalte Ultimo	Moderate Tempo	Baritone	Bb2	C4	Lead	Romantic Lead Male
Candide	Bernstein, Leonard	1956	Ensemble	Voltaire Chorale	Moderate Tempo	SATB			Ensemble	Adults
Candide	Bernstein, Leonard	1956	Candide	Life Is Happiness Indeed*	Moderate Tempo	Tenor	F3	G4	Lead	Ingenue Male
Candide	Bernstein, Leonard	1956	Maximillion	Life Is Happiness Indeed*	Moderate Tempo	Tenor	D3	F4	Lead	Romantic Lead Male
Candide	Bernstein, Leonard	1956	Cunegonde	Life Is Happiness Indeed	Moderate Tempo	Soprano	F4	C6	Lead	Ingenue Female
Candide	Bernstein, Leonard	1956	Ensemble	The Best Of All Possible Worlds	Uptempo	SATB			Ensemble	Adults
Candide	Bernstein, Leonard	1956	Ensemble	Universal Good	Ballad	SATB			Ensemble	Adults
Candide	Bernstein, Leonard	1956	Candide & Cunegonde	Oh Happy We	Uptempo	Tenor/Sop			Duet	IM/IF

* = Music Edit Required
+ = Ethnic Specific

Show	Composer	Year	Role	Song	Tempo	Vocal Type	Range-Bottom	Range-Top	Category	Character Type
Candide	Bernstein, Leonard	1956	Candide	It Must Be So	Ballad	Tenor	D3	E4	Lead	Ingenue Male
Candide	Bernstein, Leonard	1956	Candide	Candide's Lament	Ballad	Tenor	C3	F4	Lead	Ingenue Male
Candide	Bernstein, Leonard	1956	Dr. Pangloss	Dear Boy	Uptempo	Tenor	Bb2	F#4	Lead	Antagonist Male
Candide	Bernstein, Leonard	1956	Cunegonde	Glitter And Be Gay	Moderate Tempo	Soprano	B2	E6	Lead	Ingenue Female
Candide	Bernstein, Leonard	1956	Ensemble	Auto-da-fe	Moderate Tempo	SATB			Ensemble	Adults
Candide	Bernstein, Leonard	1956	Candide & Cunegonde	You Were Dead, You Know	Moderate Tempo	Tenor/Sop			Duet	IM/IF
Candide	Bernstein, Leonard	1956	Old Lady	I Am Easily Assimilated*	Moderate Tempo	Soprano	D4	A5	Lead	Mature Female
Candide	Bernstein, Leonard	1956	Ensemble	I Am Easily Assimilated	Moderate Tempo	SATB			Ensemble	Adults
Candide	Bernstein, Leonard	1956	Ensemble	Quartet Finale	Moderate Tempo	SATB			Ensemble	Adults
Candide	Bernstein, Leonard	1956	Cunegonde & Old Lady	We Are Women	Uptempo	Sop/Sop			Duet	IF/MF
Candide	Bernstein, Leonard	1956	Governor	My Love*	Moderate Tempo	Tenor	C3	A4	Lead	Romantic Lead Male
Candide	Bernstein, Leonard	1956	Cunegonde & Governor	My Love	Moderate Tempo	Sop/Tenor			Duet	IF/RLM
Candide	Bernstein, Leonard	1956	Ensemble	Alleluia	Moderate Tempo	SATB			Ensemble	Adults
Candide	Bernstein, Leonard	1956	Ensemble	Ballad of Eldorado	Moderate Tempo	SATB			Ensemble	Adults
Candide	Bernstein, Leonard	1956	Vanderdenur	Bon Voyage*	Uptempo	Tenor	C3	Bb4	Supporting	Antagonist Male
Candide	Bernstein, Leonard	1956	Ensemble	Bon Voyage	Uptempo	SATB			Ensemble	Adults
Candide	Bernstein, Leonard	1956	Candide	It Must Be Me	Ballad	Tenor	D3	E4	Lead	Ingenue Male
Candide	Bernstein, Leonard	1956	Martin	Words, Words, Words	Moderate Tempo	Tenor	A2	F4	Supporting	Mature Male
Candide	Bernstein, Leonard	1956	Ensemble	Money, Money, Money	Moderate Tempo	SATB			Ensemble	Adults
Candide	Bernstein, Leonard	1956	Dr. Pangloss	The Venice Gavotte*	Uptempo	Tenor	C3	F4	Lead	Antagonist Male
Candide	Bernstein, Leonard	1956	Ensemble	The Venice Gavotte	Uptempo	SATB			Ensemble	Adults
Candide	Bernstein, Leonard	1956	Candide	Nothing More Than This	Moderate Tempo	Tenor	D3	F#4	Lead	Ingenue Male
Candide	Bernstein, Leonard	1956	Ensemble	What's The Use?	Uptempo	SATB			Ensemble	Adults
Candide	Bernstein, Leonard	1956	Ensemble	The Kings' Barcarolle	Moderate Tempo	TTBBB			Ensemble	Adults
Candide	Bernstein, Leonard	1956	Candide	Universal Good Reprise*	Ballad	Tenor	Db3	Db4	Lead	Ingenue Male
Candide	Bernstein, Leonard	1956	Ensemble	Universal Good Reprise	Ballad	SATB			Ensemble	Adults
Candide	Bernstein, Leonard	1956	Ensemble	Make Our Garden Grow	Moderate Tempo	SATB			Ensemble	Adults
Caroline or Change	Jeanine Tesori	2004	Caroline+ & Washing Machine	16 Feet Beneath The Sea (10-49)	Ballad	Alto/Alto			Duet	AF/CF
Caroline or Change	Jeanine Tesori	2004	Caroline+ & Noah	Gonna Pass Me a Law	Moderate Tempo	Alto/Alto			Duet	AF/JM
Caroline or Change	Jeanine Tesori	2004	Ensemble	Santa Comin' Caroline	Uptempo	SSAA				Ensemble
Caroline or Change	Jeanine Tesori	2004	Ensemble	1943	Moderate Tempo	SSAA				Ensemble
Caroline or Change	Jeanine Tesori	2004	Ensemble	Little Reward	Uptempo	SSAA				Ensemble
Caroline Or Change	Jeanine Tesori	2004	Caroline+ & Rose	Mr. Gellman's Shirt	Moderate Tempo	Alto/Alto			Duet	AF/CF
Caroline Or Change	Jeanine Tesori	2004	Caroline+ & Dotty	Sunday Morning	Ballad	Alto/Alto			Duet	AF/CF
Caroline Or Change	Jeanine Tesori	2004	Ensemble	Laundry Quintet	Moderate Tempo	SAT			Ensemble	Adults
Caroline Or Change	Jeanine Tesori	2004	Ensemble	Laundry Quintet Finish	Moderate Tempo	SAT			Ensemble	Adults
Caroline, Or Change	Jeanine Tesori	2004	Caroline Thibodeaux +	16 Feet Beneath the Sea (10-49)	Ballad	Alto	B3	D4	Lead	Antagonist Female
Caroline, Or Change	Jeanine Tesori	2004	Caroline Thibodeaux +	I Got Four Kids (ms 1-114)	Moderate Tempo	Alto	B3	Bb4	Lead	Antagonist Female
Caroline, Or Change	Jeanine Tesori	2004	Caroline Thibodeaux +	Lot's Wife (ms 67-151)	Moderate Tempo	Alto	F3	Eb5	Lead	Antagonist Female
Caroline, Or Change	Jeanine Tesori	2004	Caroline Thibodeaux +	Gonna Pass Me A Law (ms 1-37)	Ballad	Alto	G3	G4	Lead	Antagonist Female
Caroline, Or Change	Jeanine Tesori	2004	Caroline Thibodeaux +	Noah Go To Sleep (ms 60-98)	Moderate Tempo	Alto	Gb3	Db5	Lead	Antagonist Female
Caroline, Or Change	Jeanine Tesori	2004	Caroline Thibodeaux +	Underwater (ms 43-74)	Ballad	Alto	G3	F4	Lead	Antagonist Female
Caroline, Or Change	Jeanine Tesori	2004	Dotty Moffett +	Lot's Wife (ms 6-42)	Moderate Tempo	Alto	G3	B4	Supporting	Character Female

Shows

Songs by Character Type

Show	Composer	Year	Role	Song	Tempo	Vocal Type	Range-Bottom	Range-Top	Category	Character Type
Caroline, Or Change	Tesori, Jeanine	2004	Emmie Thibodeaux +	Duets: Nigh Mamma (ms 71-89)	Ballad	Soprano	F#4	C5	Supporting	Ingenue Female
Caroline, Or Change	Tesori, Jeanine	2004	Emmie Thibodeaux +	I Hate The Bus (ms 6-36)	Ballad	Soprano	G3	F#5	Supporting	Ingenue Female
Caroline, Or Change	Tesori, Jeanine	2004	Emmie Thibodeaux +	Epilogue-Emmie's Dream (ms 9-73)	Uptempo	Soprano	Ab3	Db4	Supporting	Ingenue Female
Caroline, Or Change	Tesori, Jeanine	2004	Emmie Thibodeaux +	The Bus (ms 71-89)	Ballad	Soprano	Bb2	Bb4	Supporting	Ingenue Female
Caroline, Or Change	Tesori, Jeanine	2004	Mr. Stopnick	A Twenty Dollar Bill and Why (ms 41-78	Ballad	Baritone	C3	F4	Supporting	Mature Male
Caroline, Or Change	Tesori, Jeanine	2004	Noah Gellman	Noah Downstairs (ms 1-46)	Moderate Tempo	Alto	Bb3	Cb5	Lead	Juvenile Male
Caroline, Or Change	Tesori, Jeanine	2004	Rose Stopnick Gellman	Long Distance (ms 1-74)	Moderate Tempo	Alto	Bb3	D5	Supporting	Character Female
Caroline, Or Change	Tesori, Jeanine	2004	Rose Stopnick Gellman	Noah Has A Problem (ms 6-59)	Uptempo	Alto	Ab3	Cb5	Supporting	Character Female
Caroline, Or Change	Tesori, Jeanine	2004	Rose Stopnick Gellman	Rose Recovers (ms 3-27)	Ballad	Alto	G3	C5	Supporting	Character Female
Caroline, Or Change	Tesori, Jeanine	2004	Rose Stopnick Gellman	Inside/Out (ms 11-54)	Uptempo	Alto	C4	D5	Supporting	Character Female
Caroline, Or Change	Tesori, Jeanine	2004	Stuart Gellman	Moon, Emmie, Stuart Trio (ms 6-76)	Ballad	Baritone	Bb2	Eb4	Supporting	Paternal
Caroline, Or Change	Tesori, Jeanine	2004	Stuart Gellman	There Is No God, Noah (ms 1-31)	Moderate Tempo	Baritone	E3	C#4	Supporting	Paternal
Caroline, Or Change	Tesori, Jeanine	2004	The Dryer +	The Dryer (ms 1-24)	Moderate Tempo	Tenor	Bb2	C5	Supporting	Character Male
Caroline, Or Change	Tesori, Jeanine	2004	The Moon +	Moon Change (ms 1-12)	Ballad	Tenor	Bb2	G4	Supporting	Character Male
Caroline, Or Change	Tesori, Jeanine	2004	The Radio +	No One Waitin' (ms 1-18)	Alto	Alto	G3	D5	Supporting	Character Female
Carousel	Rodgers, Richard	1945	Billy Bigelow	If I Loved You *	Ballad	Baritone	Bb2	Gb4	Lead	Romantic Antagonist Male
Carousel	Rodgers, Richard	1945	Billy Bigelow	Soliloquy	Moderate Tempo	Baritone	B2	G4	Lead	Romantic Antagonist Male
Carousel	Rodgers, Richard	1945	Billy Bigelow	If I Loved You Reprise	Ballad	Baritone	Eb3	Gb4	Lead	Romantic Antagonist Male
Carousel	Rodgers, Richard	1945	Billy Bigelow	The Highest Judge Of All	Moderate Tempo	Baritone	D3	G4	Lead	Romantic Antagonist Male
Carousel	Rodgers, Richard	1945	Carrie Pipperidge	You're A Queer One Julie Jordan	Moderate Tempo	Alto	D4	E5	Lead	Character Ingenue Female
Carousel	Rodgers, Richard	1945	Carrie Pipperidge	When I Marry Mr. Snow	Ballad	Alto	D4	F5	Lead	Character Ingenue Female
Carousel	Rodgers, Richard	1945	Carrie Pipperidge	When I Marry Mr. Snow Reprise	Ballad	Alto	F#3	A4	Lead	Character Ingenue Female
Carousel	Rodgers, Richard	1945	Carrie Pipperidge	When The Children Are Asleep *	Moderate Tempo	Alto	Eb3	C5	Lead	Character Ingenue Female
Carousel	Rodgers, Richard	1945	Enoch Snow	When I Marry Mr. Snow Reprise	Ballad	Tenor	C4	D5	Lead	Character Ingenue Male
Carousel	Rodgers, Richard	1945	Enoch Snow	When The Children Are Asleep *	Moderate Tempo	Tenor	Eb3	C5	Lead	Character Ingenue Male
Carousel	Rodgers, Richard	1945	Enoch Snow	Geranium In The Window *	Ballad	Tenor	D3	F#4	Lead	Character Ingenue Male
Carousel	Rodgers, Richard	1945	Ensemble	June Is Bustin' Out All Over	Uptempo	Unison			Ensemble	Adults
Carousel	Rodgers, Richard	1945	Ensemble	You'll Never Walk Along Reprise	Ballad	SATB			Ensemble	Children/Adults
Carousel	Rodgers, Richard	1945	Jigger Craigin	Stonecutter Cut It On Stone Reprise	Uptempo	Baritone	C3	F4	Lead	Romantic Antagonist Male
Carousel	Rodgers, Richard	1945	Julie Jordan	If I Loved You *	Ballad	Soprano	C4	Gb5	Lead	Character Ingenue Female
Carousel	Rodgers, Richard	1945	Julie Jordan	What's The Use In Wonderin'	Ballad	Soprano	C4	F5	Lead	Character Ingenue Female
Carousel	Rodgers, Richard	1945	Nettie Fowler	June Is Bustin' Out All Over *	Uptempo	Soprano	D4	G5	Lead	Mature Female
Carousel	Rodgers, Richard	1945	Nettie Fowler	You'll Never Walk Alone	Moderate Tempo	Soprano	C4	G5	Lead	Mature Female
Carousel	Rodgers, Richard	1945	Nettie Fowler	June Is Bustin Out All Over Reprise	Uptempo	Soprano	E4	E5	Lead	Mature Female
Carousel	Rodgers, Richard	1945	Nettie Fowler	June...Finale Act One	Uptempo	Soprano	E4	E5	Lead	Mature Female
Carousel	Rodgers, Richard	1945	Carrie & Julie	You're A Queer One Julie Jordan	Uptempo	Alto/Sop			Duet	CIF/CIF
Carousel	Rodgers, Richard	1945	Billy & Julie	If I Loved You	Ballad	Bar/Sop			Duet	RAM/CIF
Carousel	Rodgers, Richard	1945	Carrie & Enoch	When The Children Are Asleep	Moderate Tempo	Alto/Tenor			Duet	CIF/CM
Cats	Webber, Andrew Lloyd	1981	Asparagus	Gus: The Theatre Cat	Ballad	Baritone	A2	D4	Supporting	Mature Male
Cats	Webber, Andrew Lloyd	1981	Bombalurina	Macavity	Moderate Tempo	Alto	A3	C5	Supporting	Romantic Lead Female
Cats	Webber, Andrew Lloyd	1981	Bustopher Jones	Bustopher Jones *	Uptempo	Baritone	C3	C4	Supporting	Mature Male
Cats	Webber, Andrew Lloyd	1981	Demeter	Macavity	Moderate Tempo	Alto	A3	C5	Supporting	Romantic Lead Female

Shows

Songs by Character Type

* = Music Edit Required
\+ = Ethnic Specific

Show	Composer	Year	Role	Song	Tempo	Vocal Type	Range-Bottom	Range-Top	Category	Character Type
Cats	Webber, Andrew Lloyd	1981	Ensemble	Jellicle Songs for Jellicle Cats	Moderate Tempo	SATB			Ensemble	Adults
Cats	Webber, Andrew Lloyd	1981	Ensemble	The Journey to the Heaviside Layer	Uptempo	SATB			Ensemble	Adults
Cats	Webber, Andrew Lloyd	1981	Grizabella	Grizabella the Glamour Cat	Ballad	Alto	G3	C5	Lead	Mature Female
Cats	Webber, Andrew Lloyd	1981	Grizabella	Memory	Ballad	Alto	G3	E5	Lead	Mature Female
Cats	Webber, Andrew Lloyd	1981	Jellylorum	Gus: The Theatre Cat	Ballad	Soprano	A3	D5	Supporting	Mature Female
Cats	Webber, Andrew Lloyd	1981	Jennyanydots	Bustopher Jones *	Uptempo	Soprano	B3	F5	Supporting	Ingenue Female
Cats	Webber, Andrew Lloyd	1981	Mr. Mistoffolees	Mr. Mistoffolees	Uptempo	Baritone	C3	E♭4	Supporting	Mature Male
Cats	Webber, Andrew Lloyd	1981	Mungojerrie	Mongojerrie and Rumpleteezer	Uptempo	Baritone	E3	E4	Supporting	Ingenue Male
Cats	Webber, Andrew Lloyd	1981	Munkustrap	The Old Gumbie Cat	Moderate Tempo	Baritone	E3	F4	Lead	Romantic Lead Male
Cats	Webber, Andrew Lloyd	1981	Munkustrap	Old Deuteronomy *	Ballad	Tenor	B2	G4	Lead	Romantic Lead Male
Cats	Webber, Andrew Lloyd	1981	Old Deuteronomy	Old Deuteronomy *	Ballad	Tenor	B2	G4	Lead	Mature Male
Cats	Webber, Andrew Lloyd	1981	Old Deuteronomy	The Moments of Happiness	Ballad	Tenor	B3	G5	Lead	Mature Male
Cats	Webber, Andrew Lloyd	1981	Old Deuteronomy	The Ad-Dressing of Cats	Moderate Tempo	Tenor	B♭2	G4	Lead	Mature Male
Cats	Webber, Andrew Lloyd	1981	Rum Tum Tugger	Rum Tum Tugger	Uptempo	Baritone	B2	F4	Supporting	Character Male
Cats	Webber, Andrew Lloyd	1981	Rum Tum Tugger	Old Deuteronomy *	Ballad	Baritone	B2	G4	Lead	Character Male
Cats	Webber, Andrew Lloyd	1981	Rum Tum Tugger	Mr. Mistoffolees	Uptempo	Baritone	C3	E♭4	Lead	Character Male
Cats	Webber, Andrew Lloyd	1981	Rumpleteezer	Mongojerrie and Rumpleteezer	Uptempo	Alto	E4	G5	Supporting	Ingenue Female
Cats	Webber, Andrew Lloyd	1981	Skimbleshanks	Skimbleshanks	Uptempo	Tenor	A2	F4	Supporting	Ingenue Male
Cats	Webber, Andrew Lloyd	1981	Mungojerrie & Rumpleteezer	Mongojerrie and Rumpleteezer	Uptempo	Bar/Alto			Duet	IM/IF
Cats	Webber, Andrew Lloyd	1981	Asparagus & Jellylorum	Gus: The Theatre Cat	Ballad	Bar/Sop			Duet	MM/MF
Cats	Webber, Andrew Lloyd	1981	Mistoffolees & Rum Tum Tigge	Mr. Mistoffolees	Uptempo	Bar/Bar			Duet	IM/CM
Cats	Webber, Andrew Lloyd	1981	Grizabella & Victoria	Memory Reprise	Ballad	Alto/Sop			Duet	MF/IF
Chess	Andersson and Ulvaeus	1988	Anatoly	Where I Want To Be	Moderate Tempo	Tenor	E3	G4	Lead	Romantic Lead Male
Chess	Andersson and Ulvaeus	1988	Anatoly	Anthem	Moderate Tempo	Tenor	C3	G4	Lead	Romantic Lead Male
Chess	Andersson and Ulvaeus	1988	Anatoly	You and I	Ballad	Tenor	G2	G4	Lead	Romantic Lead Male
Chess	Andersson and Ulvaeus	1988	Anatoly	You and I Reprise	Ballad	Tenor	G3	F5	Lead	Romantic Lead Male
Chess	Andersson and Ulvaeus	1988	Arbiter	The Story of Chess	Moderate Tempo	Tenor	B2	G4	Supporting	Antagonist Male
Chess	Andersson and Ulvaeus	1988	Arbiter	The Arbiter	Uptempo	Tenor	E3	A4	Supporting	Antagonist Male
Chess	Andersson and Ulvaeus	1988	Arbiter	The Arbiter Reprise	Uptempo	Tenor	E3	A4	Supporting	Antagonist Male
Chess	Andersson and Ulvaeus	1988	Ensemble	Hymn of Chess	Ballad	SATB			Ensemble	Adults
Chess	Andersson and Ulvaeus	1988	Ensemble	Hungarian Folk Song	Moderate Tempo	SATB			Ensemble	Adults
Chess	Andersson and Ulvaeus	1988	Florence	Someone Else's Story	Ballad	Alto	F3	C5	Lead	Character Ingenue Female
Chess	Andersson and Ulvaeus	1988	Florence	Nobody's Side	Uptempo	Alto	E3	E4	Lead	Character Ingenue Female
Chess	Andersson and Ulvaeus	1988	Florence	Heaven Help My Heart	Ballad	Alto	A3	A4	Lead	Character Ingenue Female
Chess	Andersson and Ulvaeus	1988	Florence	You and I*	Ballad	Alto	G3	E♭5	Lead	Character Ingenue Female
Chess	Andersson and Ulvaeus	1988	Florence	I Know Him So Well	Ballad	Alto	F3	D5	Lead	Character Ingenue Female
Chess	Andersson and Ulvaeus	1988	Florence	You and I Reprise	Ballad	Alto	G2	G4	Lead	Character Ingenue Female
Chess	Andersson and Ulvaeus	1988	Florence	Anthem Reprise	Moderate Tempo	Alto	A♭3	D5	Lead	Character Ingenue Female
Chess	Andersson and Ulvaeus	1988	Freddie	Endgame*	Uptempo	Tenor	C#3	G#4	Lead	Romantic Antagonist Male
Chess	Andersson and Ulvaeus	1988	Freddie	Florence Quits	Uptempo	Tenor	B2	B4	Lead	Romantic Antagonist Male
Chess	Andersson and Ulvaeus	1988	Freddie	One Night In Bangkok	Uptempo	Tenor	F3	A4	Lead	Romantic Antagonist Male
Chess	Andersson and Ulvaeus	1988	Freddie	Pity The Child	Ballad	Tenor	B♭2	D♭5	Lead	Romantic Antagonist Male
Chess	Andersson and Ulvaeus	1988	Molokov	The Soviet Machine	Uptempo	Baritone	A2	D4	Supporting	Mature Male

Shows

Songs by Character Type

* = Music Edit Required
+ = Ethnic Specific

Show	Composer	Year	Role	Song	Tempo	Vocal Type	Range-Bottom	Range-Top	Category	Character Type
Chess	Andersson and Ulvaeus	1988	Svetlana	You and I*	Ballad	Soprano	G3	Eb5	Supporting	Character Female
Chess	Andersson and Ulvaeus	1988	Svetlana	I Know Him So Well	Ballad	Soprano	F3	D5	Supporting	Character Female
Chess	Andersson and Ulvaeus	1988	Florence & Freddie	Commie Newpapers	Uptempo	Alto/Tenor			Duet	CIF/RAM
Chess	Andersson and Ulvaeus	1988	Florence & Freddie	You Want To Loose Your Only Friend	Uptempo	Alto/Tenor			Duet	CIF/RAM
Chess	Andersson and Ulvaeus	1988	Anatoly & Florence	Terrace Duet	Moderate Tempo	Tenor/Alto			Duet	RLM/CIF
Chess	Andersson and Ulvaeus	1988	Florence & Freddie	So You Got What You Want	Uptempo	Alto/Tenor			Duet	CIF/RAM
Chess	Andersson and Ulvaeus	1988	Molokov & Walter	Endgame II	Uptempo	Bar/Bar			Duet	MM/MM
Chess	Andersson and Ulvaeus	1988	Anatoly & Freddie	Talking Chess	Uptempo	Tenor/Tenor			Duet	RLM/RAM
Chess	Andersson and Ulvaeus	1988	Anatoly & Svetlana	Endgame III	Moderate Tempo	Tenor/Alto			Duet	RLM/CF
Chess	Andersson and Ulvaeus	1988	Anatoly & Florence	You and I	Ballad	Tenor/Alto			Duet	RLM/CIF
Chess	Andersson and Ulvaeus	1988	Anatoly & Florence	You and I Reprise	Ballad	Tenor/Alto			Duet	RLM/CIF
Chess	Andersson and Ulvaeus	1988	Anatoly	Endgame*	Uptempo	Tenor	C3	A4	Lead	Romantic Lead Female
Chicago	Kander, John	1975	Amos Hart	Mister Cellophane	Ballad	Baritone	C3	F4	Lead	Character Male
Chicago	Kander, John	1975	Billy Flynn	All I Care About Is Love	Moderate Tempo	Baritone	A2	F#4	Lead	Romantic Antagonist Male
Chicago	Kander, John	1975	Billy Flynn	Razzle Dazzle	Uptempo	Baritone	D3	F4	Lead	Romantic Antagonist Male
Chicago	Kander, John	1975	Ensemble	Cell Block Tango	Moderate Tempo	Unison			Ensemble	Adults
Chicago	Kander, John	1975	Mama Morton	When You're Good To Mama	Moderate Tempo	Alto	F#3	A4	Lead	Character Female
Chicago	Kander, John	1975	Mama Morton	Class*	Ballad	Alto	F3	B4	Lead	Character Female
Chicago	Kander, John	1975	Mary Sunshine	A Little Good In Everyone	Moderate Tempo	Soprano	F3	B5	Supporting	Character Female
Chicago	Kander, John	1975	Roxie Hart	Funny Honey	Ballad	Alto	F3	Bb4	Lead	Character Ingenue Female
Chicago	Kander, John	1975	Roxie Hart	Roxie	Moderate Tempo	Alto	G3	Bb4	Lead	Character Ingenue Female
Chicago	Kander, John	1975	Roxie Hart	My Own Best Friend	Moderate Tempo	Alto	E3	A4	Lead	Character Ingenue Female
Chicago	Kander, John	1975	Roxie Hart	Me and My Baby	Uptempo	Alto	Bb3	C4	Lead	Character Ingenue Female
Chicago	Kander, John	1975	Velma Kelly	Nowadays	Moderate Tempo	Alto	F#3	D5	Lead	Character Ingenue Female
Chicago	Kander, John	1975	Velma Kelly	All That Jazz	Moderate Tempo	Alto	G2	Db5	Lead	Romantic Antagonist Female
Chicago	Kander, John	1975	Velma Kelly	I Can't Do It Alone	Uptempo	Alto	Bb3	D4	Lead	Romantic Antagonist Female
Chicago	Kander, John	1975	Velma Kelly	My Own Best Friend	Moderate Tempo	Alto	G3	A4	Lead	Romantic Antagonist Female
Chicago	Kander, John	1975	Velma Kelly	I Know A Girl	Uptempo	Alto	E3	A4	Lead	Romantic Antagonist Female
Chicago	Kander, John	1975	Velma Kelly	Class*	Ballad	Alto	F3	B4	Lead	Romantic Antagonist Female
Chicago	Kander, John	1975	Velma Kelly	Nowadays	Moderate Tempo	Alto	F#3	D5	Lead	Romantic Antagonist Female
Chicago	Kander, John	1975	Roxie & Velma	My Own Best Friend	Moderate Tempo	Alto/Alto			Duet	CIF/RAF
Chicago	Kander, John	1975	Matron & Velma	Class	Moderate Tempo	Alto/Alto			Duet	CF/RAF
Chicago	Kander, John	1975	Roxie & Velma	Nowadays Reprise	Ballad	Alto/Alto			Duet	CIF/RAF
Children of Eden	Schwartz, Stephen	1991	Abel	Lost in The Wilderness Reprise *	Moderate Tempo	Tenor	G3	G4	Supporting	Ingenue Male
Children of Eden	Schwartz, Stephen	1991	Adam	A World Without You *	Moderate Tempo	Tenor	Db3	Ab4	Lead	Character Male
Children of Eden	Schwartz, Stephen	1991	Adam	Grateful Children *	Moderate Tempo	Tenor	B2	D#3	Lead	Character Male
Children of Eden	Schwartz, Stephen	1991	Cain	Lost In The Wilderness *	Moderate Tempo	Tenor	D3	G4	Lead	Antagonist Male
Children of Eden	Schwartz, Stephen	1991	Ensemble	In The Beginning*	Moderate Tempo	SATB			Ensemble	Adults
Children of Eden	Schwartz, Stephen	1991	Ensemble	Children of Eden*	Moderate Tempo	SATB			Ensemble	Adults
Children of Eden	Schwartz, Stephen	1991	Ensemble	Generations*	Moderate Tempo	SATB			Ensemble	Adults
Children of Eden	Schwartz, Stephen	1991	Eve	The Spark of Creation	Uptempo	Alto	G#3	Eb5	Lead	Maternal
Children of Eden	Schwartz, Stephen	1991	Eve	Grateful Children *	Moderate Tempo	Alto	B3	D#4	Lead	Maternal

Shows

Songs by Character Type

Show	Composer	Year	Role	Song	Tempo	Vocal Type	Range-Bottom	Range-Top	Category	Character Type
Children of Eden	Schwartz, Stephen	1991	Eve	The Spark of Creation Reprise	Uptempo	Alto	Ab3	Db5	Supporting	Maternal
Children of Eden	Schwartz, Stephen	1991	Eve	Children Of Eden	Moderate Tempo	Alto	Ab3	Eb5	Lead	Maternal
Children of Eden	Schwartz, Stephen	1991	Father	Father's Day	Moderate Tempo	Baritone	B2	E4	Lead	Romantic Lead Male
Children of Eden	Schwartz, Stephen	1991	Father	The Mark of Cain	Moderate Tempo	Baritone	B2	F4	Lead	Romantic Lead Male
Children of Eden	Schwartz, Stephen	1991	Father	Precious Children	Ballad	Baritone	Bb2	Eb4	Lead	Romantic Lead Male
Children of Eden	Schwartz, Stephen	1991	Father	The Hardest Part Of Love *	Uptempo	Baritone	D3	G4	Lead	Romantic Lead Male
Children of Eden	Schwartz, Stephen	1991	Mama Noah	The Spark Of Creation Reprise 2	Uptempo	Alto	A3	A4	Lead	Maternal
Children of Eden	Schwartz, Stephen	1991	Mama Noah	Ain't It Good	Moderate Tempo	Alto	A3	A5	Lead	Maternal
Children of Eden	Schwartz, Stephen	1991	Noah	Blind Obedience	Ballad	Tenor	D3	A3	Lead	Paternal
Children of Eden	Schwartz, Stephen	1991	Noah	Noah's Lullaby	Ballad	Tenor	C3	D4	Lead	Paternal
Children of Eden	Schwartz, Stephen	1991	Noah	The Hardest Part Of Love *	Uptempo	Tenor	D3	G4	Lead	Paternal
Children of Eden	Schwartz, Stephen	1991	Yonah	Stranger To The Rain	Ballad	Alto	A3	D4	Supporting	Character Ingenue Female
Children of Eden	Schwartz, Stephen	1991	Yonah	Sailor Of The Skies	Ballad	Alto	G3	Bb4	Supporting	Character Ingenue Female
Children of Eden	Schwartz, Stephen	1991	Abel & Cain	Lost In The Wilderness	Moderate Tempo	Tenor/Bar			Duet	IM/AM
Children of Eden	Schwartz, Stephen	1991	Japeth & Yonah	In Whatever Time We Have	Moderate Tempo	Tenor/Alto			Duet	CIF/AM
Chitty Chitty Bang Bang	Sherman and Sherman	2005	Baron Bomburst	Chu-Chi Face	Moderate Tempo	Tenor	C3	G4	Supporting	Character Male
Chitty Chitty Bang Bang	Sherman and Sherman	2005	Baroness Bomburst	The Bombie Samba	Uptempo	Soprano	B3	Eb5	Supporting	Character Female
Chitty Chitty Bang Bang	Sherman and Sherman	2005	Baroness Bomburst	Chu-Chi Face	Moderate Tempo	Soprano	C4	F5	Supporting	Character Female
Chitty Chitty Bang Bang	Sherman and Sherman	2005	Boris	Act English *	Moderate Tempo	Tenor	C3	G4	Supporting	Antagonist Male
Chitty Chitty Bang Bang	Sherman and Sherman	2005	Caratacus Potts	Hushabye Mountain	Ballad	Baritone	D#3	F4	Lead	Character Male
Chitty Chitty Bang Bang	Sherman and Sherman	2005	Caratacus Potts	Truly Scrumptious Reprise	Ballad	Baritone	Db3	Db4	Lead	Character Male
Chitty Chitty Bang Bang	Sherman and Sherman	2005	Caratacus Potts	You Two	Moderate Tempo	Baritone	D3	E4	Lead	Character Male
Chitty Chitty Bang Bang	Sherman and Sherman	2005	Caratacus Potts	Toot Sweets *	Uptempo	Baritone	E3	G4	Lead	Character Male
Chitty Chitty Bang Bang	Sherman and Sherman	2005	Caratacus Potts	Teamwork *	Moderate Tempo	Baritone	D3	E4	Lead	Character Male
Chitty Chitty Bang Bang	Sherman and Sherman	2005	Childcatcher	Kiddy Widdy Winkies	Moderate Tempo	Baritone	D3	E4	Supporting	Antagonist Male
Chitty Chitty Bang Bang	Sherman and Sherman	2005	Childcatcher	Childcatcher as Grandpa	Moderate Tempo	Baritone	C3	C4	Supporting	Antagonist Male
Chitty Chitty Bang Bang	Sherman and Sherman	2005	Children	Teamwork *	Uptempo	Alto	C4	Eb5	Featured Ensemble	Juvenile Female
Chitty Chitty Bang Bang	Sherman and Sherman	2005	Children	Chitty Chitty Bang Bang	Uptempo	SATB			Featured Ensemble	Children/Adults
Chitty Chitty Bang Bang	Sherman and Sherman	2005	Ensemble	Vulgarian National Anthem	Uptempo	SATB			Ensemble	Adults
Chitty Chitty Bang Bang	Sherman and Sherman	2005	Ensemble	Teamwork* (Children)	Uptempo	SATB			Ensemble	Children/Adults
Chitty Chitty Bang Bang	Sherman and Sherman	2005	Ensemble	Chitty Flies Home Finale	Uptempo	SATB			Ensemble	Children/Adults
Chitty Chitty Bang Bang	Sherman and Sherman	2005	Goan	Act English *	Moderate Tempo	Baritone	C3	E4	Supporting	Antagonist Male
Chitty Chitty Bang Bang	Sherman and Sherman	2005	Grandpa Potts	Them Three	Uptempo	Baritone	C3	C4	Supporting	Mature Male
Chitty Chitty Bang Bang	Sherman and Sherman	2005	Grandpa Potts	Posh	Moderate Tempo	Baritone	C3	C4	Supporting	Mature Male
Chitty Chitty Bang Bang	Sherman and Sherman	2005	Jemima Potts	Truly Scrumptious	Ballad	Soprano	C4	C5	Lead	Juvenile Female
Chitty Chitty Bang Bang	Sherman and Sherman	2005	Jemima Potts	Truly Scrumptious	Moderate Tempo	Soprano	C4	C5	Lead	Juvenile Female
Chitty Chitty Bang Bang	Sherman and Sherman	2005	Jeremy Potts	Us Two	Ballad	Soprano	C4	C5	Lead	Juvenile Male
Chitty Chitty Bang Bang	Sherman and Sherman	2005	Jeremy Potts	Us Two	Ballad	Soprano	C4	C5	Lead	Juvenile Male
Chitty Chitty Bang Bang	Sherman and Sherman	2005	Truly Scrumptious	Truly Scrumptious	Moderate Tempo	Soprano	C4	C5	Lead	Romantic Lead Female
Chitty Chitty Bang Bang	Sherman and Sherman	2005	Truly Scrumptious	Music Box	Ballad	Soprano	D4	Eb5	Lead	Romantic Lead Female
Chitty Chitty Bang Bang	Sherman and Sherman	2005	Truly Scrumptious	Toot Sweets *	Uptempo	Soprano	D4	Eb5	Lead	Romantic Lead Female

Shows

Songs by Character Type

Show	Composer	Year	Role	Song	Tempo	Vocal Type	Range-Bottom	Range-Top	Category	Character Type
Chitty Chitty Bang Bang	Sherman and Sherman	2005	Baron & Baroness	Chu-Chi Face	Moderate Tempo	Tenor/Sop			Duet	CM/CF
Chitty Chitty Bang Bang	Sherman and Sherman	2005	Caratacus & Truly	Music Box/Truly	Moderate Tempo	Bar/Sop			Duet	CM/RLF
Chitty Chitty Bang Bang	Sherman and Sherman	2005	Jeremia & Jeremy	Us Two/Chitty Prayer	Moderate Tempo	Sop/Sop			Duet	JF/JM
Cinderella (2013)	Rodgers, Richard	1940	Topher	Loneliness Of Evening*	Ballad	Tenor	Eb3	A4	Lead	Ingenue Male
Cinderella (2013)	Rodgers, Richard	1949	Jean-Michel	Now Is the Time*	Uptempo	Tenor	Eb3	F4	Supporting	Character Male
Cinderella (2013)	Rodgers, Richard	1949	Jean-Michel	Now Is The Time Reprise*	Uptempo	Tenor	C3	A4	Supporting	Character Male
Cinderella (2013)	Rodgers, Richard	1957	Charlotte	Stepsister's Lament*	Uptempo	Alto	C4	D5	Supporting	Character Female
Cinderella (2013)	Rodgers, Richard	1957	Ella	In My Own Little Corner	Uptempo	Soprano	C4	C5	Lead	Ingenue Female
Cinderella (2013)	Rodgers, Richard	1957	Ella	In My Own Little Corner Reprise	Uptempo	Soprano	C4	C5	Lead	Ingenue Female
Cinderella (2013)	Rodgers, Richard	1957	Ella	Impossible*	Uptempo	Soprano	Bb2	D5	Lead	Ingenue Female
Cinderella (2013)	Rodgers, Richard	1957	Ella	Ten Minutes Ago*	Moderate Tempo	Soprano	C#4	D5	Lead	Ingenue Female
Cinderella (2013)	Rodgers, Richard	1957	Ella	Do I Love You...*	Ballad	Soprano	A4	E5	Lead	Ingenue Female
Cinderella (2013)	Rodgers, Richard	1957	Ella	When You're Driving...*	Uptempo	Soprano	B2	Bb4	Lead	Ingenue Female
Cinderella (2013)	Rodgers, Richard	1957	Ella	A Lovely Night*	Uptempo	Soprano	Bb3	Bb4	Lead	Ingenue Female
Cinderella (2013)	Rodgers, Richard	1957	Ella	A Lovely Night*	Uptempo	Soprano	C4	C5	Lead	Ingenue Female
Cinderella (2013)	Rodgers, Richard	1957	Ella	It's Possible	Uptempo	Soprano	C4	B4	Lead	Ingenue Female
Cinderella (2013)	Rodgers, Richard	1957	Fairy Godmother (Marie)	Impossible*	Uptempo	Soprano	F3	F4	Supporting	Character Female
Cinderella (2013)	Rodgers, Richard	1957	Fairy Godmother (Marie)	Fol-De-Rol	Uptempo	Soprano	A2	F#4	Supporting	Character Female
Cinderella (2013)	Rodgers, Richard	1957	Gabrielle	Stepsister's Lament*	Uptempo	Alto	C4	D5	Supporting	Character Ingenue Female
Cinderella (2013)	Rodgers, Richard	1957	Gabrielle	A Lovely Night*	Uptempo	Alto	B3	D5	Supporting	Character Ingenue Female
Cinderella (2013)	Rodgers, Richard	1957	Joy	A Lovely Night*	Uptempo	Alto	B3	D5	Supporting	Character Female
Cinderella (2013)	Rodgers, Richard	1957	Stepmother (Madam)	A Lovely Night*	Uptempo	Alto	B3	D5	Supporting	Romantic Antagonist Female
Cinderella (2013)	Rodgers, Richard	1957	Topher	Ten Minutes Ago*	Moderate Tempo	Tenor	C3	D4	Lead	Ingenue Male
Cinderella (2013)	Rodgers, Richard	1957	Topher	Do I Love You...*	Ballad	Tenor	A3	Eb4	Lead	Ingenue Male
Cinderella (2013)	Rodgers, Richard	1957	Topher	Ten Minutes Ago Reprise	Moderate Tempo	Tenor	C3	D4	Lead	Ingenue Male
Cinderella (2013)	Rodgers, Richard	1957	Ella & Marie	In My Own Little Corner Reprise	Uptempo	Sop/Sop			Duet	IF/CF
Cinderella (2013)	Rodgers, Richard	1957	Ella & Marie	Impossible	Uptempo	Sop/Sop			Duet	IF/CF
Cinderella (2013)	Rodgers, Richard	1957	Ella & Marie	It's Possible	Uptempo	Sop/Sop			Duet	IF/CF
Cinderella (2013)	Rodgers, Richard	1957	Ella & Topher	Ten Minutes Ago	Moderate Tempo	Sop/Tenor			Duet	IM/IF
Cinderella (2013)	Rodgers, Richard	1957	Ella & Gabrielle	A Lovely Night Reprise	Moderate Tempo	Sop/Alto			Duet	IF/CIF
Cinderella (2013)	Rodgers, Richard	1957	Ella & Topher	Loneliness Of Evening	Ballad	Sop/Alto			Duet	IF/IM
Cinderella (2013)	Rodgers, Richard	1962	Ella	The Sweetest Sounds*	Moderate Tempo	Soprano	C#4	C5	Lead	Ingenue Female
Cinderella (2013)	Rodgers, Richard	1962	Topher	The Sweetest Sounds*	Moderate Tempo	Tenor	E3	E4	Lead	Ingenue Male
Cinderella (2013)	Rodgers, Richard	1962	Topher	The Sweetest Sounds Reprise	Moderate Tempo	Tenor	A2	Fb4	Lead	Ingenue Male
Cinderella (2013)	Rodgers, Richard	1985	Topher	Me, Who Am I*	Moderate Tempo	Tenor	B2	G4	Lead	Ingenue Male
Cinderella (2013)	Rodgers, Richard	1997	Ensemble	There's Music In You	Moderate Tempo	SATB			Ensemble	Adults
Cinderella (2013)	Rodgers, Richard	1997	Fairy Godmother (Marie)	There's Music In You*	Ballad	Soprano	C4	F5	Lead	Character Female
Cinderella (2013)	Rodgers, Richard	2013	Ella	He Was Tall	Ballad	Soprano	D4	C#5	Lead	Ingenue Female
Cinderella (2013)	Rodgers, Richard	2013	Gabrielle & Jean-Michel	Now it the Time Reprise	Moderate Tempo	Alto/Tenor			Duet	CF/CM
City of Angels	Coleman, Cy	1989	Bobbi	With Every Breath I Take	Ballad	Alto	E3	Db5	Lead	Romantic Lead Female
City of Angels	Coleman, Cy	1989	Bobbi	With Every Breath I Take Reprise *	Ballad	Alto	D#3	C5	Lead	Romantic Lead Female
City of Angels	Coleman, Cy	1989	Buddy Fiddler	The Buddy System	Moderate Tempo	Baritone	C3	D4	Lead	Character Male
City of Angels	Coleman, Cy	1989	Buddy Fiddler	Double Talk (Buddy)	Moderate Tempo	Baritone	C3	G4	Lead	Character Male

Shows

Songs by Character Type

* = Music Edit Required
+ = Ethnic Specific

Show	Composer	Year	Role	Song	Tempo	Vocal Type	Range-Bottom	Range-Top	Category	Character Type
City of Angels	Coleman, Cy	1989	Ensemble	Everybody's Gotta Be Somewhere	Uptempo	SATB			Ensemble	Adults
City of Angels	Coleman, Cy	1989	Gabby	What You Don't Know About Women *	Moderate Tempo	Alto	G3	F5	Lead	Romantic Lead Female
City of Angels	Coleman, Cy	1989	Gabby	It Needs Work	Moderate Tempo	Alto	G#3	Cb5	Lead	Romantic Lead Female
City of Angels	Coleman, Cy	1989	Jimmy Powers	Ya Gotta Look Out For Yourself	Uptempo	Tenor	C3	D4	Supporting	Romantic Lead Male
City of Angels	Coleman, Cy	1989	Jimmy Powers	Stay With Me	Ballad	Tenor	C3	G4	Supporting	Romantic Lead Male
City of Angels	Coleman, Cy	1989	Mallory	Lost And Found	Ballad	Alto	G#3	F#5	Supporting	Romantic Antagonist Female
City of Angels	Coleman, Cy	1989	Munoz +	All You Have To Do Is Wait	Moderate Tempo	Baritone	F#3	D4	Supporting	Character Male
City of Angels	Coleman, Cy	1989	Oolie	What You Don't Know About Women *	Moderate Tempo	Alto	G3	F5	Lead	Character Female
City of Angels	Coleman, Cy	1989	Oolie/Donna	You Can Always Count On Me	Moderate Tempo	Alto	Bb3	Db5	Supporting	Character Female
City of Angels	Coleman, Cy	1989	Stine	You're Nothing Without Me *	Uptempo	Baritone	D3	G4	Lead	Romantic Lead Male
City of Angels	Coleman, Cy	1989	Stine	Funny	Moderate Tempo	Baritone	Bb2	F4	Lead	Romantic Lead Male
City of Angels	Coleman, Cy	1989	Stine	Double Talk (Stine)	Moderate Tempo	Baritone	F3	G4	Lead	Romantic Lead Male
City of Angels	Coleman, Cy	1989	Stine	I'm Nothing Without You *	Uptempo	Baritone	F3	G4	Lead	Romantic Lead Male
City of Angels	Coleman, Cy	1989	Stone	Double Talk	Uptempo	Baritone	A#2	D4	Lead	Romantic Antagonist Male
City of Angels	Coleman, Cy	1989	Stone	You're Nothing Without Me *	Uptempo	Baritone	E3	G4	Lead	Romantic Antagonist Male
City of Angels	Coleman, Cy	1989	Stone	With Every Breath I Take Reprise *	Ballad	Baritone	G#2	F4	Lead	Romantic Antagonist Male
City of Angels	Coleman, Cy	1989	Stone	I'm Nothing Without You *	Uptempo	Baritone	F3	G4	Lead	Romantic Antagonist Male
City of Angels	Coleman, Cy	1989	Buddy & Stine	Double Talk	Uptempo	Bar/Bar			Duet	CM/RLM
City of Angels	Coleman, Cy	1989	Gabby & Oolie	What You Don't Know About Women	Uptempo	Alto/Alto			Duet	RLF/CF
City of Angels	Coleman, Cy	1989	Alaura & Stone	The Tennis Song	Uptempo	Bar/Bar			Duet	RLF/RAM
City of Angels	Coleman, Cy	1989	Stine & Stone	You're Nothing Without Me	Uptempo	Alto/Bar			Duet	RLM/RAM
City Of Angels	Coleman, Cy	1989	Bobbi & Stone	With Every Breath I Take Reprise	Ballad	Alto/Bar			Duet	RLF/RAM
Closer Than Ever	Maltby Jr., Richard	1989	Ensemble	Doors	Uptempo	SATB			Ensemble	Adults
Closer Than Ever	Maltby Jr., Richard	1989	Ensemble	There's Nothing Like It	Uptempo	SATB			Ensemble	Adults
Closer Than Ever	Maltby Jr., Richard	1989	Ensemble	Next Time/Wouldn't Go Back	Uptempo	SATB			Ensemble	Adults
Closer Than Ever	Maltby Jr., Richard	1989	Ensemble	The March of Time	Uptempo	SATB			Ensemble	Adults
Closer Than Ever	Maltby Jr., Richard	1989	Man One	She Loves Me Not *	Ballad	Tenor	Bb2	A4	Lead	Ingenue Male
Closer Than Ever	Maltby Jr., Richard	1989	Man One	What Am I Doin'	Uptempo	Tenor	C3	A4	Lead	Ingenue Male
Closer Than Ever	Maltby Jr., Richard	1989	Man One	One Of The Good Guys	Ballad	Tenor	B2	C4	Lead	Ingenue Male
Closer Than Ever	Maltby Jr., Richard	1989	Man One	Another Wedding Song *	Uptempo	Tenor	D3	G4	Lead	Ingenue Male
Closer Than Ever	Maltby Jr., Richard	1989	Man Three (Pianist)	Father of Fathers *	Ballad	Baritone	B2	E4	Lead	Adults
Closer Than Ever	Maltby Jr., Richard	1989	Man Two	Father of Fathers *	Ballad	Baritone	C3	E4	Lead	Paternal
Closer Than Ever	Maltby Jr., Richard	1989	Man Two	There *	Moderate Tempo	Baritone	A2	F4	Lead	Paternal
Closer Than Ever	Maltby Jr., Richard	1989	Man Two	If I Sing	Ballad	Baritone	A2	Eb4	Lead	Paternal
Closer Than Ever	Maltby Jr., Richard	1989	Man Two	Father of Fathers *	Ballad	Baritone	D3	F4	Lead	Paternal
Closer Than Ever	Maltby Jr., Richard	1989	Woman One	She Loves Me Not *	Ballad	Soprano	Bb3	Eb5	Lead	Maternal
Closer Than Ever	Maltby Jr., Richard	1989	Woman One	The Bear, the Tiger, the Hampster...	Uptempo	Soprano	Ab3	Db4	Lead	Maternal
Closer Than Ever	Maltby Jr., Richard	1989	Woman One	Life Story	Moderate Tempo	Soprano	Bb3	C5	Lead	Maternal
Closer Than Ever	Maltby Jr., Richard	1989	Woman One	Patterns	Ballad	Soprano	Bb3	Eb5	Lead	Maternal
Closer Than Ever	Maltby Jr., Richard	1989	Woman One	It's Never That Easy *	Ballad	Soprano	B3	G5	Lead	Maternal
Closer Than Ever	Maltby Jr., Richard	1989	Woman Two	You Want To Be My Friend	Uptempo	Alto	D4	E5	Lead	Character Female

Shows

Songs by Character Type

Show	Composer	Year	Role	Song	Tempo	Vocal Type	Range-Bottom	Range-Top	Category	Character Type
Closer Than Ever	Maltby Jr., Richard	1989	Woman Two	Miss Bird	Moderate Tempo	Alto	F3	Eb5	Lead	Character Female
Closer Than Ever	Maltby Jr., Richard	1989	Woman Two	There *	Moderate Tempo	Alto	A3	D5	Lead	Character Female
Closer Than Ever	Maltby Jr., Richard	1989	Woman Two	Another Wedding Song *	Ballad	Alto	B3	B4	Lead	Character Female
Closer Than Ever	Maltby Jr., Richard	1989	Woman Two	Back On Base	Moderate Tempo	Alto	G3	G5	Lead	Character Female
Closer Than Ever	Maltby Jr., Richard	1989	Woman Two	I've Been Here Before *	Ballad	Alto	Gb3	Cb5	Lead	Character Female
Closer Than Ever	Shire, David	1989	Man Two & Woman One	Fandango	Uptempo	Bar/Sop			Duet	P/M
Color Purple, The	Bray, Russell and Willis	2005	Celie+	Somebody Gonna Love You	Ballad	Alto	F3	A4	Lead	Character Female
Color Purple, The	Bray, Russell and Willis	2005	Celie+	What About Love *	Ballad	Alto	B2	D5	Lead	Character Female
Color Purple, The	Bray, Russell and Willis	2005	Celie+	I'm Here	Ballad	Alto	E3	G5	Lead	Character Female
Color Purple, The	Bray, Russell and Willis	2005	Celie+	Bring My Nettie Back	Uptempo	Alto	G3	G5	Lead	Character Female
Color Purple, The	Bray, Russell and Willis	2005	Celie+	Dear God (Sofia)	Moderate Tempo	Alto	G3	G4	Lead	Character Female
Color Purple, The	Bray, Russell and Willis	2005	Celie+	Dear God (Shug)	Moderate Tempo	Alto	F3	B4	Lead	Character Female
Color Purple, The	Bray, Russell and Willis	2005	Celie+	With These Hands	Moderate Tempo	Alto	Ab3	Eb5	Lead	Character Female
Color Purple, The	Bray, Russell and Willis	2005	Ensemble	The Color Purple Reprise	Ballad	SATB			Ensemble	Adults
Color Purple, The	Bray, Russell and Willis	2005	Harpo+	Brown Betty *	Moderate Tempo	Tenor	E3	G4	Lead	Character Ingenue Male
Color Purple, The	Bray, Russell and Willis	2005	Mister+	Big Dog	Uptempo	Tenor	F3	Ab4	Lead	Antagonist Male
Color Purple, The	Bray, Russell and Willis	2005	Mister+	Mister's Song (2005)	Moderate Tempo	Tenor	E3	G4	Lead	Antagonist Male
Color Purple, The	Bray, Russell and Willis	2005	Mister+	Mister's Song (2015)	Moderate Tempo	Tenor	F3	Ab4	Lead	Antagonist Male
Color Purple, The	Bray, Russell and Willis	2005	Shug Avery+	Too Beautiful For Words *	Ballad	Alto	E3	F4	Lead	Romantic Antagonist Female
Color Purple, The	Bray, Russell and Willis	2005	Shug Avery+	Push Da Button	Moderate Tempo	Alto	A3	Eb5	Lead	Romantic Antagonist Female
Color Purple, The	Bray, Russell and Willis	2005	Shug Avery+	What About Love *	Ballad	Alto	E3	D5	Lead	Romantic Antagonist Female
Color Purple, The	Bray, Russell and Willis	2005	Shug Avery+	The Color Purple	Ballad	Alto	F#3	Db5	Lead	Romantic Antagonist Female
Color Purple, The	Bray, Russell and Willis	2005	Sofia+	Hell No *	Moderate Tempo	Alto	E3	C5	Lead	Antagonist Female
Color Purple, The	Bray, Russell and Willis	2005	Celie+ & Shug+	What About Love	Ballad	Alto/Alto			Duet	CF/RAF
Color Purple, The	Bray, Russell, and Willis	2005	Harpo+ & Sofia+	Any Little Thing	Moderate Tempo	Tenor/Alto			Duet	CM/CF
Company	Sondheim, Stephen	1970	April & Robert	Barcelona	Ballad	Sop/Tenor			Duet	CF/RLM
Company (Revival)	Sondheim, Stephen	1970	Ensemble	Side By Side	Moderate Tempo	SATB			Ensemble	Adults
Company (Revival)	Sondheim, Stephen	1970	Ensemble	What Would We Do Without You	Uptempo	Unison			Ensemble	Adults
Company (Revival)	Sondheim, Stephen	1970	Amy	Not Getting Married Today	Uptempo	Soprano	C#4	Ab5	Supporting	Character Ingenue Female
Company (Revival)	Sondheim, Stephen	1970	April	You Could Drive a Person Crazy	Uptempo	Soprano	C#4	A5	Supporting	Character Female
Company (Revival)	Sondheim, Stephen	1970	David	Sorry Grateful	Ballad	Baritone	B2	E4	Supporting	Character Male
Company (Revival)	Sondheim, Stephen	1970	David	Have I Got A Girl For You	Uptempo	Baritone	B5	Gb7	Supporting	Character Male
Company (Revival)	Sondheim, Stephen	1970	Harry	Sorry Grateful	Ballad	Baritone	B2	E4	Supporting	Character Male
Company (Revival)	Sondheim, Stephen	1970	Harry	Have I Got A Girl For You	Uptempo	Baritone	B6	Gb8	Supporting	Character Male
Company (Revival)	Sondheim, Stephen	1970	Joanne	The Little Things We Do Together	Uptempo	Alto	F3	A4	Supporting	Antagonist Female
Company (Revival)	Sondheim, Stephen	1970	Joanne	The Ladies Who Lunch	Moderate Tempo	Alto	F3	Bb4	Supporting	Antagonist Female
Company (Revival)	Sondheim, Stephen	1970	Kathy	You Could Drive a Person Crazy	Uptempo	Soprano	C#4	A5	Supporting	Ingenue Female
Company (Revival)	Sondheim, Stephen	1970	Larry	Sorry Grateful	Ballad	Baritone	B2	E4	Supporting	Mature Male
Company (Revival)	Sondheim, Stephen	1970	Larry	Have I Got A Girl For You	Uptempo	Baritone	B2	Gb4	Supporting	Mature Male
Company (Revival)	Sondheim, Stephen	1970	Marta	You Could Drive a Person Crazy	Uptempo	Alto	C#4	A5	Supporting	Character Ingenue Female
Company (Revival)	Sondheim, Stephen	1970	Marta	Another Hundred People	Uptempo	Alto	A3	D5	Supporting	Character Ingenue Female
Company (Revival)	Sondheim, Stephen	1970	Paul	Have I Got A Girl For You	Uptempo	Baritone	B4	Gb6	Supporting	Character Ingenue Male

Shows

Show	Composer	Year	Role	Song	Tempo	Vocal Type	Range-Bottom	Range-Top	Category	Character Type
Company (Revival)	Sondheim, Stephen	1970	Peter	Have I Got A Girl For You	Uptempo	Baritone	B3	Gb5	Supporting	Romantic Lead Male
Company (Revival)	Sondheim, Stephen	1970	Robert	Company	Uptempo	Tenor	A2	Ab4	Lead	Romantic Lead Male
Company (Revival)	Sondheim, Stephen	1970	Robert	Someone Is Waiting	Ballad	Tenor	B2	E4	Lead	Romantic Lead Male
Company (Revival)	Sondheim, Stephen	1970	Robert	Being Alive	Moderate Tempo	Tenor	D3	F4	Lead	Romantic Lead Male
Crazy For You (1992)	Gershwin, George	1924	Irene Roth	Naughty Baby	Moderate Tempo	Alto	Ab3	D#4	Supporting	Romantic Lead Female
Crazy For You (1992)	Gershwin, George	1926	Polly Baker	Someone To Watch Over Me	Ballad	Alto	Ab2	C4	Lead	Character Ingenue Female
Crazy For You (1992)	Gershwin, George	1930	Ensemble	I Got Rhythm	Uptempo	Unison/2 Part			Ensemble	Adults
Crazy For You (1992)	Gershwin, George	1930	Polly Baker	Could You Use Me	Uptempo	Alto	A2	Eb4	Lead	Character Ingenue Female
Crazy For You (1992)	Gershwin, George	1930	Polly Baker	Embraceable You	Ballad	Alto	A3	B4	Lead	Character Ingenue Female
Crazy For You (1992)	Gershwin, George	1930	Polly Baker	I Got Rhythm	Uptempo	Alto	Bb3	Eb4	Lead	Character Ingenue Female
Crazy For You (1992)	Gershwin, George	1930	Polly Baker	But Not For Me	Ballad	Alto	Bb3	C5	Lead	Character Ingenue Female
Crazy For You (1992)	Gershwin, George	1930	Bobby & Polly	Could You Use Me	Uptempo	Tenor/Alto			Duet	IM/CIF
Crazy For You (1992)	Gershwin, George	1930	Bobby & Polly	Embraceable You	Ballad	Tenor/Alto			Duet	IM/CIF
Crazy For You (1992)	Gershwin, George	1937	Bobby Child	I Can't Be Bothered Now	Uptempo	Tenor	D3	F4	Lead	Ingenue Male
Crazy For You (1992)	Gershwin, George	1937	Bobby Child	Things Are Looking Up	Uptempo	Tenor	C3	D4	Lead	Ingenue Male
Crazy For You (1992)	Gershwin, George	1937	Bobby Child	Shall We Dance	Uptempo	Tenor	D3	Fb4	Lead	Ingenue Male
Crazy For You (1992)	Gershwin, George	1937	Bobby Child	They Can't Take That Away	Moderate Tempo	Tenor	Bb2	Eb4	Lead	Ingenue Male
Crazy For You (1992)	Gershwin, George	1937	Bobby Child	Nice Work If You Can Get It	Uptempo	Tenor	D3	C4	Lead	Ingenue Male
Crazy For You (1992)	Gershwin, George	1937	Eugene Fodor	Stiff Upper Lip	Uptempo	Baritone	D3	F4	Supporting	Character Male
Crazy For You (1992)	Gershwin, George	1937	Patricia Fodor	Stiff Upper Lip	Uptempo	Soprano	D4	F5	Supporting	Character Female
Crazy For You (1992)	Gershwin, George	1992	Bela Zangler	What Causes That*	Uptempo	Baritone	C3	F#4	Supporting	Mature Male
Crazy For You (1992)	Gershwin, George	1992	Bobby Child	Krazy For You	Uptempo	Tenor	Eb3	Eb4	Lead	Ingenue Male
Curtains	Gershwin, George	1992	Ensemble	Tonight's The Night	Uptempo	Unison/2 Part			Ensemble	Adults
Curtains	Gershwin, George	1992	Bela & Bobby	What Causes That	Uptempo	Bar/Tenor			Duet	IM/MM
Curtains	Kander, John		Ensemble	Wide Open Spaces	Uptempo	Unison/2 Part			Ensemble	Adults
Curtains	Kander, John	2007	Ensemble	What Kind of Man	Moderate Tempo	Unison/2 Part			Ensemble	Adults
Curtains	Kander, John	2007	Ensemble	The Woman's Dead	Ballad	SATB			Ensemble	Adults
Curtains	Kander, John	2007	Ensemble	Show People*	Uptempo	Unison			Ensemble	Adults
Curtains	Kander, John	2007	Ensemble	He Did It	Uptempo	Unison/3 Part			Ensemble	Adults
Curtains	Kander, John	2007	Cioffi & Nikki	In The Same Boat Parts 1-6	Uptempo	SATB			Ensemble	Adults
Curtains	Kander, John	2007	Cioffi & Nikki	A Tough Act To Follow	Uptempo	Bar/Sop			Duet	CF/CIF
Curtains	Kander, John	2007	Aaron & Georgia	Thinking Of Him Reprise	Moderate Tempo	Tenor/Alto			Duet	RLM/RLF
Curtains	Kander, John	2007	Aaron Fox	I Miss The Music	Ballad	Tenor	C3	Gb4	Lead	Romantic Lead Male
Curtains	Kander, John	2007	Aaron Fox	Thinking of Him Reprise*	Ballad	Tenor	A2	Gb4	Lead	Romantic Lead Male
Curtains	Kander, John	2007	Carmen Bernstein	It's A Business	Moderate Tempo	Alto	Eb3	Bb4	Lead	Character Female
Curtains	Kander, John	2007	Carmen Bernstein	Show People	Moderate Tempo	Alto	G3	Ab4	Lead	Character Female
Curtains	Kander, John	2007	Carmen Bernstein	Show People Reprise *	Moderate Tempo	Alto	G3	Bb4	Lead	Character Female
Curtains	Kander, John	2007	Georgia Hendricks	Thinking of Him	Ballad	Alto	G3	Db5	Lead	Romantic Lead Female
Curtains	Kander, John	2007	Georgia Hendricks	Thataway *	Uptempo	Alto	B#3	B4	Lead	Romantic Lead Female
Curtains	Kander, John	2007	Lieutenant Frank Cioffi	Show People	Moderate Tempo	Baritone	A2	F4	Lead	Character Male
Cutains	Kander, John	2007	Lieutenant Frank Cioffi	Coffe Shop Nights	Ballad	Baritone	Ab2	D3	Lead	Character Male

Shows

Songs by Character Type

* = Music Edit Required
+ = Ethnic Specific

Show	Composer	Year	Role	Song	Tempo	Vocal Type	Range-Bottom	Range-Top	Category	Character Type
Cutains	Kander, John	2007	Lieutenant Frank Cioffi	A Tough Act To Follow *	Ballad	Baritone	A2	E♭4	Lead	Character Male
Cutains	Kander, John	2007	Lieutenant Frank Cioffi	Show People Reprise *	Moderate Tempo	Baritone	B2	B♭3	Lead	Character Male
Damn Yankees	Adler and Ross	1955	Applegate	Those Were The Good Old Days	Uptempo	Baritone	A#2	D#4	Lead	Antagonist Male
Damn Yankees	Adler and Ross	1955	Applegate	Good Old Day Reprise	Uptempo	Baritone	A#2	E4	Lead	Antagonist Male
Damn Yankees	Adler and Ross	1955	Ensemble	Six Months Out Of Every Year	Uptempo	SATB			Ensemble	Adults
Damn Yankees	Adler and Ross	1955	Ensemble	Heart	Moderate Tempo	TB			Ensemble	Adults
Damn Yankees	Adler and Ross	1955	Ensemble	The Game	Uptempo	TB			Ensemble	Adults
Damn Yankees	Adler and Ross	1955	Gloria Thorpe	Shoeless Joe From Hannibal, Mo	Uptempo	Alto	B♭3	D♭5	Supporting	Character Female
Damn Yankees	Adler and Ross	1955	Joe Boyd	Goodbye Old Girl	Ballad	Baritone	D3	E4	Lead	Mature Male
Damn Yankees	Adler and Ross	1955	Joe Boyd	Near To You*	Ballad	Baritone	C3	C4	Supporting	Mature Male
Damn Yankees	Adler and Ross	1955	Joe Hardy	A Man Doesn't Know	Ballad	Tenor	C3	G♭4	Lead	Ingenue Male
Damn Yankees	Adler and Ross	1955	Joe Hardy	Near To You*	Ballad	Tenor	C3	C4	Lead	Ingenue Male
Damn Yankees	Adler and Ross	1955	Joe Hardy	Goodbye Old Girl	Ballad	Tenor	E♭3	F#4	Lead	Ingenue Male
Damn Yankees	Adler and Ross	1955	Lola	Whatever Lola Wants	Moderate Tempo	Alto	G3	D♭5	Lead	Romantic Antagonist Female
Damn Yankees	Adler and Ross	1955	Lola	A Little Brains A Little Talent	Uptempo	Alto	A3	B4	Lead	Romantic Antagonist Female
Damn Yankees	Adler and Ross	1955	Lola	Who's Got The Pain*	Uptempo	Alto	A3	B4	Lead	Romantic Antagonist Female
Damn Yankees	Adler and Ross	1955	Meg Boyd	Six Months Out of Every Year	Uptempo	Soprano	A3	D5	Supporting	Mature Female
Damn Yankees	Adler and Ross	1955	Meg Boyd	A Man Doesn't Know	Ballad	Soprano	G3	D♭5	Supporting	Mature Female
Damn Yankees	Adler and Ross	1955	Meg Boyd	There's Something About An Empty Ch	Ballad	Soprano			Supporting	Mature Female
Damn Yankees	Adler and Ross	1955	Meg Boyd	Near To You*	Ballad	Soprano	B3	E♭5	Supporting	Mature Female
Damn Yankees	Adler and Ross	1955	Meg Boyd	A Man Doesn't Know Reprise	Ballad	Soprano	G3	D5	Supporting	Mature Female
Damn Yankees	Adler and Ross	1955	Sohovic	Who's Got The Pain	Uptempo	Baritone	G#3	D#4	Supporting	Ingenue Male
Damn Yankees	Adler and Ross	1955	Joe Hardy & Meg	A Man Doesn't Know Reprise	Ballad	Tenor/Sop			Duet	IM/MF
Damn Yankees	Adler and Ross	1955	Lola & Sohovik	Who's Got The Pain	Uptempo	Alto/Bar			Duet	RAF/IM
Damn Yankees	Adler and Ross	1955	Hardy & Meg	Near To You	Ballad	Tenor/Sop			Duet	IM/MF
Damn Yankees	Adler and Ross	1955	Boyd & Meg	A Man Doesn't Know Reprise 2	Moderate Tempo	Bar/Bar			Duet	MF/MM
Dear World	Herman, Jerry	1969	President	The Spring Of Next Year*	Moderate Tempo	Baritone	G2	D4	Supporting	Character Male
Dear World	Herman, Jerry	1969	Ensemble	The Spring Of Next Year	Moderate Tempo	SATB			Ensemble	Adults
Dear World	Herman, Jerry	1969	Madame Constance	Memory	Moderate Tempo	Soprano	A3	F5	Lead	Mature Female
Dear World	Herman, Jerry	1969	Countess Aurelia	Through The Bottom Of The Glass	Moderate Tempo	Soprano	E3	A4	Lead	Mature Female
Dear World	Herman, Jerry	1969	President	Just A Little Bit More*	Uptempo	Baritone	G2	F♭4	Supporting	Character Male
Dear World	Herman, Jerry	1969	Ensemble	Just A Little But More	Uptempo	TTB			Ensemble	Adults
Dear World	Herman, Jerry	1969	President	Just A Little Bit More Reprise*	Uptempo	Baritone	G♭3	E♭4	Supporting	Character Male
Dear World	Herman, Jerry	1969	Ensemble	Just A Little Bit More Reprise	Uptempo	TTB			Ensemble	Adults
Dear World	Herman, Jerry	1969	Countess Aurelia	Each Tomorrow Morning	Moderate Tempo	Alto	E3	B♭4	Lead	Mature Female
Dear World	Herman, Jerry	1969	Ensemble	Each Tomorrow Morning Reprise 1	Moderate Tempo	SATB			Ensemble	Adults
Dear World	Herman, Jerry	1969	Countess Aurelia	I Don't Want To Know	Moderate Tempo	AAB	G#3	A4	Lead	Mature Female
Dear World	Herman, Jerry	1969	Julian & Countess Aurelia	Each Tomorrow Morning Reprise 2	Moderate Tempo	Tenor/Alto			Duet	IM/MF
Dear World	Herman, Jerry	1969	Nina	I've Never Said I Love You	Ballad	Alto	B♭3	E♭5	Lead	Ingenue Female
Dear World	Herman, Jerry	1969	Sewerman	Pretty Garbage*	Moderate Tempo	Baritone	B2	E4	Supporting	Character Male
Dear World	Herman, Jerry	1969	Sewerman	Ugly Garbage*	Moderate Tempo	Baritone	A3	E4	Supporting	Character Male
Dear World	Herman, Jerry	1969	Countess Aurelia	One Person*	Uptempo	Alto	F3	B♭4	Lead	Mature Female

Shows

406

* = Music Edit Required
\+ = Ethnic Specific

Show	Composer	Year	Role	Song	Tempo	Vocal Type	Range-Bottom	Range-Top	Category	Character Type
Dear World	Herman, Jerry	1969	Ensemble	One Person	Uptempo	SATB			Ensemble	Adults
Dear World	Herman, Jerry	1969	Gabrielle & Aurelia	Pearls	Ballad	Sop/Alto			Duet	MF/MF
Dear World	Herman, Jerry	1969	Madame Constance	Voices	Uptempo	Soprano	F4	E5	Lead	Mature Female
Dear World	Herman, Jerry	1969	Madame Gabrielle	Dickie	Uptempo	Soprano	G3	E5	Lead	Mature Female
Dear World	Herman, Jerry	1969	Countess Aurelia	Thoughts	Uptempo	Alto	G3	D5	Lead	Mature Female
Dear World	Herman, Jerry	1969	Ensemble	Tea Party Trio	Uptempo	SSA			Ensemble	Adults
Dear World	Herman, Jerry	1969	Countess Aurelia	And I Was Beautiful	Ballad	Alto	G3	D5	Lead	Mature Female
Dear World	Herman, Jerry	1969	Countess Aurelia	Dear World*	Moderate Tempo	Alto	E3	A4	Lead	Mature Female
Dear World	Herman, Jerry	1969	Ensemble	Dear World	Moderate Tempo	SATB			Ensemble	Adults
Dear World	Herman, Jerry	1969	Ensemble	The Spring Of Next Year Reprise	Ballad	TB			Ensemble	Adults
Dear World	Herman, Jerry	1969	Countess Aurelia	Kiss Her Now	Moderate Tempo	Alto	G#3	A4	Lead	Mature Female
Dear World	Herman, Jerry	1969	Ensemble	Finale-Tomorrow Morning	Moderate Tempo	SATB			Ensemble	Adults
Dear World	Herman, Jerry	1969	Ensemble	Bows-Medley	Uptempo	SATB			Ensemble	Adults
Dirty Rotten Scoundrels	Yazbek, David	2005	Christine & Freddy	Nothing Is Too Wonderful	Moderate Tempo	Sop/Tenor			Duet	RLF/CM
Dirty Rotten Scoundrels	Yazbek, David	2005	Andre & Muriel	Like Zis/Like Zat	Moderate Tempo	Bar/Alto			Duet	CM/RLF
Dirty Rotten Scoundrels	Yazbek, David	2005	Andre Thibault	A Chimp In A Suit	Uptempo	Baritone	C3	E4	Supporting	Character Male
Dirty Rotten Scoundrels	Yazbek, David	2005	Andre Thibault	Like Zis/Like Zat *	Moderate Tempo	Baritone	Bb3	Eb4	Supporting	Character Male
Dirty Rotten Scoundrels	Yazbek, David	2005	Christine Colgate	Here I Am	Uptempo	Soprano	F3	E5	Lead	Romantic Lead Female
Dirty Rotten Scoundrels	Yazbek, David	2005	Christine Colgate	Nothing Is Too Wonderful To Be True	Ballad	Soprano	A3	F5	Lead	Romantic Lead Female
Dirty Rotten Scoundrels	Yazbek, David	2005	Freddy Benson	Great Big Stuff	Uptempo	Tenor	D3	F#4	Lead	Character Male
Dirty Rotten Scoundrels	Yazbek, David	2005	Jolene Oakes	Oklahoma	Uptempo	Alto	G#3	C5	Supporting	Romantic Lead Female
Dirty Rotten Scoundrels	Yazbek, David	2005	Lawrence Jameson	Give Them What They Want *	Moderate Tempo	Baritone	C3	Eb4	Lead	Romantic Lead Male
Dirty Rotten Scoundrels	Yazbek, David	2005	Lawrence Jameson	All About Ruprecht	Uptempo	Baritone	D3	E4	Lead	Romantic Lead Male
Dirty Rotten Scoundrels	Yazbek, David	2005	Lawrence Jameson	Ruffjousin' Mit Shuffhousen	Uptempo	Baritone	C3	A4	Lead	Romantic Lead Male
Dirty Rotten Scoundrels	Yazbek, David	2005	Lawrence Jameson	Love Sneaks In	Ballad	Baritone	G2	D4	Lead	Romantic Lead Male
Dirty Rotten Scoundrels	Yazbek, David	2005	Lawrence Jameson	The More We Dance	Uptempo	Baritone	D3	G4	Lead	Romantic Lead Male
Dirty Rotten Scoundrels	Yazbek, David	2005	Lawrence Jameson	Dirty Rotten Number	Moderate Tempo	Baritone	C3	F4	Lead	Romantic Lead Male
Dirty Rotten Scoundrels	Yazbek, David	2005	Muriel Eubanks	What's A Woman To Do	Moderate Tempo	Alto	G2	D4	Supporting	Romantic Lead Female
Dirty Rotten Scoundrels	Yazbek, David	2005	Muriel Eubanks	What's Was A Woman To Do Reprise	Moderate Tempo	Alto	E3	Bb4	Supporting	Romantic Lead Female
Dirty Rotten Scoundrels	Yazbek, David	2005	Muriel Eubanks	Like Zis/Like Zat *	Moderate Tempo	Alto	E3	Bb4	Supporting	Romantic Lead Female
Dreamgirls	Krieger, Henry	1981	CC White +	Family	Ballad	Baritone	D3	E4	Lead	Ingenue Male
Dreamgirls	Krieger, Henry	1981	Curtis Taylor, Jr +	Cadilac Car	Uptempo	Baritone	F3	G4	Lead	Romantic Lead Male
Dreamgirls	Krieger, Henry	1981	Curtis Taylor, Jr +	When I First Saw You	Ball	Baritone	C3	E4	Lead	Romantic Lead Male
Dreamgirls	Krieger, Henry	1981	Deena Jones +	Heavy	Uptempo	Soprano	D3	D4	Lead	Ingenue Female
Dreamgirls	Krieger, Henry	1981	Deena Jones +	One Night Only	Uptempo	Soprano	Ab3	D5	Lead	Ingenue Female
Dreamgirls	Krieger, Henry	1981	Effie White +	I Am Changing	Ballad	Alto	Eb4	F5	Lead	Character Female
Dreamgirls	Krieger, Henry	1981	Effie White +	One Night Only	Ballad	Alto	Ab3	D5	Lead	Character Female
Dreamgirls	Krieger, Henry	1981	Ensemble	Cadilac Car	Moderate Tempo	TB			Ensemble	Adults
Dreamgirls	Krieger, Henry	1981	James Thunder Early +	Fake Your Way to the Top	Uptempo	Tenor	F3	Ab4	Supporting	Character Male
Dreamgirls	Krieger, Henry	1981	James Thunder Early +	I Want You Baby	Ballad	Tenor	Eb3	Db4	Lead	Character Male
Dreamgirls	Krieger, Henry	1981	James Thunder Early +	I Meant You No Harm	Ballad	Tenor	Bb2	G4	Lead	Character Male
Dreamgirls	Krieger, Henry	1981	Lorelle Robinson +	Ain't No Party *	Uptempo	Soprano	Bb3	E4	Lead	Character Ingenue Female

* = Music Edit Required
+ = Ethnic Specific

Show	Composer	Year	Role	Song	Tempo	Vocal Type	Range-Bottom	Range-Top	Category	Character Type
Dreamgirls	Krieger, Henry	1981	Curtis & Deena	When I First Saw You	Ballad	Bar/Sop			Duet	RLM/IF
Drowsy Chaperon, The	Lambert and Morrison	2006	Adolpho	I Am Adolpho *	Moderate Tempo	Tenor	E2	A5	Lead	Romantic Lead Male
Drowsy Chaperon, The	Lambert and Morrison	2006	Drowsy Chaperone	As We Stumble Along	Moderate Tempo	Alto	F3	D5	Lead	Character Female
Drowsy Chaperon, The	Lambert and Morrison	2006	Drowsy Chaperone	Show Off Encore	Uptempo	Soprano	A3	A5	Lead	Character Female
Drowsy Chaperon, The	Lambert and Morrison	2006	Gangster	Toledo Surprise *	Uptempo	Tenor	C3	G♭4	Supporting	Character Male
Drowsy Chaperon, The	Lambert and Morrison	2006	Janet Van de Graff	Show Off *	Uptempo	Soprano	G3	C5	Lead	Ingenue Female
Drowsy Chaperon, The	Lambert and Morrison	2006	Janet Van de Graff	Accident Waiting To Happen *	Moderate Tempo	Soprano	C4	D5	Lead	Ingenue Female
Drowsy Chaperon, The	Lambert and Morrison	2006	Janet Van de Graff	Bride's Lament *	Ballad	Soprano	A♭3	F5	Lead	Ingenue Female
Drowsy Chaperon, The	Lambert and Morrison	2006	Mrs. Tottendale	Love Is Always Lovely *	Moderate Tempo	Alto	G3	B♭4	Supporting	Mature Female
Drowsy Chaperon, The	Lambert and Morrison	2006	Robert Martin	Accident Waiting To Happen *	Moderate Tempo	Tenor	E♭3	A4	Lead	Ingenue Male
Drowsy Chaperon, The	Lambert and Morrison	2006	Robert Martin	Cold Feets *	Uptempo	Tenor	C3	A♭4	Lead	Ingenue Male
Drowsy Chaperon, The	Lambert and Morrison	2006	Trix	I Do, I Do In The Sky	Uptempo	Soprano	A3	A5	Lead	Character Female
Drowsy Chaperone	Lambert and Morrison	2006	George & Robert	Cold Feets	Moderate Tempo	Tenor/Tenor			Duet	CM/IM
Drowsy Chaperone	Lambert and Morrison	2006	Janet & Robert	Accident Waiting To Happen	Moderate Tempo	Sop/Tenor			Duet	IF/IM
Evita	Webber, Andrew Lloyd	1978	Che Guevara	Oh What A Circus	Uptempo	Tenor	B2	E4	Lead	Antagonist Male
Evita	Webber, Andrew Lloyd	1978	Che Guevara	Goodnight and Thank You	Uptempo	Tenor	B2	F4	Lead	Antagonist Male
Evita	Webber, Andrew Lloyd	1978	Che Guevara	Peron's Latest Flame	Uptempo	Tenor	F2	F4	Lead	Romantic Antagonist Male
Evita	Webber, Andrew Lloyd	1978	Che Guevara	High Flying Adored	Moderate Tempo	Tenor	B♭2	G4	Lead	Antagonist Male
Evita	Webber, Andrew Lloyd	1978	Che Guevara	Rainbow Tour	Uptempo	Tenor	C3	E4	Lead	Antagonist Male
Evita	Webber, Andrew Lloyd	1978	Che Guevara	And the Money Kept Rolling In	Uptempo	Tenor	A2	G4	Lead	Antagonist Male
Evita	Webber, Andrew Lloyd	1978	Che Guevara	Waltz for Eva and Che	Uptempo	Tenor	D3	G4	Lead	Antagonist Male
Evita	Webber, Andrew Lloyd	1978	Eva Peron	Buenos Aires	Uptempo	Alto	E3	F5	Lead	Romantic Antagonist Female
Evita	Webber, Andrew Lloyd	1978	Eva Peron	I'd Be Surprisingly Good For You	Moderate Tempo	Alto	G#3	F5	Lead	Romantic Antagonist Female
Evita	Webber, Andrew Lloyd	1978	Eva Peron	Another Suitcase In Another Hall	Ballad	Alto	A3	E5	Supporting	Romantic Antagonist Female
Evita	Webber, Andrew Lloyd	1978	Eva Peron	Don't Cry For Me Argentina	Alto	Alto	A♭3	E♭5	Lead	Romantic Antagonist Female
Evita	Webber, Andrew Lloyd	1978	Eva Peron	Rainbow High	Uptempo	Alto	G3	E5	Lead	Romantic Antagonist Female
Evita	Webber, Andrew Lloyd	1978	Eva Peron	The Actress Hasn't Learned the Lines	Ballad	Alto	G#3	D#5	Lead	Romantic Antagonist Female
Evita	Webber, Andrew Lloyd	1978	Eva Peron	Waltz for Eva and Che	Uptempo	Alto	A♭3	F5	Lead	Romantic Antagonist Female
Evita	Webber, Andrew Lloyd	1978	Eva Peron	Eva's Final Broadcast	Ballad	Alto	A♭3	D♭5	Lead	Romantic Antagonist Female
Evita	Webber, Andrew Lloyd	1978	Eva Peron	Lament	Ballad	Alto	B♭3	D♭5	Lead	Romantic Antagonist Female
Evita	Webber, Andrew Lloyd	1978	Juan Peron	The Art of the Possible	Moderate Tempo	Baritone	B♭2	D4	Lead	Romantic Lead Male
Evita	Webber, Andrew Lloyd	1978	Juan Peron	She's A Diamond	Moderate Tempo	Baritone	A2	F4	Lead	Romantic Lead Male
Evita	Webber, Andrew Lloyd	1978	Magaldi	On This Nigh of a Thousand Stars	Ballad	Tenor	B♭2	G4	Supporting	Romantic Lead Male
Evita	Webber, Andrew Lloyd	1978	Mistress	Another Suitcase In Another Hall	Ballad	Soprano	A3	E5	Supporting	Ingenue Female
Evita	Webber, Andrew Lloyd	1978	Eva & Peron	I'd Be Surprisingly Good For You	Moderate Tempo	Alto/Bar			Duet	RAF/RLM
Evita	Webber, Andrew Lloyd	1978	Eva & Eva	High Flying Adore	Uptempo	Tenor/Alto			Duet	RAM/RAF
Evita	Webber, Andrew Lloyd	1978	Che & Eva	Waltz of Eva And Che	Uptempo	Tenor/Alto			Duet	RAM/RAF
Evita	Webber, Andrew Lloyd	1978	Eva & Peron	Dice Are Rolling	Moderate Tempo	Alto/Bar			Duet	RAF/RLM
Fame	Webber, Andrew Lloyd	1988	Carmen & Schlomo	Bring On Tomorrow	Moderate Tempo	Alto/Bar			Duet	CIF/CM
Fame	Margoshes, Steve	2003	Carmen	There She Goes *	Uptempo	Alto	A3	C5	Lead	Character Ingenue Female
Fame	Margoshes, Steve	2003	Carmen	Fame! *	Uptempo	Alto	E♭4	E♭5	Lead	Character Ingenue Female

Shows

Songs by Character Type

* = Music Edit Required
\+ = Ethnic Specific

Show	Composer	Year	Role	Song	Tempo	Vocal Type	Range-Bottom	Range-Top	Category	Character Type
Fame	Margoshes, Steve	2003	Carmen	Bring In Tomorrow *	Ballad	Alto	D4	D	Lead	Character Ingenue Female
Fame	Margoshes, Steve	2003	Carmen	In LA	Ballad	Alto	Bb3	Eb5	Lead	Character Ingenue Female
Fame	Margoshes, Steve	2003	Ensemble	Hard Work	Uptempo	SATB			Ensemble	Adults
Fame	Margoshes, Steve	2003	Joe	I Can't Keep It Down *	Uptempo	Tenor	C3	Bb4	Supporting	Character Male
Fame	Margoshes, Steve	2003	Mabel	Mabel's Prayer	Moderate Tempo	Alto	D4	E5	Supporting	Character Female
Fame	Margoshes, Steve	2003	Miss Sherman	These Are My Children	Ballad	Alto	F3	C5	Supporting	Mature Female
Fame	Margoshes, Steve	2003	Nick	I Want To Make Magic	Moderate Tempo	Tenor	C3	G4	Lead	Ingenue Male
Fame	Margoshes, Steve	2003	Nick	Let's Play A Love Scene Reprise *	Ballad	Tenor	Db3	G4	Lead	Ingenue Male
Fame	Margoshes, Steve	2003	Schlomo	Bring In Tomorrow *	Ballad	Baritone	D3	F4	Lead	Character Male
Fame	Margoshes, Steve	2003	Serena	Let's Play A Love Scene	Ballad	Alto	G#3	D#5	Lead	Character Female
Fame	Margoshes, Steve	2003	Serena	Think of Meryl Streep	Uptempo	Alto	B3	D5	Lead	Character Female
Fame	Margoshes, Steve	2003	Serena	Let's Play A Love Scene Reprise *	Ballad	Alto	A3	B4	Lead	Character Female
Fame	Margoshes, Steve	2003	Tyrone+	Tyrone's Rap	Uptempo	Tenor	Bb3	Bb4	Lead	Antagonist Male
Fame	Margoshes, Steve	2003	Tyrone+	Dancin' On The Sidewalk	Uptempo	Tenor	Bb2	Bb4	Lead	Antagonist Male
Fantasticks, The	Schmidt, Harvey	2003	Bell & Sherman	Teacher's Argument	Uptempo	Alto/Alto			Duet	MF/MF
Fantasticks, The	Schmidt, Harvey	2003	Nick & Serena	Let's Play A Love Scene Reprise	Moderate Tempo	Tenor/Alto			Duet	IM/CF
Fantasticks, The	Schmidt, Harvey	1960	Luis & Matt	Metaphor	Moderate Tempo	Tenor/Sop			Duet	IF/IM
Fantasticks, The	Schmidt, Harvey	1960	Bellomy & Hucklebee	Never Say No	Moderate Tempo	Bar/Bar			Duet	P/P
Fantasticks, The	Schmidt, Harvey	1960	Luisa & Matt	Soon It's Gonna Rain	Moderate Tempo	Sop/Tenor			Duet	IF/IM
Fantasticks, The	Schmidt, Harvey	1960	El Gallo & Matt	I Can See It	Uptempo	Bar/Tenor			Duet	RLM/IM
Fantasticks, The	Schmidt, Harvey	1960	Bellomy & Hucklebee	Plant A Radish	Uptempo	Bar/Bar			Duet	P/P
Fantasticks, The	Schmidt, Harvey	1960	Luisa & Matt	They Were You	Ballad	Sop/Tenor			Duet	IF/IM
Fantasticks, The	Schmidt, Harvey	1960	Bellomy	Never Say No *	Uptempo	Baritone	G3	E4	Supporting	Paternal
Fantasticks, The	Schmidt, Harvey	1960	Bellomy	Plant A Raddish *	Uptempo	Baritone	C3	F4	Supporting	Paternal
Fantasticks, The	Schmidt, Harvey	1960	Bellomy	It Depends On What You Pay Reprise *	Uptempo	Baritone	D3	G4	Supporting	Paternal
Fantasticks, The	Schmidt, Harvey	1960	El Gallo	Try To Remember *	Ballad	Baritone	A2	C4	Lead	Romantic Lead Male
Fantasticks, The	Schmidt, Harvey	1960	El Gallo	Try To Remember Reprise	Moderate Tempo	Baritone	B2	C4	Lead	Romantic Lead Male
Fantasticks, The	Schmidt, Harvey	1960	El Gallo	I Depends On What You Pay	Uptempo	Baritone	A2	G4	Lead	Romantic Lead Male
Fantasticks, The	Schmidt, Harvey	1960	El Gallo	Round and Round *	Ballad	Baritone	Ab2	F4	Lead	Romantic Lead Male
Fantasticks, The	Schmidt, Harvey	1960	Ensemble	Happy Ending	Uptempo	SATB			Ensemble	Adults
Fantasticks, The	Schmidt, Harvey	1960	Huckabee	Never Say No *	Uptempo	Baritone	C3	E4	Supporting	Paternal
Fantasticks, The	Schmidt, Harvey	1960	Huckabee	Plant A Raddish *	Uptempo	Baritone	C3	F4	Supporting	Paternal
Fantasticks, The	Schmidt, Harvey	1960	Huckabee	It Depends On What You Pay Reprise *	Uptempo	Baritone	D3	G4	Supporting	Paternal
Fantasticks, The	Schmidt, Harvey	1960	Luisa	Much More	Uptempo	Soprano	B3	F5	Lead	Ingenue Female
Fantasticks, The	Schmidt, Harvey	1960	Luisa	Metaphor *	Uptempo	Soprano	Eb4	G5	Lead	Ingenue Female
Fantasticks, The	Schmidt, Harvey	1960	Luisa	Soon It's Gonna Rain *	Moderate Tempo	Soprano	B2	F4	Lead	Ingenue Female
Fantasticks, The	Schmidt, Harvey	1960	Luisa	They Were You *	Ballad	Soprano	B3	D5	Lead	Ingenue Female
Fantasticks, The	Schmidt, Harvey	1960	Matt	Metaphor *	Uptempo	Tenor	Cb3	Eb4	Lead	Ingenue Male
Fantasticks, The	Schmidt, Harvey	1960	Matt	Soon It's Gonna Rain *	Moderate Tempo	Baritone	D4	Ab5	Lead	Ingenue Male
Fantasticks, The	Schmidt, Harvey	1960	Matt	I Can See It *	Uptempo	Tenor	B2	E4	Lead	Ingenue Male
Fantasticks, The	Schmidt, Harvey	1960	Matt	They Were You *	Ballad	Tenor	B2	D4	Lead	Ingenue Male
Fantasticks, The	Schmidt, Harvey	1960	Matt	Metaphor Reprise *	Uptempo	Tenor	B2	D4	Lead	Ingenue Male
Fiddler On The Roof	Bock, Jerry	1964	Ensemble	Anatevka	Ballad	SATB			Ensemble	Adults

Shows

409

* = Music Edit Required
+ = Ethnic Specific

Show	Composer	Year	Role	Song	Tempo	Vocal Type	Range-Bottom	Range-Top	Category	Character Type
Fiddler on The Roof	Bock, Jerry	1964	Golde	Sabbath Prayer	Ballad	Alto	D4	C5	Lead	Maternal
Fiddler on The Roof	Bock, Jerry	1964	Golde	Sunrise Sunset	Ballad	Alto	C4	D5	Lead	Maternal
Fiddler on The Roof	Bock, Jerry	1964	Hodel	Far From The Home I Love	Ballad	Alto	C4	E5	Supporting	Character Ingenue Female
Fiddler on The Roof	Bock, Jerry	1964	Motel	Miracle of Miracles	Uptempo	Tenor	E3	F#4	Supporting	Character Male
Fiddler on The Roof	Bock, Jerry	1964	Perchik	Now I Have Everything	Uptempo	Baritone	B2	E4	Supporting	Antagonist Male
Fiddler on The Roof	Bock, Jerry	1964	Tevye	If I Were A Rich Man	Moderate Tempo	Baritone	Db3	F4	Lead	Paternal
Fiddler on The Roof	Bock, Jerry	1964	Tevye	Sabbath Prayer	Ballad	Baritone	D3	C4	Lead	Paternal
Fiddler on The Roof	Bock, Jerry	1964	Tevye	Sunrise Sunset	Ballad	Baritone	C3	D4	Lead	Paternal
Fiddler on The Roof	Bock, Jerry	1964	Tevye	Chavaleh	Ballad	Baritone	C3	C4	Lead	Paternal
Fiddler on The Roof	Bock, Jerry	1964	Tevye	Tevye's Monologue	Moderate Tempo	Baritone	Ab2	E4	Lead	Paternal
Fiddler on The Roof	Bock, Jerry	1964	Tevye	Tevye's Rebuttal	Moderate Tempo	Baritone	Ab2	E4	Lead	Paternal
Fiddler On The Roof	Bock, Jerry	1964	Hodel & Perchik	Now I Have Everything	Uptempo	Alto/Bar			Duet	CIF/RAM
Fiddler On The Roof	Bock, Jerry	1964	Golde & Tevye	Do You Love Me	Moderate Tempo	Alto/Bar			Duet	M/P
Flower Drum Song 2002	Rodgers, Richard	1958	Wang Ta+	You Are Beautiful	Ballad	Tenor	Eb3	G4	Lead	Ingenue Male
Flower Drum Song 2002	Rodgers, Richard	1958	Wu Mei-Li+	A Hundred Million Miracles*	Moderate Tempo	Alto	C4	Eb5	Lead	Ingenue Female
Flower Drum Song 2002	Rodgers, Richard	1958	Ensemble	A Hundred Million Miracles	Moderate Tempo	SATB			Ensemble	Adults
Flower Drum Song 2002	Rodgers, Richard	1958	Wu Mei-Li+	I Am Going To Like It Here	Moderate Tempo	Alto	Bb3	Bb4	Lead	Ingenue Female
Flower Drum Song 2002	Rodgers, Richard	1958	Ensemble	Jazz Bit	Moderate Tempo	SATB			Ensemble	Adults
Flower Drum Song 2002	Rodgers, Richard	1958	Linda Low+	I Enjoy Being A Girl	Uptempo	Alto	A3	B4	Lead	Romantic Lead Female
Flower Drum Song 2002	Rodgers, Richard	1958	Linda Low+	I Enjoy Being A Girl Encore*	Moderate Tempo	Alto	A3	Cb5	Lead	Romantic Lead Female
Flower Drum Song 2002	Rodgers, Richard	1958	Linda Low+	I Enjoy Being A Girl Playoff*	Moderate Tempo	Alto	Bb3	Eb5	Lead	Romantic Lead Female
Flower Drum Song 2002	Rodgers, Richard	1958	Ensemble	I Enjoy Being A Girl Playoff*	Moderate Tempo	ATB	D4	D5	Ensemble	Adults
Flower Drum Song 2002	Rodgers, Richard	1958	Wang Ta+	You Are Beautiful Reprise*	Ballad	Alto	F3	G4	Lead	Ingenue Female
Flower Drum Song 2002	Rodgers, Richard	1958	Wang Ta+ & Wu Mei-Li	You Are Beautiful Reprise*	Ballad	Tenor			Duet	Ingenue Male
Flower Drum Song 2002	Rodgers, Richard	1958	Wang Ta+ & Wu Mei-Li	Flower Boat	Ballad	Tenor/Alto			Duet	IM/IF
Flower Drum Song 2002	Rodgers, Richard	1958	Madam Rita Liang	Grant Avenue*	Moderate Tempo	Alto	A3	C5	Lead	Romantic Antagonist Female
Flower Drum Song 2002	Rodgers, Richard	1958	Ensemble	Grant Avenue	Moderate Tempo	SATB			Ensemble	Adults
Flower Drum Song 2002	Rodgers, Richard	1958	Wang Ta+	Sunday	Moderate Tempo	Tenor	C#4	D5	Lead	Ingenue Male
Flower Drum Song 2002	Rodgers, Richard	1958	Wu Mei-Li+	I Enjoy Being A Girl Reprise	Ballad	Alto	Bb3	B4	Lead	Ingenue Female
Flower Drum Song 2002	Rodgers, Richard	1958	Linda Low+	Fan Tan Fannie*	Uptempo	Alto	B3	D5	Lead	Romantic Lead Female
Flower Drum Song 2002	Rodgers, Richard	1958	Ensemble	Fan Tan Fannie	Uptempo	SATB			Ensemble	Adults
Flower Drum Song 2002	Rodgers, Richard	1958	Chi-Yang Wang+	Gliding Through My Memory*	Moderate Tempo	Baritone	D3	G4	Lead	Romantic Lead Male
Flower Drum Song 2002	Rodgers, Richard	1958	Ensemble	Gliding Through My Memory	Moderate Tempo	TB			Ensemble	Adults
Flower Drum Song 2002	Rodgers, Richard	1958	Wu Mei-Li+	A Hundred Million Miracles Reprise*	Moderate Tempo	Alto	Ab3	Bb4	Lead	Ingenue Female
Flower Drum Song 2002	Rodgers, Richard	1958	Ensemble	A Hundred Million Miracles Reprise	Moderate Tempo	SATB			Ensemble	Adults
Flower Drum Song 2002	Rodgers, Richard	1958	Chi-Yang Wang+	Chop Suey*	Moderate Tempo	Tenor	B2	D#4	Lead	Romantic Lead Male
Flower Drum Song 2002	Rodgers, Richard	1958	Ensemble	Chop Suey	Moderate Tempo	SATB			Ensemble	Adults
Flower Drum Song 2002	Rodgers, Richard	1958	Chin+	My Best Love*	Ballad	Baritone	D#3	E4	Lead	Mature Male
Flower Drum Song 2002	Rodgers, Richard	1958	Ensemble	I Am Going To Like It Here Reprise	Ballad	SATB			Ensemble	Adults
Flower Drum Song 2002	Rodgers, Richard	1958	Wang+ & Liang+	Don't Marry Me	Uptempo	Bar/Alto			Duet	RLM/RAF
Flower Drum Song 2002	Rodgers, Richard	1958	Wu Mei-Li+	Love, Look Away (Ab Maj)	Ballad	Alto	G3	C5	Lead	Ingenue Female

Songs by Character Type

* = Music Edit Required
+ = Ethnic Specific

Show	Composer	Year	Role	Song	Tempo	Vocal Type	Range-Bottom	Range-Top	Category	Character Type
Flower Drum Song 2002	Rodgers, Richard	1958	Helen Chao+	Love, Look Away (C Maj)	Ballad	Alto	B3	E5	Lead	Romantic Lead Female
Flower Drum Song 2002	Rodgers, Richard	1958	Wang Ta+	Like A God	Uptempo	Tenor	C#3	G#4	Lead	Ingenue Male
Flower Drum Song 2002	Rodgers, Richard	1958	Wang Ta+	Like A God	Moderate Tempo	Tenor	B2	G4	Lead	Ingenue Male
Flower Drum Song 2002	Rodgers, Richard	1958	Ensemble	Finale: A Hundred Million Mirac	Moderate Tempo	SATB			Ensemble	Adults
Follies	Sondheim, Stephen	1971	Benjamin Stone	The Road You Didn't Take *	Uptempo	Baritone	A2	E4	Lead	Romantic Lead Male
Follies	Sondheim, Stephen	1971	Benjamin Stone	Too Many Mornings *	Ballad	Baritone	C3	E4	Lead	Romantic Lead Male
Follies	Sondheim, Stephen	1971	Benjamin Stone	Live, Laugh, Love	Uptempo	Baritone	C#3	F4	Lead	Romantic Lead Male
Follies	Sondheim, Stephen	1971	Buddy Plummer	The Right Girl *	Uptempo	Baritone	C3	F4	Lead	Character Male
Follies	Sondheim, Stephen	1971	Buddy Plummer	Buddy's Blues	Uptempo	Baritone	Db3	F4	Lead	Character Male
Follies	Sondheim, Stephen	1971	Carolotta Champion	I'm Still Here	Moderate Tempo	Alto	Eb3	C5	Supporting	Romantic Lead Female
Follies	Sondheim, Stephen	1971	Emily Whitman	Rain On The Roof *	Uptempo	Soprano	Bb3	D5	Supporting	Mature Female
Follies	Sondheim, Stephen	1971	Ensemble	Loveland	Uptempo	Unison			Ensemble	Adults
Follies	Sondheim, Stephen	1971	Hattie Walker	Broadway Baby	Moderate Tempo	Alto	A3	Bb4	Supporting	Antagonist Female
Follies	Sondheim, Stephen	1971	Heidi Schiller	One More Kiss *	Ballad	Soprano	D4	F5	Supporting	Mature Female
Follies	Sondheim, Stephen	1971	Phyllis Rogers Stone	Could I Leave You	Moderate Tempo	Alto	F#3	Bb4	Lead	Romantic Antagonist Female
Follies	Sondheim, Stephen	1971	Roscoe	Beautiful Girls	Moderate Tempo	Tenor	D3	A4	Supporting	Mature Male
Follies	Sondheim, Stephen	1971	Sally Durant	In Buddy's Eyes *	Ballad	Alto	F#3	D5	Lead	Character Female
Follies	Sondheim, Stephen	1971	Sally Durant	Too Many Mornings *	Ballad	Soprano	C4	G#5	Lead	Character Female
Follies	Sondheim, Stephen	1971	Sally Durant	Losing My Mind	Ballad	Soprano	F3	B4	Lead	Character Female
Follies	Sondheim, Stephen	1971	Sally Durant	The Story of Lucy and Jesse	Uptempo	Soprano	G3	Bb4	Lead	Character Female
Follies	Sondheim, Stephen	1971	Solange LaFitte	Don't Look At Me*	Uptempo	Soprano	A3	B4	Lead	Romantic Lead Female
Follies	Sondheim, Stephen	1971	Stella Deems	Ah, Paris *	Uptempo	Alto	C3	G4	Supporting	Mature Female
Follies	Sondheim, Stephen	1971	Theodore Whitman	Who's That Woman *	Uptempo	Alto	E3	A4	Supporting	Mature Female
Follies	Sondheim, Stephen	1971	Theodore Whitman	Rain On The Roof *	Uptempo	Baritone	Bb2	D4	Supporting	Mature Male
Follies	Sondheim, Stephen	1971	Ben & Sally	Don't Look At Me	Uptempo	Bar/Sop			Duet	RLM/CF
Follies	Sondheim, Stephen	1971	Emily & Theodore	Rain On The Roof	Uptempo	Alto/Bar			Duet	MF/MM
Follies	Sondheim, Stephen	1971	Ben & Sally	Too Many Mornings	Moderate Tempo	Bar/Sop			Duet	RLM/CF
Follies	Sondheim, Stephen	1971	Heidi & Young Heidi	One More Kiss	Ballad	Sop/Sop			Duet	MF/IF
Follies	Sondheim, Stephen	1971	Young Ben & Young Phyllis	You're Gonna Love Tomorrow	Uptempo	Tenor/Alto			Duet	IM/IF
Follies	Sondheim, Stephen	1971	Young Buddy & Young Sally	Love Will See Us Through	Uptempo	Bar/Alto			Duet	CIM/CIF
Footloose	Snow, Tom	1998	Ariel Moore	Holding Out For A Hero	Uptempo	Alto	C4	C5	Lead	Character Ingenue Female
Footloose	Snow, Tom	1998	Ariel Moore	Almost Paradise*	Ballad	Alto	G3	C5	Lead	Character Ingenue Female
Footloose	Snow, Tom	1998	Chuck Cranston	The Girl Gets Around	Uptempo	Tenor	G#3	A4	Supporting	Romantic Antagonist Male
Footloose	Snow, Tom	1998	Ren McCormick	Footloose (Finale)	Uptempo	SATB			Ensemble	Teens
Footloose	Snow, Tom	1998	Ethel McCormick	Learning To Be Silent	Ballad	Alto	Ab3	D5	Lead	Maternal
Footloose	Snow, Tom	1998	Featured Ensemble	Somebody's Eyes Are Watching	Ballad	Alto	Ab3	Bb4	Supporting	Character Ingenue Female
Footloose	Snow, Tom	1998	Irene	Let's Make Believe We're In Love	Moderate Tempo	Alto	G3	D4	Supporting	Character Female
Footloose	Snow, Tom	1998	Ren McCormick	I'm Free	Uptempo	Tenor	D3	C5	Lead	Character Ingenue Male
Footloose	Snow, Tom	1998	Ren McCormick	Almost Paradise*	Ballad	Tenor	G2	Ab4	Lead	Character Ingenue Male
Footloose	Snow, Tom	1998	Ren McCormick	Dancing Is Not A Crime (Rap)	Uptempo	Tenor	G2	A4	Lead	Character Ingenue Male
Footloose	Snow, Tom	1998	Rev. Shaw Moore	Heaven Help Me	Uptempo	Tenor	G2	E4	Lead	Paternal

Shows

Songs by Character Type

* = Music Edit Required
+ = Ethnic Specific

Show	Composer	Year	Role	Song	Tempo	Vocal Type	Range-Bottom	Range-Top	Category	Character Type
Footloose	Snow, Tom	1998	Rev. Shaw Moore	I Confess	Moderate Tempo	Tenor	B2	F4	Lead	Paternal
Footloose	Snow, Tom	1998	Rev. Shaw Moore	Can You Find It In Your Heart	Ballad	Tenor	A2	C4	Lead	Paternal
Footloose	Snow, Tom	1998	Rusty	Let's Hear It For the Boy	Uptempo	Alto	A3	D#5	Supporting	Character Female
Footloose	Snow, Tom	1998	Vi Moore	Learning To Be Silent	Ballad	Alto	Ab3	D5	Lead	Maternal
Footloose	Snow, Tom	1998	Vi Moore	Can You Find It In Your Heart	Ballad	Alto	A3	Db5	Supporting	Maternal
Footloose	Snow, Tom	1998	Willard Hewitt	Mama Says	Uptempo	Baritone	Bb2	G4	Lead	Antagonist Male
Footloose	Snow, Tom	1998	Ethel & Vi	Learning To Be Silent	Ballad	Alto/Alto			Duet	M/M
Footloose	Snow, Tom	1998	Ariel & Ren	Almost Paradise	Ballad	Alto/Tenor			Duet	CIF/CIM
Full Monty, The	Yazbek, David	2000	Dave & Jerry	Man	Uptempo	Bar/Tenor			Duet	CM/RLM
Full Monty, The	Yazbek, David	2000	Dave & Harold	You Rule My World	Ballad	Bar/Bar			Duet	CM/CM
Full Monty, The	Yazbek, David	2000	Ethan & Malcolm	You Walk With Me	Ballad	Tenor/Tenor			Duet	CM/CM
Full Monty, The	Yazbek, David	2000	Georgie & Vicki	You Rule My World Reprise	Ballad	Alto/Alto			Duet	CF/CF
Full Monty, The	Yazbek, David	2000	Dave Bukatinsky	You Rule My World *	Ballad	Baritone	C#3	B4	Lead	Character Male
Full Monty, The	Yazbek, David	2000	Ensemble	Let It Go	Uptempo	TB			Ensemble	Adults
Full Monty, The	Yazbek, David	2000	Georgie Bukatinsky	You Rule My World Reprise *	Ballad	Alto	G#3	D5	Supporting	Character Female
Full Monty, The	Yazbek, David	2000	Harold Nichols	You Rule My World *	Ballad	Baritone	C#3	G4	Lead	Character Male
Full Monty, The	Yazbek, David	2000	Jeanette Burmeister	Jeanette's Showbiz Number	Moderate Tempo	Alto	F3	Db5	Supporting	Mature Female
Full Monty, The	Yazbek, David	2000	Jerry Lukowski	Man *	Uptempo	Tenor	E3	B4	Lead	Romantic Lead Male
Full Monty, The	Yazbek, David	2000	Jerry Lukowski	Michael Jordan's Ball *	Uptempo	Tenor	G3	Bb4	Lead	Romantic Lead Male
Full Monty, The	Yazbek, David	2000	Jerry Lukowski	Breeze Off The River	Moderate Tempo	Tenor	C3	B4	Lead	Romantic Lead Male
Full Monty, The	Yazbek, David	2000	Jerry Lukowski	Man Reprise *	Uptempo	Tenor	E3	G4	Lead	Romantic Lead Male
Full Monty, The	Yazbek, David	2000	Malcolm MacGregor	You Walk With With Me *	Ballad	Tenor	A3	A4	Lead	Character Male
Full Monty, The	Yazbek, David	2000	Noah "Horse" Simmons	Big Black Man *	Uptempo	Baritone	F#3	A4	Lead	Antagonist Male
Full Monty, The	Yazbek, David	2000	Vicki Nichols	Life With Harold	Uptempo	Alto	G3	G4	Supporting	Character Female
Full Monty, The	Yazbek, David	2000	Vicki Nichols	You Rule My World Reprise *	Ballad	Alto	G#3	B4	Supporting	Character Female
Funny Girl	Styne, Julie	1964	Eddie Ryan	Who Taught Her Everything....*	Moderate Tempo	Baritone	C3	F4	Supporting	Character Male
Funny Girl	Styne, Julie	1964	Eddie Ryan	Rat Tat Tat*	Uptempo	Baritone	D3	F#4	Lead	Character Male
Funny Girl	Styne, Julie	1964	Eddie Ryan	If A Girl Isn't Pretty*	Moderate Tempo	Baritone	B2	F#4	Supporting	Character Male
Funny Girl	Styne, Julie	1964	Ensemble	Henry Street	Uptempo	Unison/2 Part			Ensemble	Adults
Funny Girl	Styne, Julie	1964	Fanny Brice	I'm The Greatest Start	Moderate Tempo	Alto	G#3	C5	Lead	Character Female
Funny Girl	Styne, Julie	1964	Fanny Brice	Coronet Man	Moderate Tempo	Alto	A#3	D5	Lead	Character Female
Funny Girl	Styne, Julie	1964	Fanny Brice	His Love Makes Me Beautiful*	Moderate Tempo	Alto	Bb3	Eb5	Lead	Character Female
Funny Girl	Styne, Julie	1964	Fanny Brice	People	Ballad	Alto	A3	Db5	Lead	Character Female
Funny Girl	Styne, Julie	1964	Fanny Brice	You Are Woman*	Moderate Tempo	Alto	A#3	C#5	Lead	Character Female
Funny Girl	Styne, Julie	1964	Fanny Brice	Don't Rain On My Parade	Uptempo	Alto	E3	B4	Lead	Character Female
Funny Girl	Styne, Julie	1964	Fanny Brice	Sade, Sade Married Lady	Moderate Tempo	Alto	A3	F5	Lead	Character Female
Funny Girl	Styne, Julie	1964	Fanny Brice	Who Are You Now	Ballad	Alto	Bb3	Db4	Lead	Character Female
Funny Girl	Styne, Julie	1964	Fanny Brice	The Music That Makes Me Dance	Ballad	Alto	G#3	E5	Lead	Character Female
Funny Girl	Styne, Julie	1964	Fanny Brice	Don't Rain On My Parade Reprise	Moderate Tempo	Alto	E3	B4	Lead	Character Female
Funny Girl	Styne, Julie	1964	Fanny Brice	Rat Tat Tat Part 2*	Uptempo	Alto	B3	D#5	Lead	Character Female
Funny Girl	Styne, Julie	1964	Mrs. Brice	Who Taught Her Everything....*	Moderate Tempo	Alto	A3	Eb5	Supporting	Mature Female

Shows

Songs by Character Type

Show	Composer	Year	Role	Song	Tempo	Vocal Type	Range-Bottom	Range-Top	Category	Character Type
Funny Girl	Styne, Julie	1964	Mrs. Brice	If A Girl Isn't Pretty*	Moderate Tempo	Alto	G#3	C#5	Supporting	Mature Female
Funny Girl	Styne, Julie	1964	Nick Arnstein	I Want To Be Seen With You... *	Moderate Tempo	Baritone	Ab2	Eb4	Lead	Romantic Lead Male
Funny Girl	Styne, Julie	1964	Nick Arnstein	You Are Woman*	Moderate Tempo	Baritone	A#2	E4	Lead	Romantic Lead Male
Funny Girl	Styne, Julie	1964	Nick Arnstein	Don't Rain On My Parade (Nick)	Moderate Tempo	Baritone	G3	D4	Lead	Romantic Lead Male
Funny Girl	Styne, Julie	1964	Zeigfeld Tenor	His Love Makes Me Beautiful*	Moderate Tempo	Tenor	E3	A4	Supporting	Romantic Lead Male
Funny Girl	Styne, Julie	1964	Eddie & Mrs. Brice	Who Taught Her Everything	Moderate Tempo	Bar/Alto			Duet	CM/MF
Funny Girl	Styne, Julie	1964	Fanny & Nick	I Want To Be Seen With You	Uptempo	Alto/Bar			Duet	CF/RLM
Godspell	Schwartz, Stephen	1971	Ensemble	Prepare Ye Finale	Uptempo	SATB			Ensemble	Adults
Godspell	Schwartz, Stephen	1971	Jesus	Save The People	Uptempo	Tenor	G3	G4	Lead	Character Male
Godspell	Schwartz, Stephen	1971	Jesus	Alas For You	Uptempo	Tenor	E3	G4	Lead	Character Male
Godspell	Schwartz, Stephen	1971	Jesus	Beautiful City (1972 Film)	Ballad	Tenor	E3	F#4	Lead	Character Male
Godspell	Schwartz, Stephen	1971	Jesus	All For The Best*	Uptempo	Tenor	D3	E4	Lead	Character Male
Godspell	Schwartz, Stephen	1971	John The Baptist	Prepare Ye*	Ballad	Tenor	C#3	G#4	Lead	Antagonist Male
Godspell	Schwartz, Stephen	1971	Judas	On The Willows	Ballad	Tenor	C3	F#4	Lead	Antagonist Male
Godspell	Schwartz, Stephen	1971	Judas	All For The Best*	Uptempo	Tenor	C3	D4	Lead	Antagonist Male
Godspell	Schwartz, Stephen	1971	Soloist 1	Day By Day	Ballad	Alto	C4	A4	Supporting	Character Female
Godspell	Schwartz, Stephen	1971	Soloist 2	Learn Your Lesson Well	Uptempo	Alto	G3	Eb5	Supporting	Character Female
Godspell	Schwartz, Stephen	1971	Soloist 3	O Bless The Lord*	Moderate Tempo	Alto	B3	E5	Supporting	Character Female
Godspell	Schwartz, Stephen	1971	Soloist 4	All Good Gifts	Ballad	Tenor	D3	A4	Supporting	Character Male
Godspell	Schwartz, Stephen	1971	Soloist 5	Turn Back O Man*	Moderate Tempo	Alto	D3	D5	Supporting	Character Female
Godspell	Schwartz, Stephen	1971	Jesus & Judas	All For The Best	Uptempo	Tenor/Tenor			Duet	CM/AM
Good News (1993 Revival)	Henderson, Ray	1927	Ensemble	He's A Ladies' Man	Uptempo	SA			Ensemble	Adults
Good News (1993 Revival)	Henderson, Ray	1927	Ensemble	The Varsity Drag	Uptempo	SATB			Ensemble	Adults
Good News (1993 Revival)	Henderson, Ray	1927	Ensemble	Good News	Uptempo	SATB			Ensemble	Adults
Good News (1993 Revival)	Henderson, Ray	1927	Babe O'Day	The Varsity Drag	Uptempo	Alto	Bb3	C5	Lead	Ingenue Female
Good News (1993 Revival)	Henderson, Ray	1927	Connie Lane	The Best Things In Life Are Free*	Ballad	Alto	A3	D5	Lead	Character Ingenue Female
Good News (1993 Revival)	Henderson, Ray	1927	Connie Lane	Just Imagine	Ballad	Alto	B3	E5	Lead	Character Ingenue Female
Good News (1993 Revival)	Henderson, Ray	1927	Connie Lane	Lucky In Love*	Uptempo	Alto	C4	Eb5	Lead	Character Ingenue Female
Good News (1993 Revival)	Henderson, Ray	1927	Pat	Lucky In Love*	Uptempo	Alto	A3	C5	Supporting	Ingenue Female
Good News (1993 Revival)	Henderson, Ray	1927	Pat	The Girl Of Pi Beta Phi	Moderate Tempo	Alto	G3	A4	Supporting	Ingenue Female
Good News (1993 Revival)	Henderson, Ray	1927	Tom Marlowe	The Best Things In Life Are Free*	Ballad	Baritone	C3	Eb4	Lead	Ingenue Male
Good News (1993 Revival)	Henderson, Ray	1927	Tom Marlowe	Lucky In Love*	Uptempo	Baritone	D3	F4	Lead	Ingenue Male
Good News (1993 Revival)	Henderson, Ray	1928	Babe O'Day	Button Up Your Overcoat*	Uptempo	Alto	C4	C5	Lead	Ingenue Female
Good News (1993 Revival)	Henderson, Ray	1928	Bobby Randall	Button Up Your Overcoat*	Uptempo	Baritone	E3	F#4	Supporting	Ingenue Male
Good News (1993 Revival)	Henderson, Ray	1928	Coach Johnson	You're The Cream In My Coffee*	Uptempo	Baritone	B2	Eb4	Lead	Romantic Lead Male
Good News (1993 Revival)	Henderson, Ray	1928	Coach Johnson	Together*	Ballad	Baritone	G3	B4	Lead	Romantic Lead Male
Good News (1993 Revival)	Henderson, Ray	1928	Coach Johnson	Together Part 2*	Ballad	Baritone	G2	C4	Lead	Romantic Lead Male
Good News (1993 Revival)	Henderson, Ray	1928	Connie Lane	My Lucky Star	Moderate Tempo	Alto	Bb3	Db5	Lead	Character Ingenue Female
Good News (1993 Revival)	Henderson, Ray	1928	Professor Kenyan	Together*	Ballad	Alto	G3	B4	Lead	Romantic Lead Female
Good News (1993 Revival)	Henderson, Ray	1928	Professor Kenyan	You're The Cream In My Coffee*	Uptempo	Alto	Db4	Eb5	Lead	Romantic Lead Female
Good News (1993 Revival)	Henderson, Ray	1928	Professor Kenyan	Together Part 2*	Ballad	Alto	G3	C5	Lead	Romantic Lead Female
Good News (1993 Revival)	Henderson, Ray	1929	Pooch Kearney	Keep Your Sunny Side Up*	Uptempo	Baritone	Bb2	F4	Supporting	Character Male

Shows

Songs by Character Type

* = Music Edit Required
+ = Ethnic Specific

Show	Composer	Year	Role	Song	Tempo	Vocal Type	Range-Bottom	Range-Top	Category	Character Type
Good News (1993 Revival)	Henderson, Ray	1930	Babe O'Day	Never Swat A Fly*	Uptempo	Alto	A3	C#5	Lead	Ingenue Female
Good News (1993 Revival)	Henderson, Ray	1930	Bobby Randall	Never Swat A Fly*	Uptempo	Baritone	A2	E4	Supporting	Ingenue Male
Good News (1993 Revival)	Henderson, Ray	1931	Professor Kenyan	Life Is Just A Bowl Of Cherries	Uptempo	Alto	A3	D♭5	Lead	Romantic Lead Female
Good News (1993 Revival)	Henderson, Ray	1993	Connie & Tom	The Best Things In Life Are Free	Moderate Tempo	Alto/Bar			Duet	CIF/IM
Good News (1993 Revival)	Henderson, Ray	1993	Babe & Bobby	Button Up Your Overcoat	Uptempo	Alto/Bar			Duet	IF/IM
Good News (1993 Revival)	Henderson, Ray	1993	Connie & Tom	Lucky In Love	Uptempo	Alto/Bar			Duet	CIF/IM
Good News (1993 Revival)	Henderson, Ray	1993	Coach & Kenyon	You're The Cream In My Coffee	Uptempo	Bar/Alto			Duet	RLM/RLF
Goodbye Girl, The	Hamlisch, Marvin	1993	Elliot & Paula	My Rules	Uptempo	Bar/Alto			Duet	AM/RLF
Goodbye Girl, The	Hamlisch, Marvin	1993	Lucy & Paula	Footsteps	Moderate Tempo	Alto/Alto			Duet	JF/RLF
Goodbye Girl, The	Hamlisch, Marvin	1993	Elliot & Paula	Paula	Moderate Tempo	Bar/Alto			Duet	AM/RLF
Goodbye Girl, The	Hamlisch, Marvin	1993	Actress	Too Good To Be Bad*	Moderate Tempo	Alto	A3	A4	Supporting	Romantic Lead Female
Goodbye Girl, The	Hamlisch, Marvin	1993	Billy	A Beat Behind*	Uptempo	Baritone	E3	F#4	Supporting	Character Male
Goodbye Girl, The	Hamlisch, Marvin	1993	Elliott Garfield	Elliott Garfield Grant	Uptempo	Baritone	C3	G♭4	Lead	Antagonist Male
Goodbye Girl, The	Hamlisch, Marvin	1993	Elliott Garfield	Good News, Bad News*	Moderate Tempo	Baritone	B♭3	F4	Lead	Antagonist Male
Goodbye Girl, The	Hamlisch, Marvin	1993	Elliott Garfield	Paula*	Moderate Tempo	Baritone	G#2	E4	Lead	Antagonist Male
Goodbye Girl, The	Hamlisch, Marvin	1993	Elliott Garfield	I Can Play This Part	Ballad	Baritone	G#2	E♭4	Lead	Antagonist Male
Goodbye Girl, The	Hamlisch, Marvin	1993	Lucy McFadden	Good News, Bad News*	Moderate Tempo	Alto	D♭4	D♭5	Supporting	Juvenile Female
Goodbye Girl, The	Hamlisch, Marvin	1993	Mrs. Crosby+	Too Good To Be Bad*	Uptempo	Alto	B♭3	F4	Supporting	Antagonist Female
Goodbye Girl, The	Hamlisch, Marvin	1993	Mrs. Crosby+	Too Good To Be Bad Play Off*	Uptempo	Alto	B♭3	F4	Supporting	Antagonist Female
Goodbye Girl, The	Hamlisch, Marvin	1993	Paula McFadden	No More	Moderate Tempo	Alto	G3	C5	Lead	Romantic Lead Female
Goodbye Girl, The	Hamlisch, Marvin	1993	Paula McFadden	A Beat Behind*	Uptempo	Alto	F#3	B4	Lead	Romantic Lead Female
Goodbye Girl, The	Hamlisch, Marvin	1993	Paula McFadden	My Rules	Moderate Tempo	Alto	A♭3	C5	Lead	Romantic Lead Female
Goodbye Girl, The	Hamlisch, Marvin	1993	Paula McFadden	Don't Follow In My Footsteps*	Moderate Tempo	Alto	D#3	C#5	Lead	Romantic Lead Female
Goodbye Girl, The	Hamlisch, Marvin	1993	Paula McFadden	How Can I Win	Ballad	Alto	A♭3	D5	Lead	Romantic Lead Female
Goodbye Girl, The	Hamlisch, Marvin	1993	Paula McFadden	What A Guy	Ballad	Alto	F#3	C5	Lead	Romantic Lead Female
Grease	Casey and Jacobs	1971	Betty Rizzo	Look At Me I'm Sandra Dee	Moderate Tempo	Alto	G3	E♭5	Lead	Antagonist Female
Grease	Casey and Jacobs	1971	Betty Rizzo	There Are Worse Things I Could Do	Ballad	Alto	A3	C4	Lead	Antagonist Female
Grease	Casey and Jacobs	1971	Danny Zuko	Alone at a Drive-in Movie	Moderate Tempo	Tenor	D3	D♭5	Lead	Romantic Antagonist Male
Grease	Casey and Jacobs	1971	Doody	Those Magic Changes	Uptempo	Tenor	E3	C♭5	Lead	Character Ingenue Male
Grease	Casey and Jacobs	1971	Doody	Rock N Roll Party Queen	Uptempo	Tenor	A2	A♭3	Lead	Character Ingenue Male
Grease	Casey and Jacobs	1971	Johnny Casino	Born to Hand Jive	Uptempo	Baritone	A3	F#4	Supporting	Character Ingenue Male
Grease	Casey and Jacobs	1971	Kenicke	Greased Lightening	Uptempo	Tenor	E3	B4	Lead	Antagonist Male
Grease	Casey and Jacobs	1971	Marty	Freddy My Love	Uptempo	Alto	C4	C5	Lead	Character Ingenue Female
Grease	Casey and Jacobs	1971	Miss Lynch	Born to Hand Jive	Uptempo	Alto	D4	B4	Supporting	Mature Female
Grease	Casey and Jacobs	1971	Roger	Mooning	Ballad	Tenor	F3	G4	Supporting	Character Male
Grease	Casey and Jacobs	1971	Roger	Rock N Roll Party Queen	Uptempo	Tenor	A2	A♭3	Lead	Character Male
Grease	Casey and Jacobs	1971	Sandy Dumbrowski	It's Raining on Prom Night	Ballad	Soprano	A3	D5	Lead	Ingenue Female
Grease	Casey and Jacobs	1971	Sandy Dumbrowski	Hopelessly Devoted to You	Ballad	Soprano	A3	F5	Lead	Ingenue Female
Grease	Casey and Jacobs	1971	Sandy Dumbrowski	Look At Me I'm Sandra Dee Reprise	Ballad	Soprano	A3	C#5	Lead	Ingenue Female
Grease	Casey and Jacobs	1971	Sandy Dumbrowski	Since I Don't Have You	Ballad	Soprano	A♭3	A♭5	Lead	Ingenue Female
Grease	Casey and Jacobs	1971	Teen Angel	Beauty School Dropout	Moderate Tempo	Tenor	F#3	F#5	Supporting	Romantic Lead Male

Shows

Songs by Character Type

* = Music Edit Required
+ = Ethnic Specific

Show	Composer	Year	Role	Song	Tempo	Vocal Type	Range-Bottom	Range-Top	Category	Character Type
Grease	Casey and Jacobs	1971	Jan & Roger	Mooning	Moderate Tempo	Alto/Tenor			Duet	CM/CM
Grease	Casey and Jacobs	1971	Doody & Roger	Rock N Roll Party Queen	Uptempo	Tenor/Tenor			Duet	CIM/CM
Grease	Casey and Jacobs	1972	Ensemble	Shakin' At The High School Hop	Uptempo	SATB			Ensemble	Teens
Grease	Casey and Jacobs	1972	Ensemble	We Go Together Reprise (Finale Part 2)	Uptempo	SATB			Ensemble	Teens
Grease	Casey and Jacobs	1972	Ensemble	Rock' N Roll Party Queen	Uptempo	SATB			Ensemble	Teens
Grey Gardens	Frankel, Scott	2006	Edie Beale (Act 1)	Daddy's Girl*	Uptempo	Soprano	C4	E5	Lead	Ingenue Female
Grey Gardens	Frankel, Scott	2006	Edie Beale (Act 1)	The Telegram	Moderate Tempo	Soprano	C#4	F#5	Lead	Ingenue Female
Grey Gardens	Frankel, Scott	2006	Edie Beale (Act 2)	The Revolutionary Costume*	Uptempo	Soprano	Bb3	C5	Lead	Romantic Lead Female
Grey Gardens	Frankel, Scott	2006	Edie Beale (Act 2)	Around The World	Moderate Tempo	Soprano	C4	C#5	Lead	Romantic Lead Female
Grey Gardens	Frankel, Scott	2006	Edie Beale (Act 2)	Around The World Reprise	Ballad	Soprano	C4	C#5	Lead	Romantic Lead Female
Grey Gardens	Frankel, Scott	2006	Edie Beale (Act 2)	Another Winter	Ballad	Soprano	F#3	C#5	Lead	Romantic Lead Female
Grey Gardens	Frankel, Scott	2006	Edith Beale (Act 1)	The Five Fifteen*	Uptempo	Soprano	B3	B4	Lead	Romantic Lead Female
Grey Gardens	Frankel, Scott	2006	Edith Beale (Act 1)	Hominy Grits*	Moderate Tempo	Soprano	B3	C#5	Lead	Romantic Lead Female
Grey Gardens	Frankel, Scott	2006	Edith Beale (Act 1)	The Five Fifteen Reprise*	Ballad	Soprano	C4	A4	Lead	Romantic Lead Female
Grey Gardens	Frankel, Scott	2006	Edith Beale (Act 1)	Will You?	Ballad	Soprano	C4	E5	Lead	Romantic Lead Female
Grey Gardens	Frankel, Scott	2006	Edith Beale (Act 2)	The Girl Who Has Everything*	Moderate Tempo	Alto	C4	Eb5	Lead	Mature Female
Grey Gardens	Frankel, Scott	2006	Edith Beale (Act 2)	The Cake I Had*	Moderate Tempo	Alto	E#3	A#4	Lead	Mature Female
Grey Gardens	Frankel, Scott	2006	Edith Beale (Act 2)	Jerry Likes My Corn	Moderate Tempo	Alto	G3	F5	Lead	Mature Female
Grey Gardens	Frankel, Scott	2006	Gould	Drift Away*	Ballad	Baritone	Eb3	F4	Lead	Romantic Lead Male
Grey Gardens	Frankel, Scott	2006	Joe Kennedy	Goin' Places*	Uptempo	Tenor	C3	F#4	Supporting	Ingenue Male
Grey Gardens	Frankel, Scott	2006	Major Bouvier	Marry Well*	Moderate Tempo	Baritone	A#2	E4	Supporting	Mature Male
Grey Gardens	Frankel, Scott	2006	Norman Vincent Peale	Choose To Be Happy*	Moderate Tempo	Baritone	G2	E4	Supporting	Mature Male
Grey Gardens	Frankel, Scott	2006	Edie (AI) & Edith (AI)	Peas In A Pod	Moderate Tempo	Sop/Sop			Duet	IF/RLF
Grey Gardens	Frankel, Scott	2006	Edith (AI) & Gould	Drift Away	Ballad	Sop/Bar			Duet	RLF/RLM
Guys and Dolls	Loesser, Frank	1950	Arvide	More I Cannot Wish You	Moderate Tempo	Baritone	D4	D5	Supporting	Mature Male
Guys and Dolls	Loesser, Frank	1950	Miss Adelaide	A Bushel And A Peck	Uptempo	Alto	B3	Eb5	Lead	Character Female
Guys and Dolls	Loesser, Frank	1950	Miss Adelaide	Adelaide's Lament	Moderate Tempo	Alto	Ab3	D5	Lead	Character Female
Guys and Dolls	Loesser, Frank	1950	Miss Adelaide	Adelaide's Lament Reprise	Ballad	Alto	Db4	Cb5	Lead	Character Female
Guys and Dolls	Loesser, Frank	1950	Miss Adelaide	Take Back Your Mink	Uptempo	Alto	Bb3	D5	Lead	Character Female
Guys and Dolls	Loesser, Frank	1950	Miss Adelaide	Marry The Man Today*	Uptempo	Alto	C4	Eb5	Lead	Character Male
Guys and Dolls	Loesser, Frank	1950	Nicely Nicely	Sit Down You're Rockin' The Boat*	Uptempo	Tenor	F3	C5	Supporting	Character Male
Guys and Dolls	Loesser, Frank	1950	Sarah Brown	I'll Know	Ballad	Soprano	E4	G#5	Lead	Ingenue Female
Guys and Dolls	Loesser, Frank	1950	Sarah Brown	If I Were A Bell	Uptempo	Soprano	Bb3	D5	Lead	Ingenue Female
Guys and Dolls	Loesser, Frank	1950	Sarah Brown	Marry The Man Today*	Uptempo	Soprano	C4	Eb5	Lead	Ingenue Female
Guys and Dolls	Loesser, Frank	1950	Sarah Brown	I'll Know (Finish)	Ballad	Soprano	Eb4	F5	Lead	Ingenue Female
Guys and Dolls	Loesser, Frank	1950	Sky Masterson	I'll Know*	Ballad	Baritone	B2	D#4	Lead	Romantic Lead Male
Guys and Dolls	Loesser, Frank	1950	Sky Masterson	My Time Of Day	Ballad	Baritone	Bb2	Db4	Lead	Romantic Lead Male
Guys and Dolls	Loesser, Frank	1950	Sky Masterson	Luck Be A Lady*	Uptempo	Baritone	Db3	Eb4	Lead	Romantic Lead Male
Guys And Dolls	Loesser, Frank	2006	Nathan & Sky	Travelling Light	Moderate Tempo	Bar/Bar			Duet	CM/RLM
Guys And Dolls	Loesser, Frank	2006	Sarah & Sky	I'll Know	Ballad	Sop/Bar			Duet	IF/RLM
Guys And Dolls	Loesser, Frank	2006	Sarah & Sky	I've Never Been In Love Before	Ballad	Sop/Bar			Duet	IF/RLM

Shows

Songs by Character Type

* = Music Edit Required
+ = Ethnic Specific

Show	Composer	Year	Role	Song	Tempo	Vocal Type	Range-Bottom	Range-Top	Category	Character Type
Guys And Dolls	Loesser, Frank	2006	Adelaide & Nathan	Sue Me	Moderate Tempo	Alto/Bar			Duet	CF/CM
Guys And Dolls	Loesser, Frank	2006	Adelaide & Sarah	Marry The Man Today	Uptempo	Alto/Sop			Duet	CM/IF
Gypsy	Styne, Jule	1959	June	If Momma Was Married*	Moderate Tempo	Alto	G3	C5	Lead	Ingenue Female
Gypsy	Styne, Jule	1959	June	Broadway	Uptempo	Alto	E#4	D5	Lead	Ingenue Female
Gypsy	Styne, Jule	1959	Louise	Little Lamb	Ballad	Alto	Db4	Eb5	Lead	Ingenue Female
Gypsy	Styne, Jule	1959	Louise	If Momma Was Married*	Moderate Tempo	Alto	G3	C5	Lead	Ingenue Female
Gypsy	Styne, Jule	1959	Louise	Let Me Entertain You*	Moderate Tempo	Alto	G3	C5	Lead	Ingenue Female
Gypsy	Styne, Jule	1959	Rose	Some People	Uptempo	Alto	G#3	C5	Lead	Antagonist Female
Gypsy	Styne, Jule	1959	Rose	Small World	Moderate Tempo	Alto	F#3	B4	Lead	Antagonist Female
Gypsy	Styne, Jule	1959	Rose	You'll Never Get Away From Me*	Uptempo	Alto	F#3	B4	Lead	Antagonist Female
Gypsy	Styne, Jule	1959	Rose	Everything's Coming Up Roses	Uptempo	Alto	Bb3	C5	Lead	Antagonist Female
Gypsy	Styne, Jule	1959	Rose	Rose's Turn	Moderate Tempo	Alto	G3	C5	Lead	Antagonist Female
Gypsy	Styne, Jule	1959	Rose	Some People Reprise*	Ballad	Alto	G#3	A4	Lead	Antagonist Female
Gypsy	Styne, Jule	1959	Tulsa	All I Need Is The Girl	Uptempo	Tenor	E3	G4	Lead	Ingenue Male
Gypsy	Styne, Jule	1959	Baby June & Baby Louise	May We Entertain You	Uptempo	Alto/Alto			Duet	JF/JF
Gypsy	Styne, Jule	1959	Herbie & Rose	Small World	Moderate Tempo	Bar/Alto			Duet	CM/AF
Gypsy	Styne, Jule	1959	June & Louise	If Momma Was Married	Uptempo	Alto/Alto			Duet	IF/IF
Hair	MacDermot, Galt	1968	Berger	Donna	Uptempo	Tenor	Eb3	Bb4	Lead	Antagonist Male
Hair	MacDermot, Galt	1968	Berger	Going Down	Uptempo	Baritone	C3	F4	Lead	Antagonist Male
Hair	MacDermot, Galt	1968	Claude	Manchester England	Moderate Tempo	Baritone	E3	F#4	Lead	Romantic Lead Male
Hair	MacDermot, Galt	1968	Claude	I Got Life	Uptempo	Baritone	C3	F4	Lead	Romantic Lead Male
Hair	MacDermot, Galt	1968	Claude	Where Do I Go	Moderate Tempo	Baritone	C4	F5	Lead	Romantic Lead Male
Hair	MacDermot, Galt	1968	Claude	Hair	Uptempo	Baritone	D3	G4	Lead	Romantic Lead Male
Hair	MacDermot, Galt	1968	Claude	Manchester England Reprise	Moderate Tempo	Baritone	E3	E4	Lead	Romantic Lead Male
Hair	MacDermot, Galt	1968	Crissy	Frank Mills	Ballad	Alto	A2	C5	Lead	Ingenue Female
Hair	MacDermot, Galt	1968	Ensemble	Aquarius	Uptempo	SATB			Ensemble	Adults
Hair	MacDermot, Galt	1968	Ensemble	Hashish	Ballad	Unison			Ensemble	Adults
Hair	MacDermot, Galt	1968	Ensemble	Initials	Uptempo	SATB			Ensemble	Adults
Hair	MacDermot, Galt	1968	Ensemble	The Bed	Uptempo	SATB			Ensemble	Adults
Hair	MacDermot, Galt	1968	Ensemble	Walking In Space	Ballad	SATB			Ensemble	Adults
Hair	MacDermot, Galt	1968	Hud+	Colored Spade	Uptempo	Baritone	B2	D4	Lead	Antagonist Male
Hair	MacDermot, Galt	1968	Jeanie	Air	Uptempo	Alto	G3	G4	Lead	Character Female
Hair	MacDermot, Galt	1968	Margaret Mead	My Conviction	Moderate Tempo	Alto	E3	A4	Lead	Character Female
Hair	MacDermot, Galt	1968	Ron	Aquarius	Moderate Tempo	Baritone	Eb3	Eb4	Lead	Character Male
Hair	MacDermot, Galt	1968	Sheila	I Believe In Love	Uptempo	Alto	G3	C5	Lead	Character Ingenue Female
Hair	MacDermot, Galt	1968	Sheila	Easy To Be Hard	Ballad	Alto	C4	C5	Lead	Character Ingenue Female
Hair	MacDermot, Galt	1968	Sheila	Good Morning Starshine	Uptempo	Alto	C4	C5	Lead	Character Ingenue Female
Hair	MacDermot, Galt	1968	Woof	Sodomy	Ballad	Tenor	D3	G4	Lead	Character Male
Hair	MacDermot, Galt	1968	Berger & Claude	Hair	Uptempo	Tenor/Bar			Duet	AM/RLM
Hair	MacDermot, Galt	1968	Ron & Tribe Member	What A Piece Of Work Is Man	Moderate Tempo	Bar/Bar			Duet	CM/CM
Hairspray	Shaiman, Marc	2002	Amber Von Tussle	Cooties	Uptempo	Alto	E4	E5	Lead	Romantic Antagonist Female
Hairspray	Shaiman, Marc	2002	Corny Collins	Hairspray	Uptempo	Tenor	E3	C5	Lead	Romantic Lead Male
Hairspray	Shaiman, Marc	2002	Corny Collins	Nicest Kids In Town*	Uptempo	Tenor	D3	F#4	Lead	Romantic Lead Male
Hairspray	Shaiman, Marc	2002	Corny Collins	Nicest Kids In Town Reprise	Uptempo	Tenor	B3	F#4	Lead	Romantic Lead Male

Shows

Songs by Character Type

Show	Composer	Year	Role	Song	Tempo	Vocal Type	Range-Bottom	Range-Top	Category	Character Type
Hairspray	Shaiman, Marc	2002	Edna Turnblad	Welcome To The 60s*	Uptempo	Baritone	F2	G3	Lead	Character Male
Hairspray	Shaiman, Marc	2002	Edna Turnblad	Timeless To Me*	Moderate Tempo	Baritone	F#2	D4	Lead	Character Male
Hairspray	Shaiman, Marc	2002	Ensemble	Mama I'm A Big Girl Now	Uptempo	SA			Ensemble	Teens/Adults
Hairspray	Shaiman, Marc	2002	Ensemble	The Big Doll House	Uptempo	SA			Ensemble	Teens/Adults
Hairspray	Shaiman, Marc	2002	Inez Stubs+	Run And Tell That*	Uptempo	Alto	F4	E5	Lead	Juvenile Female
Hairspray	Shaiman, Marc	2002	Link Larkin	It Takes Two	Ballad	Tenor	E3	F#4	Lead	Ingenue Male
Hairspray	Shaiman, Marc	2002	Link Larkin	Without Love*	Moderate Tempo	Tenor	C3	A4	Lead	Ingenue Male
Hairspray	Shaiman, Marc	2002	Motormouth Mabel+	Big Blonde And Beautiful*	Moderate Tempo	Alto	C4	E5	Lead	Character Female
Hairspray	Shaiman, Marc	2002	Motormouth Mabel+	I Know Where I've Been	Ballad	Alto	E3	C5	Lead	Character Female
Hairspray	Shaiman, Marc	2002	Penny Pingleton	Without Love*	Moderate Tempo	Alto	Eb3	Eb4	Lead	Character Ingenue Female
Hairspray	Shaiman, Marc	2002	Seaweed Stubs+	Run And Tell That*	Uptempo	Tenor	F3	B4	Lead	Ingenue Male
Hairspray	Shaiman, Marc	2002	Seaweed Stubs+	Without Love*	Moderate Tempo	Tenor	G3	Ab4	Lead	Ingenue Male
Hairspray	Shaiman, Marc	2002	Teen Girl	The New Kid In Town*	Uptempo	Alto	A3	D5	Featured Ensemble	Ingenue Female
Hairspray	Shaiman, Marc	2002	Tracy Turnblad	Good Morning Baltimore	Uptempo	Alto	Bb3	C#5	Lead	Character Ingenue Female
Hairspray	Shaiman, Marc	2002	Tracy Turnblad	I Can Hear The Bells	Uptempo	Alto	A3	E5	Lead	Character Ingenue Female
Hairspray	Shaiman, Marc	2002	Tracy Turnblad	Welcome To The 60s*	Uptempo	Alto	G3	C#5	Lead	Character Ingenue Female
Hairspray	Shaiman, Marc	2002	Tracy Turnblad	Good Morning Baltimore Reprise	Ballad	Alto	Ab3	Bb4	Lead	Character Ingenue Female
Hairspray	Shaiman, Marc	2002	Tracy Turnblad	Without Love*	Moderate Tempo	Alto	A3	B4	Lead	Character Ingenue Female
Hairspray	Shaiman, Marc	2002	Velma Von Tussle	Miss Baltimore Crabs	Uptempo	Alto	B3	Eb5	Lead	Romantic Antagonist Female
Hairspray	Shaiman, Marc	2002	Velma Von Tussle	Velma's Cha Cha	Moderate Tempo	Alto	Ab3	C#5	Lead	Romantic Antagonist Female
Hairspray	Shaiman, Marc	2002	Wilbur Turnblad	Timeless To Me	Moderate Tempo	Tenor	A#2	A4	Lead	Paternal
Hairspray	Shaiman, Marc	2003	Link & Tracy	It Takes Two	Ballad	Tenor/Alto			Duet	IM/CF
Hairspray	Shaiman, Marc	2003	Edna & Wilbur	Timeless To Me	Moderate Tempo	Bar/Tenor			Duet	CM/P
Heathers	Waters, Daniel	2014	Ensemble	Big Fun	Uptempo	SATB			Ensemble	Adults
Heathers	Waters, Daniel	2014	Heather Chandler	Candy*	Uptempo	Alto	Bb3	A5	Lead	Romantic Antagonist Female
Heathers	Waters, Daniel	2014	Heather McNamara	Lifeboat	Ballad	Alto	G3	Db5	Lead	Ingenue Female
Heathers	Waters, Daniel	2014	Jason Dean (JD)	Freeze Your Brain	Moderate Tempo	Tenor	Bb3	G#4	Lead	Romantic Antagonist Male
Heathers	Waters, Daniel	2014	Jason Dean (JD)	Our Love Is God	Ballad	Tenor	F#3	F#4	Lead	Romantic Antagonist Male
Heathers	Waters, Daniel	2014	Jason Dean (JD)	Meant To Be Yours	Uptempo	Tenor	G3	Ab4	Lead	Romantic Antagonist Male
Heathers	Waters, Daniel	2014	Jason Dean (JD)	I Am Damaged	Ballad	Tenor	E3	F#4	Lead	Romantic Antagonist Male
Heathers	Waters, Daniel	2014	Martha Dunnstock	Kindergarten Boyfriend	Ballad	Alto	G3	E5	Supporting	Character Female
Heathers	Waters, Daniel	2014	Mrs. Fleming	Shine A Light*	Uptempo	Soprano	G3	F5	Supporting	Maternal
Heathers	Waters, Daniel	2014	Ram Sweeney	Blue*	Uptempo	Tenor	F#3	D5	Supporting	Romantic Antagonist Male
Heathers	Waters, Daniel	2014	Ram's Dad	My Dead Gay Son	Uptempo	Tenor	C3	A4	Supporting	Paternal
Heathers	Waters, Daniel	2014	Veronica Sawyer	Beautiful	Uptempo	Alto	G3	C5	Lead	Character Ingenue Female
Heathers	Waters, Daniel	2014	Veronica Sawyer	Fight For Me	Ballad	Alto	Bb3	D5	Lead	Character Ingenue Female
Heathers	Waters, Daniel	2014	Veronica Sawyer	Dead Girl Walking*	Uptempo	Alto	A3	G5	Lead	Character Ingenue Female
Heathers	Waters, Daniel	2014	Veronica Sawyer	The Me Inside Of Me	Moderate Tempo	Alto	Ab3	D5	Lead	Character Ingenue Female
Heathers	Waters, Daniel	2014	Veronica Sawyer	Seventeen*	Ballad	Alto	A3	B4	Lead	Character Ingenue Female
Heathers	Waters, Daniel	2014	Veronica Sawyer	Dead Girls Walking Reprise	Uptempo	Alto	A3	A5	Lead	Character Ingenue Female

Shows

417

* = Music Edit Required
+ = Ethnic Specific

Show	Composer	Year	Role	Song	Tempo	Vocal Type	Range-Bottom	Range-Top	Category	Character Type
Heathers	Waters, Daniel	2014	Veronica Sawyer	Seventeen Reprise*	Moderate Tempo	Alto	A3	Gb5	Lead	Character Ingenue Female
Heathers	Waters, Daniel	2014	JD & Veronica	Seventeen	Ballad	Tenor/Alto			Duet	RAM/CIF
Heathers	Waters, Daniel	2014	JD & Veronica	I Am Damaged	Ballad	Tenor/Alto			Duet	RAM/CIF
Hello Dolly	Herman, Jerry	1964	Barnaby Tucker	Elegance*	Moderate Tempo	Baritone	C3	F4	Lead	Character Ingenue Male
Hello Dolly	Herman, Jerry	1964	Cornelius Hackl	Put On Your Sunday Clothes	Uptempo	Baritone	C3	G#4	Lead	Character Ingenue Male
Hello Dolly	Herman, Jerry	1964	Cornelius Hackl	It Only Takes A Moment*	Ballad	Baritone	Bb2	Eb4	Lead	Character Ingenue Male
Hello Dolly	Herman, Jerry	1964	Cornelius Hackl	Elegance*	Moderate Tempo	Baritone	C3	F4	Lead	Character Ingenue Male
Hello Dolly	Herman, Jerry	1964	Dolly Levi	I Put My Hand In	Uptempo	Alto	Eb3	G4	Lead	Mature Female
Hello Dolly	Herman, Jerry	1964	Dolly Levi	Motherhood*	Uptempo	Alto	D3	F4	Lead	Mature Female
Hello Dolly	Herman, Jerry	1964	Dolly Levi	Before The Parade Passes By	Moderate Tempo	Alto	D3	F4	Lead	Mature Female
Hello Dolly	Herman, Jerry	1964	Dolly Levi	Hello Dolly	Moderate Tempo	Alto	Bb2	F4	Lead	Mature Female
Hello Dolly	Herman, Jerry	1964	Dolly Levi	So Long Dearie	Uptempo	Alto	D3	G4	Lead	Mature Female
Hello Dolly	Herman, Jerry	1964	Dolly Levi	I Put My Hand In	Uptempo	Alto	Ab3	C5	Lead	Mature Female
Hello Dolly	Herman, Jerry	1964	Dolly Levi	Motherhood	Uptempo	Alto	F3	A4	Lead	Mature Female
Hello Dolly	Herman, Jerry	1964	Dolly Levi	Before The Parade Passes By	Moderate Tempo	Alto	F3	F4	Lead	Mature Female
Hello Dolly	Herman, Jerry	1964	Dolly Levi	Dancing*	Moderate Tempo	Alto	D3	D5	Lead	Mature Female
Hello Dolly	Herman, Jerry	1964	Dolly Levi	Before The Parade Passes By Reprise	Ballad	Alto	C3	F4	Lead	Mature Female
Hello Dolly	Herman, Jerry	1964	Ensemble	Hello Dolly Finale	Uptempo	SATB			Ensemble	Adults
Hello Dolly	Herman, Jerry	1964	Horace Vandergelder	It Takes A Woman	Uptempo	Baritone	B2	G5	Lead	Mature Male
Hello Dolly	Herman, Jerry	1964	Horace Vandergelder	Hello Dolly	Moderate Tempo	Baritone	B2	D4	Lead	Mature Male
Hello Dolly	Herman, Jerry	1964	Irene Molloy	Ribbons Down My Back	Ballad	Soprano	A3	D5	Lead	Romantic Lead Female
Hello Dolly	Herman, Jerry	1964	Irene Molloy	Motherhood	Uptempo	Soprano	D4	E5	Lead	Romantic Lead Female
Hello Dolly	Herman, Jerry	1964	Irene Molloy	It Only Takes A Moment*	Ballad	Soprano	Ab3	Db4	Lead	Romantic Lead Female
Hello Dolly	Herman, Jerry	1964	Irene Molloy	Ribbons Down My Back Reprise	Ballad	Soprano	B3	D5	Lead	Romantic Lead Female
Hello Dolly	Herman, Jerry	1964	Irene Molloy	Dancing*	Moderate Tempo	Soprano	G3	E5	Lead	Romantic Lead Female
Hello Dolly	Herman, Jerry	1964	Cornelius & Irene	It Only Takes A Moment	Ballad	Bar/Sop			Duet	CIM/RLF
Hello Dolly	Herman, Jerry	1970	Dolly Levi	World Take Me Back	Moderate Tempo	Alto	C4	E5	Lead	Mature Female
Hello Dolly	Herman, Jerry	1970	Dolly Levi	Love, Look In MY Window	Ballad	Alto	C4	F5	Lead	Mature Female
High School Musical	Various	2007	Ensemble	Start of Something New*	Uptempo	SATB			Ensemble	Teens/Adults
High School Musical	Various	2007	Ensemble	Stick to the Status Quo	Uptempo	SATB			Ensemble	Teens/Adults
High School Musical	Various	2007	Ensemble	We're All In This Together	Uptempo	SATB			Ensemble	Teens/Adults
High School Musical	Various	2007	Gabriella Montez	When There Was You And Me	Ballad	Alto	F#3	F5	Lead	Ingenue Female
High School Musical	Various	2007	Gabriella Montez	Breaking Free*	Ballad	Alto	Bb3	D5	Lead	Ingenue Female
High School Musical	Various	2007	Ryan Evans	What I've Been Looking For*	Uptempo	Tenor	A3	F#4	Lead	Character Ingenue Male
High School Musical	Various	2007	Troy Bolton	What I've Been Looking For Reprise*	Ballad	Tenor	G3	F#4	Lead	Ingenue Male
High School Musical	Various	2007	Troy Bolton	Breaking Free*	Ballad	Tenor	Bb2	Bb4	Lead	Ingenue Male
High School Musical	Various	2007	Ryan & Sharpay	What I've Been Looking For	Uptempo	Tenor/Alto			Duet	CIM/CIF
High School Musical	Various	2007	Gabriella & Troy	What I've Been Looking For Reprise	Ballad	Alto/Tenor			Duet	IF/IM
High School Musical	Various	2007	Gabriella & Troy	If I Can't Take My Eyes Off You	Uptempo	Alto/Tenor			Duet	IF/IM
High School Musical	Various	2007	Gabriella & Troy	Start Of Something New Reprise	Uptempo	Alto/Tenor			Duet	IF/IM
High School Musical	Various	2007	Gabriella & Troy	Breaking Free	Uptempo	Alto/Tenor			Duet	IF/IM
High Society 1998	Porter, Cole	1927	Tracy Lord	Let's Misbehave*	Uptempo	Soprano	B2	C#5	Lead	Romantic Lead Female
High Society 1998	Porter, Cole	1927	Ensemble	Let's Misbehave	Uptempo	SATB			Ensemble	Adults

Shows

Songs by Character Type

*= Music Edit Required
+ = Ethnic Specific

Show	Composer	Year	Role	Song	Tempo	Vocal Type	Range-Bottom	Range-Top	Category	Character Type
High Society 1998	Porter, Cole	1929	Uncle Willie	She's Got That Thing*	Uptempo	Tenor	G2	G4	Lead	Mature Male
High Society 1998	Porter, Cole	1929	Dexter C.K. Haven	She's Got That Thing*	Uptempo	Tenor	A2	G4	Lead	Romantic Lead Male
High Society 1998	Porter, Cole	1929	Ensemble	She's Got That Thing	Uptempo	SATB			Ensemble	Adults
High Society 1998	Porter, Cole	1929	Ensemble	She's Got That Thing Reprise	Uptempo	SATB			Ensemble	Adults
High Society 1998	Porter, Cole	1929	George Kittredge	I'll Worship You	Moderate Tempo	Baritone	G#2	F#4	Lead	Romantic Lead Male
High Society 1998	Porter, Cole	1930	Uncle Willie	I'm Getting Ready For You*	Uptempo	Tenor	Bb2	E4	Lead	Mature Male
High Society 1998	Porter, Cole	1930	Liz Imbrie	I'm Getting Ready For You*	Uptempo	Alto	A#3	E5	Lead	Character Female
High Society 1998	Porter, Cole	1930	Uncle Willie & Liz Imbrie	I'm Getting Ready For You	Uptempo	Tenor/Sop			Duet	MM/CF
High Society 1998	Porter, Cole	1930	Uncle Willie	Say It With Gin	Uptempo	Tenor	C3	C4	Lead	Mature Male
High Society 1998	Porter, Cole	1933	Dexter C.K. Haven	Once Upon A Time	Moderate Tempo	Tenor	G2	E4	Lead	Romantic Lead Male
High Society 1998	Porter, Cole	1933	Tracy Lord	Once Upon A Time	Moderate Tempo	Soprano	F3	A4	Lead	Romantic Lead Female
High Society 1998	Porter, Cole	1935	Dexter C.K. Haven	Just One Of Those Things	Uptempo	Tenor	B2	E4	Lead	Romantic Lead Male
High Society 1998	Porter, Cole	1939	Ensemble	Well Did You Evah	Uptempo	SATB			Ensemble	Adults
High Society 1998	Porter, Cole	1940	Ensemble	Throwing A Ball Tonight	Uptempo	SATB			Ensemble	Adults
High Society 1998	Porter, Cole	1943	Liz Imbrie	He's A Right Guy	Ballad	Alto	F3	A4	Lead	Character Female
High Society 1998	Porter, Cole	1953	Tracy & Dinah	I Love Paris	Moderate Tempo	Alto/Alto			Duet	RLF/JF
High Society 1998	Porter, Cole	1953	Tracy Lord	It's Alright With Me	Ballad	Soprano	C4	E5	Lead	Romantic Lead Female
High Society 1998	Porter, Cole	1955	Tracy Lord	High Society*	Uptempo	Soprano	Ab3	Eb5	Lead	Romantic Lead Female
High Society 1998	Porter, Cole	1955	Ensemble	High Society	Uptempo	SATB			Ensemble	Adults
High Society 1998	Porter, Cole	1955	Dexter C.K. Haven	Little One*	Uptempo	Tenor	A2	D4	Lead	Romantic Lead Male
High Society 1998	Porter, Cole	1955	Dexter C.K. Haven	Little On Reprise	Uptempo	Tenor	Bb2	Ab3	Lead	Romantic Lead Male
High Society 1998	Porter, Cole	1955	Dexter C.K. Haven	True Love*	Ballad	Tenor	C3	F4	Lead	Romantic Lead Male
High Society 1998	Porter, Cole	1955	Dexter & Tracy	True Love	Ballad	Tenor/Srp			Duet	RLM/RLF
High Society 1998	Porter, Cole	1955	Ensemble	High Society Act II	Moderate Tempo	SATB			Ensemble	Adults
High Society 1998	Porter, Cole	1956	Mike & Liz	Who Wants To Be A Millionaire	Moderate Tempo	Bar/Alto			Duet	RAM/CF
High Society 1998	Porter, Cole	1956	Mike Connor	You're Sensational	Ballad	Baritone	G2	F4	Lead	Romantic Antagonist Male
High Society 1998	Porter, Cole	1956	Ensemble	True Love Finale	Moderate Tempo	SATB			Ensemble	Adults
Honk	Stiles, George	1993	Bullfrog	Warts and All	Moderate Tempo	Baritone	A2	C#4	Supporting	Character Male
Honk	Stiles, George	1993	Cat	You Can Play With Your Food	Uptempo	Tenor	C3	Ab4	Supporting	Antagonist Male
Honk	Stiles, George	1993	Ida	The Joy of Motherhood*	Ballad	Alto	G#3	C#5	Lead	Maternal
Honk	Stiles, George	1993	Ida	Different Pre-Reprise	Ballad	Alto	Ab3	A4	Lead	Maternal
Honk	Stiles, George	1993	Ida	Hold Your Head Up High	Moderate Tempo	Alto	G#3	C5	Lead	Maternal
Honk	Stiles, George	1993	Ida	Every Tear a Mother Cries	Ballad	Alto	F3	A4	Lead	Maternal
Honk	Stiles, George	1993	Maureen	The Joy of Motherhood*	Uptempo	Alto	G#3	C#5	Supporting	Maternal
Honk	Stiles, George	1993	Ugly	Different	Ballad	Baritone	Db3	F4	Lead	Character Ingenue Male
Honk	Stiles, George	1993	Ugly	Hold Your Head Up High Reprise	Ballad	Baritone	C3	G4	Lead	Character Ingenue Male
Honk	Stiles, George	1993	Ugly	Now I've Seen You	Moderate Tempo	Baritone	Bb2	G4	Lead	Character Ingenue Male
Honk!	Stiles, George	1993	Drake	A Poultry Tale	Uptempo	Baritone	C3	F4	Lead	Paternal
Honk!	Stiles, George	1993	Drake	The Collage	Uptempo	Baritone	G#2	E3	Lead	Paternal
Honk!	Stiles, George	1993	Lowbutt	It Takes All Sorts*	Uptempo	Alto	C#4	D5	Supporting	Mature Female
Honk!	Stiles, George	1993	Queenie	It Takes All Sorts*	Uptempo	Alto	C#4	D5	Supporting	Mature Female
Honk!	Stiles, George	1993	Ensemble	Look At Him Reprise*	Uptempo	SATB			Ensemble	Adults
Honk!	Stiles, George	1993	Ensemble	Warts And All Reprise*	Uptempo	SATB			Ensemble	Adults

Shows

419

Songs by Character Type

* = Music Edit Required
+ = Ethnic Specific

Show	Composer	Year	Role	Song	Tempo	Vocal Type	Range-Bottom	Range-Top	Category	Character Type
Honk!	Stiles, George	1993	Ida & Maureen	The Joy Of Motherhood	Moderate Tempo	Alto/Alto			Duet	M/M
Honk!	Stiles, George	1993	Cat & Ugly	You Can Play With Your Good	Uptempo	Tenor/Bar			Duet	AM/CIM
Honk!	Stiles, George	1993	Ida & Ugly	Hold Your Head Up High Reprise	Ballad	Alto/Bar			Duet	M/CIM
Honk!	Stiles, George	1993	Lowbutt & Queenie	It Takes All Sorts	Uptempo	Alto/Alto			Duet	M/MF
How To Succeed…	Loesser, Frank	1961	Ensemble	Been A Long Day	Uptempo	SATB			Ensemble	Adults
How To Succeed…	Loesser, Frank	1961	Ensemble	Company Way Finale Act II	Uptempo	SATB			Ensemble	Adults
How To Succeed…	Loesser, Frank	1961	Bud Frump	Company Way Reprise*	Uptempo	Tenor	D3	G4	Lead	Antagonist Male
How To Succeed…	Loesser, Frank	1961	Bud Frump	Been A Long Day Reprise*	Uptempo	Baritone	Bb3	D4	Lead	Antagonist Male
How To Succeed…	Loesser, Frank	1961	Hedy La Rue	Love From A Heart Of Gold*	Ballad	Alto	B3	D5	Supporting	Romantic Lead Female
How To Succeed…	Loesser, Frank	1961	J Pierpont Finch	How To Succeed	Uptempo	Tenor	E3	E4	Lead	Character Male
How To Succeed…	Loesser, Frank	1961	J Pierpont Finch	Rosemary*	Moderate Tempo	Tenor	B2	E4	Lead	Character Male
How To Succeed…	Loesser, Frank	1961	J Pierpont Finch	I Believe In You*	Uptempo	Tenor	F3	C4	Lead	Character Male
How To Succeed…	Loesser, Frank	1961	J Pierpont Finch	Brotherhood Of Man*	Uptempo	Tenor	F3	G4	Lead	Character Male
How To Succeed…	Loesser, Frank	1961	JB Biggley	Grand Old Ivy*	Uptempo	Tenor	C3	G4	Lead	Mature Male
How To Succeed…	Loesser, Frank	1961	JB Biggley	Love From A Heart Of Gold*	Ballad	Tenor	C#3	E4	Lead	Mature Male
How To Succeed…	Loesser, Frank	1961	Miss Jones	Brotherhood Of Man*	Uptempo	Alto	A#3	G5	Featured Ensemble	Character Female
How To Succeed…	Loesser, Frank	1961	Rosemary Pillkington	Happy To Keep His Dinner Warm	Moderate Tempo	Alto	A3	Db5	Lead	Ingenue Female
How To Succeed…	Loesser, Frank	1961	Rosemary Pillkington	Paris Original*	Moderate Tempo	Alto	Bb3	D5	Lead	Ingenue Female
How To Succeed…	Loesser, Frank	1961	Rosemary Pillkington	Happy To Keep His Dinner Warm Repris	Moderate Tempo	Alto	Bb3	Db5	Lead	Ingenue Female
How To Succeed…	Loesser, Frank	1961	Rosemary Pillkington	I Believe In You Reprise*	Moderate Tempo	Alto	E4	B4	Lead	Ingenue Female
How To Succeed…	Loesser, Frank	1961	Smitty	Been A Long Day*	Uptempo	Alto	Bb3	D5	Supporting	Character Female
How To Succeed…	Loesser, Frank	1961	Twimble	Company Way*	Uptempo	Tenor	D3	G4	Supporting	Mature Male
How To Succeed…	Loesser, Frank	1961	Finch & Twimble	Company Way	Uptempo	Tenor/Tenor			Duet	CM/MM
How To Succeed…	Loesser, Frank	1961	Biggley & Finch	Grand Old Ivy	Uptempo	Tenor/Tenor			Duet	CM/MM
How To Succeed…	Loesser, Frank	1961	Finch & Rosemary	Rosemary	Moderate Tempo	Alto/Tenor			Duet	CM/IF
How To Succeed…	Loesser, Frank	1961	Biggley & Hedy	Love From A Heart Of Gold	Ballad	Tenor/Alto			Duet	MM/RLF
In The Heights	Miranda, Lin-Manuel	2008	Abuela Claudia	Paciencia Y Fe	Uptempo	Alto	F3	C5	Lead	Mature Female
In The Heights	Miranda, Lin-Manuel	2008	Benny+	Benny's Dispatch*	Uptempo	Tenor	B3	F#4	Lead	Romantic Lead Male
In The Heights	Miranda, Lin-Manuel	2008	Benny+	When You're Home*	Uptempo	Tenor	E3	G4	Lead	Romantic Lead Male
In The Heights	Miranda, Lin-Manuel	2008	Camila Rosario+	Enough*	Moderate Tempo	Alto	G3	Db5	Lead	Maternal
In The Heights	Miranda, Lin-Manuel	2008	Kevin Rosario+	Inutil	Ballad	Baritone	C3	E4	Lead	Paternal
In The Heights	Miranda, Lin-Manuel	2008	Kevin Rosario+	Atencion	Ballad	Baritone	F#3	D4	Lead	Paternal
In The Heights	Miranda, Lin-Manuel	2008	Nina Rosario+	Breathe	Moderate Tempo	Alto	F3	F5	Lead	Ingenue Female
In The Heights	Miranda, Lin-Manuel	2008	Nina Rosario+	When You're Home*	Uptempo	Alto	C#4	E5	Lead	Ingenue Female
In The Heights	Miranda, Lin-Manuel	2008	Nina Rosario+	Everything's I Know	Ballad	Alto	Bb3	Db5	Lead	Ingenue Female
In The Heights	Miranda, Lin-Manuel	2008	Nina Rosario+	Alabanza*	Ballad	Alto	A3	A4	Lead	Ingenue Female
In The Heights	Miranda, Lin-Manuel	2008	Piragua Guy+	Piragua	Uptempo	Tenor	E3	A4	Supporting	Character Male
In The Heights	Miranda, Lin-Manuel	2008	Piragua Guy+	Piragua Reprise*	Uptempo	Baritone	D3	A4	Supporting	Character Male
In The Heights	Miranda, Lin-Manuel	2008	Usnavi De La Vega+	In The Heights (Rap)*	Uptempo	Baritone	D3	G4	Lead	Character Male
In The Heights	Miranda, Lin-Manuel	2008	Usnavi De La Vega+	Finale (Rap)*	Moderate Tempo	Baritone	A3	C4	Lead	Character Male
In The Heights	Miranda, Lin-Manuel	2008	Vanessa+	It Won't Be Long Now	Uptempo	Alto	A3	E5	Lead	Romantic Lead Female
In The Heights	Miranda, Lin-Manuel	2008	Benny & Nina	Benny's Dispatch	Uptempo	Tenor/Alto			Duet	RLM/IF
In The Heights	Miranda, Lin-Manuel	2008	Usnavi & Vanessa	Champagne	Moderate Tempo	Bar/Alto			Duet	CM/RLF

Shows

Songs by Character Type

* = Music Edit Required
\+ = Ethnic Specific

Show	Composer	Year	Role	Song	Range-Bottom	Range-Top	Vocal Type	Tempo	Category	Character Type
In The Heights	Miranda, Lin-Manuel	2008	Benny & Nina	When The Sun Goes Down			Tenor/Alto	Ballad	Duet	RLM/IF
Into The Woods	Sondheim, Stephen	1987	Baker	It Takes Two	Bb2	F4	Baritone	Moderate Tempo	Lead	Character Male
Into The Woods	Sondheim, Stephen	1987	Baker	No More*	D3	Eb4	Baritone	Ballad	Lead	Character Male
Into The Woods	Sondheim, Stephen	1987	Baker's Wife	Maybe They're Magic	G#3	E5	Alto	Uptempo	Lead	Character Female
Into The Woods	Sondheim, Stephen	1987	Baker's Wife	It Takes Two	A3	D5	Alto	Moderate Tempo	Lead	Character Female
Into The Woods	Sondheim, Stephen	1987	Baker's Wife	Moments In The Woods	F3	D4	Alto	Uptempo	Lead	Character Female
Into The Woods	Sondheim, Stephen	1987	Cinderella	On The Steps Of The Palace	A3	E5	Soprano	Uptempo	Lead	Ingenue Female
Into The Woods	Sondheim, Stephen	1987	Cinderella	No One Is Alone	Bb3	Db5	Soprano	Ballad	Lead	Ingenue Female
Into The Woods	Sondheim, Stephen	1987	Cinderella	No One Is Alone (Part 2)	Bb3	Db5	Soprano	Ballad	Lead	Ingenue Female
Into The Woods	Sondheim, Stephen	1987	Cinderella's Prince	Agony*	C#3	E4	Baritone	Moderate Tempo	Lead	Romantic Lead Male
Into The Woods	Sondheim, Stephen	1987	Cinderella's Prince	Agony II*	C#3	F4	Baritone	Moderate Tempo	Lead	Romantic Lead Male
Into The Woods	Sondheim, Stephen	1987	Cinderella's Prince	Any Moment*	B2	Eb5	Baritone	Uptempo	Lead	Romantic Lead Male
Into The Woods	Sondheim, Stephen	1987	Jack	I Guess This Is Goodbye	D#3	D#4	Tenor	Ballad	Lead	Character Ingenue Male
Into The Woods	Sondheim, Stephen	1987	Jack	Giants In The Sky	C3	F#4	Tenor	Uptempo	Lead	Character Ingenue Male
Into The Woods	Sondheim, Stephen	1987	Little Red Riding Hood	I Know Things Now	C4	E5	Alto	Uptempo	Lead	Juvenile Female
Into The Woods	Sondheim, Stephen	1987	Mysterious Man	No More*	Bb2	E4	Baritone	Ballad	Lead	Mature Male
Into The Woods	Sondheim, Stephen	1987	Narrator	Act I Opening (Part 4)*	G2	E4	Baritone	Uptempo	Lead	Mature Male
Into The Woods	Sondheim, Stephen	1987	Rapunzel's Prince	Agony*	C#3	E4	Baritone	Moderate Tempo	Lead	Romantic Lead Male
Into The Woods	Sondheim, Stephen	1987	Rapunzel's Prince	Agony II*	C#3	F4	Baritone	Moderate Tempo	Lead	Romantic Lead Male
Into The Woods	Sondheim, Stephen	1987	Witch	Stay With Me	A#3	D5	Alto	Ballad	Lead	Romantic Antagonist Female
Into The Woods	Sondheim, Stephen	1987	Witch	Lament	A3	D5	Alto	Ballad	Lead	Romantic Antagonist Female
Into The Woods	Sondheim, Stephen	1987	Witch	Last Midnight	F3	Db5	Alto	Moderate Tempo	Lead	Romantic Antagonist Female
Into The Woods	Sondheim, Stephen	1987	Wolf	Hello Little Girl	Bb2	Gb4	Baritone	Uptempo	Lead	Romantic Lead Male
Into The Woods	Sondheim, Stephen	1987	Baker's Wife & Cinderella	A Very Nice Prince			Alto/Sop	Uptempo	Duet	CF/IF
Into The Woods	Sondheim, Stephen	1987	C's Prince & R's Prince	Agony			Bar/Bar	Moderate Tempo	Duet	RLM/RLM
Into The Woods	Sondheim, Stephen	1987	Baker & Baker's Wife	It Takes Two			Bar/Alto	Uptempo	Duet	CM/CF
Into The Woods	Sondheim, Stephen	1987	C's Prince & R's Prince	Agony Reprise			Bar/Bar	Moderate Tempo	Duet	RLF/RLM
Into The Woods	Sondheim, Stephen	1987	Baker's Wife & C's Prince	Any Moment			Alto/Bar	Moderate Tempo	Duet	CF/RLM
Into The Woods	Sondheim, Stephen	1987	Baker & Mysterious Man	No More			Bar/Bar	Ballad	Duet	CM/MM
Into The Woods	Sondheim, Stephen	2008	Ensemble	Into The Woods Act II Finale Part 4			Unison/3 Part	Moderate Tempo	Ensemble	Adults
Into The Woods	Sondheim, Stephen	2008	Ensemble	Children Will Listen Act II Finale Part 3			Unison/3 Part	Ballad	Ensemble	Adults
Jane Eyre	Gordon, Paul	2008	Blanche Ingram	The Finer Things	Eb4	B5	Soprano	Uptempo	Supporting	Ingenue Female
Jane Eyre	Gordon, Paul	2008	Blanche Ingram	In the Virgin Morning*	B3	F5	Soprano	Moderate Tempo	Supporting	Ingenue Female
Jane Eyre	Gordon, Paul	2000	Edward Fairfax Rochester	As Good As You	A2	E4	Tenor	Moderate Tempo	Lead	Romantic Antagonist Male
Jane Eyre	Gordon, Paul	2000	Edward Fairfax Rochester	Secret Soul*	B2	B4	Tenor	Uptempo	Lead	Romantic Antagonist Male
Jane Eyre	Gordon, Paul	2000	Edward Fairfax Rochester	Sirens	Bb2	F4	Tenor	Uptempo	Lead	Romantic Antagonist Male
Jane Eyre	Gordon, Paul	2000	Edward Fairfax Rochester	The Gypsy (Drag)	D4	A5	Tenor	Uptempo	Lead	Romantic Antagonist Male
Jane Eyre	Gordon, Paul	2000	Edward Fairfax Rochester	Farewell Good Angel	G2	G4	Tenor	Uptempo	Lead	Romantic Antagonist Male
Jane Eyre	Gordon, Paul	2000	Edward Fairfax Rochester	Brave Enough for Love			Tenor	Uptempo	Lead	Romantic Antagonist Male
Jane Eyre	Gordon, Paul	2000	Ensemble	Sympathies Exist			SATB	Ballad	Ensemble	Adults
Jane Eyre	Gordon, Paul	2000	Helen Burnes	Forgiveness	A3	C5	Soprano	Ballad	Supporting	Juvenile Female
Jane Eyre	Gordon, Paul	2000	Jane Eyre	The Graveside	A3	D5	Alto	Ballad	Lead	Character Female

Shows

Songs by Character Type

* = Music Edit Required
+ = Ethnic Specific

Show	Composer	Year	Role	Song	Tempo	Vocal Type	Range-Bottom	Range-Top	Category	Character Type
Jane Eyre	Gordon, Paul	2000	Jane Eyre	Sweet Liberty	Uptempo	Alto	A3	D5	Lead	Character Female
Jane Eyre	Gordon, Paul	2000	Jane Eyre	Secret Soul*	Uptempo	Alto	F#3	D4	Lead	Character Female
Jane Eyre	Gordon, Paul	2000	Jane Eyre	Painting Her Portrait	Uptempo	Alto	Bb3	D5	Lead	Character Female
Jane Eyre	Gordon, Paul	2000	Jane Eyre	In the Virgin Morning*	Moderate Tempo	Alto	G3	D5	Lead	Character Female
Jane Eyre	Gordon, Paul	2000	Jane Eyre	Sirens Reprise*	Moderate Tempo	Alto	G3	C5	Lead	Character Female
Jane Eyre	Gordon, Paul	2000	Jane Eyre	The Voice Across the Moors	Moderate Tempo	Alto	Ab3	E5	Supporting	Character Female
Jane Eyre	Gordon, Paul	2000	Jane Eyre	Brave Enough for Love*	Uptempo	Alto	E3	Eb5	Lead	Character Female
Jane Eyre	Gordon, Paul	2000	Mrs. Fairfax	Perfectly Nice	Uptempo	Alto	A3	C#5	Lead	Mature Female
Jane Eyre	Gordon, Paul	2000	Mrs. Fairfax	Slip of a Girl	Uptempo	Alto	F3	Bb4	Lead	Mature Female
Jane Eyre	Gordon, Paul	2000	Mrs. Reed	Forgiveness Reprise	Moderate Tempo	Alto	G#3	B4	Supporting	Mature Female
Jane Eyre	Gordon, Paul	2000	School Girl	Rain	Moderate Tempo	Soprano	Bb3	E5	Supporting	Ingenue Female
Jane Eyre	Gordon, Paul	2000	St. John Rivers	The Voice Across the Moors	Moderate Tempo	Tenor	C3	G4	Supporting	Ingenue Male
Jane Eyre	Gordon, Paul	2000	Young Jane Eyre	The Graveside	Ballad	Soprano	A3	D5	Supporting	Juvenile Female
Jane Eyre	Gordon, Paul	2000	Edward & Jane	Secret Soul	Ballad	Tenor/Alto			Duet	RAM/CF
Jane Eyre	Gordon, Paul	2000	Edward & Jane	The Pledge	Moderate Tempo	Tenor/Alto			Duet	RAM/CF
Jane Eyre	Gordon, Paul	2000	Blanche & Jane	In the Light Of The Morning	Moderate Tempo	Sop/Alto			Duet	IF/CF
Jane Eyre	Gordon, Paul	2000	Edward & Jane	The Proposal	Moderate Tempo	Tenor/Alto			Duet	RAM/CF
Jane Eyre	Gordon, Paul	2000	Edward & Jane	Siren Reprise	Moderate Tempo	Tenor/Alto			Duet	RAM/CF
Jane Eyre	Gordon, Paul	2000	Edward & Jane	Brave Enough For Love	Moderate Tempo	Tenor/Alto			Duet	RAM/CF
Jane Eyre	Gordon, Paul	2000	Edward Fairfax Rochester	Brave Enough for Love*	Uptempo	Tenor	Db3	Bb4	Lead	Romantic Lead Male
Jekyll and Hyde	Wildhorn, Frank	1997	Dr. Henry Jekyll	Lost In The Darkness	Ballad	Tenor	G2	E4	Lead	Romantic Antagonist Male
Jekyll and Hyde	Wildhorn, Frank	1997	Dr. Henry Jekyll	Take Me As I Am	Ballad	Tenor	Bb2	Eb4	Lead	Romantic Lead Male
Jekyll and Hyde	Wildhorn, Frank	1997	Dr. Henry Jekyll	This Is The Moment	Ballad	Tenor	B2	G#4	Lead	Romantic Antagonist Male
Jekyll and Hyde	Wildhorn, Frank	1997	Dr. Henry Jekyll	What Streak of Madness/Obsession	Ballad	Tenor	C3	Eb4	Lead	Romantic Antagonist Male
Jekyll and Hyde	Wildhorn, Frank	1997	Dr. Henry Jekyll	The Way Back/Angst 2	Uptempo	Tenor	B2	G4	Lead	Romantic Antagonist Male
Jekyll and Hyde	Wildhorn, Frank	1997	Dr. Henry Jekyll	Lost In The Darkness Reprise	Ball	Tenor	G2	E4	Lead	Romantic Antagonist Male
Jekyll and Hyde	Wildhorn, Frank	1997	Dr. Henry Jekyll	Confrontation*	Uptempo	Tenor	B2	A4	Lead	Romantic Antagonist Male
Jekyll and Hyde	Wildhorn, Frank	1997	Dr. Henry Jekyll	I Need To Know	Ballad	Tenor	B2	F#4	Lead	Romantic Antagonist Male
Jekyll and Hyde	Wildhorn, Frank	1997	Emma Crow	Emma's Reasons/The Engagement Part	Moderate Tempo	Soprano	Bb3	Db5	Lead	Romantic Lead Female
Jekyll and Hyde	Wildhorn, Frank	1997	Emma Crow	Take Me As I Am	Ballad	Soprano	Bb3	F5	Lead	Romantic Lead Female
Jekyll and Hyde	Wildhorn, Frank	1997	Emma Crow	Once Upon A Dream	Moderate Tempo	Soprano	B2	C#4	Lead	Romantic Lead Female
Jekyll and Hyde	Wildhorn, Frank	1997	Emma Crow	In His Eyes*	Ballad	Soprano	Bb3	F5	Lead	Romantic Lead Female
Jekyll and Hyde	Wildhorn, Frank	1997	Ensemble	Façade	Uptempo	SATB			Ensemble	Adults
Jekyll and Hyde	Wildhorn, Frank	1997	Ensemble	Murder, Murder	Uptempo	SATB			Ensemble	Adults
Jekyll and Hyde	Wildhorn, Frank	1997	Lucy Harris	No One Knows Who I Am	Ballad	Alto	C4	D5	Lead	Romantic Antagonist Female
Jekyll and Hyde	Wildhorn, Frank	1997	Lucy Harris	Good and Evil	Moderate Tempo	Alto	G#3	E5	Lead	Romantic Antagonist Female
Jekyll and Hyde	Wildhorn, Frank	1997	Lucy Harris	Someone Like You	Ballad	Alto	G2	Eb4	Lead	Romantic Antagonist Female
Jekyll and Hyde	Wildhorn, Frank	1997	Lucy Harris	Sympathy, Tenderness	Ballad	Alto	D3	C#4	Lead	Romantic Antagonist Female
Jekyll and Hyde	Wildhorn, Frank	1997	Lucy Harris	In His Eyes*	Ballad	Alto	Bb3	F5	Lead	Romantic Antagonist Female
Jekyll and Hyde	Wildhorn, Frank	1997	Lucy Harris	A New Life	Ballad	Alto	B3	D5	Lead	Romantic Antagonist Female
Jekyll and Hyde	Wildhorn, Frank	1997	Lucy Harris	Bring On The Men	Uptempo	Alto	G#3	E5	Lead	Romantic Antagonist Female

Shows

Songs by Character Type

* = Music Edit Required
+ = Ethnic Specific

Show	Composer	Year	Role	Song	Tempo	Vocal Type	Range-Bottom	Range-Top	Category	Character Type
Jekyll and Hyde	Wildhorn, Frank	1997	Lucy Harris	Sympathy, Tenderness/Lucy's Death	Ballad	Alto	C#4	C#5	Lead	Romantic Antagonist Female
Jekyll and Hyde	Wildhorn, Frank	1997	Mr. Edward Hyde	Alive	Uptempo	Tenor	B2	D4	Lead	Antagonist Male
Jekyll and Hyde	Wildhorn, Frank	1997	Mr. Edward Hyde	Confrontation*	Uptempo	Tenor	B2	A4	Lead	Antagonist Male
Jekyll and Hyde	Wildhorn, Frank	1997	Mr. Edward Hyde	Alive Reprise	Uptempo	Tenor	E3	A4	Lead	Antagonist Male
Jekyll and Hyde	Wildhorn, Frank	1997	Emma & Stride	Emma's Reasons	Moderate Tempo	Sop/Bar			Duet	RLF/RLM
Jekyll and Hyde	Wildhorn, Frank	1997	Emma & Jekyll	Take Me As I Am	Ballad	Sop/Tenor			Duet	RLF/RAM
Jekyll and Hyde	Wildhorn, Frank	1997	Emma & Danvers	Letting Go	Ballad	Sop/Bar			Duet	RLF/P
Jekyll and Hyde	Wildhorn, Frank	1997	Emma & Lucy	In His Eyes	Ballad	Sop/Alto			Duet	RLF/RAM
Jersey Boys	Gaudio, Bob	2005	Ensemble	You're the Apple of My Eye	Uptempo	TB			Ensemble	Adults
Jersey Boys	Gaudio, Bob	2005	Ensemble	Walk Like A Man	Uptempo	TB			Ensemble	Adults
Jersey Boys	Gaudio, Bob	2005	Ensemble	Dawn	Uptempo	TB			Ensemble	Adults
Jersey Boys	Gaudio, Bob	2005	Ensemble	Who Loves You	Uptempo	TB			Ensemble	Adults
Jersey Boys (2005)	Gaudio, Bob	1928	Frankie Castelluccio	I Can't Give You Anything But Love	Moderate Tempo	Tenor	E3	Ab4	Lead	Character Ingenue Male
Jersey Boys (2005)	Gaudio, Bob	1935	Frankie Valli	I'm In The Mood	Ballad	Tenor	E3	F5	Lead	Character Ingenue Male
Jersey Boys (2005)	Gaudio, Bob	1946	Frankie Castelluccio	Sunday Kind Of Love	Uptempo	Tenor	D3	E5	Lead	Character Ingenue Male
Jersey Boys (2005)	Gaudio, Bob	1954	Tommy DeVito	Earth Angel	Ballad	Tenor	Bb3	Eb4	Lead	Antagonist Male
Jersey Boys (2005)	Gaudio, Bob	1960	Frankie Valli	Stay*	Uptempo	Tenor	F3	D5	Lead	Character Ingenue Male
Jersey Boys (2005)	Gaudio, Bob	1961	Hal Miller	An Angel Cried	Uptempo	Tenor	A3	C5	Supporting	Character Male
Jersey Boys (2005)	Gaudio, Bob	1962	Frankie Valli	Sherry*	Moderate Tempo	Tenor	G4	F5	Lead	Character Ingenue Male
Jersey Boys (2005)	Gaudio, Bob	1962	Frankie Valli	Big Girls Don't Cry	Uptempo	Tenor	Eb4	F5	Lead	Character Ingenue Male
Jersey Boys (2005)	Gaudio, Bob	1963	Frankie Valli	My Mother's Eyes	Ballad	Tenor	E3	F4	Lead	Character Ingenue Male
Jersey Boys (2005)	Gaudio, Bob	1963	Frankie Valli	Walk Like A Man	Moderate Tempo	Tenor	B3	F5	Lead	Character Ingenue Male
Jersey Boys (2005)	Gaudio, Bob	1964	Frankie Valli	Rag Doll	Moderate Tempo	Tenor	Bb3	F5	Lead	Character Ingenue Male
Jersey Boys (2005)	Gaudio, Bob	1965	Frankie Valli	Bye Bye Baby	Uptempo	Tenor	C#4	D5	Lead	Character Ingenue Male
Jersey Boys (2005)	Gaudio, Bob	1965	Frankie Valli	Work My Way Back To You	Uptempo	Tenor	G3	C5	Lead	Character Ingenue Male
Jersey Boys (2005)	Gaudio, Bob	1965	Frankie Valli	Let's Hang On!*	Uptempo	Tenor	Db3	D5	Lead	Character Ingenue Male
Jersey Boys (2005)	Gaudio, Bob	1966	Bob Gaudio	Cry For Me	Ballad	Tenor	Bb2	G4	Lead	Character Male
Jersey Boys (2005)	Gaudio, Bob	1966	Frankie Valli	Don't you Worry 'Bout Me*	Uptempo	Tenor	G3	C5	Lead	Character Ingenue Male
Jersey Boys (2005)	Gaudio, Bob	1967	Frankie Valli	Beggin'*	Uptempo	Tenor	B3	Bb4	Lead	Character Ingenue Male
Jersey Boys (2005)	Gaudio, Bob	1967	Frankie Valli	Can't Take My Eyes Off You	Uptempo	Tenor	D3	G4	Lead	Character Ingenue Male
Jersey Boys (2005)	Gaudio, Bob	1975	Bob Gaudio	December 1963	Uptempo	Tenor	F3	G4	Lead	Character Male
Jersey Boys (2005)	Gaudio, Bob	1975	Frankie Valli	My Eyes Adored You	Ballad	Tenor	G3	Bb4	Lead	Character Ingenue Male
Jersey Boys (2005)	Gaudio, Bob	1976	Frankie Valli	Fallen Angel	Ballad	Tenor	Eb3	Ab4	Lead	Character Ingenue Male
Jersey Boys, The	Gaudio, Bob	2005	Bob & Frankie	Let's Hang On	Moderate Tempo	Tenor/Tenor			Duet	CM/CIM
Jesus Christ Superstar	Webber, Andrew Lloyd	1971	Jesus of Nazareth	Poor Jerusalem	Ballad	Tenor	A2	Ab4	Lead	Romantic Lead Male
Jesus Christ Superstar	Webber, Andrew Lloyd	1971	Jesus of Nazareth	Gethsemane	Ballad	Tenor	Bb2	Ab4	Lead	Romantic Lead Male
Jesus Christ Superstar	Webber, Andrew Lloyd	1971	Jesus of Nazareth	The Last Supper	Ballad	Tenor	F#2	C5	Lead	Romantic Lead Male
Jesus Christ Superstar	Webber, Andrew Lloyd	1971	Judas Iscariot	Heaven On Their Minds*	Uptempo	Tenor	D3	D5	Lead	Antagonist Male
Jesus Christ Superstar	Webber, Andrew Lloyd	1971	Judas Iscariot	Damned For All Time*	Uptempo	Tenor	D3	D5	Lead	Antagonist Male
Jesus Christ Superstar	Webber, Andrew Lloyd	1971	Judas Iscariot	Judas' Death	Uptempo	Tenor	D3	E5	Lead	Antagonist Male
Jesus Christ Superstar	Webber, Andrew Lloyd	1971	Judas Iscariot	Superstar	Uptempo	Tenor	E3	B4	Lead	Antagonist Male
Jesus Christ Superstar	Webber, Andrew Lloyd	1971	King Herod	King Herod's Song	Uptempo	Baritone	B2	G4	Supporting	Character Male

Shows

Songs by Character Type

* = Music Edit Required
+ = Ethnic Specific

Show	Composer	Year	Role	Song	Tempo	Vocal Type	Range-Bottom	Range-Top	Category	Character Type
Jesus Christ Superstar	Webber, Andrew Lloyd	1971	Mary Magdalene	Everything's Alright	Moderate Tempo	Alto	G#3	D5	Lead	Character Ingenue Female
Jesus Christ Superstar	Webber, Andrew Lloyd	1971	Mary Magdalene	Everything's Alright Reprise	Moderate Tempo	Alto	F#3	G4	Lead	Character Ingenue Female
Jesus Christ Superstar	Webber, Andrew Lloyd	1971	Mary Magdalene	I Don't Know How To Love Him	Ballad	Alto	A3	C5	Lead	Character Ingenue Female
Jesus Christ Superstar	Webber, Andrew Lloyd	1971	Mary Magdalene	Could We Start Again Please	Ballad	Alto	A3	F#5	Lead	Character Ingenue Female
Jesus Christ Superstar	Webber, Andrew Lloyd	1971	Pontius Pilate	Pilate's Dream	Ballad	Baritone	A2	Bb3	Supporting	Antagonist Male
Jesus Christ Superstar	Webber, Andrew Lloyd	1971	Pontius Pilate	Pilate and Christ	Moderate Tempo	Baritone	Bb3	G#4	Supporting	Antagonist Male
Jesus Christ Superstar	Webber, Andrew Lloyd	1971	Simon Zealots	Simon Zealots*	Uptempo	Tenor	F3	Ab4	Supporting	Antagonist Male
Jesus Christ Superstar	Webber, Andrew Lloyd	1971	Mary & Peter	Could We Start Again Please	Ballad	Alto/Tenor			Duet	CIF/AM
Joseph...Dream Coat	Webber, Andrew Lloyd	1982	Joseph	Any Dream Will Do	Ballad	Tenor	C4	F4	Lead	Ingenue Male
Joseph...Dream Coat	Webber, Andrew Lloyd	1982	Joseph	Close Every Door	Ballad	Tenor	C3	A4	Lead	Ingenue Male
Joseph...Dream Coat	Webber, Andrew Lloyd	1982	Joseph	Pharaoh's Dream Explained	Uptempo	Tenor	B2	E4	Lead	Ingenue Male
Joseph...Dream Coat	Webber, Andrew Lloyd	1982	Joseph	Any Dream Will Do Reprise	Ballad	Tenor	D3	F4	Lead	Ingenue Male
Joseph...Dream Coat	Webber, Andrew Lloyd	1982	Joseph	Any Dream Will Do (II)	Ballad	Tenor	C3	F4	Lead	Ingenue Male
Joseph...Dream Coat	Webber, Andrew Lloyd	1982	Levi	One More Angel In Heaven	Moderate Tempo	Baritone	D3	F4	Lead	Character Male
Joseph...Dream Coat	Webber, Andrew Lloyd	1982	Napthali	Benjamin Calypso	Uptempo	Baritone	F3	F4	Supporting	Character Female
Joseph...Dream Coat	Webber, Andrew Lloyd	1982	Narrator	Pharaoh Story	Moderate Tempo	Alto	A3	E5	Lead	Character Female
Joseph...Dream Coat	Webber, Andrew Lloyd	1982	Pharaoh (Elvis)	Song of the King	Uptempo	Tenor	B2	G#4	Supporting	Character Male
Joseph...Dream Coat	Webber, Andrew Lloyd	1982	Pharaoh (Elvis)	Song of the King Reprise	Uptempo	Tenor	B2	G#4	Supporting	Character Male
Joseph...Dream Coat	Webber, Andrew Lloyd	1982	Reuben (Chevalier)	Those Canaan Days	Ballad	Baritone	C3	F4	Supporting	Character Male
King and I, The	Rodgers, Richard	1951	Anna Leonowens	I Whistle A Happy Tune*	Uptempo	Soprano	D4	D5	Lead	Romantic Lead Female
King and I, The	Rodgers, Richard	1951	Anna Leonowens	Hello, Young Lovers	Ballad	Soprano	C#4	D5	Lead	Romantic Lead Female
King and I, The	Rodgers, Richard	1951	Anna Leonowens	Getting To Know You*	Moderate Tempo	Soprano	C#4	E5	Lead	Romantic Lead Female
King and I, The	Rodgers, Richard	1951	Anna Leonowens	Shall I Tell You What I Think....	Uptempo	Soprano	D3	C#5	Lead	Romantic Lead Female
King and I, The	Rodgers, Richard	1951	Anna Leonowens	Shall We Dance	Uptempo	Soprano	D4	C5	Lead	Romantic Lead Female
King and I, The	Rodgers, Richard	1951	Anna Leonowens	Hello, Young Lovers Reprise	Ballad	Soprano	C4	D5	Lead	Romantic Lead Female
King and I, The	Rodgers, Richard	1951	Ensemble	Getting To Know You*	Uptempo	Unison			Ensemble	Adults
King and I, The	Rodgers, Richard	1951	King of Siam+	A Puzzlement	Uptempo	Baritone	C3	E4	Lead	Romantic Lead Male
King and I, The	Rodgers, Richard	1951	King of Siam+	Song of the King	Moderate Tempo	Baritone	D3	D4	Lead	Romantic Lead Male
King and I, The	Rodgers, Richard	1951	Lady Thiang+	Something Wonderful	Ballad	Soprano	C#4	G5	Lead	Romantic Lead Female
King and I, The	Rodgers, Richard	1951	Lady Thiang+	Western People Funny*	Moderate Tempo	Soprano	E4	G5	Lead	Romantic Lead Female
King and I, The	Rodgers, Richard	1951	Louis Leonowens	A Puzzlement Reprise*	Uptempo	Baritone	G2	G3	Supporting	Juvenile Male
King and I, The	Rodgers, Richard	1951	Louis Leonowens	I Whistle A Happy Tune*	Uptempo	Baritone	B2	B3	Supporting	Juvenile Male
King and I, The	Rodgers, Richard	1951	Lun Tha+	We Kiss In The Shadow	Ballad	Tenor	D3	E4	Lead	Ingenue Male
King and I, The	Rodgers, Richard	1951	Lun Tha+	I Have Dreamed	Ballad	Tenor	C3	G4	Lead	Ingenue Male
King and I, The	Rodgers, Richard	1951	Prince Chulalongkorn	A Puzzlement Reprise*	Uptempo	Baritone	G2	G3	Supporting	Juvenile Male
King and I, The	Rodgers, Richard	1951	Tuptim+	My Lord And Master	Moderate Tempo	Soprano	D#4	A#5	Lead	Ingenue Female
King and I, The	Rodgers, Richard	1951	Tuptim+	We Kiss In The Shadow	Ballad	Soprano	D4	G5	Lead	Ingenue Female
King and I, The	Rodgers, Richard	1951	Tuptim+	I Have Dreamed	Ballad	Soprano	C4	G5	Lead	Ingenue Female
King and I, The	Rodgers, Richard	1951	Anna & Louis	I Whistle A Happy Tune	Uptempo	Sop/Bar			Duet	RLF/JM
King and I, The	Rodgers, Richard	1951	Lun Tha+ & Tuptim+	We Kiss In a Shadow	Ballad	Tenor/Sop			Duet	IM/IF
King and I, The	Rodgers, Richard	1951	Lun Tha+ & Tuptim+	I Have Dreamed	Ballad	Tenor/Sop			Duet	IM/IF
King and I, The	Rodgers, Richard	1951	Louis & Prince	A Puzzlement Reprise	Uptempo	Bar/Bar			Duet	JM/JM
Kinky Boots	Lauper, Cyndi	2013	Charlie Price	Take What You Got*	Uptempo	Tenor	F#3	F#4	Lead	Ingenue Male
Kinky Boots	Lauper, Cyndi	2013	Charlie Price	Step One	Uptempo	Tenor	Ab3	Ab4	Lead	Ingenue Male

Shows

Songs by Character Type

Show	Composer	Year	Role	Song	Tempo	Vocal Type	Range-Bottom	Range-Top	Category	Character Type
Kinky Boots	Lauper, Cyndi	2013	Charlie Price	Not My Father's Son*	Ballad	Tenor	F#3	F#4	Lead	Ingenue Male
Kinky Boots	Lauper, Cyndi	2013	Charlie Price	The Soul of a Man	Uptempo	Tenor	C3	Bb4	Lead	Ingenue Male
Kinky Boots	Lauper, Cyndi	2013	Charlie Price	Charlie's Soliloquy	Ballad	Tenor	Eb3	Cb4	Lead	Ingenue Male
Kinky Boots	Lauper, Cyndi	2013	Charlie Price	Charlie's Soliloquy Reprise	Uptempo	Tenor	F#3	C#4	Lead	Ingenue Male
Kinky Boots	Lauper, Cyndi	2013	Ensemble	Raise You Up	Uptempo	SATB			Ensemble	Adults
Kinky Boots	Lauper, Cyndi	2013	Harry	Take What You Got*	Uptempo	Baritone	F#3	F#4	Supporting	Character Ingenue Male
Kinky Boots	Lauper, Cyndi	2013	Lauren	The History of Wrong Guys	Uptempo	Alto	Bb3	D5	Lead	Character Female
Kinky Boots	Lauper, Cyndi	2013	Lola (Drag)	The Land of Lola	Uptempo	Tenor	F#3	F#4	Lead	Character Male
Kinky Boots	Lauper, Cyndi	2013	Lola (Drag)	The Sex Is In the Heel	Moderate Tempo	Tenor	A3	B4	Lead	Character Male
Kinky Boots	Lauper, Cyndi	2013	Lola (Drag)	Not My Father's Son*	Ballad	Tenor	E3	A4	Lead	Character Male
Kinky Boots	Lauper, Cyndi	2013	Lola (Drag)	What a Woman Wants	Moderate Tempo	Tenor	E3	A4	Lead	Character Male
Kinky Boots	Lauper, Cyndi	2013	Lola (Drag)	Hold Me In Your Heart	Ballad	Tenor	E3	Bb4	Lead	Character Male
Kinky Boots	Lauper, Cyndi	2013	Charlie & Harry	Take What You Got	Uptempo	Tenor/Bar			Duet	CIM/CIM
Kinky Boots	Lauper, Cyndi	2013	Charlie & Lola (Drag)	I'm Not My Father's Son	Ballad	Tenor/Tenor			Duet	IM/CM
Kiss Me Kate	Porter, Cole	2013	Bill Calhoun/Lucentio	Bianca*	Uptempo	Baritone	G2	F4	Lead	Character Ingenue Male
Kiss Me Kate	Porter, Cole	1948	Ensemble	Another Op'nin Another Show*	Uptempo	SATB			Ensemble	Adults
Kiss Me Kate	Porter, Cole	1948	Ensemble	We Open In Venice	Uptempo	Unison			Ensemble	Adults
Kiss Me Kate	Porter, Cole	1948	Ensemble	Too Darn Hot*	Uptempo	SATB			Ensemble	Adults
Kiss Me Kate	Porter, Cole	1948	Ensemble	Kiss Me Kate	Moderate Tempo	SATB			Ensemble	Adults
Kiss Me Kate	Porter, Cole	1948	Ensemble	Cantiamo D'Amore	Uptempo	SATB			Ensemble	Adults
Kiss Me Kate	Porter, Cole	1948	First Man	Brush Up Your Shakespeare*	Moderate Tempo	Baritone	B2	D4	Lead	Antagonist Male
Kiss Me Kate	Porter, Cole	1948	Fred Graham/Petruchio	Wunderbar*	Ballad	Baritone	C3	G4	Lead	Romantic Lead Male
Kiss Me Kate	Porter, Cole	1948	Fred Graham/Petruchio	Were Thine That Speical Face	Moderate Tempo	Baritone	C3	F4	Lead	Romantic Lead Male
Kiss Me Kate	Porter, Cole	1948	Fred Graham/Petruchio	Where Is The Life That Late I Led	Moderate Tempo	Baritone	B2	F4	Lead	Romantic Lead Male
Kiss Me Kate	Porter, Cole	1948	Fred Graham/Petruchio	So In Love Reprise	Ballad	Baritone	B2	Eb4	Lead	Romantic Lead Male
Kiss Me Kate	Porter, Cole	1948	General Howell	From This Moment On	Uptempo	Baritone	B2	C#4	Supporting	Character Male
Kiss Me Kate	Porter, Cole	1948	Hattie	Another Op'nin Another Show*	Uptempo	Alto	G3	E5	Supporting	Character Female
Kiss Me Kate	Porter, Cole	1948	Lilli Vanessi/Katherine	So In Love	Ballad	Soprano	C4	G5	Lead	Romantic Lead Female
Kiss Me Kate	Porter, Cole	1948	Lilli Vanessi/Katherine	I Hate Men	Ballad	Soprano	A3	Db5	Lead	Romantic Lead Female
Kiss Me Kate	Porter, Cole	1948	Lilli Vanessi/Katherine	I Am Ashamed That Women Are So Sim	Moderate Tempo	Alto	B3	C#5	Lead	Romantic Lead Female
Kiss Me Kate	Porter, Cole	1948	Lois Lane/Bianca	Why Can't You Behave*	Moderate Tempo	Soprano	C4	Eb5	Lead	Character Ingenue Female
Kiss Me Kate	Porter, Cole	1948	Lois Lane/Bianca	Always True To You*	Moderate Tempo	Alto	G3	Cb5	Lead	Character Ingenue Female
Kiss Me Kate	Porter, Cole	1948	Lois Lane/Bianca	Always True To You Encore	Uptempo	Alto	A3	C#5	Lead	Character Ingenue Female
Kiss Me Kate	Porter, Cole	1948	Paul	Too Darn Hot*	Uptempo	Tenor	C3	Gb4	Supporting	Character Male
Kiss Me Kate	Porter, Cole	1948	Second Man	Brush Up Your Shakespeare*	Moderate Tempo	Baritone	B2	D4	Supporting	Antagonist Male
Kiss Me Kate	Porter, Cole	1948	Fred & Lilli	Wunderbar	Moderate Tempo	Sop/Bar			Duet	RLM/RLF
Kiss Me Kate	Porter, Cole	1948	First Man & Second Man	Brush Up Your Shakespeare	Uptempo	Bar/Bar			Duet	CM/CM
Kiss Of The Spider Woman	Kander, John	1993	Molina	Her Name Is Aurora*	Moderate Tempo	Tenor	C3	C4	Lead	Character Male
Kiss Of The Spider Woman	Kander, John	1993	Aurora	Her Name Is Aurora*	Moderate Tempo	Alto	C3	A4	Lead	Romantic Antagonist Female
Kiss Of The Spider Woman	Kander, John	1993	Molina & Aurora	Her Name Is Aurora	Moderate Tempo	Tenor/Alto			Duet	CM/RAF
Kiss Of The Spider Woman	Kander, John	1993	Ensemble	Over The Wall 1	Uptempo	TB			Ensemble	Adults

Shows

Songs by Character Type

* = Music Edit Required
+ = Ethnic Specific

Show	Composer	Year	Role	Song	Tempo	Vocal Type	Range-Bottom	Range-Top	Category	Character Type
Kiss Of The Spider Woman	Kander, John	1993	Aurora	Spider Woman Fragment 1	Ballad	Alto	F3	F4	Lead	Romantic Antagonist Female
Kiss Of The Spider Woman	Kander, John	1993	Molina	Bluebloods*	Uptempo	Tenor	B2	C#4	Lead	Character Male
Kiss Of The Spider Woman	Kander, John	1993	Monlina & Valentin	Bluebloods	Uptempo	Tenor/Tenor			Duet	CM/RAM
Kiss Of The Spider Woman	Kander, John	1993	Molina	Dressing Them Up	Uptempo	Tenor	C3	F4	Lead	Character Male
Kiss Of The Spider Woman	Kander, John	1993	Monlina & Valentin	I Draw A Line	Uptempo	Tenor/Tenor			Duet	CM/RAM
Kiss Of The Spider Woman	Kander, John	1993	Mother	Dear One*	Ballad	Alto	Bb3	C5	Lead	Mature Female
Kiss Of The Spider Woman	Kander, John	1993	Marta	Dear One*	Ballad	Alto	C4	Eb5	Lead	Character Ingenue Female
Kiss Of The Spider Woman	Kander, John	1993	Valentin	Dear One*	Ballad	Tenor	Bb2	C4	Lead	Romantic Antagonist Male
Kiss Of The Spider Woman	Kander, John	1993	Molina	Dear One*	Ballad	Tenor	C3	Eb4	Lead	Character Male
Kiss Of The Spider Woman	Kander, John	1993	Ensemble	Dear One	Ballad	SATB			Ensemble	Adults
Kiss Of The Spider Woman	Kander, John	1993	Ensemble	Over The Wall 2	Uptempo	TB			Ensemble	Adults
Kiss Of The Spider Woman	Kander, John	1993	Aurora	Where You Are*	Uptempo	Alto	Eb3	Gb4	Lead	Romantic Antagonist Female
Kiss Of The Spider Woman	Kander, John	1993	Valentin	Where You Are	Uptempo	ATB			Ensemble	Adults
Kiss Of The Spider Woman	Kander, John	1993	Spider Woman	Over The Wall 3 - Marta	Moderate Tempo	Tenor	F3	A4	Lead	Romantic Antagonist Male
Kiss Of The Spider Woman	Kander, John	1993	Marta	Interrogation*	Moderate Tempo	Alto	F3	F4	Lead	Romantic Antagonist Female
Kiss Of The Spider Woman	Kander, John	1993	Aurora	I Do Miracles*	Moderate Tempo	Alto	E3	Bb4	Lead	Character Ingenue Female
Kiss Of The Spider Woman	Kander, John	1993	Aurora & Marta	I Do Miracles*	Moderate Tempo	Alto	B2	Ab4	Lead	Romantic Antagonist Female
Kiss Of The Spider Woman	Kander, John	1993	Gabriel	I Do Miracles	Moderate Tempo	Alto/Alto			Duet	RAF/CIF
Kiss Of The Spider Woman	Kander, John	1993	Valentin	Gabriel's Letter*	Moderate Tempo	Tenor	D#3	G4	Lead	Character Ingenue Male
Kiss Of The Spider Woman	Kander, John	1993	Ensemble	My First Woman*	Moderate Tempo	Tenor	C3	G4	Lead	Romantic Antagonist Male
Kiss Of The Spider Woman	Kander, John	1993	Mother	Morphine Tango	Moderate Tempo	TTB			Ensemble	Adults
Kiss Of The Spider Woman	Kander, John	1993	Molina & Spider Woman	You Could Never Shame Me	Moderate Tempo	Alto	F3	D5	Lead	Mature Female
Kiss Of The Spider Woman	Kander, John	1993	Ensemble	A Visit	Moderate Tempo	Tenor/Alto			Duet	CM/RAF
Kiss Of The Spider Woman	Kander, John	1993	Molina	Morphine Tango @	Moderate Tempo	TTB			Ensemble	Adults
Kiss Of The Spider Woman	Kander, John	1993	Aurora	She's A Woman	Ballad	Tenor	C3	E4	Lead	Character Male
Kiss Of The Spider Woman	Kander, John	1993	Aurora	Let's Make Love*	Uptempo	Alto	D3	A4	Lead	Romantic Antagonist Female
Kiss Of The Spider Woman	Kander, John	1993	Valentin	Good Times*	Uptempo	Tenor	D#3	A4	Lead	Romantic Antagonist Female
Kiss Of The Spider Woman	Kander, John	1993	Molina & Spider Woman	The Day After That*	Uptempo	Tenor	D3	Gb4	Lead	Romantic Antagonist Male
Kiss Of The Spider Woman	Kander, John	1993	Ensemble	The Day After That	Uptempo	TB			Ensemble	Adults
Kiss Of The Spider Woman	Kander, John	1993	Molina	Mama, It's Me	Moderate Tempo	Tenor	C3	E4	Lead	Character Male
Kiss Of The Spider Woman	Kander, John	1993	Ensemble	Anything For Him	Moderate Tempo	ATT			Ensemble	Adults
Kiss Of The Spider Woman	Kander, John	1993	Spider Woman	Kiss Of The Spider Woman	Uptempo	Alto	C#3	A4	Lead	Romantic Antagonist Female
Kiss Of The Spider Woman	Kander, John	1993	Ensemble	Over The Wall 4	Uptempo	TB			Ensemble	Adults
Kiss Of The Spider Woman	Kander, John	1993	Molina	Only In the Movies	Uptempo	Tenor	B2	F4	Lead	Character Male
LA Cage Aux Folles	Herman, Jerry	1983	Albin	A Little More Mascara (Drag)	Uptempo	Baritone	Bb2	D4	Lead	Character Male
LA Cage Aux Folles	Herman, Jerry	1983	Albin	I Am What I Am (Drag)	Moderate Tempo	Baritone	G#3	F4	Lead	Character Male
LA Cage Aux Folles	Herman, Jerry	1983	Albin	The Best Of Times (Drag)	Moderate Tempo	Baritone	C3	Eb4	Lead	Character Male
LA Cage Aux Folles	Herman, Jerry	1983	Albin	With You On My Arm	Moderate Tempo	Baritone	G#2	Eb4	Lead	Character Male
LA Cage Aux Folles	Herman, Jerry	1983	Albin	La Cage Aux Folles (Drag)	Moderate Tempo	Baritone	Bb2	E4	Lead	Character Male
LA Cage Aux Folles	Herman, Jerry	1983	Georges	Song On The Sand	Ballad	Baritone	Ab2	E4	Lead	Romantic Lead Male
LA Cage Aux Folles	Herman, Jerry	1983	Georges	Masculinity	Uptempo	Baritone	B2	E4	Lead	Romantic Lead Male
LA Cage Aux Folles	Herman, Jerry	1983	Georges	Look Over There	Ballad	Baritone	B2	Eb4	Lead	Romantic Lead Male

Songs by Character Type

* = Music Edit Required
+ = Ethnic Specific

Show	Composer	Year	Role	Song	Tempo	Vocal Type	Range-Bottom	Range-Top	Category	Character Type
LA Cage Aux Folles	Herman, Jerry	1983	Georges	With You On My Arm	Moderate Tempo	Baritone	G#2	Eb4	Lead	Romantic Lead Male
LA Cage Aux Folles	Herman, Jerry	1983	Georges	Song On The Sand Reprise	Ballad	Baritone	C3	D4	Lead	Romantic Lead Male
LA Cage Aux Folles	Herman, Jerry	1983	Jean-Michel	With Anne On My Arm	Moderate Tempo	Tenor	A#2	G4	Lead	Ingenue Male
LA Cage Aux Folles	Herman, Jerry	1983	Jean-Michel	Look Over There Reprise	Tenor	Baritone	Db3	Eb4	Lead	Ingenue Male
LA Cage Aux Folles	Herman, Jerry	1983	Albin & Georges	With You on My Arm Reprise	Moderate Tempo	Bar/Bar			Duet	CM/RLM
LA Cage Aux Folles	Herman, Jerry	1983	Albin & Georges	Song On The Sand Reprise	Ballad	Bar/Bar			Duet	CM/RLM
Last Five Years, The	Brown, Jason Robert	2002	Catherine Hiatt	Still Hurting	Ballad	Alto	A3	Db5	Lead	Ingenue Female
Last Five Years, The	Brown, Jason Robert	2002	Catherine Hiatt	See I'm Smiling	Ballad	Alto	E3	C#5	Lead	Ingenue Female
Last Five Years, The	Brown, Jason Robert	2002	Catherine Hiatt	I'm A Part Of That	Uptempo	Alto	Bb3	Eb5	Lead	Ingenue Female
Last Five Years, The	Brown, Jason Robert	2002	Catherine Hiatt	A Summer In Ohio	Uptempo	Alto	F#3	E5	Lead	Ingenue Female
Last Five Years, The	Brown, Jason Robert	2002	Catherine Hiatt	The Next Ten Minutes	Ballad	Alto	G#3	E#4	Lead	Ingenue Female
Last Five Years, The	Brown, Jason Robert	2002	Catherine Hiatt	Climbing Uphill/Audition	Uptempo	Alto	G3	D5	Lead	Ingenue Female
Last Five Years, The	Brown, Jason Robert	2002	Catherine Hiatt	I Can Do Better Than That	Uptempo	Alto	A3	D5	Lead	Ingenue Female
Last Five Years, The	Brown, Jason Robert	2002	Catherine Hiatt	Goodbye Until Tomorrow	Moderate Tempo	Alto	F#3	Db5	Lead	Ingenue Female
Last Five Years, The	Brown, Jason Robert	2002	Catherine Hiatt	When You Come To Me	Moderate Tempo	Alto	A3	D5	Lead	Ingenue Female
Last Five Years, The	Brown, Jason Robert	2002	Jamie Wellerstein	Shiksa Goddess	Uptempo	Tenor	A2	A4	Lead	Ingenue Male
Last Five Years, The	Brown, Jason Robert	2002	Jamie Wellerstein	Moving Too Fast	Uptempo	Tenor	C3	Bb4	Lead	Ingenue Male
Last Five Years, The	Brown, Jason Robert	2002	Jamie Wellerstein	The Schmuel Song	Uptempo	Tenor	C#3	Ab4	Lead	Ingenue Male
Last Five Years, The	Brown, Jason Robert	2002	Jamie Wellerstein	The Next Ten Minutes	Ballad	Tenor	C#3	G#4	Lead	Ingenue Male
Last Five Years, The	Brown, Jason Robert	2002	Jamie Wellerstein	If I Didn't Believe In You	Ballad	Tenor	Bb2	G4	Lead	Ingenue Male
Last Five Years, The	Brown, Jason Robert	2002	Jamie Wellerstein	Nobody Needs To Know	Ballad	Tenor	C3	A4	Lead	Ingenue Male
Last Five Years, The	Brown, Jason Robert	2002	Jamie Wellerstein	I Could Never Rescue You	Ballad	Tenor	C3	G4	Lead	Ingenue Male
Last Five Years, The	Brown, Jason Robert	2002	Jamie Wellerstein	A Miracle Would Happen	Uptempo	Tenor	A2	A4	Lead	Ingenue Male
Last Five Years, The	Brown, Jason Robert	2002	Cathy & Jamie	The Next Ten Minutes	Ballad	Alto/Tenor			Duet	IF/IM
Legally Blonde	Benjamin and O'Keefe	2007	Aaron Schultz	Harvard Variation*	Uptempo	Baritone	C3	Eb4	Supporting	Character Male
Legally Blonde	Benjamin and O'Keefe	2007	Brooke Wyndam	Whipped Into Shape*	Uptempo	Alto	A3	G5	Supporting	Romantic Lead Female
Legally Blonde	Benjamin and O'Keefe	2007	Elle Woods	So Much Better	Uptempo	Alto	G3	E5	Lead	Ingenue Female
Legally Blonde	Benjamin and O'Keefe	2007	Elle Woods	Take It Like A Man	Moderate Tempo	Alto	Gb3	E5	Lead	Ingenue Female
Legally Blonde	Benjamin and O'Keefe	2007	Elle Woods	Legally Blonde	Ballad	Alto	G3	Db5	Lead	Ingenue Female
Legally Blonde	Benjamin and O'Keefe	2007	Elle Woods	Find My Way	Moderate Tempo	Alto	G3	B4	Lead	Ingenue Female
Legally Blonde	Benjamin and O'Keefe	2007	Elle Woods	Legally Blonde Remix*	Uptempo	Alto	E4	D5	Lead	Ingenue Female
Legally Blonde	Benjamin and O'Keefe	2007	Elle Woods	What You Want	Uptempo	Alto	Bb3	Db5	Lead	Ingenue Female
Legally Blonde	Benjamin and O'Keefe	2007	Elle Woods	Chip On My Shoulder*	Uptempo	Alto	C4	Eb5	Lead	Ingenue Female
Legally Blonde	Benjamin and O'Keefe	2007	Emmett Forrest	Chip On My Shoulder*	Uptempo	Tenor	C3	A4	Lead	Character Male
Legally Blonde	Benjamin and O'Keefe	2007	Emmett Forrest	Legally Blonde (ms 101b-166)	Ballad	Tenor	E3	G4	Lead	Character Male
Legally Blonde	Benjamin and O'Keefe	2007	Enid Hoops	Harvard Variation*	Uptempo	Alto	Bb3	C5	Supporting	Character Female
Legally Blonde	Benjamin and O'Keefe	2007	Ensemble	There, Right There	Uptempo	SATB			Ensemble	Adults
Legally Blonde	Benjamin and O'Keefe	2007	Padamadan*	Harvard Variation*	Uptempo	Baritone	B2	E4	Supporting	Ingenue Male
Legally Blonde	Benjamin and O'Keefe	2007	Paulette	Ireland	Moderate Tempo	Alto	A#3	B4	Lead	Character Female
Legally Blonde	Benjamin and O'Keefe	2007	Paulette	Ireland Reprise	Moderate Tempo	Alto	C4	Bb4	Lead	Character Female
Legally Blonde	Benjamin and O'Keefe	2007	Paulette	Find My Way	Ballad	Alto	Ab3	C5	Lead	Character Female

Songs by Character Type

* = Music Edit Required
+ = Ethnic Specific

Show	Composer	Year	Role	Song	Tempo	Vocal Type	Range-Bottom	Range-Top	Category	Character Type
Legally Blonde	Benjamin and O'Keefe	2007	Professor Callahan	Blood In The Water	Moderate Tempo	Baritone	C3	F#4	Supporting	Romantic Antagonist Male
Legally Blonde	Benjamin and O'Keefe	2007	Professor Callahan	Whipped Into Shape*	Uptempo	Baritone	C3	F#4	Supporting	Romantic Antagonist Male
Legally Blonde	Benjamin and O'Keefe	2007	Vivianne Kensington	Legally Blonde Remix*	Uptempo	Alto	A3	Eb5	Lead	Antagonist Female
Legally Blonde	Benjamin and O'Keefe	2007	Warner Huntington	Serious*	Uptempo	Tenor	F3	G4	Lead	Ingenue Male
Legally Blonde	Benjamin and O'Keefe	2007	Elle & Warner	Serious	Moderate Tempo	Alto/Tenor			Duet	IF/IM
Legally Blonde	Benjamin and O'Keefe	2007	Elle & Warner	Serious Reprise	Moderate Tempo	Alto/Tenor			Duet	IF/IM
Legally Blonde	Benjamin and O'Keefe	2007	Elle & Emmett	Legally Blonde	Ballad	Alto/Tenor			Duet	IF/CM
Les Miserables	Schonberg, Claude-Michel	1987	Ensemble	At the End of the Day	Uptempo	SATB			Ensemble	Adults
Les Miserables	Schonberg, Claude-Michel	1987	Ensemble	Do You Hear the People Sing*	Moderate Tempo	SATB			Ensemble	Adults
Les Miserables	Schonberg, Claude-Michel	1987	Ensemble	One Day More*	Moderate Tempo	SATB			Ensemble	Adults
Les Miserables	Schonberg, Claude-Michel	1987	Ensemble	Drink With Me*	Ballad	SATB			Ensemble	Adults
Les Miserables	Schonberg, Claude-Michel	1987	Ensemble	Turning*	Moderate Tempo	SA			Ensemble	Adults
Les Miserables	Schonberg, Claude-Michel	1987	Ensemble	The Wedding*	Uptempo	SATB			Ensemble	Adults
Les Miserables	Schonberg, Claude-Michel	1987	Ensemble	Lovely Ladies *	Uptempo	SATB			Ensemble	Adults
Les Miserables	Schonberg, Claude-Michel	1987	Eponine	On My Own	Ballad	Alto	A3	C5	Lead	Character Ingenue Female
Les Miserables	Schonberg, Claude-Michel	1987	Eponine	A Little Fall Of Rain*	Ballad	Alto	F3	Db5	Lead	Character Ingenue Female
Les Miserables	Schonberg, Claude-Michel	1987	Fantine	I Have Dreamed (E Major)	Ballad	Alto	G3	C#5	Lead	Romantic Lead Female
Les Miserables	Schonberg, Claude-Michel	1987	Fantine	Come To Me	Ballad	Alto	C4	C5	Lead	Romantic Lead Female
Les Miserables	Schonberg, Claude-Michel	1987	Fantine	I Have Dreamed (Eb Major)	Ballad	Alto	Gb3	C5	Lead	Romantic Lead Female
Les Miserables	Schonberg, Claude-Michel	1987	Gavroche	Look Down*	Moderate Tempo	Alto	C4	Db5	Supporting	Juvenile Male
Les Miserables	Schonberg, Claude-Michel	1987	Gavroche	Little People*	Uptempo	Alto	B3	D5	Supporting	Juvenile Male
Les Miserables	Schonberg, Claude-Michel	1987	Javert	Stars	Moderate Tempo	Tenor	B2	E4	Lead	Antagonist Male
Les Miserables	Schonberg, Claude-Michel	1987	Javert	Javert's Suicide	Moderate Tempo	Tenor	C3	F#4	Lead	Antagonist Male
Les Miserables	Schonberg, Claude-Michel	1987	Jean Valjean	Soliloquy	Moderate Tempo	Tenor	C3	B4	Lead	Romantic Antagonist Male
Les Miserables	Schonberg, Claude-Michel	1987	Jean Valjean	Who Am I	Moderate Tempo	Tenor	B3	B4	Lead	Romantic Antagonist Male
Les Miserables	Schonberg, Claude-Michel	1987	Jean Valjean	Bring Him Home	Ballad	Tenor	E3	A4	Lead	Romantic Antagonist Male
Les Miserables	Schonberg, Claude-Michel	1987	Madame Thenardier	Master of the House*	Uptempo	Alto	B3	D5	Supporting	Antagonist Female
Les Miserables	Schonberg, Claude-Michel	1987	Madame Thenardier	Beggars at the Wedding	Uptempo	Alto	C#4	D5	Supporting	Antagonist Female
Les Miserables	Schonberg, Claude-Michel	1987	Male Student	Drink With Me*	Ballad	Tenor	D3	Eb4	Lead	Ingenue Male
Les Miserables	Schonberg, Claude-Michel	1987	Marius	Empty Chairs, Empty Tables (Bb Minor)	Ballad	Tenor	Bb2	Ab4	Lead	Ingenue Male
Les Miserables	Schonberg, Claude-Michel	1987	Marius	Empty Chairs, Empty Tables (A Minor)	Ballad	Tenor	A2	G4	Lead	Ingenue Male
Les Miserables	Schonberg, Claude-Michel	1987	Thenardier	Master of the House*	Uptempo	Baritone	C3	D4	Supporting	Antagonist Male
Les Miserables	Schonberg, Claude-Michel	1987	Thenardier	Dog Eats Dog	Moderate Tempo	Baritone	C3	E4	Supporting	Antagonist Male
Les Miserables	Schonberg, Claude-Michel	1987	Thenardier	Beggars at the Wedding	Uptempo	Baritone	G#2	C4	Supporting	Antagonist Male
Les Miserables	Schonberg, Claude-Michel	1987	Young Cosette	Castle On The Cloud	Ballad	Soprano	A3	C5	Lead	Juvenile Female
Les Miserables	Schonberg, Claude-Michel	1987	Fantine & Jean Valjean	Come To Me	Ballad	Alto/Tenor			Duet	RLM/CM
Les Miserables	Schonberg, Claude-Michel	1987	Eponine & Marius	A Little Fall Of Rain	Ballad	Alto/Tenor			Duet	CF/IM
Les Miserables	Schonberg, Claude-Michel	1987	M. Thenardier & Thenardier	Beggar At The Feast	Uptempo	Alto/Bar			Duet	CM/CF
Les Miserables	Schonberg, Claude-Michel	1987	Cosette & Marius	A Heart Full Of Love*	Ballad	Sop/Tenor			Duet	IF/IM
Light In The Piazza, The	Guettel, Adam	2005	Clara Johnson	The Beauty Is	Uptempo	Soprano	Cb4	G5	Lead	Ingenue Female
Light In The Piazza, The	Guettel, Adam	2005	Clara Johnson	The Light in the Piazza	Moderate Tempo	Soprano	A3	F#5	Lead	Ingenue Female
Light In The Piazza, The	Guettel, Adam	2005	Ensemble	Aiutami	Uptempo	SATB			Ensemble	Adults
Light In The Piazza, The	Guettel, Adam	2005	Fabrizio Naccarelli	Il Mondo Era Vuoto	Moderate Tempo	Tenor	Bb2	Ab4	Lead	Ingenue Male

Shows

Songs by Character Type

Show	Composer	Year	Role	Song	Tempo	Vocal Type	Range-Bottom	Range-Top	Category	Character Type
Light In The Piazza, The	Guettel, Adam	2005	Fabrizio Naccarelli	Passegiata*	Moderate Tempo	Tenor	B3	G#4	Lead	Ingenue Male
Light In The Piazza, The	Guettel, Adam	2005	Fabrizio Naccarelli	Love To Me	Moderate Tempo	Tenor	F4	F#5	Lead	Ingenue Male
Light In The Piazza, The	Guettel, Adam	2005	Franca Naccarelli	The Joy You Feel	Moderate Tempo	Soprano	C4	Gb5	Lead	Romantic Antagonist Female
Light In The Piazza, The	Guettel, Adam	2005	Margaret Johnson	Statues and Stories*	Uptempo	Soprano	A3	A5	Lead	Romantic Lead Female
Light In The Piazza, The	Guettel, Adam	2005	Margaret Johnson	Dividing Day	Ballad	Soprano	G3	E5	Lead	Romantic Lead Female
Light In The Piazza, The	Guettel, Adam	2005	Margaret Johnson	The Beauty Is Reprise	Moderate Tempo	Soprano	B#3	G5	Lead	Romantic Lead Female
Light In The Piazza, The	Guettel, Adam	2005	Margaret Johnson	Fable	Uptempo	Soprano	C#4	F#5	Lead	Romantic Lead Female
Light In The Piazza, The	Guettel, Adam	2005	Clara & Margaret	Statues And Stories	Uptempo	Sop/Sop			Duet	IF/RLF
Light In The Piazza, The	Guettel, Adam	2005	Clara & Fabrizio	Passegiata	Uptempo	Sop/Tenor			Duet	IF/IM
Light In The Piazza, The	Guettel, Adam	2005	Clara & Fabrizio	Say It Somehow	Ballad	Sop/Tenor			Duet	IF/IM
Light In The Piazza, The	Guettel, Adam	2005	Margaret & Signor	Let's Walk	Moderate Tempo	Sop/Bar			Duet	RLF/RLM
Lion King, The	John, Elton	1997	Ensemble	Weem-O-Wep	Moderate Tempo	SATB			Ensemble	Adults
Lion King, The	John, Elton	1997	Ensemble	Circle of Life*	Moderate Tempo	SATB			Ensemble	Adults
Lion King, The	John, Elton	1997	Ensemble	Hakuna Matata*	Uptempo	SATB			Ensemble	Adults
Lion King, The	John, Elton	1997	Ensemble	One By One	Uptempo	SATB			Ensemble	Adults
Lion King, The	John, Elton	1997	Ensemble	Can You Feel The Love Tonight*	Ballad	SATB			Ensemble	Adults
Lion King, The	John, Elton	1997	Ensemble	Circle of Life Finale Part 2*	Moderate Tempo	SATB			Ensemble	Adults
Lion King, The	John, Elton	1997	Ensemble	Shadowland*	Moderate Tempo	SATB			Ensemble	Adults
Lion King, The	John, Elton	1997	Mufasa	They Live In You*	Moderate Tempo	Baritone	C#3	F#4	Lead	Romantic Lead Male
Lion King, The	John, Elton	1997	Nala	Shadowland*	Ballad	Alto	E3	B4	Lead	Ingenue Female
Lion King, The	John, Elton	1997	Rafiki	Circle of Life*	Moderate Tempo	Alto	F#3	C5	Lead	Character Female
Lion King, The	John, Elton	1997	Rafiki	Rafiki Mourns (Eulogy)	Ballad	Alto	G3	Eb5	Lead	Character Female
Lion King, The	John, Elton	1997	Rafiki	He Lives In You*	Moderate Tempo	Alto	C4	E5	Lead	Character Female
Lion King, The	John, Elton	1997	Scar	Be Prepared*	Uptempo	Baritone	A2	A3	Lead	Antagonist Male
Lion King, The	John, Elton	1997	Scar	Be Prepared Reprise*	Uptempo	Baritone	A2	D3	Lead	Antagonist Male
Lion King, The	John, Elton	1997	Simba	Endless Night*	Ballad	Tenor	E4	A4	Lead	Juvenile Male
Lion King, The	John, Elton	1997	Young Simba	I Just Can't Wait To Be King*	Uptempo	Alto	C4	C5	Supporting	Juvenile Male
Lion King, The	John, Elton	1997	Zazu	The Morning Report*	Uptempo	Baritone	Eb3	F4	Supporting	Character Male
Little Me	Coleman, Cy	1962	Ensemble	The Truth	Uptempo	ATB			Ensemble	Adults
Little Me	Coleman, Cy	1962	Young Belle	Other Side Of The Tracks (Slow Version)	Ballad	Alto	B3	C5	Lead	Character Female
Little Me	Coleman, Cy	1962	Young Belle & Noble Eggleston	I Love You	Moderate Tempo	Alto/Bar			Duet	CF/CM
Little Me	Coleman, Cy	1962	Young Belle	On The Other Side Of The Tracks Reprise	Uptempo	Alto	A3	D5	Lead	Character Female
Little Me	Coleman, Cy	1962	Mr. Pinchley & Belle	Deep Down Inside*	Uptempo	Bar/Alto			Duet	CM/CF
Little Me	Coleman, Cy	1962	Ensemble	Deep Down Inside	Uptempo	SATB			Ensemble	Adults
Little Me	Coleman, Cy	1962	Benny Buchsbaum	To Be A Performer*	Uptempo	Baritone	D#3	F4	Lead	Character Male
Little Me	Coleman, Cy	1962	Bernie Buchsbaum	To Be A Performer*	Uptempo	Baritone	D#3	F4	Lead	Character Male
Little Me	Coleman, Cy	1962	Benny & Bernie	To Be A Performer	Uptempo	Bar/Bar			Duet	CM/CM
Little Me	Coleman, Cy	1962	Belle	Dimples*	Uptempo	Alto	A3	D5	Lead	Character Female
Little Me	Coleman, Cy	1962	Val DuVal	Boom Boom*	Uptempo	Baritone	C#3	F#4	Lead	Character Male
Little Me	Coleman, Cy	1962	George Musgrove	I've Got Your Number*	Moderate Tempo	Baritone	E3	Ab4	Lead	Character Male
Little Me	Coleman, Cy	1962	Fred Poitrane	Real Live Girl*	Ballad	Baritone	D3	C4	Lead	Character Male
Little Me	Coleman, Cy	1962	Ensemble	Real Live Girl		TB			Ensemble	Adults
Little Me	Coleman, Cy	1962	Young Belle	Poor Little Hollywood Star	Moderate Tempo	Alto	G#3	E5	Lead	Character Female
Little Me	Coleman, Cy	1962	Benny Buchsbaum	Be A Performer Reprise*	Uptempo	Baritone	E3	E4	Lead	Character Male

Shows

Songs by Character Type

* = Music Edit Required
+ = Ethnic Specific

Show	Composer	Year	Role	Song	Tempo	Vocal Type	Range-Bottom	Range-Top	Category	Character Type
Little Me	Coleman, Cy	1962	Bernie Buchsbaum	Be A Performer Reprise*	Uptempo	Baritone	E3	E4	Lead	Character Male
Little Me	Coleman, Cy	1962	Benny & Bernie	Be A Performer Reprise	Uptempo	Bar/Bar			Duet	CM/CM
Little Me	Coleman, Cy	1962	Young Belle	I Needed Social Position*	Moderate Tempo	Alto	Ab3	C#5	Lead	Character Female
Little Me	Coleman, Cy	1962	Belle	I Needed Social Position*	Moderate Tempo	Alto	Ab3	C#5	Lead	Character Female
Little Me	Coleman, Cy	1962	Young Belle & Belle	I Needed Social Position	Moderate Tempo	Alto/Alto			Duet	CF/CF
Little Me	Coleman, Cy	1962	Prince Cherney	Goodbye	Uptempo	Baritone	B2	F#4	Lead	Character Male
Little Me	Coleman, Cy	1962	Belle	Here's To Us*	Uptempo	Alto	F3	Bb4	Lead	Character Female
Little Me	Coleman, Cy	1962	Ensemble	Here's To Us	Uptempo	SATB			Ensemble	Adults
Little Shop of Horrors	Menken, Alan	1982	Audrey	Somewhere That's Green	Ballad	Alto	B3	C5	Lead	Character Ingenue Female
Little Shop of Horrors	Menken, Alan	1982	Audrey	Suddenly Seymour	Moderate Tempo	Alto	A2	C#4	Lead	Character Ingenue Female
Little Shop of Horrors	Menken, Alan	1982	Audrey	Somewhere That's Green Reprise	Ballad	Alto	B2	C5	Lead	Character Ingenue Female
Little Shop of Horrors	Menken, Alan	1982	Ensemble	Downtown	Moderate Tempo	SATB			Ensemble	Adults
Little Shop of Horrors	Menken, Alan	1982	Ensemble	Don't Feed The Plant*	Uptempo	SATB			Ensemble	Adults
Little Shop of Horrors	Menken, Alan	1982	Ensemble	Little Shop of Horrors	Uptempo	SA			Ensemble	Adults
Little Shop of Horrors	Menken, Alan	1982	Ensemble	Ya Never Know*	Uptempo	SA			Ensemble	Adults
Little Shop of Horrors	Menken, Alan	1982	Mr. Mushnik	Mushnik and Son*	Uptempo	Baritone	A2	F4	Lead	Mature Male
Little Shop of Horrors	Menken, Alan	1982	Mr. Mushnik	Ya Never Know*	Uptempo	Baritone	C3	C4	Lead	Mature Male
Little Shop of Horrors	Menken, Alan	1982	Orin Scrivello	Dentist!	Uptempo	Baritone	A2	F4	Lead	Antagonist Male
Little Shop of Horrors	Menken, Alan	1982	Seymour Krelborn	Grow For Me	Moderate Tempo	Tenor	Bb2	F4	Lead	Character Male
Little Shop of Horrors	Menken, Alan	1982	Seymour Krelborn	Now*	Uptempo	Tenor	B2	G4	Lead	Character Male
Little Shop of Horrors	Menken, Alan	1982	Voice of Audrey II	Git It (Feed Me)*	Moderate Tempo	Baritone	B2	G4	Lead	Antagonist Male
Little Shop of Horrors	Menken, Alan	1982	Voice of Audrey II	Suppertime*	Moderate Tempo	Baritone	G2	F4	Lead	Antagonist Male
Little Shop of Horrors	Menken, Alan	1982	Mushnik & Seymour	Mushnik And Son	Moderate Tempo	Bar/Tenor			Duet	CM/CM
Little Shop of Horrors	Menken, Alan	1982	Audrey & Seymour	Call Back In The Morning	Moderate Tempo	Alto/Tenor			Duet	CIF/CM
Little Shop of Horrors	Menken, Alan	1982	Orin & Seymour	Now	Uptempo	Bar/Tenor			Duet	AM/CM
Little Women	Howland, Jason	2005	Aunt March	Could You*	Uptempo	Alto	D3	F5	Supporting	Mature Female
Little Women	Howland, Jason	2005	Beth March	Off to Massachusettes*	Moderate Tempo	Soprano	C#4	F5	Lead	Ingenue Female
Little Women	Howland, Jason	2005	Beth March	Some Things Are Meant To Be	Uptempo	Soprano	B2	E5	Lead	Ingenue Female
Little Women	Howland, Jason	2005	John Brooke	More Than I Am*	Moderate Tempo	Baritone	E3	E4	Supporting	Ingenue Male
Little Women	Howland, Jason	2005	Josephine March	Better	Uptempo	Alto	B3	B4	Lead	Character Ingenue Female
Little Women	Howland, Jason	2005	Josephine March	Our Finest Dreams	Uptempo	Alto	F#3	Db5	Lead	Character Ingenue Female
Little Women	Howland, Jason	2005	Josephine March	Better Reprise	Uptempo	Alto	B2	B4	Lead	Character Ingenue Female
Little Women	Howland, Jason	2005	Josephine March	Astonishing	Uptempo	Alto	Ab3	Eb5	Lead	Character Ingenue Female
Little Women	Howland, Jason	2005	Josephine March	The Fire Within Me	Moderate Tempo	Alto	Ab3	Bb4	Lead	Character Ingenue Female
Little Women	Howland, Jason	2005	Josephine March	Volcano Reprise	Ballad	Alto	A3	D5	Lead	Character Ingenue Female
Little Women	Howland, Jason	2005	Laurie Laurence	Take a Chance On Me	Uptempo	Tenor	B3	Bb4	Lead	Ingenue Male
Little Women	Howland, Jason	2005	Marmee	Here Alone	Ballad	Alto	G3	Eb5	Lead	Maternal
Little Women	Howland, Jason	2005	Marmee	Days of Plenty	Ballad	Alto	Eb3	Db5	Lead	Maternal
Little Women	Howland, Jason	2005	Meg March	More Than I Am*	Moderate Tempo	Soprano	E4	E5	Lead	Ingenue Female
Little Women	Howland, Jason	2005	Professor Bhaer	How I Am	Uptempo	Baritone	A2	F#4	Supporting	Romantic Lead Male
Little Women	Howland, Jason	2005	Aunt March & Jo	Could You	Uptempo	Alto/Alto			Duet	MF/CIF
Little Women	Howland, Jason	2005	Beth & Mr. Laurence	Off To Massachusettes	Moderate Tempo	Sop/Bar			Duet	IF/MM

Shows

Songs by Character Type

* = Music Edit Required
+ = Ethnic Specific

Show	Composer	Year	Role	Song	Tempo	Vocal Type	Range-Bottom	Range-Top	Category	Character Type
Little Women	Howland, Jason	2005	Meg & John	More Than I Am	Moderate Tempo	Sop/Bar			Duet	IF/CM
Little Women	Howland, Jason	2005	Beth & Jo	Some Things Are Meant To Be	Moderate Tempo	Sop/Alto			Duet	IF/CIF
Little Women	Howland, Jason	2005	Amy & Laurie	The Most Amazing Thing	Uptempo	Sop/Tenor			Duet	IF/IM
Mack and Mabel	Herman, Jerry	1974	Ensemble	When Mabel Comes In The Room*	Uptempo	TB			Ensemble	Adults
Mack and Mabel	Herman, Jerry	1974	Lottie Ames	Big Time*	Uptempo	Alto	F#3	Eb5	Supporting	Character Female
Mack and Mabel	Herman, Jerry	1974	Lottie Ames	Tap Your Troubles Away	Uptempo	Alto	F3	Bb4	Lead	Character Female
Mack and Mabel	Herman, Jerry	1974	Mabel Normand	Look What Happened to Mabel*	Uptempo	Alto	Gb3	C5	Lead	Ingenue Female
Mack and Mabel	Herman, Jerry	1974	Mabel Normand	Mabel's Roses	Ballad	Alto	G3	D5	Lead	Ingenue Female
Mack and Mabel	Herman, Jerry	1974	Mabel Normand	Wherever He Ain't	Uptempo	Alto	A3	C5	Lead	Ingenue Female
Mack and Mabel	Herman, Jerry	1974	Mabel Normand	Time Heals Everything	Ballad	Alto	F#3	C#5	Lead	Ingenue Female
Mack and Mabel	Herman, Jerry	1974	Mack Sennett	Movies Were Movies	Uptempo	Baritone	A2	Eb4	Lead	Romantic Antagonist Male
Mack and Mabel	Herman, Jerry	1974	Mack Sennett	I Wont Send Roses	Ballad	Baritone	G2	Eb4	Lead	Romantic Antagonist Male
Mack and Mabel	Herman, Jerry	1974	Mack Sennett	Make The World Laugh*	Uptempo	Baritone	A2	G4	Lead	Romantic Antagonist Male
Mack and Mabel	Herman, Jerry	1974	Mack Sennett	Hundreds of Girls*	Uptempo	Baritone	B2	F4	Lead	Romantic Antagonist Male
Mack and Mabel	Herman, Jerry	1974	Mack Sennett	I Promise You a Happy Ending	Ballad	Baritone	G2	D4	Lead	Romantic Antagonist Male
Mame	Herman, Jerry	1966	Anges Gooch	St. Bridget*	Ballad	Soprano	G3	F5	Lead	Character Female
Mame	Herman, Jerry	1966	Mame	It's Today*	Uptempo	Alto	A3	D5	Lead	Romantic Lead Female
Mame	Herman, Jerry	1966	Mame	Open A New Window*	Uptempo	Alto	A3	D5	Lead	Romantic Lead Female
Mame	Herman, Jerry	1966	Vera Charles	The Man In The Moon	Ballad	Alto	Eb3	A4	Lead	Romantic Antagonist Female
Mame	Herman, Jerry	1966	Young Patrick Dennis	You're My Best Girl*	Ballad	Alto	A3	C5	Lead	Juvenile Male
Mame	Herman, Jerry	1966	Mame	We Need A Little Christmas*	Uptempo	Alto	F3	Bb4	Lead	Romantic Lead Female
Mame	Herman, Jerry	1966	Ensemble	Mame	Uptempo	SATB			Ensemble	Children/Adults
Mame	Herman, Jerry	1966	Young Patrick Dennis	The Letter*	Uptempo	Alto	C#4	Bb4	Lead	Juvenile Male
Mame	Herman, Jerry	1966	Patrick Dennis	The Letter*	Uptempo	Baritone	D#3	D4	Lead	Ingenue Male
Mame	Herman, Jerry	1966	Anges Gooch	Gooch's Song	Moderate Tempo	Soprano	G3	Bb5	Lead	Character Female
Mame	Herman, Jerry	1966	Patrick Dennis	My Best Girl Reprise	Ballad	Baritone	C3	E4	Lead	Ingenue Male
Mame	Herman, Jerry	1966	Mame	That's How Young I Feel*	Uptempo	Alto	G3	Bb4	Lead	Romantic Lead Female
Mame	Herman, Jerry	1966	Mame	If He Walked Into My Life	Ballad	Alto/Alto	F#3	Bb4	Lead	Romantic Lead Female
Mame	Herman, Jerry	1966	Mame & Vera	Bosom Buddies	Moderate Tempo	Alto/Alto			Duet	RLF/RAF
Mame	Herman, Jerry	1966	Mame	It's Today Reprise*	Uptempo	Alto	F3	Bb4	Lead	Romantic Lead Female
Mame	Herman, Jerry	1966	Patrick Dennis	My Best Girl Reprise 2	Ballad	Baritone	C3	E4	Lead	Ingenue Male
Mame	Herman, Jerry	1966	Ensemble	Open A New Window*	Uptempo	SATB			Ensemble	Children/Adults
Mame	Herman, Jerry	1966	Mame	It's Today Reprise 2*	Moderate Tempo	Alto	A3	Eb5	Lead	Romantic Lead Female
Mame	Herman, Jerry	1966	Mame & Young Patrick	You're My Best Girl	Ballad	Alto/Alto			Duet	RLF/JM
Mame	Herman, Jerry	1966	Mame	You're My Best Girl*	Uptempo	Alto	G3	Bb4	Lead	Romantic Lead Female
Mame	Herman, Jerry	1966	Mame	We Need A Little Christmas*	Uptempo	Alto	C#4	D5	Lead	Romantic Lead Female
Mame	Herman, Jerry	1966	Ensemble	It's Today	Uptempo	SATB Unison			Ensemble	Children/Adults
Mame	Herman, Jerry	1966	Ensemble	We Need A Little Christmas*	Uptempo	SAB			Ensemble	Children/Adults
Mame	Herman, Jerry	1966	Ensemble	The Fox Hunt	Uptempo	SATB			Ensemble	Children/Adults
Mame	Herman, Jerry	1966	Ensemble	That's How Young I Feel*	Uptempo	SATB			Ensemble	Adults
Mame	Herman, Jerry	1966	Ensemble	Curtain Call	Uptempo	SATB			Ensemble	Adults

Shows

* = Music Edit Required
+ = Ethnic Specific

Show	Composer	Year	Role	Song	Tempo	Vocal Type	Range-Bottom	Range-Top	Category	Character Type
Mamma Mia!	Andersson, Benny	2001	Sophie Sheridan	I Have A Dream	Ballad	Soprano	A♭4	B♭4	Lead	Ingenue Female
Mamma Mia!	Andersson, Benny	2001	Sophie Sheridan	Honey Honey*	Uptempo	Soprano	C4	C5	Lead	Ingenue Female
Mamma Mia!	Andersson, Benny	2001	Donna Sheridan	Money Money Money	Uptempo	Alto	G4	B♭4	Lead	Romantic Lead Female
Mamma Mia!	Andersson, Benny	2001	Harry Bright	Thank You For the Music*	Moderate Tempo	Baritone	A3	D5	Lead	Character Male
Mamma Mia!	Andersson, Benny	2001	Harry & Sophie	Thank You For the Music*	Moderate Tempo	Bar/Sop			Duet	CM/IF
Mamma Mia!	Andersson, Benny	2001	Tanya & Rosie	Chiquitita*	Ballad	Alto/Alto			Duet	CF/CF
Mamma Mia!	Andersson, Benny	2001	Donna Sheridan	Mamma Mia*	Uptempo	Alto	F#3	A4	Lead	Romantic Lead Female
Mamma Mia!	Andersson, Benny	2001	Ensemble	Dancing Queen	Uptempo	SATB			Ensemble	Adults
Mamma Mia!	Andersson, Benny	2001	Sophie & Sky	Lay All Your Love On Me	Moderate Tempo	Alto/Tenor			Duet	IF/IM
Mamma Mia!	Andersson, Benny	2001	Sophie Sheridan	Lay All Your Love On Me*	Moderate Tempo	Alto	C4	E5	Lead	Ingenue Female
Mamma Mia!	Andersson, Benny	2001	Sky	Lay All Your Love On Me*	Moderate Tempo	Tenor	G3	A♭4	Lead	Ingenue Male
Mamma Mia!	Andersson, Benny	2001	Donna Sheridan	Super Trouper*	Moderate Tempo	Alto	G3	G4	Lead	Romantic Lead Female
Mamma Mia!	Andersson, Benny	2001	Ensemble	Gimmie Gimmie Gimmie	Uptempo	SSAA			Ensemble	Adults
Mamma Mia!	Andersson, Benny	2001	Sophie Sheridan	The Name Of The Game*	Moderate Tempo	Soprano	F#3	B4	Lead	Ingenue Female
Mamma Mia!	Andersson, Benny	2001	Ensemble	Chiquitita*	Ballad	SA			Ensemble	Adults
Mamma Mia!	Andersson, Benny	2001	Sophie Sheridan	Under Attack*	Uptempo	Soprano	B3	C#5	Lead	Ingenue Female
Mamma Mia!	Andersson, Benny	2001	Donna Sheridan	One Of Us*	Moderate Tempo	Alto	A3	C5	Lead	Romantic Lead Female
Mamma Mia!	Andersson, Benny	2001	Tanya	Does Your Mother Know*	Uptempo	Alto	A3	A♭4	Lead	Character Female
Mamma Mia!	Andersson, Benny	2001	Sam Carmichael	Knowing Me, Knowing You*	Moderate Tempo	Tenor	G2	F#4	Lead	Romantic Lead Male
Mamma Mia!	Andersson, Benny	2001	Donna & Sam	SOS	Uptempo	Alto/Tenor			Duet	RLF/RLM
Mamma Mia!	Andersson, Benny	2001	Donna Sheridan	SOS*	Uptempo	Alto	F4	A4	Lead	Romantic Lead Female
Mamma Mia!	Andersson, Benny	2001	Sam Carmichael	SOS*	Uptempo	Tenor	A3	A♭4	Lead	Romantic Lead Male
Mamma Mia!	Andersson, Benny	2001	Harry Bright	One Last Summer*	Ballad	Baritone	F#3	E4	Lead	Character Male
Mamma Mia!	Andersson, Benny	2001	Donna Sheridan	One Last Summer*	Ballad	Alto	F#3	E4	Lead	Romantic Lead Female
Mamma Mia!	Andersson, Benny	2001	Donna & Harry	One Last Summer	Ballad	Alto/Bar			Duet	RLF/CM
Mamma Mia!	Andersson, Benny	2001	Donna Sheridan	Slipping Through My Fingers*	Ballad	Alto	A3	C5	Lead	Romantic Lead Female
Mamma Mia!	Andersson, Benny	2001	Donna Sheridan	The Winner Takes It All	Moderate Tempo	Alto	G3	C5	Lead	Romantic Lead Female
Mamma Mia!	Andersson, Benny	2001	Rosie	Take A Chance On Me*	Moderate Tempo	Alto	F3	B♭4	Lead	Character Female
Mamma Mia!	Andersson, Benny	2001	Donna Sheridan	I Do, I Do, I Do, I Do, I Do	Moderate Tempo	Alto	G3	C5	Lead	Romantic Lead Female
Mamma Mia!	Andersson, Benny	2001	Sophie Sheridan	I have A Dream Reprise	Ballad	Soprano	A♭3	D♭5	Lead	Ingenue Female
Mamma Mia!	Andersson, Benny	2001	Ensemble	Honey Honey*	Ballad	SATB			Ensemble	Adults
Mamma Mia!	Andersson, Benny	2001	Ensemble	Mamma Mia!	Uptempo	SA			Ensemble	Adults
Mamma Mia!	Andersson, Benny	2001	Ensemble	Lay All Your Love On Me*	Uptempo	SATB			Ensemble	Adults
Mamma Mia!	Andersson, Benny	2001	Ensemble	Super Trouper*	Moderate Tempo	SATB			Ensemble	Adults
Mamma Mia!	Andersson, Benny	2001	Ensemble	The Name Of The Game*	Moderate Tempo	SATB			Ensemble	Adults
Mamma Mia!	Andersson, Benny	2001	Ensemble	Voulez Vous	Uptempo	SATB			Ensemble	Adults
Mamma Mia!	Andersson, Benny	2001	Ensemble	Under Attack*	Uptempo	SATB			Ensemble	Adults
Mamma Mia!	Andersson, Benny	2001	Ensemble	One Of Us*	Moderate Tempo	SATB			Ensemble	Adults
Mamma Mia!	Andersson, Benny	2001	Ensemble	Does Your Mother Know*	Uptempo	SATB			Ensemble	Adults
Mamma Mia!	Andersson, Benny	2001	Ensemble	Knowing Me, Knowing You*	Moderate Tempo	SATB			Ensemble	Adults
Mamma Mia!	Andersson, Benny	2001	Ensemble	One Last Summer	Ballad	SATB			Ensemble	Adults
Mamma Mia!	Andersson, Benny	2001	Ensemble	Slipping Through My Fingers*	Ballad	SA			Ensemble	Adults
Marie Christine	La Chuisa, Michael John	1999	Ensemble	Before The Morning	Moderate Tempo	SA			Ensemble	Adults

Shows

Songs by Character Type

* = Music Edit Required
+ = Ethnic Specific

Show	Composer	Year	Role	Song	Tempo	Vocal Type	Range-Bottom	Range-Top	Category	Character Type
Marie Christine	La Chuissa, Michael John	1999	Ensemble	Mamzell' Marie	Moderate Tempo	SATB	D3	E5	Ensemble	Adults
Marie Christine	La Chuissa, Michael John	1999	Mother+	Ton Grandpere Est Le Soleil*	Moderate Tempo	Alto	G3	D5	Lead	Romantic Antagonist Female
Marie Christine	La Chuissa, Michael John	1999	Marie Christine L'Adrese+	Beautiful*	Moderate Tempo	Soprano	D4	G5	Lead	Romantic Antagonist Female
Marie Christine	La Chuissa, Michael John	1999	Marie Christine L'Adrese+	Way Back To Paradise*	Moderate Tempo	Soprano	D4	G5	Lead	Romantic Antagonist Female
Marie Christine	La Chuissa, Michael John	1999	Marie Christine+ & Lisette+	Way Back To Paradise*	Moderate Tempo	Sop/Sop	A3	G4	Duet	RAF/1F
Marie Christine	La Chuissa, Michael John	1999	Marie Christine L'Adrese+	To Find A Lover*	Uptempo	Soprano	B2	E4	Lead	Romantic Antagonist Female
Marie Christine	La Chuissa, Michael John	1999	Dante Keyes	Nothing Beats Chicago	Uptempo	Tenor	C3	A4	Lead	Romantic Antagonist Male
Marie Christine	La Chuissa, Michael John	1999	Dante Keyes	Ocean Is Different	Moderate Tempo	Tenor	D4	C#5	Lead	Romantic Antagonist Male
Marie Christine	La Chuissa, Michael John	1999	Lisette+	Tout Mi Mi	Ballad	Soprano	E3	F5	Lead	Ingenue Female
Marie Christine	La Chuissa, Michael John	1999	Mother+	Miracles and Mysteries	Moderate Tempo	Alto	Eb3	F4	Lead	Romantic Antagonist Female
Marie Christine	La Chuissa, Michael John	1999	Dante Keyes	I Don't Hear The Ocean*	Moderate Tempo	Tenor	A2	E4	Lead	Romantic Antagonist Male
Marie Christine	La Chuissa, Michael John	1999	Dante & Marie+	I Don't Hear The Ocean	Moderate Tempo	Tenor/Sop			Duet	RAM/RAF
Marie Christine	La Chuissa, Michael John	1999	Ensemble	Bird Inside The House	Uptempo	SATB			Ensemble	Adults
Marie Christine	La Chuissa, Michael John	1999	Jean L'Adrese+	All Eyes Look To You	Ballad	Baritone	Db3	F4	Lead	Ingenue Male
Marie Christine	La Chuissa, Michael John	1999	Maid #1+ & Maid #2+	A Month Ago	Uptempo	Sop/Sop			Duet	CIF/CIF
Marie Christine	La Chuissa, Michael John	1999	Dante Keyes	We Gonna Go To Chicago	Moderate Tempo	Tenor	E4	C6	Lead	Romantic Antagonist Male
Marie Christine	La Chuissa, Michael John	1999	Lisette+	Dansen Calinda	Ballad	Soprano	Bb3	Fb4	Lead	Ingenue Female
Marie Christine	La Chuissa, Michael John	1999	Marie Christine L'Adrese+	I Will Give	Ballad	Soprano	G3	F5	Lead	Romantic Antagonist Female
Marie Christine	La Chuissa, Michael John	1999	Ensemble	Finale Act I (P 1-3)	Uptempo	SATB			Ensemble	Adults
Marie Christine	La Chuissa, Michael John	1999	Dante & Marie+	I Will Love You	Ballad	Tenor/Sop			Duet	RAM/RAF
Marie Christine	La Chuissa, Michael John	1999	Magdelena	Cincinnati*	Moderate Tempo	SATB	G3	F#3	Supporting	Character Female
Marie Christine	La Chuissa, Michael John	1999	Ensemble	You're Looking At A Man*	Uptempo	Tenor			Ensemble	Adults
Marie Christine	La Chuissa, Michael John	1999	Dante Keyes	The Scorpion*	Uptempo	SSA	C3	Gb4	Lead	Romantic Antagonist Male
Marie Christine	La Chuissa, Michael John	1999	Ensemble	Lover Bring Me Summer	Ballad	SSA			Ensemble	Adults
Marie Christine	La Chuissa, Michael John	1999	Marie Christine L'Adrese+	Tell Me	Moderate Tempo	Soprano	G3	F5	Lead	Romantic Antagonist Female
Marie Christine	La Chuissa, Michael John	1999	Magdelena	Paradise Is Burning Down*	Uptempo	Alto	Eb3	Eb5	Lead	Character Female
Marie Christine	La Chuissa, Michael John	1999	Marie Christine L'Adrese+	Prison In A Prison*	Moderate Tempo	Soprano	G3	D5	Lead	Romantic Antagonist Female
Marie Christine	La Chuissa, Michael John	1999	McMahon & Leary	Better And Best	Moderate Tempo	Tenor/Tenor	G3	E4	Duet	CM/CM
Marie Christine	La Chuissa, Michael John	1999	Charles Gates	Good Looking Woman*	Moderate Tempo	Baritone	G3	E4	Lead	Antagonist Male
Marie Christine	La Chuissa, Michael John	1999	Paris L'Adrese+	No Turning Back	Ballad	Tenor	F3	Eb5	Supporting	Romantic Antagonist Male
Marie Christine	La Chuissa, Michael John	1999	Marie Christine L'Adrese+	Marie's Soliloquy	Ballad	Soprano	A3	D5	Lead	Romantic Antagonist Female
Marie Christine	La Chuissa, Michael John	1999	Magdelena	A Lovely Wedding*	Uptempo	Alto	C4	C#5	Supporting	Character Female
Marie Christine	La Chuissa, Michael John	1999	Dante & Marie+	I Will Love You Reprise	Ballad	Tenor/Sop			Duet	RAM/RAF
Marie Christine	La Chuissa, Michael John	1999	Dante Keyes	Your Name (Helena's Death)	Ballad	Tenor	G#2	A4	Lead	Romantic Antagonist Male
Marie Christine	La Chuissa, Michael John	1999	Ensemble	Innocence Dies	Moderate Tempo	SSAA			Ensemble	Adults
Marie Christine	La Chuissa, Michael John	1999	Ensemble	In An Instant	Moderate Tempo	SSA			Ensemble	Adults
Marie Christine	La Chuissa, Michael John	1999	Ensemble	Map Your Heart	Moderate Tempo	TTA			Ensemble	Adults
Marie Christine	La Chuissa, Michael John	1999	Ensemble	C'est L'Amour	Moderate Tempo	SATB			Ensemble	Adults
Marie Christine	La Chuissa, Michael John	1999	Dante Keyes	The Adventure Never Ends	Uptempo	Tenor	Bb2	Fb4	Lead	Romantic Antagonist Male
Marie Christine	La Chuissa, Michael John	1999	Dante Keyes	Danced With A Girl	Uptempo	Tenor	B2	E4	Lead	Romantic Antagonist Male
Marie Christine	La Chuissa, Michael John	1999	Lisette+	Tout Mimi Reprise	Ballad	Soprano	Bb3	Bb4	Lead	Ingenue Female
Marie Christine	La Chuissa, Michael John	1999	Ensemble	And You Would Lie	Moderate Tempo	SSAA			Ensemble	Adults
Marie Christine	La Chuissa, Michael John	1999	Ensemble	Cincinnati*	Moderate Tempo	SATB			Ensemble	Adults

Shows

* = Music Edit Required
+ = Ethnic Specific

Show	Composer	Year	Role	Song	Tempo	Vocal Type	Range-Bottom	Range-Top	Category	Character Type
Marie Christine	La Chuissa, Michael John	1999	Magdelena	There's A Rumor	Moderate Tempo	Alto	F#3	C#5	Lead	Character Female
Mary Poppins	Sherman, Richard	2006	Bert	Chim Chim Cher-ee	Moderate Tempo	Baritone	A2	D4	Lead	Character Male
Mary Poppins	Sherman, Richard	2006	George Banks	Cherry Tree Lane*	Uptempo	Baritone	Bb2	Eb4	Lead	Paternal
Mary Poppins	Sherman, Richard	2006	Ensemble	Cherry Tree Lane*	Uptempo	SATB			Ensemble	Children/Adults
Mary Poppins	Sherman, Richard	2006	Jane Banks	The Perfect Nanny*	Moderate Tempo	Alto	A3	B4	Lead	Juvenile Female
Mary Poppins	Sherman, Richard	2006	Michael Banks	The Perfect Nanny*	Moderate Tempo	Alto	A3	B4	Lead	Juvenile Male
Mary Poppins	Sherman, Richard	2006	Jane & Michael	The Perfect Nanny	Moderate Tempo	Alto/Alto			Duet	JF/JM
Mary Poppins	Sherman, Richard	2006	Ensemble	Cherry Tree Lane (Part 2)	Uptempo	SATB			Ensemble	Children/Adults
Mary Poppins	Sherman, Richard	2006	Ensemble	Practically Perfect	Moderate Tempo	SATB			Ensemble	Children/Adults
Mary Poppins	Sherman, Richard	2006	Mary Poppins	Practically Perfect*	Moderate Tempo	Soprano	A3	G#3	Lead	Romantic Lead Female
Mary Poppins	Sherman, Richard	2006	Bert	Jolly Holiday*	Uptempo	Baritone	B2	E4	Lead	Character Female
Mary Poppins	Sherman, Richard	2006	Ensemble	Jolly Holiday*	Uptempo	SATB			Ensemble	Children/Adults
Mary Poppins	Sherman, Richard	2006	Ensemble	Cherry Tree Lane Reprise	Moderate Tempo	SATB			Ensemble	Adults
Mary Poppins	Sherman, Richard	2006	Bert	Being Mrs. Banks*	Ballad	Baritone	C3	C4	Lead	Character Male
Mary Poppins	Sherman, Richard	2006	Ensemble	Winds Can Change	Uptempo	SATB			Ensemble	Children/Adults
Mary Poppins	Sherman, Richard	2006	Mary Poppins	A Spoonful Of Sugar*	Uptempo	Soprano	Cb4	Ab5	Lead	Romantic Lead Female
Mary Poppins	Sherman, Richard	2006	Bank Chairman	A Spoonful Of Sugar*	Moderate Tempo	Baritone	C3	F4	Supporting	Character Male
Mary Poppins	Sherman, Richard	2006	Ensemble	Precision And Order*	Moderate Tempo	SATB			Ensemble	Ensemble
Mary Poppins	Sherman, Richard	2006	George Banks	Precision And Order*	Ballad	Baritone	Bb2	Eb4	Lead	Paternal
Mary Poppins	Sherman, Richard	2006	Bird Woman	A Man Has Dreams	Uptempo	Soprano	Gb3	Db5	Supporting	Mature Female
Mary Poppins	Sherman, Richard	2006	Winifred Banks	Feed The Birds*	Moderate Tempo	Alto	G#3	B4	Lead	Maternal
Mary Poppins	Sherman, Richard	2006	Mary Poppins	Being Mrs. Banks*	Uptempo	Soprano	C4	E5	Lead	Romantic Lead Female
Mary Poppins	Sherman, Richard	2006	Mrs. Corry.	Supercalifragilisticexpialidocious*	Uptempo	Alto	C4	D5	Lead	Character Female
Mary Poppins	Sherman, Richard	2006	Ensemble	Supercalifragilisticexpialidocious*	Uptempo	SATB			Ensemble	Adults
Mary Poppins	Sherman, Richard	2006	Bert	Temper Temper	Moderate Tempo	Baritone	C#3	E4	Lead	Character Male
Mary Poppins	Sherman, Richard	2006	Ensemble	Chim Chim Cher-ee A1	Uptempo	SATB			Ensemble	Children/Adults
Mary Poppins	Sherman, Richard	2006	Miss Andrew	Chim Chim Cher-ee A2	Moderate Tempo	Soprano	G#3	F5	Lead	Antagonist Female
Mary Poppins	Sherman, Richard	2006	Winifred Banks	Brimstone And Treacle (P1)	Moderate Tempo	Alto	G#3	Db5	Lead	Maternal
Mary Poppins	Sherman, Richard	2006	Mary Poppins & Miss Andrews	Being Mrs. Banks*	Ballad	Sop/Sop	A2	D4	Duet	RLF/AF
Mary Poppins	Sherman, Richard	2006	Bert	Brimstone And Treacle (P2)	Moderate Tempo	Baritone	A2	D4	Lead	Character Male
Mary Poppins	Sherman, Richard	2006	Ensemble	Chim Chim Cher-ee Reprise	Uptempo	SATB			Ensemble	Adults
Mary Poppins	Sherman, Richard	2006	Bert	Step In Time*	Uptempo	Baritone	B2	F#4	Lead	Character Male
Mary Poppins	Sherman, Richard	2006	Winifred Banks	Step In Time*	Ballad	Alto	Bb2	C4	Lead	Maternal
Mary Poppins	Sherman, Richard	2006	Bert	A Man Has Dreams Reprise	Moderate Tempo	Baritone	Bb2	C#4	Lead	Character Male
Mary Poppins	Sherman, Richard	2006	Ensemble	A Spoonful Of Sugar Reprise*	Moderate Tempo	SATB			Ensemble	Children/Adults
Mary Poppins	Sherman, Richard	2006	Mary Poppins	Anything Can Happen	Moderate Tempo	Soprano	C4	D5	Lead	Romantic Lead Female
Mary Poppins	Sherman, Richard	2006	Jane Banks	Anything Can Happen*	Moderate Tempo	Alto	C4	D5	Lead	Juvenile Female
Mary Poppins	Sherman, Richard	2006	Michael Banks	Anything Can Happen*	Moderate Tempo	Alto	C4	D5	Lead	Juvenile Male
Mary Poppins	Sherman, Richard	2006	Bert	All Me Own Work	Ballad	Baritone	C#3	D#4	Lead	Character Male
Mary Poppins	Sherman, Richard	2006	Bert	Twists And Turns	Ballad	Baritone	B2	E4	Lead	Character Male
Mary Poppins	Sherman, Richard	2006	Bert	Let's Go Fly A Kite*	Moderate Tempo	Baritone	Bb2	E4	Lead	Character Male
Mary Poppins	Sherman, Richard	2006	Ensemble	Let's Go Fly A Kite*	Moderate Tempo	SATB			Ensemble	Children/Adults

Shows

Songs by Character Type

Show	Composer	Year	Role	Song	Tempo	Vocal Type	Range-Bottom	Range-Top	Category	Character Type
Meet Me In St. Louis	Ralph & Hugh	1989	Ensemble	Meet Me In St. Louis	Moderate Tempo	SATB			Ensemble	Adults
Meet Me In St. Louis	Ralph & Hugh	1989	Ensemble	Meet Me In St. Louis Reprise 6B	Moderate Tempo	SATB			Ensemble	Adults
Meet Me In St. Louis	Ralph & Hugh	1989	Esther Smith	The Boy Next Door	Ballad	Alto	A♭3	B♭4	Lead	Character Ingenue Female
Meet Me In St. Louis	Ralph & Hugh	1989	Ensemble	Skip To My Lou	Uptempo	SATB			Ensemble	Children/Teens/Adults
Meet Me In St. Louis	Ralph & Hugh	1989	Ensemble	Under The Bamboo Tree	Moderate Tempo	SATB Unison			Ensemble	Children/Teens/Adults
Meet Me In St. Louis	Ralph & Hugh	1989	Agnes Smith	Under The Bamboo Tree*	Moderate Tempo	Soprano	C4	B♭4	Lead	Ingenue Female
Meet Me In St. Louis	Ralph & Hugh	1989	Esther Smith	Under The Bamboo Tree*	Moderate Tempo	Alto	C4	B♭4	Lead	Character Ingenue Female
Meet Me In St. Louis	Ralph & Hugh	1989	Tootie Smith	Under The Bamboo Tree*	Moderate Tempo	Alto	C4	B♭4	Lead	Juvenile Female
Meet Me In St. Louis	Ralph & Hugh	1989	Lon Smith	Banjos*	Uptempo	Baritone	B♭2	F4	Lead	Ingenue Male
Meet Me In St. Louis	Ralph & Hugh	1989	Ensemble	Banjos*	Uptempo	SATB			Ensemble	Children/Teens/Adults
Meet Me In St. Louis	Ralph & Hugh	1989	Alonso Smith	Wasn't It Fun*	Ballad	Baritone	A♭2	B♭3	Lead	Paternal
Meet Me In St. Louis	Ralph & Hugh	1989	Anna Smith	Wasn't It Fun*	Ballad	Alto	F3	C4	Lead	Maternal
Meet Me In St. Louis	Ralph & Hugh	1989	Alonso & Anna Sith	Wasn't It Fun	Ballad	Bar/Alto			Duet	P/M
Meet Me In St. Louis	Ralph & Hugh	1989	Esther Smith	The Trolly Song*	Uptempo	Alto	A3	B♭4	Lead	Character Ingenue Female
Meet Me In St. Louis	Ralph & Hugh	1989	Ensemble	The Trolly Song	Uptempo	SATB			Ensemble	Adults
Meet Me In St. Louis	Ralph & Hugh	1989	Katie	A Touch Of Irish*	Uptempo	Alto	G3	B♭4	Lead	Character Female
Meet Me In St. Louis	Ralph & Hugh	1989	John Truitt	You Are For Loving*	Ballad	Baritone	D♭3	F4	Lead	Ingenue Male
Meet Me In St. Louis	Ralph & Hugh	1989	Esther Smith	You Are For Loving*	Ballad	Alto	B♭3	C5	Lead	Character Ingenue Female
Meet Me In St. Louis	Ralph & Hugh	1989	John & Esther	You Are For Loving	Ballad	Bar/Alto			Duet	IM/CIF
Meet Me In St. Louis	Ralph & Hugh	1989	Ensemble	When I'm With You	Uptempo	SAB			Ensemble	Adults
Meet Me In St. Louis	Ralph & Hugh	1989	Anna Smith	A Day In New York*	Uptempo	Alto	B3	E4	Lead	Maternal
Meet Me In St. Louis	Ralph & Hugh	1989	Esther Smith	Have Yourself A Merry Little Christmas	Ballad	Alto	G3	C5	Lead	Character Ingenue Female
Meet Me In St. Louis	Ralph & Hugh	1989	Ensemble	Finale Act I	Uptempo	SATB			Ensemble	Adults
Meet Me In St. Louis	Ralph & Hugh	1989	Anna Smith	You'll Hear A Bill	Moderate Tempo	Alto	B♭3	D5	Lead	Maternal
Meet Me In St. Louis	Ralph & Hugh	1989	Warren Sheffield	Raving Beauty*	Ballad	Baritone	C3	E♭4	Lead	Romantic Lead Male
Meet Me In St. Louis	Ralph & Hugh	1989	Rose Smith	Raving Beauty*	Ballad	Soprano	B♭3	D♭5	Lead	Ingenue Female
Meet Me In St. Louis	Ralph & Hugh	1989	Warren & Rose	Raving Beauty	Ballad	Bar/Sop			Duet	RLM/IF
Meet Me In St. Louis	Ralph & Hugh	1989	Esther Smith	Over The Banister	Moderate Tempo	Alto	B♭3	E♭5	Lead	Character Ingenue Female
Meet Me In St. Louis	Ralph & Hugh	1989	Anna Smith	You'll Hear A Bell Reprise	Moderate Tempo	SATB	B♭3	B♭4	Ensemble	Maternal
Meet Me In St. Louis	Ralph & Hugh	1989	Ensemble	The First Noel	Moderate Tempo	SATB			Ensemble	Adults
Meet Me In St. Louis	Ralph & Hugh	1989	John Truitt	The Girl Next Door	Moderate Tempo	Baritone	D3	E4	Lead	Ingenue Male
Merrily We Roll Along	Sondheim, Stephen	1994	Ensemble	Merrily Rolling Along	Moderate Tempo	SATB			Ensemble	Adults
Merrily We Roll Along	Sondheim, Stephen	1994	Mary Flynn	Old Friends	Ballad	Soprano	A3	A4	Lead	Romantic Antagonist Female
Merrily We Roll Along	Sondheim, Stephen	1981	Mary Flynn	Like It Was	Moderate Tempo	Soprano	G3	B♭4	Lead	Romantic Antagonist Female
Merrily We Roll Along	Sondheim, Stephen	1981	Charley Kringas	Franklin Shepard, Inc.	Uptempo	Tenor	C3	G4	Lead	Character Male
Merrily We Roll Along	Sondheim, Stephen	1981	Franklin Shepard	Old Friends II*	Moderate Tempo	Tenor	B♭2	D4	Lead	Romantic Antagonist Male
Merrily We Roll Along	Sondheim, Stephen	1981	Charley Kringas	Old Friends II*	Moderate Tempo	Tenor	B♭2	D4	Lead	Character Male
Merrily We Roll Along	Sondheim, Stephen	1981	Ensemble	Old Friends II	Moderate Tempo	ABB	D3	E4	Ensemble	Adults
Merrily We Roll Along	Sondheim, Stephen	1981	Beth	Not A Day Goes By	Ballad	Soprano	G3	B4	Lead	Romantic Lead Female
Merrily We Roll Along	Sondheim, Stephen	1981	Mary Flynn	Now You Know*	Uptempo	Soprano	G3	D5	Lead	Romantic Antagonist Female
Merrily We Roll Along	Sondheim, Stephen	1981	Ensemble	Now You Know	Uptempo	SATB			Ensemble	Adults

Shows

Songs by Character Type

* = Music Edit Required
+ = Ethnic Specific

Show	Composer	Year	Role	Song	Tempo	Vocal Type	Range-Bottom	Range-Top	Category	Character Type
Merrily We Roll Along 1994	Sondheim, Stephen	1981	Ensemble	It's A Hit	Uptempo	SATB			Ensemble	Adults
Merrily We Roll Along 1994	Sondheim, Stephen	1981	Charley Kringas	Good Thing Going	Ballad	Tenor	C3	F4	Lead	Character Male
Merrily We Roll Along 1994	Sondheim, Stephen	1981	Ensemble	Bobby and Jackie and Jack	Uptempo	STT			Ensemble	Adults
Merrily We Roll Along 1994	Sondheim, Stephen	1981	Ensemble	Not A Day Goes By Reprise	Ballad	SST			Ensemble	Adults
Merrily We Roll Along 1994	Sondheim, Stephen	1981	Ensemble	Opening Doors	Uptempo	SATB			Ensemble	Adults
Merrily We Roll Along 1994	Sondheim, Stephen	1981	Franklin Shepard	Our Time Part 1 & 2*	Moderate Tempo	Tenor	Db3	Bb4	Lead	Romantic Antagonist Male
Merrily We Roll Along 1994	Sondheim, Stephen	1981	Franklin & Charley	Our Time Part 1 & 2	Moderate Tempo	Tenor/Tenor			Duet	RAM/CM
Merrily We Roll Along 1994	Sondheim, Stephen	1981	Ensemble	Our Time	Moderate Tempo	SATB			Ensemble	Adults
Merrily We Roll Along 1994	Sondheim, Stephen	1994	Ensemble	That Frank	Uptempo	SATB			Ensemble	Adults
Merrily We Roll Along 1994	Sondheim, Stephen	1994	Ensemble	Transition 1	Moderate Tempo	SATB			Ensemble	Adults
Merrily We Roll Along 1994	Sondheim, Stephen	1994	Ensemble	Transition 2	Uptempo	SATB			Ensemble	Adults
Merrily We Roll Along 1994	Sondheim, Stephen	1994	Franklin Shepard	Growing Up Part I	Moderate Tempo	Tenor	D3	E4	Lead	Romantic Antagonist Male
Merrily We Roll Along 1994	Sondheim, Stephen	1994	Gussie Carnegie	Growing Up Part II	Moderate Tempo	Alto	G#3	Bb4	Lead	Romantic Antagonist Female
Merrily We Roll Along 1994	Sondheim, Stephen	1994	Ensemble	Transition 3	Moderate Tempo	SATB			Ensemble	Adults
Merrily We Roll Along 1994	Sondheim, Stephen	1994	Gussie Carnegie	Act 2 Opening	Moderate Tempo	Alto	B3	C5	Lead	Romantic Antagonist Female
Merrily We Roll Along 1994	Sondheim, Stephen	1994	Ensemble	Transition 4	Moderate Tempo	SATB Unison			Ensemble	Adults
Merrily We Roll Along 1994	Sondheim, Stephen	1994	Ensemble	The Blob I	Uptempo	SATB			Ensemble	Adults
Merrily We Roll Along 1994	Sondheim, Stephen	1994	Gussie Carnegie	The Blob II	Uptempo	Alto	Ab3	Bb4	Lead	Romantic Antagonist Female
Merrily We Roll Along 1994	Sondheim, Stephen	1994	Gussie Carnegie	Growing Up Act 2	Moderate Tempo	Alto	G3	A4	Lead	Romantic Antagonist Female
Merrily We Roll Along 1994	Sondheim, Stephen	1994	Ensemble	The Blg III	Uptempo	SATB Unison			Ensemble	Adults
Merrily We Roll Along 1994	Sondheim, Stephen	1994	Ensemble	The Blob IV	Moderate Tempo	SATB			Ensemble	Adults
Merrily We Roll Along 1994	Sondheim, Stephen	1994	Ensemble	Transition 5	Uptempo	SATB Unison			Ensemble	Adults
Merrily We Roll Along 1994	Sondheim, Stephen	1994	Tyler & Dory	Transition 6	Uptempo	Bar/Alto			Duet	RAM/RAF
Merrily We Roll Along 1994	Sondheim, Stephen	1994	Frank, Jr.	Transition 7	Moderate Tempo	Alto	B2	C5	Supporting	Juvenile Male
Merrily We Roll Along 1994	Sondheim, Stephen	1994	Ensemble	Transition 7	Moderate Tempo	SA			Ensemble	Adults
Miss Saigon	Schonberg, Claude-Michel	1991	Ensemble	The Heat Is On In Saigon	Uptempo	ATT			Ensemble	Adults
Miss Saigon	Schonberg, Claude-Michel	1991	Kim+	The Movie In My Mind*	Ballad	Soprano	Ab3	Eb5	Lead	Ingenue Female
Miss Saigon	Schonberg, Claude-Michel	1991	Gigi Van Trahn+	The Movie In My Mind*	Ballad	Alto	Ab3	Eb5	Supporting	Romantic Antagonist Female
Miss Saigon	Schonberg, Claude-Michel	1991	Chris & Kim+	This Money's Yours	Moderate Tempo	Tenor/Sop			Duet	RLM/IF
Miss Saigon	Schonberg, Claude-Michel	1991	Chris & John	The Telephone	Uptempo	Tenor/Tenor			Duet	RLM/RAM
Miss Saigon	Schonberg, Claude-Michel	1991	Chris Scott	Why God Why	Moderate Tempo	Tenor	G3	G4	Lead	Romantic Lead Male
Miss Saigon	Schonberg, Claude-Michel	1991	Ensemble	The Ceremony*	Ballad	SSAA			Ensemble	Adults
Miss Saigon	Schonberg, Claude-Michel	1991	Kim+	The Ceremony*	Ballad	Soprano	B3	D5	Lead	Ingenue Female
Miss Saigon	Schonberg, Claude-Michel	1991	Chris & Kim+	The Last Night Of the World*	Ballad	Tenor/Sop			Duet	RLM/IF
Miss Saigon	Schonberg, Claude-Michel	1991	Ensemble	The Morning Of The Dragon	Uptempo	SATB			Ensemble	Adults
Miss Saigon	Schonberg, Claude-Michel	1991	Kim+ & Ellen Scott	I Still Believe*	Ballad	Sop/Alto			Duet	IF/RLF
Miss Saigon	Schonberg, Claude-Michel	1991	Kim+	I Still Believe*	Ballad	Soprano	A3	E5	Lead	Ingenue Female
Miss Saigon	Schonberg, Claude-Michel	1991	Ellen Scott	There Is A Secret (ms 214-258)	Moderate Tempo	Alto	A3	Db5	Lead	Romantic Lead Female
Miss Saigon	Schonberg, Claude-Michel	1991	Kim+	You Will Not Touch Him (ms 20-51)	Moderate Tempo	Soprano	C4	Eb5	Lead	Ingenue Female
Miss Saigon	Schonberg, Claude-Michel	1991	Ensemble	This Is The Hour	Moderate Tempo	SATB			Ensemble	Adults
Miss Saigon	Schonberg, Claude-Michel	1991	Engineer+	If you Want To Die In Bed*	Moderate Tempo	Tenor	A2	G4	Lead	Antagonist Male
Miss Saigon	Schonberg, Claude-Michel	1991	Kim+	I'd Give My Life For You*	Ballad	Soprano	G3	E5	Lead	Ingenue Female

Shows

436

Songs by Character Type

* = Music Edit Required
+ = Ethnic Specific

Show	Composer	Year	Role	Song	Tempo	Vocal Type	Range-Bottom	Range-Top	Category	Character Type
Miss Saigon	Schonberg, Claude-Michel	1991	Ensemble	Bui-Doi	Moderate Tempo	TTB			Ensemble	Adults
Miss Saigon	Schonberg, Claude-Michel	1991	John Thomas	Bui-Doi	Moderate Tempo	Tenor	Ab2	Bb4	Lead	Romantic Antagonist Male
Miss Saigon	Schonberg, Claude-Michel	1991	Engineer+	What A Waste*	Moderate Tempo	Tenor	B2	F#4	Lead	Antagonist Male
Miss Saigon	Schonberg, Claude-Michel	1991	John & Kim+	Please	Moderate Tempo	Tenor/Sop			Duet	RAM/IF
Miss Saigon	Schonberg, Claude-Michel	1991	Kim+	Sun and Moon Reprise	Ballad	Soprano	E3	D5	Lead	Ingenue Female
Miss Saigon	Schonberg, Claude-Michel	1991	Kim+ & Ellen Scott	Room 317	Moderate Tempo	Sop/Alto			Duet	IF/RLF
Miss Saigon	Schonberg, Claude-Michel	1991	Ellen Scott	Now I've Seen Her	Ballad	Alto	G#3	E5	Lead	Romantic Lead Female
Miss Saigon	Schonberg, Claude-Michel	1991	Chris Scott	The Confrontation (ms44-79)	Uptempo	Tenor	F3	B4	Lead	Romantic Lead Male
Miss Saigon	Schonberg, Claude-Michel	1991	Engineer+	The American Dream*	Moderate Tempo	Tenor	A2	A4	Lead	Antagonist Male
Miss Saigon	Schonberg, Claude-Michel	1991	Kim+	Little God Of My Heart	Ballad	Soprano	A3	D5	Lead	Ingenue Female
Miss Saigon	Schonberg, Claude-Michel	1991	Kim+	Sun And Moon*	Ballad	Soprano	F#3	D5	Lead	Ingenue Female
Miss Saigon	Schonberg, Claude-Michel	1991	Chris Scott	Sun And Moon*	Ballad	Tenor	A2	F#4	Lead	Romantic Lead Male
Miss Saigon	Schonberg, Claude-Michel	1991	Chris & Kim+	Sun And Moon	Ballad	Tenor/Sop			Duet	RLM/IF
Miss Saigon	Schonberg, Claude-Michel	1991	Thuy+	Kim's Nightmare Part I	Uptempo	Tenor	C3	E4	Lead	Romantic Antagonist Male
Miss Saigon	Schonberg, Claude-Michel	1991	Ensemble	The Transaction	Moderate Tempo	SATT			Ensemble	Adults
Miss Saigon	Schonberg, Claude-Michel	1991	Ensemble	You Will Not Touch Him*	Moderate Tempo	SATB			Ensemble	Adults
Miss Saigon	Schonberg, Claude-Michel	1991	Ensemble	What A Waste*	Moderate Tempo	SATB			Ensemble	Adults
Most Happy Fella, The	Loesser, Frank	1956	Cleo	Ooh! My Feet!	Moderate Tempo	Alto	A#3	Bb4	Lead	Character Female
Most Happy Fella, The	Loesser, Frank	1956	Rosabella & Cleo	I Know How It Is	Moderate Tempo	Sop/Alto			Duet	CIF/CM
Most Happy Fella, The	Loesser, Frank	1956	Rosabella	I Don't Know*	Moderate Tempo	Soprano	Bb3	D5	Lead	Character Ingenue Female
Most Happy Fella, The	Loesser, Frank	1956	Postman	Somebody Somewhere	Ballad	Soprano	E4	G5	Lead	Character Ingenue Female
Most Happy Fella, The	Loesser, Frank	1956	Tony	Most Happy Fella (ms 74-109 & 131-15)	Uptempo	Baritone	Eb3	G4	Lead	Mature Male
Most Happy Fella, The	Loesser, Frank	1956	Tony & Marie	A Long Time Ago	Moderate Tempo	Bar/Alto			Duet	MM/MF
Most Happy Fella, The	Loesser, Frank	1956	Ensemble	Standing On The Corner	Moderate Tempo	TTBB			Ensemble	Adults
Most Happy Fella, The	Loesser, Frank	1956	Marie	A Long Time Ago*	Moderate Tempo	Alto	D4	Eb5	Lead	Mature Female
Most Happy Fella, The	Loesser, Frank	1956	Ensemble	The Most Happy Fella	Uptempo	SATB			Ensemble	Adults
Most Happy Fella, The	Loesser, Frank	1956	Joe	Joey, Joey, Joey	Moderate Tempo	Baritone	C3	F4	Lead	Romantic Antagonist Male
Most Happy Fella, The	Loesser, Frank	1956	Tony	Soon You Gonna Leave Me Joe	Moderate Tempo	Baritone	C#3	E4	Lead	Mature Male
Most Happy Fella, The	Loesser, Frank	1956	Tony	Rosabella	Moderate Tempo	Baritone	Eb3	G4	Lead	Mature Male
Most Happy Fella, The	Loesser, Frank	1956	Ensemble	Abbondanza	Uptempo	TTB			Ensemble	Adults
Most Happy Fella, The	Loesser, Frank	1956	Tony	Plenty Bambini	Ballad	Baritone	C#3	F#4	Lead	Mature Male
Most Happy Fella, The	Loesser, Frank	1956	Ensemble	Sposalizio	Uptempo	SATB			Ensemble	Adults
Most Happy Fella, The	Loesser, Frank	1956	Ensemble	I Seen Her At The Station	Moderate Tempo	Baritone	D3	E4	Featured Ensemble	Character Male
Most Happy Fella, The	Loesser, Frank	1956	Ensemble	Benvenuta	Moderate Tempo	TTB			Ensemble	Adults
Most Happy Fella, The	Loesser, Frank	1956	Rosabella	Aren't You Glad?	Ballad	Soprano	C4	E5	Lead	Character Ingenue Female
Most Happy Fella, The	Loesser, Frank	1956	Rosabella	No Home No Job	Uptempo	Soprano	D4	Eb5	Lead	Character Ingenue Female
Most Happy Fella, The	Loesser, Frank	1956	Joe	Don't Cry	Moderate Tempo	Baritone	Bb2	Eb4	Lead	Romantic Antagonist Male
Most Happy Fella, The	Loesser, Frank	1956	Ensemble	Fresno Beauties*	Uptempo	TB			Ensemble	Adults
Most Happy Fella, The	Loesser, Frank	1956	Tony & Rosabella	Cold And Dead	Ballad	Bar/Sop			Duet	MM/CIF
Most Happy Fella, The	Loesser, Frank	1956	The Doctor	Love and Kindness	Moderate Tempo	Tenor	E3	A4	Supporting	Character Male
Most Happy Fella, The	Loesser, Frank	1956	Tony & Rosabella	Happy To Make Your Acquaintance*	Moderate Tempo	Bar/Sop			Duet	MM/CIF
Most Happy Fella, The	Loesser, Frank	1956	Marie & Cleo	I Don't Like This Dame	Uptempo	Alto/Alto			Duet	MF/CF
Most Happy Fella, The	Loesser, Frank	1956	Herman & Cleo	Big D*	Uptempo	Tenor/Alto			Duet	CM/CF

Shows

Songs by Character Type

Show	Composer	Year	Role	Song	Tempo	Vocal Type	Range-Bottom	Range-Top	Category	Character Type
Most Happy Fella, The	Loesser, Frank	1956	Ensemble	Big D	Uptempo	SATB			Ensemble	Adults
Most Happy Fella, The	Loesser, Frank	1956	Tony & Rosabella	How Beautiful The Days*	Ballad	Bar/Sop			Duet	MM/CIF
Most Happy Fella, The	Loesser, Frank	1956	Ensemble	How Beautiful The Days	Ballad	SATB			Ensemble	Adults
Most Happy Fella, The	Loesser, Frank	1956	Ensemble	Young People*	Moderate Tempo	SATB			Ensemble	Mature Female
Most Happy Fella, The	Loesser, Frank	1956	Marie	Young People*	Moderate Tempo	Alto	C4	E5	Lead	Mature Female
Most Happy Fella, The	Loesser, Frank	1956	Rosabella	Warm All Over	Ballad	Soprano	C#4	F#5	Lead	Character Ingenue Female
Most Happy Fella, The	Loesser, Frank	1956	Tony	Old People Gotta Dance	Moderate Tempo	Baritone	C3	C4	Lead	Mature Male
Most Happy Fella, The	Loesser, Frank	1956	Herman	I Like Everybody*	Uptempo	Tenor	G3	G4	Lead	Character Male
Most Happy Fella, The	Loesser, Frank	1956	Rosabella	I Love Him*	Moderate Tempo	Soprano	D4	Eb5	Lead	Character Ingenue Female
Most Happy Fella, The	Loesser, Frank	1956	Cleo	I Know How It Is*	Moderate Tempo	Alto	Ab3	B4	Lead	Character Female
Most Happy Fella, The	Loesser, Frank	1956	Rosabella	Like A Woman Loves A Man	Moderate Tempo	Soprano	D4	G5	Lead	Character Ingenue Female
Most Happy Fella, The	Loesser, Frank	1956	Tony & Rosabella	My Heart Is So Full Of You*	Ballad	Bar/Sop			Duet	MM/CIF
Most Happy Fella, The	Loesser, Frank	1956	Tony	My Heart Is So Full Of You*	Ballad	Baritone	Db3	Gb4	Lead	Mature Male
Most Happy Fella, The	Loesser, Frank	1956	Rosabella	My Heart Is So Full Of You*	Ballad	Soprano	Db4	Gb5	Lead	Character Ingenue Female
Most Happy Fella, The	Loesser, Frank	1956	Tony	Mamma, Mamma	Moderate Tempo	Baritone	C#3	G4	Lead	Mature Male
Most Happy Fella, The	Loesser, Frank	1956	Ensemble	Abbodanza	Uptempo	TTB			Ensemble	Adults
Most Happy Fella, The	Loesser, Frank	1956	Herman & Cleo	I Like Everybody Reprise	Uptempo	Tenor/Alto			Duet	CM/CF
Most Happy Fella, The	Loesser, Frank	1956	Cleo	I Like Everybody Reprise*	Uptempo	Alto	G#3	B4	Lead	Character Female
Most Happy Fella, The	Loesser, Frank	1956	Herman	I Like Everybody Reprise*	Uptempo	Tenor	F3	G4	Lead	Character Male
Most Happy Fella, The	Loesser, Frank	1956	Ensemble	A Song Of A Summer Night*	Uptempo	SATB			Ensemble	Adults
Most Happy Fella, The	Loesser, Frank	1956	The Doctor	A Song Of A Summer Night*	Uptempo	Tenor	F3	F4	Supporting	Character Male
Most Happy Fella, The	Loesser, Frank	1956	Rosabella	Please Let Me Tell You	Uptempo	Soprano	D4	E5	Lead	Character Ingenue Female
Most Happy Fella, The	Loesser, Frank	1956	Tony	Tony's Thoughts	Ballad	Baritone	D3	F4	Lead	Mature Male
Most Happy Fella, The	Loesser, Frank	1956	Ensemble	Nobody's Ever Gonna Love You	Moderate Tempo	BAA			Ensemble	Adults
Most Happy Fella, The	Loesser, Frank	1956	Joe	Getting' Out Of Town	Ballad	Baritone	Db3	F4	Lead	Romantic Antagonist Male
Most Happy Fella, The	Loesser, Frank	1956	Herman & Cleo	I Made A Fist*	Moderate Tempo	Tenor/Alto			Duet	CM/CF
Most Happy Fella, The	Loesser, Frank	1956	Herman	I Made A Fist*	Moderate Tempo	Tenor	F3	Ab4	Lead	Character Male
Most Happy Fella, The	Loesser, Frank	1956	Tony & Rosabella	Finale-My Heart Is So Full...	Uptempo	Bar/Sop			Duet	CM/CF
Most Happy Fella, The	Loesser, Frank	1956	Ensemble	Finale	Uptempo	SATB			Ensemble	Adults
Most Happy Fella, The	Loesser, Frank	1957	Tony	I Canno' Leave You Money	Moderate Tempo	Baritone	D#3	Eb4	Lead	Mature Male
Music Man, The	Wilson, Meredith	1957	Ensemble	Rock Island	Uptempo	TB			Ensemble	Adults
Music Man, The	Wilson, Meredith	1957	Ensemble	Iowa Stubborn	Uptempo	SATB			Ensemble	Adults
Music Man, The	Wilson, Meredith	1957	Harold Hill	Trouble	Uptempo	Baritone	A2	E4	Lead	Romantic Antagonist Male
Music Man, The	Wilson, Meredith	1957	Marian Paroo & Mrs. Paroo	Piano Lesson	Uptempo	Sop/Alto			Duet	RLF/MF
Music Man, The	Wilson, Meredith	1957	Harold Hill	Seventy Six Trombones	Uptempo	Baritone	B2	F4	Lead	Romantic Antagonist Male
Music Man, The	Wilson, Meredith	1957	Ensemble	Sincere	Moderate Tempo	TTBB			Ensemble	Adults
Music Man, The	Wilson, Meredith	1957	Harold Hill	The Sadder But Wiser Girl*	Uptempo	Baritone	C3	E4	Lead	Romantic Antagonist Male
Music Man, The	Wilson, Meredith	1957	Ensemble	Pickalittle*	Uptempo	SA			Ensemble	Adults
Music Man, The	Wilson, Meredith	1957	Ensemble+	Goodnight Ladies*	Uptempo	TTBB			Ensemble	Adults
Music Man, The	Wilson, Meredith	1957	Ensemble	Pickalittle/Goodnight Ladies	Moderate Tempo	SATB			Ensemble	Adults
Music Man, The	Wilson, Meredith	1957	Harold Hill	Marian The Librarian	Moderate Tempo	Baritone	C3	F4	Lead	Romantic Antagonist Male
Music Man, The	Wilson, Meredith	1957	Marian Paroo	My White Knight	Ballad	Soprano	C#4	Ab5	Lead	Romantic Lead Female
Music Man, The	Wilson, Meredith	1957	Winthrop Paroo	Gary Indiana Reprise	Uptempo	Soprano	C4	Eb5	Lead	Juvenile Male

Shows

438

Songs by Character Type

* = Music Edit Required
+ = Ethnic Specific

Show	Composer	Year	Role	Song	Tempo	Vocal Type	Range-Bottom	Range-Top	Category	Character Type
Music Man, The	Wilson, Meredith	1957	Ensemble	The Wells Fargo Wagon	Uptempo	SATB			Ensemble	Adults
Music Man, The	Wilson, Meredith	1957	Ensemble	It's You	Ballad	TTBB			Ensemble	Adults
Music Man, The	Wilson, Meredith	1957	Ensemble	Shipoopi	Uptempo	SATB			Ensemble	Teens/Adults
Music Man, The	Wilson, Meredith	1957	Ensemble	Pickalittle Talkalittle Reprise	Uptempo	SA			Ensemble	Adults
Music Man, The	Wilson, Meredith	1957	Ensemble	Lida Rose*	Ballad	TTBB			Ensemble	Adults
Music Man, The	Wilson, Meredith	1957	Marian Paroo	Will I Ever Leave You*	Moderate Tempo	Soprano	D4	F#5	Lead	Romantic Lead Female
Music Man, The	Wilson, Meredith	1957	Ensemble	Lida Rose/Will I Ever Leave You	Moderate Tempo	STTBB			Ensemble	Adults
Music Man, The	Wilson, Meredith	1957	Ensemble	It's You Reprise	Ballad	SATB			Ensemble	Adults
Music Man, The	Wilson, Meredith	1957	Marian Paroo	Till There Was You	Ballad	Soprano	Eb4	F5	Lead	Romantic Lead Female
Music Man, The	Wilson, Meredith	1957	Harold & Marian	76 Trombones/Goodnight My Someone	Moderate Tempo	Bar/Sop			Duet	RAM/RLF
Music Man, The	Wilson, Meredith	1957	Ensemble	76 Trombones Reprise	Moderate Tempo	SATB			Ensemble	Children/Teens/Adults
Music Man, The	Wilson, Meredith	1957	Harold Hill	76 Trombones	Moderate Tempo	Baritone	G2	F4	Lead	Romantic Antagonist Male
Music Man, The	Wilson, Meredith	1957	Ensemble	Columbia Gem Of The Ocean	Moderate Tempo	SATB Unison			Ensemble	Adults
Music Man, The	Wilson, Meredith	1957	Harold Hill	Trouble Reprise	Uptempo	Baritone	A3	Eb4	Lead	Romantic Antagonist Male
Music Man, The	Wilson, Meredith	1957	Marian Paroo	Goodnight My Someone*	Ballad	Soprano	B3	E5	Lead	Romantic Lead Female
Music Man, The	Wilson, Meredith	1957	Ensemble	Shipoopi	Uptempo	SATB			Ensemble	Teens
Music Man, The	Wilson, Meredith	1957	Harold Hill	Till There Was You Reprise	Ballad	Baritone	B2	C4	Lead	Romantic Antagonist Male
Music Man, The	Wilson, Meredith	1957	Ensemble	Lida Rose Reprise	Moderate Tempo	TTBB			Ensemble	Adults
My Fair Lady	Loewe, Frederick	1956	Henry Higgins	Why Can't The English	Uptempo	Baritone	B2	D4	Lead	Romantic Lead Male
My Fair Lady	Loewe, Frederick	1956	Eliza Doolittle	Wouldn't It Be Lovely	Moderate Tempo	Soprano	C4	Eb5	Lead	Ingenue Female
My Fair Lady	Loewe, Frederick	1956	Alfred Doolittle	With A Little Bit Of Luck*	Uptempo	Baritone	G2	E4	Lead	Character Male
My Fair Lady	Loewe, Frederick	1956	Alfred Doolittle	Little Bit Of Luck Reprise	Uptempo	Baritone	G2	E4	Lead	Character Male
My Fair Lady	Loewe, Frederick	1956	Eliza Doolittle	Just You Wait	Moderate Tempo	Soprano	A3	Eb4	Lead	Ingenue Female
My Fair Lady	Loewe, Frederick	1956	Eliza Doolittle	I Could Have Danced All Night*	Uptempo	Soprano	B3	G5	Lead	Ingenue Female
My Fair Lady	Loewe, Frederick	1956	Ensemble	Ascot Gavotte	Moderate Tempo	SATB			Ensemble	Adults
My Fair Lady	Loewe, Frederick	1956	Eliza Doolittle	Just You Wait Reprise	Ballad	Soprano	D4	C5	Lead	Ingenue Female
My Fair Lady	Loewe, Frederick	1956	Freddy Eynsford Hill	On The Street Where You Live	Moderate Tempo	Tenor	C3	F4	Lead	Ingenue Male
My Fair Lady	Loewe, Frederick	1956	Freddy Eynsford Hill	On The Street Where You Live Reprise	Moderate Tempo	Tenor	C3	E4	Lead	Ingenue Male
My Fair Lady	Loewe, Frederick	1956	Eliza Doolittle	Wouldn't It Be Lovely Reprise*	Ballad	Soprano	C4	D5	Lead	Ingenue Female
My Fair Lady	Loewe, Frederick	1956	Alfred Doolittle	Get Me To The Church On Time	Uptempo	Baritone	B2	D4	Lead	Character Male
My Fair Lady	Loewe, Frederick	1956	Henry Higgins	A Hymn to Him	Uptempo	Baritone	C#3	D4	Lead	Romantic Lead Male
My Fair Lady	Loewe, Frederick	1956	Eliza Doolittle	Without You	Moderate Tempo	Soprano	B3	Eb5	Lead	Ingenue Female
My Fair Lady	Loewe, Frederick	1956	Henry Higgins	I've Grown Accustomed To Her Face	Ballad	Baritone	A2	B3	Lead	Romantic Lead Male
My Fair Lady	Loewe, Frederick	1956	Henry & Eliza	The Rain In Spain	Uptempo	Bar/Sop			Duet	RLM/IF
My Fair Lady	Loewe, Frederick	1956	Henry Higgins	I'm An Ordinary Man	Moderate Tempo	Baritone	Bb2	C4	Lead	Romantic Lead Male
My Fair Lady	Loewe, Frederick	1956	Henry & Pickering	You Did It	Uptempo	Bar/Bar			Duet	RLM/MM
My Fair Lady	Loewe, Frederick	1956	Eliza Doolittle	Show Me	Uptempo	Soprano	D4	G5	Lead	Ingenue Female
My Fair Lady	Loewe, Frederick	1956	Ensemble	With A Little Bit Of Luck*	Uptempo	SATB			Ensemble	Adults
My Fair Lady	Loewe, Frederick	1956	Ensemble	The Servants Chorus	Moderate Tempo	SATB			Ensemble	Adults
My Fair Lady	Loewe, Frederick	1956	Ensemble	I Could Have Danced All Night*	Uptempo	SA			Ensemble	Adults
My Fair Lady	Loewe, Frederick	1956	Ensemble	Wouldn't It Be Loverly Reprise*	Moderate Tempo	TBB			Ensemble	Adults
My Fair Lady	Loewe, Frederick	1956	Ensemble	Get Me To The Church On Time Reprise	Ballad	SATB			Ensemble	Adults
My Favorite Year	Flaherty, Stephen	1992	Ensemble	Twenty Million People*	Moderate Tempo	SATB			Ensemble	Adults

Shows

Songs by Character Type

Show	Composer	Year	Role	Song	Tempo	Vocal Type	Range-Bottom	Range-Top	Category	Character Type
My Favorite Year	Flaherty, Stephen	1992	Benjy Stone	Larger Than Life	Moderate Tempo	Tenor	Eb3	F4	Lead	Character Ingenue Male
My Favorite Year	Flaherty, Stephen	1992	Ensemble	Three Musketeer Sketch	Uptempo	SATB			Ensemble	Adults
My Favorite Year	Flaherty, Stephen	1992	Benjy Stone	Waldorf Reveal	Uptempo	Tenor	C3	F4	Lead	Character Ingenue Male
My Favorite Year	Flaherty, Stephen	1992	Belle Carroca	Rookie In The Ring*	Ballad	Alto	G3	Bb4	Lead	Maternal
My Favorite Year	Flaherty, Stephen	1992	Ensemble	The Gospel According To King	Uptempo	SATB			Ensemble	Adults
My Favorite Year	Flaherty, Stephen	1992	King Kaiser	The Gospel According To King*	Uptempo	Baritone	D3	C#4	Lead	Antagonist Male
My Favorite Year	Flaherty, Stephen	1992	Ensemble	Musketeer Sketch Rehearsal PII	Uptempo	TB			Ensemble	Adults
My Favorite Year	Flaherty, Stephen	1992	Swann & Benjy	Musketeer Sketch Rehearsal PI	Uptempo	Bar/Tenor			Duet	RAM/CIM
My Favorite Year	Flaherty, Stephen	1992	K.C. Downing	Funny*	Moderate Tempo	Soprano	A3	E5	Lead	Character Ingenue Female
My Favorite Year	Flaherty, Stephen	1992	K.C. & Alice	Funny	Moderate Tempo	Sop/Alto			Duet	CIF/CF
My Favorite Year	Flaherty, Stephen	1992	King & Alan	Musketeer Sketch Rehearsal PII*	Uptempo	Bar/Bar			Duet	AM/RAM
My Favorite Year	Flaherty, Stephen	1992	Ensemble	Welcome To Brooklyn*	Moderate Tempo	SATB			Ensemble	Adults
My Favorite Year	Flaherty, Stephen	1992	Alan Swann	If The World Were Like The Movies	Ballad	Baritone	Bb2	E4	Lead	Romantic Antagonist Male
My Favorite Year	Flaherty, Stephen	1992	Alan Swann	Exits	Moderate Tempo	Baritone	G2	D4	Lead	Romantic Antagonist Male
My Favorite Year	Flaherty, Stephen	1992	Benjy & K.C.	Shut Up And Dance	Moderate Tempo	Bar/Sop			Duet	CIM/CIF
My Favorite Year	Flaherty, Stephen	1992	K.C. Downing	Shut Up And Dance*	Moderate Tempo	Soprano	A3	C5	Lead	Character Ingenue Female
My Favorite Year	Flaherty, Stephen	1992	King & Alice	Professional Show Biz Comedy	Uptempo	Bar/Alto			Duet	AM/CF
My Favorite Year	Flaherty, Stephen	1992	Alan & Benjy	The Lights Come Up	Ballad	Bar/Tenor			Duet	RAM/CIM
My Favorite Year	Flaherty, Stephen	1992	Alan Swann	The Lights Come Up*	Ballad	Baritone	Bb2	C4	Lead	Romantic Antagonist Male
My Favorite Year	Flaherty, Stephen	1992	Ensemble	Maxford House	Moderate Tempo	SSA			Ensemble	Adults
My Favorite Year	Flaherty, Stephen	1992	Ensemble	My Favorite Year	Moderate Tempo	SATB			Ensemble	Adults
My Favorite Year	Flaherty, Stephen	1992	Benjy Stone	My Favorite Year*	Moderate Tempo	Tenor	C3	G4	Lead	Character Ingenue Male
My Favorite Year	Flaherty, Stephen	1992	Ensemble	Manhattan	Uptempo	SATB			Ensemble	Adults
My Favorite Year	Flaherty, Stephen	1992	Alan Swann	Manhattan*	Uptempo	Baritone	G2	Eb4	Lead	Romantic Antagonist Male
My Favorite Year	Flaherty, Stephen	1992	Ensemble	Comedy Calvacade	Moderate Tempo	SATB			Ensemble	Adults
My Favorite Year	Flaherty, Stephen	1992	Ensemble	There You Are	Uptempo	SATB			Ensemble	Adults
Mystery Of Edwin Drood, T	Holmes, Rupert	1985	Chairman	There You Are*	Uptempo	Baritone	D3	D4	Lead	Mature Male
Mystery Of Edwin Drood, T	Holmes, Rupert	1985	Drood & Jasper	Two Kinsmen	Uptempo	Sop/Tenor			Duet	CIF/AM
Mystery Of Edwin Drood, T	Holmes, Rupert	1985	John Jasper	A Man Could Go Quite Mad	Uptempo	Tenor	A2	G4	Lead	Antagonist Male
Mystery Of Edwin Drood, T	Holmes, Rupert	1985	Rosa Bud	Moonfall	Ballad	Soprano	B3	G5	Lead	Ingenue Female
Mystery Of Edwin Drood, T	Holmes, Rupert	1985	Ensemble	A British Subject	Moderate Tempo	SATB			Ensemble	Adults
Mystery Of Edwin Drood, T	Holmes, Rupert	1985	Neville & Helena	A British Subject*	Moderate Tempo	Bar/Alto			Duet	RAM/RAF
Mystery Of Edwin Drood, T	Holmes, Rupert	1985	Princess Puffer	The Wages Of Sin	Moderate Tempo	Alto	F3	C5	Lead	Antagonist Female
Mystery Of Edwin Drood, T	Holmes, Rupert	1985	Ensemble	Ceylon	Moderate Tempo	SATB			Ensemble	Adults
Mystery Of Edwin Drood, T	Holmes, Rupert	1985	Jasper & Chairman	Both Sides Of The Coin	Uptempo	Tenor/Bar			Duet	AM/MM
Mystery Of Edwin Drood, T	Holmes, Rupert	1985	Chairman	Both Sides Of The Coin*	Uptempo	Baritone	C3	F#4	Lead	Mature Male
Mystery Of Edwin Drood, T	Holmes, Rupert	1985	John Jasper	Both Sides Of The Coin*	Uptempo	Tenor	C3	E4	Lead	Antagonist Male
Mystery Of Edwin Drood, T	Holmes, Rupert	1985	Drood & Rosa Bud	Perfect Strangers	Moderate Tempo	Sop/Sop			Duet	CF/IF
Mystery Of Edwin Drood, T	Holmes, Rupert	1985	Rosa Bud	Perfect Strangers*	Moderate Tempo	Soprano	C#4	F5	Lead	Ingenue Female
Mystery Of Edwin Drood, T	Holmes, Rupert	1985	Ensemble	No Good Comes From Bad	Uptempo	SATB			Ensemble	Adults
Mystery Of Edwin Drood, T	Holmes, Rupert	1985	Jasper & Rosa Bud	The Name Of Love	Uptempo	Tenor/Sop			Duet	AM/IF
Mystery Of Edwin Drood, T	Holmes, Rupert	1985	Jasper & Rosa Bud	Moonfall Reprise	Moderate Tempo	Tenor/Sop			Duet	AM/IF
Mystery Of Edwin Drood, T	Holmes, Rupert	1985	Datchery & Puffer	Settling Up The Score	Uptempo	Alto/Alto			Duet	CF/AF

Shows

* = Music Edit Required
+ = Ethnic Specific

Show	Composer	Year	Role	Song	Tempo	Vocal Type	Range-Bottom	Range-Top	Category	Character Type
Mystery Of Edwin Drood, T	Holmes, Rupert	1985	Ensemble	Off To The Races	Uptempo	SATB			Ensemble	Adults
Mystery Of Edwin Drood, T	Holmes, Rupert	1985	Chairman	Off To The Races*	Uptempo	Baritone	C3	F4	Lead	Mature Male
Mystery Of Edwin Drood, T	Holmes, Rupert	1985	Princess Puffer	Garden Path To Hell	Ballad	Alto	G3	A4	Lead	Antagonist Female
Mystery Of Edwin Drood, T	Holmes, Rupert	1985	Ensemble	Don't Quit While You're Ahead	Moderate Tempo	SATB			Ensemble	Adults
Mystery Of Edwin Drood, T	Holmes, Rupert	1985	Princess Puffer	Don't Quit While You're Ahead*	Moderate Tempo	Alto	F3	A4	Lead	Antagonist Female
Mystery Of Edwin Drood, T	Holmes, Rupert	1985	Ensemble	Moonfall Quartet	Ballad	SSAA			Ensemble	Adults
Mystery Of Edwin Drood, T	Holmes, Rupert	1985	Bazzard	Never The Luck*	Moderate Tempo	Tenor	C3	G4	Lead	Character Male
Mystery Of Edwin Drood, T	Holmes, Rupert	1985	Dick Datchery (Drood)	Out On A Limerick	Moderate Tempo	Alto	C3	E4	Lead	Character Female
Mystery Of Edwin Drood, T	Holmes, Rupert	1985	John Jasper	Jasper's Confession	Moderate Tempo	Tenor	B2	A4	Lead	Antagonist Male
Mystery Of Edwin Drood, T	Holmes, Rupert	1985	Bazzard	Bazzard's Confession	Uptempo	Tenor	A2	G4	Lead	Character Male
Mystery Of Edwin Drood, T	Holmes, Rupert	1985	Chrisparkle	Chrisparkle's Confession	Moderate Tempo	Baritone	D3	F4	Lead	Character Male
Mystery Of Edwin Drood, T	Holmes, Rupert	1985	Durdle	Durdle's Confession	Ballad	Baritone	C3	E4	Lead	Mature Male
Mystery Of Edwin Drood, T	Holmes, Rupert	1985	Helena Landless	Helena's Confession	Moderate Tempo	Alto	G3	B4	Lead	Romantic Antagonist Female
Mystery Of Edwin Drood, T	Holmes, Rupert	1985	Neville Landless	Neville's Confession	Moderate Tempo	Baritone	G♭3	F4	Lead	Romantic Antagonist Male
Mystery Of Edwin Drood, T	Holmes, Rupert	1985	Princess Puffer	Puffer's Confession	Ballad	Alto	C4	C5	Lead	Antagonist Female
Mystery Of Edwin Drood, T	Holmes, Rupert	1985	Rosa Bud	Rosa's Confession	Uptempo	Soprano	A3	A♭5	Lead	Ingenue Female
Mystery Of Edwin Drood, T	Holmes, Rupert	1985	Ensemble	Perfect Strangers	Moderate Tempo	SATB			Ensemble	Adults
Mystery Of Edwin Drood, T	Holmes, Rupert	1985	Male & Female	Perfect Strangers*	Moderate Tempo	Bar/Alto			Duet	Any/Any
Mystery Of Edwin Drood, T	Holmes, Rupert	1985	Ensemble	The Writing On The Wall*	Uptempo	SATB	G3	G♭5	Ensemble	Adults
Mystery Of Edwin Drood, T	Holmes, Rupert	1985	Edwin Drood	The Writing On The Wall*	Uptempo	Soprano	G3	G♭5	Lead	Character Female
Next To Normal	Kitt, Tom	2009	Ensemble	Just Another Day	Uptempo	AATT			Ensemble	Adults
Next To Normal	Kitt, Tom	2009	Natalie	Everything Else	Uptempo	Alto	G3	C5	Lead	Character Ingenue Female
Next To Normal	Kitt, Tom	2009	Dan	Who's Crazy*	Moderate Tempo	Tenor	G3	F4	Lead	Character Male
Next To Normal	Kitt, Tom	2009	Diana	My Psychopharmacologist And I	Moderate Tempo	Alto	A3	C5	Lead	Romantic Lead Female
Next To Normal	Kitt, Tom	2009	Natalie & Henry	Perfect For You	Moderate Tempo	Tenor/Alto			Duet	CIF/CIM
Next To Normal	Kitt, Tom	2009	Diana	I Miss The Mountains	Moderate Tempo	Alto	G3	D5	Lead	Romantic Lead Female
Next To Normal	Kitt, Tom	2009	Ensemble	It's Gonna Be Good	Uptempo	AATTT			Ensemble	Adults
Next To Normal	Kitt, Tom	2009	Dan	He's Not Here	Ballad	Tenor	E♭3	G4	Lead	Character Male
Next To Normal	Kitt, Tom	2009	Diana	You Don't Know*	Moderate Tempo	Alto	A3	B4	Lead	Romantic Lead Female
Next To Normal	Kitt, Tom	2009	Dan	I Am The One*	Uptempo	Tenor	E3	F#4	Lead	Character Male
Next To Normal	Kitt, Tom	2009	Ensemble	I Am The One*	Uptempo	AAT			Ensemble	Adults
Next To Normal	Kitt, Tom	2009	Natalie	Superboy And The Invisible Girl	Uptempo	Alto	D4	D5	Lead	Character Ingenue Female
Next To Normal	Kitt, Tom	2009	Gabe	I'm Alive	Uptempo	Tenor	G3	B4	Lead	Character Ingenue Male
Next To Normal	Kitt, Tom	2009	Dan	I've Been	Uptempo	Tenor	E3	G4	Lead	Character Male
Next To Normal	Kitt, Tom	2009	Diana	Didn't I See This Movie	Uptempo	Alto	A3	F#5	Lead	Romantic Lead Female
Next To Normal	Kitt, Tom	2009	Dan	A Light In The Dark*	Ballad	Tenor	D3	E4	Lead	Character Male
Next To Normal	Kitt, Tom	2009	Ensemble	Wish I Were Here*	Uptempo	AATT			Ensemble	Romantic Lead Female
Next To Normal	Kitt, Tom	2009	Natalie & Henry	Song Of Forgetting	Ballad	AAT			Ensemble	Adults
Next To Normal	Kitt, Tom	2009	Ensemble	Hey #2	Uptempo	Tenor/Alto			Duet	CIF/CIM
Next To Normal	Kitt, Tom	2009	Gabe	Better Than Before	Moderate Tempo	AAT			Ensemble	Adults
Next To Normal	Kitt, Tom	2009	Diana & Dr. Madden	Aftershocks*	Uptempo	Tenor	D3	D4	Lead	Character Ingenue Male
Next To Normal	Kitt, Tom	2009	Diana	You Don't Know Reprise	Uptempo	Alto/Tenor			Duet	RLF/CM
Next To Normal	Kitt, Tom	2009	Dr. Madden	You Don't Know Reprise*	Uptempo	Alto	A3	A4	Lead	Romantic Lead Female
Next To Normal	Kitt, Tom	2009		Make Up Your Mind*	Moderate Tempo	Tenor	A♭3	A♭4	Lead	Character Male

Shows

Songs by Character Type

* = Music Edit Required
+ = Ethnic Specific

Show	Composer	Year	Role	Song	Tempo	Vocal Type	Range-Bottom	Range-Top	Category	Character Type
Next To Normal	Kitt, Tom	2009	Ensemble	Catch Me I'm Falling	Moderate Tempo	AATT			Ensemble	Adults
Next To Normal	Kitt, Tom	2009	Diana & Dan	How Could I Forget	Ballad	Alto/Tenor			Duet	RLF/CM
Next To Normal	Kitt, Tom	2009	Diana	How Could I Forget*	Ballad	Alto	B♭3	D♭5	Lead	Romantic Lead Female
Next To Normal	Kitt, Tom	2009	Dan	It's Gonna Be Good Reprise*	Uptempo	Tenor	A2	F4	Lead	Character Male
Next To Normal	Kitt, Tom	2009	Diana & Natalie	Why Stay	Uptempo	Alto/Alto			Duet	RLF/CIF
Next To Normal	Kitt, Tom	2009	Dan	A Promies*	Uptempo	Tenor	C3	F4	Lead	Character Male
Next To Normal	Kitt, Tom	2009	Gabe	I'm Alive Reprise	Uptempo	Tenor	G3	G4	Lead	Character Ingenue Male
Next To Normal	Kitt, Tom	2009	Diana	The Break	Uptempo	Alto	B3	C5	Lead	Romantic Lead Female
Next To Normal	Kitt, Tom	2009	Dr. Madden	Make Up Your Mind Reprise	Moderate Tempo	Tenor	A3	G4	Lead	Character Male
Next To Normal	Kitt, Tom	2009	Diana & Gabe	Catch Me I'm Falling Reprise	Moderate Tempo	Alto/Tenor			Duet	RLF/CIM
Next To Normal	Kitt, Tom	2009	Diana & Natalie	Maybe*	Moderate Tempo	Alto/Alto			Duet	RLF/CIM
Next To Normal	Kitt, Tom	2009	Diana	Maybe*	Moderate Tempo	Alto	E♭3	E♭5	Lead	Romantic Lead Female
Next To Normal	Kitt, Tom	2009	Natalie	Maybe*	Moderate Tempo	Alto	A♭3	D5	Lead	Character Ingenue Female
Next To Normal	Kitt, Tom	2009	Natalie & Henry	Hey #3 Reprise	Moderate Tempo	Alto/Tenor			Duet	CIF/CIM
Next To Normal	Kitt, Tom	2009	Henry	Perfect For You Reprise*	Moderate Tempo	Tenor	D3	G4	Lead	Character Ingenue Male
Next To Normal	Kitt, Tom	2009	Diana	So Anyway	Ballad	Alto	B3	C5	Lead	Romantic Lead Female
Next To Normal	Kitt, Tom	2009	Dan & Gabe	I Am The One Reprise	Moderate Tempo	Tenor/Tenor			Duet	CM/CIM
Next To Normal	Kitt, Tom	2009	Dan & Natalie	Let There Be Lifht	Moderate Tempo	Tenor/Alto			Duet	CM/CIF
Next To Normal	Kitt, Tom	2009	Dr. Madden	Open Your Eyes*	Moderate Tempo	Tenor	F3	A4	Lead	Character Male
Next To Normal	Kitt, Tom	2009	Gabe	There's A World	Ballad	Tenor	G3	G4	Lead	Character Ingenue Male
Next To Normal	Kitt, Tom	2009	Ensemble	Light	Moderate Tempo	AATTTT			Ensemble	Adults
Nick & Nora	Strouse, Charles	1991	Tracy Gardner	Everybody Wants To Do A Musical	Moderate Tempo	Soprano	E2	G#5	Lead	Romantic Lead Female
Nick & Nora	Strouse, Charles	1991	Ensemble	Not Me	Moderate Tempo	ABB			Ensemble	Adults
Nick & Nora	Strouse, Charles	1991	Ensemble	Swill	Moderate Tempo	ABTT			Ensemble	Adults
Nick & Nora	Strouse, Charles	1991	Lily Connors	People Get Hurt	Uptempo	Alto	A♭3	D♭5	Lead	Romantic Antagonist Female
Nick & Nora	Strouse, Charles	1991	Lorraine Bixby	Men*	Moderate Tempo	Alto	F3	C♭5	Lead	Mature Female
Nick & Nora	Strouse, Charles	1991	Ensemble	May The Best Man Win	Uptempo	SATB			Ensemble	Adults
Nick & Nora	Strouse, Charles	1991	Nick Charles	Look Who's Alone Now	Ballad	Baritone	A♭2	C4	Lead	Romantic Lead Male
Nick & Nora	Strouse, Charles	1991	Victor Moisa	Class	Moderate Tempo	Baritone	B2	F#4	Lead	Romantic Antagonist Male
Nick & Nora	Strouse, Charles	1991	Maria Valdex	Boom Chicka Boom*	Uptempo	Alto	A3	B♭4	Lead	Character Female
Nick & Nora	Strouse, Charles	1991	Max Bernheim & Lorraine Bixb	Max's Story	Moderate Tempo	Bar/Alto			Duet	CM/MF
Nick & Nora	Strouse, Charles	1991	Nick Charles & Nora Charles	As Long As You're Happy*	Uptempo	Baritone	A2	F4	Lead	Romantic Lead Male
Nick & Nora	Strouse, Charles	1991	Nick Charles & Nora Charles	As Long As You're Happy	Uptempo	Bar/Alto			Duet	RLM/RLF
Nick & Nora	Strouse, Charles	1991	Victor Moisa	Class Reprise	Moderate Tempo	Baritone	B2	F#3	Lead	Romantic Antagonist Male
Nick & Nora	Strouse, Charles	1991	Nick Charles	Let' Go Home Nora	Ballad	Baritone	G3	B4	Lead	Romantic Lead Male
Nick & Nora	Strouse, Charles	1991	Nick Charles & Nora Charles	Married Life	Moderate Tempo	Bar/Alto			Duet	RLM/RLF
Nick & Nora	Strouse, Charles	1991	Nick Charles & Nora Charles	Is There Anything Better Than Dancing	Moderate Tempo	Bar/Alto			Duet	RLM/RLF
Nine	Yeston, Maury	1982	Ensemble	Overture Belle Donna	Moderate Tempo	SA			Ensemble	Adults
Nine	Yeston, Maury	1982	Ensemble	Not Since Chaplin	Uptempo	SA			Ensemble	Adults
Nine	Yeston, Maury	1982	Guido Contini	Guido's Song*	Uptempo	Tenor	G#2	F#4	Lead	Romantic Antagonist Male
Nine	Yeston, Maury	1982	Ensemble	Coda Di guido	Uptempo	SSAA			Ensemble	Adults
Nine	Yeston, Maury	1982	Luisa Contini	My Husband Makes Movies	Moderate Tempo	Alto	E♭3	C5	Lead	Romantic Lead Female
Nine	Yeston, Maury	1982	Carla Albanese	A Call From The Vatican	Moderate Tempo	Soprano	A3	C6	Lead	Romantic Lead Female

Shows

Songs by Character Type

* = Music Edit Required
+ = Ethnic Specific

Show	Composer	Year	Role	Song	Vocal Type	Range-Bottom	Range-Top	Tempo	Category	Character Type
Nine	Yeston, Maury	1982	Guido Contini	Only With You	Tenor	G#2	E4	Moderate Tempo	Lead	Romantic Antagonist Male
Nine	Yeston, Maury	1982	Ensemble	Folies Bergeres*	SSAA			Uptempo	Ensemble	Adults
Nine	Yeston, Maury	1982	Liliane & Stephanie	Folies Bergeres*	Alto/Alto			Uptempo	Duet	RLF/RLF
Nine	Yeston, Maury	1982	Stephanie Necrophorus	Folies Bergeres*	Alto	B3	B4	Uptempo	Supporting	Romantic Lead Female
Nine	Yeston, Maury	1982	Liliane La Fluer	Folies Bergeres*	Alto	G#3	B4	Uptempo	Supporting	Romantic Lead Female
Nine	Yeston, Maury	1982	Guido Contini	Script	Tenor	C3	F4	Uptempo	Lead	Romantic Antagonist Male
Nine	Yeston, Maury	1982	Ensemble	Nine	SA			Moderate Tempo	Ensemble	Adults
Nine	Yeston, Maury	1982	Ensemble	Ti Voglio Bene	SA			Moderate Tempo	Ensemble	Adults
Nine	Yeston, Maury	1982	Saraghina	Ti Voglio Bene*	Alto	G3	Bb4	Moderate Tempo	Lead	Romantic Antagonist Female
Nine	Yeston, Maury	1982	Ensemble	Be Italian #4	SSAA			Moderate Tempo	Ensemble	Adults
Nine	Yeston, Maury	1982	Ensemble	The Bells Of St. Sebastian	TSSAA			Moderate Tempo	Ensemble	Adults
Nine	Yeston, Maury	1982	Guido Contini	The Bells Of St. Sebastian*	Tenor	D4	G4	Moderate Tempo	Lead	Romantic Antagonist Male
Nine	Yeston, Maury	1982	Guido & Claudia	A Man Like You	Tenor/Sop			Moderate Tempo	Duet	RAM/RLF
Nine	Yeston, Maury	1982	Claudia Nardi	Unusual Way*	Soprano	G#3	E5	Ballad	Lead	Romantic Lead Female
Nine	Yeston, Maury	1982	Guido & Claudia	Unusual Way	Tenor/Sop			Ballad	Duet	RAM/RLF
Nine	Yeston, Maury	1982	Guido Contini	The Grand Canal*	Tenor	D#3	G4	Moderate Tempo	Lead	Romantic Antagonist Male
Nine	Yeston, Maury	1982	Ensemble	The Grand Canal	SSAT			Moderate Tempo	Ensemble	Adults
Nine	Yeston, Maury	1982	Carla Albanese	Simple	Soprano	A3	E5	Ballad	Lead	Romantic Lead Female
Nine	Yeston, Maury	1982	Luisa Contini	Be On Your Own	Alto	G#3	A4	Moderate Tempo	Lead	Romantic Lead Female
Nine	Yeston, Maury	1982	Guido Contini	I Can't Make This Movie	Tenor	G3	G4	Moderate Tempo	Lead	Romantic Antagonist Male
Nine	Yeston, Maury	1982	Young Guido Contini	Getting Tall	Soprano	Ab3	F5	Moderate Tempo	Supporting	Juvenile Male
Nine	Yeston, Maury	1982	Guido Contini	Long Ago Reprise	Tenor	Bb2	Bb3	Ballad	Lead	Romantic Antagonist Male
Nine	Yeston, Maury	1982	Guido Contini	Nine Reprise	Tenor	Bb2	G4	Ballad	Lead	Romantic Antagonist Male
Nine	Yeston, Maury	1982	Ensemble	Every Girl In Venice	SSA			Moderate Tempo	Ensemble	Adults
Nine	Yeston, Maury	1982	Guido Contini	Amour	Tenor/Sop	A2	Bb4	Uptempo	Lead	Romantic Antagonist Male
Nine	Yeston, Maury	1982	Ensemble	Only You	SAT			Moderate Tempo	Ensemble	Adults
Nine	Yeston, Maury	1982	Ensemble	Be Italian Finale	SSAA			Moderate Tempo	Ensemble	Adults
Nine	Yeston, Maury	1982	Ensemble	Wester Di Guido	SSAA			Uptempo	Ensemble	Adults
No, No Nanette	Youmans, Vincent	1925	Ensemble	Too Many Rings Around Rosie	TB			Uptempo	Ensemble	Adults
No, No Nanette	Youmans, Vincent	1925	Lucille Early	Too Many Rings Around Rosie*	Alto	B3	D5	Uptempo	Lead	Romantic Lead Female
No, No Nanette	Youmans, Vincent	1925	Tom Trainor	I've Confessed To The Breeze*	Tenor	D3	F4	Moderate Tempo	Lead	Ingenue Male
No, No Nanette	Youmans, Vincent	1925	Nanette	I've Confessed To The Breeze*	Soprano	B3	F5	Moderate Tempo	Lead	Ingenue Female
No, No Nanette	Youmans, Vincent	1925	Tom Trainor & Nanette	I've Confessed To The Breeze	Tenor/Sop			Moderate Tempo	Duet	IM/IF
No, No Nanette	Youmans, Vincent	1925	Bill Early	The Call Of TheSea*	Baritone	D3	F#4	Uptempo	Lead	Romantic Lead Male
No, No Nanette	Youmans, Vincent	1925	Jimmy Smith	I Want To Be Happy*	Baritone	C#3	F#4	Uptempo	Lead	Mature Male
No, No Nanette	Youmans, Vincent	1925	Nanette	I Want To Be Happy*	Soprano	C4	E5	Uptempo	Lead	Ingenue Female
No, No Nanette	Youmans, Vincent	1925	Jimmy Smith & Nanette	I Want To Be Happy*	Bar/Sop			Uptempo	Duet	MM/IF
No, No Nanette	Youmans, Vincent	1925	Ensemble	I Want To Be Happy*	TB			Uptempo	Ensemble	Adults
No, No Nanette	Youmans, Vincent	1925	Nanette	No, No Nanette*	Soprano	Bb3	F5	Uptempo	Lead	Ingenue Female
No, No Nanette	Youmans, Vincent	1925	Tom Trainor	No, No Nanette*	Tenor	C3	Eb4	Uptempo	Lead	Ingenue Male
No, No Nanette	Youmans, Vincent	1925	Ensemble	No, No Nanette*	SATB			Uptempo	Ensemble	Adults
No, No Nanette	Youmans, Vincent	1925	Nanette	Peach On The Beach*	Soprano	F#4	A4	Uptempo	Lead	Ingenue Female

Shows

* = Music Edit Required
+ = Ethnic Specific

Show	Composer	Year	Role	Song	Tempo	Vocal Type	Range-Bottom	Range-Top	Category	Character Type
No, No Nanette	Youmans, Vincent	1925	Ensemble	Peach On The Beach	Uptempo	SATB			Ensemble	Adults
No, No Nanette	Youmans, Vincent	1925	Flora Latham	The Three Happies*	Moderate Tempo	Alto	F4	Eb5	Supporting	Character Female
No, No Nanette	Youmans, Vincent	1925	Betty Brown	The Three Happies*	Moderate Tempo	Alto	A3	C5	Supporting	Character Female
No, No Nanette	Youmans, Vincent	1925	Winnie Winslow	The Three Happies*	Moderate Tempo	Soprano	C5	G5	Supporting	Character Female
No, No Nanette	Youmans, Vincent	1925	Tom Trainor	Tea For Two*	Moderate Tempo	Tenor	Eb3	F4	Lead	Ingenue Male
No, No Nanette	Youmans, Vincent	1925	Tom Trainor & Nanette	Tea For Two	Moderate Tempo	Tenor/Sop			Duet	IM/IF
No, No Nanette	Youmans, Vincent	1925	Nanette	Tea For Two*	Moderate Tempo	Soprano	Eb4	F5	Lead	Ingenue Female
No, No Nanette	Youmans, Vincent	1925	Lucille Early	You Can Dance With Any Girl At All*	Uptempo	Alto	A3	D5	Lead	Romantic Lead Female
No, No Nanette	Youmans, Vincent	1925	Bill Early	You Can Dance With Any Girl At All*	Uptempo	Baritone	C3	F4	Lead	Romantic Lead Male
No, No Nanette	Youmans, Vincent	1925	Lucille Early & Bill Early	You Can Dance With Any Girl At All	Uptempo	Alto/Bar			Duet	RLF/RLM
No, No Nanette	Youmans, Vincent	1925	Bill Early	Telephone Girlie*	Uptempo	Baritone	C3	F4	Lead	Romantic Lead Male
No, No Nanette	Youmans, Vincent	1925	Lucille Early	Where Has My Hubby Gone Blues*	Ballad	Alto	G3	D5	Lead	Romantic Lead Female
No, No Nanette	Youmans, Vincent	1925	Ensemble	Where Has My Hubby Gone Blues	Ballad	TB			Ensemble	Adults
No, No Nanette	Youmans, Vincent	1925	Tom Trainor	Waiting For You*	Moderate Tempo	Tenor	C3	Eb4	Lead	Ingenue Male
No, No Nanette	Youmans, Vincent	1925	Nanette	Waiting For You*	Moderate Tempo	Soprano	Ab3	Eb5	Lead	Ingenue Female
No, No Nanette	Youmans, Vincent	1925	Tom Trainor & Nanette	Waiting For You	Moderate Tempo	Tenor/Sop			Duet	IM/IF
No, No Nanette	Youmans, Vincent	1925	Sue Smith	Take A Little One Step*	Uptempo	Alto	G3	Cb5	Lead	Romantic Lead Female
No, No Nanette	Youmans, Vincent	1925	Ensemble	Take A Little One Step*	Uptempo	ATB			Ensemble	Adults
No, No Nanette	Youmans, Vincent	1925	Ensemble	Finale	Uptempo	SATB			Ensemble	Adults
No, No Nanette	Youmans, Vincent	1925	Ensemble	Bows and Exit	Moderate Tempo	SATB			Ensemble	Adults
Nunsense	Goggin, Dan	1985	Ensemble	Veni Creator Spititus	Ballad	Unison			Ensemble	Adults
Nunsense	Goggin, Dan	1985	Ensemble	Nunsense Is Habit-Forming	Uptempo	SA			Ensemble	Adults
Nunsense	Goggin, Dan	1985	Ensemble	A Difficult Transition	Uptempo	SA			Ensemble	Adults
Nunsense	Goggin, Dan	1985	Mary Leo	Benedicte*	Moderate Tempo	Alto	C4	G5	Lead	Ingenue Female
Nunsense	Goggin, Dan	1985	Mary Leo & Mary Hubert	The Biggest Ain't The Best	Uptempo	Alto/Alto			Duet	IF/AF
Nunsense	Goggin, Dan	1985	Mary Robert Anne	Playing Second Fiddle	Uptempo	Alto	B3	B4	Lead	Antagonist Female
Nunsense	Goggin, Dan	1985	Mary Amnesia	So You Want To Be A Nun	Moderate Tempo	Soprano	C4	B5	Lead	Character Female
Nunsense	Goggin, Dan	1985	Ensemble	One Last Hope	Uptempo	SA			Ensemble	Adults
Nunsense	Goggin, Dan	1985	Ensemble	Mock Fifties	Uptempo	SA			Ensemble	Adults
Nunsense	Goggin, Dan	1985	Ensemble	Lilac Bring Back Memories	Moderate Tempo	SA			Ensemble	Adults
Nunsense	Goggin, Dan	1985	Mary Hubert	Tackle That Temptation*	Uptempo	Alto	A3	D5	Lead	Antagonist Female
Nunsense	Goggin, Dan	1985	Ensemble	Tackle That Temptation	Uptempo	SA			Ensemble	Adults
Nunsense	Goggin, Dan	1985	Mary Robert Anne	Growing Up Catholic*	Ballad	Alto	Ab3	Db5	Lead	Antagonist Female
Nunsense	Goggin, Dan	1985	Ensemble	Growing Up Catholic	Ballad	SA			Ensemble	Adults
Nunsense	Goggin, Dan	1985	Mary Hubert & Mother Superior	We've Got To Clean Out The Freezer Just A Coupl'a Sisters	Uptempo	Alto/Alto			Duet	AF/MF
Nunsense	Goggin, Dan	1985	Mary Robert Anne	Second Fiddle Reprise	Uptempo	Alto	E4	B4	Lead	Antagonist Female
Nunsense	Goggin, Dan	1985	Mary Robert Anne	I Just Want To Be A Star*	Uptempo	Alto	G3	C5	Lead	Antagonist Female
Nunsense	Goggin, Dan	1985	Ensemble	The Drive In	Uptempo	SA			Ensemble	Adults
Nunsense	Goggin, Dan	1985	Mary Amnesia	I Could've Gone To Nashville	Ballad	Soprano	G3	E5	Lead	Character Female
Nunsense	Goggin, Dan	1985	Ensemble	Gloria In Excelsis Deo	Moderate Tempo	SA			Ensemble	Adults
Nunsense	Goggin, Dan	1985	Mary Hubert	Holier Than Thou*	Uptempo	Alto	Bb3	F5	Lead	Antagonist Female
Nunsense	Goggin, Dan	1985	Ensemble	Holier Than Thou	Uptempo	SA			Ensemble	Adults

Shows

Songs by Character Type

Show	Composer	Year	Role	Song	Tempo	Vocal Type	Range-Bottom	Range-Top	Category	Character Type
Nunsense	Goggin, Dan	1985	Ensemble	Nunsense Reprise	Uptempo	SA			Ensemble	Adults
Of Thee I Sing	Gershwin, George	1931	Ensemble	Wintergreen For President	Uptempo	SATB			Ensemble	Adults
Of Thee I Sing	Gershwin, George	1931	Ensemble	Who Is The Lucky Girl To Be	Uptempo	SA			Ensemble	Adults
Of Thee I Sing	Gershwin, George	1931	Ensemble	The Dimple On My Knee	Uptempo	SATB			Ensemble	Adults
Of Thee I Sing	Gershwin, George	1931	Ensemble	Because, Because	Uptempo	TB			Ensemble	Adults
Of Thee I Sing	Gershwin, George	1931	Ensemble	How Beautiful	Uptempo	SATB			Ensemble	Adults
Of Thee I Sing	Gershwin, George	1931	John P Wintergreen	Some Girls Can Bake A Pie*	Uptempo	Baritone	E3	F4	Lead	Romantic Lead Male
Of Thee I Sing	Gershwin, George	1931	Ensemble	Some Girls Can Bake A Pie	Uptempo	SATB			Ensemble	Adults
Of Thee I Sing	Gershwin, George	1931	Ensemble	Love Is Sweeping The Country	Uptempo	SATB			Ensemble	Adults
Of Thee I Sing	Gershwin, George	1931	John P Wintergreen	Of Thee I Sing*	Moderate Tempo	Baritone	C3	E4	Lead	Romantic Lead Male
Of Thee I Sing	Gershwin, George	1931	Mary Turner	Of Thee I Sing*	Moderate Tempo	Soprano	C4	E5	Lead	Romantic Lead Female
Of Thee I Sing	Gershwin, George	1931	Ensemble	Of The I Sing	Uptempo	SATB			Ensemble	Adults
Of Thee I Sing	Gershwin, George	1931	John P Wintergreen	Supreme Court Judges*	Uptempo	Baritone	B2	E4	Lead	Romantic Lead Male
Of Thee I Sing	Gershwin, George	1931	Ensemble	Supreme Court Judges	Uptempo	SATB			Ensemble	Adults
Of Thee I Sing	Gershwin, George	1931	Mary Turner	A Kiss For Cinderella*	Moderate Tempo	Soprano	Ab4	G5	Lead	Romantic Lead Female
Of Thee I Sing	Gershwin, George	1931	Diana Devereaux	The Most Beautiful Blossom	Ballad	Soprano	Eb4	F5	Lead	Romantic Antagonist Female
Of Thee I Sing	Gershwin, George	1931	Ensemble	Hello Good Morning	Uptempo	SATB			Ensemble	Adults
Of Thee I Sing	Gershwin, George	1931	Ensemble	Who Cares	Uptempo	SATB			Ensemble	Adults
Of Thee I Sing	Gershwin, George	1931	Wintergreen & Mary Turner	Who Cares*	Uptempo	Bar/Sop			Duet	RLM/RLF
Of Thee I Sing	Gershwin, George	1931	French Ambassador	The Illegitimate Daughter*	Uptempo	Tenor	C#3	G4	Lead	Antagonist Male
Of Thee I Sing	Gershwin, George	1931	Ensemble	The Illegitimate Daughter	Uptempo	SATB			Ensemble	Adults
Of Thee I Sing	Gershwin, George	1931	Diana Devereaux	Because Reprise*	Moderate Tempo	Soprano	E4	F5	Lead	Romantic Antagonist Female
Of Thee I Sing	Gershwin, George	1931	Mary Turner	Who Cares Reprise*	Moderate Tempo	Soprano	C4	E5	Lead	Romantic Lead Female
Of Thee I Sing	Gershwin, George	1931	John P Wintergreen	Who Cares Reprise*	Moderate Tempo	Baritone	C3	E4	Lead	Romantic Lead Male
Of Thee I Sing	Gershwin, George	1931	Wintergreen & Mary Turner	Who Cares Reprise	Moderate Tempo	Bar/Sop			Duet	RLM/RLF
Of Thee I Sing	Gershwin, George	1931	Alexander Throttlebottom	The Senator From Minesota*	Uptempo	Baritone	Eb3	F4	Lead	Character Male
Of Thee I Sing	Gershwin, George	1931	Ensemble	The Senator From Minesota	Uptempo	TB			Ensemble	Adults
Of Thee I Sing	Gershwin, George	1931	French Ambassador	Illegitimate Daughter Reprise*	Uptempo	Tenor	D3	D4	Lead	Antagonist Male
Of Thee I Sing	Gershwin, George	1931	Diana Devereaux	Jilted*	Moderate Tempo	Soprano	D4	F5	Lead	Romantic Antagonist Female
Of Thee I Sing	Gershwin, George	1931	Ensemble	Jilted	Moderate Tempo	SATB			Ensemble	Adults
Of Thee I Sing	Gershwin, George	1931	Mary Turner	I'm About To Be A Mother*	Uptempo	Soprano	B3	A5	Lead	Romantic Lead Female
Of Thee I Sing	Gershwin, George	1931	Ensemble	Posterity Is Just Around The Corner	Uptempo	SATB			Ensemble	Adults
Of Thee I Sing	Gershwin, George	1931	Ensemble	Trumpeter Blow Your Horn	Moderate Tempo	SATB			Ensemble	Adults
Of Thee I Sing	Gershwin, George	1931	Ensemble	Finale-Of Thee I Sing Reprise*	Moderate Tempo	SATB			Ensemble	Adults
Oklahoma!	Rodgers, Richard	1943	Curly	Oh What A Beautiful Morning	Uptempo	Baritone	D3	E4	Lead	Romantic Lead Male
Oklahoma!	Rodgers, Richard	1943	Curly	The Surrey With The Fringe On Top	Uptempo	Baritone	D#3	E4	Lead	Romantic Lead Male
Oklahoma!	Rodgers, Richard	1943	Will Parker	Kansas City	Uptempo	Baritone	Eb3	F4	Lead	Character Ingenue Male
Oklahoma!	Rodgers, Richard	1943	Ado Annie Carnes	I Cain't Say No	Moderate Tempo	Alto	C4	D5	Lead	Character Ingenue Female
Oklahoma!	Rodgers, Richard	1943	Laurey	Many A New Day	Uptempo	Soprano	C#4	E5	Lead	Character Ingenue Female
Oklahoma!	Rodgers, Richard	1943	Curly & Laurey	People Will Say We're In Love	Moderate Tempo	Bar/Sop			Duet	RLM/CIF
Oklahoma!	Rodgers, Richard	1943	Curly & Jud Fry	Poor Jud	Moderate Tempo	Bar/Bar			Duet	RLM/AM
Oklahoma!	Rodgers, Richard	1943	Jud Fry	Lonley Room	Ballad	Baritone	D3	C4	Lead	Antagonist Male
Oklahoma!	Rodgers, Richard	1943	Curly	People Will Say We're In Love	Moderate Tempo	Baritone	C#3	F#4	Lead	Romantic Lead Male
Oklahoma!	Rodgers, Richard	1943	Laurey	People Will Say We're In Love	Moderate Tempo	Soprano	C#4	F#5	Lead	Character Ingenue Female

Shows

Songs by Character Type

* = Music Edit Required
+ = Ethnic Specific

Show	Composer	Year	Role	Song	Vocal Type	Range-Bottom	Range-Top	Category	Character Type
Oklahoma!	Rodgers, Richard	1943	Curly	Poor Jud*	Baritone	D#3	C#4	Lead	Romantic Lead Male
Oklahoma!	Rodgers, Richard	1943	Jud Fry	Poor Jud*	Baritone	D#3	C#4	Lead	Antagonist Male
Oklahoma!	Rodgers, Richard	1943	Ensemble	Out Of My Dreams	SA			Ensemble	Adults
Oklahoma!	Rodgers, Richard	1943	Will & Ado Annie	All 'Er Nothin'	Bar/Alto			Duet	CIM/CIf
Oklahoma!	Rodgers, Richard	1943	Curly & Laurey	People Will Say Reprise	Bar/Sop			Duet	RLM/CIf
Oklahoma!	Rodgers, Richard	1943	Ado Annie Carnes	I Cain't Say No Reprise	Alto	C4	D5	Lead	Character Ingenue Female
Oklahoma!	Rodgers, Richard	1943	Ensemble	Many A New Day	SA			Ensemble	Adults
Oklahoma!	Rodgers, Richard	1943	Ali Hakim	It's A Scandal! It's A Outrage	Baritone	B2	F#4	Lead	Character Male
Oklahoma!	Rodgers, Richard	1943	Laurey	Out Of My Dreams	Soprano	E4	F5	Lead	Character Ingenue Female
Oklahoma!	Rodgers, Richard	1943	Old Man Carnes	The Farmer And The Cowman*	Baritone	F3	F4	Supporting	Mature Male
Oklahoma!	Rodgers, Richard	1943	Ensemble	The Farmer And The Cowman	SATB Unison			Ensemble	Adults
Oklahoma!	Rodgers, Richard	1943	Ensemble	Oklahoma	SATB			Ensemble	Adults
Oklahoma!	Rodgers, Richard	1943	Ensemble	Oklahoma Encore	SATB			Ensemble	Adults
Oklahoma!	Rodgers, Richard	1943	Ensemble	Finale Ultimo	SATB Unison			Ensemble	Adults
Oliver!	Bart, Lionel	1963	Ensemble	Food Glorious Food	SAA			Ensemble	Children
Oliver!	Bart, Lionel	1963	Ensemble	Oliver	SATB			Ensemble	Adults
Oliver!	Bart, Lionel	1963	Nancy	I Shall Scream	Bar/Alto			Duet	CM/AF
Oliver!	Bart, Lionel	1963	Mr. Bumble & Widow Corney	Boy For Sale	Baritone	C3	G4	Lead	Character Male
Oliver!	Bart, Lionel	1963	Mr. Bumble	That's Your Funeral*	Bar/Alto			Duet	AM/AF
Oliver!	Bart, Lionel	1963	Mr. & Mrs. Sowerbery	Where Is Love	Soprano	C4	C5	Lead	Juvenile Male
Oliver!	Bart, Lionel	1963	Oliver Twist	Consider Yourself (Part One)*	Alto	A3	F5	Lead	Juvenile Male
Oliver!	Bart, Lionel	1963	Artful Dodger	Consider Yourself (Part One)	SATB			Ensemble	Children/Teens/Adults
Oliver!	Bart, Lionel	1963	Ensemble	Pick A Pocket Or Two	Baritone	D3	Eb4	Lead	Mature Male
Oliver!	Bart, Lionel	1963	Fagin	It's A Fine Life*	Alto	Ab3	D5	Lead	Antagonist Female
Oliver!	Bart, Lionel	1963	Nancy	I'd Do Anything	SA			Ensemble	Children/Teens/Adults
Oliver!	Bart, Lionel	1963	Ensemble	Be Back Soon	SA			Ensemble	Children/Teens/Adults
Oliver!	Bart, Lionel	1963	Ensemble	Be Back Soon*	Baritone	C3	E4	Lead	Mature Male
Oliver!	Bart, Lionel	1963	Fagin	Oom-Pah-Pah*	Alto	B3	C#5	Lead	Antagonist Female
Oliver!	Bart, Lionel	1963	Ensemble	Oom-Pah-Pah	SATB			Ensemble	Adults
Oliver!	Bart, Lionel	1963	Ensemble	My Name	Baritone	C#3	C4	Lead	Antagonist Male
Oliver!	Bart, Lionel	1963	Bill Sykes	As Long As He Needs Me	Alto	F#3	C#5	Lead	Antagonist Female
Oliver!	Bart, Lionel	1963	Nancy	Where Is Love Reprise	Alto	C#4	Bb4	Supporting	Mature Female
Oliver!	Bart, Lionel	1963	Mrs. Bedwin	Who Will Buy*	Soprano	C4	C5	Lead	Juvenile Male
Oliver!	Bart, Lionel	1963	Oliver Twist	Who Will Buy	SSAB			Ensemble	Children/Adults
Oliver!	Bart, Lionel	1963	Ensemble	Who Will Buy Part Two	SATB			Ensemble	Adults
Oliver!	Bart, Lionel	1963	Ensemble	It's A Fine Life Reprise	AABB			Ensemble	Adults
Oliver!	Bart, Lionel	1963	Ensemble	Reviewing The Situation	Baritone	C3	F4	Lead	Mature Male
Oliver!	Bart, Lionel	1963	Fagin	Oliver Reprise	Bar/Alto			Duet	CM/AF
Oliver!	Bart, Lionel	1963	Mr. Bumble & Widow Corney	As Long As He Needs Me Reprise	Alto	G#3	C#5	Lead	Antagonist Female
Oliver!	Bart, Lionel	1963	Nancy	Reviewing the Situation Reprise	Baritone	C4	Eb5	Lead	Antagonist Male
Oliver!	Bart, Lionel	1963	Fagin	Bows-Consider Yourself	SATB			Ensemble	Children/Teens/Adults
On The Town	Bernstein, Leonard	1944	Chip	Ya Got Me *	Tenor	E3	Gb4	Lead	Character Ingenue Male
On The Town	Bernstein, Leonard	1944	Claire DeLune	Carried Away	Soprano	F3	G5	Lead	Character Ingenue Female

Shows

* = Music Edit Required
+ = Ethnic Specific

Show	Composer	Year	Role	Song	Tempo	Vocal Type	Range-Bottom	Range-Top	Category	Character Type
On The Town	Bernstein, Leonard	1944	Claire DeLune	Ya Got Me *	Uptempo	Soprano	G3	Eb4	Lead	Character Ingenue Female
On The Town	Bernstein, Leonard	1944	Diana Dream	I Wish I Was Dead	Uptempo	Alto	C4	Db4	Featured Ensemble	Character Female
On The Town	Bernstein, Leonard	1944	Gabey	Lonely Town	Ballad	Tenor	C4	F5	Lead	Romantic Lead Male
On The Town	Bernstein, Leonard	1944	Gabey	Lucky To Be Me	Uptempo	Tenor	B2	A4	Lead	Romantic Lead Male
On The Town	Bernstein, Leonard	1944	Hildy	I Can Cook Too	Uptempo	Alto	A3	G#5	Lead	Character Female
On The Town	Bernstein, Leonard	1944	Hildy	Ya Got Me *	Uptempo	Alto	F3	Db5	Lead	Character Female
On The Town	Bernstein, Leonard	1944	Ozzie	Carried Away	Uptempo	Baritone	E2	F4	Lead	Character Ingenue Male
On The Town	Bernstein, Leonard	1944	Ozzie	Ya Got Me *	Uptempo	Baritone	Eb3	Fb4	Lead	Character Male
On The Town	Bernstein, Leonard	1944	Pitkin Bridgework	I Understand	Uptempo	Baritone	A2	D4	Supporting	Mature Male
On The Town	Bernstein, Leonard	1944	Chip & Hildy	Come Up To My Place	Uptempo	Tenor/Alto			Duet	CIM/CF
On The Town	Bernstein, Leonard	1944	Ensemble	Stranded*	Ballad	SATB			Ensemble	Adults
On The Twentieth Century	Coleman, Cy	1978	Owen O'Malley & Oliver Webb	Saddle Up*	Uptempo	Tenor/Bar			Duet	CM/CM
On The Twentieth Century	Coleman, Cy	1978	Ensemble	On The Twentieth Century*	Uptempo	SATB			Ensemble	Adults
On The Twentieth Century	Coleman, Cy	1978	Oscar Jaffe	I Rise Again*	Moderate Tempo	Baritone	B2	E4	Lead	Romantic Antagonist Male
On The Twentieth Century	Coleman, Cy	1978	Imelda & Mildred	Indian Maiden's Lament	Moderate Tempo	Sop/Sop			Duet	RLF/RLF
On The Twentieth Century	Coleman, Cy	1978	Lily Garland	Veronique	Uptempo	Soprano	E3	Ab6	Lead	Romantic Lead Female
On The Twentieth Century	Coleman, Cy	1978	Conductor Flanagan	I Have Written A Play	Moderate Tempo	Baritone	C3	F4	Supporting	Character Male
On The Twentieth Century	Coleman, Cy	1978	Oscar Jaffe	Together*	Uptempo	Baritone	C3	E4	Lead	Romantic Antagonist Male
On The Twentieth Century	Coleman, Cy	1978	Ensemble	Together	Uptempo	SATB			Ensemble	Adults
On The Twentieth Century	Coleman, Cy	1978	Lily Garland	Never*	Uptempo	Soprano	A3	A5	Lead	Romantic Lead Female
On The Twentieth Century	Coleman, Cy	1978	Oscar Jaffe	Our Private World*	Ballad	Baritone	A2	E4	Lead	Romantic Antagonist Male
On The Twentieth Century	Coleman, Cy	1978	Lily Garland	Our Private World*	Ballad	Soprano	A3	E5	Lead	Romantic Lead Female
On The Twentieth Century	Coleman, Cy	1978	Oscar Jaffe & Lily Garland	Our Private World	Ballad	Bar/Sop			Duet	RAM/RLF
On The Twentieth Century	Coleman, Cy	1978	Letitia Primrose	Repent	Uptempo	Alto	C4	F#5	Lead	Mature Female
On The Twentieth Century	Coleman, Cy	1978	Oscar Jaffe & Bruce Granit	Mine	Uptempo	Bar/Tenor			Duet	RAM/RLM
On The Twentieth Century	Coleman, Cy	1978	Lily Garland	I've Got It All*	Moderate Tempo	Soprano	B3	A5	Lead	Romantic Lead Female
On The Twentieth Century	Coleman, Cy	1978	Oscar Jaffe	I've Got It All*	Moderate Tempo	Baritone	B2	E5	Lead	Romantic Antagonist Male
On The Twentieth Century	Coleman, Cy	1978	Oscar Jaffe & Lily Garland	I've Got It All	Moderate Tempo	Bar/Sop			Duet	RAM/RLF
On The Twentieth Century	Coleman, Cy	1978	Ensemble	End Act I-On The Twentieth Century	Uptempo	SATB			Ensemble	Adults
On The Twentieth Century	Coleman, Cy	1978	Congressman	I Have Written A Play	Moderate Tempo	Baritone	C3	F4	Supporting	Character Male
On The Twentieth Century	Coleman, Cy	1978	Ensemble	Life Is Like A Train	Moderate Tempo	TB			Ensemble	Adults
On The Twentieth Century	Coleman, Cy	1978	Oscar Jaffe	Five Zeros*	Moderate Tempo	Baritone	Ab2	Ab4	Lead	Romantic Antagonist Male
On The Twentieth Century	Coleman, Cy	1978	Owen O'Malley	Five Zeros*	Moderate Tempo	Tenor	Ab2	Ab4	Lead	Character Male
On The Twentieth Century	Coleman, Cy	1978	Letitia Primrose	Five Zeros*	Moderate Tempo	Alto	Ab3	Eb5	Lead	Mature Female
On The Twentieth Century	Coleman, Cy	1978	Ensemble	Five Zeros	Moderate Tempo	ATB			Ensemble	Adults
On The Twentieth Century	Coleman, Cy	1978	Doctor	I Have Written A Play	Moderate Tempo	Baritone	Bb3	Eb5	Supporting	Character Male
On The Twentieth Century	Coleman, Cy	1978	Lily Garland	Sign Lily Sign*	Moderate Tempo	Soprano	B3	A5	Lead	Romantic Lead Female
On The Twentieth Century	Coleman, Cy	1978	Ensemble	Sign Lily Sign	Moderate Tempo	SATB			Ensemble	Adults
On The Twentieth Century	Coleman, Cy	1978	Ensemble	She's A Nut	Moderate Tempo	SATB			Ensemble	Adults
On The Twentieth Century	Coleman, Cy	1978	Max Jacobs	Max Jacobs	Uptempo	Baritone	Bb2	F4	Lead	Antagonist Male
On The Twentieth Century	Coleman, Cy	1978	Lily Garland	Babette	Uptempo	Soprano	F#3	F#5	Lead	Romantic Lead Female
On The Twentieth Century	Coleman, Cy	1978	Oscar Jaffe	Last Will And Testament	Moderate Tempo	Baritone	B2	F4	Lead	Romantic Antagonist Male
On The Twentieth Century	Coleman, Cy	1978	Oscar Jaffe	Because Of Her	Moderate Tempo	Baritone	B2	F4	Lead	Romantic Antagonist Male

Shows

Songs by Character Type

* = Music Edit Required
+ = Ethnic Specific

Show	Composer	Year	Role	Song	Tempo	Vocal Type	Range-Bottom	Range-Top	Category	Character Type
On The Twentieth Century	Coleman, Cy	1978	Ensemble	Finale Part II-On The Twentieth Century		SATB			Ensemble	Adults
Once On This Island	Flaherty, Stephen	1990	Ensemble+	Prologue-We Dance	Uptempo	SATB			Ensemble	Adults
Once On This Island	Flaherty, Stephen	1990	Ensemble+	One Small Girl	Moderate Tempo	SATB			Ensemble	Adults
Once On This Island	Flaherty, Stephen	1990	Mama Euralie+	Come Down From The Tree	Moderate Tempo	Alto	A3	E5	Lead	Mature Female
Once On This Island	Flaherty, Stephen	1990	Ti Moune+	Waiting For Life	Uptempo	Alto	C#4	E5	Lead	Ingenue Female
Once On This Island	Flaherty, Stephen	1990	Ensemble+	And The Gods Heard Her Prayer	Uptempo	SATB			Ensemble	Adults
Once On This Island	Flaherty, Stephen	1990	Agwe+	Rain*	Uptempo	Baritone	C#3	E4	Lead	Romantic Antagonist Male
Once On This Island	Flaherty, Stephen	1990	Ensemble+	Pray	Uptempo	SATB			Ensemble	Adults
Once On This Island	Flaherty, Stephen	1990	Ti Moune+	Forever Yours*	Ballad	Alto	A#3	C#5	Lead	Ingenue Female
Once On This Island	Flaherty, Stephen	1990	Daniel+	Forever Yours*	Ballad	Baritone	E#3	F#4	Lead	Ingenue Male
Once On This Island	Flaherty, Stephen	1990	Papa Ge+	Forever Yours*	Uptempo	Tenor	C#3	G4	Ensemble	Antagonist Male
Once On This Island	Flaherty, Stephen	1990	Ensemble+	The Sad Tale Of The Beauxhommes	Moderate Tempo	SATB			Lead	Adults
Once On This Island	Flaherty, Stephen	1990	Mama Euralie+	Ti Moune*	Ballad	Alto	Gb3	Bb4	Lead	Maternal
Once On This Island	Flaherty, Stephen	1990	Tonton Julian+	Ti Moune*	Ballad	Baritone	G2	Eb4	Lead	Paternal
Once On This Island	Flaherty, Stephen	1990	Ti Moune+	Ti Moune*	Ballad	Alto	G3	C5	Lead	Ingenue Female
Once On This Island	Flaherty, Stephen	1990	Ensemble+	Mama Will Provide*	Uptempo	AAB			Ensemble	Adults
Once On This Island	Flaherty, Stephen	1990	Asaka+	Mama Will Provide*	Uptempo	Alto	B3	G5	Lead	Character Female
Once On This Island	Flaherty, Stephen	1990	Ti Moune+	Waiting For Life Reprise	Uptempo	Alto	B3	C#5	Lead	Ingenue Female
Once On This Island	Flaherty, Stephen	1990	Ensemble+	Some Say	Ballad	SATB			Ensemble	Adults
Once On This Island	Flaherty, Stephen	1990	Erzulie+	Human Heart*	Ballad	Alto	B3	C#5	Lead	Romantic Lead Female
Once On This Island	Flaherty, Stephen	1990	Ensemble+	Pray Reprise	Uptempo	SATB			Ensemble	Adults
Once On This Island	Flaherty, Stephen	1990	Daniel+	Some Girls	Moderate Tempo	Baritone	B2	F#4	Lead	Ingenue Male
Once On This Island	Flaherty, Stephen	1990	Andrea+	Andrea Sequence*	Moderate Tempo	Alto	Bb3	C5	Lead	Romantic Lead Female
Once On This Island	Flaherty, Stephen	1990	Papa Ge+	Promises/Forever Yours Reprise*	Moderate Tempo	Tenor	C3	G4	Lead	Antagonist Male
Once On This Island	Flaherty, Stephen	1990	Ensemble+	A Part Of Us	Ballad	SATB			Ensemble	Adults
Once On This Island	Flaherty, Stephen	1990	Ensemble+	Why We Tell The Story	Uptempo	SATB			Ensemble	Adults
Once Upon A Mattress	Rodgers, Mary	1959	Minstrel	Many Moons Ago	Moderate Tempo	Tenor	D3	G4	Lead	Romantic Lead Male
Once Upon A Mattress	Rodgers, Mary	1959	Ensemble	Opening For A Princess	Uptempo	SATB			Ensemble	Adults
Once Upon A Mattress	Rodgers, Mary	1959	Sir Harry	In A Little While*	Uptempo	Baritone	Db3	F4	Lead	Romantic Lead Male
Once Upon A Mattress	Rodgers, Mary	1959	Lady Larken	In A Little While*	Uptempo	Soprano	Db4	Eb5	Lead	Romantic Lead Female
Once Upon A Mattress	Rodgers, Mary	1959	Sir Harry & Lady Larken	In A Little While	Ballad	Bar/Sop			Duet	RLM/RLF
Once Upon A Mattress	Rodgers, Mary	1959	Sir Harry	In A Little While Reprise*	Ballad	Baritone	D3	F4	Lead	Romantic Lead Male
Once Upon A Mattress	Rodgers, Mary	1959	Lady Larken	In A Little While Reprise*	Ballad	Soprano	D4	F5	Lead	Romantic Lead Female
Once Upon A Mattress	Rodgers, Mary	1959	Sir Harry & Lady Larken	In A Little While Reprise	Ballad	Bar/Sop			Duet	RLM/RLF
Once Upon A Mattress	Rodgers, Mary	1959	Princess Winifred	Shy*	Uptempo	Alto	B3	C5	Lead	Character Female
Once Upon A Mattress	Rodgers, Mary	1959	Minstrel & Jester & King	The Minstrel, The Jester and I	Uptempo	TTB			Ensemble	Adults
Once Upon A Mattress	Rodgers, Mary	1959	Queen Aggravain	Sensitivity*	Moderate Tempo	Alto	A3	B4	Lead	Romantic Antagonist Female
Once Upon A Mattress	Rodgers, Mary	1959	Minstrel	Normandy*	Uptempo	Tenor	D#3	B4	Lead	Romantic Antagonist Male
Once Upon A Mattress	Rodgers, Mary	1959	Jester	Normandy*	Uptempo	Tenor	D#3	B4	Lead	Character Male
Once Upon A Mattress	Rodgers, Mary	1959	Minstrel & Jester	Normancy	Uptempo	Tenor/Tenor			Duet	RAM/CM
Once Upon A Mattress	Rodgers, Mary	1959	Prince Dauntless	Song Of Love*	Uptempo	Baritone	C#3	Eb4	Lead	Character Ingenue Male
Once Upon A Mattress	Rodgers, Mary	1959	Dauntless & Winifred	Song of Love	Uptempo	Bar/Alto			Duet	CIM/CIF
Once Upon A Mattress	Rodgers, Mary	1959	Princess Winifred	Happily Ever After	Moderate Tempo	Alto	A3	Cb5	Lead	Character Ingenue Female

Shows

448

Songs by Character Type

* = Music Edit Required
+ = Ethnic Specific

Show	Composer	Year	Role	Song	Tempo	Vocal Type	Range-Bottom	Range-Top	Category	Character Type
Once Upon A Mattress	Rodgers, Mary	1959	Sextimus & Dauntless	Man To Man Talk	Uptempo	Bar/Mute	D3		Duet	CIF/MM
Once Upon A Mattress	Rodgers, Mary	1959	Jester	Very Soft Shoes*	Moderate Tempo	Tenor	F3	F4	Lead	Character Male
Once Upon A Mattress	Rodgers, Mary	1959	Sir Harry	Yesterday I Loved You*	Uptempo	Baritone	E4	F4	Lead	Romantic Lead Male
Once Upon A Mattress	Rodgers, Mary	1959	Lady Larken	Yesterday I Loved You*	Uptempo	Soprano		F5	Lead	Romantic Lead Female
Once Upon A Mattress	Rodgers, Mary	1959	Ensemble	Finale		SATB			Ensemble	Adults
Once Upon A Mattress	Rodgers, Mary	1959	Nightingale	Nightingale Lullaby	Moderate Tempo	Soprano	Gb4	G5	Supporting	Character Ingenue Female
Pacific Overtures	Sondheim, Stephen	1976	Female	Prologue	Ballad	Alto	D3		Lead	Character Female
Pacific Overtures	Sondheim, Stephen	1976	Male	Prologue	Ballad	Baritone	D2	Bb3	Lead	Character Male
Pacific Overtures	Sondheim, Stephen	1976	Reciter+	The Advantages Of Floating...*	Uptempo	Baritone	B2	E4	Lead	Character Male
Pacific Overtures	Sondheim, Stephen	1976	Ensemble	The Advantages Of Floating...		SATB			Ensemble	Adults
Pacific Overtures	Sondheim, Stephen	1976	Observer 1 & Observer 2+	There Is No Other Way	Ballad	Tenor/Bar			Duet	CM/CM
Pacific Overtures	Sondheim, Stephen	1976	Fisherman+	Four Black Dragons*	Uptempo	Tenor	Eb3	Gb4	Supporting	Character Male
Pacific Overtures	Sondheim, Stephen	1976	Thief+	Four Black Dragons*	Uptempo	Baritone	B2	C#4	Supporting	Antagonist Male
Pacific Overtures	Sondheim, Stephen	1976	Ensemble	Four Black Dragons	Uptempo	TB			Ensemble	Antagonist Male
Pacific Overtures	Sondheim, Stephen	1976	Mother+	Chrysanthemum Tea*	Moderate Tempo	Tenor	D3	F4	Lead	Character Male
Pacific Overtures	Sondheim, Stephen	1976	Soothsayer+	Chrysanthemum Tea*	Moderate Tempo	Baritone	F2	D4	Lead	Character Male
Pacific Overtures	Sondheim, Stephen	1976	Priest 1 & Priest 2+	Chrysanthemum Tea*	Moderate Tempo	Tenor/Tenor			Duet	CM/CM
Pacific Overtures	Sondheim, Stephen	1976	Ensemble+	Chrysanthemum Tea	Moderate Tempo	TB			Ensemble	Adults
Pacific Overtures	Sondheim, Stephen	1976	Kayama+	Poems*	Moderate Tempo	Tenor	Eb3	F4	Lead	Romantic Lead Male
Pacific Overtures	Sondheim, Stephen	1976	Manjiro+	Poems*	Moderate Tempo	Baritone	Eb3	F4	Lead	Character Male
Pacific Overtures	Sondheim, Stephen	1976	Kayama+ & Majiro+	Poems	Moderate Tempo	Tenor/Bar			Duet	RLM/CM
Pacific Overtures	Sondheim, Stephen	1976	Madam+	Welcome to Kanagawa*	Uptempo	Tenor	C3	E4	Lead	Romantic Antagonist Male
Pacific Overtures	Sondheim, Stephen	1976	Ensemble+	Someone In A Tree	Uptempo	TB			Ensemble	Adults
Pacific Overtures	Sondheim, Stephen	1976	Ensemble	Please Hello	Uptempo	TB			Ensemble	Adults
Pacific Overtures	Sondheim, Stephen	1976	Kayama+	A Bowler Hat	Moderate Tempo	Tenor	G2	Eb4	Lead	Romantic Lead Male
Pacific Overtures	Sondheim, Stephen	1976	Ensemble+	Pretty Lady	Moderate Tempo	TTB			Ensemble	Adults
Pacific Overtures	Sondheim, Stephen	1976	Ensemble	Next Part	Uptempo	SATB			Ensemble	Adults
Pajama Game	Adler, Richard	1954	Hines	The Pajama Game	Uptempo	Baritone	Db3	F4	Lead	Character Male
Pajama Game	Adler, Richard	1954	Ensemble	Racing With The Clock	Uptempo	SATB			Ensemble	Adults
Pajama Game	Adler, Richard	1954	Sid Sorokin	A New Town Is A Blue Town	Ballad	Tenor	Db3	G4	Lead	Romantic Lead Male
Pajama Game	Adler, Richard	1954	Ensemble	Racing With The Clock Reprise	Moderate Tempo	SA Unison			Ensemble	Adults
Pajama Game	Adler, Richard	1954	Babe Williams	I'm Not At All In Love*	Uptempo	Alto	A3	B4	Lead	Romantic Lead Female
Pajama Game	Adler, Richard	1954	Ensemble	I'm Not At All In Love	Uptempo	SA			Ensemble	Adults
Pajama Game	Adler, Richard	1954	Hines & Mabel	I'll Never Be Jealous Again	Uptempo	Bar/Alto			Duet	CM/CF
Pajama Game	Adler, Richard	1954	Sid Sorokin	Hey There*	Ballad	Tenor	F3	Ab4	Lead	Romantic Lead Male
Pajama Game	Adler, Richard	1954	Prez	Her Is*	Uptempo	Baritone	Db3	F4	Lead	Romantic Antagonist Male
Pajama Game	Adler, Richard	1954	Ensemble	Sleep Tite	Moderate Tempo	SATB			Ensemble	Adults
Pajama Game	Adler, Richard	1954	Sid Sorokin	Once-A-Year Day*	Uptempo	Tenor	E3	F4	Lead	Romantic Lead Male
Pajama Game	Adler, Richard	1954	Ensemble	Once-A-Year Day	Uptempo	SATB			Ensemble	Adults
Pajama Game	Adler, Richard	1954	Prez	Her Is Reprise*	Uptempo	Baritone	Ab2	F4	Lead	Romantic Antagonist Male
Pajama Game	Adler, Richard	1954	Sid Sorokin	Small Talk*	Uptempo	Tenor	Db3	Gb4	Lead	Romantic Lead Male
Pajama Game	Adler, Richard	1954	Sid & Babe	Small Talk	Uptempo	Tenor/Alto			Duet	RLM/RLF

Shows

449

Songs by Character Type

Show	Composer	Year	Role	Song	Tempo	Vocal Type	Range-Bottom	Range-Top	Category	Character Type
Pajama Game	Adler, Richard	1954	Sid Sorokin	There Once Was A Man*	Uptempo	Tenor	C#3	Gb4	Lead	Romantic Lead Male
Pajama Game	Adler, Richard	1954	Babe Williams	There Once Was A Man*	Uptempo	Alto	Bb3	Eb5	Lead	Romantic Lead Female
Pajama Game	Adler, Richard	1954	Sid & Babe	There Once Was A Man	Uptempo	Tenor/Alto			Duet	RLM/RLF
Pajama Game	Adler, Richard	1954	Sid Sorokin	Hey There-Finale Act I	Ballad	Tenor	F3	Gb4	Lead	Romantic Lead Male
Pajama Game	Adler, Richard	1954	Gladys	Steam Heat*	Uptempo	Alto	C4	Eb5	Lead	Romantic Antagonist Female
Pajama Game	Adler, Richard	1954	Ensemble	Steam Heat	Uptempo	ATB			Ensemble	Adults
Pajama Game	Adler, Richard	1954	Babe Williams	Hey There Reprise	Ballad	Alto	A#3	Bb4	Lead	Romantic Lead Female
Pajama Game	Adler, Richard	1954	Hines	Think Of The Time I Save	Uptempo	Baritone	C3	D4	Lead	Character Male
Pajama Game	Adler, Richard	1954	Gladys	Hernando's Hideaway	Moderate Tempo	Alto	B3	C5	Lead	Romantic Antagonist Female
Pajama Game	Adler, Richard	1954	Prez	Seven And A Half Cents*	Uptempo	Baritone	D3	E4	Lead	Romantic Antagonist Male
Pajama Game	Adler, Richard	1954	Babe Williams	Seven And A Half Cents*	Uptempo	Alto	A3	D5	Lead	Romantic Lead Female
Pajama Game	Adler, Richard	1954	Ensemble	Seven And A Half Cents	Uptempo	Bar/Alto			Duet	RAM/RLF
Pajama Game	Adler, Richard	1954	Sid & Babe	There Once Was A Man Reprise	Uptempo	Tenor/Alto			Duet	RLM/RLF
Pajama Game	Adler, Richard	1954	Ensemble	The Pajama Game Closing	Uptempo	SATB			Ensemble	Adults
Pal Joey	Hart, Lorenz & Rodgers	1940	Joey Evans	A Great Big Town	Uptempo	Baritone	Eb3	F4	Lead	Romantic Antagonist Male
Pal Joey	Hart, Lorenz & Rodgers	1940	Joey Evans	You Mustn't Kick It Around	Uptempo	Baritone	D3	F4	Lead	Romantic Antagonist Male
Pal Joey	Hart, Lorenz & Rodgers	1940	Gladys Bumps	You Mustn't Kick It Around Encore	Uptempo	Alto	A3	C5	Lead	Romantic Antagonist Female
Pal Joey	Hart, Lorenz & Rodgers	1940	Joey Evans	I Could Write A Book*	Moderate Tempo	Baritone	Eb3	Eb4	Lead	Romantic Antagonist Male
Pal Joey	Hart, Lorenz & Rodgers	1940	Linda English	I Could Write A Book*	Moderate Tempo	Alto	D4	D5	Lead	Ingenue Female
Pal Joey	Hart, Lorenz & Rodgers	1940	Joey & Linda	I Could Write A Book	Uptempo	Bar/Alto			Duet	RAM/IF
Pal Joey	Hart, Lorenz & Rodgers	1940	Ensemble	A Great Bit Town Reprise	Uptempo	SA			Ensemble	Adults
Pal Joey	Hart, Lorenz & Rodgers	1940	Gladys Bumps	That Terrific Rainbow	Moderate Tempo	Alto	B3	Bb4	Lead	Romantic Antagonist Female
Pal Joey	Hart, Lorenz & Rodgers	1940	Vera Simpson	What Is A Man	Moderate Tempo	Alto	D4	Eb5	Lead	Romantic Antagonist Female
Pal Joey	Hart, Lorenz & Rodgers	1940	Joey Evans	Happy Hunting Horn	Moderate Tempo	Baritone	Ab3	F4	Lead	Romantic Antagonist Male
Pal Joey	Hart, Lorenz & Rodgers	1940	Vera Simpson	Bewitched Bothered And Bewildered	Moderate Tempo	Alto	E4	D5	Lead	Romantic Antagonist Female
Pal Joey	Hart, Lorenz & Rodgers	1940	Vera Simpson	Bewitched...Encore	Moderate Tempo	Alto	F4	D5	Lead	Romantic Antagonist Female
Pal Joey	Hart, Lorenz & Rodgers	1940	Joey Evans	What Do I Care For A Dame	Uptempo	Baritone	D3	C#4	Duet	Romantic Antagonist Male
Pal Joey	Hart, Lorenz & Rodgers	1940	Louis	The Flower Garden Of My Heart*	Moderate Tempo	Tenor	Eb3	G4	Featured Ensemble	Character Male
Pal Joey	Hart, Lorenz & Rodgers	1940	Gladys Bumps	The Flower Garden Of My Heart*	Moderate Tempo	Alto	D4	F#5	Lead	Romantic Antagonist Female
Pal Joey	Hart, Lorenz & Rodgers	1940	Louis & Gladys	The Flower Garden Of My Heart	Moderate Tempo	Tenor/Alto			Duet	CM/RAF
Pal Joey	Hart, Lorenz & Rodgers	1940	Melba	Zip	Moderate Tempo	Alto	F3	G4	Supporting	Romantic Antagonist Female
Pal Joey	Hart, Lorenz & Rodgers	1940	Gladys Bumps	Plant You Now, Dig You Later	Uptempo	Alto	D4	D5	Lead	Romantic Antagonist Female
Pal Joey	Hart, Lorenz & Rodgers	1940	Vera Simpson	Den Of Iniquity*	Uptempo	Alto	G4	Eb5	Lead	Romantic Antagonist Female
Pal Joey	Hart, Lorenz & Rodgers	1940	Joey Evans	Den Of Iniquity*	Uptempo	Baritone	G3	Eb4	Lead	Romantic Antagonist Male
Pal Joey	Hart, Lorenz & Rodgers	1940	Joey & Vera	Den Of Iniquity	Uptempo	Bar/Alto			Duet	RAM/RLF
Pal Joey	Hart, Lorenz & Rodgers	1940	Linda English	Do It The Hard Way	Moderate Tempo	Baritone	C3	C4	Lead	Ingenue Female
Pal Joey	Hart, Lorenz & Rodgers	1940	Linda English	Take Him*	Moderate Tempo	Alto	C4	D5	Lead	Romantic Antagonist Male
Pal Joey	Hart, Lorenz & Rodgers	1940	Vera Simpson	Take Him*	Moderate Tempo	Alto	C4		Lead	Ingenue Female
Pal Joey	Hart, Lorenz & Rodgers	1940	Linda & Vera	Take Him	Moderate Tempo	Alto/Alto			Duet	RLF/RAF
Pal Joey	Hart, Lorenz & Rodgers	1940	Vera Simpson	Bewitched...Reprise	Moderate Tempo	Alto	D4	D5	Lead	Romantic Antagonist Female
Pal Joey	Hart, Lorenz & Rodgers	1940	Joey Evans	Finale-I Could Write A Book	Moderate Tempo	Baritone	Eb3	Eb4	Lead	Romantic Antagonist Male

Shows

* = Music Edit Required
+ = Ethnic Specific

Show	Composer	Year	Role	Song	Tempo	Vocal Type	Range-Bottom	Range-Top	Category	Character Type
Pal Joey	Hart, Lorenz & Rodgers	2008	Gladys Bumps	Zip	Moderate Tempo	Alto	F3	G4	Lead	Romantic Antagonist Female
Parade	Brown, Jason Robert	1998	Young Soldier	Old Red Hills Of Home (Part 1)	Moderate Tempo	Tenor	D3	A4	Supporting	Character Ingenue Male
Parade	Brown, Jason Robert	1998	Old Soldier	Old Red Hills Of Home (Part 2)*	Moderate Tempo	Baritone	C3	G4	Supporting	Mature Male
Parade	Brown, Jason Robert	1998	Ensemble	Old Red Hills Of Home (Part 2)	Moderate Tempo	SATB			Ensemble	Adults
Parade	Brown, Jason Robert	1998	Ensemble	The Dream Of Atlatna	Uptempo	SATB			Ensemble	Adults
Parade	Brown, Jason Robert	1998	Leo Frank	How Can I Call This Home?	Uptempo	Baritone	A2	F4	Lead	Character Male
Parade	Brown, Jason Robert	1998	Frankie Epps & Mary Phagan	The Picture Show	Uptempo	Bar/Alto			Duet	IM/IF
Parade	Brown, Jason Robert	1998	Lucille Frank	Waiting*	Moderate Tempo	Alto	A3	C5	Lead	Romantic Lead Female
Parade	Brown, Jason Robert	1998	Newt Lee+	Interrogation Sequence*	Moderate Tempo	Tenor	Bb2	C4	Lead	Antagonist Male
Parade	Brown, Jason Robert	1998	Britt Craig	Big News	Uptempo	Tenor	D3	Ab4	Lead	Antagonist Male
Parade	Brown, Jason Robert	1998	Ensemble	There Is A Fountain*	Moderate Tempo	SATB			Ensemble	Adults
Parade	Brown, Jason Robert	1998	Frankie Epps	It Don't Make Sense*	Ballad	SATB			Ensemble	Adults
Parade	Brown, Jason Robert	1998	Tom Watson	Watson's Lullaby	Ballad	Tenor	A#2	A3	Lead	Romantic Lead Male
Parade	Brown, Jason Robert	1998	Hugh Dorsey	Somethin' Ain't Right*	Moderate Tempo	Baritone	C#3	F#4	Lead	Romantic Antagonist Male
Parade	Brown, Jason Robert	1998	Britt Craig	Real Big News*	Uptempo	Tenor	F3	A4	Lead	Antagonist Male
Parade	Brown, Jason Robert	1998	Ensemble	Real Big News	Uptempo	SATB			Ensemble	Adults
Parade	Brown, Jason Robert	1998	Lucille Frank	You Don't Know this Man	Ballad	Alto	G3	Eb5	Lead	Romantic Lead Female
Parade	Brown, Jason Robert	1998	Ensemble	The Trial, Part 1: People Of Atlanta	Uptempo	SATB			Ensemble	Adults
Parade	Brown, Jason Robert	1998	Ensemble	The Trial, Part 2: Twenty From Marietta	Uptempo	SATB			Ensemble	Adults
Parade	Brown, Jason Robert	1998	Ensemble	The Trial, Part 3: Frankie's Testimony	Moderate Tempo	SATB			Ensemble	Adults
Parade	Brown, Jason Robert	1998	Ensemble	The Trial, Part 4: The Factory Girls	Moderate Tempo	AAA			Ensemble	Adults
Parade	Brown, Jason Robert	1998	Hugh Dorsey	The Trial, Part 2: Twenty From Marietta	Uptempo	Baritone	Bb2	Eb4	Lead	Romantic Antagonist Male
Parade	Brown, Jason Robert	1998	Leo Frank	Come Up To My Office*	Uptempo	Baritone	A2	F4	Lead	Character Male
Parade	Brown, Jason Robert	1998	Newt Lee+	The Trial, Part 5: Newt Lee's Testimony	Uptempo	Baritone	B2	F#3	Lead	Antagonist Male
Parade	Brown, Jason Robert	1998	Mrs. Phagan	My Child Will Forgive Me	Ballad	Alto	F#3	A4	Lead	Maternal
Parade	Brown, Jason Robert	1998	John Conley+	That's What He Said	Uptempo	Tenor	D3	G4	Lead	Romantic Antagonist Male
Parade	Brown, Jason Robert	1998	Leo Frank	It's Hard To Speak My Heart	Ballad	Baritone	B2	E4	Lead	Character Male
Parade	Brown, Jason Robert	1998	Ensemble	The Trial, Part 9: Closing Statemen/Ver	Moderate Tempo	SATB			Ensemble	Adults
Parade	Brown, Jason Robert	1998	Britt Craig	Opening Act II	Moderate Tempo	Tenor	F3	G4	Lead	Antagonist Male
Parade	Brown, Jason Robert	1998	Ensemble+	A Rumblin' And A Rollin'	Moderate Tempo	ATB			Ensemble	Adults
Parade	Brown, Jason Robert	1998	Lucille Frank	Do It Alone	Moderate Tempo	Alto	A3	E5	Lead	Romantic Lead Female
Parade	Brown, Jason Robert	1998	Judge Roan	Judge Roan's Letter	Uptempo	Baritone	Eb2	D4	Lead	Antagonist Male
Parade	Brown, Jason Robert	1998	Gov. Jack Slaton	Pretty Music*	Uptempo	Baritone	C3	G4	Lead	Romantic Lead Male
Parade	Brown, Jason Robert	1998	Leo Frank	This Is Not Over Yet*	Uptempo	Baritone	D3	F#4	Lead	Character Male
Parade	Brown, Jason Robert	1998	Leo Frank & Lucille Frank	This Is Not Over Yet	Uptempo	Bar/Alto			Duet	CM/RLF
Parade	Brown, Jason Robert	1998	John Conley+	Blues: Feel The Rain Fall*	Moderate Tempo	Tenor	D3	Bb4	Lead	Romantic Antagonist Male
Parade	Brown, Jason Robert	1998	Ensemble+	Blues: Feel The Rain Fall	Moderate Tempo	TBB			Ensemble	Adults
Parade	Brown, Jason Robert	1998	Tom Watson	Where Will You Stand....Flood Comes*	Uptempo	Tenor	B2	Eb4	Lead	Romantic Lead Male
Parade	Brown, Jason Robert	1998	Ensemble	Where Will You Stand....Flood Comes	Uptempo	SATB			Ensemble	Adults
Parade	Brown, Jason Robert	1998	Leo Frank	All The Wasted Time*	Ballad	Baritone	D3	Bb4	Lead	Character Male
Parade	Brown, Jason Robert	1998	Lucille Frank	All The Wasted Time*	Ballad	Alto	G3	Eb5	Lead	Romantic Lead Female
Parade	Brown, Jason Robert	1998	Leo Frank & Lucille Frank	All The Wasted Time	Ballad	Bar/Alto			Duet	CM/RLF

Shows

451

* = Music Edit Required
+ = Ethnic Specific

Show	Composer	Year	Role	Song	Tempo	Vocal Type	Range-Bottom	Range-Top	Category	Character Type
Parade	Brown, Jason Robert	1998	Leo Frank	Sh'ma	Ballad	Baritone	G3	Eb4	Lead	Character Male
Parade	Brown, Jason Robert	1998	Lucille Frank	Finale	Ballad	Alto	A3	C5	Lead	Romantic Lead Female
Parade	Brown, Jason Robert	1998	Ensemble	Old Red Hills Of Home Finale	Moderate Tempo	SATB			Ensemble	Adults
Parade	Brown, Jason Robert	1998	Frankie Epps	Old Red Hills Of Home Finale*	Moderate Tempo	Baritone	Eb3	Eb4	Lead	Ingenue Male
Passion	Sondheim, Stephen	1994	Clara	Happiness (Part 1)*	Moderate Tempo	Soprano	Bb3	Eb5	Lead	Romantic Lead Female
Passion	Sondheim, Stephen	1994	Giorgio Bachetti & Clara	Happiness (Part 1)	Moderate Tempo	Tenor/Sop			Duet	RLM/RLF
Passion	Sondheim, Stephen	1994	Giorgio Bachetti	Happiness (Part 2)*	Moderate Tempo	Tenor	A2	C4	Duet	Romantic Lead Male
Passion	Sondheim, Stephen	1994	Giorgio Bachetti & Clara	Happiness (Part 2)	Moderate Tempo	Tenor/Sop			Duet	RLM/RLF
Passion	Sondheim, Stephen	1994	Clara	Fourth Letter-How Could I Forget You	Moderate Tempo	Soprano	F3	Db5	Lead	Romantic Lead Female
Passion	Sondheim, Stephen	1994	Fosca	I Read	Ballad	Alto	F3	D5	Lead	Antagonist Female
Passion	Sondheim, Stephen	1994	Clara	Thinking Of You	Moderate Tempo	Soprano	Ab3	Db5	Lead	Romantic Lead Female
Passion	Sondheim, Stephen	1994	Giorgio Bachetti & Clara	Every Waking Moment	Uptempo	Tenor/Sop			Duet	RLM/RLF
Passion	Sondheim, Stephen	1994	Fosca	To Speak To Me Of Love	Moderate Tempo	Alto	E#3	C5	Lead	Antagonist Female
Passion	Sondheim, Stephen	1994	Ensemble	Transition-To Speak To Me Of Love	Moderate Tempo	TTBB			Ensemble	Adults
Passion	Sondheim, Stephen	1994	Ensemble	Fifth Letter-Trio*	Moderate Tempo	SSB			Ensemble	Adults
Passion	Sondheim, Stephen	1994	Fosca	I Wish I Could Forget You*	Ballad	Alto	F3	C5	Lead	Antagonist Female
Passion	Sondheim, Stephen	1994	Ensemble	Soldier's Gossip (Scenet 7&8)	Moderate Tempo	TTBB			Ensemble	Adults
Passion	Sondheim, Stephen	1994	Ensemble	Flashback (Parts 1-4)	Moderate Tempo	TBB			Ensemble	Adults
Passion	Sondheim, Stephen	1994	Clara	Sunrise Letter*	Moderate Tempo	Soprano	Ab3	G5	Lead	Romantic Lead Female
Passion	Sondheim, Stephen	1994	Giorgio Bachetti & Clara	Sunrise Letter*	Moderate Tempo	Tenor/Sop			Duet	RLM/RLF
Passion	Sondheim, Stephen	1994	Giorgio Bachetti	Is This What You Call Love?	Uptempo	Tenor	A#2	F4	Lead	Romantic Lead Male
Passion	Sondheim, Stephen	1994	Ensemble	Soldier's Gossip (Scene 10)	Moderate Tempo	TTBB			Ensemble	Adults
Passion	Sondheim, Stephen	1994	Ensemble	Transition-To Feel A Woman's Touch	Moderate Tempo	TTBB			Ensemble	Adults
Passion	Sondheim, Stephen	1994	Ensemble	Nightmare	Uptempo	TTBB			Ensemble	Adults
Passion	Sondheim, Stephen	1994	Clara	Forty Days	Uptempo	Soprano	Bb3	E5	Lead	Romantic Lead Female
Passion	Sondheim, Stephen	1994	Fosca	Loving You	Ballad	Alto	F#3	C5	Lead	Antagonist Female
Passion	Sondheim, Stephen	1994	Ensemble	Soldier's Gossip (Scene 11)	Moderate Tempo	TTBB			Ensemble	Adults
Passion	Sondheim, Stephen	1994	Clara	I Didn't Tell You	Ballad	Soprano	Ab3	F5	Lead	Romantic Lead Female
Passion	Sondheim, Stephen	1994	Lt. Torasso	Christmas Music	Moderate Tempo	Tenor	Eb3	F4	Lead	Character Male
Passion	Sondheim, Stephen	1994	Clara	I Am Writing To You	Moderate Tempo	Soprano	A3	C#5	Lead	Romantic Lead Female
Passion	Sondheim, Stephen	1994	Giorgio Bachetti & Clara	Just Another Love Story	Moderate Tempo	Tenor/Sop			Lead	RLM/RLF
Passion	Sondheim, Stephen	1994	Giorgio Bachetti	No One Has Ever Loved Me	Ballad	Tenor	B2	D4	Lead	Romantic Lead Male
Passion	Sondheim, Stephen	1994	Fosca	All This Happiness	Moderate Tempo	Alto	B3	A4	Lead	Antagonist Female
Passion	Sondheim, Stephen	1994	Ensemble	Finale	Uptempo	SATB			Ensemble	Adults
Peter Pan	Charlap, Mark	1954	Ensemble	Tender Shepherd	Ballad	SAT			Lead	Children/Teens/Adults
Peter Pan	Charlap, Mark	1954	Peter Pan	I've Got To Crow	Uptempo	Soprano	Bb3	C5	Lead	Character Female
Peter Pan	Charlap, Mark	1954	Peter Pan	Neverland	Moderate Tempo	Soprano	Eb3	C5	Lead	Character Female
Peter Pan	Charlap, Mark	1954	Peter Pan	I'm Flying*	Uptempo	Soprano	A3	F5	Lead	Character Female
Peter Pan	Charlap, Mark	1954	Ensemble	Pirate Song*	Moderate Tempo	TB			Ensemble	Adults
Peter Pan	Charlap, Mark	1954	Captain Hook	Hook's Tango*	Moderate Tempo	Baritone	A2	D4	Lead	Antagonist Male
Peter Pan	Charlap, Mark	1954	Peter Pan	Wendy*	Moderate Tempo	Soprano	Bb3	C5	Lead	Character Female
Peter Pan	Charlap, Mark	1954	Ensemble	Wendy	Moderate Tempo	SATB			Ensemble	Children/Teens/Adults

Shows

Songs by Character Type

Show	Composer	Year	Role	Song	Tempo	Vocal Type	Range-Bottom	Range-Top	Category	Character Type
Peter Pan	Charlap, Mark	1954	Captain Hook	Tarantella*	Uptempo	Baritone	D3	D4	Lead	Antagonist Male
Peter Pan	Charlap, Mark	1954	Ensemble	I Won't Grow Up	Uptempo	SATB			Ensemble	Children/Teens/Adults
Peter Pan	Charlap, Mark	1954	Hook & Peter Pan	Oh, My Mysterious Lady	Uptempo	Bar/Sop			Duet	AM/CF
Peter Pan	Charlap, Mark	1954	Ensemble	Ugg-A-Wugg	Uptempo	SATB			Ensemble	Children/Teens/Adults
Peter Pan	Charlap, Mark	1954	Peter Pan	Distant Melody	Ballad	Soprano	Gb3	Ab4	Lead	Character Female
Peter Pan	Charlap, Mark	1954	Captain Hook	Captain Hook's Waltz*	Moderate Tempo	Baritone	B2	G4	Lead	Antagonist Male
Peter Pan	Charlap, Mark	1954	Ensemble	I Won't Grow Up Reprise*	Uptempo	SATB			Ensemble	Children/Teens/Adults
Peter Pan	Charlap, Mark	1954	Peter Pan	Neverland Reprise	Moderate Tempo	Soprano	E3	B4	Lead	Character Female
Phantom	Yeston, Maury	1991	Christine Daee	Melody Of Paris	Uptempo	Soprano	B3	A5	Lead	Ingenue Female
Phantom	Yeston, Maury	1991	Phantom	Paris Is A Tomb	Ballad	Baritone	A2	C4	Lead	Antagonist Male
Phantom	Yeston, Maury	1991	Ensemble	Dressing For The Night	Uptempo	SATB			Ensemble	Adults
Phantom	Yeston, Maury	1991	Carlotta	This Place Is Mine	Uptempo	Soprano	Bb3	Bb5	Lead	Romantic Antagonist Female
Phantom	Yeston, Maury	1991	Phantom	Where In The World	Uptempo	Baritone	G2	F4	Lead	Antagonist Male
Phantom	Yeston, Maury	1991	Christine Daae	Home*	Moderate Tempo	Soprano	D4	A5	Lead	Ingenue Female
Phantom	Yeston, Maury	1991	Phantom	Home*	Moderate Tempo	Baritone	C3	G4	Lead	Antagonist Male
Phantom	Yeston, Maury	1991	Phantom & Christine	Home	Moderate Tempo	Bar/Sop			Duet	AM/IF
Phantom	Yeston, Maury	1991	Ensemble	Phantom Fugue	Uptempo	SATB			Ensemble	Adults
Phantom	Yeston, Maury	1991	Phantom & Christine	You Are Music	Moderate Tempo	Bar/Sop			Duet	AM/IF
Phantom	Yeston, Maury	1991	Christine Daea	The Bistro*	Uptempo	Soprano	Bb3	B5	Lead	Ingenue Female
Phantom	Yeston, Maury	1991	Ensemble	The Bistro	Uptempo	SATB			Ensemble	Adults
Phantom	Yeston, Maury	1991	Count Philippe	Who Could Have Ever Dreamed Up You	Uptempo	Baritone	Bb2	E4	Lead	Romantic Lead Male
Phantom	Yeston, Maury	1991	Christine Daae	Who Could Have Ever Dreamed Up You	Uptempo	Soprano	Bb3	Eb5	Lead	Ingenue Female
Phantom	Yeston, Maury	1991	Carlotta	This Is Mine Reprise	Moderate Tempo	Soprano	D4	G5	Lead	Romantic Antagonist Female
Phantom	Yeston, Maury	1991	Count Philippe	Without Your Music	Moderate Tempo	Baritone	C3	F4	Lead	Romantic Lead Male
Phantom	Yeston, Maury	1991	Phantom	Where In The World Reprise	Uptempo	Baritone	Bb2	F4	Lead	Antagonist Male
Phantom	Yeston, Maury	1991	Christine Daae	My True Love	Moderate Tempo	Soprano	C4	F5	Lead	Ingenue Female
Phantom	Yeston, Maury	1991	Phantom	My Mother Bore Me	Moderate Tempo	Baritone	F2	F#4	Lead	Antagonist Male
Phantom	Yeston, Maury	1991	Gerard Carriere	You Are My Own*	Moderate Tempo	Baritone	G2	D4	Lead	Mature Male
Phantom	Yeston, Maury	1991	Erik (Phantom)	You Are My Own*	Moderate Tempo	Baritone	G2	E4	Lead	Antagonist Male
Phantom	Yeston, Maury	1991	Gerard & Erik	You Are My Own	Moderate Tempo	Bar/Bar			Duet	MM/AM
Phantom	Yeston, Maury	1991	Christine Daae	Finale: You Are Music*	Ballad	Soprano	B4	G5	Lead	Ingenue Female
Phantom Of The Opera	Webber, Andrew Lloyd	1986	Raoul, Vicomte de Chagny	Prologue	Ballad	Tenor	C#3	E4	Lead	Romantic Lead Male
Phantom Of The Opera	Webber, Andrew Lloyd	1986	Carlotta Giudicelli	Hannibal Cadenza	Moderate Tempo	Soprano	C4	D6	Lead	Romantic Antagonist Female
Phantom Of The Opera	Webber, Andrew Lloyd	1986	Ensemble	Hannibal Rehearsal	Moderate Tempo	SATB			Ensemble	Adults
Phantom Of The Opera	Webber, Andrew Lloyd	1986	Carlotta Giudicelli	Think Of Me*	Moderate Tempo	Soprano	E#4	G#5	Lead	Romantic Antagonist Female
Phantom Of The Opera	Webber, Andrew Lloyd	1986	Christine Daae	Think Of Me*	Moderate Tempo	Soprano	D4	C6	Lead	Ingenue Female
Phantom Of The Opera	Webber, Andrew Lloyd	1986	Christine Daae	Angel Of Music*	Moderate Tempo	Soprano	Bb3	F#5	Lead	Ingenue Female
Phantom Of The Opera	Webber, Andrew Lloyd	1986	Phantom & Christine	Angel Of Music	Moderate Tempo	Tenor/Sop			Duet	AM/IF
Phantom Of The Opera	Webber, Andrew Lloyd	1986	Christine Daae	Phantom Of The Opera*	Moderate Tempo	Soprano	G3	E5	Lead	Ingenue Female
Phantom Of The Opera	Webber, Andrew Lloyd	1986	Phantom & Christine	Phantom Of The Opera*	Moderate Tempo	Tenor/Sop			Duet	AM/IF
Phantom Of The Opera	Webber, Andrew Lloyd	1986	Phantom	Phantom Of The Opera*	Moderate Tempo	Tenor	B2	G#4	Lead	Antagonist Male
Phantom Of The Opera	Webber, Andrew Lloyd	1986	Phantom	The Music Of The Night	Ballad	Tenor	G#2	G#4	Lead	Antagonist Male
Phantom Of The Opera	Webber, Andrew Lloyd	1986	Phantom	Stranger Than You Dreamt It*	Ballad	Tenor	D3	D4	Lead	Antagonist Male

Shows

Songs by Character Type

* = Music Edit Required
+ = Ethnic Specific

Show	Composer	Year	Role	Song	Tempo	Vocal Type	Range-Bottom	Range-Top	Category	Character Type
Phantom Of The Opera	Webber, Andrew Lloyd	1986	Monsieurs Firmin & Andre	Notes	Uptempo	Bar/Bar			Duet	MM/MM
Phantom Of The Opera	Webber, Andrew Lloyd	1986	Carlotta Giudicelli	Diva*	Moderate Tempo	Soprano	F4	E6	Lead	Romantic Antagonist Female
Phantom Of The Opera	Webber, Andrew Lloyd	1986	Monsieurs Firmin & Andre	Prima Donna*	Moderate Tempo	Bar/Bar			Duet	MM/MM
Phantom Of The Opera	Webber, Andrew Lloyd	1986	Carlotta Giudicelli	Prima Donna*	Moderate Tempo	Soprano	F4	F6	Lead	Romantic Antagonist Female
Phantom Of The Opera	Webber, Andrew Lloyd	1986	Carlotta Giudicelli	Poor Fool He Makes Me Laugh*	Moderate Tempo	Soprano	F4	C6	Lead	Romantic Antagonist Female
Phantom Of The Opera	Webber, Andrew Lloyd	1986	Ensemble	Poor Fool He Makes Me Laugh*	Moderate Tempo	SATB			Ensemble	Adults
Phantom Of The Opera	Webber, Andrew Lloyd	1986	Raoul & Christine	Why Have You Brought Us Here*	Uptempo	Tenor/Sop			Duet	IM/IF
Phantom Of The Opera	Webber, Andrew Lloyd	1986	Christine Daae	Raoul I've Been There	Moderate Tempo	Soprano	C#4	A♭5	Lead	Ingenue Female
Phantom Of The Opera	Webber, Andrew Lloyd	1986	Raoul, Vicomte de Chagny	All I Ask Of You*	Ballad	Tenor	A♭3	G4	Lead	Romantic Lead Male
Phantom Of The Opera	Webber, Andrew Lloyd	1986	Raoul & Christine	All I Ask Of You*	Ballad	Tenor/Sop			Duet	RLM/IF
Phantom Of The Opera	Webber, Andrew Lloyd	1986	Christine Daae	All I Ask Of You Reprise	Ballad	Soprano	A♭3	A♭5	Lead	Ingenue Female
Phantom Of The Opera	Webber, Andrew Lloyd	1986	Ensemble	Masquerade*	Moderate Tempo	SATB			Ensemble	Adults
Phantom Of The Opera	Webber, Andrew Lloyd	1986	Phantom	Why So Silent*	Ballad	Tenor	E♭3	G♭4	Lead	Antagonist Male
Phantom Of The Opera	Webber, Andrew Lloyd	1986	Phantom	Notes: No Doubt She'll Do Her Best	Ballad	Tenor	D#3	D#4	Lead	Antagonist Male
Phantom Of The Opera	Webber, Andrew Lloyd	1986	Christine Daae	Twisted Every Way*	Ballad	Soprano	C4	E♭5	Lead	Ingenue Female
Phantom Of The Opera	Webber, Andrew Lloyd	1986	Christine Daae	Wishing You Were Somehow Here Again	Ballad	Soprano	A3	G5	Lead	Ingenue Female
Phantom Of The Opera	Webber, Andrew Lloyd	1986	Ensemble	Whispering Child*	Moderate Tempo	STT			Ensemble	Adults
Phantom Of The Opera	Webber, Andrew Lloyd	1986	Phantom	The Point Of No Return*	Ballad	Tenor	C3	G4	Lead	Antagonist Male
Phantom Of The Opera	Webber, Andrew Lloyd	1986	Christine Daae	The Point Of No Return*	Ballad	Soprano	C4	G5	Lead	Ingenue Female
Phantom Of The Opera	Webber, Andrew Lloyd	1986	Phantom	All I Ask Of You Reprise 2*	Ballad	Tenor	D♭3	A♭4	Lead	Antagonist Male
Pippin	Schwartz, Stephen	1972	Leading Player	Magic To Do*	Uptempo	Tenor	E3	A4	Lead	Romantic Antagonist Male
Pippin	Schwartz, Stephen	1972	Ensemble	Magic To Do	Uptempo	SATB			Ensemble	Adults
Pippin	Schwartz, Stephen	1972	Pippin	Corner Of The Sky	Uptempo	Tenor	E3	C5	Lead	Ingenue Male
Pippin	Schwartz, Stephen	1972	Charles	War Is A Science*	Uptempo	Baritone	B♭2	E4	Lead	Antagonist Male
Pippin	Schwartz, Stephen	1972	Pippin	War Is A Science*	Uptempo	Tenor	B♭2	G4	Lead	Ingenue Male
Pippin	Schwartz, Stephen	1972	Charles & Pippin	War Is A Science*	Uptempo	Bar/Tenor			Duet	AM/IM
Pippin	Schwartz, Stephen	1972	Ensemble	War Is A Science	Uptempo	SATB			Ensemble	Adults
Pippin	Schwartz, Stephen	1972	Leading Player	Glory Part I & III*	Moderate Tempo	Tenor	E3	G#4	Lead	Romantic Antagonist Male
Pippin	Schwartz, Stephen	1972	Ensemble	Glory Part I & III	Moderate Tempo	SATB			Ensemble	Adults
Pippin	Schwartz, Stephen	1972	Pippin	Corner Of The Sky Reprise	Moderate Tempo	Tenor	D3	F4	Lead	Ingenue Male
Pippin	Schwartz, Stephen	1972	Berthe	No Time At All*	Uptempo	Alto	G3	A4	Lead	Maternal
Pippin	Schwartz, Stephen	1972	Ensemble	No Time At All	Uptempo	SATB			Ensemble	Adults
Pippin	Schwartz, Stephen	1972	Pippin	With You	Ballad	Tenor	C3	A♭4	Lead	Ingenue Male
Pippin	Schwartz, Stephen	1972	Fastrada	Spread A Little Sunshine	Moderate Tempo	Alto	A2	F5	Lead	Romantic Antagonist Female
Pippin	Schwartz, Stephen	1972	Pippin	Morning Glow (C Major)	Moderate Tempo	Tenor	C3	F#4	Lead	Ingenue Male
Pippin	Schwartz, Stephen	1972	Pippin	Morning Glow (D♭ Major)	Moderate Tempo	Tenor	D♭3	G4	Lead	Ingenue Male
Pippin	Schwartz, Stephen	1972	Ensemble	Morning Glow	Moderate Tempo	SATB			Ensemble	Adults
Pippin	Schwartz, Stephen	1972	Catherine	There He Was	Uptempo	Alto	G#3	B4	Lead	Romantic Lead Female
Pippin	Schwartz, Stephen	1972	Leading Player	Right On Track*	Moderate Tempo	Tenor	E♭3	A♭4	Lead	Romantic Antagonist Male
Pippin	Schwartz, Stephen	1972	Leading Player & Pippin	Right On Track	Moderate Tempo	Tenor/Tenor			Duet	RAM/IM
Pippin	Schwartz, Stephen	1972	Catherine	King Of Woman*	Moderate Tempo	Alto	A♭3	C#5	Lead	Romantic Lead Female

Shows

Songs by Character Type

Show	Composer	Year	Role	Song	Tempo	Vocal Type	Range-Bottom	Range-Top	Category	Character Type
Pippin	Schwartz, Stephen	1972	Pippin	Extraordinary	Uptempo	Tenor	C3	G4	Lead	Ingenue Male
Pippin	Schwartz, Stephen	1972	Pippin	Prayer For A Duck	Uptempo	Tenor	D3	F#4	Lead	Ingenue Male
Pippin	Schwartz, Stephen	1972	Pippin	Corner Of the Sky Last Reprise	Moderate Tempo	Tenor	D#3	F#4	Lead	Ingenue Male
Pippin	Schwartz, Stephen	1972	Catherine	I Guess I'll Miss the Man	Ballad	Alto	F#3	B4	Lead	Romantic Lead Female
Pippin	Schwartz, Stephen	1972	Pippin	Love Song*	Ballad	Tenor	B2	G#4	Lead	Ingenue Male
Pippin	Schwartz, Stephen	1972	Pippin & Catherine	Love Song	Ballad	Tenor/Alto			Duet	IM/RLF
Pippin	Schwartz, Stephen	1972	Leading Player	Think About The Sun*	Uptempo	Tenor	G3	F4	Lead	Romantic Antagonist Male
Pippin	Schwartz, Stephen	1972	Pippin	Think About The Sun*	Uptempo	Tenor	C3	G4	Lead	Ingenue Male
Pippin	Schwartz, Stephen	1972	Ensemble	Think About The Sun	Uptempo	SATB			Ensemble	Adults
Porgy and Bess	Gershwin, George	1935	Clara+	Summertime	Moderate Tempo	Soprano	F#4	B5	Lead	Ingenue Female
Porgy and Bess	Gershwin, George	1935	Ensemble+	Nobody Knows When The Lord Goin' Ca	Moderate Tempo	TTBB			Ensemble	Adults
Porgy and Bess	Gershwin, George	1935	Jim+	A Woman Is A Sometime Thing*	Moderate Tempo	Baritone	D3	F4	Lead	Character Male
Porgy and Bess	Gershwin, George	1935	Ensemble+	A Woman Is A Sometime Thing	Moderate Tempo	SATB			Ensemble	Adults
Porgy and Bess	Gershwin, George	1935	Porgy+	Lonesome Road*	Ballad	Baritone	A2	D4	Lead	Character Male
Porgy and Bess	Gershwin, George	1935	Ensemble+	Gone, Gone, Gone	Ballad	SATB			Ensemble	Adults
Porgy and Bess	Gershwin, George	1935	Ensemble+	Overflow	Moderate Tempo	SATB			Ensemble	Adults
Porgy and Bess	Gershwin, George	1935	Serena+	My Man's Gone Now*	Moderate Tempo	Soprano	E4	B5	Lead	Character Female
Porgy and Bess	Gershwin, George	1935	Ensemble+	Leavin' For The Promise Land	Uptempo	SATB			Ensemble	Adults
Porgy and Bess	Gershwin, George	1935	Ensemble+	It Takes A Long Pull To Get There	Moderate Tempo	TTBB			Ensemble	Adults
Porgy and Bess	Gershwin, George	1935	Porgy+	It Takes A Long Pull To Get There*	Moderate Tempo	Baritone	E3	G4	Lead	Character Male
Porgy and Bess	Gershwin, George	1935	Porgy+	Oh, I Got Plenty O' Nuttin'*	Uptempo	Baritone	B2	D4	Lead	Character Male
Porgy and Bess	Gershwin, George	1935	Ensemble+	Oh, I Got Plenty O' Nuttin'	Uptempo	SATB			Ensemble	Adults
Porgy and Bess	Gershwin, George	1935	Maria+	I Hates Yo' Struttin' Style (Spoken)	Uptempo	Alto			Lead	Mature Female
Porgy and Bess	Gershwin, George	1935	Porgy+	The Buzzard*	Moderate Tempo	Baritone	Bb2	E4	Lead	Character Male
Porgy and Bess	Gershwin, George	1935	Ensemble+	Lo, Bess, Goin' To The Picnic	Moderate Tempo	STB			Ensemble	Character Male
Porgy and Bess	Gershwin, George	1935	Porgy+	Bess, You Is My Woman*	Ballad	Baritone	Bb2	B5	Lead	Character Male
Porgy and Bess	Gershwin, George	1935	Bess+	Bess, You Is My Woman*	Ballad	Soprano	D4	A#5	Lead	Romantic Lead Female
Porgy and Bess	Gershwin, George	1935	Porgy+ & Bess+	Bess, You Is My Woman	Ballad	Bar/Sop			Duet	CM/RLF
Porgy and Bess	Gershwin, George	1935	Ensemble+	Oh I Can't Sit Down	Uptempo	SATB			Ensemble	Adults
Porgy and Bess	Gershwin, George	1935	Porgy+	I Got Plenty O' Nuttin' Reprise	Uptempo	Baritone	Bb2	Eb4	Lead	Character Male
Porgy and Bess	Gershwin, George	1935	Ensemble+	I Ain't Got No Shame	Uptempo	SATB			Ensemble	Adults
Porgy and Bess	Gershwin, George	1935	Sporting Life+	It Ain't Necessarily So*	Moderate Tempo	Tenor	C4	A4	Lead	Romantic Lead Male
Porgy and Bess	Gershwin, George	1935	Ensemble+	It Ain't Necessarily So	Moderate Tempo	SATB			Ensemble	Adults
Porgy and Bess	Gershwin, George	1935	Crown & Bess	Crown!	Moderate Tempo	Bar/Sop			Duet	AM/RLM
Porgy and Bess	Gershwin, George	1935	Bess+	What You Want Wid Bess*	Moderate Tempo	Soprano	Eb4	A5	Lead	Romantic Lead Female
Porgy and Bess	Gershwin, George	1935	Crown & Bess+	What You Want Wid Bess	Moderate Tempo	Bar/Sop			Duet	AM/RLM
Porgy and Bess	Gershwin, George	1935	Crown+	What You Want Wid Bess*	Moderate Tempo	Baritone	Eb3	Ab4	Lead	Antagonist Male
Porgy and Bess	Gershwin, George	1935	Ensemble+	It Takes A Long Pull To Get There Repri	Ballad	SATB			Ensemble	Adults
Porgy and Bess	Gershwin, George	1935	Strawberry Woman+	Strawberry Woman	Ballad	Alto	G4	E5	Featured Ensemble	Character Female
Porgy and Bess	Gershwin, George	1935	Honey Man+	Honeyman	Ballad	Tenor	B3	G4	Featured Ensemble	Character Male
Porgy and Bess	Gershwin, George	1935	Crab Man+	Crab Man	Ballad	Tenor	B3	G4	Featured Ensemble	Character Male
Porgy and Bess	Gershwin, George	1935	Bess+	I Loves You Porgy*	Moderate Tempo	Soprano	Bb3	A5	Lead	Romantic Lead Female
Porgy and Bess	Gershwin, George	1935	Porgy+	I Loves You Porgy*	Moderate Tempo	Baritone	Db3	Db4	Lead	Character Male

Shows

Songs by Character Type

Show	Composer	Year	Role	Song	Tempo	Vocal Type	Range-Bottom	Range-Top	Category	Character Type
Porgy and Bess	Gershwin, George	1935	Ensemble+	Dr. Jesus	Moderate Tempo	SATB			Ensemble	Adults
Porgy and Bess	Gershwin, George	1935	Clara+	Summertime Reprise	Moderate Tempo	Soprano	E4	A5	Lead	Ingenue Female
Porgy and Bess	Gershwin, George	1935	Ensemble+	Oh, Dere's Somebody Knockin'	Moderate Tempo	SATB			Ensemble	Adults
Porgy and Bess	Gershwin, George	1935	Crown+	A Red-Headed Woman	Moderate Tempo	Baritone	Db3	F4	Lead	Antagonist Male
Porgy and Bess	Gershwin, George	1935	Ensemble+	Clara, Clara	Moderate Tempo	SATB			Ensemble	Adults
Porgy and Bess	Gershwin, George	1935	Bess+	Summertime Reprise 2	Ballad	Soprano	E4	A5	Lead	Romantic Lead Female
Porgy and Bess	Gershwin, George	1935	Sporting Life+	There's A Boat That's Leaving Soon....	Moderate Tempo	Tenor	D3	Bb4	Lead	Romantic Lead Male
Porgy and Bess	Gershwin, George	1935	Ensemble+	Good Mornin' Sistuh!...*	Uptempo	SATB			Ensemble	Adults
Porgy and Bess	Gershwin, George	1935	Ensemble+	It Porgy Comoin' Home	Moderate Tempo	SATB			Ensemble	Adults
Porgy and Bess	Gershwin, George	1935	Porgy+	Oh, Bess, Oh, Where's My Bess*	Moderate Tempo	Baritone	C#3	F4	Lead	Character Male
Porgy and Bess	Gershwin, George	1935	Ensemble+	Oh, Bess, Oh, Where's My Bess	Moderate Tempo	SATB			Ensemble	Adults
Porgy and Bess	Gershwin, George	1935	Ensemble+	Oh Lawd I'm On My Way	Moderate Tempo	SATB			Ensemble	Adults
Porgy and Bess	Gershwin, George	1935	Porgy+	Oh Lawd I'm On My Way*	Moderate Tempo	Baritone	B2	E#4	Lead	Character Male
Producers, The	Brooks, Mel	2001	Ensemble	Opening Night	Uptempo	SATB			Ensemble	Adults
Producers, The	Brooks, Mel	2001	Max Bialystock	King Of Broadway*	Uptempo	Baritone	C#3	E4	Lead	Character Male
Producers, The	Brooks, Mel	2001	Ensemble	King of Broadway	Uptempo	SATB			Ensemble	Adults
Producers, The	Brooks, Mel	2001	Max Bialystock	We Can Do It*	Uptempo	Baritone	Bb2	Eb4	Lead	Character Male
Producers, The	Brooks, Mel	2001	Leo Bloom	We Can Do It*	Uptempo	Baritone	Bb2	E4	Lead	Character Male
Producers, The	Brooks, Mel	2001	Max Bialystock & Leo Bloom	We Can Do It	Uptempo	Bar/Bar			Duet	CM/CM
Producers, The	Brooks, Mel	2001	Leo Bloom	I Wanna Be A Producer*	Moderate Tempo	Baritone	A2	F4	Lead	Character Male
Producers, The	Brooks, Mel	2001	Ensemble	I Wanna Be A Producer	Moderate Tempo	SATB			Ensemble	Adults
Producers, The	Brooks, Mel	2001	Max Bialystock & Leo Bloom	We Can Do It Reprise	Uptempo	Bar/Bar			Duet	CM/CM
Producers, The	Brooks, Mel	2001	Franz Liebkind	In Old Bavaria	Moderate Tempo	Baritone	F2	D4	Lead	Antagonist Male
Producers, The	Brooks, Mel	2001	Franz Liebkind	Der Guten Tag Hop-Clop	Uptempo	Baritone	D#3	E4	Lead	Antagonist Male
Producers, The	Brooks, Mel	2001	Roger De Bris	Keep It Gay*	Uptempo	Tenor	G#2	G4	Lead	Romantic Lead Male
Producers, The	Brooks, Mel	2001	Ensemble	Keep It Gay	Uptempo	ATB			Ensemble	Adults
Producers, The	Brooks, Mel	2001	Ulla	When You've Got It Flaunt It!	Moderate Tempo	Soprano	Bb3	Eb5	Lead	Romantic Lead Female
Producers, The	Brooks, Mel	2001	Max Bialystock	Along Came Bially*	Moderate Tempo	Baritone	Bb2	Eb4	Lead	Character Male
Producers, The	Brooks, Mel	2001	Ensemble	Along Came Bially	Moderate Tempo	SATB			Ensemble	Adults
Producers, The	Brooks, Mel	2001	Ensemble	We Can Do It Reprise Act 1 Finale	Uptempo	SATB			Ensemble	Adults
Producers, The	Brooks, Mel	2001	Leo Bloom	That Face*	Uptempo	Baritone	B2	F4	Lead	Character Male
Producers, The	Brooks, Mel	2001	Leo Bloom & Ulla	That Face	Uptempo	Bar/Sop			Duet	CM/RLF
Producers, The	Brooks, Mel	2001	Max Bialystock	That Face Reprise*	Uptempo	Baritone	A2	Eb4	Lead	Character Male
Producers, The	Brooks, Mel	2001	Franz Liebkind	Haben Sie Gehort Das Deutsche Band	Uptempo	Tenor	A2	G4	Lead	Antagonist Male
Producers, The	Brooks, Mel	2001	Usherette 1 & Usherette 2	It's Opening Night Reprise*	Uptempo	Alto/Alto			Duet	IF/IF
Producers, The	Brooks, Mel	2001	Ensemble	It's Bad Luck To Say Good Luck	Uptempo	TB			Ensemble	Adults
Producers, The	Brooks, Mel	2001	Ensemble	Springtime For Hitler	Moderate Tempo	SATB			Ensemble	Adults
Producers, The	Brooks, Mel	2001	Storm Trooper	Springtime For Hitler*	Moderate Tempo	Tenor	D3	Ab4	Lead	Romantic Lead Male
Producers, The	Brooks, Mel	2001	Roger De Bris	Springtime For Hitler*	Moderate Tempo	Tenor	B2	G4	Lead	Romantic Lead Male
Producers, The	Brooks, Mel	2001	Max Bialystock	Where Did We Go Right*	Uptempo	Baritone	A2	D4	Lead	Character Male
Producers, The	Brooks, Mel	2001	Max Bialystock & Leo Bloom	Where Did We Go Right	Uptempo	Bar/Bar			Duet	CM/CM
Producers, The	Brooks, Mel	2001	Leo Bloom	Leo Goes To Rio*	Moderate Tempo	Baritone	C3	E4	Lead	Character Male
Producers, The	Brooks, Mel	2001	Max Bialystock	Betrayed	Uptempo	Baritone	B2	F4	Lead	Character Male

Shows

Songs by Character Type

* = Music Edit Required
+ = Ethnic Specific

Show	Composer	Year	Role	Song	Tempo	Vocal Type	Range-Bottom	Range-Top	Category	Character Type
Producers, The	Brooks, Mel	2001	Leo Bloom	Til Him	Ballad	Baritone	C3	F4	Lead	Character Male
Producers, The	Brooks, Mel	2001	Max Bialystock & Leo Bloom	Til Him	Ballad	Bar/Bar			Duet	CM/CM
Producers, The	Brooks, Mel	2001	Max Bialystock	Til Him	Ballad	Baritone	C3	D#4	Lead	Character Male
Producers, The	Brooks, Mel	2001	Ensemble	Prisoners Of Love	Uptempo	SATB			Ensemble	Adults
Producers, The	Brooks, Mel	2001	Ensemble	Goodbye	Uptempo	SATB Unison			Ensemble	Adults
Rags	Schwartz, Stephen	1986	Man	I Remember	Moderate Tempo	Tenor	E3	G4	Featured Ensemble	Character Male
Rags	Schwartz, Stephen	1986	American Male 1 & Male 2	Greenhorns*	Uptempo	Tenor/Bar			Duet	CM/CM
Rags	Schwartz, Stephen	1986	Rebecca Hershkowitz	Brand New World*	Moderate Tempo	Soprano	B3	G4	Lead	Romantic Lead Female
Rags	Schwartz, Stephen	1986	Rebecca Hershkowitz	Children Of The Wind	Moderate Tempo	Soprano	A3	Bb5	Lead	Romantic Lead Female
Rags	Schwartz, Stephen	1986	Rebecca Hershkowitz	If We Never Meet Again*	Ballad	Soprano	B2	C5	Lead	Romantic Lead Female
Rags	Schwartz, Stephen	1986	Bella Cohen	If We Never Meet Again*	Ballad	Alto	B2	C5	Lead	Character Ingenue Female
Rags	Schwartz, Stephen	1986	Rebecca & Bella	If We Never Meet Again	Ballad	Sop/Alto			Duet	RLF/CIF
Rags	Schwartz, Stephen	1986	Man & Woman	Children Of The Wind Reprise	Moderate Tempo	Sop/Bar			Duet	CM/CF
Rags	Schwartz, Stephen	1986	Bella Cohen	Brand New World*	Moderate Tempo	Alto	C#4	D#5	Lead	Character Ingenue Female
Rags	Schwartz, Stephen	1986	Ensemble	Brand New World	Moderate Tempo	SSA			Ensemble	Children/Adults
Rags	Schwartz, Stephen	1986	Rebecca & Bella	Brand New World Reprise	Moderate Tempo	Sop/Alto			Duet	RLF/CIF
Rags	Schwartz, Stephen	1986	Ensemble	Penny A Tune	Uptempo	SATB			Ensemble	Adults
Rags	Schwartz, Stephen	1986	Rachel Halpern	Penny A Tune	Uptempo	Alto	G3	Bb4	Lead	Mature Female
Rags	Schwartz, Stephen	1986	Rebecca Hershkowitz	Penny A Tune	Uptempo	Soprano	E4	F#4	Lead	Romantic Lead Female
Rags	Schwartz, Stephen	1986	Bella Cohen	Penny A Tune	Uptempo	Alto	B3	D5	Lead	Character Ingenue Female
Rags	Schwartz, Stephen	1986	Saul	Easy For You	Uptempo	Baritone	D3	D4	Lead	Antagonist Male
Rags	Schwartz, Stephen	1986	Ensemble	Hard To Be A Prince	Uptempo	SATB			Ensemble	Adults
Rags	Schwartz, Stephen	1986	Rebecca Hershkowitz	Blame It on The Summer Night	Moderate Tempo	Soprano	A3	D#5	Lead	Romantic Lead Female
Rags	Schwartz, Stephen	1986	Ben & Tenor	For My Mary	Moderate Tempo	Tenor/Tenor			Duet	CIM/CIM
Rags	Schwartz, Stephen	1986	Bella Cohen	Rags*	Uptempo	Alto	A3	D5	Lead	Character Ingenue Female
Rags	Schwartz, Stephen	1986	Bella & Avram Cohen	Rags	Uptempo	Alto/Bar			Duet	CIF/MM
Rags	Schwartz, Stephen	1986	Rebecca & Bella	If We Never Meet Again Reprise	Ballad	Sop/Alto			Duet	RLF/CIF
Rags	Schwartz, Stephen	1986	Nathan Hershkowitz	Uptown*	Moderate Tempo	Tenor	E3	G4	Lead	Character Male
Rags	Schwartz, Stephen	1986	Avram Cohen	Uptown*	Moderate Tempo	Soprano	C4	Eb5	Lead	Romantic Lead Female
Rags	Schwartz, Stephen	1986	Nathan & Rebecca	Uptown	Moderate Tempo	Tenor/Sop			Duet	CM/RLF
Rags	Schwartz, Stephen	1986	Rebecca Hershkowitz	Wanting*	Moderate Tempo	Soprano	A3	D#5	Lead	Romantic Lead Female
Rags	Schwartz, Stephen	1986	Saul & Rebecca	Wanting	Moderate Tempo	Bar/Sop			Duet	AM/RLF
Rags	Schwartz, Stephen	1986	Ben	The Sound Of Love*	Uptempo	Tenor	Eb3	Ab4	Lead	Character Ingenue Male
Rags	Schwartz, Stephen	1986	Ensemble	The Sound Of Love	Uptempo	SATB			Ensemble	Adults
Rags	Schwartz, Stephen	1986	Bella Cohen	Rags Reprise	Ballad	Alto	B#3	B4	Lead	Character Ingenue Female
Rags	Schwartz, Stephen	1986	Rachel Halpern	Three Sunny Rooms*	Moderate Tempo	Baritone	G3	Bb4	Lead	Mature Female
Rags	Schwartz, Stephen	1986	Avram Cohen	Three Sunny Rooms*	Moderate Tempo	Baritone	C3	D4	Lead	Paternal
Rags	Schwartz, Stephen	1986	Rachel & Avram	Three Sunny Rooms	Moderate Tempo	Alto/Bar			Duet	MF/P
Rags	Schwartz, Stephen	1986	Tim Sullivan	What's Wrong With That*	Uptempo	Tenor	A2	G4	Supporting	Character Male
Rags	Schwartz, Stephen	1986	Nathan Hershkowitz	What's Wrong With That*	Uptempo	Tenor	A2	G4	Lead	Character Male
Rags	Schwartz, Stephen	1986	Tim & Nathan	What's Wrong With That	Uptempo	Tenor/Tenor			Duet	CM/CM
Rags	Schwartz, Stephen	1986	Rebecca Hershkowitz	If We Never Meet Again Reprise 2	Ballad	Soprano	C4	D5	Lead	Romantic Lead Female
Rags	Schwartz, Stephen	1986	Ensemble	Kaddish	Moderate Tempo	STB			Ensemble	Adults

Shows

Songs by Character Type

* = Music Edit Required
+ = Ethnic Specific

Show	Composer	Year	Role	Song	Tempo	Vocal Type	Range-Bottom	Range-Top	Category	Character Type
Rags	Schwartz, Stephen	1986	Ensemble	Bread and Freedom*	Moderate Tempo	SATB			Ensemble	Adults
Rags	Schwartz, Stephen	1986	Rebecca Hershkowitz	Dancing With Fools*	Uptempo	Soprano	Bb3	Gb5	Lead	Romantic Lead Female
Ragtime	Flaherty, Stephen	1998	Ensemble	Prologue	Moderate Tempo	SATB			Ensemble	Children/Adults
Ragtime	Flaherty, Stephen	1998	Mother	Goodbye My Love	Moderate Tempo	Soprano	G3	Db5	Lead	Romantic Lead Female
Ragtime	Flaherty, Stephen	1998	Father	Journey On*	Uptempo	Baritone	B2	E4	Lead	Romantic Lead Male
Ragtime	Flaherty, Stephen	1998	Tateh	Journey On*	Uptempo	Tenor	Db3	Gb4	Lead	Paternal
Ragtime	Flaherty, Stephen	1998	Ensemble	Journey On	Uptempo	STB			Ensemble	Adults
Ragtime	Flaherty, Stephen	1998	Evelyn Nesbit	Crime Of The Century*	Uptempo	Alto	Bb3	D5	Lead	Romantic Lead Female
Ragtime	Flaherty, Stephen	1998	Mother	What Kind Of Woman*	Moderate Tempo	Soprano	Bb3	Eb5	Lead	Romantic Lead Female
Ragtime	Flaherty, Stephen	1998	Ensemble	A Shtetl Iz Amereke	Moderate Tempo	SATB			Ensemble	Children/Adults
Ragtime	Flaherty, Stephen	1998	Tateh	Success (Part 1, 2 & 5)	Uptempo	Tenor	D3	F#4	Lead	Paternal
Ragtime	Flaherty, Stephen	1998	Coalhouse Walker, Jr.+	Now She Is Haunting Me (Part 1)	Ballad	Baritone	Bb2	D4	Lead	Romantic Lead Male
Ragtime	Flaherty, Stephen	1998	Henry Ford	Henry Ford*	Uptempo	Tenor	D3	G4	Lead	Character Male
Ragtime	Flaherty, Stephen	1998	Ensemble	Henry Ford	Uptempo	SATB			Ensemble	Adults
Ragtime	Flaherty, Stephen	1998	Ensemble	Nothing Like The City	Moderate Tempo	SSST			Ensemble	Children/Adults
Ragtime	Flaherty, Stephen	1998	Sarah+	Your Daddy's Son (Bb Maj)	Ballad	Soprano	G3	F5	Lead	Character Ingenue Female
Ragtime	Flaherty, Stephen	1998	Sarah+	Your Daddy's Son (Cb Maj)	Ballad	Soprano	Ab3	Gb5	Lead	Character Ingenue Female
Ragtime	Flaherty, Stephen	1998	Father	New Music*	Ballad	Baritone	Bb2	D4	Lead	Romantic Lead Male
Ragtime	Flaherty, Stephen	1998	Mother	New Music*	Ballad	Soprano	Bb3	D5	Lead	Romantic Lead Female
Ragtime	Flaherty, Stephen	1998	Younger Brother	New Music*	Ballad	Tenor	Bb2	D4	Lead	Ingenue Male
Ragtime	Flaherty, Stephen	1998	Sarah+	New Music*	Ballad	Soprano	Bb3	D5	Lead	Character Ingenue Female
Ragtime	Flaherty, Stephen	1998	Coalhouse Walker, Jr.+	On The Wheels Of A Dream*	Moderate Tempo	Baritone	Ab2	Fb4	Lead	Romantic Lead Male
Ragtime	Flaherty, Stephen	1998	Coalhouse+ & Sarah+	On The Wheels Of A Dram	Moderate Tempo	Bar/Sop			Duet	RFM/CIF
Ragtime	Flaherty, Stephen	1998	Younger Brother	The Night That Goldman Spoke...(P 1 &	Uptempo	Tenor	B2	F#4	Lead	Ingenue Male
Ragtime	Flaherty, Stephen	1998	Tateh	Gliding (Part 1 & 2)	Moderate Tempo	Tenor	A2	F#4	Lead	Paternal
Ragtime	Flaherty, Stephen	1998	Sarah+	President (A Maj)*	Moderate Tempo	Soprano	A3	D5	Lead	Character Ingenue Female
Ragtime	Flaherty, Stephen	1998	Sarah+	President (Bb Maj)*	Moderate Tempo	Soprano	Bb3	Eb5	Lead	Character Ingenue Female
Ragtime	Flaherty, Stephen	1998	Sarah+	Justice*	Uptempo	Soprano	Ab3	C5	Lead	Character Ingenue Female
Ragtime	Flaherty, Stephen	1998	Ensemble	Till We Reach That Day	Moderate Tempo	SATB			Ensemble	Adults
Ragtime	Flaherty, Stephen	1998	Harry Houdini	Harry Houdini Master Escapist (Part 1&	Moderate Tempo	Tenor	Db3	Gb4	Lead	Character Male
Ragtime	Flaherty, Stephen	1998	Coalhouse Walker, Jr.+	Coalhouse's Soliloquoy	Moderate Tempo	Baritone	G2	F4	Lead	Romantic Lead Male
Ragtime	Flaherty, Stephen	1998	Ensemble	What A Game!	Uptempo	TB			Ensemble	Adults
Ragtime	Flaherty, Stephen	1998	Evelyn Nesbit	Atlantic City (Part 1)*	Uptempo	Alto	B3	B4	Lead	Romantic Lead Female
Ragtime	Flaherty, Stephen	1998	Ensemble	Atlantic City (Part 1)*	Uptempo	SATB			Ensemble	Adults
Ragtime	Flaherty, Stephen	1998	Evelyn Nesbit	Atlantic City (Part 3)*	Uptempo	Alto	Bb3	D5	Lead	Romantic Lead Female
Ragtime	Flaherty, Stephen	1998	Harry Houdini	Atlantic City (Part 3)*	Uptempo	Tenor	E3	G4	Lead	Character Male
Ragtime	Flaherty, Stephen	1998	Harry Houdini & Evelyn	Atlantic City (Part 3)*	Uptempo	Tenor/Sop			Duet	CM/RLF
Ragtime	Flaherty, Stephen	1998	Tateh	Buffalo Nickel Photoplay Inc.	Uptempo	Tenor	B2	F#4	Lead	Paternal
Ragtime	Flaherty, Stephen	1998	Mother & Tateh	Our Children	Moderate Tempo	Sop/Tenor			Duet	RLF/P
Ragtime	Flaherty, Stephen	1998	Coalhouse Walker, Jr.	Sarah Brown Eyes*	Moderate Tempo	Baritone	A2	E4	Lead	Romantic Lead Male
Ragtime	Flaherty, Stephen	1998	Coalhouse+ & Sarah+	Sarah Brown Eyes	Moderate Tempo	Bar/Sop			Duet	RLM/RLF

Shows

* = Music Edit Required
+ = Ethnic Specific

Show	Composer	Year	Role	Song	Tempo	Vocal Type	Range-Bottom	Range-Top	Category	Character Type
Ragtime	Flaherty, Stephen	1998	Emma Goldman	He Wanted To Say*	Moderate Tempo	Alto	G3	Bb4	Lead	Character Female
Ragtime	Flaherty, Stephen	1998	Ensemble	He Wanted To Say	Moderate Tempo	ATB			Ensemble	Adults
Ragtime	Flaherty, Stephen	1998	Mother	Back To Before	Moderate Tempo	Soprano	G3	C5	Lead	Romantic Lead Female
Ragtime	Flaherty, Stephen	1998	Coalhouse Walker, Jr.+	Make Them Hear You	Moderate Tempo	Baritone	Eb3	G#4	Lead	Romantic Lead Male
Ragtime	Flaherty, Stephen	1998	Ensemble	Epilogue Two	Moderate Tempo	SATB			Ensemble	Adults
Rent	Larson, Jonathan	1996	Ensemble	Rent	Uptempo	SATB			Ensemble	Adults
Rent	Larson, Jonathan	1996	Mark Cohen & Roger Davis	Rent*	Uptempo	Tenor/Tenor			Duet	CM/RAM
Rent	Larson, Jonathan	1996	Angel Schunard & Tom Collins	You Okay, Honey	Moderate Tempo	Tenor/Tenor			Duet	CIM/RLM
Rent	Larson, Jonathan	1996	Roger Davis	One Song Glory	Moderate Tempo	Tenor	D3	Ab4	Lead	Romantic Lead Male
Rent	Larson, Jonathan	1996	Mimi Marquez & Roger Davis	Light My Candle	Moderate Tempo	Alto/Tenor			Duet	RAF/RAM
Rent	Larson, Jonathan	1996	Angel Schunard	Today For You*	Uptempo	Tenor	Bb3	G4	Lead	Character Ingenue Male
Rent	Larson, Jonathan	1996	Ensemble	You'll See	Uptempo	TTTBB			Ensemble	Adults
Rent	Larson, Jonathan	1996	Mark Cohen & Joanne Jefferso	Tango Maureen	Moderate Tempo	Tenor/Atlo			Duet	CM/AF
Rent	Larson, Jonathan	1996	Ensemble	Life Support*	Moderate Tempo	SATB			Ensemble	Adults
Rent	Larson, Jonathan	1996	Mimi Marquez	Out Tonight	Uptempo	Alto	A3	E5	Lead	Romantic Antagonist Female
Rent	Larson, Jonathan	1996	Roger Davis	Another Day*	Uptempo	Tenor	F3	Gb4	Lead	Romantic Antagonist Male
Rent	Larson, Jonathan	1996	Mimi Marquez	Another Day*	Uptempo	Alto	B3	B4	Lead	Romantic Antagonist Female
Rent	Larson, Jonathan	1996	Roger Davis & Mimi Marquez	Another Day*	Uptempo	Tenor/Atlo			Duet	RAM/RAF
Rent	Larson, Jonathan	1996	Ensemble	Another Day	Uptempo	SATB			Ensemble	Adults
Rent	Larson, Jonathan	1996	Ensemble	Will I	Moderate Tempo	SATB			Ensemble	Adults
Rent	Larson, Jonathan	1996	Tom Collins	Sante Fe*	Moderate Tempo	Tenor	F#2	F#4	Lead	Romantic Lead Male
Rent	Larson, Jonathan	1996	Ensemble	Sante Fe	Moderate Tempo	SATB			Ensemble	Adults
Rent	Larson, Jonathan	1996	Angel Schunard	I'll Cover You*	Moderate Tempo	Tenor	G3	A4	Lead	Character Ingenue Male
Rent	Larson, Jonathan	1996	Tom Collins	I'll Cover You*	Moderate Tempo	Tenor	C3	G4	Lead	Romantic Lead Male
Rent	Larson, Jonathan	1996	Angel & Tom	I'll Cover You	Moderate Tempo	Tenor/Tenor			Duet	CIM/RLM
Rent	Larson, Jonathan	1996	Joanne Jefferson	We're Okay	Uptempo	Alto	C4	C5	Lead	Antagonist Female
Rent	Larson, Jonathan	1996	Maureen Johnson	Over The Moon	Moderate Tempo	Alto	C4	Eb5	Lead	Romantic Antagonist Female
Rent	Larson, Jonathan	1996	Ensemble	La Vie Boheme*	Uptempo	SATB			Ensemble	Adults
Rent	Larson, Jonathan	1996	Roger Davis & Mimi Marquez	I Should Tell You*	Ballad	Tenor/Atlo			Duet	RAM/RAF
Rent	Larson, Jonathan	1996	Ensemble	Seasons Of Love	Moderate Tempo	SATB			Ensemble	Adults
Rent	Larson, Jonathan	1996	Joanne Jefferson	Take Me Or leave Me*	Uptempo	Alto	C4	E5	Lead	Antagonist Female
Rent	Larson, Jonathan	1996	Maureen Johnson	Take Me Or leave Me*	Uptempo	Alto	C4	F5	Lead	Romantic Antagonist Female
Rent	Larson, Jonathan	1996	Maureen & Joanne	Take Me Or leave Me	Uptempo	Alto/Alto			Duet	RAF/AF
Rent	Larson, Jonathan	1996	Ensemble	Seasons Of Love B	Moderate Tempo	SATB			Ensemble	Adults
Rent	Larson, Jonathan	1996	Mimi Marquez	Without You*	Moderate Tempo	Alto	A3	A4	Lead	Romantic Antagonist Female
Rent	Larson, Jonathan	1996	Ensemble	Contact	Uptempo	SATB			Ensemble	Adults
Rent	Larson, Jonathan	1996	Tom Collins	I'll Cover You Reprise*	Ballad	Tenor	F#2	A4	Lead	Romantic Lead Male
Rent	Larson, Jonathan	1996	Ensemble	I'll Cover You Reprise	Ballad	SATB			Ensemble	Adults
Rent	Larson, Jonathan	1996	Mark Cohen	Halloween	Moderate Tempo	Tenor	Eb3	Eb4	Lead	Character Male
Rent	Larson, Jonathan	1996	Mimi Marquez	Goodbye Love*	Moderate Tempo	Alto	A4	C5	Lead	Romantic Antagonist Female
Rent	Larson, Jonathan	1996	Mimi Marquez & Roger Davis	Goodbye Love	Moderate Tempo	Alto/Tenor			Duet	RAF/RAM
Rent	Larson, Jonathan	1996	Mark Cohen	You Are What You Own*	Uptempo	Tenor	D3	E4	Lead	Character Male
Rent	Larson, Jonathan	1996	Mark Cohen & Roger Davis	You Are What You Own	Uptempo	Tenor/Tenor			Duet	CM/RAM

Shows

Songs by Character Type

Show	Composer	Year	Role	Song	Tempo	Vocal Type	Range-Bottom	Range-Top	Category	Character Type
Rent	Larson, Jonathan	1996	Roger Davis	Your Eyes*	Ballad	Tenor	B2	G4	Lead	Romantic Antagonist Male
Rent	Larson, Jonathan	1996	Ensemble	Finale B-Medley	Moderate Tempo	SATB			Ensemble	Adults
Romance/Romance	Herrmann, Keith	1987	Ensemble	So Glad I Married	Moderate Tempo	SATB			Ensemble	Adults
Romance/Romance	Herrmann, Keith	1987	Barb & Lenny	Small Craft Warning	Moderate Tempo	Sop/Bar			Duet	RLF/RLM
Romance/Romance	Herrmann, Keith	1987	Monica	How Did I End Up Here	Uptempo	Alto	F3	C5	Lead	Romantic Antagonist Female
Romance/Romance	Herrmann, Keith	1987	Sam	There Are Things He Doesn't Say	Ballad	Tenor	Ab2	G4	Lead	Romantic Antagonist Male
Romance/Romance	Herrmann, Keith	1987	Barb & Lenny	My Love For You	Uptempo	Bar/Sop			Duet	RLF/RLM
Romance/Romance	Herrmann, Keith	1987	Sam	Moonlight Passing Through A Window	Ballad	Tenor	D3	F4	Lead	Romantic Antagonist Male
Romance/Romance	Herrmann, Keith	1987	Monica	Now	Uptempo	Alto	A3	D5	Lead	Romantic Antagonist Female
Romance/Romance	Herrmann, Keith	1987	Ensemble	Romantic Notions	Ballad	SATB			Ensemble	Adults
Romance/Romance	Herrmann, Keith	1987	Sam	Romantic Notions*	Ballad	Tenor	B3	E4	Lead	Romantic Antagonist Male
Romance/Romance	Herrmann, Keith	1987	Alfred & Josephine	Little Comedy	Moderate Tempo	Tenor/Atlo			Duet	RAM/RAF
Romance/Romance	Herrmann, Keith	1987	Josephine Weninger	Goodbye Emil	Uptempo	Alto	A3	F5	Lead	Romantic Antagonist Female
Romance/Romance	Herrmann, Keith	1987	Josephine Weninger	Goodbye Emil Reprise	Uptempo	Alto	Bb3	E5	Lead	Romantic Antagonist Female
Romance/Romance	Herrmann, Keith	1987	Alfred Von Wilmers	It's Not Too Late*	Moderate Tempo	Tenor	Bb2	F4	Lead	Romantic Antagonist Male
Romance/Romance	Herrmann, Keith	1987	Josephine Weninger	It's Not Too Late*	Moderate Tempo	Alto	G3	Cb5	Lead	Romantic Antagonist Female
Romance/Romance	Herrmann, Keith	1987	Alfred & Josephine	It's Not Too Late	Moderate Tempo	Tenor/Atlo			Duet	RAM/RAF
Romance/Romance	Herrmann, Keith	1987	Alfred & Josephine	Great News	Uptempo	Tenor/Atlo			Duet	RAM/RAF
Romance/Romance	Herrmann, Keith	1987	Alfred & Josephine	A Performance*	Moderate Tempo	Tenor	A2	F#4	Lead	Romantic Antagonist Male
Romance/Romance	Herrmann, Keith	1987	Josephine Weninger	A Performance*	Moderate Tempo	Alto	G3	D#5	Lead	Romantic Antagonist Female
Romance/Romance	Herrmann, Keith	1987	Alfred & Josephine	A Performance	Moderate Tempo	Tenor/Atlo			Duet	RAM/RAF
Romance/Romance	Herrmann, Keith	1987	Alfred Von Wilmers	I'll Remember The Song*	Uptempo	Tenor	B2	E4	Lead	Romantic Antagonist Male
Romance/Romance	Herrmann, Keith	1987	Josephine Weninger	I'll Remember The Song*	Uptempo	Alto	B3	D4	Lead	Romantic Antagonist Female
Romance/Romance	Herrmann, Keith	1987	Alfred & Josephine	I'll Remember The Song	Uptempo	Tenor/Atlo			Duet	RAM/RAF
Romance/Romance	Herrmann, Keith	1987	Alfred Von Wilmers	Happy, Happy, Happy	Ballad	Tenor	Bb2	F#4	Lead	Romantic Antagonist Male
Romance/Romance	Herrmann, Keith	1987	Alfred Von Wilmers	Women Of Vienna	Moderate Tempo	Tenor	C3	F#4	Lead	Romantic Antagonist Male
Romance/Romance	Herrmann, Keith	1987	Josephine Weninger	Yes, It's Love	Uptempo	Alto	Ab3	C5	Lead	Romantic Antagonist Female
Romance/Romance	Herrmann, Keith	1987	Alfred Von Wilmers	A Rustic Country Inn*	Uptempo	Tenor	C3	F4	Lead	Romantic Antagonist Male
Romance/Romance	Herrmann, Keith	1987	Josephine Weninger	A Rustic Country Inn*	Uptempo	Alto	G3	E5	Lead	Romantic Antagonist Female
Romance/Romance	Herrmann, Keith	1987	Alfred & Josephine	A Rustic Country Inn	Uptempo	Tenor/Atlo			Duet	RAM/RAF
Romance/Romance	Herrmann, Keith	1987	Monica	The Night It Had To End	Ballad	Alto	Ab3	Db5	Lead	Romantic Antagonist Female
Romance/Romance	Herrmann, Keith	1987	Alfred & Josephine	A Little Comedy Finale	Moderate Tempo	Tenor/Atlo			Duet	RAM/RAF
Romance/Romance	Herrmann, Keith	1987	Ensemble	Summer Share	Uptempo	SATB			Ensemble	Adults
Romance/Romance	Herrmann, Keith	1987	Barb & Lenny	Think Of The Odds	Moderate Tempo	Sop/Bar			Duet	RLF/RLM
Romance/Romance	Herrmann, Keith	1987	Sam	It's Not Too Late Reprise*	Moderate Tempo	Tenor	Bb2	A4	Lead	Romantic Antagonist Male
Romance/Romance	Herrmann, Keith	1987	Sam & Monica	It's Not Too Late Reprise	Moderate Tempo	Tenor/Atlo			Duet	RAM/RAF
Romance/Romance	Herrmann, Keith	1987	Monica	Plan A and B	Uptempo	Alto	Ab3	A4	Lead	Romantic Antagonist Female
Romance/Romance	Herrmann, Keith	1987	Barb & Lenny	Let's Not Talk About It	Ballad	Sop/Bar			Duet	RAM/RAF
Scarlet Pimpernel, The	Wildhorn, Frank	1997	Ensemble	Storybook	Moderate Tempo	SATB			Ensemble	Adults
Scarlet Pimpernel, The	Wildhorn, Frank	1997	Marguerite St. Just	Storybook*	Moderate Tempo	Alto	A3	E5	Lead	Romantic Lead Female
Scarlet Pimpernel, The	Wildhorn, Frank	1997	Chauvelin	Madame Guillotine*	Uptempo	Baritone	B2	F4	Lead	Romantic Antagonist Male
Scarlet Pimpernel, The	Wildhorn, Frank	1997	Ensemble	Madame Guillotine	Uptempo	SATB			Ensemble	Adults
Scarlet Pimpernel, The	Wildhorn, Frank	1997	Marguerite St. Just	You Are My Home*	Ballad	Alto	C#4	F#5	Lead	Romantic Lead Female

Shows

Songs by Character Type

* = Music Edit Required
+ = Ethnic Specific

Show	Composer	Year	Role	Song	Tempo	Vocal Type	Range-Bottom	Range-Top	Category	Character Type
Scarlet Pimpernel, The	Wildhorn, Frank	1997	Percy Blakeney	You Are My Home*	Ballad	Tenor	B2	G4	Lead	Romantic Lead Male
Scarlet Pimpernel, The	Wildhorn, Frank	1997	Ensemble	You Are My Home	Ballad	SATB			Ensemble	Adults
Scarlet Pimpernel, The	Wildhorn, Frank	1997	Percy & Marguerite	You Are My Home*	Ballad	Tenor/Alto			Duet	RLM/RLF
Scarlet Pimpernel, The	Wildhorn, Frank	1997	Percy Blakeney	Prayer*	Ballad	Tenor	Bb2	Ab4	Lead	Romantic Lead Male
Scarlet Pimpernel, The	Wildhorn, Frank	1997	Percy Blakeney	Into The Fire*	Uptempo	Tenor	D3	Ab4	Lead	Romantic Lead Male
Scarlet Pimpernel, The	Wildhorn, Frank	1997	Ensemble	Into The Fire	Uptempo	TB			Ensemble	Adults
Scarlet Pimpernel, The	Wildhorn, Frank	1997	Chauvelin	Falcon In The Dive*	Uptempo	Baritone	G2	G4	Lead	Romantic Antagonist Male
Scarlet Pimpernel, The	Wildhorn, Frank	1997	Ensemble	Scarlet Pimpernel	Moderate Tempo	SATB			Ensemble	Adults
Scarlet Pimpernel, The	Wildhorn, Frank	1997	Marguerite St. Just	When I Look At You	Ballad	Alto	B3	E5	Lead	Romantic Lead Female
Scarlet Pimpernel, The	Wildhorn, Frank	1997	Percy Blakeney	When I Look At You Reprise	Ballad	Tenor	Db3	F4	Lead	Romantic Lead Male
Scarlet Pimpernel, The	Wildhorn, Frank	1997	Chauvelin	Where's The Girl	Moderate Tempo	Baritone	B2	G4	Lead	Romantic Antagonist Male
Scarlet Pimpernel, The	Wildhorn, Frank	1997	Marguerite & Armad	You Are My Home (Garden Reprise)	Ballad	Alto/Tenor			Duet	RLF/IM
Scarlet Pimpernel, The	Wildhorn, Frank	1997	Ensemble	The Creation Of Man	Moderate Tempo	SATB			Ensemble	Adults
Scarlet Pimpernel, The	Wildhorn, Frank	1997	Chauvelin	The Riddle Part 1	Moderate Tempo	Baritone	A2	D4	Lead	Romantic Antagonist Male
Scarlet Pimpernel, The	Wildhorn, Frank	1997	Chauvelin & Marguerite	The Riddle Part 3*	Moderate Tempo	Bar/Alto			Duet	RAM/RLF
Scarlet Pimpernel, The	Wildhorn, Frank	1997	Ensemble	The Riddle Part 3	Moderate Tempo	SATB			Ensemble	Adults
Scarlet Pimpernel, The	Wildhorn, Frank	1997	Ensemble	They Seek Him Here	Moderate Tempo	SATB			Ensemble	Adults
Scarlet Pimpernel, The	Wildhorn, Frank	1997	Percy Blakeney	She Was There	Ballad	Tenor	C#3	G#4	Lead	Romantic Lead Male
Scarlet Pimpernel, The	Wildhorn, Frank	1997	Percy Blakeney	She Was There Tag	Moderate Tempo	Tenor	A3	G4	Lead	Romantic Lead Male
Scarlet Pimpernel, The	Wildhorn, Frank	1997	Chauvelin	Where Is The Girl Reprise	Moderate Tempo	Baritone	B2	G4	Lead	Romantic Antagonist Male
Scarlet Pimpernel, The	Wildhorn, Frank	1997	Ensemble	Into The Fire Reprise	Uptempo	SATB			Ensemble	Adults
Scarlet Pimpernel, The	Wildhorn, Frank	1997	Marguerite St. Just	I'll Foget You	Ballad	Alto	G#3	D5	Lead	Romantic Lead Female
Scarlet Pimpernel, The	Wildhorn, Frank	1997	Percy & Marguerite	Finale-When I Look At You	Moderate Tempo	Tenor/Atlo			Duet	RLM/RLF
Scarlet Pimpernel, The	Wildhorn, Frank	1997	Percy & Marguerite	Believe	Moderate Tempo	Tenor/Atlo			Duet	RLM/RLF
Scarlet Pimpernel, The	Wildhorn, Frank	1997	Ensemble	Vivez	Moderate Tempo	SATB			Ensemble	Adults
Scarlet Pimpernel, The	Wildhorn, Frank	1997	Marguerite St. Just	Vivez*	Moderate Tempo	Alto	C#4	E5	Lead	Romantic Lead Female
Scarlet Pimpernel, The	Wildhorn, Frank	1997	Percy & Marguerite	Believe Reprise	Moderate Tempo	Tenor/Atlo			Duet	RLM/RLF
Scarlet Pimpernel, The	Wildhorn, Frank	1997	Helen & Chloe	Lullabye	Ballad	Sop/Sop			Duet	MF/JF
Scarlet Pimpernel, The	Wildhorn, Frank	1997	Marguerite St. Just	Only Love	Ballad	Alto	Bb3	E5	Lead	Romantic Lead Female
Secret Garden, The	Simon, Lucy	1991	Ensemble	There's A Girl	Uptempo	SATB			Ensemble	Adults
Secret Garden, The	Simon, Lucy	1991	Ensemble	The House Upon A Hill*	Moderate Tempo	SATB			Ensemble	Adults
Secret Garden, The	Simon, Lucy	1991	Ensemble	I Heard Someone Crying	Moderate Tempo	SATB			Ensemble	Adults
Secret Garden, The	Simon, Lucy	1991	Martha	If I Had A Fine White Horse	Uptempo	Alto	G3	D5	Lead	Character Female
Secret Garden, The	Simon, Lucy	1991	Archibald & Lily	A Girl In The Vallet	Moderate Tempo	Tenor/Sop			Duet	CM/RLF
Secret Garden, The	Simon, Lucy	1991	Ensemble	It's A Maze	Uptempo	SATB			Ensemble	Adults
Secret Garden, The	Simon, Lucy	1991	Dickon	Winter's On The Wing	Uptempo	Tenor	D3	F#4	Lead	Character Ingenue Male
Secret Garden, The	Simon, Lucy	1991	Mary Lennox	Show Me The Key (ms 52-92)	Uptempo	Alto	B3	C#5	Lead	Juvenile Female
Secret Garden, The	Simon, Lucy	1991	Dickon & Mary	Show Me The Key	Moderate Tempo	Tenor/Atlo			Duet	CIM/JF
Secret Garden, The	Simon, Lucy	1991	Dickon	Winter's On The Wing Reprise	Ballad	Tenor	D3	E4	Lead	Character Ingenue Male
Secret Garden, The	Simon, Lucy	1991	Archibald Craven	A Bit of Earth*	Moderate Tempo	Baritone	D3	E4	Lead	Character Male
Secret Garden, The	Simon, Lucy	1991	Ensemble	Storm I	Uptempo	SATB			Ensemble	Adults
Secret Garden, The	Simon, Lucy	1991	Archibald & Neville	Lily's Eyes	Moderate Tempo	Bar/Bar			Duet	CM/RLM
Secret Garden, The	Simon, Lucy	1991	Mary Lennox	Storm III*	Moderate Tempo	Alto	B3	E5	Lead	Juvenile Female
Secret Garden, The	Simon, Lucy	1991	Colin Craven	Round-Shouldered Man	Uptempo	Soprano	A3	D5	Lead	Juvenile Male

Shows

Songs by Character Type

Show	Composer	Year	Role	Song	Tempo	Vocal Type	Range-Bottom	Range-Top	Category	Character Type
Secret Garden, The	Simon, Lucy	1991	Ensemble	Storm Final	Uptempo	SATB			Ensemble	Adults
Secret Garden, The	Simon, Lucy	1991	Mary Lennox	The Girl I Mean To Be	Uptempo	Alto	A♭3	C5	Lead	Juvenile Female
Secret Garden, The	Simon, Lucy	1991	Ensemble	Quartet	Uptempo	SATB			Ensemble	Adults
Secret Garden, The	Simon, Lucy	1991	Archibald Craven	Race You To The Top Of The Morning	Uptempo	Tenor	E♭3	A♭4	Lead	Character Male
Secret Garden, The	Simon, Lucy	1991	Dickon	Wick*	Uptempo	Tenor	F3	G4	Lead	Character Ingenue Male
Secret Garden, The	Simon, Lucy	1991	Dickon & Mary	Wick	Uptempo	Tenor/Alto			Duet	CIM/JF
Secret Garden, The	Simon, Lucy	1991	Lily	Come To My Garden*	Moderate Tempo	Soprano	C4	G5	Lead	Romantic Lead Female
Secret Garden, The	Simon, Lucy	1991	Colin Craven	Come To My Garden*	Moderate Tempo	Soprano	C4	E5	Lead	Juvenile Male
Secret Garden, The	Simon, Lucy	1991	Lily & Colin	Come To My Garden	Moderate Tempo	Sop/Sop			Duet	RLF/JM
Secret Garden, The	Simon, Lucy	1991	Ensemble	Come Spirit Come Charm	Uptempo	SATB			Ensemble	Children/Adults
Secret Garden, The	Simon, Lucy	1991	Ensemble	A Bit Of Earth Reprise	Moderate Tempo	SAT			Ensemble	Adults
Secret Garden, The	Simon, Lucy	1991	Neville Craven	Disppear*	Moderate Tempo	Baritone	C3	F4	Lead	Romantic Lead Male
Secret Garden, The	Simon, Lucy	1991	Martha	Hold On	Uptempo	Alto	F#3	B4	Lead	Character Female
Secret Garden, The	Simon, Lucy	1991	Mary Lennox	Letter Song*	Moderate Tempo	Alto	B♭3	C5	Lead	Juvenile Female
Secret Garden, The	Simon, Lucy	1991	Archibald Craven	Where In The World	Uptempo	Tenor	F3	F♭4	Lead	Character Male
Secret Garden, The	Simon, Lucy	1991	Lily	How Could I Ever Know*	Ballad	Soprano	B♭3	A5	Lead	Romantic Lead Female
Secret Garden, The	Simon, Lucy	1991	Lily & Archibald	How Could I Ever Know	Ballad	Sop/Tenor			Duet	RLF/CM
Secret Garden, The	Simon, Lucy	1991	Ensemble	Finale-Come To My Garden	Moderate Tempo	SATB			Ensemble	Adults
Seussical	Flaherty, Stephen	2000	Ensemble	Oh, The thinks You Can Think	Uptempo	SATB			Ensemble	Adults
Seussical	Flaherty, Stephen	2000	Horton	Horton Hears A Who (ms 17-119)	Moderate Tempo	Baritone	A2	E4	Lead	Character Male
Seussical	Flaherty, Stephen	2000	Ensemble	Horton Hears A Who	Moderate Tempo	SATB			Ensemble	Adults
Seussical	Flaherty, Stephen	2000	Sour Kangaroo	Biggest Blame Fool (ms 9-29)*	Uptempo	Alto	B♭3	D♭5	Lead	Antagonist Female
Seussical	Flaherty, Stephen	2000	Ensemble	Biggest Blame Fool	Uptempo	SATB			Ensemble	Adults
Seussical	Flaherty, Stephen	2000	The Mayor	We're Whos Here Part 1*	Uptempo	Baritone	E3	E4	Supporting	Character Male
Seussical	Flaherty, Stephen	2000	Ensemble	We're Whos Here Part 1-4	Uptempo	SATB			Ensemble	Children/Adults
Seussical	Flaherty, Stephen	2000	The Cat In The Hat	A Day For The Cat In The Hat*	Uptempo	Baritone	E3	E4	Lead	Character Male
Seussical	Flaherty, Stephen	2000	The Cat In The Hat	A Day For The Cat In The Hat*	Uptempo	Alto	E3	E4	Lead	Character Female
Seussical	Flaherty, Stephen	2000	Ensemble	It's Possible*	Uptempo	SATB			Ensemble	Adults
Seussical	Flaherty, Stephen	2000	Mrs. Mayor	How To Raise A Child*	Uptempo	Alto	A3	B♭4	Lead	Character Female
Seussical	Flaherty, Stephen	2000	The Mayor	How To Raise A Child*	Uptempo	Baritone	A2	E4	Lead	Character Male
Seussical	Flaherty, Stephen	2000	The Mayor & Mrs. Mayor	How To Raise A Child	Uptempo	Bar/Alto			Duet	CM/CF
Seussical	Flaherty, Stephen	2000	Genghis Kahn Schmitz	The Military*	Uptempo	Baritone	G2	F4	Supporting	Antagonist Male
Seussical	Flaherty, Stephen	2000	Ensemble	The Military	Uptempo	TB			Ensemble	Adults
Seussical	Flaherty, Stephen	2000	Horton	Alone In The Universe*	Moderate Tempo	Baritone	B2	E4	Lead	Character Male
Seussical	Flaherty, Stephen	2000	JoJo	Alone In The Universe*	Moderate Tempo	Alto	A♭3	A♭4	Lead	Juvenile Male
Seussical	Flaherty, Stephen	2000	Horton & JoJo	Alone In The Universe	Moderate Tempo	Bar/Alto			Duet	CM/JM
Seussical	Flaherty, Stephen	2000	Gertrude McFuzz	The One Feather Tail	Moderate Tempo	Soprano	G3	C5	Lead	Character Ingenue Female
Seussical	Flaherty, Stephen	2000	Mayzie LaBird	Amayzing Mayzie*	Uptempo	Alto	G#3	D5	Lead	Romantic Antagonist Female
Seussical	Flaherty, Stephen	2000	Ensemble	Amayzing Mayzie	Uptempo	SA			Ensemble	Adults
Seussical	Flaherty, Stephen	2000	Gertrude McFuzz	Amayzing Gertrude*	Uptempo	Soprano	C#4	D6	Lead	Character Ingenue Female
Seussical	Flaherty, Stephen	2000	Ensemble	Amayzing Gertrude	Uptempo	SA			Ensemble	Adults
Seussical	Flaherty, Stephen	2000	Ensemble	Monkey Around	Uptempo	TB			Ensemble	Adults
Seussical	Flaherty, Stephen	2000	Ensemble	Chasing The Whos	Uptempo	SATB			Ensemble	Adults

Shows

* = Music Edit Required
+ = Ethnic Specific

Show	Composer	Year	Role	Song	Tempo	Vocal Type	Range-Bottom	Range-Top	Category	Character Type
Seussical	Flaherty, Stephen	2000	The Cat In The Hat	How Lucky You Are	Moderate Tempo	Baritone	D3	F4	Lead	Character Male
Seussical	Flaherty, Stephen	2000	The Cat In The Hat	How Lucky You Are	Moderate Tempo	Alto	D3	F4	Lead	Character Female
Seussical	Flaherty, Stephen	2000	Gertrude McFuzz	Notice Me, Horton*	Uptempo	Soprano	G3	C5	Lead	Character Ingenue Female
Seussical	Flaherty, Stephen	2000	Gertrude & Horton	Notice Me, Horton	Uptempo	Sop/Bar			Duet	CIF/CM
Seussical	Flaherty, Stephen	2000	Mayzie LaBird	How Lucky You Are Reprise	Moderate Tempo	Alto	Bb3	D5	Lead	Romantic Antagonist Female
Seussical	Flaherty, Stephen	2000	Ensemble	Finale: Horton Sits On An Egg	Moderate Tempo	SATB			Ensemble	Adults
Seussical	Flaherty, Stephen	2000	Ensemble	Egg, Nest, And Tree	Uptempo	SATB			Ensemble	Adults
Seussical	Flaherty, Stephen	2000	Mayzie LaBird	Mayzie In Palm Beach*	Uptempo	Alto	G3	C5	Lead	Romantic Antagonist Female
Seussical	Flaherty, Stephen	2000	Horton	Alone In The Universe Reprise	Moderate Tempo	Baritone	C3	C5	Lead	Character Male
Seussical	Flaherty, Stephen	2000	Ensemble	Solla Sollew	Moderate Tempo	SATB			Ensemble	Adults
Seussical	Flaherty, Stephen	2000	Horton	Solla Sollew*	Moderate Tempo	Baritone	C3	D4	Lead	Character Male
Seussical	Flaherty, Stephen	2000	The Cat In The Hat	Havin' A Hunch*	Uptempo	Baritone	C#3	E4	Lead	Character Male
Seussical	Flaherty, Stephen	2000	The Cat In The Hat	Havin' A Hunch*	Uptempo	Alto	C#4	E5	Lead	Character Female
Seussical	Flaherty, Stephen	2000	Gertrude McFuzz	For You*	Uptempo	Soprano	F3	C5	Lead	Character Ingenue Female
Seussical	Flaherty, Stephen	2000	Ensemble	For You	Uptempo	SA			Ensemble	Adults
Seussical	Flaherty, Stephen	2000	Ensemble	The People Versus Horton The Elephant	Uptempo	SATB			Ensemble	Adults
Seussical	Flaherty, Stephen	2000	Ensemble	Finale-Oh, The Thinks You Can Think	Uptempo	SATB			Ensemble	Adults
Seven Brides/Seven Brothe	de Paul, Kaska, Hirshchbor	1982	Adam	Bless Your Beautiful Hide*	Moderate Tempo	Baritone	B2	G4	Lead	Romantic Lead Male
Seven Brides/Seven Brothe	de Paul, Kaska, Hirshchbor	1982	Adam	Get A Wife*	Moderate Tempo	Baritone	F3	G4	Lead	Romantic Lead Male
Seven Brides/Seven Brothe	de Paul, Kaska, Hirshchbor	1982	Milly	Wonderful Day*	Moderate Tempo	Alto	Ab3	Db5	Lead	Character Ingenue Female
Seven Brides/Seven Brothe	de Paul, Kaska, Hirshchbor	1982	Ensemble	Wonderful Day	Moderate Tempo	SA			Ensemble	Adults
Seven Brides/Seven Brothe	de Paul, Kaska, Hirshchbor	1982	Milly	I'm Jumpin' In*	Moderate Tempo	Alto	Ab3	Bb4	Lead	Character Ingenue Female
Seven Brides/Seven Brothe	de Paul, Kaska, Hirshchbor	1982	Milly	One Man*	Moderate Tempo	Alto	G3	Bb4	Lead	Character Ingenue Female
Seven Brides/Seven Brothe	de Paul, Kaska, Hirshchbor	1982	Milly	I Married Seven Brothers*	Moderate Tempo	Alto	G3	Bb4	Lead	Character Ingenue Female
Seven Brides/Seven Brothe	de Paul, Kaska, Hirshchbor	1982	Milly	Goin' Co'tin*	Moderate Tempo	Alto	Bb3	Eb5	Lead	Character Ingenue Female
Seven Brides/Seven Brothe	de Paul, Kaska, Hirshchbor	1982	Adam	Love Never Goes Away*	Ballad	Baritone	E3	E4	Lead	Romantic Lead Male
Seven Brides/Seven Brothe	de Paul, Kaska, Hirshchbor	1982	Gideon	Love Never Goes Away*	Ballad	Tenor	D3	G4	Lead	Ingenue Male
Seven Brides/Seven Brothe	de Paul, Kaska, Hirshchbor	1982	Milly	Love Never Goes Away	Ballad	Alto	G3	B5	Lead	Character Ingenue Female
Seven Brides/Seven Brothe	de Paul, Kaska, Hirshchbor	1982	Ensemble	Sobbin' Women	Uptempo	ATB			Ensemble	Adults
Seven Brides/Seven Brothe	de Paul, Kaska, Hirshchbor	1982	Ensemble	Sobbin' Women*	Uptempo	TB			Ensemble	Adults
Seven Brides/Seven Brothe	de Paul, Kaska, Hirshchbor	1982	Adam	Suitors Lament	Ballad	Baritone	C3	F4	Lead	Romantic Lead Male
Seven Brides/Seven Brothe	de Paul, Kaska, Hirshchbor	1982	Ensemble	A Woman Ought To Know Her Place	Uptempo	TB			Ensemble	Adults
Seven Brides/Seven Brothe	de Paul, Kaska, Hirshchbor	1982	Ensemble	We Gotta Make It Through The Winter	Uptempo	TB			Ensemble	Adults
Seven Brides/Seven Brothe	de Paul, Kaska, Hirshchbor	1982	Milly	Lonesome Polecat	Ballad	TB			Ensemble	Adults
Seven Brides/Seven Brothe	de Paul, Kaska, Hirshchbor	1982	Milly	We Gotta Make It Through…Reprise*	Ballad	Alto	A3	A4	Lead	Character Ingenue Female
Seven Brides/Seven Brothe	de Paul, Kaska, Hirshchbor	1982	Adam & Gideon	A Woman Ought To Know…Reprise	Uptempo	Bar/Alto			Duet	RLM/CIF
Seven Brides/Seven Brothe	de Paul, Kaska, Hirshchbor	1982	Milly	Glad That You Were Born*	Ballad	Alto	Db4	Bb4	Lead	Character Ingenue Female
Seven Brides/Seven Brothe	de Paul, Kaska, Hirshchbor	1982	Adam	Love Never Goes Away Tag	Ballad	Baritone	B3	D4	Lead	Romantic Lead Male
Seven Brides/Seven Brothe	de Paul, Kaska, Hirshchbor	1982	Adam & Milly	Wonderful Day Reprise	Moderate Tempo	Bar/Alto			Duet	RLM/CIF
Seven Brides/Seven Brothe	de Paul, Kaska, Hirshchbor	1982	Ensemble	Goin' Co'tin/Wonderful, Wonderful	Moderate Tempo	SATB			Ensemble	Adults
She Loves Me	Bock, Jerry	1963	Ensemble	Good Morning Good Day	Moderate Tempo	SATB			Ensemble	Adults
She Loves Me	Bock, Jerry	1963	Ensemble	Sound While Selling	Moderate Tempo	SATB			Ensemble	Adults

* = Music Edit Required
+ = Ethnic Specific

Show	Composer	Year	Role	Song	Tempo	Vocal Type	Range-Bottom	Range-Top	Category	Character Type
She Loves Me	Bock, Jerry	1963	Mr. Maraczek	Days Gone By*	Uptempo	Baritone	Bb2	C4	Lead	Mature Male
She Loves Me	Bock, Jerry	1963	Amalia Balash	No More Candy*	Moderate Tempo	Soprano	Db4	Fb5	Lead	Romantic Lead Female
She Loves Me	Bock, Jerry	1963	Georg Nowack	Three Letters*	Moderate Tempo	Baritone	D#3	E4	Lead	Romantic Lead Female
She Loves Me	Bock, Jerry	1963	Amalia & Ilona	I Don't Know His Name	Moderate Tempo	Sop/Alto			Duet	RLF/RAM
She Loves Me	Bock, Jerry	1963	Amalia Balash	I Don't Know His Name*	Moderate Tempo	Soprano	B#3	D#5	Lead	Romantic Lead Female
She Loves Me	Bock, Jerry	1963	Ladislav Sipos	Perpective	Uptempo	Baritone	D3	C#4	Lead	Character Male
She Loves Me	Bock, Jerry	1963	Ensemble	Goodby Georg	Moderate Tempo	SATB			Ensemble	Adults
She Loves Me	Bock, Jerry	1963	Amalia Balash	Will He Like Me	Ballad	Soprano	Bb3	F5	Lead	Romantic Lead Female
She Loves Me	Bock, Jerry	1963	Steven Kodaly	Ilona*	Moderate Tempo	Tenor	C3	E4	Lead	Romantic Antagonist Male
She Loves Me	Bock, Jerry	1963	Ilona Ritter	I Resolve	Uptempo	Alto	Ab3	Bb4	Lead	Romantic Antagonist Female
She Loves Me	Bock, Jerry	1963	Headwaiter	A Romantic Atmosphere (G Maj)	Moderate Tempo	Tenor	C#3	B4	Supporting	Character Male
She Loves Me	Bock, Jerry	1963	Amalia Balash	Dear Friend	Uptempo	Soprano	C4	F5	Lead	Romantic Lead Female
She Loves Me	Bock, Jerry	1963	Arpad Lazslo	Try Me	Uptempo	Tenor	B2	E4	Lead	Character Ingenue Male
She Loves Me	Bock, Jerry	1963	Mr. Maraczek	Days Gone By Reprise	Uptempo	Baritone	B2	E4	Lead	Mature Male
She Loves Me	Bock, Jerry	1963	Amalia Balash	Where's My Shoe (B Maj)*	Uptempo	Soprano	E4	G5	Lead	Romantic Lead Female
She Loves Me	Bock, Jerry	1963	Amalia & Georg	Where's My Shoe	Uptempo	Bar/Sop			Duet	RLF/RLM
She Loves Me	Bock, Jerry	1963	Amalia Balash	Vanilla Ice Cream	Uptempo	Soprano	D4	B5	Lead	Romantic Lead Female
She Loves Me	Bock, Jerry	1963	Georg Nowack	She Loves Me	Uptempo	Baritone	Eb3	F4	Lead	Romantic Lead Male
She Loves Me	Bock, Jerry	1963	Ilona Ritter	A Trip To The Library	Moderate Tempo	Alto	G3	C#5	Lead	Romantic Antagonist Female
She Loves Me	Bock, Jerry	1963	Steven Kodaly	Grand Knowing You	Uptempo	Tenor	D3	A4	Lead	Romantic Antagonist Male
She Loves Me	Bock, Jerry	1963	Ensemble	Twelve Days Of Christmas	Uptempo	SATB			Ensemble	Adults
She Loves Me	Bock, Jerry	1963	Headwaiter	A Romantic Atmosphere (D Maj)	Moderate Tempo	Baritone	G2	F4	Lead	Character Male
She Loves Me	Bock, Jerry	1963	Amalia Balash	Mr. Norwack, Will You Please	Moderate Tempo	Soprano	C4	E5	Lead	Romantic Lead Female
She Loves Me	Bock, Jerry	1963	Amalia Balash	Where's My Shoe (G Maj)	Uptempo	Soprano	C#4	F5	Lead	Romantic Lead Female
She Loves Me	Bock, Jerry	1963	Ensemble	A Christmas Carol	Uptempo	SATB			Ensemble	Adults
She Loves Me	Bock, Jerry	1963	Georg & Amalia	Finale Act II	Uptempo	Bar/Sop			Duet	RLM/RLF
Show Boat	Kern, Jerome	1927	Ensemble	Cotton Blossom	Uptempo	SATB			Ensemble	Adults
Show Boat	Kern, Jerome	1927	Gaylord Ravenal	Where's The Mate For Me	Ballad	Tenor	D3	F#4	Lead	Romantic Lead Male
Show Boat	Kern, Jerome	1927	Gaylord Ravenal	Make Believe*	Ballad	Tenor	C3	G4	Lead	Romantic Lead Male
Show Boat	Kern, Jerome	1927	Gaylord & Magnolia	Make Believe	Ballad	Tenor/Sop			Duet	RLM/IF
Show Boat	Kern, Jerome	1927	Magnolia	Make Believe	Ballad	Soprano	D4	Bb5	Lead	Ingenue Female
Show Boat	Kern, Jerome	1927	Joe+	Ol' Man River	Ballad	Bass	F2	D4	Lead	Character Male
Show Boat	Kern, Jerome	1927	Julie	Can't Help Lovin' Dat Man	Moderate Tempo	Alto	Eb3	Ab4	Lead	Romantic Lead Female
Show Boat	Kern, Jerome	1927	Ellie	Life Upon The Wicked Stage*	Uptempo	Alto	G3	D5	Lead	Character Ingenue Female
Show Boat	Kern, Jerome	1927	Queenie+	Can't Help Lovin' Dat Man*	Moderate Tempo	Alto	C3	D4	Lead	Character Female
Show Boat	Kern, Jerome	1927	Ensemble	Can't Help Lovin' Dat Man	Uptempo	SATB			Ensemble	Adults
Show Boat	Kern, Jerome	1927	Joe+	Ol' Man River Reprise	Ballad	Bass	F2	D4	Lead	Character Male
Show Boat	Kern, Jerome	1927	Ensemble	Life Upon The Wicked Stage*	Uptempo	SATB			Ensemble	Adults
Show Boat	Kern, Jerome	1927	Gaylord Ravenal	You Are Love*	Ballad	Tenor	D3	Bb4	Lead	Romantic Lead Male
Show Boat	Kern, Jerome	1927	Magnolia	You Are Love*	Ballad	Soprano	D4	Bb5	Lead	Ingenue Female
Show Boat	Kern, Jerome	1927	Gaylord & Magnolia	You Are Love	Ballad	Tenor/Sop			Duet	RLM/IF
Show Boat	Kern, Jerome	1927	Ensemble	Finale Act I - The Wedding	Moderate Tempo	SATB			Ensemble	Adults
Show Boat	Kern, Jerome	1927	Ensemble	At The Fair	Uptempo	SATB			Ensemble	Adults

Shows

Songs by Character Type

* = Music Edit Required
+ = Ethnic Specific

Show	Composer	Year	Role	Song	Tempo	Vocal Type	Range-Bottom	Range-Top	Category	Character Type
Show Boat	Kern, Jerome	1927	Gaylord & Magnolia	Why Do I Love You	Moderate Tempo	Tenor/Sop			Duet	RLM/IF
Show Boat	Kern, Jerome	1927	Ensemble	Dahomey	Uptempo	SATB			Ensemble	Adults
Show Boat	Kern, Jerome	1927	Julie	Bill	Ballad	Alto	F#3	G#4	Lead	Romantic Lead Female
Show Boat	Kern, Jerome	1927	Magnolia	Can't Help Reprise	Ballad	Soprano	Ab3	Eb5	Lead	Ingenue Female
Show Boat	Kern, Jerome	1927	Frank & Ellie	Goodbye My Lady Love	Uptempo	Bar/Alto			Duet	IM/CIF
Show Boat	Kern, Jerome	1927	Magnolia	After The Ball	Moderate Tempo	Soprano	D4	Ab5	Lead	Ingenue Female
Show Boat	Kern, Jerome	1927	Gaylord Ravenal	You Are Love Reprise	Ballad	Tenor	C3	Ab4	Lead	Romantic Lead Male
Show Boat	Kern, Jerome	1927	Ensemble	Ol' Man River	Ballad	TB			Ensemble	Adults
Show Boat	Kern, Jerome	1927	Ensemble	Montage 1	Moderate Tempo	SATB			Ensemble	Adults
Show Boat	Kern, Jerome	1927	Ensemble	Life Upon The Wicked Stage	Uptempo	SATB			Ensemble	Adults
Show Boat	Kern, Jerome	1927	Ensemble	Till Good Luck Comes My Way	Uptempo	TTBB			Ensemble	Adults
Show Boat	Kern, Jerome	1927	Ensemble	Can't Help Lovin' Dat Man*	Moderate Tempo	SATB			Ensemble	Adults
Show Boat	Kern, Jerome	1927	Ensemble	At The Fair	Uptempo	SATB			Ensemble	Adults
Show Boat	Kern, Jerome	1927	Queenie*	Misery*	Ballad	Alto	A3	Eb5	Lead	Character Female
Show Boat	Kern, Jerome	1927	Ensemble+	Misery*	Ballad	SATB			Ensemble	Adults
Show Boat	Kern, Jerome	1927	Gaylord Ravenal	I Have The Room Above Her	Moderate Tempo	Tenor	E3	Eb4	Lead	Romantic Lead Male
Show Boat	Kern, Jerome	1927	Queenie+	Bally-Hoo*	Uptempo	Alto	A3	Eb5	Lead	Character Female
Show Boat	Kern, Jerome	1927	Ensemble+	Bally-Hoo*	Uptempo	SATB			Ensemble	Adults
Show Boat	Kern, Jerome	1927	Joe+	Ol' Man River - Act II	Ballad	Bass	Ab2	F4	Lead	Character Male
Show Boat	Kern, Jerome	1927	Magnolia	Dance The Night Away*	Uptempo	Soprano	G3	C5	Lead	Ingenue Female
Show Boat	Kern, Jerome	1927	Ensemble	Ol' Man River	Ballad	SATB			Ensemble	Adults
Singin' In The Rain	Brown, Nacio Herb	1983	Don Lockwood & Cosmo Brown	Fit As A Fiddle*	Uptempo	Bar/Tenor			Duet	RLM/CM
Singin' In The Rain	Brown, Nacio Herb	1983	Ensemble	All I Do Is Dream Of You*	Uptempo	SA			Ensemble	Adults
Singin' In The Rain	Brown, Nacio Herb	1983	Ensemble	You Stepped Out Of A Dream	Moderate Tempo	SATB			Ensemble	Adults
Singin' In The Rain	Brown, Nacio Herb	1983	Don Lockwood	You Stepped Out Of A Dream*	Moderate Tempo	Baritone	C3	C4	Lead	Romantic Lead Male
Singin' In The Rain	Brown, Nacio Herb	1983	Don Lockwood	You Stepped Out Of A Dream Reprise	Moderate Tempo	Baritone	C3	G4	Lead	Romantic Lead Male
Singin' In The Rain	Brown, Nacio Herb	1983	Cosmo Brown	Make "Em Laugh	Uptempo	Tenor	C3	G4	Lead	Character Male
Singin' In The Rain	Brown, Nacio Herb	1983	Production Tenor	Beautiful Girl	Moderate Tempo	Tenor	F3	Bb4	Supporting	Romantic Lead Male
Singin' In The Rain	Brown, Nacio Herb	1983	Kathy Seldon	Lucky Star	Moderate Tempo	Soprano	Bb3	Eb5	Lead	Ingenue Female
Singin' In The Rain	Brown, Nacio Herb	1983	Don Lockwood	You Were Meant For Me	Moderate Tempo	Baritone	Bb2	Db4	Lead	Romantic Lead Male
Singin' In The Rain	Brown, Nacio Herb	1983	Don Lockwood	Meant For Me Playoff	Moderate Tempo	Baritone	C3	Db4	Lead	Romantic Lead Male
Singin' In The Rain	Brown, Nacio Herb	1983	Don Lockwood & Cosmo Brown	Moses Supposes	Uptempo	Bar/Tenor			Duet	RLM/CM
Singin' In The Rain	Brown, Nacio Herb	1983	Ensemble	Good Morning	Uptempo	ABT			Ensemble	Adults
Singin' In The Rain	Brown, Nacio Herb	1983	Don Lockwood	Singin' In The Rain	Uptempo	Baritone	D3	D4	Lead	Romantic Lead Male
Singin' In The Rain	Brown, Nacio Herb	1983	Kathy Seldon	Kathy's Would You	Moderate Tempo	Soprano	G3	C5	Lead	Ingenue Female
Singin' In The Rain	Brown, Nacio Herb	1983	Don Lockwood	Don's Would You	Moderate Tempo	Baritone	G2	C4	Lead	Romantic Lead Male
Singin' In The Rain	Brown, Nacio Herb	1983	Lina Lamont	What's Wrong With Me? (Eb Maj)	Moderate Tempo	Alto	C4	Eb5	Lead	Romantic Antagonist Female
Singin' In The Rain	Brown, Nacio Herb	1983	Lina Lamont	What's Wrong With Me? (C Maj)	Moderate Tempo	Alto	A3	C5	Lead	Romantic Antagonist Female
Singin' In The Rain	Brown, Nacio Herb	1983	Cosmo Brown	Broadway Melody* (ms 1-30)	Uptempo	Tenor	Bb3	F4	Lead	Character Male
Singin' In The Rain	Brown, Nacio Herb	1983	Don Lockwood	Broadway Rhythm* (ms 115-182)	Uptempo	Baritone	C3	F4	Lead	Romantic Lead Male
Singin' In The Rain	Brown, Nacio Herb	1983	Don Lockwood & Cosmo Brown	Lucky Star Reprise (Eb Maj)	Moderate Tempo	Bar/Tenor			Duet	RLF/CM
Singin' In The Rain	Brown, Nacio Herb	1983	Ensemble	Singin' In The Rain Finale	Uptempo	SATB			Ensemble	Adults

Songs by Character Type

Show	Composer	Year	Role	Song	Tempo	Vocal Type	Range-Bottom	Range-Top	Category	Character Type
Song & Dance	Webber, Andrew Lloyd	1985	Emma	Take That Look Off Your Face	Uptempo	Alto	B3	D5	Lead	Character Ingenue Female
Song & Dance	Webber, Andrew Lloyd	1985	Emma	Let Me Finish	Moderate Tempo	Alto	G#3	Eb5	Lead	Character Ingenue Female
Song & Dance	Webber, Andrew Lloyd	1985	Emma	So Much To Do In New York	Moderate Tempo	Alto	Ab3	Eb5	Lead	Character Ingenue Female
Song & Dance	Webber, Andrew Lloyd	1985	Emma	1st Letter Home	Moderate Tempo	Alto	A3	D5	Lead	Character Ingenue Female
Song & Dance	Webber, Andrew Lloyd	1985	Emma	English Girls	Uptempo	Alto	G3	C5	Lead	Character Ingenue Female
Song & Dance	Webber, Andrew Lloyd	1985	Emma	Capped Teeth And Ceasar Salad	Moderate Tempo	Alto	A3	B4	Lead	Character Ingenue Female
Song & Dance	Webber, Andrew Lloyd	1985	Emma	You Made Me Think You Were In Love	Uptempo	Alto	A3	Bb4	Lead	Character Ingenue Female
Song & Dance	Webber, Andrew Lloyd	1985	Emma	Capped Teeth And Ceasar Salad Reprise	Ballad	Alto	Ab3	Bb4	Lead	Character Ingenue Female
Song & Dance	Webber, Andrew Lloyd	1985	Emma	So Much To Do In New York #2	Moderate Tempo	Alto	G3	Eb5	Lead	Character Ingenue Female
Song & Dance	Webber, Andrew Lloyd	1985	Emma	2nd Letter Home	Moderate Tempo	Alto	A3	A4	Lead	Character Ingenue Female
Song & Dance	Webber, Andrew Lloyd	1985	Emma	The Last Man In My Life	Ballad	Alto	G3	Eb5	Lead	Character Ingenue Female
Song & Dance	Webber, Andrew Lloyd	1985	Emma	Unexpectied Song	Ballad	Alto	F3	G5	Lead	Character Ingenue Female
Song & Dance	Webber, Andrew Lloyd	1985	Emma	Come Back With The Same Look...	Uptempo	Alto	A3	C5	Lead	Character Ingenue Female
Song & Dance	Webber, Andrew Lloyd	1985	Emma	Take That Look Off Your Face Reprise	Uptempo	Alto	B3	E5	Lead	Character Ingenue Female
Song & Dance	Webber, Andrew Lloyd	1985	Emma	Tell Me On A Sunday	Ballad	Alto	G3	E5	Lead	Character Ingenue Female
Song & Dance	Webber, Andrew Lloyd	1985	Emma	I Love New York	Moderate Tempo	Alto	F3	Bb4	Lead	Character Ingenue Female
Song & Dance	Webber, Andrew Lloyd	1985	Emma	So Much To Do In New York #3	Moderate Tempo	Alto	A3	Eb5	Lead	Character Ingenue Female
Song & Dance	Webber, Andrew Lloyd	1985	Emma	Married Man	Moderate Tempo	Alto	G#3	C5	Lead	Character Ingenue Female
Song & Dance	Webber, Andrew Lloyd	1985	Emma	I'm Very You	Uptempo	Alto	A#3	C5	Lead	Character Ingenue Female
Song & Dance	Webber, Andrew Lloyd	1985	Emma	3rd Letter Home	Moderate Tempo	Alto	G3	Eb5	Lead	Character Ingenue Female
Song & Dance	Webber, Andrew Lloyd	1985	Emma	Nothing Like You've Ever Known	Ballad	Alto	G3	C5	Lead	Character Ingenue Female
Song & Dance	Webber, Andrew Lloyd	1985	Emma	Let Me Finish Finale	Moderate Tempo	Alto	G#3	Eb5	Lead	Character Ingenue Female
Songs For A New World	Brown, Jason Robert	1995	Ensemble	A New World	Uptempo	SATB			Ensemble	Adults
Songs For A New World	Brown, Jason Robert	1995	Man 1	On The Deck Of A Spanish Sailing Ship	Ballad	Tenor	F3	Bb4	Lead	Romantic Antagonist Male
Songs For A New World	Brown, Jason Robert	1995	Ensemble	On The Deck Of A Spanish Sailing Ship	Ballad	SATB			Ensemble	Adults
Songs For A New World	Brown, Jason Robert	1995	Woman 2	Just One Step	Uptempo	Alto	F3	C#5	Lead	Character Female
Songs For A New World	Brown, Jason Robert	1995	Woman 1	I'm Not Afraid Of Anything	Moderate Tempo	Soprano	A3	E5	Lead	Romantic Lead Female
Songs For A New World	Brown, Jason Robert	1995	Man 1	The River Won't Flow*	Uptempo	Tenor	G3	C5	Lead	Romantic Antagonist Male
Songs For A New World	Brown, Jason Robert	1995	Man 2	The River Won't Flow*	Uptempo	Baritone	D3	A4	Lead	Romantic Lead Female
Songs For A New World	Brown, Jason Robert	1995	Ensemble	The River Won't Flow*	Uptempo	SATB			Ensemble	Adults
Songs For A New World	Brown, Jason Robert	1995	Woman 2	Stars And The Moon	Moderate Tempo	Alto	A3	D5	Lead	Character Female
Songs For A New World	Brown, Jason Robert	1995	Man 2	She Cries	Uptempo	Baritone	C3	G#4	Lead	Romantic Lead Male
Songs For A New World	Brown, Jason Robert	1995	Man 1	Steam Train*	Uptempo	Tenor	F3	C5	Lead	Romantic Antagonist Male
Songs For A New World	Brown, Jason Robert	1995	Ensemble	Steam Train*	Uptempo	SATB			Ensemble	Adults
Songs For A New World	Brown, Jason Robert	1995	Woman 1 & Man 2	The World Was Dancing*	Moderate Tempo	Sop/Bar			Duet	RLF/RLM
Songs For A New World	Brown, Jason Robert	1995	Ensemble	The World Was Dancing*	Moderate Tempo	SATB			Ensemble	Adults
Songs For A New World	Brown, Jason Robert	1995	Woman 2	Surabaya Santa	Moderate Tempo	Alto	G3	Eb4	Lead	Character Female
Songs For A New World	Brown, Jason Robert	1995	Woman 1	Christmas Lullaby	Ballad	Soprano	A3	E5	Lead	Romantic Lead Female
Songs For A New World	Brown, Jason Robert	1995	Man 1	King Of the World	Uptempo	Tenor	E3	C5	Lead	Romantic Antagonist Male
Songs For A New World	Brown, Jason Robert	1995	Man 2	I'd Give It All For You*	Moderate Tempo	Baritone	F#2	G4	Lead	Romantic Lead Male
Songs For A New World	Brown, Jason Robert	1995	Woman 1	I'd Give It All For You*	Moderate Tempo	Soprano	A3	F4	Lead	Romantic Lead Female
Songs For A New World	Brown, Jason Robert	1995	Woman 1 & Man 2	I'd Give It All For You*	Moderate Tempo	Sop/Bar			Duet	1F/RLM

Shows

Songs by Character Type

Show	Composer	Year	Role	Song	Tempo	Vocal Type	Range-Bottom	Range-Top	Category	Character Type
Songs For A New World	Brown, Jason Robert	1995	Woman 2	The Flagmaker 1775	Moderate Tempo	Alto	A3	E5	Lead	Character Female
Songs For A New World	Brown, Jason Robert	1995	Man 1	Flying Home*	Ballad	Tenor	D#3	F4	Lead	Romantic Antagonist Male
Songs For A New World	Brown, Jason Robert	1995	Woman 2	Hear My Song*	Moderate Tempo	Alto	A3	B4	Lead	Character Female
Songs For A New World	Brown, Jason Robert	1995	Woman 1	Hear My Song*	Moderate Tempo	Soprano	A3	G4	Lead	Romantic Lead Female
Songs For A New World	Brown, Jason Robert	1995	Man 1	Hear My Song*	Moderate Tempo	Tenor	D3	C4	Lead	Romantic Antagonist Male
Songs For A New World	Brown, Jason Robert	1995	Man 2	Hear My Song*	Moderate Tempo	Baritone	F3	E4	Lead	Romantic Lead Male
Songs For A New World	Brown, Jason Robert	1995	Ensemble	One Moment	Moderate Tempo	SATB			Ensemble	Adults
Sound Of Music, The	Rodgers, Richard	1959	Ensemble	The Sound Of Music	Moderate Tempo	SATB			Ensemble	Adults
Sound Of Music, The	Rodgers, Richard	1959	Maria Rainer	Maria	Uptempo	Soprano	B3	B4	Lead	Character Ingenue Female
Sound Of Music, The	Rodgers, Richard	1959	Ensemble	My Favorite Things*	Uptempo	SA			Ensemble	Adults
Sound Of Music, The	Rodgers, Richard	1959	Maria & Mother Superior	Do-Re-Mi	Uptempo	Sop/Sop			Duet	CIF/MF
Sound Of Music, The	Rodgers, Richard	1959	Ensemble	You Are Sixteen*	Moderate Tempo	SAT			Ensemble	Children/Teens/Adults
Sound Of Music, The	Rodgers, Richard	1959	Liesl von Trapp	You Are Sixteen*	Moderate Tempo	Alto	B3	C#5	Lead	Ingenue Female
Sound Of Music, The	Rodgers, Richard	1959	Rolf Gruber	You Are Sixteen	Moderate Tempo	Baritone	D3	E4	Lead	Ingenue Male
Sound Of Music, The	Rodgers, Richard	1959	Liesl & Rolf	The Lonely Goatherd	Uptempo	Alto/Bar			Duet	IF/IM
Sound Of Music, The	Rodgers, Richard	1959	Maria Rainer	The Sound Of Music Reprise	Ballad	Soprano	C4	Bb5	Lead	Character Ingenue Female
Sound Of Music, The	Rodgers, Richard	1959	Ensemble	So Long Farewell	Moderate Tempo	SATB			Ensemble	Children/Teens/Adults
Sound Of Music, The	Rodgers, Richard	1959	Ensemble	Climb Every Mountain	Ballad	SAT			Ensemble	Children/Teens
Sound Of Music, The	Rodgers, Richard	1959	Mother Abbess	No Way To Stop It	Uptempo	Soprano	C4	Ab5	Lead	Mature Female
Sound Of Music, The	Rodgers, Richard	1959	Ensemble	Ordinary People	Ballad	SBB			Ensemble	Adults
Sound Of Music, The	Rodgers, Richard	1959	Maria & Captain	Ordinary People*	Ballad	Sop/Bar			Duet	CIF/RLM
Sound Of Music, The	Rodgers, Richard	1959	Maria Rainer	The Concert	Uptempo	Soprano	B3	D5	Lead	Character Ingenue Female
Sound Of Music, The	Rodgers, Richard	1959	Ensemble	Edelweiss	Ballad	SATB			Ensemble	Children/Teens/Adults
Sound Of Music, The	Rodgers, Richard	1959	Captain von Trapp	So Long Reprise	Uptempo	Baritone	E3	F4	Lead	Romantic Lead Male
Sound Of Music, The	Rodgers, Richard	1959	Ensemble	Lonely Goatherd*	Uptempo	SATB Unison			Ensemble	Children/Teens/Adults
Sound Of Music, The	Rodgers, Richard	1959	Ensemble	How Can Love Survive	Uptempo	SAT			Ensemble	Children/Teens/Adults
Sound Of Music, The	Rodgers, Richard	1959	Elsa Schraeder	Finale Ultimo	Moderate Tempo	Soprano	D4	F5	Lead	Romantic Lead Female
Sound Of Music, The	Rodgers, Richard	1959	Ensemble	Preludium	Ballad	SSMA			Ensemble	Adults
Sound Of Music, The	Rodgers, Richard	1959	Ensemble	Confitemini	Uptempo	SSMA			Ensemble	Adults
Sound Of Music, The	Rodgers, Richard	1959	Ensemble	Alleluia	Uptempo	SSMA			Ensemble	Adults
Sound Of Music, The	Rodgers, Richard	1959	Ensemble	Processional	Uptempo	SSMA			Ensemble	Adults
Sound Of Music, The	Rodgers, Richard	1959	Ensemble	Morning Hymn	Moderate Tempo	SA Unison			Ensemble	Adults
Sound Of Music, The	Rodgers, Richard	1959	Ensemble	My Favorite Things Reprise	Uptempo	SAT			Ensemble	Children/Teens/Adults
Sound Of Music, The	Rodgers, Richard	1959	Ensemble	Gaudeamus	Uptempo	SSMA			Ensemble	Adults
South Pacific	Rodgers, Richard	1949	Jerome & Ngana	Dites-Moi Pourquoi	Moderate Tempo	Sop/Sop	D4	C5	Duet	JM/JF
South Pacific	Rodgers, Richard	1949	Jerome	Dites-Moi Pourquoi*	Moderate Tempo	Soprano	D4	C5	Supporting	Juvenile Male
South Pacific	Rodgers, Richard	1949	Ngana	Dites-Moi Pourquoi*	Moderate Tempo	Soprano	A3	C5	Supporting	Juvenile Female
South Pacific	Rodgers, Richard	1949	Nellie Forbush	A Cockeyed Optimist	Uptempo	Alto			Lead	Romantic Lead Female
South Pacific	Rodgers, Richard	1949	Emile & Nellie	Twin Soliloquies	Moderate Tempo	Bar/Alto			Duet	RLM/RLF
South Pacific	Rodgers, Richard	1949	Emile De Becque	Some Enchanted Evening	Ballad	Baritone	C3	E4	Lead	Romantic Lead Male
South Pacific	Rodgers, Richard	1949	Ensemble	Bloody Mary	Uptempo	BT			Ensemble	Adults
South Pacific	Rodgers, Richard	1949	Ensemble	There Is Nothing Like A Dame	Uptempo	BT			Ensemble	Adults
South Pacific	Rodgers, Richard	1949	Bloody Mary	Bali Ha'i	Ballad	Alto	G3	G4	Lead	Character Female

Shows

Songs by Character Type

Show	Composer	Year	Role	Song	Tempo	Vocal Type	Range-Bottom	Range-Top	Category	Character Type
South Pacific	Rodgers, Richard	1949	Bloody Mary	Bali Ha'I Reprise	Ballad	Alto	D3	E4	Lead	Character Female
South Pacific	Rodgers, Richard	1949	Nellie Forbush	I'm Gonna Wash That Man*	Uptempo	Alto	D3	E5	Lead	Romantic Lead Female
South Pacific	Rodgers, Richard	1949	Ensemble	I'm Gonna Wash That Man*	Uptempo	SA			Ensemble	Adults
South Pacific	Rodgers, Richard	1949	Emile & Nellie	Some Enchanted Evening Reprise	Moderate Tempo	Bar/Alto			Duet	RLM/RLF
South Pacific	Rodgers, Richard	1949	Lt. Jospeh Cable	Younger Than Springtime*	Ballad	Tenor	E3	G4	Lead	Ingenue Male
South Pacific	Rodgers, Richard	1949	Emile & Nellie	Cockeyed Optimist Reprise	Uptempo	Bar/Alto			Duet	RLM/RLF
South Pacific	Rodgers, Richard	1949	Emile De Becque	Some Enchanted Evening Reprise 2	Ballad	Baritone	C3	E4	Lead	Romantic Lead Male
South Pacific	Rodgers, Richard	1949	Bloody Mary	Happy Talk	Uptempo	Alto	A3	C5	Lead	Character Female
South Pacific	Rodgers, Richard	1949	Nellie Forbush	Honey Bun	Uptempo	Alto	Bb3	Bb4	Lead	Romantic Lead Female
South Pacific	Rodgers, Richard	1949	Lt. Jospeh Cable	You've Got To Be Carefully Taught	Uptempo	Tenor	E3	G4	Lead	Ingenue Male
South Pacific	Rodgers, Richard	1949	Luther Billis	Honey Bun Reprise	Uptempo	Baritone	Bb2	B3	Lead	Character Male
South Pacific	Rodgers, Richard	1949	Emile De Becque	This Nearly Was Mine	Ballad	Baritone	B2	D4	Lead	Romantic Lead Male
South Pacific	Rodgers, Richard	1949	Nellie Forbush	Some Enchanted Evening Reprise 2	Ballad	Alto	Ab3	Bb4	Lead	Romantic Lead Female
South Pacific	Rodgers, Richard	1949	Ensemble	Im In Love...Wonderful Guy	Uptempo	SA Unison			Ensemble	Adults
South Pacific	Rodgers, Richard	1949	Nellie Forbush	Im In Love...Wonderful Guy*	Uptempo	Alto	B3	Db5	Lead	Romantic Lead Female
South Pacific	Rodgers, Richard	1949	Ensemble	Bali Ha'i	Uptempo	SA			Ensemble	Adults
South Pacific	Rodgers, Richard	1949	Emile & Nellie	Cockeyed Optimist Reprise	Uptempo	Bar/Alto			Duet	RLM/RLF
South Pacific	Rodgers, Richard	1949	Nellie Forbush	Im In Love...Wonderful Guy Reprise	Uptempo	Alto	B3	C5	Lead	Romantic Lead Female
South Pacific	Rodgers, Richard	1949	Ensemble	Honey Bun	Uptempo	SATB Unison			Lead	Adults
South Pacific	Rodgers, Richard	1949	Emile De Becque	You've Got To Be Carefully Taught Repri	Moderate Tempo	Baritone	C#3	E4	Lead	Romantic Lead Male
Spamalot	Du Pres and Idle	2005	Ensemble	Fisch Schlapping Dance	Moderate Tempo	SATB			Ensemble	Adults
Spamalot	Du Pres and Idle	2005	Dad	I Am Not Dead Yet	Uptempo	Baritone	C3	E4	Lead	Paternal
Spamalot	Du Pres and Idle	2005	Ensemble	I Am Not Dead Yet	Uptempo	TB			Ensemble	Adults
Spamalot	Du Pres and Idle	2005	Ensemble	Monks Chat	Ballad	TB			Ensemble	Adults
Spamalot	Du Pres and Idle	2005	The Lady Of The Lake	Come With Me*	Moderate Tempo	Alto	A3	C5	Lead	Romantic Antagonist Female
Spamalot	Du Pres and Idle	2005	Sir Galahad & Lady of the Lake	The Song That Goes Like This	Moderate Tempo	Bar/Alto			Duet	RLM/RAF
Spamalot	Du Pres and Idle	2005	Ensemble	We Are Not Dead Yet Reprise	Uptempo	TB			Ensemble	Adults
Spamalot	Du Pres and Idle	2005	Sir Bedevere	Burn Her*	Uptempo	Baritone	F3	E4	Lead	Character Male
Spamalot	Du Pres and Idle	2005	Ensemble	All For One	Uptempo	SATB			Ensemble	Adults
Spamalot	Du Pres and Idle	2005	Ensemble	Knights Of The Round Table*	Uptempo	SATB			Ensemble	Adults
Spamalot	Du Pres and Idle	2005	The Lady Of The Lake	The Song That Goes Like This Reprise*	Moderate Tempo	Alto	Ab3	Eb5	Lead	Romantic Antagonist Female
Spamalot	Du Pres and Idle	2005	Ensemble	Find Your Grail	Moderate Tempo	SATB			Ensemble	Adults
Spamalot	Du Pres and Idle	2005	The Lady Of The Lake	Find Your Grail*	Moderate Tempo	Alto	C#4	E5	Lead	Romantic Antagonist Female
Spamalot	Du Pres and Idle	2005	Marlene Cow	The Cow Song*	Moderate Tempo	Alto	F3	B4	Featured Ensemble	Character Female
Spamalot	Du Pres and Idle	2005	Ensemble	The Cow Song	Moderate Tempo	SATB			Ensemble	Adults
Spamalot	Du Pres and Idle	2005	Ensemble	Run Away	Uptempo	TB			Ensemble	Adults
Spamalot	Du Pres and Idle	2005	Patsy	Always Lok On The Bright Side of Life*	Moderate Tempo	Tenor	B2	F4	Supporting	Character Male
Spamalot	Du Pres and Idle	2005	King Arthur	Always Lok On The Bright Side of Life*	Moderate Tempo	Baritone	C3	D4	Lead	Antagonist Male
Spamalot	Du Pres and Idle	2005	Ensemble	Always Lok On The Bright Side of Life	Moderate Tempo	TB			Ensemble	Adults
Spamalot	Du Pres and Idle	2005	Minstrel	Brave Sir Robin	Moderate Tempo	Tenor	A3	D4	Supporting	Character Male
Spamalot	Du Pres and Idle	2005	Sir Robin	You Won't Succeed On Broadway*	Uptempo	Baritone	D3	E4	Lead	Character Male
Spamalot	Du Pres and Idle	2005	Minstrel	Brave Sir Robin Reprise	Moderate Tempo	Tenor	A3	D4	Supporting	Character Male

Shows

Songs by Character Type

* = Music Edit Required
+ = Ethnic Specific

Show	Composer	Year	Role	Song	Tempo	Vocal Type	Range-Bottom	Range-Top	Category	Character Type
Spamalot	Du Pres and Idle	2005	The Lady Of The Lake	Whatever Happened To My Part	Moderate Tempo	Alto	F#3	Eb5	Lead	Romantic Antagonist Female
Spamalot	Du Pres and Idle	2005	Herbert	Here You Are*	Moderate Tempo	Baritone	G2	Bb3	Supporting	Character Male
Spamalot	Du Pres and Idle	2005	Ensemble	Lancelot	Uptempo	SATB			Ensemble	Adults
Spamalot	Du Pres and Idle	2005	King Arthur	I'm All Alone*	Ballad	Baritone	A2	A3	Lead	Antagonist Male
Spamalot	Du Pres and Idle	2005	King Arthur & Patsy	I'm All Alone	Ballad	Bar/Tenor			Duet	AM/CM
Spamalot	Du Pres and Idle	2005	The Lady Of The Lake	Why Does He Never Notice Me	Ballad	Alto	F3	Db5	Lead	Romantic Antagonist Female
Spamalot	Du Pres and Idle	2005	King Arthur & Lady of the Lake	Twice In Every Show	Moderate Tempo	Bar/Alto			Duet	AM/RAM
Spamalot	Du Pres and Idle	2005	Ensemble	Finale Ensemble	Uptempo	SATB			Ensemble	Adults
Spitfire Grill	Valcq, James	2001	Percy Talbott	A Ring Around The Moon	Moderate Tempo	Alto	A3	E5	Lead	Character Ingenue Female
Spitfire Grill	Valcq, James	2001	Hannah Ferguson	Hannah's Harangue	Moderate Tempo	Alto	G3	A4	Lead	Antagonist Female
Spitfire Grill	Valcq, James	2001	Ensemble	Something's Cooking	Uptempo	SATB			Ensemble	Adults
Spitfire Grill	Valcq, James	2001	Percy Talbott	Coffee Cups And Gossip	Uptempo	Alto	C4	C5	Lead	Character Ingenue Female
Spitfire Grill	Valcq, James	2001	Percy Talbott	Out Of The Frying Pan	Uptempo	Alto	A3	D5	Lead	Character Ingenue Female
Spitfire Grill	Valcq, James	2001	Shelby Thorpe	Hannah Had A Son	Ballad	Soprano	D4	D5	Lead	Ingenue Female
Spitfire Grill	Valcq, James	2001	Shelby Thorpe	When Hope Goes	Ballad	Soprano	A3	D5	Lead	Ingenue Female
Spitfire Grill	Valcq, James	2001	Ensemble	Ice And Snow	Uptempo	ATB			Ensemble	Adults
Spitfire Grill	Valcq, James	2001	Percy & Shelby	The Colors of Paradise	Uptempo	Alto/Sop			Duet	CIF/IF
Spitfire Grill	Valcq, James	2001	Percy Talbott	The Colors of Paradise*	Uptempo	Alto	G3	F5	Lead	Character Ingenue Female
Spitfire Grill	Valcq, James	2001	Caleb Thorpe	Digging Stone	Moderate Tempo	Tenor	B2	G4	Lead	Romantic Antagonist Male
Spitfire Grill	Valcq, James	2001	Joe Sutter	This Wide Woods Part 2	Uptempo	Tenor	E3	F4	Lead	Character Male
Spitfire Grill	Valcq, James	2001	Percy Talbott	This Wide Woods Part 3	Moderate Tempo	Alto	E3	C#5	Lead	Character Ingenue Female
Spitfire Grill	Valcq, James	2001	Percy & Joe	This Wide Woods Part 4	Moderate Tempo	Alto/Tenor			Duet	CIF/CM
Spitfire Grill	Valcq, James	2001	Hannah Ferguson	Forgotten Lullaby	Ballad	Alto	G3	G4	Lead	Antagonist Female
Spitfire Grill	Valcq, James	2001	Ensemble	Shoot The Moon P1&P2	Moderate Tempo	SATB			Ensemble	Adults
Spitfire Grill	Valcq, James	2001	Hannah Ferguson	Come Alive Again Part 2	Moderate Tempo	Alto	G3	A4	Lead	Antagonist Female
Spitfire Grill	Valcq, James	2001	Joe Sutter	Forest For The Trees	Uptempo	Tenor	D3	A4	Lead	Character Male
Spitfire Grill	Valcq, James	2001	Shelby Thorpe	Wild Bird	Ballad	Soprano	C4	D5	Lead	Ingenue Female
Spitfire Grill	Valcq, James	2001	Percy Talbott	Shine	Ballad	Alto	G3	E5	Lead	Character Ingenue Female
Spitfire Grill	Valcq, James	2001	Hannah Ferguson	Way Back Home	Ballad	Alto	E3	B4	Lead	Antagonist Female
Spitfire Grill	Valcq, James	2001	Ensemble	The Colors of Paradise Reprise	Moderate Tempo	AAS			Ensemble	Adults
Spring Awakening	Sheik, Duncan	2006	Wendla	Mama Who Bore Me	Moderate Tempo	Soprano	G3	A4	Lead	Ingenue Female
Spring Awakening	Sheik, Duncan	2006	Ensemble	Mama Who Bore Me Reprise	Uptempo	SAA			Ensemble	Adult
Spring Awakening	Sheik, Duncan	2006	Melchior	All That's Known	Moderate Tempo	Tenor	D3	E4	Lead	Romantic Antagonist Male
Spring Awakening	Sheik, Duncan	2006	Moritz	The Bitch Of Living*	Uptempo	Tenor	C3	D4	Lead	Antagonist Male
Spring Awakening	Sheik, Duncan	2006	Georg	The Bitch Of Living	Uptempo	Baritone	F3	D4	Lead	Character Ingenue Male
Spring Awakening	Sheik, Duncan	2006	Ensemble	The Bitch Of Living	Uptempo	TB			Ensemble	Adult
Spring Awakening	Sheik, Duncan	2006	Ensemble	My Junk	Uptempo	SATB			Ensemble	Adult
Spring Awakening	Sheik, Duncan	2006	Female Solo	My Junk*	Uptempo	Alto	A3	E5	Featured Ensemble	Character Female
Spring Awakening	Sheik, Duncan	2006	Ensemble	Touch Me	Moderate Tempo	SATB			Ensemble	Adult
Spring Awakening	Sheik, Duncan	2006	Wendla & Melchior	The Word Of Your Body	Ballad	Sop/Tenor			Duet	IF/RAM
Spring Awakening	Sheik, Duncan	2006	Martha	The Dark I Know Well*	Moderate Tempo	Alto	A3	A4	Lead	Character Ingenue Female
Spring Awakening	Sheik, Duncan	2006	Ilse	The Dark I Know Well*	Moderate Tempo	Alto	A3	A4	Lead	Character Ingenue Female
Spring Awakening	Sheik, Duncan	2006	Martha & Ilse	The Dark I Know Well	Moderate Tempo	Alto/Alto			Duet	CIF/CIF
Spring Awakening	Sheik, Duncan	2006	Georg & Otto	The World Of You Body Reprise	Ballad	Bar/Bar			Duet	CIM/CM

Shows

Songs by Character Type

Show	Composer	Year	Role	Song	Tempo	Vocal Type	Range-Bottom	Range-Top	Category	Character Type
Spring Awakening	Sheik, Duncan	2006	Ensemble	And Then There Were None	Uptempo	TB			Ensemble	Adult
Spring Awakening	Sheik, Duncan	2006	Moritz	And Then There Were None*	Uptempo	Tenor	E3	G#4	Lead	Antagonist Male
Spring Awakening	Sheik, Duncan	2006	Ensemble	The Mirror-Blue Nigh	Moderate Tempo	TB			Ensemble	Adult
Spring Awakening	Sheik, Duncan	2006	Ensemble	I Believe	Moderate Tempo	SATB			Ensemble	Adult
Spring Awakening	Sheik, Duncan	2006	Moritz	Don't Do Sadness	Uptempo	Tenor	B2	A4	Lead	Antagonist Male
Spring Awakening	Sheik, Duncan	2006	Ilse	Blue Wind	Ballad	Alto	G3	A4	Lead	Character Ingenue Female
Spring Awakening	Sheik, Duncan	2006	Moritz & Ilse	Don't Do Sadness/Blue Wind	Uptempo	Tenor/Alto			Duet	AM/CIF
Spring Awakening	Sheik, Duncan	2006	Ensemble	The Guilty One	Moderate Tempo	SATB			Ensemble	Adult
Spring Awakening	Sheik, Duncan	2006	Wendla	The Guilty One*	Moderate Tempo	Soprano	G3	A4	Lead	Ingenue Female
Spring Awakening	Sheik, Duncan	2006	Melchoir	The Guilty One*	Moderate Tempo	Tenor	G2	A3	Lead	Romantic Antagonist Male
Spring Awakening	Sheik, Duncan	2006	Melchoir	Left Behind	Ballad	Tenor	E3	B4	Lead	Romantic Antagonist Male
Spring Awakening	Sheik, Duncan	2006	Ensemble	Totally Fucked	Uptempo	SATB			Ensemble	Adult
Spring Awakening	Sheik, Duncan	2006	Melchoir	Totally Fucked*	Uptempo	Tenor	Bb3	G4	Lead	Romantic Antagonist Male
Spring Awakening	Sheik, Duncan	2006	Ensemble	Word Of Your Body Reprise 2	Ballad	SATB			Ensemble	Adult
Spring Awakening	Sheik, Duncan	2006	Ernst & Hanschen	Word Of Your Body Reprise 2*	Ballad	Tenor/Bar			Duet	IM/RAM
Spring Awakening	Sheik, Duncan	2006	Hanschen	Word Of Your Body Reprise 2*	Ballad	Baritone	C3	E#4	Lead	Romantic Antagonist Male
Spring Awakening	Sheik, Duncan	2006	Wendla	Whispering	Ballad	Soprano	B3	A4	Lead	Ingenue Female
Spring Awakening	Sheik, Duncan	2006	Moritz	Those You've Known*	Ballad	Tenor	D3	E4	Lead	Antagonist Male
Spring Awakening	Sheik, Duncan	2006	Wendla	Those You've Known*	Moderate Tempo	Soprano	C4	D5	Lead	Ingenue Female
Spring Awakening	Sheik, Duncan	2006	Melchoir	Those You've Known*	Moderate Tempo	Tenor	D3	F4	Lead	Romantic Antagonist Male
Spring Awakening	Sheik, Duncan	2006	Ensemble	Those You've Known	Moderate Tempo	STT			Ensemble	Adult
Spring Awakening	Sheik, Duncan	2006	Ilse	Song of Purple Summer*	Moderate Tempo	Alto	G3	A4	Lead	Character Ingenue Female
Spring Awakening	Sheik, Duncan	2006	Ensemble	Song of Purple Summer	Moderate Tempo	SATB			Ensemble	Adult
State Fair 1996	Rodgers, Richard	1945	Margy Frake	It Might As Well Be Spring	Moderate Tempo	Alto	Bb3	Bb4	Lead	Ingenue Female
State Fair 1996	Rodgers, Richard	1945	Wayne Frake	That's For Me	Moderate Tempo	Baritone	C3	F4	Lead	Ingenue Male
State Fair 1996	Rodgers, Richard	1945	Pat Gilbert	Isn't It Kinda Fun*	Uptempo	Baritone	C#3	D4	Lead	Romantic Antagonist Male
State Fair 1996	Rodgers, Richard	1945	Pat Gilbert & Margy Frake	Isn't It Kinda Fun	Uptempo	Bar/Alto			Duet	RAM/IF
State Fair 1996	Rodgers, Richard	1945	Margy Frake	It Might As Well Be Spring Reprise	Moderate Tempo	Alto	Bb3	Bb4	Lead	Ingenue Female
State Fair 1996	Rodgers, Richard	1945	Pat Gilbert	Isn't It Kinda Fun Reprise	Moderate Tempo	Baritone	C3	G#4	Lead	Romantic Antagonist Male
State Fair 1996	Rodgers, Richard	1947	Wayne Frake	So Far*	Moderate Tempo	Baritone	D3	E4	Lead	Ingenue Male
State Fair 1996	Rodgers, Richard	1947	Wayne Frake & Emily Arden	So Far	Moderate Tempo	Bar/Alto			Duet	IM/RAM
State Fair 1996	Rodgers, Richard	1947	Ensemble	A Grand Night For Singing	Uptempo	SATB			Ensemble	Adults
State Fair 1996	Rodgers, Richard	1947	Emily Arden	All I Owe Ioway	Moderate Tempo	SATB			Ensemble	Romantic Antagonist Female
State Fair 1996	Rodgers, Richard	1953	Emily Arden	You Never Had It So Good	Uptempo	Alto	Bb3	Bb4	Lead	Adults
State Fair 1996	Rodgers, Richard	1996	Ensemble	Our State Fair*	Uptempo	SATB			Ensemble	Adults
State Fair 1996	Rodgers, Richard	1996	Abel Frake & Melissa Frake	When I Go Out Walking With My Baby	Moderate Tempo	Bar/Alto			Duet	P/M
State Fair 1996	Rodgers, Richard	1996	Ensemble	More Than Just A Friend	Moderate Tempo	TTBB			Ensemble	Adults
State Fair 1996	Rodgers, Richard	1996	Wayne Frake	The Man I Used To Be*	Moderate Tempo	Baritone	C3	Eb4	Lead	Ingenue Male
State Fair 1996	Rodgers, Richard	1996	Pat Gilbert	The Man I Used To Be Reprise	Moderate Tempo	Baritone	C3	Eb4	Lead	Romantic Antagonist Male
State Fair 1996	Rodgers, Richard	1996	Emily Arden	That's The Way It Happens*	Moderate Tempo	Alto	B3	D5	Lead	Romantic Antagonist Female
State Fair 1996	Rodgers, Richard	1996	Abel Frake	Boys And Girls Like You And Me*	Moderate Tempo	Baritone	Bb2	C4	Lead	Paternal
State Fair 1996	Rodgers, Richard	1996	Abel Frake & Melissa Frake	Boys And Girls Like You And Me	Moderate Tempo	Bar/Alto			Duet	P/M
State Fair 1996	Rodgers, Richard	1996	Margy Frake	The Next Time It Happens	Uptempo	Alto	Bb3	D5	Lead	Ingenue Female

Shows

Show	Composer	Year	Role	Song	Tempo	Vocal Type	Range-Bottom	Range-Top	Category	Character Type
State Fair 2016	Rodgers, Richard	1996	Ensemble	State Fair Bows	Uptempo	SATB		C5	Ensemble	Adults
Steel Pier	Kander, John	1997	Rita Racine	Willing To Ride	Uptempo	Alto	Gb3	F4	Lead	Romantic Lead Female
Steel Pier	Kander, John	1997	Mick Hamilton	Everybody Dance Part 1*	Uptempo	Baritone	D3		Lead	Romantic Antagonist Male
Steel Pier	Kander, John	1997	Ensemble	Everybody Dance Part 1	Uptempo	SATB		E4	Ensemble	Adults
Steel Pier	Kander, John	1997	Bill Kelly	Second Chance	Uptempo	Tenor	B2	E4	Lead	Romantic Lead Male
Steel Pier	Kander, John	1997	Ensemble	Steel Pier	Uptempo	SAA			Ensemble	Adults
Steel Pier	Kander, John	1997	Mick Hamilton	It's A Powerful Thing*	Uptempo	Baritone	C3	E4	Lead	Romantic Antagonist Male
Steel Pier	Kander, John	1997	Mick Hamilton	Dance With Me*	Uptempo	Baritone	Db3	Eb4	Lead	Romantic Antagonist Male
Steel Pier	Kander, John	1997	Bill Kelly	The Last Girl*	Moderate Tempo	Tenor	Bb2	G4	Lead	Romantic Lead Male
Steel Pier	Kander, John	1997	Ensemble	The Last Girl	Moderate Tempo	SATB			Ensemble	Adults
Steel Pier	Kander, John	1997	Shelby Stevens	Everybody's Girl	Uptempo	Alto	G3	C5	Lead	Mature Female
Steel Pier	Kander, John	1997	Shelby Stevens	Everybody's Girl Encore	Uptempo	Alto	G3	Bb4	Lead	Mature Female
Steel Pier	Kander, John	1997	Bill & Rita	Wet	Uptempo	Tenor/Alto			Duet	RLM/RLF
Steel Pier	Kander, John	1997	Ensemble	Fralenger's Commercial	Moderate Tempo	SAA			Ensemble	Adults
Steel Pier	Kander, John	1997	Rita Racine	Love Bird*	Moderate Tempo	Alto	G3	C5	Lead	Romantic Lead Female
Steel Pier	Kander, John	1997	Bill Kelly	Leave The World Behind*	Moderate Tempo	Tenor	D3	Eb4	Lead	Romantic Lead Male
Steel Pier	Kander, John	1997	Ensemble	Leave The World Behind	Uptempo	SSAA			Ensemble	Adults
Steel Pier	Kander, John	1997	Ensemble	Leave The World Behind	Moderate Tempo	SATB			Ensemble	Adults
Steel Pier	Kander, John	1997	Shelby Stevens	Somebody Older	Moderate Tempo	Alto	G3	Bb4	Lead	Mature Female
Steel Pier	Kander, John	1997	Rita Racine	Willing To Ride Reprise	Moderate Tempo	Alto	Ab3	B4	Lead	Romantic Lead Female
Steel Pier	Kander, John	1997	Precious McGuire	Two Little Words	Uptempo	Soprano	C4	E6	Lead	Character Ingenue Female
Steel Pier	Kander, John	1997	Bill Kelly	First You Dream*	Uptempo	Tenor	C3	F4	Lead	Romantic Lead Male
Steel Pier	Kander, John	1997	Mick Hamilton	Steel Pier Reprise*	Uptempo	Baritone	Bb2	E4	Lead	Romantic Antagonist Male
Steel Pier	Kander, John	1997	Rita Racine	Steel Pier Reprise*	Uptempo	Alto	Ab3	Db5	Lead	Romantic Lead Female
Steel Pier	Kander, John	1997	Ensemble	Steel Pier Reprise	Uptempo	SATB			Ensemble	Adults
Sugar	Styne, Julie	1972	Sugar Kane	Open Chicago	Uptempo	Alto	A3	C5	Lead	Romantic Lead Female
Sugar	Styne, Julie	1972	Jerry	Penniless Bums*	Uptempo	Baritone	C3	E4	Lead	Character Male
Sugar	Styne, Julie	1972	Joe	Penniless Bums*	Uptempo	Baritone	C3	E4	Lead	Romantic Lead Male
Sugar	Styne, Julie	1972	Jerry & Joe	Penniless Bums	Uptempo	Bar/Bar			Duet	CM/RLM
Sugar	Styne, Julie	1972	Jerry	The Beauty That Drives Men Mad*	Uptempo	Baritone	D3	F4	Lead	Character Male
Sugar	Styne, Julie	1972	Joe	The Beauty That Drives Men Mad*	Uptempo	Baritone	D3	F4	Lead	Romantic Lead Male
Sugar	Styne, Julie	1972	Jerry & Joe	The Beauty That Drives Men Mad	Uptempo	Bar/Bar			Duet	CM/RLM
Sugar	Styne, Julie	1972	Jerry & Sugar	We Could Be Close	Moderate Tempo	Bar/Alto			Duet	CM/RLF
Sugar	Styne, Julie	1972	Ensemble	Sun On My Face	Uptempo	SATB			Ensemble	Adults
Sugar	Styne, Julie	1972	Jerry	Doin' It For Sugar*	Moderate Tempo	Baritone	B3	E4	Lead	Character Male
Sugar	Styne, Julie	1972	Joe	Doin' It For Sugar*	Moderate Tempo	Baritone	B3	E4	Lead	Romantic Lead Male
Sugar	Styne, Julie	1972	Jerry & Joe	Doin' It For Sugar	Moderate Tempo	Bar/Bar			Duet	CM/RLM
Sugar	Styne, Julie	1972	Joe	Shell Oil	Moderate Tempo	Baritone	D3	B3	Lead	Romantic Lead Male
Sugar	Styne, Julie	1972	Sugar Kane	Hey Why Not!*	Uptempo	Alto	Bb3	Bb4	Lead	Romantic Lead Female
Sugar	Styne, Julie	1972	Ensemble	Hey Why Not!	Uptempo	TB			Ensemble	Adults
Sugar	Styne, Julie	1972	Sir Osgood	Beautiful Through and Through*	Moderate Tempo	Baritone	C#3	Eb4	Lead	Mature Male
Sugar	Styne, Julie	1972	Jerry	Beautiful Through and Through*	Moderate Tempo	Baritone	C#3	E4	Lead	Character Male

Shows

Songs by Character Type

* = Music Edit Required
+ = Ethnic Specific

Show	Composer	Year	Role	Song	Tempo	Vocal Type	Range-Bottom	Range-Top	Category	Character Type
Sugar	Styne, Julie	1972	Sir Osgood & Jerry	Beautiful Through and Through	Moderate Tempo	Bar/Bar			Duet	MM/CM
Sugar	Styne, Julie	1972	Joe	What Do You Give To A Man...*	Uptempo	Baritone	C3	E4	Lead	Romantic Lead Male
Sugar	Styne, Julie	1972	Joe & Sugar	What Do You Give To A Man....	Uptempo	Bar/Alto			Duet	RLM/RLF
Sugar	Styne, Julie	1972	Jerry	Magic Nights	Moderate Tempo	Baritone	E3	F4	Lead	Character Male
Sugar	Styne, Julie	1972	Joe	It Always Love	Uptempo	Baritone	C3	D4	Lead	Romantic Lead Male
Sugar	Styne, Julie	1972	Sweet Sue	When You Meet A Man...*	Uptempo	Alto	Ab3	Eb5	Lead	Romantic Antagonist Female
Sugar	Styne, Julie	1972	Ensemble	When You Meet A Man....	Uptempo	SATB			Ensemble	Adults
Sunday...Park With Geroge	Sondheim, Stephen	1984	Dot	Sunday In The Park With George	Moderate Tempo	Alto	E3	Db5	Lead	Romantic Lead Female
Sunday...Park With Geroge	Sondheim, Stephen	1984	Jules & Yvonne	No Life	Moderate Tempo	Bar/Alto			Duet	RAM/RAF
Sunday...Park With Geroge	Sondheim, Stephen	1984	George	Color And Light (Part 1)	Uptempo	Tenor	Bb2	Eb4	Lead	Romantic Antagonist Male
Sunday...Park With Geroge	Sondheim, Stephen	1984	Dot	Color And Light (Part 2)	Moderate Tempo	Alto	B3	C5	Lead	Romantic Lead Female
Sunday...Park With Geroge	Sondheim, Stephen	1984	George	Color And Light (Part 3)*	Uptempo	Tenor	D3	G4	Lead	Romantic Antagonist Male
Sunday...Park With Geroge	Sondheim, Stephen	1984	Dot	Color And Light (Part 3)*	Uptempo	Alto	E4	E5	Lead	Romantic Lead Female
Sunday...Park With Geroge	Sondheim, Stephen	1984	George & Dot	Color And Light (Part 3)	Uptempo	Bar/Alto			Duet	RAM/RLF
Sunday...Park With Geroge	Sondheim, Stephen	1984	Ensemble	Gossip Sequence	Uptempo	SATB			Ensemble	Adults
Sunday...Park With Geroge	Sondheim, Stephen	1984	George	The Day Off (Part 1)	Uptempo	Tenor	A#2	G4	Lead	Romantic Antagonist Male
Sunday...Park With Geroge	Sondheim, Stephen	1984	George	The Day Off (Part 2)	Moderate Tempo	Tenor	D#3	D#4	Lead	Romantic Antagonist Male
Sunday...Park With Geroge	Sondheim, Stephen	1984	Nurse	The Day Off (Part 3)*	Moderate Tempo	Alto	B3	D5	Supporting	Character Female
Sunday...Park With Geroge	Sondheim, Stephen	1984	Franz	The Day Off (Part 5)*	Moderate Tempo	Tenor	C3	Eb4	Lead	Character Male
Sunday...Park With Geroge	Sondheim, Stephen	1984	Boatman	The Day Off (Part 6)	Moderate Tempo	Baritone	E2	C4	Supporting	Antagonist Male
Sunday...Park With Geroge	Sondheim, Stephen	1984	Franz & Frieda	The Day Off (Part 5)	Moderate Tempo	Tenor/Atlo			Duet	CM/CF
Sunday...Park With Geroge	Sondheim, Stephen	1984	Ensemble	The Day Off (Part 7)	Uptempo	SATB			Ensemble	Adults
Sunday...Park With Geroge	Sondheim, Stephen	1984	Dot	Everybody Loves Lois	Uptempo	Alto	A#3	C#5	Lead	Romantic Lead Female
Sunday...Park With Geroge	Sondheim, Stephen	1984	Ensemble	The One On The Left	Uptempo	SATB			Ensemble	Adults
Sunday...Park With Geroge	Sondheim, Stephen	1984	George	Finishing The Hat	Moderate Tempo	Tenor	Bb2	Ab5	Lead	Romantic Antagonist Male
Sunday...Park With Geroge	Sondheim, Stephen	1984	Dot	We Do Not Belong Together*	Moderate Tempo	Alto	G3	D5	Lead	Romantic Lead Female
Sunday...Park With Geroge	Sondheim, Stephen	1984	George	We Do Not Belong Together*	Moderate Tempo	Tenor	A2	E4	Lead	Romantic Antagonist Male
Sunday...Park With Geroge	Sondheim, Stephen	1984	Dot & George	We Do Not Belong Together	Moderate Tempo	Alto/Tenor			Duet	RLF/RAM
Sunday...Park With Geroge	Sondheim, Stephen	1984	Old Lady	Beautiful*	Ballad	Alto	F#3	B4	Supporting	Mature Female
Sunday...Park With Geroge	Sondheim, Stephen	1984	George	Beautiful*	Ballad	Tenor	C#3	F#4	Lead	Romantic Antagonist Male
Sunday...Park With Geroge	Sondheim, Stephen	1984	George & Old Lady	Beautiful	Ballad	Tenor/Atlo			Duet	RAM/MF
Sunday...Park With Geroge	Sondheim, Stephen	1984	Ensemble	Sunday	Moderate Tempo	SATB			Ensemble	Children/Adults
Sunday...Park With Geroge	Sondheim, Stephen	1984	Ensemble	It's Hot Up Here	Moderate Tempo	SATB			Ensemble	Children/Adults
Sunday...Park With Geroge	Sondheim, Stephen	1984	Ensemble	Putting It Together (Part 2 & 3)	Uptempo	SATB			Ensemble	Adults
Sunday...Park With Geroge	Sondheim, Stephen	1984	George	Putting It Together (Part 7 & 9)	Uptempo	Tenor	D4	Gb4	Lead	Romantic Antagonist Male
Sunday...Park With Geroge	Sondheim, Stephen	1984	Ensemble	Putting It Together (Part 8)	Uptempo	SATB			Ensemble	Adults
Sunday...Park With Geroge	Sondheim, Stephen	1984	Ensemble	Putting It Together (Part 16)	Uptempo	SATB			Ensemble	Adults
Sunday...Park With Geroge	Sondheim, Stephen	1984	George	Putting It Together (Part 16)*	Uptempo	Tenor	Db3	Gb4	Lead	Romantic Lead Female
Sunday...Park With Geroge	Sondheim, Stephen	1984	Marie	Children And Art*	Ballad	Alto	Gb3	Db5	Lead	Romantic Lead Female
Sunday...Park With Geroge	Sondheim, Stephen	1984	George	Lesson #8	Ballad	Tenor	G#2	Eb4	Lead	Romantic Antagonist Male
Sunday...Park With Geroge	Sondheim, Stephen	1984	George	Move On*	Ballad	Tenor	D#3	G4	Lead	Romantic Antagonist Male
Sunday...Park With Geroge	Sondheim, Stephen	1984	Dot	Move On*	Ballad	Alto	G#3	C#5	Lead	Romantic Lead Female
Sunday...Park With Geroge	Sondheim, Stephen	1984	George & Dot	Move On	Ballad	Tenor/Atlo			Duet	RAM/RLF

Shows

Songs by Character Type

* = Music Edit Required
+ = Ethnic Specific

Show	Composer	Year	Role	Song	Tempo	Vocal Type	Range-Bottom	Range-Top	Category	Character Type
Sunday...Park With Geroge	Sondheim, Stephen	1984	Ensemble	Sunday Finale	Ballad	SATB			Ensemble	Children/Adults
Sunset Boulevard	Webber, Andrew Lloyd	1994	Joe Gillis	Prologue	Moderate Tempo	Tenor	D3	G4	Lead	Romantic Antagonist Male
Sunset Boulevard	Webber, Andrew Lloyd	1994	Joe Gillis	Let Me Take You Back Six Months	Moderate Tempo	Tenor	C3	Eb4	Lead	Romantic Antagonist Male
Sunset Boulevard	Webber, Andrew Lloyd	1994	Ensemble	Let's Have Lunch	Moderate Tempo	SATB			Ensemble	Adults
Sunset Boulevard	Webber, Andrew Lloyd	1994	Joe Gillis & Betty Schaefer	Betty's Pitch	Moderate Tempo	Tenor/Sop			Duet	RAM/CIF
Sunset Boulevard	Webber, Andrew Lloyd	1994	Norma Desmond	Surrender	Ballad	Alto	F3	Bb4	Lead	Romantic Antagonist Female
Sunset Boulevard	Webber, Andrew Lloyd	1994	Norma Desmond	Once Upon A Time	Uptempo	Alto	A3	A4	Lead	Romantic Antagonist Female
Sunset Boulevard	Webber, Andrew Lloyd	1994	Norma Desmond	With One Look	Moderate Tempo	Alto	G3	D5	Lead	Romantic Antagonist Female
Sunset Boulevard	Webber, Andrew Lloyd	1994	Joe Gillis & Norma Desmond	Salome	Moderate Tempo	Tenor/Atlo			Duet	RAM/RAF
Sunset Boulevard	Webber, Andrew Lloyd	1994	Max Von Mayerling	The Grestest Star Of All	Moderate Tempo	Baritone	B2	Gb4	Lead	Character Male
Sunset Boulevard	Webber, Andrew Lloyd	1994	Ensemble	Let's Have Lunch Reprise	Moderate Tempo	SATB			Ensemble	Adults
Sunset Boulevard	Webber, Andrew Lloyd	1994	Joe Gillis & Betty Schaefer	Girl Meets Boy	Moderate Tempo	Tenor/Sop			Duet	RAM/CIF
Sunset Boulevard	Webber, Andrew Lloyd	1994	Joe Gillis	I Started Work	Uptempo	Tenor	C3	G4	Lead	Romantic Antagonist Male
Sunset Boulevard	Webber, Andrew Lloyd	1994	Norma Desmond	New Ways To Dream	Ballad	Alto	B3	C5	Lead	Romantic Antagonist Female
Sunset Boulevard	Webber, Andrew Lloyd	1994	Manfred	The Lady's Paying*	Uptempo	Baritone	C3	F4	Lead	Character Male
Sunset Boulevard	Webber, Andrew Lloyd	1994	Ensemble	The Lady's Paying	Uptempo	ATB			Ensemble	Adults
Sunset Boulevard	Webber, Andrew Lloyd	1994	Norma Desmond	The Perfect Year*	Moderate Tempo	Alto	A3	Eb5	Lead	Romantic Antagonist Female
Sunset Boulevard	Webber, Andrew Lloyd	1994	Joe Gillis	The Perfect Year*	Moderate Tempo	Tenor	A2	D4	Lead	Romantic Antagonist Male
Sunset Boulevard	Webber, Andrew Lloyd	1994	Joe Gillis	I Had To Get Out	Uptempo	Tenor	C3	Eb4	Lead	Romantic Antagonist Male
Sunset Boulevard	Webber, Andrew Lloyd	1994	Ensemble	This Time Next Year	Moderate Tempo	SATB			Ensemble	Adults
Sunset Boulevard	Webber, Andrew Lloyd	1994	Ensemble	Auld Lang Syne	Moderate Tempo	SATB			Ensemble	Adults
Sunset Boulevard	Webber, Andrew Lloyd	1994	Joe Gillis	Sunset Boulevard	Uptempo	Tenor	C3	G4	Lead	Romantic Antagonist Male
Sunset Boulevard	Webber, Andrew Lloyd	1994	Norma Desmond	As If We Never Said Goodbye	Moderate Tempo	Alto	G#3	C#5	Lead	Romantic Antagonist Female
Sunset Boulevard	Webber, Andrew Lloyd	1994	Norma Desmond	There's Been A Call*	Uptempo	Alto	C4	D5	Lead	Romantic Antagonist Female
Sunset Boulevard	Webber, Andrew Lloyd	1994	Joe Gillis	It Took Her Three Days	Uptempo	Tenor	A2	E4	Lead	Romantic Antagonist Male
Sunset Boulevard	Webber, Andrew Lloyd	1994	Ensemble	Paramount Conversations	Moderate Tempo	SATB			Ensemble	Adults
Sunset Boulevard	Webber, Andrew Lloyd	1994	Joe Gillis	Girl Meets Boy Reprise*	Uptempo	Tenor	D3	E4	Lead	Romantic Antagonist Male
Sunset Boulevard	Webber, Andrew Lloyd	1994	Betty Schaefer	Girl Meets Boy Reprise*	Uptempo	Soprano	A3	E5	Lead	Character Ingenue Female
Sunset Boulevard	Webber, Andrew Lloyd	1994	Cecil B. DeMille	Surrender Reprise	Ballad	Baritone	Ab2	Db4	Supporting	Mature Male
Sunset Boulevard	Webber, Andrew Lloyd	1994	Ensemble	A Little Suffering	Uptempo	SA			Ensemble	Adults
Sunset Boulevard	Webber, Andrew Lloyd	1994	Joe Gillis	I Should Have Stayed There	Uptempo	Tenor	A3	E4	Lead	Romantic Antagonist Male
Sunset Boulevard	Webber, Andrew Lloyd	1994	Betty Schaefer	Too Much In Love To Care*	Moderate Tempo	Soprano	A3	G5	Lead	Character Ingenue Female
Sunset Boulevard	Webber, Andrew Lloyd	1994	Joe Gillis	Too Much In Love To Care*	Moderate Tempo	Tenor	F3	G4	Lead	Romantic Antagonist Male
Sunset Boulevard	Webber, Andrew Lloyd	1994	Joe Gillis & Betty Schaefer	Too Much In Love To Care	Moderate Tempo	Tenor/Sop			Duet	RAM/CIF
Sunset Boulevard	Webber, Andrew Lloyd	1994	Max Von Mayerling	New Ways To Dream Reprise	Ballad	Baritone	G2	E4	Lead	Character Male
Sunset Boulevard	Webber, Andrew Lloyd	1994	Norma Desmond	Phone Call	Moderate Tempo	Alto	F3	Ab4	Lead	Romantic Antagonist Female
Sunset Boulevard	Webber, Andrew Lloyd	1994	Joe Gillis	Sunset Blvd Reprise-What's Going On J	Uptempo	Tenor	C#3	Gb4	Lead	Romantic Antagonist Male
Sunset Boulevard	Webber, Andrew Lloyd	1994	Joe Gillis & Betty Schaefer	Sunset Blvd Reprise-What's Going On J	Uptempo	Tenor/Sop			Duet	RAM/CIF
Sunset Boulevard	Webber, Andrew Lloyd	1994	Norma & Max	The Final Scene	Ballad	Alto/Bar			Duet	RAF/CM
Sweeney Todd	Sondheim, Stephen	1979	Ensemble	The Ballad Of Sweeney Todd	Moderate Tempo	SATB			Ensemble	Adults
Sweeney Todd	Sondheim, Stephen	1979	Sweeney Todd	The Barber And His Wife	Ballad	Baritone	F3	Ab4	Lead	Antagonist Male
Sweeney Todd	Sondheim, Stephen	1979	Mrs. Lovett	The Worst Pies In London	Uptempo	Alto	B3	Eb5	Lead	Character Female
Sweeney Todd	Sondheim, Stephen	1979	Mrs. Lovett	Poor Thing	Uptempo	Alto	F#3	B4	Lead	Character Female

Shows

473

* = Music Edit Required
+ = Ethnic Specific

Show	Composer	Year	Role	Song	Tempo	Vocal Type	Range-Bottom	Range-Top	Category	Character Type
Sweeney Todd	Sondheim, Stephen	1979	Sweeney & Mrs. Lovett	My Friends	Ballad	Bar/Alto			Duet	AM/CF
Sweeney Todd	Sondheim, Stephen	1979	Johannah	Green Finch And Linnet Bird*	Uptempo	Soprano	C4	G5	Lead	Ingenue Female
Sweeney Todd	Sondheim, Stephen	1979	Anthony Hope	Ah, Miss (I & III)	Uptempo	Tenor	C3	F4	Lead	Ingenue Male
Sweeney Todd	Sondheim, Stephen	1979	Anthony Hope	Johanna	Ballad	Tenor	C3	Eb4	Lead	Ingenue Male
Sweeney Todd	Sondheim, Stephen	1979	Tobias Ragg	Perelli's Miracle Elixir*	Uptempo	Tenor	B2	A4	Lead	Character Ingenue Male
Sweeney Todd	Sondheim, Stephen	1979	Adolfo Pirelli	The Contest	Moderate Tempo	Tenor	B2	C4	Lead	Character Male
Sweeney Todd	Sondheim, Stephen	1979	Mrs. Lovett	Wait	Moderate Tempo	Alto	Bb2	Eb5	Lead	Character Female
Sweeney Todd	Sondheim, Stephen	1979	Anthony & Johanna	Kiss Me (I & II)	Uptempo	Tenor/Sop			Duet	IM/IF
Sweeney Todd	Sondheim, Stephen	1979	The Beadle	Ladies In Their Sensitivities	Ballad	Tenor	D3	A4	Lead	Character Male
Sweeney Todd	Sondheim, Stephen	1979	Ensemble	Quintet	Ballad	SATB			Ensemble	Adults
Sweeney Todd	Sondheim, Stephen	1979	Sweeney & Judge Turpin	Pretty Women (I & II)	Ballad	Bar/Bar			Duet	AM/AM
Sweeney Todd	Sondheim, Stephen	1979	Sweeney Todd	Epiphany*	Uptempo	Baritone	Bb2	F4	Lead	Antagonist Male
Sweeney Todd	Sondheim, Stephen	1979	Mrs. Lovett	By The Sea	Uptempo	Alto	G3	E5	Lead	Character Female
Sweeney Todd	Sondheim, Stephen	1979	Tobias Ragg	Not While I'm Around*	Ballad	Tenor	Eb3	Ab4	Lead	Character Ingenue Male
Sweeney Todd	Sondheim, Stephen	1979	Ensemble	God That's Good	Moderate Tempo	SATB			Ensemble	Adults
Sweeney Todd	Sondheim, Stephen	1979	Sweeney Todd	My Friends*	Ballad	Baritone	Bb2	Eb4	Lead	Antagonist Male
Sweeney Todd	Sondheim, Stephen	1979	Sweeney & Mrs. Lovett	A Little Priest	Uptempo	Bar/Alto			Duet	AM/CF
Sweeney Todd	Sondheim, Stephen	1979	Ensemble	Ballad Of Sweeney Todd #1	Moderate Tempo	SATB			Ensemble	Adults
Sweeney Todd	Sondheim, Stephen	1979	Ensemble	Ballad Of Sweeney Todd #5	Moderate Tempo	SATB			Ensemble	Adults
Sweeney Todd	Sondheim, Stephen	1979	Ensemble	Ballad Of Sweeney Todd #10B	Moderate Tempo	SATB			Ensemble	Adults
Sweeney Todd	Sondheim, Stephen	1979	Ensemble	Ballad Of Sweeney Todd #10B	Moderate Tempo	SATB			Ensemble	Adults
Sweeney Todd	Sondheim, Stephen	1979	Ensemble	Ballad Of Sweeney Todd #12C	Moderate Tempo	TTT			Ensemble	Adults
Sweeney Todd	Sondheim, Stephen	1979	Ensemble	Ballad Of Sweeney Todd #22	Moderate Tempo	SATB			Ensemble	Adults
Sweeney Todd	Sondheim, Stephen	1979	Ensemble	Ballad Of Sweeney Todd #25 Fogg's As'	Moderate Tempo	SATB			Ensemble	Adults
Sweeney Todd	Sondheim, Stephen	1979	Ensemble	Ballad Of Sweeney Todd #27A	Moderate Tempo	SATB Unison			Ensemble	Adults
Sweeney Todd	Sondheim, Stephen	1979	Ensemble	Ballad Of Sweeney Todd #29B	Moderate Tempo	SATB			Ensemble	Adults
Sweeney Todd	Sondheim, Stephen	1979	Adolfo Pirelli	Pirelli's Death	Moderate Tempo	Tenor	Eb3	C5	Lead	Character Male
Sweeney Todd	Sondheim, Stephen	1979	Sweeney Todd	Johanna II*	Moderate Tempo	Baritone	A2	Eb4	Lead	Antagonist Male
Sweeney Todd	Sondheim, Stephen	1979	Sweeney & Anthony	Johanna II	Moderate Tempo	Bar/Tenor			Duet	AM/IM
Sweeney Todd	Sondheim, Stephen	1979	The Beadle	Parlor Songs	Moderate Tempo	Tenor	D3	G4	Lead	Character Male
Sweeney Todd	Sondheim, Stephen	1979	Ensemble	City On Fire	Uptempo	SATB			Ensemble	Adults
Sweeney Todd	Sondheim, Stephen	1979	Sweeney Todd	Finale Scene II	Uptempo	Baritone	G2	C4	Lead	Antagonist Male
Sweet Charity	Coleman, Cy	1966	Charity Hope Valentine	You Should See Yourself	Uptempo	Alto	Bb3	Bb4	Lead	Character Ingenue Female
Sweet Charity	Coleman, Cy	1966	Ensemble	Big Spender	Moderate Tempo	SA			Ensemble	Adults
Sweet Charity	Coleman, Cy	1966	Dance Hall Girl	Big Spender*	Moderate Tempo	Alto	F3	B4	Featured Ensemble	Antagonist Female
Sweet Charity	Coleman, Cy	1966	Charity Hope Valentine	Charity's Soliloquy	Moderate Tempo	Alto	F3	Ab4	Lead	Character Ingenue Female
Sweet Charity	Coleman, Cy	1966	Charity Hope Valentine	If My Friends Could See Me Now	Uptempo	Alto	G#3	Bb4	Lead	Character Ingenue Female
Sweet Charity	Coleman, Cy	1966	Vittorio Vidal	Too Many Tomorrows	Ballad	Tenor	Bb2	G4	Lead	Romantic Lead Male
Sweet Charity	Coleman, Cy	1966	Nickie	There's Gotta Be Something Better...*	Uptempo	Alto	A3	Db4	Lead	Romantic Antagonist Female
Sweet Charity	Coleman, Cy	1966	Ensemble	There's Gotta Be Something Better...	Uptempo	AAA			Ensemble	Adults
Sweet Charity	Coleman, Cy	1966	Helene	There's Gotta Be Something Better...*	Uptempo	Alto	A3	Db5	Lead	Romantic Antagonist Female
Sweet Charity	Coleman, Cy	1966	Charity Hope Valentine	There's Gotta Be Something Better...*	Uptempo	Alto	Bb3	Db5	Lead	Character Ingenue Female

Shows

Songs by Character Type

* = Music Edit Required
+ = Ethnic Specific

Show	Composer	Year	Role	Song	Tempo	Vocal Type	Range-Bottom	Range-Top	Category	Character Type
Sweet Charity	Coleman, Cy	1966	Charity Hope Valentine	I'm The Bravest Individual	Uptempo	Alto	C4	Eb5	Lead	Character Ingenue Female
Sweet Charity	Coleman, Cy	1966	Daddy Brubeck	The Rhythm Of Life*	Uptempo	Tenor	B2	G4	Lead	Character Male
Sweet Charity	Coleman, Cy	1966	Ensemble	The Rhythm Of Life	Uptempo	SATB			Ensemble	Adults
Sweet Charity	Coleman, Cy	1966	Nickie & Helene	Baby Dream Your Dream	Moderate Tempo	Alto/Alto			Duet	RAF/RAF
Sweet Charity	Coleman, Cy	1966	Oscar Lindquist	Sweet Charity	Moderate Tempo	Baritone	Bb2	E4	Lead	Character Male
Sweet Charity	Coleman, Cy	1966	Charity Hope Valentine	Where Am I Going	Moderate Tempo	Alto	A3	A4	Lead	Character Ingenue Female
Sweet Charity	Coleman, Cy	1966	Charity Hope Valentine	I'm A Brass Band*	Uptempo	Alto	A#3	G#4	Lead	Character Ingenue Female
Sweet Charity	Coleman, Cy	1966	Herman	I Love To Cry At Weddings*	Uptempo	Tenor	D3	B4	Lead	Antagonist Male
Sweet Charity	Coleman, Cy	1966	Herman & Wedding Guest	I Love To Cry At Weddings	Uptempo	Tenor/Tenor			Duet	AM/CM
Sweet Smell Of Success	Hamlisch, Marvin	2002	Ensemble	The Column	Moderate Tempo	SATB			Ensemble	Adults
Sweet Smell Of Success	Hamlisch, Marvin	2002	Sidney	I Can Get You In JJ	Uptempo	Tenor	Db3	Ab4	Lead	Romantic Antagonist Male
Sweet Smell Of Success	Hamlisch, Marvin	2002	Dallas	I Cannot Hear The City	Ballad	Tenor	A3	G4	Lead	Romantic Lead Male
Sweet Smell Of Success	Hamlisch, Marvin	2002	Ensemble	Welcome To The Night	Uptempo	SATB			Ensemble	Adults
Sweet Smell Of Success	Hamlisch, Marvin	2002	Zanzibar Singer	Laughin' All The Way To The Bank	Uptempo	Alto	G#3	D4	Supporting	Romantic Antagonist Female
Sweet Smell Of Success	Hamlisch, Marvin	2002	Sidney	At The Fountain	Moderate Tempo	Tenor	F3	A4	Lead	Romantic Antagonist Male
Sweet Smell Of Success	Hamlisch, Marvin	2002	Sidney	Welcome To The Night Reprise*	Uptempo	Tenor	Db4	F4	Lead	Romantic Antagonist Male
Sweet Smell Of Success	Hamlisch, Marvin	2002	Ensemble	Psalm 151	Ballad	SATB			Ensemble	Adults
Sweet Smell Of Success	Hamlisch, Marvin	2002	Dallas	Don't Know Where You Leave Off*	Moderate Tempo	Tenor	A2	G4	Lead	Romantic Lead Male
Sweet Smell Of Success	Hamlisch, Marvin	2002	Dallas & Susan	Don't Know Where You Leave Off	Moderate Tempo	Tenor/Sop			Duet	RLM/IF
Sweet Smell Of Success	Hamlisch, Marvin	2002	Susan	What If*	Uptempo	Soprano	A3	F5	Lead	Ingenue Female
Sweet Smell Of Success	Hamlisch, Marvin	2002	JJ Hunsecker	For Susan*	Moderate Tempo	Baritone	C3	Eb4	Lead	Antagonist Male
Sweet Smell Of Success	Hamlisch, Marvin	2002	Dallas	One Track Mind	Uptempo	Tenor	E3	A4	Lead	Romantic Lead Male
Sweet Smell Of Success	Hamlisch, Marvin	2002	Ensemble	I Cannot Hear The City (Act 1 Finale)	Ballad	SATB			Ensemble	Adults
Sweet Smell Of Success	Hamlisch, Marvin	2002	Dallas	I Cannot Hear The City (Act 1 Finale)	Ballad	Tenor	A2	Bb4	Lead	Romantic Lead Male
Sweet Smell Of Success	Hamlisch, Marvin	2002	Ensemble	Break It Up	Uptempo	SATB			Ensemble	Adults
Sweet Smell Of Success	Hamlisch, Marvin	2002	Sidney	Break It Up*	Uptempo	Tenor	E3	F4	Lead	Romantic Antagonist Male
Sweet Smell Of Success	Hamlisch, Marvin	2002	Rita	Rita's Tune	Moderate Tempo	Alto	A3	Eb5	Lead	Romantic Antagonist Female
Sweet Smell Of Success	Hamlisch, Marvin	2002	Ensemble	Dirt	Moderate Tempo	SATB			Ensemble	Adults
Sweet Smell Of Success	Hamlisch, Marvin	2002	Sidney	I Could Get You In JJ Reprise	Moderate Tempo	Tenor	D3	G#4	Lead	Romantic Antagonist Male
Sweet Smell Of Success	Hamlisch, Marvin	2002	Susan	I Cannot Hear The City Reprise*	Ballad	Soprano	Ab3	G5	Lead	Ingenue Female
Sweet Smell Of Success	Hamlisch, Marvin	2002	Dallas & Susan	I Cannot Hear The City Reprise*	Ballad	Tenor/Sop			Duet	RLM/IF
Sweet Smell Of Success	Hamlisch, Marvin	2002	JJ Hunsecker	Don't Look Now*	Moderate Tempo	Baritone	C3	G4	Lead	Antagonist Male
Sweet Smell Of Success	Hamlisch, Marvin	2002	Ensemble	Don't Look Now	Moderate Tempo	TB			Ensemble	Adults
Sweet Smell Of Success	Hamlisch, Marvin	2002	Sidney	At The Fountain Reprise*	Moderate Tempo	Tenor	A2	F4	Lead	Romantic Antagonist Male
Sweet Smell Of Success	Hamlisch, Marvin	2002	Ensemble	At The Fountain Reprise	Moderate Tempo	SATB			Ensemble	Adults
Sweet Smell Of Success	Hamlisch, Marvin	2002	Sidney	Finale*	Uptempo	Tenor	E3	F4	Lead	Romantic Antagonist Male
Sweet Smell Of Success	Hamlisch, Marvin	2002	Ensemble	Finale (Part 3)	Moderate Tempo	TB			Ensemble	Adults
The Little Mermaid	Menken, Alan	2007	Ensemble	The Fathoms Below	Uptempo	SSA			Ensemble	Adults
The Little Mermaid	Menken, Alan	2007	Ensemble	Daughters Of Triton	Uptempo	Soprano	A3	C5	Ensemble	Adults
The Little Mermaid	Menken, Alan	2007	Ariel	The World Above	Uptempo	Soprano	A3	C5	Lead	Ingenue Female
The Little Mermaid	Menken, Alan	2007	Scuttle	Human Stuff*	Uptempo	Tenor	B2	G4	Lead	Character Male
The Little Mermaid	Menken, Alan	2007	Ursula	I Want The Good Times Back	Moderate Tempo	Soprano	F#3	A5	Lead	Antagonist Female
The Little Mermaid	Menken, Alan	2007	Ursula	Daddy's Little Angel	Moderate Tempo	Soprano	Eb3	C5	Lead	Antagonist Female

* = Music Edit Required
+ = Ethnic Specific

Show	Composer	Year	Role	Song	Tempo	Vocal Type	Range-Bottom	Range-Top	Category	Character Type
The Little Mermaid	Menken, Alan	2007	Ariel	Part Of Your World	Uptempo	Soprano	C4	C5	Lead	Ingenue Female
The Little Mermaid	Menken, Alan	2007	Ensemble	She's In Love	Uptempo	SSA			Ensemble	Adults
The Little Mermaid	Menken, Alan	2007	Prince Eric	Her Voice	Moderate Tempo	Tenor	C3	G4	Lead	Ingenue Male
The Little Mermaid	Menken, Alan	2007	Sebastian & King Triton	The World Above Reprise	Moderate Tempo	Tenor/Bar			Duet	CM/RLM
The Little Mermaid	Menken, Alan	2007	Sebastian	The World Above Reprise	Moderate Tempo	Tenor	C3	E4	Lead	Character Male
The Little Mermaid	Menken, Alan	2007	Flotsam & Jetsom	Sweet Child	Ballad	Tenor/Tenor			Duet	AM/AM
The Little Mermaid	Menken, Alan	2007	Flotsam	Sweet Child	Ballad	Tenor	C3	C5	Supporting	Antagonist Male
The Little Mermaid	Menken, Alan	2007	Jetsom	Sweet Child	Ballad	Tenor	C3	C5	Supporting	Antagonist Male
The Little Mermaid	Menken, Alan	2007	Ursula	Poor Unfortunate Soul	Moderate Tempo	Soprano	C4	A5	Lead	Antagonist Female
The Little Mermaid	Menken, Alan	2007	Scuttle	Positoovity	Uptempo	Tenor	G2	A4	Lead	Character Male
The Little Mermaid	Menken, Alan	2007	Ensemble	Positoovity	Uptempo	SAT			Ensemble	Adults
The Little Mermaid	Menken, Alan	2007	Flounder	She's In Love*	Uptempo	Soprano	G3	A#5	Lead	Juvenile Male
The Little Mermaid	Menken, Alan	2007	Flounder	She's In Love*	Uptempo	Tenor	G2	A#4	Lead	Ingenue Male
The Little Mermaid	Menken, Alan	2007	Chef Louis	Les Poisons	Uptempo	Baritone	Eb3	D4	Lead	Character Male
The Little Mermaid	Menken, Alan	2007	Prince Eric	One Step Closer	Moderate Tempo	Tenor	B3	F#5	Lead	Ingenue Male
The Little Mermaid	Menken, Alan	2007	Ursula	I Want The Good Time Back Reprise	Moderate Tempo	Soprano	F#3	A5	Lead	Antagonist Female
The Little Mermaid	Menken, Alan	2007	Sebastian	Kiss The Girl	Moderate Tempo	Tenor	D3	F4	Lead	Character Male
The Little Mermaid	Menken, Alan	2007	Ensemble	If Only	Ballad	STTB			Ensemble	Adults
The Little Mermaid	Menken, Alan	2007	Ursula	Her Voice Reprise	Moderate Tempo	Soprano	Db3	Eb4	Lead	Antagonist Female
The Little Mermaid	Menken, Alan	2007	Ensemble	The Contest	Uptempo	SATB			Ensemble	Adults
The Little Mermaid	Menken, Alan	2007	Ensemble	Human Stuff	Uptempo	TTB			Ensemble	Adults
The Little Mermaid	Menken, Alan	2007	Ensemble	Under The Sea	Uptempo	SATB			Ensemble	Adults
The Little Mermaid	Menken, Alan	2007	Ursula	Ursula's Incantation*	Moderate Tempo	Soprano	G4	F#5	Lead	Antagonist Female
The Little Mermaid	Menken, Alan	2007	Ariel	Ursula's Incantation (Ahs)*	Moderate Tempo	Soprano	F#4	E5	Lead	Ingenue Female
The Little Mermaid	Menken, Alan	2007	Ensemble	Kiss The Girl	Moderate Tempo	SATB			Ensemble	Adults
The Little Mermaid	Menken, Alan	2007	Sebastian	Kiss The Girl*	Moderate Tempo	Tenor	A2	C4	Lead	Character Male
They're Playing Our Song	Hamlisch, Marvin	1974	Vernon Gersch	Falling	Moderate Tempo	Baritone	A2	D4	Lead	Romantic Antagonist Male
They're Playing Our Song	Hamlisch, Marvin	1974	Sonia Walsk	If He Really Knew Me*	Ballad	Alto	E3	A4	Lead	Romantic Lead Female
They're Playing Our Song	Hamlisch, Marvin	1974	Vernon Gersch	If She Really Knew Me*	Ballad	Baritone	C3	F4	Lead	Romantic Antagonist Male
They're Playing Our Song	Hamlisch, Marvin	1974	Vernon Gersch	They're Playing My Song*	Uptempo	Baritone	G3	B4	Lead	Romantic Antagonist Male
They're Playing Our Song	Hamlisch, Marvin	1974	Sonia Walsk	They're Playing My Song*	Uptempo	Alto	B2	Cb5	Lead	Romantic Lead Female
They're Playing Our Song	Hamlisch, Marvin	1974	Vernon Gersch	Workin' It Out*	Uptempo	Baritone	C3	F4	Lead	Romantic Antagonist Male
They're Playing Our Song	Hamlisch, Marvin	1974	Ensemble	Workin' It Out	Uptempo	SATB			Ensemble	Adults
They're Playing Our Song	Hamlisch, Marvin	1974	Vernon Gersch & Sonia Walsk	Workin' It Out*	Uptempo	Bar/Alto			Duet	RAM/RLF
They're Playing Our Song	Hamlisch, Marvin	1974	Sonia Walsk	If He Really Knew Me*	Ballad	Alto	G3	Cb5	Lead	Romantic Lead Female
They're Playing Our Song	Hamlisch, Marvin	1974	Sonia Walsk	Falling Reprise	Moderate Tempo	Alto	C3	D4	Lead	Romantic Lead Female
They're Playing Our Song	Hamlisch, Marvin	1974	Vernon Gersch	If She Really Knew Me Reprise*	Ballad	Baritone	G3	Ab4	Lead	Romantic Antagonist Male
They're Playing Our Song	Hamlisch, Marvin	1974	Sonia Walsk	If He Really Knew Me Reprise*	Ballad	Alto	A3	G4	Lead	Romantic Lead Female
They're Playing Our Song	Hamlisch, Marvin	1974	Vernon Gersch & Sonia Walsk	Right*	Uptempo	Bar/Alto			Duet	RAM/RLF
They're Playing Our Song	Hamlisch, Marvin	1974	Sonia Walsk	Right	Uptempo	SA			Ensemble	Adults
They're Playing Our Song	Hamlisch, Marvin	1974	Ensemble	Just For Tonight	Ballad	Alto	G3	A4	Lead	Romantic Lead Female
They're Playing Our Song	Hamlisch, Marvin	1974	Vernon Gersch & Sonia Walsk	When You're In My Arms*	Uptempo	Bar/Alto			Duet	RAM/RLF
They're Playing Our Song	Hamlisch, Marvin	1974	Ensemble	When You're In My Arms	Uptempo	SATB			Ensemble	Adults

Shows

* = Music Edit Required
+ = Ethnic Specific

Show	Composer	Year	Role	Song	Tempo	Vocal Type	Range-Bottom	Range-Top	Category	Character Type
Thoroughly Modern Millie	Tesori, Jeanine	2002	Millie Dillmount	Not For The Life Of Me	Uptempo	Alto	Ab3	C5	Lead	Character Ingenue Female
Thoroughly Modern Millie	Tesori, Jeanine	2002	Ensemble	Thoroughly Modern Millie	Uptempo	SATB			Ensemble	Adults
Thoroughly Modern Millie	Tesori, Jeanine	2002	Ensemble	Not For The Life Of Me Reprise	Uptempo	SA			Ensemble	Adults
Thoroughly Modern Millie	Tesori, Jeanine	2002	Millie & Dorothy	How The Other Half Lives	Uptempo	Alto/Sop			Ensemble	Adults
Thoroughly Modern Millie	Tesori, Jeanine	2002	Ching Ho & Bun Foo	Not For The Life Of Me Reprise II	Uptempo	Bar/Bar			Duet	CM/CM
Thoroughly Modern Millie	Tesori, Jeanine	2002	Mrs. Meers	They Don't Know	Moderate Tempo	Alto	D#3	F4	Lead	Character Female
Thoroughly Modern Millie	Tesori, Jeanine	2002	Jimmy Smith	What Do I Need With Love	Uptempo	Tenor	D3	G4	Lead	Ingenue Male
Thoroughly Modern Millie	Tesori, Jeanine	2002	Muzzy Van Hossmere	Only In New York	Ballad	Alto	G#3	B4	Lead	Romantic Lead Female
Thoroughly Modern Millie	Tesori, Jeanine	2002	Millie Dillmount	Jimmy	Uptempo	Alto	B3	D#4	Lead	Character Ingenue Female
Thoroughly Modern Millie	Tesori, Jeanine	2002	Ensemble	Forget About The Boy	Uptempo	SA			Ensemble	Adults
Thoroughly Modern Millie	Tesori, Jeanine	2002	Millie Dillmount	Forget About The Boy*	Uptempo	Alto	A3	Db5	Lead	Character Ingenue Female
Thoroughly Modern Millie	Tesori, Jeanine	2002	Trevor & Dorothy	I'm Falling In Love With Someone	Ballad	Tenor/Sop			Duet	IM/IF
Thoroughly Modern Millie	Tesori, Jeanine	2002	Trevor & Dorothy	Ah! Sweet Myster Of Life	Moderate Tempo	Tenor/Sop			Duet	IM/IF
Thoroughly Modern Millie	Tesori, Jeanine	2002	Jimmy Smith	I Turned The Corner	Moderate Tempo	Tenor	C#3	Ab4	Lead	Ingenue Male
Thoroughly Modern Millie	Tesori, Jeanine	2002	Muzzy Van Hossmere	Long As I'm Here With You*	Uptempo	Alto	A3	C#5	Lead	Romantic Lead Female
Thoroughly Modern Millie	Tesori, Jeanine	2002	Millie Dillmount	Gimmie Gimmie	Uptempo	Alto	Ab3	D5	Lead	Character Ingenue Female
Thoroughly Modern Millie	Tesori, Jeanine	2002	Ensemble	Thoroughly Modern Millie Reprise	Uptempo	SATB			Ensemble	Adults
Thoroughly Modern Millie	Tesori, Jeanine	2002	Millie Dillmount	How The Other Half Lives*	Moderate Tempo	Alto	B3	Eb5	Lead	Character Ingenue Female
Thoroughly Modern Millie	Tesori, Jeanine	2002	Dorothy Brown	How The Other Half Lives	Moderate Tempo	Soprano	B3	Eb5	Lead	Ingenue Female
Thoroughly Modern Millie	Tesori, Jeanine	2002	Ensemble	Long As I'm Here With You*	Uptempo	ATB			Ensemble	Adults
Thoroughly Modern Millie	Tesori, Jeanine	2002	Millie & Jimmy	I Turned The Corner	Moderate Tempo	Alto/Tenor			Duet	CIF/IM
Thoroughly Modern Millie	Tesori, Jeanine	2002	Trevor & Millie	The Speed Test	Uptempo	Tenor/Alto			Duet	RLM/CIF
Thoroughly Modern Millie	Tesori, Jeanine	2002	Trevor Graydon	The Speed Test*	Uptempo	Tenor	A2	F4	Lead	Romantic Lead Male
Thoroughly Modern Millie	Tesori, Jeanine	2002	Millie Dillmount	The Speed Test*	Uptempo	Alto	A3	E5	Lead	Character Ingenue Female
Thoroughly Modern Millie	Tesori, Jeanine	2002	Ensemble	Falling In Love With Love Reprise	Ballad	SATB			Ensemble	Adults
Thoroughly Modern Millie	Tesori, Jeanine	2002	Ensemble	Muquin (My Mammy)	Uptempo	SATB			Ensemble	Adults
Unsinkable Molly Brown, Th	Willson, Meredith	1960	Molly Tobin	I Ain't Down Yet*	Uptempo	Soprano	Ab3	F5	Lead	Romantic Antagonist Female
Unsinkable Molly Brown, Th	Willson, Meredith	1960	Ensemble	I Ain't Down Yet	Uptempo	STB			Ensemble	Adults
Unsinkable Molly Brown, Th	Willson, Meredith	1960	Ensemble	Belly Up To The Bar Boys	Uptempo	STB			Ensemble	Adults
Unsinkable Molly Brown, Th	Willson, Meredith	1960	Johnny Brown	Colorado My Home	Moderate Tempo	Tenor	B2	F4	Lead	Romantic Lead Male
Unsinkable Molly Brown, Th	Willson, Meredith	1960	Johnny Brown	I've A'ready Started In	Moderate Tempo	Tenor	G3	E4	Lead	Romantic Lead Male
Unsinkable Molly Brown, Th	Willson, Meredith	1960	Johnny Brown	I'll Never Say No	Ballad	Tenor	Db3	F4	Lead	Romantic Lead Male
Unsinkable Molly Brown, Th	Willson, Meredith	1960	Molly Tobin	My Own Brass Bed	Ballad	Soprano	G3	Bb4	Lead	Romantic Antagonist Female
Unsinkable Molly Brown, Th	Willson, Meredith	1960	Ensemble	The Denver Police	Moderate Tempo	SATB			Ensemble	Adults
Unsinkable Molly Brown, Th	Willson, Meredith	1960	Molly Tobin	Beautiful People Of Denver	Uptempo	Soprano	F3	Bb4	Lead	Romantic Antagonist Female
Unsinkable Molly Brown, Th	Willson, Meredith	1960	Molly Tobin	Are You Sure*	Uptempo	Soprano	G3	Db5	Lead	Romantic Antagonist Female
Unsinkable Molly Brown, Th	Willson, Meredith	1960	Ensemble	Are You Sure	Uptempo	SATB			Ensemble	Adults
Unsinkable Molly Brown, Th	Willson, Meredith	1960	Johnny Brown & Molly Tobin	I Ain't Down Yet Reprise	Uptempo	Bar/Sop		Bb4	Duet	RLM/RAF
Unsinkable Molly Brown, Th	Willson, Meredith	1960	Ensemble	Happy Birthday, Mrs. JJ Brown	Moderate Tempo	SATB			Ensemble	Adults
Unsinkable Molly Brown, Th	Willson, Meredith	1960	Ensemble	Bon Jour	Uptempo	SATB			Ensemble	Adults
Unsinkable Molly Brown, Th	Willson, Meredith	1960	Johnny Brown	If I Knew	Ballad	Tenor	C3	F4	Lead	Romantic Lead Male
Unsinkable Molly Brown, Th	Willson, Meredith	1960	Johnny Brown	Chick-A-Pen	Ballad	Tenor	Db3	F4	Lead	Romantic Lead Male

Shows

* = Music Edit Required
+ = Ethnic Specific

Show	Composer	Year	Role	Song	Tempo	Vocal Type	Range-Bottom	Range-Top	Category	Character Type
Unsinkable Molly Brown	Willson, Meredith	1960	Molly Tobin	Chick-A-Pen	Ballad	Soprano	G3	B4	Lead	Romantic Antagonist Female
Unsinkable Molly Brown	Willson, Meredith	1960	Ensemble	Keep-A-Hoppin'	Uptempo	SATB			Ensemble	Adults
Unsinkable Molly Brown	Willson, Meredith	1960	Johnny Brown	Leadville Johnny Brown Soliloquy	Moderate Tempo	Tenor	C3	E4	Lead	Romantic Lead Male
Unsinkable Molly Brown	Willson, Meredith	1960	Prince Delong	Dolce Far Niente*	Ballad	Tenor	C3	Eb4	Lead	Romantic Antagonist Male
Unsinkable Molly Brown	Willson, Meredith	1960	Prince Delong & Molly Tobin	Dolce Far Niente	Ballad	Tenor/Sop			Duet	RAM/RAF
Unsinkable Molly Brown	Willson, Meredith	1960	Prince Delong	Dolce Far Niente Reprise	Ballad	Tenor	D3	Eb4	Lead	Romantic Antagonist Male
Unsinkable Molly Brown	Willson, Meredith	1960	Ensemble	I Ain't Down Yet Fnale	Uptempo	SATB			Ensemble	Adults
Victor/Victoria	Mancini, Henry	1995	Toddy	Paris By Night*	Moderate Tempo	Baritone	Bb2	Eb4	Lead	Character Male
Victor/Victoria	Mancini, Henry	1995	Ensemble	Paris By Night	Moderate Tempo	TB			Ensemble	Adults
Victor/Victoria	Mancini, Henry	1995	Victoria	If I Were A Man	Uptempo	Soprano	G3	A4	Lead	Romantic Lead Female
Victor/Victoria	Mancini, Henry	1995	Toddy	Trust Me*	Uptempo	Baritone	A2	D4	Lead	Character Male
Victor/Victoria	Mancini, Henry	1995	Jazz Singer	Le Jazz Hot*	Moderate Tempo	Soprano	D3	F#4	Lead	Romantic Lead Male
Victor/Victoria	Mancini, Henry	1995	Victor	Le Jazz Hot	Moderate Tempo	Soprano	G#3	D5	Lead	Romantic Lead Female
Victor/Victoria	Mancini, Henry	1995	Ensemble	Le Jazz Hot	Moderate Tempo	SATB			Ensemble	Adults
Victor/Victoria	Mancini, Henry	1995	Norma Cassidy	Paris Makes Me Horny	Moderate Tempo	Soprano	Bb3	A5	Lead	Romantic Antagonist Female
Victor/Victoria	Mancini, Henry	1995	Victoria	Crazy World	Ballad	Soprano	Eb3	C5	Lead	Romantic Lead Female
Victor/Victoria	Mancini, Henry	1995	Victor	Louis Says*	Uptempo	Soprano	E3	F4	Lead	Romantic Lead Female
Victor/Victoria	Mancini, Henry	1995	Ensemble	Louis Says	Uptempo	SATB			Ensemble	Adults
Victor/Victoria	Mancini, Henry	1995	King Marchan	King's Dilemma*	Uptempo	Baritone	A2	D4	Lead	Romantic Lead Male
Victor/Victoria	Mancini, Henry	1995	Toddy & Victor	You And Me*	Moderate Tempo	Bar/Sop			Duet	CM/RLF
Victor/Victoria	Mancini, Henry	1995	Parisienne	Paris By Night Reprise	Moderate Tempo	Alto	A3	C5	Supporting	Romantic Lead Female
Victor/Victoria	Mancini, Henry	1995	Victoria	Almost A Love Song*	Ballad	Soprano	G#3	C5	Lead	Romantic Lead Female
Victor/Victoria	Mancini, Henry	1995	King Marchan	Almost A Love Song*	Ballad	Baritone	G#2	Eb4	Lead	Romantic Lead Male
Victor/Victoria	Mancini, Henry	1995	King & Victoria	Almost A Love Song	Ballad	Bar/Sop			Duet	RLM/RLF
Victor/Victoria	Mancini, Henry	1995	Norma Cassidy	Chicago Illinois*	Uptempo	Soprano	A#3	E5	Lead	Romantic Antagonist Female
Victor/Victoria	Mancini, Henry	1995	Ensemble	Chicago Illinois	Uptempo	SA			Ensemble	Adults
Victor/Victoria	Mancini, Henry	1995	Victoria	Living In The Shadows	Ballad	Soprano	E3	A4	Lead	Romantic Lead Female
Victor/Victoria	Mancini, Henry	1995	Victoria	Living In The Shadows	Moderate Tempo	Soprano	E3	D5	Lead	Romantic Lead Female
Victor/Victoria	Mancini, Henry	1995	Ensemble	Victor/Victoria	Uptempo	SATB			Ensemble	Adults
West Side Story	Bernstein, Leonard	1957	Tony	Something's Coming	Uptempo	Tenor	F#3	Bb4	Lead	Ingenue Male
West Side Story	Bernstein, Leonard	1957	Tony	Maria	Ballad	Tenor	B2	Bb4	Lead	Ingenue Male
West Side Story	Bernstein, Leonard	1957	Tony & Maria+	Tonight	Moderate Tempo	Tenor/Sop			Duet	IM/IF
West Side Story	Bernstein, Leonard	1957	Ensemble+	America	Uptempo	SA			Ensemble	Adults
West Side Story	Bernstein, Leonard	1957	Riff	Cool	Moderate Tempo	Tenor	C3	Eb4	Lead	Antagonist Male
West Side Story	Bernstein, Leonard	1957	Tony & Maria+	One Hand, One Heart	Ballad	Tenor/Sop			Duet	IM/IF
West Side Story	Bernstein, Leonard	1957	Ensemble	Tonight Quintet	Uptempo	SATB			Ensemble	Adults
West Side Story	Bernstein, Leonard	1957	Maria+	I Feel Pretty*	Uptempo	Soprano	C4	F5	Lead	Ingenue Female
West Side Story	Bernstein, Leonard	1957	Female Shark+	Somewhere	Ballad	Soprano	B3	F#5	Featured Ensemble	Ingenue Female
West Side Story	Bernstein, Leonard	1957	Ensemble	Gee, Officer Krupke	Uptempo	TB			Ensemble	Adults
West Side Story	Bernstein, Leonard	1957	Anita+ & Maria+	A Boy Like That	Moderate Tempo	Alto/Sop	Eb3	Cb5	Duet	RLF/IF
West Side Story	Bernstein, Leonard	1957	Anita+	A Boy Like That*	Moderate Tempo	Alto	Eb3	Cb5	Lead	Romantic Lead Female
West Side Story	Bernstein, Leonard	1957	Maria+	I Have A Love*	Ballad	Soprano	Bb3	Bb5	Lead	Ingenue Female

Shows

Songs by Character Type

Show	Composer	Year	Role	Song	Tempo	Vocal Type	Range-Bottom	Range-Top	Category	Character Type
West Side Story	Bernstein, Leonard	1957	Ensemble	I Feel Pretty*	Uptempo	SA			Ensemble	Adults
West Side Story	Bernstein, Leonard	1957	Riff	The Jet Song*	Uptempo	Tenor	Bb2	G4	Lead	Antagonist Male
West Side Story	Bernstein, Leonard	1957	Ensemble	The Jet Song*	Uptempo	TB			Ensemble	Adults
White Christmas	Berlin, Irving	2008	Bob Wallace & Phil Davis	Happy Holiday	Uptempo	Bar/Bar			Duet	RLM/CM
White Christmas	Berlin, Irving	2008	Bob Wallace & Phil Davis	Happy Holiday/Let Yourself Go	Uptempo	Bar/Bar			Duet	RLM/CM
White Christmas	Berlin, Irving	2008	Ensemble	Happy Holiday/Let Yourself Go	Uptempo	SATB			Ensemble	Adults
White Christmas	Berlin, Irving	2008	Bob Wallace	Love And The Weather*	Uptempo	Baritone	Db3	E4	Lead	Romantic Lead Male
White Christmas	Berlin, Irving	2008	Betty Haynes	Love And The Weather*	Uptempo	Alto	A3	C5	Lead	Romantic Lead Female
White Christmas	Berlin, Irving	2008	Bob Wallace & Betty Haynes	Love And The Weather	Uptempo	Bar/Alto			Duet	RLM/RLF
White Christmas	Berlin, Irving	2008	Betty Haynes & Judy Haynes	Sisters	Uptempo	Alto/Alto			Duet	RLM/IF
White Christmas	Berlin, Irving	2008	Phil Davis	The Best Things...Dancing	Moderate Tempo	Baritone	Db3	F4	Lead	Character Male
White Christmas	Berlin, Irving	2008	Ensemble	Snow	Moderate Tempo	SATB			Ensemble	Adults
White Christmas	Berlin, Irving	2008	Ensemble	What Can You With A General	Moderate Tempo	ATB			Ensemble	Adults
White Christmas	Berlin, Irving	2008	Martha Watson	Let Me sing And I'm Happy	Moderate Tempo	Soprano	F3	G4	Lead	Mature Female
White Christmas	Berlin, Irving	2008	Bob Wallace	Count Your Blessings*	Moderate Tempo	Baritone	C3	D4	Lead	Romantic Lead Male
White Christmas	Berlin, Irving	2008	Bob Wallace & Betty Haynes	Count Your Blessings	Moderate Tempo	Bar/Alto			Duet	RAM/RLF
White Christmas	Berlin, Irving	2008	Bob Wallace	Blue Skies (Part 1-3)*	Moderate Tempo	Baritone	E3	F4	Lead	Romantic Lead Male
White Christmas	Berlin, Irving	2008	Ensemble	Blue Skies (Part 1-3)	Moderate Tempo	SATB			Ensemble	Adults
White Christmas	Berlin, Irving	2008	Ensemble	I've Got My Love To Keep Me Warm	Uptempo	SATB			Ensemble	Adults
White Christmas	Berlin, Irving	2008	Phil Davis & Judy Haynes	I Love A Piano*	Moderate Tempo	Bar/Alto			Duet	CM/IF
White Christmas	Berlin, Irving	2008	Ensemble	I Love A Piano	Moderate Tempo	SA			Ensemble	Adults
White Christmas	Berlin, Irving	2008	Martha Watson	Falling Out Of Love Can Be Fun*	Uptempo	Soprano	G3	C5	Lead	Mature Female
White Christmas	Berlin, Irving	2008	Betty Haynes	Falling Out Of Love Can Be Fun*	Uptempo	Alto	G3	C5	Lead	Romantic Lead Female
White Christmas	Berlin, Irving	2008	Judy Haynes	Falling Out Of Love Can Be Fun*	Uptempo	Alto	G3	C5	Lead	Ingenue Female
White Christmas	Berlin, Irving	2008	Ensemble	Falling Out Of Love Can Be Fun	Uptempo	AAA			Ensemble	Adults
White Christmas	Berlin, Irving	2008	Bob Wallace & Phil Davis	Sisters Reprise	Moderate Tempo	Bar/Bar			Duet	RLM/CM
White Christmas	Berlin, Irving	2008	Betty Haynes	Love, You Didn't Do Right By Me	Moderate Tempo	Alto	A3	Bb4	Lead	Romantic Lead Female
White Christmas	Berlin, Irving	2008	Bob Wallace	How Deep Is The Ocean	Ballad	Baritone	C#3	D4	Lead	Romantic Lead Male
White Christmas	Berlin, Irving	2008	Ensemble	The Old Man	Moderate Tempo	TB			Ensemble	Adults
White Christmas	Berlin, Irving	2008	Bob Wallace & Betty Haynes	How Deep Is The Ocean Reprise	Moderate Tempo	Bar/Alto			Duet	RLM/RLF
White Christmas	Berlin, Irving	2008	Susan Waverly	Let Me sing And I'm Happy Reprise	Uptempo	Alto	B3	B4	Lead	Juvenile Female
White Christmas	Berlin, Irving	2008	Ensemble	White Christmas	Moderate Tempo	SATB			Ensemble	Adults
Wicked	Schwartz, Stephen	2003	Glinda	Openning*	Moderate Tempo	Soprano	A3	A5	Lead	Romantic Lead Female
Wicked	Schwartz, Stephen	2003	Glinda	No One Mourns The Wicked*	Moderate Tempo	Soprano	C#4	B5	Lead	Romantic Lead Female
Wicked	Schwartz, Stephen	2003	Father	No One Mourns The Wicked*	Moderate Tempo	Tenor	D3	G4	Supporting	Character Male
Wicked	Schwartz, Stephen	2003	Salesman	No One Mourns The Wicked*	Moderate Tempo	Baritone	D3	E4	Supporting	Character Male
Wicked	Schwartz, Stephen	2003	Ensemble	No One Mourns The Wicked	Moderate Tempo	SATB			Ensemble	Adults
Wicked	Schwartz, Stephen	2003	Ensemble	Dear Old Shiz	Moderate Tempo	SATB			Ensemble	Adults
Wicked	Schwartz, Stephen	2003	Madame Morrible	The Wizard And I*	Moderate Tempo	Alto	Gb3	Bb4	Lead	Mature Female
Wicked	Schwartz, Stephen	2003	Elphaba	The Wizard And I	Moderate Tempo	Alto	G3	E5	Lead	Character Female
Wicked	Schwartz, Stephen	2003	Morrible & Elphaba	The Wizard and I	Moderate Tempo	Alto/Alto			Duet	MF/CF
Wicked	Schwartz, Stephen	2003	Glinda & Elphaba	What Is This Feeling*	Uptempo	Sop/Alto			Duet	RLF/CF
Wicked	Schwartz, Stephen	2003	Doctor Dillamond	Something Bad*	Moderate Tempo	Baritone	C#3	Db4	Lead	Character Male

Shows

Songs by Character Type

Show	Composer	Year	Role	Song	Tempo	Vocal Type	Range-Bottom	Range-Top	Category	Character Type
Wicked	Schwartz, Stephen	2003	Fiyero	Dancing Through Life*	Uptempo	Tenor	C3	A4	Lead	Romantic Lead Male
Wicked	Schwartz, Stephen	2003	Fiyero & Glinda	Dancing Through Life*	Uptempo	Tenor/Sop			Duet	RLM/RLF
Wicked	Schwartz, Stephen	2003	Nessarose	Dancing Through Life*	Uptempo	Alto	A3	B4	Lead	Character Ingenue Female
Wicked	Schwartz, Stephen	2003	BOQ	Dancing Through Life*	Uptempo	Tenor	G3	G4	Lead	Character Ingenue Male
Wicked	Schwartz, Stephen	2003	Nessarose & BOQ	Dancing Through Life*	Uptempo	Alto/Tenor			Duet	CIF/CIM
Wicked	Schwartz, Stephen	2003	Glinda	Popular*	Moderate Tempo	Soprano	G3	C5	Lead	Romantic Lead Female
Wicked	Schwartz, Stephen	2003	Elphaba	I'm Not That Girl	Ballad	Alto	E3	B4	Lead	Character Female
Wicked	Schwartz, Stephen	2003	Elphaba	The Wizard and I Reprise	Moderate Tempo	Alto	A3	C5	Lead	Character Female
Wicked	Schwartz, Stephen	2003	Ensemble	One Short Day	Uptempo	SATB			Ensemble	Adults
Wicked	Schwartz, Stephen	2003	Wizard	A Sentimental Man	Moderate Tempo	Baritone	B2	F#4	Lead	Character Male
Wicked	Schwartz, Stephen	2003	Elphaba	Defying Gravity*	Uptempo	Alto	G3	F5	Lead	Character Female
Wicked	Schwartz, Stephen	2003	Elphaba & Glinda	Defying Gravity	Uptempo	Alto/Sop			Duet	CF/RLF
Wicked	Schwartz, Stephen	2003	Ensemble	Opening Act II	Uptempo	SATB			Ensemble	Adults
Wicked	Schwartz, Stephen	2003	Ensemble	Thank Goodness (Part 1-3)	Uptempo	SATB			Ensemble	Adults
Wicked	Schwartz, Stephen	2003	Glinda	Thank Goodness (Part 3)	Uptempo	Soprano	Bb3	A5	Lead	Romantic Lead Female
Wicked	Schwartz, Stephen	2003	Madame Morrible	Thank Goodness (Part 3)	Uptempo	Alto	A3	B4	Lead	Mature Female
Wicked	Schwartz, Stephen	2003	Ensemble	Thank Goodness (Part 1-3)	Uptempo	SATB			Ensemble	Adults
Wicked	Schwartz, Stephen	2003	Wizard	Wonderful*	Ballad	Baritone	B2	E4	Lead	Character Male
Wicked	Schwartz, Stephen	2003	Glinda	I'm Not That Girl Reprise	Ballad	Soprano	G3	D5	Lead	Romantic Lead Female
Wicked	Schwartz, Stephen	2003	Elphaba	As Long As You're Mine*	Moderate Tempo	Alto	Bb3	Db5	Lead	Character Female
Wicked	Schwartz, Stephen	2003	Fiyero	As Long As You're Mine*	Moderate Tempo	Tenor	G3	Bb4	Lead	Romantic Lead Male
Wicked	Schwartz, Stephen	2003	Elphaba & Fiyero	As Long As You're Mine	Moderate Tempo	Alto/Tenor			Duet	CF/RLM
Wicked	Schwartz, Stephen	2003	Elphaba	No Good Deed	Uptempo	Alto	A3	D#5	Lead	Character Female
Wicked	Schwartz, Stephen	2003	Ensemble	March Of The Witch Hunters	Uptempo	SATB			Ensemble	Adults
Wicked	Schwartz, Stephen	2003	BOQ	March Of The Witch Hunters*	Uptempo	Tenor	G#3	G4	Lead	Character Ingenue Male
Wicked	Schwartz, Stephen	2003	Elphaba	For Good*	Ballad	Alto	Ab3	Db5	Lead	Character Female
Wicked	Schwartz, Stephen	2003	Glinda	For Good*	Ballad	Soprano	Ab3	Db5	Lead	Romantic Lead Female
Wicked	Schwartz, Stephen	2003	Elphaba & Glinda	For Good	Ballad	Alto/Sop			Duet	CF/RLF
Wicked	Schwartz, Stephen	2003	Fiyero	Which Way Is The Party*	Uptempo	Tenor	C#3	A4	Lead	Romantic Lead Male
Wicked	Schwartz, Stephen	2003	Ensemble	Which Way Is The Party	Moderate Tempo	SATB			Ensemble	Adults
Will Rogers Follies	Coleman, Cy	1991	Ensemble	Let's Go Flying	Uptempo	SATB			Ensemble	Adults
Will Rogers Follies	Coleman, Cy	1991	Ziegfield's Favorite	Will-A-Mania	Uptempo	Alto	G3	D5	Supporting	Romantic Lead Female
Will Rogers Follies	Coleman, Cy	1991	Ensemble	Will-A-Mania	Uptempo	SATB			Ensemble	Adults
Will Rogers Follies	Coleman, Cy	1991	Will Rogers	Never Met A Man I Didn't Like (Act 1)	Moderate Tempo	Baritone	B2	Bb3	Lead	Romantic Antagonist Male
Will Rogers Follies	Coleman, Cy	1991	Will Rogers	Give A Man Enough Rope	Moderate Tempo	Baritone	Bb2	F4	Lead	Romantic Antagonist Male
Will Rogers Follies	Coleman, Cy	1991	Clem Rogers	It's A Boy	Uptempo	Baritone	C#3	E4	Lead	Antagonist Male
Will Rogers Follies	Coleman, Cy	1991	Clem Rogers	It's A Boy Reprise	Uptempo	Baritone	D#3	E4	Lead	Antagonist Male
Will Rogers Follies	Coleman, Cy	1991	Will Rogers	So Long Pa	Ballad	Baritone	B2	D4	Lead	Romantic Antagonist Male
Will Rogers Follies	Coleman, Cy	1991	Betty Blake	My Unknown Someone	Ballad	Alto	Ab3	C5	Lead	Romantic Lead Female
Will Rogers Follies	Coleman, Cy	1991	Clem Rogers	Clem's Retur	Moderate Tempo	Baritone	C#3	D#4	Lead	Antagonist Male
Will Rogers Follies	Coleman, Cy	1991	Ensemble	The St. Louis Fair	Moderate Tempo	SAA			Ensemble	Adults
Will Rogers Follies	Coleman, Cy	1991	Will Rogers	The Big Time*	Moderate Tempo	Baritone	G#2	D#4	Lead	Romantic Antagonist Male
Will Rogers Follies	Coleman, Cy	1991	Betty Blake	The Big Time*	Moderate Tempo	Alto	B3	D#5	Lead	Romantic Lead Female

Shows

* = Music Edit Required
+ = Ethnic Specific

Show	Composer	Year	Role	Song	Tempo	Vocal Type	Range-Bottom	Range-Top	Category	Character Type
Will Rogers Follies	Coleman, Cy	1991	Will Rogers & Betty Blake	The Big Time*	Moderate Tempo	Bar/Alto			Duet	RAM/RLF
Will Rogers Follies	Coleman, Cy	1991	Ensemble	The Big Time	Moderate Tempo	SATB		D5	Ensemble	Children/Adults
Will Rogers Follies	Coleman, Cy	1991	Betty Blake	My Big Mistake	Moderate Tempo	Alto	F3		Lead	Romantic Lead Female
Will Rogers Follies	Coleman, Cy	1991	Will Rogers	Marry Me Now*	Moderate Tempo	Baritone	Eb3	Eb4	Lead	Romantic Antagonist Male
Will Rogers Follies	Coleman, Cy	1991	Betty Blake	With You	Moderate Tempo	Alto	Eb4	C5	Lead	Romantic Lead Female
Will Rogers Follies	Coleman, Cy	1991	Will Rogers & Betty Blake	Marry Me Now/Without You	Moderate Tempo	Bar/Alto			Duet	RAM/RLF
Will Rogers Follies	Coleman, Cy	1991	Ensemble	Give A Man Enough Rope Reprise	Uptempo	TB			Ensemble	Adults
Will Rogers Follies	Coleman, Cy	1991	Will Rogers	Look Around	Ballad	Baritone	C#5	D4	Lead	Romantic Antagonist Male
Will Rogers Follies	Coleman, Cy	1991	Will Rogers	The Campaign: Our Favorite Son	Moderate Tempo	Baritone	C3	Eb4	Lead	Romantic Antagonist Male
Will Rogers Follies	Coleman, Cy	1991	Ensemble	The Campaign: Our Favorite Son	Moderate Tempo	SATB			Ensemble	Adults
Will Rogers Follies	Coleman, Cy	1991	Betty Blake	No Man Left For Me	Moderate Tempo	Alto	A3	C5	Lead	Romantic Lead Female
Will Rogers Follies	Coleman, Cy	1991	Will Rogers	Presents For Mrs. Rogers	Moderate Tempo	Baritone	B2	D4	Lead	Romantic Antagonist Male
Will Rogers Follies	Coleman, Cy	1991	Ensemble	Presents For Mrs. Rogers	Moderate Tempo	SATB			Ensemble	Adults
Will Rogers Follies	Coleman, Cy	1991	Ensemble	Will-A-Mania Reprise	Ballad	SATB			Ensemble	Adults
Will Rogers Follies	Coleman, Cy	1991	Clem Rogers & Will Rogers	Will-A-Mania Reprise*	Ballad	Bar/Bar			Duet	RAM/AM
Will Rogers Follies	Coleman, Cy	1991	Will Rogers	Never Met A Man I Didn't Like Reprise	Moderate Tempo	Baritone	Bb2	D4	Lead	Romantic Antagonist Male
Will Rogers Follies	Coleman, Cy	1991	Ensemble	Never Met A Man I Didn't Like Reprise	Moderate Tempo	SATB			Ensemble	Adults
Wiz, The	Small, Charlie	1974	Aunt Em	The Feeling We Once Had	Moderate Tempo	Alto	G3	C5	Supporting	Maternal
Wiz, The	Small, Charlie	1974	Addaperle	He's The Wiz*	Moderate Tempo	Alto	F3	C5	Lead	Character Female
Wiz, The	Small, Charlie	1974	Ensemble	He's The Wiz	Moderate Tempo	SATB			Ensemble	Adults
Wiz, The	Small, Charlie	1974	Dorothy	Soon As I Get Home	Uptempo	Soprano	C4	C#5	Lead	Character Ingenue Female
Wiz, The	Small, Charlie	1974	Dorothy	Home	Uptempo	Soprano	Bb3	D5	Lead	Character Ingenue Female
Wiz, The	Small, Charlie	1974	Scarecrow	I Was Born On The Day Before Yesterday	Moderate Tempo	Tenor	E3	A4	Lead	Character Male
Wiz, The	Small, Charlie	1974	Ensemble	I Was Born On The Day Before Yesterday	Moderate Tempo	SATB			Ensemble	Adults
Wiz, The	Small, Charlie	1974	Ensemble	Ease On Down The Road #1	Uptempo	SATB			Ensemble	Adults
Wiz, The	Small, Charlie	1974	Tin Man	Slide Some Oil To Me	Uptempo	Tenor	Eb3	Bb4	Lead	Character Male
Wiz, The	Small, Charlie	1974	Ensemble	Ease On Down The Road #2	Uptempo	SATB			Ensemble	Adults
Wiz, The	Small, Charlie	1974	Lion	Mean Ole Lion	Uptempo	Tenor	G2	Bb4	Lead	Antagonist Male
Wiz, The	Small, Charlie	1974	Ensemble	Ease On Down The Road #3	Uptempo	SATB			Ensemble	Adults
Wiz, The	Small, Charlie	1974	Dorothy	Be A Lion*	Ballad	Soprano	Bb3	Bb5	Lead	Character Ingenue Female
Wiz, The	Small, Charlie	1974	Lion	Be A Lion*	Ballad	Tenor	Ab3	Ab4	Lead	Antagonist Male
Wiz, The	Small, Charlie	1974	Dorothy & Lion	Be A Lion	Ballad	Sop/Tenor			Duet	IF/AM
Wiz, The	Small, Charlie	1974	The Wiz	So You Wanted To Meet The Wizard	Uptempo	Tenor	E3	G4	Lead	Romantic Antagonist Male
Wiz, The	Small, Charlie	1974	Tin Man	What Would I Do If I Could Feel	Ballad	Tenor	D3	A4	Lead	Character Male
Wiz, The	Small, Charlie	1974	Evillene	Don't Nobody Bring Me No Bad News	Uptempo	Alto	Bb3	Db5	Lead	Antagonist Female
Wiz, The	Small, Charlie	1974	Ensemble	Everybody Rejoice	Uptempo	SATB			Ensemble	Adults
Wiz, The	Small, Charlie	1974	Ensemble	Who Do You Think You Are	Uptempo	SATB			Ensemble	Adults
Wiz, The	Small, Charlie	1974	The Wiz	Y'all Got It	Uptempo	Tenor	G3	A4	Lead	Romantic Antagonist Male
Wiz, The	Small, Charlie	1974	The Wiz	Believe In Yourself (F Major)	Moderate Tempo	Tenor	C4	G5	Lead	Romantic Antagonist Male
Wiz, The	Small, Charlie	1974	The Wiz	Believe In Yourself (Bb Major)	Moderate Tempo	Tenor	F3	D5	Lead	Romantic Antagonist Male
Wiz, The	Small, Charlie	1974	Glinda	A Rested Body Is A Rested Mind	Moderate Tempo	Alto	C4	C5	Lead	Romantic Lead Female
Wiz, The	Small, Charlie	1974	Dorothy	Home Reprise	Moderate Tempo	Alto	G3	E5	Lead	Character Ingenue Female

Shows

Songs by Character Type

* = Music Edit Required
+ = Ethnic Specific

Show	Composer	Year	Role	Song	Tempo	Vocal Type	Range-Bottom	Range-Top	Category	Character Type
Wizard Of Oz 1987	Stothart, Herbert	1939	Dorothy	Over The Rainbow	Ballad	Alto	G3	C5	Lead	Character Ingenue Female
Wizard Of Oz 1988	Stothart, Herbert	1939	Glenda	Come Out*	Moderate Tempo	Soprano	G3	C5	Lead	Romantic Lead Female
Wizard Of Oz 1989	Stothart, Herbert	1939	Dorothy	Come Out*	Moderate Tempo	Alto	C4	D5	Lead	Character Ingenue Female
Wizard Of Oz 1990	Stothart, Herbert	1939	Ensemble	Munchkinland Sequence	Moderate Tempo	SATB			Ensemble	Adults
Wizard Of Oz 1991	Stothart, Herbert	1939	Ensemble	Yellow Brick Road	Uptempo	SATB			Ensemble	Adults
Wizard Of Oz 1992	Stothart, Herbert	1939	Ensemble	If I Only Had A Brain	Moderate Tempo	TB			Ensemble	Adults
Wizard Of Oz 1993	Stothart, Herbert	1939	Scarecrow	If I Only Had A Brain*	Moderate Tempo	Baritone	D3	F#4	Lead	Character Male
Wizard Of Oz 1994	Stothart, Herbert	1939	Ensemble	We're Off To See The Wizard	Uptempo	Unison			Ensemble	Adults
Wizard Of Oz 1995	Stothart, Herbert	1939	Tin Man	If I Only Had A Heart*	Moderate Tempo	Tenor	D3	G4	Lead	Character Male
Wizard Of Oz 1996	Stothart, Herbert	1939	Ensemble	If I Only Had A Heart	Moderate Tempo	SAA			Ensemble	Adults
Wizard Of Oz 1997	Stothart, Herbert	1939	Cowardly Lion	If I Only Had The Nerve*	Moderate Tempo	Baritone	Bb2	D4	Lead	Antagonist Male
Wizard Of Oz 1998	Stothart, Herbert	1939	Ensemble	Poppies	Moderate Tempo	SATB			Ensemble	Adults
Wizard Of Oz 1999	Stothart, Herbert	1939	Ensemble	You're Out Of The Woods Reprise	Uptempo	SAA			Ensemble	Adults
Wizard Of Oz 2000	Stothart, Herbert	1939	Ensemble	Mary Old Land Of Oz Reprise*	Uptempo	SATB			Ensemble	Adults
Wizard Of Oz 2001	Stothart, Herbert	1939	Cowardly Lion	King Of The Forest*	Moderate Tempo	Baritone	C3	F4	Lead	Antagonist Male
Wizard Of Oz 2002	Stothart, Herbert	1939	Dorothy	The Jitterbug*	Uptempo	Alto	Ab3	D5	Lead	Character Ingenue Female
Wizard Of Oz 2003	Stothart, Herbert	1939	Ensemble	The Jitterbug	Uptempo	SATB			Ensemble	Adults
Wizard Of Oz 2004	Stothart, Herbert	1939	Dorothy	Over The Rainbow Reprise*	Ballad	Alto	B3	C#5	Lead	Character Ingenue Female
Wizard Of Oz 2005	Stothart, Herbert	1939	Ensemble	Ding Dong! The Witch Is Dead	Uptempo	Unison			Ensemble	Adults
Wonderful Town	Bernstein, Leonard	1953	Ensemble	Christopher Street	Uptempo	SATB			Ensemble	Adults
Wonderful Town	Bernstein, Leonard	1953	Eileen & Ruth	Ohio	Ballad	Sop/Alto			Duet	IF/CF
Wonderful Town	Bernstein, Leonard	1953	Ruth Sherwood	One Hundred Easy Ways To Lose A Man	Moderate Tempo	Alto	G3	A4	Lead	Character Female
Wonderful Town	Bernstein, Leonard	1953	Robert Baker	What A Waste*	Uptempo	Baritone	Ab2	F#4	Lead	Romantic Lead Male
Wonderful Town	Bernstein, Leonard	1953	1st Editor	What A Waste*	Uptempo	Baritone	A2	D4	Lead	Character Male
Wonderful Town	Bernstein, Leonard	1953	2nd Editor	What A Waste*	Uptempo	Baritone	Bb2	Eb4	Lead	Character Male
Wonderful Town	Bernstein, Leonard	1953	Ensemble	What A Waste	Uptempo	BBB			Ensemble	Adults
Wonderful Town	Bernstein, Leonard	1953	Eileen Sherwood	A Little Bit In Love	Moderate Tempo	Soprano	C4	C#5	Lead	Ingenue Female
Wonderful Town	Bernstein, Leonard	1953	Wreck	Pass The Football	Moderate Tempo	Baritone	Ab2	E4	Lead	Antagonist Male
Wonderful Town	Bernstein, Leonard	1953	Eileen Sherwood	Conversation Piece*	Uptempo	Soprano	D4	B4	Lead	Ingenue Female
Wonderful Town	Bernstein, Leonard	1953	Ensemble	Conversation Piece	Uptempo	SATB			Ensemble	Adults
Wonderful Town	Bernstein, Leonard	1953	Robert Baker	A Quiet Girl	Ballad	Baritone	G2	C4	Lead	Romantic Lead Male
Wonderful Town	Bernstein, Leonard	1953	Ruth Sherwood	Quiet Ruth	Ballad	Alto	F3	E4	Lead	Character Female
Wonderful Town	Bernstein, Leonard	1953	Ruth Sherwood	Conga*	Uptempo	Alto	F3	A4	Lead	Character Female
Wonderful Town	Bernstein, Leonard	1953	Ensemble	My Darlin' Eileen	Ballad	TTBBB			Ensemble	Adults
Wonderful Town	Bernstein, Leonard	1953	Ruth Sherwood	Swing*	Uptempo	Alto	E3	E4	Lead	Character Female
Wonderful Town	Bernstein, Leonard	1953	Ensemble	Swing	Uptempo	SATB			Ensemble	Adults
Wonderful Town	Bernstein, Leonard	1953	Eileen & Ruth	Ohio Reprise	Ballad	Sop/Alto			Duet	IF/CF
Wonderful Town	Bernstein, Leonard	1953	Robert Baker	It's Love*	Moderate Tempo	Baritone	A2	F#4	Lead	Romantic Lead Male
Wonderful Town	Bernstein, Leonard	1953	Ensemble	It's Love	Moderate Tempo	SATB			Ensemble	Adults
Wonderful Town	Bernstein, Leonard	1953	Eileen & Ruth	The Wrong Note Rag*	Uptempo	Sop/Alto			Duet	IF/CF
Wonderful Town	Bernstein, Leonard	1953	Ensemble	The Wrong Note Rag	Uptempo	SATB			Ensemble	Adults
Wonderful Town	Bernstein, Leonard	1953	Ensemble	It's Love Reprise	Moderate Tempo	SATB			Ensemble	Adults
You're A Good Man Charlie	Gesner, Clark	1971	Ensemble	You're A Good Man Charlie Brown	Moderate Tempo	SATB			Ensemble	Adults
You're A Good Man Charlie	Gesner, Clark	1971	Lucy Van Pelt	Schroeder	Moderate Tempo	Alto	G3	E5	Lead	Antagonist Female

Songs by Character Type

Show	Composer	Year	Role	Song	Tempo	Vocal Type	Range-Bottom	Range-Top	Category	Character Type
You're A Good Man Charlie	Gesner, Clark	1971	Snoopy	Snoopy	Ballad	Tenor	B2	G4	Lead	Character Male
You're A Good Man Charlie	Gesner, Clark	1971	Linus Van Pelt	My Blanket And Me	Moderate Tempo	Baritone	B2	D4	Lead	Character Ingenue Male
You're A Good Man Charlie	Gesner, Clark	1971	Charlie Brown	The Kite	Uptempo	Baritone	Bb2	Eb4	Lead	Character Male
You're A Good Man Charlie	Gesner, Clark	1971	Charlie Brown & Lucy	The Doctor Is In	Moderate Tempo	Bar/Alto			Duet	CM/AF
You're A Good Man Charlie	Gesner, Clark	1971	Ensemble	Book Report	Moderate Tempo	SATB			Ensemble	Adults
You're A Good Man Charlie	Gesner, Clark	1971	Ensemble	The Baseball Game	Uptempo	SATB Unison			Ensemble	Adults
You're A Good Man Charlie	Gesner, Clark	1971	Ensemble	Glee Club Rehearsal	Moderate Tempo	SATB			Ensemble	Adults
You're A Good Man Charlie	Gesner, Clark	1971	Ensemble	Little Known Facts	Uptempo	SATB			Ensemble	Adults
You're A Good Man Charlie	Gesner, Clark	1971	Snoopy	Suppertime*	Uptempo	Tenor	C3	A4	Lead	Character Male
You're A Good Man Charlie	Gesner, Clark	1971	Ensemble	Happiness	Ballad	SATB			Ensemble	Adults
You're A Good Man Charlie	Lippa, Andrew	1999	Ensemble	Beethoven Day	Uptempo	SATB			Ensemble	Adults
You're A Good Man Charlie	Lippa, Andrew	1999	Sally	My New Philosophy	Uptempo	Alto	B3	E5	Lead	Ingenue Female

Shows

483

The Musical Theatre Codex Works Cited

Theophrastus, Bennett, Charles E., and William A. Hammond. *The Characters of Theophrastus; A Translation with Introduction.* New York: Longmans, Green, and Co. 1902. Print.

Law, Jonathan, John Wright, Mark Salad, Alan Isaacs, David Pickering, Rosalind Fergusson, Fran Alexander, Amanda Isaacs, Jenny Roberts, Lynn Thomson, and Peter Lewis. *Cassell Companion To Theatre.* New York: Sterling Publsihing Co., Inc. 1999. Print.

Edwards, Sherman. 1776. Composed by Sherman Edwards. 1969. New York: Music Theatre International. 1969. Print.

Jones, Tom. 110 in the Shade. Composed by Harvey Schmidt. 1963. New York: Tams-Witmark Music Library. 1963. Print.

Brown, Jason Robert. 13. Composed by Jason Robert Brown. 2008. New York: MTI Enterprises. 2008. Print.

Finn, William. The 25th Annual Putnam County Spelling Bee. Composed by William Finn. 2005. New York: Music Theatre International. 2005

Kleban, Edward. A Chorus Line. Composed by Marvin Hamlisch. 1975. New York: Tams-Witmark Music Libary. 1975. Print.

Ahrens, Lynn. A Christmas Carol. Composed by Alan Menken. 1994. New York: Music Theatre International. 1994. Print.

Sondheim, Stephen. A Little Night Music. Composed by Stephen Sondheim. 1973. New York: Music Theatre International. 1973. Print.

Ahrens, Lynn. A Man of No Importance. Composed by Stephen Flaherty. 2002. New York: Music Theatre International. 2002. Print.

Reale, Willie. A Year With Frog and Toad. Composed by Willie Reale. 2003. New York: Music Theatre International. 2003. Print.

Lippa, Andrew. The Addams Family. Composed by Andrew Lippa. 2010. New York: Theatrical Rights Worldwide. 2010. Print.

Rice, Tim. Aida. Composed by Elton John. 2000. New York: Music Theatre International. 2000. Print.

Waller, Fats. <u>Ain't Misbehavin'</u>. Composed by Fats Waller, Harry Brooks, Harry Link, and Herman Autry. 1978. New York: Music Theatre International. 1978. Print.

Presley, Elvis. <u>All Shook Up</u>. Composed by Elvis Presley. 2005. New York: Theatrical Rights Worldwide. 2005. Print.

Charnin, Martin. <u>Annie</u>. Composed by Charles Strouse. 1977. New York: Music Theatre International. 1977. Print.

Berlin, Irving. <u>Annie Get Your Gun</u>. Composed by Irving Berlin. 1946. New York: Rodgers and Hammerstein Organization. 1946. Print.

Sondheim, Stephen. <u>Anyone Can Whistle</u>. Composed by Stephen Sondheim. 1964. New York: Music Theatre International. 1964. Print.

Porter, Cole. <u>Anything Goes</u>. Composed by Cole Porter. 1934. New York: Tams-Witmark Music Library. 1934. Print.

Adams, Lee. <u>Applause</u>. Composed by Charles Strouse. 1970. New York: Tams-Witmark Music Library. 1970. Print.

Harnick, Sheldon. <u>The Apple Tree</u>. Composed by Jerry Bock. 1966. New York: Music Theatre International. 1966. Print.

Sondheim, Stephen. <u>Assassins</u>. Composed by Stephen Sondheim. 1992. New York: Music Theatre International. 1992. Print.

Lopez, Robert and Jeff Marx. <u>Avenue Q</u>. Composed by Robert Lopez and Jeff Marx. New York: Music Theatre International. 2003. Print.

Hart, Lorenz. <u>Babes In Arms</u>. Composed by Richard Rodgers. 1937/1998. New York: Rodgers and Hammerstein Organization. 1937/1998. Print

Ashman, Howard and Tim Rice. <u>The Beauty and the Beast</u>. Composed by Alan Menken. New York: 1994. Print.

Comden, Betty and Adolph Green. <u>Bells Are Ringing</u>. Composed by Jule Styne. 1956. New York: Tams-Witmark Music Library. 1956. Print.

Hall, Carol. <u>The Best Little Whorehouse In Texas</u>. Composed by Carol Hall. 1978. New York: Samuel French, Inc. 1978. Print.

Maltby Jr., Richard. <u>Big</u>. Composed by David Shire. 1996. New York: Music Theatre International. 1996. Print.

Miller, Roger. Big River. Composed by Roger Miller. 1985. New York: Rogers and Hammerstein Organization. 1985. Print.

Hall, Lee. Billy Elliot. Composed by Elton John. 2008. New York: Music Theatre International. 2008. Print.

Russell, Willy. Blood Brothers. Composed by Willy Russell. 1993. New York: Samuel French, Inc. 1993. Print.

Lerner, Alan Jay. Brigadoon. Composed by Frederick Loewe. 1947. New York: Tams-Witmark Music Library. 1947. Print.

Adams, Lee. Bye Bye Birdie. Composed by Charles Strouse. 1960. New York: Tams-Witmark Music Library. 1960. Print.

Ebb, Fred. Cabaret. Composed by John Kander. 1966. New York: Tams-Witmark Music Library. 1966. Print.

Berlin, Irving. Call Me Madam. Composed by Irving Berlin. 1950. New York: Rodgers and Hammerstein Organization. 1950. Print.

Lerner, Alan Jay. Camelot. Composed by Frederick Loewe. 1960. New York: Tams-Witmark Music Library. 1960. Print.

La Touche, John, Dorothy Parker, and Richard Wilbur. Candide. Composed by Leonard Bernstein. 1956. New York: Music Theatre International. 1956 & 1999. Print.

Kushner, Tony. Caroline or Change. Composed by Jeanine Tesori. 2004. New York: Music Theatre International. 2004. Print.

Hammerstein II, Oscar. Carousel. Composed by Richard Rodgers. 1945. New York: Rodgers and Hammerstein Organization. 1945. Print.

Rice, Tim. Chess. Composed by Benny Andersson, and Bjorn Ulvaeus. 1988. New York: Samuel French, Inc. 1988. Print.

Ebb, Fred. Chicago. Composed by John Kander. 1975. New York: Samuel French, Inc. 1975. Print.

Schwartz, Stephen. Children of Eden. Composed by Stephen Schwartz. 1991. New York: Music Theatre International. 1991. Print.

Sherman, Richard M. and Robert B. Sherman. Chitty Chitty Bang Bang. Composed by Richard M. Sherman and Robert B. Sherman. New York: Music Theatre International. 2005. Print.

Hammerstein II, Oscar. <u>Rodger and Hammerstein's Cinderella</u>. Composed by Richard Rodgers. 2013. New York: Rodgers and Hammerstein Organization. 2013. Print.

Zippel, David. <u>City of Angels</u>. Composed by Cy Coleman. 1989. New York: Tams-Witmark Music Library. 1989. Print.

Maltby Jr., Richard. <u>Closer Than Ever</u>. Composed by David Shire. 1989. New York: Music Theatre International. 1989. Print.

Bray, Stephen, Brenda Russell, Allee Willis, <u>The Color Purple</u>. Composed by Stephen Bray, Brenda Russell, and Allee Willis. 2005. Theatrical Rights Worldwide. 2005. Print.

Sondheim, Stephen. <u>Company</u>. Composed by Stephen Sondheim. 1970. New York: Music Theatre International. 1970. Print.

Gershwin, George and Ira Gershwin. <u>Crazy For You</u>. Composed by George Gershwin and Richard Rodgers. 1992. New York: Tams-Witmark Music Library. 1992. Print.

Ebb, Fred. <u>Curtains</u>. Composed by John Kander. 2007. New York: Theatrical Rights Worldwide. 2007. Print.

Adler, Richard and Jerry Ross. <u>Damn Yankees</u>. Composed by Richard Adler. 1955. New York: Music Theatre International. 1955. Print.

Herman, Jerry. <u>Dear World</u>. Composed by Jerry Herman. 1964. New York: Tams-Witmark Music Library. 1969. Print.

Yazbek, David. <u>Dirty Rotten Scoundrel</u>. Composed by David Yazbek. 2005. New York: Music Theatre International. 2005. Print.

Eyen, Tom. <u>Dreamgirls</u>. Composed by Henry Krueger. 1981. New York: Tams-Witmark Music Library. 1981. Print.

Lambert, Lisa, and Greg Morrison. <u>The Drowsy Chaperone</u>. Composed by Lisa Lambert and Greg Morrison. 2006. New York: Music Theatre International. 2006. Print.

Rice, Tim. <u>Evita</u>. Composed by Webber, Andrew Lloyd. 1979. New York: Rodgers and Hammerstein Organization. 1979. Print.

Harnick, Sheldon. <u>Fiddler On the Roof</u>. Composed by Jerry Bock. 1964. New York: Music Theatre International. 1964. Print.

Hammerstein II, Oscar. <u>Flower Drum Song</u>. Composed by Richard Rodgers. 1958. New York: Rodgers and Hammerstein Organization. 1958. Print.

Sondheim, Stephen. <u>Follies</u>. Composed by Stephen Sondheim. 1971. New York: Music Theatre International. 1971. Print.

Pritchard, Dean. <u>Footloose</u>. Composed by Tom Snow. 1998. New York: Rodgers and Hammerstein Organization. 1998. Print.

Yazbek, David. <u>The Full Monty</u>. Composed by David Yazbek. 2000. New York: Music Theatre International. 2000. Print.

Merrill, Bob. <u>Funny Girl</u>. Composed by Jule Styne. 1964. New York: Tams-Whitmark Music Library. 1964. Print.

Sondheim, Stephen. <u>A Funny Thing Happened On The Way To The Forum</u>. Composed by Stephen Sondheim. 1962. New York: Music Theatre International. 1962. Print.

Schwartz, Stephen. <u>Godspell</u>. Composed by Stephen Schwartz. 1976. New York: Music Theatre International. 1976. Print.

Brown, Lew and B.G. DeSylva. <u>Good News</u>. Composed by Ray Henderson. 1993. New York: Tams-Witmark Music Library. 1993. Print.

Zippel, David. <u>The Goodbye Girl</u>. Composed by Marvin Hamlisch. 1993. New York: Music Theatre International. 1993. Print.

Casey, Warren and Jim Jacobs. <u>Grease!</u>. Composed by Warren Casey and Jim Jacobs. (1994). New York: Samuel French, Inc. 1994.

Korie, Michael. <u>Grey Gardens</u>. Composed by Scott Frankel. 2006. New York: Dramatists Play Service. 2006. Print.

Loesser, Frank. <u>Guys and Dolls</u>. Composed by Frank Loesser. 1950. New York: Music Theatre International. 1950. Print.

Sondheim, Stephen. <u>Gypsy</u>. Composed by Jule Styne. 1959. New York: Tams-Witmark Music Library. 1959. Print.

Rado, James and Gerome Ragni. <u>Hair</u>. Composed by Galt MacDermot. 1968. New York: Tams Witmark Music Library. 1968. Print.

Shaiman, Marc and Scott Wittman. <u>Hairspray</u>. Composed by Marc Shaiman. 2002. New York: Music Theatre International. 2002. Print.

Murphy, Kevin and Laurence O'Keefe. <u>The Heathers</u>. Composed by Kevin Murphy and Laurence O'Keefe. 2014. New York: Samuel French, Inc. 2014. Print.

Herman, Jerry. <u>Hello Dolly</u>. Composed by Jerry Herman. 1964. New York: Tams Witmark Music Library. 1964. Print.

Porter, Cole. <u>High Society</u>. Composed by Cole Porter. 1988. New York: Tams-Witmark Music Library. 1988. Print.

Gerard, Matthew, Robbie Nevil, Ray and Greg Cham, Drew Seeley, Randy Petersen, Kevin Quinn, Andy Dodd, Adam Watts, Bryan Louiselle, David N. Lawrence, Faye Greenberg and Jamie Houston. <u>High School Musical On Stage!</u> Composed by Gerard, Matthew, Robbie Nevil, Ray and Greg Cham, Drew Seeley, Randy Petersen, Kevin Quinn, Andy Dodd, Adam Watts, Bryan Louiselle, David N. Lawrence, Faye Greenberg and Jamie Houston. 2007. New York: Music Theatre International. 2007. Print.

Drewe, Anthony. <u>Honk!</u>. Composed by George Stiles. 1993. New York: Music Theatre International. 1993. Print.

Loesser, Frank. <u>How to Succeed in Business Without Really Trying</u>. Composed by Frank Loesser. 1961. New York: Music Theatre International. 1961. Print.

Miranda, Lin-Manuel. <u>In The Heights</u>. Composed by Lin-Manuel Miranda. 2008. New York: Rodgers and Hammerstein Organization. 2008. Print.

Sondheim, Stephen. <u>Into The Woods</u>. Composed by Stephen Sondheim. 1987. New York: Music Theatre International. 1987. Print.

Gordon, Paul. <u>Jane Eyre</u>. Composed by Paul Gordon. 2000. New York: Music Theatre International. 2000. Print.

Bricusse, Leslie. <u>Jekyll & Hyde</u>. Composed by Frank Wildhorn. 1997. New York: Music Theatre International. 1997. Print.

Crewe, Bob. <u>Jersey Boys</u>. Composed by Bob Gaudio. 2005. New York: Samuel French. 2005. Print.

Rice, Tim. <u>Jesus Christ Superstar</u>. Composed by Andrew Lloyd Webber. 1971. New York: Rodgers and Hammerstein Organization. 1971. Print.

Rice, Tim. <u>Joseph and the Amazing Technicolor Dreamcoat</u>. Composed by Andrew Lloyd Webber. 1982. New York: Rodgers and Hammerstein Organization. 1982. Print.

Hammerstein II, Oscar. <u>The King and I</u>. Composed by Richard Rodgers. 1951. New York: Rodgers and Hammerstein Organization. 1951. Print.

Lauper, Cyndi. <u>Kinky Boots</u>. Composed by Cyndi Lauper. 2013. New York: Music Theatre International. 2013. Print.

Porter, Cole. <u>Kiss Me Kate</u>. Composed by Cole Porter. 1948. New York: Tams-Witmark Music Library. 1948. Print.

Ebb, Fred. <u>Kiss of the Spider Woman</u>. Composed by John Kander. 1993. New York: Samuel French, Inc. 1993. Print.

Herman, Jerry. <u>La Cage Aux Folles</u>. Composed by Jerry Herman. 1983. New York: Samuel French, Inc. 1983. Print.

Brown, Jason Robert. <u>The Last 5 Years</u>. Composed by Jason Robert Brown. 2002. New York: Music Theatre International. 2002. Print.

Benjamin, Nell and Laurence O'Keefe. <u>Legally Blonde</u>. Composed by Nell Benjamin. 2007. New York: Music Theatre International. 2007. Print.

Kretzmer, Herbert. <u>Les Miserables</u>. Composed by Schonberg, Claude-Michael. 1987. New York: Music Theatre International. 1987. Print.

Guettel, Adam. <u>The Light in the Piazza</u>. Composed by Adam Guettel. 1987. New York: Music Theatre International. 1987. Print.

Rice, Tim. <u>The Lion King</u>. Composed by Elton John. 1997. New York: Music Theatre International. 1997. Print.

Menken, Alan. <u>The Little Mermaid</u>. Composed by Ashman, Howard and Glenn Slater. 2003. New York: Music Theatre International. 2003. Print

Ashman, Howard. <u>Little Shop of Horrors</u>. Composed by Alan Menken. 1982. New York: Music Theatre International. 1982. Print.

Dickstein, Mindi. <u>Little Women</u>. Composed by Jason Howland. 2005. New York: Music Theatre International. 2005. Print.

Herman, Jerry. <u>Mack and Mabel</u>. Composed by Jerry Herman. 1974. New York: Samuel French, Inc. 1974. Print.

Herman, Jerry. Mame. Composed by Jerry Herman. 1966. New York: Tams-Witmark Music Library. 1966. Print.

Blane, Ralph and Hugh Martin. Meet Me In St. Louis. Ralph Blane and Hugh Martin. 1989. New York: Tams-Witmark Music Library. 1989. Print.

Sondheim, Stephen. Merrily We Roll Along. Composed by Stephen Sondheim. 1981. New York: Music Theatre International. 1981. Print.

Boublil, Alain and Richard Maltby, Jr. Miss Saigon. Composed by Schonberg. 1991. New York: Music Theatre International. 1991. Print.

Loesser, Frank. Most Happy Fella. Composed by Frank Loesser. 1956. New York: Music Theatre International. 1956. Print.

Willson, Meredith. The Music Man. Composed by Meredith Willson. 1957. New York: MTI Enterprises, Inc. 1957. Print.

Lerner, Alan Jay. My Fair Lady. Composed by Frederick Loewe. 1956. New York: Tams-Witmark Music Library. 1956. Print.

Ahrens, Lynn. My Favorite Year. Composed by Stephen Flaherty. 1992. New York: Music Theatre International. 1992. Print.

Holmes, Rupert. The Mystery of Edwin Drood. Composed by Rupert Holmes. 1985. New York: Tams-Witmark Music Library. 1985. Print.

Yorkey, Brian. Next To Normal. Composed by Tom Kitt. 2009. New York: Music Theatre Internatinal. 2009. Print.

Maltby Jr., Richard. Nick and Nora. Composed by Charles Strouse. 1991. New York: Music Theatre International. 1991. Print.

Yeston, Maury. Nine. Composed by Maury Yeston. 2003. New York: Samuel French, Inc. 2003. Print.

Caesar, Irving and Otto Harback. No No Nanette. Composed by Vincent Youmans. 1925. New York: Tams-Witmark Music Library. 1925. Print.

Goggin, Dan. Nunsense. Composed by Dan Goggin. 1985. New York: Samuel French, Inc. 1985. Print.

Gershwin, Ira. Of Thee I Sing. Composed by George Gershwin. 1931. New York: George Gershwin. 1931. Print.

Hammerstein II, Oscar. Oklahoma. Composed by Richard Rodgers. 1943. New York: Rodgers and Hammerstein Organization. 1943. Print.

Bart, Lionel. <u>Oliver!</u>. Composed by Lionel Bart. 1963. New York: Music Theatre International. 1963. Print.

Comden, Betty and Adolph Green. <u>On The Town</u>. Composed by Leonard Bernstein. 1944. New York: Tams-Witmark Music Library. 1944. Print.

Comden, Betty and Adolph Green. <u>On The Twentieth Century</u>. Composed by Cy Coleman. 1978. New York: Samuel French, Inc. 1978. Print.

Ahrens, Lynn. <u>Once On This Island</u>. Composed by Stephen Flaherty. 1990. New York: Music Theatre International. 1990. Print.

Barer, Marshall. <u>Once Upon A Mattress</u>. Composed by Mary Rodgers. 1959. New York: Rodgers and Hammerstein Organization. 1959. Print.

Sondheim, Stephen. <u>Pacific Overtures</u>. Composed by Stephen Sondheim. 1976. New York: Music Theatre International. 1976. Print.

Adler, Richard and Jerry Ross. <u>The Pajama Game</u>. Composed by Richard Adler and Jerry Ross. 1954. New York: Music Theatre International. 1954. Print.

Hart, Lorenz. <u>Pal Joey</u>. Composed by Richard Rodgers. 1940. New York: Rodgers and Hammerstein Organization. 1940. Print.

Brown, Jason Robert. <u>Parade</u>. Composed by Jason Robert Brown. 1998. New York: Music Theatre International. 1998. Print.

Sondheim, Stephen. <u>Passion</u>. Composed by Stephen Sondheim. 1994. New York: Music Theatre International. 1994. Print.

Carolyn Leigh. <u>Peter Pan</u>. Composed by Mark Charlap. 1954. New York: MTI Enterprises, Inc. 1954. Print.

Hart, Charles. <u>Phantom of the Opera</u>. Composed by Andrew Lloyd Webber. 1986. New York: Rodgers and Hammerstein Organization. 1988. Print.

Gershwin, Ira and DuBose Heyward. <u>Porgy and Bess</u>. Composed by George Gershwin. 1935. New York: Tams-Witmark Music Library. 1935. Print.

Brooks, Mel. <u>The Producers</u>. Composed by Mel Brooks. 1959. New York: Music Theatre International. 1959. Print.

Schwartz, Stephen. <u>Rags</u>. Composed by Charles Strouse. 1986. New York: Samuel French, Inc. 1984. Print.

Ahrens, Lynn. <u>Ragtime</u>. Composed by Stephen Flaherty. 1998. New York: Music Theatre International. 1998. Print.

Larson, Jonathan. <u>Rent</u>. 1996. Composed by Jonathan Larson. 1996. New York: Music Theatre International. 1996. Print.

Harman, Barry. <u>Romance Romance</u>. Composed by Keith Herrmann. 1987. New York: Samuel French, Inc. 1987. Print.

Knighton, Nan. <u>Scarlet Pimpernel</u>. Composed by Frank Wildhorn. 1997. New York: Tams-Witmark Music Library. 1997. Print.

Norman, Marsha. <u>The Secret Garden</u>. Composed by Lucy Simon. 1997. New York: Samuel French, Inc. 1997. Print.

Ahrens, Lynn. <u>Seusical The Musical</u>. Composed by Stephen Flaherty. 2000. New York: Musical Theatre International. 2000. Print.

Mercer, Johnny, Al Kaska and Joel Hirshcborn. <u>Seven Brides for Seven Brothers</u>. Composed by Gene de Paul. 1982. New York: Musical Theatre International. 1982. Print.

Harnick, Sheldon. <u>She Loves Me</u>. Composed by Jerry Bock. 1963. New York: MTI Enterprises, Inc. 1963. Print.

Hammerstein II, Oscar. <u>Showboat</u>. Composed by Jerome Kern. 1927. New York: Rodgers and Hammerstein Organization, 1927. Print.

Freed, Arthur. <u>Singin' in the Rain</u>. Composed by Nacio Herb Brown. 1983. New York: Music Theatre International. 1985. Print.

Black, Don. <u>Song and Dance</u>. Composed by Andrew Lloyd Webber. 1985. New York: Samuel French, Inc. 1985. Print.

Brown, Jason Robert. <u>Songs For A New World</u>. Composed by Jason Robert Brown. 1995. New York: Music Theatre International. 1995. Print

Hammerstein II, Oscar. <u>The Sound of Music</u>. Composed by Richard Rodgers. 1959. New York: Rodgers and Hammerstein Organization. 1959. Print.

Hammerstein II, Oscar. <u>South Pacific</u>. Composed by Richard Rodgers. 1949. New York: Rodgers and Hammerstein Organization. 1949. Print

Idle, Eric. <u>Spamalot</u>. Composed by John Du Prey and Eric Idle. 2005. New York: Theatrical Rights Worldwide. 2005. Print.

Sater, Steven. <u>Spring Awakening</u>. Composed by Duncan Sheik. 2006. New York: Music Theatre International. 2006. Print.

Hammerstein II, Oscar. <u>State Fair</u>. Composed by Richard Rodgers. 1996. New York: Rodgers and Hammerstein Organization. 1996. Print.

Ebb, Fred. <u>Steel Pier</u>. Composed by John Kander. 1997. New York: Samuel French, Inc. 1997. Print.

Sondheim, Stephen. <u>Sunday In The Park With George</u>. Composed by Stephen Sondheim. 1984. New York: Music Theatre International. 1984. Print.

Merrill, Bob. <u>Sugar</u>. Composed by Jule Styne. 1972. New York: Tams-Witmark Music Library. 1972. Print.

Black, Dan and Christopher Hampton. <u>Sunset Boulevard</u>. Composed by Andrew Lloyd Webber. 1994. New York: Rodgers and Hammerstein Organization. 1994. Print.

Sondheim, Stephen. <u>Sweeney Todd</u>. Composed by Stephen Sondheim. 1979. New York: MTI Enterprises, Inc. 1979. Print.

Fields, Dorothy. <u>Sweet Charity</u>. Composed by Cy Coleman. 1966. New York: Tams-Witmark Music Library. 1966. Print.

Carnelia, Craig. <u>Sweet Smell of Success</u>. Composed by Marvin Hamlisch. 2002. New York: Samuel French, Inc. 2002. Print.

Sager, Carol Bayer. <u>They're Playing Our Song</u>. Composed by Marvin Hamlisch. 1979. New York: Samuel French, Inc. 1979. Print.

Scanian, Dick. <u>Thoroughly Modern Millie</u>. Composed by Jeanine Tesori. 2002. New York: MTI Enterprises, Inc. 2002. Print.

Wilson, Meredith. <u>The Unsinkable Molly Brown</u>. Composed by Meredith Wilson. 1960. New York: Music Theatre International. 1960. Print.

Bricusse, Leslie. <u>Victor Victoria</u>. Composed by Henry Mancini. 1995. New York: Tams-Witmark Music Library. 1995. Print.

Sondheim, Stephen. <u>West Side Story</u>. Composed by Stephen Sondheim. 1957. New York: MTI Enterprises, Inc. 1957. Print.

Berlin, Irving. <u>White Christmas</u>. Composed by Irving Berlin. 2008. New York: Rodgers and Hammerstein Organization. 2008. Print.

Schwartz, Stephen. <u>Wicked</u>. Composed by Stephen Schwartz. 2003. New York: MTI Enterprises, Inc. 2003. Print.

Comden, Betty and Adolph Green. <u>Will Rogers Follies</u>. Composed by Betty Comden and Adolph Green. 1991. New York: Tams-Witmark Music Library. 1991. Print.

Smalls, Charlie. <u>The Wiz</u>. Composed by Charlie Smalls. 1975. New York: Samuel French, Inc. 1975. Print.

Harburg, E. Y. <u>The Wizard of Oz</u>. Composed by Harold Arlen. 1987. New York: Tams-Witmark music Library. 1987. Print.

Comden, Betty and Adolph Green. <u>Wonderful Town</u>. Composed by Leonard Bernstein. 1953. New York: Tams-Witmark Music Library. 1953. Print.

Gesner, Clark. <u>You're A Good Man Charlie Brown</u>. Composed by Clark Gesner. 1971. New York: Tams-Witmark Music Library. 1971. Print.

Made in the USA
Lexington, KY
09 January 2018